Edwin Abbott

A Concordance to the Works of Alexander Pope

Edwin Abbott

A Concordance to the Works of Alexander Pope

ISBN/EAN: 9783337091491

Printed in Europe, USA, Canada, Australia, Japan

Cover: Foto ©Thomas Meinert / pixelio.de

More available books at **www.hansebooks.com**

A CONCORDANCE

TO THE

WORKS

OF

ALEXANDER POPE

BY

EDWIN ABBOTT,
FORMERLY HEAD-MASTER OF THE PHILOLOGICAL SCHOOL.

With an Introduction

BY

EDWIN A. ABBOTT, D.D.,
AUTHOR OF "A SHAKESPEARIAN GRAMMAR," ETC., ETC.

NEW YORK:
D. APPLETON & CO.
1875.

INTRODUCTION.

In the course of revising the proofs of this Concordance, I noted a few peculiarities of Grammar and Metre; and these, at the Compiler's request, are now collected and prefixed by way of Introduction to his work.

Every student of Modern English, and indeed every Englishman who wishes to use English words correctly, will find help from knowing how Pope used them. Pope's own words:

"Correct with spirit,"

exactly express the merits of his style. "A man may correct his verses," says Walsh, Pope's early patron and able critic, "till he takes away the true spirit of them:" but, with Pope, every correction was an improvement in "spirit" as well as in correctness. The instances given by Johnson in his Lives of the Poets are extremely interesting as proofs of the fastidiousness with which each syllable was weighed by the Poet before a couplet was finally dismissed as complete. The motive of each change can generally be traced; and, although in many cases the later version may depart further from the original than the earlier, yet there cannot be a doubt that, in each case, euphony and force are gained by the correction. Take as a specimen Iliad, book viii., v. 687:

1st version—"As when in stillness of the silent night."

Here the pause on "when" is excessive, and the repetition of the same vowel sound in "silent" and "night" is objectionable. Hence:—

2nd version—"As when the moon in all her lustre bright."

There is a little want of pause and dignity here: and the collocation of the *l*-sounds is not euphonious. Hence:—

3rd and last version—"As when the moon, refulgent lamp of night."

The second line of the couplet is:—

1st version—"O'er Heaven's clear azure sheds her silver light."

"Sheds" is not so suitable to "o'er" as "spreads:" and "pure" suggests itself as alliterative with the *p* and *r* in "spreads." Hence:—

2nd version—"O'er Heaven's pure azure spreads her sacred light."

But here we are met with an unpleasant repetition in "pure" and "azure," and consequently "clear" is once more restored.

3rd version—"O'er Heaven's clear azure spreads her sacred light."

a 2

"Of these specimens," adds Dr. Johnson, "every man who has cultivated poetry, or who delights to trace the mind from the rudeness of its first conceptions to the elegance of its last, will naturally desire a greater number; but most other readers are already tired, and I am not writing only to poets and philosophers."

It might have been feared that euphony, where so carefully studied, might occasionally interfere with correctness of language. But no such danger need be apprehended in Pope, at least not in Pope's original Poems. The Iliad and Odyssey, no doubt, are injured by an excessive avoidance of colloquial terms and an excessive use of the conventional phraseology current in the elevated poetry of the eighteenth century: in the Odyssey, for example, a man is a " swain," a woman is a " fair," a bed is an " alcove," a cloak is a " vest," and Eumæus "launches the purple tide" from the throats of two pigs with his "cutlass." But there are few faults of this kind in Pope's original Poems, especially in the Satires and Essays: there the language is entirely subordinated to the thought, in accordance with Pope's own definition of wit—"justness of thought and facility of expression." The " Song by a Person of Quality " is a sufficient proof that Pope was not one of those who

> " — by Numbers judge a Poet's song,
> And smooth or rough, with them is right or wrong.
> In the bright Muse though thousand charms conspire,
> Her voice is all these tuneful fools admire." *E.C.* 340.

Equally sober was he in rejecting conceits and quaintnesses of style. He will not for a moment tolerate Wycherley's hint that method is inconsistent with Poetry : "I must take notice of what you say of 'my pains to make your dulness methodical;' and of your hint that 'the sprightliness of wit despises method.' This is true enough, no doubt, if by wit you mean no more than fancy or conceit; but in the better notion of wit considered as propriety, surely method is not only necessary for perspicuity and harmony of parts, but gives beauty even to the minute and particular thoughts which receive an additional advantage from those which precede or follow in their due place. You remember a simile Mr. Dryden used in conversation, of feathers in the crowns of the wild Indians, which they not only choose for the beauty of their colours, but place them in such a manner as to reflect a lustre on each other." To the same effect he writes to Walsh, "To bestow heightening on every part is monstrous; some parts ought to be lower than the rest; and nothing looks more ridiculous than a work, where the thoughts, however different in their own nature, seem all on a level. . . . People seek for what they call wit on all subjects and in all places; not considering that nature loves truth so well that it hardly ever admits of flourishing. Conceit is to nature what paint is to beauty: it is not only needless, but impairs what it would improve."

Pope's English is not only correct, it is also, as Dryden's is, modern. There is no substantial difference between it and the English of the present day, except that Pope is more exact than most modern authors in the use of words. It would be an interesting subject to consider the causes that originated the subtle differences that effectually distinguish the English of Shakespeare and the English of Milton from the English of Dryden, who is the first author of the Period of Modern English. Bunyan, De Foe, Fox, are all more archaic and less modern than Dryden. Set a passage from " Pilgrim's Progress" by the side of another from Dryden, and you would take Dryden's to be the later by a century. To what extent French influence and court influence may have modified the language, or the introduction of the rhyming drama may have simplified the idiom by the exclusion of the old Elizabethan Periodic structure, this is not the

INTRODUCTION. v

place to consider, but whatever the causes may have been, the fact is certain, that we may glance down page after page of this Concordance without finding a line or phrase that might not have been written in the nineteenth century.

It is Pope's modernness, as well as correctness, that makes him so valuable a model for the student of modern English. I know few better or more valuable lessons in the choice of English words than, after reading a passage of Pope, to shut the book and to have the verses repeated with blanks here and there for the student to fill up. By comparing one's failures with the original, one learns to appreciate the unerring exactitude with which Pope elaborated every couplet till it reached absolute perfection. Pope is one of the few poets whose lines cannot be misquoted with impunity. Many of his couplets would be seriously impaired by the change of an epithet, the transformation of a word, nay, even the alteration of a vowel or consonant. Byron was probably not far wrong in calling Pope a "poet of a thousand years." Pope's ideal of a poet was not a noble one, but, such as it was, he rose to its full height. "It seems," he says, in a letter to Walsh, "not so much the perfection of sense to say those things that have never been said before, as to express those best that have been said oftenest." This Pope has done: he has expressed the common-places of criticism and of morality in such language as is recognised to be not only the best, but, now, the only possible way of expressing them. We pass to some of the peculiarities of Pope's language. It will be convenient to classify them under Words, Idioms, Metre.

WORDS. *Spelling.* Words are often abbreviated by Pope to an extent not now customary. Thus *Penny-worth* is pronounced *penn'orth, casuistry* is pronounced as a trisyllable and *influence* as a disyllable. (Stúrgeón is an exception.)

This abbreviation is often expressed in the spelling. Hence *confus'dly; cov'nant; dev'l* as well as *devil; clam'rous; di'mond* as well as *diamond; flatt'rer* (except twice); *gall'ry; gen'ral* seventeen times, *general* once; *ign'rance; immac'late; intemp'rate; int'rest; Marybone; 'Pothecaries.* Though is, I believe, almost always spelt *tho'*, and *through, thro'*.

Many of these abbreviated pronunciations are common in the Elizabethan Poets. The Possessive inflection of a Noun in *s* is now represented by *'s*, except in polysyllabic words. Pope does not appear to have recognised this rule. He has *Cynthus', Lewis', mistress', Nilus', Parnassus', Peleus', Phœbus', Rabelais', Rufus', Thames'*. On the other hand he has three times *Thames's*, once *Pegasus's*, and also *Pythagoras's. Mexico's* is once used as a Plural.

Under the head of spelling it may be worth while saying a word about Pope's use of capitals. They are irregularly used, but seem occasionally intended to express emphasis, serving much the same purpose as modern Italics. Thus:—

"Let Us be fix'd and our own Masters still." *S.* ii. 180.

"Man never Is but always to be blest." *E.M.* i. 96.

"Who copies Yours or Oxford's better part." *M.E.* iii. 243.

"Why should not We be wiser than our Sires?" *S.* v. 44.

"As in the gentle reign of My Queen Anne." *I.H.* iii. 4.

"That rails at dear Lepell and You." *Mi.* vi. 10.

Occasionally antithesis seems to suggest sufficient emphasis for capitals:—

"To squander These and Those to hide again." *M.E.* iii. 14.

But in many cases there is manifest inconsistency. Compare:—

"When love is liberty and nature Law." *E.A.* 92.

and—

"When Love was Liberty and Nature Law." *E.M.* iii. 208.

Old forms of words. The Participial form without final *n* is * occasionally found: "I had *chose*," *Mi.* ix. 51; "more had she *spoke*," *D.* iv. 605; "Or what was *spoke* at Cressy or Poitiers," *S.* iii. 100; "are *spoke*," *S.* v. 308; "have I *swore*," *Mi.* ix. 67; "You've played and lov'd and *eat* and *drank* your fill," *S.* vi. 323. The Participial use of *drank* in the last instance is perhaps a slip. As a rule Pope avoids the use of the forms in *a* even as Past Tenses. Thus *rang* and *sang* do not occur, and, as in Milton, *sung* and *rung* are used to represent both the Passive Participle and the Active Past Tense.†

Occasionally Pope discards *strong* forms in favour of *weak* forms that have not been sanctioned by modern usage: *shin'd, thriv'd.*

The rule observed by the Translators of our Bible that *ye* is the Subjective and *you* the Objective form, is disregarded by Pope, no less than by Shakespeare:

"I'll tell *ye.*" *E.* vi. 26.   "Horace long before *ye.*" *E.S.* i. 7.

'Em is not uncommonly used for *them*, even in serious passages. There are indications that it was thought more appropriate for women than for men. It is twice used in the last line of Pope's most impassioned poem:—

"The well-sung woes will sooth my pensive ghost;
He best can paint '*em* who shall feel '*em* most." *E.A.* 366.

See also *ib.* 86; *W.F.* 104; *D.* ii. 116.

It is, as is now generally known, a contraction not of *them*, but of the old form *hem*, and, although not common in Shakespeare, is very frequent in the "Henry VIII." and in other plays of Fletcher and contemporary dramatists.

Words used in peculiar senses. Pope is exact but not pedantical in his use of words. Hence his use is generally the modern use. In a few cases, as in the well-known *opinion*—which has only during the last generation acquired the meaning of *judgment*—slight changes are discernible:—

"Take Nature's path and mad *Opinion's* leave." *E.M.* iv. 29.

"They talk of principles, but *notions* prize." *E.C.* 265.

Enormous appears to be used for that which is *out of measure* or *anomalous* in:—

"Th' *enormous* faith of many made for one." *E.M.* iii. 242.

Complacence seems used for *complaisance* in:—

"With mean *complacence* ne'er betray your trust." *E.C.* 580.

Flagrant is used literally in:—

"And Tutchin *flagrant* from the scourge below." *D.* ii. 148

---

* The *n* had been occasionally dropped as early as the Thirteenth Century.

† In the *Plural* of the Past Tense, the forms *rung*, *sung*, are sanctioned by the usage of early English. But neither Milton nor Pope limits their use to the Plural:

"Next Ægon *sung* while Windsor groves admired." *A.* 55.

INTRODUCTION.

IDIOMS. It is Pope's custom—and a custom that has manifest conveniences in spite of its antagonism to the established rules of grammar—to use a Plural Verb after a series of singular Nouns connected by *or*. Pope seems justified by logic. A negation when made about several subjects, seems to justify a Plural Verb. At all events Pope's ungrammatical idiom is much better English than it would be if made modernly grammatical.

> "There where no Passion, Pride, or Shame *transport*." *R.S.* i. 97.
>
> "And scarce *are* seen the prostrate Nile or Rhine." *M.E.* v. 28.
>
> "Snuff or the fan *supply* each pause of chat." *R.L.* iii. 17.
>
> "Whose table Wit or modest Merit *share*." *M.E.* iii. 241.

The same notion of an *implied Plural* probably justifies *yield* (which is not likely to be Subjunctive) in :—

> "Try what the open, what the covert *yield*." *E.M.* i. 10.

Was is used for *were* :—

> "Pity you *was* not Druggerman at Babel. *S.* viii. 33.

The preposition *but* is treated as though it were a conjunction with the ellipsis of a verb :—

> "And perish all *but she*." *A.* 34.

Than is treated as a Preposition governing an object :—

> "And lin'd with Giants deadlier *than 'em* all." *S.* viii. 275.
>
> "The king of dykes *than whom* no sluice of Mud." *D.* ii. 273.

On the other hand :—

> "But thinks his neighbour further gone *than he*." *E.M.* ii. 223.

Very seldom are there such irregularities as :—

> "This *to* disclose is all thy guardian can." *R.L.* iii. 17.
>
> "And drink the falling tears *each other* sheds." *E.A.* 350.

Gallicisms. Pope's use of *the* is perhaps a result of French influence :—

> "Where London's column pointing at the skies,
> Like a tall bully lifts *the* head and lies." *M.E.* iii. 340.
>
> "Ev'n mitred Rochester would nod *the* head." *P.S.* 140.
>
> "You might have held *the* pretty head aside." *E.J.S.* 3.
>
> "Rous'd by the light, old Dulness heav'd *the* head." *D.* i. 257 ; *R.L.* 33.

The use of *critic'd* for *criticized* is perhaps also French. Add also "the most strong," and the accentuation of the last syllable in *essáy* (noun), *effórt*, *virtú* (of which the two first are similarly accented by Dryden). Add the pronunciation of *barrier* in :

> "'Twixt that and Reason what a nice *barrier*,
> For ever sep'rate, yet for ever near." *E.M.* i. 223.

The frequent use of certain Adjectives after their nouns, e.g., *divine*, is probably also a result, in part at least, of French influence.

Abbreviated constructions. Abundant specimens might be given of these. The following are a few of the more striking :—

> "'Gainst Pallas, Mars ; ('gainst) Latona, Hermes arms." *R.L.* v. 47.

INTRODUCTION.

> " Alive, ridiculous, and dead, forgot." *M.E.* ii. 248.
> " No place so sacred from such fops is barr'd." *E.C.* 622.

The use of *but* for the Objective Relative with *not* is rare, as in :—

> " Who ne'er knew joy *but* Friendship might divide." *Ep.* iii. 3.
> " The sot a hero, (the) lunatic a king." *E.M.* ii. 268.

The use of the Relative for the Relative and Antecedent is probably a Latinism :—

> " Who cannot flatter, and detest (those) *who* can." *S.* viii. 198.
> " In *who* obtain defence or who defend." *E.M.* iv. 59.
> " 'Tis thus we riot while *who* sow it starve." *M.E.* iii. 24.
> " Not but there are *who* merit other palms." *S.* v. 229.

The use of a Relative after an Antecedent implied in a preceding Possessive Adjective is not uncommon :—

> " Yet shun *their* fault *who* scandalously nice." *E.C.* 556.

Archaisms. These are very rare. Pope uses once at least the old prefix *y-* in *y-fed;* he has once " *a* God's name." It is rare for him to dispense with *self* as in :—

> " The poor contents *him* with the care of heaven." *E.M.* ii. 266.

The use of *which* after *same* is perhaps archaic in :—

> " The *same which* in a Sire the sons obeyed." *E.M.* ii. 213.

The sounding of *-ed* final is rare : it is sounded in *forkèd*, *P.S.* 231, and *wingèd E.C.* 86. The pronunciation of *satellites* as a quadrisyllable seems also archaic. Add :—

> " At last Centlivre felt her voice *to* fail." *D.* ii. 411.

But Pope's principle archaism is the forcible use of the Subjunctive, which is one of his great beauties :—

> " *Rise* Alps between us ! and whole oceans *roll*." *E.A.* 290.
> " Swift *fly* the years and *rise* th' expected morn." *M.* 21.

In other cases after *till, before*, &c. Pope uses the Subjunctive more sparingly, though more frequently than we now use it :—

> " Ridotta sips and dances till she *see*." *S.* i. 47.
> " Choose a firm cloud before it *fall*." *M.E.* ii. 19.
> " Suffice that Reason *keep* to Nature's Road." *E.M.* ii. 115.

"*That*" and "*who*." The Elizabethan distinction between *that* and *who* or *which* was that (1) *that* introduced something essential to complete the Antecedent, while (2) *who* or *which* introduced a new fact about the Antecedent. This valuable distinction was unfortunately unknown in Addison's time ; and the excessive use of *that* caused a reaction, which found a humorous expression in No. 78 of the Spectator.

> " To Mr. SPECTATOR.
> " *The humble Petition of* WHO *and* WHICH.

" Sheweth,

> " THAT your Petitioners, being in a forlorn and destitute Condition, know not to whom we should apply ourselves for Relief, because there is hardly any Man alive who hath not injured us. . . .

INTRODUCTION. ix

We are descended of ancient Families, and kept up our Dignity and Honour many Years, till the Jacksprat THAT supplanted us. How often have we found ourselves slighted by the Clergy in their Pulpits, and the Lawyers at the Bar. Nay, how often have we heard in one of the most polite and august Assemblies in the Universe, to our great Mortification, these words, *That THAT that noble L—d urged;* which, if one of us had Justice done, would have sounded nobler thus, *That WHICH that noble L—d urged.*"

 This Prayer is based upon a mistake; for *that* is the legitimate sovereign, while *who* and *which* are the Jacksprats. But Addison's example and possibly a general sense of the ambiguity arising from the use of *that* as a Relative Pronoun and Conjunction, stimulated the use of *who* and *which* even where, as is occasionally the case in Pope, they are not only incorrect but inelegant.

 It would be useless to enumerate the instances where Pope uses *who* or *which* for *that:* they are legion, as the following references will shew:—

  E.M. ii. 139; M.E. v. 9; S. viii. 182; MI. ii. 22; S. iii. 57; S. v. 296; E.C. 631; S. iv. 131; E.M. i. 12; E.C. 514; M.E. ii. 130; D. iii. 53; D. iv. 95; E.S. i. 172; D. ii. 281; M.E. iii. 196; S. viii. 33; P.S. 41; S. vi. 244; E.C. 392; S. v. 131; A. 30; E.C. 201; S. vii. 40; M.E. i. 62.

 I know but one instance where Pope seems to recognise the Elizabethan distinction:—

  " Abuse the City's best good men in metre,
  And laugh at Peers *that* put their trust in Peter." *S.* i. 40.

  " And taught his Romans in much better metre,
  To laugh at Fools *who* put their trust in Peter." *E.S.* i. 10.

 In the first case *that* is essential to the Antecedent. Pope does not laugh at Peers, but only at *Peers that put their trust,* &c. In the second case, Pope laughs at Fools, *because* they, *since* they, put their trust in Peter; and therefore *who* is correct. Pope once at least uses *who* after *such:*—

  " Let *such* teach others *who* themselves excel." *E.C.* 15.

 Antithesis. Some specimens of Pope's Antithetical style may be useful as evidences of the paucity of types in which he moulded his verses. Over and over again the same kind of antithesis occurs. For example:—

  " Good without noise; without pretension, great." *Ep.* vii. 4.
  " Soft without weakness; without glaring, gay." *E.* iii. 66.
  " Heady, not strong; o'erflowing, though not full." *D.* iii. 172.
  " Plain, but not sordid; tho' not splendid, clear." *S.* ii. 48.
  " Sincere, tho' prudent; constant, yet resign'd." *Ep.* ii. 2.
  " So firm, yet soft; so strong, yet so refin'd." *Ep.* vi. 8.
  " In action faithful, and in honour clear." *M.E.* v. 68.
  " Compos'd in suff'rings, and in joy sedate." *Ep.* vii. 3.
  " Tho' stale, not ripe; tho' thin, yet never clear." *D.* iii. 170.

Some of these types of antithesis seem copied from Denham's well-known description of the Thames:—

  " Though deep, yet clear; though gentle, yet not dull.
  Strong without rage; without o'erflowing, full."

Other instances of the double antithesis in a line are:—

  " Teach oaths to gamesters, and to Nobles wit." *D.* i. 204.
  " So sweetly mawkish, and so smoothly dull." *D.* iii. 171.
  " Wit that can creep, and pride that licks the dust." *P.S.* 333.

INTRODUCTION.

A less justifiable method of producing an antithetical effect is to repeat some word unnecessarily, so as to supply as it were the missing fourth term in the rhetorical proportion. Pope is almost too fond of this device:—

"*By strangers* honour'd and *by strangers* mourn'd." *U.L.* 54.
"*A hireling* scribbler or *a hireling* peer." *P.S.* 364.
"*At once* the chaser and *at once* the prey." *W.F.* 81.
"Or tir'd in *search of* wit or *search of* rhyme." *S.* ii. 86.
"Sacred to *social* life and *social* love." *I.H.* iii. 22.
"*Who rules in* Cornwall or *who rules in* Berks." *S.* iv. 104.
"*Who sings so* loudly and *who sings so* long." *D.* ii. 268.
"*The slave that* digs it and *the slave that* hides." *M.E.* iii. 110.
"But what will *grow on* pride and *grow on* shame." *E.M.* ii. 191.

An ingenious and rare form of antithesis is:—

"Less wit than Mimic, more a wit than wise." *M.E.* ii. 48.

Imitations of Shakespeare and Milton:—

"Come with petitions fairly penn'd." *I.H.* ii. 65, ».
"Break Priscian's head." *D.* iii. 162.
"And makes night hideous." *D.* iii. 166.
"All sly, slow things." *E.M.* iv. 226.
"The stuff of which our dream is wrought." *M.E.* 148.
"This vault of air, this congregated ball."* *S.* iv. 27.
"Her tresses staring from Poetic dreams."† *D.* iii. 17.
"Puff'd nobility."‡ *S.* viii. 201.
"The strong connections, nice dependencies." *E.M.* i. 30.
"Is blest in what it gives and what it takes." *R.L.* iii. 168.

There are few imitations of Milton. In:—

"The yellow carp in scales bedropp'd with gold." *W.F.* 144.

there is perhaps a reminiscence of Milton's:—

"Shew to the sun their wav'd coats dropp'd with gold,"

and—

"Bernard rows his state." *D.* xii. 63.

is probably borrowed from Milton's description of the Swan, which:—

"Between her white wings mantling proudly *rows*
Her *state* with oary feet."

Lastly,

"This subtle thief of life, this paltry time." *S.* vi. 76.

recals:—

"How soon hath Time, the subtle thief of youth."

But there is not much of Milton's style in Pope, and the estimation in which

---

* *Hamlet*, ii. 2, 310-15.
† "With hair *up-staring*." *Tempest*, i. 2, 213.
‡ *Hamlet*, i. 2, 49.

Milton was held at the time may perhaps be illustrated by the following extract from Atterbury to Pope, in a letter dated July 15, 1722:—

"I hope you won't utterly forget what pass'd in the coach about Samson Agonistes. I shall not press you as to time, but some time or other I wish you would review and polish that piece. If upon a new perusal of it (which I desire you to make) you think as I do, that it is written in the very spirit of the Ancients, it deserves your care, and is capable of being improved with little trouble into a perfect model and standard of Tragick poetry."

METRE. Words. A few words are accented by Pope on a different syllable from that which is now accented: *effórt; essáy* (noun); *convérse* (noun) *E.C.* 641, *cónverse E.M.* iv. 379; *Córneille, S.* v. 374, *Cornéille, D.* i. 285; *Poitiérs, S.* iii. 100; *enérvate, S.* v. 153; *cónfessor* (so Dryden and Shakespeare); *virtú; gázette* once (so Dryden once); *gazéttes* once (so Dryden all but once). The Verb *dictate* is always accented on the first syllable.

Versification. Pope's versification receives much illustration from the following letter elaborated by Pope, for the purpose of publication, from a letter to Cromwell, dated Nov. 25, 1710, and "grafted upon Mr. Walsh's stock." It expresses many of the rules on which Pope constructed his verses.

"Oct. 26, 1706.*

"After the thoughts I have already sent you on the subject of English Versification, you desire my opinion as to some further particulars. There are indeed certain Niceties, which, tho' not much observed even by correct versifiers, I cannot but think deserve to be better regarded.

"It is not enough that nothing offends† the ear, but a good Poet will adapt the very Sounds, as well as Words, to the things he treats of. So that there is (if one may express it so) a Style of Sound. As in describing a gliding stream, the numbers should run easy and flowing; in describing a rough ‡ torrent or deluge, sonorous and swelling; and so of the rest. . . .

"2. Every nice ear must (I believe) have observ'd that in any smooth English verse of ten syllables, there is naturally a Pause at the fourth, fifth, or sixth syllable. It is upon these that the ear rests, and upon the judicious change and management of which depends the variety of versification. For example,

"At the fifth:
  'Where'er thy navy | spreads her canvass wings.'

"At the fourth:
  'Homage to thee | and peace to all she brings.'

"At the sixth:
  'Like tracks of leverets | in morning snows.'

"Now I fancy that, to preserve an exact Harmony and variety, the Pause at the 4th or 6th should not be continued above three lines together, without the interposition of another; else it will be apt to weary the ear with one continued tone, at least it does mine. That at the 5th runs quicker, and carries not quite so dead a weight, so tires not so much, tho' it be continued longer.

"3. Another nicety is in relation to Expletives, whether words or syllables, which are made use of purely to supply a vacancy; *do*§ before verbs plural is absolutely such; and it is not improbable

---

* The "Essay on Criticism" was published in 1711. But 1706 (see above) is probably not the true date of the letter.

† "'Tis not enough, no harshness gives offence,
 The sound must seem an echo to the sense." *E.C.* 364.

‡ "Soft is the strain when Zephyr gently blows,
 And the smooth stream in smoother numbers flows;
 But when loud surges lash the sounding shore,
 The hoarse rough verse should like the torrent roar." *Ib.* 376-9.

§ "While expletives their feeble aid *do* join." *E.C.* 346.

INTRODUCTION.

but future refiners may explode *did* and *does** in the same manner, which are almost always used for the sake of rhyme. The same cause has occasioned the promiscuous use of *you* and *thou* to the same person, which can never be found so graceful as either one or the other.

"4. I would also object to the irruption of Alexandrine† verses of twelve syllables, which, I think, should never be allow'd but when some remarkable beauty or propriety in them atones for the liberty. Mr. Dryden has been too free of these, especially in his latter works.‡ I am of the same opinion as to Triple Rhimes.

"5. I could equally object to the repetition of the same Rhimes§ within four or six lines of each other, as tiresome to the ear thro' their Monotony.

"6. Monosyllable ‖ Lines unless very artfully managed, are stiff, or languishing; but may be beautiful to express Melancholy, Slowness, or Labour.¶

"7. To come to the Hiatus, or Gap between two words, which is caus'd by two vowels opening ** on each other (upon which you desire me to be particular); I think the rule in this case is either to use the Cæsura, or admit the Hiatus, just as the ear is least shock'd by either; for the Cæsura sometimes offends the ear more than the Hiatus itself, and our language is naturally over-charg'd with consonants. As for example; if in this verse,

    '*The old have Int'rest ever in their eye,*'

we should say, to avoid the Hiatus,

    '*But th' old have int'rest.*'

The Hiatus which has the worst effect, is when one word ends with the same vowel that begins the following; and next to this, those vowels whose sounds come nearest each other, are most to be avoided. . . . . To conclude, I believe the Hiatus should be avoided with more care in poetry than in Oratory; and I would constantly try to prevent it, unless where the cutting it off is more prejudicial to the sound than the Hiatus itself."

From the rules in the first five paragraphs of this letter Pope seldom deviates. Except in the Messiah, Alexandrines are rarely found, and he generally observes the rule of the varied pause.

The following are instances of his use of monosyllabic or nearly monosyllabic lines, which he often employs to denote contempt :—

    "Of hairs, or straws, or dirt, or grubs, or worms." *P.S.* 170.
    "She saw poor Phillips creep like Tate's poor page." *D.* i. 105.
    "And strains from hard-bound brains eight lines a year." *P.S.* 182.

In order to break what would otherwise be a monotonous smoothness, Pope often

---

* Dryden is a great offender in this point:
    "In shipping such as this the Irish kern
    And untaught Indian on the stream *did* glide
    Ere sharp-keeled boats to stem the flood *did* learn
    Or fin-like oars *did* spread from either side."
                                                    Annus Mirabilis, 1666.

Smilinda (Mi. ix. 22) says :—
    "She all the cares of Love and Play *does* know."
But *Smilinda* is not supposed to speak in the choicest verse. Compare, as more to the purpose :—
    "Ev'n rival wits *did* Voiture's death deplore." *E.* iv. 15.

† "A needless Alexandrine ends the song,
    That, like a wounded snake, drags its slow length along." *E.C.* 356.

‡ Pope expresses his eulogy on Dryden in an Alexandrine :—
        "But Dryden taught to join
    The varying verse, the full-resounding line
    The long majestic March, and Energy divine." *S.* v. 269.

§ "While they ring round the same unvary'd chimes
    With sure returns of still expected rhymes." *E.C.* 349.

‖ "And ten low words oft creep in one dull line." *Ib.* 347.

¶ "When Ajax strives some rock's vast weight to throw." *Ib.* 370.

** "Though oft the ear the open vowels tire." *Ib.* 345.

lays a metrical accent on an unemphatic syllable short in quantity, placing after it an emphatic monosyllable, long in quantity, without the metrical accent:—

"Where one step broken *thé great* scale's destroyed." *E.M.* i. 244.
"Down with the Bible, up with *thé Pope's* arms." *D.* ii. 82.
"Now night descending *thé proud* scene was o'er." *D.* i. 89.
"Swears, like Albutius *á good* cook away." *S.* ii. 64.
"The lines, tho' touch'd but faint*ly áre* drawn right." *E.C.* 22.
"Drive to St. James's *á whole* herd of swine." *M.E.* iii. 74.
"When num'rous wax-lights *in bright* order blaze." *R.E.* iii. 68.

Less frequently a trochee is found in the middle of the verse, or, as it might be better expressed in the case of Pope's verses, the metrical accent is laid on an unemphatic and short syllable, while the preceding syllable is long and emphatic :—

"At night would swear him dropp'd *out of* the moon." *S.* viii. 33.
"Is the great chain that draws *all to* agree." *E.M.* i. 33.
"And chiefless armies doz'd *out the* campaign." *D.* iv. 617.
"Some rising genius sins *up to* my song." *E.S.* ii. 9.
"O'er a *learn'd un*intelligible place." *S.* vii. 102.

For many of these harshnesses there is a special reason beside the general desire to gain variety. For example, there seems a wish to express a combination of *carelessness* and *care* in the following :—

"Divided *bétween* carelessness and care." *S.* vi. 291.

As regards Pope's use of Alliteration it may be worth while pointing out that his verses depend for their force and beauty almost more upon the artful combination of the vowel sounds than on the more obvious alliteration of the consonants. The use of the *o* sound to express solemnity is frequent.

"Ye nymphs of Solyma begin the song." *M.* 1.
"An honest man's the noblest work of God." *E.M.* iv. 248.
"And swelling organs lift the rising soul." *E.A.* 272.

On the other hand a prevalence of *ŭ* is always a sign of contempt or disgust : —

"Then number'd with the puppies in the mud." *D.* ii. 308.
"The clam'rous crowd is hush'd with mugs of Mum." *D.* ii. 385.
"With Guns, Drums, Trumpets, Blunderbuss and Thunder." *S.* i. 28.
"And suck'd all o'er like an industrious Bug." *D.* i. 130.

I believe it would be found that, as a rule, in Pope's more serious and solemn verses, he prefers to have a long vowel sound in the final rhyme (the way sometimes being prepared for it by a short vowel sound of a similar nature) :—

"The shrines all trembled and the *lamps* grew *pale.*" *E.A.* 112.

On the other hand, to produce a mock-heroic effect, the final rhyme is often a short vowel sound. A comparison of the rhymes of the Dunciad and Eloisa and Abelard would shew this to be generally true. A short vowel at the end following long and solemn

INTRODUCTION.

sounding vowels in the middle gives an effect of bathos very appropriate to the Dunciad :—

"Loud thunder to its bottom shook the bog." *D.* i. 329.
"Slow rose a form in majesty of Mud." *Ib.* ii. 326.
"Now Henley lay inspir'd beside a sink
And to mere mortals seem'd a Priest in drink." *Ib.* ii. 426.

As regards Hiatus, Pope often elides *e* in *the, but not, as Milton does, before a metrically accented syllable.* At least I have not noted an instance like Milton's "*th'* other," "from *th'* egg," &c.

"*Th'* enormous faith of many made for one." *E.M.* iii. 242.
"And love *th'* offender yet detest *th'* offence." *E.A.* 192, &c.

But :—

"Adieu to all the follies of *the* age." *S.* viii. 2.
"Admires the jay *the* insect's gilded wings." *E.M.* iii. 55, &c.

The use of *thine* and *mine* might have prevented Hiatus in the following instances; but Pope very rarely uses these forms.

"*Thy* offspring, Thames." *W.F.* 172; "And make a long posterity *thy* own." *D.* iv. 334; "*Thy own* point." *E.M.* i. 283; "*Thy own* lord." *Mi.* ix. 48; "Lamented in *thy* end." *Ep.* xi. 8; "*Thy* eyes." *M.* 86; "*Thy enemies.*" *E.M.* iv. 356; "*Thy* eye." *E.A.* 122; "*My eye,*" *E.A.* 278, 332; "*Thy infant* thought." *R.L.* i. 29; "*Thy instructions.*" *E.M.* iii. 172; "*Thy honour.*" *W.* 84; "*Thy own* importance know." *R.L.* i. 35; "*Thy* image." *E.A.* 268.

Add :—

"Admire we then what earth's *low* entrails hold." *S.* iv. 11.
"Ah! quit not the *free* innocence of life." *E.* iv. 45.

Pope seems to have had a great aversion to *thine* and *mine* as archaic. He uses *thine* once in the Essay on Criticism, with the Metrical accent. But in the two passages where it is found in the Dunciad, without the Metrical accent; it seems intended to produce a bombastic and mock-heroic effect.

"The world's just wonder and ev'n *thine,* O Rome." *E.C.* 248.
"Flow, Welsted, flow, like *thine* inspirer, Beer." *D.* iii. 169.
"Far Eastward cast *thine* eye from whence the Sun." *Ib.* iii. 73.

Before taking leave of the subject of Pope's alliteration, it may be worth while to note his love of the sound of *s*. There are, I believe, nearly twice as many entries in the Concordance under *s,* as under any other letter. Possibly it is the combination of this sound with the exquisite variety of vowels, that induced Pope to select out of all his verses this couplet, as the "one by which he declared his ear to be most gratified"* :—

"Lo where Mœotis sleeps, and hardly flows
The freezing Tanais through a waste of snows." *D.* iii. 87.

For Pope's Rhymes, see page xvii.

With these remarks—which owe their insertion to the Compiler's request, and not to the writer's sense of the necessity of an introduction—I venture to commend the following pages to all those who wish to be able to know at any moment how Pope used any English word in his Original Poems. However close may be our acquaintance with the best English Authors, a knowledge of Pope's "use" must always be of value : and an Englishman may wait more patiently for the ideal Dictionary of his native tongue if he can see before him, on a shelf in his library, next to the Concordance of Shakespeare, the Concordance to the Original Poems of Pope.—E. A. A.

March, 1875.

---

* "The reason of this preference," adds Dr. Johnson, " I cannot discover."

EXPLANATION OF ABBREVIATIONS,
ETC.

Reference.		Number of Verses.	Reference.		Number of Verses.
A.	Autumn	100	Ep. xvi.	Epitaph on the same	8
D. i.	Dunciad, Book I.	330	I.H. i.	Imitation of Horace, Ep. i. 7.	84
D. ii.	,, ,, II.	428	I.H. ii.	,, ,, Sat. ii. 6.	221
D. iii.	,, ,, III.	340	I.H. iii.	,, ,, Odes iv. 1.	48
D. iv.	,, ,, IV.	656	I.H. iv.	,, ,, ,, iv. 9.	16
E. i.	Epistle to Harley	40	M.	Messiah	108
E. ii.	,, Craggs	17	M.E.	Moral Essays:	
E. iii.	,, Jervas	78	M.E. i.	Ep. I. to Cobham	265
E. iv.	,, Miss Blount	80	M.E. ii.	Ep. II. to a Lady	292
E. v.	,, the same	50	M.E. iii.	Ep. III. to Bathurst	402
E. vi.	,, Lady F. Shirley	32	M.E. iv.	Ep. IV. to Boyle	204
E.A.	Eloisa to Abelard	366	M.E. v.	Ep. V. to Addison	72
E.C.	Essay on Criticism	744	Mi.	Miscellaneous.	
E.J.S.	Epilogue to "Jane Shore"	50	Mi. i.	On Verses by Buckingham	8
E.M. i.	Essay on Man, Ep. I.	294	Mi. ii.	Prologue for Dennis	24
E.M. ii.	,, ,, ,, II.	294	Mi. iii.	Macer	26
E.M. iii.	,, ,, ,, III.	318	Mi. iv.	To Moore, the Worm-Doctor	40
E.M. iv.	,, ,, ,, IV.	398			
E.S. i.	Epilogue to Sat., Dial. I.	172	Mi. v.	To Mrs. M. B.	20
E.S. ii.	,, ,, Dial. II.	255	Mi. vi.	Answer to Mrs. Howe	10
Ep. i.	Epitaph on Dorset	14	Mi. vii.	Song, by a Person of Quality	32
Ep. ii.	,, Trumbal	12	Mi. viii.	On a certain Lady at Court	12
Ep. iii.	,, Harcourt	8	Mi. ix.	The Basset-Table	112
Ep. iv.	,, Craggs	6	Mi. x.	On his Grotto	14
Ep. v.	,, Rowe	4	Mi. xi.	Verbatim from Boileau	12
Ep. vi.	,, Mrs. Corbet	10	Mi. xii.	To Southern	14
Ep. vii.	,, R. Digby	20	O. i.	Ode on St. Cecilia's Day	134
Ep. viii.	,, Kneller	8	O. ii.	Chorus of Athenians	32
Ep. ix.	,, Withers	12	O. iii.	Chorus of Youths and Virgins	44
Ep. x.	,, Fenton	10	O. iv.	Ode on Solitude	20
Ep. xi.	,, Gay	12	O. v.	Dying Christian to his Soul	18
Ep. xii.	,, Newton	2	P.C.	Prologue to "Cato"	46
Ep. xiii.	,, Atterbury	8	P.S.	,, to Satires, to Arbuthnot	419
Ep. xiv.	,, Buckingham	14	R.L. i.	Rape of the Lock, Canto I.	148
Ep. xv.	,, One who would not be buried in Westminster Abbey	4	R.L. ii.	,, ,, ,, II.	142
			R.L. iii.	,, ,, ,, III.	178
			R.L. iv.	,, ,, ,, IV.	176
			R.L. v.	,, ,, ,, V.	150

EXPLANATION OF ABBREVIATIONS, ETC.

Reference.				Number of Verses.	Reference.		Number of Verses.
S. i.	- - - -Sat.	I. from Hor. Sat.	II., i.	156	S. viii.-	-Sat. VIII. Donne versified, S. IV.	287
S. ii.	- - -,,	II.	,, Sat. II., ii.	180	Sp. . . .	Spring - - - - - - - - -	102
S. iii.	-,,	III.	,, Ep. I., i.	188	Su. - - - -	Summer -	98
S. iv.	- - -,,	IV.	,, Ep. I., vi.	133	U.L. - - -	Elegy on an Unfortunate Lady	82
S. v.	- - -,,	V.	,, Ep. II., i.	419	U.P. - - -	Universal Prayer - - - - - -	52
S. vi.	- - -,,	VI.	,, Ep. II., ii.	327	W. - -	Winter - - - - - - - - -	92
S. vii.	-,,	VII. Donne versified, S. II.		128	W.F. - - -	Windsor Forest - - - - - -	434

(*rep.*) denotes that the word recurs in the next line. Sometimes, but rarely, the recurrence is in the next line but one. This abbreviation has been borrowed from Mrs. Cowden Clarke's "Concordance to Shakspere."

s, after a reference, means that the verse quoted was written by Swift.

A whole line in Italics denotes a grammatical change in the heading word, but the inflections of a verb stand as separate headings.

Compound words *formed with a hyphen* will be found under the heading of their first constituent: e.g., "air-built" under "air."

A word used only in the plural occupies the position the singular would have occupied, had it occurred: thus "antics" stands before "antichrist," &c.

⁂ *This Concordance applies to all the Poems contained in the first authorised edition of Pope's Completed Works, edited by Warburton in 1751, except the Translations from Greek and Latin, the Adaptations of Chaucer, and the Imitations of English Poets. It contains every word in these poems, so that a glance will show whether or not Pope uses a given word. For example, "also" never occurs, nor does "towards." Of the minor poems found in subsequent editions, several are more or less doubtful and none were thought worthy of the poet by the friend to whom he bequeathed the care of his reputation.* At first I intended to include them, and I had transcribed the necessary slips, but further consideration led me to the conclusion that they did not deserve a place in a work professing to extend the knowledge of Pope's diction and style. Curiosity may be gratified, but assuredly Art will not be elevated by attempts to disinter or embalm the failures and follies of Genius.*

Into a work containing forty thousand references some errors will almost of necessity find their way. A list of "Corrigenda" will be found at p. 366. It is too long, and even now, perhaps, is not complete. To any one that will take the trouble to send the publisher additional corrections I shall be very grateful.

I cannot take leave of a work which has been my close companion for nearly three years, without expressing an earnest hope that it may do something to spread the knowledge of our noble Mother-tongue, or without acknowledging my obligations to the printers for the pains and care they have taken in producing a handsome volume.

E. A.

March, 1875.

---

* One of them was avowedly rescued from the "rubbish and sweepings" of Pope's study.

EXAMPLES OF IRREGULAR OR UNUSUAL RHYMES.

₊ *Rhymes to the eye, such as* caprice, nice, *are not included. A number in brackets after a word denotes how often the rhyme occurs.*

Word		Rhymes with	Reference	Word	Rhymes with	Word	Rhymes with	Reference
Abhor	{ rhymes with }	more	S. iii. 65	Ear { rhymes with }		parterre	M.E iv. 173
air	,,	atmosphere	D. iv. 423	effort	,,	Earl's-Court.	S. vi. 112
,,	,,	star	R.L. i. 107	endu'd	,,	good	E.M. iii. 13
appear'd	,,	reward	D. ii. 25	enjoy	,,	luxury	E.M. iii. 61
awake	,,	speak	D. iv. 609	essays (*noun*)	,,	ways	D. ii. 361
Baal	,,	call	,, ,, 93	eyes	,,	precipice	E.C. 158
barrier	,,	near	E.M. i. 223	Face	,,	brass	M.E. v. 57
beat	,,	set	S. v. 21	,,	,,	mass	E. iii. 15
Berks	,,	remarks	S. iv. 103	fault (9)	,,	thought,&c.	E.C. 422, &c.
besiege ye	,,	oblige ye	I.H. i. 29	feast (2)	,,	guest	S. ii. 75, &c.
besieg'd	,,	oblig'd	P.S. 207	,,	,,	rest	I.H. i. 25
bohea	,,	way	R.L. iv. 155	field	,,	impelled	M.E. i. 107
born = borne	,,	adorn	W.F. 31	fierce (2)	,,	verse	S. i. 23, &c.
,,	,,	return	E.M. iii. 19	figure	,,	bigger	S. vi. 298
,,	,,	scorn	M.E. ii. 59	Fleury	,,	fury	E.S. i. 51
,,	,,	torn	D. iv. 123	flood	,,	nod	D. iv. 241
boy	,,	Blois	S. vi. 3	fool	,,	cowl	E.M. iv. 199
break	,,	crack	P.S. 85	,,	,,	dull	E.S. ii. 132
breath	,,	teeth	S. vi. 300	,,	,,	owl	D. i. 271
Care	,,	war	S. v. 272	,,	,,	ridicule(3)	M.E. ii 119, &c.
chac'd	,,	pass'd	E.C. 709	,,	,,	skull	E.J.S. 7
chariots	,,	garrets	D. ii. 23	Gate	,,	eat	M.E. iii. 195
chaste	,,	last	S. iv. 79	get	,,	meat	S. vii. 25
cheat	,,	forget	,, ,, 93	glare	,,	war	D. iii. 235
choir	,,	Prior	D. ii. 123	God	,,	abode	D. iii. 133
city	,,	fit ye	E.J.S. 41	,,	,,	road	D. iv. 471
civil (4)	,,	devil	S. v. 41, &c.	,,	,,	unaw'd	D. iii. 223
come	,,	room	S. viii. 214	,,	,,	wood	E.M. iii. 155
compelling	,,	Helen	M.E. ii. 193	grot	,,	thought	Mi. x. 9
compose	,,	vows	Mi. ix. 87	guest	,,	beast	S. viii. 166
conceive	,,	give	E.M. iv. 163	Hear	,,	pray'r	M.E. iv. 141
Corneille	,,	Ozell	D. i. 285	heart	,,	desert	E.M. iv. 253
Death	,,	breathe	E. iv. 19	,,	,,	pert	Mi. ix. 65
desert	,,	heart	E.C. 731	heav'n	,,	ev'n	E.A. 213
dictionary	,,	said I	S. viii. 68	,,	,,	giv'n (8).	E.M. ii. 265, &c.
die	,,	Paduasoy	S. viii. 112	,,	,,	uneven	M.E. iv. 143
draws	,,	was	P.C. 17	hell	,,	prevail	O. i. 87
dull	,,	school	S. vi. 200	join (14)	,,	vine, &c.	D. i. 304, &c.

xviii EXAMPLES OF IRREGULAR OR UNUSUAL RHYMES.

join'd (7)	⎱rhymes⎰ ⎰ with ⎱	mind, &c.	- *D.* iii. 179, &c.	Race	⎱rhymes⎰ ⎰ with ⎱	pass	- *D.* iii. 155
joins	,,	mines	- *M.E.* iii. 131	,,	,,	peace	*S.* vi. 147
Knew	,,	too	- - *S.* vii. 1	relieves	,,	gives	*M.E.* iii. 269
known	,,	one	- *E.M.* iii. 229	remain'd	,,	land	- *R.L.* iv. 154
Laugh	,,	safe	- - *E.C.* 450	return	,,	unborn	- *D.* i. 241
least	,,	jest	- *S.* iv. 108	revere	,,	star	- *M.E.* i. 89
Lintot	,,	print it	- *P.S.* 61	rêver'd	,,	heard	- *S.* v. 27
Man	,,	plain	- *E.M.* i. 47	Rome (3)	,,	doom, &c.	*E.C.* 685, &c.
martyr	,,	quarter	- *S.* iii. 150	rows	,,	billet-doux	- *R.L.* i. 138
martyrs	,,	Chartres	- *M.E.* ii. 63	Satires	,,	dedicators	- *E.C.* 592
mast	,,	plac'd	- *R.L.* ii. 69	says Sir	,,	praise her	- *Mi.* viii. 9
merit (3)	,,	spirit	- *S.* v. 384, &c.	seem	,,	him	- *E.* iv. 3
minute	,,	in it	- *M.E.* ii. 19	serve (2)	,,	starve	- *P.S.* 247, &c.
Molière	,,	here	- *D.* i. 131	shade	,,	dead	- *E.M.* iv. 243
mourn	,,	adorn	- *E.* i. 3	shadows	,,	Meadows	*Mi.* vi. 3
,,	,,	burn (2)	- *E.M.* i. 277, &c.	share	,,	commissioner	*D.* iii. 183
,,	,,	return	- *D.* iii. 147	shew	,,	do	*M.E.* i. 101
,,	,,	urn (3)	*M.E.* iv. 125, &c.	short (2)	,,	court	- *S.* i. 91, &c.
News	,,	shoes	- *S.* iii. 155	sluice	,,	Arethuse	- *D.* ii. 341
night	,,	doit	- *S.* vi. 35	sphere	,,	care	- *D.* iv. 431
Out-weighs	,,	huzzas	- *E.M.* iv. 255	,,	,,	fair	*E.M.* ii. 23
own	,,	gone	- *S.* v. 33	spoke	,,	look	- *D.* iv. 51
,,	,,	none	- *S.* iii. 179	state	,,	eat	*M.E.* iv. 157
,,	,,	shone	- *S.* v. 276	,,	,,	that	- *S.* ii. 61
,,	,,	son	- *S.* ii. 173	stone	,,	on	*D.* iii. 294
Paris	,,	Maries	- *D.* ii. 135	strong	,,	tongue	*S.* vi. 172
pass	,,	place	- *S.* vii. 101	succeeds	,,	spreads	- *E.M.* iv. 365
,,	,,	was	- *S.* viii. 74	sudden	,,	pudden	*Mi.* xii. 11
peer	,,	shire	- *P.S.* 364	swells	,,	conceals	- *M.E.* ii. 189
peers	,,	Poitiers	- *S.* iii. 99	Take	,,	weak	*E.M.* iv. 227
plac'd	,,	last	- *S.* vi. 302	tea	,,	away	*R.L.* i. 62
poor	,,	endure	- *S.* iii. 45	,,	,,	obey	- *R.L.* iii. 7
,,	,,	secure	- *S.* viii. 140	,,	,,	stay	*Mi.* ix. 27
,,	,,	sour	- *S.* ii. 33	tears	,,	theirs	- *S.* viii. 284
,,	,,	store	- *S.* ii. 117	Thames (3)	,,	beams, &c.	*R.L.* ii. 3, &c.
,,	,,	yore	*M.E.* iii. 351	throne	,,	down	*D.* i. 29
pours	,,	show'rs	*D.* ii. 3	turn	,,	morn	*M.E.* iii. 379
pow'r	,,	more	- *E.S.* i. 161	,,	,,	worn	*E.C.* 446
precise	,,	immortalize	*S.* v. 53	Urn	,,	horn	- *D.* ii. 11
preferr'd	,,	guard	- *E.M.* ii. 161	Vernon	,,	concern one	- *S.* ii. 166
prepar'd	,,	reward	*M.E.* iii. 335	Walls	,,	capitals	*P.S.* 215
priest	,,	undrest	*E.M.* iii. 157	wit	,,	delight	- *E.C.* 237
prince	,,	hence	- *E.S.* ii. 60	,,	,,	forget	*E.S.* ii. 84
proud	,,	good	- *S.* viii. 19	,,	,,	yet	*S.* v. 354
Race	,,	grass	- *E.M.* i. 210	won	,,	shown	- *Mi.* ix. 39
,,	,,	Lucrece	- *E.M.* iv. 207				

CONCORDANCE

TO THE POETICAL WORKS

OF

ALEXANDER POPE.

A, AN—ABSURD.

A, An.—*Passim.* **A'.**
To sound or sink in *cano* O or *A. D.* iv. 221
And let, *a'* God's name ev'ry Fool and Knave *E.S.* i. 85

Aaron.
Like *A.'s* serpent, swallows up the rest *E.M.* ii. 132

Abandon'd.
There are as mad *a.* Critics too *E.C.* 611

Abate.
Nothing to add, and nothing to *a. E.M.* i. 184

Abbots.
Where slumber *A.* purple as their wines *D.* iv. 302

Abchurch-Lane.
O learned Friend of *A. Mi.* iv. 33

Abdicated.
Much future Ode, and *a.* Play *D.* i. 122

A-bed.
The moon was up, and men *a. I.H.* ii. 194

Abel.
That righteous *A.* was destroy'd by Cain *E.M.* iv. 118

Abelard.
Yet, yet I love! From *A.* it came *E.A.* 7
All is not Heav'n's while *A.* has part *E.A.* 25
And is my *A.* less kind than they *E.A.* 44
And once the lot of *A.* and me *E.A.* 98
And make my soul quit *A.* for God *E.A.* 128
Come, *A.!* for what hast thou to dread *E.A.* 257
Thou, *A.! the last sad office pay *E.A.* 321
And ev'n my *A.* be lov'd no more *E.A.* 334

Abhor.
Blockheads with reason wicked wits *a. D.* iii. 175
'Tis the first Virtue, Vices to *a. S.* iii. 65
A. a Perpetuity should stand *S.* vi. 247

Abhorr'd.
The fiery soul *a.* in Catiline *E.M.* ii. 199

Abhors.
That all beside, one pities, not *a. S.* vii. 5

Abides.
But in my breast the serpent Love *a. Su.* 68

Abject.
To what base ends, and by what *a.* ways *E.C.* 520

Able.
Reason, however *a.*, cool at best *E.M.* iii. 85
Till I cry'd out: "You prove yourself so *a.*" *S.* viii. 82

Ablest.
God knows may hurt your very *a.* head *S.* vi. 103

Aboard.
They hire their sculler, and when once *a. S.* iii. 159

Abode.
With reams abundant this *a.* supply *D.* ii. 90

Surveys around her in the blest *a. D.* iii. 133
Full in my view set all the bright *a. E.A.* 127
Snatch me, just mounting, from the blest *a. E.A.* 287
Oh worthy thou of Ægypt's wife a—s *D.* iii. 207
Pride still is aiming at the blest *a. E.M.* i. 125
Here fix'd the dreadful, there the blest *a. E.M.* iii. 255
On rifted rocks, the dragon's late *a. M.* 71
Ambition first sprung from the blest *a. U.L.* 13
As thine, which visits Windsor's fam'd *a. W.F.* 229

Abortion.
Round him much Embryo, much *A.* lay *D.* i. 121
For now a—s, *all ye pregnant fair D.* iii. 314

Abound.
Words are like leaves, and where they most *a. E C.* 309

Abounds.
Barnard in spirit, sense, and truth *a. S.* iii. 85

About.—*Passim.*
And write *a.* it, Goddess, and *a.* it *D.* iv. 252

Abroad.
Did some more sober Critic come *a. P.S.* 157
On wings of winds came flying all *a. P.S.* 218
Half froth, half venom, spits himself *a. P.S.* 370
Your wine lock'd up, your butler stroll'd *a. S.* ii. 13
Your Country, chief in Arms, *a.* defend *S.* v. 3

Abs-court.
Delightful *A.*, if its fields afford *S.* vi. 232

Absence.
Say is not *a.* death to those who love *A.* 30
Condemned whole years in *a.* to deplore *E.A.* 361

Absent.
This mourned a faithless, that an *a.* love *A.* 3
For their defrauded *a.* foals they make *D.* ii. 249
Nor *a.* they, no members of her state *D.* iv. 91
A. or dead, still let a friend be dear (*rep.*) *E.* i. 13
Brutus for *a.* Portia sighs *O.* iii. 15
Yet *a.* wounds an honest author's fame *P.S.* 292
But Delia always; *a.* from her sight *Sp.* 79
And *a.* trees that tremble in the floods *W.F.* 214

Absolute.
Lest God himself should seem too *a. E.C.* 549

Absolves.
For God, not man *a.* our frailties here *E.A.* 316

Absorbs.
What is this *a.* me quite *O.* v. 9

Abstract.
A. what others feel, what others think *E.M.* iv. 45

Absurd.
This arch *A.*, that wit and fool delights *D.* i. 221
Just as *a.* for any part to claim (*rep.*) *E.M.* i. 263
'Tis phrase *a.* to call a Villain Great *E.M.* iv. 230
Of all mankind, the creatures most *a. S.* v. 359

B

ABUNDANT—ACTS.

Abundant.
With reams *a.* this abode supply *D.* ii. 90.
In one *a.* shower of Cent. per Cent. *M.E.* iii. 372

Abuse.
A., on all he lov'd, or lov'd him, spread *P.S.* 354
Let the two Curlls of Town and Court a. P.S. 380
A. the City's best good men in metre *S.* i. 39

Abus'd.
This hour she's idolis'd, the next *a. E.C.* 433
Still by himself *a.*, or disabus'd *E.M.* ii. 14
Vice, thus *a.*, demands a Nation's care *E.S.* i. 128

Abusive.
And more *a.*, calls himself my friend *P.S.* 112

Abyss.
Shot to the black *a.*, and plung'd downright *D.* ii. 288
Draw forth the monsters of th' *a.* profound *E.M.* iii. 221

Academic.
Or wanders wild in *A.* Groves *D.* iv. 490

Accent.
What's long or short, each *a.* where to place *S.* v. 207
Of whose best phrase and courtly *a.* join'd *S.* viii. 48

Accept.
Osborne and Curl *a.* the glorious strife *D.* ii. 167
A., O GARTH, the Muse's early lays *Su.* 9
A. the wreath which you deserve alone *Su.* 57

Accepted.
Each pray'r *a.*, and each wish resign'd *E.A.* 210

Accepting.
Charms by *a.*, by submitting sways *M.E.* ii. 263

Accepts.
Pleas'd, she *a.* the Hero and the Dame *D.* iv. 335

Accidents.
For ills or *a.* that chance to all *E.M.* iv. 98

Accomplish.
Proud to *a.* what such hands design'd *M.E.* iv. 196

Accomplish'd.
Receive, great Empress! thy *a.* Son *D.* iv. 282

Accord.
Ready, by force, or of your own *a. S.* vi. 250

Accorded.
The lights and shades, whose well *a.* strife *E.M.* ii. 121

According.
Th' *a.* music of a well-mix'd State *E.M.* iii. 294
Then each *a.* to the rank they bore *R.L.* iii. 34

Account.
Bring then these blessings to a strict *a. E.M.* iv. 269
This day TOM's fair *a.* has run *Mi.* xii. 3
A. for moral, as for nat'ral things E.M. i. 162
Shall we, or shall we not, *a.* him so *S.* v. 51

Accurst.
Well might you wish for change by those *a. E.* iv. 39
Oh fact *a.!* what tears has Albion shed *W.F.* 321

Accus'd.
Th' *A.* stood forth, and thus address'd the Queen *D.* iv. 420

Accuser.
A sharp *a.*, but a helpless friend *E.M.* ii. 154

Ace.
An *A.* of Hearts steps forth: the King unseen *R.L.* iii. 95
And falls like thunder on the prostrate *A. R.L.* iii. 98

Achilles.
To touch *A.'* only tender part *D.* ii. 218

Aching.
No craving void left *aking* in the breast *E.A.* 94
With honest anguish, and an *aching* head *P.S.* 38

Acid.
Where bile, and wind, and phlegm, and *a.* jar *S.* ii. 71

A-clock.
And breaks our rest, to tell us what's *a. D.* iv. 444

Acquir'd.
Spoil'd his own language, and *a.* no more *D.* iv. 320
Good from each object, from each place *a. E.M.* iv. 321

Acquires.
Mourn not, my SWIFT, at aught our realm *a. D.* i. 26

Acquit.
Why charge we Heav'n in those, in these *a. E.M.* i. 163

Acre.
To grant me this, and t'other *A. I.H.* ii. 185
Piecemeal they win this *a.* first, then that *S.* vii. 91
His Father's *A*—s *who enjoys in peace M.E.* iv. 181
A few paternal *a.* bound *O.* iv. 2
Than in five *a.* now of rented land *S.* ii. 136

Act.
But as in graceful *a.*, with awful eye *D.* iv. 199
The rising tempest puts in *a.* the soul *E.M.* ii. 105
And when in *a.* they cease, in prospect rise *E.M.* ii. 124
Th' Eternal *A.* educing good from ill *E.M.* ii. 175
Oh wealth ill-fated! which no *a.* of fame *E.M.* iv. 299
Between each *A.* the trembling salvers ring *M.E.* iv. 161
That single *a.* gives half the world the spleen *R.L.* iv. 78
And gets an *A.* of Parliament to rob *S.* viii. 143
Re-judge his a—s and dignify disgrace E. i. 30
With Edward's *a.* adorn the shining page *W.F.* 303
And a., and be, a coxcomb with success D. i. 110
Then build a new, or *a.* it in a plain *E.C.* 284
Is not to *a.* or think beyond mankind *E.M.* i. 190
He hangs between; in doubt to *a.* or rest *E.M.* ii. 7
So two consistent motions *a.* the Soul *E.M.* iii. 315
A. well your part, there all the honour lies *E.M.* iv. 191
Must *a.* on motives powerful, tho' unknown *M.E.* iii. 112
Conscious they *a.* a true Palladian part *M.E.* iv. 37
Who sees him *a.*, but envies ev'ry deed *P.C.* 25
On various tempers *a.* by various ways *R.L.* iv. 61
To *a.* consistent with himself an hour *S.* iii. 137
Shall I, in London, *a.* this idle part *S.* vi. 125
A. sins which Prisca's Confessor scarce hears *S.* vii. 40
To *a.* a Lover's or a Roman's part *U.L.* 8

Acting.
See then the *a.* and comparing pow'rs *E.M.* iii. 95
His pride in Reasoning, not in *A.* lies *M.E.* i. 118
Amphibious thing! that *a.* either part *P.S.* 326

Action.
Man, but for that, no *a.* could attend *E.M.* ii. 61
The *a.* of the stronger to suspend *E.M.* ii. 77
Some place the bliss in *a.*, some in ease *E.M.* iv. 21
His principle of *a.* once explore *M.E.* i. 27
One spring of *a.* to ourselves is lost *M.E.* i. 42
One *a.*, conduct; one, heroic love *M.E.* i. 134
Too rash for Thought, for *A.* too refin'd *M.E.* i. 201
In *a.* faithful, and in honour clear *M.E.* v. 68
Which Betterton's grave *a.* dignify'd *S.* v. 122
The Play stands still; damn *a.* and discourse *S.* v. 314
Inclines our *a.*, not constrains our will *S.* vi. 281
On human a—s reason tho' you can M.E. i. 25
Not always *A.* shew the man; we find *M.E.* i. 109
But grant that *a.* best discover man *M.E.* i. 119
By *A.!* those uncertainty divides *M.E.* i. 168
Watch all their ways and all their *a.* guide *R.L.* ii. 88
Your Arms, your *A.*, your repose to sing *S.* v. 395
And dreads more *a.*, hurries from a jail *S.* viii. 183
His a—s', passions', being's, use and end E.M. i. 66

Active.
No crab more *a.* in the dirty dance *D.* ii. 319
And, but for this, were *a.* to no end *E.M.* ii. 62
A. its task, it prompts, impels, inspires *E.M.* ii. 68
On morning wings how *a.* springs the Mind *S.* ii. 81
Sometimes a Patriot, *a.* in debate *S.* iii. 27

Actor.
Sinks the lost *A.* in the tawdry load *S.* v. 333
Himself a dinner, makes an *A.* live *S.* vii. 14
For these are a—s too, as well as those S. viii. 223

Acts.
Perhaps *a.* second to some sphere unknown *E.M.* i. 58
A. not by partial, but by gen'ral laws *E.M.* i. 146 & iv. 36

Self-love, the spring of motion, *a.* the soul *E.M.* ii. 59
And in one interest body *a.* with mind *E.M.* ii. 180
A. to one end, but *a.* by various laws *E.M.* iii. 2
You'll find if once the monarch *a.* the monk *E.M.* iv. 201
She speaks, behaves, and *a.* just as she ought *M.E.* ii. 161

Acute.
You miss my aim, I mean the most *a. S.* viii. 70

Adam.
A thing which *A.* had been pos'd to name *S.* viii. 25

Adamantine.
In *a.* chains shall Death be bound *M.* 47
Arm'd in *a.* chains *Mi.* vii. 18

Add.
This glorious Youth, and *a.* one Venus more *D.* iv. 330
Proud to my list to *a.* one Monarch more *D.* iv. 600
Nothing to *a.*, and nothing to abate *E.M.* i. 184
A. Health, and Pow'r, and ev'ry earthly thing *E.M.* iv. 159
But let me *a.*, Sir ROBERT's mighty dull *E.S.* ii. 133
Or *a.* one Patriot to the sinking state *Ep.* xiv. 4
A. Nature's, Custom's, Reason's, Passion's strife *M.E.* i. 21
To change a Flounce, or *a.* a Furbelow *R.L.* ii. 100
A. one round hundred, and (if that's not fair) (*rep.*) *S.* iv. 75
And *a.* new lustre to her silver star *W.F.* 290

Added.
An *a.* pudding solemniz'd the Lord's *M.E.* iii. 346
With *a.* years if life bring nothing new *Mi.* v. 5

Adder.
Fierce as a startled *A.*, swell'd and said *D.* iv. 373

Addison.
She deck'd like Congreve, *A.*, and Prior *D.* ii. 124
And we too boast our Garth and *A. D*, ii. 140
A Virgil here, and there an *A. M.E.* v. 62
And swear not *A.* himself was safe *P.S.* 192
No whiter page than *A.* remains *S.* v. 216

Address.
Each eager to present their first *A, D.* iv. 136
Like the last Gazette, or the last *A. E.S.* ii. 227
Th' *A.*, the Delicacy, stoops at once *M.E.* ii. 85
As some coy nymph her-lover's warm *a. W.F.* 19

Address'd.
Th' Accus'd stood forth, and thus *a.* the Queen *D.* iv. 420
Then thus *a.* the pow'r, "Hail, wayward Queen *R.L.* iv. 57
There to her Heart sad Tragedy *a—t D.* iv. 37

Adds.
That Casting-weight pride *a.* to Emptiness *P.S.* 177
Which *a.* new glory to the shining sphere *R.L.* v. 142
A. to Christ's pray'r the *Pow'r & Glory* clause *S.* vii. 108
That *a.* this wreath of Ivy to thy Bays *Su.* 10

Adieu.
Farewell, ye woods ! *a.* the light of day *A.* 94
Long lov'd, ador'd ideas, all *a. E.A.* 296
A. Distinction, Satire, Warmth and Truth *E.S.* i. 64
WITHERS *a. !* yet not with thee remove *Ep.* ix. 7
A., fond hope of mutual fire *I.H.* iii. 33
A., the heart-expanding bowl *I.H.* iii. 35
'Twas a fat Oyster—Live in peace—*A. Mi.* xi. 12
A. to Virtue, if you're once a Slave *S.* iii. 118
A., if this advice appear the worst *S.* iv. 130
A. to all the follies of the age *S.* viii. 2
A., ye vales, ye mountains, streams and groves (*rep*) *W.* 89

Adjourn.
Our fate thou only canst *a. Mi.* iv. 37

Adjust.
A. their clothes, and to confession draw *S.* viii. 242

Administer'd.
Whate'er is best *a.* is best *E.M.* iii. 304

Admiration.
His gardens next your *a.* call *M.E.* iv. 113

Admire.
The Senior's judgment all the crowd *a. D.* ii. 289
See now, what Dulness and her sons *a. D.* iii. 228
A. new light thro' holes yourselves have made *D* iv. 126
And taught the world with reason to *a. E.C.* 101
T' *a.* superior sense, and doubt their own *E.C.* 200
Her voice is all these tuneful fools *a. E.C.* 340
For fools *a.*, but men of sense approve *E.C.* 391
What, they *a.* him for his jokes *I.H.* ii. 107 s
Enough if all around him but *a. M.E.* i. 190
Not with those toys the female world *a. Mi.* v. 3
Not to *a.* is all the art I know *S.* iv. 1
A. we then what Earth's low entrails hold *S.* iv. 11
In either case, believe me, we *a. S.* iv. 21
Go then, and if you can, *a.* the state *S.* iv. 28
To form, not to *a.* but be admir'd *S.* iv. 41
A. whate'er the maddest can *a. S.* iv. 68
Show'd us that France had something to *a. S.* v. 275
Nor the vain itch t' *a.* and be admir'd *S.* viii. 10
And naked youths and painted chiefs *a. W.F.* 405

Admired.
Next Ægon sung, while Windsor groves *a. A.* 55
Oh just beheld and lost ! *a.* and mourn'd *E.* i. 3
Then most our trouble still when most *a. E.C.* 502
And Vice *a.* to find a flatt'rer there *E.C.* 551
A. such wisdom in an earthly shape *E.M.* ii. 33
No Arts essay'd, but not to be *a. Ep.* vi. 4
Th' advent'rous Baron the bright locks *a. R.L.* ii. 29
To form, not to admire, but be *a. S.* iv. 41
Nor the vain itch t' admire, and be *a. S.* viii. 10
Such was the life great Scipio once *a. W.F.* 257

Admirer.
Seek an *a.*, or would fix a friend *E.M.* iv. 44
Their happy Spots the nice *a.* take *M.E.* ii. 44

Admiring.
All comes united to th' *a.* eyes *E.C.* 250
Fanes, which *a.* Gods with pride survey *M.E.* v. 9

Admires.
A. the jay the insect's gilded wings *E.M.* iii. 55
A Nymph of Quality *a.* our Knight *M.E.* iii. 383
And ease thy heart of all that it *a. S.* iii. 76
That less *a.* the Palace than the Park *S.* iii. 113
Tho' justly Greece her eldest Sons *a. S.* v. 43
Mistake him not, he envies, not *a. S.* v. 133

Admit.
A. your Law to spare the Knight requires *E.S.* ii. 30
These shelves *a.* not any modern book *M.E.* iv. 140
Does not one table Bavius still *a. P.S.* 99
And part *a.* and part exclude the day *W.F.* 18

Admitted.
But thinks, *a.* to that equal sky *E.M.* i. 111

Admits.
Whate'er of mongrel no one class *a. D.* iv. 89
Or Change *a.* or Nature lets it fall *E.M.* iv. 115
A., and leaves them, Providence's care *M.E.* iii. 106

Adonis.
He struts *A.* and affects grimace *D.* ii. 202
Or soft *A.*, so perfum'd and fine *M.E.* iii. 73
Mourn'd *A.*, darling Youth *Mi.* vii. 10
In woods bright Venus with *A.* stray'd *Su.* 61
And break your bows, as when *A.* died *W.* 24

Adopt.
A. him Son, or Cousin at the least *S.* iv. 108

Adore.
Hear Jove! whose name my bards and I *a, D* ii. 79
Bid her be all that makes mankind *a. E.* iii. 53
Wait the great teacher Death, and God *a. E.M.* i. 92
Are what ten thousand envy and *a. E.S.* i. 166
But die, and she'll *a.* you. Then the Bust *M.E.* ii. 139
Th' inscription value, but *a.* the rust *M.E.* v. 36
Which Jews might kiss, and Infidels *a. R.L.* ii. 8

Ador'd.
In peace, great Goddess, ever be *a. D.* iii. 119
Whole years neglected, for some months *a. E.* iv. 43
Long lov'd, *a.* ideas, all adieu *E.A.* 296
Be crown'd as Monarchs, or as Gods *a. E.M.* iii. 198
One great first father, and that first *a. E.M.* iii. 226
I joyless make my once *a. Alpin Mi.* ix. 5
Her last good man dejected Rome *a. P.C.* 35
Propitious Heav'n, and ev'ry pow'r *a. R.L.* ii. 36
Why Angels call'd, and Angel-like *a. R.L.* v. 12

In ev'ry Clime *a. U.P.* 2
Or raise old warriors, whose *a.* remains *W.F.* 301

Adores.
Her too receive (for her my soul *a. D.* iv. 331
That NATURE our Society *a. D.* iv. 491
As the rapt Seraph that *a.* and burns *E.M.* i. 278
Then turns repentant, and his God *a. M.E.* i. 188
First, rob'd in white, the Nymph intent *a. R.L.* i. 123

Adorn.
Let op'ning roses knotted oaks *a. A.* 37
Till Peter's keys some christen'd Jove *a. D.* iii. 109
And a new Cibber shall the stage *a. D.* iii. 142
And shameless *Billingsgate* her robes *a. D.* iv. 26
But ev'n those clouds at last *a.* its way *E.C.* 472
The spiry fir and shapely box *a. M.* 74
See a long race thy spacious courts *a. M.* 87
Proud Vice to brand, and injur'd Worth *a. S.* v. 227
These are the talents that *a.* them all *S.* vii. 79
Now leaves the trees, and flow'rs *a.* the ground *Sp.* 43
And with fresh bays her rural shrine *a. W.* 20
Like verdant isles the sable waste *a. W.F.* 28
And realms commanded which those trees *a. W.F.* 32
With Edward's acts *a.* the shining page *W.F.* 303

Adorn'd.
With softest manners, gentlest acts *a.* E i. 4
By foreign hands thy humble grave *a. U.L.* 53

Adriatic.
Where, eas'd of Fleets, the *A.* main *D.* iv. 309

Advance.
She sees a Mob of Metaphors *a. D.* i. 67
Downward to climb, and backward to *a. D.* ii. 320
But who, weak rebels, more *a.* her cause *D.* iv. 86
Dunce scorning Dunce beholds the next *a. D.* iv. 137
Show all his paces, not a step *a. D.* iv. 266
But wherefore waste I words? I see *a. D.* iv. 271
Some ne'er *a.* a judgment of their own *E.C.* 408
Thence Arts o'er all the northern world *a. E.C.* 711
Nor one that Temperance *a. I.H.* i. 61
See lofty Lebanon his head *a. M.* 25
Tho' what he learns he speaks, and may *a. M.E.* i. 3
Spontaneous beauties all around *a. M.E.* iv. 67
See, shady forms *a. O.* i. 65
Not to go back, is somewhat to *a. S.* iii. 53
A. thy golden Mountain to the skies *S.* iv. 73
A. and conquer! go where glory calls *S.* vi. 47

Advanc'd.
But more *a.* behold with strange surprise *E.C.* 223
Old Father Thames *a.* his reverend head *W.F.* 330

Advances.
No thought *a.* but her Eddy Brain *M.E.* ii. 121
My Lord *a.* with majestic mien *M.E.* iv. 127

Advantage.
True Wit is Nature to *a.* dress'd *E.C.* 297
Count all th' *a.* prosp'rous Vice attains *E.M.* iv. 89
In Parts superior what *a.* lies *E.M.* iv. 259
For, mark th' *a.*, just so many score *S.* iv. 77

Advent'rous.
Th' *a.* Baron the bright locks admired *R.L.* ii. 29
Burns to encounter two *a.* Knights *R.L.* iii. 26

Advice.
Produc'd his Play, and begg'd the Knight's *a. E.C.* 274
Be niggards of *a.* on no pretence *E.C.* 578
And good Simplicius asks of her *a. M.E.* ii. 32
A., and (as you use) without a Fee *S.* i. 10
Adieu, if this *a.* appear the worst *S.* iv. 130
None should, by my *a.*, learn Virtue there *S.* viii. 97

Advise.
Form'd but to check, delib'rate, and *a. E.M.* ii. 70
But talk with Celsus, Celsus will *a. S.* i. 19
I'll do what Mead and Cheselden *a. S.* iii. 51

Advis'd.
And well (he thought) *a.* him, "Live like me" *M.E.* iii. 316

Advocate.
The Frail one's *a.*, the Weak one's friend *M.E.* ii. 30
And a—s *for folly dead and gone S.* v. 34

Adust.
No meagre, muse-rid mope, *a.* and thin *D.* ii. 37
The same *a.* complexion has impell'd *M.E.* i. 107

Ægon.
Hylas and Æ. sung their rural lays *A.* 2
Next Æ. sung, while Windsor groves admir'd *A.* 55
Hylas and Æ.'s rural lays I sing A. 6

Æneas.
Safe and unseen the young Æ. past *D.* iv. 290

Aerial.
And all th' *a.* audience clap their wings *Sp.* 16
Soft o'er the shrouds *a.* whispers breathe *R.L.* ii. 57
By laws eternal to th' *a.* kind *R.L.* ii. 76
Soon as she spreads her hand, th' *a.* guard *R.L.* iii. 31
There towns *a.* on the waving tree *E.M.* iii. 182
Or fetch th' *a.* eagle to the ground *E.M.* iii. 222

Æson.
A new edition of old Æ. gave *D.* iv. 122

Æschylus.
Another Æ. appears! prepare *D.* iii. 313

Æther.
Whate'er of life all-quick'ning *æ.* keeps *E.M.* iii. 115
Some in the fields of purest Æ. play *R.L.* ii. 77

Æthereal, *see* Ethereal.
Th' Æ. spirit o'er its leaves shall move *M.* 11

Ætna.
Shall burning Æ. if a sage requires *E.M.* iv. 123
Thou wert from Æ.'s burning entrails torn A. 91

Afar.
Held from *a.*, aloft, th' immortal prize *E.C.* 96

Affair.
About some great *A.* at Two *I.H.* ii. 74 s
A hundred other men's *a*—s *I.H.* ii. 69 s
I was not born for Courts or great *a. P.S.* 267

Affectation.
There *A.* with a sickly mien *R.L.* iv. 31
Or A—s *quite reverse the soul M.E.* i. 66

Affect.
Let Friend *a.* to speak as Terence spoke *D.* iv. 223
Why pique all mortals, yet *a.* a name *M.E.* ii. 61

Affected.
Or damn all Shakespear, like th' *a.* Fool *S.* v. 105

Affects.
He struts Adonis, and *a.* grimace *D.* ii. 202
In wit, as nature, what *a.* our hearts *E.C.* 243
That Fop, whose pride *a.* a patron's name *P.S.* 291
Spenser himself *a.* the Obsolete *S.* v. 97
Takes God to witness he *a.* your cause *S.* vii. 76
He past it o'er; *a.* an easy smile *S.* viii. 122

Affections.
Desires compos'd, *a.* ever ev'n *E.A.* 213
Of Manners gentle, of *A.* mild *Ep.* xi. 1

Affirm.
A. 'twas Travel made them what they were *S.* viii. 79

Affliction.
Of all *a.* taught a lover yet *E.A.* 189

Affluence.
Let Joy or Ease, let *A.* or Content *Mi.* v. 11

Afford.
And for those Arts mere Instinct could *a. E.M.* iii. 197
Let Courtly Wits to Wits *a.* supply *E.S.* ii. 171
Some ends of Verse his Betters might *a. Mi.* iii. 5
Why deck'd with all that land and sea *a. R.L.* v. 11
Shades, that to Bacon could retreat *a. S.* ii. 175
Delightful Abs-court, if its fields *a. S.* vi. 232
Buy ev'ry pullet tbey *a.* to eat *S.* vi. 243

Affords.
Nature *a.* at least a glimm'ring light *E.C.* 21
Has what the frugal, dirty soil *a. E.S.* ii. 174
And see what comfort it *a.* our end *M.E.* iii. 298

AFFORDS—AIM.

One solid dish his week-day meal *a. M.E.* iii. 345
But gudgeons, flounders, what my Thames *a. S.* ii. 142
What dear delights to Britons Farce *a. S.* v. 310

Affright.
What happier natures shrink at with *a. E.M.* ii. 229

Affrighted.
And screams of horror rend th' *a.* skies *R.L.* iii. 156

Affrights.
A. the beggar whom he longs to eat *M.E.* iii. 196

Affront.
But when he heard th' *A.* the fellow gave *E.S.* ii. 152
Hold, Sir ! for God's sake where's th' *A.* to you *E.S.* ii. 157
When Truth or Virtue an *A.* endures (*rep.*) *E.S.* ii. 199
But why insult the poor, *a.* the great *P.S.* 360

Afraid.
Still pleas'd to praise, yet not *a.* to blame *E.C.* 742
Men not *a.* of God, *a.* of me *E.S.* ii. 209
Willing to wound, and yet *a.* to strike *P.S.* 203
I quak'd at heart ; and still *a.*, to see *S.* viii. 180

Afric.
Of Asia's troops, and *A. 's* sable sons *R.L.* iii. 82
A verier monster, than on *A.* shore, *S.* viii. 28

After.—*Passim.*

Afterward, Afterwards.—*Passim.*

Again.—*Passim.*

Against.—*Passim.*

Age.
To hatch a new Saturnian *a.* of lead *D.* i. 28
The Classics of an *A.* that heard of none *D.* i. 148
Thus visit not thy own ! on this blest *a. D.* iii. 121
Divides a friendship long confirm'd by *a. D.* iii. 174
Preacher at once and Zany of thy *a. D.* iii. 206
The third mad passion of thy doting *a. D.* iii. 304
And promis'd vengeance on a barb'rous *a. D.* iv. 40
Like them to shine thro' long succeeding *a. E.* iii. 11
Her modest cheek shall warm a future *a. E.* iii. 56
Custom grown blind with *A.*, must be your guide *E.* iv. 33
Those, *A.* or Sickness soon or late disarms *E.* iv. 60
Religion, Country, genius of his *A. E.C.* 121
Destructive War, and all-involving *A. E.C.* 184
No longer now that golden *a.* appears *E.C.* 478
In the fat *a.* of pleasure, wealth and ease *E.C.* 534
And the same *a.* saw Learning fall, and Rome *E.C.* 686
Stemm'd the wild torrent of a barb'rous *a. E.C.* 695
See some fit Passion ev'ry *a.* supply *E.M.* ii. 273
And beads and pray'r-books are the toys of *a. R.M.* ii. 280
That pointed back to youth, this on to *a. E.M.* iii. 144
Shall then this verse to future *a.* pretend *E.M.* iv. 339
A Patriot is a Fool in ev'ry *a. E.* i. 41
Filled with the Sense of *A.*, the Fire of Youth *Ep.* ii. 7
O soft Humanity, in *A.* beloved *Ep.* ix. 4
Still leave some ancient virtues to our *a. Ep.* ix. 10
Form'd to delight at once and lash the *a. Ep.* xi. 4
The promis'd father of the future *a. M.* 56
From loveless youth to unrespected *a. M.* ii. 125
As leaves them scarce a subject in their *A. M.E.* ii. 222
A Youth of Frolics, an old *A.* of Cards *M.E.* ii. 244
The Crown of Poland, venal twice an *a. M.E.* iii. 127
Where *A.* and Want sit smiling at the gate *M.E.* iii. 266
Another *a.* shall see the golden Ear *M.E.* iv. 173
Some felt the silent stroke of mould'ring *a. M.E.* v. 11
If there's a Senior, who contemns this *a. Mi.* ii. 22
In ev'ry *a.*, in ev'ry state *O.* ii. 30
Commanding tears to stream thro' ev'ry *a. P.C.* 6
The good man walk'd innoxious thro' his *a. P.S.* 395
To rock the cradle of reposing *a. P.S.* 409
Charm'd the small-pox, or chas'd old *a.* away *R.L.* v. 20
Publish the present *a.* ; but where my text *S.* i. 59
Whether Old *A.*, with faint but cheerful ray *S.* i. 93
In flow'r of *a.* you perish for a song *S.* i. 102
And more the sickness of long life, Old *A.* (*rep.*) *S.* ii. 88
Public too long, ah let me hide my *a. S.* iii. 5
Say at what *a.* a Poet grows divine *S.* v. 30
From eldest Heywood, down to Cibber's *A. S.* v. 88
Has sanctify'd whole poems for an *a. S.* v. 114
And swear all shame is lost in George's *A. S.* v. 126

Has *a.* but melted those rough parts away *S.* vi. 318
Walk sober off ; before a sprightlier *a. S.* vi. 321
Adieu to all the follies of the *a. S.* viii. 2
Most souls, 'tis true, but peep out once an *a. U.L.* 17
Father of All ! in ev'ry *A. U.P.* 1
Surrey, the Granville of a former *a. W.F.* 292
Stretch his long triumphs down thro' ev'ry *a. W.F.* 304
It grows their *A. 's prudence to pretend M.E.* ii. 236
Heav'ns ! what a pile ! whole a—s perish there ! D. iii. 77
To future *a.* may thy dulness last *D.* iii. 289
Thro' twilight *a.* hunt th' Athenian fowl *D.* iv. 361
Nor tears for *a.* taught to flow io vain *E.A.* 28
Then, *a.* hence, when all my woes are o'er *E.A.* 345
Whose honours with increase of *a.* grow *E.C.* 191
Which from the first has shone on *a.* past *E.C.* 402
Athens and Rome in better *a.* knew *E.C.* 644
Now for two *a.* having snatch'd from fate *Ep.* viii. 3
Thro' climes and *a.*, bear each form and name *E.M.* v. 32
Then future *a.* with delight shall see *M.E.* v. 59
Or wedg'd whole *a.* in a bodkin's eye *R.L.* ii. 128
And stretch the Ray to *A.* yet unborn *S.* v. 228
Or bid the new be English, *a.* hence *S.* vi. 169
Not thus the land appear'd in *a.* 'past *W.F.* 43
Consults the dead and lives past *a.* o'er *W.F.* 248

Ago.—*Passim.*

Agonize.
To smart and *a.* at ev'ry pore *E.M.* i. 198

Agree.
Is the great chain that draws all to *a. E.M.* i. 33
But first consider how those Just *a. E.M.* iv. 134
How Plato's, Bacon's, Newton's looks *a. M.E.* v. 60
Careless how ill I with myself *a. S.* iii. 175
They had, and greater Virtues, I'll *a. S.* v. 96
The wisest man might blush, I must *a. S.* vi. 228
The bleating sheep with my complaints *a. Su.* 19
And where, tho' all things differ, all *a. W.F.* 16

Agreeable.
Soft and *A.* come never there *M.E.* iv. 102

Agreed.
But where th' Extreme of Vice, was ne'er *a. E.M.* ii. 221
Heroes are much the same, the point 's *a. E.M.* iv. 219
But hear me further. Japhet, 'tis *a. E.S.* ii. 185
But you are tired—I'll tell a tale—*A. M.E.* iii. 338

Agrees.
A. as ill with Rufa studying Locke *M.E.* ii. 23

Aggravates.
But ah ! what *a.* the killing smart *Mi.* ix. 53

Ah.—*Passim.*

Aid.
If Music meanly borrows *a.* from sense *D.* iv. 64
And Metaphysic calls for *a.* on sense *D.* iv. 646
Heav'n first taught letters for some wretch's *a. E.A.* 51
Tho' meant each other's *a.*, like man and wife *E.C.* 83
Some drily plain, without invention's *a. E.C.* 114
While expletives their feeble *a.* do join *E.C.* 346
Made Beast in *a.* of Man, and Man of Beast *E.M.* iii. 24
Then shar'd the Tyranny, then lent it *a. E.M.* iii. 247
It raises Armies in a Nation's *a. M.E.* iii. 31
Sad chance of war ! now destitute of *a. R.L.* iii. 63
GRANVILLE commands ; your *a.*, O Muses, bring *W.F.* 5
In vain on Father Thames she calls for *a. W.F.* 197
What a—s, what armies to assert her cause D. iii. 128
To a. our cause if Heav'n thou canst not bend D. iii. 307
No more these scenes my meditation *a. E.A.* 161
Pride then was not ; nor Arts that Pride to *a. E.M.* iii. 151
All fear, none *a.* you, and few understand *E.M.* iv. 266
Spirit of Arnall ! *a.* me while I lie *E.S.* ii. 129
The sick and weak the healing plant shall *a. M.* 15

Aid-de-Camp.
And thou ! his *A.*, lead on my sons *D.* i. 305

Ail.
Or heal, old Narses, thy obscener *a. M.E.* iii. 89
Ev'n those you touch not, hate you. What should *a.* them *S.* i. 41

Aim.
Which, as more pond'rous, made its *a.* more true *D.* i. 171

AIM—ALFRED.

Those, that imparted, court a nobler *a. E.M.* ii. 99
Oh Happiness ! our being's end and *a. E.M.* iv. 1
That REASON, PASSION, answer one great *a. E.M.* iv. 395
Than ev'n that Passion, if it has no *A. M.E.* iii. 156
You miss my *a.*, I mean the most acute *S.* viii. 70
But see how oft ambitious *a*—s are cross'd *R.L.* v. 107
Let others *a.* : '*tis yours to shake the soul* D. ii. 225
A. not at Joy, but rest content with Ease *E.* iv. 48
Shall parts so various *a.* at nothing new *M.E.* i. 286
Bulls *a.* their horns, and Asses lift their heels *S.* i. 86
That when I *a.* at praise, they say I bite *S.* v. 409

Aim'd.
Thrice Budgel *a.* to speak, but thrice supprest *D.* ii. 397
Had *a.*, like him, by Chastity at praise *M.E.* i. 217

Aiming.
Pride still is *a.* at the blest abodes *E.M.* i. 125

Air.
Whether thou choose Cervantes' serious *a. D.* i. 21
She form'd this image of well-body'd *a. D.* ii. 42
A place there is betwixt earth, *a.*, and seas *D.* ii. 83
His papers light fly diverse, tost to *a. D.* ii. 114
As from the blanket, high in *a.*, he flies *D.* ii. 152
And one bright blaze turos Learning into *a. D.* iii. 78
But lo ! to dark encounter in mid *a. D.* iii. 265
Foreign her *a.*, her robe's discordant pride *D.* iv. 47
There mov'd Montalto with superior *a. D.* iv. 105
And last turn'd *A.*, the Echo of a Sound *D.* iv. 322
Suckled, and cheer'd, with *a.*, and sun, and show'r *D.* iv. 406
Once brightest shin'd this child of Heat and *A. D.* iv. 424
Match Raphael's grace with thy lov'd Guido's *a. E.* iii. 36
And breathe an *a.* divine on ev'ry face *E.* iii. 72
Drags from the Town to wholesome Country *a. E.* v. 2
Love, free as *a.*, at sight of human ties *E.* i. 75
That never *a.* or ocean felt the wind *E.M.* i. 167
See, thro' this *a.*, this ocean, and this earth *E.M.* i. 233
Go, measure earth, weigh *a.*, and state the tides *E.M.* ii. 20
Or breathes thro' *a.*, or shoots beneath the deeps *E.M.* iii. 116
The young dismiss'd to wander earth or *a. E.M.* iii. 127
On *a.* or sea new motions he imprest *E.M.* iv. 125
Seeks freshest pasture and the purest *a. M.* 99
Dip in the Rainbow, trick her off in *a. M.E.* ii. 18
But the good Bishop, with a meeker *a. M.E.* iii. 105
Rous'd by the Prince of *A.*, the whirlwinds sweep *M.E.* iii. 353
The well-bred cuckolds in St. James's *a. M.E.* iii. 388
So proud, so grand ; and that stupendous *a. M.E.* iv. 101
And whisper with that soft deluding *a. Mi.* ix. 7
In broken *a.*, trembling, the wild music floats *O.* i. 17
Content to breathe his native *a. O.* iv. 3
Of thousand bright Inhabitants of *A. R.L.* i. 28
Think what an equipage thou hast in *A. R.L.* i. 45
From earthly vehicles to these of *a. R.L.* i. 50
And sport and flutter in the fields of *A. R.L.* i. 66
Late, as I rang'd the crystal wilds of *a. R.L.* i. 107
The rest, the winds dispers'd in empty *a. R.L.* ii. 46
He summons strait his Denizens of *a. R.L.* ii. 55
Or suck the mists in grosser *a.* below *R.L.* ii. 83
Chang'd to a bird, and sent to flit in *a. R.L.* ii. 123
While fish in streams or birds delight in *a. R.L.* iii. 163
Here in a grotto, shelter'd close from *a. R.L.* iv. 21
The Goddess with a discontented *a. R.L.* iv. 79
Sooner let earth, *a.*, sea to Chaos fall *R.L.* iv. 119
That while my nostrils draw the vital *a. R.L.* iv. 137
Now Jove suspends his golden scales in *a. R.L.* v. 71
A sudden star, it shot thro' liquid *a. R.L.* v. 127
The temp'rate sleeps, and spirits light as *a. S.* ii. 74
If such a Doctrine, in St. James's *a. S.* iii. 110
This vault of *A.*, this congregated Ball *S.* iv. 5
Or snatch me, o'er the earth, or thro' the *a. S.* v. 346
Stept from its pedestal to take the *a. S.* vi. 122
Whose *a.* cries Arm ! whose very look's an oath *S.* viii. 261
The Sun's mild lustre warms the vital *a. Sp.* 74
As into *a.* the purer spirits flow *U.L.* 25
Shall list'ning in mid *a.* suspend their wings *W.* 54
Who claim'd the skies, dispeopled *a.* and floods *W.F.* 47
And high in *a.* Britannia's standard flies *W.F.* 110
They fall, and leave their little lives in *a. W.F.* 134
And now his shorter breath, with sultry *a. W.F.* 195
She looks, and breathes herself into their *a*—s *D.* ii. 264
As breathe, or pause, by fits the *a.* divine *D.* ii. 394
Ungrateful wretch, with mimic *a.* grown pert *Mi.* ix. 65

Exalts her in enliv'ning *a. O.* i. 27
While solemn *a.* improve the sacred fire *O.* i. 129
Assist their blushes, and inspire their *a. R.L.* ii. 98
Faints into *a.* and laoguishes with pride *R.L.* iv. 34
When *a.*, and flights, and screams, and scolding fail *R.L.* v. 32
Let vernal *a.* thro' trembling osiers play *Sp.* 5
The *a.*-built *Castle, and the golden Dream D.* iii. 10

Airy.
Thee, drest in Fancy's *a.* beam *I.H.* iii. 41
Of *a.* Elves by moonlight shadows seen *R.L.* i. 31
Loose to the wind their *a.* garments flew *R.L.* ii. 63
Straight hover round the Fair her *a.* band *R.L.* iii. 113
But *a.* substance soon unites again *R.L.* iii. 152
If e'er with *a.* horns I planted heads *R.L.* iv. 71
Oft as in *a.* rings they skim the heath *W.F.* 131
Here was she seen o'er *a.* wastes to rove *W.F.* 167

Aisles.
Long-sounding *a.*, and intermingled graves *E.A.* 164

Ajax.
When *A.* strives some rock's vast weight to throw *E.C.* 370
But stern as *A.*' spectre, strode away *D.* iv. 274

Aking, see Aching.

Alans.
Great nurse of Goths, of *A.*, and of Huns *D.* iii. 90

Alaric.
See *A.'s* stern port ! the martial frame *D.* iii. 91

Alarm.
Who felt the wrong, or fear'd it, took th' *a. S.* v. 255.
And all Olympus rings with loud a—s *R.L.* v. 48

Alarm'd.
'Twas thus Calypso once each heart *a. M.E.* ii. 45

Alas.—*Passim.*

Albion.
When *A.* sends her eager sons to war *W.F.* 106
Whom not th' extended *A.* could contain *W.F.* 315
Oh fact accurst ! what tears has *A.* shed *W.F.* 321
And A.'s cliffs resound the rural lay Sp. 6
Touch the fair fame of *A.* golden days *W.F.* 424

Albutius.
Swears, like *A.*, a good cook away *S.* ii. 64

Alcides.
The great *A.*, ev'ry labour past *S.* v. 17

Alcove.
Gallant and gay in Cliveden's proud *a. M.E.* iii. 307

Alders.
And verdant *a.* form'd a quiv'ring shade *Su.* 4
The Loddon slow, with verdant *a.* crown'd *W.F.* 342

Alderman.
So by each Bard an *A.* shall sit *D.* iv. 131
Tho' my own A.-men conferr'd the bays D. iii. 279
Appear'd Apollo's May'r and *A. D.* iv. 116
Two *A.* dispute it with an Ass *S.* vi. 105

Aldgate.
There all from Paul's to *A.* drink and sleep *D.* ii. 346

Aldus.
These *A.* printed, those Du Sueil has bound *M.E.* iv. 136

Ale-house.
Not sulphur-tipt, emblaze an *A.* fire *D.* i. 235
Thee shall each *a.*, thee each gill-house mourn *D.* iii. 147

Alexandrine.
A needless *A.* ends the song *E.C.* 356

Alexis.
While your *A.* pines in hopeless love *Su.* 24
He said ; *A.*, take this pipe, the same *Su.* 41
But your *A.* knows no sweets but you *Su.* 70
Here shall I try the sweet A.' strain W. 11

Alfred.
And virtuous *A.*, a more sacred Name *S.* v. 8

ALIKE—ALPS.

Alike.—*Passim*.

Alive.

We'd be the best good-natur'd things *a*. *E.J.S.* 14
Or touch, if tremblingly *a*. all o'er *E.M.* i. 197
Would Chloe know if you're *a*. or dead *M.E.* ii. 177
A., ridiculous, and dead, forgot *M.E.* ii. 248
Statues of Men, scarce less *a*. than they *M.E.* v. 10
And both the struggling figures seem *a*. *Mi.* ix. 32
Nor know, if Dennis be *a*. or dead *P.S.* 270
Her joy in gilded Chariots, when *a*. *R.L.* i. 55
Not youthful kings in battle seiz'd *a*. *R.L.* iv. 3
And burn in Cupid's flames, but burn *a*. *R.L.* v. 102
Indebted to no Prince or Peer *a*. *S.* vi. 69

All.—*Passim*.

The great directing Mind of *A*. ordains *E.M.* i. 266
With singing, laughing, ogling, and *a*. *that R.L.* iii. 18
Oh *A*.-accomplished *St. John* deck thy shrine *E.S.* ii. 139
Chatting and laughing *all-a-row I.H.* ii. 136
Some emanation of th' *a*.-*beauteous* mind *E.A.* 62
A.-*bounteous*, fragrant Grains and Golden show'rs *D.* ii. 4
In vain, in vain, the *a*.-*composing* Hour *D.* iv. 627
Oh curst, dear horrors of *a*.-*conscious* night *E.A.* 229
See the wide waste of *a*.-*devouring* years *M.E.* v. 1
Tho' the same sun with *a*.-*diffusive* rays *M.E.* i. 145
O Death *a*.-*eloquent!* you only prove *E.A.* 335
One *a*.-*extending*, all-preserving Soul *E.M.* iii. 22
Destructive War, and *a*.-*involving* Age *E.C.* 184
One all-extending, *a*.-*preserving* Soul *E.M.* iii. 22
Whate'er of life *a*.-*quick'ning* æther keeps *E.M.* iii. 115
A.-*seeing* in thy mists, we want no guide *D.* iv. 469
Sleep's *a*.-*subduing* charms who dares defy *D.* ii. 373

Allegiance.

Love all the faith, and all th' *a*. then *E.M.* iii. 235

Alien.

Let humble *A*., with an awkward Shame *E.S.* i. 135

Alley.

Grove nods to grove, each *A*. has a brother *M.E.* iv. 117
Now sweep those *A*—s they were born to shade *M.E.* iv. 98

Allow.

Then share thy pain, *a*. that sad relief *E.A.* 49
The pow'r of Music all our hearts *a*. *E.C.* 382
All may *a*.; but seek your friendship too *E.C.* 565
Whom all Lord Chamberlains *a*. the Stage *E.S.* i. 42
They too may be corrupted, you'll *a*. *E.S.* ii. 126
A. him but his plaything of a Pen *S.* v. 193
Or, I'm content, *a*. me Dryden's strains *S.* vi. 145
But that the cure is starving, all *a*. *S.* vii. 10
These as good works, 'tis true, we all *a*. *S.* vii. 121
What tho' no sacred earth *a*. thee room *U.L.* 61

Allure.

If Parts *a*. thee, think how Bacon shin'd *E.M.* iv. 281

Alluring.

Fair Coursers, Vases, and *a*. Dames *M.E.* iii. 70

Ally.

Wants, frailties, passions, closer still *a*. *E.M.* ii. 253

Ally'd.

Remembrance and reflection how *a*. *E.M.* i. 225
The virtue nearest to our vice *a*. *E.M.* ii. 196
Reserve with Frankness, Art with Truth *a*. *M.E.* ii. 277

Alma Mater.

And *A*. lie dissolv'd in Port *D*. iii. 338

Almighty.

No ('tis reply'd), the first *A*. Cause *E.M.* i. 145
Preserve *A*. Providence *I.H.* ii. 23 *s*

Almost.—*Passim*.

Alms.

Gave *a*. at Easter, in a Christian trim *M.E.* ii. 57
There broken vows and death-bed *a*. are found *R.L.* v. 117
He feeds you *A*.-house, neat but void of state *M.E.* iii. 265

Aloft.

Held from afar, *a*., th' immortal prize *E.C.* 96

Returning Justice lift *a*. her scale *M*. 18
The light Coquettes in Sylphs *a*. repair *R.L.* i. 65

Alone.

Fear held them mute. *A*., untaught to fear *D*. ii. 57
And modest as the maid that sips *a*. *D*. iii. 144
Not those *a*. who passive own her laws *D*. iv. 85
Words are Man's province, Words we teach *a*. *D*. iv. 150
Give law to Words, or war with Words *a*. *D*. iv. 178
That which my Priests, and mine *a*. maintain *D*. iv. 135
O Muse! relate (for you can tell *a*. *D*. iv. 619
Who seek in love for aught but love *a*. *E.A.* 84
Fill my fond heart with God *a*., for he (*rep*.) *E.A.* 205
A fool might once himself *a*. expose *E.C.* 7
And which a master-hand *a*. can reach *E.C.* 145
Some to Conceit *a*. their taste confine *E.C.* 289
These equal syllables *a*. require *E.C.* 344
Which not *a*. the southern wit sublimes *E.C.* 400
In youth *a*. its empty praise we boast *E.C.* 496
That not *a*. what to your sense is due *E.C.* 564
So Man, who here seems principal *a*. *E.M.* i. 57
If Man *a*. engross not Heav'n's high care (*rep*.) *E.M.* i. 119
Is Heav'n unkind to Man and Man *a*. *E.M.* i. 186
The pow'rs of all subdu'd by thee *a*. *E.M.* i. 231
Nor God *a*. in the still calm we find *E.M.* ii. 109
All serv'd, all serving: nothing stands *a*. *E.M.* iii. 25
Is thine *a*. the seed that strews the plain *E.M.* iii. 37
Not man *a*., but all that roam the wood *E.M.* iii. 119
Each loves itself, but not itself *a*. *E.M.* iii. 121
He sees, why Nature plants in Man *a*. *E.M.* iii. 345
But Health consists in Temperance *a*. *E.M.* iv. 81
But fools the Good *a*. unhappy call *E.M.* iv. 97
Virtue *a*. is Happiness below *E.M.* iv. 310
Yet touch'd and sham'd by Ridicule *a*. *E.S.* ii. 211
My Lord *a*. knows how to live *I.H.* ii. 209
A., in company: in place, or out *M.E.* i. 27
Search then the RULING PASSION: there, *a*. *M.E.* i. 174
When 'tis by that *a*. she can be borne *M.E.* ii. 60
Some flying stroke *a*. can hit 'em right *M.E.* ii. 154
A Woman's seen in Private life *a*. *M.E.* ii. 200
Yet hate repose, and dread to be *a*. *M.E.* ii. 228
Rare monkish Manuscripts for Hearne *a*. *M.E.* iv. 9
'Tis Use alone that sanctifies Expense *M.E.* iv. 179
Were lovely SHARPER mine, and mine *a*. *Mi.* ix. 16
All *a*. O. i. 101
Such Plays *a*. should win a British ear *P.C.* 45
Should such a man, too fond to rule *a*. *P.S.* 197
Dryden *a*. (what wonder?) came not nigh (*rep*.) *P.S.* 245
Satire be kind, and let the wretch *a*. *S*. iii. 135
That very night he longs to lie *a*. *S*. iii. 149
Will any mortal let himself *a*. *S*. iv. 55
If wealth *a*. then make and keep us blest *S*. iv. 95
The Cordial Drop of Life is Love *a*. *S*. iv. 127
A. deserves the favour of the Great *S*. v. 349
There all *a*., and compliments apart *S*. vi. 210
Is known *a*. to that Directing Pow'r *S*. vi. 278
For such *a*. the Great rebukes endure *S*. viii. 282
To Maids *a*. and Children are reveal'd *R.L.* i. 38
But ev'ry eye was fixed on her *a*. *R.L.* ii. 6
The sister-lock now sits uncouth, *a*. *R.L.* iv. 171
To Proculus *a*., confessed in view *R.L.* v. 126
A heap of dust *a*. remains of thee *U.L.* 73
Or think The Lord *a*. of Man *U.P.* 23
And arms employ'd on birds and beasts *a*. *W.F.* 374

Along.—*Passim*.

Aloud.

I call *a*., it hears not what I say *E.A.* 237
And others roar *a*., "Subscribe, subscribe" *P.S.* 114
And maids turn'd bottles, call *a*. for corks *R.L.* iv. 54
Sing thy sonorous verse, but not *a*. *S*. vi. 109

Alpen.

I joyless make my once ador'd *A*. *Mi.* ix. 5

Alphabet.

While tow'ring o'er the *A*., like Saul *D*. iv. 217

Alpheus.

As under seas *A*.' secret sluice *D*. ii. 341

Alps.

Together o'er the *A*. methinks we fly *E*. iii. 25
Rise *A*. between us! and whole oceans roll *E.A.* 290
So pleas'd at first the tow'ring *A*. we try *E.C.* 225
Hills peep o'er Hills, and *A*. on *A*. arise *E.C.* 232

Already.—*Passim.*

Alsop.
And *A.* never but like Horace joke *D.* iv. 224

Altar.
Inspired he seizes; these an *a.* raise *D.* i. 157
That *a.* crowns; a folio Common place *D.* i. 159
Love finds an *a.* for forbidden fires *E.A.* 182
Rise in the grove, before the *a.* rise *E.A.* 265
Still green with Bays each ancient *a.* stands *E.C.* 181
Should'ring God's *a.* a vile image stands *M.E.* iii. 293
But chiefly Love—to Love an *a.* built *R.L.* ii. 37
Whose *A.*, Earth, Sea, Skies *U.P.* 50
When *victims at yon* a's *foot we lay E.A.* 108
Th' inferior Priestess, at her *a.* side *R.L.* i. 117
Yet then, to those dread—s as I drew *E.A.* 115
While *A.* blaze and Angels tremble round *E.A.* 176
Nay, fly to *A.*, there they'll talk you dead *E.C.* 624
A. grew marble then, and reek'd with gore *E.M.* iii. 264
See thy bright *a.* throng'd with prostrate kings *M.* 93
On shining *A.* of Japan they raise *R.L.* iii. 107
As Heav'n's own Oracles from *A.* heard *S.* v. 28
A milk-white bull shall at your *a.* stand *Sp.* 47

Alter.
What's Property? dear Swift, you see it *a.* *S.* ii. 167

Alter'd.
The Case is *a.*—you may then proceed *S.* i. 154

Alters.
It gilds all objects, but it *a.* none *E.C.* 317

Alternate.
And bid *a.* passions fall and rise *E.C.* 375
And Taunts *a.* innocently flew *S.* v. 250
His swelling waters and *a.* tides *W.F.* 334

Although.—*Passim.*

Alum.
Or *A.* styptics with contracting pow'r *R.L.* ii. 131

Always.—*Passim.*

Am, &c.—*Passim.*

Amain.
Vice with such Giant strides comes on *a.* *E.S.* ii. 6

Amaranthine.
Or *A.* bow'rs *O.* i. 76
There while you rest in *A.* bow'rs *W.* 73

Amaze.
In Tot'nham fields the brethren with *a.* *D.* ii. 261
And pay the Great our homage of *A.* *S.* iv. 17
A. th' unlearn'd, and make the learned smile E.C. 327
Escape in Monsters, and *a.* the town *D.* i. 38

Amaz'd.
Convinc'd, *a.*, he checks the bold design *E.C.* 136
They stand *a.* and think me grown *I.H.* ii. 123
A., confus'd, he found his pow'r expir'd *R.L.* iii. 145
Sudden they seize th' *a.*, defenceless prize *W.F.* 109

Amazement.
Not more *a.* seiz'd on Circe's guests *S.* viii. 166

Amazing.
Alike essential to th' *a.* whole *E.M.* i. 248

Amazon.
His warlike *A.* her host invades *R.L.* iii. 67

Amber.
And liquid *a.* drop from ev'ry thorn *A.* 38
Pretty! in *a.* to observe the forms *P.S.* 169
Sir Plume of *a.* snuff-box justly vain *R.L.* iv. 123
And trees weep *a.* on the banks of Po *Sp.* 62
The weeping *a.* or the balmy tree *W.F.* 30
For me the balm shall bleed, and *a.* flow *W.F.* 393

Ambergrise.
In heaps, like *A.*, a stink it lies *M.E.* iii. 235

Ambition.
How quick *A.* hastes to ridicule *D.* iv. 547

What Charms could Faction, what *A.* lull *D.* iv. 623
By vain *a.* still to make them move *E.C.* 65
To low *a.*, and the pride of kings *E.M.* i. 2
Pours fierce *A.* in a Cæsar's mind *E.M.* i. 159
The same *a.* can destroy or save *E.M.* ii. 201
To one Man's pow'r, *a.*, lucre, lust *E.M.* iii. 270
If all, united, thy *a.* call *E.M.* iv. 285
'Tis Av'rice all, *A.* is no more *E.S.* i. 162
When black *A.* stains a public Cause *E.S.* ii. 228
Were means not ends; *A.* was the vice *M.E.* i. 215
Glorious *A.*! Peter, swell thy store *M.E.* iii. 125
A. sigh'd: she found it vain to trust *M.E.* v. 19
'Twas all th' *A.* his high soul could feel *Mi.* iii. 3
Fools grant whate'er *A.* craves *O.* ii. 27
And wild *A.* well deserves its woe *P.C.* 12
A. humbled, mighty Cities storm'd *S.* v. 11
His whole *a.* was to serve a Lord *S.* vi. 14
Has yet a strange *a.* to look worse *S.* viii. 269
A. first sprung from your blest abodes *U.L.* 13
Not Lucre's madman, nor *A.*'s tool *P.S.* 335

Ambitious.
Or helps th' *a.* hill the heav'ns to scale *M.E.* iv. 59
Removed from all th' *A.* scene *I.H.* ii. 27
But see how oft *a.* aims are cross'd *R.L.* v. 107

Ambitiously.
Not meanly, nor *a.* pursued *M.E.* iii. 221

Ambrose Philips.
Lo! *A. P.* is preferr'd for Wit *D.* ii. 326

Ambrosia.
Where, from *A.*, Jove retires for ease *D.* ii. 84

Amelia.
Lull with *A.*'s liquid name the Nine *S.* i. 31

Amend.
At home with Morals, Arts, and Laws *a.* *S.* v. 4

Amends.
He has a Husband that will make *a.* *E.J.S.* 26

Amice.
On some a Priest succinct in *a.* white *D.* iv. 549

Amicable.
Enter each mild, each *a.* guest *E.A.* 301

Amid, Amidst.—*Passim.*

Amiss.
Ten censure wrong for one who writes *a.* *E.C.* 6

Ammon.
Witness great *A.* by whose horns I swore *D.* iv. 387
Or turns young *A.* loose to scourge mankind *E.M.* i. 160
And what young *A.* wish'd, but wish'd in vain *E.S.* ii. 117
A.'s *great son one shoulder had too high P.S.* 117

Among, Amongst.—*Passim.*

Am'rous.
Oft on the rind I carv'd her *a.* vows *A.* 67
O pious fraud of *a.* charity *E.A.* 150
Papilia, wedded to her *a.* spark *M.E.* ii. 37
What dire offence from *a.* causes springs *R.L.* i. 1
And breathes three *a.* sighs to raise the fire *R.L.* ii. 42
At *a.* Flavio is the stocking thrown *S.* iii. 148
Each *a.* nymph prefers her gifts in vain *Sw.* 53

Amount.
The whole *a.* of that enormous fame *E.M.* iv. 307

Amphibious.
A. thing! that acting either part *P.S.* 327

Amphitrite.
Here *A.* sails thro' myrtle bow'rs *M.E.* iv. 123

Ample.
Her *a.* presence fills up all the place *D.* i. 261
Together let us beat this *a.* field *E.M.* i. 9
Far as Creation's *a.* range extends *E.M.* i. 207
Whose *a.* Lawns are not asham'd to feed *M.E.* iv. 185
What life in all that *a.* body, say *S.* ii. 77
Let old Arcadia boast her *a.* plain *W.F.* 159
Their *a.* bow, a new Whitehall ascend *W.F.* 380

Ampler.
My life gave a. lessons to mankind *D.* i. 192

Amplest.
Of these twelve volumes, twelve of a. size *D.* i. 155
To him we grant our a. pow'rs to sit *D.* ii. 375

Amply.
But having a. stuff'd his skin *I.H.* i. 53

Amus'd.
A. he reads, and then returns the bills *D.* ii. 91

Amusements.
My Life's a. have been just the same *S.* ii. 153
In one our Frolics, our A. end *S.* vi. 74

Amusing.
There sober thought pursu'd th' a. theme *S.* viii. 188

Analysed.
Criticis'd your wine, and a. your meat *M.E.* ii. 81

Anarch.
Thy hand, great A.! lets the curtain fall *D.* iv. 655

Anarchy.
She rul'd, in native A., the mind *D.* i. 76
And a. without confusion know *E.M.* iii. 186

Ancestors.
Sire, A., himself. One cast his eyes *D.* iv. 519
Our rural A., with little blest *S.* v. 241

Ancient.
Dulness possess'd o'er all her a. right *D.* i. 11
Much she revolves their arts, their a. praise *D.* i. 97
Or rob Rome's a. geese of all their glories *D.* i. 211
He sleeps among the dull of a. days *D.* i. 294
This, this is he, foretold by a. rhymes *D.* iii. 319
In a. Sense if any needs will deal *D.* iv. 229
Be rich in a. brass, tho' not in gold *D.* iv. 365
Rattling an a. Sistrum at his head *D.* iv. 374
Some on the leaves of a. authors prey *E.C.* 112
Learn hence for a. rules a just esteem *E.C.* 139
Still green with bays each a. Altar stands *E.C.* 181
And but so mimic a. wits at best *E.C.* 331
Rome's a. Genius, o'er its ruins spread *E.C.* 699
Their a. bounds the banish'd Muses pass'd *E.C.* 710
Who durst assert the juster a. cause *E.C.* 721
Relum'd her a. light, not kindled new *E.M.* iii. 287
Go! if your a., but ignoble blood *E.M.* iv. 211
From a. story learn to scorn them all *E.M.* iv. 286
Still leave some a. Virtues to our age *Ep.* ix. 10
Sleep, or peruse some a. Book *I.H.* ii. 130
All crimes shall cease, and a. fraud shall fail *M.* 17
The Saviour comes! by a. bards foretold *M.* 37
To White's he carry'd, as to a. games *M.E.* ii. 69
That a. Worm the Devil *Mi.* iv. 12
He bids your breasts with a. ardour rise *P.C.* 15
For Sylphs, yet mindful of their a. race *R.L.* iii. 35
Nnt a. ladies when refus'd a kiss *R.L.* iv. 6
Here stood Ill-nature like an a. maid *R.L.* iv. 27
The same, his a. personage to deck *R.L.* v. 89
But a. friends (tho' poor, or out of play) *S.* ii. 139
And shall we deem him A., right and sound *S.* v. 58
Had a. times conspir'd to disallow (*rep.*) *S.* v. 135
Those a. words that shaded all the ground *S.* vii. 110
Of a. writ unlocks the learned store *W.F.* 247
And call the Muses to their a. seats *W.F.* 284
First the fam'd authors of his a. name *W.F.* 339
Know well each A.'s *proper character E.C.* 119
But th' the A—s thus their rules invade *E.C.* 161
A. in phrase, mere moderns in their sense *E.C.* 325
The A. only, or the Moderns prize *E.C.* 395
I melt down A. like a heap of snow *S.* v. 65

And.—*Passim.*

Anew.
And builds imaginary Rome a. *E.* iii. 32
I sit and dream I see my CRAGGS a. *E.S.* ii. 69
And all her faded garlands bloom a. *M.E.* v. 48
He spins the slight, self-pleasing thread a. *P.S.* 90
To paint a. the flow'ry sylvan scenes *W.F.* 285

Angel.
A. of Dulness, sent to scatter round *D.* iii. 257

Nor wish'd an A. whom I lov'd a Man *E.A.* 70
And little less than A. would be more *E.M.* i. 174
Nature's ethereal, human, a., man *E.M.* i. 238
Beast, Man, or A., Servant, Lord, or King *E.M.* iii. 302
An a. Tongue, which no man can persuade *M.E.* i. 199
In Quibbles A. and Archangel join *S.* v. 101
An A.'s *sweetness, or Bridgewater's eyes E.* iii. 46
He asks no A. wing, no Seraph's fire *E.A.* i. 10
And whisp'ring A—s prompt her golden dreams E.A. 216
While Altars blaze, and A. tremble round *E.A.* 276
Bright clouds descend, and A. watch thee round *E.A.* 340
For Fools rush in where A. fear to tread *E.C.* 625
Men would be A., A. would be Gods (*rep.*) *E.M.* i. 126
Let ruling A. from their spheres be hurl'd *E.M.* i. 253
And stoops from A. to the Dregs of Earth *E.S.* i. 142
With simp'ring A., Palms, and Harps divine *M.E.* ii. 14
And A. guard him in the golden Mean *M.E.* iii. 246
And A. lean from heav'n to hear *O.* i. 130
Hark! they whisper; A. say *O.* v. 7
And crystal domes and a. in machines *R.L.* iv. 46
Why A. call'd, and Angel-like ador'd *R.L.* v. 12
Paint A. trembling round his falling Horse *S.* i. 28
When golden A. cease to cure the Evil *S.* vi. 218
The glorious fault of A. and of Gods *U.L.* 14
While A. with their silver wings o'ershade *U.L.* 67
Why Angels call'd, *and* A.-*like ador'd R.L.* v. 12
Or virgins visited by A.-pow'rs *R.L.* i. 33

Angelic.
My fancy form'd thee of a. kind *E.A.* 61

Anger.
Fear not the a. of the wise to raise *E.C.* 582
See a., zeal, and fortitude supply *E.M.* ii. 187
His A. moral, and his Wisdom gay *Ep.* i. 6
These you but a., *and you mend not those E.S.* i. 54

Anger'd.
It a. TURENNE, once upon a day *E.S.* ii. 150
Aud itch most hurts when a. to a sore *S.* viii. 119

Angle.
Intent, his a. trembling in his hand *W.F.* 138

Angry.
A fool quite a. is quite innocent *P.S.* 107
Were others a. : I excus'd them too *P.S.* 173

Anguish.
With honest a., and an aching head *P.S.* 38

Animal.
Nay, feasts the a. he dooms his feast *E.M.* iii. 65

Animate.
Exalt the dance, and a. the song *I.H.* iii. 28

Animated.
Warriors she fires with a. sounds *O.* i. 28
Lely on a. Canvas stole *S.* v. 149

Anne.
But now (so A. and Piety ordain *D.* ii. 29
As in the gentle reign of my Queen A. *I.H.* iii. 4
And France reveng'd of A.'s *and* EDWARD'S *arms M.E.* iii. 144
Here thou, great A—a! whom three realms obey *R.L.* iii. 7
While A. begg'd and Dido rag'd in vain *R.L.* v. 6
At length great A. said, "Let Discord cease" *W.F.* 327
In A.'s *wars, a Soldier poor and old S.* vi. 33

Annius.
But A., crafty Seer, with ebon wand *D.* iv. 347
(Reply'd soft A.) "this our paunch before *D.* iv. 388

Annoys.
Whose buzz the witty and the fair a. *P.S.* 311

Annual.
Their a. trophies, and their monthly wars *D.* iii. 282
Or issue Members of an A. feast *D.* iv. 574
A. for me the grape, the rose renew *E.M.* i. 135
So bought an a. Rent or two *I.H.* i. 71
With a. joy the redd'ning shoots to greet *M.E.* iv. 91
Indulg'd the day that hous'd their a. grain *S.* v. 243

Anodyne.
The daily A., and nightly draught *M.E.* ii. 111

ANOINTED—APPEARS.

Anointed.
The Goddess then, o'er his *a*. head *D*. i. 287
On Dulness' lap th' *A*. head repos'd *D*. iii. 2
No Lord's *a*., but a Russian Bear *S*. v. 389

Another.—*Passim*.

Anstis.
Than such as *A*. casts into the Grave *E.S.* ii. 237
Venus shall give him Form, and *A*. Birth *S*. iv. 82

Answer.
Faith, I shall give the *a*. Reynard gave *S*. iii. 114
Each prompt to query, *a*., and debate *D*. ii. 381
And makes night hideous. *A*. him, ye Owls *D*. iii. 166
Some lucky License *a*. to the full *E.C.* 148
That REASON, PASSION, *a*. one great aim *E.M*. iv. 395
Why, *a*. LYTTLETON, and I'll engage *E.S.* i. 47
Cæsar perhaps might *a*. he was drunk *M.E.* i. 132
The woods shall *a*. and their echo ring *Su*. 16

Answer'd.
"My Sons!" (she *a*.), "both have done your parts *D*. iv. 437
I never *a*.—I was not in debt *P.S.* 154
Heard, noted, *a*., as in full debate *S*. vi. 187

Answ'ring.
And *a*. gin-shops sourer sighs return *D*. iii. 148
Parts *a*. parts shall slide into a whole *M.E.* iv. 66

Answers.
"Not so by Heav'n" (he *a*. in a rage) *E.C.* 281
Earth for whose use? Pride *a*., "'Tis for mine *E.M*. i. 132
She who ne'er *a*. till a Husband cools *M.E.* ii. 261

Ant.
The *A*.'s republic, and the realm of Bees *E.M*. iii. 184

Antedate.
And *a*. the bliss above *O*. i. 123

Antics.
To see those *a*., Fopling and Courting *S*. viii. 237

Antichrist.
Thron'd on seven hills, the *A*. of wit *D*. ii. 16

Antipathy.
The strong *A*. of Good to Bad *E.S.* ii. 198

Antipodes.
And ev'n th' *A*. Virgilius mourn *D*. iii. 106

Antiquaries.
With sharpen'd sight pale *A*. pore *M.E.* v. 35

Antithesis.
And he himself one vile *A*. *P.S.* 325
Light-arm'd with Points, A—es, and Puns *D*. i. 306

Any.—*Passim*.

Anxious.
A. and trembling for the birth of Fate *R.L.* ii. 142
Just in that instant *a*. Ariel sought *R.L.* iii. 139
But *a*. cares the pensive nymph oppress'd *R.L.* iv. 1

Aonian.
The dreams of Pindus and th' *A*. maid *M*. 4

Apace.
'Tis true : but Winter comes *a*. *I.H.* i. 16
The Baron now his Diamonds pours *a*. *R.L.* iii. 75

Apart.
But let me die, all raillery *a*. *E.J.S.* 11
There all alone, and compliments *a*. *S*. vi. 210

Apathy.
In lazy *A*. let Stoics boast *E.M*. ii. 101

Ape.
Less human genius than God gives an *a*. *D*. i. 282
Became, when seiz'd, a puppy, or an *a*. *D*. ii. 130
And shew'd a NEWTON as we shew an *A*. *E.M*. ii. 34
As a—s our grandsires, in their doublets drest *E.C.* 332

Ape-and-Monkey.
Not sail with Ward to *A*. climes *D*. i. 233

Apelles.
Or Phidias broken, and *A*. burn'd *D*. iii. 112

A-piece.
A peck of coals *a*. shall glad the rest *D*. ii. 282

Apocrypha.
Howe'er what's now *A*., my Wit *S*. viii. 286

Apollo.
Bright *A*. lead thy Choir *Mi*. vii. 16
Proud as *A*. on his forked hill *P.S.* 231
Appear'd A.'s *May'r and Aldermen D*. iv. 116
If Mævius scribble in *A*. spite *E.C.* 34

Apostles.
Nay troth th' *A*. (tho' perhaps too rough) *S*. viii. 76

Apothecary—*see* 'Pothecaries.

Apparel.
Such was the wight ; th' *a*. on his back *S*, viii. 38

Apparent.
Would from the *a*. What conclude the Why *M.E.* i. 100

Appal.
Does neither Rage inflame, nor Fear *a*. *S*. vi. 303

Appeal.
To-morrow my *A*. comes on *I.H.* ii. 71 5
And aspect ardent to the Throne *a*. *D*. iv. 402

Appeal'd.
A. to Law, and Justice lent her arm *S*. v. 256

Appear.
Dry bodies of Divinity *a*. *D*. i. 152
Did on the stage my Fops *a*. confin'd *D*. i. 191
There in his seat two spacious vents *a*. *D*. ii. 85
A. more glorious, as more hack'd and torn *D*. iv. 124
Let mine an innocent gay farce *a*. *E*. iv. 25
What scenes *a*. where'er I turn my view *E.A.* 263
A. in writing or in judging ill *E.C.* 2
Some figures monstrous and mis-shap'd *a*. *E.C.* 171
Th' eternal snows *a*. already past *E.C.* 227
No monstrous height, or breadth, or length *a*. *E.C.* 251
Better for Us, perhaps, it might *a*. *E.M*. i. 165
What crops of wit and honesty *a*. *E.M*. ii. 185
But Heav'ns just balance equal will *a*. *E.M*. iv. 69
Not twice a twelvemonth you *a*. in Print *E.S.* i. 1
Just write to make his barrenness *a*. *P.S.* 181
And Garters, Stars, and Coronets *a*. *R.L.* i. 85
The various off'rings of the world *a*. *R.L.* i. 130
In me what spots (for spots I have) *a*. *S*. i. 55
Adieu—if this advice *a*. the worst *S*. iv. 130
There mingled forms and pyramids *a*. *S*. vi. 259
Four figures rising from the work *a*. *Sp*. 37
See what delights in sylvan scenes *a*. *Su*. 59
What tho' no friends in sable weeds *a*. *U.L.* 55
Now hung with pearls the dropping trees *a*. *W*. 31
Where, in their blessings, all those Gods *a*. *W.F.* 36
Hills, vales, and floods *a*. already cross'd *W.F.* 153
And future navies on thy shores *a*. *W.F.* 222
No seas so rich, so gay no banks *a*. *W.F.* 225
Still in thy song should vanquish'd France *a*. *W.F.* 309

Appear'd.
All who true Dunces in her cause *a*. *D*. ii. 25
All as the vest, *a*. the wearer's frame *D*. iii. 39
A. Apollo's May'r and Aldermen *D*. iv. 116
What scenes *a*. *O*. i. 54
Not thus the land *a*. in ages past *W.F.* 43
Grav'd on his urn *a*. the moon, that guides *W.F.* 333
The god *a*. ; he turn'd his azure eyes *W.F.* 351

Appears.
Wond'ring he gaz'd : When lo ! a Sage *a*. *D*. iii. 35
Another Æschylus *a*. ! prepare *D*. iii. 313
How finish'd with illustrious toil *a*. *E*. iii. 39
O write it not my hand—the name *a*. *E.A.* 13
A. more decent, as more suitable *E.C.* 319
No longer now that golden age *a*. *E.C.* 478
And always list'ning to himself *a*. *E.C.* 615
Now looking downwards, just as griev'd *a*. *E.M*. i. 175
Prepare the way ! a God, a God *a*. *M*. 30
Or who in sweet vicissitude *a*. *M.E.* ii. 109
How Rome her own sad Sepulchre *a*. *M.E.* v. 2

Such unfeign'd Passion in his looks *a. Mi.* ix. 93
A heav'nly image in the glass *a. R.L.* i. 125
The hoary Majesty of Spades *a. R.L.* iii. 56
Then see ! the nymph in beauteous grief *a. R.L.* iv. 143
Mark where a bold expressive phrase *a. S.* vi. 165
Say, Daphnis, say in what glad soil *a. Sp.* 85
The silver flood, so lately calm, *a. W.* 65
Now fainting, sinking, pale, the nymph *a. W.F.* 191
The blue, transparent Vandalis *a. W.F.* 345

Appetite.
With hounds and horns go hunt an *A. S.* iv. 114

Appius.
But *A.* reddens at each word you speak *E.C.* 585

Applaud.
And worlds *a.* that must not yet be found *E.C.* 194
And now the Punk *a.*, and now the Friar *M.E.* i. 191

Applauds.
Rough Satyrs dance, and Pan *a.* the song *Su.* 50

Applause.
The last, not least in honour or *a. D.* iv. 577
A. in spite of trivial faults is due *E.C.* 258
And rapid Severn hoarse *a.* resounds *M.E.* iii. 252
And sit attentive to his own *a. P.S.* 210
While yet in Britain Honour had *a. P.S.* 389
So spoke the Dame, but no *a.* ensu'd *R.L.* v. 35
In Life's cool Ev'ning satiate of *A. S.* iii. 9
And say, to which shall our *a.* belong *S.* iii. 97
These fools demand not pardon, but *A. S.* v. 118
To make poor Pinky eat with vast *a. S.* v. 293
To court *a.* by printing what I write *S.* vi. 150
The Mob's a—s, or the gifts of Kings *S.* iv. 15

Apples.
Yet sigh'st thou now for *a.* and for cakes *E.M.* iv. 176

Application.
Sir, you may spare your *A. I.H.* i. 59

Applies.
Kind Self-conceit to some her glass *a. D.* iv. 533
Music her soft assuasive voice *a. O.* i. 25

Apply.
Prescribe, *a.*, and call their masters fools *E.C.* 111
A. to me; to keep them mad or vain *P.S.* 22
But ask not to what Doctors I *a. S.* iii. 23
Nor once to Chanc'ry, nor to Hale *a. S.* iii. 173

Apply'd.
Thus Wit, like Faith, by each man is *a. E.C.* 396
That, happy frailties to all ranks *a. E.M.* ii. 241
Know, there are Rhymes,which fresh and fresh *a. S,* iii.59

Apprentice—see Prentice.

Apprentic'd.
Him portion'd maids, *a.* orphans blest *M.E.* iii. 267

Approach.
Thus sung the shepherds till th' *a.* of night *A.* 97
Thus at his felt *a.*, and secret might *D.* iv. 639
But soft,—by regular *a.*,—not yet *M.E.* iv. 129
A ! Great NATURE studiously behold *Mi.* x. 7
A. ; but awful ! Lo, th' Egerian Grot *Mi.* x. 9
Tell at your Levee, as the Crowds *a. S.* iv. 101

Approach'd.
Each with some wond'rous gift *a.* the Pow'r *D.* iv. 309
When Love *a.* me under Friendship's name *E.A.* 60

Approaching.
Prudence, whose glass presents th' *a.* jail *D.* i. 51
The rocks proclaim th' *a.* Deity *M.* 32
She sees, and trembles at th' *a.* ill *R.L.* iii. 91

Approve.
For fools admire, but men of sense *a. E.C.* 391
Love's purer flames the Gods *a. O.* iii. 13
If I *a.*, "Commend it to the Stage" *P.S.* 58
Who can *your* merit *selfishly* *a. P.S.* 293
If She inspire, and He *a.* my lays *R.L.* i. 6
Such as Sir Robert would *a.* Indeed *S.* i. 153

Approv'd.
O born to Arms ! O Worth in Youth *a. Ep.* ix. 3
The living Virtue now had shone *a. Ep.* xiv. 7
Ennobled by himself, by all *a. M.E.* v. 71
Britons, attend : be worth like this *a. P.C.* 37
Happy my studies, when by these *a. P.S.* 143

Approving.
The damning critic, half *a.* wit *P.S.* 344

Approves.
A Tyrant to the wife his heart *a. M.E.* i. 102
Sheffield *a.*, consenting Phœbus bends *Mi.* i. 7
Happy the man whom this bright court *a. W.F.* 235

Apron'd.
The cobbler *a.*, and the parson gown'd *E.M.* iv. 197

Apropos.
A Tale extremely à *p. I.H.* 254
See BETTY LOVET ! very à *p. Mi.* ix. 21

Apt.
Dulness is ever *a.* to magnify *E.C.* 393

Aptly.
Is *a.* term'd a Glow-worm *Mi.* iv. 16

Arabia.
And all *A.* breathes from yonder box *R.L.* i. 134

Arabian.
His conq'ring tribes th' *A.* prophet draws *D.* iii. 97
A. shores, or Indian seas infold *S.* iv. 12

Arachne.
Or draw to silk *A.'s* subtile line *D.* iv. 590

Arbitrary.
'Tis in the shade of *A.* Sway *D.* iv. 182

Arbuthnot.
To second, *A.* ! thy Art and Care *P.S.* 133

Arcs.
Turn *A.* of triumph to a Garden-gate *M.E.* iv. 30

Arcades.
Shall call the winds thro' long *a.* to roar *M.E.* iv. 35

Arcadia.
Let old *A.* boast her ample plain *W.F.* 159
A.'s Countess, here in ermin'd pride *M.E.* ii. 7

Arcadians.
Mild *A.*, ever blooming *Mi.* vii. 5

Arch.
To rear the Column, or the *A.* to bend *M.E.* iv. 48
Bid the broad *A.* the dangerous Flood contain *M.E.* iv. 199
Now scantier limits the proud *A.* confine *M.E.* v. 27
Where awful a—es make a noon-day night *E.A.* 143
The trophy'd *a.*, story'd halls invade *E.M.* iv. 103
With nodding *a.*, broken temples spread *M.E.* v. 3
And how triumphal *a.* to the ground *R.L.* iii. 176
This *a.* Absurd, that wit and fool delights *D.* i. 221
Build on the wave, or *a.* beneath the sand *E.M.* iii. 102

Archangel.
In Quibbles Angel and *A.* join *S.* v. 101

Arch'd.
Lost the *a.* eye-brow or Parnassian sneer *P.S.* 96

Archer.
And under his, and under *A.'s* wing *D.* i. 309

Arcturus.
Now bright *A.* glads the teeming grain *A.* 72
Nor yet, when moist *A.* clouds the sky *W.F.* 119

Ardent.
And aspect *a.* to the Throne appeal *D.* iv. 402
An *a.* Judge, who zealous in his trust *E.C.* 677
Nor *a.* warriors meet with hateful eyes *M.* 58
Then prostrate falls, and begs with *a.* eyes *R.L.* ii. 43
Not *a.* lovers robb'd of all their bliss *R.L.* iv. 5

ARDOUR—ARRAIGN.

Ardour.
All gaze with *a*, ; some a poet's name *D.* ii. 51
He bids your breasts with ancient *a.* rise *P.C.* 15
Wounds, Charms, and A—s were no sooner read *R.L.* i. 119

Arduous.
And pointed out those *a*, paths they trod *E.C.* 95

Area.
Amid that *a.* wide they took their stand *D.* ii. 27

Arede.
Right well mine eyes *a.* the myster wight *D.* iii. 187

Arethuse.
Bears Pisa's off'rings to his *A. D.* ii. 342

Aretine.
Few are the Converts *A.* has made *S.* viii. 95

Argent.
Or ask of yonder *a.* fields above *E.M.* i. 41

Argo.
While *A.* saw her kindred trees *O.* i. 40

Arguments.
Thicker than *a*, temptations throng *E.M.* ii. 75

Argus.
And boasts Ulysses' ears with *A.*' eyes *D.* ii. 374
As *A.*'s eyes by Hermes' wand opprest *D.* iv. 637

Argyll.
A., the State's whole Thunder born to wield *E.S.* ii. 86

Ariel.
A watchful sprite, and *A.* is my name *R.L.* i. 106
Superior by the head, was *A.* plac'd *R.L.* ii. 70
A. himself shall be the guard of Shock *R.L.* ii. 116
First *A.* perch'd upon a Matadore *R.L.* iii. 33
Just in that instant, anxious *A.* sought *R.L.* iii. 139
And *A.* weeping from Belinda flew *R.L.* iv. 12

Arise.
Let spring attend, and sudden flow'rs *a. A.* 36
Ye soft illusions, dear deceits, *a. E.A.* 240
Clouds interpose, waves roar, and winds *a. E.A.* 246
Hills peep o'er hills, and Alps on Alps *a. E.C.* 232
New Blackmores and new Milbourns must *a. E.C.* 463
From Jesse's root behold a branch *a. M.* 9
In crowding ranks on ev'ry side *a. M.* 89
A., and tell me, was thy death more bless'd *M.E.* iii. 322
If in the breast tumultuous joys *a. O.* i. 24
While thousand grateful thoughts *a. O.* iii. 30
Sees by degrees a purer blush *a. R.L.* i. 143
Strange phantoms rising as the mists *a. R.L.* iv. 40
Nor morning odours from the flow'rs *a. W.* 46
A., the pines a noxious shade diffuse *W.* 86
Thin trees *a.* that shun each other's shades *W.F.* 22
And midst the desert fruitful fields *a. W.F.* 26

Aristarch.
Before them march'd that *A. D.* iv. 203
Avaunt—is *A—us* yet unknown *D.* iv. 210

Aristippus.
Sometimes with *A.* or St. Paul *S.* iii. 31

Aristotle.
A hundred heads of *A.*'s friends *D.* iv. 192
Who durst depart from *A.* rules *E.C.* 272

Ark.
Noah had refus'd it lodging in his *A. S.* viii. 26

Arm.
Whirlpools and storms his circling *a.* invest *D.* ii. 317
His stretch'd-out *a.* display'd a volume fair *D.* iv. 106
Here living Tea-pots stand, one *a.* held out *R.L.* iv. 49
While mighty WILLIAM's thund'ring *a.* prevail'd *S.* vi. 63
There, stamp'd with *a—s* Newcastle shines complete *D.* i. 142
With *a.* expanded Bernard rows his state *D.* ii. 67
And Milo-like surveys his *a.* and hands *D.* ii. 284
His blunted *A.* by Sophistry are borne *D.* iv. 25
Strong in new *A.*, lo! Giant Handel stands *D.* iv. 65
Take at this hand celestial *a. E.* vi. 4

'Tis Venus, Venus gives these *a. E.* vi. 27
Oh born to *A.* / O Worth in Youth approv'd *E.* ix. 3
And round thy phantom glue my clasping *a. E.A.* 234
I stretch my empty *a.*, ; it glides away *E.A.* 238
Against the Poets their own *a.* they turn'd *E.C.* 106
Thus useful *a.* in magazines we place *E.C.* 671
But soon by impious *a.* from Latium chas'd *E.C.* 709
Ah! if she lend not *a.* as well as rules *E.M.* ii. 151
'Twas VIRTUE ONLY (or in arts or *a. E.M.* iii. 211
In hearts of Kings, or *a.* of Queens who lay *E.M.* iv. 289
Dragg'd in the dust! his *a.* hang idly round *E.S.* i. 153
And now you burst (ah cruel!) from my *a. I.H.* iii. 44
The tender lambs he raises in his *a. M.* 53
And France reveng'd of ANNE's and EDWARD's *a. M.E.* iii. 144
I yield at once, and sink into his *a. Mi.* ix. 96
Sloth unfolds her *a.* and wakes *O.* i. 32
But when our Country's cause provokes to *a. O.* i. 36
To *a.*, to *a.*, to *a. O.* i. 48
With open *a.* receiv'd one Poet more *P.S.* 142
Now awful Beauty puts on all its *a. R.L.* i. 139
And guard with *A.* divine the British Throne *R.L.* ii. 90
Straight the three bands prepare in *a.* to join *R.L.* iii. 29
Sunk in Thalestris' *a.* the nymph he found *R.L.* iv. 89
"To *a.*, to *a.*!" the fierce Virago cries *R.L.* v. 37
With *A.*, and GEORGE, and BRUNSWICK crowd the verse *S.* i. 24
In peace provides fit *a.* against a war *S.* ii. 128
Your Country, chief, in *A.* abroad defend *S.* v. 3
Appeal'd to law, and Justice lent her *a. S.* v. 256
Her Arts victorious triumph'd o'er our *A. S.* v. 264
Your *A.*, your Actions, your repose to sing *S.* v. 395
And *a.* employ'd on birds and beasts alone *W.F.* 374
But less to please the ear than *a.* the hand *E.C.* 673
Whose air cries *A.* / whose very look's an oath *S.* viii. 261
Present the spear and *a.* him for the fight *R.L.* iii. 130
Let barb'rous Ganges *a.* a servile train *W.F.* 365

Armed.
By the hero's armed shades *O.* i. 77
A.'d in adamantine Chains *Mi.* vii. 18
Tho' stiff with hoops, and *a.* with ribs of whale *R.L.* ii. 120
What? *a.* for Virtue when I point the pen *S.* i. 105
He's *a.* without that's innocent within *S.* iii. 94
Here *a.* with silver bows in early dawn *W.F.* 169

Armour.
Old Edward's *a.* beams on Cibber's breast *S.* v. 319

Arms.
'Gainst Pallas, Mars ; Latona, Hermes *a. R.L.* v. 47

Army.
Around him wide a sable *A.* stand *D.* ii. 355
Ye Tradesmen vile, in *A.*, Court, or Hall *E.S.* ii. 17
A single leaf shall waft an *A.* o'er *M.E.* iii. 43
Thus when dispersed a routed *A.* runs *R.L.* iii. 81
Save but our *A.*! and let Jove encrust *S.* i. 73
It brought (no doubt) th' *Excise* and *A.* in *S.* vii. 8
And suckle a—ies and dry-nurse the land D. i. 316
What aids, what *a.* to assist his cause *D.* iii. 128
And chiefless *A.* doz'd out the Campaign *D.* iv. 617
It raises *A.* in a Nation's aid *M.E.* iii. 31
And mow'd down *a.* in the fights of Lu *R.L.* iii. 62
Thus far both *a.* to Belinda yield *R.L.* iii. 65
Before and after Standing *A.* came *S.* ii. 254

Arnall.
Not so bold *A.* ; with a weight of skull *D.* ii. 315
Spirit of *A.* / aid me while I lie *E.S.* ii. 129

Aromatic.
Die of a rose in *a.* pain *E.M.* i. 200
And draws the *a.* souls of flow'rs *W.F.* 244

Arose.
They led him soft ; each rev'rend Bard *a. D.* ii. 348
Assist me, heav'n! but whence *a.* that pray'r *E.A.* 179
All eyes may see from what the change *a. M.E.* ii. 35

Around.—*Passim.*

A-row.
A little House, with trees *a. I.H.* i. 77

Arraign.
A. no mightier Thief than wretched *Wild E.S.* ii. 39

Arrant'st.
Will cure the *a.* Puppy of his Pride *S.* iii. 60

Array.
Demand new bodies, and in Calf's *a. D.* iii. 29
His pow'rs in equal ranks, and fair *a. E.C.* 176

Array'd.
Her wrinkled form in black and white *a. R.L.* iv. 28

Arrest.
A. him, Empress; or you sleep no more *D.* iv. 69

Arriv'd.
Of some Express at Court *a. I.H.* ii. 110

Arrogance.
Mother of *A.,* and Source of Pride *D.* iv. 470

Art.
The *a.* of Terence, and Menander's fire *A.* 8
Then he: "Great Tamer of all human *a. D.* i. 163
As, taught by Venus, Paris learnt the *a. D.* ii. 277
With Shakespear's nature, or with Jonson's *a. D.* ii. 224
Dennis and Dissonance, and captious *A. D.* ii. 239
Each *A.* he prompts, each Charm he can create *D.* iii. 227
Not touch'd by Nature, and not reach'd by *A. D.* iii. 230
Bounded by Nature, narrow'd still by *A. D.* iv. 503
A. after *A.* goes out, and all is *Night D.* iv. 640
Fresnoy's close *A.,* and Dryden's native Fire *E.* iii. 8
While Images reflect from *a.* to *a. E.* iii. 90
His easy *A.* may happy Nature seem *E.* iv. 3
So vast is *a.,* so narrow human wit *E.C.* 61
At once the source, and end, and test of *a. E.C.* 73
So modern 'Pothecaries, taught the *a. E.C.* 108
And snatch a grace beyond the reach of *a. E.C.* 153
Most Critics, fond of some subservient *A. E.C.* 263
And hide with ornaments their want of *a. E.C.* 296
True ease in writing comes from *a.,* not chance *E.C.* 362, *and S.* vi. 178
The treach'rous colours the fair *a.* betray *E.C.* 492
Tho' wit and *a.* conspire to move your mind *E.C.* 531
Fancy and *a.* in gay Petronius please *E.C.* 667
All Nature is but *A.,* unknown to thee *E.M.* i. 289
Uncheck'd may rise, and climb from *a.* to *a. E.M.* ii. 40
These mix'd with *a.,* and to due bounds confin'd *E.M.* ii. 119
Imagination plies her dang'rous *a. E.M.* ii. 143
See him from Nature rising slow to *A. E.M.* iii. 169
That urg'd by thee, I turn'd the tuneful *a. E.M.* iv. 391
Smile without *A.,* and win without a Bribe *E.S.* i. 32
Whose *A.* was Nature, and whose Pictures Thought *Ep.* viii. 2
In whom a Race, for Courage fam'd and *A. Ep.* xiv. 11
Thus with each gift of nature and of *a. M.E.* i. 192
Reserve with Frankness, *A.* with Truth ally'd *M.E.* ii. 277
The sense to value Riches, with the *A. M.E.* iii. 219
And, if they starve, they starve by rules of *a. M.E.* iv. 38
Still follow Sense, of ev'ry *A.* the Soul *M.E.* iv. 65
And *A.* reflected images to *A. M.E.* v. 52
Nature must give way to *A. Mi.* vii. 4
Oh heav'n-born sisters! source of *a. O.* ii. 9
To wake the soul by tender strokes of *a. P.C.* 1
To second, Arbuthnot, thy *A.* and Care *P.S.* 133
Blest with each talent and each *a.* to please *P.S.* 195
Unlearn'd, he knew no schoolman's subtle *a. P.S.* 398
Sudden he view'd in spite of all her *a. R.L.* iii. 143
Then all your Muse's softer *a.* display *S.* i. 29
What, and how great, the Virtue and the *A. S.* ii. 1
Not to admire, is all the *A.* I know *S.* iv. 1
Forget his Epic, nay Pindaric *A. S.* v. 77
Not one but nods, and talks of Jonson's *A. S.* v. 81 (92)
Forms the soft bosom with the gentlest *a. S.* v. 219
The last and greatest *A.,* the *A.* to blot *S.* v. 281
Enrage, compose, with more than magic *a. S.* v. 344
The better *a.* to know the good from bad *S.* vi. 55
Ah wretched shepherd, what avails thy *a. Su.* 33
With chymic *a.* exalts the min'ral pow'rs *W.F.* 243
Much she revolves their a—s, their ancient praise D. i. 97
Such happy *a.* attention can command *D.* ii. 229
The soil that *a.* and infant letters bore *D.* iii. 96
Of *a.,* but thund'ring against human lore *D.* iii. 102
Vain of Italian *A.,* Italian Souls *D.* iv. 300
Live happy both, and long promote our *a. D.* iv. 438
Others import yet nobler *a.* from France *D.* iv. 597
With softest manners, gentlest *A.* adorn'd *E.* i. 4
The kindred *A.* shall in their praise conspire *E.* iii. 69
Not only bounded to peculiar *a. E.C.* 62

In fearless youth we tempt the heights of *A. E.C.* 220
Form short Ideas; and offend in *a. E.C.* 287
And *A.* still follow'd where her Eagles flew *E.C.* 684
Thence *A.* o'er all the northern world advance *E.C.* 711
Of all our Vices have created *A. E.M.* ii. 50
Pride then was not; nor *A.* that Pride to aid *E.M.* iii. 151
Thy *a.* of building from the bee receive *E.M.* iii. 175
And for those *A.* mere Instinct could afford *E.M.* iii. 197
'Twas Virtue only (or in *a.* or arms *E.M.* iii. 211
Condemn'd in bus'ness or in *a.* to drudge *E.M.* iv. 263
Patron of *A.,* and Judge of Nature, died *Ep.* i. 2
No *A.* essay'd, but not to be admir'd *Ep.* vi. 4
He, with a hundred *A.* refin'd *I.H.* iii. 15
You too proceed! make falling *A.* your care *M.E.* iv. 191
By whose vile *a.* this heavy grief I bear *Mi.* ix. 56
See *A.* her savage sons control *O.* ii. 21
Freedom and *A.* together fall *O.* ii. 26
And *A.* but soften us to feel thy flame *O.* iii. 4
Rome learning *a.* from Greece, whom she subdu'd *P.C.* 40
And hate for *a.* that caus'd himself to rise *P.S.* 200
With lenient *a.* extend a Mother's breath *P.S.* 410
The Knave of Diamonds tries his wily *a. R.L.* iii. 87
At home, with Morals, *A.,* and Laws amend *S.* v. 4
Her *A.* victorious triumph'd o'er our Arms *S.* v. 264
Or praise malignly *A.* I-cannot reach *S.* v. 339

Art—see also Sister-arts.

Artful.
An *a.* Manager, that crept between *E.S.* i. 21
Fair to no purpose, *a.* to no end *M.E.* ii. 245
No *a.* wildness to perplex the scene *M.E.* iv. 116

Arthur.
By potent *A.,* knock'd his chin and breast *D.,* ii. 398
A., whose giddy son neglects the Laws *P.S.* 23

Articles.
Indentures, Cov'nants, *A.* they draw *S.* vii. 94

Artill'ry.
The whole *A.* of the terms of War *S.* viii. 54
Charge them with Heav'n's *A.,* bold Divine *S.* viii. 281

Artist.
The wild Mæander wash'd the *a.'s* face *D.* ii. 176
'Tis well—but *A*—s! *who can paint or write M.E.* ii. 187
A. must choose his Pictures, Music, Meats *M.E.* iv. 6

Artless.
Their *a.* passions, and their tender pains *A.* 12
But clear and *a.* pouring thro' the plain *M.E.* iii. 257

As.—*Passim.*

Ascend.
Go, purify'd by flames, *a.* the sky *D.* i. 227
A., and recognize their Native Place *D.* i. 268
A. this hill, whose cloudy point commands *D.* iii. 67
Bid Temples, worthier of the God, *a. M.E.* iv. 198
There wrapt in clouds the blueish hills *a. W.F.* 24
Their ample bow, a new Whitehall *a. W.F.* 380

Ascendant.
A. Phœbus watch'd that hour with care *M.E.* ii. 285

Ascending.
Behold! th' *a.* Villas on my side *W.F.* 375

Ascends.
The scale of sensual, mental pow'rs *a. E.M.* i. 208
Is it for thee the lark *a.* and sings *E.M.* iii. 31
And while the muse now stoops, or now *a. E.M.* iv. 375
All mild *a.* the Moon's more sober light *M.E.* ii. 254
And all the Thunder of the Pit *a. S.* v. 237

Ascribe.
A. all Good; to their improper, Ill *E.M.* ii. 58

Ascribes.
A. his gettings to his parts and merit *M.E.* iii. 376

Asham'd.
A. of any Friend, not ev'n of Me *E.* ii. 15
If not, 'tis I must be *a.* of You *E.* ii. 17
I'm quite *a.,* 'tis mighty rude *I.H.* ii. 206
A. to own they gave delight before *M.E.* ii. 237
No, 'twas thy righteous end, *a.* to see *M.E.* iii. 147
Whose ample Lawns are not *a.* to feed *M.E.* iv. 185

Ashes.
What tho' no weeping Loves thy *a.* grace *U.L.* 59

Asia.
Of *A.'s* troops and Afric's sable sons *R.L.* iii. 82
And *A.* Tyrants tremble at your Throne *S.* v. 403

Asian.
I kept, like *A.* Monarchs, from their sight *P.S.* 220

Aside.
What can I now? my Fletcher cast *a. D.* i. 199
His never-blushing head he turn'd *a. D.* iii. 231
In patch-work flutt'ring, and her head *a. D.* iv. 48
Walker with rev'rence took and laid *a. D.* iv. 206
Nor yet the last to lay the old *a. E.C.* 336
And never shock'd, and never turn'd *a. E.C.* 629
You might have held the pretty head *a. E.J.S.* 3
HAZARDIA blush'd, and turn'd her Head *a. Mi.* ix. 41
Practis'd to lisp, and hang the head *a. R.L.* iv. 33
Turns you from sound Philosophy *a. S.* ii. 6

Ask.
A. ye their names? I could as soon disclose *D.* ii. 309
To *a.*, to guess, to know, as they commence *D.* iv. 155
A. them the cause; they're wiser still, they say *E.C.* 436
A. of thy mother earth, why oaks are made *E.M.* i. 39
Or *a.* of yonder argent fields above *E.M.* i. 41
A. for what end the heavenly bodies shine *E.M.* i. 131
A. your own heart, and nothing is so plain *E.M.* i. 215
A. where's the North? at York, 'tis on the Tweed *E.M.* ii. 222
A. of the Learn'd the way? The Learn'd are blind *E.M.* iv. 19
Who *a.* and reason thus will scarce conceive *E.M.* iv. 163
If any *a.* you, "Who's the Man, so near *E.S.* i. 45
A. you what Provocation I have had *E.S.* ii. 197
I *a.* not to increase my store *I.H.* ii. 8 s
A. why from Britain Cæsar would retreat *M.E.* i. 129
A. Men's opinions; Scoto now shall tell *M.E.* i. 158
A. you why Wharton broke thro' ev'ry rule *M.E.* I. 206
A. you why Phryne the whole Auction buys *M.E.* iii. 119
A. we what makes one keep, and one bestow *M.E.* iii. 163
I want a Patron; *a.* him for a Place *P.S.* 50
Few *a.*, if fraud or force attain'd his ends *R.L.* ii. 34
But *a.* not, to what Doctors I apply *S.* iii. 23
All that we *a.* is but a patient Ear *S.* iii. 64
If I but *a.*, if any weed can grow *S.* v. 120
Nay vents to *a.* for Verse at such a time *S.* vi. 31
I *a.* these sober questions of my heart *S.* vi. 211

Askapart.
Each man an *A.* of strength to toss *S.* viii. 276

Ask'd.
Pan came, and *a.*, what magic caus'd my smart *A.* 81
This weeping marble had not *a.* thy tear *Ep.* xiv. 5
Who first his judgment *a.*, and then a place *P.S.* 238
Why am I *a.* what next shall see the light *P.S.* 271
A. for a groat, he gives a hundred pounds *S.* iv. 86

Asking.
Explore the thought, explain the *a.* eye *P.S.* 412

Asks.
He *a.* no angel's wing, no Seraph's fire *E.M.* i. 110
Each mother *a.* it for her booby Son (ref.) *E.S.* ii. 107
And good Simplicius *a.* of her advice *M.E.* ii. 32
Nor *a.* of God, but of her Stars, to give *M.E.* ii. 89
A. no firm hand, and no unerring line *M.E.* ii. 152
He *a.* "What News?" I tell him of new Plays *S.* viii. 124

Asleep.
And lash'd so long, like tops, are lash'd *a. E.C.* 601
A., and naked as an Indian lay *M.E.* iii. 361

Aspect.
And *a.* ardent to the Throne appeal *D.* iv. 402
With *a.* open shall erect his head *M.E.* v. 65

Aspers'd.
To please a Mistress one *a.* his life *P.S.* 376

Asphodel.
In yellow meads of *A. O.* i. 75

Aspire.
Self-love and Reason to one end *a. E.M.* ii. 87
Borne on the swelling notes our souls *a. O.* i. 128
We see no new-built palaces *a. S.* vii. 111
Why bade ye else, ye Pow'rs! her soul *a. U.L.* 11

Aspir'd.
Or hand, to toil, *a.* to be the head *E.M.* i. 260
He saw, he wish'd, and to the prize *a. R.L.* ii. 30

Aspires.
Whose pious hope *a.* to see the day *D.* iv. 461

Aspiring.
'Tis thus *a.* Dulness ever shines *D.* iv. 19
A. to be Gods, if Angels fell (ref.) *E.M.* i. 127
See, all our Fools *a.* to be Knaves *E.S.* i. 164

Ass.
Drowns the loud clarion of the braying *A. D.* ii. 234
So swells each wind-pipe; *A.* intones to *A. D.* ii. 253
As not to stick at fool or *a. E.* vi. 23
As heavy mules are neither horse nor *a. E.C.* 39
No *A.* so meek, no *A.* so obstinate *M.E.* ii. 102
That secret to each fool, that he's an *A. P.S.* 80
Compared to this a Minister's an *A. S.* iii. 96
Two Aldermen dispute it with an *A. S.* vi. 105
Hath made him an Attorney of an *A. S.* vii. 50
Sporus, that mere white curd of A.'s *milk P.S.* 306
Keep close to Ears, and those let a—s *prick P.S.* 77
Bulls aim their horns, and *A.* lift their heels *S.* i. 86

Assail.
Let crowds of Critics now my verse *a. Mi.* i. 3

Assails.
All books he reads, and all he reads *a. E.C.* 616
In vain Thalestris with reproach *a. R.L.* v. 3

Assassin.
But, dreadful too, the dark *A.* hires *M.E.* iii. 28

Assault.
A well-bred Lord t' *a.* a gentle Belle *R.L.* i. 8

Assembled.
Tho' Gods *a.* grace his tow'ring height *W.F.* 34

Assembly.
Thy choicer mists on this *a.* shed *D.* iv. 357
She went from Op'ra, Park, *A.*, Play *E.* v. 13
Some keep A—*ies, and would keep the Stews S.* iii. 129

Assent.
With Laws, to which you gave your own *a. S.* vi. 30
Damn with faint praise, a. with civil leer P.S. 201

Assert.
What aids, what armies, to *a.* his cause *D.* iii. 128
Guard my Prerogative, *a.* my Throne *D.* iv. 583
Who durst *a.* the juster ancient cause *E.C.* 721
Dare to have sense yourselves; *a.* the stage *P.C.* 43

Assignations.
While nymphs take treats, or *a.* give *R.L.* iii. 169

Assign'd.
The proper organs, proper pow'rs, *a. E.M.* i. 180
Great standing miracle! that Heav'n *a. E.M.* iii. 77
As well as dream such titles are *a. E.M.* iv. 179
To some a dry rehearsal was *a. P.S.* 243
Ye know the spheres and various tasks *a. R.L.* ii. 75
A. his figure to Bernini's care *S.* v. 381

Assist.
A. me heav'n! but whence arose that pray'r *E.A.* 179
A. the fiends, and tear me from my God *E.A.* 288
And strongest motive to *a.* the rest *E.M.* iv. 352
A. their blushes, and inspire their airs *R.L.* ii. 98
So Ladies in Romance *a.* their Knight *R.L.* iii. 129
The growing combat, or *a.* the fray *R.L.* v. 56

Assistance.
Bids each on other for *a.* call *E.M.* ii. 251
Let him to-night his just *a.* lend *Mi.* ii. 23

Assisted.
So shall each youth *a.* by our eyes *D.* iv. 359

ASSISTS—ATTILA.

Assists.
Verse cheers their leisure, Verse *a.* their work *S.* v. 235

Assuasive.
Music her soft, *a.* voice applies *O.* i. 25

Assume.
A. what sexes and what shapes they please *R.L.* i. 70

Astræa.
The stage how loosely does *A.* tread *S.* v. 290

Astride.
A. his cheese Sir Morgan we might meet *M.E.* iii. 61

Asturian.
And one fate buries in th' *A.* Mines *M.E.* iii. 132

Asunder.
Rend with tremendous sound your ears *a. S.* i. 27

At.—*Passim.*
Disputes of *Me* or *Te*, of *aut* or *a. D.* ii. 220

Atalantis.
As long as *A.* shall be read *R.L.* iii. 165

Ate—*see* **Eat.**
Yet *a.* in dreams, the custard of the day *D.* i. 92
He *a.* himself the rind and paring *I.H.* ii. 170

Atheism.
And *A.* and Religion take their turns *M.E.* ii. 66

Atheists.
Ye Rev'rend *A.* Scandal! name them! Who *E.S.* ii. 18

Athenian.
Thro' twilight ages hunt th' *A.* fowl *D.* iv. 361
Yes, I beheld th' *A.* Queen *E.* vi. 1
A. Queen! and *sober charms E.* vi. 25

Athens.
A. and Rome in better ages knew *E.C.* 644
When *A.* sinks by fates unjust *O.* ii. 17
And *A.* rising near the pole *O.* ii. 22
Some *A.* perishes, some Tully bleeds *O.* ii. 32
And learned *A.* to our art must stoop *S.* v. 47
To Thebes, to *A.*, when he wills, and where *S.* v. 347

Athwart.
Pursue the stars that shoot *a.* the night *R.L.* ii. 82

A-tilt.
Stood just *a.*, the Minister came by *S.* viii. 175

Atlantic.
Say, will you bless the bleak *A.* shore *O.* ii. 15

Atmosphere.
Or swings along the fluid *a. D* iv. 423

Atom.
The Gnomes direct, to ev'ry *a.* just *R.L.* v. 83
Those venial sins, an *a.* or a straw *S.* viii. 243
A—s *or systems into ruin hurl'd E.M.* i. 89
The single *a.* each to other tend *E.M.* iii. 10

Atone.
Or where the pictures for the page *a. W.* i. 139
What cannot copious Sacrifice *a. D.* ii. 557
What can *a.* (oh, ever-injur'd shade!) *U.L.* 47

Atones.
A. not for that envy which it brings *E.C.* 495

Atossa.
A., curs'd with ev'ry granted pray'r *M.E.* ii. 147
But what are these to great *A.*'s mind *M.E.* ii. 115

Attack.
All side in parties, and begin th' *A. R.L.* v. 39
All my demurs but double his A—s *P.S.* 65
But, Friend, take heed *whom you a. E.* vi. 17

Attack'd.
The Rights a Court *a.*, a Poet sav'd *S.* v. 224

Attain'd.
But those *a.* we tremble to survey *E.C.* 229
Few ask, if fraud or force *a.* his ends, *R.L.* ii. 34

Attains.
The heart, and all its end at once *a. E.C.* 155
Count all th' advantage prosp'rous Vice *a. E.M.* iv. 89

Attemper'd.
High Sound, *a.* to the vocal nose *D.* ii. 256

Attemp'ring.
Those smiling eyes *a.* ev'ry ray *E.A.* 63

Attempt.
Oh sons of earth! *a.* ye still to rise *E.M.* iv. 73

Attempts.
(Her guide now lost) no more *a.* to rise *E.C.* 737

Attend.
Let spring *a.*, and sudden flow'rs arise *A.* 36
Yet oh, my sons, a father's words *a. D.* iii. 213
A. the trial we propose to make *D.* iii. 371
Of ever-listless Loit'rers that *a. D.* iv. 339
For him thou oft hast bid the World *a. E.* i. 7
Parties in Wit *a.* on those of State *E.C.* 456
Man, bad for that, no action could *a. E.M.* ii. 61
Reason still use, to Reason still *a. E.M.* ii. 78
See some strange comfort ev'ry state *a. E.M.* ii. 271
Thus beast and bird the common charge *a. E.M.* iii. 125
A. the shade of gentle Buckingham *Ep.* xiv. 10
Since Harley bid me first *a. I.H.* ii. 85 s
See barb'rous nations at thy gates *a. M.* 91
The frugal Crone, whom praying priests *a. M.E.* i. 242
When Hopkins dies, a thousand lights *a. M.E.* iii. 291
Envy, be silent and *a. Mi.* viii. 2
A. and yield to what I now decide *Mi.* ix. 109
What various joys on one *a. O.* iii. 27
Britons, *a.*: be worth like this approv'd *P.C.* 37
On cares like these if length of days *a. P.S.* 414
More honours, more rewards, *a.* the brave *S.* vi. 48
Sing then, and Damon shall *a.* the strain *Sp.* 29
The hills and rocks *a.* my doleful lay *Su.* 17
Let other swains *a.* the rural care *Su.* 35
And mad Ambition, shall *a.* her there *W.F.* 416

Attendant.
When thus th' *a.* Orator begun *D.* iv. 281
Say shall my little bark *a.* sail *E.M.* iv. 385
And thou, blest Maid! *a.* on his doom *Ep.* vii. 11
The laugh, the jest, a—s on the bowl S. v. 247

Attended.
And if it lose, *a.* with no pain *E.M.* iv. 316

Attends.
A.; all flesh is nothing in his sight *D.* iv. 550
The Muse *a.* thee to thy silent shade *E.* i. 28
What greater bliss *a.* their close of life *E.M.* iv. 301
Prescribes, *a.*, the med'cine makes, and gives *M.E.* iii. 270
For when success a Lover's toil *a. R.L.* ii. 33
A. to gild the Ev'ning of my day *S.* i. 94
Besides, a fate *a.* on all I write *S* v. 408
Who there his Muse, or self, or soul *a. S.* vi. 90
A. the duties of the wise and good *W.F.* 250

Attention.
Such happy arts *a.* can command *D.* ii. 229
A., habit and experience gains *E.M.* ii. 79

Attentive.
And sit *a.* to his own applause *P.S.* 270
Tell, tell your griefs; *a.* will I stay *Mi.* ix. 27

Atterbury.
Nor has one *A.* spoil'd the flock *D.* iv. 246
How pleasing A.'s softer hour E.S. ii. 82

Attic.
For *A.* Phrase in Plato let them seek *D.* iv. 227
While Roman Spirit charms and *A.* Wit *E.S.* ii. 84

Atticus.
Who would not weep, if *A.* were he *P.S.* 214
Thus *A.*, and Trumbal thus retir'd *W.F.* 258

Attila.
Of Genseric! and *A.*'s dread name *D.* iii. 92

Attire.
Thy joy, thy pastime, *a.*, thy food *E.M.* iii. 28
Whose flocks supply him with *a. O.* iv. 6
Our speech, our colour, and our strange *a. W.F.* 406

Attorney.
Hath made him an *A.* of an Ass *S.* vii. 50
And vile A—s, *now an useless race M.E.* iii. 274

Attract.
A., *a—ed* to, the next in place *E.M.* iii. 11

Attraction.
None need a guide, by sure *a.* led *D.* iv. 75

Attracts.
A. each light gay meteor of a Spark *M.E.* ii. 22

Attribute.
Heav'n's *A.* was Universal Care *E.M.* iii. 159
Whose a—s *were Rage, Revenge, or Lust E.M.* iii. 258

Attys.
Now see an *A.*, now a Cecrops clear *D.* iv. 363

Auction.
Ask you why Phryne the whole *A.* buys *M.E.* iii. 119

Audacious.
But when by Man's *a.* labour won *M.E.* iii. 11

Audience.
She said, the pitying *a.* melt in tears *R.L.* v. 1
Had he beheld an *a.* gape so wide *S.* v. 321
And all the aërial *a.* clap their wings *Sp.* 16

Aught.
Mourn not, my SWIFT, at *a.* our Realm requires *D.* i. 26
Then first (if Poets *a.* of truth declare) *D.* ii. 77
And sure, if *a.* below the seats divine *E.* i. 21
Who seek in love for *a.* but love alone *E.A.* 84
At *a.* thy Wisdom has decoy'd (*rep.*) *U.P.* 35

Augment.
Reflect new glories, and *a.* the day *E.C.* 473

Augments.
And with celestial tears *a.* the waves *W.F.* 210

August.
Chang'd it to *A.*, and in short *I.H.* i. 3
A. her deed, and sacred be her fame E.A. 78
The forms *a.*, of King, or conqu'ring Chief *S.* v. 391

Augusta.
And on their banks *A.* rose in gold *W.F.* 336
Behold A.'s *glitt'ring spires increase W.F.* 377

Augustus.
Th' *A.* born to bring Saturnian times *D.* iii. 320
Could please at Court, and make *A.* smile *E.S.* i. 20

Aunts.
Old fashion'd halls, dull *A.*, and croaking rooks *E.* v. 12

Aurelia.
Gilding my *A.'s* brows *Mi.* vii. 22

Aurelius.
Like good *A.* let him reign, or bleed *E.M.* iv. 235

Auspicious.
Oh spring to light, *a.* Babe, be born *M.* 22

Auster.
Language, which Boreas might to *A.* hold *S.* vii. 61

Aut.
Disputes of *Me* or *Te*, of *a.* or *at D* ii. 220

Author.
A. of something yet more great than letter *D.* iv. 216
And let the *A.* of the whole escape *D.* iv. 456
With the same spirit that its *a.* writ *E.C.* 234
Our *A.*, happy in a judge so nice *E.C.* 273
But each ill *A.* is as bad a Friend *E.C.* 559
Will needs mistake an *a.* into vice *E.C.* 557
Well, if our *A.* in the Wife offends *F.J.S.* 25
Once (says an *A.* ; where I need not say) *Mi.* xi. 1

Our *a.* shuns by vulgar springs to move *P.C.* ix.
Happier their *a.* when by these belov'd *P.S.* 144
I weigh what a*.'s heaviness prevails D.* ii. 368
And dead, as living, 'tis our *A.* pride *E.* iv. 79
And ev'ry *a.* merit but his own *E.C.* 728
Yet absent, wounds an honest *a.* fame *P.S.* 292
With A—s, *Stationers obey'd the call D.* ii. 31
But now for *A.* nobler palms remain *D.* ii. 191
Yet lo! in me what *a.* have to brag on *D.* iii. 285
A. are partial to their wit, 'tis true *E.C.* 17
Some on the leaves of ancient *a.* prey *E.C.* 112
And *a.* think their reputation safe *E.C.* 450
With him, most *a.* steal their works or buy *E.C.* 618
His study! with what *A.* is it stor'd (*rep.*) *M.E.* ii. 133
A., like coins, grow dear, as they grow old *S.* v. 35
And estimating *A.* by the year *S.* v. 67
Think of those *A.*, Sir, who would rely *S.* v. 350
First the fam'd *a.* of his ancient name *W.F.* 339
Some *judge of* a—s' *names, not works, and then E.C.* 412

Autumn.
In spring the fields, in *a.* hills I love *Sp.* 77
Sylvia's like *a.* ripe, yet mild as May *Sp.* 81
When milder *a.* summer's beat succeeds *W.F.* 97
Ye trees that fade when *a.*-heats remove *A.* 29

Avail.
Alas, my BATHURST! what will they *a. S.* vi. 256
Ah what *a.* the beauties nature wore *W.* 35
Ah! what *a.* his glossy varying dyes *W.F.* 115

Avails.
Ah! what *a.* it me the flocks to keep *A.* 79
Ah wretched shepherd, what *a.* thy art *Su.* 33
How lov'd, how honour'd once *a.* thee not *U.L.* 71

Avarice.
For the worst *a.* is that of sense *E.C.* 579
As Pride in Slaves, and *A.* in Kings *E.S.* i. 110
In this thy Lust, in that thy *A. M.E.* i. 214
Poor *A.* one torment more would find *M.E.* iii. 59
As wild as mad: the *A.* of pow'r *S.* vi. 307
Ev'n *av'rice*, prudence ; sloth, philosophy *E.M.* ii. 188
'Tis *A.* all, Ambition is no more *E.S.* i. 162
Congenial souls, whose life one *A.* joins *M.E.* iii. 131
Shall deluge all ; and *A.* creeping on *M.E.* iii. 137
With wretched *A.*, or as wretched Love *S.* iii. 56
And rarely *A.* taints the tuneful mind *S.* v. 192
But why all this of *A.*? I have none *S.* vi. 304

Avaunt.
A.— is Aristarchus yet unknown *D.* iv. 210

Avenger.
And ev'ry death its own *a.* breeds *E.M.* iii. 166

Avenues.
Link towns to towns with *a.* of oak *S.* vi. 260

Averse.
A. alike to flatter, or offend *E.C.* 743

Aversion.
Pain their *a.*, Pleasure their desire *E.M.* ii. 88

Avert.
A. it, Heav'n! that thou, my Cibber, e'er *D.* iii. 287

Averted.
Then lights the structure with *a.* eyes *D.* i. 247
A. half your Parents' simple Pray'r *M.E.* ii. 286

Averting.
Diffusing blessings, or *a.* harms *E.M.* iii. 212

Avidien.
A., or his wife (no matter which *S.* ii. 49

Avoid.
T' *a.* great errors, must the less commit *E.C.* 260
A. Extremes ; and shun the fault of such *E.C.* 384

Avon.
On *A.'s* bank, where flow'rs eternal blow *S.* v. 119

Await.
On whom three hundred gold-capt youths *a. D.* iv. 117

Awake.

Oh born to see what none can see *a. D.* iii. 43
Serves but to keep fools pert, and knaves *a. D.* iv. 442
Then catch'd the Schools, the Hall scarce kept *a. D.* iv. 609
How shall he keep, what, sleeping or *a. E.M.* iii. 275
A moan so loud that all the guild *a. D.* ii. 250
A., my St. John, leave all meaner things *E.M.* i. 1
And sleepless lovers just at twelve *a. R.L.* i. 16

Awakens.

That well-known name *a.* all my woes *E.A.* 30
Repairs her smiles, *a.* ev'ry grace *R.L.* i. 141

Awakes.

Where life *a.*, and dawns at ev'ry line *E.* iii. 4

Away.—*Passim*.

Awe.

Jacob, the scourge of Grammar, mark with *a. D.* iii. 149
Till Superstition taught the tyrant *a. E.M.* iii. 246
All, all look up with reverential *a. E.S.* i. 167
Tim'rous by nature, of the rich in *a. S.* i. 7
Confounds the civil, keeps the rude in *a. S.* viii. 270

Aw'd.

A., on my bended knees I fell *E.* vi. 9
A. without Virtue, without Beauty charm'd *M.E.* ii. 46
A. by his Nobles, by his Commons curst *W.F.* 73

Awful.

A veil of fogs dilates her *a.* face *D.* i. 262
But as in graceful act, with *a.* eye *D.* iv. 109
Before them march'd that *a.* Aristarch *D.* iv. 203
In these deep solitudes and *a.* cells *E.A.* 1
Where *a.* arches make a noon-day night *E.A.* 143
Nay, should great Homer lift his *a.* head *E.C.* 464
And sacred, place by DRYDEN'S *a.* dust *EA.* v. 2
When *a.* Love seems melting in his eyes *Mi.* ix. 90
Approach; but *a.* ! Lo! th' Egerian Grot *Mi.* x. 9
Now *a.* Beauty puts on all its arms *R.L.* i. 139

Awhile.—*Passim*.

Awkward.

These sparks with *a.* vanity display *E.C.* 329
Let humble ALLEN, with an *a.* Shame *E.S.* i. 135
See I sportive fate, to punish *a.* pride *M.E.* iv. 19
A. and supple each devoir to pay *Mi.* iii. 17
An *a.* Thing, when first she came to Town *Mi.* ix. 59

Awry.

Not Cynthia, when her mantle's pinn'd *a. R.L.* iv. 8
Yet hang your lip, to see a Seam *a. S.* iii. 174
And with a face as red, and as *a. S.* viii. 266

Axis.

On their own *A.* as the Planets run *E.M.* iii. 313

Azure.

He rais'd his *a.* wand and thus begun *R.L.* ii. 72
In the clear *a.* gleam the flocks are seen *W.F.* 215
The god appear'd: he turn'd his *a.* eyes *W.F.* 351

B.

So K.* so B.** sneak'd into the grave *D.* iv. 511

Baal.

Who, false to Phœbus, bow the knee to *B. D.* iv. 93

Babbling.

But all such *b.* blockheads in his stead *P.S.* 304

Babe.

Oh spring to light, auspicious *B.*, be born *M.* 22
"The Man of Ross," each lisping *b.* replies *M.E.* ii. 26a
Two b—s of love close clinging to her waist *D.* ii. 158

Babel.

Pity! you was not Druggerman at *B. S* viii. 83

Bacchanals.

Carthusian fasts, and fulsome *B. S.* vii. 118
Hark! Hæmus resounds with the B——s' cries *O.* i. 111

Back, *adv.*—*Passim*.

With each a sickly brother at his *b. D.* ii. 306
Such was the wight; th' apparel on his *b. S.* viii. 38
To all their dated B——he turns you round *M.C.* iv. 135
It ought to bring all courtiers on their *b. S.* viii. 207
And jingling down the b.-stairs told the crew *M.E.* iii. 73

Backward, Backwards.—*Passim*.

Bacon.

And *B.* trembling for his brazen head *D.* iii. 104
'Tis yours a *B.* or a Locke to blame *D.* iii. 215
If Parts allure thee, think how *B.* shin'd *E.M.* iv. 281
The Beans and *B.* set before 'em *I.H.* ii. 137
He brought him *B.* nothing lean *J.H.* ii. 265
Shades, that to *B.* could retreat afford *S.* ii. 175
Words that wise *B* or brave Raleigh spake *S.* vi. 168
The source of Newton's Light, of *B*.'s Sense *D.* iii. 218
How Plato's, *B.*, Newton's looks agree *M.E.* v. 60

Bad.

For each ill author is as *b.* a friend *E.C.* 519
Nor this a good, nor that a *b.* we call *E.M.* ii. 55
The good or *b.* the gifts of Fortune gain *E.M.* iv. 83
And grant the *b.* what happiness they would *E.M.* iv. 91
The *b.* must miss; the good, untaught, will find *E.M.* iv. 330
You make men desp'rate if they once are *b. E.S.* ii. 59
The strong Antipathy of Good to *B. E.S.* ii. 198
My lady falls to play; so *b.* her chance *M.E.* ii. 395
One, one *b. Deal*, Three *Septlevas* have lost *Mi* ix. 12
Would all my gold in one *b.* Deal were gone *Mi* ix. 15
And He, whose fustian's so sublimely *b. P.S.* 187
Nor stops, for one *b.* cork, his butler's pay *S.* ii. 63
Thus good or *b.* to one extreme betray *S.* iv. 24
When works are censur'd, not as *b.* but new *S.* v. 116
Could you complain, my Friend, he prov'd so *b. S.* vi. 22
The better art to know the good from *b. S.* vi. 55
In vain *b.* Rhymers all mankind reject *S.* vi. 153
Call, if you will, *b.* rhyming a disease *S.* vi. 182

Bade.

Say how the Goddess *b.* Britannia sleep *D.* i. 7
And *b.* the nimblest racer seize the prize *D.* i. 36
And *b.* thee live to crown Britannia's praise *D.* iii. 211
When, warm in youth, I *b.* the world farewell *E.A.* 110
Or moving spirit *b.* the waters flow *E.A.* 254
And *b.* Self-love and Social be the same *E.M.* iii. 318
From the dry rocks who *b.* the waters flow *M.E.* iii. 254
All these, my modest Satire *b. translate P.S.* 189
Why *b.* ye else, ye Pow'rs! her soul expire *U.L.* 11
For these perhaps (ere Nature *b.* her die *U.L.* 23
And *b.* his willows learn the moving song *W.* 14

Bag.

From the crack'd *b.* the dropping guinea spoke *M.E.* iii. 36
A wond'rous *B.* with both her hands she binds *R.L.* iv. 81
Full o'er their heads the swelling *b.* he rent *R.L.* iv. 91
A motley mixture! in long wigs, in b—s *D.* ii. 21

Bagatelle—see Vive.

Bagnios.

Thro' Taverns, Stews, and *B.* take our round *S.* iv. 119

Bail.

Ran out as fast as one who pays his *b. S.* viii. 182

Balaam—*see also* Sir Balaam.

A plain good man, and *B.* was his name *M.E.* iii. 342
A hundred smart in Timon, and in *B. S.* i. 42

Balance.

Where in nice *b.*, truth with gold she weighs *D.* i. 53
Snatch from his hand the *b.* and the rod *E.M.* i. 121
Reason's comparing *b.* rules the whole *E.M.* ii. 60
Make and maintain the *b.* of the mind *E.M.* ii. 120
But Heaven's just *b.* equal will appear *E.M.* iv. 69
Trims Europe's *b.*, tops the statesman's part *S.* viii. 154
At Sense and Virtue, b. all again *E.S.* i. 60
You *b.* not the many in the dark *M.E.* i. 122
To *b.* Fortune by a just expense *M.E.* iii. 223

Balanc'd.

The *b.* World, and open all the Main *S.* v. 2

c

BALANCING—BARE.

Balancing.
Tuning his voice, and *b*. his hands *D*. iii. 200

Balbus.
(Cries prating *B*.) "something will come out" *P.S.* 274

Bald.
Men bearded, *b*., cowl'd, uncowl'd, shod, unshod *D*. iii. 114

Bales.
Huge *b*. of British cloth blockade the door *M.E.* iii. 57

Balk'd.
B. are the Courts, and contest is no more *M.E.* iii. 272

Ball.
How little, mark ! that portion of the *b*. *D*. iii. 83
A fire, a jig, a battle, and a *b*. *D*. iii. 239
The Senator at Cricket urge the *B*. *D*. iv. 592
Drunk at a Borough, civil at a *B*. *M.E.* i. 75
With Truth and Goodness, as with Crown and *B*. *M.E.* ii. 184
Ye Gods ! what justice rules the *b*. *O*. ii. 25
To one man's treat, but for another's *b*. *R.L.* i. 96
Or lose her heart, or necklace, at a *b*. *R.L.* ii. 109
Who gave the *b*. or paid the visit last *R.L.* iii. 12
This Vault of Air, this congregated *B*. *S*. iv. 5.
The busy, idle blockheads of the *b*. *S*. viii. 203
Thus if eternal justice rules the *b*. *U.L.* 35
She glares in B—s, *front Boxes, and the Ring E*. iv. 53
Thus vanish sceptres, coronets, and *b*. *E*. v. 39
In courtly *b*., and nightly masquerades *R.L.* i. 72
Mere household trash f of birthrights, *b*., and shows, *S*. viii. 130

Balm.
But Welsted most the Poet's healing *b*. *D*. ii. 207
The *b*. of Dulness trickling in the ear *D*. iv. 544
Pours *b*. into the bleeding lover's wounds *O*. i. 29
For me the *b*. shall bleed, and amber flow *W.F.* 393

Balmy.
Not *b*. sleep to lab'rers faint with pain *A*. 44
The juice nectareous, and the *b*. dew *E.M.* l. 136
Her guardian SYLPH prolong'd the *b*. rest *R.L.* i. 20
The *b*. Zephyrs, silent since her death *W*. 49
The weeping amber or the *b*. tree *W.F.* 30

Band.
Fatten the courtier, starve the learned *b*. *D*. i. 315
They summon all her race : an endless *b*. *D*. ii. 19.
Here fortun'd Curl to slide ; loud shout the *b*. *D*. ii. 73
A low-born, cell-bred, selfish, servile *b*. *D*. ii. 356
Known by the *b*. and suit which Settle wore *D*. iii. 37
Four Knaves in garbs succinct, a trusty *b*. *R.L.* iii. 41
Straight hover round the Fair her airy *b*. *R.L.* iii. 113
Safe past the Gnome thro' this fantastic *b*. *R.L.* iv. 55
My wig all powder, and all snuff my *b*. *S*. iii. 262
With *b*. of Lily, and with cheek of Rose *S*. viii. 251
As flow'ry b—s *in wantonness are worn E*. iv. 65
That longer care contracts more lasting *b*. *E.M.* iii. 132
And boys in flow'ry *b*. the tiger lead *M*. 78
Next goes his wool, to clothe our valiant *b*. *M.E.* iii. 211
Straight the three *b*. prepare in arms to join *R.L.* iii. 29

Bandit.
No *B*. fierce, no Tyrant mad with pride *E.M.* iv. 41

Banish.
Beaux *b*. beaux, and coaches drive *R.L.* i. 102

Banish'd.
Some *b*. lover, or some captive maid *E.A.* 52
Their ancient bounds the *b*. Muses pass'd *E.C.* 710
B. the doctor, and expell'd the friend *M.E.* iii. 330
That both extremes were *b*. from their walls *S*. vii. 117
Ah, Cynthia ! ah, tho' *b*. from thy train *W.F.* 200

Bank.
On Avon's *b*., where flow'rs eternal blow *S*. v. 119
Expos'd in glorious heaps the tempting *B*. *Mi*. ix. 78
Well *purg'd, and worthy* Settle, B—s *and* Broome *D*. i. 146
Thence to the *b*. where rev'rend Bards repose *D*. ii. 347
Millions and millions on these *b*. he views *D*. iii. 31
Where bask on sunny *b*. the simple sheep *D*. iv. 552
As half-formed insects on the *b*. of Nile *E.C.* 41
While on thy *b*. Sicilian Muses sing *Sp*. 4

And trees weep amber on the *b*. of Po *Sp*. 62
No seas so rich, so gay no *b*. appear *W.F.* 225
Like the bright Beauties on thy *b*. below *W.F.* 232
To Thames's *b*., which fragrant breezes fill *W.F.* 263
When the sad pomp along his *b* was led *W.F.* 274
And on their *b*. Augusta rose in gold *W.F.* 336
Let Volga's *b*. with iron squadrons shine *W.F.* 363
A lost B.-bill *or heard their son was drown'd S*. ii. 56

Bankrupt.
In vain at Court the *B*. pleads his cause *M.E.* iii. 217

Banners.
Glad chains, warm furs, broad *b*. and broad faces *D*. i. 88

Bansted-down.
To Hounslow-heath I point and *B*. *S*. ii. 143

Bar.
Safe from the *B*., the Pulpit, and the Throne *E.S.* ii. 210
And (all those plagues in one) the brawling *B*. *S*. viii. 55

Barbarian.
B., stay ! that bloody stroke restrain *E.A.* 103
B. blindness, Christian zeal conspire *M.E.* v. 13
When wild B—s *spurn her dust O*. ii. 18

Barb'rous.
But fool with fool is *b*. civil war *D*. iii. 176
And promis'd Vengeance on a *b*. age *D*. iv. 40
More glorious yet, for *b*. hands to keep *D*. iv. 379
Stemm'd the wild torrent of a *b*. age *E.C.* 695
See *b*. nations at thy gates attend *M*. 91
What tho' (the use of *b*. spits forgot) *M.E.* iii. 171
Spite of his haughty mien, and *b*. pride *R.L.* iii. 70
How *b*. rage subsided at your word *S*. v. 398
Our haughty Norman boasts that *b*. name *W.F.* 63
Let *b*. Ganges arm a servile train *W.F.* 365
In brazen bonds shall *b*. Discord dwell *W.F.* 414

Barbecu'd.
Cries "Send me, Gods ! a whole hog *b*." *S*. ii. 26

Barber.
They change their weekly *B*., weekly News *S*. iii. 155
Your *B*., Cook, Upholst'rer, what you please *S*. vi. 10

Bares.
Or gives to Zembla fruits, to *B*. flow'rs *D*. i. 74

Bard.
Swift as a *b*. a bailiff leaves behind *D*. ii. 61
There march'd the *b*. and blockhead, side by side *D*. iv. 101
So by each *B*. an Alderman shall sit *D*. iv. 131
Else some some *B*. to our eternal praise *D*. iv. 171
And sure, if fate some future *b*. shall join *E.A.* 359
A certain *b*. encount'ring on the way *E.C.* 268
Or grant the *B*. whose Distich all commend *E.S.* ii. 160
Then southward let your *B*. retire *J.H.* i. 17
Rapt into future times, the *B*. began *M*. 7
And grace, altho' a *b*., devout *Ms*. xii. 14
The *B*. whom pilfer'd Pastorals renown *P.S.* 179
The silly *b*. grows fat or falls away *S*. v. 303
Here a lean *B*. whose wit could never give *S*. vii. 13
Hence B—s, *like Proteus long in vain tied down D*. i. 37
But such a bulk as no twelve *b*. could raise (*rep*.) *D*. ii. 39
Hear, Jove ! whose name my *b*. and I adore *D*. ii. 79
Thence to the banks where rev'rend *B*. repose (*rep*.) *D*. ii. 347
Why should I sing, what *b*. the nightly Muse *D*. ii. 421
Hail, *B*. triumphant ! born in happier days *E.C.* 189
Such shameless *B*. we have ; and yet 'tis true *E.C.* 610
The Saviour comes ! by ancient *b*. foretold *M*. 37
Or in fair series laurell'd *B*. be shown *M.E.* v. 61
He paid some *b*. with port, and some with praise *P.S.* 242
When British *b*. begin t' immortalize *S*. v. 54
Extols old *B*., or Merlin's Prophecy *S*. v. 132
How match the *b*. whom none e'er match'd before *S*. vi. 115

Bare.
And *b*. three-score is all ev'n that can boast *E.C.* 481
Nor over dress, nor leave her wholly *b*. *M.E.* iv. 52
Then by the rule that made the horse-tail *b*. *S*. v. 63
Tho' coarse, was rev'rend, and tho' *b*. was black *S*. viii. 39
B. *the mean heart that lurks beneath a Star S*. i. 108

Barge.
They stop the chariot, and they board the *b. P.S.* 10

Bark.
Say, shall my little *b.* attendant sail *E.M.* iv. 385
O you ! whom Vanity's light *b.* conveys *S.* v. 296
And *b. at Honour not confer'd by Kings E.S.* ii. 243

Barnard.
B. in spirit, sense, and truth abounds *S.* iii. 85
B., thou art a Cit, with all thy worth *S.* iii. 89

Baron.
The learned *B.* butterflies design *D.* iv. 589
Th' advent'rous *B.* the bright locks admir'd *R.L.* ii. 29
Now to the *B.* fate inclines the field *R.L.* iii. 66
The *B.* now his Diamonds pours apace *R.L.* iii. 75
See, fierce Belinda on the *B.* flies *R.L.* v. 75
Sent up in vapours to the *B.*'s brain *R.L.* iii. 119
But Fate and Jove had stopp'd the *B.* ears *R.L.* v. 2

Barr'd.
No place so sacred from such fops is *b. E.C.* 622

Barren.
The swain in *b.* deserts with surprise *M.* 67
A teeming Mistress, but a *b.* Bride *M.E.* ii. 72

Barrenness.
Just writes to make his *b.* appear *P.S.* 181

Barrier.
Guard the sure *b.* between that and Sense *D.* i. 178
'Twixt that, and Reason what a nice *b. E.M.* i. 223

Barrister.
Call himself *B.* to ev'ry wench *S.* vii. 79

Barrow.
Nor could a *B.* work on ev'ry block *D.* iv. 245

Base.
Founds the whole pile, of all his works the *b. D.* i. 160
Up starts a Palace ; lo, th' obedient *b. S.* iii. 140
On the broad *b.* of fifty thousand rise *S.* iv. 74
Speak'st thou of Syrian Princes ! Traitor b. D. iv. 375
To what *b.* ends, and by what abject ways *E.C.* 520
But were his Verses vile, his whisper *b. E.S.* i. 49
Th' unwilling Gratitude of *b.* mankind *S.* v. 14
B. Fear becomes the guilty, not the free *S.* viii. 194

Basilisk.
The crested *b.* and speckled snake *M.* 82

Bask.
Where *b.* on sunny banks the simple sheep *D.* iv. 352
And *b.* and whiten in the blaze of day *R.L.* ii. 78

Bass.
And his this Drum, whose hoarse, heroic *b. D.* ii. 233
And *b.* and treble voices strike the skies *R.L.* v. 42

Basset.
To gaze on *B.*, and remain unmov'd *Mi.* ix. 76
Look upon *B.*, you who Reason boast *Mi.* ix. 85
To *B.*'s *heavenly Joys, and pleasing Cares Mi.* ix. 102
The *B.*-table *spread, the Tallier come Mi.* ix. 1

Bastard.
T' enrich a *B.*, or a Son they hate *M.E.* iii. 98

Bastardy.
Not more of *B.* in heirs to Crowns *S.* vii. 82

Basto.
Him *B.* follow'd, but his fate more hard *R.L.* iii. 53

Bath.
Each Cygnet sweet, of *B.* and Tunbridge rage *D.* iii. 155

Bath'd.
All *b.* in tears—" Oh odious, odious Trees" *M.E.* ii. 46
There purple Vengeance *b.* in gore retires *W.F.* 417

Bathes.
And *b.* the forest where she rang'd before *W.F.* 208

Bathurst.
O teach us, *B. !* yet unspoil'd by wealth *M.E.* iii. 226
Who plants like *B.*, or who builds like Boyle *M.E.* iv. 178
Alas, my *B. !* what will they avail *S.* vi. 256

Battalions.
The pierc'd *b.* disunited fall *R.L.* iii. 85

Batter.
Next pleas'd his Excellence a town to *b. S* vi. 44

Batter'd.
By names of Toasts retails each *b.* jade *D.* ii. 134
And in four months a *b.* Harridan *Mi.* iii. 24
At the *Groom-Porter's b.* Bullies play *Mi.* ix. 99
See Ward by *b.* Beaux invited over *S.* iv. 56

Batt'ring-rams.
Like *b.* beats open ev'ry door *S.* viii. 265

Battle.
A fire, a jig, a *b.*, and a ball *D.* iii. 239
Not youthful Kings in *b.* seiz'd alive *R.L.* iv. 3
Mix with the World, and b. *for the State S.* iii. 28

Bauble.
Pleas'd with this *b.* still, as that before *E.M.* ii. 281

Bavius.
Old *B.* sits to dip poetic souls *D.* iii. 24
The hand of *B.* drench'd thee o'er and o'er *D.* iii. 46
Now *B.* take the poppy from thy brow *D.* iii. 317
Does not one table *B.* still admit *P.S.* 99
May ev'ry *B.* have his BUFO still *P.S.* 250

Bawd.
To *b.* for others, and go shares with Punk *Mi.* iii. 26

Bawdry.
Let *B.*, Billingsgate, my daughters dear *D.* i. 307

Bawl.
And Hungerford re-echoes *b.* for *b. D.* ii. 266

Bawling.
And (all those plagues in one) the *b.* Bar *S.* viii. 55

Bay.
Bring, bring the madding *B.*, the drunken Vine *D.* i. 303
Smote ev'ry Brain, and wither'd ev'ry *B. D.* iv. 10
To the last honour of the Butt and B—s *D.* i. 168
Mix'd the Owl's Ivy with the Poet's *b. D.* iii. 54
Tho' my own Aldermen confer'd the *b. D.* iii. 279
See, see, our own true Phœbus wears the *b. D.* iii. 323
Ev'n now, she shades thy Ev'ning walk with *b. E.* i. 35
Still green with *b.* each ancient Altar stands *E.C.* 181
Starts from her trance and trims her wither'd *b. E.C.* 698
The Poet's *b.* and Critic's ivy grow *E.C.* 706
A table with a cloth of *b. Mi.* xii. 6
You'll gain at least a *Knighthood*, or the *B. S.* i. 22
To Gammer Garton if it give the *b. S.* v. 91
Sons, Sires, and Grandsires all will wear the *b. S.* v. 171
Roscommon only boasts unspotted *b. S.* v. 214
That adds this wreath of Ivy to thy *B. Su.* 10
Embrace my Love, and bind my brows with *b. Su.* 38
And with fresh *b.* her rural shrine adorn *W.* 20
But chief in BAYS's monster-breeding breast (*rep.*) *D.* i. 108

Bayonne.
Thy Truffles, Perigord ! thy Hams, *B. D.* iv. 558

Be.—*Passim. See also* **To be.**

Bead.
With every *b.* I drop too soft a tear *E.A.* 270
And b—s *and pray'r-books are the toys of age E.M.* ii. 280
When doom'd to say his *b.* and even-song *S.* vii. 106

Beagles.
To plains with well-bred *b.* we repair *W.F.* 121

Beam.
So from the Sun's broad *b.* in shallow urns *D.* ii. 11
The mole's dim curtain, and the lynx's *b. E.M.* i. 212
As Heav'n's blest *b.* turns vinegar more sour *E.M.* ii. 148
Thee, drest in Fancy's airy *b. I.H.* iii. 41

BEAMING—BEAUTEOUS.

Or Fancy's *b.* enlarges, multiplies *M.E.* i. 35
So when the Sun's broad *b.* has tired the sight *M.E.* ii. 253
While ev'ry *b.* new transient colours flings *R.L.* ii. 67
The doubtful *b.* long nods from side to side *R.L.* v. 73
Oppress'd we feel the *b.* directly beat *S.* v. 221
And then a nodding *b.*, or pig of lead *S.* vi. 102
Where faint at best, the b—s of Science fall *D.* iii. 84
Grace shines around her with serenest *b. E.A.* 215
Where *b.* of warm imagination play *E.C.* 58
When first that sun too pow'rful *b.* displays *E.C.* 470
Thao, issu'd forth, the rival of his *b. R.L.* ii. 3
Defence from Phœbus', not from Cupid's *b. Su.* 14
Or b., good *DIGBY*, from a heart like thine *E.S.* ii. 241

Beaming.

The body's harmony, the *b.* soul *D.* iv. 236
Of *b.* diamonds, and reflected plate *S.* iv. 29

Beams.

That *b.* on earth, each Virtue he inspires *D.* iii. 220
Old Edward's armour *b.* on Cibber's breast *S.* v. 319

Beans.

The *B.* and Bacon set before 'em *I.H.* ii. 137

Bear.

Each growing lump, and brings it to a *B. D.* i. 102
At once the *B.* and Fiddle of the town *D.* i. 224
The fur that warms a monarch, warm'd a *b. E.M.* iii. 44
A Switz, a High-dutch, or a Low-dutch *B. S.* iii. 63
Call for the Farce, the *B.*, or the Black-joke *S.* v. 309
Let *B.* or Elephant be e'er so white *S.* v. 327
That *B.* or Elephant shall heed thee more *S.* v. 325
No Lord's anointed, but a Russian *B. S.* v. 389
'Tis a *B.*'s talent not to kick but hug *S.* i. 87
To want the strength of bulls, the fur of b—s *E.M.* i. 176
Go, gentle gales, and b. my sighs away *A.* 17, 23, &c.
And cease, ye gales,.to *b.* my sighs away *A.* 54
Our hearts may *b.* its slender chain a day *E.* iv. 64
And justly *b.* a Critic's noble name *E.C.* 47
Those best can *b.* reproof, who merit praise *E.C.* 583
But what his nature and his state can *b. E.M.* i. 292
Secure to be as blest as thou canst *b. E.M.* i. 286
On savage stocks inserted, learn to *b. E.M.* i. 182
For which we *b.* to live, or dare to die *E.M.* iv. 4
This, this, my friend, I cannot, must not *b. E.S.* i. 127
A Virgin shall conceive, a Virgin *b.* a Son *M.* 8
Court-virtues *b.*, like gems, the highest rate *M.E.* i. 141
Matter too soft a lasting mark to *b. M.E.* ii. 3
What then ? let Blood and Body *b.* the fault *M.E.* ii 73
B. home six Whores, and make his Lady weep *M.E.* iii. 72
Sufficient sap at once to *b.* and rot *Mi.* iii. 12
Alas ! far lesser losses than I *b. Mi.* ix. 45
By whose vile arts this heavy grief I *b. Mi.* ix. 56
My Passions rise, and will not *b.* the rein *Mi.* ix. 84
And teach the Being you preserv'd, to *b. P.S.* 134
B., like the Turk, no brother near the Throne *P.S.* 198
Oh cruel nymph ! a living death I *b. R.L.* v. 61
They scarce can *b.* their *Laureate* twice a year *S.* i. 34
In all debates where Critics *b.* a part *S.* i. 81
Is what two souls so gen'rous cannot *b. S.* iii. 58
Talkers I've learn'd to *b.* ; Motteux I knew *S.* viii. 50
These I could *b.* ; but not a rogue so civil *S.* viii. 56
B. me, some God ! oh quickly *b.* me hence *S.* viii. 184
To *b.* too tender, or too firm, a heart *U.L.* 7
And *b.* about the mockery of woe *U.L.* 57
B. me, O *b.* me to sequester'd scenes *W.F.* 261
B. Britain's thunder, and her Cross display *W.F.* 387

Beard.

With hoary whiskers, and a forky *b. R.L.* iii. 38

Bearded.

Men *b.*, bald, cowl'd, uncowl'd, shod, unshod *D.* iii. 114
Shall tend the flocks, or reap the *b.* grain *W.F.* 370

Bearings.

But of this frame, the *b.*, and the ties *E.M.* i. 29

Bears.

He *b.* no token of the sabler streams *D.* ii. 297
And Monumental brass this record *b. D.* ii. 313
B. Pisa's off'rings to his Arethuse *D.* ii. 342
To whom Time *b.* me on his rapid wing *D.* iv. 6
Still *b.* them faithful ; and that thus I eat *D.* iv. 389

Much injur'd Blunt ! why *b.* he Britain's hate *M.E.* iii. 133
She *b.* a Coronet and P—x for life *M.E.* iii. 392
The Lab'rer *b.* : what his hard heart denies *M.E.* iv. 171
Thro' climes and ages *b.* each form and name *M.E.* v. 32
The Gnome rejoicing *b.* her gifts away *R.L.* iv. 87
A wond'rous Tree that sacred Monarchs *b. S*⁄. 85
Still *b.* the name the hapless virgin bore *W.F.* 207

Beast.

Then thus. "Since Man from *b.* by Words is known *D.* iv. 149
Each *b.*, each insect happy in its own *E.M.* i. 185
B., bird, fish, insect, what no eye can see *E.M.* i. 239
In doubt to deem himself a God or *B. E.M.* ii. 8
Made *B.* in aid of Man, and Man of *B. E.M.* iii. 24
Thus *b.* and bird their common charge attend *E.M.* iii. 125
Man walked with *b.*, joint tenant of the shade *E.M.* iii. 152
B., Man, or Angel, Servant, Lord, or King *E.M.* iii. 302
I'm no such *B.*, nor his Relation *I.H.* i. 60
Full many a *B.* goes in, but none come out *S.* iii. 117
The People are a many-headed *B. S.* iii. 121
What wonder then, a *b.* or subject slain *W.F.* 57
But while the subject starv'd, the *b.* was fed *W.F.* 60
To b—s his pastures, and to fish his floods *E.M.* iii. 58
Learn from the *b.* the physic of the field *E.M.* iii. 174
Some sunk to *b.* find pleasure end in pain *E.M.* iv. 23
As *B.* of Nature may we hunt the Squires *E.S.* ii. 31
Return well-travell'd, and transform'd to *B. S.* iv. 193
Some *b.* were killed, tho' not whole hecatombs *S.* vii. 116
To see themselves fall endlong into *b. S.* viii. 167
To savage *b.* and savage laws a prey *W.F.* 45
What could be free, when lawless *b.* obey'd *W.F.* 51
A waste for *b.*, himself deny'd a grave *W.F.* 80
B., urg'd by us, their fellow-*b.* pursue *W.F.* 123
And arms employ'd on *b.* and birds alone *W.F.* 374

Beastly.

This filthy simile, this *b.* line *E.S.* ii. 181
And *b.* Skelton Heads of Houses quote *S.* v. 38

Beat.

When this rebellious heart shall *b.* no more *E.A.* 346
Together let us *b.* this ample field *E.M.* i. 9
To find an honest man I *b.* about *E.S.* ii. 102
Cæsar himself might whisper he was *b. M.E.* i. 130
Oppress'd we feel the beam directly *b. S.* v. 221
And, pawing, seems to *b.* the distant plain *W.F.* 152

Beating.

With *b.* hearts the dire event they wait *R.L.* ii. 141

Beats.

What bosom *b.* not in his country's cause *P.C.* 24
While clogg'd he *b.* his silken wings in vain *R.L.* ii. 130
Like batt'ring-rams *b.* open ev'ry door *S.* viii. 265
Flutters in blood, and panting *b.* the ground *W.F.* 114
With eager b. his Mechlin Cravat moves *Mi.* ix. 91

Beau.

No rag, no scrap of all the *b.* or wit *D.* ii. 119
Soft SIMPLICETTA doats upon a *B. Mi.* ix. 103
A Youth more glitt'ring than a Birth-night *B. R.L.* i. 23
And little hearts to flutter at a *B. R.L.* i. 90
And bids her *b.* demand the precious hairs *R.L.* iv. 122
A *B.* and Witling perish'd in the throng *R.L.* v. 59
But at her smile, the *b.* reviv'd again *R.L.* v. 70
You laugh, half *B.*, half Sloven if I stand *S.* iii. 261
Or h.'s in snuff-boxes and tweezer-cases *R.L.* v. 116
In various shapes of Parsons, Critics, B—s *E.C.* 459
Misers are Muck-worms, Silk-worms *B. Mi.* iv. 23
B—x banish b., and coaches coaches drive *R.L.* i. 102
Why round our coaches crowd the white-gloved *B. R.L.* v. 13
See Ward by batter'd *B.* invited over *S.* iv. 56
Of all b.-kind the best proportioned fools *S.* viii. 241
This the *B.-monde* shall from the Mall survey *R.L.* v. 133

Beaumont.

How *B.*'s judgment check'd what Fletcher writ *S.* v. 84

Beauteous.

And where it fix'd the *b.* bird I seiz'd *D.* iv. 430
Or blend in *b.* tints the coloured mass *E.* iii. 5
Whate'er was *b.*, or whate'er was great *Ep.* viii. 4
And once inclos'd in Woman's *b.* mould *R.L.* i. 48

Or raise a pimple on a *b.* face *R.L.* iv. 68
Then see, the nymph in *b.* grief appears *R.L.* iv. 143
Where twelve fair Signs in *b.* order lie *Sp.* 40
Oh ever *b.*, ever friendly! tell *U.L.* 5
And Temples rise, the *b.* works of Peace *W.F.* 378

Beautifully.
Let then the Fair one *b.* cry *M.E.* ii. 11

Beautify.
Those painted clouds that *b.* our days *E.M.* ii. 284

Beauty.
Thence *B.*, waking all her forms, supplies *E.* iii. 45
B., frail flow'r that ev'ry season fears *E.* iv. 57
Love, rais'd on *B.*, will like that decay *E.* iv. 63
Life, force, and *b.*, must to all impart *E.C.* 72
'Tis not a lip, or eye, we *b.* call *E.C.* 245
Her Birth, her *B.*, Crowds and Courts confess *E.S.* i. 145
Aw'd without Virtue, without *B.* charm'd *M.E.* ii. 46
Pow'r all their end, but *B.* all their means *M.E.* ii. 220
Still round and round the Ghosts of *B.* glide *M.E.* ii. 241
And gave you *B.*, but deny'd the Pelf *M.E.* ii. 287
And of one *b.* many bhuoders make *M.E.* iv. 28
Let not each *b.* ev'rywhere be spy'd *M.E.* iv. 53
Seen with Wit and *B.* seldom *Mi.* vi. 2
Yet wit ne'er tastes, and *b.* ne'er enjoys *P.S.* 312
B. that shocks you, parts that none will trust *P.S.* 332
Now awful *B.* puts on all its arms *R.L.* i. 139
And *b.* draws us with a single hair *R.L.* ii. 28
Unless good sense preserve, what *b.* gains *R.L.* v. 16
But since, alas! frail *b.* must decay *R.L.* v. 25
Procure her *B.*, make that *b.* chaste *S.* iv. 79
Just as one *B.* mortifies another *S.* viii. 259
What once had *b.*, titles, wealth and fame *U.L.* 70
Their *b.* wither'd, and their verdure lost *W.* 10
Like them in *b.*, should be like in fame *W.F.* 10
She scorn'd the praise of *b.*, and the care *W.F.* 177
And Quarles is sav'd by B—ies not his own D. i. 140
And other *B.* envy Wortley's Eyes *E.* iii. 60
With other *b.* charm my partial Eyes *E.A.* 126
Some *b.* yet no Precepts can declare *E.C.* 141
Those freer *b.* ev'n in them, seem faults *E.C.* 170
And call new *b.* forth from ev'ry line *E.C.* 666
That counts your *B.* only by your Stains *E.S.* ii. 221
They please as *b.*, here as wonders strike *M.E.* i. 144
B., like Tyrants, old and friendless grown *M.E.* ii. 227
Spontaneous *b.* all around advance *M.E.* iv. 67
Gods, Emp'rors, Heroes, Sages, *B.* lie *M.E.* v. 34
When rival *B.* for the Present strove *Mi.* ix. 38
Once gave new *b.* to the snowy neck *R.L.* iv. 170
Say why are *b.* prais'd and honour'd most *R.L.* v. 9
B. in vain their pretty Eyes may roll *R.L.* v. 33
Not that I'd lop the *B.* from his book *S.* v. 103
Such wits and *b.* are not prais'd for nought (*rep.*) *S.* viii. 234
Blest Thames's shores the brightest *b.* yield *Sp.* 63
And in one garland all their *b.* join *Su.* 56
In whom all *b.* are comprised in one *Su.* 58
Ah what avail the *b.* Nature wore (*rep.*) *W.* 35
Eternal *b.* grace the shining scene *W.* 71
Like the bright *B.* on thy banks below *W.F.* 231

Beaver.
Or round a Quaker's *B.* cast a Glory *E.S.* ii. 97

Beaver'd.
His *b.* brow a birchen garland wears *D.* iv. 141

Becalm'd.
Perhaps Prosperity *b.* his breast *M.E.* i. 111

Became.
B., when seiz'd, a puppy or an ape *D.* ii. 130
Zeal then, not charity, *b.* the guide *E.M.* iii. 261

Because.—*Passim.*

Becca-ficos.
Till *B.* sold so dev'lish dear *S.* ii. 39

. Beckon.
Sudden you mount, you *b.* from the skies *E.A.* 245

Beckoning.
What *b.* ghost, along the moonlight shade *U.L.* 1

Beckons.
Me gentle Delia *b.* from the plain *Sp.* 53

Become.
So shall each hostile name *b.* our own *D.* ii. 139
Contending wits *b.* the sport of fools *E.C.* 517
To patch, nay ogle, might *b.* a Saint *R.L.* v. 213
B. the portion of a booby Lord *S.* ii. 176

Becomes.
Ev'n mean Self-love *b.*, by force divine *E.M.* ii. 291
The same Self-love, in all, *b.* the cause *E.M.* iii. 271
Then better sure it Charity *b. E.S.* ii. 48
B. the stuff of which our dream is wrought *M.E.* i. 48
And which it much *b.* you to forget *S.* iv. 94
Base Fear *b.*, the guilty, not the free *S.* viii. 194

Becoming.
On the rich quilt sinks with *b.* woe *R.L.* iv. 35

Bed.
Then snatch'd a sheet of Thule from her *b. D.* i. 258
On Codrus' old, or Dunton's modern *b. D.* ii. 144
In flames, like Semele's, be brought to *b. D.* iii. 315
F'air from its humble *b.* I rear'd this Flow'r *D.* iv. 405
The same his table, and the same his *b. E.M.* iii. 153
The George and Garter dangling from that *b. M.E.* iii. 303
Morpheus rouses from his *b. O.* i. 31
Say for my comfort, languishing in *b. P.S.* 121
Make Languor smile, and smooth the *b.* of Death *P.S.* 411
'Twas He had summon'd to her silent *b. R.L.* i. 21
Or the small pillow grace a lady's *b. R.L.* iii. 166
She sighs for ever on her pensive *b. R.L.* iv. 23
Who fairly puts all Characters to *b. S.* v. 291
In that blest moment from his oozy *b. W.F.* 329
The shining robes, rich jewels, b—*s of state E.* iv. 51
A waving Glow the bloomy *b.* display *M.E.* iv. 83
The Furies sink upon their iron *b. O.* i. 69
Or rumpled petticoats, or tumbled *b. R.L.* iv. 72
Discharge their Garrets, move their *b.*, and run *S.* iii. 157
Faith, gallants, board with saints, and b. *with sinners E. J.S.* 24

Bedford-head.
I'll have a party at the *B. S.* ii. 42

Bedlam.
All *B.*, or Parnassus, is let out *P.S.* 4
I wag'd no war with *B.* or the *Mint P.S.* 156
In durance, exile, *B.*, or the Mint *S.* i. 99
Befringe the rails of *B.* and Soho *S.* v. 419
Hence, from the straw where B.*'s Prophet nods D.* iii. 7

Bedropp'd.
The Priest whose Flattery *b.* the Crown *E.S.* ii. 164
The yellow carp, in scales *b.* with gold *W.F.* 144

Bee.
Not show'rs to larks, nor sun-shine to the *b. A.* 45
In the nice *b.*, what sense so subtly true *E.M.* i. 219
Thy arts of building from the *b.* receive *E.M.* iii. 175
As thick as b—*s o'er vernal blossoms fly D.* iii. 33
The buzzing *B.* about their dusky Queen *D.* iv. 80
The Ant's republic, and the realm of *B. E.M.* iii. 184
Like *b.*, are humming in my ears *I.H.* ii. 70 *s*
Here *b.* from blossoms sip the rosy dew *Su.* 69
Th' industrious *b.* neglect their golden store *W.* 51

Beech.
Beneath the shade a spreading *E.* displays *A.* 1
The shady b—es, *and the cooling streams Su.* 13

Beef.
Roast *b.*, though old, proclaims him stout *Mi.* xii. 13

Been.—*Passim.*

Beer.
Flow, Welsted, flow! like thine inspirer, *B. D.* iii. 169
Is there a Parson, much bemus'd in *b. P.S.* 15

Beeves.
B. at his touch at once to jelly turn *D.* iv. 551

Before.—*Passim.*

Befriend.
Be thou the first true merit to *b. E.C.* 474

Befringe.
B. the rails of Bedlam and Soho *S.* v. 419

Beg.
Ye shall not *b.* like gratis-given Bland *D.* i. 331
Some *b.* an eastern, some a western wind *D.* ii. 88
But, Sir, I *b.* you (for the Love of Vice) *E.S.* ii. 42
Wants reach all states; they *b.* but better drest *S.* viii. 224

Began.
Next o'er his Books his eyes *b.* to roll *D.* i. 127
With whom my Muse *b.*, with whom shall end *D.* i. 166
With me *b.* this genius, and shall end *D.* ii. 55
Thou gav'st that ripeness, which so soon *b. D.* iv. 287
But candid, free, sincere, as you *b. E.* ii. 13
Stones leap'd to form, and rocks *b.* to live *E.C.* 702
As who *b.* a thousand years ago *E.M.* i. 76
Th' exceptions few; some change since all *b. E.M.* i. 147
The gen'ral ORDER, since the whole *b. E.M.* i. 171
Vast chain of Being! which from God *b. E.M.* i. 237
Saw helpless him from whom their life *b. E.M.* iii. 142
Self-love and Social at her birth *b. E.M.* iii. 249
The Fury-passions from that blood *b. E.M.* iii. 167
'Till drooping, sick'ning, dying, they *b. E.M.* iii. 223
And knows where Faith, Law, Morals, all *b. E.M.* iv. 339
Alas! alas! pray end what you *b. E.S.* ii. 254
But just endures the winter she *b. Mi.* iii. 23
'Tis sung, when Midas' ears *b.* to spring *P.S.* 69
Silence ensu'd, and thus the nymph *b. R.L.* v. 8
Go work, hunt, exercise! (he thus *b.*) *S.* ii. 11
Whereat the gentleman *b.* to stare *S.* vi. 194
Proud Nimrod first the bloody chase *b. W.F.* 61

See also **Begun.**

Beget.
All that on Folly Frenzy could *b. D.* i. 125

Beggar.
See the blind *b.* dance, the cripple sing *E.M.* ii. 167
Affrights the *b.* whom he longs to eat *M.E.* iv. 196
Call'd happy Dog! the *B.* at his door *S.* iv. 116
As needy *B*—s *sing at doors for meat S.* vii. 26

Begged.
The Mother *b.* the blessing of a Rake *D.* iv. 286
Produc'd his Play, and *b.* the Knight's advice *E.C.* 274
And *b.* he'd take the pains to kick the rest *E.S.* ii. 155
While Anna *b.* and Dido rag'd in vain *R.L.* v. 6
I bought no benefice, I *b.* no place *S.* viii. 11

Begging.
See all our Nobles *b.* to be Slaves *E.S.* i. 163

Begin.
Now sighs steal out, and tears *b.* to flow *E.C.* 379
Ye Nymphs of Solyma! *b.* the song *M.* 1
Now leave complaining, and *b.* your *Tea Mi.* ix. 112
All side in parties, and *b.* th' attack *R.L.* v. 39
When British bards *b.* t' immortalize *S.* v. 54
B., the vales shall ev'ry note rebound *Sp.* 44
If Delia smile, the flow'rs *b.* to spring *Sp.* 71
B.; this charge the dying Daphne gave *W.* 17

Beginning.
Explain his own *b.,* or his end *E.M.* ii. 38

Begins.
And each bold figure just *b.* to live *E.C.* 491
Where ends the Virtue, or *b.* the Vice *E.M.* ii. 210
All that we feel of it *b.* and ends *E.M.* iv. 241
Here honest Nature ends as she *b. M.E.* i. 227
Trembling *b.* the sacred rites of Pride *R.L.* i. 128
Bows and *b.*—" This Lad, Sir, is of Blois *S.* vi. 4

Begot.
For Use will father what 's *b.* by Sense *S.* vi. 170
To whom related, or by whom *b. U.L.* 72

Begs.
Physic of *Metaphysic b.:* defence *D.* iv. 645
That *b.* my int'rest for a Place *I.H.* ii. 68 *s*
Now he *b.* Verse, and the wag *b.* gets commends *Mi.* iii. 13
Then prostrate falls, and *b.* with ardent eyes *R.L.* ii. 43
A Poet *b.* me, I will hear him read *S.* vi. 93

Begun.
Bland and familiar as in life *b. D.* iii. 41
And orient Science their bright course *b. D.* iii. 74
When thus th' attendant Orator *b. D.* iv. 281
And the Monks finish'd what the Goths *b. E.C.* 692
But when his own great work is but *b. E.M.* ii. 41
Or plain tradition that this All *b. E.M.* iii. 227
Rapt into future times, the Bard *b. M.* 7
Shall finish what his short-liv'd Sire *b. M.* 64
So morning Insects that in muck *b. M.E.* ii. 27
He rais'd his azure wand, and thus *b., R.L.* ii. 72

Behaves.
She speaks, *b.,* and acts just as she ought *M.E.* ii. 161

Beheld.
And South *b.* that Master-piece of Man *D.* iv. 174
Oh just *b.* and lost! admir'd and mourn'd *E.* i. 3
Yes, I *b.* th' Athenian Queen *E.* vi. 1
Consider'd singly, or *b.* too near *E.C.* 172
Had he *b.* an Audience gape so wide *S.* v. 321
B. such scenes of envy, sin, and hate *S.* viii. 193
Hast thou, oh Sun! *b.* an emptier sort *S.* viii. 204

Behind.—*Passim.*

Behold.
Here pleas'd *b.* her mighty wings outspread *D.* i. 27
Stood dauntless Curl; "*B.* that rival here *D.* ii. 58
B. the wonders of th' oblivious Lake *D.* iii. 44
B. yon Isle, by Palmers, Pilgrims trod *D.* iii. 113
Now look thro' Fate! *b.* the scene she draws *D.* iii. 127
B., and count them, as they rise to light *D.* iii. 130
B. an hundred sons, and each a Dunce *D.* iii. 138
B. yon Pair, in strict embraces join'd *D.* iii. 179
Yet would'st thou more? in yonder cloud *b. D.* iii. 253
Now prostrate! dead! *b.* that Caroline *D.* iv. 413
She comes! she comes! the sable Throne *b. D.* iv. 629
And image charms he must *b.* no more *E.A.* 362
But more advanc'd, *b.* with strange surprise *E.C.* 223
Where slaves once more their native land *b. E.M.* i. 107
B. the child, by Nature's kindly law *E.M.* ii. 275
Look round our World! *b.* the chain of Love *E.M.* iii. 7
Now Europe's laurels on their brows *b. E.M.* iv. 295
B. the place, where if a Poet *I.H.* ii. 187
From Jesse's root *b.* a branch arise *M.* 9
Hear him ye deaf, and all ye blind, *b. M.* 38
B.! If Fortune or a Mistress frowns *M.E.* i. 103
B. a rev'rend sire, whom want of grace *M.E.* i. 232
B. the market-place with poor o'erspread *M.E.* iii. 263
B. what blessings Wealth to life can lend *M.E.* iii. 297
The Dev'l was piqu'd such saintship to *b. M.E.* iii. 349
B. Sir Balaam, now a man of spirit *M.E.* iii. 375
B. Villario's ten years' toil complete *M.E.* iv. 79
On ev'ry side you look, *b.* the Wall *M.E.* iv. 114
B. this *Equipage,* by *Mathers* wrought *Mi.* ix. 29
Approach! Great Nature studiously *b. Mi.* x. 7
Live o'er each scene, and be what they *b. P.C.* 4
B., four Kings in majesty rever'd *R.L.* iii. 37
B. the first in virtue as in face *R.L.* v. 78
The Sylphs *b.* it kindling as it flies *R.L.* v. 131
Could she *b.* us tumbling thro' a hoop *S.* v. 48
B. the band that wrought a Nation's cure *S.* v. 225
Scarce was I enter'd, when, *b.!* there came *S.* viii. 24
B. the groves that shine with silver frost *W.* 9
B. us kindly, who your name implore *W.* 75
Tho' Tiber's streams immortal Rome *b. W.F.* 357
B.! th' ascending Villas on my side (rep.) *W.F.* 375
Earth's distant ends our glory shall *b. W.F.* 401
Peru once more a race of Kings *b. W.F.* 411

Beholds.
Here she *b.* the Chaos dark and deep *D.* i. 55
B. thro' fogs, that magnify the scene *D.* ii. 80
Padua, with sighs, *b.* her Livy burn *D.* iii. 105
Dunce scorning Dunce *b.* the next advance *D.* iv. 137
B. himself a Patriot, Chief or Saint *D.* iv. 536
B. thee glorious only in thy Fall *E.* i. 20
And Heav'n *b.* its image in his breast *E.M.* iv. 372

Being.
All this thou wert, and *b.* this before *E.* ii. 8
What vary'd *B.* peoples ev'ry star *E.M.* i. 27
Or who could suffer *B.* here below *E.M.* i. 80
Vast chain of *B.!* which from God began *E.M.* i. 237
B. on *B.* wreck'd, and world on world *E.M.* i. 254

A *B.* darkly wise, and rudely great *E.M.* ii. 4
Connects each *b.*, greatest with the least *E.M.* iii. 23
And, till he ends the *b.*, makes it blest *E.M.* iii. 66
To each unthinking *b.* Heav'n, a friend *E.M.* iii. 72
God in the nature of each *b.* founds *E.M.* iii. 109
A sov'reign *b.* but a sov'reign good *E.M.* iii. 238
Sees that no *B.* any bliss can know *E.M.* iv. 335
Prov'd by the ends of *b.* to have been *M.E.* iii. 290
And teach the *B.* you preserv'd, to bear *P.S.* 134
One Chorus let all *B.* raise *U.P.* 51
His actions, passions, b—'s *use and end E.M.* i. 66
Oh Happiness! our *b.* end and aim *E.M.* iv. 1
Superior b—s *when of late they saw E.M.* ii. 31
All vocal *b.* hymn'd their equal God *E.M.* iii. 156
As now your own, our *b.* were of old *R.L.* i. 47

Beldam.

What is PRUDERY? 'Tis a *B. Mi.* vi. 1

Belerium.

From old *B.* to the northern main *W.F.* 316

Belief.

To kings presumption, and to crowds *b. E.M.* ii. 244

Belies.

B. his features, nay extends his hands *M.E.* iii. 294

Believe.

And all the western world *b.* and sleep *D.* iii. 100
And, form'd like tyrants, tyrants would *b. E.M.* iii. 260
And yet, *b.* me, good as well as ill *M.E.* ii. 269
I pay my debts, *b.*, and say my pray'rs *P.S.* 268
Hear and *b.!* thy own importance know *R.L.* i. 35
The Fair and Innocent shall still *b. R.L.* i. 40
In either case, *b.* me, we admire *S.* iv. 21
B. me, many a German prince is worse *S.* iv. 83

Believ'd.

Heav'n scarce *b.* the conquest it survey'd *E.A.* 113
Oh wretch! *b.* the spouse of God in vain *E.A.* 177
Much was *b.*, but little understood *E.C.* 689
How many curs'd the moment they *b. Mi.* ix. 72
In mystic visions, now *b.* too late *R.L.* iv. 166

Believers.

So Schismatics the plain *B.* quit *E.C.* 428

Believes.

Go just alike, yet each *b.* his own *E.C.* 10
Whom, when they praise, the world *b.* no more *E.C.* 594
One who *b.* as Tindal leads the way *S.* iv. 64

Belinda.

As when *B.* rais'd my strain *I.H.* i. 50
This ev'n *B.* may vouchsafe to view *R.L.* i. 4
B. still her downy pillow prest *R.L.* i. 19
'Twas then, *B.*, if report say true *R.L.* i. 117
B. smil'd, and all the world was gay *R.L.* ii. 52
B. now, whom thirst of fame invites *R.L.* iii. 25
Thus far both armies to *B.* yield *R.L.* iii. 65
And Ariel weeping from *B.* flew *R.L.* iv. 12
Hear me, and touch *B.* with chagrin *R.L.* iv. 77
B. burns with more than mortal ire *R.L.* iv. 93
For who can move when fair *B.* fails *R.L.* v. 4
B. frown'd, Thalestris call'd her prude *R.L.* v. 36
See fierce *B.* on the Baron flies *R.L.* v. 72
Now meet thy fate, incensed *B.* cry'd *R.L.* v. 87
Which long she wore, and now *B.* wears *R.L.* v. 96
And soft B.'s blush for ever glow E. iii. 62
This just behind *B.* neck he spread *R.L.* iii. 133
And 'midst the stars inscribe *B.* name *R.L.* v. 150

Belisarius.

But pitied *B.* old and blind *Mi.* ii. 6

Bell.

Now sunk in sorrows with a tolling *b. D.* ii. 228
And now the Chapel's silver *b.* you hear *M.E.* iv. 141
Who to the *Dean,* and *silver b.* can swear *P.S.* 299
Thrice rung the *b.*, the slipper knock'd the ground *R.L.* i. 17
That touch my *b.*, I cannot turn away *S.* ii. 140
Far as loud Bow's stupendous b—s *resound D.* iii. 278
The *b.* she jingled, and the whistle blew *R.L.* v. 94

Belle.

A well-bred Lord t' assault a gentle *B. R.L.* i. 8
Could make a gentle *B.* reject a Lord *R.L.* i. 10
Might hide her faults, if B—s had faults to hide R.L. ii. 16

Bellow.

Or such as *b.* from the deep Divine *D.* ii. 257

Bellows.

Blue Neptune storms, the *b.* deeps resound *R.L.* v. 50

Bellowing.

Heard by the breath th' inspiring *b.* blow (*rep.*) *S.* vii. 19

Belly.

Then snapt his box, and strok'd his *b.* down *D.* iv. 495
A salmon's *b.*, Helluo, was thy fate *M.E.* i. 238

Belong.

To heav'nly themes sublimer strains *b. M.* 2
Whether the name *b.* to Pope or Vernon *S.* ii. 166
And say to which shall our applause *b. S.* iii. 97

Belonging.

Which one *b.* to the House *I.H.* i. 55

Belongs.

Thus far was right, the rest *b.* to Heav'n *P.S.* 419

Belov'd.

To dress her charms, and make her more *b. E.C.* 103
That only makes superior sense *b. E.C.* 577
She's still the same, *b.*, contented thing *E.S.* i. 140
O soft Humanity in Age *b. Ep.* ix. 4
Thus gracious CHANDOS is *b.* at sight *M.E.* i. 54
Happier their author, when by these *b. P.S.* 144

Below.—*Passim.*

Belt.

A *b.* her waist, a fillet binds her hair *W.F.* 178

Bemoan.

The silver swans her hapless fate *b. W.* 39

Bemus'd.

Is there a Parson, much *b.* in beer *P.S.* 15

Ben.

And each true Briton is to *B.* so civil *S.* v. 41
B., old and poor, as little seem'd to heed *S.* v. 73
What boy but hears the sayings of old *B. S.* v. 80
Which made old *B.*, and surly Deonis swear *S.* v. 388

Bench.

And woo in language of the Pleas and *B. S.* vii. 60
Still break the b—es, *Henley! with thy strain D.* iii. 203

Bend.

To aid our cause, if Heav'n thou canst not *b. D.* iii. 307
Did here the trees mount ruddier burdens *b. E.M.* iii. 203
She taught the weak to *b.*, the proud to pray *E.M.* iii. 251
But useless lances into scythes shall *b. M.* 61
Walk in thy light, and in thy temple *b. M.* 92
To rear the Column, and the Arch to *b. M.E.* iv. 48
The Gods and Brutus *b.* to love *O.* iii. 14
But when to mischief mortals *b.* their will *R.L.* iii. 125
And swelling clusters *b.* the curling vines *Sp.* 36
I see, I see, where two fair cities *b. W.F.* 379
Once more to *b.* before a BRITISH QUEEN *W.F.* 384

Bended.

Next bidding all draw near on *b.* knees *D.* iv. 565
Aw'd, on my *b.* knees I fell *E.* vi. 9

Bending.

While she with garlands hung the *b.* boughs *A.* 68
Lo, earth receives him from the *b.* skies *M.* 33
And eyes the dancing cork, and *b.* reed *W.F.* 140

Bends.

And here the groaning shelves Philemon *b. D.* i. 154
Sheffield approves, consenting Phœbus *b. Mi.* i. 7
To that she *b.*, to that her eyes she rears *R.L.* i. 126
As o'er the fragrant streams she *b.* her head *R.L.* iii. 134

Beneath.—*Passim.*

24 BENEFICE—BESTOW.

Benefice.
I bought no *b.*, I begg'd no place *S.* viii. 12

Benefit.
The blessed *b.*, not there confin'd *E.S.* ii. 177

Benefits.
Sometimes the Folly *b.* Mankind *S.* v. 191

Benevolence.
That graft *b.* on charities *E.M.* iii. 138
Ev'n Kings learn'd justice and *b. E.M.* iii. 280
In one close system of *B. E.M.* iv. 358
One, driv'n by strong *B.* of soul *S.* vi. 276

Benighted.
And all who since, in mild *b.* days *D.* iii. 53
B. wanderers, the forest o'er *M.E.* iii. 193

Benigner.
B. influence on thy nodding head *D.* iv. 346

Benlowes.
B., propitious still to blockheads, bows *D.* iii. 21

Benson.
Composed he stood, bold *B.* thrust him by *D.* iv. 110
Manners with Candour are to *B.* giv'n *E.S.* ii. 72
On Poets' tombs see *B*—'s titles writ *D.* iii. 325

Bent.
Tho' strong the *b.*, and quick the turns of mind *M.E.* i. 64
Just as the Twig is *b.*, the Tree 's inclin'd *M.E.* i. 150
One *b.*; the handle this, and that the spout *R.L.* iv. 50

Bentley.
B. his mouth with classic flatt'ry opes *D.* ii. 205
Where *B.* late tempestuous wont to sport *D.* iv. 201
From slashing *B.* down to pidling Tibalds *P.S.* 164
Like slashing *B.* with his desp'rate hook *S.* v. 104

Bequeath'd.
Inspir'd when living, and *b.* in death *Sw.* 40

Berecynthia.
As *B.*, while her offspring vie *D.* iii. 131

Berenice.
Not *B.'s* locks first rose so bright *R.L.* v. 129

Be-rhym'd.
Poems I heeded (now *b.* so long) *P.S.* 221

Berkeley.
To *B.*, ev'ry Virtue under Heav'n *E.S.* ii. 73

Berks.
Who rules in Cornwall, or who rules in *B. S.* iv. 104

Bernard.
With arms expanded *B.* rows his state *D.* ii. 67
And "*B.! B.!*" rings thro' all the Strand *D.* ii. 74

Bernini.
Assign'd his figure to *B.'s* care *S.* v. 381

Berries.
Now blushing *b.* paint the yellow grove *A.* 75
The *b.* crackle, and the mill turns round *R.L.* iii. 106

Bertrand.
It came from *B.'s*, not the skies *E.* vi. 15

Besaleel, *see also* **Morris.**
Breval, Bond, *B.*, the varlets caught *D.* ii. 126

Beset.
Now range the hills, the gameful woods *b. W.F.* 95
Secure they trust th' unfaithful field *b. W.F.* 103

Beside, Besides.—*Pass'm.*

Besiege.
Thus Fools with Compliments *b.* ye *I.H.* i. 29
And frequent hearses shall *b.* your gates *U.L.* 38

Besieg'd.
Dreading ev'n fools, by Flatterers *b. P.S.* 207

Besought.
And feels that grace his pray'r *b.* in vain *S.* v. 238

Bespangling.
The heav'ns *b.* with dishevell'd light *R.L.* v. 130

Bespread.
Or should one pound of powder less *b. S.* viii. 246

Besprent.
Of sober face, with learned dust *b. D.* iii. 186

Besprinkles.
And soft *b.* with Cimmerian dew *D.* iii. 4

Bess.
Was velvet in the youth of good Queen *B. S.* viii. 41

Best.
The Goddess then: "Who *b.* can send on high *D.* ii. 161
He wins this Patron, who can tickle *b. D.* ii. 196
Here prove who *b.* can dash thro' thick and thin *D.* ii. 276
A pig of lead to him who dives the *b. D.* ii. 282
Where, faint at *b.*, the beams of Science fall *D.* iii. 84
And loves you *b.* of all things—but his horse *E.* v. 30
There died the *b.* of passions, Love and Fame *E.A.* 40
He *b.* can paint 'em, who shall feel 'em most *E.A.* 366
And but so mimic ancient wits at *b. E.C.* 331
Those heads, as stomachs, are not sure the *b. E.C.* 388
Those *b.* can bear reproof, who merit praise *E.C.* 583
'Tis *b.* sometimes your censure to restrain *E.C.* 596
We'd be the *b.* good-natur'd things alive *E.J.S.* 14
That Wisdom infinite must form the *b. E.M.* i. 44
At *b.* more watchful this, but that more strong *E.M.* ii. 76
Grafts on this Passion our *b.* principle *E.M.* ii. 176
And ev'n the *b.*, by fits, what they despise *E.M.* ii. 214
Know, all enjoy that pow'r which suits them *b. E.M.* iii. 80
Reason, however able, cool at *b. E.M.* iii. 85
Whate'er is *b.* administer'd, is *b. E.M.* iii. 304
Who sees and follows that great scheme the *b.* (rep.) *E.M.* iv. 95
The very *b.* will variously incline *E.M.* iv. 143
Each widow asks it for the *B. of Men E.S.* ii. 108
Be satisfied, I'll do my *b. I.H.* ii. 78 s
And what the very *b.* of all *I.H.* ii. 152
He did his *b.* to seem to eat *I.H.* ii. 173
But grant that actions *b.* discover man *M.E.* i. 119
And *b.* distinguish'd by black, brown, or fair *M.E.* ii. 4
Because she 's honest, and the *b.* of Friends *M.E.* ii. 104
Woman's at *b.* a contradiction still *M.E.* ii. 270
Its last *b.* work, but forms a softer man *M.E.* ii. 272
Blest paper-credit, last and *b.* supply *M.E.* iii. 39
Which snatch'd my *b.*, my fav'rite curl away *R.L.* iv. 148
Abuse the city's *b.* good men in metre *S.* i. 39
There my retreat the *b.* Companions grace *S.* i. 125
For I, who hold sage Homer's rule the *b. S.* ii. 159
At *b.*, it falls to some ungracious son *S.* ii. 173
Who counsels *b.*? who whispers, "Be but great *S.* iii. 101
And promise our *b.* Friends to rhyme no more *S.* v. 178
Observe how seldom ev'n the *b.* succeed *S.* v. 286
Ah think, what Poet *b.* may make them known *S.* v. 377
Of whose *b.* phrase and courtly accent join'd *S.* viii. 48
"But the *b.* words?" "Oh Sir, the *Dictionary*" *S.* viii. 69
And all is splendid poverty at *b. S.* viii. 225
Of all beau-kind the *b.* proportion'd fools *S.* viii. 241
Thou know'st if *b.* bestow'd or not *U.P.* 47

Bestia.
And better got, than *B.'s* from the throne *P.S.* 391

Bestow.
Each pleasing Blount shall endless smiles *b. E.* iii. 61
Those still at least are left thee to *b. E.A.* 120
But where 's the man, who counsel can *b. E.C.* 631
How those in common all their wealth *b. E.M.* iii. 185
What War could ravish, Commerce could *b. E.M.* iii. 205
See the sole bliss Heav'n could on all *b. E.M.* iv. 327
'Tis with distinction you *b. I.H.* i. 22
Ask we what makes one keep, and one *b. M.E.* iii. 163
Unpolish'd Gems no ray on Pride *b. Mi.* x. 5
Nay oft, in dreams, invention we *b. R.L.* ii. 99
B. a Garland only on a Bier *S.* v. 68
Fit to *b.* the Laureate's weighty place *S.* v. 379
Indeed, could wealth *b.* or wit or merit *S.* vi. 226
There shall the morn her earliest tears *b. U.L.* 65

BESTOW'D—BIDS.   25

Bestow'd.
And Pride b. on all a common friend *E.M.* ii. 272
Thou hast at least b. one penny well *S.* ii. 110
Unless the Gods b. a proper Muse *S.* v. 234
Or when from Court a birth-day suit b. *S.* v. 332
Thou know'st if best b. or not *U.P.* 47

Bestows.
Of blindness, weakness, Heav'n b. on thee *E.M.* i. 284
What nature wants, commodious gold b. *M.E.* iii. 21
But how unequal it b., observe *M.E.* iii. 23
And harvests on a hundred realms b. *W.F.* 360

Bestride.
The bounding steed you pompously b. *E.M.* iii. 35

Bet.
Newmarket-fame, and judgment at a b. *M.E.* i. 86

Bethel.
Oh blameless B.! to relieve thy breast *E.M.* iv. 126
Thus B. spoke, who always speaks his thought *S.* ii. 129
Hear B.'s *Sermon, one not vers'd in schools S.* ii. 9

Betides.
Damn'd to the Mines, an equal fate b. *M.E.* iii. 109

Betimes.
And 'tis but just to let them live b. *E.C.* 477
I've had my Purgatory here b. *S.* viii. 5

Betray.
How happy! those to ruin, these b. *E.M.* iv. 290
The treach'rous colours the fair art b. *E.C.* 492
With mean complacence ne'er b. your trust *E.C.* 580
And, if he lie not, must at least b. *P.S.* 298
Eternal smiles his emptiness b. *P.S.* 315
With hairy springes we the birds b. *R.L.* ii. 25
By force to ravish, or by fraud b. *R.L.* ii. 32
Thus good or bad to one extreme b. *S.* iv. 24
But when the tainted gales the game b. *W.F.* 101

Betray'd.
And once b. me into common sense *D.* i. 188
All Europe sav'd, yet Britain not b. *M.E.* i. 84
But bribes a Senate, and the Land's b. *M.E.* iii. 32
By love of Courts to numerous ills b. *R.L.* iv. 152

Betrays.
Such rage without b. the fire within *E.J.S.* 17
Murders their species, and b. his own *E.M.* iii. 164

Better.
Take up the Bible, once my b. guide *D.* i. 200
My b. and more Christian progeny *D.* i. 228
Taylor, their b. Charon, lends an oar *D.* iii. 19
Points him two ways, the narrower is the b. *D.* iv. 152
Roman and Greek Grammarians I know your B. *D.* iv. 215
What tho' we let some b. sort of fool *D.* iv. 255
Your silence there is b. than your spite *E.C.* 598
Athens and Rome in b. ages knew *E.C.* 644
Of those who less presum'd, and b. knew *E.C.* 720
B. for Us, perhaps, it might appear *E.M.* iv. 72
But future views of b., or of worse *E.M.* iv. 72
Contents us not. A b. shall we have *E.M.* iv. 132
Is Virtue's prize: a b. would you fix *E.M.* iv. 169
When what t' oblivion b. were resign'd *E.M.* iv. 251
And taught his Romans, in much b. metre *E.S.* i. 9
So much the b., you may laugh the more *E.S.* i. 56
Then b. sure it Charity becomes *E.S.* ii. 48
Still b. Ministers; or, if the thing *E.S.* ii. 50
And there I'll die, no worse nor b. *I.H.* i. 80
What good, what b., we may call *I.H.* ii. 151
Who copies Your's or OXFORD's b. part *M.E.* iii. 243
He finds at last he b. likes a Field *M.E.* iv. 88
Informs you, Sir, 'twas when he knew no b. *P.S.* 52
That not for Fame, but Virtue's b. end *P.S.* 342
And b. got thus Bestia's from the throne *P.S.* 391
B. be Cibber, I'll maintain it still *S.* i. 37
The world's good word is b. than a song *S.* ii. 102
Surpris'd at b., or surpris'd at worse *S.* iv. 23
Or b. Precepts if you can impart *S.* iv. 132
What b. teach a Foreigner the tongue *S.* v. 205
The b. art to know the good from bad *S.* vi. 55
B. (say I) be pleas'd, and play the fool *S.* vi. 181
He bought at thousands, what with b. wit *S.* vi. 236

The Ship itself may make a b. figure *S.* vi. 298
Not, Sir, my only, I have b. still *S.* viii. 114
Wants reach all states; they beg but b. drest *S.* viii. 224
A Shepherd's Boy (he seeks no b. name) *Su.* 1
To find that b. way *U.P.* 32
Some Ends of verse his B—s might afford *Mi.* iii. 5
All that disgrac'd my B., met in me *P.S.* 120
Who to disturb their B. mighty proud *S.* v. 307

Betterton.
Which B.'s grave action dignify'd *S.* v. 122

Betty.
And—B.—give this Cheek a little Red *M.E.* i. 251
See B. LOVET! very à propos *Mi.* ix. 21
Dear B. shall th' important point decide *Mi.* ix. 23
And B.'s prais'd for labours not her own *R.L.* i. 148

Between.—*Passim.*

Betwixt.—*Passim.*

Beware.
Moderns b.! or if you must offend *E.C.* 163
Warn'd by the Sylph, oh pious maid, b. *R.L.* i. 112
B. of all, but most b. of Man *R.L.* i. 114
Your Plea is good; but still I say, b. *S.* i. 143

Bewilder'd.
Some are b. in the maze of schools *E.C.* 26

Bewitch'd.
Her Tongue b. as oddly as her Eyes *M.E.* ii. 47

Bewray'd.
Obscene with filth the miscreant lies b. *D.* ii. 75

Beyond.—*Passim.*

Bias.
To this our head like b. to the bowl *D.* i. 170
What the weak head with strongest b. rules *E.C.* 203
Reason the b. turns from good to ill *E.M.* ii. 196
Have still a secret b. to a Knave *E.S.* ii. 101

Bible.
Take up the B. once my better guide *D.* i. 200
Down with the B., up with the Pope's Arms *D.* ii. 82
Puffs, Powders, Patches, B—s, Billet-doux *R.L.* i. 138

Bickerstaff.
Dean, Drapier, B., or Gulliver *D.* i. 20

Bid.
B. me with Pollio sup, as well as dine *D.* iv. 392
For him thou oft hast b. the world attend *E.* i. 7
When the last ling'ring friend has b. farewell *E.* i. 34
B. her be all that cheers or softens life *E.* iii. 51
B. her be all that makes mankind adore *E.* iii. 53
Yet should the Muses b. my numbers roll *E.* iii. 73
And b. alternate passions fall and rise *E.* 375
Who b. the stork, Columbus-like, explore *E.M.* iii. 105
Why that 's the thing you b. me not to do *E.S.* ii. 19
Speak out, and b. me blame no rogues at all *E.S.* ii. 53
Since Harley b. me first attend *I.H.* ii. 85 s
And b. new music charm th' unfolding ear *M.* 42
Can they, in gems b. pallid Hippia glow *M.E.* iii. 87
B. Harhours open, public Ways extend (*rep.*) *M.E.* iv. 197
Or b. the furious Gaul be rude no more *O.* ii. 16
Or b. the new be English, ages hence *S.* vi. 169

Bidden.
Teach Infant-cheeks a b. blush to learn *R.L.* i. 89

Bidding.
Next, b. all draw near on bended knees *D.* iv. 565

Bids.
She b. him wait her to her sacred Dome *D.* i. 265
And b. them make mistaken mortals groan *E.A.* 83
And Reason b. us for our own provide *E.M.* ii. 96
B. each on other for assistance call *E.M.* ii. 251
This b. to serve, and that to shun mankind *E.M.* iv. 20
Pride guides his steps, and b. him shun the great *M.E.* i. 114
She b. her Footman put it in her head *M.E.* ii. 178
That Pow'r who b. the Ocean ebb and flow (*rep.*) *M.E.* iii. 164

BIDST—BLACK.

B. Bubo build, and sends him such a Guide *M.E.* iv. 40
He *b.* your breasts with ancient ardour rise *P.C.* 15
And *b.* her beau demand the precious hairs *R.L.* iv. 122
Or he, who *b.* thee face with steady view *S.* iii. 107
And, while he *b.* thee, sets th' example too *S.* iii. 109
B. his free soul expatiate in the skies *W.F.* 254
Where Peace descending *b.* her olives spring *W.F.* 429

Bidst.
Or *b.* thou rather Party to embrace *D.* i. 205

Bier.
Bestow a Garland only on a *B. S.* v. 68
Pleas'd thy pale ghost, or grac'd thy mournful *b. U.L.* 50
Their faded honours scatter'd on her *b. W.* 32

Big.
Like a *b.* wife at sight of loathsome meat *S.* viii. 156

Bigger.
But I that sail am neither less nor *b, S.* vi. 299

Bigot.
The throne a *B.* keep, a Genius quit *M.E.* i. 91
Flatt'rers and B—s ev'n in Louis' reign *S.* i. 112

Bile.
Where *b.*, and wind, and phlegm, and acid jar *S.* ii. 71

Bill.
Shakespeare (whom you and ev'ry Play-house *b. S.* v. 69
Amus'd he reads, and then returns the b—s *D.* ii. 91
By Doctor's *b.* to play the Doctor's part *E.C.* 109

Billet-doux.
Thy eyes first open'd on a *B. R.L.* i. 118
Puffs, Powders, Patches, Bibles, B. *R.L.* i. 138
With tender *B.* he lights the pyre *R.L.* ii. 41

Billingsgate.
Let Bawdry, *B.*, my daughters dear *D.* i. 307
And shameless *B.* her Robes adorn *D.* iv. 26

Bind.
Too mad for mere material chains to *b. D.* iv. 32
B. rebel Wit, and double chain on chain *D.* iv. 158
With the same CEMENT, ever sure to *b. D.* iv. 267
Or *b.* in Matter, or diffuse in Space *D.* iv. 476
Could he, whose rules the rapid Comet *b. E.M.* ii. 35
Of Honour, *B.* me not to maul his Tools *E.S.* ii. 147
Embrace my Love, and *b.* my brows with bays *Su.* 38

Binding.
And *b.* Nature fast in Fate *U.P* 11

Binds.
This *b.* in ties more easy, yet more strong *E.* iv. 67
A wond'rous Bag with both her hands she *b. R.L.* iv. 81
And what is that, which *b.* the radiant sky *Sp.* 39
A belt her waist, a fillet *b.* her hair *W.F.* 178

Birch.
Till *B.* shall blush with noble blood no more *D.* iii. 334

Birchen.
His beaver'd brow a *b.* garland wears *D.* iv. 141

Bird.
And lo! her *b.* (a monster of a fowl *D.* i. 289
And where it fix'd, the beauteous *b.* I seiz'd *D.* iv. 430
Beast, *b.*, fish, insect, what no eye can see *E.M.* iii. 125
Thus beast and *b.* their common charge attend *E.M.* iii. 125
The coxcomb *b.*, so talkative and grave *M.E.* i. 5
A *b.* of passage! gone as soon as found *M.E.* i. 97
See the *B.* of Juno stooping *Mi.* vii. 31
Chang'd to a *b.*, and sent to flit in air *R.L.* iii. 123
The captive *b.* that sings within thy bow'r *Su.* 46
Ye b—s that, left by summer, cease to sing *A.* 28
The *b.* shall cease to tune their ev'ning song *A.* 40
Who visits with a Gun, presents you *b. E.* 25
The *b.* of heav'n shall vindicate their grain *E.M.* iii. 38
Man cares for all: to *b.* he gives his woods *E.M.* iii.
Learn from the *b.* what food the thickets yield *E.M.* iii. 173
Pleasures the sex, as children B., pursue *M.E.* ii. 231
With hairy springes we the *b.* betray *R.L.* ii. 149
While fish in streams, or *b.* delight in air *R.L.* iii. 163
Hear how the *b.*, on ev'ry bloomy spray *Sp.* 23

Hush'd are the *b.*, and clos'd the drooping flow'rs (*rep.*) *Sp.* 70
Your praise the *b.* shall chant in ev'ry grove *Su.* 79
While silent *b.* forget their tuneful lays *W.* 7
No more the *b.* shall imitate her lays *W.* 55
And arms employ'd on *b.* and beasts alone *W.F.* 374

Birth.
Thine from the *b.*, and sacred from the rod *D.* iv. 283
And, at their second *b.*, they issue mine *D.* iv. 386
Mark'd out for Honours, honour'd for their *B. D.* iv. 507
All matter quick, and bursting into *b. E.M.* i. 234
Self-love and Social at her *b.* began *E.M.* iii. 149
Vice is undone, if she forgets her *B. E.S.* i. 141
Her *B.*, her Beauty, Crowds and Courts confess *E.S.* i. 145
Sages and Chiefs long since had *b. I.H.* iv. 9
Who, with herself, or others, from her *b. M.E.* ii. 117
Old Cotta sham'd his fortune and his *b. M.E.* iii. 177
Man is a very worm by *b. Mi.* iv. 5
Anxious, and trembling for the *b.* of Fate *R.L.* ii. 142
Why had not I in those good times my *b. S.* ii. 97
In me 'tis noble, suits my *b.* and state *S.* ii. 113
Shall Que whom Nature, Learning, *B.*, conspir'd *S.* iv. 40
Venus shall give him Form, and Anstis *B. S.* iv. 82
When servile Chaplains cry, that *b.* and place *S.* vi. 220
A twisted B.-day Ode completes the spire *S.* i. 162
And thrice he lifted high the *B.* brand *D.* i. 245
Is that a *B.!* 'tis alas! too clear *Mi.* iv. 5
Be ev'ry *B.* more a winner *Mi.* v. 9
No more than thou, great GEORGE, a *b.* song *P.S.* 222
Our *B.* Nobles' splendid Livery *S.* iv. 33
Or when from Court a *b.* suit bestow'd *S.* v. 332
And count each *b.* with a grateful mind *S.* vi. 315
A Youth more glitt'ring than a *B.*-night Beau *R.L.* i. 23
Mere household trash! of b—s, balls, and shows *S.* viii. 130

Bishop.
The *B.* stow (Pontific Luxury!) *D.* iv. 593
Why drew Marseilles' good *b.* purer breath *E.M.* iv. 107
To save a *B.*, may I name a Dean *E.S.* ii. 32
Ev'n in a *B.* I can spy desert *E.S.* ii. 70
A Gownman learn'd; a *B.*, what you will *M.E.* i. 138
From Peer or *B.* 'tis no easy thing *M.E.* ii. 195
But the good *B.*, with a meeker air *M.E.* iii. 105
Still to one *B.* Philips seems a wit *P.S.* 100
Such as a King might read, a *B.* write *S.* i. 152
And whether to a *B.*, or a Whore *S.* viii. 137
In rev'rend B—s note some small Neglects *E.S.* i. 16
Chaste Matrons praise her, and grave *B.* bless *E.S.* i. 146
And Judges job, and *B.* bite the town *M.E.* iii. 141
Peers, Heralds, *B.*, Ermine, Gold and Lawn *S.* v. 317

Bit.
Sees hairs and pores, examines *b.* by *b. D.* iv. 234
Our courtier scarce could touch a *b. I.H.* ii. 171
You pledge as you want, and, *b.* by *b. S.* vi. 237
But murder first, and mince them all to b—s *D.* iv. 120
That, lac'd with *b.* of rustic, makes a front *M.E.* iv. 34
So kept the Di'mond, and the rogue was b. *M.E.* iii. 364
Sappho can tell you how this man was *b. P.S.* 369

Bitch.
For him you'll call a dog, and her a *b. S.* ii. 50

Bite.
I know the *B.*, yet to my Ruin run *Mi.* ix. 69
It is the slaver kills, and not the *b. P.S.* 106
And Judges job, and Bishops b. the town *M.E.* iii. 141
'Tis nothing. Nothing? if they *b.* and kick *P.S.* 78
In mumbling of the game they dare not *b. P.S.* 314
That when I am at praise, they say I *b. S.* v. 409
And much must flatter, if the whim should *b. S.* vi. 149
There Faction roar, Rebellion *b.* her chain *W.F.* 421

Bitter.
Or plung'd in lakes of *b.*, washes lie *R.L.* ii. 127
He calls for something *b.*, something sour *S.* ii. 33

Black.
From her *b.* grottos near the Temple-wall *D.* ii. 98
The very worsted shall look *b.* and blue *D.* ii. 150
Shot to the *b.* abyss, and plung'd downright *D.* ii. 288
Nigrina *b.*, and Merdamante brown *D.* ii. 334

Rolls the *b.* troop, and overshades the street *D.* ii. 360
Thick and more thick the *b.* blockade extends *D.* iv. 191
Red, Blue, and Green, nay, white and *b. E.* vi. 19
B. Melancholy sits, and round her throws *E.A.* 165
If white and *b.* blend, soften, and unite (*rep.*) *E.M.* ii. 213
Hear her *b.* Trumpet thro' the Land proclaim *E.S.* i. 159
When *b.* Ambition stains a public Cause *E.S.* ii. 228
And best distinguish'd by *b.*, brown, or fair *M.E.* ii. 4
Chameleons who can paint in white and *b. M.E.* ii. 156
This day *b.*, Omens threat the brightest Fair *R.L.* ii. 101
The Club's *b.* Tyrant first her Victim dy'd *R.L.* iii. 69
Her wrinkled form in *b.* and white array'd *R.L.* iv. 28
Spreads his *b.* wings, and slowly mounts to day *R.L.* iv. 86
Or Death's *b.* wing already be display'd *S.* i. 95
Not the *b.* fear of death, that saddens all *S.* vi. 309
Not more of Simony beneath *b.* gowns *S.* vii. 81
Tho' coarse was rev'rend, and tho' bare was *b. S.* viii. 39
Call for the Farce, the Bear, or the B.-joke *S.* v. 309

Blacken.
While the long funerals *b.* all the way *U.L.* 40

Blacken'd.
The morals *b.* when the writings scape *P.S.* 352

Black'ning.
Then thick as Locusts *b.* all the ground *D.* iv. 397
And Fun'rals *b.* all the Doors *I.H.* i. 9

Blackens.
There's nothing *b.* like the ink of fools *S.* v. 411

Blackmore, see also Sir Richard.
Not everlasting *B.* this denies *D.* ii. 302
You limp, like *B.* on a Lord Mayor's horse *S.* iii. 16
One knighted *B.*, and one pension'd Quarles *S.* v. 387
B. himself for any grand effort *S.* vi. 112
And Eusden ehe out B.*'s endless line D.* i. 104
But far o'er all sonorous *B.* strain *D.* ii. 259
My H—ley's periods, and my *B.* members *D.* ii. 370
New B—s *and new Milbourns must arise E.C.* 463

Bladder.
Than such as swell this *b.* of a Court *S.* viii. 205

Blade.
And half unsheath'd the shining *b. O.* i. 46

Bladen.
Wash *B.* white, and expiate Hays's strain *D.* iv. 560

Blame.
'Tis yours a Bacon or a Locke to *b. D.* iii. 215
Something to *b.*, and something to commend *E.* iii. 22
We cannot *b.* indeed—but we may sleep *E.C.* 242
But *b.* the false, and value still the true *E.C.* 407
Nor praise, nor *b.* the writings, but the men *E.C.* 413
Some praise at morning what they *b.* at night *E.C.* 430
Who justly knew to *b.* or to commend *E.C.* 730
Still pleas'd to praise, yet not afraid to *b. E.C.* 742
Our proper bliss depends on what we *b. E.M.* i. 282
We ought to *b.* the culture, not the soil *E.M.* iv. 14
Speak out, and bid me *b.* no Rogues at all *E.S.* ii. 53
But pray, when others him, do I *b. E.S.* ii. 136
Whoever borrow'd, could not be to *b. E.S.* ii. 169
No zealous Pastor *b.* a failing Spouse *E.S.* ii. 193
Why, Virtue, dost thou *b.* desire *O.* iii. 9
Alike reserv'd to *b.*, or to commend *P.S.* 205

Blameless.
How happy is the *b.* Vestal's lot *E.A.* 207
Unbrib'd, unbloody stood the *b.* priest *E.M.* iii. 158
Oh *b.* Bethel! to relieve thy breast *E.M.* iv. 126
Of all thy *b.* life the sole return *P.S.* 259

Bland.
Ye shall not beg, like gratis-given *B. D.* i. 231
As, tho' the pride of Middleton and *B. E.S.* i. 75
B. and familiar, as in life, begun D. iii. 41
B. and familiar to the throne he came *D.* iv. 497

Blank.
'Tis all *b.* sadness, or continued tears *E.A.* 148

Blank'd.
B. his bold visage, and a thin Third day *D.* i. 114

Blanket.
As, from the *b.*, high in air, he flies *D.* ii. 152

Blankettings.
Our purgings, pumpings, *b.*, and blows *D.* ii. 154

Blaspheme.
Than ridicule all Taste, *b.* Quadrille *S.* i. 38

Blasphem'd.
B. his Gods, the Dice, and damn'd his Fate *D.* i. 116

Blasphemer.
And each *B.* quite escape the rod *E.S.* ii. 195

Blasphemies.
And the press groan'd with licens'd *b. E.C.* 553
Or spite, or smut, or rhymes, or *b. P.S.* 322

Blast.
The rage of Pow'r, the *b.* of public breath *R.* i. 25
These cheeks now fading at the *b.* of death *U.L.* 32
Good Heav'n forbid, that I should b. *their glory E.S.* i. 105
Oh *b.* it, South-winds! till a stench exhale *S.* ii. 27

Blaze.
When the last *b.* sent Ilion to the skies *D.* i. 256
And one bright *b.* turns learning into air *D.* iii. 78
Such vary'd light in one promiscuous *b. D.* iv. 412
She 'midst the light'ning's *b.*, and thunder's sound *E.M.* iii. 249
One tide of glory, one unclouded *b. M.* 102
Blush, Grandeur, blush! proud Courts withdraw your *b. M.E.* iii. 281
And bask and whiten in the *b.* of day *R.L.* ii. 78
While Altars b., *and Angels tremble round E.A.* 276
Blush in the Rose, and in the Di'mond *b. M.E.* i. 146
The silver lamp; the fiery spirits *b. R.L.* iii. 108
When num'rous wax-lights in bright order *b. R.L.* iii. 168
On that rapacious hand for ever *b. R.L.* iv. 116
The Greatest can but *b.*, and pass away *S.* iv. 47

Blazing.
The lilies *b.* on the regal shield *W.F.* 306

Bleak.
Keen, hollow winds howl thro' the *b.* recess *D.* i. 35
Say, will you bless the *b.* Atlantic shore *O.* ii. 15

Bleating.
The *b.* sheep with my complaints agree *Su.* 19

Bled.
In vain they schem'd, in vain they *b. I.H.* iv. 15
They *b.*, they cupp'd, they purg'd; in short they cur'd *S.* vi. 193
Have *b.* and purg'd me to a simple Vote *S.* vi. 197
Both doom'd alike, for sportive tyrants *b. W.F.* 59
Heav'ns, what new wounds! and bow her old have *b. W.F.* 322

Bleed.
The lamb thy riot dooms to *b.* to-day *E.M.* i. 81
Like good Aurelius let him reign, or *b. E.M.* iv. 285
Who hears him groan, and does not wish to *b. P.C.* 26
To thee, bright goddess, oft a lamb shall *b. W.* 81
And *b.* for ever under Britain's spear *W.F.* 310
For me the balm shall *b.*, and amber flow *W.F.* 393

Bleeding.
A naked Lover bound and *b.* lies *E.A.* 100
Pours balm into the *b.* lover's wounds *O.* i. 29
Nor fond of *b.*, ev'n in BRUNSWICK's cause *S.* iii. 10
'Tis she! but why that *b.* bosom gor'd *U.L.* 3

Bleeds.
See Sidney *b.* amid the martial strife *E.M.* iv. 101
Some Athens perishes, some Tully *b. O.* ii. 32
B. in the Forest like a wounded hart *W.F.* 84

Blend.
Did Nature's pencil ever *b.* such rays *D.* iv. 411
Or *b.* in beauteous tints the colour'd mass *E.* iii. 5
If white and black *b.*, soften, and unite *E.M.* ii. 213

Blended.
And *b.* lie th' oppressor and opprest *W.F.* 318

Blends.

A Tale, that *b.* their glory with their shame *E.M.* iv. 308
B., in exception to all general rules *M.E.* ii. 275

Bless.

Bays, form'd by Nature, Stage and Town to *b.* *D.* i. 109
Some gentle JAMES to *b.* the land again *D.* iv. 176
Might he return, and *b.* once more our eyes *E.C.* 462
And *b.* their Critic with a Poet's fire *E.C.* 676
But as he fram'd a Whole, the Whole to *b.* *E.M.* iii. 111
And all of God, that *b.* Mankind or mend *E.M.* iii. 310
Chaste Matrons praise her, and grave Bishops *b.* *E.S.* i. 146
And two rich shipwrecks *b.* the lucky shore *M.E.* iii. 356
Just at his Study-door he'll *b.* your eyes *M.E.* iv. 132
From soup to sweet-wine, and God *b.* the King *M.E.* iv. 162
Whose cheerful Tenants *b.* their yearly toil *M.E.* iv. 183
Say, will you *b.* the bleak Atlantic shore *O.* ii. 15
B. me! a packet. "'Tis a stranger sues *P.S.* 55
May some choice patron *b.* each gray goose quill *P.S.* 249
May Heav'n, to *b.* those days, preserve my friend *P.S.* 425
Come, lovely nymph, and *b.* the silent hours *Su.* 63
Whose raptures fire me, and whose visions *b.* *W.F.* 260
'Tis yours, my Lord, to *b.* our soft retreats *W.F.* 283

Blessed, Bless'd, Blest.

The *b.* benefit not there confin'd *E.S.* ii. 177
B.'d *with his father's front, his mother's tongue* D. ii. 416
Be pleas'd with nothing if not *b.* with all *E.M.* i. 188
Without satiety, tho' e'er so *b. E.M.* iv. 317
Never dejected, while another's *b. E.M.* iv. 324
With soups unbought, and salads *b.* his board *M.E.* iii. 182
Arise, and tell me was thy death more *b. M.E.* iii. 322
Great without Title, without Fortune *b. S.* iii. 181
Or peaceably forget, at once be b—t *D.* i. 239
With all the might of gravitation *b. E.* ii. 318
Thus visit not thy own! on this *b.* age *D.* iii. 121
Surveys around her, in the *b.* abode *D.* iii. 133
With all thy Father's virtues *b.*, be born *D.* iii. 141
B. in one Niger, till he knows of two *D.* iv. 370
Whose Heads she partly, whose completely, *b.* *D.* iv. 622
B. in each science, *b.* in ev'ry strain *E.* i. 5
Snatch me, just mounting, from the *b.* abode *E.A.* 287
B. with a taste exact, yet unconfin'd *E.C.* 639
The *b.* to-day is as completely so *E.M.* i. 75
Man never Is, but always To be *b. E.M.* i. 96
Pride still is aiming at the *b.* abodes *E.M.* i. 125
Secure to be as *b.* as thou canst bear *E.M.* i. 286
As Heav'n's *b.* beam turns vinegar more sour *E.M.* ii. 148
Supremely *b.*, the Poet in his Muse *E.M.* ii. 270
And, till he ends the being, makes it *b. E.M.* iii. 66
Whether with Reason, or with Instinct *b. E.M.* iii. 79
Here fix'd the dreadful, there the *b.* abodes *E.M.* iii. 255
And, in proportion as it blesses, *b. E.M.* iii. 300
Of Vice or Virtue, whether *b.* or curst *E.M.* iv. 87
Best knows the blessing, and will most be *b. E.M.* iv. 96
Nor with one system can they all be *b. E.M.* iv. 142
And which more *b.!* who chain'd his country, say *E.M.* iv. 147
Is *b.* in what it takes, and what it gives *E.M.* iv. 314
At once his own bright prospect to be *b. E.M.* iv. 351
Earth smiles around, with boundless bounty *b. E.M.* iv. 371
All Parts perform'd, and *all* the Children *b. E.S.* i. 82
B. Satirist! who touch'd the Mean so true *Ep.* i. 7
B. Courtier! who could King and Country please *Ep.* i. 9
B. Peer! his great Forefathers' ev'ry grace *Ep.* i. 11
B. with plain Reason and with sober Sense *Ep.* vi. 2
And thou, *b.* Maid! attendant on his doom *Ep.* vii. 11
A Poet, *b.* beyond a Poet's fate *Ep.* x. 3
Oh! *b.* with Temper, whose unclouded ray *M.E.* ii. 257
Picks from each sex, to make the Fav'rite *b. M.E.* ii. 273
B. paper-credit! last and best supply *M.E.* iii. 39
Him portion'd maids, apprentic'd orphans *b. M.E.* iii. 267
Oh be thou *b.* with all that Heav'n can send *Mi.* v. 1
B., who can unconcern'dly find *O.* iv. 9
B. with each talent and each art to please *P.S.* 195
B. be the Great! for those they take away *P.S.* 255
With such a prize no mortal must he *b. R.L.* v. 111

This the *b.* Lover shall for Venus take *R.L.* v. 135
Or *b.* with little, whose preventing care *S.* ii. 127
Would ye be *b.?* despise low Joys, low Gains *S.* iv. 60
If Wealth alone then make and keep us *b. S.* iv. 95
Our rural Ancestors, with little *b. S.* v. 241
Let but the Ladies smile, and they are *b. S.* viii. 254
B. Thames's shores the brightest beauties yield *Sp.* 63
But *b.* with her, 'tis spring throughout the year *Sp.* 84
B. Swains, whose nymphs in ev'ry grace excel (*rep.*) *Sp.* 95
Ambition first sprung from your *b.* abodes *U.L.* 13
Some thoughtless Town, with ease and plenty *b. W.F.* 107
In that *b.* moment from his oozy bed *W.F.* 329

Blesses.

And, in proportion as it *b.*, blest *E.M.* iii. 300

Blessing.

The Mother begg'd the *b.* of a Rake *D.* iv. 286
Meanly they seek the *b.* to confine *E.C.* 308
But gives that Hope to be the *b.* now *E.M.* i. 94
The bliss of Man (could Pride that *b.* find) *E.M.* i. 189
The extensive *b.* of his luxury *E.M.* iii. 62
There's not a *b.* Individuals find *E.M.* iv. 39
One common *b.*, as one common soul *E.M.* iv. 62
Best knows the *b.*, and will most be blest *E.M.* iv. 96
If Calvin feel Heav'n's *b.*, or its rod *E.M.* iv. 139
Gives thee to make thy neighbour's *b.* thine *E.M.* iv. 354
The mighty *b.*, "while we live, to live" *M.E.* ii. 90
Give Harpax' self the *b.* of a friend *M.E.* iii. 92
What late he call'd a *B.*, now was Wit *M.E.* ii. 377
But, like a Sieve, let ev'ry *b.* thro' *Mi.* v. 6
Whether that *b.* be deny'd or giv'n *P.S.* 418
The *b.* thrills thro' all the lab'ring throng *S.* v. 239
Calm Temperance, whose b—*s those partake D.* i. 42
Diffusing *b.*, or averting harms *E.M.* iii. 212
Bring them these *b.* to a strict account *E.M.* iv. 269
Behold what *b.* Wealth to life can lend *E.M.* iii. 297
Now hear what *b.* Temperance can bring *S.* ii. 67
What *B.* thy free Bounty knows *U.P.* 17
Where, in their *b.*, all those Gods appear *W.F.* 36
Be mine the *b.* of a peaceful reign *W.F.* 356
And scatters *b.* from her dove-like wing *W.F.* 430
Then, b. *all,* "Go, Children of my care *D.* iv. 579

Blew.

The bells she jingl'd, and the whistle *b. R.L.* v. 94

Blind.

Laborious, heavy, busy, bold, and *b. D.* i. 15
The names of these *b.* puppies as of those *D.* ii. 310
But *b.* to former as to future fate *D.* iii. 47
Or chew'd by *b.* old Scholiasts o'er and o'er *D.* iv. 232
Custom, grown *b.* with Age, must be your Guide *E.* iv. 33
Why form'd so weak, so little, and so *b. E.M.* i. 36
See the *b.* beggar dance, the cripple sing *E.M.* i. 267
Ask of the Learn'd the way? The Learn'd are *b. E.M.* iv. 19
Oh *b.* to truth, and God's whole scheme below *E.M.* iv. 93
Yet poor with fortune, and with learning *b. E.M.* iv. 329
Hear him, ye deaf, and all ye *b.*, behold *M.* 38
But pitied Belisarius, old and *b. Mi.* ii. 6
Oh *b.* to truth! the Sylphs contrive it all *R.L.* i. 104
Oh thoughtless mortals! ever *b.* to fate *R.L.* iii. 101
Sigh, while his Chloe, *b.* to wit and worth *S.* iv. 42
And that myself am *b. U.P.* 8
Of all the Causes which conspire to b. *E.C.* 201

Blinder.

Why form'd no weaker, *b.*, and no less *E.M.* i. 38

Blindly.

Not dully prepossessed, nor *b.* right *E.C.* 634
Of all who *b.* creep, or sightless soar *E.M.* i. 12
Nor think, in NATURE'S STATE they *b.* trod *E.M.* iii. 147

Blindness.

Oh *b.* to the future! kindly giv'n *E.M.* i. 85
Of *b.*, weakness, Heav'n bestows on them *E.M.* i. 284
Barbarian *b.*, Christian zeal conspire *M.E.* v. 13

Bliss.

And, to complete her *b.*, a Fool for Mate *E.* iv. 52
This sure is *b.* (if *b.* on earth there be) *E.A.* 97
What future *b.*, he gives not thee to know *E.M.* 1. 93
The *b.* of Man (could Pride that blessing find) *E.M.* i. 189
Our proper *b.* depends on what we blame *E.M.* i. 282
To *b.* alike by that direction tend *E.M.* iii. 81
Its proper *b.*, and sets its proper bounds *E.M.* iii. 110

BLISSFUL—BLUEISH.

That Virtue only makes our *b.* below *E.M.* iii. 397
Some place the *b.* in action, some in ease *E.M.* iv. 21
B. is the same in subject or in king *E.M.* iv. 58
Who fancy *B.* to Vice, to Virtue Woe *E.M.* iv. 94
What greater *b.* attends their close of life *E.M.* iv. 301
The only point where human *b.* stands still *E.M.* iv. 311
See the sole *b.* Heav'n could on all bestow *E.M.* iv. 327
Sees that no Being any *b.* can know *E.M.* iv. 335
It pours the *b.* that fills up all the mind *E.M.* iv. 344
Hope of known *b.*, and Faith in *b.* unknown *E.M.* iv. 346
His greatest Virtue, and his greatest *B. E.M.* iv. 350
And height of *B.* but height of Charity *E.M.* iv. 360
Go then, where only *b.* sincere is known *Ep.* vii. 15
And antedate the *b.* above *O.* i. 123
Oh the pain, the *b.* of dying *O.* v. 4
O Friend! may each domestic *b.* be thine *P.S.* 406
Not ardent lovers robb'd of all their *b. R.L.* iv. 5

Blissful.
Nor blush to sport on Windsor's *b.* plains *Sp.* 2

Block.
So when Jove's *b.* descended from on high *D.* i. 327
Nor could a BARROW work on ev'ry *b. D.* iv. 245
And hew the *B.* off, and get out the Man *D.* iv. 270

Blockade.
Thick, and more thick the black *b.* extends *D.* iv. 191
Huge bales of British cloth b. *the door M.E.* iii. 57

Blockhead.
But lick up ev'ry *b.* in the way *D.* iii. 294
There march'd the bard and *b.*, side by side *D.* iv. 101
The bookful *b.*, ignorantly read *E.C.* 612
The *B.* is a Slow-worm *Mi.* iv. 14
Just as a *b.* rubs his thoughtless skull *E.J.S.* 7
Benlowes, propitious still to b—s, *bows D.* iii. 21
B. with reason wicked wits abhor *D.* iii. 175
But all such babbling *b.* in his stead *P.S.* 304
The busy, idle *b.* of the ball *S.* viii. 203

Blois.
Bows, and begins—"This lad, Sir, is of *B. S.* vi. 4

Blood.
Till Birch shall blush with noble *b.* no more *D.* iii. 334
Dropping with Infants' *b.*, and Mothers' tears *D.* iv. 142
No pulse that riots, and no *b.* that glows *E.A.* 252
What wants in *b.* and spirits, swell'd with word *E.C.* 208
As bodies perish thro' excess of *b. E.C.* 304
With manners gen'rous as his noble *b. E.C.* 726
To see a piece of failing flesh and *b. E.J.S.* 47
And licks the hand just rais'd to shed his *b. E.M.* i. 84
The Fury-passions from that *b.* began *E.M.* iii. 167
Next his grim idol smear'd with human *b. E.M.* iii. 266
Boast the pure *b.* of an illustrious race *E.M.* iv. 207
Go! if your ancient, but ignoble *b. E.M.* iv. 211
Alas! not all the *b.* of all the HOWARDS *E.M.* iv. 216
But stain'd with *b.*, or ill exchang'd for gold *E.M.* iv. 296
What then? let *B.* and Body bear the fault *M.E.* ii. 73
Unspotted long with human *b. O.* ii. 6
Of gentle *b.* (part shed in honour's cause *P.S.* 388
At this, the *b.* the virgin's cheek forsook *R.L.* iii. 89
Say, does thy *b.* rebel, thy bosom move *S.* iii. 55
Thou mean deserter of thy brother's *b. U.L.* 30
Ye vig'rous swains! while youth ferments your *b. W.F.* 93
Flutters in *b.*, and panting beats the ground *W.F.* 114
And silent Darent, stain'd with Danish *b. W.F.* 348
No more my sons shall dye with British *b. W.F.* 367
Of war or *b.*, but in the sylvan chase *W.F.* 372
And gasping Furies thirst for *b.* in vain *W.F.* 422

Bloodless.
Pomps without guilt, of *b.* swords and maces *D.* i. 87

Bloody.
Barbarian, stay! that *b.* stroke restrain *E.A.* 103
Proud Nimrod first the *b.* chase began *W.F.* 61
Whom ev'n the Saxon spar'd and *b.* Dane *W.F.* 77

Bloom.
Poor W * * nipt in folly's broadest *b. D.* iv. 513
Now warm in love, now with'ring in my *b. E.A.* 37
While op'ning b—s *diffuse their sweets around Sp.* 100
For me the vernal garlands b. *no more I.H.* ii. 32
And all her faded garlands *b.* anew *W.F.* 48
Left me to see neglected Genius *b. P.S.* 257
Like roses, that in deserts *b.* and die *R.L.* iv. 158

Blooming.
Fresh *b.* Hope, gay daughter of the sky *E.A.* 299
That gaily blooms, but ev'n in *b.* dies *E.C.* 499
And ev'ry op'ning Virtue *b.* round *Ep.* xiv. 2
There spread round MURRAY all your *b.* loves *I.H.* iii. 10
Mild *Arcadians*, ever *b. Mi.* vii. 5

Blooms.
B. in thy colours for a thousand years *E.* iii. 58
For her th' unfading rose of Eden *b. E.C.* 217
That gaily *b.*, but ev'n in blooming dies *E.C.* 499

Bloomsbury-square.
At ten for certain, Sir, in *B. S.* vi. 95

Bloomy.
A waving Glow of *b.* beds display *M.E.* iv. 83
Hear how the birds on ev'ry *b.* spray *Sp.* 23

Blossom.
Fade ev'ry *b.*, wither ev'ry tree *A.* 33
As thick as bees o'er vernal b—s *fly D.* iii. 33
Here bees from *b.* sip the rosy dew *Su.* 69
Now hawthorns b., *now the daisies spring Sp.* 42

Blossoms.
Glows in the stars, and *b.* in the trees *E.M.* i. 272

Blot.
(Without a *b.*) to eighty-one *Mi.* xii. 4
To *b. out Order, and extinguish Light D.* iv. 14
B. out each bright Idea of the skies *E.A.* 284
Spread like a low-born mist, and *b.* the Sun *M.E.* iii. 138
The last and greatest Art, the Art to *b. S.* v. 281

Blots.
With deeper sable *b.* the silver flood *D.* ii. 274

Blotted.
Wish'd he had *b.* for himself before *D.* i. 134

Blount.
Each pleasing *B.* shall endless smiles bestow *E.* iij. 61
If *B.* despatch'd himself, he play'd the man *E.S.* i. 123

Blow.
Yes, strike that *Wild*, I'll justify the *b. E.S.* ii. 54
The *b.* unfelt, the tear he never shed *P.S.* 349
Of hisses, b—s, *or want, or loss of ears D.* i. 48
Our purgings, pumpings, blankettings, and *b. D.* ii. 154
In cold December fragrant chaplets b. *D.* i. 77
Their heads, and lift them as they cease to *b. D.* ii. 392
Still as the sea ere winds were taught to *b. E.A.* 253
For thee Idume's spicy forests *b. M.* 95
Our fates and fortunes, as the winds shall *b. M.E.* iii. 46
The deep, majestic, solemn organs *b. O.* 1, 11
By the fragrant winds that *b. O.* i, 72
A thousand wings, by turns, *b.* back the hair *R.L.* iii. 136
On Avon's bank, where flow'rs eternal *b. S.* v. 119
Heav'd by the breath th' inspiring bellows *b. S.* vii. 19
Here western winds on breathing roses *b. Sp.* 32
There the first roses of the year shall *b. U.L.* 66

Blown.
Like the vile straw that's *b.* about the streets *D.* iii. 289
And now had Fame's posterior Trumpet *b. D.* iv. 71
The trumpet sleeps, while cheerful horns are *b. W.F.* 373

Blows.
Such as from lab'ring lungs th' Enthusiast *b. D.* ii. 255
Soft is the strain when Zephyr gently *b. E.C.* 366
The dreaded East is all the wind that *b. R.L.* iv. 20
Sharp Boreas *b.*, and Nature feels decay *W.* 87

Blue.
The very worsted still look black and *b. D.* ii. 150
Him close she curtains round with Vapours *b. D.* iii. 3
Red, *B.*, and Green, nay, white and black *E.* vi. 19
Chequer'd with Ribbons *b.* and green *I.H.* ii. 49 5
When these *b.* eyes first open'd on the sphere *M.E.* ii. 284
This the *b.* varnish, that the green endears *M.E.* v. 37
B. Neptune storms, the bellowing deeps resound *R.L.* v. 50
Here the bright crocus and *b.* vi'let glow *Sp.* 31
The *b.*, transparent Vandalis appears *W.F.* 345

Blueish.
There wrapt in clouds the *b.* hills ascend *W.F.* 24

Blunders.

And of one beauty many *b.* make *M.E.* iv. 28
Means not, but b. round about a meaning P.S. 186

Blunderbuss.

Nor less revere him, *b.* of Law *D.* iii. 150
With Gun, Drum, Trumpet, *B.,* and Thunder *S.* i. 26
From this thy *b.* discharg'd on me *S.* viii. 65

Blunt.

B. could do Bus'ness, H——ggins knew the Town *E.S.* i. 14
" God cannot love (says *B.* with tearless eyes) *M.E.* iii. 103
Much injur'd *B.!* why bears he Britain's hate *M.E.* iii. 133
And b. the sense, and fit it for a skull D. iii. 25
B. truths more mischief than nice falsehoods do E.C. 573

Blunted.

His *b.* Arms by Sophistry are born *D.* iv. 25
Her weapons *b.,* and extinct her fires *W.F.* 418

Blush.

Gone ev'ry *b.,* and silent all reproach *D.* iv. 563
And strikes a *b.* thro' frontless Flattery *E.* ii. 7
And soft Belinda's *b.* for ever glow *E.* iii. 62
Or sees the *b.* of soft Parthenia rise *E.* v. 46
Excuse the *b.,* and pour out all the heart *E.A.* 56
Teach Infant-cheeks a bidden *b.* to know *R.L.* i. 89
Sees by degrees a purer *b.* arise *R.L.* i. 143
Let tears and burning b——es speak the rest E.A. 106
Then, when he trembles! when his *b.* rise *Mi.* ix. 89
Marcus with *b.,* owns he loves *O.* iii. 7
Assist their *b.,* and inspire their airs *R.L.* ii. 98
Fresh rising *b.* paint the wat'ry glass *Sw.* 28
Till Birch shall b. with noble blood no more D. iii. 334
Whose sons shall *b.* their fathers were thy foes *E.M.* iii. 388
No cheek is known to *b.,* no heart to throb *E.S.* i. 103
Do good by stealth, and *b.* to find it Fame *E.S.* i. 136
Let Horace *b.,* and Virgil too *Ep.* xv. 4
B. in the Rose, and in the Di'mond blaze *M.E.* i. 146
B., Grandeur, *b.!* proud Courts withdraw your blaze *M.E.* iii. 281
Nor *b.,* these studies thy regard engage *M.E.* v. 49
Shall cease to *b.* with stranger's gore *O.* ii. 50
Well may he *b.,* who gives it or receives *S.* v. 414
The wisest man might *b.,* I must agree *S.* vi. 228
Nor *b.* to sport on Windsor's blissful plains *Sp.* 2

Blush'd.

And Virgins smil'd at what they *b.* before *E.C.* 543
Hazardia *b.,* and turn'd her Head aside *Mi.* ix. 41

Blushing.

Now *b.* berries paint the yellow grove *A.* 75
The skies yet *b.* with departing light *A.* 98
Religion b. veils her sacred fires *D.* iv. 649
B. in bright diversities of day *M.E.* iv. 84
The dawn now *b.* on the mountain's side *Sp.* 21
Where'er you tread, the *b.* flow'rs shall rise *Su.* 75
Here *b.* Flora paints th' enamel'd ground *W.F.* 38

Boar.

And the huge *b.* is shrunk into an urn *D.* iv. 552
Him the *B,* in silence creeping *Mi.* vii. 11

Board.

The *b.* with specious miracles he loads *D.* iv. 553
A constant Critic at the great man's *b. E.C.* 416
Receiv'd a Town Mouse at his *B. I.H.* ii. 159
With soups unbought, and salads bless'd his *b. M.E.* iii. 182
And lo! two puddings smok'd upon the *b. M.E.* iii. 360
Fop at the toilet, flatt'rer at the *b. P.S.* 328
Led off two captive trumps and swept the *b. R.L.* iii. 50
For lo! the *b.* with cups and spoons is crown'd *R.L.* iii. 105
'Tis true no Turbots dignify my *b——s. S.* ii. 141
Faith, gallants, b. *with saints, and bed with sinners E.J.S.* 24
They stop the chariot, and they *b.* the barge *P.S.* 10

Boarding.

He *b.* her, she striking sail to him *S.* viii. 231

Boast.

Hence Miscellanies spring, the weekly *b. D.* i. 39
How sweet an Ovid, Murray was our *b. D.* iv. 169
Virtue, I grant you, is an empty *b. E.S.* i. 113
Edward and Henry, now the *B.* of Fame *S.* v. 7
And we too b. *our Garth and Addison D.* ii. 140
And bare threescore is all ev'n that can *b. E.C.* 481
In youth alone its empty praise we *b. E.C.* 496
Ah ne'er so dire a thirst of glory *b. E.C.* 522
Cremona now shall ever *b.* thy name *E.C.* 707
In lazy Apathy let Stoics *b. E.M.* ii. 101
B. the pure blood of an illustrious race *E.M.* iv. 207
Look upon Basset, you who Reason *b. Mi.* ix. 85
Think of that moment, you who Prudence *b. Mi.* ix. 97
"*B.* not my fall" (he cry'd), "insulting foe *R.L.* v. 97
Not all the tresses that fair head can *b. R.L.* v. 143
Fortune not much of humbling me can *b. S.* ii. 151
And carrying with you all the world can *b. Sp.* 9
Let India *b.* her plants, nor envy we *W.F.* 29
Let old Arcadia *b.* her ample plain *W.F.* 159

Boastful.

B. and rough, your first Son is a Squire *M.E.* 151

Boasts.

And *b.* Ulysses' ear with Argus' eye *D.* ii. 374
Roscommon only *b.* unspotted bays *S.* v. 214
And *b.* a Warmth that from no Passion flows *E.* ii. 4
Our haughty Norman *b.* that barb'rous name *W.F.* 63

Bodkin.

The *b.,* comb, and essence to prepare *R.L.* iv. 98
Propp'd on their *b.* spears, the Sprites survey *R.L.* v. 55
And drew a deadly *b.* from her side *R.L.* v. 88
Then in a *b.* grac'd her mother's hairs *R.L.* v. 95
Or wedg'd whole ages in a b.'s eye R.L. ii. 128

Body.

In some fair *b.* thus th' informing soul *E.C.* 76
As that the *b.,* this enslav'd the mind *E.C.* 688
No pow'rs of *b.* or of soul to share *E.M.* i. 191
Whose *b.* Nature is, and God the soul *E.M.* i. 268
In doubt his Mind or *B.* to prefer *E.M.* ii. 9
The whole employ of *b.* and of mind *E.M.* ii. 126
Soon flows to this, in *b.* and in soul *E.M.* ii. 140
And in one interest *b.* acts with mind *E.M.* ii. 180
As Justice tears his *b.* from the grave *E.M.* iv. 250
What then? let Blood and *B.* bear the fault *M.E.* ii. 73
Th' exactest traits of *B.* or of Mind *M.E.* ii. 191
In health of *b.,* peace of mind *O.* iv. 11
His father, mother, *b.* soul, and muse *P.S.* 381
See him with pains of *b.,* pangs of soul *S.* iii. 71
Tho' his soul's bullet, and his *b.* buff *S.* viii. 263
The b.'s *harmony, the beaming soul D.* iv. 236
Th' opposing *b.* grossness, not its own *E.C.* 469
Dull sullen pris'ners in the *b.* cage *U.L.* 18
Dry b——s of Divinity appear D. i, 157
Demand new *b.,* and in Calf's array *D.* iii. 29
As *b.* perish thro' excess of blood *E.C.* 304
Ask for what end the heavenly *b.* shine *E.M.* i. 131
Their fluid *b.* half dissolv'd in light *R.L.* ii. 62
Of *b.* chang'd to various forms by Spleen *R.L.* iv. 48

Bœotia.

From thy *B.* tho' her Pow'r retires *D.* i. 25

Bœotian.

Might from *B.* to *B.* roll *D.* iii. 50

Bog.

Loud thunder to its bottom shook the *b. D.* i. 329
So clouds replenish'd from some *b.* below *D.* ii. 363

Bohea.

To part her time 'twixt reading and *b. E.* v. 15
Where none learn Ombre, none e'er taste *B. R.L.* iv. 156

Boil.

The vulgar *b.,* the learned roast an egg *S.* vi. 85

Boileau.

And *B.* still in right of Horace sways *E.C.* 714
Nor *B.* turn the Feather to a Star *E.S.* ii. 237
Could pension'd *B.* lash in honest strain *S.* i. 111
As once for Louis, *B.,* and Racine *S.* v. 375

Boil'd.

A tomb of *b.* and roast, and flesh and fish *S.* ii. 70

BOLD—BOROUGH.

Bold.

Laborious, heavy, busy, *b.*, and blind *D.* i. 15
Blank'd his *b.* visage, and a thin Third day *D.* i. 114
Not so *b.* Arnall ; with a weight of skull *D.* ii. 315
See the *b.* Ostrogoths on Latium fall *D.* iii. 93
Like *b.* Briareus, with a hundred hands *D.* iv. 66
Compos'd he stood, *b.* Benson thrust him by *D.* iv. 110
All flesh is humbled, Westminster's *b.* race *D.* iv. 145
Then taught by Hermes, and diviocly *b. D.* iv. 381
B. in the practice of mistaken rules *E.C.* 110
Convinc'd, amaz'd, he checks the *b.* design *E.C.* 136
The Whole at once is *b.*, and regular *E.C.* 252
And each *b.* figure just begins to live *E.C.* 491
Did all the dregs of *b.* Socinus drain *E.C.* 545
What crowds of these, impenitently *b. E.C.* 604
Modestly *b.*, and humanly severe *E.C.* 636
Thee, *b.* Longinus ! all the Nine inspire *E.C.* 675
Fierce for the liberties of wit, and *b. E.C.* 717
Tom struts a Soldier, open, *b.*, and brave *M.E.* i. 153
And heads the *b.* Train-Bands, and burns a Pope *M.E.* iii. 214
Here, rising *b.*, the Patriot's honest face *M.E.* v. 57
Exulting in triumph now swell the *b.* notes *O.* i. 16
So when the first *b.* vessel dar'd the seas *O.* i. 38
To make mankind in conscious virtue *b. P.C.* 3
In tasks so *b.*, can little men engage *R.L.* i. 2
So when *b.* Homer makes the Gods engage *R.L.* v. 45
When *b.* Sir Plume bad drawn Clarissa down *R.L.* v. 67
But this *b.* Lord with manly strength endu'd *R.L.* v. 79
There are to whom my Satire seems too *b. S.* i. 2
Brand the *b.* front of shameless guilty man *S.* i. 106
Here, Wisdom calls : " Seek Virtue first, be *b. S.* iii. 77
Prevent the greedy, and out-bid the *b. S.* iv. 72
Not with such majesty, such *b.* relief *S.* v. 390
Mark where a *b.* expressive phrase occurs *S.* vi. 165
Charge them with Heav'n's Artill'ry, *b.* Divine *S.* viii. 281
See the *b.* youth strain up the threat'ning steep *W.F.* 155
B. in the lists, and graceful in the dance *W.F.* 294

Bolder.

But he 's a *b.* man who dares be well *M.E.* ii. 130
Our *b.* Talents in full light display'd *M.E.* ii. 201

Boldly.

May *b.* deviate from the common track *E.C.* 151
Might *b.* censure, as be *b.* writ *E.C.* 658

Bolts.

Presume thy *b.* to throw *U.P.* 26

Bon.

Que ça est b. ! Ah goutes ça *I.H.* ii. 201

Bond.

Breval, *B.*, Besaleel the varlets caught *D.* ii. 126
Is it for *B.*, or Peter, (paltry things) *E.S.* i. 121
B. damns the Poor, and hates them from his heart *M.E.* iii. 100
B. is but one, but Harpax is a score *S.* i. 44
Union the *b.* of all things, and of Man *E.M.* iii. 150
But held in tenfold b—s the Muses lie *D.* iv. 35
In brazen *b.* shall barb'rous Discord dwell *W.F.* 414

Booby.

Each Mother asks it for her *b.* Son *E.S.* ii. 107
Become the portion of a *b.* Lord *S.* ii. 176

Book.

Heav'n from all creatures hides the *b.* of Fate *E.C.* i. 77
Sleep, or peruse some ancient *B. I.H.* ii. 130
These shelves admit not any modern *b. M.E.* iv. 140
Not that I'd lop the Beauties from his *b. S.* v. 103
Enjoys his garden and his *b.* in quiet *S.* v. 199
Next d'er his B—s his eyes began to roll *D.* i. 127
The pond'rous *b.* two gentle readers bring *D.* ii. 383
Then down are rolled the *b.* ; stretch'd o'er 'em lies *D.* ii. 403
Her grey-hair'd Synods damning *b.* unread *D.* iii. 103
A Lumber-house of *b.* in ev'ry head *D.* iii. 193
With wit well-natur'd, and with *b.* well-bred *E.* i. 8
And value *b.*, as women, for their dress *E.C.* 306
All *b.* he reads, and all he reads assails *E.C.* 616
A knowledge both of *b.* and human kind *E.C.* 640
Learn from their *B.*, to hang himself and wife *E.S.* i. 126

Yes, you despise the man to *b.* confin'd *M.E.* i. 1
Men may be read as well as *B.*, too much *M.E.* i. 10
Tenets with *B.*, and Principles with Times *M.E.* i. 173
In *B.*, not Authors, curious is my Lord *M.E.* iii. 134
And *B.* for Mead, and butterflies for Sloane *M.E.* iv. 10
From these the world will judge of men and *b. P.S.* 145
And see what friends, and read what *b.* I please *P.S.* 264
To *b.* and study give seven years complete *S.* vi. 117
The learn'd themselves we b.-worms name *Mi.* iv. 13

Book of Martyrs.

Now deep in Taylor and the *B. M.E.* ii. 63

Bookful.

The *b.* blockhead, ignorantly read *E.C.* 612

Booth.

B. in his cloudy tabernacle shrin'd *D.* iii. 267
Or well-mouth'd *B.* with emphasis proclaims *S.* v. 123
B. enters—hark ! the Universal peal *S.* v. 334
Till rais'd from b—s to Theatre, to Court *D.* iii. 297

Boots.

What *b.* the regal circle on his head *R.L.* 71

Bore.

The soil that arts and infant letters *b. D.* iii. 96
The verse and sculpture *b.* an equal part *M.E.* v. 51
Then each, according to the rank they *b. R.L.* iii. 34
And bravely *b.* the double loads of lead *R.L.* iv. 102
The sun e'er got, or slimy Nilus *b. S.* viii. 49
Still bears the name the hapless virgin *b. W.F.* 207
Oh wouldst thou sing what heroes Windsor *b. W.F.* 293

Boreas.

Language, which *B.* might to Auster hold *S.* vii. 61
Sharp *B.* blows, and Nature feels decay *W.* 87

Borgia.

Why then a *B.* or a Catiline *E.M.* i. 156

Born.

Got by fierce whirlwinds, and in thunder *b. A.* 92
For, *b.* a Goddess, Dulness never dies *D.* i. 18
O *b.* in sin, and forth in folly brought *D.* i. 225
Oh *b.* to see what none can see awake *D.* iii. 43
With all thy father's virtues blest, be *b. D.* iii. 141
Th' Augustus *b.* to bring Saturnian times *D.* iii. 320
B. for First Ministers, as Slaves for Kings *D.* iv. 602
See all in *Self*, and but for self be *b. D.* iv. 480
These *b.* to judge, as well as those to write *E.C.* 14
Hail, Bards triumphant ! *b.* in happier days *E.C.* 189
The rules a nation, *b.* to serve, obeys *E.C.* 713
B. but to die, and reas'ning but to err *E.M.* ii. 10
Passions, like Elements, tho' *b.* to fight *E.M.* ii. 111
And thanks his stars he was not *b.* a fool *E.Y.S.* 8
Argyll, the State's whole Thunder *b.* to wield *E.S.* ii. 86
Oh *b.* to Arms ! O worth in Youth approv'd *Ep.* ix. 3
Oh spring to light, auspicious Babe, be *b. M.* 22
B. where Heav'n's influence scarce can penetrate *M.E.* i. 142
B. with whate'er could win it from the Wise *M.E.* i. 182
That very Cæsar, *b.* in Scipio's days *M.E.* i. 216
Go, search it there, where to be *b.* and die *M.E.* iii. 287
Now sweep those Alleys they were *b.* to shade *M.E.* iv. 98
If there's a *Briton* then, true bred and *b. Mi.* ii. 19
And *b.* to write, converse, and live with ease *P.S.* 196
I was not *b.* for Courts or great affairs *P.S.* 267
Heav'ns ! was I *b.* for nothing but to write *P.S.* 272
B. to no Pride, inheriting no Strife *P.S.* 392

Borns, Born.

B—e on the swelling notes our souls aspire *O.* i. 128
For ever sunk too low or *b.* too high *S.* v. 209
Led by new stars, and *b.* by spicy gales *W.F.* 392
His blunted Arms by Sophistry are b—n *D.* iv. 25
Let standard-authors, thus, like trophies, *b. D.* iv. 123
Like bubbles on the sea of matter *b. E.M.* iii. 19
When 'tis by that alone she can be *b. M.E.* ii. 60
While by our oaks the precious loads are *b. W.F.* 31

Borough.

And, if a *B.* choose him not, undone *D.* iv. 328
Drunk at a *B.*, civil at a Ball *M.E.* i. 75

Borrow'd.
Whoever *b.* could not be to blame *E.S.* ii. 169
W. *b.* Pins, and Patches not her own *Mi.* iii. 22

Borrows.
If Music meanly *b.* aid from sense *D.* iv. 64
And Splendour *b.* all her rays from Sense *M.E.* iv. 180

Bosom.
In Shadwell's *b.* with eternal Rest *D.* i. 240
Feeds from his hand, and in his *b.* warms *M.* 54
What has not fir'd her *b.* or her brain *M.E.* ii. 77
How martial music ev'ry *b.* warms *O.* i. 37
What *b.* beats not in his Country's cause *P.C.* 24
Launch'd on the *b.* of the silver Thames *R.L.* ii. 4
Her hand is fill'd; her *b.* with lampoons *R.L.* iv. 30
On her heav'd *b.* hung her drooping head *R.L.* iv. 145
Say, does thy blood rebel, thy *b.* move *S.* iii. 55
Forms the soft *b.* with the gentlest art *S.* v. 219
'Tis she! but why that bleeding *b.* gor'd *U.L.* 3
Striking their *pensive* b—s. Here *lies* GAY *Ep.* xi. 12
And in soft *b.* dwells such mighty rage *R.L.* i. 12

Bosom'd.
To happy Convents, *b.* deep in vines *D.* iv. 301

Botanists.
Some *B.*, some Florists at the least *D.* iv. 573

Both.—*Passim.*

Bottle.
Expect thy dog, thy *b.*, and thy wife *E.M.* iv. 178
Scarsdale his *b.*, Darty his Ham-pie *S.* i. 46
One half-pint *b.* serves them both to dine *S.* ii. 53
And maids turn'd b—s, *call aloud for corks R.L.* iv. 54

Bottom.
Plung'd for his sense, but found no *b.* there *D.* i. 119
Loud thunder to its *b.* shook the bag *D.* i. 329
True to the *b.* see Concanen creep *D.* ii. 299
He brings up half the *b.* on his head *D.* ii. 321
Upon the *b.* shines the Queen's bright face *Mi.* ix. 33

Boughs.
While she with garlands hung the bending *b. A.* 68

Bought.
I *b.* them shrouded in their living shrine *D.* iv. 385
'Tis never to be *b.*, but always free *E.M.* iv. 17
Judges and Senates have been *b.* for gold *E.M.* iv. 187
So *b.* an Annual Rent or two *I.H.* i. 71
With Fifty Guineas (a great Pen'worth) *b. Mi.* ix. 30
Your Country's Peace, how oft, how dearly *b. S.* v. 397
He *b.* at thousands, what with better wit *S.* vi. 236
The lands are *b.*, but where are to be found *S.* vii. 109
For both the beauty and the wit are *b. S.* viii. 235

Bouncing.
The Cat comes *b.* on the floor *I.H.* ii. 213

Bound.
Or, at one *b.* o'erleaping all his laws *D.* iv. 477
In these lone walls (their days eternal.) *E.A.* 141
Tho' each by turns the other's *b.* invade *E.M.* ii. 207
Form a strong line about the silver *b. R.L.* ii. 121
From vulgar b—s *with brave disorder part E.C.* 152
Their ancient *b.* the banish'd Muses pass'd *E.C.* 710
These mix'd with art, and to due *b.* confin'd *E.M.* ii. 119
Its proper bliss, and sets its proper *b. E.M.* iii. 110
Pleas'd Vaga echoes thro' her winding *b. M.E.* iii. 251
Surprises, varies, and conceals the *B. M.E.* iv. 56
Back to his *b.* their subject Sea command *M.E.* iv. 201
But when thro' all th' infernal *b. O.* i. 49
Teach ev'ry thought within its *b.* to roll *S.* vi. 204
The stream, be his the Weekly Journals b. *D.* ii. 280
There foamed rebellious *Logic*, gagg'd and *b. D.* iv. 23
Tho' not too strictly *b.* in Time and Place *E.* iv. 28
Or *b.* in formal, or in real chains *E.* iv. 42
A naked Lover *b.* and bleeding lies *E.A.* 100
In adamantine chains shall death be *b. M.* 47
Opine, that Nature, as in duty *b. M.E.* iii. 9
These Aldus printed, those Du Sueil has *b. M.E.* iv. 136
Tho' fate has fast *b.* her *O.* i. 90
A few paternal acres *b. O.* iv. 2
Three things another's modest wishes *b. P.S.* 47
Nor *b.* thy narrow views to things below *R.L.* i. 36
For this your locks in paper durance *b. R.L.* iv. 99

And lovers' vows with ends of riband *b. R.L.* v. 118
Matures my present, and shall *b.* my last *S.* iii. 2
Milton's strong pinion now not Heav'n can *b. S.* v. 99
At length, by wholesome dread of statutes *b. S.* v. 257
Thy Goodness let me *b. U.P.* 22

Bounded.
B. by Nature, narrow'd still by Art *D.* iv. 503
Not only *b.* to peculiar arts *E.C.* 62
While from the *b.* level of our mind *E.C.* 221
Why *b.* Pow'r? why private? why no king *E.M.* iv. 160

Bounding.
The *b.* steed you pompously bestride *E.M.* iii. 35
And leap exulting like the *b.* roe *M.* 44
To fix him graceful on the *b.* Steed *S.* v. 383

Boundless.
Her *b.* empire over seas and lands *D.* iii. 68
When first young Maro in his *b.* mind *E.C.* 130
Is this too little for the *b.* heart *E.M.* iv. 355
Earth smiles around, with *b.* bounty blest *E.M.* iv. 371
What mines, to swell that *b.* charity *M.E.* iii. 278
One *b.* Green, or flourish'd Carpet views *M.E.* iv. 95
Or roll the planets thro' the *b.* sky *R.L.* ii. 80

Bounds.
He, whose long wall the wand'ring Tartar *b. D.* iii. 76
He fills, he *b.*, connects, and equals all *E.M.* i. 280
Before his lord the ready spaniel *b. W.F.* 99

Bounteous.
In flow'rs and pearls by *b.* Kirkall dress'd *D.* ii. 160
But souse the cabbage with a *b.* heart *S.* ii. 60

Bounty.
Earth smiles around with boundless *b.* blest *E.M.* iv. 371
If one, from Nature's *B.* or his Lord's *E.S.* ii. 173
A constant *B.* which no friend has made *M.E.* i. 198
To Worth or Want well-weigh'd, be *B.* giv'n *M.E.* iii. 229
There, English *B.* yet awhile may stand *M.E.* iii. 247
Then, like the Sun, let *B.* spread her ray *S.* ii. 115
'Tis such a *b.* as was never known *S.* vii. 65
What Blessings thy free *B.* gives *U.P.* 17

Bourbon.
Pours at great *B.*'s feet her silken sons *D.* iv. 298

Bousy.
Rous'd at his name, up rose the *b.* sire *D.* iv. 493

Bow.
As Jove's bright *b.* displays its wat'ry round *D.* ii. 173
Or dip their pinions in the painted *b. R.L.* ii. 84
And wits take lodgings in the sound of *B. R.L.* iv. 118
Their ample *b.*, a new Whitehall ascend *W.F.* 380
Far as loud B.'s *stupendous bells resound D.* iii. 278
And break your b—s, *as when Adonis died W.* 24
Here arm'd with silver *b.*, in early dawn *W.F.* 169
As to soft gales top-heavy pines b. *low D.* ii. 391
And place it here | here all ye Heroes *b. D.* iii. 318
Who false to Phoebus, *b.* the knee to Baal *D.* iv. 93
Instructed thus you *b.*, embrace, protest *S.* iv. 107
No wonder some folks *b.* and think them kings *S.* viii. 211

Bow'd.
Yet silent *b.* to *Christ's No kingdom here D.* ii. 400
Thro' both he pass'd, and *b.* from side to side *D.* iv. 108
Low *b.* the rest: He, kingly, did but nod *D.* iv. 207
Then *b.* and spoke; the winds forget to roar *W.F.* 353

Bow'r.
Sick was the Sun, the Owl forsook his *b. D.* iv. 11
I saw, and started from its vernal *b. D.* iv. 425
The *b.* of wanton Shrewsbury and love *M.E.* iii. 308
The Naiads wept in ev'ry wat'ry *b. Su.* 7
The captive bird that sings within thy *b. Su.* 46
Vied for his love in jetty b—s *below D.* ii. 35
I come, I come | prepare your roseate *b. E.A.* 317
Here Amphitrite sails thro' myrtle *b. M.E.* iv. 123
Or Amaranthine *b. O.* i. 76
Now rise, and haste to yonder woodhine *b. Sp.* 97
When swains from shearing seek their nightly *b. Su.* 64
There while you rest in Amaranthine *b. W.* 73

Bow'ry.
The *b.* mazes and surrounding greens *W.F.* 262

BOWL—BREACH.

Bowl.
To this our head like bias to the *b. D.* i. 170
Adieu, the heart-expanding *b. I.H.* iii. 35
Lucretia's dagger, Rosamunda's *b. M.E.* ii. 92
But who the *B.* or rattling Dice compares *Mi.* ix. 101
There St. John mingles with my friendly *b. S.* i. 127
And the brain dances to the mantling *b. S.* ii. 8
The laugh, the jest, attendants on the *b. S.* v. 247
And I this *b.*, where wanton Ivy twines *Sp.* 35
The *b.* to Strephon, and the lamb to thee *Sp.* 94
Some Dukes at Mary-bone *b. Time away Mi.* ix. 100

Bows.
Benlowes, propitious still to blockheads, *b. D.* iii. 21
He marries, *b.* at Court, and grows polite *M.E.* iii. 386
Why *b.* the side-box from its inmost rows *R.L.* v. 14
B., and begins—"This Lad, Sir, is of Blois *S.* vi. 4
B. and votes on, in Court and Parliament *S.* vi. 275
To him he flies, and *b.*, and *b.* again *S.* viii. 176

Box.
This *b.* my Thunder, this right hand my God *D.* i. 202
Then snapt his *b.*, and strok'd his belly down *D.* iv. 495
The spiry fir and shapely *b.* adorn *M.* 74
Peeress and Butler share alike the *B. M.E.* iii. 340
Pit, *b.*, and gall'ry in convulsions hurl'd *P.S.* 87
Hang o'er the *B.*, and hover round the Ring *R.L.* i. 44
And all Arabia breathes from yonder *b. R.L.* i. 134
"Give her the hair," he spoke, and rapp'd his *b. R.L.* iv. 130
For what? to have a *b.* where Eunuchs sing *S.* iii. 105
She glares in Balls, front B—es, and the Ring E. v. 53
How chang'd from him who made the *B.* groan *Mi.* ii. 15

Boy.
And ceas'd so soon, he ne'er was *B.*, nor Man *D.* iv. 288
And *B.* and Man an individual makes *E.M.* iv. 175
The Rhymes or Rattles of the Man or *B. S.* ii. 18
What *b.* but hears the saying of old Ben *S.* v. 80
A Frenchman comes, presents you with his *B. S.* vi. 3
Glad, like a *B.*, to snatch the first good play *S.* vi. 294
A Shepherd's *B.* (he seeks no better name) *Su.* 1
All B—s may read, and Girls may understand *E.S.* i. 76
What? rob your *B.*? those pretty rogues *I.H.* i. 27
And *B.* in flow'ry bands the tiger lead *M.* 78
Virtue, brave *b.*! 'tis Virtue makes a King *S.* iii. 92
The *B.* and Girls whom charity maintains *S.* v. 231
The *b.* flock round him, and the people stare *S.* vi. 120
I'll e'en leave verses to the *b.* at school *S.* vi. 201
Scarecrow to *b.*, the breeding woman's curse *S.* viii. 268
The pale B.-Senator yet tingling stands *D.* iv. 147

Boyer.
B. the State, and Law the Stage gave o'er *D.* ii. 413

Boyle.
Who plants like Bathurst, or who builds like *B. M.E.* iv. 178
Kind *B.* before his poet lays *Mi.* xii. 5
While *Jones*' and *B.*'s united Labours fall *D.* iii. 328

Brag.
Yet lo! in me what authors have to *b.* on *D.* iii. 285

Braggart.
For huffing, *b.*, puff'd Nobility *S.* viii. 201

Brahmins.
Than *B.*, Saints, and Sages did before *M.E.* iii. 184

Brain.
Cibberian forehead, and Cibberian *b. D.* i. 218
A *b.* of feathers, and a heart of lead *D.* ii. 44
And let the past and future fire thy *b. D.* ii. 66
Smote ev'ry *B.*, and wither'd ev'ry Bay *D.* iv. 10
We ply the Memory, we load the *B. D.* iv. 157
Yet by some object ev'ry *b.* is stirr'd *D.* iv. 445
Extracts his *b.*; and Principle is fled *D.* iv. 522
There shallow draughts intoxicate the *b. E.C.* 217
Ev'n to the dregs and squeezings of the *B. E.C.* 607
Or quick effluvia darting thro' the *b. E.M.* i. 199
Or tricks to shew the stretch of human *B. M.E.* ii. 47
What has not fir'd her bosom or her *b. M.E.* ii. 77
No Thought advances, but her Eddy *B. M.E.* ii. 121
'Twas no Court-badge, great Scriv'ner! fir'd thy *b. M.E.* iii. 145

Then gay ideas crowd the vacant *b. R.L.* i. 83
Sent up in vapours to the Baron's *b. R.L.* iii. 119
And the *b.* dances to the mantling bowl *S.* ii. 8
And strains, from hard-bound b—s, eight lines a year *P.S.* 182

Brainless.
Great Cibber's brazen, *b.* brothers stand *D.* i. 32

Brake.
See! from the *b.* the whirring pheasant springs *W.F.* 111

Branch.
A *b.* of Styx here rises from the Shades *D.* ii. 338
From Jesse's root behold a *b.* arise *M.* 9
A *b.* of healing Spleenwort in his hand *R.L.* iv. 56
Now golden fruits on loaded b—es shine *A.* 73
Or see the stretching *b.* long to meet *M.E.* iv. 92

Brand.
And thrice he lifted high the Birth-day *b. D.* i. 245
B. the bold front of shameless guilty men S. i. 106
Proud Vice to *b.*, and injur'd Worth adorn *S.* v. 227

Brandies.
With all their *b.*, and with all their wines *M.E.* iii. 52

Brangling.
And Noise and Norton, *B.* and Breval *D.* ii. 238

Brass.
Harmonic twang! of leather, horn, and *b. D.* ii. 254
And monumental *b.* this record bears *D.* ii. 313
Be rich in ancient *b.*, tho' not in gold *D.* iv. 365
There Warriors shining in historic *b. M.E.* v. 58
Be this thy Screen, and this thy wall of *b. S.* iii. 95

Brave.
'Tis hers, the *b.* man's latest steps to trace *E.* i. 29
From vulgar bounds with *b.* disorder part *E.C.* 152
But we, *b.* Britons, foreign laws despis'd *E.C.* 715
Is emulation in the learn'd and *b. E.M.* ii. 192
Who wickedly is wise, or madly *b. E.M.* iv. 231
There, other Trophies, deck the truly *b. E.S.* ii. 236
Due to his Merit, and *b.* Thirst of praise *Ep.* viii. 6
Who combats bravely is not therefore *b. M.E.* i. 115
Tom struts a Soldier, open, bold, and *b. M.E.* i. 153
And you, *b.* Cobham, to the latest breath *M.E.* i. 262
Could France or Rome divert our *b.* designs *M.E.* iii. 51
A *b.* man struggling in the storms of fate *P.C.* 21
Virtue, *b.* boys! 'tis Virtue makes a King *S.* iii. 92
His wealth *b.* Timon gloriously confounds *S.* iv. 85
More honours, more rewards, attend the *b. S.* vi. 48
Words that wise Bacon, or *b.* Raleigh spake *S.* vi. 168

Brav'd.
Encourag'd thus, Wit's Titans *b.* the skies *E.C.* 552
Had *b.* the *Goth*, and many a *Vandal* slain *Mi.* ii. 2

Bravely.
Who combats *b.* is not therefore brave *M.E.* i. 115
And *b.* bore the double loads of lead *R.L.* iv. 102
For those who greatly think, or *b.* die *U.L.* 10

Bravest.
Here, Withers, rest! thou *b.*, gentlest mind *Ep.* ix. 1

Brawn.
Some win rich Widows by the Chine and *B. S.* iii. 131

Bray.
Sore sighs Sir Gilbert starting at the *b. D.* ii. 251
Walls, steeples, skies b. back to him again *D.* ii. 160

Brayers.
Sound forth, my *B.*, and the welkin rend *D.* ii. 246

Braying.
Drowns the loud clarion of the *b.* Ass *D.* ii. 234

Brazen.
Great Cibber's *b.*, brainless brothers stand *D.* i. 32
This *B.* Brightness, to the 'Squire so dear *D.* i. 219
And Bacon trembling for his *b.* head *D.* iii. 104
The *b.* trumpets kindle rage no more *M.* 60
In *b.* bonds shall harb'rous Discord dwell *W.F.* 414

Breach.
In days of old they pardon'd *b.* of vows *E.J.S.* 29

D

BREAD—BREECHES.

Bread.
What then? is the reward of Virtue *b.* *E.M.* iv. 150
My *B.*, and Independency *I.H.* i. 70
A crust of *B.*, and Liberty *I.H.* ii. 221
'Tis thus we eat the *b.* another sows *M.E.* iii. 22
The MAN of Ross divides the weekly *b.* *M.E.* iii. 264
Health to himself, and to his infants *b.* *M.E.* iv. 170
Whose herds with milk, whose fields with *b.* *O.* iv. 5
If then plain *b.*, and milk will do the feat *S.* ii. 15
What few can of the living, Ease and *B. S.* viii. 107
This day be *B.* and Peace my lot *U.P.* 45

Breadth.
No monstrous height, or *b.*, or length appear *E.C.* 251

Break.
Up, up! cries Gluttony; 'tis *b.* of day *S.* iv. 112
B. Priscian's head, and Pegasus's neck D. iii. 162
Still *b.* the benches, Henley! with thy strain *D.* iii. 203
B. all their nerves, and fritter all their sense *D.* iv. 56
Death, only death, can *b.* the lasting chain *E.A.* 173
If plagues and earthquakes *b.* not Heav'n's design *E.M.* i. 155
All this dread ORDER *b.*—for whom? for thee *E.M.* i. 257
They rise, they *b.*, and to that sea return *E.M.* iii. 20
Once *b.* their rest, or stir them from their Place *E.S.* i. 100
To *b.* my Windows, if I treat a Friend *E.S.* ii. 11
And *b.* upon thee in a flood of day *M.* 98
Then never *b.* your heart when Chloe dies *M.E.* ii. 180
Cutler saw tenants *b.*, and houses fall *M.E.* iii. 323
The Mole projected *b.* the roaring Main *M.E.* iv. 200
And pointed Crystals *b.* the sparkling Rill *Mi.* x. 4
Let peals of laughter, Codrus, round thee *b. P.S.* 85
Who shames a Scribbler? *b.* one cobweb thro' *P.S.* 89
Whether the nymph shall *b.* Diana's law *R.L.* ii. 105
These in two sable ringlets taught to *b. R.L.* iv. 169
Why will you *b.* the Sabbath of my days *S.* iii. 3
While if our Elders *b.* all reason's laws *S.* v. 117
Tho' faith, I fear, 'twill *b.* his Mother's heart *S.* vi. 16
And *b.* your bows, as when Adonis died *W.* 24

Breaks.
B. out refulgent, with a heav'n its own *D.* iii. 242
And *b.* our rest, to tell us what's a-clock *D.* iv. 444
Truth *b.* upon us with resistless day *E.C.* 212
But rattling nonsense in full volleys *b. E.C.* 628
When the dull Ox, why now be *b.* the clod *E.M.* i. 63
Tenth, or ten thousandth, *b.* the chain alike *E.M.* i. 246
Touch'd with the Flame that *b.* from Virtue's Shrine, *E.S.* ii. 233
Who *b.* with her, provokes Revenge from Hell *M.E.* ii. 129
Now *b.*, or now directs, th' intending Lines *M.E.* iv. 63
Who *b.* a butterfly upon a wheel *P.S.* 308
He *b.* the Vial whence the sorrows flow *R.L.* iv. 142
And idle Cibber, how he *b.* the laws *S.* v. 92
Straight a short thunder *b.* the frozen sky *W.F.* 130

Breast.
But chief in BAVS's monster-breeding *b. D.* i. 108
By potent Arthur, knock'd his chin and *b. D.* ii. 398
The dagger wont to pierce the Tyrant's *b. D.* iv. 38
Then take them all, oh take them to thy *b. D.* iv. 515
The living image in the painter's *b. E.* iii. 42
No craving void left aking in my *b. E.A.* 94
Still on that *b.* enamour'd let me lie *E.A.* 121
Hope springs eternal in the human *b. E.M.* i. 95
Contracted all, retiring to their *b. E.M.* ii. 103
And hence one MASTER PASSION in the *b. E.M.* ii. 131
Oh blameless Bethel, to relieve thy *b. E.M.* iv. 126
And Heav'n beholds its image in his *b. E.M.* iv. 372
Again? new Tumults in my *B. I.H.* iii. 1
Perhaps Prosperity becalm'd his *b. M.E.* i. 111
She, while her Lover pants upon her *b. M.E.* ii. 167
But of what marble must that *b.* be form'd *Mi.* ix. 75
If in the *b.* tumultuous joys arise *O.* i. 24
The prudent, learn'd, and virtuous *b. O.* iii. 2
The mild and gen'rous *b. O.* iii. 12
On her white *b.* a sparkling Cross she wore *R.L.* ii. 7
Th' impending woe sat heavy on his *b. R.L.* ii. 54
And swells her *b.* with conquests yet to come *R.L.* iii. 28
As on the nosegay in her *b.* reclin'd *R.L.* iii. 141
And secret passions labour'd in her *b. R.L.* iv. 2
Old Edward's armour beams on Cibber's *b. S.* v. 319
Tis he who gives my *b.* a thousand pains *S.* v. 342
Look in that *b.*, most dirty D—! be fair *S.* vi. 222

But in my *b.* the serpent Love abides *Su.* 68
Cold is that *b.* which warm'd the world before *U.L.* 33
So perish all, whose *b.* ne'er learn'd to glow *U.L.* 45
And the green turf lie lightly on thy *b. U.L.* 64
These, were my *b.* inspir'd with equal flame *W.F.* 9
His painted wings and *b.* that flames with gold *W.F.* 118
Where flames refin'd in *b*—s seraphic glow *E.A.* 320
He bids your *b.* with ancient ardour rise *P.C.* 15
And heav'nly *b.* with human passions rage *R.L.* v. 46
And in the *b.* of Kings and Heroes glows *U.L.* 16

Breath.
Confine the thought, to exercise the *b. D.* iv. 159
The rage of Pow'r, the blast of public *b. E.* i. 25
Till fate scarce felt his gentle *b.* suppress *E.* iv. 13
Suck my last *b.*, and catch my flying soul *E.A.* 324
Till ev'ry motion, pulse, and *b.* be o'er *E.A.* 333
As Man, perhaps, the moment of his *b. E.M.* ii. 133
By turns we catch the vital *b.*, and die *E.M.* iii. 18
Why drew Marseilles' good bishop purer *b. E.M.* iv. 107
What's Fame? a fancy'd life is others' *b. E.M.* iv. 237
Collects her *b.*, as ebbing life retires *M.E.* i. 244
And you I brave Cobham, to the latest *b. M.E.* i. 262
Drowns my spirits, draws my *b. O.* v. 11
With lenient arts extend a Mother's *b. P.S.* 410
Think not, when Woman's transient *b.* is fled *R.L.* i. 51
Just where the *b.* of life his nostrils drew *R.L.* v. 81
Friend Pope! be prudent, let your Muse take *b. S.* iii. 13
All human Virtue to its latest *b. S.* v. 15
A *b.* revives him, or a *b.* o'erthrows *S.* v. 301
I neither strut with ev'ry fav'ring *b. S.* vii. 300
Heav'd by the *b.* th' inspiring bellows blow *S.* vii. 19
That flute is mine which Colin's tuneful *b. Su.* 39
See on these ruby lips the trembling *b. U.L.* 31
Since quick'ned by thy *B. U.P.* 42
Lament the ceasing of a sweeter *b. W.* 50
And now his shorter *b.*, with sultry air *W.F.* 195

Breathe.
The winds to *b.*, the waving woods to move *A.* 41
As *b.*, or pause, by fits, the airs divine *D.* ii. 394
And *b.* an air divine on ev'ry face *E.* iii. 72
But that for ever in his lines they *b. E.* iv. 20
They live, they speak, they *b.* what love inspires *E.A.* 53
Content to *b.* his native air *O.* iv. 3
Soft o'er the shrouds a‘rial whispers *b. R.L.* ii. 57
When husbands, or when lap-dogs *b.* their last *R.L.* iii. 158
Where cooling vapours *b.* along the mead *W.F.* 136

Breath'd.
Still *b.* in sighs, still usher'd with a tear *E.A.* 32
The Soldier *b.* the Gallantries of France *S.* v. 145
When the tir'd Nation *b.* from civil war *S.* v. 273
What Kings first *b.* upon her winding shore *W.F.* 300

Breathing.
Yet still her charms in *b.* paint engage *E.* iii. 55
With all the incense of the *b.* spring *M.* 24
The *b.* instruments inspire *O.* i. 2
Here western winds on *b.* roses blow *Sp.* 32

Breathless.
Faint, *b.*, thus she pray'd, nor pray'd in vain *W.F.* 199

Breathes.
She looks, and *b.* herself into their airs *D.* i. 264
And *b.* a browner horror on the woods *E.A.* 170
B. in our soul, informs our mortal part *E.M.* i. 275
Or *b.* thro' air, or shoots beneath the deeps *E.M.* iii. 116
Heav'n *b.* thro' ev'ry member of the whole *E.M.* iv. 61
And, as the prompter *b.*, the puppet squeaks *P.S.* 318
And all Arabia *b.* from yonder box *R.L.* i. 134
And *b.* three am'rous sighs to raise the fire *R.L.* ii. 42

Bred.
I know thee, Love! on foreign mountains *b. A.* 89
By common sense to common knowledge *b. D.* iv. 467
Thus *b.*, thus taught, how many have I seen *D.* iv. 505
B. to disguise, in public 'tis you hide *M.E.* ii. 203
If there's a *Briton* then, true *b.* and born *Mi.* 19
B. up at home, full early I begun *S.* vi. 52

Breeches.
Dishonest sight! his *b.* rent below *D.* iii. 198
And holds his *b.* close with both his hands *D.* iv. 148
You laugh if coat and *b.* strangely vary *S.* iii. 163

BREED—BRING.

Breed.
If teeming ewes increase my fleecy *b*. *W*. 82
With looks unmov'd, he hopes the scaly *b*. *W.F.* 139

Breeder.
He'd recommend her as a special *b*. *E.J.S.* 34

Breeding.
As men of *b*., sometimes men of wit *E.C.* 259
Without Good *B*., truth is disapprov'd *E.C.* 576
But show'd his *B*. and his Wit *I.H.* ii. 172
Scarecrow to boys, the *b*. woman's curse *S.* viii. 268

Breeds.
And ev'ry death its own avenger *b*. *E.M.* iii. 166
One, one man only *b*. my just offence *S.* vii. 45

Breeze.
The lakes that quiver to the curling *b*. *E.A.* 160
Where'er you find "the cooling western *b*." *E.C.* 350
Warms in the sun, refreshes in the *b*. *E.M.* i. 271
A puny insect, shiv'ring at a *b*. *M.E.* iv. 108
Waft on the *b*., or sink in clouds of gold *R.L.* ii. 60
No cheerful *b*. this sullen region knows *R.L.* iv. 19
Her fate is whisper'd by the gentle *b*. *W.* 61
In some still ev'ning when the whisp'ring *b*. *W.* 79
To *Thames's banks which fragrant* b—s *fill W.F.* 263

Breth'ren.
In Tot'nham.fields the *b*. with amaze *D.* ii. 261

Breval.
B., Bond, Besaleel, the varlets caught *D.* ii. 126
And Noise and Norton, Brangling and *B. D.* ii. 238

Brew. .
Or *b*. fierce tempests on the wintry main *R.L.* ii. 85

Briareus.
Like bold *B*. with a hundred hands *D.* iv. 66

Bribe.
Improve we these. Three Cat-calls be the *b. D.* ii. 231
Smile without Art, and win without a *B. E.S.* i. 23
Alas ! the small Discredit of a *B. E.S.* ii. 46
He must repair it ; takes a *b*. from France *M.E.* iii. 396
This prints my *Letters*, that expects a *b. P.S.* 113
Oh ! that such bulky b—s *as all might see M.E.* iii. 49

Brib'd.
Here *b*. the rage of ill-requited heav'n *E.A.* 138
Be *b*. as often, and as often lie *E.S.* i. 118
The *b*. Elector.—There you stoop too low *E.S.* ii. 25

Bribing.
The *b*. Statesman.—Hold, too high you go *E.S.* ii. 24

Bribes.
But *b*. a Senate, and the Land's betray'd *M.E.* iii. 32

Brick.
On passive paper, or on solid *b. D.* iv. 130
Thinks that but words, and this but *b*. and stones *S.* iv. 66

Bridal.
For her the Spouse prepares the *b*. ring *E.A.* 219

Bride.
To headless Phœbe his fair *b*. postpone *D.* iv. 367
A teeming Mistress, but a barren *B. M.E.* ii. 72
Sighs for an Otho, and neglects his *b. M.E.* v. 44

Bridewell.
This labour past, by *B*. all descend *D.* ii. 269

Bridge.
Who builds a *B*. that never drove a pile *S.* v. 185
Make Quays, build B—s, *or repair Whitehall S.* ii. 120

Bridgewater.
With Zeuxis' Helen thy *B*. vie *E.* iii. 75
An Angel's sweetness, or B.'s *eyes E.* iii. 46

Bright.
Now setting Phœbus shone serenely *b. A.* 13
Now *b*. Arcturus glads the teeming grain *A.* 72
As Jove's *b*. bow displays its wat'ry round *D.* ii. 173
And orient Science their *b*. course begun *D.* iii. 74
And one *b*. blaze turns learning into air *D.* iii. 78

B. with the gilded button tipt its head *D.* iv. 408
Or that *b*. Image to our fancy draw *D.* iv. 487
Full in my view set all the *b*. abode *E.A.* 127
Blot out each *b*. Idea of the skies *E.A.* 284
B. clouds descend, and Angels watch thee round *E.A.* 340
Unerring NATURE, still divinely *b. E.C.* 70
In the *b*. Muse tho' thousand charms conspire *E.C.* 339
Some *b*. Idea of the master's mind *E.C.* 485
And all the *b*. creation fades away *E.C.* 493
At once his own *b*. prospect to be blest *E.M.* iv. 351
See thy *b*. altars throng'd with prostrate kings *M.* 93
Blushing in *b*. diversities of day *M.E.* iv. 85
B. Apollo, lend thy Choir *Mi.* vii. 16
Upon the bottom shines the Queen's *b*. Face *Mi.* ix. 33
In *b*. Confusion open *Rouleaux* lie *Mi.* ix. 81
And the *b*. flame was shot thro' Marchmont's Soul *Mi.* x. 12
To *b*. Cecilia greater pow'er is giv'n *O.* i. 132
Of thousand *b*. inhabitants of Air *R.L.* i. 28
B., as the sun, her eyes the gazers strike *R.L.* ii. 13
Th' advent'rous Baron the *b*. locks admir'd *R.L.* ii. 29
When num'rous wax-lights in *b*. order blaze *R.L.* iii. 168
Or *b*. as visions of expiring maids *R.L.* iv. 42
Not Berenice's Locks first rose so *b. R.L.* v. 129
Then cease, *b*. Nymph ! to mourn thy ravish'd hair *R.L.* v. 141
Sir Job sail'd forth, the ev'ning *b*. and still *S.* iii. 138
Be struck with *b*. Brocade, or Tyrian dye *S.* iv. 32
B. thro' the rubbish of some hundred years *S.* vi. 166
Here the *b*. crocus and blue vi'let grew *Sp.* 31
More *b*. than noon, yet fresh as early day *Sp.* 82
In woods *b*. Venus with Adonis stray'd *Su.* 61
Is there no *b*. reversion in the sky *U.L.* 9
To thee, *b*. goddess, oft a lamb shall bleed *W.* 81
As *b*. a Goddess, and as chaste a Queen *W.F.* 162
Like the *b*. Beauties on thy banks below *W.F.* 232
Happy the man whom this *b*. court approves *W.F.* 235
Fair Geraldine, *b*. object of his vow *W.F.* 297
To the *b*. regions of the rising day *W.F.* 388
The b.-ey'd *perch with fins of Tyrian dye W.F.* 142

Brighten.
The skies to *b*. and the birds to sing *Sp.* 72

Brighten'd.
And gleams of glory *b*. all the day *E.A.* 146
It *b. Craggs's*, and may darken thine *S.* iv. 45

Brightens.
How the wit *b.* ! how the style refines *E.C.* 421

Brighter.
A *b*. wash ; to curl the waving hairs *R.L.* ii. 97

Brightest.
Once *b*. shin'd this child of Heat and Air *D.* iv. 424
Voiture was wept by all the *b*. Eyes *E.* iv. 18
The *b*. eyes of France inspir'd his Muse (*rep.*) *E.* iv. 77
The wisest, *b*., meanest of mankind *E.M.* iv. 282
This day black Omens threat the *b*. Fair *R.L.* iv. 101
Which not the tears of *b*. eyes could ease *R.L.* iv. 76
Blest Thames's shores the *b*. beauties yield *Sp.* 63

Brightness.
This brazen *B*., to the 'Squire so dear *D.* i. 219

Brillante.
The drops to thee, *B*., we consign *R.L.* ii. 113

Brilliants.
This *Snuff-Box*,—on the Hinge see *B*. shine *Mi.* ix. 43

Bring.
Ye Mantuan Nymphs, your sacred succour *b. A.* 5
B., *b*. the madding Bay, the drunken Vine *D.* i. 303
Support his front, and Oaths *b*. up the rear *D.* i. 308
The pond'rous books two gentle readers *b. D.* ii. 383
Roll all their fates ; then back their circles *b. D.* iii. 56
Th' Augustus born to *b*. Saturnian times *D.* iii. 320
And *b*. Saturnian days of Lead and Gold *D.* iv. 16
We *b*. to one dead level ev'ry mind *D.* iv. 268
You'll *b*. a House (I mean of Peers) *E.* vi. 18
Thence form your judgment, thence your maxims *b. E.C.* 126
See, from each clime the learn'd their incense *b. E.C.* 185
Draw to one point, and to one centre *b. E.M.* iii. 301

D 2

Rewards, that either would to Virtue *b*. *E.M.* iv. 181
B. then these blessings to a strict account *E.M.* iv. 269
See Nature hastes her earliest wreaths to *b. M.* 23
Is there no hope ? Alas ! then *b.* the jowl *M.E.* i. 241
And *b.* all Paradise before your eye *M.E.* iv. 148
With added years if life *b.* nothing new *Mi.* v. 5
Now hear what blessings Temperance can *b. S.* ii. 67
Add fifty more, and *b.* it to a square *S.* iv. 76
It ought to *b.* all courtiers on their backs *S.* viii. 207
Their early fruit, and milk-white turtles *b. Su.* 52
Let Nymphs and Sylvans cypress garlands *b. W.* 22
GRANVILLE commands ; your aid, O Muses, *b. W.F.* 5
And *b.* the schemes of op'ning fate to light *W.F.* 426

Bringing.
But grave *Epistles*, *b.* Vice to light *S.* i. 151

Brings.
The Mighty Mother, and her Son, who *b. D.* i. 1
Each growling lump, and *b.* it to a Bear *D.* i. 102
He *b.* up half the bottom on his head *D.* ii. 321
While fancy *b.* the vanish'd piles to view *E.* iii. 31
If ever chance two waud'ring lovers *b. E.A.* 347
Atones not for that envy which it *b. E.C.* 495
For me, the mine a thousand treasures *b. E.M.* i. 137
As *b.* all Brobdignag before your thought *M.E.* iv. 104
These Honours Peace to happy Britain *b. M.E.* iv. 203
And *b.* all natural events to pass *S.* vii. 49

Brink.
As when she touch'd the *b.* of all we hate *M.E.* ii. 52
And from the *b.* his dancing shade surveys *Sp.* 34

Brisk.
The *b.* Example never fail'd to move *D.* i. 194
When the *b.* Minor pants for twenty-one *S.* iii. 38

Brisker.
Here *b.* vapours o'er the TEMPLE creep *D.* ii. 345

Britain.
That once was *B.*—Happy ! had she seen *D.* iii. 117
The brightest eyes of *B.* now peruse *E.* iv. 78
And Chiefs or Sages long to *B.* giv'n *Ep.* xiv. 13
All Europe sav'd, yet *B.* not betray'd *M.E.* i. 84
Ask why from *B.* Cæsar would retreat *M.E.* i. 129
And *B.*, if not Europe, is undone *M.E.* i. 161
See *B.* sunk in lucre's sordid charms *M.E.* iii. 143
And shall not *B.* now reward his toils (*rep.*) *M.E.* iii. 215
These Honours Peace to happy *B.* brings *M.E.* iv. 203
Oh when shall *B.*, conscious of her claim *M.E.* v. 53
While yet in *B.* Honour had applause *P.S.* 389
But *B.*, changeful as a Child at play *S.* v. 155
B. to soft refinements less a foe *S.* v. 265
Much injur'd Blunt ! why bears he *B.*'s hate *M.E.* iii. 133
In *B.* Senate he a seat obtains *M.E.* iii. 393
Perhaps ev'n *B.* utmost shore *O.* ii. 19
Here *B.* statesmen oft the fall foredoom *R.L.* iii. 5
Newmarket's Glory rose, as *B.* fell *S.* v. 144
And bleed for ever under *B.* spear *W.F.* 310
Bear *B.* thunder, and her Cross display *W.F.* 387

Britannia.
Say how the Goddess bade *B.* sleep *D.* i. 7
And bade thee live to crown B.'s *praise D.* iii. 211
Fair Liberty, *B.* Goddess, rears *W.F.* 91
And high in air *B.* standard flies *W.F.* 110

British.
Huge bales of *B.* cloth blockade the door *M.E.* iii. 57
When *B.* sighs from dying WYNDHAM stole *Mi.* x. 11
And calls forth Roman drops from *B.* eyes *P.C.* 16
Such plays alone should win a *B.* ear *P.C.* 45
And guard with Arms divine the *B.* throne *R.L.* ii. 90
One speaks the glory of the *B.* Queen *R.L.* iii. 73
Or in a coach and six the *B.* Fair *R.L.* iii. 164
When *B.* bards begin t' immortalize *S.* v. 54
See ! where the *B.* youth, engag'd no more *S.* viii. 212
Thou, too, great father of the *B.* floods *W.F.* 219
No more my sons shall dye with *B.* blood *W.F.* 367
Once more to bend before a *B.* QUEEN *W.F.* 384

Briton.
The last true *B.* lies beneath this stone *Ep.* ix. 12
If there's a *B.* then, true bred and born *Mi.* ii. 19
And each true *B.* is to Ben so civil *S.* v. 41

And be the Critic's, B.'s, *Old Man's Friend Mi.* ii. 24
But *we*, brave B—s, *foreign laws despis'd B.C.* 715
Here, last of *B.*, let your Names be read *E.S.* ii. 250
Such, such emotions should in *B.* rise *Mi.* ii. 9
B. attend : be worth like this approv'd *P.C.* 37
What dear delight to *B.* Farce affords *S.* v. 310

Broad.
Glad chains, warm furs, *b.* banners, and *b.* faces *D.* i. 28
So from the Sun's *b.* beam in shallow urns *D.* ii. 11
He grins, and looks *b.* nonsense with a stare *D.* ii. 194
By his *b.* shoulders known, and length of ears *D.* iii. 36
In *b.* Effulgence all below reveal'd *D.* iv. 18
B. hats, and hoods, and caps, a sable shoal *D.* iv. 190
Spread thy *b.* wing, and souse on all the kind *E.S.* ii. 15
And the *b.* falchion in a plough-share end *M.* 62
So when the Sun's *b.* beam has tir'd the sight *M.E.* ii. 253
Bid the *b.* Arch the dang'rous flood contain *M.E.* iv. 199
Shines a *b.* Mirror thro' the shadowy Cave *Mi.* x. 2
With his *b.* sabre next, a chief in years *R.L.* iii. 55
On the *b.* base of fifty thousand rise *S.* iv. 74

Broadest.
Poor W** nipt in folly's *b.* bloom *D.* iv. 513
The *b.* mirth unfeeling Folly wears *E.M.* iv. 319

Brobdignag.
As brings all *B.* before your thought *M.E.* iv. 104

Brocade.
One flaunts in rags, one flutters in *b. E.M.* iv. 196
Or stain her honour, or her new *b. R.L.* ii. 107
Trembling, and conscious of the rich *b. R.L.* iii. 116
Be struck with bright *B.*, or Tyrian dye *S.* iv. 32

Broccoli.
On *b.* and mutton, round the year *S.* ii. 138

Broke.
Ere Wit oblique had *b.* that steady light *E.M.* iii. 231
Then see them *b.* with toils, or sunk in ease *E.M.* iv. 297
Ask you why Wharton *b.* thro' ev'ry rule *M.E.* i. 206
Who *b.* no promise, serv'd no private end *M.E.* v. 69
No duty *b.* , no father disobey'd *P.S.* 130
And thus *b.* out—" My Lord, why, what the devil *R.L.* iv. 127
Or say our Fathers never *b.* a rule *S.* v. 93

Broken.
Or Phidias *b.*, and Apelles burn'd *D.* iii. 112
Where, one step *b.*, the great scale 's destroy'd *E.M.* i. 244
Light quirks of Music, *b.* and uneven *M.E.* iv. 143
With nodding arches, *b.* temples spread *M.E.* v. 3
In *b.* air, trembling, the wild music floats *O.* i. 17
Lull'd by soft Zephyrs thro' the *b.* pane *P.S.* 42
Of *b.* troops an easy conquest find *R.L.* iii. 78
There *b.* vows and death-bed alms are found *R.L.* v. 117
Round *b.* columns clasping ivy twin'd *W.F.* 69
And Persecution mourn her *b.* wheel *W.F.* 420

Bronze.
Embrown'd with native *b.*, lo ! Henley stands *D.* iii. 199
New edge their dulness, and new *b.* their *face D.* ii. 10

Brood.
Still as one *b.*, and as another rose *E.M.* iii. 139

Brook.
There, leaning near a gentle *b. I.H.* ii. 129
She went, to plain-work, and to *purling b*—s *E.* v. 11
The lowing herds to murm'ring *b.* retreat *Su.* 86

Broome.
Well purg'd, and worthy Settle, Banks, and *B. D.* i. 146

Broomsticks.
The thriving plants, ignoble *b.* made *M.E.* iv. 97

Brother.
With each a sickly *b.* at his back *D.* ii. 306
The Judge to dance his *b.* Sergeant call *D.* iv. 591
Come thou, my father, *b.*, husband, friend *E.A.* 152
Oft have you hinted to your *b.* Peer *M.E.* iv. 39
Grove nods at grove, each Alley has a *b. M.E.* iv. 117
As son, as father, *b.*, husband, friend *O.* iii. 28
Bear, like the Turk, no *b.* near the Throne *P.S.* 198

F. loves the Senate, Hockley-hole his *b. S.* i. 49
The Temple late two *b,* Sergeants saw *S.* vi. 127
Nature made ev'ry Fop to plague his *b. S.* viii. 258
There, where no Father's, B.'s, Friend's disgrace *E.S.* i. 99
Thou mean deserter of thy *b.* blood *U.L.* 30
Great Cibber's brazen, brainless b—s stand *D.* i. 32
Peel'd, patch'd, and pyebald, linsey-wolsey *b. D.* iii. 115
Why, of two *b.,* rich and restless one *S.* vi. 270
Around his throne the sea-born *b.* stood *W.F.* 337

Brotherhood.
Here all his suff'ring *b.* retire *D.* i. 143

Brought.
O born in sin, and forth in folly *b. D.* i. 225
A second effort *b.* but new disgrace *D.* ii. 175
In flames, like Semele's, be *b.* to bed *D.* iii. 315
All which, exact to rule, were *b.* about *E.C.* 277
He *b.* him Bacon (nothing lean) *I.H.* ii. 165
Just *b.* out this, when scarce his tongue could stir *M.E.* i. 254
What *b.* Sir Visto's ill-got wealth to waste *M.E.* iv. 15
It *b.* (no doubt) th' *Excise* and *Army* in *S.* vii. 8
'Twas only Suretyship that *b.* 'em there *S.* vii. 70

Brow.
Lo P—p—le's *b.,* tremendous to the town *D.* iii. 151
Now, Bavius, take the poppy from thy *b. D.* iii. 317
His beaver'd *b.* a birchen garland wears *D,* iv. 141
Vex'd to be still in town, I knit my *b. E.* v. 49
Immortal Vida : on whose honour'd *b. E.C.* 705
Who hung with woods yon mountain's sultry *b. M.E.* iii. 253
Smooth'd ev'ry *b.,* and open'd ev'ry soul *S.* v. 248
Shaking the horrors of his sable b—s *D.* ii. 327
And Shadwell nods the poppy on his *b. D.* iii. 22
Now Europe's laurels on their *b.* behold *E.M.* iv. 295
Without a staring Reason on his *b. E.S.* ii. 194
Gilding my Aurelia's *B. Mi.* vii. 22
Embrace my Love, and bind my *b.* with bays *Sw.* 38

Brown.
Nor heeds the *b.* dishonours of his face *D.* ii. 108
Nigrina black, and Merdamente *b. D.* ii. 334
And best distinguish'd by black, *b.,* or fair *M.E.* iv. 2

Brown and Mears.
Where *B.* and *M.* unbar the gates of light *D.* iii. 28

Browner.
And breathes a *b.* horror on the woods *E.A.* 170

Bruin.
So watchful *B.* forms with plastic care *D.* i. 101

Bruis'd.
Not Chaos-like together crush'd and *b. W.F.* 13

Brunswick.
With ARMS, and GEORGE, and *B.* crowd the verse *S.* i. 24
Nor fond of bleeding, ev'n in B.'s cause *S.* iii. 10

Brush.
The Muse's wing shall *b.* you all away *E.S.* ii. 223

Brussels.
No, let a charming Chintz, and *B.* Lace *M.E.* i. 248

Brutes.
From *b.* what men, from men what spirits know *E.M.* i. 79
For wiser *b.* were backward to be slaves *W.F.* 50

Brutus.
Cutler and *B.* dying both exclaim *M.E.* iii. 333
And *B.* tenderly reproves *O.* iii. 8
The Gods and *B.* bend to love *O.* iii. 14

Bu—.
Why one like *B,* with pay and scorn content *S.* vi. 274

Bubble.
And now a *b.* burst, and now a world *E.M.* i. 90
In Folly's cup still laughs the *b.* joy *E.M.* ii. 288
Like b—s on the sea of Matter born *E.M.* iii. 19

Bubbling.
Not *b.* fountains to the thirsty swain *A.* 43

Bubo.
B. observes, he lash'd no sort of *Vice E.S.* i. 12
The flow'rs of *B.,* and the flow of Y—g *E.S.* i. 68
Bids *B.* build, and sends him such a Guide *M.E.* iv. 20
The first Lampoon *Sir Will* or *B.* makes *P.S.* 280

Buck.
Not so : a *B.* was then a week's repast *S.* ii. 93
Some with fat B—s on childless dotards fawn *S.* iii. 130

Buckhursts.
Where other *B.,* other DORSETS shine *Ep.* i. 13

Buckingham.
Attend the shade of gentle *B. Ep.* xiv. 10
And thou shalt live, for *B.* commends *Mi.* i. 2
And Helmsley, once proud B.'s delight *S.* ii. 177

Buckle.
In Fulvia's *b.* ease the throbs below *M.E.* iii. 88
Eternal *b.* takes in Parian stone *M.E.* iii. 296
Form'd a vast *b.* for his widow's gown *R.L.* v. 92

Budgel.
Thrice *B.* aim'd to speak, but thrice suppest *D.* ii. 397
Let *B.* charge low *Grubstreet* on his quill *P.S.* 378
Like Lee or *B.,* I will rhyme and point *S.* i. 100
Henley himself I've heard, and *B.* too *S.* viii. 51
Or nobly wild, with B.'s fire and force *S.* i. 27

Buff.
Tho' his soul's bullet, and his body *b. S.* viii. 263

Buffet.
The rich *B.* well-colour'd Serpents grace *M.E.* iv. 153
Not when a gilt B.'s reflected pride *S.* ii. 5

Buffoon.
Otho a warrior, Cromwell a *b. M.E.* i. 88
Without a Fiddler, Flatt'rer, or *B. M.E.* iii. 240

Bufo.
To *B.* left the whole Castalian state *P.S.* 230
Sat full-blown *B.,* puff'd by ev'ry quill *P.S.* 232
May ev'ry Bavius have his *B.* still *P.S.* 250

Bug.
And suck'd all o'er, like an industrious *B. D.* i. 130
Yet let me flap this *b.* with gilded wings *P.S.* 309
As *B.* now has, and Dorimant would have *S.* iii. 88
But *B.* and D * l, Their *Honours,* and so forth *S.* iii. 90

Bugbear.
But to the world no *b.* is so great *S.* iii. 67

Build.
Then *b.* a new, or act it in a plain *E.C.* 284
And *b.* on wants, and on defects of mind *E.M.* ii. 247
These *b.* as fast as knowledge can destroy *E.M.* ii. 287
B. on the wave, or arch beneath the sand *E.M.* iii. 102
For very want ; he could not *b.* a wall *M.E.* iii. 324
Bids Bubo *b.,* and sends him such a Guide *M.E.* iv. 20
To *b.,* to plant, whatever you intend *M.E.* iv. 47
Make Quays, *b.* Bridges, or repair Whitehall *S.* ii. 120
Pity ! to *b.* without a son or wife *S.* ii. 163
I plant, root up ; I *b.,* and then confound *S.* iii. 169
We *b.,* we paint, we sing, we dance as well *S.* v. 46

Builder.
In vain th' observer eyes the *b.'s* toil *M.E.* i. 220

Building.
Thy arts of *b.* from the bee receive *E.M.* iii. 175
To compass this, his *b.* is a Town *M.E.* iv. 105
And pompous b—s once were things of Use *M.E.* iv. 24
But future *B.,* future Navies grow *M.E.* iv. 188

Builds.
And *b.* imaginary Rome anew *E.* iii. 32
B. Life on Death, on Change Duration founds *M.E.* iii. 167
Who *b.* a Church to God, and not to Fame *M.E.* iii. 285
Who plants like BATHURST, or who *b.* like BOYLE *M.E.* iv. 178
Who *b.* a Bridge that never drove a pile *S.* v. 185

Built.

Tho' long my Party *b*. on me their hopes *D*. iii. 283
On mutual Wants *b*. mutual Happiness *E.M*. iii. 112
Cities were *b*., Societies were made *E.M*. iii. 200
And hell was *b*. on spite, and heav'n on pride *E.M*. iii. 262
For what has Virro painted, *b*., and planted *M.E*. iv. 13
But chiefly Love—to Love an Altar *b*. *R.L*. ii. 37

Bulk.

But such a *b*. as no twelve bards could raise *D*. ii. 39
And stretch'd on *b*—s, *as usual, Poets lay D*. ii. 420

Bulky.

Oh! that such *b*. Bribes as all might see *M.E*. iii. 49

Bull.

His Grace will game: to White's a *b*. be led *M.E*. iii. 67
A milk-white *b*. shall at your altars stand *Sp*. 47
To want the strength of *b*—s, the fur of bears *E.M*.i.176
B. aim their horns, and Asses lift their heels *S*. i. 86

Bullet.

Tho' his soul's *b*., and his body buff *S*. viii. 263

Bully.

Like a tall *b*., lifts the head, and lies *M.E*. iii. 340
At the Groom-Porter's batter'd *B*—ies *play Mi*. ix. 99

Bulrush.

The green reed trembles, and the *b*. nods *M*. 72

Bulwark.

A desp'rate *B*., sturdy, firm, and fierce *Mi*. ii. 13

Buoy.

For rising merit will *b*. up at last *E.C*. 461

Buoyant.

Sons of a Day! just *b*. on the flood *D*. ii. 307

Buoys.

Like *b*—s that never sink into the flood *D*. iv. 241
He b. *up instant, and returns to light D*. ii. 296

Burdens.

Did here the trees with ruddier *b*. bend *E.M*. iii. 203

Burgersdyck.

On German Crouzaz, and Dutch *B. D*. iv. 198

Buried, see Bury'd.

Buries.

And universal Darkness *b*. All *D*. iv. 656
And *b*. madmen in the heaps they raise *E.M*. iv. 76
And one fate *b*. in th' Asturian Mines *M.E*. iii. 132

Burman.

Are things which Kuster, *B*., Wasse shall see *D*. iv. 237

Burn.

His rapid waters in their passage *b. D*. ii. 184
Padua, with sighs, beholds her Livy *b. D*. iii. 105
Ah hopeless, lasting flames! like those that *b. E.A*. 261
With choice we fix, with sympathy we *b. E.M*. iii. 135
And *b*. for ever one *O*. iii. 22
And *b*. in Cupid's flames—but *b*. alive *R.L*. v. 102
B. thro' the Tropic, freeze beneath the Pole *S*. iii. 72
Dim lights of life, that *b*. a length of years *U.L*. 19

Burn'd.

Or Phidias broken, and Apelles *b. D*. iii. 112

Burnet.

And Oldmixon and *B*. both out-lie *S*. viii. 61
Not from the *B*—s, Oldmixons, and Cookes *P.S*. 146

Burning.

Thou wert from Ætna's *b*. entrails torn *A*. 91
Where spices smoke beneath the *b*. line *D*. iii. 70
Let tears, and *b*. blushes speak the rest *E.A*. 106
From *b*. suns when livid deaths descend *E.M*. i. 142
Shall *b*. Ætna, if a sage requires *E.M*. iv. 123
In fumes of *b*. Chocolate shall glow *R.L*. ii. 135
The sun obliquely shoots his *b*. ray *R.L*. iii. 20
Pan saw and lov'd, and *b*. with desire *W.F*. 183

Burns.

Now flames the Cid, and now Perolla *b. D*. i. 250

The torch of Venus *b*. not for the dead *E.A*. 258
Each *b*. alike, who can, or cannot write *E.C*. 30
Now *b*. with glory, and then melts with love *E.C*. 377
As the rapt Seraph that adores and *b. E.M*. i. 278
Now Conscience chills her, and now Passion *b. M.E*. ii. 65
And heads the bold Train-Bands, and *b*. a Pope *M.E*. iii. 214
His heart now melts, now leaps, now *b. O*. iii. 35
B. to encounter two advent'rous knights *R.L*. iii. 26
Belinda *b*. with more than mortal ire *R.L*. iv. 93
Ploughs, *b*., manures, and toils from sun to sun *S*. vi. 271
The sultry Sirius *b*. the thirsty plains *Su*. 21
By night he scorches, as he *b*. by day *Su*. 92

Burst.

When, lo! a *b*. of thunder shook the flood *D*. ii. 325
And now a bubble *b*., *and now a world E.M*. i. 290
And now you *b*. (ah cruel!) from my arms *I.H*. iii. 44
And men and dogs shall drink him till they *b. M.E*. iii. 176
(Some say his Queen) was forc'd to speak, or *b. P.S*. 72
'Twould *b*. ev'n Heraclitus with the spleen *S*. viii. 236

Bursting.

Thence *b*. glorious, all at once let down *D*. iv. 291
All matter quick, and *b*. into birth *E.M*. i. 234
She from the rending earth, and *b*. skies *E.M*. iii. 253
Thou stand'st unshook amidst a *b*. world *P.S*. 88

Bursts.

And the puff'd orator *b*. out in tropes *D*. ii. 206
B. out, resistless, with a thund'ring tide *E.C*. 630

Burthen.

And the sad *b*. of some merry song *S*. i. 80

Bury.

Deep Harvests *b*. all his pride has plann'd *M.E*. iv. 175
He help'd to *b*. whom he help'd to starve *P.S*. 248

Bury'd.

Some *b*. marble half preserves a name *M.E*. v. 16
Why then for ever *b*. in the shade *S*. viii. 87

Business, Bus'ness.

Life's instant *b*. to a future day *S*. iii. 42
In crowds, and courts, law, *b*., feasts, and friends *S*.vi.91
Or will you think, my Friend, your *b*. done *S*. vi. 320
Life's idle *b*. at one gasp be o'er *U.L*. 81
O thou! of *Bus'ness* the directing soul *D*. i. 169
Condemn'd in *b*. or in arts to drudge *E.M*. iv. 263
Blunt could *do B*., H—ggins *knew the Town E.S*. i. 14
Early at *b*., and at Hazard late *M.E*. i. 73
Some plunge in *b*., others shave their crowns *M.E*. i. 104
And totter on in *b*. to the last *M.E*. i. 229
Men, some to *B*., some to Pleasure take *M.E*. ii. 215

Buskin'd.

Her *b*. Virgins trac'd the dewy lawn *W.F*. 170

Buss.

Then gives a smacking *b*., and cries, "No words" *E*.v.26

Bust.

These are thy Honours! not that here thy *B. Ep*. xi. 9
But die, and she'll adore you. Then the *B. M.E*. ii. 139
The faithless column, and the crumbling *B. M.E*. v. 20
His Library (where *b*—s *of Poets dead P.S*. 235

Busy.

Laborious, heavy, *b*., bold, and blind *D*. i. 15
Seldom at Church ('twas such a *b*. life) *M.E*. iii. 381
The *b*. Sylphs surround their darling care *R.L*. i. 145
The *b*., idle blockheads of the ball *S*. viii. 203

But.—Passim.

Butcher.

And "Coll!" each *B*. roars at Hockley-hole *D*. i. 326
Of half that live the *b*. and the tomb *E.M*. iii. 162
Where Dukes and B—s *join to wreathe my crown D*. i. 223
But fate with *b*. plac'd thy priestly stall *D*. iii. 209
His *b*. Henley? his free-masons Moore *P.S*. 98

Butler.

Rush Chaplain, *B*., Dogs and all *I.H.* ii. 211
Peeress and *B*. share alike the Box *M.E.* iii. 140
Your wine lock'd up, your *b*. stroll'd abroad *S.* ii. 13
Nor stops, for one bad cork, his *b*.'s pay *S.* ii. 63

Butt.

To the last honours of the *B*. and Bays *D.* i. 168

Butterfly.

Fair ev'n in death, this peerless *B. D.* iv. 436
Who breaks a *b*. upon a wheel *P.S.* 308
The learned Baron B—ies design *D.* iv. 589
Me and the *B*. together *I.H.* i. 20
And Books for Mead, and *B*. for Sloane *M.E.* iv. 10
The Fops are painted *B. Mi.* iv. 17
Dry'd *b*., and tomes of casuistry *R.L.* v. 122

Butting.

With spurning heels, and with a *b*. head *M.E.* iii. 68

Button.

Bright with the gilded *b*. tipt its head *D.* iv. 408
Ev'n B.'s *Wits to worms shall turn Mi.* iv. 39

Buy.

With him, most authors steal their works, or *b. E.C.* 618
To *b*. both sides, and give thy Country peace *M.E.* iii. 150
A certain truth, which many *b*. too dear *M.E.* iv. 40
And *b*. a rope, that future times may tell *S.* ii. 109
Just half the land would *b*., and half be sold *S.* iii. 125
B. ev'ry stick of wood that loods them heat (*rep.*) *S.* vi. 242

Buys,

That *b*. your sex a Tyrant o'er itself *M.E.* ii. 288
And silent sells a King, or *b*. a Queen *M.E.* iii. 48
Ask why Phryne the whole Auction *b. M.E.* iii. 119
First, for his Son a gay commission *b. M.E.* iii. 389
He *b*. for Topham, Drawings and Designs *M.E.* iv. 7

Buzz.

Shine, *b*., and fly-blow in the setting sun *M.E.* ii. 28
Whose *b*. the witty and the fair annoys *P.S.* 311

Buzzing.

The *b.* Bees about their dusky Queen *D.* iv. 80

By.—*Passim.*

C.

Or give up Cicero to *C* or *K D.* iv. 222
Great *C**, H**, P**, R**, K** *D.* iv. 545

Cabbage.

But souse the *c*. with a bounteous heart *S.* ii. 60

Cackling.

And *c*. save the Monarchy of Tories *D.* i. 212

Cæsar.

Great *C*. roars, and hisses in the fire *D.* i. 251
Was made for *C*.—but for Titus too *E.M.* iv. 146
An Eugene living, as a *C*. dead *E.M.* iv. 244
Than *C*. with a senate at his heels *E.M.* iv. 258
Ere *C*. was, or Newton nam'd *I.H.* iv. 10
Ask why from Britain *C*. would retreat (*rep.*) *M.E.* i. 129
C. perhaps might answer he was drunk *M.E.* i. 132
When *C*. made a noble dame a whore *M.E.* i. 213
That very *C*., born in Scipio's days *M.E.* i. 216
C. and Tall-boy, Charles and Charlemagne *M.E.* ii. 78
Ev'n when proud *C*. 'midst triumphal cars *P.C.* 27
And honour'd *C*. less than Cato's sword *P.C.* 36
And justly *C*. scorns the Poet's lays *S.* i. 35
Not *C*.'s *empress would I design to prove E.A.* 87
Pours fierce Ambition on a *C*. mind *E.M.* i. 159
Or if you needs must write, write *C*. praise *S.* i. 21
See other C—s, other *Homers rise D.* iv. 360

Cage.

That from his *c*. cries Cuckold, Whore, and Knave *M.E.* i. 6
Dull sullen pris'ners in the body's *c. U.L.* 18
C—s *for gnats, and chains to yoke a flea R.L.* v. 121

Cain.

That righteous Abel was destroy'd by *C. E.M.* iv. 118

Caitiff.

The *c*. Vaticide conceiv'd a pray'r *D.* ii. 78

Cajole.

Ah gentle Sir! you courtiers so *c*. us *S.* viii. 90

Cakes.

Yet sigh'st thou now for apples and for *c. E.M.* iv. 176

Calf.

Whose gentle progress makes a *c*. an ox *S.* vii. 48
Demand new bodies, and in C.'s army *D.* iii. 29

Calista.

To her, *C*. prov'd her conduct nice *M.E.* ii. 31

Call.

With Authors, Stationers obey'd the *c. D.* ii. 31
Or, impious, preach his word without a *c. D.* iv. 94
Prompt at the *c*. around the Goddess roll *D.* iv. 189
The first thus open'd: "Hear thy suppliant's *c. D.* iv. 403
Not grace, or zeal, love only was my *c. E.A.* 117
The hog that ploughs not, nor obeys thy *c. E.M.* iii. 41
The moving mountains hear the pow'rful *c. Sw.* 83
C. forth each mass, a Poem, or a Play *D.* i. 58
Oft had the Goddess heard her servants *c. D.* ii. 97
All look, all sigh, all *c*. on Smedley lost *D.* ii. 293
A Page, a Grave, that they can *c*. their own *D.* iv. 128
Which Chalcis Gods, and mortals *c*. an Owl *D.* iv. 362
The Judge to dance his brother Sergeant *c. D.* iv. 591
Or deeming meanest what we greatest *c. E.* i. 19
Or from the canvass *c*. the mimic face *E.* iii. 6
C. round her tomb each object of desire *E.* iii. 49
I *c*. aloud ; it hears not what I say *E.A.* 237
Unfinish'd things, one knows not what to *c. E.C.* 42
Prescribe, apply, and *c*. their masters fools *E.C.* 111
'Tis not a lip, or eye, we beauty *c. E.C.* 245
With some unmeaning thing they *c*. a thought *E.C.* 355
And *c*. new beauties forth from ev'ry line *E C.* 666
Respecting Man, whatever wrong we *c. E.M.* i. 52
C. imperfection what thou fancy'st such *E.M.* i. 115
Made for his use all creatures if he *c. E.M.* i. 177
Shall he alone, whom rational we *c. E.M.* i. 187
Or quitting sense *c*. imitating God *E.M.* ii. 26
Nor this a good, nor that a bad we *c. E.M.* ii. 55
Modes of Self-love the Passions we may *c. E.M.* ii. 93
Bids each on other for assistance *c. E.M.* ii. 251
Stays till we *c*., and then not often near *E.M.* iii. 87
Those *c*. it Pleasure, and Contentment these *E.M.* iv. 22
And makes what Happiness we justly *c. E.M.* iv. 37
But fools the Good alone unhappy *c. E.M.* iv. 97
'Tis phrase absurd to *c*. a Villain Great *E.M.* iv. 230
Think, and if still the things thy envy *c. E.M.* iv. 275
If all, united, thy ambition *c. E.M.* iv. 285
I only *c*. those Knaves, who are so now *E.S.* ii. 127
C. Verres, Wolsey, any odious name *E.S.* ii. 137
What good, what better, we may *c. I.H.* ii. 151
Shall *c*. the smiling Loves, and young Desires *I.H.* iii. 26
Tho' many a passenger he rightly *c. M.E.* i. 7
'Twas all for fear the Knaves should *c*. him Fool *M.E.* i. 207
For tho' such motives Folly you may *c. M.E.* iii. 157
Shall *c*. the winds thro' long arcades to roar *M.E.* iv. 35
His Gardens next your admiration *c. M.E.* iv. 113
But hark ! the chiming Clocks to dinner *c. M.E.* iv. 151
Till Kings *c*. forth th' Ideas of your mind *M.E.* iv. 195
Then shall thy CRAGGS (and let me *c*. him mine) *M.E.* v. 63
Sometimes to *c*. a minister my friend *P.S.* 266
Who has the vanity to *c*. you friend *P.S.* 295
It was a sin to *c*. our neighbour fool *P.S.* 383
This erring mortals Levity may *c. R.L.* i. 103
And maids turn'd bottles, *c*. aloud for corks *R.L.* iv. 54
While Tories *c*. me Whig, and Whigs a Tory *S.* i. 68
For him you'll *c*. a dog, and her a bitch *S.* ii. 50
What right, what true, what fit, we justly *c. S.* iii. 19
And *c*. for pen and ink to show our Wit *S.* v. 180
C. for the Farce, the Bear, or the Black Joke *S.* v. 309
C. Tibbald Shakespear, and he'll swear the Nine *S.* vi. 337
C., if you will, bad rhyming a disease *S.* vi. 182
Yet these are Wights, who fondly *c*. their own *S.* vi. 244

Whether you *c.* them Villa, Park, or Chase *S.* vi. 255
C. himself Barrister to ev'ry wench *S.* vii. 59
And *c.* the Muses to their ancient seats *W.F.* 284

Call'd.

C. to this work by Dulness, Jove, and Fate *D.* i. 4
A Wit it was, and *c.* the phantom Moore *D.* ii. 50
Led up the Youth, and *c.* the Goddess Dame *D.* iv. 493
He from the wond'ring furrow *c.* the food *E.M.* iii. 219
And these be happy *c.*, unhappy those *E.M.* iv. 68
The doctor *c.*, declares all help too late *M.E.* i. 239
What late he *c.* a Blessing, now was Wit *M.E.* iii. 377
Why Angels *c.*, and Angel-like ador'd *R.L.* v. 12
Belinda frown'd, Thalestris *c.* her Prude *R.L.* v. 36
C. happy Dog! the Beggar at his door *S.* iv. 116
Be *c.* to Court to plan some work divine *S.* v. 374
That *c.* the list'ning Dryads to the plain *W.* 12

Calling.

I left no *c.* for this idle trade *P.S.* 129

Calls.

And *Metaphysic c.* for aid on *Sense D.* iv. 646
When Int'rest *c.* off all her sneaking train *E.* i. 31
In each low mind methinks a Spirit *c. E.A.* 305
Who *c.* the council, states the certain day *E.M.* iii. 107
This *c.* the Church to deprecate our Sin *E.S.* i. 129
C. in the Country, catches op'ning glades *M.E.* vi. 61
And *c.* her ghost *O.* i. 104
And *c.* forth Roman drops from British eyes *P.C.* 16
And more abusive, *c.* himself my friend *P.S.* 112
And *c.* forth all the wonders of her face *R.L.* i, 142
He *c.* for something bitter, something sour *S.* ii. 33
Here Wisdom *c.:* "Seek Virtue first, be bold *S.* iii. 77
That Man divine whom Wisdom *c.* her own *S.* iii. 180
Now *c.* in Princes, and now turns away *S.* v. 156
Advance and conquer! go where glory *c. S.* vi. 47
In vain on father Thames she *c.* for aid *W.F.* 197

Calm.

C. Temperance, whose blessings those partake *D.* i. 49
Immortal Rich! how *c.* he sits at ease *D.* iii. 261
Eyes the *c.* Sun-set of thy various day *E.* i. 38
Thy life a long dead *c.* of fix'd repose *E.A.* 251
But all is *c.* in this eternal sleep *E.A.* 313
As Men for ever temp'rate, *c.*, and wise *E.M.* i. 154
Nor God alone in the still *c.* we find *E.M.* ii. 109
The soul's *c.* sunshine, and the heart-felt joy *E.M.* iv. 168
CARLETON's *c.* Sense, and STANHOPE's noble Flame *E.S.* ii. 80
No Names! be *c.!* learn prudence of a friend *P.S.* 102
The Man, who, stretch'd in Isis' *c.* retreat *S.* vi. 116
The silver flood, so lately *c.*, appears *W.* 65
C. ev'ry thought, inspirit ev'ry grace *Mi.* v. 13

Calmly.

To welcome death, and *c.* pass away *E.M.* ii. 260
C. he look'd on either life, and here *Ep.* x. 7

Calvin.

One thinks on *C.* Heav'n's own spirit fell *E.M.* iv. 137
If *C.* feel Heav'n's blessing, or its rod *E.M.* iv. 139

Calypso.

'Twas thus *C.* once each heart alarm'd *M.E.* ii. 45

Cam.

May you, may *C.* and Isis, preach it long *D.* iv. 187
Isis and *C.* made DOCTORS of her LAWS *D.* iv. 578
Or else where *C.* his winding vales divides *Su.* 26

Came.

Pan *c.*, and ask'd, what magic caus'd my smart *A.* 81
Three College Sophs, and three pert Templars *c. D.* ii. 379
On two unequal crutches propt he *c. D.* iv. 111
C. whip and spur, and dash'd thro' thin and thick *D.* iv. 197
The first *c.* forwards, with as easy mien *D.* iv. 279
C., cramm'd with capon, from where Pollio dines *D.* iv. 350
Bland and familiar to the throne he *c. D.* iv. 497
Smit with the love of Sister-Arts we *c. E.* iii. 13
It *c.* from Bertrand's, not the skies *E.* iv. 51
Yet, yet I love! From Abelard it *c. E.A.* 7
And truths divine *c.* mended from that tongue *E.A.* 66

But when t' examine ev'ry part he *c. E.C.* 134
The Mind's disease, its RULING PASSION *c. E.M.* ii. 138
And he return'd a friend, who *c.* a foe *E.M.* iii. 206
'Faith, it imports not much from whom it *c. E.S.* ii. 168
As pure a mess almost as it *c.* in *E.S.* ii. 176
Lean as you *c.*, Sir, you must go *I.H.* i. 58
An awkward Thing, when first she *c.* to Town *Mi.* ix. 59
I lisp'd in numbers, for the numbers *c. P.S.* 128
On wings of winds *c.* flying all abroad *P.S.* 218
Dryden alone (what wonder?) *c.* not nigh *P.S.* 245
Before, and after, Standing Armies *c. S.*. ii. 154
He *c.* by sure transition to his own *S.* v. 81
Scarce was I enter'd, when, behold I there *c. S.* viii. 24
Stood just a-tilt, the Minister *c.* by *S.* viii. 175

Camilla.

Not so, when swift *C.* scours the plain *E.C.* 372

Campaign.

And chiefless Armies doz'd out the *C. D.* iv. 617
As when that Hero, who in each *C. Mi.* ii. 1

Can, Canst.—*Passim.*

Canal.

Or softly glide by the *C. I.H.* iii. 46
The walls, the woods, and long *c.*—s reply *R.L.* iii. 100

Cancel.

She e'er should *c.*—but she may forget *M.E.* ii. 172
A tongue that can cheat widows, *c.* scores *S.* viii. 58

Cancer.

Now *C.* glows with Phœbus' fiery car *W.F.* 147

Candid.

But *c.*, free, sincere, as you began *E.* ii. 12
Laugh where we must, be *c.* where we can *E.M.* i. 15

Candle.

Curse the sav'd *c.*, and unop'ning door *M.E.* iii. 194
The wretch, who living sav'd a *c.*'s end *M.E.* iii. 292

Candour.

In all you speak let truth and *c.* shine *E.C.* 563
Manners with *C.* are to Benson giv'n *E.S.* ii. 72
Indulge my *c.*, and grow all to all *S.* iii. 32

Cane.

And the nice conduct of a clouded *c. R.L.* iv. 124

Canker'd.

False as his Gems, and *c.* as his Coins *D.* iv. 349

Cannot.—*Passim.*

Cano.

To sound or sink in *c.*, O or A *D.* iv. 221

Canon.

See! still thy own, the heavy *c.* roll *D.* iv. 247

Canonist.

Of whose strange crimes no *C.* can tell *S.* vii 43

Canons.

And sees at *C.* what was never there *P.S.* 300

Canopy.

My foot-stool earth, my *c.* the skies *E.M.* i. 140

Cant.

And (last and worst) with all the *c.* of wit *D.* iv. 99

Canvas.

And from the *c.* call the mimic face *E.* iii. 6
Lely on animated *c.* stole *S.* v. 149

Cap.

In Folly's *C.*, than Wisdom's grave disguise *D.* iv. 240
The *C.* and Switch be sacred to his Grace *D.* iv. 585
Broad hats, and hoods, and *c.*—s, a sable shoal *D.* iv. 190
C. on their heads, and halberts in their hand *R.L.* iii. 42

Capacious.

Fill the *c.* Squire, the deep Divine *M.E.* iii. 204

Capitals.

Or plaister'd posts, with claps, in *c. P.S.* 216

CAPITOL—CARNAL.   41

Capitol.
Rome in her *C.* saw Querno sit *D.* ii. 15

Capon.
Came, cramm'd with *c.* from where Pollio dines *D.* iv. 350

Caprice.
Thus Critics, of less judgment than *c. E.C.* 285
That counter-works each folly and *c. E.M.* ii. 239

Captain.
But here's the *C.* that will plague them both *S.* viii. 260
The *C.'s* honest, Sirs, and that's enough *S.* viii. 262

Captious.
Dennis and Dissonance, and *c.* Art *D.* ii. 339

Captive.
Some banish'd lover, or some *c.* maid *E.A.* 52
Led off two *c.* trumps, and swept the board *R.L.* iii. 90
Lurk'd in her hand, and mourned his *c.* Queen *R.L.* iii. 96
The *c.* bird that sings within thy bow'r *Su.* 46
We conquer'd France, but felt our *C.'s* chains *S.* v. 263

Car.
And while on Fame's triumphal *C.* they ride *D.* iv. 133
Lo! at the wheels of her Triumphal *C. E.S.* i. 151
Dash the proud Gamester in his gilded *C. S.* i. 107
Ev'n to their own S—r—v—nce in a *C. S.* vi. 107
Now Cancer glows with Phœbus' fiery *c. W.F.* 147
Ev'n when proud Cæsar 'midst triumphal c—s *P.C.* 27

Cara.
O *C.! C.!* silence all that train *D.* iv. 53

Caracci.
C.'s strength, Correggio's softer line *E.* iii. 37

Card.
Reason the *c.,* but Passion is the gale *E.M.* ii. 108
'Twas my own Lord that drew the fatal *C. Mi.* ix. 48
Descend, and sit on each important *c. R.L.* iii. 32
Gain'd but one trump and one Plebeian *c. R.L.* iii. 54
A *Youth of Frolics,* an old age of C—s *M.E.* ii. 244
And mighty Dukes pack *C.* for half-a-crown *M.E.* ii. 142
And tho' she plays no more, n'erlocks the *c. R.L.* i. 54
By c—s' Ill Usage, or by Lovers Lost *Mi.* ix. 26

Cardelia.
The *Snuff-Box* to *C.* I decree *Mi.* ix. 111

Care.
You by whose *c.,* in vain decry'd and curst *D.* i. 5
So watchful Bruin forms, with plastic *c. D.* i. 101
First in my *c.,* and ever at my heart *D.* i. 164
To seize his papers, Curl, was next thy *c. D.* ii. 113
Receiv'd each Demi-God with pious *c. D.* iv. 383
Rose or Carnation was below my *c. D.* iv. 431
To your fraternal *c.* our sleeping friends *D.* iv. 449
Then, blessing all, "Go, children of my *c. D.* iv. 579
Thus Yoiture's early *c.* still shone the same *E.* iv. 69
As some fond Virgin, whom her mother's *c. E.* v. 1
Ah, think at least thy flock deserves thy *c. E.A.* 129
Divine oblivion of low-thoughted *c. E.A.* 298
For there's a happiness as well as *c. E.C.* 14
Others for *Languege* all their *c.* express *E.C.* 305
When love was all an easy Monarch's *c. E.C.* 536
If Man alone engross not Heav'n's high *c. E.M.* i. 119
List under Reason, and deserve her *c. E.M.* ii. 98
As fruits, ungrateful to the planter's *c. E.M.* ii. 181
The poor contents him with the *c.* of Heav'n *E.M.* ii. 266
Know, Nature's children all divide her *c. E.M.* iii. 43
There stops the Instinct, and there ends the *c. E.M.* iii. 128
A longer *c.* Man's helpless kind demands (rep.) *E.M.* iii. 131
Heav'n's attribute was Universal *c. E.M.* iii. 159
The good must merit God's peculiar *c. E.M.* iv. 135
Vice, thus abus'd, demands a Nation's *c. E.S.* i. 128
Is there on Earth one *c.,* one wish beside *Ep.* xiii. 7
As the good shepherd tends his fleecy *c. M.* 49
Thus shall mankind his guardian *c.* engage *M.* 55
Ascendant Phœbus watch'd that hour with *c. M.E.* ii. 285
Admits and leaves them, Providence's *c. M.E.* iii. 106
And ease, or emulate, the *c.* of Heav'n *M.E.* iii. 230
You too proceed! make falling Arts your *c. M.E.* iv. 191

A Lover lost, is but a common *c. Mi.* ix. 17
Happy the man whose wish and *c. O.* iv. 1
To second, Arbuthnot! thy Art and *C. P.S.* 133
Fairest of mortals, thou distinguish'd *c. R.L.* i. 27
The busy Sylphs surround their darling *c. R.L.* i. 145
Of these the chief the *c.* of Nations own *R.L.* ii. 89
Not a less pleasing, tho' less glorious *c. R.L.* ii. 92
That e'er deserv'd a watchful spirit's *c. R.L.* ii. 103
The flutt'ring fan be Zephyretta's *c. R.L.* ii. 112
The skilful Nymph reviews her force with *c. R.L.* iii. 45
Was it for this you took such constant *c. R.L.* iv. 97
Laws are explain'd by Men—so have a *c. S.* i. 144
Or blest with little, whose preventing *c. S.* ii. 127
Let this be all my *c.*—for this is All *S.* iii. 20
To worship like his Fathers was his *c. S.* v. 165
Ease of their toil, and partners of their *c. S.* v. 246
Late, very late, correctness grew our *c. S.* v. 272
Assign'd his figure to Bernini's *c. S.* v. 381
Sure I should want the *c.* of ten Monroes *S.* vi. 70
That wants or force, or light, or weight, or *c. S.* vi. 160
"My friends!" he cry'd, "p—x take you for your *c. S.* vi. 195
Who, if they have not, think not worth their *c. S.* vi. 267
Divided between carelessness and *c. S.* vi. 291
Pour'd o'er the whitening vale their fleecy *c. Sp.* 19
Let other swains attend the rural *c. Su.* 35
Whose *c.,* like hers, protects the sylvan reign *W.F.* 163
She scorn'd the praise of beauty, and the *c. W.F.* 177
Gigantic Pride, pale Terror, gloomy *c. W.F.* 415
What is this Wit, which must our c—s employ E.C. 500
Those *c.* that haunt the Court and Town *I.H.* ii. 132
'Tis strange the Miser should his *C.* employ *M.E.* iv. 1
She all the *c.* of Love and Play does know *Mi.* ix. 22
To Basset's heav'nly Joys, and pleasing *C. Mi.* ix. 102
Or when the soul is press'd with *c. O.* i. 26
On *c.* like these if length of days attend *P.S.* 414
But anxious *c.* the pensive nymph oppress'd *R.L.* iv. 1
Who would not scorn what housewife's *c.* produce *R.L.* v. 21
You give the things you never *c.* for *I.H.* i. 34
C. if a liv'ry'd Lord or smile or frown *S.* viii. 197

Car'd.
Lies one who ne'er *c.,* and still cares not a pin *Ep.* xvi. 5

Careful.
Then *c.* Heav'n supply'd two sorts of Men *M.E.* iii. 13
All but the Sylph—with *c.* thoughts opprest *R.L.* ii. 53
Some o'er her lap their *c.* plumes display'd *R.L.* iii. 115

Careless.
Who, *c.* now of Int'rest, Fame or Fate *E.* i. 17
Thus wisely *c.,* innocently gay *E.* iv. 11
C. of censure, nor too fond of fame *E.C.* 741
Whatever spirit, *c.* of his charge *R.L.* ii. 123
C. how ill I with myself agree *S.* iii. 175
Ev'n I more sweetly pass my *c.* days *W.F.* 431

Careless Husband.
And yet deny the *C.* praise *S.* v. 92

Carelessness.
Divided between *c.* and care *S.* vi. 291

Cares.
Lies one who ne'er car'd, and still *c.* not a pin *Ep.* xvi. 5
Man *c.* for all: to birds he gives his woods *E.M.* iii. 151
C. not for service, or but serves when prest *E.M.* iii. 86
But *c.* not if a thousand are undone *M.E.* ii. 176

Caress'd.
Treated, *c.,* and tir'd, I take my leave *M.E.* iv. 165

Carew.
Sprat, *C.,* Sedley, and a hundred more *S.* v. 109

Cargo.
K—l's lewd *C.,* or Ty—y's Crew *S.* iv. 121

Carleton.
C.'s calm Sense, and Stanhope's noble Flame *E.S.* ii. 80

Carmel.
And *C.'s* flow'ry top perfumes the skies *M.* 28

Carnal.
A very Heathen in the *c.* part *M.E.* ii. 67

Carnation.
Dismiss my soul, where no *C.* fades *D.* iv. 418
Rose, or *C.*, was below my care *D.* iv. 431

Carolina.
Let *C.* smooth the tuneful lay *S.* i. 30
Hang the sad Verse on *C.'s* Urn *E.S.* i. 80

Caroline.
Then thron'd in glass, and nam'd it *C. D.* iv. 409
Now prostrate ! dead ! behold that *C. D.* iv. 413

Carouse.
From tail to mouth, they feed and they *c. E.S.* ii. 179

Carp.
The yellow *c.*, in scales bedropp'd with gold *W.F.* 144
Of *c—s and mullets why prefer the great S.* ii. 21

Carpet.
The Napkins white, the *C.* red *I.H.* ii. 195
One boundless Green, or flourish'd *C.* views *M.E.* iv. 95

Carry.
Secure, thro' her, the noble prize to *c. D.* ii. 219
To fetch and *c.* nonsense for my Lord *E.C.* 417
Can pocket States, can fetch or *c.* Kings *M.E.* iii. 42
To fetch and *c.* sing-song up and down *P.S.* 226
Where winds can *c.*, or where waves can roll *S.* iv. 70

Carry'd.
And *c.* off in some dog's tail at last *D.* iii. 292
To White's be *c.*, as to ancient games *M.E.* iii. 69

Carrying.
And *c.* with you all the world can boast *Sp.* 9

Carted.
Coach'd, *c.*, trod upon, now loose, now fast *D.* iii. 291
And see pale Virtue *c.* in her stead *E.S.* i. 150

Carthusian.
C. fasts, and fulsome Bacchanals *S.* vii. 118

Carv'd.
Oft on the rind I *c.* her am'rous vows *A.* 67
Thus, as the pipes of some *c.* Organ move *S.* vii. 17

Caryl.
I sing—this verse to *C.*, Muse ! is due *R.L.* i. 3

Case.
With that she gave him (piteous of his *c. D.* ii. 141
You'd quickly find him in Lord Fanny's *c. E.S.* i. 50
The Dog-days are no more the *c. I.H.* i. 15
This, humbly offers me his *C. I.H.* ii. 67 s
And is not mine, my friend, a sorer *c. P.S.* 73
A two-edg'd weapon from her shining *c. R.L.* iii. 128
He first the snuff-box open'd, then the *c. R.L.* iv. 126
The *C.* is alter'd—you may then proceed *S.* i. 154
Or in pure equity (the *c.* not clear) *S.* ii. 171
You think this Madness but a common *c. S.* iii. 172
In either *c.*, believe me, we admire *S.* iv. 21
The *c.* is easier in the Mind's disease *S.* iv. 58
Faith, in such *c.*, if you should prosecute *S.* vi. 23
All vast possessions (just the same the *c. S.* vi. 254

Cash.
Who sent the Thief that stole the *C.* away *S.* vi. 25

Cashiers.
Flight of *C.*, or Mobs, he'll never mind *S.* v. 195

Casket.
This *c.* India's glowing gems unlocks *R.L.* i. 133

Cassius.
And sterner *C.* melts at Junia's eyes *O.* iii. 16

Cassock.
Gave him the *c.*, surcingle, and vest *D.* ii. 350

Cast.
What can I now ? my Fletcher *c.* aside *D.* i. 199
Old scenes of glory, times long *c.* behind *D.* ii. 63
Far eastward *c.* thine eye, from whence the sun *D.* iii. 73
C. on the prostrate Nine a scornful look *D.* iv. 51
Sire, Ancestors, Himself. Once *c.* his eyes *D.* iv. 519
So, *c.* and mingled with his very frame *E.M.* ii. 137

Or round a Quaker's Beaver *c.* a Glory *E.S.* ii. 97
And all Opinion's colours *c.* on life *M.E.* i. 22
On the *c.* ore, another Pollio shine *M.E.* v. 64
Not louder shouts to pitying Heav'n are *c. R.L.* iii. 157
A mournful glance Sir Fopling upwards *c. R.L.* v. 63
But having *c.* his cowl, and left those laws *S.* vii. 107
Ready to *c.*, I yawn, I sigh, and sweat *S.* viii. 157
Let me not *c.* away *U.P.* 18
Lodona's fate, in long oblivion *c. W.F.* 173

Castalia.
And never washed, but in *C.'s* streams *D.* iii. 18

Castalian.
To Bufo left the whole *C.* state *P.S.* 230

Casting-weight.
That *C.* pride adds to emptiness *P.S.* 177

Castle.
The air-built *C.*, and the golden Dream *D.* iii. 10
Let him take *C—s who has ne'er a great S.* vi. 51
He leap'd the trenches, scal'd a *C.*-wall *S.* vi. 40

Casts.
Turn'd to the Sun, she *c.* a thousand dyes *D.* iv. 539
Than such as Anstis *c.* into the Grave *E.S.* ii. 237

Casuistry.
Chicane in Furs, and *C.* in Lawn *D.* iv. 28
Mountains of *C.* heap'd o'er her head *D.* iv. 642
Dry'd butterflies, and tomes of *c. R.L.* v. 122

Casuists.
And soundest *c.* doubt, like you and me *M.E.* ii. 2

Cat.
The *C.* comes bouncing on the floor *I.H.* ii. 213
Die, and endow a College or a *C. M.E.* iii. 96
Let me extol a *C.*, on oysters fed *S.* ii. 41
Sound, sound, ye Viols, be the *C.*-call dumb *D.* i. 302
"Hold" (cry'd the Queen) "a *C.* each shall win *D.* ii. 243
Improve we these. Three C—s be the bribe D. ii. 231

Catch.
Suck my last breath, and *c.* my flying soul *E.A.* 324
But *c.* the spreading notion of the Town *E.C.* 409
And *c.* the Manners living as they rise *E.M.* i. 14
By turns we *c.* the vital breath, and die *E.M.* iii. 18
Spread the thin oar, and *c.* the driving gale *E.M.* iii. 178
C. ere she change, the Cynthia of this minute *M.E.* ii. 20
Sure, if they *c.*, to spoil the Toy at most *M.E.* ii. 233
Proud to *c.* cold at a Venetian door *M.E.* iv. 36
Happy to *c.* me just at Dinner-time *P.S.* 14
If once he *c.* you at your *Jesu ! Jesu ! S.* viii. 257

Catch'd.
Then *c.* the Schools ; the Hall scarce kept awake *D.* iv. 609
My good old Lady *c.* a cold, and died *M.E.* iii. 384
C. like the Plague, or Love, the Lord knows how *S.* vii. 9

Catches.
Calls in the Country, *c.* op'ning glades *M.E.* iv. 61

Catechised.
And *c.* in ev'ry street *I.H.* ii. 112

Cates.
Her ev'ning *c.* before his neighbour's shop *D.* ii. 72

Catiline.
Why then a Borgia, or a *C. E.M.* i. 156
The fiery soul abhorr'd in *C. E.M.* ii. 199
When *C.* by rapine swell'd his store *M.E.* i. 212

Catius.
C. is ever moral, ever grave *M.E.* i. 77

Cato.
Pluto with *C.* thou for this shalt join *D.* iii. 309
Tells us that *C.* dearly lov'd his wife *E.J.S.* 32
There many an honest man may copy *C. E.J.S.* 43
To *C.*, Virgil pay'd one honest line *E.S.* ii. 120
Old *C.* is as great a Rogue as you *M.E.* iii. 38
What Plato thought, and godlike *C.* was *P.C.* 18
While *C.* gives his little Senate laws *P.C.* 23
With honest scorn the first fam'd *C.* view'd *P.C.* 39
Like *C.*, give his little Senate laws *P.S.* 209

CAUGHT—CELESTIAL.

Stern C.'s self was no relentless spouse *E.J.S.* 30
Show'd Rome her C. figure drawn in state *P.C.* 30
And honour'd Cæsar less than C. sword *P.C.* 36
As C. self had not disdain'd to hear *P.C.* 46
C. long wig, flower'd gown, and lacquer'd chair *S.* v. 337

Caught—*see also* Catch'd.
Breval, Bond, Besaleel, the varlets *c. D.* ii. 126
Once (and but once) I c. him in a lie *S.* vi. 17

Cause.
Dulness! whose good old *c*, I yet defend *D.* i. 165
To serve his c., O Queen! is serving thine *D.* i. 214
All who true Dunces in her c. appear'd *D.* ii. 95
What aids, what armies to assert her *c. D.* iii. 128
To aid our c., if Heav'n thou canst not bend *D.* iii. 307
But who, weak rebels, more advance her *c. D.* iv. 86
No C., no Trust, no Duty, and no Friend *D.* iv. 340
And last, to Nature's C. thro' Nature led *D.* iv. 468
Thrust some Mechanic C. into his place *D. M.E.* iv. 475
Make God Man's Image, Man the final *C. D.* iv. 478
Shrinks to her second c., and is no more *D.* iv. 644
That *c.* of all my guilt, and all my joy *E.A.* 338
Ask them the *c.*; they're wiser still, they say *E.C.* 436
Who durst assert the juster ancient *c. E.C.* 721
Of ORDER, sins against th' Eternal *C. E.M.* i. 130
"No" ('tis reply'd) "the first Almighty *C. E.M.* i. 145
Here then we rest: "The Universal *C. E.M.* iii. 1
T' invest the world, and counter-work its *C. E.M.* iii. 244
The same Self-love, in all, becomes the *C. E.M.* iii. 271
Remember, Man, "the Universal *C. E.M.* iv. 35
Think we, like some weak Prince, th' Eternal *C. E.M.* iv. 121
And for that very *c.* I print to-day *E.S.* ii. 3
When black Ambition stains a public *C. E.S.* ii. 228
And for that *C.* which made your Fathers shine *E.S.* iii. 232
Without your help the *C.* is gone *I.H.* ii. 72
Is thus, perhaps, the *c.* of most we do *M.E.* i. 50
Why Shylock wants a meal, the *c.* is found *M.E.* iii. 115
His oxen perish in his country's *c. M.E.* iii. 206
In vain at Court the Bankrupt pleads his *c. M.E.* iii. 217
Is this the *c.* of your Romantic strains *Mi.* ix. 9
Explain'd the matter, and would win the *c. Mi.* xi. 6
The *c.* of strife remov'd so rarely well *Mi.* xi. 11
But when our Country's *c.* provokes to Arms *O.* i. 36
Here tears shall flow from a more gen'rous *c. P.C.* 13
What bosom beats not in his Country's *c. P.C.* 24
Imputes to me, and my damn'd works the *c. P.S.* 24
Of gentle blood (part shed in Honour's *c. P.S.* 388
O say what stranger *c.*, yet unexplor'd *R.L.* i. 9
Can there be wanting to defend Her *c. S.* i. 109
I will, or perish in the gen'rous *c. S.* i. 117
This is my plea, on this I rest my *c. S.* i. 141
In such a *c.* the Plaintiff will be hiss'd *S.* i. 155
Nor fond of bleeding ev'n in BRUNSWICK's *c. S.* iii. 10
Free as young Lyttleton, her *C.* pursue *S.* iii. 29
Effects unhappy from a Noble *C. S.* v. 160
Let Ireland tell, how Wit upheld her *c. S.* v. 221
Before the Lords, at twelve, my *C.* comes on *S.* vi. 96
Takes God to witness he affects your *c. S.* vii. 76
Thou Great First *C.*, least understood *U.P.* 5
Where nameless Somethings in their *c—s sleep D.* i. 56
Of all the *c.* which conspire to blind *E.C.* 201
What dire offence from am'rous *c.* springs *R.L.* i. .
Curs'd be the fields that *c.* my Delia's stay *A.* 32
Say, what can *c.* such impotence of mind *M.E.* ii. 93
Who *c.* the proud their visits to delay *R.L.* iv. 63

Caus'd.
Pan came, and ask'd, what magic *c.* my smart *A.* 81
Emblem of Music *c.* by Emptiness *D.* i. 36
Not that their Pleasures *c.* her Discontent *E.* v. 9
And hate for arts that *c.* himself to rise *P.S.* 200
That ev'n in slumber *c.* her cheek to glow *R.L.* i. 24
Or *c.* suspicion when no soul was rude *R.L.* iv. 73
Roar'd for the handkerchief that *c.* his pain *R.L.* v. 106

Causeway.
Whose *c.* parts the vale with shady rows *M.E.* iii. 259

Caution.
Which nor to Guilt or Fear, its *C.* owes *E.* ii. 3
Distrustful sense with modest *c.* speaks *E.C.* 626

Cautious.
A pleasing Form; a firm, yet *c.* mind *Ep.* ii. 1

Cave.
The *C.* of Poverty and Poetry *D.* i. 34
Shines a broad Mirror thro' the shadowy *C. Mi.* x. 2
Repair'd to search the gloomy *C.* of Spleen *R.L.* iv. 16
I cannot like, dread Sir, your Royal *C. S.* iii. 114
When Merlin's *C.* is half unfurnish'd yet *S.* v. 355
Lord! how we strut thro' Merlin's *C.*, to see *S.* vi. 139
The Nymphs, forsaking ev'ry *c.* and spring *Su.* 57
Thro' rocks and *c—s the name of Delia sounds* (*rep.*) *A.* 49
But o'er the twilight groves and dusky *c. E.A.* 163
In hollow *c.* sweet Echo silent lies *W.* 41
Cities laid waste, they storm'd the dens and *c. W.F.* 49

Cavern.
See skulking Truth to her old *c.* fled *D.* iv. 641
Ye grots and *c—s shagg'd with horrid thorn E.A.* 20

Cavern'd.
No *c.* Hermit rests self-satisfy'd *E.M.* iv. 42

Cavil.
To *c.*, censure, dictate, right or wrong *D.* ii. 377
C. you may, but never criticize *E.C.* 123

Caxton.
There C. slept, with Wynkyn at his side *D.* i. 149

Cease.
Ye birds that, left by summer, *c.* to sing *A.* 28
The birds shall *c.* to tune their ev'ning song *A.* 40
And streams to murmur, e'er (*ere*) I *c.* to love *A.* 42
She comes, my Delia comes! Now *c.* my lay (*rep.*) *A.* 53
Their heads, and lift them as they *c.* to blow *D.* ii. 392
C. then, nor ORDER Imperfection name *E.M.* i. 281
And when in act they *c.*, in prospect rise *E.M.* ii. 124
Shall gravitation *c.*, if you go by *E.M.* iv. 128
All crimes shall *c.*, and ancient fraud shall fail *M.* 17
And nobly wishing Party-rage to *c. M.E.* iii. 149
C. your Contention, which has been too long *Mi.* ix. 107
C. fond Nature, *c.* thy strife *O.* v. 5
And the long labours of the Toilet *c. R.L.* iii. 24
O *c.*, rash youth! desist ere 'tis too late *R.L.* iii. 121
Then *c.*, bright Nymph! to mourn thy ravish'd hair *R.L.* v. 141
To sing, or *c.* to sing, we never know *S.* v. 361
When golden Angels *c.* to cure the Evil *S.* vi. 218
C. to contend, for Daphnis, I decree *Sp.* 93
At length great Anna said, "Let Discord *c.*" *W.F.* 327
Till Conquest *c.*, and Slav'ry be no more *W.F.* 408
Here *c.* thy flight, nor with unhallow'd lays *W.F.* 423

Ceas'd.
She *c.* Then swells the Chapel-royal throat *D.* i. 319
He *c.*, and spread the robe; the crowd confess *D.* ii. 353
And *c.* so soon, he ne'er was Boy, nor Man *D.* iv. 288
He *c.* and wept. With innocence of mien *D.* iv. 419
The triumph *c.*, tears gush'd from ev'ry eye *P.C.* 33

Ceasing.
Lament the *c.* of a sweeter breath *W.* 50

Cecilia.
Or drest in smiles of sweet *c.* shine *M.E.* ii. 13
This the divine *C.* found *O.* i. 124
To bright *C.* greater pow'r is given *O.* i. 132

Cecrops.
Now see an Attys, now a *C.* clear *D.* iv. 363
One grasps a *C.* in ecstatic dreams *M.E.* v. 40

Cedars.
With heads declin'd, ye *c.* homage pay *M.* 35

Ceilings.
On painted *C.* you devoutly stare *M.E.* iv. 145

Celestial.
Take at this hand *c.* arms *E.* vi. 4
Shone sweetly lambent with *c.* day *E.A.* 64
C. palms, and ever-blooming flow'rs *E.A.* 318
Oh may some spark of your *c.* fire *E.C.* 195
Plant of *c.* seed! if dropt below *E.M.* iv. 7
C. Venus haunts Idalian groves *Sp.* 65
And with *c.* tears augments the waves *W.F.* 210
'Tis but their Sylph, the wise *C—s know R.L.* i. 77

Cell.

One *C.* there is conceal'd from vulgar eye *D.* i. 33
She waits, or to the scaffold, or the *c. E.* i. 33
See in her *c.* sad Eloisa spread *E.A.* 303
Shrink back to my paternal *C. I.H.* i. 76
Depriv'd us soon of our paternal *C. S.* vi. 59
In these deep solitudes, and awful c—s E.A. 1
Their sep'rate *c.* and properties maintain *E.M.* iii. 188
A low-born, c.-bred, selfish, servile band D. ii. 356

Celsus.

But talk with *C., C.* will advise *S.* i. 19

Cement.

With the same *C.* ever sure to bind *D.* iv. 267

Cements.

The dross *c.* what else were too refin'd *E.M.* ii. 179

Censer.

When from the *c.* clouds of fragrance roll *E.A.* 271

Censure.

'Tis best sometimes your *c.* to restrain *E.C.* 596
Careless of *c.*, nor too fond of praise *E.C.* 741
To 'scape my *C.*, not expect my Praise *E.S.* ii. 113
But spare your *c.*, Silia does not drink *M.E.* ii. 34
To cavil, c., dictate, right or wrong D. ii. 377
Ten *c.* wrong for one who writes amiss *E.C.* 6
And *c.* freely who have written well *E.C.* 16
Might boldly *c.*, as he boldly writ *E.C.* 658
Suppose I *c.*—you know what I mean *E.S.* ii. 32

Censur'd.

When works are *c.*, not as bad, but new *S.* v. 116

Cent.

In one abundant shower of *C. per C. M.E.* iii. 372
With rhymes of this *per C.* and that *per year S.* vii. 56

Centlivre.

At last *C.* felt her voice to fail *D.* ii. 411

Central.

Down to the *c.* earth, his proper scene *R.L.* iv. 15

Centre.

None want a place, for all their *C.* found *D.* iv. 77
Heav'n's whole foundations to their *c.* nod *E.M.* i. 255
Press to one *c.* still, the gen'ral Good *E.M.* iii. 14
Draw to one point, and to one *c.* bring *E.M.* iii. 301
The *c.* mov'd, a circle straight succeeds *E.M.* iv. 365
Thron'd in the *c.* of his thin designs *P.S.* 93
Shall in thee c., from thee circulate D. iii. 60

Century.

Who lasts a *c.* can have no flaw *S.* v. 55

Ceres.

And laughing *C.* re-assume the land *M.E.* iv. 176
Diana Cynthus, *C.* Hybla loves *Sp.* 66
And crown'd with corn their thanks to *C.* yield *Su.* 66
Here C.' gifts in waving prospect stand W.F. 39

Certain.

Of naught so *c.* as our *Reason* still *D.* iv. 481
A *c.* bard encount'ring on the way *E.C.* 268
If to be perfect in a *c.* sphere *E.M.* i. 73
This drives them constant to a *c.* coast *E.M.* ii. 168
Lust, thro' some *c.* strainers well refin'd *E.M.* ii. 189
Who calls the council, states the *c.* day *E.M.* iii. 107
Ingratitude's the *c.* crop *I.H.* i. 32
You may for *c.*, if you please *I.H.* ii. 80 s
One *c.* Portrait may (I grant) be seen *M.E.* ii. 181
A *c.* truth, which many buy too dear *M.E.* iv. 40
In them, as *c.* to be lov'd as seen *S.* i. 53
And *c.* Laws. by suff'rers thought unjust *S.* vi. 60
At ten for *c.*, Sir, in Bloomsb'ry Square *S.* vi. 95

Cervantes.

Whether thou choose *C.'* serious air *D.* i. 21

Chafe.

How did they fume, and stamp, and roar, and *c. P.S.* 191

Chagrin.

Hear me, and touch Belinda with *c. R.L.* iv. 77

Chain.

Bind rebel Wit, and double *c.* on *c. D.* iv. 158
Our hearts may bear its slender *c.* a day *E.* iv. 64
Death, only death, can break the lasting *c. E.A.* 173
Is the great *c.* that draws all to agree *E.M.* i. 33
Vast *c.* of Being I which from God began *E.M.* i. 237
From Nature's *c.* whatever link you strike (*rep.*) *E.M.* i. 245
Look round our World ; behold the *c.* of Love *E.M.* iii. 7
The *c.* holds on, and where it ends, unknown *E.M.* iii. 26
Pursues that *C.* which links th' immense design *E.M.* iv. 333
There Faction roar, Rebellion bite her *c. W.F.* 421
Or thy griev'd Country's copper c—s unbind D. i. 24
Glade, warm furs, broad banners, and broad faces *D.* i. 88
Beneath her footstool, *Science* groans in *C. D.* iv. 21
Too mad for mere material *c.* to bind *D.* iv. 32
Joys in my jigs, and dances in my *c. D.* iv. 62
Or bound in formal, or in real *c. E.* iv. 42
Or failing, smiles in exile or in *c. E.M.* iv. 234
In golden *C.* the willing World she draws *E.S.* i. 147
In adamantine *c.* shall Death be bound *M.* 47
Arm'd in adamantine *C. Mi.* vii. 28
And mighty hearts are held in slender *c. R.L.* ii. 24
Cages to gnats, and *c.* to yoke a flea *R.L.* v. 121

Chain'd.

And which more blest ? Who *c.* his country, say *E.M.* iv. 147
Draw monarchs *c.*, and Cressi's glorious field *W.F.* 305

Chair.

Or laugh and shake in Rab'lais' easy *c. D.* i. 22
Six huntsmen with a shout precede his *c. D.* ii. 193
To stick the Doctor's *C.* into the Throne *D.* iv. 177
Stretch'd on the rack of a too easy *c. D.* iv. 342
I saw him stand behind OMBRELIA's *c. Mi.* ix. 6
And view with scorn two Pages and a *C. R.L.* i. 46
Cry'd Dapperwit, and sunk beside his *c. R.L.* v. 62
This may be troublesome, is near the *C. S.* iv. 105
Cato's long wig, flower'd gown, and lacquer'd *c. S.* v. 337
And the wise *Justice*, starting from his *c. S.* viii. 36
Streets, C—s, and Coxcombs, rush upon my sight E. v. 48

Chair'd.

Or *c.* at White's, amidst the Doctors sit *D.* i. 203

Chaise.

They know not whither, in a *c.* and one *S.* iii. 158

Chalcis.

Which *C.* Gods, and mortals call an Owl *D.* iv. 362

Chalky.

And *c.* Wey, that rolls a milky wave *W.F.* 344

Chambermaid.

Trudges to town, and first turns *C. Mi.* iii. 16

Chameleons.

C. who can paint in black and white *M.E.* ii. 156

Champion.

Fierce *c.* Fortitude, that knows no fears *D.* i. 47
The *C.* too ! and, to complete the jest *S.* v. 318

Chance.

If ever *c.* two wand'ring lovers brings *E.A.* 347
True ease in writing comes from art, not *c. E.C.* 362
By *c.* go right, they purposely go wrong *E.C.* 427
All *C.*, Direction, which thou canst not see *E.M.* i. 290
Some gen'ral maxims, or be right by *c. M.E.* i. 4
My Lady falls to play, so bad her *c. M.E.* iii. 395
Start ev'n from Difficulty, strike from *C. M.E.* iv. 68
Sad *c.* of war ! now destitute of aid *R.L.* iii. 63
And wins (oh shameful *c.* I) the Queen of Hearts *R.L.* iii. 88
But ease in writing flows from Art, not *c. S.* vi. 178
How random thoughts now meaning c. to find D. i. 275
For ills or accidents that *c.* to all *E.M.* iv. 98
Should *c.* to make the well-drest Rabble stare *S.* iii. 111
A hackney coach may *c.* to spoil a thought *S.* vi. 101

Chanc'd.

Which Curl's Corinna *c.* that morn to make *D.* ii. 70
That what we *c.*, was what we meant to do *M.E.* i. 102
Or *c.* to meet a Minister that frown'd *M.E.* i. 165
It *c.*, as eager of the chase, the maid *W.F.* 181

Chanc'llor.
A Judge is just, a C. juster still *M.E.* i. 137

Chanc'ry.
The C. takes your rents for twenty year *S.* ii. 172
Nor once to C., nor to Hale apply *S.* iii. 173
Long C.—lane *retentive* rolls the sound *D.* ii. 263

Chandos.
Thus gracious C. is belov'd at sight *M.E.* i. 54

Change.
Well might you wish for *c.* by those accurst *E.* iv. 39
While, at each *c.*, the son of Libyan Jove *E.C.* 376
Th' exceptions few ; some *c.* since all began *E.M.* i. 147
Or C. admits, or Nature lets it fall *E.M.* iv. 115
All eyes may see from what the *c.* arose *M.E.* ii. 35
Builds Life on Death, on C. Duration founds *M.E.* iii. 167
Constant at Church and C.; his gains were sure *M.E.* iii. 347
And prudent Nymphs against that *c.* prepare *Mi.* ix. 18
But let all Satire in all C—s spare *E.S.* i. 91
'Twixt sense and nonsense daily *c. their side E.C.* 435
Not one will *c.* his neighbour with himself *E.M.* ii. 262
Good Mr. Dean, go *c.* your gown *I.H.* ii. 43 s
Find if you can, in what you cannot *c. M.E.* i. 171
Catch, ere she *c.*, the Cynthia of this minute *M.E.* ii. 20
Things *c.* their titles, as our manners turn *M.E.* iii. 379
Colours that *c.* whene'er they wave their wings *R.L.* ii. 68
To *c.* a Flounce, or add a Furbelow *R.L.* ii. 100
Or *c.* complexions at a losing game *R.L.* iv. 70
Who thinks that Fortune cannot *c.* his mind *S.* ii. 123
They *c.* their weekly Barber, weekly News *S.* iii. 155
You never *c.* one muscle of your face *S.* iii. 171
By sale, at least by death, to *c.* their lord *S.* vi. 251
Let nature *c.*, let heav'n and earth deplore *W.* 27
Might *c.* Olympus for a nobler hill *W.F.* 234

Chang'd.
And Montausier was only *c.* in name *E.* iv. 70
Alas, how *c. !* what sudden horrors rise *E.A.* 99
That, *c.* thro' all, and yet in all the same *E.M.* i. 269
Who never *c.* his Principle, or Wig *E.S.* i. 40
C. it to August, and (in short) *I.H.* i. 3
Alas ! in truth the man but *c.* his mind *M.E.* i. 127
Great Villiers lies—alas ! how *c.* from him *M.E.* iii. 305
How *c.* from him who made the boxes groan *Mi.* 15
C. to a bird, and sent to flit in air *R.L.* iii. 123
Of bodies *c.* to various forms by Spleen *R.L.* iv. 48
Now times are *c.*, and one Poetic Itch *S.* v. 169
'Tis *c.*, no doubt, from what it was before *S.* vii. 31

Changeful.
Gods partial, *c.*, passionate, unjust *E.M.* iii. 257
But Britain, *c.* as a Child at play *S.* v. 155

Changes.
So Time, that *c.* all things, had ordain'd *S.* viii. 43

Channel.
Nor cross the C. twice a year *I.H.* ii. 31 s

Chant.
The Thrush may *c.* to the forsaken groves *Sp.* 14
Your praise the birds shall *c.* in ev'ry grove *Su.* 79

Chaos.
Daughter of C. and eternal Night *D.* i. 12
Here she beholds the C. dark and deep *D.* i. 55
Indulge, dread C. *!* and eternal Night *D.* iv. 2
Then rose the seed of C. and of Night *D.* iv. 13
Joy to great C. *!* let Division reign *D.* iv. 54
Of Night primæval, and of C. old *D.* iv. 630
Lo ! thy dread Empire, C. *!* is restor'd *D.* iv. 653
One glaring C. and wild heap of wit *E.C.* 292
C. of Thought and Passion, all confus'd *E.M.* ii. 13
This light and darkness in our *c.* join'd *E.M.* ii. 203
Sooner let earth, air, sea, to C. fall *R.L.* iv. 119
Not C.-like *together crush'd and bruis'd W.F.* 13

Chapel.
And now the *c.*'s silver bell you bear *M.E.* iv. 141
Churches and C—s instantly it reach'd *D.* iv. 607
She ceas'd. Then *swells* the C.-royal throat *D.* i. 319

Chaplain.
Who praises now? his C. on his Tomb *D.* iv. 514
Scolds with her maid, or with her *c.* crams *E.J.S.* 22
Rush C., Butler, Dogs and all *I.H.* ii. 211
So first to preach a white-glov'd C. goes *S.* viii. 250
When servile C—s cry that birth and place *S.* vi. 220

Chaplets.
In cold December fragrant *c.* blow *D.* i. 77
With thy flow'ry C. crown'd *Mi.* vii. 28

Character.
Know well each ANCIENT's proper *c. E.C.* 119
The few that glare, each C. must mark *M.E.* i. 121
Must then at once (the *c.* to save) *M.E.* i. 125
Most women have no C. at all *M.E.* i. 2
Till show'rs of Sermons, C—s, Essays *D.* ii. 361
Come, harmless C., that no one hit *E.S.* i. 65
But these plain C. we rarely find *M.E.* i. 63
'Tis from high Life high C. are drawn *M.E.* i. 135
Who fairly puts all C. to bed *S.* v. 291

Charcoal.
With desp'rate *c.* round his darken'd walls *P.S.* 20

Charge.
Thus beast and bird their common *c.* attend *E.M.* iii. 125
The Medal, faithful to its *c.* of fame *M.E.* v. 31
By land, by water, they renew the *c. P.S.* 9
Haste, then, ye spirits ! to your *c.* repair *R.L.* ii. 111
We trust th' important *c.*, the Petticoat *R.L.* ii. 118
Whatever spirit, careless of his *c. R.L.* ii. 123
A *c.* of Snuff the wily virgin threw *R.L.* v. 82
But thou false guardian of a *c.* too good *U.L.* 29
Begin ; this *c.* the dying Daphne gave *W.* 17
Why *c. we Heav'n in those, in these acquit E.M.* i. 163
Let *Budget c.* low *Grubstreet* on his quill *P.S.* 378
C. them with Heav'n's Artill'ry, bold Divine *S.* viii. 281

Charing-cross.
Might be proclaim'd at C. *I.H.* ii. 100 s
For Quoits, both Temple-bar and C. *S.* viii. 277

Chariot.
They stop the *c.*, and they board the barge *P.S.* 10
Whose C.'s that we left behind *I.H.* ii. 90 s
Where the gilt C. never marks the way *R.L.* iv. 155
On horse, on foot, in hacks, and gilded *c*—s' *D.* ii. 24
Her joy in gilded C., when alive *R.L.* i. 55
For not in C. *Peter* puts his trust *S.* vii. 74

Charitable.
His *c.* Vanity supplies *M.E.* iv. 172

Charitably.
And *c.* let the dull be vain *E.C.* 597
And *c.* comfort Knave and Fool *E.S.* i. 62

Charity.
O pious fraud of am'rous *c. E.A.* 150
Zeal then, not *c.*, became the guide *E.M.* iii. 261
But all Mankind's concern is C. *E.M.* iii. 308
And height of Bliss, but height of C. *E.M.* iv. 360
Then better sure it C. becomes *E.S.* ii. 48
Who suffer thus, mere C. should own *M.E.* iii. 111
With Splendour, C.; with Plenty, Health *M.E.* iii. 225
What Mines to swell that boundless *c. M.E.* iii. 278
The Boys and Girls whom *c.* maintains *S.* v. 231
In downright *c.* revive the dead *S.* v. 164
I die in *c.* with fool and knave *S.* viii. 3
Who makes a Trust or C. a Job *S.* viii. 142
That *graft benevolence* on *c*—ies *M.E.* iii. 138

Charlemagne.
Cæsar and Tall-boy, Charles and C. *M.E.* ii. 78

Charles.
C. to the Convent, Philip to the Field *M.E.* i. 108
Cæsar and Tall-boy, C. and Charlemagne *M.E.* ii. 78
Yet neither C. nor James be in a rage *S.* i. 114
Was sheath'd, and *Luxury* with C. restor'd *S.* v. 140
C., to late times to be transmitted fair *S.* v. 380
The Hero William, and the Martyr C. *S.* v. 386
But for the Wits of either C—s days *S.* v. 107
Unhappy Dryden ! In all C. days *S.* v. 213
Make sacred C. tomb for ever known *W.F.* 319

Charm.

Each Art he prompts, each C. he can create D. iii. 221
Pity! the c. works only in our wall D. iv. 165
That C. shall grow, while what fatigues the Ring M.E. ii. 252
Great in her c—s! as when on Shrieves and Mayors D. i. 263
Sleep's all-subduing c. who dares defy D. ii. 373
See what the c. that smite the simple heart D. iii. 229
Her magic c. o'er all unclassic ground D. iii. 258
What C. could Faction, what Ambition lull D. iv. 623
Yet still her c. in breathing paint engage E. iii. 55
Strong as their c., and gentle as their soul E. iii. 74
Trust not too much your new resistless c. E. iv. 59
Good humour only teaches c. to last E. iv. 61
Descend in all her sober c. E. vi. 2
Athenian Queen! and *sober c.* E. vi. 25
And image c. he must behold no more E.A. 362
To dress her c., and make her more belov'd E.C. 103
In the bright Muse tho' thousand c. conspire E.C. 339
All spread their c., but charm not all alike E.M. i. 127
Nor circle sober fifty with thy C. I.H. iii. 6
Now, now I seize, I clasp your c. I.H. iii. 43
'Tis to their changes half their c. we owe M.E. ii. 42
She who can love a Sister's c., or hear M.E. ii. 259
See Britain sunk in lucre's sordid c. M.E. iii. 143
She owes to me the very c. she wears Mi. ix. 58
My panting breast confesses all his c. Mi. ix. 95
Enflam'd with glory's c. O. i. 44
Wounds, C., and Ardors were no sooner read R.L. i. 119
The fair each moment rises in her c. R.L. i. 140
Not scornful virgins who their c. survive R.L. iv. 4
There kept my c. conceal'd from mortal eye R.L. v. 157
C. strike the sight, but merit wins the soul R.L. v. 34
And gaze on Parian C. with learned eyes S. iv. 31
We conquer'd France, but felt our Captive's c. S. v. 263
Dear Countess! you have c. all hearts to hit S. viii. 232
'Tis done, and nature's various c. decay W. 29
Sure to c. all was his peculiar fate E. iv. 5
By this ev'n now they live, ev'n now they c. E. iv. 71
Still to c. those who c. the world beside E. iv. 80
With other beauties c. my partial eyes E.A. 196
To c. the Mistress, or to fix the Friend I.H. iii. 14
And bid new music c. th' unfolding ear M. 42
Lucullus, when Frugality could c. M.E. i. 218
Music the fiercest grief can c. O. i. 118
Who c. the sense, or mend the heart O. ii. 10
And vanquish'd nature seems to c. no more Sp. 76
Who now shall c. the shades where Cowley strung W.F. 279

Charm'd.

The gen'rous pleasure to be c. with Wit E.C. 238
Aw'd without Virtue, without Beauty c. M.E. ii. 46
C. the small-pox, or chas'd old age away R.L. v. 20
But, c. to silence, listens while she sings Sp. 15

Charmer.

Whether the c. sinner it, or saint it M.E. ii. 15

Charming.

Are half so c. as thy sight to me A. 46
Each maid cry'd, C.! and each youth, Divine D. iv. 410 and 414
Come, if thou dar'st, all c. as thou art E.A. 281
O c. Noons! and Nights divine I.H. ii. 133
No let a c. Chintz, and Brussels lace M.E. i. 248
Sighs for the shades—"How c. is a Park!" M.E. ii. 38
Cries, "Ah! how c., if there's no such place!" M.E. ii. 108
And one describes a c. Indian screen R.L. iii. 14
For Sylvia, c. Sylvia, shall be thine Sp. 92

Charms.

Whose sense instructs us, and whose humour c. A. 9
I hear thee, view thee, gaze o'er all thy c. E.A. 233
Horace still c. with graceful negligence E.C. 653
Is gentle love, and c. all womankind E.M. ii. 190
In Decius's, in Curtius is divine E.M. ii. 200
While Roman Spirit c., and Attic Wit E.S. ii. 84
While one there is who c. us with his Spleen M.E. i. 62
C. by accepting, by submitting sways M.E. ii. 263
Whom Nature c., and whom the Muse inspires W.F. 238

Charon.

Taylor, their better C., lends an oar D. iii. 19

Charron.

What made (say Montagne, or more sage C.) M.E. i. 87

Chartres.

Writ not, and C. scarce could write or read E.S. ii. 186
Now drinking citron with his Grace and C. M.E. ii. 64
To Ward, to Waters, C., and the Devil M.E. iii. 20
To C., Vigour; Japhet, Nose and Ears M.E. iii. 86
And something said of C. much too rough S. i. 4
To drink with Walters, or with C. eat S. i. 89
Go dine with C., in each Vice out-do S. iv. 120
Who live like S—tt—n, or who die like C. S. vii. 36
For C.'s *head reserve the hanging wall* E.M. iv 130

Chartreux.

Like some lone C. stands the good old Hall M.E. iii. 187

Chase.

Whether you call them Villa, Park, or C. S. vi. 255
Proud Nimrod first the bloody c. began W.F. 61
It chanc'd, as eager of the c., the maid W.F. 181
Or as the god, more furious, urg'd the c. W.F. 190
Of war or blood, but in the sylvan c. W.F. 371
Marriage may all those petty Tyrants c. E. iv. 37

Chas'd.

When Sallee Rovers c. him on the deep D. iv. 380
The rising game, and c. from flow'r to flow'r D. iv. 426
But soon by impious arms from Latium c. E.C. 709
Charm'd the small-pox, or old age away R.L. v. 20

Chaser.

At once the c., and at once the prey W.F. 81

Chaste.

Of Curll's c. press, and Lintot's rubric post D. i. 40
C. Matrons praise her, and grave Bishops bless E.S. i. 146
C. to her Husband, frank to all beside M.E. ii. 71
C. as cold Cynthia's virgin light O. ii. 2
Know further yet; whoever fair and c. R.L. i. 67
Procure her Beauty, make that beauty c. S. iv. 79
And c. Diana haunts the forest-shade Su. 62
As bright a Goddess, and as c. a Queen W.F. 162
In her c. current oft the goddess laves W.F. 209

Chastity.

Ev'n here where frozen C. retires E.A. 181
Had aim'd, like him, by C. at praise M.E. i. 217

Chat.

Snuff, or the fan, supply each pause of c. R.L. iii. 17
Would take me in his Coach to c. I.H. ii. 87

Chatt'ring.

Of him, whose c. shames the monkey-tribe D. ii. 232
'Twas c., grinning, mouthing, jabbering all D. ii. 237

Chatting.

C. and laughing all-a-row I.H. ii. 136

Chaucer.

And such as C. is, shall Dryden be E.C. 483
C.'s *worst ribaldry is learn'd by rote* S. v. 37

Cheap.

C. eggs, and herbs, and olives still we see S. ii. 35

Cheat.

Have you less pity for the needy C. E.S. ii. 44
A Knave this morning, and his Will a C. M.E. ii. 142
The Wit of C—s, *the Courage of a Whore* E.S. i. 165
Grant, gracious Goddess! I grant me still to c. D. iv. 355
But grant that those can conquer, these can c. E.M. iv. 229
Unthought-of Frailties c. us in the Wise M.E. i. 69
What made Directors c. in South-sea year M.E. iii. 117
And those feign'd sighs which c. the list'ning Fair Mi. ix. 8
They'll never poison you, they'll only c. S. i. 90
Something, which for your Honour they may c. S. iv. 93
To c. a Friend, or Ward, he leaves to Peter S. v. 197
A tongue that can c. Widows, cancel scores S. viii. 58

Cheats.

The Wretch that trusts them, or the Rogue that c. M.E. iii. 238
And c. th' unknowing Widow, and the Poor S. viii. 141

CHECK—CHIN.

Check.
Some free from rhyme or reason, rule or *c*. *D.* iii. 161
Oh filthy *c*. on all industrious skill *M.E.* iii. 75
Shows most true mettle when you *c*. his course *E.C.* 87
Form'd but to *c*., delib'rate, and advise *E.M.* ii. 70
Thus Nature gives us (let it *c*. our pride) *E.M.* ii. 195

Check'd.
Nature stands *c*. ; Religion disapproves *E.A.* 259
Why doing, suff'ring, *c*., impell'd ; and why *E.M.* i. 67
How Beaumont's judgment *c*. what Fletcher writ *S.* v. 84

Checks.
Convinc'd, amaz'd, he *c*. the bold design *E.C.* 136
Nature that Tyrant *c*. ; he only knows *E.M.* iii. 51

Cheek—*see also* Infant-Cheek.
Her modest *c*. shall warm a future age *E.* iii. 56
See from my *c*. the transient roses fly *E.A.* 331
No *c*. is known to blush, no heart to throb *E.S.* i. 103
Steals down my *c*. th' involuntary Tear *I.H.* iii. 38
And—Betty—give this *C*. a little Red *M.E.* i. 251
That ev'n in slumber caus'd her *c*. to glow *R.L.* i. 24
At this, the blood the virgin's *c*. forsook *R.L.* iii. 89
Shows in her *c*. the roses of eighteen *R.L.* iv. 30
With band of Lily, and with *c*. of Rose *S.* viii. 251
Upon her sallow *c*—s, enliv'ning red *Mi.* ix. 62
Like Citron-waters matrons' *c*. inflame *R.L.* iv. 69
These *c*. now fading at the blast of death *U.L.* 32

Cheer.
Rouse the fleet hart, and *c*. the op'ning hound *W.F.* 150

Cheer'd.
Suckled, and *c*., with air, and sun, and show'r *D.* iv. 406

Cheerful.
C. he play'd the trifle, Life, away *E.* iv. 12
Can make to-morrow *c*. as to-day *M.E.* ii. 258
Is there a Lord, who knows a *c*. noon *M.E.* ii. 239
Whose *c*. Tenants bless their yearly toil *M.E.* iv. 183
Preserve him social, *c*., and serene *P.S.* 416
No *c*. breeze this sullen region knows *R.L.* iv. 19
Whether Old age, with faint but *c*. ray *S.* i. 93
To live on little, with a *c*. heart *S.* ii. 2
Then *c*. healths (your Mistress shall have place) *S.* ii. 149
See gloomy clouds obscure the *c*. day *W.* 30
Her *c*. head, and leads the golden years *W.F.* 92
The trumpet sleep, while *c*. horns are blown *W.F.* 373

Cheers.
Bid her be all that *c*. or softens life *E.* iii. 51
Hark ! a glad voice the lonely desert *c*. *M.* 29
Verse *c*. their leisure, Verse assists their work *S.* v. 235

Cheese.
C. such as men in Suffolk make *I.H.* ii. 167
Astride his *c*. Sir Morgan we might meet *M.E.* iii. 61

Chemist.
The starving *c*. in his golden views *E.M.* ii. 269
The Maids romantic wish, the C.'s flame D. iii. 11

Cheops.
Who like his *C*. stinks above the ground *D.* iv. 372

Chequered.
And you, my Critics ! in the *c*. shade *D.* iv. 195
C. with ribbons blue and green *I.H.* ii. 40 s
Here waving groves a *c*. scene display *W.F.* 17

Cherub.
A *C*.'s face, a reptile all the rest *P.S.* 331

Cheselden.
I'll do what Mead and *C*. advise *S.* iii. 51

Chest.
Can mark the figures on an Indian *c*. *M.E.* ii. 168
He spits fore-right, his haughty *c*. before *S.* viii. 264

Chesterfield.
Nor couldst thou, *C*. / a tear refuse *D.* iv. 43
How can I Pult'ney, *C*. forget *E.S.* ii. 84

Chew.
Old politicians *c*. on wisdom past *M.E.* i. 228

Chew'd.
Or *c*. by blind old Scholiasts o'er and o'er *D.* iv. 232

Chicane.
C. in Furs, and *Casuistry* in Lawn *D.* iv. 28

Chicks.
Thence comes your mutton, and these *c*. my own *S.* ii. 144

Chief.
This China Jordan let the *c*. o'ercome *D.* ii. 165
Beholds himself a Patriot, *C*., or Saint *D.* iv. 536
A prudent *c*. not always must display *E.C.* 175
Tho' with the Stoic *C*. our stage may ring *E.J.S.* 37
Fear to the Statesman, rashness to the *c*. *E.M.* ii. 243
A Wit's a feather, and a *C*.'s a rod *E.M.* iv. 247
Was there a *C*. but melted at the sight *Mi.* ii. 7
Each *c*. his sev'nfold shield display'd *O.* i. 45
Ye Sylphs and Sylphids to your *c*. give ear *R.L.* ii. 73
With his broad sabre next, a *c*. in years *R.L.* iii. 55
Nor fear'd the *C*. th' unequal fight to try *R.L.* v. 77
The forms august of King, or conquering *C*. *S.* v. 391
Vain was the C.'s, the Sage's pride I.H. iv. 13
Himself among the story'd c—s appears D. ii. 151
And *C*. or Sages long to Britain giv'n *Ep.* xiv. 13
Sages and *C*. long since had birth *I.H.* iv. 9
And *c*. contend till all the prize is lost *R.L.* v. 108
C. out of war, and Statesmen out of place *S.* i. 126
And naked youths and painted *c*. admire *W.F.* 403
But *c*. in Bays's monster-breeding breast *D.* i. 103
And Milbourn *c*., deputed by the rest *D.* ii. 349
But *c*. her shrine where naked Venus keeps *D.* iv. 307
Nature's *c*. Master-piece is writing well *E.C.* 724
Of these the *c*. the care of Nations own *R.L.* ii. 89
Your country, *c*., in Arms abroad depend *S.* v. 3

Chiefless.
And *C*, Armies doz'd out the Campaign *D.* iv. 617

Chiefly.
But *c*. Love—to Love an Altar built *R.L.* ii. 37

Child.
Once brightest shin'd this *c*. of Heat and Air *D.* iv. 424
Then dupe to Party ; *c*. and man the same *D.* iv. 502
But she, good Goddess, sent to ev'ry *c*. *D.* iv. 529
In Wit, a Man ; Simplicity, a *C*. *Ep.* xi. 2
Behold the *c*., by Nature's kindly law *E.M.* 275
'Twas what I said to Craggs and *C*. *I.H.* i. 67
And ev'ry *c*. hates Shylock, tho' his soul *M.E.* i. 55
Europe a Woman, *C*., or Dotard rule *M.E.* i. 93
To make a wash would hardly stew a *c*. *M.E.* ii. 54
As yet a *c*., nor yet a fool to fame *P.S.* 127
This painted *c*. of dirt, that stinks and stings *P.S.* 310
Men prove with *c*., as pow'rful fancy works *R.L.* iv. 53
Yet ev'ry *c*. another song will sing *S.* iii. 91
But Britain, changeful as a *C*. at play *S.* v. 155
What will a *C*. learn sooner than a song *S.* v. 205
Here strip, my c—ren l *here at once leap in D.* ii. 275
Fast by, like Niobe (her *c*. gone) *D.* ii. 311
Her *c*. first of more distinguish'd sort *D.* iv. 567
Then, blessing all, " Go, *C*. of my care *D.* iv. 579
Plants of thy hand, and *c*. of thy pray'r *E.A.* 130
Know Nature's *c*. all divide her care *E.M.* ii. 43
All Parts perform'd, and *all* her *C*. blest *E.S.* i. 82
Childless, with all her *C*., wants an Heir *M.E.* ii. 148
Pleasures the sex, as *c*. Birds, pursue *M.E.* ii. 231
Of Debts, and Taxes, Wife and *C*. clear *M.E.* iii. 279
To Maids alone and *C*. are reveal'd *R.L.* i. 38
And *c*. sacred held a Martin's nest *S.* ii. 38
Thus shall your wives, and thus your *c*. fall *U.L.* 36

Childless.
C. with all her children, wants an Heir *M.E.* ii. 148
Some with fat Bucks on *c*. dotards fawn *S.* iii. 130

Chills.
Now Conscience *c*. her, and now Passion burns *M.E.* ii. 65

Chimes.
While they ring round the same unvary'd *c*. *E.C.* 348

Chiming.
But hark ! the *c*. Clocks to dinner call *M.E.* iv. 151

Chin.
First he relates, how sinking to the *c*. *D.* ii. 331
By potent Arthur, knock'd his *c*. and breast *D.* ii. 398

China.
This *C.* Jordan let the chief o'ercome *D.* ii. 165
And Mistress of herself, tho' *C.* fall *M.E.* ii. 268
Or some frail *C.* jar receive a flaw *R.L.* i. 106
Or when rich *C.* vessels fall'n from high *R.L.* iii. 159
The tott'ring *C.* shook without a wind *R.L.* iv. 163
While C.'s *earth receives the smoking tide R.L.* iii. 110

China.
Some win rich Widows by the *C.* and Brawn *S.* iii. 131

Chink.
In at a Corn-loft thro' a *C. I.H.* i. 52
For your damn'd Stucco has no *c. I.H.* ii. 217

Chinks.
He *c.* his purse, and takes his seat of state *D.* ii. 197

Chintz.
No, let a charming *C.,* and Brussels lace *M.E.* i. 248
Observes how much a *C.* exceeds Mohair *M.E.* ii. 170

Chirping.
He takes his *c.* pint, and cracks his jokes *M.E.* iii. 358

Chloe.
(Thy Grecian Form) and *C.* lend the Face *I.H.* iii. 20
Yet *C.* sure was form'd without a spot *M.E.* ii. 157
Say, what can *C.* want? She wants a Heart *M.E.*ii.160
Would *C.* know if you're alive or dead *M.E.* ii. 177
C. is prudent. Would you too be wise (*rep.*) *M.E.* ii. 179
C. stepp'd in, and kill'd him with a frown *R.L.* v. 68
Sigh, while his *C.* blind to Wit and Worth *S.* iv. 42
Safe is your secret still in C.'s ear (*rep.*) *M.E.* ii. 173

Chocolate.
In fumes of burning *C.* shall glow *R.L.* ii. 135

Choice.
The *c.* we make, or justify it made *E.M.* ii. 156
With *c.* we fix, with sympathy we burn *E.M.* iii. 135
Some in their *c.* of Friends (nay, louk not grave) *E.S.* ii. 100
May some c. patron bless each graygoose quill P.S. 249

Choicer.
Thy *c.* mists on this assembly shed *D.* iv. 357

Choicest.
My *c.* Hours of Life are lost *I.H.* ii. 126

Choir—*see also* Quire.
Three wicked imps of her own Grubstreet *c. D.* ii. 113
From the full *c.* when loud Hosannas rise *E.A.* 353
Bright Apollo, lead thy *C. Mi.* vii. 16

Chok'd.
Streets pav'd with Heroes, Tiber *c.* with Gods *D.* iii. 108

Choose.
Whether thou *c.* Cervantes' serious air *D.* i. 21
And, if a Borough *c.* him not, undone *D.* iv. 328
To shun their poison, and to *c.* their food *E.M.* iii. 100
Virtue may *c.* the high or low degree *E.S.* i. 137
Whether we ought to *c.* our Friends *I.H.* ii. 149
C. a firm cloud before it fall, and in it *M.E.* ii. 19
Artists must *c.* his Pictures, Music, Meats *M.E.* iv. 6
Poor guiltless I I and can I *c.* but smile *P.S.* 281
Will *c.* a pheasant still before a hen *S.* ii. 18
That makes three members, this can *c.* a May'r *S.* iii. 126
Or *c.* at least some Minister of Grace *S.* v. 378

Chorus.
And fill the gen'ral *c.* of mankind *E.C.* 188
Let *Envy* howl, while Heav'n's whole *C.* sings *E.S.*ii.243
One *C.* let all Being raise *U.P.* 51

Chose.
And *c.* me for an humble friend *I.H.* ii. 86 s
The *Knave* won *Sonica,* which I had *c. Mi.* ix. 51

Chosen.
Here to her *C.* all her works she shews *D.* i. 273
To fifty *c.* Sylphs, of special note *R.L.* ii. 47

Christ.
Adds to *C.'s* pray'r, the *Power and Glory* clause *S.*vii.108
Tho' *C.*-church *long kept prudishly away D.* iv. 194

Christ's Kirk o' the Green.
A Scot will fight for *C. S.* v. 40

Christ's No Kingdom Here.
Yet silent bow'd to *C. D.* ii. 400

Christen'd.
Till Peter's keys some *c.* Jove adorn *D.* iii. 129

Christian.
Yet still a sad, good *C.* at her heart *M.E.* ii. 68
See *C—s, Jews, one heavy sabbath keep D.* iii. 99
No fiends torment, no *C.* thirst for gold *E.M.* i. 108
My better and more *c.* progeny *D.* i. 228
And gather'd ev'ry Vice on *C.* ground *D.* iv. 312
Gave alms at Easter, in a *C.* trim *M.E.* ii. 65
Barbarian blindness, *C.* zeal conspire *M.E.* v. 13

Christmas-tide.
There (so the Dev'l ordain'd) one *C. M.E.* iii. 383

Chromatic.
C. tortures soon shall drive them hence *D.* iv. 55

Chuck.
Shortly no lad shall *c.,* or lady vole *S.* viii. 146

Church.
A *C.* collects the saints of Drury-lane *D.* ii. 30
Wake the dull *C.,* and lull the ranting Stage *D.* iv. 58
Unseen at *C.,* at Senate, or at Court *D.* iv. 338
Not mend their minds; as some to *C.* repair *E.C.* 342
Nor is Paul's *c.* more safe than Paul's church-yard *E.C.* 623
This calls the *C.* to deprecate our Sin *E.S.* i. 129
He dies, sad outcast of each *c.* and state *M.E.* i. 204
Or her, whose life the *C.* and Scandal share *M.E.* ii. 105
Who builds a *C.* to God, and not to Fame *M.E.* iii 285
Constant at *C.* and Change ; his gains were sure *M.E.* iii. 347
Where once I went to *C.,* I'll now go twice *M.E.* iii. 367
Seldom at *C.* ('twas such a busy life) *M.E.* iii. 381
Load some vain *C.* with old Theatric state *M.E.* iv. 29
No place is sacred, not the *C.* is free *P.S.* 11
Lights of the *C.,* or Guardians of the Laws *S.* i. 110
Who Virtue and a *C.* alike disowns *S.* iv. 65
Now all for Pleasure, now for *C.* and State *S.* v. 158
And send his Wife to *c.,* his Son to school *S.* v. 164
These Madmen never hurt the *C.* or State *S.* v. 190
You go to *c.* to hear these Flatt'rers preach *S.* vi. 225
Are Fathers of the *C.* for writing less *S.* vii. 98
Stretch'd o'er the Poor and *C.* his iron rod *W.F.* 75
C—es and Chapels instantly it reach'd D. iv. 607
Shall half the new-built *C.* round thee fall *S.* ii. 119

Churchill.
Thus *C.'s* race shall other hearts surprise *E.* iii. 59

Churchman.
In Soldier, *C.,* Patriot, Man in Pow'r *E.S.* i. 161
Is he a *C.?* then he's fond of pow'r *M.E.* i. 155

Churchyard.
Nor is Paul's church more safe than Paul's *c. E.C.* 623

Chymic.
With *c.* art exalts the min'ral pow'rs *W.F.* 243

Cibber.
Can make a *C.,* Tibbald, or Ozell *D.* i. 285
Thou, *C.!* thou, his Laurel shall support *D.* i. 299
"God save King *C.!*" mounts in ev'ry note *D.* i. 318
Great *C.* sate. The proud Parnassian sneer *D.* ii. 5
And a new *C.* shall the stage adorn *D.* iii. 142
New wizards rise ; I see my *C.* there *D.* iii. 266
Avert it, Heav'n! that thou my *C.* e'er *D.* iii. 287
As Jansen, Fleetwood, *C.* shall think fit *D.* iv. 326
Has drunk with *C.,* nay has rhym'd for *Moore P.S.* 373
Better be *C.,* I'll maintain it still *S.* i. 37
See, Modest *C.* now has left the stage *S.* iii. 6
And idle *C.,* how he breaks the laws *S.* v. 29a
Dear *C.!* never match'd one ode of thine *S.* vi. 138
Great C.'s brasen, brainless brothers stand D. i. 32
Ye Gods! shall *C.* son, without rebuke *E.S.* i. 115
From eldest Heywood, down to *C.* Age *S.* v. 88
Old Edward's Armour beams on *C.* breast *S.* v. 319

Cibberian.
C. forehead, and C. brain *D.* i. 218
C. forehead, or Cimmerian gloom *D.* iv. 532

Cicero.
Or give up C. to C or K *D.* iv. 222

Ciceronian.
O come, that easy C. style *E.S.* i. 73

Cid.
Now flames the C., and now Perolla burns *D.* i. 250

Cimmerian.
And soft besprinkles with C. dew *D.* iii. 4
Cibberian forehead, or C. gloom *D.* iv. 532

Cimon.
Like C., triumph'd both on land and wave *D.* i. 86

Circe.
Not more amazement seiz'd on C.'s guests *S.* viii. 166

Circean.
From Latian Syrens, French C. Feasts *S.* iv. 122

Circle.
But lofty Lintot in the c. rose *D.* ii. 53
See in the c. next Eliza plac'd *D.* ii. 157
One c. first, and then a second makes *D.* ii. 406
Like motion, from one c. to the rest *D.* ii. 408
Now running round the C. finds it square *D.* iv. 34
That each may fill the c. mark'd by Heav'n *E.M.* i. 86
Yet make at once their c. round the Sun *E.M.* iii. 314
The centre mov'd, a c. straight succeeds *E.M.* iv. 365
In the small c. of our foes or friends *E.M.* iv. 242
Hemm'd by a triple c. round *I.H.* ii. 48 s
Thro' all the giddy c. they pursue *R.L.* ii. 93
Amid the c., on the gilded mast *R.L.* ii. 69
What boots the regal c. on his head *R.L.* ii. 71
Long as the Year's dull c. seems to run *S.* iii. 37
And foremost in the C. eye a King *S.* iii. 106
Next Smedley div'd; slow c—s dimpled o'er D. ii. 291
Roll all their tides; then back their c. bring *R.L.* ii. 56
As Eastern priests in giddy c. run *E.M.* ii. 27
And other planets c. other suns D. iii. 244
What other planets c. other suns *E.M.* i. 26
Nor c. sober fifty with thy charms *I.H.* iii. 6

Circled.
With scarlet hats wide-waving c. round *D.* ii. 14
The silver token, and the c. green *R.L.* i. 32

Circling.
Whirlpools and storms his c. arm invest *D.* ii. 317
In c. fleeces whiten all the ways *D.* ii. 362
Or scoops in c. theatres the Vale *M.E.* iv. 60
And heighten'd by the diamond's c. rays *R.L.* iv. 115
And trace the mazes of the c. hare *W.F.* 122

Circulate.
Shall in thee centre, from thee c. *D.* iii. 60

Circumference.
And guard the wide c. around *R.L.* ii. 122

Circumspectivo.
All sly slow things, with c. eyes *E.M.* iv. 226

Circumstance.
Condition,'c., is not the thing *E.M.* iv. 57

Circus.
Sooner shall grass in Hyde-park C. grow *R.L.* iv. 117

Cirque.
See the C. falls, th' unpillar'd Temple nods *D.* iii. 107

Cit.
Barnard, thou art a C., with all thy worth *S.* iii. 89
Why Turnpikes rise, and now no C. nor clown *S.* viii. 144
Leaves the dull C—s, and joins (to please the Fair) M.E. iii. 387

Citizen.
There dwelt a C. of sober fame *M.E.* iii. 341
What Squire his lands, what C. his wife *S.* viii. 149

Citron.
Now drinking C. with his Grace and Chartres *M.E.* ii. 64
Like c.-waters *matrons' cheeks inflame R.L.* iv. 69

City.
But the kind cuckold might instruct the c. *E.J.S.* 42
Has seiz'd the Court and C., poor and rich *S.* v. 170
And here, while town, and court, and c. roars *S.* vi. 123
What C. Swans once sung within the walls D. i. 96
Nor lordly Luxury, nor C. Gain *M.E.* iii. 146
Rise from a Clergy, or a C. Feast *S.* ii. 76
Slides to a Scriv'ner or a c. Knight *S.* ii. 178
Abuse the C.'s best good men in metre *S.* i. 39
Here subterranean works and c—ies see E.M. iii. 181
C. were built, societies were made *E.M.* iii. 200
Ambition humbled, mighty C. storm'd *S.* v. 11
C. laid waste, Pride from Morn to Eve *W.F.* 49
From men their c., and from Gods their fanes *W.F.* 66
I see, I see, where two fair c. bend *W.F.* 379
Or C.-heir *in mortgage melts away S.* vii. 89

Civet-cats.
And all your courtly C. can vent *E.S.* ii. 183

Civil.
But fool with fool is barb'rous c. war *D.* iii. 176
Nor be so c. as to prove unjust *E.C.* 581
Drunk at a Borough, c. at a Ball *M.E.* i. 75
Sick of his c. Pride from Morn to Eve *M.E.* iv. 166
And c. madness tears them from the land *O.* ii. 24
Oh curs'd effects of c. hate *O.* ii. 29
Damn with faint praise, assent with c. leer *P.S.* 201
Stranger to c. and religious rage *P.S.* 394
Z—ds! damn the lock! 'fore Gad, you must be c. *R.L.* iv. 128
And each true Briton is to Ben so c. *S.* v. 41
When the tir'd Nation breath'd from c. war *S.* v. 273
Fond of his Friend, and c. to his Wife *S.* vi. 189
Than C. Codes, with all their Glosses, are *S.* vii. 96
These I could bear; but not a rogue so c. *S.* viii. 56
Confounds the c., keeps the rude in awe *S.* viii. 270

Civility.
I sit with sad c., I read *P.S.* 37

Civilly.
So well-bred spaniels c. delight *P.S.* 313

Claim.
Nor is his c. to plenty, but content *E.M.* iv. 156
Oh when shall Britain, conscious of her c. *M.E.* v. 53
Alas! how little from the grave we c. E. iii. 77
Just as absurd for any part to c. *E.M.* i. 263
Ev'n such small Critics some regard may c. *P.S.* 167
Of these am I, who thy protection c. *R.L.* i. 105
My Liege! why Writers little c. your thought *S.* v. 356

Claim'd.
Who c. the skies, dispeopled air and floods *W.F.* 47

Claims.
No merit now the dear Nonjuror c. *D.* i. 253
And loudly c. the Journals and the Lead *D.* ii. 322
A sigh the absent c., the dead a tear *E.* i. 14
No Pow'r, when Virtue c. it, can withstand *E.S.* ii. 119

Clam'rous.
The c. lapwings feel the leaden death *W.F.* 132

Clamour.
Before her each with c. pleads the Laws *Mi.* xi. 5

Clap.
Time, that at last matures a c. to pox *S.* vii. 47
Or plaister'd posts, with c—s, in capitals P.S. 216
A Rat, a Rat! c. to the door I.H. ii. 212
Then c. four slices of Pilaster on't *M.E.* iv. 33
Glad of a quarrel, straight I c. the door *P.S.* 67
Fans c., silks rustle, and tough whalebones crack *R.L.* v. 40
And all th' aërial audience c. their wings *Sp.* 16

Clapp'd.
C. his glad wings, and sate to view the fight *R.L.* v. 54

Clare-hall.
To lull the sons of Marg'ret and C. *D.* iv. 200

Clarion.
Drowns the loud c. of the braying Ass *D.* ii. 234

Clarissa.

Just then *C.* drew with tempting grace *R.L.* iii. 127
Then grave *C.* graceful wav'd her fan *R.L.* v. 7
When bold Sir Plume had drawn *C.* down *R.L.* v. 67

Clarke.

Nor in an Hermitage set Dr. *C. M.E.* iv. 78

Clasp.

Now, now I seize, I *c.* your charms *I.H.* iii. 43

Clasp'd.

One *c.* in wood, and one in strong cow-hide *D.* i. 150

Clasping.

And round thy phantom glue my *c.* arms *E.A.* 234
Round broken columns *c.* ivy twin'd *W.F.* 69

Class.

Whate'er of mongrel no one *c.* admits *D.* iv. 89

Classic.

Bentley his mouth with *c.* flatt'ry opes *D.* ii. 205
All *C.* learning lost on *C.* ground *D.* ii. 321
I hold that Wit a *C.*, good in law *S.* v. 56
The *C—s* of an Age that heard of none *D.* i. 148

Clatt'ring.

C. their sticks before ten lines are spoke *S.* v. 308

Clause.

Adds to Christ's pray'r the *Pow'r and Glory c. S.* vii. 108

Clay.

What heav'nly particle inspires the *c. S.* ii. 128

Clean.

Plain, but not sordid; tho' not splendid, *c. S.* ii. 48
Observe his shape how *c.* / his locks how curl'd *S.* vi. 5
I have but one, I hope the fellow's *c. S.* viii. 111

Clear.

Tho' stale, not ripe; tho' thin, yet never *c. D.* iii. 170
Now see an Attys, now a Cecrops *c. D.* iv. 363
To prove me, Goddess! *c.* of all design *D.* iv. 391
One *c.*, unchang'd, and universal light *E.C.* 71
One truth is *c.*, WHATEVER IS, IS RIGHT *E.M.* i. 294
Whose life is healthful, and whose conscience *c. E.M.* iv. 191
Oft, in the *c.*, still Mirror of Retreat *E.S.* ii. 78
I've often wish'd that I had *c. I.H.* ii. 1 s
But *c.* and artless, pouring thro' the plain *M.E.* iii. 257
Of Debts, and Taxes, Wife and Children *c. M.E.* iii. 279
And am so *c.* too of all other vice *M.E.* iii. 368
In action faithful, and in honour *c. M.E.* v. 68
Is that a Birth-day? 'Tis alas! too *c. Mi.* v. 9
Hark ! the numbers soft and *c. O.* i. 12
In the *c.* Mirror of thy ruling star *R.L.* l. 108
Will prove at least the medium must be *c. S.* i. 56
Or in pure Equity (the case not *c.*) *S.* ii. 171
And tho' the Court show Vice exceeding *c. S.* viii. 96
Why sit we sad when Phosphor shines so *c. Sp.* 97
Seek the *c.* spring, or haunt the pathless grove *W.F.* 168
In the *c.* azure gleam the flocks are seen *W.F.* 215
No lake so gentle, and no spring so *c. W.F.* 226
'Tis he th' obstructed paths of sound shall *c. M.* 41
Those words, that would against them *c.* the doubt *S.* vii. 104

Clearer.

And see now *c.* and now darker days *E.C.* 405
Where *c.* flames glow round the frozen pole *W.F.* 390

Clearest.

The justest rules, and *c.* method joined *E.C.* 670
The *c.* head, and the sincerest heart *E.C.* 732

Clears.

C., and improves whate'er it shines upon *E.C.* 316
The prospect *c.*, and Wharton stands confest *M.E.* i. 179

Cleaves.

When the firce eagle *c.* the liquid sky *W.F.* 186

Clenches.

Here one poor word an hundred *c.* makes *D.* i. 63

Clergy.

Rise from a *C.*, or a City feast *S.* ii. 76

Clerk.

Each gentle *c.*, and mutt'ring seals his eyes *D.* ii. 404
" Be that my task," replies a gloomy *C. D.* iv. 459
A *C.*, foredoom'd his father's soul to cross *P.S.* 17
Then mount the c—s, and in one lazy tone *D.* ii. 387

Clever.

I can't but think 'twould sound more *c. I.H.* ii. 11 s

Cliff.

One leap from yonder *c.* shall end my pains *A.* 95
And Albion's c—s resound the rural lay *Sp.* 6

Climate.

Grow sick, and damn the *c.*—like a Lord *S.* iii. 160

Climb.

Downward to *c.*, and backward to advance *D.* ii. 320
Uncheck'd may rise, and *c.* from art to art *E.M.* ii. 40
Who *c.* their mountain, or who taste their spring *S.* v. 353

Climb'd.

He said, and *c.* a lighter's stranded height *D.* ii. 287

Clime.

See, from each *c.* the learn'd their incense bring *E.C.* 185
To what new *c.*, what distant sky *O.* ii. 13
In ev'ry *c.* ador'd *U.P.* 2
Not sail with Ward to Ape-and-Monkey c—s *D.* i. 233
But ripeos spirits in cold northern *c. E.C.* 401
Manners with Fortunes, Humours turn with *c. M.E.* i. 172
Thro' *c.* and ages bears each form and name *M.E.* v. 32

Clinging.

Two babes of love close *c.* to her waist *D.* ii. 158

Clipp'd.

C. from the lovely head where late it grew *R.L.* iv. 136

Cliveden.

Gallant and gay, in *C.*'s proud alcove *M.E.* iii. 307

Cloacina.

In office here fair *C.* stands *D.* ii. 93

Cloak.

Once, we confess, beneath the Patriot's *c. M.E.* iii. 35

Clock.

Count the slow *c.*, and dine exact at noon *E.* v. 18
As c—s to weight their nimble motion owe *D.* i. 183
But hark! the chiming *C.* to dinner call *M.E.* iv. 151

Clod.

When the dull Ox, why now he breaks the *c. E.M.* i. 63

Clogg'd.

While *c.* he beats his silken wings in vain *R.L.* ii. 130

Close.

When at the *c.* of each sad sorrowing day *E.A.* 225
What greater bliss attends their *c.* of life *E.M.* iv. 301
A gentler exercise to *c.* the games *D.* ii. 356
To dream once more I *c.* my willing eyes *E.A.* 239
Shall hail the rising, *c.* the parting day *I.H.* iii. 30
Hartshorn, or something that shall *c.* your eyes *S.* i. 20
C. to those walls where Folly holds her throne *D.* i. 29
'Twixt Prince and People *c.* the Curtain draw *D.* i. 313
Two babes of love *c.* clinging to her waist *D.* ii. 158
Him *c.* she curtains round with Vapours blue *D.* iii. 3
But who is he in closet *c.* y-pent *D.* iii. 185
And holds his breeches *c.* with both his hands *D.* iv. 148
Fresnoy's *c.* Art, and Dryden's native Fire *E.* iii. 8
Hide it, my heart, within that *c.* disguise *E.A.* 11
Some dire misfortune follows *c.* behind *E.A.* 34
In some *c.* corner of the soul, they sin *E.S.* 18
In one *c.* system of Benevolence *E.M.* iv. 358
Drops to the third, who nuzzles *c.* behind *E.S.* ii. 178
Others so very *c.*, they're hid from none *M.E.* i. 52
Keep *c.* to Ears, and those let asses prick *P.S.* 77
"I found him *c.* with Swift "—" Indeed ! no doubt " *P.S.* 275
C., by those meads, for ever crown'd with flow'rs *R.L.* iii. 1
The *c.* recesses of the Virgin's thought *R.L.* iii. 140
Here in a grotto, shelter'd *c.* from air *R.L.* iv. 21
Then, *c.* as Umbra, joins the dirty train *S.* viii. 177
And *c.* confin'd to their own palace, sleep *U.L.* 22
Couch'd *c.* he lies, and meditates the prey *W.F.* 102
Now *c.* behind, his sounding steps she hears *W.F.* 192

Clos'd.

The quaking mud, that *c.*, and op'd no more *D.* ii. 292
Withdrew his hand, and *c.* the pompous page *D.* iv. 114
C. one by one to everlasting rest *D.* iv. 638
Recall those nights that *c.* thy toilsome days *E.* i. 15
Ev'n then, before the fatal engine *c. R.L.* iii. 149
C. their long Glories with a sigh, to find *S.* v. 13
Hush'd are the birds, and *c.* the drooping flow'rs *Sp.* 70
By foreign hands thy dying eyes were *c. U.L.* 51

Closely.

Yet if we look more *c.*, we shall find *E.C.* 19

Closer.

Not *c.*, orb in orb, conglob'd are seen *D.* iv. 79
Wants, frailties, passions, *c.* still ally *E.M.* ii. 253
"But, Sir, of writers?" Swift, for *c.* style *S.* viii. 72
To *c.* shades the panting flocks remove *Su.* 87

Closest.

The *c.* mortal ever known *I.H.* ii. 124 s

Closet.

But who is he in *c.* close y-pent *D.* iii. 185

Closing.

While the spread fan o'ershades the *c.* eyes *E.* v. 37
Then from his *c.* eyes thy form shall part *U.L.* 79
Near, and more near, the *c.* lines invest *W.F.* 108

Cloth.

Huge bales of British *c.* blockade the door *M.E.* iii. 57
A table, with a *c.* of bays *Mi.* xii. 6
The musty wine, foul *c.*, or greasy glass *S.* ii. 66

Clothe.

Next goes his wool—to *c.* our valiant bands *M.E.* iii. 211
C. spice, line trunks, or, flutt'ring in a row *S.* v. 418

Cloth'd.

No murder *c.* him, and no murder fed *E.M.* iii. 154
Yet hence the Poor are *c.*, the Hungry fed *M.E.* iv. 1

Clothes.

Meat, Fire, and *C.* What more? Meat, *C.*, and Fire *M.E.* iii. 80
And why not players strut in courtiers' *c. S.* viii. 222
Adjust their *c.*, and to confession draw *S.* viii. 242

Cloud.

But soon the *c.* return'd—and thus the Sire *D.* iii. 227
Yet wouldst thou more? in yonder *c.* behold *D.* iii. 253
She mounts the Throne: her head a *c.* conceal'd *D.* iv. 17
Thro' School and College, thy kind *c.* o'ercast *D.* iv. 289
O may thy *c.* still cover the deceit *D.* iv. 396
Thro' Fortune's *c.* one truly great can see *E.* i. 39
If once right reason drives that *c.* away *E.C.* 211
Choose a firm *c.*, before it fall, and in it *M.E.* ii. 19
And fleecy c—s were streak'd with purple light A. 14
The op'ning *c.* disclose each work by turns *D.* i. 249
Like forms in *c.*, or visions of the night *D.* ii. 112
So *c.*, replenish'd from some bog below *D.* ii. 363
Embody'd dark, what *c.* of Vandals rise *D.* iii. 86
There, dim in *c.*, the poring Scholiasts mark *D.* iii. 191
Before her, *Fancy's* gilded *c.* decay *D.* iv. 631
C. interpose, waves roar, and winds arise *E.A.* 246
Whee from the censer *c.* of fragrance roll *E.A.* 271
Bright *c.* descend, and Angels watch thee round *E.A.* 340
And the first *c.* and mountains seem the last *E.C.* 228
But ev'n those *c.* at last adorn its way *E.C.* 472
Sees God in *c.*, or hears him in the wind *M.E.* i. 100
Those painted *c.* that beautify our days *E.M.* ii. 284
See spicy *c.* from lowly Saron rise *M.* 27
On gilded *c.* in fair expansion lie *M.E.* iv. 147
Waft on the breeze, or sink in *c.* of gold *R.L.* ii. 60
See gloomy *c.* obscure the cheerful day *W.* 30
Above the *c.*, above the starry sky *W.* 70
There wrapt in *c.*, the blueish hills ascend *W.F.* 24
When thro' the *c.* he drives the trembling doves *W.F.* 188
All these and more the c.-compelling Queen D. i. 79
Behind the *c.-topt* hill an humbler heav'n *E.M.* i. 104

Clouded.

In *c.* Majesty here Dulness shone *D.* i. 45
And the nice conduct of a *c.* cane *R.L.* iv. 124

Cloudless.

As much eternal springs and *c.* skies *E.M.* i. 153
This Partridge soon shall view in *c.* skies *R.L.* v. 137

Clouds.

And labours till it *c.* itself all o'er *D.* iv. 254
A Fit of Vapours *c.* this Demi-God *S.* iii. 188
Nor yet, when moist Arcturus *c.* the sky *W.F.* 119

Cloudy.

Ascend this hill, whose *c.* point commands *D.* iii. 67
Booth in his *c.* tabernacle shrin'd *D.* iii. 267

Clown.

Is like a *c.* in regal purple dress'd *E.C.* 321
Why turnpikes rise, and now no Cit nor *c. S.* viii. 144

Club.

The *C.* must hail him master of the joke *M.E.* i. 185
The *C.'s black Tyrant first her victim dy'd R.L.* iii. 69
The *c—s of Quidnuncs, or her own Guildhall D.* i. 270
The KNAVE OF *C.* thrice lost: Oh! who could guess *Mi.* ix. 19
C., Diamonds, Hearts, in wild disorder seen *R.L.* iii. 79
Will *c.* their Testers, now, to take your life *S.* i. 104

Clubb'd.

A common Soldier, but who *c.* his Mite *Mi.* ii. 8

Clue.

This *c.* once found, unravels all the rest *M.E.* i. 178

Clusters.

And grateful *c.* swell with floods of wine *A.* 74
And swelling *c.* bend the curling vines *Sp.* 36

Coach.

Contending Princes mount them in their *C. D.* iv. 564
Gave the gilt *C.* and dappled Flanders Mares *E.* iv. 50
Then give Humility a *c.* and six *E.M.* iv. 170
Would take me in his *C.* to chat *I.H.* ii. 87 s
And scorn a rascal and a *c. Mi.* xii. 20
Or in a *c.* and six the British Fair *R.L.* iii. 164
To whom to nod, whom take into your *C. S.* iv. 102
A hackney *c.* may chance to spoil a thought *S.* vi. 101
Beaux banish beaux, and c—s c. drive R.L. i. 102
Why round our *c.* crowd the white-glov'd Beaux *R.L.* v. 13

Coach'd.

C., carted, trod upon, now loose, now fast *D.* iii. 291

Coals.

A peck of *c.* a-piece shall glad the rest *D.* ii. 282
And Worldly crying *c.* from street to street *M.E.* ii. 62

Coarse.

Whose laughs are hearty, tho' his jests are *c. E.* v. 29
To some *c.* Country Wench, almost decay'd *Mi.* iii. 15
Tho' *c.*, was reverend, and tho' bare, was black *S.* viii. 39
And *c.* of phrase—your English all are so *S.* viii. 109
But as *c.* iron, sharpen'd, mangles more *S.* viii. 118

Coast.

"Smedley" in vain resounds thro' all the *c. D.* ii. 294
Now crown'd with Myrtle on th' Elysian *c. E.* iv. 73
This drives them constant to a certain *c. E.M.* ii. 168
O'e'r all the dreary *c—s O.* i. 55

Coat.

You laugh, if *c.* and breeches strangely vary *S.* iii. 163

Cobbler.

The *c.* apron'd, and the parson gown'd *E.M.* iv. 197
Or *c.-like the parson will be drunk E.M.* iv. 202

Cobham.

C.'s a Coward, POLWARTH is a Slave E.S. ii. 130
And you, brave *C.*, to the latest breath *M.E.* i. 262
Lo! *C.* comes, and floats them with a lake *M.E.* iv. 74
Dear Col'nel, *C.'s and your country's Friend S.* vi. 1

Cobweb.

And hang some curious *c.* in its stead *D.* i. 180
Who shames a Scribbler? break one *c.* thro' *P.S.* 89
Amidst their kindred c—s in Duck-lane E.C. 445
Spin all your *C.* o'er the Eye of Day *E.S.* ii. 222

Cochinel.

Like frigates fraught with spice and *c. S.* viii. 227

Cock.
Spurts in the gard'ner's eyes who turns the c. *D.* ii. 178
Cockle-kind.
Congenial matter in the *C. D.* iv. 448
Codes.
Than Civil *C.*, with all their glosses, are *S.* vii. 96
Codille.
Disdains all loss of Tickets or *C. M.E.* ii. 266
Just in the jaws of ruin and *C. R.L.* iii. 92
Codrus.
Let peals of laughter, *C. l* round thee break *P.S.* 85
On *C.* old, or Dunton's modern bed *D.* ii. 144
Coffee.
Or o'er cold *c.* trifle with the spoon *E.* v. 17
C., (which makes the politician wise *R.L.* iii. 117
Coher'd.
Hung to the Goddess, and *c.* around *D.* iv. 78
Coherent.
Where all must full or not *c.* be *E.M.* i. 45
Coin.
And all her triumphs shrink into a *C. M.E.* v. 24
False as his Gems, and canker'd as his *C—s D.* iv. 349
For Pembroke, Statues, dirty Gods and *C. M.E.* iv. 8
Authors, like *c.*, grow dear as they grow old *S.* v. 35
Cold.
My good old Lady catch'd a *c.*, and died *M.E.* iii. 384
Proud to catch *c.* at a Venetian door *M.E.* iv. 36
He starves with *c.* to save them from the fire *S.* vii. 72
In *c.* December fragrant chaplets blow *D.* i. 77
A *c.* long-winded native of the deep *D.* ii. 300
There sunk Thalia, nerveless, *c.*, and dead *D.* iv. 41
Or o'er *c.* coffee trifle with the spoon *E.* v. 17
Tho' *c.* like you, unmov'd and silent grown *E.A.* 23
As with *c.* lips I kiss'd the sacred veil *E.A.* 111
And here, ev'n then, shall my *c.* dust remain *E.A.* 174
Ev'n thou art *c.*—yet Eloïsa loves *E.A.* 260
Glance on the stone where our *c.* relics lie *E.A.* 356
Correctly *c.*, and regularly low *E.C.* 240
But ripens spirits in *c.* northern climes *E.C.* 401
Wrap my *c.* limbs, and shade my lifeless face *M.E.* i. 249
Chaste as *c.* Cynthia's virgin light *O.* iii. 23
C. is that breast which warm'd the world before *U.L.* 33
Coldly.
Can hearken *c.* to my SHARPER's vows *Mi.* ix. 88
Coldness.
The silver stream her virgin *c.* keeps *W.F.* 205
Cole.
C., whose dark streams his flowery islands lave *W.F.* 343
Colepepper.
Had *C.*'s whole wealth been hops and hogs *M.E.* iii. 65
Colin.
That flute is mine which *C.*'s tuneful breath *Sw.* 39
Coll.
And "*C. l*" each Butcher roars at Hockley-hole *D.* i. 326
Collects.
A Church *c.* the saints of Drury-lane *D.* ii. 30
C. her breath, as ebbing life retires *M.E.* i. 244
There she *c.* the force of female lungs *R.L.* iv. 83
College.
Whate'er of dunce in *C.* or in Town *D.* iv. 87
Thro' School and College, by kind cloud o'ercast *D.* iv. 289
Die, and endow a *C.* or a Cat *M.E.* iii. 96
From drawing-rooms, from c—s, from garrets *D.* ii. 93
Three *C.* Sophs, and three pert Templars came *D.* ii. 379
Colley.
Familiar White's, "God save King *C. l*" cries (*rep.*) *D.* i. 319
And has not *C.* still his Lord, and whore *P.S.* 97
Col'nel.
Dear *C.*, Cobham's and your country's Friend *S.* vi. 1

Colour.
Gives all the strength and *c.* of your life *E.M.* ii. 122
Our speech, our *c.*, and our strange attire *W.F.* 406
And as she turns, the c—s fall or rise *D.* iv. 540
Like friendly *c.* found them both unite *E.* iii. 15
Blooms in thy *c.* for a thousand years *E.* iii. 58
Oh lasting as those *c.* may they shine *E.* iii. 63
Its gaudy c—s spreads on ev'ry place *E.C.* 322
When the ripe *c.* soften and unite *E.C.* 488
The treach'rous *c.* the fair art betray *E.C.* 492
And all Opinion's *c.* cast on life *M.E.* i. 22
Come then, the *c.* and the ground prepare *M.E.* ii. 17
For how should equal *C.* do the knack *M.E.* ii. 155
While ev'ry beam new transient *c.* flings (*rep.*) *R.L.* ii. 67
To draw fresh *c.* from the vernal flow'rs *R.L.* ii. 95
Then, from her roofs when Verrio's *c.* fall *W.F.* 307
Colour'd.
Or blend in beauteous tints the *c.* mass *E.* iii. 5
Till Fancy *c.* it, and form'd a dream *S.* viii. 189
Columbus-like.
Who bid the stork, *C.*, explore *E.M.* iii. 105
Column.
Where London's *c.*, pointing at the skies *M.E.* iii. 339
To rear the *C.*, or the Arch to bend *M.E.* iv. 48
The faithless *C.*, and the crumbling Bust *M.E.* v. 20
Not to the skies in useless *C—s* tost *M.E.* iii. 255
Round broken *c.* clasping ivy twin'd *W.F.* 69
Comb.
The bodkin, *c.*, and essence to prepare *R.L.* iv. 98
Transform'd to c—s, the speckled and the white *R.L.* i. 136
Combat.
Were but a *C.* in the lists left out (*rep.*) *E.C.* 278
And swift as lightning to the *c.* flies *R.L.* v. 38
The growing *c.*, or assist the fray *R.L.* v. 56
Draw forth to *c.* on the velvet plain *R.L.* iii. 44
Combats.
Who *c.* bravely is not therefore brave *M.E.* i. 115
Combin'd.
While pleasure, gratitude, and hope, *c. E.M.* iii. 145
And his refulgent Queen with pow'rs *c. R.L.* iii. 77
Combining.
C. all below and all above *E.M.* iii. 8
Come.
C., Delia, *c.*; ah, why this long delay *A.* 48
Lift up your Gates, ye Princes I see him *c. D.* i. 301
C., if you'll be a quiet soul *E.* vi. 29
C. with thy looks, thy words, relieve my woe *E.A.* 119
C. thou, my father, brother, husband, friend *E.A.* 152
Oh *c.!* oh teach me nature to subdue *E.A.* 203
C., Abelard! for what hast thou to dread *E.A.* 257
C., if thou dar'st, all charming as thou art *E.A.* 283
C., with one glance of those deluding eyes *E.A.* 283
Ah, *c.* not, write not, think not once of me *E.A.* 291
C., sister, *c. !* (it said, or seem'd to say) (*rep.*) *E.A.* 309
I *c.*, I *c. l* prepare your roseate bow'rs *E.A.* 317
Here in crowds, and stare the strumpet down *E.Y.S.* 50
Rests and expatiates in a life to *c. E.M.* i. 98
Which serv'd the past, and must the times to *c. E.M.* ii.
52
Ah l how unlike the man of times to *c. E.M.* iii. 161
C. then, my Friend ! my Genius ! *c.* along *E.M.* iv. 373
And never laugh for all my life to *c. E.S.* i. 28
C., *c.*, at all I laugh, he laughs, no doubt *E.S.* i. 35
C. harmless Characters, that no one hit (*rep.*) *E.S.* i. 63
O *c.*, that easy Ciceronian style *E.S.* i. 73
C. on thee, Satire ! gen'ral, unconfin'd *E.S.* ii. 14
If merely to *c.* in, Sir, they go out *E.S.* ii. 124
Is that too little ? *C.* then, I'll comply *E.S.* ii. 128
I must by all means *c.* to town *I.H.* ii. 33 s
Let my Lord know you're *c.* to town *I.H.* ii. 44 s
C. with petitions fairly penn'd *I.H.* 65 s
For God's sake, *c.*, and live with Men *I.H.* ii. 176
Away they *c.*, thro' thick and thin *I.H.* ii. 183
Or *c.* discolour'd thro' our Passions shown *M.E.* i. 34
C. then, the colours, and the ground prepare *M.E.* ii. 17
Soft and Agreeable *c.* never there *M.E.* iv. 102
And wake to Raptures in a Life to *c. Mi.* v. 20

COMEDY—COMMON. 53

The *Basset Table* spread, the *Tallier* c. *Mi.* ix. 1
Sister Spirit, c. away *O.* v. 8
Did some more sober Critic c. abroad *P.S.* 157
(Cries prating Balbus) "something will c. out *P.S.* 276
And swells her breast with conquests yet to c. *R.L.* iii. 28
I c. to Counsel learned in the Law *S.* i. 8
More pleas'd to keep it till their friends could c. *S.* ii. 95
Full many a Beast goes in, but none c. out *S.* iii. 117
The Life to c., in ev'ry Poet's Creed *S.* v. 74
The season, when to c., and when to go *S.* v. 360
Wisdom (curse on it) will c. soon or late *S.* vi. 199
Swears ev'ry place entail'd for years to c. *S.* viii. 160
Pay their last duty to the Court, and c. *S.* viii. 214
In time to c. may pass for holy writ *S.* viii. 287
C., lovely nymph, and bless the silent hours *Sw.* 63
The World's great Oracle in times to c. *W.F.* 382
The time shall c., when, free as seas or wind *W.F.* 397

Comedy.

How Tragedy and C. embrace *D.* i. 69
A long, exact, and serious C. *E.* iv. 22
The humbler Muse of C. requires *S.* v. 283

Comes.

She c., my Delia c.! Now cease my lay *A.* 53
To stir, to rouse, to shake the soul he c. *D.* iv. 67
She c.! she c.! the sable Throne behold *D.* iv. 629
Or with his hound c. hollowing from the stable *E.* v. 27
All c. united to th' admiring eyes *E.C.* 250
True ease in writing c. from art, not chance *E.C.* 362
But honest Instinct c. a volunteer *E.M.* iii. 88
Plays round the head, but c. not to the heart *E.M.* iv. 254
And when it c., the Court see nothing in't *E.S.* i. 2
Vice with such Giant strides c. on amain *E.S.* ii. 6
'Tis true; but Winter c. apace *J.H.* i. 16
And not to ev'ry one that c. *J.H.* i. 23
To-morrow my appeal c. on *J.H.* ii. 71
The Cat c. bouncing on the floor *J.H.* iii. 213
The Saviour c.! by ancient bards foretold *M.* 37
And what c. then is master of the field *M.E.* i. 44
To town he c., completes the nation's hope *M.E.* iii. 213
Lo! COBHAM c., and floats them with a Lake *M.E.* iv. 73
Thence c. your mutton, and these chicks my own *S.* ii. 144
None c. too early, none departs too late *S.* ii. 158
A Frenchman c., presents you with his Boy *S.* vi. 3
Before the Lords at twelve my Cause c. *S.* vi. 96
C. titt'ring on, and shoves you from the stage *S.* vi. 325

Comet.

Could he whose rules the rapid C. bind *E.M.* ii. 35
C—s are regular, and Wharton plain *M.E.* i. 209

Comfort.

See some strange c. ev'ry state attend *E.M.* ii. 271
See! and confess, one c. still must rise *E.M.* ii. 293
And see, what c. it affords our end *M.E.* iii. 298
Say for my c., languishing in bed *P.S.* 121
And feel some c. not to be a fool *S.* iii. 48
Above life's weakness, and its c—s too E.M. iv. 268
And charitably c. Knave and Fool *E.S.* i. 62

Coming.

How c. to the Poet ev'ry Muse *S.* ii. 84
Welcome the c., speed the going guest *S.* ii. 160

Commas.

C. and points they set exactly right *P.S.* 161

Command.

How Time himself stands still at her c. *D.* i. 71
Her poniard, had oppos'd the dire c. *E.A.* 102
Where a new world leaps out at his c. *E.C.* 486
Still fit for use, and ready at c. *E.C.* 674
Or dubb'd Historians, by express c. *S.* v. 372
All my c—s are easy, short, and full D. iv. 581
Such happy arts attention can c. *D.* ii. 29
Tyrant Supreme! shall three estates c. *D.* iv. 603
Each might his sev'ral province well c. *E.C.* 66
Taught to c. the fire, control the flood *E.M.* iii. 220
No Pow'r the Muse's Friendship can c. *E.S.* ii. 118
Back to his bounds their subject Sea c. *M.E.* iv. 201
C. old words that have long slept, to wake *S.* vi. 167

Commanded.

And realms c. which those trees adorn *W.F.* 32

Commander.

"Prodigious well;" his great C. cry'd *S.* vi 42

Commanding.

C. tears to stream thro' ev'ry age *P.C.* 6

Commandment.

In what C.'s large contents they dwell *S.* vii. 44

Commands.

Ascend this hill, whose cloudy point c. *D.* iii. 67
Jests like a licens'd fool, c. like law *S.* viii. 271
GRANVILLE c.; your aid, O Muses, bring *W.F.* 5

Commence.

Now at his head the dext'rous task c. *D.* ii. 199
But soon, ah soon, Rebellion will c. *D.* iv. 63
To ask, to guess, to know, as they c. *D.* iv. 155
Ah let not Learning too c. its foe *E.C.* 509

Commend.

Something to blame, and something to c. *E.* iii. 22
His praise is lost, who stays till all c. *E.C.* 475
But still the worst with most regret c. *E.C.* 518
Who justly knew to blame or to c. *E.C.* 730
Or grant the Bard whose distich all c. *E.S.* ii. 160
If I approve, "C. it to the Stage" *P.S.* 58
Alike reserv'd to blame, or to c. *P.S.* 205
The World beside may murmur or c. *S.* i. 122

Commended.

Then why so few c.? Not so fierce *E.S.* ii. 104

Commends.

And thou shalt live, for Buckingham c. *Mi.* i. 2
Now he begs Verse, and what he gets c. *Mi.* iii. 13

Comment.

And let your c. be the Mantuan Muse *E.C.* 129
And Pope's, ten years to c. and translate *D.* iii. 332

Commentator.

No C. can more silly pass *S.* vii. 101

Commerce.

What War could ravish, C. could bestow *E.M.* iii. 205

Commission.

First, for his Son a gay C. buys *M.E.* iii. 389
There (thank my stars) my whole C. ends *P.S.* 59
I hop'd for no c. from his Grace *S.* viii. 11

Commissioner.

That shines a Consul, this C. *D.* iii. 184

Commit.

T' avoid great errors, must the less c. *E.C.* 260
To him c. the hour, the day, the year *S.* iv. 9

Committee.

The Vapour mild o'er each C. crept *D.* iv. 615

Committing.

To me c. their eternal praise *D.* iii. 280

Commodious.

What Nature wants, c. Gold bestows *M.E.* iii. 21

Common.

And once betray'd me into c. sense *D.* i. 188
Great Queen, and c. Mother of us all *D.* iv. 404
The c. Soul, of Heav'n's more frugal make *D.* iv. 441
By c. sense to c. knowledge bred *D.* iv. 467
The crime was c., c. be the pain *E.A.* 104
In search of wit where lose their c. sense *E.C.* 28
May boldly deviate from the c. track *E.C.* 151
Which out of c. order rise *E.C.* 157
The c. int'rest, or endear the tie *E.M.* ii. 154
And Pride bestow'd on all a c. friend *E.M.* ii. 278
Thus beast and bird their c. charge attend *E.M.* iii. 125
How those in c. all their wealth bestow *E.M.* iii. 185
Till c. int'rest plac'd the sway in one *E.M.* iii. 210
Equal is C. Sense, and C. Ease *E.M.* iv. 34
That such are happier, shocks all c. sense *E.M.* iv. 52
One c. blessing, as one c. soul *E.M.* iv. 62
'Tis Education forms the c. mind *M.E.* i. 149
With too much Thinking to have c. Thought *M.E.* ii. 98
A c. Soldier, but who clubb'd his Mite *Mi.* ii. 8
A Lover lost is but a c. case *Mi.* ix. 17

COMMONS—CONCEAL'D.

No *c.* object to your sight displays *P.C.* 19
No *c.* weapons in your hands are found *R.L.* v. 43
You think this madness but a *c.* case *S.* iii. 172
Good *c.* linguists, and so Panurge was *S.* viii. 75
That altar crowns: *a folio C.*-place *D.* i. 159

Commons.
Aw'd by his Nobles, by his *C.* curst *W.F.* 73

Commonweal.
O'er head and ears plunge for the *C. D.* i. 210

Companion.
A safe *C.* and an easy Friend *Ep.* xi. 7
A safe *C.*, and a free *I.H.* i. 40
There, my retreat the best *C—s grace S.* i. 125

Company.
His faithful dog shall bear him *C. E.M.* i. 112
Alone, in *c.*; in place, or out *M.E.* i. 72
I nod in *c.*, I wake at night *S.* i. 13

Compare.
Each heav'nly piece unwearied we *c. E.* iii. 35
Is that the grief which you *c.* with mine *Mi.* ix. 13
Thus (if small things we may with great *c.*) *W.F.* 105

Compar'd.
Still with itself *c.*, his text peruse *E.C.* 128
C., half-reas'ning elephant, with thine *E.M.* i. 222
C., and knew their gen'rous End the same *E.S.* ii. 81
C. to this, a Minister's an Ass *S.* iii. 96

Compares.
But who the Bowl, or rattling Dice *c. Mi.* ix. 101

Comparing.
Reason's *c.* balance rules the whole *E.M.* ii. 60
Sedate and quiet the *c.* lies *E.M.* ii. 69
See then the acting and *c.* pow'rs *E.M.* iii. 95

Compass.
Since none can *c.* more than they intend *E.C.* 256
Gold, imp'd by thee, can *c.* hardest things *M.E.* iii. 41
To *c.* this, his building is a Town *M.E.* iv. 105
Till, like the Sea, they *c.* all the land *S.* vii. 85

Compassion.
Which meets contempt, or which *c.* first *E.M.* iv. 88
The flocks around a dumb *c.* show *Su.* 6

Compel.
Say what strange motive, Goddess, could *c. R.L.* i. 7

Compell'd.
Let it be seldom, and *c.* by need *E.C.* 165

Compelling.
If QUEENSBURY to strip there's no *c. M.E.* ii. 193

Compensated.
Each seeming want *c.* of course *E.M.* i. 181

Competence.
Lie in three words, Health, Peace, and *C. E.M.* iv. 80
Just what you gave me, *C. I.H.* ii. 245

Complacence.
With mean *c.* ne'er betray your trust *E.C.* 580

Complain.
Of perjur'd Doris, dying I *c. A.* 58
We just as wisely might of Heav'n *c. E.M.* iv. 117
Let the warbling lute *c. O.* i. 6
Could you *c.*, my Friend, he prov'd so bad *S.* vi. 22

Complaining.
Now leave *c.*, and begin your Tea *Mi.* ix. 112

Complains.
Whence hapless Monsieur much *c.* at Paris *D.* ii. 135
How all things listen, while thy Muse *c. W.* 77

Complaint.
No friend's *c.*, no kind domestic tear *U.L.* 49
The bleating sheep with my *c—s* agree *Su.* 19

Complaisance.
But Fop shews Fop superior *c. D.* iv. 138
In *c.*, I took the *Queen* he gave *Mi.* ix. 49

Complaisant.
Scarce to wise Peter *c.* enough *S.* i. 3

Complaisantly.
And *c.* help'd to all I hate *M.E.* iv. 164

Complete.
There, stamp'd with arms, Newcastle shines *c. D.* i. 142
See the false scale of Happiness *c. E.M.* iv. 288
Behold Villario's ten years' toil *c. M.E.* iv. 79
To books and study gives seven years *c. S.* vi. 117
And to *c.* her bliss, a Fool for Mate *E.* iv. 52
The Champion too ! and to *c.* the jest *S.* v. 318

Completely.
Whose Heads she partly, whose *c.* blest *D.* iv. 622
The blest to-day is as *c.* so *E.M.* i. 75

Completes.
A twisted Birth-day Ode *c.* the spire *D.* i. 162
With Fool of Quality *c.* the quire *D.* i. 298
To town he comes, *c.* the nation's hope *M.E.* iii. 213

Complexion.
The same adust *c.* has impell'd *M.E.* i. 107
Or change *c—s* at a losing game *R.L.* iv. 70

Compliment.
Thus Fools with *c—s* besiege ye *I.H.* i. 29
There all alone, and *c.* apart *S.* vi. 210
Whose tongue will *c.* you to the devil *S.* viii. 57

Comply.
But with th' occasion and the place *c. E.C.* 177
Is that too little ? Come then, I'll *c. E.S.* ii. 128

Compose.
Soft creeping, words on words, the sense *c. D.* ii. 389
See worlds on worlds *c.* one universe *E.M.* i. 24
And let me in these shades *c. I.H.* ii. 25
What more than marble must that heart *c. Mi.* ix. 87
Enrage, *c.*, with more than magic Art *S.* v. 344

Compos'd.
C. he stood, bold Benson thrust him by *D.* iv. 110
Desires *c.*, affections ever ev'n *E.A.* 213
So unaffected, so *c.* a mind *Ep.* vi. 7
C. in suff'rings, and in joy sedate *Ep.* vii. 3
By foreign hands thy decent limbs *c. U.L.* 52

Composes.
But what *c.* Man, can Man destroy *E.M.* ii. 114

Composing.
C. songs, for Fools to get by heart *S.* vi. 126

Compound.
Subject, *c.* them, follow her and God *E.M.* ii. 116
Suppose he wants a year, will you *c. S.* v. 57

Comprehend.
Then shall Man's pride and dulness *c. E.M.* i. 65
T' inspect a mite, not *c.* the heav'n *E.M.* i. 196

Comprehensive.
His *c.* head ! all Int'rests weigh'd *M.E.* i. 83

Compris'd.
In whom all beauties are *c.* in one *Su.* 58

Compute.
C. the morn and ev'ning to the day *E.M.* iv. 306

Concanen.
Cook shall be Prior, and *C.* Swift *D.* ii. 138
True to the bottom see *C.* creep *D.* ii. 299

Conceal.
C., disdain,—do all things but forget *E.A.* 200
C. his force, nay sometimes seem to fly *E.C.* 178

Conceal'd.
One Cell there is, *c.* from mortal eye *D.* i. 33
She mounts the throne: her head a cloud *c. D.* iv. 17
The hour *c.*, and so remote the fear *E.M.* iii. 75
Riches, like insects, when *c.* they lie *M.E.* iii. 169
Some secret truths, from learned pride *c. E.* i. 37
The rest his many-colour'd robe *c. R.L.* iii. 58
There kept my charms *c.* from mortal eye *R.L.* iv. 157

Conceals.
None see what Parts of Nature it *c. M.E.* ii. 190
Surprises, varies, and *c.* the Bounds *M.E.* iv. 56

Conceit.
Some to *C.* alone their taste confine *E.C.* 289
A vile *c.* in pompous words express'd *E.C.* 320

Conceive.
Such as the souls of cowards might *c. E.M.* iii. 259
All states can reach it, and all heads *c. E.M.* iv. 30
Who ask and reason thus, will scarce *c. E.M.* iv. 163
A Virgin shall *c.*, a Virgin bear a Son *M.* 8

Conceiv'd.
The caitiff Vaticide *c.* a pray'r *D.* ii. 78

Concern.
But all Mankind's *c.* is Charity *E.M.* iii. 308
But something much more our *c. I.H.* ii. 145
Well, if the use be mine, can it c. one S. ii. 165

Concert.
There Youths and Nymphs in *c.* gay *I.H.* iii. 29

Conclude.
Thus the soft gifts of Sleep *c.* the day *D.* ii. 419
They reason and *c.* by precedent *E.C.* 410
Would from th' apparent What *c.* the Why *M.E.* i. 100

Concludes.
And the rich feast *c.* extremely poor *S.* ii. 34

Concluding.
C. all were desp'rate sots and fools *E.C.* 271

Conclusion.
And Major, Minor, and *C.* quick *D.* ii. 242

Concur.
Extremes in Man *c.* to gen'ral use *M.E.* iii. 162

Condemn'd.
C. whole years of absence to deplore *E.A.* 361
C. in bus'ness or in arts to drudge *E.M.* iv. 263
The Thief *c.*, in law already dead *S.* vii. 15

Condescend.
Above a Patron, tho' I *c. P.S.* 265

Condition.
C., circumstance, is not the thing *E.M.* iv. 57
Honour and shame from no *c.* rise *E.M.* iv. 193
Thus Worms suit all c—s Mi. iv. 22

Conduce.
Which most *c.* to soothe the soul in slumbers *D.* ii. 369

Conduct.
And if the means be just, the *c.* true *E.C.* 257
One action, *C.*; one, heroic Love *M.E.* i. 131
To her Calista prov'd her *c.* nice *M.E.* ii. 31
And the nice *c.* of a clouded cane *R.L.* iv. 124

Conferr'd.
Tho' my own Aldermen *c.* the bays *D.* iii. 279
And bark at Honour not *c.* by Kings *E.S.* ii. 243

Confers.
The Queen *c.* her *Titles* and *Degrees D.* iv. 556

Confess.
He ceas'd, and spread the robe; the crowd *c. D.* ii. 353
Roll in her Vortex, and her pow'r *c. D.* iv. 84
Shrink, and *c.* the genius of the place *D.* iv. 146
And heard thy everlasting yawn *c. D.* iv. 343
See! and *c.*, one comfort still must rise *E.M.* ii. 293
Some swell'd to Gods, *c.* ev'n Virtue vain *E.M.* iv. 24
Heav'n to Mankind impartial we *c. E.M.* iv. 53
Her Birth, her Beauty, Crowds and Courts *c. E.S.* i. 145
When I *c.*, there is who feels for Fame *E.S.* ii. 64
That each from other differs, first *c. M.E.* i. 19
Once, we *c.*, beneath the Patriot's cloak *M.E.* iii. 35
This dreaded Sat'rist *Dennis* will *c. P.S.* 370
C. as well your Folly, as Disease *S.* vi. 215
So vast, our new Divines, we must *c. S.* vii. 97
Survey the region, and *c.* her home *W.F.* 256

Confess'd, Confest.
Well pleas'd he enter'd, and *c.* his home *D.* i. 266
Fair as before her works she stands *c. D.* ii. 159
C. within the slave of love and man *E.A.* 178
Thy life more wretched, Cutler, was *c. M.E.* iii. 321
Virtue *c.* in human shape he draws *P.C.* 17
To Proculus alone *c.* in view *R.L.* v. 126
Of Systems possible if 'tis *c—t E.M.* i. 43
ORDER is Heav'n's first law, and this *c. E.M.* iv. 49
The prospect clears, and Wharton stands *c. M.E.* i. 179
Just in one instance, be it yet *c. S.* v. 31

Confesses.
My panting heart *c.* all his charms *Mi.* ix. 95
Their fruits to you, *c.* you its lord *S.* vi. 233

Confession.
Adjust their clothes, and to *c.* draw *S.* viii. 242

Confessor.
Act sins which Prisca's *C.* scarce hears *S.* vii. 40
Display'd the fates her c—s endure D. ii. 146
I pass o'er all those *C.* and Martyrs *S.* vii. 35

Confidence.
One on his manly *c.* relies *D.* ii. 169

Confine.
C. the thought, to exercise the breath *D.* iv. 159
And rules as strict his labour'd work *c. E.C.* 137
Some to *Conceit* alone their taste *c. E.C.* 289
Meanly they seek the blessing to *c. E.C.* 398
To Vice and Folly to *c.* the jest *E.S.* i. 57
Now scantier limits the proud Arch *c. M.E.* v. 27

Confin'd.
Did on the stage my Fops appear *c. D.* i. 191
Too much your Sex is by their Forms *c. E.* iv. 31
But oft in those *c.* to single parts *E.C.* 63
The soul, uneasy and *c.* from home *E.M.* i. 97
These mix'd with art, and to due bounds *c. E.M.* ii. 119
The blessed benefit, not there *c. E.S.* ii. 177
Yes, you despise the man to Books *c. M.E.* i. 1
And to her Maker's praise *c.* the sound *O.* i. 125
To rules of Poetry no more *c. S.* vi. 202
And close *c.* to their own palace, sleep *U.L.* 22
Who all my Sense *c. U.P.* 6

Confirm'd.
Divides a friendship long *c.* by age *D.* iii. 174

Confirms.
This nod *c.* each privilege your own *D.* iv. 584

Conflagration.
Till one wide *c.* swallows all *D.* iii. 240

Conflict.
Dire is the *c.*, dismal is the din *D.* iii. 269

Confound.
Or puzzling Contraries *c.* the whole *M.E.* i. 65
What could they more, than Knights and Squires *c. M.E.* iii. 53
Steel could the works of mortal pride *c. R.L.* iii. 175
I plant, root up; I build, and then *c.*; *S.* iii. 169
Or shall we ev'ry Decency *c. S.* iv. 118
Mistake, *c.*, object at all he spoke *S.* viii. 117

Confounded.
Despairing, *c. O.* i. 107
To stop my ears to their *c.* stuff *S.* vi. 152

Confounds.
One god-like Monarch all that pride *c. D.* iii. 75
He gains all points, who pleasingly *c. M.E.* iv. 55
His Wealth brave Timon gloriously *c. S.* iv. 85
C. the civil, keeps the rude in awe *S.* viii. 270

Confus'd.
Chaos of Thought and Passion, all *c. E.M.* ii. 13
Amaz'd, *c.*, he found his pow'r expir'd *R.L.* iii. 145
But, as the world, harmoniously *c. W.F.* 14

Confus'dly.
Heroes' and Heroines' shouts *c.* rise *R.L.* v. 41

Confusion.
The least *c.* but in one, not all *E.M.* i. 249
And Anarchy without *c.* know *E.M.* iii. 186
In bright *C.* open *Rouleaux* lie *Mi.* ix. 81
With like *c.* different nations fly *R.L.* iii. 83

Confuted.
And none had sense enough to be *c. E.C.* 443

Congenial.
C. matter in the cockle-kind *D.* iv. 448
And met *c.*, mingling flame with flame *E.* iii. 14
C. souls! whose life one Av'rice joins *M.E.* iii. 131
With equal talents, their *c.* souls *S.* vi. 129
So flew the soul to its *c.* place *U.L.* 27

Congregated.
This Vault of Air, this *c.* Ball *S.* iv. 5

Congreve.
She deck'd like *C.*, Addison, and Prior *D.* ii. 124
And *C.* lov'd, and Swift endur'd my lays *P.S.* 138
Tell me if C.'s Fools are Fools indeed S. v. 287

Conglob'd.
Not closer, orb in orb, *c.* are seen *D.* iv. 79

Coningsby.
The House impeach him, *C.* harangues *M.E.* iii. 397

Connects.
He fills, he bounds, *c.*, and equals all *E.M.* i. 280
C. each being, greatest with the least *E.M.* iii. 23
Wise is her present; she *c.* in this *E.M.* iv. 349

Connexions.
The strong *c.*, nice dependencies *E.M.* i. 30

Connivance.
Nay hints, 'tis by *c.* of the Court *S.* viii. 164

Conquer.
But grant that those can *c.*, these can cheat *E.M.* iv. 229
In Youth they *c.*, with so wild a rage *M.E.* ii. 221
Advance and *c.* I go where glory calls *S.* vi. 47

Conquer'd.
Who *c.* Nature, should preside o'er Wit *E.C.* 652
Almost as quickly as he *c.* Spain *S.* i. 132
Finds Envy never *c.* but by Death *S.* v. 16
We *c.* France, but felt our Captive's charms *S.* v. 263

Conqu'ring.
His *c.* tribes th' Arabian prophet draws *D.* iii. 97
The *c.* force of unresisted steel *R.L.* iii. 178
The Forms august, of King or *c.* Chief *S.* v. 391

Conqu'ror.
Justice a *C.'s* sword, or Truth a gown *E.M.* iv. 171
And Gods of *C—s, Slaves of Subjects made E.M.* iii. 248

Conquers.
The ruling Passion *c.* Reason still *M.E.* iii. 154
Time *c.* all, and we must Time obey *W.* 88

Conquest.
Heav'n scarce believ'd the *C.* it survey'd *E.A.* 113
Proud of an easy *c.* all along *E.M.* ii. 157
Force first made *C.*, and that *c.*, Law *E.M.* iii. 245
A narrow orb each crowded *c.* keeps *M.E.* v. 25
A *c.* how hard and how glorious *O.* i. 89
Of broken troops an easy *c.* finds *R.L.* iii. 78
And give the *c.* to thy Sylvia's eyes *Sp.* 88
Till *C.* cease, and Slav'ry be no more *W.F.* 408
Still makes new c—s, and maintains the past E. iv. 62
Like kings we lose the *c.* gain'd before *E.C.* 64
No *C.* she, but o'er herself, desir'd *Ep.* vi. 3
Shall stretch thy *c.* over half the kind *I.H.* iii. 16
And swells her breast with *c.* yet to come *R.L.* iii. 28

Conscience.
Then *c.* sleeps, and leaving nature free *E.A.* 227
Whose life is healthful, and whose *c.* clear *E.M.* iv. 191
Now *C.* chills her, and now Passion burns *M.E.* ii. 65
Their *C.* is a Worm within *Mi.* iv. 27
And the gay *C.* of a life well spent *Mi.* v. 13
What *C.* dictates to be done *U.P.* 13

Conscious.
The *c.* simper, and the jealous leer *D.* ii. 6
And nobly *c.*, Princes are but things *D.* iv. 601
C. they act a true Palladian part *M.E.* iv. 37
Oh when shall Britain, *c.* of her claim *M.E.* v. 53
To make mankind in *c.* virtue bold *P.C.* 3
Some nymphs there are, too *c.* of their face *R.L.* i. 79
Trembling, and *c.* of the rich brocade *R.L.* iii. 16
True, *c.* Honour is to feel no sin *S.* iii. 93
And secret transport touch'd the *c.* swain *W.F.* 90

Consecrate.
This Lock, the Muse shall *c.* to fame *R.L.* v. 149

Consecrated.
I seem thro' *c.* walks to rove *W.F.* 267

Consent.
The Goddess smiling seem'd to give *c. D.* iv. 395
From Order, Union, full *C.* of things *E.M.* iii. 296

Consented.
He sung, and hell *c. O.* i. 83
And Jove *c.* in a silent show'r *Su.* 8

Consenting.
Hear, in all tongues *c.* Pæans ring *E.C.* 186
Sheffield approves, *c.* Phœbus bends *Mi.* i. 7

Consequence.
Reason, the future and the *c. E.M.* ii. 74

Consider.
But first *c.* how those Just agree *E.M.* iv. 134
The matter's weighty, pray *c.* twice *E.S.* ii. 43
You ne'er *c.* whom you shove *I.H.* ii. 58 s
C., 'tis my first request *I.H.* ii. 77 s
C., Mice, like Men, must die *I.H.* ii. 177
C. then, and judge me in this light *S.* vi. 27

Consider'd.
C. singly, or beheld too near *E.C.* 172
And that they ne'er *c.* yet *I.H.* ii. 42 s

Consid'ring.
C. what a gracious Prince was next *E.S.* i. 108

Consign.
The drops to thee, Brillante, we *c. R.L.* ii. 113

Consist.
If in the Pomp of Life *c.* the joy *S.* iv. 98

Consistent.
So two *c.* motions act the soul *E.M.* iii. 315
The Fool *c.*, and the False sincere *M.E.* i. 176
C. in our follies and our sins *M.E.* i. 226
To act *c.* with himself an hour *S.* iii. 137

Consists.
But Health *c.* with Temperance alone *E.M.* iv. 81

Console.
And empty heads *c.* with empty sound *D.* iv. 542

Consort.
Th' imperial *c.* of the crown of Spades *R.L.* iii. 68

Conspicuous.
C. scene! another yet is nigh *S.* iv. 50

Conspire.
Grubstreet! thy fall should men and Gods *c. D.* iii. 311
Read their instructive leaves, in which *c. E.* iii. 7
The kindred Arts shall in their praise *c. E.* iii. 69
Of all the Causes which *c.* to blind *E.C.* 201
In the bright Muse tho' thousand charms *c. E.C.* 339
Tho' wit and art *c.* to move your mind *E.C.* 531
Barbarian blindness, Christian zeal *c.*, *M.E.* v. 13

Conspir'd.
In equal curls, and well *c.* to deck *R.L.* ii. 21
Shall One whom Nature, Learning, Birth, *c. S.* iv. 40
Had ancient times *c.* to disallow *S.* v. 135

Conspires.
When all the World *c.* to praise her *Mi.* viii. 11

Constant.

A *c.* Critic at the great man's board *E.C.* 416
As much that end a *c.* course requires *E.M.* i. 151
This drives them *c.* to a certain coast *E.M.* ii. 168
Where only Merit *c.* pay receives *E.M.* iv. 313
Sincere, tho' prudent ; *c.*, yet resign'd *Ep.* ii. 2
The Wild are *c.*, and the Cunning known *M.E.* i. 175
A *c.* Bounty which no friend has made *M.E.* i. 198
C. at Church and Change ; his gains were sure *M.E.* iii. 347
C. faith, fair hope, long leisure *O.* iii. 42
A *c.* Vapour o'er the palace flies *R.L.* iv. 39
Was it for this you took such *c.* care *R.L.* iv. 97

Constitution.

To give me back my *C. I.H.* i. 44

Constrains.

Led by some rule that guides, but not *c. E.* iii. 67
Inclines our action, not *c.* our will *S.* vi. 281

Constraint.

Still in *c.* your suff'ring Sex remains *E.* iv. 41

Constru'd.

And to be dull was *c.* to be good *E.C.* 690

Consul.

That shines a *C.*, this Commissioner *D.* iii. 184

Consult.

C. the Genius of the Place in all *M.E.* iv. 57
C. the Statute : *quart*, I think, it is *S.* i. 147

Consults.

C. the dead, and lives past ages o'er *W.F.* 248

Consuming.

See my weary Days *c. Mi.* vii. 7

Contain.

So vast a throng the stage can ne'er *c. E.C.* 283
Look'd thro'? or can a part *c.* the whole *E.M.* i. 32
Bid the broad Arch the dang'rous Flood *c. M.E.* iv. 199
Or Sloane or Woodward's wond'rous shelves *c. S.* viii. 30
Whom not th' extended Albion could *c. W.F.* 315

Contains.

Relentless walls ! whose darksome round *c. E.A.* 17
In weeping vaults her hallow'd earth *c. W.F.* 302

Contemns.

If there 's a Senior, who *c.* this age *Mi.* ii. 22

Contemplation.

Where heav'nly-pensive *c.* dwells *E.A.* 2
Where *C.* prunes her ruffled wings *S.* viii. 186

Contempt.

Which meets *c.*, or which compassion first *E.M.* iv. 88
Was this their Virtue, or *C.* of Life *E.M.* iv. 102
And most contemptible, to shun *c. M.E.* i. 195

Contemptible.

And most *c.*, to shun contempt *M.E.* i. 195

Contend.

He spoke : and who with Lintot shall *c. D.* ii. 56
And chiefs *c.* till all the prize is lost *R.L.* v. 108
Cease to *c.*, for, Daphnis, I decree *Sp.* 93

Contending.

C. Theatres our Empire raise *D.* iii. 271
C. Princes mount them in their Coach *D.* iv. 564
C. Wits become the sport of fools *E.C.* 517

Contends.

The bard inhabitant *c.* is right *E.M.* ii. 230
And strength of Shade *c.* with strength of Light *M.E.* iv. 82

Content.

The Sense, they humbly take upon *c. E.C.* 308
Good, Pleasure, Ease, *C. !* whate'er thy name *E.M.* iv. 2
God in Externals could not place *C. E.M.* iv. 66
Nor is his claim to plenty, but *c. E.M.* iv. 156
C., or Pleasure, but the Good and Just *E.M.* iv. 186
Let Joy or Ease, let Affluence or *C. Mi.* v. 11
C., *each Emanation of his fires D.* iii. 219
Aim not at Joy, but rest *c.* with Ease *E.* iv. 48
C. if hence th' unlearn'd their wants may view *E.C.* 739

C. with Science in the Vale of Peace *Ep.* x. 6
In short, I'm perfectly *c. I.H.* ii. 29 s
C. to dwell in Decencies for ever *M.E.* ii. 164
C. to breathe his native air *O.* iv 3
Oh hadst thou, cruel ! been *c.* to seize *R.L.* iv. 175
C. with little, I can piddle here *S.* ii. 137
In dirt and darkness, hundreds stink *c. S.* iii. 133
Or, I'm *c.*, allow me Dryden's strains *S.* vi. 145
Why one like Bu—, with pay and scorn *c. S.* vi. 274

Contented.

Crown'd with the Jordan, walks *c.* home *D.* ii. 190
She's still the same belov'd, *c.* thing *E.S.* i. 140

Contention.

Cease your *c.*, which has been too long *Mi.* ix. 107

Contentment.

But now no face divine *c.* wears *E.A.* 147
Those call it Pleasure, and *C.* these *E.M.* iv. 22

Contents.

In what Commandment's large *c.* they dwell *S.* vii. 44
To-Be c. *his natural desire E.M.* i. 109
The poor *c.* him with the care of Heav'n *E.M.* ii. 266
C. us not. A better shall we have *E.M* iv. 132

Contest.

Balk'd are the Courts, and *c.* is no more *M.E.* iii. 272
What mighty c—s *rise from trivial things R.L.* i. 2
For Forms of Government let fools *c. E.M.* iii. 303
And each were equal, must not all *c. E.M.* iv. 64
So heav'n decrees I with heav'n who can *c. R.L.* v. 112

Continual.

Tis all blank sadness, or *c.* tears *E.A.* 148

Continu'd.

Or if your life be one *c.* Treat *S.* iv. 110

Contract.

And each from each *c.* new strength and light *E.* iii. 16

Contracted.

A trifling head, and a *c.* heart *D.* iv. 504
C. all, retiring to their breast *E.M.* ii. 103
Yet not to Earth's *c.* Span *U.P.* 21

Contracting.

Or Alum styptics with *c.* pow'r *R.L.* ii. 131

Contracts.

Shall Ward draw *C.* with a Statesman's skill *E.S.* i. 119
That longer care c. *more lasting bands B.M.* iii. 132
C., inverts, and gives ten thousand dyes *M.E.* i. 36
Convinc'd, she now *c.* her vast design *M.E.* v. 23

Contradiction.

Woman's at best a *C.* still *M.E.* ii. 270

Contraries.

Or puzzling *C.* confound the whole *M.E.* i. 65

Contrary.

Our Critics take a *c.* extreme *E.C.* 661

Contrive.

And did not wicked custom so *c. E.J.S.* 13
Oh blind to truth ! the Sylphs *c.* it all *R.L.* i. 104

Contriving.

C. never to oblige ye *I.H.* i. 30

Control.

Grant that the pow'rful still the weak *c. E.M.* iii. 49
Taught to command the fire, *c.* the flood *E.M.* iii. 220
See Arts her savage sons *c. O.* ii. 21
Know, there are Words, and Spells which can *c. S.* iii. 57

Controls.

A matchless Youth ! his nod these worlds *c. D.* ii. 255

Convent.

Charles to the *C.*, Philip to the Field *M.E.* i. 108
Lost in a c.'s *solitary gloom E.A.* 38
To happy C—s, *bosom'd deep in vines D.* iv. 301

Converse.

Gen'rous *c.* ; a soul exempt from pride *E.C.* 641
C. and Love mankind might strongly draw *E.M.* iii. 207

CONVERS'D—CORRUPTION.

Form'd by thy *c.*, happily to steer *E.M.* iv. 379
And *born to write*, *c.*, *and live with ease P.S.* 196

Convers'd.
Still with esteem no less *c.* than read *E.* iv. 7
She first *c.* with her own Kind *Mi.* iv. 11

Converts.
Few are the *C.* Aretine has made *S.* viii. 95

Convey.
To Delia's ear, the tender notes *c. A.* 18
Did slumb'ring visit, and *c.* to shews *D.* ii. 422
Will, like a friend, familiarly *c. E.C.* 655

Convey'd.
And now on Fancy's easy wing *c. D.* iii. 13
C. unbroken faith from sire to son *E.M.* iii. 228

Conveys.
Rolli the feather to his ear *c. D.* iii. 203
O you! whom Vanity's light bark *c. S.* v. 296

Convict.
C. a Papist he, and I a Poet *S.* vi. 67

Convicted.
C. of that mortal crime, a hole *S.* viii. 245

Convinc'd.
C., amaz'd, he checks the bold design *E.C.* 136
Something, whose truth *c.* at sight we find *E.C.* 299
Receiv'd his laws; and stood *c.* 'twas fit *E.C.* 651
C. that Virtue only is our own *Ep.* vi. 6
C., she now contracts her vast design *M.E.* v. 23

Convocation.
The *C.* gap'd, but could not speak *D.* iv. 610

Convulsions.
Pit, box, and gall'ry in *c.* hurl'd *P.S.* 87

Cook.
C. shall be Prior, and Concanen Swift *D.* ii. 138
Swears, like Albutius, a good *c.* away *S.* ii. 64
Your Barber, *C.*, Upholst'rer, what you please *S.* vi. 10
Not from the Burnets, Oldmixons, and *C*—s *P.S.* 146

Cool.
If modest Youth, with *c.* Reflection crown'd *E.* xiv. 1
A *c.* suspense from pleasure and from pain *E.A.* 250
Reason, however able, *c.* at best *E.M.* iii. 85
In Life's *c.* Ev'ning, satiate of Applause *S.* iii. 9
Where'er you walk, *c.* gales shall fan the shade *Su.* 73
To the *c.* ocean, where his journey ends *Su.* 90

Cooling.
Where'er you find "thus *c.* western breeze" *E.C.* 350
Ye shady beeches, and ye *c.* streams *Su.* 13
Where *c.* vapours breathe along the mead *W.F.* 136

Coolness.
Yet judg'd with *c.*, tho' he sung with fire *E.C.* 659
His kitchen vied in *c.* with his grot *M.E.* iii. 180

Cools.
She who ne'er answers till a Husband *c. M.E.* ii. 261

Cooper's Hill.
Or where ye Muses sport on *C.* (*rep.*) *W.F.* 264

Copies.
Who *c.* Your's or Oxford's better part *M.E.* iii. 243
Who writes a Libel, or who *c.* out *P.S.* 290

Copious.
What cannot *c.* Sacrifice atone *D.* iv. 557
In grave Quintilian's *c.* work we find *E.C.* 669
Ev'n *c.* Dryden wanted or forgot *S.* v. 280

Copper.
Or thy griev'd Country's *c.* chains unbind *D.* i. 24

Copse.
As when a dab-chick waddles thro' the *c. D.* ii. 63

Copy.
A fool, so just a *c.* of a wit *D.* ii. 48
To c. Nature is to c. them E.C. 140
There many an honest man may *c.* Cato *E.J.S.* 43

To *c.* Instinct then was Reason's part *E.M.* iii. 170
Alas! I *c.* (or my draught would fail) *M.E.* ii. 197
His equal mind I *c.* what I can *S.* ii. 131

Coquettes.
The light *C.* in Sylphs aloft repair *R.L.* i. 65
Instruct the eyes of young *C.* to roll *R.L.* i. 88

Coral.
The *c.* redden, and the ruby glow *W.F.* 394

Cord.
Gasps as they straiten at each end the *c. D.* iv. 29

Cordial.
What ev'n deny'd a *c.* at his end *M.E.* iii. 329
The *C.* Drop of Life is Love alone *S.* iv. 126
For fainting Age what *c.* drop remains *S.* ii. 89

Corinna.
Which Curl's *C.* chanc'd that morn to make *D.* ii. 70

Cork.
Nor stops, for one bad *c.*, his butler's pay *S.* ii. 63
And eyes the dancing *c.*, and bending reed *W.F.* 140
And maids turn'd bottles, call aloud for *c*—s *R.L.* iv. 54

Corn.
Flies o'er th' unbending *c.*, and skims along the main *E.C.* 373
And crown'd with *c.* their thanks to Ceres yield *Su.* 66
That crown'd with tufted trees, and springing *c. W.F.* 27
In at a *C.* loft thro' a Chink *I.H.* i. 52

Cornbury
Disdain whatever *C.* disdains *S.* iv. 61

Corneille.
'Twixt Plautus, Fletcher, Shakespear, and *C. D.* i. 285
Exact Racine, and C.'s noble fire S. v. 274

Corner.
In some close *c.* of the soul, they sin *E.J.S.* 18

Cornish.
Then full against his *C.* lands they roar *M.E.* iii. 355

Cornus.
Poor *C.* sees his frantic wife elope *P.S.* 25

Cornwall.
Who rules in *C.*, or who rules in Berks *S.* iv. 104

Coronations.
See *C.* rise on ev'ry green *E.* v. 34

Coronet.
She bears a *C.* and P—x for life *M.E.* iii. 392
Thus vanish sceptres, *c*—*s*, and balls *E.* v. 39
And Garters, Stars, and *C.* appear *R.L.* i. 85

Correct.
C. with spirit, eloquent with ease *E.M.* iv. 381
You grow *c.*, that once with Rapture writ *E.S.* i. 3
C. old Time, and regulate the Sun E.M. ii. 22

Corrected.
Thus finish'd and *c.* to a hair *S.* viii. 248

Correctly.
C. cold, and regularly low *E.C.* 240

Correctness.
Late, very late, *c.* grew our care *S.* v. 272

Correggio.
Caracci's strength, *C.*'s softer line *E.* iii. 37

Corrupt.
Knight of the post *c.*, or of the shire *P.S.* 365
But Times *c.*, and Nature, ill-inclin'd *S.* v. 251

Corrupted.
That NOT TO BE *C.* IS THE SHAME *E.S.* i. 160
They too may be *c.*, you'll allow *E.S.* ii. 126
The trifling head, or the *c.* heart *P.S.* 387
The modern language of *c.* Peers *S.* iii. 99

Corruption.
Amidst *C.*, Luxury, and Rage *Ep.* ix. 9
That lends *C.* lighter wings to fly *M.E.* iii. 40
At length *C.*, like a gen'ral flood *M.E.* iii. 135

Corrupts.
But lures the Pirate, and c. the Friend *M.E.* iii. 30

Corticelli.
At *C.'s* he the Raffle won *Mi.* ix. 39

Cosmetic.
With head uncover'd, the *C.* pow'rs *R.L.* i. 124

Cost.
I curse such lavish c., and little skill *M.E.* iv. 167
How much of other each is sure to c. *E.M.* iv. 271
Or let it c. five hundred pound *I.H.* ii. 39 *s*
Alas! they fear a man will c. a plum *M.E.* iii. 122

Costive.
Or e'er to c. lap-dog gave disease *R.L.* iv. 75

Costs.
'Tis to mistake them, c. the time and pain *E.M.* ii. 216

Cotswood.
Join *C.* hills to Saperton's fair dale *S.* vi. 257

Cotta.
Old *C.* sham'd his fortune and his birth (*rep.*) *M.E.* iii. 177
If *C.* liv'd on pulse, it was no more *M.E.* iii. 183

Cottage.
Nor saw displeas'd the peaceful c. rise *W.F.* 86

Couch'd.
C. close he lies, and meditates the prey *W.F.* 102

Cough.
I c., like Horace, and tho' lean, am short *P.S.* 116

Could, Couldst.—*Passim.*

Council.
And turn the *C.* to a Grammar School *D.* iv. 180
Seldom at c., never in a war *E.C.* 537
What Pope or *C.* can they need beside *E.M.* iii. 84
Who calls the *C.*, states the certain day *E.M.* iii. 107
Or just as gay, at *C.*, in a ring *M.E.* ii. 309
If not so pleas'd, at C.-board rejoice S. iv. 34

Counsel.
Tis not enough, your c. still be true *E.C.* 572
But where 's the man, who c. can bestow *E.C.* 631
This saving c. "Keep your piece nine years" *P.S.* 40
Dost sometimes c. take—and sometimes Tea *R.L.* iii. 8
I come to *C.* learned in the Law *S.* i. 8
What saith my *C.*, learned in the laws *S.* i. 142
E'en take the c. which I gave you first *S.* iv. 131
My c. sends to execute a deed *S.* vi. 92

Counsels.
Who c. best? who whispers "Be but great *S.* iii. 101

Count.
Behold, and c. them, as they rise to light *D.* iii. 130
C. the slow clock, and dine exact at noon *E.* v. 18
C. all th' advantage prosp'rous Vice attains *E.M.* iv. 89
C. me those only who were good and great *E.M.* iv. 210
And c. each birth-day with a grateful mind *S.* vi. 315

Counter-work.
T' invest the world, and c. its Cause *E.M.* iii. 244

Counter-works.
That c. each folly and caprice *E.M.* ii. 239

Countess.
Arcadia's *C.*, here, in ermin'd pride *M.E.* ii. 7
Dear *C.!* you have charms all hearts to hit *S.* viii. 232

Counting-house.
His *C.* employ'd the Sunday-morn *M.E.* iii. 380

Country.
See to my c. happy I restore *D.* iv. 329
Lost is his God, his *C.*, ev'ry thing *D.* iv. 523
Yes, SAVE MY *C.*, HEAV'N—He said and died *E.* xiii. 8
Religion, *C.*, Genius of his Age *E.C.* 121
As sev'ral garbs with c., town, and court *E.C.* 323
And lov'd his c.—but what's that to you *E.J.S.* 40
And which more blest? who chain'd his c., say *E.M.* iv. 147

His *c.* next; and next all human race *E.M.* iv. 368
And offer *C.*, Parent, Wife, or Son *E.S.* i. 158
Or if a Court or *C.*'s made a job *E.S.* ii. 40
Blest Courtier! who could King and *C.* please *Ep.* i. 9
Just to his Prince, and to his *C.* true *Ep.* v. 2
Drags from the town to wholesome *C.* air *Ep.* v. 2
O more than Fortune, Friends, or *C.* lost *Ep.* xiii. 6
The Senate heard him, and his *C.* lov'd *Ep.* xiv. 8
Writ underneath the *C.* signs *I.H.* ii. 92 *s*
Oh, could I see my *C.* Seat *I.H.* ii. 128
A *C.* Mouse, right hospitable *I.H.* ii. 158
"Oh, save my *C.*, Heav'n!" shall be your last *M.E.* i. 265
To buy both sides, and give thy *C.* peace *M.E.* iii. 350
No noon-tide bell invites the *C.* round *M.E.* iii. 190
His thankless *C.* leaves him to her Laws *M.E.* iii. 218
Calls in the *C.*, catches op'ning glades *M.E.* iv. 61
First shade a *C.*, and then raise a Town *M.E.* iv. 190
Now drain'd a distant *C.* of her Floods *M.E.* v. 8
So some coarse *C.* wench, almost decay'd *Mi.* iii. 15
Who dare to love their *C.*, and be poor *Mi.* x. 14
Or to thy c. let that heap be lent *S.* ii. 121
Renounce our *C.*, and degrade our Name *S.* iv. 125
Your *C.*, chief, in Arms abroad defend *S.* v. 3
How could Devotion touch the *C.* pews *S.* v. 233
Soon as I enter at my c. door *S.* vi. 206
Cau gratis see the c., or the town *S.* viii. 145
His Sov'reign favours, and his *C.* loves *W.F.* 236
Or thy griev'd *C.*'s copper chains unbind *D.* i. 24
O let my *C.* friends illumine mine *E.S.* ii. 121
So odd, my *C.* Ruin makes me grave *E.S.* ii. 207
Thy *C.* friend, but more of human-kind *Ep.* i. 2
In lavish streams to quench a *C.* thirst *M.E.* iii. 177
His oxen perish in his c. cause *M.E.* ii. 206
Last, for his *C.* love, he sells his Lands *M.E.* iii. 212
But when our *C.* cause provokes to arms *O.* i. 36
What bosom beats not in his *C.* cause *P.C.* 24
Their *C.* wealth our mightier Misers drain *S.* iii. 126
Where MURRAY (long enough his *C.* pride) *S.* iv. 52
Your *C.* Peace, how oft, how dearly bought *S.* v. 327
Dear Col'nel, Cobham's and your c. Friend *S.* vi. 1

Counts.
That c. your Beauties only by your Stains *E.S.* ii. 221

Couplet.
Then, at the last and only c. fraught *E.C.* 354

Courage.
The man had c., was a sage, 'tis true *E.J.S.* 39
The Wit of Cheats, the *C.* of a Whore *E.S.* i. 165
In whom a Race, for *C.* fam'd and Art *Ep.* xi. 21
C. with Softness, Modesty with Pride *M.E.* ii. 278
A grain of c., or a spark of spirit *S.* vi. 227

Course.
As oil'd with magic juices for the c. *D.* ii. 104
And orient Science their bright c. begun *D.* iii. 74
Shows most true mettle when you check his c. *E.C.* 87
You then whose judgment the right c. would steer *E.C.* 118
Still humming on, their drowsy c. they keep *E.C.* 600
His fiery c., or drives him o'er the plains *E.M.* i. 62
As much that end a constant c. requires *E.M.* i. 157
Each seeming want compensated of c. *E.M.* i. 181
Steer'd the same c. to the same quiet shore *Ep.* vii. 13
Bids seed-time, harvest, equal c. maintain *M.E.* iii. 165
So quick retires each flying c., you'd swear *M.E.* iv. 159
Some guide the c. of wand'ring orbs on high *R.L.* ii. 79
With what a shifting gale your c. you ply *S.* v. 298
Now marks the c. of rolling orbs on high *W.F.* 245

Courser.
The winged c., like a gen'rous horse *E.C.* 86
Th' impatient c. pants in ev'ry vein *W.F.* 151
Fair *C*—s, *Vases, and alluring Dames M.E.* iii. 70
Hang o'er their c—s' *heads with eager speed W.F.* 157

Court.
Or praise the *C.*, or magnify Mankind *D.* i. 23
Folly, my Son, has still a Friend at *C. D.* i. 300
Till rais'd from booths, to Theatre, to *C. D.* iii. 299
Saw ev'ry *C.*, heard ev'ry King declare *D.* iv. 313
Unseen at Church, at Senate, or at *C. D.* iv. 338
Who study Shakespear at the Inns of *C. D.* iv. 568

As sev'ral garbs with country, town, and c. *E.C.* 323
And when it comes, the *C.* see nothing in't *E.S.* i. 2
Could please at *C.*, and make AUGUSTUS smile *E.S.* i. 20
Lull'd with the sweet Nepenthe of a *C. E.S.* i. 98
Ye Tradesmen vile, in Army, *C.*, or Hall *E.S.* ii. 17
Or if a *C.* or Country's made a job *E.S.* ii. 40
But does the *C.* a worthy Man remove *E.S.* ii. 74
Ye tinsel Insects ! whom a *C.* maintains *E.S.* ii. 220
Have kept it—as you do at *C. I.H.* i. 4
And a thin *C.* that wants your Face *I.H.* i. 12
Of some Express arriv'd at *C. I.H.* ii. 110 s
Cares that haunt the *C.* and Town *I.H.* ii. 132
This doctrine, Friend, I learnt at *C. I.H.* ii. 160
His *c.* with nettles, moats with cresses stor'd *M.E.* iii. 181
In vain at *C.* the Bankrupt pleads his cause *M.E.* iii. 217
He marries, bows at *C.*, and grows polite *M.E.* iii. 386
The *C.* forsake him, and Sir Balaam hangs *M.E.* iii. 398
There are, who to my person pay their *c. P.S.* 115
Sporus at *c.*, or *Japhet* in a jail *P.S.* 362
Let the two *Curlls* of Town and *C. P.S.* 380
To taste awhile the pleasures of a *C. R.L.* ii. 10
Whate'er my fate,—or well or ill at *C. S.* i. 92
I'd never doubt at *C.* to make a friend *S.* ii. 44
This new *C.* jargon, or the good old song *S.* iii. 98
Send her to *C.*, you send her to her grave *S.* iii. 119
At *c.*, who hates whate'er he read at school *S.* v. 106
The willing Muses were debauch'd at *C. S.* v. 152
Has seiz'd the *C.* and City, poor and rich *S.* v. 170
To please a lewd or unbelieving *C. S.* v. 212
The Rights a *C.* attack'd, a Poet sav'd *S.* v. 224
Or when from *C.* a birth-day suit bestow'd *S.* v. 332
Be call'd to *C.* to plan some work divine *S.* v. 374
And here, while town, and *c.*, and city roars *S.* vi. 123
Nay tho' at *C.* (perhaps) it may find grace *S.* vi. 162
Bows and votes 00, in *C.* and Parliament *S.* vi. 275
Let no *C.* Sycophant pervert my sense *S.* vii. 126
Yet went to *C. I* the Dev'l would have it so *S.* viii. 14
Who live at *C.*, for going once that way *S.* viii. 23
And tho' the *C.* show Vice exceeding clear *S.* viii. 96
Nay hints, 'tis by connivance of the *C. S.* viii. 164
All the *C.* fill'd with stranger things but *S.* viii. 181
And forc'd ev'n me to see the damn'd at *C. S.* viii. 191
Than such as swell this bladder of a *c.* (*rep.*) *S.* viii. 205
Pay their last duty to the *C.*, and come *S.* viii. 214
Our *C.* may justly to our stage give rules *S.* viii. 220
To deluge sin, and drown a *C.* in tears *S.* viii. 285
Happy the man whom this bright *c.* approves *W.F.* 235
Fair op'ning to some c.'s propitious shine E.M. iv. 9
And *c*—s to *c*—s *return it round and round D.* ii. 264
Senates and *C.* with Greek and Latin rule *D.* iv. 179
Her Birth, her Beauty, Crowds and *C.* confess *E.S.* i. 145
In all the *C.* of Pindus guiltless quite *E.S.* ii. 187
DORSET, the Grace of *C.*, the Muses' Pride *Ep.* i. 1
See a long race thy spacious *c.* adorn *M.* 87
O'erflow thy *c.* : the light himself shall shine *M.* 103
Balk'd are the *C.*, and coolest is no more *M.E.* iii. 272
Blush, Grandeur ! blush, proud *C.*, withdraw your blaze *M.E.* iii. 281
I was not born for *C.* or great affairs *P.S.* 267
No *C.* he saw, no suits would ever try *P.S.* 396
By love of *C.* to nom'rous ills betray'd *R.L.* iv. 152
Say with what Eyes we ought at *C.* to gaze *S.* iv. 16
In ev'ry taste of foreign *C.* improv'd *S.* v. 141
In crowds, and *c.*, law, business, feasts, and friends *S.* vi. 91
Obliging Sir, for *C.* you sure were made *S.* viii. 86
And as for *C.*, forgive me, if I say *S.* viii. 92
C. are too much for wits so weak as mine *S.* viii. 280
Those, that imparted, *c. a nobler aim E.M.* ii. 99
I shun his Zenith, *c.* his mild Decline *E.S.* ii. 76
And love him, *c.* him, praise him, in or out *E.S.* ii. 103
To *c.* applause, by printing what I write *S.* vi. 130
Or *c.* a Wife, spread out his wily parts *S.* vii. 57
Twas no C.-badge, great Scriv'ner! fir'd thy brain M.E. iii. 145
C.-virtues bear, like Gems, the highest rate M.E. i. 141

Courtesy.
By *c.* of England, he may do *S.* v. 62

Courtier.
Fatten the *C.*, starve the learned band *D.* i. 315
Thee shall the Patriot, thee the *C.* taste *D.* iii. 297
God knows, I praise a *C.* when I can *E.S.* ii. 63
Blest *C. !* who could King and Country please *Ep.* i. 9

An honest *C.*, yet a Patriot too *Ep.* ii. 5
And the gay *C.* feels the sigh sincere *Ep.* ix. 6
Our *C.* scarce could touch a bit *I.H.* ii. 171
Our *C.* walks from dish to dish *I.H.* ii. 198
The *C.* smooth, who forty years had shin'd *M.E.* i. 252
If thou couldst make the *C.* void *Mi.* iv. 31
And ev'ry flow'ry *C.* writ Romance *S.* v. 146
But some excising *C.* will have toll *S.* vii. 147
The Fair sat panting at a C.'s play E.C. 540
The scholar's learning, with the *c.* ease *E.C.* 668
The *c.* promises, and sick man's pray'rs *R.L.* v. 119
So like, that critics said, and c—s *swore D.* ii. 49
C. and Patriots in two ranks divide *D.* iv. 107
Ah gentle Sir ! you *C.* so cajole us *S.* viii. 90
It ought to bring all *c.* on their backs *S.* viii. 207
And why not players strut in c—s' *clothes S.* viii. 222

Courtin.
To see those antics, Fopling and *C. S.* viii. 237

Courtly.
The creeping, dirty, *c.* Ivy join *D.* i. 304
The *c. Talbot, Somers, Sheffield read P.S.* 139
And all the well-whipt Cream of *C.* Sense *E.S.* i. 70
Let *C.* Wits to Wits afford supply *E.S.* ii. 171
And all your *c.* Civet-cats can vent *E.S.* ii. 183
In *c.* balls, and midnight masquerades *R.L.* i. 72
And in our own (excuse some *C.* stains) *S.* v. 215
Of whose best phrase and *c.* accent join'd *S.* viii. 48

Cousin.
Adopt him Son, or *C.* at the least *S.* iv. 108

Coute qui coute.
On just occasion, *c. I.H.* 264

Cov'nants.
Indentures, *C.*, Articles they draw *S.* vii. 94

Cover.
Shade him from Light, and *c.* him from Law *D.* i. 314
O may thy cloud still *c.* the deceit *D.* iv. 356
With gold and jewels *c.* ev'ry part *E.C.* 295
Fond to spread friendships, but to *c.* heats *S.* i. 136

Cover'd.
And all the nations *c.* in her shade *D.* iii. 72
Nor fields with gleaming steel be *c.* o'er *M.* 59
The levell'd towns with weeds lie *c.* o'er *W.F.* 67

Covert.
Try what the open, what the *c.* yield *E.M.* i. 10

Covet.
His Passion still, to *c.* gen'ral praise *M.E.* i. 196
To *c.* flying, and regret when lost *M.E.* ii. 234

Cow.
One clasp'd in wood, and one in strong *c.*-hide *D.* i. 150
With *c.-like* udders, and with ox-like eyes *D.* ii. 164

Coward.
COBHAM'S a *C.*, POLWARTH is a Slave *E.S.* ii. 130
Such as the souls of c—s *might conceive E.M.* iii. 259
What can ennoble sots, or slaves, or *c. E.M.* iv. 215

Cowl.
What differ more (you cry) than crown and *c. E.M.* iv. 199
But having cast his *c.*, and left those laws *S.* vii. 107

Cowl'd.
Men bearded, bald, *c.*, uncowl'd, shod, unshod *D.* iii. 114

Cowley.
Who now reads *C. ?* if he pleases yet *S.* v. 75
Who now shall charm the shades where *C.* strung *W.F.* 279
Nor pensive C.'s moral lay I.H. iv 8
Of Shakespear's Nature, and of *C.* Wit *S.* v. 83
There the last numbers flow'd from *C.* tongue *W.F.* 272

Cowper.
Yours, *C.'s manner"—and "yours, Talbot's sense" S.* vi. 134

Cowslip-wine.
Lettuce and *c. ; Probatum est S.* i. 18

Coxcomb.
And act, and be, a *C.* with success *D.* i. 110
Or, if to Wit a *c.* make pretence *D.* i. 177
The *c.* bird, so talkative and grave *M.E.* i. 5
That never *C.* reach'd Magnificence *M.E.* iv. 2a
When ev'ry *C.* perks them in my face *P.S.* 74
When ev'ry *C.* knows me by my Style *P.S.* 282
The *C.* hit, or fearing to be hit *P.S.* 345
Who think a *C.'s Honour like his Sense E.S.* ii. 202
On him, and crowds turn *C—s as they gaze D.* ii. 8
Streets, Chairs, and *C.* rush upon my sight *E.* v. 48
And some made *c.* Nature meant but fools *E.C.* 27
Ere *c.*-pies, or *c—s were on earth S.* ii. 98

Coy.
As some *c.* nymph her lover's warm address *W.F.* 19

Cozen.
Make Scots speak treason, *c.* subtlest whores *S.* vlii. 59

Cozens.
And, by my int'rest, *C.* made her stays *Mi.* ix. 64

Crab.
No *c.* more active in the dirty dance *D.* ii. 319

Crack.
Thou unconcern'd canst hear the mighty *c. P.S.* 86
That slipp'd thro' *C—s and Zig-zags of the Head D.* i. 124
Fans clap, silks rustle, and tough whalebones *c. R.L.* v. 40
Or ev'n to *c.* live Crawfish recommend *S.* ii. 43

Crack'd.
From the *c.* bag the dropping Guinea spoke *M.E.* iii. 36

Crackle.
The berries *c.*, and the mill turns round *R.L.* iii. 106

Cracks.
He takes his chirping pint, and *c.* his jokes *M.E.* iii. 358

Cradle.
To rock the *c.* of reposing Age *P.S.* 409

Crafty.
But Annius, *c.* Seer, with ebon wand *D.* iv. 347
The plain rough Hero turn a *c.* Knave *M.E.* i. 126

Craggs.
I sit and dream I see my *C.* anew *E.S.* ii. 69
Then shall thy *C.* (and let me call him mine) *M.E.* v. 63
'Twas what I said to *C.* and Child *I.H.* i. 67
It brighten'd *C.'s, and may darken thine S.* iv. 45

Cram.
To *c.* the Rich was prodigal expense *M.E.* iii. 185

Cramm'd.
Came, *c.* with capon, from where Pollio dines *D.* iv. 350
C. to the throat with Ortolans *I.H.* i. 62
First Health : The stomach (*c.* from ev'ry dish *S.* ii. 69

Crams.
Scolds with her maid, or with her chaplain *c. E.J.S.* 22

Craps.
A Saint in *C.* is twice a Saint in Lawn *M.E.* i. 136
In silks, in *c—s, in Garters, and in Rags D.* ii. 22

Cravat.
With eager beats his Mechlin *C.* moves *Mi.* ix. 91

Crave.
If, when the more you drink, the more you *c. S.* vi. 212
To *c.* your sentiments, if—'s your name *S.* viii. 67

Craves.
Fools grant whate'er Ambition *c. O.* ii. 27
A noble superfluity it *c. S.* iv. 91

Craving.
Dext'rous the *c.* fawning crowd to quit *E.* i. 11
No *c.* void left aking in the breast *E.A.* 94

Crawfish.
Or ev'n to crack live *C.* recommend *S.* ii. 43

Crawl.
And learn to *c.* upon poetic feet *D.* i. 62
Before her dance : behind her *c.* the Old *S.* i. 156

Crawls.
Still to his wench he *c.* on knocking knees *M.E.* i. 236
A while he *c.* upon the Earth *Mi.* iv. 7

Craz'd.
Pity mistakes for some poor tradesman *c. M.E.* iii. 64

Cream.
And all the well-whipt *C.* of Courtly Sense *E.S.* i. 90

Create.
Each Art he prompts, each Charm he can *c. D.* iii. 221
Till jarring int'rests of themselves *c. E.M.* iii. 293
Yet ne'er so sure our passion to *c. M.E.* ii. 51

Created.
And what *c.* perfect ? Why then Man *E.M.* i. 148
C. half to rise, and half to fall *E.M.* ii. 15
Of all our Vices have *c.* Arts *E.M.* ii. 50

Creation.
With self-applause her wild *c.* views *D.* i. 82
And last, to give the whole *c.* grace *D.* iii. 247
And all the bright *c.* fades away *E.C.* 493
Or in the full *c.* leave a void *E.M.* i. 243
Far as *C.'s ample range extends E.M.* i. 207

Creature.
The Play may pass—but that strange *C.*, Shore *E.J.S.* 5
Go, wond'rous *c.* ! mount where Science guides *E.M.* ii. 19
No *c.* owns it in the first degree *E.M.* iii. 225
The *c.* had his feast of life before *E.M.* iii. 69
And *c.* link'd to *c.*, man to man *E.M.* iii. 114
Take ev'ry *c.* in, of ev'ry kind *E.M.* iv. 370
Or any good *c.* shall lay o'er my head *Ep.* xvi. 4
No *c.* smarts so little as a fool *P.S.* 84
The *c.'s* at his dirty work again *P.S.* 92
Its proper power to hurt, each *c.* feels *S.* i. 85
And helps, another *c.'s wants and woes E.M.* iii. 52
And sure such kind good *c—s may be living E.J.S.* 28
Heav'n from all *c.* hides the book of Fate *E.M.* i. 77
Destroy all *C.* for thy sport or gust *E.M.* i. 117
Made for his use all *c.* if he call *E.M.* i. 177
Go, from the *c.* thy instruction take *E.M.* iv. 172
Yet go ! and thus o'er all the *c.* sway *E.M.* iii. 195
Like following life thro' *c.* you dissect *M.E.* i. 29
Of all mad *c.*, if the learn'd are right *P.S.* 105
Go on, obliging *c.*, make me see *P.S.* 119
Of all mankind, the *c.* most absurd *S.* v. 359

Credit.
What tho' no *c.* doubting Wits may give *R.L.* i. 39
Shall walk the World in *c.*, to his grave *S.* i. 120
Who having lost his *c.*, pawn'd his rent *S.* viii. 138

Creech.
So take it in the very words of *C. S.* iv. 4

Creed.
The Life to come, in ev'ry Poet's *C. S.* v. 74

Creep.
She saw slow Philips *c.* like Tate's poor page *D.* i. 105
True to the bottom see Concanen *c. D.* ii. 299
Here brisker vapours o'er the TEMPLE *c. D.* ii. 345
Soft as the wily Fox is seen to *c. D.* iv. 351
Let others *c.* by timid steps, and slow *D.* iv. 465
And ten low words oft *c.* in one dull line *E.C.* 347
If crystal streams "with pleasing murmurs *c." E.C.* 352
Of all who blindly *c.*, or sightless soar *E.M.* i. 12
Wit that can *c.*, and pride that licks the dust *P.S.* 333

Creeping.
The *c.*, dirty, courtly Ivy join *D.* i. 304
Soft *c.*, words on words, the sense compose *D.* ii. 389
Shall deluge all ; and Av'rice, *c.* on *M.E.* iii. 137
Him the Boar in Silence *c. Mi.* vii. 11

Creeps.
Where round some mould'ring Tower pale ivy *c. E.A.* 243

Cremona.
C. now shall ever boast thy name *E.C.* 707

CREPT—CROSS.

Crept.
The Vapour mild o'er each Committee *c.* *D.* iv. 615
Has *c.* thro' scoundrels ever since the flood *E.M.* iv. 212
An artful Manager, that *c.* between *E.S.* i. 21

Crescent.
But by the *c.* and the golden zone *W.F.* 176

Cresses.
His court with nettles, moats with *c.* stor'd *M.E.* iii. 181

Cressy, Cressi.
Or what was spoke at *C.* and POITIERS *S.* iii. 100
Draw monarchs chain'd, and C—*i's glorious field W.F.* 305

Crest.
His purple *c.*, and scarlet-circled eyes *W.F.* 116

Crested.
The *c.* basilisk and speckled snake *M.* 82

Crew.
Stands in the streets, abstracted from the *c.* *E.* v. 43
And jingling down the back-stairs, told the *c.* *M.E.* iii. 37
K—l's lewd Cargo, or Ty—y's *C.* *S.* iv. 121
Adieu, my flocks, farewell the sylvan *c.* *W.* 91

Crib.
The steer and lion at one *c.* shall meet *M.* 79

Cricket.
The Senator at *C.* urge the Ball *D.* iv. 592

Cried—*see* Cry'd.

Cries.
Familiar White's, "God save King Colley!" *c.* *D.* i. 319
"Now turn to diff'rent sports" (the Goddess *c.*) *D.* ii. 221
"What pow'r," he *c.*, "What pow'r these wonders wrought?" *D.* iii. 250
"Enough! enough!" the raptur'd Monarch *c.* *D.* iii. 339
No maid *c.*, Charming! and no youth, Divine *D.* iv. 214
Then gives a smacking buss, and *c.*, "No words!" *E.* v. 26
"What *well!* what *weapons?*" (Flavia *c.*) *E.* vi. 13
This *c.* there is, and that, there is no God *E.M.* iv. 140
That from his cage *c.*, Cuckold, Whore, and Knave *M.E.* i. 6
"Mercy!" *c.* Helluo, "mercy on my soul!" *M.E.* i. 240
C., "Ah! how charming, if there's no such place!" *M.E.* ii. 108
"All this is madness," *c.* a sober sage *M.E.* iii. 151
"Nine years!" *c.* he, who high in Drury-lane *P.S.* 41
(*C.* prating Balbus) "something will come out *P.S.* 276
"To arms, to arms!" the fierce Virago *c.* *R.L.* v. 37
"Restore the lock!" she *c.*; and all around *R.L.* v. 103
C. "Send me, Gods! a whole Hog barbecu'd!" *S.* ii. 26
"Right," *c.* his Lordship, "for a rogue in need *S.* ii. 111
"Pray heav'n it last" (*c.* Swift) "as you go on *S.* ii. 161
Who *c.*, "My father's damn'd, and all's my own *S.* ii. 174
Up, up! *c.* Gluttony, 'tis break of day *S.* iv. 112
"Permit" (he *c.*) "no stranger to your fame *S.* viii. 66
Whose air *c.* Arm! whose very look's an oath *S.* viii. 261

Crime.
The *c.* was common, common be the pain *E.A.* 104
I view my *c.*, but kindle at the view *E.A.* 185
How the dear object from the *c.* remove *E.A.* 193
It will be then no *c.* to gaze on me *E.A.* 330
No *c.* was thine, if 'tis no *c.* to love *O.* i. 96
Convicted of that mortal *c.*, a hole *S.* viii. 245
Is it, in heav'n, a *c.* to love too well *U.L.* 6
Discharge that rage on more provoking *c*—s *E.C.* 528
At *C.* that 'scape, or triumph o'er the Land *E.S.* i. 168
All *c.* shall cease, and ancient fraud shall fail *M.* 17
Of whose strange *c.* no Canonist can tell *S.* vii. 121
Whom *c.* gave wealth, and wealth gave Impudence *S.* vii. 46
Were equal *c.* in a despotic reign *W.F.* 58

Crimson.
Swift trouts, diversified with *c.* stains *W.F.* 145

Cripple.
See the blind beggar dance, the *c.* sing *E.M.* ii. 267

Crispissa.
Do thou, *C.*, tend her fav'rite Lock *R.L.* ii. 115

Criterion.
By what *C.* do you eat, d'ye think *S.* ii. 29

Critic.
The gen'rous *C.* fann'd the Poet's fire *E.C.* 100
The *C.* else proceeds without remorse *E.C.* 167
Neglect the rules each verbal *C.* lays *E.C.* 261
A constant *C.* at the great man's board *E.C.* 416
Nor in the *C.* let the Man be lost *E.C.* 523
And make each day a *C.* on the last *E.C.* 571
And bless their *C.* with a Poet's fire *E.C.* 676
If there's a *C.* of distinguish'd rage *Mi.* ii. 21
Did some more sober *C.* come abroad *P.S.* 157
The damning *c.*, half approving wit *P.S.* 344
The *c.* Eye, that microscope of Wit *D.* iv. 233
True Taste as seldom is the *C.*'s share *E.C.* 12
And justly bear a *C.* noble name *E.C.* 47
Perhaps he seem'd above the *c.* law *E.C.* 132
The Poet's bays and *C.* ivy grow *E.C.* 706
And be the *C.*, Briton's, Old Man's Friend *Mi.* ii. 24
Safe, where no *C*—s damn, no duns molest *D.* i. 295
So like, that *c.* said, and courtiers swore *D.* ii. 49
Ye *C.!* in whose heads, as equal scales *D.* ii. 367
And you, my *C.!* in the chequer'd shade *D.* iv. 125
C. like me shall make it prose again *D.* iv. 214
C. in Wit or Life, are hard to please *E.* iv. 29
But are not *C.* to their judgment too *E.C.* 18
And then turn *C.* in their own defence *E.C.* 29
Turn'd *C.* next, and prov'd plain fools at last (*rep.*) *E.C.* 37
And rise to faults true *C.* dare not mend *E.C.* 160
Most *C.*, fond of some subservient art *E.C.* 263
Thus *C.*, of less judgment than caprice *E.C.* 285
In various shapes of Parsons, *C.*, Beaus *E.C.* 459
These monsters, *C.!* with your darts engage *E.C.* 554
Learn then what MORALS *C.* ought to show *E.C.* 560
'Twere well might *c.* still this freedom take *E.C.* 584
There are as mad abandon'd *C.* too *E.C.* 611
Such once were *C.*; such the happy few *E.C.* 643
Our *C.* take a contrary extreme *E.C.* 661
By Wits, than *C.*, in as wrong Quotations *E.C.* 664
Thus long succeeding *C.* justly reigned *E.C.* 681
Let crowds of Critics now my verse assail *Mi.* i. 3
Ev'n such small *C.* some regards may claim *P.S.* 167
In all debates where *C.* bear a part *S.* v. 81
By learned *C.*, of the mighty Dead *S.* v. 198
Nor glad vile Poets with true C—*s gore D.* iii. 178
But *C.*-learning *flourish'd most in France E.C.* 712

Critic'd.
C. your wine, and analys'd your meat *M.E.* ii. 81

Criticise.
Then *C.* the Muses' handmaid prov'd *E.C.* 102

Criticize.
Cavil you may, but never *c.* *E.C.* 123

Croak'd.
And the hoarse nation *c.*, "God save King Log!" *D.* i. 330

Croaking.
Old-fashion'd halls, dull Aunts, and *c.* rooks *E.* v. 12

Crocus.
Here the bright *c.* and blue vi'let glow *Sp.* 31

Cromwell.
See *C.* damn'd to everlasting fame *E.M.* iv. 284
Otho a warrior, *C.* a buffoon *M.E.* i. 88

Crone.
The frugal *C.*, whom praying priests attend *M.E.* i. 242

Crop.
Ingratitude's the certain *c.* *I.H.* 32
What *c*—s *of wit and honesty appear E.M.* ii. 185

Crops.
Pleas'd to the last he *c.* the flow'ry food *E.M.* i. 83

Cropt.
Who *c.* our Ears, and sent them to the King *E.S.* i. 18

Cross.
Not on the *C.* my eyes were fix'd, but you *E.A.* 116
Present the *C.* before my lifted eye *E.A.* 327
On her white breast a sparkling *C.* she wore *R.L.* ii. 7
Bear Britain's thunder, and her *C.* display *W.F.* 387
A Clerk, foredoom'd *his father's wish to c. P.S.* 17
Nor *c.* the Channel twice a year *I.H.* ii. 31
Or *c.*, to plunder Provinces, the Main *S.* iii. 127

Cross'd.

As you by Love, so I by Fortune *c. Mi.* ix. 11
But see how oft ambitious aims are *c. R.L.* v. 107
Hills, vales, and floods appear already *c. W.F.* 153

Crousaz.

On German *C.*, and Dutch Burgersdyck *D.* iv. 198

Crowd.

The Senior's judgment all the *c.* admire *D.* ii. 289
He ceas'd, and spread the robe; the *c.* confess *D.* ii. 353
The clam'rous *c.* is hush'd with mugs of Mum *D.* ii. 385
Dext'rous the craving, fawning *c.* to quit *E.* i. 11
So much they scorn the *c.*, that if the throng *E.C.* 426
To jostle here among a *c. I.H.* ii. 54 s
A senseless, worthless, and unhonour'd *c. S.* v. 306
Go, lofty Poet! and in such a *c. S.* vi. 108
On him, and C—s turn Coxcombs as they gaze *D.* ii. 8
Now *c.* on *c.* around the Goddess press *D.* iv. 135
KNIGHT lifts the head, for what are *c.* undone *D.* iv. 561
What *c.* of these, impenitently bold *E.C.* 604
Come here in *c.*, and stare the strumpet down *E.J.S.* 50
To Kings presumption, and to *c.* belief *E.M.* ii. 244
Her Birth, her Beauty, *C.* and Courts confess *E.S.* i. 145
Let *C.* of Critics now my verse assail *Mi.* i. 3
Tell at your levee, as the *C.* approach *S.* iv. 101
In *c.* and courts, law, business, feasts and friends *S.* vi. 91
All *c. who foremost shall be damn'd to fame D.* iii. 158
Then gay ideas *c.* the vacant brain *R.L.* i. 83
Why round our coaches *c.* the white-gloved Beaux *R.L.* v. 13
With ARMS, and GEORGE, and BRUNSWICK *c.* the verse *S.* i. 24
Trees, where you sit, shall *c.* into a shade *Su.* 74
And feather'd people *c.* my wealthy side *W.F.* 404

Crowded.

A narrow orb each *c.* conquest keeps *M.E.* v. 25
These, only these, support the *c.* stage *S.* v. 87

Crowding.

In *c.* ranks on ev'ry side arise *M.* 89

Crown.

Where Dukes and Butchers join to wreathe my *c. D.* i. 223
Perch'd on his *c.* "All hail! and hail again *D.* i. 291
Or give from fool to fool the Laurel *c. D.* iv. 98
Now, they who reach Parnassus' lofty *c. E.C.* 514
Or Public Spirit its great cure, a *C. M.* iv. 172
What differ more (you cry) than *c.* and cowl *E.M.* iv. 199
Horace would say, Sir Billy *serv'd the C. E.S.* i. 73
Must great Offenders, once escap'd the *C. E.S.* ii. 28
The Priest whose Flattery be-dropt the *C. E.S.* ii. 64
'Tis for the service of the *C. I.H.* ii. 34 s
With Truth and Goodness, as with *C.* and Ball *M.E.* ii. 184
The *C.* of Poland, venal twice an age *M.E.* iii. 127
His wealth, yet dearer, forfeit to the *C. M.E.* iii. 400
And with a borrow'd Play, out-did poor *C. Mi.* iii. 8
Th' imperial consort of the *C.* of Spades *R.L.* iii. 68
Who turns a Persian tale for half a *C. P.S.* 180
Expect a place or Pension from the *C. S.* v. 371
C—s *were reserv'd to grace the soldiers too E.C.* 513
Some plunge in bus'ness, others shave their *c. M.E.* i. 104
With golden *c.* and wreaths of heav'nly flow'rs *R.L.* i. 34
Weave laurel *C.*, and take what names we please *S.* vi. 142
Not more of bastardy in heirs to *C. S.* vii. 82
And bade thee live to *c. Britannia's praise D.* iii. 211
To *c.* thy forests with immortal green *W.F.* 286

Crown'd.

Not with more glee by hands pontific *c. D.* ii. 13
C. with the Jordan, walks contented home *D.* ii. 190
Not with less glory mighty Dulness *c. D.* iii. 135
A tribe, with weeds and shells fantastic *c. D.* iv. 398
Now *c.* with Myrtle, on th' Elysian coast *E.* iv. 73
These moss-grown domes with spiry turrets *c. E.A.* 142
Be *c.* as Monarchs, or as Gods ador'd *E.M.* iii. 198
Till then, by Nature *c.*, each Patriarch sate *E.M.* iii. 215
The friar hooded, and the monarch *c. E.M.* iv. 198
The Number may be hang'd, but not be *c. E.S.* ii. 111
Lies *c.* with Princes' benefits, Poets' lays *Ep.* viii. 5
If modest Youth, with cool Reflection *c. Ep.* xiv. 1
Rise, *c.* with light, imperial Salem, rise *M.* 85
A few grey hairs his rev'rend temples *c. M.E.* iii. 327
With thy flow'ry Chaplets *c. Mi.* vii. 28
Close by those meads for ever *c.* with flow'rs *R.L.* iii. 1

For lo! the board with cups and spoons is *c. R.L.* iii. 105
The turf with rural dainties shall be *c. Sp.* 99
And *c.* with corn their thanks to Ceres yield *Su.* 66
That *c.* with tufted trees and springing corn *W.F.* 27
The Loddon slow, with verdant alders *c. W.F.* 342

Crowns.

That Altar *c.*; A folio Common-place *D.* i. 159
'Tis GEORGE and LIBERTY that *c.* the cup *M.E.* iii. 207

Crucify'd.

The Frippery of *c.* Molière *D.* i. 132

Cruel.

As erst Medea (*c.*, so to save) *D.* iv. 121
And now you burst (ah *c.!*) from my arms *I.H.* iii. 44
The *c.* thought that stabs me to the heart *Mi.* ix. 54
You think this *c.!* take it for a rule *P.S.* 83
Oh hadst thou, *c.!* been content to seize *R.L.* iv. 175
Oh *c.* nymph! a living death I bear *R.L.* v. 61

Crumbling.

The faithless Column, and the *c.* Bust *M.E.* v. 20

Crush'd.

Not Chaos-like together *c.* and bruis'd *W.F.* 13

Crust.

A *c.* of Bread, and Liberty *I.H.* ii. 221

Crutch.

The dumb shall sing, the lame his *c.* forego *M.* 43
On two unequal *c*—*es propt he came D.* iv. 111

Cry.

The shepherds *c.*, "Thy flocks are left a prey" *A.* 78
How new-born nonsense first is taught to *c. D.* i. 60
And all thy yawning daughters *c.*, *encore D.* iv. 60
Yet *c.*, if Man's unhappy, God's unjust *E.M.* i. 118
What differ more (you *c.*) than crows and cowl *E.M.* iv. 199
Let then the Fair one beautifully *c. M.E.* ii. 11
Where all *c.* out, "What sums are thrown away" *M.E.* iv. 100
And SWIFT *c.* wisely, "Vive la Bagatelle!" *S.* iv. 128
And then, unwhipp'd, he had the grace to *c. S.* iv. 18
When servile Chaplains *c.*, that birth and place *S.* vi. 220
C.: "By your Priesthood tell me what you are" *S.* viii. 37
And *c—es of tortur'd ghosts O.* i. 62
Hark! Hæmus resounds with the Bacchanal's *c. O.* i. 111
Succeeding monarchs heard the subjects' *c. W.F.* 85

Cry'd.

And "Oh!" (he *c.*) "what street, what lane but knows *D.* ii. 153
"Hold!" (*c.* the Queen) "a Cat-call each shall win *D.* ii. 243
"Oh" (*c.* the Goddess) "for some pedant Reign *D.* iv. 175
Each maid *c.*, Charming! and each youth, Divine *D.* iv. 410
Peep'd in your fans, been serious thus, and *c. E.J.S.* 4
Observing, *c.*, "You 'scape not so *I.H.* i. 57
Give me, I *c.*, (enough for me) *I.H.* i. 69
And *c.*, "I vow you're mighty neat *I.H.* ii. 174
"The Manor, Sir!" "the Manor I hold," he *c. M.E.* i. 260
Nor at Rehearsals, sweat, and mouth'd, and *c. P.S.* 227
(The victor *c.*) the glorious Prize is mine *R.L.* iii. 162
"O wretched maid!" she spread her hands, and *c. R.L.* iv. 95
C. Dapperwit, and sunk beside his chair *R.L.* v. 62
Now meet thy fate, incens'd Belinda *c. R.L.* v. 87
"Boast not my fall" (he *c.*) "insulting foe *R.L.* v. 97
"No place on earth (he *c.*) like Greenwich hill" *S.* iii. 139
"Prodigious well;" his great Commander *c. S.* vi. 42
Go on, my Friend (he *c.*) see yonder walls *S.* vi. 46
"My Friends!" (he *c.*) "p—x take you for your care *S.* vi. 195
Till I *c.* out; You prove yourself so able *S.* viii. 182

Crying.

And Worldly *c.* coals from street to street *M.E.* iii. 62
I grant that Poetry's a *c.* sin *S.* vii. 7

Crystal.

Expos'd thro' c. to the gazing eyes *R.L.* iv. 114
If c. streams " with pleasing murmurs creep" *E.C.* 352
Lead me to the C. Mirrors *Mi.* vii. 19
Late, as I rang'd the c. wilds of air *R.L.* i. 107
And c. domes and angels in machines *R.L.* iv. 46
As in the c. spring I view my face *Su.* 27
Ye gentle Muses, leave your c. spring *W.* 21
Project long shadows o'er the c. tide *W.F.* 376
And pointed C—s break the sparkling Rill *Mi.* x. 4

Cuckold.

But the kind c. might instruct the city *E.J.S.* 42
That from his cage cries, C., Whore, and Knave *M.E.* i. 6
The well-bred c—s in St. James's air *M.E.* iii. 388

Cudgell'd.

There Ridpath, Roper, c. you might view *D.* ii. 149

Culls.

From each she nicely c. with curious toil *R.L.* i. 131

Culture.

We ought to blame the c., not the soil *E.M.* iv. 14

Cunning.

And in the C., Truth itself's a lie *M.E.* i. 68
The Wild are constant, and the C. known *M.E.* i. 175

Cup.

With that, a WIZARD OLD his C. extends *D.* iv. 517
In Folly's c. still laughs the bubble, joy *E.M.* ii. 288
'Tis GEORGE and LIBERTY that crowns the c. *M.E.* iii. 207
For lo! the board with c—s and spoons is crown'd *R.L.* iii. 105
And frequent c. prolong the rich repast *R.L.* iii. 112

Cupid.

Gentle C., o'er my Heart *Mi.* vii. 2
See on the Tooth-pick, Mars and C. strive *Mi.* ix. 31
And burn in C.'s flames—but burn alive *R.L.* v. 102
Defence from Phœbus', not from C. beams *Su.* 14
And C—s ride the Lion of the Deeps *D.* iv. 308
Two C. squirt before ; a Lake behind *M.E.* iv. 111
In the same shades the C. tun'd his lyre *W.F.* 295

Cupp'd.

They bled, they c., they purg'd ; in short they cur'd *S.* vi. 193

Curb'd.

And wisely c. proud man's pretending wit *E.C.* 53

Curd.

Sporus, that mere white c. of Ass's milk *P.S.* 306

Cure.

Or Public Spirit its great c., a Crown *E.M.* iv. 172
Behold the hand that wrought a Nation's c. *S.* v. 225
But that the c. is starving, all allow *S.* vii. 10
Will c. the arrant'st Puppy of his Pride *S.* iii. 60
When golden Angels cease to c. the Evil *S.* vi. 218
From Love, the sole disease thou canst not c. *Su.* 12
To c. thy lambs, but not to heal thy heart *Su.* 34

Cur'd.

There all Men may be c., whene'er they please *S.* iv. 59
They bled, they cupp'd, they purg'd ; in short they c. *S.* vi. 193

Curio.

And C., restless by the Fair one's side *M.E.* v. 43

Curious.

And hang some c. cobweb in its stead *D.* i. 180
C. not knowing, not exact but nice *E.C.* 286
Mere c. pleasure, or ingenious pain *E.M.* ii. 47
In Books, not Authors, c. is my Lord *M.E.* iv. 134
From each she nicely culls with c. toil *R.L.* i. 131
Preach as I please, I doubt our c. men *S.* ii. 17

Curl.

Which snatch'd my best, my fav'rite c. away *R.L.* iv. 148
In equal c—s, and well conspir'd to deck *R.L.* ii. 27
A brighter wash ; to c. their waving hairs *R.L.* ii. 97

Curl, Curll.

Stood dauntless C.; " Behold that rival here *D.* ii. 58
Here fortun'd C. to slide ; loud shout the band *D.* ii. 73

To seize his papers, C., was next thy care *D.* ii. 113
C. stretches after Gay, but Gay is gone *D.* ii. 127
Osborne and C. accept the glorious strife *D.* ii. 167
Not so from shameless C.; impetuous spread *D.* ii. 179
The Pindars and the Miltons of a C. *D.* iii. 164
Dare you refuse him ? C—l invites to dine *P.S.* 53
Of C.'s chaste press, and Lintot's rubric post *D.* i. 40
Which C. Corinna chanc'd that morn to make *D.* ii. 70
Or that where on her C—s the Public pours *D.* ii. 3
Let the two C—ls of Town and Court abuse *P.S.* 380

Curl'd.

C. or uncurl'd, since locks will turn to grey *R.L.* v. 26
Observe his shape how clean ! his locks how c. *S.* vi. 5

Curling.

While c. smokes from village-tops are seen *A.* 63
The lakes that quiver to the c. breeze *E.A.* 160
And swelling clusters bend the c. vines *Sp.* 36

Current.

In her chaste c. oft the goddess laves *W.F.* 209
While led along the skies his c. strays *W.F.* 228
The c. folly proves the ready wit *E.C.* 449

Curse.

Nor present good or ill, the joy or c. *E.M.* iv. 71
Superiors ? death ! and Equals ? what a c. *M.E.* ii. 135
Whether we joy or grieve, the same the c. *S.* iv. 22
So when you plague a fool, 'tis still the c. *S.* viii. 120
Scarecrow to boys, the breeding woman's c. *S.* viii. 268
Despairing quacks with c—s fled the place *M.E.* iii. 273
The Gods to c. Pamela with her pray'rs *E.* iv. 49
C. on all laws but those which love has made *E.A.* 74
Now think of thee, and c. my innocence *E.A.* 188
C. the sav'd candle, and unop'ning door *M.E.* iii. 194
I c. such lavish cost, and little skill *M.E.* iv. 167
Wisdom (c. on it) will come soon or late *S.* vi. 199

Curs'd, Curst.

C. be the fields that cause my Delia's stay *A.* 32
Atossa, c. with ev'ry granted pray'r *M.E.* ii. 147
Oh c. effects of civil hate *O.* ii. 29
This c. Ombrelia, this undoing Fair *Mi.* ix. 55
How many c. the moment they believ'd *Mi.* ix. 72
And c. for ever this victorious day *R.L.* iii. 104
For ever c. be this detested day *R.L.* iv. 147
C. be thy neighbours, thy trustees, thyself *S.* ii. 106
C. be the wretch, so venal and so vain *S.* vii. 63
And c. with hearts unknowing how to yield *D.* i. 5
You by whose care, in vain decry'd and c—t *D.* i. 5
Oh c., dear horrors of all-conscious night *E.A.* 229
Of Vice or Virtue, whether blest or c. *E.M.* iv. 87
Experience, this ; by Man's oppression c. *M.E.* ii. 213
C. be the verse, how well soe'er it flow *P.S.* 283
Aw'd by his Nobles, by his Commons c. *W.F.* 73

Curses.

And sad Sir Balaam c. God and dies *M.E.* iii. 402
And c. Wit, and Poetry, and Pope *P.S.* 26

Curtain.

'Twixt Priest and People close the C. draw *D.* i. 313
Thy hand, great Anarch, lets the c. fall *D.* iv. 655
The mole's dim c., and the lynx's beam *E.M.* i. 212
With tape-ty'd c—s never meant to draw *M.E.* iii. 302
Sol thro' white c. shot a tim'rous ray *R.L.* i. 13

Curtains.

Him close she c. round with Vapours blue *D.* iii. 3

Curtius.

Shall I, like C., desp'rate in my zeal *D.* i. 209
In Decius charms, in C. is divine *E.M.* ii. 200

Curve.

It rose, and labour'd to a c. at most *D.* ii. 172

Custard.

Yet ate, in dreams, the c. of the day *D.* i. 92

Custom.

C., grown blind with Age, must be your Guide *E.* iv. 33
And did not wicked c. so contrive *E.J.S.* 13
Add Nature's, C.'s, Reason's, Passion's strife *M.E.* i. 21

Cut.

And pond'rous slugs c. swiftly thro' the sky *D.* i. 182
Sure, if they cannot c., it may be said *E.S.* ii. 148

Or c. wide views thro' Mountains to the Plain *M.E.* iv. 75
Trees c. to Statues, Statues thick as trees *M.E.* iv. 120
Fate urg'd the Shears, and c. the Sylph in twain *R.L.* v. 151
Then, learned Sir! (to c. the matter short) *S.* i. 91
Tho' c. in pieces ere my Lord can eat *S.* ii. 22

Cutler.
His Grace's fate sage C. could foresee *M.E.* iii. 315
Thy life more wretched, C., was confess'd *M.E.* iii. 321
C. saw tenants break, and houses fall *M.E.* iii. 323
C. and Brutus, dying, both exclaim *M.E.* iii. 333

Cygnet.
Each C. sweet, of Bath and Tunbridge race *D.* iii. 155

Cynthia.
Silence, ye Wolves! while Ralph to C. howls *D.* iii. 165
Another C. her new journey runs *D.* iii. 243
Nor ev'ning C. fill her silver horn *M.* 100
Catch, ere she change, the C. of this minute *M.E.* ii. 20
C., tune harmonious Numbers *Mi.* vii. 13
Not C. when her manteau's pinn'd awry *R.L.* iv. 8
Ah, C.! ah—tho' banish'd from thy train *W.F.* 200
Now shown by C.'s *silver ray I.H.* iii. 47
Chaste as cold C. virgin light *O.* iii. 23

Cynthus.
Diana C., Ceres Hybla loves (*rep.*) *Sp.* 66
And C.' *top forsook for Windsor shade W.F.* 166

Cypress.
Mournful C., verdant Willow *Mi.* vii. 21
Let Nymphs and Sylvans c. garlands bring *W.* 22

Cyprian.
Thus the C. Goddess weeping *Mi.* vii. 9

D.

Look in that breast, most dirty *D.*! be fair *S.* vi. 222
If *D* *** lov'd sixpence more than he *S.* vi. 229
But Bug and *D—l*, Their *Honours* and so forth *S.* iii. 90

Dab-chick.
As when a d. waddles thro' the copse *D.* ii. 63

Dæmon.
Some *D.* stole my pen (forgive th' offence) *D.* i. 187
Till all the *D.* makes his full descent *M.E.* iii. 371
Some d. whisper'd, "Visto! have a Taste" *M.E.* iv. 16
Provoking *D—s all restraint remove E A.* 232
Fays, Fairies, Genii, Elves, and *D.* hear *R.L.* ii. 74

Dagger.
The d. wont to pierce the Tyrant's breast *D.* iv. 38
Lucretia's d., Rosamunda's bowl *M.E.* ii. 92

Daggled.
Nor, like a puppy, d. thro' the town *P.S.* 225

Daily.
'Twixt sense and nonsense d. change their tide *E.C.* 435
While Truth, Worth, Wisdom, d. they decry *E.S.* i. 169
The d. Anodyne, and nightly Draught *M.E.* ii. 111

Dainties.
The turf with rural d. shall be crown'd *Sp.* 99

Daisies.
Now hawthorns blossom, now the d. spring *Sp.* 42

Dale.
Join Cotswold hills to Saperton's fair d. *S.* vi. 257

Dame.
As the sage d., experienc'd in her trade *D.* ii. 133
And the pleas'd d., soft smiling, lead'st away *D.* ii. 188
Pleas'd, she accepts the Hero, and the *D. D.* iv. 335
Led up the Youth, and call'd the Goddess *D. D.* iv. 498
Let wealth, let honour, wait the wedded d. *E.A.* 77
The godly d., who fleshly failings damns *E.J.S.* 21
The poisoning *D.*—You mean—I don't—You do *E.S.* ii. 22
When Cæsar made a noble d. a whore *M.E.* i. 213

While Scale in hand *D. Justice* past along *Mi.* xi. 4
D. Justice weighing long the doubtful Right *Mi.* xi. 7
So spoke the *D.*, but no applause ensu'd *R.L.* v. 35
Fair Coursers, Vases, and alluring D—s *M.E.* iii. 70

Damn.
Safe, where no Critics d., no duns molest *D.* i. 295
Prompt or to guard or stab, to saint or d. *D.* ii. 357
How, Sir? not d. the Sharper, but the Dice *E.S.* ii. 13
D. with faint praise, assent with civil leer *P.S.* 201
Z—ds, d. the lock! 'fore Gad, you must be civil *R.L.* iv. 128
Grow sick, and d. the climate—like a Lord *S.* iii. 160
Or d. to all eternity at once *S.* v. 59
Or d. all Shakespear, like th' affected Fool *S.* v. 105
The Play stands still; d. action and discourse *S.* v. 314

Damnation.
And deal d. round the land *U.P.* 27

Damn'd.
Blasphem'd his Gods, the Dice, and d. his Fate *D.* i. 116
Works d., or to be d.! (your father's fault) *D.* i. 226
All crowd, who foremost shall be d. to fame *D.* iii. 158
To one small sect, and all are d. beside *E.C.* 397
And are but d. far having too much wit *E.C.* 429
See Cromwell, d. to everlasting fame *E.M.* iv. 284
For your d. Stucco has no chink *I.H.* i. 217
D. to the Mines, an equal fate betides *M.E.* iii. 109
Imputes to me and my d. works the cause *P.S.* 24
Who cries, "My father's d., and all's my own" *S.* ii. 174
Him the d. Doctors and his Friends immur'd *S.* vi. 192
And forc'd ev'n me to see the d. at Court *S.* viii. 191

Damning.
Her grey-hair'd Synods d. books unread *D.* iii. 103
The d. critic, half approving wit *P.S.* 344

Damns.
And d. implicit faith, and holy lies *D.* iv. 463
The godly dame, who fleshly failings d. *E.J.S.* 21
Bond d. the Poor, and hates them from his heart *M.E.* iii. 100

Damon.
Sing then, and *D.* shall attend the strain *Sp.* 29
If gentle *D.* did not squeeze her hand *R.L.* i. 98

Dan Prior.
Our Friend, *D.*, told (you know) *I.H.* ii. 153

Dance.
Pleas'd with the madness of the mazy d. *D.* i. 68
No crab more active in the dirty d. *D.* ii. 319
Exalt the d., or animate the song *I.H.* iii. 28
No rafter'd roofs with d. and tabor sound *M.E.* iii. 189
Bold in the lists, and graceful in the d. *W.F.* 294
To midnight d—s, *and the public show U.L.* 58
Hell rises, Heav'n descends, and d. on Earth *D.* iii. 237
The forests d., the rivers upwards rise *D.* iii. 245
The Judge to d. his brother Sergeant call *D.* iv. 591
Teach Kings to fiddle, or make Senates d. *D.* iv. 598
As those move easiest who have learn'd to d. *E.C.* 363 ; (*rep.*) *S.* vi. 179
See the blind beggar d., the cripple sing *E.M.* ii. 267
Before her d.: behind her crawl the Old *E.S.* i. 156
See nodding forests on the mountains d. *M.* 26
Make the soul d. upon a Jig to Heav'n *M.E.* iv. 144
And the pale spectres d. *O.* i. 68
Oh! if to d. all night, and dress all day *R.L.* v. 19
The doubling Lustres d. as fast as she *S.* i. 48
And men must walk at least before they d. *S.* iii. 54
We build, we paint, we sing, we d. as well *S.* v. 46
Nor dare to practise till they've learn'd to d. *S.* v. 184
The gilded puppets d. and mount above *S.* vii. 18
The wond'ring forests soon shall d. again *Su.* 82

Dances.
Joys in my jigs, and d. in my chains *D.* iv. 62
Ridotta sips and d., till she see *S.* i. 47
And the brain d. to the mantling bowl *S.* ii. 8

Dancing.
And lest we err by Wit's wild d. light *D.* i. 175
To lands of singing, or of d. slaves *D.* iv. 305
As sober Lanesb'row d. in the gout *M.E.* i. 231
When music softens, and when d. fires *R.L.* i. 76
And from the brink his d. shade surveys *Sp.* 34

F

When *d.* sun-beams on the water play'd *Su.* 3
And eyes the *d.* cork, and bending reed *W.F.* 140

Dane.
Whom ev'n the Saxon spar'd, and bloody *D. W.F.* 77

Danger.
And hear a spark, yet think no *d.* nigh *E.* v. 4
The toil, the *d.* of the Seas *I.H.* ii. 37
D—s, *doubts, delays, surprises O.* iii. 39

Dang'rous.
But, of the two, less *d.* is th' offence *E.C.* 3
A *little learning* is a *d.* thing *E.C.* 215
Leave *d.* truths to unsuccessful Satires *E.C.* 592
Imagination plies her *d.* art *E.M.* ii. 143
Bid the broad Arch the *d.* Flood contain *M.E.* iv. 199
Good friend, forbear ! you deal in *d.* things *P.S.* 75

Dangling.
The George and Garter *d.* from that bed *M.E.* iii. 303

Daniel.
She saw old Pryn in restless *D.* shine *D.* i. 103
Norton, from *D.* and Ostræa sprung *D.* ii. 415

Danish.
And silent Darent, stain'd with *D.* blood *W.F.* 348

Dante.
Not *D.* dreaming all th' infernal state *S.* viii. 192

Daphne.
Begin ; this charge the dying *D.* gave *W.* 17
Fair *D.*'s dead, and love is no more (*varied*) *W.* 2,&c.
No more the mounting larks, while *D.* sings *W.* 53
D., our grief! our glory now no more *W.* 68
D., our Goddess, and our grief no more *W.* 76
D., farewell, and all the world adieu *W.* 92
O *sing* of D.'s *fate, and* D.'s *praise W.* 8

Daphnis.
Thus *D.* spoke, and Strephon thus reply'd *Sp.* 22
Say, *D.,* say, in what glad soil appears *Sp.* 85
Cease to contend, for, *D.,* I decree *Sp.* 93

Dapperwit.
Cry'd *D.,* and sunk beside his chair *R.L.* v. 62

Dappled.
Gave the gilt Coach, and *d.* Flanders Mares *E.* iv. 50

Dare.
And rise to faults true Critics *d.* not mend *E.C.* 160
For which we bear to live, or *d.* to die *E.M.* iv. 4
The only diff'rence is I *d.* laugh out *E.S.* i. 36
D., they to hope a Poet for their Friend *E.S.* ii. 115
Who *d.* to love their Country, and be poor *Mi.* x. 14
Fires that scorch, yet *d.* not shine *O.* iii. 40
D. to have sense yourselves : assert the stage *P.C.* 43
D. you refuse him? Curll invites to dine *P.S.* 53
In mumbling of the game they *d.* not bite *P.S.* 314
One tragic sentence if I *d.* deride *S.* v. 121
Nor *d.* to practise till they've learn'd to dance *S.* v. 184
Yet these were all poor Gentlemen! I *d. S.* viii. 78

Dar'd.
So when the first bold vessel *d.* the seas *O.* i. 38
Nor *d,* an Oath, nor hazarded a Lie *P.S.* 397

Darent.
And silent *D.* stain'd with Danish blood *W.F.* 348

Dares.
Sleep's all-subduing charms who *d.* defy *D.* ii. 373
Nor *public* Flame, nor *private, d.* to shine *D.* iv. 651
And if a Vice *d.* keep the field *E.* vi. 7
That *d,* tell neither Truth nor Lies *E.* vi. 30
But he's a bolder man who *d.* be well *M.E.* ii. 130
She *d.* to steal my Fav'rite Lover's heart *Mi.* ix. 66
The rebel knave, who *d.* his prince engage *R.L.* iii. 59

Dar'st.
Come, if thou *d.,* all charming as thou art *E.A.* 281
How *d.* thou let one worthy man be poor *S.* ii. 118

Daring.
Perhaps more high some *d.* son may soar *D.* iv. 599
Tho' *d.* Milton sits sublime *I.H.* iv. 5
Safe from the treach'rous friend, the *d.* spark *R.L.* i. 73

Dark.
Here she beholds the Chaos *d.* and deep *D.* i. 55
Or *d.* dexterity of groping well *D.* ii. 278
Mount in *d.* volumes, and descend in snow *D.* ii. 364
Embody'd *d.,* what clouds of Vandals rise *D.* iii. 85
Wits, who, like owls, see only in the *d. D.* iii. 192
But lo ! to *d.* encounter in mid air *D.* iii. 265
Sworn foe to Myst'ry, yet divinely *d. D.* iv. 460
And LYTTLETON a *d.,* designing Knave *E.S.* ii. 131
You balance not the many in the *d. M.E.* i. 122
But, dreadful too, the *d.* assassin hires *M.E.* iii. 28
The glance by day, the whisper in the *d. R.L.* i. 74
Yet gave me in this *d.* Estate *U.P.* 9
Cole, whose *d.* streams his flow'ry islands lave *W.F.* 343

Darken.
It brighten'd *Cragg's*, and may *d.* thine *S.* iv. 45

Darken'd.
The pomp was *d.,* and the day o'ercast *P.C.* 32
With desp'rate charcoal round his *d.* walls *P.S.* 20
Whether the *d.* room to muse invite *S.* i. 97

Darkens.
Shades ev'ry flow'r, and *d.* ev'ry green *E.A.* 168
His Quincunx *d.,* his Espaliers meet *M.E.* iv. 80

Darker.
And see now clearer, and now *d.* days *E.C.* 405

Darkly.
A Being *d.* wise, and rudely great *E.M.* ii. 4

Darkness.
Half thro' the solid *d.* of his soul *D.* iii. 226
Of *d.* visible so much be lent *D.* iv. 3
And universal *D.* buries All *D.* iv. 656
This light and *d.* in one chaos join'd *E.M.* ii. 203
So *D.* strikes the sense no less than Light *M.E.* i. 53
In dirt and *d.,* hundreds stink content *S.* iii. 133

Darksome.
Relentless walls ! whose *d.* round contains *E.A.* 17
The *d.* pines that o'er yon rock reclin'd *E.A.* 155

Darling.
Mourn'd *Adonis, d.* Youth *Mi.* vii. 10
The busy Sylphs surround their *d.* care *R.L.* i. 145

Dart.
Lo Rufus, tugging at the deadly *d. W.F.* 83
And with her *d.* the flying deer she wounds *W.F.* 180
These monsters, Critics ! with your d—s *engage E.C.* 556
And with your golden *d.,* now useless grown *W.* 25
Or what ill eyes malignant glances *d. A.* 82

Dartineuf.
When Oldfield loves, what *D.* detests *S.* vi. 87

Darting.
Or quick effluvia *d.* thro' the brain *E.M.* i. 199

Darts.
That *d.* severe upon a rising lie *E.* ii. 6

Darty.
Scarsdale his bottle, *D.* his Ham-pie *S.* i. 46

Dash.
Ev'n Guthry saves half Newgate by a *D. E.S.* ii. 11
Here prove who best can d. *thro' thick and thin D.* ii. 276
Stood up to *d.* each vain PRETENDER'S hope *Mi.* ii. 17
D. the proud Gamester in his gilded Car *S.* i. 107

Dash'd.
Then gnaw'd his pen, then *d.* it on the ground *D.* i. 117
Never was *d.* out, at one lucky hit *D.* ii. 47
Came whip and spur, and *d.* thro' thin and thick *D.* iv. 297

Date.
Heav'n had decreed these works a longer *d. D.* i. 196
All nonsense thus, of old or modern *d. D.* iii. 59
Short is the *d.,* alas, of modern rhymes *E.C.* 476
What Time would spare, from Steel receives its *d. R.L.* iii. 171
My foes shall wish my Life a longer *d. S.* i. 61

Dated.
To all their *d.* Backs he turns you round *M.E.* iv. 135

Daughter.

D. of Chaos and eternal Night *D.* i. 12
Laid this gay d. of the Spring in dust *D.* iv. 416
The tender sister, d., friend, and wife *E.* iii. 52
Ah let thy handmaid, sister, d., move *E.A.* 153
Fresh blooming Hope, gay d. of the sky *E.A.* 299
Sighs for a d. with unwounded ear *M.E.* ii. 260
His only d. in a stranger's pow'r *M.E.* iii. 325
His D. flaunts a Viscount's tawdry wife *M.E.* iii. 391
Wife, son, and d., Satan I are thine own *M.E.* iii. 399
Let Bawdry, Billingsgate, my d—s dear D. i. 307
And all thy yawning d. cry, encore *D.* iv. 60
See future sons, and d. yet unborn *M.* 88
Our Wives read Milton, and our D. plays *S.* v. 172

Dauntless.

Stood d. Curl; "Behold that rival here *D.* ii. 58
A d. infant! never scar'd with God *D.* iv. 284

Dawn.

Such was her wont at early d. to drop *D.* ii. 71
The d. now blushing on the mountain's side *Sp.* 21
Here arm'd with silver bows, in early d. *W.F.* 169
Soon as they d. *from Hyperborean skies D.* iii. 85

Dawning.

And d. grace is op'ning on my soul *E.A.* 280
With joyous musick wake the d. day *Sp.* 24

Dawns.

Where Life awakes, and d. at ev'ry line *E.* iii. 4

Day—see also To-day.

Beneath yon poplar oft we past the d. *A.* 66
Farewell, ye woods, adieu the light of d. *A.* 94
Till genial Jacob, or a warm Third d. *D.* i. 57
'Twas on the d. when * * rich and grave *D.* i. 85
But liv'd in Settle's numbers one d. more *D.* i. 90
Yet ate, in dreams, the custard of the d. *D.* i. 92
Blank'd his bold visage, and a thin Third d. *D.* i. 114
Thou triumph'st, Victor of the high-wrought d. *D.* ii. 187
Sons of a D.! just buoyant on the flood *D.* ii. 307
Thus the soft gifts of Sleep conclude the d. *D.* ii. 419
Rush to the world, impatient for the d. *D.* iii. 30
A Poet the first d. he dips his quill *D.* iv. 163
For sure if Dulness sees a grateful D. *D.* iv. 181
Nor wert thou, Isis! wanting to the d. *D.* iv. 193
Whose pious hope aspires to see the d. *D.* iv. 461
Eyes the calm Sun-set of thy various D. *E.* i. 38
How oft in pleasing tasks we wear the d. *E.* iii. 17
Our hearts may bear its slender chain a d. *E.* iv. 64
To morning-walks, and pray'rs three hours a d. *E.* v. 14
Shone sweetly lambent with celestial d. *E.A.* 64
Canst thou forget that sad, that solemn d. *E.A.* 107
And gleams of glory brighten'd all the d. *E.A.* 146
And melts in visions of Eternal d. *E.A.* 222
When at the close of each sad sorrowing d. *E.A.* 225
And smooth my passage to the realms of d. *E.A.* 322
Read them by d., and meditate by night *E.C.* 125
Truth breaks upon us with resistless d. *E.C.* 212
Reflect new glories, and augment the d. *E.C.* 473
And make each d. a Critic on the last *E.C.* 571
Let this great truth be present night and d. *E.M.* iii. 5
Who calls the council, states the certain d. *E.M.* iii. 107
Or he whose Virtue sigh'd to lose a d. *E.M.* iv. 148
Compute the morn and ev'ning to the d. *E.M.* iv. 306
What? shall each spur-gall'd Hackney of the d. *E.S.* ii. 140
It anger'd Turenne, once upon a d. *E.S.* ii. 150
Spin all your Cobwebs o'er the Eye of D. *E.S.* ii. 222
Shall hail the rising, close the parting d. *I.H.* iii. 30
And on the sightless eye-ball pour the d. *M.* 40
By d. o'ersees them, and by night protects *M.* 52
And break upon thee in a flood of d. *M.* 98
Reveal'd, and God's eternal d. be thine *M.* 104
Blushing in bright diversities of d. *M.E.* iv. 84
At Timon's Villa let us pass a d. *M.E.* iv. 99
And swear no D. was ever past so ill *M.E.* iv. 168
She flatters her good lady twice a d. *Mi.* iii. 18
That gnaws them Night and D. *Mi.* iv. 28
This d. Tom's fair account has run *Mi.* xii. 3
Quiet by d. *O.* iv. 12
The pomp was darken'd, and the d. o'ercast *P.C.* 32
Fed with soft Dedication all d. long *P.S.* 233
And flatter'd ev'ry d., and some days eat (rep.) *P.S.* 240
And op'd those eyes that must eclipse the d. *R.L.* i. 14
The glance by d., the whisper in the dark *R.L.* i. 74

And bask and whiten in the blaze of d. *R.L.* ii. 78
This d. black Omens threat the brightest Fair *R.L.* ii. 101
Meanwhile declining from the noon of d. *R.L.* iii. 19
And curs'd for ever this victorious d. *R.L.* iii. 104
Spreads his black wings, and slowly mounts to d. *R.L.* iv. 88
For ever curs'd be this detested d. *R.L.* iv. 147
Oh! if to dance all night, and dress all d. *R.L.* v. 19
And the pale ghosts start at the flash of d. *R.L.* v. 52
Lord Fanny spins a thousand such a d. *S.* i. 6
Attends to gild the Ev'ning of my d. *S.* i. 94
But on some lucky d. (as when they found *S.* ii. 55
What ev'ry d. will want, and most, the last *S.* iii. 22
Long, as to him who works for debt, the d. *S.* iii. 35
Life's instant business to a future d. *S.* iii. 42
To him commit the hour, the d., the year *S.* iv. 9
And what is Fame? the Meanest have their D. *S.* iv. 46
Takes the whole House upon the Poet's D. *S.* iv. 88
Up, Up! cries Gluttony, 'tis break of d. *S.* iv. 112
Indulg'd the d. that hous'd the annual grain *S.* v. 243
Years following years, steal something ev'ry d. *S.* vi. 72
Each prais'd within, is happy all d. long *S.* vi. 156
Glad, like a Boy, to snatch the first good d. *S.* vi. 294
He, ev'ry d., from King to King can walk *S.* viii. 104
In sure succession to the d. of doom *S.* vii. 161
With joyous musick wake the dawning d. *Sp.* 24
More bright than noon, yet fresh as early d. *Sp.* 82
By night he scorches, as he burns by d. *Su.* 92
The gaze of fools, and pageant of a d. *U.L.* 44
And part admit, and part exclude the d. *W.F.* 18
To the bright regions of the rising d. *W.F.* 388
Such this d.'s *doctrine—in another fit M.E.* ii. 75
As, when a Statesman wants a d. defence *P.S.* 251
And screen'd in shades from d. detested glare *R.L.* iv. 22
Thro' this d. Life or Death (rep.) *U.P.* 44
And sure succession down from Heywood's d—s *D.* i. 98
He sleeps among the dull of ancient d. *D.* i. 294
Twelve starv'ling bards of these degenerate d. *D.* ii. 40
And all who since, in mild benighted d. *D.* iii. 53
In Toland's, Tindal's, and in Woolston's d. *D.* iii. 213
Proceed, great d.! till Learning fly the shore *D.* iii. 333
And bring Saturnian d. of Lead and Gold *D.* iv. 16
In twice ten thousand rhyming nights and d. *D.* iv. 172
Recall those nights that clos'd thy toilsome d. *E.* i. 15
In these lone walls (their d. eternal bound) *E.A.* 141
Hail, Bards triumphant! born in happier d. *E.C.* 189
And see now clearer, and now darker d. *E.C.* 405
But see! each Muse, in Leo's golden d. *E.C.* 57
In d. of old, they pardon'd breach of vows *E.J.S.* 29
Those painted clouds that beautify our d. *E.M.* iv. 284
Why, full of d. and honour, lives the Sire *E.M.* iv. 106
Enough for half the Greatest of these d. *E.S.* ii. 112
Wharton, the scorn and wonder of our d. *M.E.* i. 180
That very Cæsar, born in Scipio's d. *M.E.* i. 216
See my weary D. consuming *Mi.* vii. 7
D. of ease, and nights of pleasure *O.* iii. 43
Hours, d., and years slide soft away *O.* iv. 10
I ne'er with wits or writings pass'd my d. *P.S.* 223
And flatter'd ev'ry day, and some d. eat (rep.) *P.S.* 240
On cares like these if length of d. attend (rep.) *P.S.* 414
While visits shall be paid on solemn d. *R.L.* iii. 167
Alas young man! your d. can ne'er be long *S.* i. 101
In South-sea d. not happier, when surmis'd *S.* ii. 133
Why will you break the Sabbath of my d. *S.* iii. 3
But for the Wits of either Charles's d. *S.* v. 107
In D. of Ease, when now the weary Sword *S.* v. 139
Unhappy Dryden! In all Charles's d. *S.* v. 213
How free or frugal, I shall pass my d. *S.* vi. 289
But, as the Fool that in reforming d. *S.* viii. 15
'Tis true, far ten d. hence 'twill be King Lear's *S.* viii. 219
Oh! how I long with you to pass my d. *Su.* 77
Hail, sacred peace! hail, long-expected d. *W.F.* 355
Touch the fair fame of Albion's golden d. *W.F.* 424
Ev'n I more sweetly pass my careless d. *W.F.* 431

Dazzle.

Ah! Friend! to d. let the Vain design *M.E.* ii. 249

Dazzled,

Alas! not d. with their noontide ray *E.M.* iv. 305

Dead.

Did the d. letter unsuccessful prove *D.* i. 193
Rolls the large tribute of d. dogs to Thames *D.* ii. 272

DEADLIER—DEATH.

And all was hush'd as Folly's self lay *d. D.* ii. 418
Sense, speech, and measure, living tongues and *d. D.* iii. 167
There sunk Thalia, nerveless, cold, and *d. D.* iv. 41
Patrons who sneak from living worth to *d. D.* iv. 95
We bring to one *d.* level ev'ry mind *D.* iv. 268
Now prostrate I *d. l* behold that Caroline *D.* iv. 413
Absent or *d.*, still let a friend be dear (*rep.*) *E.* i. 13
Those tears eternal, that embalm the *E.* iii. 48
And *d.*, as living, 'tis our Author's pride *E.* iv. 79
A death-like silence, and a *d.* repose *E.A.* 166
Thy life a long *d.* calm of fix'd repose *E.A.* 251
The torch of Venus burns not for the *d. E.A.* 258
To light the *d.*, and warm th' unfruitful urn *E.A.* 262
Propt on some tomb, a neighbour of the *d. E.A.* 304
Zoilus again would start up from the *d. E.C.* 465
Nay, fly to Altars ; there they'll talk you *d. E.C.* 624
An Eugene living, as a Cæsar *d. E.M.* iv. 244
Are none, none living? let me praise the *D. E.S.* ii. 251
They had no Poet, and are *d. I.H.* iv. 16
One would not, sure, be frightful when one's *d. M.E.* i. 250
Would Chloe know if you're alive or *d. M.E.* ii. 177
Alive, ridiculous, and *d.* forgot *M.E.* ii. 248
The very tombs now vanish'd like their *d. M.E.* v. 4
To the pale nations of the *d. O.* i. 52
As her *d.* Father's rev'rend image past *P.C.* 31
Tie up the knocker, say I'm sick, I'm *d. P.S.* 2
If foes, they write, if friends, they read me *d. P.S.* 32
His Library (where busts of Poets *d. P.S.* 235
Nor know, if *Dennis* be alive or *d. P.S.* 270
A friend in exile, or a father, *d. P.S.* 355
That all her vanities at once are *d. R.L.* i. 52
And Advocates for Folly *d.* and gone *S.* v. 34
By learned Critics, of the mighty *d. S.* v. 138
In downright charity revive the *d. S.* vi. 164
The Thief condemn'd, in law already *d. S.* vii. 15
And yet, by speaking truth of monarchs *d. S.* viii. 106
Fair Daphne's *d.*, and love is now no more *W.* 28, &c.
Consults the *d.*, and lives past ages o'er *W.F.* 248
All, all but Truth drops d.-born *from the Press E.S.* ii. 226

Deadlier.
And lin'd with Giants *d.* than 'em all *S.* viii. 275

Deadly.
And drew a *d.* bodkin from her side *R.L.* v. 88
For hung with *d.* sins I see the wall *S.* viii. 274
Lo Rufus, tugging at the *d.* dart *W.F.* 83

Deaf.
Hear him, ye *d.*, and all ye blind, behold *M.* 38
The Woman's *d.*, and does not hear *Mi.* viii. 12
To you I mourn, nor to the *d.* I sing *Su.* 15
D. the prais'd ear, and mute the tuneful tongue *U.L.* 76

Deal.
One, one bad *D.*, three *Septievas* have lost *Mi.* ix. 12
Would all my gold in one bad *D.* were gone *Mi.* ix. 15
In ancient Sense *if any needs will d. D.* iv. 229
Good friend, forbear I you *d.* in dang'rous things *P.S.* 75
In shillings and in pence at first they *d. S.* vii. 83
And *d.* damnation round the land *U.P.* 27

Deals.
Who in the secret, *d.* in Stocks secure *S.* viii. 140

Dean.
D., Drapier, Bickerstaff, or Gulliver *D.* i. 20
To save a Bishop, may I name a *D.* (*rep.*) *E.S.* ii. 33
Lewis, the *D.*, will be of use *I.H.* ii. 35 *s*
Good Mr. *D.*, go change your gown *I.H.* ii. 43 *s*
I thought the *D.* had been too proud *I.H.* ii. 53 *s*
How think you of our Friend the *D. I.H.* ii. 103 *s*
Pudding, that might have pleas'd a *D. I.H.* ii. 166
To rest, the Cushion and soft *D.* invite *M.E.* iv. 149
Who to the *D.* and *silver bell* can swear *P.S.* 299

Dear.
To Dulness Ridpath is as *d.* as Mist *D.* i. 208
This brazen Brightness, to the 'Squire so *d. D.* i. 219
No merit now the *d.* Nonjuror claims *D.* i. 253
Let Bawdry, Billingsgate, my daughters *d. D.* i. 307
D. to the Muse ! to HARLEY *d.*, in vain *E.* i. 6
Absent or dead, still let a friend be *d. E.* i. 13
From the *d.* man unwilling she must sever *E.* v. 5
So when your Slave, at some *d.* idle time *E.* v. 41

D. fatal name ! rest ever unreveal'd *E.A.* 9
Oh name for ever sad ! for ever *d. E.A.* 31
How the *d.* object from the crime remove *E.A.* 193
Oh curst, *d.* horrors of all-conscious night *E.A.* 229
Ye soft illusions, *d.* deceits, arise *E.A.* 240
The *d.* Ideas, where I fly, pursue *E.A.* 264
How strangely you expose yourself, my *d. E.J.S.* 10
D. Sir, forgive the Prejudice of Youth *E.S.* i. 63
Here lies the Friend most lov'd, the Son most *d. Ep.* iii. 2
May Heav'n, *d.* Father ! now have all thy Heart *Ep.* xiii. 2
Till you are dust like me—*D.* Shade ! I will *Ep.* xiii. 4
Mother too fierce of *d.* Desires *I.H.* iii. 7
But why ! ah tell me, ah too *d. I.H.* iii. 37
Pictures like these, *d.* Madam, to design *M.E.* ii. 151
To live on Ven'son when it sold so *d. M.E.* iii. 118
A certain truth, which many buy too *d. M.E.* iv. 40
D. BETTY shall th' important point decide *Mi.* ix. 23
And trust me, *d. l* good humour can prevail *R.L.* v. 31
Peace is my *d.* delight—not Fleury's more *S.* i. 75
Till Becca-ficos sold so dev'lish *d. S.* ii. 39
What's Property ? *d.* Swift ! you see it alter *S.* ii. 167
For Snug's the word : my *d. l* we'll live in town *S.* iii. 147
Plain truth, *d.* MURRAY, needs no flow'rs of speech *S.* iv. 3
Authors; like coins, grow *d.* as they grow old *S.* v. 35
What *d.* delight to Britons Farce affords *S.* v. 316
D. Col'nel, COBHAM's and your country's Friend *S.* vi. 1
D. Cibber ! never match'd one Ode of thine *S.* vi. 138
My *d.* Tibullus !" if that will not do *S.* vi. 143
D. Countess I you have charms all hearts to hit *S.* viii. 232
Of all her D—s she never slander'd one M.E. ii. 175

Dearer.
This the Great Mother *d.* held than all *D.* i. 269
His wealth, yet *d.*, forfeit to the Crown *M.E.* iii. 400

Dearly.
Tells us that Cato *d.* lov'd his wife *E.J.S.* 32
She *d.* pays for Nisus' injur'd hair *R.L.* iii. 124
Your Country's Peace, how oft, how *d.* bought *S.* v. 397
Had *d.* earn'd a little purse of gold *S.* vi. 34

Dearth.
Nor fear a *d.* in these flagitious times *E.C.* 529

Death.
Say, is not absence *d.* to those who love *A.* 30
And keep them in the pale of Words till *d. D.* iv. 160
Fair ev'n in *d.*, this peerless *Butterfly D.* iv. 436
Till *D.* untimely stopp'd his tuneful tongue *E.* i. 2
The lust of Lucre, and the dread of *D. E.* i. 26
Ev'n rival Wits did Voiture's *d.* deplore *E.* iv. 15
The Smiles and Loves had died in Voiture's *d. E.* iv. 19
D., only *d.*, can break the lasting chain *E.A.* 173
O *D.* all-eloquent ! you only prove *E.A.* 335
Wait the great teacher *D.*; and God adore *E.M.* i. 92
Receives the lurking principle of *d. E.M.* ii. 134
To welcome *d.*, and calmly pass away *E.M.* ii. 260
D. still draws nearer, never seeming near *E.M.* iii. 76
And ev'ry *d.* its own avenger breeds *E.M.* iii. 166
When Nature sicken'd, and each gale was *d. E.M.* iv. 108
A thing beyond us, ev'n before our *d. E.M.* iv. 238
Fame but from *d.* a villain's name can save *E.M.* iv. 249
In adamantine chains shall *D.* be bound *M.* 47
Shall feel your ruling passion strong in *d. M.E.* i. 263
Then all for *D.*, that Opiate of the Soul *M.E.* ii. 91
Superiors! *d. l* and Equals ! what a curse *M.E.* ii. 135
Builds Life on *D.*, on Change, Duration founds *M.E.* iii. 167
Wealth in the gross is *d.*, but life diffus'd *M.E.* iii. 233
Arise, and tell me, was thy *d.* more bless'd *M.E.* iii. 322
Till *D.* unfelt that tender frame destroy *Mi.* v. 17
Love, strong as *d.*, the Poet led *O.* i. 51
O'er *d.*, and o'er hell *O.* i. 88
Yet ev'n in *d.* Eurydice he sung *O.* i. 113
Tell me, my Soul, can this be *D. O.* v. 12
O *D. l* where is thy Sting *O.* v. 18
If I dislike it, "Furies, *d.*, and rage !" *P.S.* 57
His *d.* was instant, and without a groan *P.S.* 403
Make Langour smile, and smooth the bed of *D. P.S.* 411
And love of Ombre, after *d.* survive *R.L.* i. 56
And scatters *d.* around from both her eyes *R.L.* v. 58
Oh cruel nymph ! a living *d.* I bear *R.L.* v. 61
And never gallop Pegasus to *d. S.* iii. 14
Finds Envy never conquer'd but by *D. S.* v. 16

DEBASE—DEDICATES.   69

By sale, at least by *d.*, to change their lord *S.* vi. 251
Inexorable *D.* shall level all *S.* vi. 262
Not the black fear of *d.*, that saddens all *S.* vi. 309
No rat is rhym'd to *d.*, nor maid to love *S.* vii. 22
Inspir'd when living, and bequeath'd in *d. Su.* 40
These cheeks now fading at the blast of *d. U.L.* 32
Thro' this day's Life or *D. U.P.* 44
The balmy Zephyrs, silent since her *d. W.* 49
The winds and trees and floods her *d.* deplore *W.* 67
The clam'rous lapwings feel the leaden *d. W.F.* 132
Or *d.*'s *black wing already be display'd S.* i. 95
From burning suns when livid *d*—s descend *E.M.* i. 142
She saw her sons with purple *d.* expire *W.F.* 323
He dreads a *d.*-bed *like the meanest slave M.E.* i. 116
There broken vows, and *d.* alms are found *R.L.* v. 117
A *d.-like* silence, and a dead repose *E.A.* 166

Debase.
And to *d.* the Sons, exalt the Sires *S.* v. 134

Debate.
'Tis true on Words is still our whole *d. D.* iv. 219
'Twas on the night of a *D. I.H.* ii. 185
Mad at a Fox-chase, wise at a *D. M.E.* i. 74
Sometimes a Patriot, active in *d. S,* iii. 27
Heard, noted, answer'd, as in full *d. S.* vi. 187
In all *d*—s *where critics bear a part S.* v. 81
Each prompt to query, answer, and d. *D.* ii. 381

Debauch'd.
The willing Muses were *d.* at Court *S.* v. 152

Debt.
Who starves a Sister, or forswears a *D. E.S.* i. 112
Who starv'd a Sister, who forswore a *D. E.S.* ii. 20
It is but so much more in *d. I.H.* ii. 41 *s*
Forbid it Heav'n, a Favour or a *D. M.E.* ii. 171
I never answer'd—I was not in *d. P.S.* 154
Long, as to him who works for *d.*, the day *S.* iii. 35
As deep in *d.*, without a thought to pay *S.* viii. 21
To *pay their D*—s, *or keep their Faith, like Kings E.S.* i. 122
Of *D.*, and Taxes, Wife and Children clear *M.E.* iii. 279
I pay my *d.*, believe, and say my pray'rs *P.S.* 268

Debtor.
There died my Father, no man's *d. I.H.* i. 79

Decay.
Taught half by Reason, half by mere *d. E.M.* ii. 259
D. of Parts, alas! we all must feel *E.S.* i. 5
Sharp Boreas blows, and Nature feels *d. W.* 87
Tho' each may feel increases and *d*—s *E.C.* 404
So dies her love, and so my hopes d. *A.* 70
How Prologues into Prefaces *d. D.* i. 277
When Moral Evidence shall quite *d. D.* iv. 462
Before her, *Fancy's* gilded clouds *d. D.* iv. 631
Love, rais'd on Beauty, will like that *d. E.* iv. 63
The seas shall waste, the skies in smoke *d. M.* 105
And in a Worm *d. Mi.* iv. 20
The strains *d. O.* i. 19
As winter-fruits grow mild ere they *d. S.* vi. 319
Our sons shall see it leisurely *d. S.* viii. 54
But since, alas! frail beauty must *d. R.L.* v. 25
'Tis done, and nature's various charms *d. W.* 29

Decay'd.
So some coarse Country Wench almost *d. Mi.* iii. 15

Deceit.
O may thy cloud still cover the *d. D.* iv. 356
Ye *soft illusions, dear* d—s, *arise E.A.* 240
Hence false tears, *d.*, disguises *O.* iii. 38

Deceiv'd.
D. by Shows and Forms *Mi.* iv. 2
How many Maids have SHARPER's vows *d. Mi.* ix. 71

Deceivers.
And all the kind *D.* of the soul *I.H.* iii. 36

December.
In cold *D.* fragrant chaplets blow *D.* i. 77

Decency.
O! shall we ev'ry *D.* confound *S.* iv. 118
Content to dwell in D—ies *for ever M.E.* ii. 164

Decent.
A *d.* priest, where monkeys were the gods *D.* iii. 208
The *d.* Knight retir'd with sober rage *D.* iv. 113
Appears more *d.*, as more suitable *E.C.* 319
Secker is *d., Rundel* has a heart *E.S.* ii. 71
With ev'ry sprightly, ev'ry *d.* part *I.H.* iii. 12
When *Kings, Queens, Knaves,* are set in *d.* rank *Mi.* ix. 77
By foreign hands thy *d.* limbs compos'd *U.L.* 52

Decently.
Where half the skill is *d.* to hide *M.E.* iv. 54

Decide.
Who shall *d.*, when Doctors disagree *M.E.* iii. 1
Dear BETTY shall th' important point *d. Mi.* ix. 23
Attend, and yield to what I now *d. Mi.* ix. 109
At Ombre singly to *d.* their doom *R.L.* iii. 27
I think Sir Godfrey should *d.* the suit *S.* vi. 24

Decius.
In *D.* charms, in Curtius is divine *E.M.* ii. 200

Deck.
Oh All-accomplish'd ST. JOHN! *d.* thy shrine *E.S.* ii. 139
There other trophies *d.* the truly brave *E.S.* ii. 236
And Patriots still, or Poets, *d.* the Line *Ep.* i. 14
In equal curls, and well conspir'd to *d. R.L.* iii. 27
The same, his ancient personage to *d. R.L.* v. 89

Deck'd.
When falling dews with spangles *d.* the glade *A.* 99
She *d.* like Congreve, Addison, and Prior *D.* ii. 124
Why *d.* with all that land and sea afford *R.L.* v. 11

Decks.
And *d.* the Goddess with the glitt'ring spoil *R.L.* i. 132

Declaim.
Must never Patriot then *d.* at Gin *E.S.* ii. 191

Declare.
Then first (if Poets aught of truth *d.*) *D.* ii. 77
Saw ev'ry Court, heard ev'ry King *d. D.* iv. 313
Some beauties yet no Precepts can *d. E.C.* 141
That instant, I *d.*, he has my Love *E.S.* ii. 75
I never (to my sorrow I *d.*) *E.S.* ii. 98
And tho' I solemnly *d. I.H.* ii. 121 *s*
Why then *d.* Good-nature is her scorn *M.E.* ii. 59

Declares.
Then thus the wonders of the deep *d. D.* ii. 330
The doctor call'd, *d.* all help too late *M.E.* i. 239

Decline.
Yet from the same we learn, in its *d. E.M.* ii. 257
I shun his Zenith, court his mild *d. E.S.* ii. 76
Thus oft they rear, and oft the head d. *D.* ii. 393

Declin'd.
With heads *d.*, ye cedars homage pay *M.* 35

Declines.
And unobserv'd the glaring Orb *d. M.E.* ii. 256

Declining.
Meanwhile, *d.* from the noon of day *R.L.* iii. 19

Decorum.
The Grace-cup serv'd with all *d. I.H.* ii. 138

Decree.
The *Snuff-Box* to CARDELIA I *d. Mi.* ix. 111
Cease to contend, for Daphnis, I *d. Sp.* 93

Decreed.
Yet sure had Heav'n *d.* to save the state (*rep.*) *D.* i. 195
And great Nassau to Kneller's hand *d., S.* v. 382

Decrees.
So heav'n *d.!* with heav'n who can contest *R.L.* v. 112

Decry.
While Truth, Worth, Wisdom, daily they *d. E.S.* i. 169

Decry'd.
You by whose care, in vain *d.* and curst *D.* i. 5

Dedicates.
One *d.* in high heroic prose *P.S.* 109

Dedication.
Fed with soft *d.* all day long *P.S.* 233
Dedicators.
With ready quills the *d.* wait *D.* ii. 198
And flattery to fulsome *D. E.C.* 593
Deduct.
D. what is but Vanity, or Dress *E.M.* ii. 45
Deductions.
Make fair *d.*; see to what they mount *E.M.* iv. 270
Deed.
August her *d.*, and sacred be her fame *E.A.* 78
Because the *D.* he forg'd was not my own *E.S.* ii. 190
Infer the Motive from the *D.*, and shew *M.E.* i. 101
Who sees him act, but envies ev'ry *d. P.C.* 25
My council sends to execute a *d. S.* vi. 92
The d—s, and dext'rously omits ses heires *S.* vii. 700
Deem.
In doubt to *d.* himself a God, or Beast *E.M.* ii. 8
And shall we *d.* him Ancient, right and sound *S.* v. 58
Deem'd.
Th' embroider'd suit at least he *d.* his prey *D.* ii. 117
Who *d.* each other Oracles of Law *S.* vi. 128
Deeming.
Or, *d.* meanest what we greatest call *E.* i. 19
Deems.
Another *d.* him instrument of hell *E.M.* iv. 138
Deep.
And with *d.* murmurs fill the sounding shores *A.* 20
And pour'd her spirit o'er the land and *d. D.* i. 8
Here she beholds the Chaos dark and *d.* L. 55
Or such as bellow from the *d.* Divine *D.* ii. 257
A cold, long-winded native of the *d. D.* ii. 300
Then thus the wonders of the *d.* declares *D.* ii. 330
As half to shew, half veil, the *d.* Intent *D.* iv. 4
Plough'd was his front with many a *d.* Remark *D* iv. 204
To happy Convents, bosom'd *d.* in vines *D.* iv. 301
When Sallee Rovers chas'd him on the *d. D.* iv. 380
D. in his Entrails—I rever'd them there *D.* iv. 384
Some, *d.* Free-Masons, join the silent race *D.* iv. 571
In these *d.* solitudes and awful cells *E.A.* 1
Drink *d.*, or taste not the Pierian spring *E.C.* 216
Towns to one grave, whole nations to the *d. E.M.* i. 144
Around, how wide! how *d.* extend below *E.M.* i. 236
Or *d.* with di'monds in the flaming mine *E.M.* iv. 10
Now *d.* in Taylor, and the Book of Martyrs *M.E.* ii. 3
And when she sees her Friend in *d.* despair *M.E.* ii. 169
D. hid the shining mischief under ground *M.E.* iii. 10
Fill the capacious Squire, and *d.* Divine *M.E.* iii. 204
The surge, and plunge his Father in the *d. M.E.* iii. 354
Sinks *d.* within him, and possesses whole *M.E.* iii. 373
D. harvests bury all his pride has plann'd *M.E.* iv. 175
The *d.*, majestic, solemn organs blow *O.* i. 11
He, who to seem more *d.* than you or I *S.* v. 131
Howl to the roarings of the Northern *d. S.* v. 329
How, when you nodded, o'er the land and *d. S.* v. 402
As *d.* in debt, without a thought to pay *S.* viii. 21
And Cupids ride the Lion of the D—s *D.* iv. 308
And low-brow'd rocks hung nodding o'er the *d. E.A.* 244
Spread all his sails, and durst the *d.* explore *E.C.* 646
Or breathes thro' air, or shoots beneath the *d. E.M.* iii. 16
Blue Neptune storms, the bellowing *d.* resound *R.L.* v. 50
Deepens.
D. the murmur of the falling floods *E.A.* 169
Deeper.
With *d.* sable blots the silver flood *D.* ii. 274
Who but to sink the *d.*, rose the higher *D.* ii. 290
Deepest.
Who knew most Sentences, was *d.* read *E.C.* 441
Exil'd by thee from earth to *d.* hell *W.F.* 413
Deer.
Go drive the *D.*, and drag the finny prey *S.* iv. 113
And with her dart the flying *d.* she wounds *W.F.* 180

Defac'd.
So by false learning is good sense *d. E.C.* 25
Defame.
And who unknown *d.* me, let them be *S.* i. 139
Default.
Regardless of our merit or *d. D.* iv. 486
Defeated.
Strange! by the Means *d.* of the Ends *M.E.* ii. 243
Defect.
Fine by *d.*, and delicately weak *M.E.* ii. 43
Trust not yourself; but your *d*—s to know *E.C.* 213
And build on wants, and on *d.* of mind *E.M.* ii. 247
Defence.
Physic of Metaphysic begs *d. D.* iv. 645
And then turn Critics in their own *d. E.C.* 29
Pride, where wit fails, steps in to our *d. E.C.* 209
In who obtain *d.*, or who defend *E.M.* iv. 59
O sacred weapon! left for Truth's *d. E.S.* ii. 212
So, when a Statesman wants a day's *d. P.S.* 251
D. from Phœbus', not from Cupid's beams *Su.* 14
Defenceless.
Sudden they seize th' amaz'd, *d.* prize *W.F.* 109
Defend.
Dulness! whose good old cause I yet *d. D.* i. 165
The mothers nurse it, and the sires *d. E.M.* iii. 126
In who obtain defence, or who *d. E.M.* iv. 59
Equal, the injur'd to *d. I.H.* iii. 13
At last, to follies Youth could scarce *d. M.E.* ii. 235
One from all Grubstreet will my fame *d. P.S.* 111
Yet wants the honour, injur'd, to *d. P.S.* 296
How shall I, then, your helpless fame *d. R.L.* iv. 111
Can there be wanting, to *d.* Her cause *S.* i. 109
Your Country, chief, in Arms abroad *d. S.* v. 3
Then too we hurt ourselves, when to *d. S.* v. 364
Define.
Who thus *d.* it, say they more or less *E.M.* iv. 27
Defin'd.
Try'd all *hors d'œuvres*, all *liqueurs d. D.* iv. 317
De Foe—see also Daniel.
Earless on high, stood unabash'd *D. D.* ii. 147
Defraud.
An hour, and not *d.* the Public Weal *S.* v. 6
Defrauded.
Redeem'd from tapers and *d.* pies *D.* i. 156
For their *d.* absent foals they make *D.* ii. 249
Defy.
Sleep's all-subduing charms who dares *d. D.* ii. 373
Defy'd.
We still *d.* the Romans as of old *E.C.* 718
Their Quibbles routed, and *d.* their Puns *Mi.* ii. 12
Degen'rate.
Twelve starv'ling bards of these *d.* days *D.* ii. 40
Fall by the Votes of their *d.* line *E.S.* ii. 153
Senates *d.*, Patriots disagree *M.E.* iii. 148
Degrade.
Renounce our Country, and *d.* our Name *S.* iv. 125
Such they'll *d.*; and sometimes in its stead *S.* vi. 163
Degraded.
Already see you a *d.* toast *R.L.* iv. 109
Degrades.
But 'tis the Fall *d.* her to a Whore *E.S.* i. 143
Yet Time ennobles, or *d.* each Line *S.* iv. 44
Degree.
Be not, exalted to whate'er *d. E.* ii. 14
And all that rises, rise in due *d. E.M.* i. 46
Know thy own point: This kind, this due *d. E.M.* i. 283
No creature owns it in the first *d. E.M.* ii. 225
Few in th' extreme, but all in the *d. E.M.* ii. 232
Happier as kinder, in whate'er *d. E.M.* iv. 359
Virtue may choose the high or low *d. E.S.* i. 337
The Queen confers her Titles and D—s *D.* iv. 366

DEIGN—DENNIS. 71

As without learning they can take *D. E.C.* 521
Here with *d.* of swiftness, there of force *E.M.* i. 182
Till, by *d.*, remote and small *O.* i. 18
Sees by *d.* a purer blush arise *R.L.* i. 143

Deign.
Not Cæsar's empress would I *d.* to prove *E.A.* 87
Oh *d.* to visit our forsaken seats *Su.* 71

Deign'd.
Walker! our hat—nor more he *d.* to say *D.* iv. 273
Yet on plain Pudding *d.* at home to eat *M.E.* ii. 62

Deign'st.
Say in what mortal soil thou *d.* to grow *E.M.* iv. 8

Deigns.
When this Heroics only *d.* to praise *S.* vi. 82
If PETER *d.* to help you to your *own S.* vii. 66

Deity.
This hour a slave, the next a *d. E.M.* i. 68
The rocks proclaim th' approaching *D. M.* 32

Dejected.
Never *d.*, while another's bless'd *E.M.* iv. 324
Her last good man *d.* Rome ador'd *P.C.* 35
Too soon *d.*, and too soon elate *R.L.* iii. 102
Her eyes *d.* and her hair unbound *R.L.* iv. 90

Dejects.
Nor think, to die *d.* my lofty mind *R.L.* v. 99

Delay.
Come, Delia, come; ah, why this long *d. A.* 48
Dangers, doubts, d—s, *surprises O.* iii. 39
Who cause the *proud their visits to* d. *R.L.* iv. 63
That keep me from myself; and still *d. S.* iii. 41

Delay'd.
And says our wars thrive ill, because *d. S.* viii. 163

Delia.
Thus, far from *D.*, to the winds I mourn *A.* 21
What have I said? where'er my *D.* flies *A.* 35
Come, *D.*, come; ah, why this long delay *A.* 48
Me gentle *D.* beckons from the plains *Sp.* 55
If *D.* smile, the flow'rs begin to spring *Sp.* 71
But *D.* always; absent from her sight *Sp.* 79
And *D.'s name and Doris' fill'd the Grove A.* 4
To *D.* ear the tender notes convey *A.* 18
Curs'd be the fields that cause my *D.* stay *A.* 32
Slander or prison dread from *D.* rage *S.* i. 81
Inspire me, Phœbus, in my *D.* praise *Sp.* 45

Delib'rate.
Form'd but to check, *d.*, and advise *E.M.* ii. 70

Delicacy.
Th' address, the *D.*—stoops at once *M.E.* ii. 85
Weakness or *D.*; all so nice *M.E.* ii. 205

Delicate.
But Horace, Sir, was *d.*, was nice *E.S.* i. 11

Delicately.
Fine by defect, and *d.* weak *M.E.* ii. 43

Delicious.
Still drink *d.* poison from thy eye *E.A.* 122

Delight.
Some Squire, perhaps you take *d.* to rack *E.* v. 23
How glowing guilt exalts the keen *d. E.A.* 230
Be Homer's works your study and *d. E.C.* 124
Nor lose, for that malignant dull *d. E.C.* 237
Some livelier plaything gives his youth *d. E.M.* ii. 277
Say in pursuit of profit or *d. E.M.* iv. 85
To draw the Naked is your true *d. M.E.* ii. 188
Asham'd to own they gave *d.* before *M.E.* ii. 237
Then future ages with *d.* shall see *M.E.* v. 59
Peace is my dear *d.*—not Fleury's more *S.* i. 75
And Helmsley, once proud Buckingham's *d. S.* ii. 177
What dear *d.* to Britons Farce affords *S.* v. 310
See what d—s in sylvan scenes appear Su. 59
Tears that d., *and sighs that waft to heav'n E.A.* 214
Form'd to *d.* at once and lash the age *Ep.* xi. 4
D. no more—O thou my voice inspire *M.* 5
So well-bred spaniels civilly *d. P.S.* 313
While fish in streams, or birds *d.* in air *R.L.* iii. 163

If Windsor-shades *d.* the matchless maid *Sp.* 67
Nor plains at morn, nor groves at noon *d. Sp.* 80

Delighted.
List'ning *d.* to the jest unclean *D.* ii. 99
Or sat *d.* in the thick'ning shade *M.E.* iv. 90
Who, tho' the House was up, *d.* sate *S.* vi. 186

Delightful.
D. Abscourt, if its fields afford *S.* vi. 232

Delights.
This arch Absurd, that wit and fool *d. D.* i. 221

Deluding.
Come, with one glance of those *d.* eyes *E.A.* 283
And whisper with that soft *d.* air *Mi.* ix. 7

Deluge.
A second *d.* Learning thus o'er-run *E.C.* 691
Shall d. *all; and* Av'rice *creeping on M.E.* iii. 137
To *d.* sin, and drown a Court in tears *S.* viii. 285

Delusive.
Mears, Warner, Wilkins run; *d.* thought *D.* ii. 125

De Lyra.
D. there a dreadful front extends *D.* l. 153

Demand.
But grant him Riches, your *D.* is o'er *E.M.* iv. 157
Immense the pow'r, immense were the *D. E.M.* iv. 165
Or *simple pride for flatt'ry makes* d—a *P.S.* 253
D. new bodies, and in Calf's array D. iii. 29
And bids her beau *d.* the precious hairs *R.L.* iv. 122
These fools *d.* not pardon, but Applause *S.* v. 118

Demanding.
D. life, impatient for the skies *M.* 90

Demands.
A fading Fresco here *d.* a sigh *E.* iii. 34
Love but d. *what else were shed in pray'r E.A.* 46
Vice, thus abus'd, *d.* a Nation's care *E.S.* i. 128
A longer care Man's helpless kind *d. E.M.* iii. 131
Uncurl'd it hangs, the fatal shears *d. R.L.* iv. 173

Demi-God.
Receiv'd each *D.*, with pious care *D.* iv. 383
A Fit of Vapours clouds this *D. D. S.* iii. 188
Transported d—s *stood round O.* i. 42

Democritus.
With laughter sure *D.* had died *S.* v. 320

Demoivre.
Sure as *D.*, without rule or line *E.M.* iii. 104

Demon—*see* Dæmon.

Demonstration.
And *D.* thin, and Theses thick *D.* ii. 241

Demurs.
All my *d.* but double his Attacks *P.S.* 65

Dens.
Cities laid waste, they storm'd the *d.* and caves *W.F.* 49

Denham.
Here his first lays majestic *D.* sung *W.F.* 271
His living harp, and lofty *D.* sung *W.F.* 280
Where *D.'s strength, and Waller's sweetness join E.C.* 361

Denied—*see* Deny'd.

Denies.
Not everlasting Blackmore this *d. D.* ii. 302
Alike in what it gives and whist *d. E.M.* i. 206
"The wretch he starves"—and piously *d. M.E.* iii. 104
The Lab'rer bears: What his hard Heart *d. M.E.* iv. 171
And what a solemn face if he *d. S.* vii. 68

Denizens.
He summons straight his *D.* of air *R.L.* ii. 55

Dennis.
And all the mighty Mad in *D.* rage *D.* i. 106
D. and Dissonance, and captious Art *D.* ii. 239
Ah *D.!* Gildon ah! what ill-starr'd rage *D.* iii. 173
As e'er could *D.*, of the Grecian stage *E.C.* 270

DENY—DESERVES.

Let *D.* write, and nameless numbers rail *Mi.* i. 4
When press'd by want and weakness *D.* lies (*rep.*) *Mi.* ii. 10
Yet then did *D.* rave in furious fret *P.S.* 153
Nor know, if *D.* be alive or dead *P.S.* 270
This dreaded Sat'rist *D.* will confess *P.S.* 370
Which made old Ben, and surly *D.* swear *S.* v. 388

Deny.
For her, the limes their pleasing shades *d. A.* 25
For me what Virgil, Pliny may *d. D.* iv. 225
'Tis all in vain, *d.* it as I will *P.S.* 277
Each mortal has his pleasures: none *d. S.* i. 45
And yet *d.* the Careless Husband praise *S.* v. 92
The woods and fields their pleasing toils *d. W.F.* 120

Deny'd.
Whatever nature has in worth *d. E.C.* 205
To all but Heav'n-directed hands *d. E.S.* ii. 214
And gave you Beauty, but *d.* you Pelf *M.E.* ii. 287
What ev'n *d.* a cordial at his end *M.E.* iii. 329
Whether that blessing be *d.* or giv'n *P.S.* 418
When offers are disdain'd, and love *d. R.L.* i. 82
Or fish *d.* (your river yet unthaw'd) *S.* ii. 14
D. all posts of profit or of trust *S.* vi. 61
At aught thy Wisdom has *d. U.P.* 35
A waste for beasts, himself *d.* a grave *W.F.* 80

Depart.
Who durst *d.* from Aristotle's rules *E.C.* 272

Departing.
The skies yet blushing with *d.* light *A.* 98

Departs.
None comes too early, none *d.* too late *S.* ii. 158

Depend.
But why should I on others pray'rs *d. E.A.* 151
Still make the Whole *d.* upon a Part *E.C.* 264
Heav'n forming each on other to *d. E.M.* ii. 249

Dependant.
But as the Flatt'rer or *D.* paint *D.* iv. 535
But an Inferior not *d.*? worse *M.E.* ii. 136

Dependencies.
The strong connexions, nice *d. E.M.* i. 30

Depends.
Our proper bliss *d.* on what we blame *E.M.* i. 282
On one nice Trick *d.* the gen'ral fate *R.L.* iii. 94

Deplore.
Ev'n rival Wits did Voiture's death *d. E.* iv. 15
Condemn'd whole years of absence to *d. E.A.* 361
When sick of Muse, our follies we *d. S.* v. 177
Let nature change, let heav'n and earth *d. W.* 27
The winds, and trees, and floods her death *d. W.* 67

Deplores.
As some sad Turtle his lost love *d. A.* 19

Deprecate.
This calls the Church to *d.* our Sin *E.S.* i. 129

Depriv'd.
D. us soon of our paternal Cell *S.* vi. 59

Depth.
Launch not beyond your *d.*, but be discreet *E.C.* 50
Some safer world in *d.* of woods embrac'd *E.M.* i. 105
Our *d—s who fathoms*, or our *shallows finds M.E.* i. 23

Deputed.
And Milbourn chief, *d.* by the rest *D.* ii. 349

Deride.
All fools have still an itching to *d. E.C.* 32
One Tragic sentence if I dare *d. S.* v. 121

Derive.
Both must alike from Heav'n *d.* their light *E.C.* 13

Deriv'd.
She drew from them what they *d.* from Heav'n *E.C.* 99

Descend.
This labour past, by Bridewell all *d. D.* ii. 269
Mount in dark volumes, and *d.* in snow *D.* ii. 364
D. in all her sober charms *E.* vi. 2
Bright clouds *d.*, and Angels watch thee round *E.A.* 340
From burning suns when livid deaths *d. E.M.* i. 142
Who saw its fires here rise, and there *d. E.M.* ii. 37
And there the streams in purer rills *d. E.M.* iii. 204
Saw Gods *d.*, and fiends infernal rise *E.M.* iii. 254
And may *d.* to Mordington from STAIR *E.S.* ii. 239
And white-rob'd Innocence from heav'n *d. M.* 20
D., ye Nine! *d.* and sing *O.* i. x
D. from Pelion to the main *O.* i. 41
Ere to the main this morning sun *d. R.L.* i. 110
He spoke; the spirits from the sails *d. R.L.* ii. 137
D., and sit on each important card *R.L.* iii. 32
And from the Pleiads fruitful show'rs *d. Sp.* 102
No grateful dews *d.* from ev'ning skies *W.* 45

Descended.
So when Jove's block *d.* from on high *D.* i. 327

Descending.
Now Night *d.*, the proud scene was o'er *D.* i. 89
The King *d.* views th' Elysian Shade *D.* iii. 14
D. Gods have found Elysium here *Su.* 60
Where Peace *d.* bids her olives spring *W.F.* 429

Descends.
Hell rises, Heav'n *d.*, and dance on Earth *D.* iii. 237
While Wren with sorrow to the grave *d. D.* iii. 239
And on its top *d.* the mystic Dove *M.* 12
To Heirs unknown *d.* th' unguarded store *M.E.* ii. 149
But soon the sun with milder rays *d. Su.* 89

Descent.
Till all the Dæmon makes his full *d. M.E.* iii. 371

Describe.
D. or fix one movement of his Mind *E.M.* ii. 36

Describ'd.
THE SAME FOR EVER! and *d.* by all *M.E.* ii. 183

Describes.
And one *d.* a charming Indian screen *R.L.* iii. 14

Description.
Here gay *D.* Egypt glads with show'rs *D.* i. 73
Shin'd in *D.*, he might show it *I.H.* ii. 188
While pure *D.* held the place of Sense? *P.S.* 148
Live in *d.*, and look green in song *W.F.* 8

Descry.
As things seem large which we thro' mists *d. E.C.* 392

Desert.
This golden lance shall guard *D. E.* vi. 6
You rais'd these hallow'd walls; the *d.* smil'd *E.A.* 133
To failings mild, but zealous for *d. E.C.* 731
All fame is foreign, but of true *d. E.M.* iv. 253
Ev'n in a Bishop I can spy *D. E.S.* ii. 70
Hark! a glad voice the lonely *d.* cheers *M.* 29
Who would not praise Patritio's high *d. M.E.* i. 81
See, wild as the winds, o'er the *d.* he flies *O.* i. 110
In the dry *d.* of a thousand lines *S.* v. 112
And 'midst the *d.* fruitful fields arise *W.F.* 26
A dreary *d.*, and a gloomy waste *W.F.* 44
In vain to D—s *thy retreat is made E.* i. 27
By thee to mountains, wilds, and *d.* led *E.A.* 132
The swain in barren *d.* with surprise *M.* 67
Like roses, that in *d.* bloom and die *R.L.* iv. 158
And all th' oblig'd d., *and all the vain E.* i. 32
And Nero's Terraces *d.* their walls *M.E.* iv. 72

Deserter.
Thou mean *d.* of thy brother's blood *U.L.* 30

Deserve.
List under Reason, and *d.* her care *E.M.* ii. 98
Accept the wreath which you *d.* alone *Su.* 57
To sing those honours you *d.* to wear *W.F.* 289

Deserv'd.
That e'er *d.* a watchful spirit's care *R.L.* ii. 102

Deserves.
Ah, think at least thy flock *d.* thy care *E.A.* 129
The knave *d.* it, when he tills the soil (*rep.*) *E.M.* iv. 152
And wild Ambition well *d.* its woe *P.C.* 12
Alone *d.* the favour of the Great *S.* v. 349

DESERVING—DEVIATE. 73

Deserving.
Part pays, and justly, the *d.* steer *E.M.* iii. 40
Yet sure, of qualities *d.* praise *M.E.* iii. 201
The milky heifer, and *d.* steed *M.E.* iv. 186

Design.
To prove me, Goddess! clear of all *d. D.* iv. 391
Whether thy hand strike out some free *d. E.* iii. 3
Convinc'd, amaz'd, he checks the bold *d. E.C.* 136
If plagues or earthquakes break not Heav'n's *d. E.M.* i. 155
Pursues that Chain which links th' immense *d. E.M.* iv. 333
Convinc'd she now contracts her vast *d. M.E.* v. 23
Since 'twas no form'd *d.* of serving God *S.* viii. 18
Could France or Rome divert our brave *d*—*M.E.* iii. 51
He buys for Topham, Drawings and *D. M.E.* iv. 7
Thron'd in the centre of his thin *d. P.S.* 93
The learn'd Baron Butterflies d. *D.* iv. 589
Who made the spider parallels *d. E.M.* iii. 103
Pictures like these, dear Madam, to *d. M.E.* ii. 151
Ah! Friend! to dazzle let the Vain *d. M.E.* ii. 249
For you the swains the fairest flow'rs *d. Su.* 55

Design'd.
Whate'er the talents, or howe'er *d. D.* iv. 161
A work t' outlast immortal Rome *d. E.C.* 131
So when the faithful pencil has *d. E.C.* 484
Proud to accomplish what such hands *d. M.E.* iv. 196

Designing.
And LYTTLETON a dark, *d.* knave *E.S.* ii. 131

Designs.
Plants as you plant, and as you work *d. M.E.* iv. 64

Desire.
Call round the Tomb each object of *d. E.* iii. 49
To Be, contents his natural *d. E.M.* i. 109
Pain their aversion, Pleasure their *d. E.M.* ii. 88
The still-believing, still-renew'd *d. I.H.* iii. 34
Your love of Pleasure, our *d.* of Rest *M.E.* ii. 274
Why, Virtue, dost thou blame *d. O.* iii. 9
A vapour fed from wild *d. O.* iii. 19
Fly then on all the wings of wild *d. S.* iv. 67
Above the vulgar flight of low *d. U.L.* 12
Pan saw and lov'd, and, burning with *d. W.F.* 183
To the same notes, of love, and soft *d. W.F.* 296
D—s compos'd, affections ever ev'n *E.A.* 213
Of show'rs and sunshine, as of man's *d. E.M.* i. 152
Mother too fierce of dear *D. I.H.* iii. 7
Shall call the smiling Loves, and young *D. I.H.* iii. 26
When kind occasion prompts their warm *d. R.L.* i. 75
To stop thy foolish views, thy long *d. S.* iii. 75
What I d. *the world should know I.H.* ii. 62 *s*
Whether we dread, or whether we *d. S.* iv. 20

Desir'd.
No Conquests she, but o'er herself, *d. Ep.* vi. 3

Desires.
Each sex *d.* alike, till two are one *E.M.* iii. 122
All join to guard what each *d.* to gain *E.M.* iii. 278

Desiring.
D. I would stand their friend *I.H.* ii. 66 *s*

Desist.
Ah, cease, rash youth! *d.* ere 'tis too late *R.L.* iii. 121

Despair.
Yet wrote and flounder'd on in mere *d. D.* i. 120
A youth unknown to Phœbus, in *d. D.* ii. 213
Sprung it from piety, or from *d. E.A.* 180
And when she sees her Friend in deep *d. M.E.* ii. 169
And make *d.* and madness please *O.* i. 121
E'er felt such rage, resentment, and *d. R.L.* iv. 9
How often hope, d., *resent, regret E.A.* 199

Despairing.
D. Quacks with curses fled the place *M.E.* iii. 273
D., confounded *O.* i. 107

Despatch'd.
If Blount *d.* himself, he play'd the man *E.S.* i. 123

Desp'rate.
Shall I, like Curtius, *d.* in my zeal *D.* i. 209
Next plung'd a feeble, but a *d.* pack *D.* ii. 305
Concluding all were *d.* sots and fools *E.C.* 271
You make men *d.* if they once are bad *E.S.* ii. 59
A *d. Bulwark,* sturdy, firm, and fierce *M.* ii. 13
With *d.* charcoal round his darken'd walls *P.S.* 20
And *d.* Misery lays hold on Dover *S.* iv. 57
Like slashing Bentley with his *d.* hook *S.* v. 104
This put the man in such a *d.* mind *S.* vi. 37

Despise.
Some foreign writers, some our own *d. E.C.* 394
And ev'n the best, by fits, what they *d. E.M.* ii. 234
Yes, you *d.* the man to Books confin'd *M.E.* i. 1
That task, which as we follow, or *d. S.* iii. 43
Would ye be blest? *d.* low Joys, low Gains *S.* iv. 60
D. the known, nor tremble at th' unknown *S.* vi. 311

Despis'd.
For SWIFT and him *d.* the farce of state *E.* i. 9
But we, brave Britons, foreign laws *d. E.C.* 715
For ever silent, since *d.* by thee *Su.* 44

Despite.
And grow Immortal in his own *d. S.* v. 72

Despotic.
Were equal crimes in a *d.* reign *W.F.* 58

Dessert.
This same *D.* is not so pleasant *I.H.* ii. 219

Destin'd.
Are *d.* Hymen's willing Victim too *E.* iv. 58

Destitute.
Sad chance of war! now *d.* of aid *R.L.* iii. 63

Destroy.
Then too, when fate shall thy fair frame *d. E.A.* 337
But what composes Man, can Man *d. E.M.* ii. 114
The same ambition can *d.* or save *E.M.* ii. 221
These build as fast as knowledge can *d. E.M.* ii. 287
What nothing earthly gives, or can *d. E.M.* iv. 167
As Fits give vigour, just when they *d. M.E.* i. 223
Till Death unfelt that tender frame *d. Mi.* v. 17
D. his fit or sophistry, in vain *P.S.* 91
Steel could the labours of the Gods *d. R.L.* iii. 173

Destroy'd.
Where things *d.* are swept to things unborn *D.* i. 242
Where, one step broken, the great scale's *d. E.M.* i. 244
Destroying others, by himself *d. E.M.* ii. 66
That righteous Abel was *d.* by Cain *E.M.* iv. 118

Destroying.
D. others, by himself destroy'd *E.M.* ii. 66

Destruction.
This Nymph, to the *d.* of mankind *R.L.* ii. 19

Destructive.
D. War, and all-involving Age *E.C.* 184
No joy, or be *d.* of the thing *E.M.* iv. 182

Detains.
Love in their labyrinths his slaves *d. R.L.* ii. 23

Detect.
You lose it in the moment you *d. M.E.* i. 30

Determin'd.
Tir'd, not *d.*, to the last we yield *M.E.* i. 43

Detest.
And love th' offender, yet *d.* th' offence *E.A.* 192
Who cannot flatter, and *d.* who can *S.* viii. 198

Detested.
And screen'd in shades from day's *d.* glare *R.L.* iv. 22
For ever curs'd be this *d.* day *R.L.* iv. 147

Detests.
When Oldfield loves, what Dartineuf *d. S.* vi. 87

Develop.
Then take him to *d.*, if you can *D.* iv. 269

Deviate.
May boldly *d.* from the common track *E.C.* 151

DEVIATES—DIE.

Deviates.
Then Nature d., and can Man do less *E.M.* i. 150
There d. Nature, and here wanders Will *E.M.* iv. 112

Devil, 'Dev'l.
Back to the D. the last echoes roll *D.* i. 325
To Ward, to Waters, Chartres, and the D. *M.E.* iii. 20
The D. and the King divide the prize *M.E.* iii. 401
That ancient Worm, the D. *Mi.* iv. 72
But wonder how the d. they got there *P.S.* 172
And thus broke out—"My Lord, why, what the d. *R.L.* iv. 127
He swears the Muses met him at the D. *S.* v. 42
You give all royal Witchcraft to the D. *S.* vi. 219
Whose tongue will compliment you to the d. *S.* viii. 57
The D.'l was piqu'd such saintship to behold *M.E.* iii. 349
There (so the D. ordain'd) one Christmas-tide *M.E.* iii. 383
The d. is in you if you cannot dine *S.* ii. 148
Now let some whimsy, or that D. within *S.* iii. 143
Half that the D. o'erlooks from Lincoln town *S.* vi. 245
And scorn the flesh, the d., and all but gold *S.* vii. 94
Yet went to Court!—the D. would have it so *S.* viii. 14
Fear made her D—s, and weak Hope her Gods E.M. iii. 256
In spite of witches, d., dreams, and fire *S.* vi. 313

Dev'lish.
Till Becca-ficos sold so d. dear *S.* ii. 39

Devise.
I give and I d. (old Euclio said) *M.E.* i. 256

Devis'd.
Those RULES of old discover'd, not d. *E.C.* 88

Devoir.
Awkward and supple, each d. to pay *Mi.* iii. 17

Devotion.
And him and his if more d. warms *D.* ii. 81
How could D. touch the country pews *S.* v. 233
D.'s *self shall steal a thought from Heav'n E.A.* 357

Devour.
But greedy That, its object would d. *E.M.* ii. 89

Devour'd.
Poor Vadius, long with learned spleen d. *M.E.* v. 41

Devout.
And grace, altho' a bard, d. *Mi.* xii. 14

Devoutly.
On painted Ceilings you d. stare *M.E.* iv. 145

Dew.
And soft besprinkles with Cimmerian d. *D.* iii. 4
The juice nectareous, and the balmy d. *E.M.* i. 136
From pois'nous herbs extracts the healing d. *E.M.* i. 220
The gracious D. of Pulpit Eloquence *E.S.* i. 69
Thin glittering textures of the filmy d. *R.L.* ii. 64
And ev'ry plant that drinks the morning d. *Su.* 32
Here bees from blossoms sip the rosy d. *Su.* 69
When falling d—s with spangles deck'd the glade A. 99
Thick as the stars of night, or morning d. *D.* iii. 32
Soon as the flocks shook off the nightly d. *Sp.* 17
No grateful d. descend from ev'ning skies *W.* 45
But see, Orion sheds unwholesome d. *W.* 85
His tresses dropp'd with d., and o'er the stream *W.F.* 332

Dewy.
Ye Heav'ns! from high the d. nectar pour *M.* 13
Her buskin'd Virgins trac'd the d. lawn *W.F.* 170

Dexterity.
Or dark d. of groping well *D.* ii. 278
With all the rash d. of wit *E.M.* ii. 84

Dext'rous.
Now at his head the d. task commence *D.* ii. 199
D. the craving, fawning crowd to quit *E.* i. 11

Dext'rously.
The deeds, and d. omits *see heires S.* vii. 100

Diadem'd.
Not when so d. with rays divine *E.S.* ii. 232

Dialogue.
What pert, low D. has Farquhar writ *S.* v. 288

Diamond, Di'mond.
And thrice they twitch'd the d. in her ear *R.L.* iii. 137
And heighten'd by the d.'s circling rays R.L. iv. 115
The Baron now his d—s pours apace R.L. iii. 75
Clubs, D., Hearts, in wild disorder seen *R.L.* iii. 79
The Knave of D. tries his wily arts *R.L.* iii. 87
Of beaming d., and reflected plate *S.* iv. 29
Blush in the rose, and in the d.'d blaze *M.E.* i. 146
So kept the D., and the rogue was bit *M.E.* iii. 364
Or deep with d—s in the flaming mine E.M. iv. 10
As Sappho's d. with her dirty smock *M.E.* ii. 24

Diana.
D. Cynthus, Ceres Hybla loves *Sp.* 66
And chaste D. haunts the forest-shade *Su.* 62
Here too, 'tis sung, of old D. stray'd *W.F.* 165
Nor could D. help her injur'd maid *W.F.* 198
Whether the nymph shall break D.'s *laws R.L.* ii. 105

Dice.
Blasphem'd his Gods, the D., and damn'd his Fate *D.* i. 116
Let thy heart, next Drabs and D. engage *D.* iii. 303
How, Sir! not damn the Sharper, but the D. *E.S.* ii. 13
But who the Bowl, or rattling D. compares *Mi.* ix. 101

Dictate.
To cavil, censure, d. right or wrong *D.* ii. 377

Dictates.
Nature, whose d. to no other kind *E.M.* iv. 347
Where Tindal d., and Silenus snores D. iv. 492
Her heart still d., and her hand obeys *E.A.* 16
What conscience d. to be done *U.P.* 13

Dictator.
As Helluo, late D. of the Feast *M.E.* ii. 79

Dictionary.
"But the best *words!*" "O Sir, the D." *S.* viii. 69

Did—*Passim*.

Didius.
And be what Rome's great D. was before *M.E.* iii. 126

Dido.
While Anna begg'd, and D. rag'd in vain *R.L.* v. 6

Die.
For her, the lilies hang their heads, and d. *A.* 26
D. ev'ry flow'r, and perish all, but she *A.* 34
And all its varying Rainbows d. away *D.* iv. 632
In vain I they gaze, turn giddy, rave, and d. *D.* iv. 648
And these be sung till Granville's Mira d. *Æ.* iii. 76
Teach me at once, and learn of me to d. *E.A.* 328
But let me d., all raillery apart *E.Y.S.* ft
Than just to look about us and to d. *E.M.* i. 4
D. of a rose in aromatic pain *E.M.* i. 200
Born but to d., and reas'ning but to err *E.M.* ii. 10
Hope travels thro', nor quits us when we d. *E.M.* ii. 274
By turns we catch the vital breath, and d. *E.M.* iii. 18
For which we bear to live, or dare to d. *E.M.* iv. 4
So—Satire is no more—I feel it d. *E.S.* i. 83
Her Priestless Muse forbids the Good to d. *E.S.* ii. 234
Her works; and dying, fears herself may d. *Ep.* viii. 8
And there I'll d., no worse nor better *I.H.* i. 80
All this is mine but till I d. *I.H.* ii. 10 s
Consider, Mice, like Men, must d. *I.H.* ii. 177
Lest you should think that verse shall d. *I.H.* iv. 1
And d. of nothing but a Rage to live *M.E.* ii. 100
But d., and she'll adore you—Then the Bust *M.E.* ii. 139
Nor leave one sigh behind them when they d. *M.E.* ii. 230
Toasts live a scorn, and Queens may d. a jest *M.E.* ii. 282
But thousands d. without or this or that (*rep.*) *M.E.* iii. 95
Go, search it there, where to be born and d. *M.E.* iii. 287
There Gladiators fight, or d. in flow'rs *M.E.* iv. 124
Resign'd to live, prepar'd to d. *Mi.* xii. 1
Thus unlamented let me d. *O.* iv. 18
And when I d., be sure you let me know *P.S.* 123
Neglected d., and tell it on his tomb *P.S.* 258
Oh let me live my own, and d. so too (*rep.*) *P.S.* 261
O grant me, thus to live, and thus to d. *P.S.* 404
And soften'd sounds along the waters d. *R.L.* iii. 50
Not tyrants fierce that unrepenting d. *R.L.* iv. 7

DIED—DIN. 75

Like roses, that in deserts bloom and *d. R.L.* iv. 158
And she who scorns a man, must *d.* a maid *R.L.* v. 28
Who sought no more than on his foe to *d. R.L.* v. 78
Nor think, to *d.* dejects my lofty mind *R.L.* v. 99
When, after millions slain, yourself shall *d. R.L.* v. 146
Who live like S—tt—n, or who *d.* like Chartres *S.* vii. 36
I *d.* in charity with fool and knave *S.* viii. 3
Oh ! Sir, politely so ! nay, let me *d. S.* viii. 112
For those who greatly think, or bravely *d. U.L.* 10
From these perhaps (ere Nature bade her *d.*) *U.L.* 23
With her they flourish'd, and with her they *d. W.* 34
I hear soft music *d.* aloog the grove *W.F.* 268

Died.

The Smiles and Loves had *d.* in Voiture's death *E.* iv. 19
There *d.* the best of passions, Love and Fame *E.A.* 40
And when three Sov'reigns *d.*, could scarce be vext *E.S.* i. 107
Patron of Arts, and Judge of Nature, *d. Ep.* i. 2
Or gave his Father Grief but when he *d. Ep.* iii. 4
The Saint sustain'd it, but the Woman *d. Ep.* vi. 10
Thank'd Heav'n that he had liv'd, and that he *d. Ep.*x.10
Yes, SAVE MY COUNTRY, HEAV'N—He said, and *d. Ep.* xiii. 8
There *d.* my Father, no man's Debtor *I.H.* i. 79
They had no Poet, and they *d. I.H.* iv. 14
" Not that—I cannot part with that," and *d. M.E.* i. 261
And haunt the places where their Honour *d. M.E.* ii. 242
My good old Lady catch'd a cold, and *d. M.E.* iii. 364
By the youths that *d.* for love *O.* i. 79
Great Homer *d.* three thousand years ago *P.S.* 124
The Club's black Tyrant first her victim *d. R.L.* iii. 69
One *d.* in metaphor, and one in song *R.L.* v. 60
Who *d.*, perhaps, an hundred years ago *S.* v. 52
With laughter sure Democritus had *d. S.* v. 320
And break your bows, as when Adonis *d. W.* 24

Dies.

So *d.* her love, and so my hopes decay *A.* 70
For, born a Goddess, Dulness never *d. D.* i. 18
Gay *d.* unpension'd with a hundred friends *D.* iii. 330
And *d.*, when Dulness gives her Page the word *D.* iv. 30
Which as it *d.* or lives, we fall, or reign *D.* iv. 186
Up to a *Star*, and like Endymion *d. D.* iv. 520
Light *d.* before thy uncreating word *D.* iv. 654
To sounds of heav'nly harps she *d.* away *E.A.* 221
That gaily blooms, but ev'n in blooming *d. E.C.* 499
See Falkland *d.*, the virtuous and the just *E.M.* iv. 99
Women and Fools must like him or he *d. M.E.* i. 183
He *d.*, sad outcast of each church and state *M.E.* i. 204
Then never break your heart when Chloe *d. M.E.* ii. 180
When Hopkins *d.*, a thousand lights attend *M.E.* iii. 291
Who drinks, whores, fights, and in a duel *d. M.E.* iii. 390
And sad Sir Balaam curses God and *d. M.E.* iii. 402
The Worm that never *d. Mi.* iv. 32
Again she falls, again she *d.*, she *d. O.* i. 94
Ah see, he *d. O.* i. 112
At ev'ry word a reputation *d. R.L.* iii. 16
Th' expiring Swan, and as he sings, he *d. R.L.* v. 66
For matrimonial solace *d.* a martyr *S.* iii. 151
Pants on the leaves, and *d.* upon the trees *W.* 80
And famish'd *d.* amidst his ripen'd fields *W.F.* 56

Diet.

And then—a perfect Hermit in his *d. S.* v. 200

Differ.

What *d.* more (you cry) than crown and cowl *E.M.* i. 199
And where, tho' all things *d.*, all agree *W.F.* 16

Diff'rence.

And oft so mix, the *d.* is too nice *E.M.* ii. 209
All Nature's *d.* keeps all Nature's peace *E.M.* iv. 56
Fortune in Men has some small *d.* made *E.M.* iv. 195
The only *d.* is I dare laugh out *E.S.* i. 36
But makes a *d.* in his thought *I.H.* i. 37
Yet more; the *d.* is as great between *M.E.* i. 31
Now, or long since, what *d.* will be found *S.* vi. 238

Diff'rent.

'Tis the same rope at *d.* ends they twist *D.* i. 207
" Now turn to *d.* sports " (the Goddess cries) *D.* ii. 221
For *d.* styles with *d.* subjects sort *E.C.* 322
If Faith itself has *d.* dresses worn *E.C.* 446
On *d.* senses *d.* objects strike (*rep.*) *E.M.* ii. 128
And *d.* men directs to *d.* ends *M.E.* iii. 160
With like confusion *d.* nations fly *R.L.* iii. 83

Diff'ring.

But *d.* far in figure and in face *R.L.* iv. 26

Differs.

That each from other *d.*, first confess *M.E.* i. 19

Difficulty.

Start ev'n from *D.*, strike from Chance *M.E.* iv. 68

Diffidence.

And speak, tho' sure, with seeming *d. E.C.* 567

Diffuse.

Or bind in Matter, or *d.* in Space *D.* iv. 476
While op'ning blooms *d.* their sweets around *Sp.* 100
Arise, the pines a noxious shade *d. W.* 86

Diffus'd.

Thy eyes *d.* a reconciling ray *E.A.* 145
Wealth in the gross is death, but life *d. M.E.* iii. 233
His shining horns *d.* a golden gleam *W.F.* 332

Diffusing.

D. languor in the panting gales *D.* iv. 304
D. blessings, or averting harms *E.M.* iii. 212

Digamma.

Stands our *D.*, and o'ertops them all *D.* iv. 218

Digby.

Lamented *D.* ! sunk thee to the grave *E.M.* iv. 104

Digest.

Which nauseate all, and nothing can *d. E.C.* 389
D. his thirty-thousandth dinner *Mi.* xii. 18

Digested.

For food *d.* takes another name *S.* vii. 34

Digestion.

His rank *d.* makes it wit no more *S.* vii. 32

Dignify.

Rejudge his acts, and *d.* disgrace *E.* i. 30
'Tis true no Turbots *d.* my boards *S.* ii. 141

Dignify'd.

Which Betterton's grave action *d. S.* v. 122

Dignity.

Shine in the *D.* of F.R.S. *D.* iv. 570
To fall with *d.*, with temper rise *E.M.* iv. 378
But shall the *D.* of *Vice* be lost *E.S.* i. 114
Maintain a Poet's *d.* and ease *P.S.* 263

Digs.

The Slave that *d.* it, and the Slave that hides *M.E.* iii. 110

Dilates.

A veil of fogs *d.* her awful face *D.* i. 262

Dilemma.

A dire *d.* ! either way I'm sped *P.S.* 31

Dim.

There *d.* in clouds, the poring Scholiasts mark *D.* iii. 191
Yet, yet a moment, one *d.* Ray of Light *D.* iv. 1
D. and remote the joys of saints I see *E.A.* 71
And the *d.* windows shed a solemn light *E.A.* 144
The mole's *d.* curtain, and the lynx's beam *E.M.* i. 212
Something as *d.* to our internal view *M.E.* i. 49
D. lights of life, that burn a length of years *U.L.* 19
For thee we *d.* the eyes, and stuff the head *D.* iv. 249

Diminish'd.

Ye little Stars ! hide your *d.* rays *M.E.* iii. 282

Dimly.

Why *d.* gleams the visionary sword *U.L.* 4

Dimpled.

Next Smedley div'd; slow circles *d.* o'er *D.* ii. 191

Dimpling.

As shallow streams run *d.* all the way *P.S.* 316

Din.

Now thousand tongues are heard in one loud *d. D.* ii. 235
Equal your merits ! equal is your *d. D.* ii. 244

DINE—DISCHARG'D.

Dire is the conflict, dismal is the *d. D.* iii. 269
Know, all the distant *d.* that world can keep *S.* i. 123

Dine.

Bid me with Pollio sup, as well as *d. D.* iv. 302
Count the slow clock, and *d.* exact at noon *E.* v. 18
Or when I sup, or when I *d. I.H.* ii. 134
To wear red stockings, and to *d.* with *Steele Mi.* iii. 4
Dare you refuse him? Curll invites to *d. P.S.* 53
And wretches hang that jury-men may *d. R.L.* ii. 22
Let's talk, my friends, but talk before we *d. S.* ii. 4
One half-pint bottle serves them both to *d. S.* ii. 53
The dev'l is in you if you cannot *d. S.* ii. 148
Plead much, read more, *d.* late, or not at all *S.* iv. 37
Go *d.* with Chartres, in each Vice out-do *S.* iv. 120

Din'd.

Judicious drank, and greatly daring *d. D.* iv. 318
D. with the MAN of ROSS or my LORD MAV'R *E.S.* ii. 99
Perhaps was sick, in love, or had not *d. M.E.* i. 128

Dines.

Came, cramm'd with capon from where Pollio *d. D.* iv. 250

Dinner.

Save just at *d.*—then, prefers, no doubt *M.E.* i. 79
But hark! the chiming Clocks to *d.* call *M.E.* iv. 151
Is this a *d.!* this a Genial room *M.E.* iv. 155
Digest his thirty-thousandth *d. Mi.* xii. 18
I wish'd the man a *d.*, and sat still *P.S.* 152
Then scorn a homely *d.*, if you can *S.* ii. 12
Himself a *d.*, makes an Actor live *S.* vii. 14
Would you enjoy soft nights, and solid d—s E.J.S. 23
Happy to catch me just at D.-*time P.S.* 14

Dionysius.

See *D.* Homer's thoughts refine *E.C.* 665

Dip.

Old Bavius sits to *d.* poetic souls *D.* iii. 24
Full in the midst of Euclid *d.* at once *D.* iv. 263
One *d.* the pencil, and one string the lyre *E.* iii. 70
Pray, *d.* your Whiskers and your Tail in *I.H.* ii. 203
D. in the Rainbow, trick her off in Air *M.E.* ii. 18
Or *d.* their pinions in the painted bow *R.L.* ii. 84

Dips.

A Poet the first day he *d.* his quill *D.* iv. 163

Dipt.

Instant, when *d.*, away they wing their flight *D.* iii. 27
And *d.* them in the sable Well *E.* vi. 11
D. me in ink, my parents', or my own *P.S.* 126
D. in the richest tincture of the skies *R.L.* ii. 65

Dire.

D. is the conflict, dismal is the din *D.* iii. 269
Some *d.* misfortune follows close behind *E.A.* 34
Her poniard, had oppos'd the *d.* command *E.A.* 102
Ah ne'er so *d.* a thirst of glory boast *E.C.* 522
When his lewd father gave the *d.* disease *E.M.* iv. 120
A *d.* dilemma, either way I'm sped *P.S.* 31
What *d.* offence from am'rous causes springs *R.L.* i. 1
Some *d.* disaster, or by force, or slight *R.L.* ii. 103
With beating hearts the *d.* event they wait *R.L.* ii. 141

Direct.

Mix in his look: All eyes *d.* their rays *d. O.* ii. 7
D. my Plough to find a Treasure *I.H.* ii. 20 s
To *Number five d.* your doves *I.H.* ii. 9
The Gnomes *d.*, to ev'ry atom just *R.L.* v. 83
Can they *d.* what measures to pursue *S.* iii. 122

Directing.

O thou! of Bus'ness the *d.* soul *D.* i. 169
Thou, only thou, *d.* all our way *D.* iv. 296
The great *d.* MIND of ALL ordains *E.M.* i. 266
Is known alone to that *D.* Pow'r *S.* vi. 278

Direction.

All Chance, *D.*, which thou canst not see *E.M.* i. 290
A mightier Pow'r the strong *d.* sends *E.M.* ii. 165
To bliss alike by that *d.* tend *E.M.* iii. 81

Directly.

Oppress'd we feel the beam *d.* beat *S.* v. 21

Director.

Then dubs *D.*, and secures his soul *M.E.* iii. 374
To tax D—s, *who (thank God) have Plums E.S.* ii. 49
What made *D.* cheat in South-sea year *M.E.* iii. 117
Thieves, Supercargoes, Sharpers, and *D. S.* i. 72
Plums and *D.*, Shylock and his Wife *S.* i. 103

Directs.

Then his nice taste *d.* our Operas *D.* ii. 204
Rides in the whirlwind, and *d.* the storm *D.* iii. 264
For, Vice or Virtue, Self *d.* it still *E.M.* ii. 236
In this 'tis God *d.*, in that 'tis Mae *E.M.* iii. 98
Explores the lost, the wand'ring sheep *d. M.* 51
And diff'rent men *d.* to diff'rent ends *M.E.* iii. 160
Now breaks, or now *d.*, th' intending lines *M.E.* iv. 63

Dirge.

Nor hallow'd *d.* be mutter'd o'er thy tomb *U.L.* 62

Dirt.

And who the most in love of *d.* excel *D.* ii. 277
Is yellow *d.* the passion of thy life *E.M.* iv. 279
From *d.* and sea-weed as proud Venice rose *E.M.* iv. 292
But 'twas my Guest at whom they threw the *d. E.S.* ii. 145
Of hairs, or straws, or *d.*, or grubs, or worms *P.S.* 170
This painted child of *d.*, that stinks and stings *P.S.* 310
In *d.* and darkness, hundreds stink content *S.* iii. 133

Dirty.

The creeping, *d.*, courtly Ivy join *D.* i. 304
No crab more active in the *d.* dance *D.* ii. 319
Has what the frugal, *d.* soil affords *E.S.* ii. 174
As Sappho's di'monds with her *d.* smock *M.E.* ii. 24
Where tawdry yellow strove with *d.* red *M.E.* iii. 304
For Pembroke, Statues, *d.* Gods, and Coins *M.E.* iv. 8
The creature's at his *d.* work again *P.S.* 92
And when I flatter, let my *d.* leaves *S.* v. 415
Look in that breast, most *d.* D—! be fair *S.* vi. 222
Then, close as Umbra, joins the *d.* train *S.* viii. 177

Disabus'd.

Still by himself abus'd, or *d. E.M.* ii. 14

Disagree.

In Faith and Hope the world will *d. E.M.* iii. 307
What will you do with such as *d. M.E.* i. 123
Who shall decide, when Doctors *d. M.E.* i. 1
Senates degen'rate, Patriots *d. M.E.* iii. 148

Disallow.

Had ancient times conspir'd to *d. S.* v. 135

Disappears.

The world recedes; it *d. O.* v. 13

Disappointment.

And oh! what makes the *d.* hard *Mi.* ix. 47

Disappoints.

That *d.* th' effect of ev'ry vice *E.M.* ii. 240

Disapprov'd.

Without Good Breeding, truth is *d. E.C.* 576

Disapproves.

Nature stands check'd; Religion *d. E.A.* 259

Disarm.

And fate's severest rage *d. O.* i. 119

Disarm'd.

Poor and *d.*, and hardly worth your hate *S.* vii. 12

Disarms.

Those Age or Sickness soon or late *d. E.* iv. 60

Disaster.

Some dire *d.*, or by force, or slight *R.L.* ii. 103

Discerning.

But Kings in Wit may want *d.* Spirit *S.* v. 385

Discharge.

D. that rage on more provoking crimes *E.C.* 528
D. their garrets, move their beds, and run *S.* ii. 157

Discharg'd.

From this thy blunderbuss *d.* on me *S.* viii. 65

Disclaim.
Tell me but this, and I'll d. the prize Sp. 87

Disclose.
The op'ning clouds d. each work by turn D. i. 249
Ask ye their names? I could as soon d. D. ii. 309
This to d. is all thy guardian can R.L. i. 113
Her lively looks a sprightly mind d. R.L. ii. 9

Discolour'd.
Or come d. thro' our Passions shown M.E. i. 34

Discompos'd.
That never passion d. the mind E.M. i. 168
Or d. the head-dress of a Prude R.L. iv. 74

Discontent.
Not that their Pleasures caus'd her d. E. v. 9
You said the same, and are you d. S. vi. 29
Or impious D. U.P. 34

Discontented.
The Goddess with a d. air R.L. iv. 79

Discord.
All D., Harmony not understood E.M. i. 291
Nor marrying D. in a noble wife P.S. 393
At length great Anna said, "Let D. cease!" W.F. 327
In brazen bonds shall barb'rous D. dwell W.F. 414

Discordant.
The monkey-mimics rush d. in D. ii. 236
Foreign her air, her robe's d. pride D. iv. 47

Discourse.
The Play stands still; damn action and d. S. v. 314

Discours'd.
D. in terms as just, with looks as sage E.C. 269

Discover.
But grant that Actions best d. man M.E. i. 119

Discover'd.
Those RULES of old d., not devis'd E.C. 88
He steer'd securely, and d. far E.C. 647
And shake all o'er, like a d. spy S. viii. 279

Discredit.
Alas! the small D. of a Bribe E.S. ii. 46

Discreet.
Launch not beyond your depth, but be d. E.C. 50
Satire's my weapon, but I'm too d. S. i. 69

Discreetly.
The most recluse, d. open'd, find D. iv. 447

Discretion.
Fair D. string the Lyre Mi. vii. 15

Disdain.
Not yet purg'd off, of spleen and sour d. E.C. 527
Shew there was one who held it in d. E.S. i. 172
Conceal, d.,—do all things but forget E.A. 200
Fir'd by the sight, all Reason I d. Mi. ix. 83
D. whatever CORNBURY disdains S. iv. 61

Disdain'd.
As Cato's self had not d. to hear P.C. 46
When offers are d., and love deny'd R.L. i. 82

Disdains.
'Tis but what Virtue flies from and d. E.M. iv. 90
D. all loss of Tickets, or Codille M.E. ii. 266
A nymph there is, that all thy pow'r d. R.L. iv. 65
Disdain whatever CORNBURY d. S. iv. 61
But Verse, alas! your Majesty d. S. v. 404

Disease.
The young d. that must subdue at length E.M. ii. 135
The Mind's d., its RULING PASSION came E.M. ii. 138
But just d. to luxury succeeds E.M. iii. 165
When his lewd father gave the dire d. E.M. iv. 120
To help me thro' this long d., my Life P.S. 132
When each new night-dress gives a new d. R.L. iv. 38
Or e'er to costive lap-dogs gave d. R.L. iv. 75
The case is easier in the Mind's d. S. iv. 58
Call, if you will, bad rhyming a d. S. vi. 182

Confess as well your Folly, as D. S. vi. 215
From Love, the sole d. thou canst not cure Su. 12

Disemboguing.
To where Fleet-ditch with d. streams D. ii. 271

Disgrace.
A second effort brought but new d. D. ii. 175
Rejudge his acts, and dignify d. E. i. 30
If, after all, you think it a d. E.J.S. 45
You still may lash the greatest—in D. E.S. i. 88
There, where no Father's, Brother's, Friend's d. E.S. i. 99

Disgrac'd.
Is by ill-colouring but the more d. E.C. 24
All that d. my Betters, met in me P.S. 120
You'd think no Fools d. the former reign S. v. 127

Disguise.
In Folly's Cap, than Wisdom's grave d. D. iv. 240
I tell the naked fact without d. D. iv. 433
Hide it, my heart, within that close d. E.A. 11
Bred to d., in Public 'tis you hide M.E. ii. 203
Praise undeserv'd is scandal in d. S. v. 413
Hence false tears, deceits, d—s O. iii. 38

Dish.
Our Courtier walks from d. to d. I.H. ii. 198
One solid d. his week-day meal affords M.E. iii. 345
First Health: The stomach (cramm'd from ev'ry d. S. ii. 69

Dishabille.
And this you see is but my d. S. viii. 115

Dishevell'd.
The heav'ns bespangling with d. light R.L. v. 130

Dishonest.
D. sight! his breeches rent below D. iii. 198
Inglorious triumphs, and d. scars W.F. 326

Dishonours.
Nor heeds the brown d. of his face D. ii. 108

Dislike.
Just hint a fault, and hesitate d. P.S. 204
If I d. it, "Furies, death, and rage!" P.S. 57

Dismal.
Dire is the conflict, d. is the din D. iii. 279
D. screams O. i. 57
And in a vapour reach'd the d. dome R.L. iv. 18

Dismiss.
Mistress! d. that rabble from your throne D. iv. 209
D. my soul, where no Carnation fades D. iv. 418

Dismiss'd.
My Lords the Judges laugh, and you're d. S. i. 156
The young d. to wander earth or air E.M. iii. 127

Disobey'd.
No duty broke, no father d. P.S. 230

Disorder.
From vulgar bounds with brave d. pass E.C. 152
Clubs, Diamonds, Hearts, in wild d. seen R.L. iii. 79

Disowns.
Who Virtue and a Church alike d. S. iv. 65

Dispensary.
Garth did not write his own D. E.C. 619

But oh! with One, immortal One d. D. iii. 217
As Kings d. with laws themselves have made E.C. 162

Dispeopled.
Who claim'd the skies, d. air and floods W.F. 47

Disperse.
'Tis one thing madly to d. my store S. vi. 292

Dispers'd.
The rest the winds d. in empty air R.L. ii. 46
Thus when d. a routed army runs R.L. iii. 81

Display.
There all thy gifts and graces we d. *D.* iv. 295
New graces yearly like thy works d. *E.* iii. 65
These leave the sense, their learning to d. *E.C.* 116
A prudent chief not always must d. *E.C.* 175
These sparks with awkward vanity d. *E.C.* 329
See heav'n its sparkling portals wide d. *M.* 97
A waving Glow the bloomy beds d. *M.E.* iv. 83
Gods! shall the ravisher d. your hair *R.L.* iv. 103
Then all your Muse's softer art d. *S.* i. 29
Here waving groves a chequer'd scene d. *W.F.* 17
Bear Britain's thunder, and her Cross d. *W.F.* 387

Display'd.
D. the fates her confessors endure *D.* ii. 146
(Earth's wide extremes) her sable flag d. *D.* iii. 71
His stretch'd-out arm d. a volume fair *D.* iv. 106
Our bolder talents in full light d. *M.E.* ii. 201
Each chief his sev'n-fold shield d. *O.* i. 45
And now, unveil'd, the Toilet stands d. *R.L.* i. 121
Some o'er her lap their careful plumes d. *R.L.* iii. 115
Or Death's black wing already be d. *S.* i. 95
Tho' in his pictures Lust be full d. *S.* viii. 94

Displays.
Beneath the shade a spreading Beech d. *A.* 1
So Jove's bright bow d. its wat'ry round *D.* ii. 173
When first that sun too pow'rful beams d. *E.C.* 470
No common object to your sight d. *P.C.* 19
Ev'n the wild heath d. her purple dyes *W.F.* 25

Displeas'd.
Nor saw d. the peaceful cottage rise *W.F.* 86

Displeases.
Ev'n spring d., when she shines not here *Sp.* 83

Disports.
Where light d. in ever-mingling dyes *R.L.* ii. 66

Dispose.
Fortune her gifts may variously d. *E.M.* iv. 67
Thus we d. of all poetic merit *S.* vi. 135

Dispos'd.
All rang'd in order, and d. with grace *E.C.* 672

Disposing.
Safe in the hand of one d. Pow'r *E.M.* i. 287

Disputs.
Plague with *D.*, or persecute with Rhyme *D.* iv. 260
Like Doctors thus, when much d. has past *M.E.* iii. 15
Both fierce, both hungry; the d. grew strong *Mi.* xi. 3
End all d.; and fix the year precise *S.* v. 53
"And perfect *Speaker*?" "Onslow, past d." *S.* viii. 71
D— *of Me or Te, of aut or at D.* iv. 220
That Name the learn'd with fierce d. pursue *M.E.* v. 17
Where Heav'n's free subjects might their rights d. *E.C.* 548
Oppose thyself to heav'n; d. my heart *E.A.* 282
Two Aldermen d. it with an Ass *S.* vi. 105

Disputed.
Faith, Gospel, all, seem'd made to be d. *E.C.* 442

Dissect.
Like following life thro' creatures you d. *M.E.* i. 29

Dissemblers.
Priests, Princes, Women, no d. here *M.E.* i. 177

Dissever.
The meeting points the sacred hair d. *R.L.* iii. 153

Dissimulation.
By Passions? these *D.* hides *M.E.* i. 169

Dissolv'd.
And Alma Mater lie d. in Port *D.* iii. 318
All Ties d., and ev'ry Sin forgiv'n *E.S.* i. 94
But lost, d. in thy superior rays *M.* 101
Their fluid bodies half d. in light *R.L.* ii. 62
In a soft, silver stream d. away *W.F.* 204

Dissolves.
The link d., each seeks a fresh embrace *E.M.* iii. 129

Dissolving.
See life d. vegetate again *E.M.* iii. 16

Dissonance.
Dennis and *D.*, and captious Art *D.* ii. 239

Dissuades.
Tho' this his Son d., and that his Wife *D.* ii. 168

Distance.
Due d. reconciles to form and grace *E.C.* 174
Reason's at d., and in prospect lie *E.M.* ii. 72
Heroes and Kings! your d. keep *Ep.* xv. 1

Distant.
Slept first; the d. nodded to the hum *D.* ii. 402
New d. scenes of endless science rise *E.C.* 224
Or ship off Senates to a d. Shore *M.E.* iii. 44
Now drain'd a d. country of her Floods *M.E.* v. 8
To what new clime, what d. sky *O.* ii. 13
The d. threats of vengeance on his head *P.S.* 348
In some lone isle, or d. Northern land *R.L.* iv. 154
Know, all the d. din that world can keep *S.* i. 123
Feed here my lambs, I'll seek no d. field *Sp.* 64
And, pawing, seems to beat the d. plain *W.F.* 152
Earth's d. ends our glory shall behold *W.F.* 401

Distastes.
Hence guilty joys, d., surmises *O.* iii. 37

Distemper'd.
And now (as oft in some d. State) *R.L.* iii. 93

Distich.
Or grant the Bard whose *D.* all commend *E.S.* ii. 160

Distil, Distill.
Or o'er the glebe d. the kindly rain *R.L.* ii. 86
Where ling'ring drops from min'ral Roofs d—l *Mi.* x. 3

Distill'd.
Soft show'rs d., and suns grew warm in vain *W.F.* 54

Distils.
Sign'd with that Ichor which from Gods d. *D.* ii. 92

Distinct.
The worker from the work d. was known *E.M.* iii. 229

Distinction.
And plac'd it next him, a d. rare *D.* ii. 96
All glares alike, without d. gay *E.C.* 314
Adieu *D.*, Satire, Warmth, and Truth *E.S.* i. 64
'Tis with *D.* you bestow *I.H.* i. 22

Distinguish.
Or how d. penitence from love *E.A.* 194
There none d. 'twixt your Shame or Pride *M.E.* ii. 204

Distinguish'd.
Her children first of more d. sort *D.* iv. 567
And best d. by black, brown, and fair *M.E.* ii. 4
If there's a Critic of d. rage *Mi.* ii. 21
Fairest of mortals, thon d. care *R.L.* i. 27
That from a Patriot of d. note *S.* vi. 196

Distract.
But oh! what terrors must d. the soul *S.* viii. 244

Distress.
By Wealth of Follow'rs! without one d. *M.E.* ii. 145
This fatal stroke, this unforeseen *D. Mi.* ix. 20
Insults fall'n worth, or Beauty in d. *P.S.* 288
Foe to his pride, but friend to his d. *P.S.* 371

Distress'd.
And but more relish'd, as the more d. *E.M.* iv. 318

Distrust.
What Nature wants (a phrase I much d.) *M.E.* iii. 25

Distrustful.
D. sense with modest caution speaks *E.C.* 626

Disturb.
Who, to d. their betters mighty proud *S.* v. 307

Dis-united.
The pierc'd battalions d. fall *R.L.* iii. 85

Div'd.
Next Smedley d.; slow circles dimpled o'er *D.* ii. 291

DIVER—DOIT.

Diver.
If perseverance gain the *d.'s* prize *D.* ii. 301

Diverse.
His papers light fly *d.*, tost in air *D.* ii. 114

Diversely.
On life's vast ocean *d.* we sail *E.M.* ii. 107

Diversified.
Swift trouts *d.* with crimson stains *W.F.* 145

Diversities.
Blushing in bright *d.* of day *M.E.* iv. 84

Divert.
D. his eyes with pictures in the fire *E.* v. 19
Could France or Rome *d.* our brave designs *M.E.* iii. 51

Diverting.
And more *d.* still than regular *E.* iv. 26

Dives.
A pig of lead to him who *d.* the best *D.* ii. 281
Furious he *d.*, precipitately dull *D.* ii. 316
Where Folly fights for kings, or *d.* for gain *E.M.* iv. 154

Divide.
Courtiers and Patriots in two ranks *d. D.* iv. 107
What thin partitions Sense from Thought *d. E.M.* i. 226
More studious to *d.* than to unite *E.M.* ii. 82
But since not ev'ry good we can *d., E.M.* ii. 95
What shall *d.* ? The God within the mind *E.M.* ii. 204
Know, Nature's children all *d.* her care *E.M.* iii. 43
Who ne'er knew Joy, but Friendship might *d. Ep.* ii. 3
In Women, two almost *d.* the kind *M.E.* ii. 208
The Devil and the King *d.* the prize *M.E.* iii. 401
These set the head, and those *d.* the hair *R.L.* i. 146
T' inclose the lock; now joins it, to *d. R.L.* iii. 148
And seas but join the regions they *d. W.F.* 400

Divided.
D. between carelessness and care *S.* vi. 291

Divides.
D. a friendship long confirm'd by age *D.* iii. 174
By Actions? those Uncertainty *d.* i. 168
The Man of Ross *d.* the weekly bread *M.E.* iii. 264
Or else where Cam his winding vales *d. Su.* 26

Divine.
Or such as bellow from the deep *D. D.* ii. 257
Dulness is sacred in a sound *d. D.* ii. 352
Fill the capacious Squire, and deep *D. M.E.* iii. 204
He'll write a *Journal*, or he'll turn *D. P.S.* 54
No young *d.*, new benefic'd, can be *S.* vii. 51
Charge them with Heav'n's Artill'ry, bold *D. S.* viii. 281
To seem but mortal, ev'n in sound D—*s S.* ii. 80
So vast, our new *D.*, we must confess *S.* vii. 97
Or, in quotation, shrewd *D.* leave out *S.* vii. 103
Till Senates nod to lullabies d. D. i. 317
Persist, by all *d.* in Man unaw'd *D.* iii. 293
These Fate reserv'd to grace thy reign *d. D.* iii. 275
The Right *D.* of Kings to govern wrong *D.* iv. 188
Each maid cry'd, Charming, and each youth *D. D.* iv. 410 & 414
Nor human Spark is left, nor Glimpse *d. D.* iv. 652
And sure if aught below the seats *d. E.* i. 21
Paulo's free stroke, and Titian's warmth *d. E.* iii. 38
And breathe an air *d.* on ev'ry face *E.* iii. 102
And truths *d.* came mended from that tongue *E.A.* 66
But now no face *d.* contentment wears *E.A.* 147
And wings of Seraphs shed *d.* perfumes *E.A.* 218
D. oblivion of low-thoughted care *E.A.* 298
To err is human, to forgive, *d. E.C.* 525
In Decius charms, in Curtius is *d. E.M.* ii. 200
For Nature knew no right *d.* in Men *E.M.* ii. 236
Ev'n mean Self-love becomes, by force *d. E.M.* ii. 291
Joins heav'n and earth, and mortal and *d. E.M.* iv. 334
Self-love thus push'd to social, to *d. E.M.* iv. 353
Not so, when diadem'd with rays *d. E.S.* ii. 232
Go, and exalt thy Moral to *D. Ep.* vii. 10
O charming Noons! and Nights *d. I.H.* ii. 133
With simp'ring Angels, Palms, and Harps *d. M.E.* ii. 14
The Metal, and the Workmanship, *d. Mi.* ix. 36
This the *d.* Cecilia found *O.* i. 124
And guard with Arms *d.* the British Throne *R.L.* ii. 90

That Man *d.* whom Wisdom calls her own *S.* iii. 18
Say at what age a Poet grows *d. S.* v. 50
Style the *d.*, the matchless, what you will *S.* v. 70
The long majestic March, and Energy *d. S.* v. 269
Be call'd to Court to plan some work *d. S.* v. 374
In hues as gay, and odours as *d. S.* viii. 216

Divinely.
Then taught by Hermes, and *d.* bold *D.* iv. 381
Sworn foe to Myst'ry, yet *d.* dark *D.* iv. 460
Unerring Nature, still *d.* bright *E.C.* 70
Serenely pure, and yet *d.* strong *S.* vi. 172

Diving.
And sullen Mole, that hides his *d.* flood *W.F.* 347

Divinity.
Dry bodies of *D.* appear *D.* i. 152
Hist'ry her Pot, *D.* her Pipe *D.* iii. 196
And much *D.* without a Noũs *D.* iv. 244

Division.
Joy to great Chaos! let *D.* reign *D.* iv. 54

Divorce.
Or wed to what he must *d.*, a Muse *D.* iv. 262

Do.—*Passim*.
At last he whispers, "*D.*; and we go snacks" *P.S.* 66

Doats.
Soft Simplicetta *d.* upon a Beau *Mi.* ix. 103

Doctor.
The *d.* fancies he has driv'n them out *E.M.* ii. 160
Ah *D.*, how you love to jest *I.H.* ii. 175
The *d.* call'd, declares all help too late *M.E.* i. 239
Or find some *D.* that would save the life *M.E.* ii. 93
Banish'd the *d.*, and expell'd the friend *M.E.* iii. 330
Sancho's dread *D.* and his Wand were there *M.E.* iv. 160
You tell the *D.*; when the more you have *S.* vi. 213
To stick the D.'*s chair into the Throne D.* iv. 177
By *D.* bills to play the *d.* part *E.C.* 109
The *D.* Wormwood style, the Hash of tongues *S.* viii. 52
Or chair'd at White's amidst the D—*s sit D.* i. 203
Isis and Cam made *D.* of her Laws *D.* iv. 578
Who shall decide, when *D.* disagree *M.E.* iii. 1
Like *D.* thus, when much dispute has past *M.E.* iii. 15
But ask not to what *D.* I apply *S.* iii. 23
Ev'n Radcliffe's *D.* travel first to France *S.* v. 183
Him the damn'd *D.* and his Friends immur'd *S.* vi. 192

Doctrine.
Not for the *d.*, but the music there *E.C.* 343
Out-do Llandaff in *D.*,—yea in Life *E.S.* i. 134
This *d.*, Friend, I learnt at Court *I.H.* ii. 180
Such this day's *d.*—in another fit *M.E.* ii. 75
A *d.* sage, but truly none of mine *S.* ii. 3
This, this the saving *d.* preach'd to all *S.* iii. 81
If such a *D.*, in St. James's air *S.* iii. 110

Dog.
His faithful *d.* shall bear him company *E.M.* i. 112
Expect thy *d.*, thy bottle, and thy wife *E.M.* iv. 178
For him you'll call a *d.*, and her a bitch *S.* ii. 50
Call'd happy *D.* ! the Beggar at his door *S.* vi. 116
He slept, poor *d.* ! and lost it, to a doit *S.* vi. 36
And carry'd off in some d.'s tail at last D. iii. 292
Rolls the large tribute of dead d—*s to Thames D.* ii. 272
To run with Horses, or to hunt with *D. D.* iv. 526
And ev'n the very *D.* at ease *I.H.* ii. 140
Rush Chaplain, Butler, *D.* and all *I.H.* ii. 211
Could he himself have sent it to the *d. M.E.* iii. 66
And men and *d.* shall drink him till they burst *M.E.* iii. 178
The d.*-days are no more the case I.H.* i. 15
On some patch'd *d.-hole* ek'd with ends of wall *M.E.* iv. 32
The *d.-star* rages ! nay 'tis past a doubt *P.S.* 3
Now flam'd the *d.'s* unpropitious ray *D.* iv. 9

Dogmatize.
Prompt to impose, and fond to *d. D.* iv. 464

Doing.—*Passim*.

Doit.
He slept, poor dog! and lost it, to a *d. S.* vi 36

Doleful.
The hills and rocks attend my *d*. lay *Su.* 17

Dolphins.
Whales sport in woods, and *d*. in the skies *D.* iii. 246

Dome.
She bids him wait her to her sacred *D. D.* i. 265
Thus when we view some well-proportion'd *d. E.C.* 247
And in a vapour reach'd the dismal *d. R.L.* iv. 18
And the high *d.* re-echoes to his nose *R.L.* v. 86
These *moss-grown* d—s *with spiry turrets crown'd E.A.* 142
And crystal *d.* and angels in machines *R.L.* iv. 46
Well, I could wish, that still in lordly *d. S.* vii. 115
Her sacred *d.* involv'd in rolling fire *W.F.* 324

Domestic.
O Friend! may each *d.* bliss be thine *P.S.* 406
No friend's complaint, no kind *d.* tear *U.L.* 49

Dominions.
I a Slave in thy *D. Mi.* vii. 3

Done.—*Passim.*

Doom.
From the same foes, at last, both felt their *d. E.C.* 685
And thou, blest Maid! attendant on his *d. Ep.* vii. 11
At Ombre singly to decide their *d. R.L.* iii. 27
In sure succession to the day of *d. S.* viii. 161
There mighty Nations shall inquire their *d. W.F.* 381

Doom'd.
Or whether Heav'n has *d.* that Shock must fall *R.L.* ii. 110
When *d.* to say his beads and Even-song *S.* vii. 106
Both *d.* alike, for sportive Tyrants bled *W.F.* 59

Dooms.
The lamb thy riot *d.* to bleed to-day *E.M.* i. 81
Nay, feasts the animal he *d.* his feast *E.M.* iii. 65

Door.
Plac'd at the *d.* of Learning, youth to guide *D.* iv. 153
A Rat, a Rat! clap to the *d. I.H.* ii. 212
Huge bales of British cloth blockade the *d. M.E.* iii. 57
Curse the sav'd candle, and unop'ning *d. M.E.* iii. 194
Is there a variance? enter but his *d. M.E.* iii. 271
Proud to catch cold at a Venetian *d. M.E.* iv. 36
Shut, shut the *d.*, good John! fatigu'd, I said *P.S.* 1
Glad of a quarrel, straight I clap the *d. P.S.* 67
So humble, he has knock'd at *Tibbald's d. P.S.* 372
As drives the storm, at any *d.* I knock *S.* iii. 25
Call'd happy Dog! the Beggar at his *d. S.* iv. 116
Soon as I enter at my country *d. S.* vi. 206
The good old landlord's hospitable *d. S.* vii. 114
Like batt'ring-rams, beats open ev'ry *d. S.* viii. 265
And Fun'rals *black'ning all the* D—s *I.H.* i. 9
Palladian walls, Venetian *d. I.H.* 191
With mobs, and duns, and soldiers at their *d. S.* vi. 124
As needy beggars sing at *d.* for meat *S.* vii. 26

Dorimant.
As Bug now has, and *D.* would have *S.* iii. 88

Doris.
Of perjur'd *D.* dying I complain *A.* 58
And *Delia's* name and *D.' fill'd the Grove A.* 4

Dorset.
D., the Grace of Courts, the Muses' Pride *Ep.* i. 1
Where other *BUCKHURSTS*, other D—s *shine Ep.* i. 13

Dotage.
Fate in their *d.* this fair Idiot gave *D.* i. 13

Dotard.
Europe a Woman, Child, or *D.* rule *M.E.* i. 93
Some with fat Bucks on childless d—s *fawn S.* iii. 130

Dote.
What dust we *d.* on, when 'tis man we love *E.A.* 336

Doting.
The third mad passion of thy *d.* age *D.* iii. 304

Double.
O'er-look'd, seen *d.*, by the fool, and wise *E.M.* iv. 6

When Paxton gives him *d.* Pots and Pay *E.S.* ii. 141
And bravely bore the *d.* loads of lead *R.L.* v. 102
Tho' *d.* tax'd, how little have I lost *S.* ii. 152
Bind rebel Wit, and *d. chain on chain D.* iv. 158
All my demurs but *d.* his Attacks *P.S.* 65
Procure a TASTE to *d.* the surprise *S.* iv. 30

Doubles.
And public faction *d.* private hate *E.C.* 457

Doublets.
As apes our grandsires, in their *d.* drest *E.C.* 332

Doubling.
The *d.* Lustres dance as fast as she *S.* i. 48

Doubly.
A vile Encomium *d.* ridicules *S.* v. 410

Doubt.
Our wiser sons, no *d.*, will think us so *E.C.* 439
Come, come, at all I laugh, he laughs, no *d. E.S.* i. 35
He hangs between; in *d.* to act or rest (*rep.*) *E.M.* ii. 7
Save just at dinner—then, prefers, no *d. M.E.* ii. 79
The Dog-star rages! nay 'tis past a *d. P.S.* 3
"I found him close with Swift"—Indeed, no *d. P.S.* 275
It brought (no *d.*) th' *Excise* and *Army* in *S.* vii. 8
'Tis chang'd, no *d.*, from what it was before *S.* vii. 31
Those words, that would against them clear the *d. S.* vii. 104
Dangers, d—s, *delays, surprises O.* iii. 39
For these explain *a thing till all men d.* it *D.* iv. 251
And reason downward, till we *d.* of God *D.* iv. 472
T' admire superior sense, and *d.* their own *E.C.* 200
Be silent always when you *d.* your sense *E.C.* 566
To trust in ev'ry thing, or *d.* of all *E.M.* iv. 26
I *d.* not, if his lordship knew *I.H.* ii. 81 s
And soundest Casuists *d.*, like you and me *M.E.* iii. 2
Preach as I please, I *d.* our curious men *S.* ii. 17
I'd never *d.* at Court to make a friend *S.* ii. 44
Some *d.*, if equal pains, or equal fire *S.* v. 282

Doubtful.
Of naught so *d.* as of *Soul* and *Will D.* iv. 482
When Reason *d.*, like the Samian letter *D.* iv. 151
Dame *Justice* weighing long the *d.* Right *Mi.* xi. 7
The *d.* beam long nods from side to side *R.L.* v. 73

Doubting.
What tho' no credit *d.* Wits may give *R.L.* i. 39

Doughty.
She smil'd to see the *d.* hero slain *R.L.* v. 69

Douglas.
And *D.* lend his soft, obstetric hand *D.* iv. 394

Dove.
Smit with her varying plumage, spare the *d. E.M.* iii. 54
And on its top descends the mystic *D. M.* 12
To *Number five direct your* d—s *I.H.* iii. 9
Where *d.* in flocks the leafless trees o'ershade *W.F.* 127
Not half so swift the trembling *d.* can fly (*rep.*) *W.F.* 185
*D.-*like *she gathers to her wings again D.* iii. 126
And scatters blessing from her *d.* wing *W.F.* 430

Dover.
And desp'rate Misery lays hold on *D. S.* iv. 57
From *Scots to Wight, from Mount to* D.'s *strand S.* vii. 86

Dow'r.
For very want; he could not pay a *d. M.E.* iii. 326

Down.—*Passim.*
How young Lutetia, softer than the *d. D.* ii. 333
His pond an Ocean, his parterre a *D. M.E.* iv. 106
Let his plantations stretch from *d.* to *d. M.E.* iv. 189
Enclose whole d—s *in walls, 'tis all a joke S.* vi. 261

Downright.
Shot to the black abyss, and plung'd *d. D.* ii. 288
As *d.* SHIPPEN, or as old Montaigne *S.* i. 52
In *d.* charity revive the dead *S.* vi. 164

Downward, Downwards.—*Passim.*

Downy.
Belinda still her *d.* pillow prest *R.L.* i. 19

Doze.

Would drink and *d.* at Tooting or Earl's-Court *S.* vi. 113
At ev'ry line they stretch, they yawn, they *d. D.* ii. 390

Doz'd.

And Chiefless Armies *d.* out the Campaign *D.* iv. 617

Drabs.

Let her thy heart, next *D.* and Dice, engage *D.* iii. 303
Paltry and proud, as *d.* in Drury-lane *S.* vii. 64

Drag.

Go drive the Deer, and *d.* the finny prey *S.* iv. 113

Dragg'd.

D. in the dust ! his arms hang idly round *E.S.* i. 153
And when up ten steep slopes you've *d.* your thighs *M.E.* iv. 131

Dragoman *see* Druggerman.

Dragon.

Reduc'd at last to hiss in my own *d. D.* iii. 286
On rifted rocks, the *d.*'s late abodes *M.* 71
All sudden, Gorgons hiss, and D—s glare *D.* iii. 235
On grinning *d.* thou shalt mount the wind *D.* iii. 268

Dragoons.

Who holds *D.* and wooden shoes in scorn *Mi.* ii. 20

Drags.

D. from the Town to wholesome Country air *E.* v. 2
That, like a wounded snake, *d.* its slow length along *E.C.* 357

Drain.

Did all the dregs of bold Socinus *d. E.C.* 545
Their Country's wealth our mightier Misers *d. S.* iii. 126

Drain'd.

Now *d.* a distant country of her Floods *M.E.* v. 8

Drains.

If our intemp'rate Youth the vessel *d., S.* ii. 90

Drams.

From the strong fate of *d.* if thou get free *D.* iii. 145

Drank.

Judicious *d.*, and greatly-daring din'd *D.* iv. 318
You've play'd, and lov'd, and eat, and *d.* your fill *S.* vi. 323

Drapier.

Dean, *D.*, Bickerstaff, or Gulliver *D.* i. 20

Draught.

The daily Anodyne, and nightly *D. M.E.* ii. 111
Alas ! I copy (or my *d.* would fail) *M.E.* ii. 197
Greatness, with Timon, dwells in such a *d. M.E.* iv. 103
There shallow d—s intoxicate the brain *E.C.* 217

Draw.

'Twixt Prince and People close the Curtain *d. D.* i. 313
Heav'n's twinkling Sparks *d.* light, and point their horns *D.* ii. 12
How keen the war, if Dulness *d.* the sword *D.* iii. 120
Or that bright Image to our fancy *d. D.* iv. 487
Next, bidding all *d.* near on bended knees *D.* iv. 565
Or *d.* to silk Arachne's subtile line *D.* iv. 590
Oh ! happy state ! where souls each other *d. E.A.* 91
And but from Nature's fountains scorn'd to *d. E.C.* 133
To *d.* nutrition, propagate, and rot *E.M.* ii. 64
In vain thy Reason finer webs shall *d. E.M.* iii. 191
Converse and Love mankind might strongly *d. E.M.* iii. 207
D. forth the monsters of th' abyss profound *E.M.* iii. 221
D. to one point, and to one centre bring *E.M.* iii. 301
Shall Ward *d.* contracts with a Statesman's skill *E.S.* i. 119
Yes, the last Pen for Freedom let me *d. E.S.* ii. 248
To this sad shrine, whoe'er thou art i *d.* near *Ep.* iii. 1
To *d.* the Naked is your true delight *M.E.* ii. 188
To *d.* the man who loves his God, or King *M.E.* ii. 196
With tape-ty'd curtains, never meant to *d. M.E.* iii. 302
Yet then did *Gildon d.* his venal quill *P.S.* 151
To *d.* fresh colours from the vernal flow'rs *R.L.* ii. 95
D. forth to combat on the velvet plain *R.L.* iii. 44
That while my nostrils *d.* the vital air *R.L.* iv. 137
Shall *d.* such envy as the Lock you lost *R.L.* v. 144

Drawings.

Indentures, Cov'nants, Articles they *d. S.* vii. 94
Nor sly informer watch these words to *d. S.* vii. 127
Adjust their clothes, and to confusion *d. S.* viii. 242
D. monarchs chain'd, and Cressi's glorious field *W.F.* 305

Drawings.

He buys for Topham, *D.* and Designs *M.E.* iv. 7
Who random *d.* from your sheets shall take *M.E.* iv. 27

Drawing-room.

All fresh and fragrant from the *d. S.* viii. 215
From d—s, from colleges, from garrets *D.* ii. 23

Drawl.

Thro' the long, heavy, painful page *d.* on *D.* ii. 388

Drawn.

Morality, by her false Guardians *d. D.* iv. 27
Who gently *d.*, and struggling less and less *D.* iv. 83
The lines, tho' touch'd but faintly, are *d.* right *E.C.* 22
And *d.* supports, upheld by God, or thee *E.M.* i. 34
Maxims are *d.* from Notions, these from Guess *M.E.* i. 14
'Tis from high Life high Characters are *d. M.E.* i. 135
Show'd Rome her Cato's figure *d.* in state *P.C.* 30
When bold Sir Plume had *d.* Clarissa down *R.L.* v. 67
Pageants on Pageants, in long order *d. S.* v. 316
Has life no sourness, *d.* so near its end *S.* vi. 316

Draws.

His conqu'ring tribes th' Arabian prophet *d. D.* iii. 97
Now look thro' Fate ! behold the scene she *d. D.* iii. 127
It *d.* up vapours which obscure its rays *E.C.* 472
And is himself that great Sublime he *d. E.C.* 680
He *d.* him gentle, tender, and forgiving *E.J.S.* 27
Is the great chain that *d.* all to agree *E.M.* i. 33
Death still *d.* nearer, never seeming near *E.M.* iii. 76
In golden Chains the willing World she *d. E.S.* i. 147
A Monarch's sword when mad Vain-glory *d. E.S.* ii. 229
Yet no mean motive this profusion *d. M.E.* iii. 205
Drowns my spirit, *d.* my breath *O.* v. 11
Virtue confess'd in human shape he *d. P.C.* 17
And beauty *d.* us with a single hair *R.L.* ii. 28
And *d.* the aromatic souls of flow'rs *W.F.* 244

Dread.

The Lust of Lucre, and the *d.* of Death *E.* i. 26
Sole *D.* of Folly, Vice, and Insolence *E.S.* ii. 313
At length, by wholesome *d.* of statutes bound *S.* v. 257
Of *Generic I* and *Attila's* d. name *D.* iii. 92
Indulge, *d.* Chaos, and eternal Night *D.* iv. 2
As one by one, at *d.* Medea's strain *D.* iv. 635
Lo ! thy *d.* Empire, CHAOS ! is restor'd *D.* iv. 653
Yet then to those *d.* altars as I drew *E.A.* 115
All this *d.* ORDER break—for whom ? for thee *E.M.* i. 257
Sancho's *d.* Doctor and his Wand were there *M.E.* iv. 160
I saw, alas ! some *d.* event impend *R.L.* i. 109
I cannot like, *d.* Sir, your Royal Cave *S.* iii. 115
Come, Abelard ! for what hast thou to *d. E.A.* 257
Yet hate repose, and *d.* to be alone *M.E.* ii. 228
A lash like mine no honest man shall *d. P.S.* 303
Like Gods they fight, nor *d.* a mortal wound *R.L.* v. 44
All that I *d.* is leaving you behind *R.L.* v. 100
Slander or Poison *d.* from Delia's rage *S.* i. 81
Whether we *d.*, or whether we desire *S.* iv. 20

Dreaded.

This *d.* Sat'rist *Dennis* will confess *P.S.* 370
The *d.* East is all the wind that blows *R.L.* iv. 20

Dreadful.

De Lyra there a *d.* front extends *D.* i. 153
Held forth the virtue of the *d.* wand *D.* iv. 140
And swell the pomp of *d.* sacrifice *E.A.* 354
Here fix'd the *d.*, there the blest abodes *E.M.* iii. 255
But, *d.* too, the dark Assassin hires *M.E.* iii. 28
D. gleams *O.* i. 56
D. as hermit's dreams in haunted shades *R.L.* iv. 41
Prepares a *d.* jest for all mankind *S.* ii. 124
And view this *d.* All without a fear *S.* vi. 10
A *d.* series of intestine wars *W.F.* 325

Dreading.

D. ev'n fools, by Flatterers besieg'd *P.S.* 207

Dreads.

And *Wit d.* Exile, Penalties, and Pains *D.* iv. 22
As, while he *d.* it, makes him hope it too *E.M.* iii. 74

DREAM—DROPT.

He *d.* a death-bed like the meanest slave *M.E.* i. 116
And *d.* more actions, hurries from a jail *S.* viii. 183

Dream.
The air-built Castle, and the golden *D. D.* iii. 10
Absent I follow thro' th' extended *d. I.H.* iii. 42
Becomes the stuff of which our *d.* is wrought *M.E.* i. 48
Till Fancy colour'd it, and form'd a *D. S.* viii. 189
Yet ate, in d—s, *the custard of the day D.* i. 92
From *d.* of millions, and three groats to pay *D.* ii. 252
And wafting Vapours from the Land of *d. D.* ii. 340
Her tresses staring from Poetic *d. D.* iii. 17
Or wait inspiring *D.* at Maro's Urn *E.* iii. 28
And whisp'ring Angels prompt her golden *d. E.A.* 216
Far other *d.* my erring soul employ *E.A.* 223
The *d.* of Pindus and th' Aonian maids *M.* 4
But nobler scenes Maria's *d.* unfold *M.E.* iii. 129
One grasps a Cecrops in ecstatic *d. M.E.* v. 40
Nay oft, in *d.*, invention we bestow *R.L.* i. 99
Dreadful as hermit's *d.* in haunted shades *R.L.* iv. 41
In spite of witches, devils, *d.*, and fire *S.* vi. 323
Do lovers d., *or is my Delia kind A.* 52
You *d.* of triumphs in the rural shade *E.* v. 32
Give all thou canst—and let me *d.* the rest *E.A.* 124
To *d.* once more I close my willing eyes *E.A.* 239
Nor is it Homer nods, but we that *d. E.C.* 180
As well as *d.* such trifles are assign'd *E.M.* iv. 179
I sit and *d.* I see my Craggs anew *E.S.* ii. 69

Dreaming.
Not Dante *d.* all th' infernal state *S.* viii. 192

Dreary.
Thro' *d.* wastes, and weep each other's woe *E.A.* 242
O'er all the *d.* coasts *O.* i. 55
A *d.* desert, and a gloomy waste *W.F.* 44

Dregs.
But if in noble minds some *d.* remain *E.C.* 526
Did all the *d.* of bold Socinus drain *E.C.* 545
Ev'n to the *d.* and squeezings of the brain *E.C.* 607
And stoops from Angels to the *d.* of Earth *E.S.* i. 142
And sep'rate from their kindred *d.* below *U.L.* 26

Drench.
Go *d.* a Pick-pocket, and join the Mob *E.S.* ii. 41

Drench'd.
The hand of Bavius *d.* thee o'er and o'er *D.* iii. 46

Dress.
The rev'rend Flamen in his lengthen'd *d. D.* ii. 354
And value books, as women men, for *d. E.C.* 306
Expression is the *d.* of thought, and still *E.C.* 318
Deduct what is but Vanity, or *D. E.M.* ii. 45
Kind to my *d.*, my figure, not to Me *S.* iii. 176
Of hollow gew-gaws, only *d.* and face *S.* viii. 209
If Faith itself has diff'rent d—es *worn E.C.* 446
To *d. her charms, and make her more belov'd E.C.* 103
Oh! if to dance all night and *d.* all day *R.L.* v. 19

Dress'd, Drest.
In flow'rs and pearls by bounteous Kirkall *d. D.* ii. 160
True Wit is Nature to advantage *d. E.C.* 297
Is like a clown in regal purple *d. E.C.* 321
Or their fond parents d—t in red and gold *D.* i. 138
As apes our grandsires, in their doublets *d. E.C.* 332
Thee, *d.* in Fancy's airy beam *I.H.* iii. 41
Or *d.* in smiles of sweet Cecilia shine *M.* ii. 13
Wants reach all states ; they beg but better *d. S.* viii. 224
Yet shall thy grave with rising flow'rs be *d. U.L.* 63

Dressing-Room.
Why stays *Smilinda* in the *D. Mi.* ix. *

Drew.
Such as Lucretius *d.*, a God like thee *D.* iv. 484
Yet then, to those dread altars as I *d., E.A.* 115
She *d.* from them what they deriv'd from Heav'n *E.C.* 99
If not God's image, yet his shadow *d. E.M.* iii. 288
Why *d.* Marseilles' good bishop purer breath *E.M.* iv. 107
'Twas my own Lord that *d.* the *fatal Card Mi.* ix. 48
Just then Clarissa *d.* with tempting grace *R.L.* i. 127
Thrice she look'd back and thrice the foe *d.* near *R.L.* iii. 138
Just where the breath of life his nostrils *d. R.L.* v. 81

And *d.* a deadly bodkin from her side *R.L.* v. 88
And *d.* behind a radiant trail of hair *R.L.* v. 128

Drily.
Some *d.* plain, without invention's aid *E.C.* 114

Drink.
And to mere mortals seem'd a Priest in *d. D.* ii. 426
There, all *from Paul's to Aldgate* d. *and sleep D.* ii. 346
Still *d.* delicious poison from thy eye *E.A.* 122
And *d.* the falling tears each other sheds *E.A.* 350
Or *d.* deep, or taste not the Pierian spring *E.C.* 216
But spare your censure ; Silia does not *d. M.E.* ii. 34
And men and dogs shall *d.* him till they burst *M.E.* iii. 278
You *d.* by measure, and to minutes eat *M.E.* iv. 158
So *d.* with Walters, or with Chartres eat *S.* i. 89
Would *d.* and doze at Tooting or Earl's-Court *S.* vi. 113
If, when the more you *d.*, the more you crave *S.* vi. 212

Drinking.
And *d.* largely sobers us again *E.C.* 218
Now *d.* citron with his Grace and Chartres *M.E.* ii. 64

Drinks.
With the same spirit that he *d.* and whores *M.E.* i. 189
Who *d.*, whores, fights, and in a duel dies *M.E.* iii. 390
And ev'ry plant that *d.* the morning dew *Su.* 32

Drive.
Chromatic tortures soon shall *d.* them hence *D.* iv. 55
D. to St. James's a whole herd of swine *M.E.* iii. 74
Beaux banish beaux, and coaches coaches *d. R.L.* i. 102
Go *d.* the Deer, and drag the finny prey *S.* iv. 113

Driv'n.
The doctor fancies he has *d.* them out *E.M.* ii. 160
One, *d.* by strong Benevolence of soul *S.* vi. 276

Drives.
If once right reason *d.* that cloud away *E.C.* 211
His fiery course, or *d.* him o'er the plains *E.M.* i. 62
This *d.* them constant to a certain coast *E.M.* ii. 168
So *d.* Self-love, thro' just and thro' unjust *E.M.* iii. 269
As *d.* the storm, at any door I knock *S.* iii. 25
When thro' the clouds he *d.* the trembling doves *W.F.* 188

Driving.
Spread the thin oar, and catch the *d.* gale *E.M.* iii. 178

Droop.
Ye flow'rs that *d.*, forsaken by the spring *A.* 27

Drooping.
Till *d.*, sick'ning, dying, they began *E.M.* iii. 223
Un-water'd see the *d.* sea-horse mourn *M.* iv. 125
Thus when *Philomela d. Mi.* vii. 29
On her heav'd bosom hung her *d.* head *R.L.* iv. 145
Hush'd are the birds, and clos'd the *d.* flow'rs *Sp.* 70
His *d.* swans on ev'ry note expire *W.F.* 275

Drop.
What *D.* or *Nostrum* can this plague remove *P.S.* 29
Oil, tho' it stink, they *d.* by *d.* impart *S.* ii. 59
For fainting Age what cordial *d.* remains *S.* ii. 89
The cordial *D.* of Life is Love alone *S.* iv. 127
Ward try'd on Puppies, and the Poor, his *D. S.* v. 182
Between each *d.* it gives, stays half a minute *S.* viii. 127
Kind, virtuous d—s *just gathering in my eye E.A.* 278
Where ling'ring *d.* from min'ral Roofs distill *Mi.* x. 3
And calls forth Roman *d.* from British eyes *P.C.* 16
The *d.* to thee, Brillante, we consign *R.L.* ii. 113
And liquid amber d. *from ev'ry thorn A.* 38
Such was her wont at early dawn to *d. D.* ii. 71
With ev'ry bead I *d.* too soft a tear. *E.A.* 270
One human tear shall *d.* and be forgiv'n *E.A.* 358
Then *d.* into thyself, and be a fool *E.M.* ii. 30
And *d.* at last, but in unwilling ears *P.S.* 39
To steal from rainbows ere they *d.* in show'rs *R.L.* ii. 96

Dropp'd, Dropt.
His tresses *d.* with dews, and o'er the stream *W.F.* 331
And thrice he *d—t* it from his quiv'ring hand *D.* i. 246
But pious Needham *d.* the name of God *D.* i. 324
What Dulness *d.* among her sons imprest *D.* ii. 407
D. the dull lumber of the Latin store *D.* iv. 319
Plant of celestial seed! if *d.* below *E.M.* iv. 7

And Nations wonder'd while they *d*. the sword *S*. v. 399
My mind resumes the thread it *d*. before *S*. vi. 207
At night, would swear him *d*. out of the Moon *S*. viii. 33

Dropping.

D. with Infant's blood, and Mother's tears *D*. iv. 142
The Honey *d*. from Favonio's tongue *E.S*. i. 67
From the crack'd bag the *d*. Guinea spoke *M.E*. iii. 36
Now hung with pearls the *d*. trees appear *W*. 31
Strain out the last dull d—s of their sense E.C. 608

Drops.

The meteor *d*., and in a flash expires *D*. iv. 634
D. to the third, who nuzzles close behind *E.S*. ii. 178
All, all but Truth, *d*. dead-born from the Press *E.S*. ii. 226
For thee the hardy Vet'ran *d*. a tear *Ep*. ix. 5
List'ning Envy *d*. her snakes *O*. i. 33
In one a Mistress *d*., in one a Friend *S*. vi. 75
By little and by little, *d*. his lies *S*. viii. 129

Dross.

The *d*. cements what else were too refin'd *E.M*. ii. 179
Kept *D*. for Duchesses, the world shall know it *M.E*. ii. 291

Drought.

Thro' reconcil'd extremes of *d*. and rain *M.E*. iii. 166

Drove.

She heard, and *d*. him to th' Hibernian shore *D*. iv. 70
And *d*. those holy Vandals off the stage *E.C*. 695
Who builds a Bridge that never *d*. a pile *S*. v. 185

Drown.

And *d*. his lands and Manors in a Soupe (*sic*) *D*. iv. 596
And there in sweet oblivion *d*. *I.H*. ii. 131
To deluge sin, and *d*. a Court in tears *S*. viii. 285

Drown'd.

Sure sign that no spectator shall be *d*. *D*. ii. 174
Some would have spoken, but the voice was *d*. *D*.iv.277
Till *d*. was Sense, and Shame, and Right, and Wrong *D*. iv. 625
In seas of flame my plunging soul is *d*. *E.A*. 275
In trance ecstatic may thy pangs be *d*. *E.A*. 339
A lost Bank-bill, or beard their Son was *d*. *S*. ii. 56

Drowns.

D. the loud clarion of the braying Ass *D*. ii. 234
D. my spirits, draws my breath *O*. v. 11

Drowsy.

As verse, or prose, infuse the *d*. God *D*. ii. 396
A *d*. Watchman, that just gives a knock *D*. iv. 443
Still humming on, their *d*. course they keep *E.C*. 600

Drudge.

Condemn'd in bus'ness or in arts to *d*. *E.M*. iv. 263

Drug.

Or quicken'd a Reversion by a *d*. *S*. viii. 135

Druggerman.

Pity you was not *D*. at Babel *S*. viii. 83

Drum.

And his this *D*., whose deep heroic Bass *D*. ii. 233
With Gun, *D*., Trumpet, Blunderbuss and Thunder *S*. i. 28
And Jove's own Thunders follow Mars's d—s *D*. iv. 68

Drunk.

Or, cobbler-like, the parson will be *d*. *E.M*. iv. 202
D. at a Borough, civil at a Ball *M.E*. i. 75ˡ
Cæsar perhaps might answer he was *d*. *M.E*. i. 132
See Sin in State, majestically *d*. *M.E*. ii. 69
Has *d*. with Cibber, nay has rhym'd for Moore *P.S*. 373
Be furious, envious, slothful, mad, or *d*. *S*. iii. 61

Drunken.

Bring, bring the madding Bay, the *d*. Vine *D*. i. 303

Drury.

Here shouts all *D*., there all Lincoln's-inn *D*. iii. 270
"*God save King Colley!*" *D*.-lane replies *D*.·i. 320
A Church collects the saints of *D*. *D*. ii. 30
"Nine years!" cries he, who high in *D*. *P.S*. 41
Paltry and proud, as drabs in *D*. *S*. vii. 64

Dry.

D. bodies of Divinity appear *D*. i. 152
From the *d*. rock who bade the waters flow *M.E*. iii. 254
To some a *d*. rehearsal was assign'd *P.S*. 243
In the *d*. desert of a thousand lines *S*. v. 112
And suckle armies, and d.-*nurse the land D*. i. 316

Dryads.

Foe to the *D*. of his Father's groves *M.E*. iv. 94
That call'd the list'ning *D*. to the plain *W*. 12

Dryden.

And what Timotheus was, is *D*. now *E.C*. 383
Pride, Malice, Folly, against *D*. rose *E.C*. 458
And such as Chaucer is, shall *D*. be *E.C*. 483
D. alone (what wonder?) came not nigh (*rep*.) *P.S*. 245
Could Laureate *D*. Pimp and Friar engage *S*. i. 113
Unhappy *D*.!—In all Charles's days *S*. v. 213
Waller was smooth; but *D*. taught to join *S*. v. 267
Ev'n copious *D*. wanted, or forgot *S*. v. 280
Fresnoy's close Art, and D.'s native Fire E. iii. 8
In *D*. Virgil see the print *E*. vi. 28
From *D*. Fables down to Durfey's Tales *E.C*. 617
And sacred, place by *D*. awful dust *Ep*. v. 2
And *St. John's* self (great *D*. friend before) *P.S*. 141
Or, I'm content, allow me *D*. strains *S*. vi. 145

Dry'd.

D. butterflies, and tomes of casuistry *R.L*. v. 122

Dubb'd.

A Man of wealth is *d*. a Man of worth *S*. iv. 81
Or *d*. Historians, by express command *S*. v. 372

Dubs.

Then *d*. Director, and secures his Soul *M.E*. iii. 374

Duchess.

She sighs, and is no *D*. at her heart *E*. iv. 56
Of wrongs from D—*es and Lady Maries D*. ii. 136
Kept dross for *D*., the world shall know it *M.E*. ii. 291

Duck-lane.

Amidst their kindred cob-webs in *D*. *E.C*. 445

Ductile.

And *d*. Dulness new mæanders takes *D*. i. 64

Due.

And give to Titus old Vespasian's *d*. *M.E*. v. 18
Well might they rage, I gave them but their *d*. *P.S*. 174
Such with their shelves as d. proportion hold D. i. 137
D. distance reconciles to form and grace *E.C*. 174
Applause, in spight of trivial faults, is *d*. *E.C*. 258
Tho' triumphs were to gen'rals only *d*. *E.C*. 512
That not alone what to your sense is *d*. *E.C*. 564
And all that rises, rise in *d*. degree *E.M*. i. 46
Know thy own point: This kind, this *d*. degree *E.M*. i. 283
These mix'd with art, and to *d*. bounds confin'd *E.M*. ii. 119
Taught Pow'r's *d*. use to People and to Kings *E.M*. iii. 289
D. to his Merit, and brave Thirst of praise *Ep*. viii. 6
I sing. This verse to CARYL, Muse! is *d*. *R.L*. i. 3

Duel.

Stol'n from a *D*., follow'd by a Nun *D*. iv. 327
Who drinks, whores, fights, and in a *d*. dies *M.E*. iii. 390

Duke.

Swear like a Lord, or Rich out-whore a *D*. *E.S*. i. 116
But rudely press before a *D*. *I.H*. ii. 59 s
The *D*. expects my Lord and you *I.H*. ii. 73 s
Or when a *D*. to *Jansen* punts at White's *S*. vii. 88
Where D—s *and Butchers join to wreathe my crown D*. i. 293
Of Lords, and Earls, and *D*., and garter'd Knights *E*. v. 36
And mighty *D*. pack cards for half-a-crown *M.E*. iii. 142
Some *D*. at *Marybone* bowl Time away *Mi*. ix. 100
While Peers, and *D*., and all their sweeping train *R.L*. i. 84

Dull.

Fruits of *d*. Heat, and Sooterkins of Wit *D*. i. 126

DULLER—DUST.

He sleeps among the *d.* of ancient days *D.* i. 294
Furious he dives, precipitately *d. D.* ii. 316
Of solid proof, impenetrably *d. D.* iii. 26
So sweetly mawkish, and so smoothly *d. D.* iii. 171
See! the *d.* stars roll round and re-appear *D.* iii. 322
Of *d.* and veal a new World to mould *D.* iv. 15
Wake the *d.* Church, and lull the racing Stage *D.* iv. 58
Or vest *d.* Flatt'ry in the sacred Gown *D.* iv. 97
Made Horace *d.*, and humbled Milton's strains *D.* iv. 212
Dropt the *d.* lumber of the Latin store *D.* iv. 319
The *d.* may waken to a humming-bird *D.* iv. 446
My Sons! be proud, be selfish, and be *d. D.* iv. 582
The Venal quiet, and entrance the *d. D.* iv. 624
For the *d.* glory of a virtuous Wife *E.* iv. 46
Old-fashion'd halls, *d.* Aunts, and croaking rooks *E.* v. 12
Write *d.* receipts how poems may be made *E.C.* 115
Nor lose, for that malignant *d.* delight *E.C.* 237
And ten low words oft creep in one *d.* line *E.C.* 347
Leave such to tune their own *d.* rhymes, and know *E.C.* 358
Whose right it is, uncensur'd, to be *d. E.C.* 589
And charitably let the *d.* be vain *E.C.* 597
Strain out the last *d.* droppings of their sense *E.C.* 608
And to be *d.* was constru'd to be good *E.C.* 690
When the *d.* Ox, why now he breaks the clod *E.M.* i. 63
But let me add, Sir ROBERT's mighty *d. E.S.* ii. 133
The *D.*, flat falsehood serves for policy *M.E.* i. 67
Leaves the *d.* Cits, and joins (to please the fair) *M.E.* iii. 387
Lintot, *d.* rogue! will think your price too much *P.S.* 63
The *d.*, the proud, the wicked, and the mad *P.S.* 347
Long as the Year's *d.* circle seems to run *S.* iii. 37
There is a time when Poets will grow *d. S.* vi. 200
D. sullen pris'ners in the body's cage *U.L.* 18

Duller.

And ev'ry year be *d.* than the last *D.* iii. 296

Dully.

Not *d.* prepossess'd, nor blindly right *E.C.* 634

Dulness.

Call'd to this work by *D.*, Jove, and Fate *D.* i. 4
D. possess'd o'er all her ancient right *D.* i. 11
For, born a Goddess, *D.* never dies *D.* i. 18
In clouded Majesty here *D.* shone *D.* i. 45
And ductile *D.* new mæanders takes *D.* i. 64
D. with transport eyes the lively Dunce *D.* i. 111
D.! whose good old cause I yet defend *D.* i. 165
Me Emptiness and *D.* could inspire *D.* i. 185
To *D.* Ridpath is as dear as Mist *D.* i. 208
Rous'd by the light, old *D.* heav'd the head *D.* i. 257
New edge their *d.*, and new bronze their face *D.* ii. 10
And gentle *D.* ever loves a joke *D.* ii. 34
D., good Queen, repeats the jest again *D.* ii. 122
His Honour's meaning *D.* thus exprest *D.* ii. 195
D. is sacred to a sound divine *D.* ii. 352
What *D.* dropt among her sons imprest *D.* ii. 407
How keen the war, if *D.* draw the sword *D.* iii. 120
Not with less glory mighty *D.* crown'd *D.* iii. 135
To future ages may thy *d.* last (*rep.*) *D.* iii. 189
See now what *D.* and her sons admire *D.* iii. 228
Angel of *D.*, sent to scatter round *D.* iii. 257
Thy giddy *D.* still shall lumber on *D.* iii. 294
Her seat imperial *D.* shall transport *D.* iii. 298
'Tis thus aspiring *D.* ever shines *D.* iv. 19
And dies, when *D.* gives her Page the word *D.* iv. 30
When *D.*, smiling—"Thus revive the Wits *D.* iv. 119
For sure, if *D.* sees a grateful day *D.* iv. 181
Ah, think not, Mistress, more true *D.* lies *D.* iv. 239
The balm of *D.* trickling in their ear *D.* iv. 544
And mark that point where sense and *d.* meet *E.C.* 51
D. is ever apt to magnify *E.C.* 393
That in proud *d.* joins with Quality *E.C.* 415
But *D.* with Obscenity must prove *E.C.* 532
Then shall Man's pride and *d.* comprehend *E.M.* i. 65
Th' imputed trash, and *d.* not his own *P.S.* 351
Weds the rich *D.* of some Son of earth *S.* iv. 43
That all the shot of *d.* now must be *S.* viii. 64
On *D.*' *lap* th' Anointed head repos'd *D.* iii. 2

Duly.

But *d.* sent his family and wife *M.E.* iii. 382

Dumb.

Sound, sound, ye Viols! be the Cat-call *d. D.* i. 302

The *d.* shall sing, the lame his crutch forego *M.* 43
The flocks around a *d.* compassion show *Su.* 6

Dun.

In a *d.* night-gown of his own loose skin *D.* ii. 38
Safe where no Critics damn, no d—s molest D. i. 295
With mobs, and *d.*, and soldiers at their doors *S.* vi. 124

Dunce.

Still *D.* the second reigns like *D.* the first *D.* i. 6
Dulness with transport eyes the lively *D. D.* i. 111
Behold an hundred sons, and each a *D. D.* iii. 138
Whate'er of *D.* in College or in Town *D.* iv. 87
D. scorning *D.* beholds the next advance *D.* iv. 137
And petrify a Genius to a *D. D.* iv. 264
What turns him now a stupid silent *D. M.E.* i. 163
And makes her hearty meal upon a *d. M.E.* ii. 86
May *d.* by *d.* be whistled off my hands *P.S.* 254
At ninety-nine, a Modern and a *D. S.* v. 60
All who true D—s in her cause appear'd (*rep.*) *D.* ii. 25
But learn, ye *D.*! not to scorn your God *D.* iii. 224
A wit with *d.*, and a dunce with wits *D.* iv. 90
Wits have short memories, and *d.* none *D.* iv. 620

Dunciad.

And MAKE ONE MIGHTY *D.* OF THE LAND *D.* iv. 604
Out with it, *D.*! let the secret pass *P.S.* 79

Dung.

The floors of plaister, and the walls of *d. M.E.* iii. 300

Dunkirk.

That Spain robs on, and *D.*'s still a Port *S.* viii. 165

Dunton.

On Codrus' old, or *D.*'s modern bed *D.* ii. 144

Dupe.

Then *d.* to Party, child and man the same *D.* iv. 502
Yet soft by nature, more a *d.* than wit *P.S.* 368

Dup'd.

Faithless thro' Piety, and *d.* thro' Wit *M.E.* i. 92

Durance.

For this your locks in paper *d.* bound *R.L.* iv. 99
In *d.*, exile, Bedlam or the Mint *S.* i. 99

Duration.

Builds Life on Death, on Change *D.* founds *M.E.* iii. 167

Durer.

See them survey their limbs by *D.*'s rules *S.* viii. 240

Durfey.

Another *D.*, Ward! shall sing in thee *D.* iii. 146
From Dryden's Fables down to D.'s Tales E.C. 617

Durst.

Who *d.* depart from Aristotle's rules *E.C.* 272
Spread all his sails, and *d.* the deep explore *E.C.* 646
Who *d.* assert the juster ancient cause *E.C.* 721
Th' oppressor rul'd tyrannic where he *d. W.F.* 74

Dusky.

And the fleet shades glide o'er the *d.* green *A.* 64
Here in a *d.* vale where Lethe rolls *D.* iii. 23
The buzzing Bees about their *d.* Queen *D.* iv. 80
But o'er the twilight groves and *d.* caves *E.A.* 163
Umbriel, a *d.*, melancholy sprite *R.L.* iv. 13

Dust.

Of sober face with learned *d.* besprent *D.* iii. 186
Laid this gay daughter of the Spring in *d. D.* iv. 416
And here, e'en then, must my cold *d.* remain *E.A.* 174
While praying, trembling, in the *d.* I roll *E.A.* 279
What *d.* we dote on, when 'tis man we love *E.A.* 336
Shakes off the *d.*, and rears his rev'rend head *E.C.* 700
What if the foot, ordain'd the *d.* to tread *E.M.* i. 259
See godlike TURENNE prostrate on the *d. E.M.* iv. 100
When statesmen, heroes, kings, in *d.* repose *E.M.* iv. 387
Dragg'd in the *d.*! his arms hang idly round *E.S.* i. 153
And sacred, place by DRYDEN's awful *d. Ep.* v. 2
Is mix'd with Heroes, and with Kings thy *d. Ep.* xi. 10
Till you are *d.* like me. Dear Shade! I will (*rep.*) *Ep.* xiii. 4

DUSTY—EAR.

And what a *d.* in ev'ry place *I.H.* i. 11
Rocks fall to *d.*, and mountains melt away *M.* 106
And Temple rise—then fall again to *d. M.E.* ii. 140
When wild Barbarians spurn her *d. O.* ii. 28
Wit that can creep, and pride that licks the *d. P.S.* 333
In glitt'ring *d.*, and painted fragments lie *R.L.* iii. 160
And strike to *d.* th' imperial tow'rs of Troy *R.L.* iii. 174
The pungent grains of titillating *d. R.L.* v. 84
And all those tresses shall be laid in *d. R.L.* v. 148
See ! strew'd with learned *d.*, her night-cap on *S.* vi. 118
For you he walks the streets in rain and *d. S.* vii. 73
A heap of *d.* alone remains of thee *U.L.* 73

Dusty.
And swallows roost in Nilus' *d.* urn *M.E.* iv. 126

Du Sueil.
These Aldus printed, those *D.* has bound *M.E.* iv. 136

Dutch.
On German Crouzaz, or *D.* Burgersdyck *D.* iv. 198

Dutchman.
As what a *D.* plumps into the lakes *D.* ii. 405
How many D—n *she vouchsaf'd to thrid D.* iii. 51

Duty.
No Cause, no Trust, no Duty, and no Friend *D.* iv. 340
Opine that Nature, as in *d.* bound *M.E.* iii. 9
No *d.* broke, no father disobey'd *P.S.* 130
Pay their last *d.* to the Court, and come *S.* viii. 214
Attends the d—ies of the wise and good W.F. 250

Dwell.
Ev'n those who *d.* beneath its very zone *E.M.* ii. 227
Obvious her goods, in no extreme they *d. E.M.* iv. 31
D. in a Monk, or light upon a King *E.S.* i. 139
Content to *d.* in Decencies for ever *M.E.* ii. 164
By those happy souls who *d. O.* i. 74
In what Commandment's large contents they *d. S.* vii. 44
In brazen bonds shall barb'rous Discord *d. W.F.* 414

Dwells.
And is there magic but what *d.* in love. *A.* 84
Where heav'nly-pensive contemplation *d. E.A.* 2
And fled from monarchs, ST. JOHN, *d.* with thee *E.M.* iv. 18
Greatness, with Timon, *d.* in such a draught *M.E.* iv. 103
And in soft bosoms *d.* such mighty Rage *R.L.* i. 12
He *d.* amidst the royal Family *S.* viii. 103

Dwelt.
There *d.* a Citizen of sober fame *M.E.* iii. 341

Dye.
Of various habit, and of various *d. R.L.* iii. 84
Be struck with bright Brocade, or Tyrian *D. S.* iv. 32
Paint, Marble, Gems, and robes of Persian *d. S.* vi. 265
The bright-ey'd perch, with fins of Tyrian *d. W.F.* 142
Turned to the Sun, she casts a thousand d—s *D.* iv. 539
Contracts, inverts, and gives ten thousand *d. M.E.* i. 36
Where light disports in ever-mingling *d. R.L.* ii. 66
Ev'n the wild heath displays her purple *d. W.F.* 25
Ah ! what avail his glossy, varying *d. W.F.* 115
No more my sons shall d. with British blood W.F. 367

Dying.
Of perjur'd Doris *d.* I complain *A.* 58
No silver saints by *d.* misers giv'n *E.A.* 137
The *d.* gales that pant upon the trees *E.A.* 159
Here as I watch'd the *d.* lamps around *E.A.* 307
See *d.* vegetables life sustain *E.M.* ii. 15
Till drooping, sick'ning, *d.,* they began *E.M.* iii. 223
Her works ; and *d.,* fears herself may die *Ep.* viii. 8
But who, living and *d.,* serene still and free *Ep.* xvi. 7
What can they give? to *d.* Hopkins, Heirs *M.E.* iii. 85
Cutler and Brutus, *d.* both exclaim *M.E.* iii. 333
Hear me pay my *d.* Vows *Mi.* vii. 24
Where British sighs from *d.* WYNDHAM stole *Mi.* x. 11
In a *d.,* fall *O.* i. 21
Oh the pain, the bliss of *d. O.* v. 4
Such Tears as Patriots shed for *d.* Laws *P.C.* 14
By foreign hands thy *d.* eyes were clos'd *U.L.* 51
Begin ; this charge the *d.* Daphne gave *W.* 17

Dykes.
The king of *d.,* ! than whom no sluice of mud *D.* ii. 273

E.

Each.—*Passim.*

Eager.
And now the victor stretch'd his *e.* hand *D.* ii. 109
Each *e.* to present their first address *D.* iv. 136
So *e.* to express your love *I.H.* ii. 57 s
With *e.* beats his Mechlin cravat moves *Mi.* ix. 91
He springs to vengeance with an *e.* pace *R.L.* iii. 97
Then hid in shades eludes her *e.* swain *Sp.* 54
When Albion sends her *e.* sons to war *W.F.* 106
The youth rush *e.* to the sylvan war *W.F.* 148
Hang o'er their coursers' heads with *e.* speed *W.F.* 157
It chanc'd, as *e.* of the chase, the maid *W.F.* 181

Eagle.
Or fetch th' aërial *e.* to the ground *E.M.* iii. 222
When the fierce *e.* cleaves the liquid sky (*rep.*) *W.F.* 186
And little E—s *wave their wings in gold M.E.* v. 30
And Arts still follow'd where her *E.* flew *E.C.* 684

Ear.
To Delia's *e.*, the tender notes convey *A.* 18
The Smithfield Muses to the *e.* of Kings *D.* i. 2
O Thou ! whatever title please thine *e. D.* i. 19
On this he sits, to. that he leans his *e. D.* ii. 86
Rolli the feather to his *e.* conveys *D.* ii. 203
And boasts Ulysses' *e.* with Argus' eye *D.* ii. 374
Nay, Mahomet ! the Pigeon at thine *e. D.* iv. 364
The balm of Dulness trickling in their *e. D.* iv. 544
Who haunt Parnassus but to please their *e. E.C.* 341
Tho' oft the *e.* the open vowels tire *E.C.* 345
What if the head, the eye, the *e.* repin'd *E.M.* i. 261
His Prince, that writes in Verse, and has his *e. E.S.* i.46
A word, pray, in your Honour's *e. I.H.* i. 42
And bid new music charm th' unfolding *e. M.* 42
New falls of water murm'ring in his *e. M.* 70
Safe is your secret still in Chloe's *e. M.E.* ii. 173
Sighs for a daughter with unwounded *e. M.E.* ii. 260
Another age shall see the golden *e. M.E.* iv. 173
Gently steal upon the *e. O.* i. 13
Th' immortal pow'rs incline their *e. O.* i. 127
Such Plays alone should win a British *e. P.C.* 45
Or at the *e.* of Eve, familiar Toad *P.S.* 319
Perhaps, yet vibrates in his SOV'REIGN's *e.' P.S.* 357
He gain his Prince's *e.,* or lose his own *P.S.* 367
Seem'd to her *e.* his winning lips to lay *R.L.* i. 25
And in soft sounds, Your Grace salutes their *e. R.L.* i. 86
The pow'rs gave *e.,* and granted half his pray'r *R.L.* ii. 45
Ye Sylphs and Sylphids, to your chief give *e. R.L.* ii. 73
Some hung upon the pendants of her *e. R.L.* ii. 140
And thrice they twitch'd the diamond in her *e. R.L.* iii. 137
Alas ! few verses touch their nicer *e. S.* i. 33
That sweetest music to an honest *e. S.* ii. 100
A voice there is that whispers in my *e. S.* iii. 11
All that we ask is but a patient *e. S.* iii. 64
For him whose quills stand quiver'd at his *e. S.* iii. 83
Pierce the soft labyrinth of a lady's *e. S.* vii. 55
When half his nose is in his Prince's *e. S.* vii. 179
Deaf the prais'd *e.,* and mute the tuneful tongue *U.L.* 76
Of hisses, blows, or want, or loss of e—s *D.* i. 48
O'er head and *e.* plunge for the Commonwealth *D.* i. 210
Prick all their *e.* up, and forget to graze *D.* ii. 262
By his broad shoulders known, and length of *e. D.* iii. 36
So may the fates preserve the *e.* you lend *D.* iii. 214
L—* and all about your *e. Æ.* vi. 20
With his own tongue still edifies his *e. E.C.* 614
If oature thunder'd in his op'ning *e. E.M.* ii. 201
Who cropt our *E.,* and sent them to the King *E.S.* i. 18
Ev'n Peter trembles only for his *E. E.S.* ii. 57
Like bees, are humming in my *e. I.H.* ii. 70 s
To Chartres, Vigour ; Japhet, Nose and *E. M.E.* iii. 86
Who never mentions Hell to *e.* polite *M.E.* iv. 150
Heav'n opens on my eyes ! my *e. O.* v. 14
And drop at last, but in unwilling *e. P.S.* 39
'Tis sung, when Midas' *E.* began to spring *P.S.* 69
Keep close to *E.,* and those let asses prick *P.S.* 77
But Fate and Jove had stopp'd the Baron's *e. R.L.* v. 4
Rend with tremendous sounds your *e.* asunder *S.* i. 27
From heads to *e.,* and now from *e.* to eyes *S.* v. 313
To stop my *e.* to their confounded stuff *S.* vi. 152
Then might my voice thy list'ning *e.* employ *Su.* 47
The Flatterer an E.-wig *grows Mi.* iv. 21

Earl.
From Stage to Stage the licens'd *E.* may run *D.* iv. 587
Of *Lords,* and *E—s, and Dukes, and garter'd Knights E.* v. 36

Earl's-Court.
Would drink and doze at Tooting or *E. S.* vi. 113

Earless.
E. on high, stood unabash'd De Foe *D.* ii. 147

Earliest.
See Nature hastes her *e.* wreaths to bring *M.* 23
There shall the morn her *e.* tears bestow *U.L.* 65

Early.
Such was her wont at *e.* morn to drop *D.* ii. 71
Thus Voiture's *e.* care still shone the same *E.* iv. 69
From the false world in *e.* youth they fled *E.A.* 131
And Faith, our *e.* immortality *E.A.* 300
Like some fair flow'r the *e.* spring supplies *E.C.* 735
The Muse, whose *e.* voice you taught to sing *E.C.* 735
E. at Bus'ness and at Hazard late *M.E.* i. 73
Well-natur'd *Garth* inflam'd with *e.* praise *P.S.* 137
'Tis these that *e.* taint the female soul *R.L.* i. 87
None comes too *e.*, none departs too late *S.* ii. 158
The Harvest *e.*, but mature the praise *S.* v. 24
Bred up at home, full *e.* I begun *S.* vi. 52
Yes ; thank my stars ! as *e.* as I know *S.* vii. 1
Wicked as Pages, who in *e.* years *S.* vii. 39
Why sit we mute when *e.* linnets sing *Sp.* 25
More bright than noon, yet fresh as *e.* day *Sp.* 82
Accept, O GARTH, the Muse's *e.* lays *Su.* 9
Their *e.* fruit, and milk-white turtles bring *Su.* 52
Fate snatch'd her *e.* to the pitying sky *U.L.* 24
Here arm'd with silver bows, in *e.* dawn *W.F.* 169
Oh *e.* lost ! what tears the river shed *W.F.* 273

Earn'd.
Had dearly *e.* a little purse of gold *S.* vi. 34

Earnest.
But far the foremost, two, with *e.* zeal *D.* iv. 401
As weak, as *e.*, and as gravely out *M.E.* i. 230
With *e.* eyes, and round unthinking face *R.L.* iv. 125

Earth.
A place there is, betwixt *e.*, air, and seas *D.* ii. 83
That beams on *e.*, each Virtue he inspires *D.* iii. 220
Hell rises, Heav'n descends, and dance on *E. D.* iii. 237
To thee the most rebellious things on *E. D.* iv. 508
This sure is bliss (if bliss on *e.* there be) *E.A.* 97
Ask of thy mother *e.*, why oaks are made *E.M.* i. 39
E. for whose use ? Pride answers, "'Tis for mine *E.M.* i. 132
My footstool *e.*, my canopy the skies *E.M.* i. 140
See, thro' this air, this ocean, and this *e. E.M.* i. 233
Let *E.* unbalanc'd from her orbit fly *E.M.* i. 251
Great in the *e.*, as in th' ethereal frame *E.M.* i. 270
Go, measure *e.*, weigh air, and state the tides *E.M.* ii. 20
Or pours profuse on *e.*, one nature feeds *E.M.* iii. 117
The young dismissed to wander *e.* or air *E.M.* iii. 127
She, from the rending *e.* and bursting skies *E.M.* iii. 253
Oh sons of *e. !* attempt ye still to rise *E.M.* iv. 73
Why is not Man a God, and *E.* a Heav'n *E.M.* iv. 162
Joins heav'n and *e.*, and mortal and divine *E.M.* iv. 334
E. smiles around, with boundless beauty blest *E.M.* iv. 371
And stoops from Angels to the Dregs of *E. E.S.* i, 142
Such this Man was ; who now from *E.* removed *Ep.* ii. 11
Is there on *e.* one care, one wish beside *Ep.* xiii. 7
These rais'd new Empires o'er the *E. I.H.* iv. 11
Lo, *e.* receives him from the bending skies *M.* 33
Finds all his life one warfare upon *e. M.E.* ii. 218
Awhile he crawls upon the *E. Mi.* iv. 7
In search of mischief still on *E.* to roam *R.L.* i. 64
Others on *e.* o'er human race preside *R.L.* ii. 87
While China's *e.* receives the smoking tide *R.L.* iii. 110
Down to the central *e.*, his proper scene *R.L.* iv. 15
Sooner let *e.*, air, sea, to chaos fall *R.L.* iv. 119
E. shakes her nodding tow'rs, the ground gives way *R.L.* v. 51
Since all things lost on *e.* are treasur'd there *R.L.* v. 114
Ere coxcomb-pies or coxcombs were on *e. S.* ii. 98
No place on *e.* (he cry'd) like Greenwich hill *S.* iii. 139
Weds the rich Dulness of some Son of *e. S.* iv. 43
Or snatch me o'er the *e.*, or thro' the air *S.* v. 346
Thence to their images on *e.* it flows *U.L.* 15

What tho' no sacred *e.* allow thee room *U.L.* 61
Whose Altar, *E.*, Sea, Skies *U.P.* 50
Let nature change, let heav'n and *e.* deplore *W.* 27
See, where on *e.* the flow'ry glories lie *W.* 33
Here *e.* and water seem to strive again *W.F.* 12
And *e.* rolls back beneath the flying steed *W.F.* 158
In weeping vaults her hallow'd *e.* contains *W.F.* 302
Exil'd by thee from *e.* to deepest hell *W.F.* 413
(*E.*'s *wide extremes*) *her sable flag display'd D.* iii. 71
Admire we then what *E.* low entrails hold *S.* iv. 11
Till *e.* extremes your mediation own *S.* v. 402
Yet not to *e.* contracted Span *U.P.* 21
The *E.* fair light, and empress of the main *W.F.* 164
E. distant ends one glory shall behold *W.F.* 401

Earthly.
O ! if my sons may learn one *e.* thing *D.* iv. 183
Admir'd such wisdom in an *e.* shape *E.M.* ii. 33
Add Health, and Pow'r, and every *e.* thing *E.M.* iv. 159
What nothing *e.* gives, or can destroy *E.M.* iv. 167
From *e.* vehicles to those of air *R.L.* i. 50
An *e.* lover lurking at her heart *R.L.* iii. 144
Or who would learn one *e.* thing of use *R.L.* v. 22
Oh ! 'tis the sweetest of all *e.* things *S.* viii. 100
To grace the mansion of our *e.* Gods *W.F.* 230

Earthquakes.
When *e.* swallow, or when tempests sweep *E.M.* L 143
If plagues and *e.* break not Heav'n's design *E.M.* i. 155

Ease.
Where from Ambrosia, Jove retires for *e. D.* ii. 84
Immortal Rich ! how calm he sits at *e. D.* iii. 261
Have Humour, Wit, and native *E.*, and Grace *E.* iv. 27
Aim not at Joy, but rest content with *E. E.* iv. 48
True *e.* in writing comes from art, not chance *E.C.* 362
Whose fame with pains we guard, but lose with *e. E.C.* 504
In the fat age of pleasure, wealth, and *e. E.C.* 534
The scholar's learning, with the courtier's *e. E.C.* 668
Or (oft more strong than all) the love of *e. E.M.* ii. 170
Good, Pleasure, *E.*, Content ! whate'er thy name *E.M.* iv. 2
Some place the bliss in action, some in *e. E.M.* iv. 21
Equal in Common Sense, and Common *E. E.M.* iv. 34
As that the virtuous son is ill at *e. E.M.* iv. 119
How sometimes life is risk'd, and always *e. E.M.* iv. 274
Then see them broke with toils, or sunk in *e. E.M.* iv. 297
Correct with spirit, eloquent with *e. E.M.* iv. 381
Yet sacred keep his Friendships, and his *E. Ep.* i. 10
Foe to loud Praise, and Friend to learned *E. Ep.* x. 5
Leave me but Liberty and *E. I.H.* i. 66
And ev'n the very Dogs at *e. I.H.* ii. 240
With too much Spirit to be e'er at *e. M.E.* ii. 96
Let Joy or *E.*, let Affluence or Content *Mi.* v. 11
With *e.*, the smiles of Fortune I resign *Mi.* ix. 14
Music can soften pain to *e. O.* i. 120
Days of *e.*, and nights of pleasure *O.* iii. 43
Sound sleep by night ; study and *e. O.* iv. 13
And born to write, converse, and live with *e. P.S.* 196
Maintain a Poet's dignity and *e. P.S.* 263
For Spirits, freed from mortal laws, with *e. R.L.* i. 69
Yet graceful *e.*, and sweetness void of pride *R.L.* ii. 15
E., pleasure, virtue, all our sex resign *R.L.* iv. 106
The Mob of Gentlemen who write with *E. S.* v. 108
In Days of *E.*, when now the weary Sword *S.* v. 139
E. of their toil, and partners of their care *S.* v. 246
Mere wax as yet, you fashion him with *e. S.* vi. 9
To *e.* and silence, ev'ry Muse's son *S.* vi. 111
Walk with respect behind, while we at *e. S.* vi. 141
Then polish all, with so much life and *e. S.* vi. 176
But *e.* in writing flows from art, not chance *S.* vi. 178
It gives men happiness, or leaves them *e. S.* vi. 183
The more you want ; why not with equal *e. S.* vi. 214
Leave such to trifle with more grace and *e. S.* vi. 326
What few can of the living, *E.* and Bread *S.* viii. 107
Some thoughtless Town, with *e.* and plenty blest *W.F.* 107
Successive study, exercise, and *e. W.F.* 240
To *e.* the *soul of one oppressive weight M.E.* i. 105
In Fulvia's buckle, *e.* the throbs below *M.E.* iii. 86
And *e.*, or emulate, the care of Heav'n *M.E.* iii. 230
To *e.* th' oppress'd, and raise the sinking heart *M.E.* iii. 244
The Muse but serv'd to *e.* some friend, not Wife *P.S.* 131

EAS'D—EFFECT.   87

Which not the tears of brightest eyes could *e. R.L.* iv. 76
And *e.* thy heart of all that it admires *S.* iii. 76

Eas'd.
Where, *e.* of Fleets, the Adriatic main *D.* iv. 309
Some scruple rose, but thus he *e.* his thought *M.E.* iii. 365

Easier.
The care is *e.* in the Mind's disease *S.* iv. 58

Easiest.
As those move *e.* who have learn'd to dance *E.C.* 363 *and S.* vi. 179
The truest notions in the *e.* way *E.C.* 656

East.
Perhaps the Wind just shifted from the *e. M.E.* i. 112
The dreaded *E.* is all the wind that blows *R.L.* iv. 20

Easter.
No fiercer sons, had *E.* never been *D.* iii. 118
Gave alms at *E.*, in a Christian trim *M.E.* ii. 57

Eastern.
Some by an *e.*, some a western wind *D.* ii. 88
As *E.* priests in giddy circles run *E.M.* ii. 27
Like *E.* kings a lazy state they keep *U.L.* 21

Eastward.
Far *e.* cast thine eye, from whence the Sun *D.* iii. 73

Easy.
Or laugh and shake in Rabelais' *e.* chair *D.* i. 22
And now on Fancy's *e.* wing convey'd *D.* iii. 13
The first came forwards, with as *e.* mien *D.* iv. 279
Stretch'd on the rack of a too *e.* chair *D.* iv. 342
All my commands are *e.*, short, and full *D.* iv. 581
His *e.* Art may happy Nature seem *E.* iv. 3
This binds in ties more *e.*, yet more strong *E.* iv. 67
And praise the *e.* vigour of a line *E.C.* 360
When love was all an *e.* Monarch's care *E.C.* 536
Proud of an *e.* conquest all along *E.M.* ii. 157
O come, that *e.* Ciceronian style *E.S.* i. 73
A safe Companion, and an *e.* Friend *E.P.* xi. 7
From Peer or Bishop 'tis no *e.* thing *M.E.* ii. 195
Of broken troops an *e.* conquest find *R.L.* iii. 78
How *e.* ev'ry labour it pursues *S.* i. 83
He past it o'er; affects an *e.* smile *S.* viii. 122

Eat.
Still bears them faithful; and that thus I *e. D.* iv. 389
E. some and pocket up the rest *I.H.* i. 26
He did his best to seem to *e. I.H.* ii. 173
To *e.* so much—but all's so good *I.H.* ii. 207
Yet on plain Pudding deign'd at home to *e. M.E.* ii. 82
'Tis thus we *e.* the bread another sows *M.E.* iii. 22
Affrights the beggar whom he longs to *e. M.E.* iii. 196
You drink by measure, and to minutes *e. M.E.* iii. 158
Since worms shall *e.* ev'n thee *Mi.* iv. 36
And flatter'd ev'ry day, and some days *e. P.S.* 240
So drink with Walters, or with Chartres *e. S.* i. 89
Except you *e.* the feathers green and gold *S.* ii. 20
Tho' cut in pieces ere my Lord can *e. S.* ii. 22
By what Criterion do ye *e.*, d'ye think *S.* ii. 29
Than *e.* the sweetest by themselves at home *S.* ii. 96
If to live well means nothing but to *e. S.* iv. 115
So Russel did, yet could not *e.* at night *S.* iv. 115
To make poor Pinky *e.* with vast applause *S.* v. 293
Buy ev'ry pullet they afford to *e. S.* vi. 243
You've play'd, and lov'd, and *e.*, and drank your fill *S.* vi. 323

Eats.
And seal for that great House which *e.* him up *M.E.* iii. 208
Who starves by Nobles, or with Nobles *e. M.E.* iii. 237
Not for himself he sees, or hears, or *e. M.E.* iv. 5

Ebb.
One *e.* and flow of follies all my life *S.* iii. 168
But in such lays, as neither *e.* nor flow *E.C.* 239
That Pow'r who bids the Ocean *e.* and flow *M.E.* iii. 164

Ebbing.
Collects her breath, as *e.* life retires *M.E.* i. 244

Ebon.
But Annius, crafty Seer, with *e.* wand *D.* iv. 347

Echo.
And last turn'd *Air*, the *E.* of a Sound *D.* iv. 322
The sound must seem an *E.* to the sense *E.C.* 365
The woods shall answer, and their *e.* ring *Su.* 16
In hollow Caves sweet *E.* silent lies *W.* 41
Back to the Devil the last *e*—*es* roll *D.* i. 325
And more than *E.* talk along the walls *E.A.* 306
The shrill *e.* rebound *O.* i. 9
While Hampton's *e.* "Wretched maid!" reply'd *R.L.* iv. 96
Griefs to thy griefs, and e. sighs to thine E.A. 42
The grots that *e.* to the tinkling rills *E.A.* 158

Echoes.
Pleas'd Saga *e.* thro' her winding bounds *M.E.* iii. 251

Echoing.
Delia, each cave and *e.* rock rebounds *A.* 50

Eclipse.
And op'd those eyes that must *e.* the day *R.L.* i. 14

Eclips'd.
For envy'd Wit, like Sol *e.*, makes known *E.C.* 468

Economy.
Join with *E.*, Magnificence *M.E.* iii. 224

Ecstatic.
Now to pure space lifts his *e.* stare *D.* iv. 33
In trance *e.*, may thy pangs be drown'd *E.A.* 339
One grasps a Cecrops in *e.* dreams *M.E.* v. 40

Eddy.
No Thought advances, but her *E.* Brain *M.E.* ii. 121
Quick whirls, and shifting e—s, of our minds M.E. i. 24

Eden.
For her th' unfading rose of *E.* blooms *E.A.* 217
The Groves of *E.* vanish'd now so long *W.F.* 7

Edge.
Reason itself but gives it *e.* and pow'r *E.M.* ii. 147
When Truth stands trembling on the *e.* of Law *E.S.* ii. 249
New *e.* their dulness, and new bronze their face *D.* ii. 10

Edg'd.
Whose sars'net skirts are *e.* with flamy gold *D.* iii. 254

Edifies.
With his own tongue still *e.* his ears *E.C.* 614

Edify.
What shocks one part, will *e.* the rest *E.M.* iv. 141

Edition.
A new *E.* of old Æson gave *D.* iv. 122

Education.
Tho' *E.* forms the common mind *M.E.* i. 149

Educing.
Th' Eternal Act *e.* good from ill *E.M.* ii. 175

Edward.
E. and Henry, now the Boast of Fame *S.* v. 7
And, fast beside him, once-fear'd *E.* sleeps *W.F.* 314
That *E.*'s Miss thus perks it in your face *E.J.S.* 46
And France reveng'd of Anne's and *E.* arms *M.E.* iii. 144
Old *E.* Armour beams on Cibber's breast *S.* v. 319
With *E.* acts adorn the shining page *W.F.* 303
Of all our Harries, all our *E—s* talk *S.* viii. 105

Edwardi.
E. sext. or *prim. et quint. Elis. S.* i. 148

Eel.
Yet holds the *e.* of science by the tail *D.* i. 280
The silver *e.* in shining volumes roll'd *W.F.* 143
The Kennet swift, for silver e—s renown'd W.F. 341

Efface.
Judge we by Nature? Habit can *e. M.E.* i. 166

Effac'd.
And fluent Shakespear scarce *e.* a line *S.* v. 279

Effect.
That disappoint th' *e.* of ev'ry vice *E.M.* ii. 240
Both fairly owning, Riches, in *e. M.E.* iii. 17

EFFLUVIA—EMBALM

Itself unseen, but in th' e—s remains E.C. 79
Oh curs'd *e.* of civil hate O. ii. 29
E. unhappy from a Noble Cause S. v. 160

Effluvia.
Vig'rous he rises, from th' *e.* strong D. ii. 105
Or quick *e.* darting thro' the brain E.M. i. 199

Effort.
A second *e.* brought but new disgrace D. ii. 175
We prize the stronger *e.* of his pow'r M.E. i. 147
Blackmore himself, for any grand *e.* S. vi. 112

Effulgence.
In broad E. all below reveal'd D. iv. 18

Egerian.
Approach; but awful! Lo! th' E. Grot Mi. x. 9

Egg.
Lo! one vast E. produces human race D. iii. 248
And shall no E. in Japhet's face be thrown E.S. ii. 189
Like in all else, as one E. to another S. i. 50
The vulgar boil, the learned roast an *e.* S. vi. 85
As thick as e—s at Ward in pillory D. iii. 34
Cheap *e.,* and herbs, and olives still we see S. ii. 35

Egregious.
How much, *e. Moore*, are we Mi. iv. 1
And hence th' *e.* wizard shall foredoom. R.L. v. 139

Egypt, Egypt.
Here gay description E. glads with show'rs D. i. 73
Oh worthy thou of Æ.'s wise abodes D. iii. 207
Is now a victim, and now E. God E.M. i. 64

Eight.
And strains, from hard-bound brains *e.* lines a year P.S. 182

Eighteen.
Shows in her cheek the roses of *e.* R.L. iv. 32

Eighty-one.
(Without a blot) to *e.* Mi. xii. 4

Either.—*Passim.*

Eke.
And Eusden *e.* out Blackmore's endless line D. i. 104

Ek'd.
On some patch'd dog-hole *e.* with ends of wall M.E. iv. 32

Elasticity.
And were my E. and Fire D. i. 186

Elate.
Too soon dejected, and too soon *e.* R.L. iii. 102

Elated.
Never *e.,* while one man's oppress'd E.M. iv. 323

Elbow.
In some fair ev'ning on your *e.* laid E. v. 31

Elder.
Point she to Priest or E., Whig or Tory E.S. ii. 96
Till Isis' E—s *reel, their pupils' sport* D. iii. 337
While if our E. break all reason's laws S. v. 117

Eldest.
In *e.* time, ere mortals writ or read D. i. 9
The *e.* is a fool, the youngest wise S. iii. 44
Tho' justly Greece her *e.* sons admires S. v. 43
From *e.* Heywood, down to Cibber's age S. v. 88

Elect.
No Grace of Heav'n or token of th' E. M.E. iii. 18

Elector.
The brib'd E.—There you stoop too low E.S. ii. 25

Elegant.
Trifles themselves are *e.* in him E. iv. 4
"How *e.* your Frenchmen?" "Mine, d'ye mean S. viii. 110

Elegiac.
Hence hymning Tyburn's *e.* lines D. i. 41

Elements.
And Passions are the *e.* of life E.M. i. 170
Passions, like E., tho' born to fight E.M. ii. 111
To their first E. their Souls retire R.L. i. 58
And ev'n the *e.* a tyrant sway'd W.F. 52

Elemental.
But ALL subsists by *e.* strife E.M. i. 169
And sip, with Nymphs, their *e.* Tea R.L. i. 62

Elephant.
Compar'd, half-reas'ning E., with thine E.M. i. 222
The Tortoise here and E. unite R.L. i. 135
Let Bear or E. he e'er so white S. v. 322
That Bear or E. shall heed thee more S. v. 325

Elevates.
Joy tunes his voice, joy *e.* his wings E.M. iii. 32

Elves.
Of airy E. by moonlight shadows seen R.L. i. 31
Fays, Fairies, Genii, E., and Dæmons, hear! R.L. ii. 74

Eliz.
Edwardi sext. or *prim. et quint.* E. S. i. 148

Eliza.
See in the circle next, E. plac'd D. ii. 157

Eloïsa, Eloise.
And E. yet must kiss the name E.A. 8
In vain lost E. weeps and prays E.A. 15
Ev'n thou art cold—yet E. loves E.A. 260
See in her cell sad E. spread E.A. 303
Ah then, thy once-lov'd E. see E.A. 329
Where, where was E—e? her voice, her hand E.A. 101

Elope.
Poor Cornus sees his frantic wife *e.* P.S. 25

Elopes.
The Fool, whose Wife *e.* some thrice a quarter S. iii. 150

Eloquence.
False E., like the prismatic glass E.C. 311
The gracious Dew of Pulpit E. E.S. i. 69
How vain is Reason, E. how weak Ep. iii. 5
'Twas "Sir, your law"—and "Sir, your *e.*" S. vi. 133
Pour the full tide of *e.* along S. vi. 171

Eloquent.
Correct with spirit, *e.* with ease E.M. iv. 381

Else.—*Passim.*

Eludes.
Then hid in shades, *e.* her eager swain Sp. 54

Elysian.
The king descending views th' E. shade D. iii. 14
Oh punish him, or to th' E. shades D. iv. 417
Now crown'd with Myrtle, on th' E. coast E. iv. 73
Wat'ring soft E. plains Mi. vii. 20
O'er the E. flow'rs O. i. 73
Now lakes of liquid gold, E. scenes R.L. iv. 45

Elysium.
Descending Gods have found E. here Su. 60

'Em.
And whisk '*e.* back to Evans, Young, and Swift D. ii. 116
Then down are roll'd the books; stretch'd o'er '*e.* lies D. ii. 403
Himself, his throne, his world, I'd scorn '*e* all E.A. 86
He best can paint '*e.* who shall feel '*e.* most E.A. 366
To tell '*e.*, would a hundred tongues require E.C. 44
But beans and bacon set before '*e.* I.H. ii. 137
Some flying stroke alone can hit '*e.* right M.E. ii. 154
Look on her face, and you'll forget '*e.* all R.L. ii. 18
'Twas only Suretyship that brought '*e.* there S. vii. 70
And lin'd with Giants deadlier than '*e.* all S. viii. 275
Till hov'ring o'er '*e.* sweeps the swelling net W.F. 104

Emanation.
Content, each E. of his fires D. iii. 219
Some *e.* of th' all-beauteous Mind E.A. 62

Embalm.
Those tears eternal, that *e.* the dead E. iii. 48

Embark.
Where all the Race of Reptiles might *e*. *S.* viii. 27

Emblaze.
Not sulphur-tipt *e*. an Ale-house fire *D.* i. 235
Our shrines irradiate, or *e*. the floors *E.A.* 136

Emblem.
E. of Music caus'd by Emptiness *D.* i. 36
Th' expressive *e*. of their softer pow'r *R.L.* iii. 40

Embody'd.
E. dark, what clouds of Vandals rise *D.* iii. 86

Embosom'd.
His House, *e*. in the Grove *I.H.* iii. 21

Embrace.
Nor ends the pleasure with the fierce *e*. *E.M.* iii. 123
The link dissolves, each seeks a fresh *e*. *E.M.* iii. 129
The strength he gains is from th' *e*. he gives *E.M.* iii. 212
For life predestin'd to the Goomes' *e*. *R.L.* i. 80
Behold yon Pair, in strict e—s join'd D. iii. 179
How tragedy and comedy e. *D.* i. 69
Or bidst thou rather Party to *e*. *D.* i. 205
E., e., my sons! be foes no more *D.* ii. 177
And saints *e*. thee with a love like mine *E.A.* 342
We first endure, then pity, then *e*. *E.M.* ii. 220
Form'd and impell'd its neighbour to *e*. *E.M.* iii. 12
Friend, parent, neighbour, first it will *e*. *E.M.* iv. 367
Slopes at its foot, the woods its sides *e*. *S.* iii. 141
Instructed thus, you bow, *e*., protest *S.* iv. 107
E. my Love, and bind my brows with bays *Su.* 38

Embrac'd.
Some safer world in depth of woods *e*. *E.M.* i. 105
Rejects mankind,—is by some Sylph *e*. *R.L.* i. 68

Embroider'd.
Th' *e*. suit at least he deem'd his prey *D.* ii. 117
In flow'd at once a gay *e*. race *D.* iv. 275
Th' *e*. King who shows but half his face *R.L.* iii. 76

Embroid'ry.
With all th' *e*. plaister'd at thy tail *M.E.* iii. 90

Embroils.
This quits an Empire, that *e*. a State *M.E.* i. 106

Embrown.
E. the Slope, and nod on the Parterre *M.E.* iv. 174

Embrown'd.
E. with native bronze, lo! Healey stands *D.* iii. 199

Embryo.
How hints, like spawn, scarce quick in *e*. lie *D.* i. 59
Round him much *E.*, much Abortion lay *D.* i. 121

Em'rald.
And well dissembled *e*. on his hand *D.* iv. 348

Emotions.
Such, such *e*. should in *Britons* rise *Mi.* ii. 9

Emp'ror.
Inform us, will the *E*. treat *I.H.* ii. 113 *s*
Gods, E—s, *Heroes*, *Sages*, *Beauties lie* M.E. v. 34

Emphasis.
Or well mouth'd Booth with *e*. proclaims *S.* v. 123

Empire.
Still her old *E*. to restore she tries *D.* i. 17
Her boundless *e*. over seas and lands *D.* iii. 68
Contending Theatres our *e*. raise *D.* iii. 271
Lo! thy dread *E*., Chaos! is restor'd *D.* iv. 653
Learning and Rome alike in *e*. grew *E.C.* 683
This quits an *E*., that embroils a State *M.E.* i. 106
Why risk the world's great *e*. for a Punk *M.E.* i. 131
The shady *e*. shall retain no trace *W.F.* 371
As toys and e—s, for a godlike mind E.M. iv. 180
These rais'd new *E*. o'er the Earth *I.H.* iv. 11

Employ.
The whole *e*. of body and of mind *E.M.* ii. 126
Far other dreams my erring soul e. *E.A.* 223
What is this Wit, which must our cares *e*. *E.C.* 500

E. their pains to spurn some others down *E.C.* 515
These 'tis enough to temper and *e*. *E.M.* ii. 113
'Tis strange the Miser should his Cares *e*. *M.E.* iv. 1
Then might my voice thy list'ning ears *e*. *Su.* 47

Employ'd.
His Counting-house *e*. the Sunday-morn *M.E.* iii. 380
Ah *Moore!* thy skill were well *e*. *Mi.* iv. 9
And arms *e*. on birds and beasts alone *W.F.* 374

Employs.
To gain Pescennius one *e*. his schemes *M.E.* v. 39

Empress.
Arrest him, *E*.; or you sleep no more *D.* iii. 69
Receive, great *E*.! thy accomplish'd Son *D.* iv. 282
Prop thine, O *E*.! like each neighbour Throne *D.* iv. 333
Not Cæsar's *e*. would I deign to prove *E.A.* 87
The Earth's fair light, and *E*. of the main *W.F.* 164

Emptier.
Hast thou, oh Sun! beheld an *e*. sort *S.* viii. 204

Emptiness.
Emblem of Music caus'd by *E. D.* i. 36
Me *E*. and Dulness could inspire *D.* i. 185
That Casting-weight Pride adds to *e*. *P.S.* 177
Eternal smiles his *e*. betray *P.S.* 315

Empty.
Or solid pudding against *e*. praise *D.* i. 54
And *e*. words she gave, and sounding strain *D.* ii. 45
He grants an *e*. Joseph for a John *D.* ii. 128
And *e*. heads console with *e*. sound *D.* iv. 542
Nor let false Shows, or *e*. Titles please *E.* iv. 47
And leave you in lone woods, or *e*. walls *E.* v. 49
I stretch my *e*. arms, it glides away *E.A.* 238
In youth alone its *e*. praise we boast *E.C.* 496
A little louder, but as *e*. quite *E.M.* ii. 278
To all beside as much ao *e*. shade *E.M.* iv. 243
Virtue, I grant you, is an *e*. boast *E.S.* i. 113
Want with a full, or with ac *e*. purse *M.E.* iii. 320
The rest, the winds dispers'd in *e*. air *R.L.* ii. 46
But show no mercy to ao *e*. line *S.* vi. 175
To this were trifles, toys, and *e*. names *S.* viii. 8
The lonely lords of *e*. wilds and woods *W.F.* 48
Pleas'd in the silent shade with *e*. praise *W.F.* 432

Empyreal.
Go, soar with Plato to th' *e*. sphere *E.M.* ii. 23

Emulate.
And left-legg'd Jacob seems to *e*. *D.* ii. 68
And ease, or *e*., the care of Heav'n *M.E.* iii. 230
No kitchens *e*. the vestal fire *S.* vii. 112
Nor polish'd marble *e*. thy face *U.L.* 60

Emulation.
Is *e*. in the learn'd or brave *E.M.* ii. 192

Emulous.
Stand *e*. of Greek and Roman fame *M.E.* v. 54

Enabled.
Thrice happy man! *e*. to pursue *M.E.* iii. 275

Enamell'd.
Of all th' *e*. race, whose silv'ry wing *D.* iv. 421
Here blushing Flora paints th' *e*. ground *W.F.* 38

Enamour'd.
Wafts the smooth Eunuch, and *e*. swain *D.* iv. 310
Still on that breast *e*. let me lie *E.A.* 121

Enclose.
E. whole downs in walls, 'tis all a joke *S.* vi. 261

Enclos'd.
But in her Temple's last recess *e*. *D.* iii. 1

Encomium.
A vile *E*. doubly ridicules *S.* v. 410

Encore.
And all thy yawning daughters cry, *e*. *D.* iv. 60

Encounter.
But lo! to dark *e*. in mid air *D.* iii. 265
Burns to e. *two advent'rous knights R.L.* iii. 26

ENCOUNT'RING—ENFLAM'D.

Encount'ring.
A certain bard *e.* on the way *E.C.* 268

Encourag'd.
E. thus, Wit's Titans brav'd the skies *E.C.* 552

Encroach.
Make Nature still *e.* upon his plan *D.* iv. 473

Encrust.
Save but our *Army!* and let Jove *e. S.* i. 73

Encumber'd.
Still, as of old, *e.* Villainy *M.E.* iii. 50

End.
Gasps as they straiten at each *e.* the cord *D.* iv. 29
At once the source, and *e.*, and test of Art *E.C.* 73
Since rules were made but to promote their *e. E.C.* 147
The heart, and all its *e.* at once attains *E.C.* 155
Against the precept, ne'er transgress its *E. E.C.* 164
In ev'ry work regard the writer's *E. E.C.* 255
In God's, one single can its *e.* produce *E.M.* i. 55
His actions, passions, being's, use and *e. E.M.* i. 66
Ask for what *e.* the heav'nly bodies shine *E.M.* i. 131
But errs not Nature from this gracious *e. E.M.* i. 141
If the great *e.* be human Happiness *E.M.* i. 149
As much that *e.*, a constant course requires *E.M.* i. 151
Explain his own beginning or his *e. E.M.* ii. 38
Each works its *e.*, to move or govern all *E.M.* ii. 56
And, but for this, were active to no *e. E.M.* ii. 62
Self-love and Reason to one *e.* aspire *E.M.* ii. 87
Acts to one *e.*, but acts by various laws *E.M.* iii. *
See plastic Nature working to this *e. E.M.* iii. 9
Gives not the useless knowledge of its *e. E.M.* iii. 72
To find the means proportion'd to their *e. E.M.* iii. 82
All must be false that thwart this One great *e. E.M.* iii. 309
Oh Happiness! our being's *e.* and aim *E.M.* iv. 1
The joy unequall'd, if its *e.* it gain *E.M.* iv. 315
Compar'd, and knew their gracious *E.* the same *E.S.* ii. 81
Unblam'd thro' Life, lamented in thy *E. Ep.* xi. 8
A River at my Garden's *e. I.H.* ii. 4
Still tries to save the hallow'd taper's *e. M.E.* i. 243
Pow'r all their *e.*, but Beauty all the means *M.E.* ii. 220
Fair to no purpose, artful to no *e. M.E.* ii. 245
No, 'twas thy righteous *e.*, asham'd to see *M.E.* iii. 147
The wretch, who living, sav'd a candle's *e. M.E.* iii. 292
And see, what comfort it affords our *e. M.E.* iii. 298
What ev'n deny'd a cordial at his *e. M.E.* iii. 329
Who broke no promise, serv'd no private *e. M.E.* v. 69
That not for Fame, but Virtue's better *e. P.S.* 342
Wilt thou do nothing for a nobler *e. S.* iii. 73
Patient of labour, when the *e.* was rest *S.* v. 242
Each individual: His great *E.* the same *S.* vi. 283
Has life no sourness, drawn so near its *e. S.* vi. 316
To follow nature, and regard his *e. W.F.* 252
'Tis the same rope at different *e*—s they twist *D.* i. 207
To what base *e.*, and by what abject ways *E.C.* 520
And sev'ral men impels to sev'ral *e. E.M.* ii. 166
Extremes in Nature equal *e.* produce *E.M.* ii. 205
That, Virtue's *e.* from Vanity can raise *E.M.* ii. 245
Who noble *e.* by noble means obtains *E.M.* iv. 233
To Man's low passions, or their glorious *e. E.M.* iv. 376
For their own Worth, or our own *E. I.H.* ii. 150
Were means not *e.*; Ambition was the vice *M.E.* i. 215
Strange! by the Means defeated of the *E. M.E.* ii. 143
And diff'rent men direct to diff'rent *e. M.E.* iii. 160
Prov'd by the *e.* of being, to have been *M.E.* iii. 290
On some patch'd dog-hole ek'd with *e.* of wall *M.E.* iv. 32
Some *e.* of Verse his Betters might afford *Mi.* iii. 5
Few ask if fraud or force attain'd his *e. R.L.* ii. 34
The little engine on his fingers' *e. R.L.* iii. 132
And lovers' hearts with *e.* of riband bound *R.L.* v. 118
Earth's distant *e.* our glory shall behold *W.F.* 401
One leap from yonder cliff shall *e.* my pains *A.* 95
With whom my Muse began, with whom shall *e. D.* i. 166
With me began this genius, and shall *e. D.* ii. 55
But that this well-disputed game may *e. D.* ii. 245
As morning pray'r and flagellation *e. D.* ii. 270
And, till he *e.* the being, makes it blest *E.M.* iii. 66
Some sunk to Beasts, find pleasure *e.* in pain *E.M.* iv. 23
All *e.*, in LOVE OF GOD, and LOVE OF MAN *E.M.* iv. 340
And if yet higher the proud list should *e. E.S.* ii. 92
Alas! alas! pray *e.* what you began *E.S.* ii. 254
And the broad falchion in a plough-share *e. M.* 62

Or which must *e.* one, a Fool's wrath or love *P.S.* 30
E. all dispute; and fix the year precise *S.* ii. 53
In one our Frolics, our Amusements *e. S.* vi. 74

Endear.
The common int'rest, or *e.* the tie *E.M.* ii. 254

Endears.
This the blue varnish, that the green *e. M.E.* v. 57

Endeavour.
Virtue she finds too painful so *e. M.E.* ii. 163

Endeavour'd.
And such were prais'd who but *e.* well *E.C.* 511

Ending.
So Spirits *e.* their terrestrial race *D.* i. 267

Endless.
And Eusden eke out Blackmore's *e.* line *D.* i. 104
They summon all her Race: an *e.* band *D.* ii. 19
Thence *e.* streams of fair Ideas flow *E.* iii. 43
Each pleasing Blount shall *e.* smiles bestow *E.* iii. 61
New distant scenes of *e.* science rise *E.C.* 224
Sole judge of Truth, in *e.* Error hurl'd *E.M.* ii. 17

Endlong.
To see themselves fall *e.* into beasts *S.* viii. 167

Endow.
Die, and *e.* a College, or a Cat *M.E.* iii. 196

Ends.
A needless Alexandrine *e.* the song *E.C.* 356
Where *e.* the Virtue, or begins the Vice *E.M.* ii. 210
The chain holds on, and where it *e.*, unknown *E.M.* iii. 26
Nor *e.* tho pleasure with the fierce embrace *E.M.* iii. 123
There stops the Instinct, and there *e.* the care *E.M.* iii. 128
All that we feel of it begins and *e. E.M.* iv. 241
E. in the milder merit of the Heart *Ep.* xiv. 12
Here honest Nature *e.* as she begins *M.E.* i. 227
And fame, this lord of useless thousands *e. M.E.* iii. 314
Muse, 'tis enough: at length thy labour *e. Mi.* i. 1
Rhymes ere he wakes, and priots before *Term e. P.S.* 43
There (thank my stars) my whole Commission *e. P.S.* 59
To the cool ocean, where his journey *e. Su.* 90

Endue.
E. a Peer, with honour, truth, and grace *S.* vi. 221

Endu'd.
See Matter next, with various life *e. E.M.* iii. 13
But this bold Lord with manly strength *e. R.L.* v. 79
Oldfield with more than Harpy throat *e. S.* ii. 25

Endure.
Display'd the fates her confessors *e. D.* ii. 146
We first *e.*, then pity, then embrace *E.M.* ii. 220
Which done, the poorest can no wants *e. S.* iii. 45
Canst thou *e.* a foe, forgive a friend *S.* vi. 317
From such alone the Great rebukes *e. S.* viii. 282
Hear what from Love unpractis'd hearts *e. Su.* 11

Endur'd.
But just *e.* the winter she began *Mi.* iii. 23
And *Congreve* lov'd, and *Swift e.* my lays *P.S.* 138
After a Life of gen'rous Toils *e. S.* v. 9

Endures.
When Truth or Virtue an Affront *e. E.S.* ii. 199
Thinks who *e.* a knave, is next a knave *M.E.* i. 78

Endymion.
Up to a *Star*, and like *E.* dies *D.* iv. 520

Enemy.
Or make an *e.* of all mankind *E.M.* iv. 222
Extend it, let thy *e*—ies have part *E.M.* iv. 356

Energy.
The long majestic March, and *E.* divine *S.* v. 269

Enervate.
On each *e.* string they taught the note *S.* v. 153

Enflam'd.
E. with glory's charms *O.* i. 44

Engage.
Let her thy heart, next Drabs and Dirt, *e. D.* iii. 303
Yet still her charms in breathing paint *e. E.* iii. 55
These monsters, Critics! with your darts *e. E.C.* 554
Mem'ry and fore-cast just returns *e. E.M.* iii. 143
Why, answer LYTTLETON, and I'll *e. E.S.* i. 47
Thus shall mankind his guardian care *e. M.* 55
Nor blush these studies thy regard *e. M.E.* v. 49
Me, let the tender office long *e. P.S.* 408
In tasks so bold, can little men *e. R.L.* i. 11
The rebel Knave, who dares his prince *e. R.L.* iii. 59
So when bold Homer makes the Gods *e. R.L.* v. 45
Could Laureate Dryden Pimp and Friar *e. S.* i. 113
Ill health some just indulgence may *e. S.* ii. 87

Engag'd.
See! where the British youth, *e.* no more *S.* viii. 212

Engaging.
Th' *e.* Smile, the Gaiety *I.H.* i. 46

Engine.
And play'd the God an *e.* on his foe *E.M.* iii. 268
The little *e.* on his fingers' ends *R.L.* iii. 132
Ev'n then, before the fatal *e.* clos'd *R.L.* iii. 149
To serve mere e—s to the ruling Mind E.M. i. 262

England.
By courtesy of *E.*, he may do *S.* v. 62
Old *E.*'s *Genius, rough with many a Scar E.S.* i. 152

English.
So Latin, yet so *E.* all the while *E.S.* i. 74
Nor let us say (those *E.* glories gone) *Ep.* ix. 11
There *E.* Bounty yet awhile may stand *M.E.* iii. 247
Or bid the new be *E.*, ages hence *S.* vi. 169
And coarse of phrase—your *E.* all are so *S.* viii. 109

Englishman.
Time was, a sober *E.* would knock *S.* v. 161

Engrav'd.
And leave on SWIFT this graceful verse *e. S.* v. 223

Engross.
If Man alone *e.* not Heav'n's high care *E.M.* i. 118
But all our praises why should Lords *e. M.E.* iii. 249
Who pens a Stanza, when he should *e. P.S.* 18

Enjoy.
The owner's wife, that other men *e. E.C.* 501
Would you *e.* soft nights and solid dinners *E.J.S.* 23
All feed on one vain Patron, and *e. E.M.* iii. 61
Know, all *e.* that pow'r which suits them best *E.M.* iii. 80
Go, where to love and to *e.* are one *Ep.* vii. 16
In this one Passion man can strength *e. M.E.* i. 222
T' *e.* them, and the Virtue to impart *M.E.* iii. 220
To gain those riches he can ne'er *e. M.E.* iv. 2
E. them, you! Villario can no more *M.E.* v. 86
Why, you'll *e.* it only all your life *S.* ii. 164
A part I will *e.*, as well as keep *S.* vi. 285
E. the glory to be great no more *Sp.* 8
And I those kisses he receives, *e. Su.* 48
T' *e.* is to obey *U.P.* 20

Enjoys.
At length *e.* that Liberty he lov'd *Ep.* ii. 12
His Father's Acres who *e.* in peace *M.E.* iv. 181
Yet wit ne'er tastes, and beauty ne'er *e. P.S.* 312
E. his garden, and his book in quiet *S.* v. 199

Enlarges.
Or Fancy's beam *e.*, multiplies *M.E.* i. 35

Enlarging.
As streams roll down, *e.* as they flow *E.C.* 192

Enlights.
E. the present, and shall warm the last *E.C.* 403

Enliv'ning.
Upon her sallow cheeks *e.* red *Mi.* ix. 62
Exalts her in *e.* airs *O.* i. 27

Ennoble.
What can *e.* sots, or slaves, or cowards *E.M.* iv. 215

Ennobled.
E. by himself, by all approv'd *M.E.* v. 71

Ennobles.
Yet Time *e.*, or degrades each line *S.* iv. 44

Enormous.
Th' *e.* faith of many made for one *E.M.* iii. 242
The whole amount of that *e.* fame *E.M.* iv. 307

Enough.—*Passim.*

Enquire—*see also* Inquire.
What Riches give us let us then *e. M.E.* iii. 79

Enquiring.
I never nam'd : the Town's *e.* yet *E.S.* ii. 21
To which thy Tomb shall guide *e.* eyes *Ep.* v. 4

Enrage.
E., compose, with more than magic Art *S.* v. 344

Enrag'd.
While thro' the press *e.* Thalestris flies *R.L.* v. 57

Enrich.
T' *e.* a Bastard, or a Son they hate *M.E.* iii. 98
Loth to *e.* me with too quick replies *S.* viii. 128

Enroll.
T' *e.* your Triumphs o'er the seas and land *S.* v. 373

Enroll'd.
In living medals see her wars *e. M.E.* v. 55

Enslav'd.
As that the body, this *e.* the mind *E.C.* 688
Who first taught souls *e.*, and realms undone *E.M.* iii. 241

Ensnare.
Fair tresses man's imperial race *e. R.L.* ii. 27

Ensu'd.
Silence *e.*, and thus the nymph began *R.L.* v. 8
So spoke the Dame, but no applause *e. R.L.* v. 35

Entail'd.
Swears ev'ry place *e.* for years to come *S.* viii. 160

Entangle.
E. Justice in her net of Law *E.M.* iii. 192

Enter.
E., each mild, each amicable guest *E.A.* 301
Knights, squires, and steeds must *e.* on the stage *E.C.* 282
Is there a variance? *e.* but his door *M.E.* iii. 271
Back fly the scenes, and *e.* foot and horse *S.* v. 315
Soon as I *e.* at my country door *S.* vi. 206
Whole nations *e.* with each swelling tide *W.F.* 399

Enter'd.
Well pleas'd, he *e.*, and confess'd his home *D.* i. 266
Scarce was I *e.*, when, behold! there came *S.* viii. 24

Ent'ring.
But *e.* learns to be sincere *O.* iii. 6

Enters.
Love, soft intruder, *e.* here *O.* iii. 5
Booth *e.*—hark! the Universal peal *S.* v. 334

Entertains.
Such tattle often *e. I.H.* ii. 95 *l*

Enthrones.
And saving Ignorance *e.* by Laws *D.* iii. 98

Enthusiast.
Such as from lab'ring lungs th' *E.* blows *D.* ii. 255

Entire.
Survey both worlds, intrepid and *e. S.* vi. 312
His *Office* keeps your Parchment fates *e. S.* vii. 71

Entrails.
Thou wert from Ætna's burning *e.* torn *A.* 91
Deep in his *E.*—I reuer'd them there *D.* ii. 384
Who sett'st our *E.* free *Mi.* iv. 34
Admire we then what Earth's low *e.* hold *S.* iv. 11

Entrance.
The Venal quiet, and *e.* the Dull *D.* iv. 624

Entranc'd.
At this *e.*, he lifts his hands and eyes *S.* viii. 98

Envies.
And *e.* ev'ry sparrow that he sees *M.E.* i. 237
Who sees him act, but *e.* ev'ry deed *P.C.* 25
Mistake him not, he *e.*, not admires *S.* v. 133

Envious.
'Tis an ugly *e.* Shrew *Mi.* vi. 9
Be furious, *e.*, slothful, mad, or drunk *S.* iii. 61

Envy.
With holy *e.* gave one Layman place *D.* ii. 324
E. will merit, as its shade, pursue *E.C.* 456
Atones not for that *e.* which it brings *E.C.* 495
E., to which th' ignoble mind's a slave *E.M.* ii. 191
Think, and if still the things thy *e.* call *E.M.* iv. 275
Let *E.* howl, while Heav'n's whole Chorus sings *E.S.* ii. 242
Yet some I know with *e.* swell *I.H.* ii. 101 s
E., he silent, and attend *Mi.* viii. 2
Has she no faults then (*E.* says) Sir *Mi.* viii. 9
A Rival's *e.* (all in vain) to hide *Mi.* ix. 42
List'ning *E.* drops her snakes *O.* i. 33
Or *E.* holds a whole week's war with Sense *P.S.* 252
Shall draw such *e.* as the Lock you lost *R.L.* v. 144
E. must own, I live among the Great *S.* i. 133
Now sick alike of *E.* and of Praise *S.* iii. 4
Finds *E.* never conquer'd but by Death *S.* v. 16
Beheld such scenes of *e.*, sin, and hate *S.* viii. 193
There hateful *E.* her own snakes shall feel *W.F.* 419
Watch'd both by *E.*'s and by Flattery's eye *D.* iv. 36
Secure from Flames, from *E.* fiercer rage *E.C.* 183
And other Beauties *e.* Worsley's eyes *E.* iii. 60
Nor *e.* them that heav'n I lose for thee *E.A.* 72
That virtuous ladies *e.* while they rail *E.J.S.* 16
Are what ten thousand *e.* and adore *E.S.* l. 166
While the Fops *e.*, and the ladies stare *R.L.* iv. 104
Let India boast her plains, nor *e.* we *W.F.* 29
Nor *e.*, Windsor ! since thy shades have seen *W.F.* 161

Envy'd.
For *e.* Wit, like Sol eclips'd, makes known *E.C.* 468
And *e.* Thirst and Hunger to the Poor *S.* iv. 117

Epic.
How Farce and *E.* get a jumbled race *D.* i. 70
Forget his *E.*, nay Pindaric Art *S.* v. 77

Epicurus.
And *E.* lay inspir'd *O.* ii. 4

Epigrams.
Songs, sonnets, *e.* the winds uplift *D.* ii. 115

Epistles.
But grave *E.*, bringing Vice to light *S.* l. 151
We needs will write *E.* to the King *S.* v. 369

Equal.
E. your merits ! *e.* is your din *D.* ii. 244
Ye Critics ! in whose heads, as *e.* scales *D.* ii. 367
Till all, tun'd *e.*, send a gen'ral hum *D.* ii. 386
There rival flames with *e.* glory rise *D.* iii. 80
E. in wit, and equally polite *D.* iii. 181
Labour and rest, that *e.* periods keep *E.A.* 211
And urg'd the best by *e.* steps to rise *E.C.* 97
His pow'rs in *e.* ranks and fair array *E.C.* 176
These *e.* syllables alone require *E.C.* 344
Who sees with *e.* eyes, as God of all *E.M.* i. 87
But thinks, admitted to that *e.* sky *E.M.* i. 111
Extremes in Nature *e.* ends produce *E.M.* ii. 205
All vocal beings hymn'd their *e.* God *E.M.* iii. 156
E. is Common Sense, and Common Ease *E.M.* iv. 34
If all are *e.* in their Happiness *E.M.* iv. 54
And each were *e.*, must not all contest *E.M.* iv. 64
But Heav'n's just balance *e.* will appear *E.M.* iv. 69
In each how guilt and greatness *e.* ran *E.M.* iv. 293
E., the injur'd to defend *I.H.* iii. 13
Make but his Riches *e.* to his Wit *I.H.* iii. 18
For how should *e.* Colours do the knack *M.E.* ii. 155
Damn'd to the Mines, an *e.* fate betides *M.E.* iii. 193
Extremes in Nature *e.* good produce *M.E.* iii. 161
Bids seed-time, harvest, *e.* course maintain *M.E.* iii. 165
The verse and sculpture bore an *e.* part *M.E.* v. 51
An *e.* mixture of good Humour *Mi.* viii. 7

By Music, minds an *e.* temper know *O.* i. 22
In *e.* curls, and well conspir'd to deck *R.L.* ii. 21
And thousands more in *e.* mirth maintains *R.L.* iv. 66
His *e.* mind I copy what I can *S.* il. 131
Some doubt if *e.* pains, or *e.* fire *S.* v. 282
With *e.* talents, these congenial souls *S.* vi. 129
And keep the *e.* measure of the Soul *S.* vi. 205
The more you want ; why not with *e.* care *S.* vi. 214
These, were my breast inspir'd with *e.* flame *W.F.* 9
Were *e.* crimes in a despotic reign *W.F.* 58
Superiors! death! and E—s! what a curse *M.E.* ii. 135

Equally.
Equal in wit, and *e.* polite *D.* iii. 181
The Stews and Palace *e.* explor'd *D.* iv. 315

Equals.
He fills, he bounds, connects, and *e.* all *E.M.* i. 280

Equipage.
First strip off all her *e.* of Pride *E.M.* ii. 44
Behold this *E.* by Mathers wrought *Mi.* ix. 29
The *E.* shall grace SMILINDA's side *Mi.* ix. 110
Think what an *e.* thou hast in Air *R.L.* i. 45

Equity.
Or in pure *e.* (the case not clear) *S.* ii. 171

Equivocal.
Their generation's so *e. E.C.* 43

Erasmus.
At length *E.*, that great injur'd name *E.C.* 693
Like good *E.* in an honest Mean *S.* i. 66

Ere.—Passim.

Erect.
E. new wonders, and the old repair *M.E.* iv. 192
With aspect open shall *e.* his head *M.E.* v. 65

Eridanus.
E. his humble fountain scorns *D.* ii. 182

Ermine.
Peers, Heralds, Bishops, *E.*, Gold and Lawn *S.* v. 317

Ermin'd.
Arcadia's Countess, here, in *e.* pride *M.E.* ii. 7

Err.
And, lest we *e.* by Wit's wild dancing light *D.* i. 175
Some few in that, but numbers *e.* in this *E.C.* 5
The Vulgar thus thro' Imitation *e. E.C.* 424
To *e.* is human, to forgive, divine *E.C.* 525
Born but to die, and reas'ning but to *e. E.M.* ii. 10

Err'd.
Nature in her then *e.* not, but forgot *M.E.* ii. 158

Erring.
Far other dreams my *e.* soul employ *E.A.* 223
Man's *e.* judgment, and misguide the mind *E.C.* 202
And spite of Pride, in *e.* Reason's spite *E.M.* i. 293
Shew'd *e.* Pride, WHATEVER IS, IS RIGHT *E.M.* iv. 394
This *e.* mortals Levity may call *R.L.* i. 103

Error.
Those oft are stratagems which *e.* seem *E.C.* 179
In Pride, in reas'ning Pride, our *e.* lies *E.M.* i. 123
Sole judge of Truth, in endless *E.* hurl'd *E.M.* ii. 17
Nor lets, like Nævius, ev'ry *e.* pass *S.* ii. 65
T' avoid great *e—s*, must the less commit *E.C.* 260
But you, with pleasure own your *e.* past *E.C.* 570
If to her share some female *e.* fall *R.L.* ii. 17

Errs.
But *e.* not Nature from this gracious end *E.M.* i. 141

Erst.
As *e.* Medea (cruel, so to save !) *D.* iv. 121

Escape, 'Scape.
E. in Monsters, and amaze the Town *D.* i. 38
And let the Author of the Whole *e. D.* iv. 456
But sad example ! never to *e. D.* iv. 527
And each Blasphemer quite *e.* the rod *E.S.* ii. 195
And *'s.* the martyrdom of jakes and fire *D.* i. 144
How with less reading than makes felons *'s. D.* i. 281

And pleas'd to 's. from Flattery to Wit *E.* i. 12
At Crimes that 's., or triumph o'er the Law *E.S.* i. 168
To 's. my Censure, not expect my Praise *E.S.* ii. 113
Observing, cry'd " You 's. not so *I.H.* i. 57
The morals blacken'd, when the writings 's. *P.S.* 352
Hear this, and tremble! you, who 's. the Laws *S.* i. 118

Escap'd.
Must great offenders, once *e.* the Crown *E.S.* ii. 28
Dryden alone *e.* this judging Eye *P.S.* 246

Esdras.
Out-cant old *E.*, or out-drink his heir *S.* vii. 37

Esher.
Pleas'd let me own, in *E.*'s peaceful Grove *E.S.* ii. 66

Espalier.
And figs from standard and *e.* join *S.* ii. 147
His Quincunx darkens, his *E*—s meet *M.E.* iv. 80

Esquire—see Squire.

Essay'd.
Then * *e.;* scarce vanish'd out of sight *D.* ii. 295
No Arts *e.*, but not to be admir'd *Ep.* vi. 4

Essays.
Till show'rs of Sermons, Characters, *E. D.* ii. 361
And write next winter more *E. on Man E.S.* ii. 255

Essence.
Shrink his thin *e.* like a rivel'd flow'r *R.L.* ii. 132
The bodkin, comb, and *e.* to prepare *R.L.* iv. 98
Nor let th' imprison'd *e*—s exhale *R.L.* ii. 94

Essenc'd.
Painted for sight, and *e.* for the smell *S.* viii. 226

Essential.
To three *e.* Partridges in one *D.* iv. 562
Alike *e.* to th' amazing Whole *E.M.* i. 248

Establish'd.
Or Laws *e.*, and the world reform'd *S.* v. 12

Estate.
As much *E.*, and Principle, and Wit *D.* iv. 325
Above Temptation, in a low *E. Ep.* xi. 5
As want of figure, and a small *E. S.* iii. 68
Glean on, and gather up the whole *e. S.* vii. 92
Yet gave me in this dark *E. U.P.* 9
Tyrant Supreme! shall three E—s command *D.* iv. 603
Our Gen'rals now, retir'd to their *E. S.* iii. 7
E. have wings, and bang in Fortune's pow'r *S.* vi. 248

Esteem.
Still with *e.* no less convers'd than read *E.* iv. 7
Learn hence for ancient rules a just *e. E.C.* 139
E. and Love were never to be sold *E.M.* iv. 188
Yet for small Turbots such *e.* profess *S.* ii. 23
What Speech *e.* you most!" "The King's," said *I. S.* viii. 68

Estimating.
And *e.* Authors by the year *S.* v. 67

Eternal.
Daughter of Chaos, and *e.* Night *D.* i. 12
There painted valleys of *e.* green *D.* i. 76
In Shadwell's bosom with *e.* Rest *D.* i. 240
Full and *e.* privilege of tongue *D.* ii. 378
And Poet's vision of *e.* Fame *D.* iii. 12
To me committing their *e.* praise *D.* iii. 280
Indulge, dread Chaos, and *e.* Night *D.* iv. 2
Else sure some Bard, to our *e.* praise *D.* iv. 171
Those tears *e.*, that embalm the dead *E.* iii. 48
In these lone walls (their days *e.* bound) *E.A.* 141
E. sunshine of the spotless mind *E.A.* 209
And melts in visions of *e.* day *E.A.* 222
Receive and wrap me in *e.* rest *E.A.* 302
But all is calm in this *e.* sleep *E.A.* 313
Th' *e.* snows appear already past *E.C.* 227
Hope springs *e.* in the human breast *E.M.* i. 95
Of Order, sins against th' *E.* Cause *E.M.* i. 130
As much *e.* springs and cloudless skies *E.M.* i. 153
Go, teach *E.* Wisdom how to rule *E.M.* ii. 29
Th' *E.* Act educing good from ill *E.M.* ii. 175
So from the first *e.* Order ran *E.M.* iii. 113

That something still which prompts th' *e.* sigh *E.M.* iv. 3
Think we, like some weak Prince, th' *E.* Cause *E.M.* iv. 121
Go live! for Heav'n's *E.* year is thine *Ep.* vii. 9
And Hell's grim Tyrant feel th' *e.* wound *M.* 48
Reveal'd, and God's *e.* day be thine *M.* 104
And gives th' *e.* wheels to know their rounds *M.E.* iii. 168
E. buckle takes in Parian stone *M.E.* iii. 296
E. smiles his emptiness betray *P.S.* 315
By laws *e.* to th' aërial kind *R.L.* ii. 76
On Avon's bank, where flow'rs *e.* blow *S.* v. 119
Taste, that *e.* wanderer, which flies *S.* v. 312
How shall I rhyme in this *e.* roar *S.* vi. 114
While in thy heart *e.* winter reigns *Su.* 22
Thus, if *E.* justice rules the ball *U.L.* 35
E. beauties grace the shining scene *W.* 71
On Cooper's Hill *e.* wreaths shall grow *W.F.* 265
And palms *e.* flourish round his urn *W.F.* 312

Eternity.
And opes the Temple of *E. E.S.* ii. 235
Or damn to all *e.* at once *S.* v. 59

Ethereal, Etherial—see also Æthereal.
The sick'ning stars fade off th' *e.* plain *D.* iv. 636
Natures *e.*, human, angel, man *E.M.* i. 238
Great in the earth as in th' *e.* frame *E.M.* i. 270
Than favour'd Man by touch *e.* slain *E.M.* iii. 68
Then sacred seem'd th' *e.* vault no more *E.M.* iii. 263
Not with more glories, in th' *e*—*ial* plain *R.L.* ii. 1

Eton.
E. and Winton shake thro' all their sons *D.* iv. 144
Till Thames see *E.*'s sons for ever play *D.* iii. 335

Euclid.
Full in the midst of *E.* dip at once *D.* iv. 263

Euclio.
I give and I devise (old *E.* said) *M.E.* i. 256

Eugene.
An *E.* living, as a Cæsar dead *E.M.* iv. 244

Eunuch.
Wafts the smooth *E.*, and enamour'd swain *D.* iv. 310
Or with a Rival's, or an *E.*'s spite *E.C.* 31
To pant, or tremble thro' an *E.* throat *S.* v. 154
For what! to have a Box where E—s sing *S.* iii. 105
New *E.*, Harlequins, and Operas *S.* viii. 125

Euphrates.
A small *E.* thro' the piece is roll'd *M.E.* v. 29

Europe.
E. he saw, and *E.* saw him too *D.* iv. 294
Led by my hand, he saunter'd *E.* round *D.* iv. 311
All *E.* sav'd, yet Britain not betray'd *M.E.* i. 84
E. a Woman; Child, or Dotard rule *M.E.* i. 93
And Britain, if not *E.*, is undone *M.E.* i. 161
Now *E.*'s laurels on their brows behold *E.M.* iv. 295
Trims *E.* balance, tops the statesman's part *S.* viii. 154

Eurydice.
Restore, restore *E.* to life *O.* i. 81
Yet ev'n in death *E.* he sung (rep.) *O.* i. 113

Eusden.
And *E.* eke out Blackmore's endless line *D.* i. 104
Know, *E.* thirsts no more for sack or praise *D.* i. 293
As *E.*, Philips, Settle, writ of Kings *S.* v. 417

Evans.
And whisk 'em back to *E.*, Young, and Swift *D.* ii. 116

Eve.
Sick of his civil Pride, from Morn to *E. M.E.* iv. 166
Or at the ear of *E.*, familiar Toad *P.S.* 319
E.'s tempter thus the Rabbins have exprest *P.S.* 330

Even.—Passim.

Even-song.
When doom'd to say his beads and *E. S.* vii. 106

Ev'ning.
Her *e.* cates before his neighbour's shop *D.* ii. 72
A morning's pleasure, and at *e.* torn *E.* iv. 66
The birds shall cease to tune their *e.* song *A.* 40

EVENT—EXCLAIM.

In some fair *e.*, on your elbow laid *E.* v. 31
Compute the morn and *e.* to the day *E.M.* iv. 305
Nor *e.* Cynthia fill her silver horn *M.* 100
With Sappho fragrant at an *e.* Masque *M.E.* ii. 26
Attends to gild the *E.* of my day *S.* i. 94
In Life's cool *E.* satiate of Applause *S.* iii. 9
Sir Job sail'd forth, the *e.* bright and still *S.* iii. 138
No grateful dews descend from *e.* skies *W.* 45
In some still *e.*, when the whisp'ring breeze *W.* 79
Ev'n now, she shades thy E.-walk *with bays E.* i. 35

Event.
I saw, alas! some dread *e.* impend *R.L.* i. 109
With beating hearts the dire *e.* they wait *R.L.* ii. 141
And brings all natural *e—s to pass S.* vii. 49

Ever.—*Passim.*
Yet here for *e., e.* must I stay *E.A.* 171
For *e., e., e.* lost *O.* i. 105
From the fair head, for *e.*, and for *e. R.L.* iii. 154
Man! and *for e.!* wretch! what wouldst thou have *S.* vi. 252
Celestial palms, and e.-blooming *flow'rs E.A.* 318
What can atone (oh *e.-injur'd* shade!) *U.L.* 47
Of *e.-listless* Loit'rers that attend *D.* iv. 339
Where light disports in *e.-mingling* dyes *R.L.* ii. 66
And *e.-musing* melancholy reigns *E.A.* 3
Soothe my *e.-waking* Slumbers *Mi.* vii. 15

Everlasting.
Not *e.* Blackmore this denies *D.* ii. 302
And heard thy *e.* yawn confess *D.* iv. 343
Clos'd one by one to *e.* rest *D.* iv. 638
See Cromwell damn'd to *e.* fame *E.M.* iv. 284
Swords, pikes, and guns, with *e.* rust *S.* i. 74

Ev'ry, Ev'rywhere.—*Passim.*

Ev'rything.
More wise, more learn'd, more just, more *e. M.E.* i. 140

E'sham = Evesham.
Lords of fat *E.*, or of Lincoln fen *S.* vi. 241

Evidence.
When Moral *E.* shall quite decay *D.* iv. 462

Evil.
All partial *E.*, universal Good *E.M.* i. 292
Our greatest *e.*, or our greatest good *E.M.* ii. 92
Giv'n to the Fool, the Mad, the Vain, the *E. M.E.* iii. 19
E'er since our Grandam's *e. Mi.* iv. 10
When golden Angels cease to cure the *E. S.* vi. 218

Ewes.
If teeming *e.* increase my fleecy breed *W.* 82

Exact.
All which, *e.* to rule, were brought about *E.C.* 277
Curious not knowing, not *e.* but nice *E.C.* 286
Blest with a taste *e.*, yet unconfin'd *E.C.* 639
A long, *e.*, and serious Comedy *E.* iv. 22
Count the slow clock, and dine *e.* at noon *E.* v. 18
All in *e.* proportion to the state *E.M.* i. 183
E. Racine, and Corneille's noble fire *S.* v. 274
There's a Rehearsal, Sir, *e.* at one *S.* vi. 97

Exactest.
Th' *e.* traits of Body or of Mind *M.E.* ii. 191

Exactly.
Maggots half-form'd in rhyme *e.* meet *D.* i. 61
Would you know when? *e.* when they fall *E.S.* i. 90
Commas and points they set *e.* right *P.S.* 161

Exactness.
Is not th' *e.* of peculiar parts *E.C.* 244

Exalt.
E. their kind, and take some Virtue's name *E.M.* ii. 100
Go, and *e.* thy Moral to Divine *Ep.* vii. 10
E. the dance, or animate the song *I.H.* iii. 28
E. thy tow'ry head, and lift thy eyes *M.* 86
These swell their prospects, and *e.* their pride *R.L.* i. 81
Or under southern skies *e.* their sails *W.F.* 391

Exalted.
Thro' half the heav'ns he pours th' *e.* urn *D.* ii. 183

Be not, *e.* to whate'er degree *E.* ii. 14
And each *e.* stanza teems with thought *E.C.* 423
And Peers give way, *e.* as they are *S.* vi. 106

Exalts.
How glowing guilt *e.* the keen delight *E.A.* 230
E. her in enliv'ning airs *O.* i. 27
And to debase the Sons, *e.* the Sires *S.* v. 134
With chymic art *e.* the min'ral pow'rs *W.F.* 243

Examine.
But when t' *e.* ev'ry part he came *E.C.* 134

Examines.
Sees hairs and pores, *e.* bit by bit *D.* iv. 234

Example.
The brisk *E.* never fail'd to move *D.* i. 194
But, sad *e.*, never to escape *D.* iv. 527
Whose own *e.* strengthens all his laws *E.C.* 679
Who now that obsolete *E.* fears *E.S.* ii. 56
Go! fair *e.* of untainted youth *Ep.* vii. 1
And, while he bids thee, sets th' *E.* too *S.* iii. 109
All, by the King's *E.*, liv'd and lov'd *S.* v. 142
Just precepts thus from great e—s giv'n E.C. 98
Those strange *e.* ne'er were made to fit ye *E.J.S.* 41
Did not some grave *E.* yet remain *S.* v. 128

Exceed.
Not but that we may *e.*, some holy time *S.* ii. 85

Exceeding.
Will sneaks a Scriv'ner, an *e.* knave *M.E.* i. 154
And tho' the Court show Vice *e.* clear *S.* viii. 96

Exceeds.
Observes how much a Chintz *e.* Mohair *M.E.* ii. 170
And to be grave, *e.* all Pow'r of face *P.S.* 36

Excel.
And who the most in love of dirt *e, D.* ii. 277
Let such teach others, who themselves *e. E.C.* 15
Of old, those met rewards who could *e. E.C.* 510
Let modest FOSTER, if he will, *e. E.S.* i. 131
To help who want, to forward who *e. S.* i. 137
In ev'ry Public virtue we *e. S.* v. 45
Thea Peers grew proud in Horsemanship t' *e. S.* v. 143
Blest Swains, whose Nymphs in ev'ry grace *e. Sp.* 95

Excellence.
Next pleas'd his *E.* a town to batter *S.* vi. 44

Excellent.
Their praise is still,—the Style is *e. E.C.* 307

Excellently.
One Giant-Vice, so *e.* ill *S.* vii. 4

Except.—*Passim.*

Exception.
That proud *e.* to all Nature's laws *E.M.* iii. 243
Blends, in *e.* to all gen'ral rules *M.E.* ii. 275
Th' *e—s few; some change since all began E.M.* i. 147

Excess.
As bodies perish thro' *e.* of blood *E.C.* 304
Between *E.* and Famine lies a mean *S.* ii. 47

Exchange.
The merchant from th' *E.* returns in peace *R.L.* iii. 23

Exchang'd.
But stain'd with blood, or ill *e.* for gold *E.M.* iv. 296

Exchequer.
One lull'd th' *E.*, and one stunn'd the Rolls *S.* vi. 130

Excise.
Phryne foresees a general *E. M.E.* iii. 120
It brought (no doubt) th' *E.* and Army in *S.* vii. 8

Excis'd.
The Lord of Thousands, than if now *B. S.* ii. 134

Excising.
But some *e.* Courtier will have toll *S.* viii. 147

Exclaim.
Cutler and Brutus, dying both *e. M.E.* iii. 333

EXCLAIMS—EXPLORES. 95

Exclaims.
"What! leave the Combat out!" *e.* the Knight *E.C.* 279
While Man *e.*, "See all things for my use!" *E.M.* 45

Exclude.
And part admit, and part *e.* the day *W.F.* 18

Excrement.
Perfume to you, to me is *E. E.S.* ii. 184

Excrescent.
Expunge the whole, or lop th' *e.* parts *E.M.* ii. 49

Excursions.
It still looks home, and short *e.* makes *E.C.* 627
But in low numbers short *e.* tries *E.C.* 738

Excuse.
Send for him up, take on *e. I.H.* ii. 36 *s*
E. for writing, and for writing ill *S.* vii. 28
And to *e.* it, need but shew the prize *D.* iv. 434
E. the blush, and pour out all the heart *E.A.* 56
And in our own (*e.* some Courtly strains) *S.* v. 215

Excus'd.
Were others angry? I *e.* them too *P.S.* 173

Execute.
My counsel sends to *e.* a deed *S.* vi. 92

Execution.
As men from Jails to *e.* go *S.* viii. 273

Exempt.
Gen'rous converse; a soul *e.* from pride *E.C.* 641
Grown all to all, from no one vice *e. M.E.* i. 194

Exercise.
A gentler *e.* to close the games *D.* ii. 366
But strength of mind is *E.*, not Rest *E.M.* ii. 104
Healthy by temp'rance, and by *e. P.S.* 401
Successive study, *e.*, and ease *W.F.* 240
Confine the thought, to *e.* the breath *D.* iv. 159
Go work, hunt, *e.!* (he thus began) *S.* ii. 11

Exercis'd.
For ever *e.*, yet never tir'd *E.M.* iv. 322

Exhale.
Nor let th' imprison'd essences *e. R.L.* ii. 94
Oh blast it, South winds! till a stench *e. S.* ii. 27

Exhaust.
Here point your thunder, and *e.* your rage *E.C.* 555

Exigencies.
Now, in such *e.* not to need *S.* iv. 89

Exile.
And *Wit* dreads *E.*, Penalties, and Pains *D.* iv. 22
Or failing, smiles in *e.* or in chains *E.M.* iv. 234
A friend in *e.*, or a father, dead *P.S.* 355
In durance, *e.*, Bedlam, or the Mint *S.* i. 99

Exil'd.
And more true joy Marcellus *e.* feels *E.M.* iv. 257
At home, tho' *e.*; free, tho' in the Tower *S.* iii. 184
E. by thee from earth to deepest hell *W.F.* 413

Exotic.
He forms one tongue, *e.* and refin'd *S.* viii. 49

Expanded.
With arms *e.* Bernard rows his state *D.* ii. 67
E. flies, and gathers all its fame *E.M.* iv. 384

Expansion.
On gilded clouds in fair *e.* lie *M.E.* iv. 147

Expatiate.
E. free o'er all this scene of Man *E.M.* i. 5
Bids his free soul *e.* in the skies *W.F.* 254

Expatiates.
Rests and *e.* in a life to come *E.M.* i. 98

Expect.
E. thy dog, thy bottle, and thy wife *E.M.* iv. 178

To 'scape my Censure, not *e.* my Praise *E.S.* ii. 113
E. a place, or pension from the Crown *S.* v. 371

Expected.
With sure returns of still *e.* rhymes *E.C.* 349
Swift fly the years, and rise th' *e.* morn *M.* 21

Expects.
My son, the promis'd land *e.* thy reign *D.* i. 292
The Duke *e.* my Lord and you *I.H.* ii. 73 *s.*
This prints my Letters, that *e.* a bribe *P.S.* 113

Expel.
And old impertinence *e.* by new *R.L.* i. 94

Expell'd.
Banish'd the doctor, and *e.* the friend *M.E.* iii. 330

Expelling.
Each fierce Logician, still *e.* Locke *D.* iv. 196

Expense.
Thro' life 'tis follow'd ev'n at life's *e. E.M.* ii. 171
To cram the Rich was prodigal *e. M.E.* iii. 185
To balance Fortune by a just *e. M.E.* iii. 223
A standing sermon at each year's *e. M.E.* iv. 21
Something there is more needful than *e. M.E.* iv. 41
'Tis Use alone that sanctifies *E. M.E.* iv. 179

Experience.
On plain *E.* lay foundations low *D.* iv. 466
Attention, habit and *e.* gains *E.M.* i. 79
E., this; by Man's oppression curst *M.E.* ii. 213
By Nature honest, by *E.* wise *P.S.* 400

Experienc'd.
As the sage dame *e.* in her trade *D.* ii. 133

Expiate.
Wash Bladen white, and *e.* Hays's stain *D.* iv. 560

Expire.
Down sink the flames, and with a hiss *e. D.* i. 260
Tell me, if Virtue made the son *e. E.M.* iv. 105
For when the Fair in all their pride *e. R.L.* i. 57
His drooping swans on ev'ry note *e. W.F.* 275
She saw her sons with purple deaths *e. W.F.* 323

Expir'd.
Amaz'd, confus'd, he found his pow'r *e. R.L.* iii. 145

Expires.
King John in silence modestly *e. D.* i. 252
The meteor drops, and in a flash *e. D.* iv. 634
And unawares Morality *e. D.* iv. 650
For one puff more, and in that puff *e. M.E.* i. 245

Expiring.
Or bright, as visions of *e.* maids *R.L.* iv. 42
Th' *e.* Swan, and as he sings he dies *R.L.* v. 66

Explain.
For thee *e.* a thing till all men doubt it *D.* iv. 251
And those *e.* the meaning quite away *E.C.* 117
E. his own beginning, or his end *E.M.* ii. 38
Explore the thought, *e.* the asking eye *P.S.* 412

Explain'd.
E. the matter, and would win the cause *Mi.* xi. 6
Laws are *e.* by Men—so have a care *S.* i. 144

Explains.
E. the *Sève* and *Verdeur* of the Vine *D.* iv. 556

Expletives.
While *e.* their feeble aid do join *E.C.* 346

Explore.
Spread all his sails, and durst the deeps *e. E.C.* 646
The latest tracts, the giddy heights *e. E.M.* i. 11
The learn'd is happy nature to *e. E.M.* ii. 263
Who bid the stork, Columbus-like, *e. E.M.* iii. 105
His Principle of action once *e. M.E.* i. 27
E. the thought, explain the asking eye *P.S.* 412

Explor'd.
The Stews and Palace equally *e. D.* iv. 315
Then, looking up from sire to sire, *e. E.M.* iii. 225

Explores.
E. the lost, the wand'ring sheep directs *M.* 51

Expose.
A fool might once himself alone e. *E.C.* 7
How strangely you e. yourself, my dear *E.J.S.* 10
Spare then the Person, and e. the Vice *E.S.* ii. 12
Fair to e. myself, my foes, my friends *S.* i. 58

Expos'd.
E. in glorious heaps the tempting Bank *Mi.* ix. 78
E. thro' crystal to the gazing eyes *R.L.* iv. 114

Exposing.
Shines in e. Knaves, and painting Fools *M.E.* ii. 119

Express.
Of some E. arriv'd at Court *I.H.* ii. 110 s.
Others for Language all their cares e. *E.C.* 305
So eager to e. your love *I.H.* ii. 57 s.
Or dubb'd Historians by e. command *S.* v. 372

Express'd, Exprest.
What oft was thought, but ne'er so well e. *E.C.* 298
A vile conceit in pompous words e. *E.C.* 320
In each she marks her Image full e—t *D.* i. 107
His Honour's meaning Dulness thus e. *D.* ii. 155
Yet still how faint by precept is e. *E.* iii. 41
Eve's tempter thus the Rabbins have e. *P.S.* 330

Expression.
But true e., like th' unchanging Sun *E.C.* 315
E. is the dress of thought, and still *E.C.* 318

Expressive.
Th' e. emblem of their softer pow'r *R.L.* iii. 40
Mark where a bold e. phrase appears *S.* vi. 165

Expunge.
E. the whole, or lop th' excrescent parts *E.M.* ii. 49

Exquisitely.
The spider's touch, how e. fine *E.M.* i. 217

Extasy.
In some soft Dream, or E. of joy *Mi.* v. 18

Extend.
Thence to the south e. thy gladden'd eyes *D.* iii. 79
If, where the rules not far enough e. *E.C.* 146
Around, how wide! how deep e. below *E.M.* i. 236
At once e. the int'rest, and the love *E.M.* iii. 134
E. it, let thy enemies have part *E.M.* iv. 356
Peace o'er the World her olive wand e. *M.* 19
Trade it may help, Society e. *M.E.* iii. 29
Bid Harbours open, public Ways e. *M.E.* iv. 197
With lenient Arts e. a Mother's breath *P.S.* 410
Here files of pins e. their shining rows *R.L.* i. 137
Some, orb in orb, around the nymph e. *R.L.* ii. 138
Here in full light the russet plains e. *W.F.* 23

Extended.
Absent I follow thro' th' e. dream *I.H.* iii. 42
Whom not th' e. Albion could contain *W.F.* 315

Extends.
De Lyra there a dreadful front e. *D.* i. 153
Thick and more thick the black blockade e. *D.* iv. 191
With that, a WIZARD OLD his Cup e. *D.* iv. 517
Far as Creation's ample range e. *E.M.* i. 207
Lives thro' all life, e. thro' all extent *E.M.* i. 273
E. to Luxury, e. to Lust *M.E.* iii. 26
Belies his features, nay e. his hands *M.E.* iii. 294
Favours to none, to all she smiles e. *R.L.* ii. 11
He takes the gift with rev'rence, and e. *R.L.* iii. 131
While all its throats the Gallery e. *S.* v. 326

Extensive.
Th' e. blessing of his luxury *E.M.* iii. 62

Extent.
Lives thro' all life, extends thro' all e. *E.M.* i. 273
Proud of a vast e. of flimsy lines *P.S.* 94

External.
Nay, why e. for internal giv'n *E.M.* iv. 161
God in E—s could not place Content *E.M.* iv. 66

Extinct.
Her weapons blunted, and e. her fires *W.F.* 418

Extinguish.
To blot out Order, and e. Light *D.* iv. 14

Extol.
Let me e. a Cat, on oysters fed *S.* ii. 41

Extoll'd.
Much they e. his pictures, much his seat *P.S.* 239

Extols.
E. old Bards, or Merlin's Prophecy *S.* v. 132

Extract.
Strives to e. from his soft, giving palm *D.* ii. 208

Extracts.
E. his brain; and Principle is fled *D.* iv. 522
From pois'nous herbs e. the healing dew *E.M.* i. 220

Extreme.
Our Critics take a contrary e. *E.C.* 661
What modes of sight betwixt each wide e. *E.M.* i. 211
But where th' E. of Vice, was ne'er agreed *E.M.* ii. 221
Few in th' e., but all in the degree *E.M.* ii. 232
Or indolent, to each e. they fall *E.M.* iv. 25
Obvious her goods, in no e. they dwell *E.M.* iv. 31
Thus good or bad, to one e. betray *S.* iv. 24
(Earth's wide e—s) her sable flag display'd *D.* iii. 71
Avoid E.; and shun the fault of such *E.C.* 384
E. in Nature equal ends produce *E.M.* ii. 205
And yet the fate of all e. is such *M.E.* i. 9
E. in Nature equal good produce (rep.) *M.E.* iii. 161
Thro' reconcil'd e. of drought and rain *M.E.* iii. 166
That secret rare, between th' e. to mark *M.E.* iii. 227
Till earth's e. your mediation own *S.* v. 202
That both e. were banish'd from their walls *S.* vii. 117

Extremely.
E. ready to resign *I.H.* i. 63
A Tale e. à propos *I.H.* ii. 154
And the rich feast concludes e. poor *S.* ii. 34
Like rich old wardrobes, things e. rare *S.* vii. 123

Exulting.
And leap e. like the bounding roe *M.* 44
E. in triumph now swell the bold notes *O.* i. 16
The nymph e. fills with shouts the sky *R.L.* iii. 99
And mounts e. on triumphant wings *W.F.* 112

Eye.
One Cell there is, conceal'd from vulgar e. *D.* i. 33
And boasts Ulysses' ear, with Argus' e. *D.* ii. 374
Thy mental e., for thou hast much to view *D.* iii. 62
Far eastward cast thine e., from whence the Sun *D.* iii. 73
Horneck's fierce e., and Roome's funereal frown *D.* iii. 152
Watch'd both by Envy's, and by Flatt'ry's e. *D.* iv. 36
With mincing step, small voice, and languid e. *D.* iv. 46
But as in graceful act, with awful e. *D.* iv. 109
The critic E., that microscope of Wit *D.* iv. 233
Whose spoils this paper offers to your e. *D.* iv. 435
A Face untaught to feign, a judging E. *E.* ii. 5
Here thy well-study'd marbles fix our e. *E.* iii. 33
Just when she learns to roll a melting e. *E.* v. 3
Still drink delicious poison from thy e. *E.A.* 122
Kind, virtuous drops just gath'ring in my e. *E.A.* 278
Present the Cross before my lifted e. *E.A.* 327
See the last sparkle languish in my e. *E.A.* 332
Amid that scene if some relenting e. *E.A.* 355
'Tis not a lip, or e., we beauty call *E.C.* 245
As all looks yellow to the jaundic'd e. *E.C.* 559
And stares, tremendous, with a threat'ning e. *E.C.* 586
But less to please the e., than arm the hand *E.C.* 673
Who sees with equal e., as God of all *E.M.* i. 87
Why has not Man a microscopic e. *E.M.* i. 193
Beast, bird, fish, insect, what no e. can see *E.M.* i. 240
What if the head, the e., the ear repin'd *E.M.* i. 261
Their law his e., their oracle his tongue *E.M.* iii. 218
Spin all your Cobwebs o'er the E. of Day *E.S.* ii. 222
The sprightly Wit, the lively E. *I.H.* i. 45
In vain the Sage, with retrospective e. *M.E.* i. 99
In Magdalen's loose hair, and lifted e. *M.E.* ii. 12
Rufa, whose e. quick-glancing o'er the Park *M.E.* ii. 21
Worn out in public, weary ev'ry e. *M.E.* ii. 229
The suff'ring e. inverted Nature sees *M.E.* iv. 119
And bring all Paradise before your e. *M.E.* iv. 148
In one short view subjected to our e. *M.E.* v. 33
They strike the Soul, and glitter in the e. *Mi.* ix. 82

EYES—FACE.

Or meets his spouse's fonder *e. O.* iii. 31
The triumph ceas'd, tears gush'd from ev'ry *e. P.C.* 33
Fire in each *e.*, and papers in each hand *P.S.* 5
Such Ovid's nose, and " Sir ! you have an *E." P.S.* 118
Dryden alone escap'd this judging *e. P.S.* 246
Explore the thought, explain the asking *e. P.S.* 412
But ev'ry *e.* was fix'd on her alone *R.L.* i. 9
Or wedg'd whole ages in a bodkin's *e. R.L.* ii. 128
There kept my charms conceal'd from mortal *e. R.L.* iv. 157
Sudden, with starting tear each *e.* o'erflows *R.L.* v. 85
For, after all the murders of your *e. R.L.* v. 145
The sleeping *E.* that spoke the melting soul *S.* v. 150
More on a Reader's sense, than Gazer's *e. S.* v. 351
He lifts the tube, and levels with his *e. W.F.* 129
O'er figur'd worlds now travels with his *e. W.F.* 246
Or what ill *e—s malignant glances dart (rep.) A.* 82
Next o'er his Books his *e.* began to roll *D.* i. 127
Then lights the structure, with averted *e. D.* i. 247
Tears gush'd again as from pale Priam's *e. D.* i. 255
Mix in his look ; All *e.* direct their rays *D.* ii. 7
A Poet's form she plac'd before their *e. D.* ii. 35
With pert flat *e.* she window'd well its head *D.* ii. 43
With cow-like udders, and with ox-like *e. D.* ii. 164
Spirts in the gard'ner's *e.* who turns the cock *D.* ii. 178
Swift as it mounts, all follow with their *e. D.* ii. 185
Each gentle clerk, and mutt'ring seals his *e. D.* ii. 404
Thence to the south extend thy gladdeo'd *e. D.* iii. 79
Right well mine *e.* arede the myster wight *D.* iii. 187
For thee we dim the *e.*, and stuff the bead *D.* iv. 249
So shall each youth, assisted by our *e. D.* iv. 359
O ! would the Sons of Men once think their *E. D.* iv. 453
Sire, Ancestors, Himself. One casts his *e. D.* iv. 519
Which no one looks in with another's *e. D.* iv. 534
As Argus' *e.* by Hermes' wand oppress *D.* iv. 637
An Angel's sweetness, or Bridgewater's *e. E.* iii. 46
And other Beauties envy Worsley's *e. E.* iii. 60
Voiture was wept by all the brightest *E. E.* iv. 18
The brightest *e.* of France inspir'd his Muse *(rep.) E.*iv.77
Divert her *e.* with pictures in the fire *E.* v. 19
While the spread fan o'ershades your closing *e. E.* v. 37
Just when his fancy points your sprightly *e. E.* v. 45
Of those that sing of these poor *e. E.* vi. 32
Line after line my gushing *e.* o'erflow *E.A.* 35
No happier task these faded *e.* pursue *E.A.* 47
Those smiling *e.*, attemp'ring ev'ry ray *E.A.* 63
Not on the Cross my *e.* were fix'd, but you *E.A.* 116
With other beauties charm my partial *e. E.A.* 126
Thy *e.* diffus'd a reconciling ray *E.A.* 145
To dream once more I close my willing *e. E.A.* 239
Stain all my soul, and wanton in my *e. E.A.* 266
Come, with one glance of those deluding *e. E.A.* 283
Fair *e.* and tempting looks (which yet I view) *E.A.* 295
Without all these at once before your *e. E.C.* 122
In prospects thus, some objects please our *e. E.C.* 156
Th' increasing prospect tires our wand'ring *e. E.C.* 231
All comes united to th' admiring *e. E.C.* 250
Now his fierce *e.* with sparkling fury glow *E.C.* 378
Might he return, and bless once more our *e. E.C.* 462
Pleasures are ever in our hands or *e. E.M.* ii. 123
All sly slow things, with circumspective *e. E.M.* iv. 226
All tears are wip'd for ever from all *e. E.S.* i. 102
To which thy Tomb shall guide enquiring *e. Ep.* v. 4
Nor ardent warriors meet with hateful *e. M.* 58
Exalt thy tow'ry head, and lift thy *e. M.* 86
All *e.* may see from what the change arose *(rep.) M.E.*ii.35
Her tongue bewitch'd as oddly as her *E. M.E.* ii. 47
When those blue *e.* first open'd on the sphere *M.E.*ii.284
" God cannot love," says Blunt with tearless *e. M.E.* iii. 103
Just at his Study-door he'll bless your *e. M.E.* iv. 132
When awful Love seems melting in his *E. Mi.* ix. 90
But soon, too soon, the lover turns his *e. O.* i. 93
And sterner Cassius melts at Junia's *e. O.* iii. 16
Heav'n opens on my *e. /* my ears *O.* v. 14
And calls forth Roman drops from British *e. P.C.* 16
View him with scornful, yet with jealous *e. P.S.* 199
And op'd those *e.* that must eclipse the day *R.L.* i. 14
Instruct thine *e.* of young Coquettes to roll *R.L.* i. 88
Thy *e.* first open'd on a Billet-doux *R.L.* i. 118
To that she bends, to that her *e.* she rears *R.L.* i. 126
And keener lightnings quicken in her *e. R.L.* i. 144
Quick as her *e.*, and as unfix'd as those *R.L.* ii. 10
Bright as the sun, her *e.* the gazers strike *R.L.* ii. 13

Then prostrate falls, and begs with ardent *e. R.L.* ii. 43
A third interprets motions, looks, and *e. R.L.* iii. 15
And see thro' all things with his half-shut *e. R.L.* iii. 118
Then flash'd the living lightning from her *e. R.L.* iii. 155
Which not the tears of brightest *e.* could ease *R.L.* iv. 76
Her *e.* dejected, and her hair unbound *R.L.* iv. 90
Expos'd thro' crystal to the gazing *e. R.L.* iv. 114
With earnest *e.* and round unthinking face *R.L.* iv. 125
Here. half-languishing, half-drown'd in tears *R.L.* iv. 144
If Hampton Court these *e.* had never seen *R.L.* iv. 150
Beauties in vain their pretty *e.* may roll *R.L.* v. 33
And scatters death around from both her *e. R.L.* v. 58
"Those *e.* were made so killing "—was his last *R.L.* v. 64
With more than usual lightning in her *e. R.L.* v. 76
Tho' mark'd by none but quick, poetic *e. R.L.* v. 124
When next he looks thro' Galileo's *e. R.L.* v. 138
Hartshorn, or something that shall close your *e. S.* i. 20
With *e.* that pry not, toogue that ne'er repeats *S.* i. 135
To keep these limbs, and to preserve these *e. S.* iii. 52
There are, my Friend ! whose philosophic *e. S.* iv. 7
Say with what *e.* we ought at Courts to gaze *S.* iv. 16
And gaze on Parian charms with learned *e. S.* iv. 31
Wonder of Kings ! like whom, to mortal *e. S.* v. 29
From heads to ears, and now from ears to *e. S.* v. 313
For vulgar *e.*, and point out ev'ry line *S.* v. 367
At this entrance'd, he lifts his hands and *e. S.* viii. 98
And make my tongue victorious as her *e. Sp.* 50
How much at variance are her feet and *e. Sp.* 60
And give the conquest to thy Silvia's *e. Sp.* 88
But since those graces please thy *e.* no more *Su.* 29
And all things flourish where you turn your *e. Su.* 76
By foreign hands thy dying *e.* were clos'd *U.L.* 51
Then from his closing *e.* thy form shall part *U.L.* 79
His purple crest, and scarlet-circled *e. W.F.* 116
Or looks on heav'n with more than mortal *e. W.F.* 253
The god appear'd : he turn'd his azure *e. W.F.* 351
E. Nature's walks, shoot Folly as it flies E.M. i. 13
And *e.* the Mine without a wish for Gold *Mi.* x. 8
And foremost in the Circle *e.* a King *S.* iii. 106
And on the sightless *e.*-ball *pour the day M.* 40
See my lips tremble, and my e—s roll E.A. 323
Not when from plate to plate your *e.* roll *S.* ii. 7
Lost the arch'd *e.-brow*, or Parnassian sneer *P.S.* 96

Eyes.

Dulness with transport *e.* the lively dunce *D.* i. 111
E. the calm sun-set of thy various Day *E.* i. 38
In vain th' observer *e.* the builders toil *M.E.* i. 220
Sail in the Ladies ; how each pirate *e. S.* viii. 228
And *e.* the dancing cork, and bending reed *W.F.* 140

F.

F. loves the Senate, Hockley-hole his brother *S.* i. 49
That first was H—vy's, F's next, and then E.S. i. 71

F.R.S.
Shine in the Dignity of *F.R.S. D.* iv. 570

Fable.
His *f.*, subject, scope in ev'ry page *E.C.* 120
Once on a time (so runs the *F.*) *I.H.* ii. 157
From Dryden's F—s down to Durfey's Tales E.C. 617

Fabling.
Nor Po so swells the *f.* Poet's lays *W.F.* 227

Face.
Stole from the Master of the sev'n-fold *F. D.* i. 244
A veil of fogs dilates her awful *f. D.* i. 262
New edge their dulness, and new bronze their *f. D.* ii. 10
Nor heeds the brown dishonours of his *f. D.* ii. 108
Yet smiling at his rueful length of *f. D.* ii. 142
The wild Mæander wash'd the Artist's *f. D.* ii. 176
Now gentle touches wanton o'er his *f. D.* ii. 201
And thrusts his person full into your *f. D.* iii. 140
Of sober *f.*, with learned dust besprent *D.* iii. 186
A *F.* untaught to feign, a judging Eye *E.* ii. 5
Or from the canvas call the mimic *f. E.* ii. 6
And breathe an air divine on ev'ry *f. E.* iii. 72
Thou but preserv'st a *F.*, and I a Name *E.* ii. 78
But now no *f.* divine contentment wears *E.A.* 147
The *f.* of Nature we no more survey *E.C.* 313
That Edward's Miss thus perks it in your *f. E.J.S.* 46

H

FACT—FAIR.

Yet seen too oft, familiar with her *f. E.M.* ii. 219
And shall no Egg in Japhet's *f.* be thrown *E.S.* ii. 289
And a thin Court that wants your *F. I.H.* i. 12
(T by Grecian Form) and Chloe knew the *F. I.H.* iii. 20
From ev'ry *f.* he wipes off ev'ry tear *M.* 46
Wrap my cold limbs, and shade my lifeless *f. M.E.* i. 249
And gaping Tritons spew to wash your *f. M.E.* iv. 154
Here, rising bold, the Patriot's honest *f. M.E.* v. 57
Glow in thy heart, and smile upon thy *f. Mi.* v. 14
Upon the bottom shines the Queen's bright *F. Mi.* ix. 33
Her Shape unfashion'd, and her *F.* unknown *Mi.* ix. 60
And to be grave, exceeds all Pow'r of *f. P.S.* 36
When ev'ry coxcomb perks them in my *f. P.S.* 74
And wonder with a foolish *f.* of praise *P.S.* 212
A Cherub's *f.*, a reptile all the rest *P.S.* 331
Some nymphs there are, too conscious of their *f. R.L.* i. 79
And calls forth all the wonders of her *f. R.L.* i. 142
Look on her *f.*, and you'll forget 'em all *R.L.* ii. 18
Th' embroider'd King who shows but half his *f. R.L.* iii. 76
As ever sully'd the fair *f.* of light *R.L.* iv. 14
But diff'ring far in figure and in *f. R.L.* iv. 26
Or raise a pimple on a beauteous *f. R.L.* iv. 68
With earnest eyes, and round unthinking *f. R.L.* iv. 125
Behold the first in virtue as in *f. R.L.* v. 18
The silver Thames reflects its marble *f. S.* iii. 142
You never change one muscle of your *f. S.* iii. 171
Two of a *f.*, as soon as of a mind *S.* vi. 269
Various of temper, as of *f.* or frame *S.* vi. 282
And what a solemn *f.* if he denies *S.* vii. 68
What Lady's *f.* is not a whited wall *S.* viii. 151
Of hollow gew-gaws, only dress and *f. S.* viii. 209
And with a *f.* as red, and as awry *S.* viii. 266
As in the crystal spring I view my *f. Su.* 27
Nor polish'd marble emulate thy *f. U.L.* 60
Glad chains, warm furs, broad banners, and broad *f*—s *D.* i. 88
Or he who bids thee f. with steady view S. iii. 107

Fact.

I tell the naked *f.* without disguise *D.* iv. 433
Oh *f.* accurst! what tears has Albion shed *W.F.* 321

Faction.

What Charms could *F.*, what Ambition lull *D.* iv. 623
And public *f.* doubles private hate *E.C.* 457
There *F.* roar, Rebellion bite her chain *W.F.* 421
And giddy f—s hear away their rage O. i. 35

Factor.

An honest *f.* stole a Gem away *M.E.* iii. 362

Faculties.

Wit, Spirit, *F.*, but make it worse *E.M.* ii. 146

Fade.

Ye trees that *f.* when autumn-heats remove *A.* 29
F. ev'ry blossom, wither ev'ry tree *A.* 33
The garlands *f.*, the vows are worn away *A.* 69
The sick'ning stars *f.* off th' ethereal plain *D.* iv. 636
Since painted, or not painted, all shall *f. R.L.* v. 27

Faded.

No happier task these *f.* eyes pursue *E.A.* 47
And all her *f.* garlands bloom anew *M.E.* v. 48
Their *f.* honours scatter'd on her bier *W.* 32

Fades.

Dismiss my soul, where no Carnation *f. D.* iv. 418
And all the bright creation *f.* away *E.C.* 493
Each state of meaner merit *f.* away *S.* v. 20

Fading.

A *f.* Fresco here demands a sigh *E.* iii. 34
These cheeks now *f.* at the blast of death *U.L.* 32

Faery Queen.

One likes no language but the *F, S.* v. 39

Fail.

At last Centlivre felt her voice to *f. D.* ii. 411
All crimes shall cease, and ancient fraud shall *f. M.* 137
Alas! I copy (or my draught would) *f. M.E.* ii. 197
Alike my scorn, if he succeed or *f. P.S.* 362
Oft have we known that seven-fold fence to *f. R.L.* ii. 119

When airs, and flights, and screams, and scoldings *f. R.L.* v. 32
And then such Friends as cannot *f.* to last *S.* iv. 80

Fail'd.

The brisk Example never *f.* to move *D.* i. 194
From lips like those, what precept *f.* to move *E.A.* 67
But Otway *f.* to polish or refine *S.* v. 278
Hopes after hopes of pious Papists *f. S.* vi. 62

Failing.

Our sons their fathers' *f.* language see *E.C.* 482
To see a piece of *f.*, flesh and blood *E.J.S.* 47
Or *f.*, smiles in exile or in chains *E.M.* iv. 234
No zealous Pastor blame a *f.* Spouse *E.S.* ii. 193
To f—s mild, but zealous for desert *E.C.* 731
The godly dame, who fleshly *f.* damns *E.J.S.* 21
In Sappho touch the *F. of the Sex E.S.* i. 15

Fails.

The solid pow'r of understanding *f. E.C.* 57
Pride, where wit *f.*, steps in to our defence *E.C.* 209
For who can move when fair Belinda *f. R.L.* v. 4

Fain.

And *f.* would be upon the laughing side *E.C.* 33
I *f.* would please you, if I knew with what *E.S.* ii. 26

Faint.

Not balmy sleep to lab'rers *f.* with pain *A.* 44
Where, *f.* at best, the beams of Science fall *D.* iii. 84
Yet still how *f.* by precept is exprest *E.* iii. 41
Damn with *f.* praise, assent with civil leer *P.S.* 201
Whether Old age with *f.* but cheerful hue *S.* i. 93
F., breathless, thus she pray'd, nor pray'd in vain *W.F.* 199

Fainting.

A Vial next she fills with *f.* fears *R.L.* iv. 85
For *f.* Age what cordial drop remains *S.* ii. 89
Now *f.*, sinking, pale, the nymph appears *W.F.* 191

Faintly.

The lines, tho' touch'd but *f.*, are drawn right *E.C.* 22

Faints.

F. into airs, and languishes with pride *R.L.* iv. 34

Fair.

Shouldst wag a serpent-tail in Smithfield *f. D.* iii. 288
For new abortions, all ye pregnant *F. D.* iii. 314
His royal Sense of Op'ras or the *F. D.* iv. 314
Who without flatt'ry pleas'd the *f.* and great *E.* iv. 6
His time the Muse, the witty, and the *f. E.* iv. 10
The *F.* sate panting at a Courtier's play *E.C.* 540
To the first good, first perfect, and first *f. E.M.* ii. 24
A Park is purchas'd, but the *F.* he sees *M.E.* ii. 39
As hard a science to the *F.* as Great *M.E.* ii. 226
Leaves the dull Cits, and joins (to please the *f.) M.E.* iii. 387
But treat the Goddess like a modest *f. M.E.* iv. 51
And those same sighs which cheat the list'ning *F. Mi.* ix. 8
This curs'd OMBRELIA, this undoing *F. Mi.* ix. 55
And gave him back the *f, O.* i. 86
Whose bugs the witty and the *f.* annoys *P.S.* 311
The *F.* and Innocent shall still believe *R.L.* i. 40
For when the *F.* in all their pride expire *R.L.* i. 57
The *f.* each moment rises in her charms *R.L.* i. 140
Our humbler province is to tend the *F. R.L.* ii. 91
This day, black Omens threat the brightest *F. R.L.* ii. 101
His post neglects, or leaves the *f.* at large *R.L.* ii. 124
Straight hover round the *F.* her airy band *R.L.* iii. 113
Or in a coach and six the British *F. R.L.* iii. 164
One sings the *F.*; but songs no longer move *S.* vii. 21
They march, to prate their hour before the *F. S.* viii. 249
And by that laugh the willing *f.* is found *S6.* 56
Fate in their dotage this f. *Idiot gave D.* i. 13
All as a partridge plump, full-fed, and *f. D.* ii. 41
In office here *f.* Cloacina stands *D.* ii. 93
F. as before her works she stands confess'd *D.* ii. 159
As Hylas *f.* was ravish'd long ago *D.* ii. 336
There, stript, *f.* Rhet'ric languish'd on the ground *D.* iv. 24
His stretch'd-out arm display'd a volume *f. D.* iv. 106
To headless Phœbe his *f.* bride postpone *D.* iv. 367
F. from its humble bed I rear'd this Flow'r *D.* iv. 405
F., ev'n in death I this peerless *Butterfly D.* iv. 436

FAIRER—FALL.

Fir'd with Ideas of *f.* Italy *E.* iii. 26
Thence endless streams of *f.* Ideas flow *E.* iii. 43
Thus from the world *f.* Zephalinda flew *E.* v. 7
In some *f.* ev'ning, on your elbow laid *E.* v. 31
F. eyes, and tempting looks (which yet I view) *E.A.* 295
Oh Grace serene ! oh virtue heav'nly *f. E.A.* 297
Then too, when fate shall thy *f.* frame destroy *E.A.* 337
In some *f.* body thus th' informing soul *E.C.* 76
His pow'rs in equal ranks, and *f.* array *E.C.* 176
The treach'rous colours the *f.* art betray *E.C.* 492
Like some *f.* flow'r the early spring supplies *E.C.* 498
Passions, tho' selfish, if their means be *f. E.M.* ii. 97
Love, Hope, and Joy, *f.* Pleasure's smiling train *E.M.* ii. 117
The rogue and fool by fits is *f.* and wise *E.M.* ii. 233
F. op'ning to some Court's propitious shine *E.M.* iv. 9
Make *f.* deductions; see to what they mount *E.M.* iv. 270
Thy relics, *Rowe*, to this *f.* Urn we trust *Ep.* v. 1
Go ! *f.* example of untainted youth *Ep.* vii. 1
And best distinguish'd by black, brown, and *f. M.E.* ii. 4
F. to no purpose, artful to no end *M.E.* ii. 245
F. Coursers, Vases, and alluring Dames *M.E.* iii. 70
On gilded clouds in *f.* expansion lie *M.E.* iv. 147
Or in *f.* series laurell'd bards be shown *M.E.* v. 61
F. Discretion, string the lyre *Mi.* vii. 14
This day TOM's *f.* account has run *Mi.* xii. 3
Who lead *f.* Virtue's train along *O.* ii. 11
Constant faith, *f.* hope, long leisure *O.* iii. 42
True Genius kindles, and *f.* Fame inspires *P.S.* 194
Welcome for thee, *f. Virtue!* all the past (*rep.*) *P.S.* 358
Know forther yet ; whoever *f.* and chaste *R.L.* i. 67
F. Nymphs, and well-drest Youths around her shone *R.L.* ii. 5
F. tresses man's imperial race ensnare *R.L.* ii. 27
And four *f.* Queens whose hands sustain a flow'r *R.L.* iii. 39
From the *f.* head for ever and for ever *R.L.* iii. 154
What wonder then, *f.* nymph ! thy hairs should feel *R.L.* iii. 177
As ever sully'd the *f.* face of light *R.L.* iv. 14
For who can move when *f.* Belinda fails *R.L.* v. 4
Not all the tresses that *f.* head can boast *R.L.* v. 143
When those *f.* suns shall set, as set they must *R.L.* v. 147
F. to expose myself, my foes, my friends *S.* i. 58
Add one round hundred, and (if that's not *f. S.* iv. 75
And full in Shakespear, *f.* in Otway shone *S.* v. 277
Charles, to late times to be transmitted *f. S.* v. 380
Look in that breast, most dirty D—l be *f. S.* vi. 222
Join Cotswold hills to Saperton's *f.* dale *S.* vi. 257
O my *f.* mistress Truth ! shall I quit thee *S.* viii. 200
As the *f.* fields they sold to look so fine *S.* viii. 217
F. Thames, flow gently from thy sacred spring *Sp.* 3
Fresh as the morn, and us the season *f. Sp.* 20
Where twelve *f.* Signs in beauteous order lie *Sp.* 40
All nature laughs, the groves are fresh and *f. Sp.* 73
In those *f.* fields where sacred Isis glides *Su.* 25
F. Daphne's dead, and love is now no more (*refrain*) *W.* 28 &c.
F. Liberty, Britannia's Goddess, rears *W.F.* 91
The Earth's *f.* light, and Empress of the main *W.F.* 164
Thy offspring, Thames ! the *f.* Lodona nam'd *W.F.* 172
Thro' the *f.* scene roll slow the ling'ring streams *W.F.* 217
F. Geraldine, bright object of his vow *W.F.* 297
I see, I see, where two *f.* cities bend *W.F.* 379
Thy trees, *f.* Windsor ! now shall leave their woods *W.F.* 385
O stretch thy reign, *f.* Peace ! from shore to shore *W.F.* 407
Touch the *f.* fame of Albion's golden days *W.F.* 424
Let then the F.-one *beautifully cry M.E.* ii. 11
And Curio, restless by the F.'s side *M.E.* iv. 43
To kill those foes to F—s, *Time and Thought M.E.* ii. 112
The *f.* feel such maladies as these *R.L.* iv. 37

Fairer.
And finds a *f.* Rambouillet in you *E.* iv. 76
Feed *f.* flocks, or richer fleeces shear *Su.* 36

Fairest.
The virtues open *f.* in the shade *M.E.* ii. 202
F. of mortals, thou distinguish'd care *R.L.* i. 27
For you the swains the *f.* flow'rs design *Sn.* 55

Fairly.
The last full *f.* gives it to the *House E.S.* ii. 180
Unless, good man ! he has been *f.* in *E.S.* ii. 192
Come with Petitions *f.* penn'd *I.H.* ii. 65 s.
Both *f.* owning, Riches, in effect *M.E.* iii. 17
Who *f.* puts all Characters to bed *S.* v. 291
The fault he has I *f.* shall reveal *S.* vi. 19
Learn to live well, or *f.* make your will *S.* vi. 322

Fairies.
Fays, F., Genii, Elves, and Dæmons, hear *R.L.* ii. 73

Faith.
Meek modern *f.* to murder, hack, and maul *D.* iii. 210
And damns implicit *f.*, and holy lies *D.* iv. 463
A gen'rous *F.*, from superstition free *Ep.* ii. 9
And *F.*, our early immortality *E.A.* 300
Thus Wit, like *F.*, by each man is apply'd *E.C.* 396
F., Gospel, all, seem'd made to be disputed *E.C.* 442
If *F.* itself has diff'rent dresses worn *E.C.* 446
Convey'd unbroken *f.* from sire to son *E.M.* iii. 228
Love all the *f.*, and all th' allegiance then *E.M.* iii. 235
True *f.*, true policy, united ran *E.M.* iii. 239
Th' enormous *f.* of many made for one *E.M.* iii. 242
The *F.* and Moral, Nature gave before *E.M.* iii. 286
For Modes of *F.* let graceless zealots fight *E.M.* iii. 305
In *F.* and Hope the world will disagree *E.M.* iii. 307
And knows, where *F.*, Law, Morals all began *E.M.* iv. 339
Till lengthen'd on to *F.*, and unconfin'd *E.M.* iv. 343
Hope of known bliss, and *F.* in bliss unknown *E.M.* iv. 346
To pay their Debts, or keep their *F.*, like kings *E.S.* i. 122
Constant *f.*, fair hope, long leisure *O.* iii. 42
F., *gallants*, *board with saints*, *and bed with sinners E.J.S.* 24
F., let the modest Matrons of the town *E.S.* 49
But *f.* your very friends will soon be sore *E.S.* i. 23
Not yet, my Friend ! to-morrow *f.* it may *E.S.* ii. 2
What are you thinking ? *f.* the thought 's no sin *E.S.* ii. 122
F., it imports not much from whom it came *E.S.* ii. 168
F., Sir, you owe as much as I *I.H.* i. 116 s
For *f.*, Lord Fanny, you are in the wrong *S.* ii. 101
F., I shall give the answer Reynard gave *S.* iii. 131
Tho' *f.*, I fear, 'twill break his Mother's heart *S.* vi. 16
F., in such case, if you should prosecute *S.* vi. 23

Faithful.
Still bears them, *f.*; and that thus I eat *D.* iv. 389
Warm from the soul, and *f.* to its fires *E.A.* 54
So when the *f.* pencil has designed *E.C.* 484
His *f.* dog shall bear him company *E.M.* i. 112
The Medal, *f.* to its charge of fame *M.E.* v. 31
In action *f.*, and in honour clear *M.E.* v. 68

Faithless.
This mourn'd a *f.*, that an absent Love *A.* 3
Friendly at Hackney, *f.* at Whitehall *M.E.* i. 76
F. thro' Piety, and dup'd thro' Wit *M.E.* i. 92
The *f.* Column, and the crumbling Bust *M.E.* v. 20

Falchion.
And the broad *f.* in a plough-share end *M.* 62

Falcon.
Say, will the *f.* stooping from above *E.M.* iii. 53

Falkland.
See *F.* dies, the virtuous, and the just *E.M.* iv. 99

Fall.
Grubstreet ! thy *f.* should men and Gods conspire *D.* iii. 311
Beholds thee glorious only in thy *F. E.* i. 20
Or some old temple nodding to its *f. E.M.* iv. 129
And tastes the good without the *f.* to ill *E.M.* iv. 312
But 'tis the *F.* degrades her to a Whore *E.S.* i. 143
In a dying, dying *f. O.* i. 21
Beside the *f.* of fountains *O.* i. 98
Here Britain's statesmen oft the *f.* foredoom *R.L.* iii. 5
"Boast not my *f.*," (he cry'd) "insulting foe *R.L.* v. 97
The fate of Louis, and the *f.* of Rome *R.L.* v. 140
And headlong streams hang list'ning in their *f. Su.* 84
New f—s of water murm'ring in his ear M. 70
Or in proud *f.* magnificently lost *M.E.* iii. 90

FALL'N—FAM'D.

Sees momentary monsters rise and l. *D.* i. 83
Where, faint at best, the beams of Science *f. D.* iii. 84
See the bold Ostrogoths on Latium *f. D.* iii. 93
While Jones' and Boyle's united Labours *f. D.* iii. 328
Which as it dies, or lives, we *f.*, or reign *D.* iv. 186
As many quit the streams that murm'ring *f. D.* iv. 199
And as she turns, the colours *f.* or rise *D.* iv. 540
Thy hand, great Anarch, lets the curtain *f. D.* iv. 655
Should at my feet the world's great master *f. E.A.* 85
And bid alternate passions *f.* and rise *E.C.* 375
And the same age saw Learning *f.*, and Rome *E.C.* 686
A hero perish, or a sparrow *f. E.M.* i. 88
That system only, but the Whole must *f. E.M.* i. 250
Created half to rise, and half to *f. E.M.* ii. 15
Fools! who from hence into the notion *f. E.M.* ii. 211
And just as short of reason he must *f. E.M.* iii. 47
Or indolent, to each extreme they *f. E.M.* iv. 25
Or Change admits, or Nature lets it *f. E.M.* iv. 115
Say, wouldst thou be the Man to whom they *f. E.M.* iv. 276
To *f.* with dignity, with temper rise *E.M.* iv. 378
Would you know when? exactly when they *f. E.S.* i. 90
Stop! stop! Must Satire, then, nor rise nor *f. E.S.* ii. 52
F. by the Votes of their degen'rate Line *E.S.* ii. 253
Rocks *f.* to dust, and mountains melt away *M.* 106
Nothing so true as what you once let *f. M.E.* ii. 1
Choose a firm Cloud, before it *f.*, and in it *M.E.* ii. 19
And Temple rise—then *f.* again to dust *M.E.* ii. 140
And Mistress of herself, tho' China *f. M.E.* ii. 268
Since then, my Lord, on such a World we *f. M.E.* iii. 77
Cutler saw tenants break, and houses *f. M.E.* iii. 323
That tells the Waters or to rise or *f. M.E.* iv. 58
Freedom and Arts together *f. O.* ii. 26
What tender maid but must a victim *f. R.L.* i. 95
If to her share some female errors *f. R.L.* ii. 17
Or whether Heav'n has doom'd that Shock must *f. R.L.* ii. 110
The pierc'd battalions dis-united *f. R.L.* iii. 85
Sooner let earth, air, sea, to Chaos *f. R.L.* v. 119
About one vice, and *f.* into the other *S.* ii. 46
Shall half the new-built Churches round thee *f. S.* ii. 119
From yon old walnut-tree a show'r shall *f. S.* ii. 145
Self-center'd Sun, and Stars that rise or *f. S.* v. 6
And trees, and stones, and farms, and farmer *f. S.* vi. 263
To see themselves *f.* endlong into beasts *S.* viii. 167
Thus shall your wives, and thus your children *f. U.L.* 36
Poets themselves must *f.*, like those they sung *U.L.* 75
They *f.*, and leave their little lives in air *W.F.* 134
Then, from her roofs when Verrio's colours *f. W.F.* 307

Fall'n.

This prose on stilts, that poetry *f.* lame *D.* i. 190
F. in the plash his wickedness had laid *D.* ii. 76
Insults *f.* worth, or Beauty in distress *P.S.* 288
Or when rich China vessels *f.* from high *R.L.* iii. 159

Falling.

When *f.* dews with spangles deck'd the glade *A.* 99
Deepens the murmur of the *f.* floods *E.A.* 169
And drink the *f.* tears each other sheds *E.A.* 350
You too proceed! make *f.* Arts your care *M.E.* iv. 191
And greatly *f.*, with a *f.* state *P.C.* 22
Paint Angels trembling round his *f.* Horse *S.* i. 28

Falls.

See the Cirque *f.*, th' unpillar'd temple nods *D.* iii. 107
Resistless *f.*: the Muse obeys the Pow'r *D.* iv. 628
Then presently he *f.* to tease *I.H.* ii. 79 s
Tell how the Moon-beam trembling *f. I.H.* ii. 189
My Lady *f.* to play; so bad her chance *M.E.* iii. 395
Without it, proud Versailles! thy glory *f. M.E.* iv. 71
Again she *f.*, again she dies, she dies *O.* i. 94
Then prostrate *f.*, and begs with ardent eyes *R.L.* ii. 43
F. undistinguish'd by the victor spade *R.L.* iii. 64
And *f.* like thunder on the prostrate Ace *R.L.* iii. 98
At best, it *f.* to some ungracious son *S.* ii. 173
The silly bard grows fat, or *f.* away *S.* v. 303

False.

Morality, by her *f.* Guardians drawn *D.* iv. 27
Who, *f.* to Phœbus, bow the knee to Baal *D.* iv. 93
F. as his Gems, and canker'd as his Coins *D.* iv. 349
Nor let *f.* Shows, or empty Titles please *E.* iv. 47
From the *f.* world in early youth they fled *E.A.* 131
So by *f.* learning is good sense defac'd *E.C.* 25
F. Eloquence, like the prismatic glass *E.C.* 311

But blame the *f.*, and value still the true *E.C.* 407
F. steps but help them to renew the race *E.C.* 602
All must he *f.* that thwart this One great End *E.M.* iii. 309
See the *f.* scale of Happiness complete *E.M.* iv. 288
For Wit's *f.* mirror held up Nature's light *E.M.* iv. 393
Mine as a Foe profess'd to *f.* Pretence *E.S.* ii. 201
The Fool consistent, and the *F.* sincere *M.E.* i. 176
Hence *f.* tears, deceits, disguises *O.* iii. 38
As vain, as idle, and as *f.*, as they *S.* viii. 22
But thou, *f.* guardian of a charge too good *U.L.* 29

Falsehood.

The dull, flat *F.* serves for policy *M.E.* i. 67
Blunt truths more mischief than nice f—s do E.C. 573
Yet his known *F.* could no Warning prove *Mi.* ix. 73

Fame.

And Poet's vision of eternal *F. D.* iii. 12
All crowd, who foremost shall be damn'd to *f. D.* iii. 158
No more, alas! the voice of *F.* they hear *D.* iv. 543
Who, careless now of Int'rest, *F.*, or Fate *E.* i. 17
And reading wish, like them, our fate and *f. E.* iii. 9
By Nature yielding, stubborn but for *f. E.* iv. 35
The fount of *F.* or Infamy *E.* vi. 12
There died the best of passions, Love and *F. E.A.* 40
August her deed, and sacred be her *f. E.A.* 78
F., wealth and honour! what are you to Love *E.A.* 80
And graft my love immortal on thy *f. E.A.* 344
But you who seek to give and merit *f. E.C.* 46
Seizes your *f.*, and puts his laws in force *E.C.* 168
Some by old words to *f.* have made pretence *E.C.* 324
Now length of *F.* (our second life) is lost *E.C.* 480
Whose *f.* with pains we guard, but lose with ease *E.C.* 504
As next in place to Mantua, next in *f. E.C.* 708
Careless of censure, nor too fond of *f. E.C.* 741
Whate'er the Passion, knowledge, *f.*, or pelf *E.M.* ii. 261
What's *F.*? a fancy'd life in others' breath *E.M.* iv. 237
F. but from death a villain's name can save *E.M.* iv. 249
All *f.* is foreign, but of true desert *E.M.* iv. 253
See Cromwell damn'd to everlasting *f. E.M.* iv. 284
Oh wealth ill-fated! which do act of *f. E.M.* iv. 299
The whole amount of that enormous *f. E.M.* iv. 307
Expanded flies, and gathers all its *f. E.M.* iv. 480
When I confess, there is who feels for *F. E.S.* ii. 64
Do good by stealth, and blush to find it *F. E.S.* ii. 136
Yet softer Honours, and less noisy *F. Ep.* xiv. 9
A fool to Pleasure, yet a slave to *F. M.E.* ii. 62
Be this a Woman's *F.*: with this unblest *M.E.* ii. 281
Who builds a Church to God, and not to *F. M.E.* iii. 285
And *f.*, this lord of useless thousands ends *M.E.* iii. 314
There dwelt a citizen, of sober *f. M.E.* iii. 341
The Medal, faithful to its charge of *f. M.E.* v. 31
Stand emulous of Greek and Roman *f. M.E.* v. 54
One from all Grubstreet will my *f.* defend *P.S.* 111
As yet a child, nor yet a fool to *f. P.S.* 127
True Genius kindles, and fair *F.* inspires *P.S.* 194
Yet absent, wounds an honest author's *f. P.S.* 292
That not for *F.*, but Virtue's better end *P.S.* 342
Belinda now, whom thirst of *f.* invites *R.L.* iii. 25
How shall I, them, your helpless *f.* defend *R.L.* iv. 111
This Lock, the Muse shall consecrate to *f. R.L.* v. 149
Unworthy he, the voice of *F.* to hear *S.* ii. 99
For *F.*, for Riches, for a noble Wife *S.* iv. 39
And what is *F.*? the Meanest have their day *S.* iv. 46
Edward and Henry, now the Boast of *F. S.* v. 7
Above all Greek, above all Roman *F. S.* v. 26
"Permit," (he cries) "no stranger to your *f. S.* viii. 66
What once had beauty, titles, wealth, and *f. U.L.* 70
Like them in beauty, should be like in *f. W.F.* 10
Lost in my *f.*, as in the sea their streams *W.F.* 362
Touch the fair *f.* of Albion's golden days *W.F.* 424
And now had F.'s posterior Trumpet blown D. iv. 71
And while on *F.* triumphal Car they ride *D.* iv. 133
On *F.* mad voyage by the wind of praise *S.* v. 297

Fam'd.

Where o'er the gates by his *f.* father's hand *D.* i. 31
So *f.* like thee for turbulence and horns *D.* ii. 181
Thro' Lud's *f.* gates, along the well-known Fleet *D.* ii. 359
To some *f.* round-house, ever open gate *D.* ii. 424
There in the rich, the honour'd, *f.*, and great *E.M.* iv. 287
In whom a Race, for Courage *f.*, and Art *Ep.* xiv. 11

With honest scorn the first *f.* Cato view'd *P.C.* 39
Above the rest a rural nymph was *f. W.F.* 171
As thine, which visits Windsor's *f.* abodes *W.F.* 229
First the *f.* authors of his ancient name *W.F.* 339

Familiar.
F. White's, "God save King Colley!" cries *D.* i. 319
Bland and *f.* as in life, begun *D.* iii. 41
Bland and *f.* to the throne he came *D.* iv. 497
Yet seen tno oft, *f.* with her face *E.M.* ii. 219
Or at the ear of Eve, *f.* Toad *P.S.* 319
Amid her kindred stars *f.* roam *W.F.* 255

Familiarly.
Will, like a friend, *f.* convey *E.C.* 655

Family.
Hate, Fear, and Grief, the *f.* of pain *E.M.* ii. 118
Go I and pretend your *f.* is young *E.M.* iv. 213
But duly sent his *f.* and wife *M.E.* iii. 382
With all the mournful *f.* of Yews *M.E.* iv. 96
Hear this, and spare his *f.*, James Moore *P.S.* 385
Instruct his *f.* in ev'ry rule *S.* v. 163
He dwells amidst the royal *F. S.* viii. 103
Till friend with friend, and f—ies at strife S. v. 253

Famine.
He saves from *f.*, from the savage saves *E.M.* iii. 64
Some War, some Plague, some *F.* they foresee *M.E.* iii. 113
Between Excess and *F.* lies a mean *S.* ii. 47

Famish'd.
And *f.* dies amidst his ripen'd fields *W.F.* 56

Famous.
Yet surely, surely, these were *f.* men *S.* v. 79

Fan.
While the spread *f.* o'ershades your closing eyes *E.* v. 37
The modest *f.* was lifted up no more *E.C.* 542
The flutt'ring *f.* be Zephyretta's care *R.L.* ii. 112
Snuff, or the *f.*, supply each pause of chat *R.L.* iii. 17
Then grave Clarissa graceful wav'd her *f. R.L.* v. 7
Peep'd in your f—s, been serious, thus, and cry'd E. J.S. 4
F. clap, silks rustle, and tough whalebones crack *R.L.* v. 40
Where'er you walk, cool gales shall f. the glade *Su.* 73

Fancies.
The doctor *f.* he has driv'n them out *E.M.* ii. 160

Fancy.
There motley images her *f.* strike *D.* i. 65
And, instant, *f.* feels th' imputed sense *D.* ii. 200
When *f.* flags, and sense is at a stand *D.* ii. 230
As *F.* opens the quick springs of Sense *D.* iv. 156
Or that bright Image to our *f.* draw *D.* iv. 487
What flatt'ring scenes our wand'ring *f.* wrought *E.* iii. 23
While *f.* brings the vanish'd pile to view *E.* iii. 31
Just when his *f.* points your sprightly eyes *E.* v. 45
My *f.* form'd thee of angelic kind *E.A.* 61
F. restores what vengeance snatch'd away *E.A.* 226
F. and art in gay Petronius please *E.C.* 667
From sounds to things, from *f.* to the heart *E.M.* iv. 392
When Sense subsides, and *F.* sports in sleep *M.E.* i. 46
Fix'd Principles, with *F.* ever new *M.E.* ii. 279
Men prove with child, as pow'rful *f.* works *R.L.* iv. 53
Till *F.* colour'd it, and form'd a Dream *S.* viii. 189
And now on F.'s easy wing convey'd D. iii. 13
Before her *F.* gilded clouds decay *D.* iv. 631
Thee, drest in *F.* airy beam *I.H.* iii. 41
Or *F.* beam enlarges, multiplies *M.E.* i. 35
That not in *F.* maze he wander'd long *P.S.* 340
Who *f. Bliss to Vice, to Virtue Woe E.M.* iv. 94

Fancy'd.
In pensive thought recall the *f.* scene *E.* v. 33
What's Fame? a *f.* life in others' breath *E.M.* iv. 237

Fancy'st.
Call imperfection what thou *f.* such *E.M.* i. 115

Fanes.
F., which admiring Gods with pride survey *M.E.* v. 9
From men their cities, and from Gods their *f. W.F.* 66

Fann'd.
The gen'rous Critic *f.* the Poet's fire *E.C.* 100
Some, as she sipp'd, the fuming liquor *f. R.L.* iii. 114

Fannia.
Here *F.*, leering on her own good man *M.E.* ii. 9

Fannius.
Not *F.*' self more impudently near *S.* viii. 178

Fanny—*see also* Lord Fanny.
Like gentle *F.'s* was my flow'ry theme *P.S.* 140

Fans.
And fierce Thalestris *f.* the rising fire *R.L.* iv. 93
Pants on her neck, and *f.* her parting hair *W.F.* 196

Fantastic.
A tribe, with weeds and shells *f.* crown'd *D.* iv. 398
Alike *f.*, if too new, or old *E.C.* 334
Safe past the Gnome, thro' this *f.* band *R.L.* iv. 55

Far, Farther, Further, Farthest.—*Passim.*
The salient spout *f.-streaming* to the sky *D.* ii. 162

Farce.
How *F.* and Epic get a jumbled race *D.* i. 70
For Swift and him despis'd the *f.* of state *E.* i. 9
Let mine an innocent gay *f.* appear *E.* iv. 25
Call for the *F.*, the Bear, or the Black-joke (*rep.*) *S.* v. 309
Jilts rul'd the state, and statesmen f—s writ E.C. 538

Fare.
Remembers oft the School-boy's simple *f. S.* ii. 73

Farewell.
F., ye woods! adieu the light of day *A.* 94
When the last ling'ring friend has bid *f. E.* i. 34
When, warm in youth, I bade the world *f. E.A.* 110
F., then Verse, and Love, and ev'ry Toy *S.* iii. 17
f. the stage ! if just as thrives the play *S.* v. 302
Adieu, my flocks, *f.* the light of day (*rep.*) *W.* 91

Farm.
Had roasted turnips in the Sabine *f. M.E.* i. 219
There mingled f—s and pyramids appear S. vi. 259
And trees, and stones, and *f.*, and farmer fall *S.* vi. 263
The rest, some f. the Poor-box, some the Pews *S.* iii. 128

Farmer.
Just as a *F.* might a Lord *I.H.* ii. 160
And trees, and stones, and farms, and *f.* fall *S.* vi. 263

Farquhar.
What pert, low Dialogue has *F.* writ *S.* v. 288

Farthings.
His givings rare, save *f.* to the poor *M.E.* iii. 348

Fashion.
These nothing hurts; they keep their *f.* still *E.S.* i. 43
But oh ! these works are not in *f.* now *S.* vii. 122
The suit, if by the *f.* one might guess *S.* viii. 40
Not Fortune's worshipper, nor *F.'s fool P.S.* 334
In words, as f—s, the same rule will hold E.C. 333
Mere wax as yet, you *f.* him with ease *S.* vi. 9

Fast.
F. by, like Niobe (her children gone) *D.* ii. 311
Coach'd, carted, trod upon, now loose, now *f. D.* iii. 291
These build as *f.* as knowledge can destroy *E.M.* ii. 287
It hurries all too *f.* to mark their way *M.E.* i. 38
Tho' fate had *f.* bound her *O.* i. 90
The doubling Lustres dance as *f.* as she *S.* i. 48
Ran out as *f.* as one who pays his bail *S.* viii. 182
And binding Nature *f.* in Fate *U.P.* 11
And, *f.* beside him, once-fear'd Edward sleeps *W.F.* 314

Faster.
The more thou ticklest, gripes his fist the *f. D.* ii. 210

Fasts.
Nor pray'rs nor *f.*, its stubborn pulse restrain *E.A.* 27
Silence without, and *F.* within the wall *M.E.* iii. 188
Carthusian *f.*, and fulsome Bacchanals *S.* vii. 118

Fat.

In the *f.* age of pleasure, wealth, and ease *E.C.* 534
'Twas a *f.* Oyster. Live in Peace. Adieu *Mi.* xi, 12
Some with *f.* Bucks on childless dotards fawn *S.* iii. 130
The silly bard grows *f.*, or falls away *S.* v. 303
Lords of *f.* E'sham, or of Lincoln fen *S.* vi. 241

Fatal.

Dear *f.* name I rest ever unreveal'd *E.A.* 9
This *f.* stroke, this unforeseen Distress *Mi.* ix. 20
'Twas my own Lord that drew the *f.* Card *Mi.* ix. 48
How wilt thou now the *f.* sisters move *O.* i. 95
Ev'n then, before the *f.* engine clos'd *R.L.* iii. 149
Uncurl'd it hangs, the *f.* shears demands *R.L.* iv. 173

Fate.

Call'd to this work by Dulness, Jove, and *F. D.* i. 4
F. in their dotage this fair Idiot gave *D.* i. 13
Blasphem'd his Gods, the Dice, and damn'd his *F. D.* i. 116
But blind to former, as to future *f. D.* iii. 47
Now look thro' *F.* I behold the scene she draws *D.* iii. 127
From the strong *f.* of drams if thou get free *D.* iii. 145
But *f.* with butchers plac'd thy priestly stall *D.* iii. 209
These *F.* reserv'd to grace thy reign divine *D.* iii. 275
Hibernian Politics, O Swift! thy *f. D.* 331
Who, careless now of Int'rest, Fame, or *F. E.* i. 17
And reading wish, like theirs, our *f.* and fame *E.* iii. 9
Sure to charm all was his peculiar *f. E.* iv. 5
Till *f.* scarce felt his gentle breath suppress *E.* iv. 13
Then too, when *f.* shall thy fair frame destroy *E.A.* 337
And sure, if *f.* some future bard shall join *E.A.* 359
Heav'n from all creatures hides the book of *F. E.M.* ii. 77
Laws wise as Nature, and as fix'd as *F. E.M.* iii. 190
Now for two ages having snatch'd from *f. Ep.* viii. 3
A Poet, blest beyond a Poet's *f. Ep.* x. 3
Could save a Parent's justest Pride from *f. Ep.* xiv. 3
And yet the *f.* of all extremes is such *M.E.* i. 9
A salmon's belly, Helluo, was thy *f. M.E.* i. 238
But mark the *f.* of a whole Sex of Queens *M.E.* ii. 219
To some indeed, Heav'n grants a happier *f. M.E.* iii. 87
Damn'd to the mines, an equal *f.* betides *M.E.* iii. 109
And one *f.* buries in th' Asturian Mines *M.E.* iii. 132
A wizard told him in these words our *f. M.E.* iii. 134
His Grace's *f.* sage Cutler could foresee *M.E.* iii. 315
See! sportive *f.*, to punish awkward pride *M.E.* iv. 19
Our *F.* thou only canst adjourn *Mi.* iv. 37
Melody resigns to *F. Mi.* vii. 32
Though *f.* had fast bound her *O.* i. 90
A brave man struggling in the storms of *f. P.C.* 21
Anxious and trembling for the birth of *F. R.L.* i, 142
Him Basto follow'd, but his *f.* more hard *R.L.* iii. 53
Now to the Baron *f.* inclined the field *R.L.* iii. 66
In heaps on heaps; one *f.* o'erwhelms them all *R.L.* iii. 86
On one nice Trick depends the gen'ral *f. R.L.* iii. 94
Oh thoughtless mortals! ever blind to *f. R.L.* iii. 101
Fear the just Gods, and think of Scylla's *F. R.L.* iii. 122
Resign'd to *f.*, and with a sigh retir'd *R.L.* iii. 146
F. urged the shears, and cut the Sylph in twain *R.L.* iii. 152
And monuments, like men, submit to *f. R.L.* iii. 172
A Sylph too warn'd me of the threats of *f. R.L.* iv. 165
And in its fellow's *f.* foresees its own *R.L.* iv. 172
But *F.* and Jove had stopp'd the Baron's ears *R.L.* v. 2
Now meet thy *f.*, incens'd Belinda cry'd *R.L.* v. 87
The *f.* of Louis, and the fall of Rome *R.L.* v. 140
And ev'ry friend the less lament my *f. S.* i. 62
From furious Sappho scarce a milder *f. S.* i. 83
Whate'er my *f.*, or well or ill at Court *S.* i. 92
With Praise or Infamy leave that to *f. S.* iii. 102
Sure *f.* of all, beneath whose rising ray *S.* v. 19
Besides, a *f.* attends on all I write *S.* v. 408
Well, on the whole, plain Prose must be my *f. S.* vi. 198
F. snatch'd her early to the pitying sky *U.L.* 24
Thy *f.* unpity'd, and thy rites unpaid *U.L.* 48
And binding Nature fast in *F. U.P.* 11
Oh sing of Daphne's *f.*, and Daphne's praise *W.* 8
The silver swan her hapless *f.* bemoan *W.* 39
Her *f.* is whisper'd by the gentle breeze *W.* 61
Her *f.* remurmur to the silver flood *W.* 64
Lodona's *f.*, in long oblivion cast *W.F.* 173
Since *f.* relentless stopp'd their heav'nly voice *W.F.* 277
And bring the scenes of op'ning *f.* to light *W.F.* 426
And *f.*'s severest rage disarm *O.* i. 119
Display'd the *f—s her confessors endure D.* ii. 145
So may the *f.* preserve the ears you lend *D.* iii. 214
But, Madam, if the *f.* withstand, and you *E.* iv. 57
For thee the *f.*, severely kind, ordain *E.A.* 249
Our *f.* and fortunes, as the winds shall blow *M.E.* iii. 46
When Athens sinks by *f.* unjust *O.* ii. 17
But what, or where, the *f.* have wrapt in night *R.L.* ii. 104
His *Office* keeps your Parchment *f.* entire *S.* vii. 71

Father.

To the mild Limbo of our *F.* Tate *D.* i. 238
Thus the great *F.* to the greater Son *D.* iii. 42
Come then, my *f.*, brother, husband, friend *E.A.* 152
A Prince the *F.* of a People made *E.M.* iii. 214
Our great first *f.*, and that first ador'd *E.M.* iii. 226
And own'd a *F.* when he own'd a God *E.M.* iii. 234
When his lewd *f.* gave the dire disease *E.M.* iv. 120
Or gave his *F.* Grief but when he died *Ep.* iii. 4
'Tis all a *F.*, all a Friend can give *Ep.* vii. 20
May Heav'n, dear *F.* I now have all thy Heart *Ep.* xiii. 2
There died my *F.*, no man's Debtor *I.H.* i. 79
The promis'd *f.* of the future age *M.* 56
Has made the *f.* of a nameless race *M.E.* i. 233
The surge, and plunge his *F.* in the deep *M.E.* iii. 354
As son, as *f.*, brother, husband, friend *O.* iii. 28
No duty broke, no *f.* disobey'd *P.S.* 130
A friend in exile, or a *f.* dead *P.S.* 355
His *f.*, mother, body, soul, and muse (*rep.*) *P.S.* 381
Who cries, "My *f.*'s damn'd, and all's my own" *S.* ii. 174
And God the *F.* turns a School-divine *S.* v. 102
Who scorn a Lad should teach his *f.* skill *S.* v. 129
Besides, my *F.* taught me from a lad *S.* vi. 54
F. of All! in ev'ry Age *U.P.* 1
In vain on *f.* Thames she calls for aid *W.F.* 197
Thou, too, great *f.* of the British floods *W.F.* 219
Old *f.* Thames advanc'd his rev'rend head *W.F.* 330
When o'er the gates by his fam'd *f.*'s hand *D.* i. 31
Works damn'd, or to be damn'd! (your *f.* fault) *D.* i. 226
Bless'd with his *f.* front, his mother's tongue *D.* ii. 416
Yet oh, my sons, a *f.* words attend *D.* iii. 213
No weeping orphan saw his *f.* stores *E.A.* 135
There, where no *F.*, Brother's, Friend's disgrace *E.S.* i. 99
And, with a *F.* sorrows, mix his own *Ep.* iii. 8
Foe to the Dryads of his *F.* groves *M.E.* iv. 94
His *F.* Acres who enjoys in peace *M.E.* iv. 181
As her dead *F.* rev'rend image past *P.C.* 31
A Clerk, foredoom'd his *f.* soul to cross *P.S.* 17
In forest planted by a *f.* hand *S.* ii. 135
My lands are sold, my *f.* house is gone *S.* ii. 155
We think our f—s fools, so wise we grow E.C. 438
Nor own your *f.* have been fools so long *E.M.* iv. 214
Whose sons shall blush their *f.* were thy foes *E.M.* iv. 388
And for that cause which made your *F.* shine *E.S.* ii. 252
They pleas'd the *F.* of poetic rage *M.E.* v. 50
Our *F.* prais'd rank Ven'son. You suppose (*rep.*) *S.* ii. 91
Or say our *F.* never broke a rule *S.* v. 93
How will our *F.* rise up in a rage *S.* v. 125
To worship like his *F.* was his care *S.* v. 165
Are *F.* of the Church for writing less *S.* vii. 98
Our sons their f—s' failing language see E.C. 482
But by your *f.* worth if yours you rate *E.M.* iv. 209
For Use will f. what's begot by Sense S. vi. 170

Fathoms.

Our depths who *f.*, or our shallows finds *M.E.* i. 23

Fatigu'd.

"Shut, shut the door, good John!" *f.*, I said *P.S.* 1

Fatigues.

That Charm shall grow, while what *f.* the Ring *M.E.* ii. 251

Fatten.

F. the Courtier, starve the learned band *D.* i. 315

Fault.

Works damn'd, or to be damn'd! (your father's *f.*) *D.* i. 226
I mourn the lover, not lament the *f. E.A.* 185
Avoid extremes; and shun the *f.* of such *E.C.* 384
Before his sacred name flies ev'ry *f. E.C.* 422

FAULTLESS—FEATHER'D.

Yet shun their *f.*, who, scandalously nice *E.C.* 556
Then say not Man's imperfect, Heav'n in *f. E.M.* i. 69
By any Trick, or any *F. I.H.* ii. 144
What then? let Blood and Body bear the *f. M.E.* ii. 73
Is but to please, can Pleasure seem a *f. M.E.* ii. 212
Mend Fortune's *f.*, and justify her grace *M.E.* iii. 232
Just hint a *f.*, and hesitate dislike *P.S.* 204
I guess; and, with their leave, will tell the *f. S.* v. 357
The *f.* he has I fairly shall reveal *S.* vi. 19
The glorious *f.* of Angels and of Gods *U.L.* 14
To hide the *F.* I see *U.P.* 38
And rise to f—s true Critics dare not mend *E.C.* 160
Those freer beauties, ev'n in them, seem *f. E.C.* 170
Survey the Whole, nor seek slight *f.* to find *E.C.* 235
That shunning *f.*, one quiet tenour keep *E.C.* 241
Applause, in spite of trivial *f.*, is due *E.C.* 258
Nay show'd his *f.*—but when would Poets mend *E.C.* 621
Who to a friend his *f.* can freely show *E.C.* 637
Not free from *f.*, nor yet too vain to mend *E.C.* 744
To see all others' *f.*, and feel our own *E.M.* iv. 262
Or her, that owns her *f.*, but never mends *M.E.* ii. 103
"Has she no *f.* then (Envy says), Sir?" *Mi.* viii. 9
Might hide her *f.*, if Belles had *f.* to hide *R.L.* ii. 16
But let them own that greater *F.* than we *S.* v. 95

Faultless.
Free as thy stroke, yet *f.* as thy line *E.* iii. 64
Whoever thinks a *f.* piece to see *E.C.* 253

Faustus.
Hell thou shalt move; for *F.* is our friend *D.* iii. 308

Favonio.
The honey dropping from *F.*'s tongue *E.S.* i. 67

Favour.
Unbiass'd or by *f.* or by spite *E.C.* 633
Forbid it Heav'n, a *F.* or a Debt *M.E.* ii. 171
Alone deserves the *F.* of the Great *S.* v. 349
But sure no statute in his *f.* says *S.* vi. 288
My Lord, your F—s well I know *I.H.* i. 21
Scatter your *F.* on a Fop *I.H.* i. 31
F. to none, to all she smiles extends *R.L.* ii. 11

Favour'd.
She oft had *f.* him, and favours yet *D.* ii. 102
Than *f.* Man by touch ethereal slain *E.M.* iii. 68

Fav'ring.
I neither strut with ev'ry *f.* breath *S.* vi. 300

Favourite, Fav'rite.
Like a King's *F.* or like a King *S.* vii. 78
With royal F—s in flatt'ry vie *S.* viii. 60
This f——e Isle, long sever'd from her reign *D.* iii. 125
In this weak queen some *f.* still obey *E.M.* ii. 150
Picks from each sex, to make the *F.* blest *M.E.* ii. 273
She dares to steal my *F.* Lover's heart *Mi.* ix. 66
Do thou, Crispissa, tend her *f.* Lock *R.L.* ii. 115
Who snatch'd my best, my *f.* curl away *R.L.* iv. 148
A F.'s Porter with his Master vie *E.S.* i. 117
Prone for his f—s to reverse the laws *E.M.* iv. 122

Favours.
She oft had favour'd him, and *f.* yet *D.* ii. 102
His Sov'reign *f.*, and his Country loves *W.F.* 236

Fawn.
Who for thy table feeds the wanton *f. E.M.* iii. 29
Some with fat Bucks on childless dotards f. *S.* iii. 130

Fawning.
Dext'rous the craving, *f.* crowd to quit *E.* i. 11
The *f.* Servant turns a haughty Lord *E.* iv. 44

Fays.
F., Fairies, Genii, Elves, and Dæmons, hear *R.L.* ii. 74

Fear.
Which nor to Guilt nor *F.*, its Caution owes *E.* ii. 3
Ev'n superstition loses ev'ry *f. E.A.* 315
Hate, *F.*, and Grief, the family of Pain *E.M.* ii. 118
From spleen, from obstinacy, hate, or *f. M.E.* ii. 186
F. to the statesman, rashness to the chief *E.M.* ii. 243
The hour conceal'd, and so remote the *f. E.M.* iii. 75
Grew by like means, and join'd thro' love or *f. E.M.* iii. 202

F. made her Devils, and weak Hope her Gods *E.M.* iii. 256
While those are plac'd in Hope, and these in *F. E.M.* iv. 70
'Twas all for *f.* the Knaves should call him Fool *M.E.* i. 207
Without a Pain, a Trouble, or a *F. Mi.* v. 16
'Tis a *f.* that starts at shadows *Mi.* vi. 3
Give Virtue scandal, Innocence a *f. P.S.* 285
And view this dreadful All without a *f. S.* iv. 10
The *f.* to want them is as weak a thing *S.* iv. 19
Does neither Rage inflame, nor *F.* appal (rep.) *S.* vi. 308
Base *F.* becomes the guilty, not the free *S.* viii. 194
Fierce champion Fortitude, that knows no f—s *D.* i. 47
The virgin's wish without her *f.* impart *E.A.* 55
I lose all Mem'ry of my former *F. Mi.* ix. 94
A Vial next she fills with fainting *f. R.L.* iv. 85
Fear held them mute. Alone untaught to f. *D.* ii. 57
'Tis what the vicious *f.*, the virtuous shun *E.C.* 506
Nor *f.* a dearth in these flagitious times *E.C.* 529
F. not the anger of the wise to raise *E.C.* 582
F. most to tax an Honourable fool *E.C.* 588
For Fools rush in where Angels *f.* to tread *E.C.* 625
No ill could *f.* in God; and understood *E.M.* iii. 237
All *f.*, none aid yon, and few understand *E.M.* iv. 266
Saw nothing to regret, or there to *f. Ep.* x. 8
Alas! they *f.* a man will cost a plum *M.E.* iii. 122
F. the just Gods, and think of Scylla's Fate *R.L.* iii. 122
Tho' faith, 1 *f.*, 'twill break his mother's heart *S.* vi. 16

Fear'd.
Living, great Nature *f.* he might outvie *Ep.* viii. 7
Nor *f.* the Chief th' unequal fight to try *R.L.* v. 76
Who felt the wrong, or *f.* it, took th' alarm *S.* v. 255

Fearful.
How soft is Silia 1 *f.* to offend *M.E.* ii. 29

Fearing.
The coxcomb hit, or *f.* to be hit *P.S.* 345

Fearless.
In *f.* youth we tempt the heights of Arts *E.C.* 220

Fears.
Nor *f.* to tell, that Mortimer is he *E.* i. 40
Beauty, frail flow'r that ev'ry season *f. E.* ii. 57
Who now that obsolete Example *f. E.S.* ii. 56
Her works; and dying, *f.* herself may die *Ep.* viii. 8

Feast.
Much to the mindful Queen the *f.* recalls *D.* i. 95
Or issue Members of an Annual *f. D.* iv. 574
Nay, feasts the animal he dooms his *f. E.M.* iii. 65
The creature had his *f.* of life before (rep.) *E.M.* iii. 69
From Nature's temp'rate *f.* rose satisfy'd *Ep.* x. 9
Pray take them, Sir.—Enough's a *F. I.H.* i. 25
As Helino, late Dictator of the *F. M.E.* ii. 79
The *f.* his tow'ring genius marks *Mi.* xii. 9
The *F.* of Reason, and the Flow of Soul *S.* i. 128
And the rich *f.* concludes extremely poor *S.* ii. 34
At such a *f.*, old vinegar to spare *S.* ii. 57
Rise from a Clergy, or a City *f. S.* ii. 76
From Latian Syrens, French Circean f—s *S.* iv. 122
With *f.*, and off'rings, and a thankful strain *S.* v. 244
In crowds, and courts, law, business, *f.*, and friends *S.* vi. 91

Feasts.
Nay, *f.* the animal he dooms his feast *E.M.* iii. 65

Feat.
If then plain bread and milk will do the *f. S.* ii. 15

Feather.
Rolli the *f.* to his ear conveys *D.* ii. 203
A *F.* shooting from another's head *D.* iv. 521
A Wit's a *f.*, and a Chief's a rod *E.M.* iv. 247
Nor Boileau turn the *F.* to a Star *E.S.* ii. 231
A brain of f—s, and a heart of lead *D.* ii. 44
Except you eat the *f.* green and gold *S.* ii. 20

Feather'd.
For her, the *f.* quires neglect their song *A.* 24
And *f.* people crowd my wealthy side *W.F.* 404

Feature.

And each ferocious *f.* grim with ooze *D.* ii. 328
'Tis a Virgin, hard of *F. Mi.* vi. 5
Belies his f—s, nay extends his hand *M.E.* iii. 294

Fed.

Wolves gave thee suck, and savage Tigers *f. A.* 90
No murder cloth'd him, and no murder *f. E.M.* iii. 154
But sometimes Virtue starves, while Vice is *f. E.M.* iv. 149
Yet hence the Poor are cloth'd, the Hungry *f. M.E.* iv. 169
A vapour *f.* from wild desire *O.* iii. 19
F. with soft dedication all day long *P:S.* 233
Let me extol a Cat, on oysters *f. S.* ii. 41
But while the subject starv'd, the beast was *f. W.F.* 60
Then gath'ring flocks on unknown mountains *f. W.F.* 87

Fee.

Advice; and (as you use) without a *F. S.* i. 10

Feeble.

Next plung'd a *f.*, but a desp'rate pack *D.* iii. 305
While expletives their *f.* aid do join *E.C.* 346

Feed.

Each vital humour which should *f.* the whole *E.M.* ii. 139
All *f.* on one vain Patron, and enjoy *E.M.* iii. 61
From tail to mouth, they *f.* and they carouse *E.S.* ii. 179
Whose ample Lawns are not asham'd to *f. M.E.* iv. 185
F. here my lambs, I'll seek no distant field *Sp.* 64
F. fairer flocks, or richer fleeces shear *Su.* 36

Feeds.

With spirits *f.*, with vigour fills the whole *E.C.* 77
Who for thy table *f.* the wanton fawn *E.M.* iii. 29
Or pours profuse on earth, one nature *f. E.M.* iii. 117
F. from his band, and in his bosom warms *M.* 54
He *f.* yon Alms-house, neat, but void of state *M.E.* iii. 265
And in the new-shorn field the partridge *f. W.F.* 98

Feel.

The young, the old, who *f.* her inward sway *D.* iv. 73
He best can paint 'em who shall *f.* 'em most *E.A.* 366
Tho' each may *f.* increases and decays *E.C.* 404
Or never *f.* the rage, or never own *E.M.* ii. 228
Abstract what others *f.*, what others think *E.M.* iv. 45
If Calvin *f.* Heav'n's blessing, or its rod *E.M.* iv. 139
All that we *f.* of it begins and ends *E.M.* iv. 241
To see all others' faults, and *f.* our own *E.M.* iv. 262
Decay of Parts, alas! we all must *f. E.S.* i. 5
So—Satire is no more—I *f.* it die *E.S.* i. 83
When I confess, there is who *f.* for Fame *E.S.* ii. 64
And mine as Man, who *f.* for all mankind *E.S.* ii. 204
And Hell's grim Tyrant *f.* th' eternal wound *M.* 48
Shall *f.* your ruling passion strong in death *M.E.* i. 263
Yet numbers *f.* the want of what he had *M.E.* iii. 332
'Twas all th' Ambition his high soul could *f. M.E.* iii. 3
And Arts but soften us to *f.* thy flame *O.* iii. 4
Satire or sense, alas! can *Sporus f., P.S.* 307
Shall *f.* sharp vengeance soon o'ertake his sins *R.L.* ii. 125
Or, as Ixion fix'd, the wretch shall *f. R.L.* ii. 133
What wonder then, fair nymph! thy hairs should *f. R.L.* iii. 177
The fair ones *f.* such maladies as these *R.L.* iv. 37
And *f.* some comfort, not to be a fool *S.* iii. 48
True, conscious Honour is to *f.* no sin *S.* iii. 93
Oppress'd we *f.* the beam directly beat *S.* v. 21
Can make me *f.* each Passion that he feigns *S.* v. 343
Men only *f.* the Smart, but not the Vice *S.* vi. 217
Teach me to *f.* another's woe *U.P.* 37
The clam'rous lapwings *f.* the leaden death *W.F.* 132
There hateful Envy her own snakes shall *f. W.F.* 419

Feels.

And instant, fancy *f.* th' imputed sense *D.* ii. 200
Why *f.* my heart its long-forgotten heat *E.A.* 6
F. at each thread, and lives along the line *E.M.* i. 218
Which sees no more the stroke, or *f.* the pain *E.M.* iii. 67
And more true joy Marcellus exil'd *f. E.M.* iv. 257
Which who but *f.* can taste, but thinks can know *E.M.* iv. 282
And the gay Courtier *f.* the sigh sincere *Ep.* ix. 6
Its proper pow'r to hurt, each creature *f. S.* i. 85

And *f.* that grace his pray'r besought in vain *S.* v. 238
Satan himself *f.* far less joy than they *S.* vii. 90
Sharp Boreas blows, and Nature *f.* decay *W.* 87
Short is his joy; he *f.* the fiery wound *W.F.* 113

Feet—*see* Foot.

Feign.

A Face untaught to *f.*, a judging Eye *E.* ii. 5
F. what I will, and paint it e'er so strong *E.S.* ii. 8
Reduc'd to *f.* it, when they give no more *M.E.* ii. 238
Nay all that lying Travellers can *f. S.* viii. 31

Feign'd.

And those *f.* sighs which cheat the list'ning Fair *Mi.* ix. 8

Feigns.

Can make me feel each Passion that he *f. S.* v. 343
But *f.* a laugh, to see me search around *Sp.* 55

Fell.

Aw'd, on my bended knees I *f. E.* vi. 9
Canst thou forget what tears that moment *f. E.A.* 109
Aspiring to be Gods, if Angels *f. E.M.* i. 127
One thinks on Calvin Heav'n's own spirit *f. E.M.* iv. 137
Thrice from my trembling hand the patch-box *f. R.L.* iv. 162
Newmarket's Glory rose, as Britain's *f. S.* v. 144
Not quite a madman, tho' a pasty *f. S.* vi. 190

Fellow.

Worth makes the man, the want of it the *f. E.M.* iv. 203
But when he heard th' Affront the *F.* gave *E.S.* ii. 152
And gave the harmless *f.* a good word *Mi.* iii. 6
I have but one, I hope the *f.*'s clean *S.* viii. 111
And in its f.'s *fate foresees its own R.L.* iv. 172
Beasts, urg'd by us, their f.-beasts *pursue W.F.* 123
Pair'd with his *F.-Charioteer* the Sun *D.* iv. 588

Felons.

How with less reading than makes *f.* 'scape *D.* i. 281
At Fig's, at White's, with *f.*, or a whore *S.* viii. 213

Felt.

At last Centlivre *f.* her voice to fail *D.* ii. 411
The moon-struck Prophet *f.* the madding hour *D.* iv. 12
Thus at her *f.* approach, and secret might *D.* iv. 639
Till fate scarce *f.* his gentle breath supprest *E.* iv. 13
Nor share one pang of all I *f.* for thee *E.A.* 292
From the same foes, at last, both *f.* their doom *E.C.* 685
That never air or ocean *f.* the wind *E.M.* ii. 167
Some *f.* the silent stroke of mould'ring age *M.E.* v. 11
E'er *f.* such rage, resentment and despair *R.L.* v. 9
Who *f.* the wrong, or fear'd it, took th' alarm *S.* v. 255
We conquer'd France, but *f.* our Captive's charms *S.* v. 263
I *f.* th' infection slide from him to me *S.* viii. 170
Here noble Surrey *f.* the sacred rage *W.F.* 291

Female.

Nor Virtue, male or *f.*, can we name *E.M.* ii. 193
Not with those toys the *f.* world admire *Mi.* v. 3
'Tis these that early taint the *f.* soul *R.L.* i. 87
If to her share some *f.* errors fall *R.L.* ii. 17
Parent of vapours and of *f.* wit *R.L.* iv. 59
There she collects the force of *f.* lungs *R.L.* iv. 83

Fen.

Lords of fat E'sham, or of Lincoln *f. S.* vi. 241

Fence.

Oft have we known that sev'n-fold *f.* to fail *R.L.* ii. 119

Fencing.

Then strongly *f.* ill-got wealth by law *S.* vii. 93

Ferments.

Ye vig'rous swains, while youth *f.* your blood *W.F.* 93

Ferocious.

And each *f.* feature grim with ooze *D.* ii. 328

Fetch.

To *f.* and carry nonsense for my Lord *E.C.* 417
Or *f.* the aërial eagle to the ground *E.M.* iii. 42
Can pocket States, can *f.* or carry Kings *M.E.* iii. 42
To *f.* and carry sing-song up and down *P.S.* 226

FEVER—FIGURE.

Fever.
Between the Fits this *F.* of the soul *S.* iii. 58
And F—s *raging up and down* I.H. i. 13

Few, Fewer.—*Passim.*

Fib.
Nor stop at Flattery or *F. E.* vi. 24
Destroy his *f.* or sophistry, in vain *P.S.* 91
Not ——'s *self e'er tells more* F—s *than I S.* v. 176

Fibre.
Some unmark'd *f.*, or some varying vein *M.E.* i. 16

Fickle.
A Spark too *f.*, or a Spouse too kind *M.E.* ii. 94

Fiction.
Make Satire a Lampoon, and *F.*, Lie *P.S.* 302

Fiddle.
At once the Bear and *F.* of the town *D.* i. 224
Teach Kings to *f.*, or make Senates dance *D.* iv. 598

Fiddler.
Without a *F.*, Flatt'rer, or Buffoon *M.E.* iii. 240

Field.
In their loose traces from the *f.* retreat *A.* 62
The *f.* of glory is a *f.* for all *D.* ii. 32
And if a Vice dares keep the *f. E.* vi. 7
Together let us beat this ample *f. E.M.* i. 9
Who taught the nations of the *f.* and wood *E.M.* iii. 99
Learn from the beasts the physic of the *f. E.M.* iii. 174
Or reap'd in iron harvests of the *f. E.M.* iv. 12
And shake alike the Senate and the *F. E.S.* ii. 87
And the same hand that sow'd shall reap the *f. M.* 66
And what comes then is master of the *f. M.E.* i. 44
Charles to the Convent, Philip to the *F. M.E.* i. 108
He finds at last be better likes a *F. M.E.* iv. 88
And march'd a victor from the verdant *f. R.L.* iii. 52
Now to the Baron fate inclines the *f. R.L.* iii. 66
Feed here my lambs, I'll seek no distant *f. Sp.* 64
When weary reapers quit the sultry *f. Su.* 65
And swell the future harvest of the *f. W.* 16
No rich perfumes refresh the fruitful *f. W.* 47
And in the new-shorn *f.* the partridge feeds *W.F.* 98
Secure they trust the unfaithful *f.* beset *W.F.* 103
Draw monarchs chain'd, and Cressi's glorious *f. W.F.* 305
Curs'd be the *f*—s *that cause my Delia's stay A.* 32
In Tot'nham *f.* the brethren with amaze *D.* ii. 261
Or ask of yonder argent *f.* above *E.M.* i. 41
Nor *f.* with gleaming steel be cover'd o'er *M.* 59
Whose herds with milk, whose *f.* with bread *O.* iv. 5
And sport and flutter in the *f.* of Air *R.L.* i. 66
Some in the *f.* of purest Æther play *R.L.* ii. 77
What seas you travers'd, and what *f.* you fought *S.* v. 396
Delightful Abs-court, if its *f.* afford *S.* vi. 232
Large as the *f.* themselves, and larger far *S.* vii. 95
As the fair *f.* they sold to look so fine *S.* viii. 217
First in these *f.* I try the sylvan strains *Sp.* 1
In spring the *f.*, in autumn hills I love *Sp.* 77
Nay tell me first, in what more happy *f. Sp.* 89
In those fair *f.* where sacred Isis glides *Su.* 25
F. ever fresh, and groves for ever green *W.* 72
And midst the desert fruitful *f.* arise *W.F.* 26
And famish'd dies amidst his ripen'd *f. W.F.* 56
The *f.* are ravish'd from th' industrious swains *W.F.* 65
The woods and *f.* their pleasing toils deny *W.F.* 120
And of their fragrant physic spoils the *f. W.F.* 242
First in these *f.* I sung the sylvan strains *W.F.* 434

Fiends.
And ten-horn'd *f.* and Giants rush to war *D.* iii. 236
Assist the *f.*, and tear me from my God *E.A.* 288
No *f.* torment, no Christians thirst for gold *E.M.* 1. 108
Saw Gods descend, and *f.* infernal rise *E.M.* iii. 254
Now glaring *f.*, and snakes on rolling spires *R.L.* iv. 43
The Poet's hell, its tortures, *f.*, and flames *S.* viii. 7

Fierce.
Got by *f.* whirlwinds, and in thunder born *A.* 92
F. champion Fortitude, that knows no fears *D.* i. 47
See the *f.* Visigoths in Spain and Gaul *D.* iii. 94
Horneck's *f.* eye, and Roome's funereal frown *D.* iii. 152
Mid snows of paper, and *f.* hail of pease *D.* iii. 262
Each *f.* Logician, still expelling Locke *D.* iv. 196
F. as a startled Adder, swell'd and said *D.* iv. 373
Now his *f.* eyes with sparkling fury glow *E.C.* 378
Like some *f.* Tyrant in old tapestry *E.C.* 587
F. for the liberties of wit, and bold *E.C.* 717
Pours *f.* Ambition in a Cæsar's mind *E.M.* i. 159
Nor ends the pleasure with the *f.* embrace *E.M.* iii. 123
No Bandit *f.*, no Tyrant mad with pride *E.M.* iv. 41
Then why so few commended? Not so *f. E.S.* ii. 104
Mother too *f.* of dear Desires *I.H.* iii. 7
That name the learn'd with *f.* disputes pursue *M.E.* v. 17
A desp'rate *Bulwark*, sturdy, firm, and *f. Mi.* ii. 13
Or brew *f.* tempests on the wintry main *R.L.* ii. 85
Not tyrants *f.* that unrepenting die *R.L.* iv. 7
And *f.* Thalestris fans the rising fire *R.L.* iv. 94
"To arms, to arms!" the *f.* Virago cries *R.L.* v. 37
See, *f.* Belinda on the Baron flies *R.L.* v. 75
Not *f.* Othello in so loud a strain *R.L.* v. 105
What? like Sir Richard, rumbling, rough, and *f. S.* i. 23
When the *f.* eagle cleaves the liquid sky *W.F.* 186

Fiercer.
No *f.* sons, had Easter never been *D.* iii. 118
Secure from Flames, from Envy's *f.* rage *E.C.* 183
And turn'd on Man a *f.* savage, Man *E.M.* iii. 168
On me love's *f.* flames for ever prey *Su.* 91

Fiercest.
Music the *f.* grief can charm *O.* i. 118

Fiery.
His *f.* course, or drives him o'er the plains *E.M.* i. 62
The *f.* soul abhorr'd in Catiline *E.M.* ii. 199
The Sprites of *f.* Termagants in Flame *R.L.* i. 59
The silver lamp; the *f.* spirits blaze *R.L.* iii. 108
Short is his joy; he feels the *f.* wound *W.F.* 113
Now Cancer glows with Phœbus' *f.* car *W.F.* 147

Fifteen.
Who rule the sex to fifty from *f. R.L.* iv. 58

Fifty.
Near *f.*, and without a Wife *I.H.* i. 73
Nor circle sober *f.* with thy Charms *I.H.* iii. 6
He thinks a Loaf will rise to *f.* pound *M.E.* iii. 116
With *F.* Guineas (a great Pen'worth) bought *Mi.* ix. 30
To *f.* chosen Sylphs, of special note *R.L.* i. 77
Who rule the sex to *f.* from fifteen *R.L.* iv. 58
On the broad base of *f.* thousand rise *S.* iv. 74
Add *f.* more, and bring it to a square *S.* iv. 76

Fig.
At *F.'s*, at White's, with felons, or a whore *S.* viii. 213
And f—s *from standard and espalier join S.* ii. 147

Fight.
Present the spear and arm him for the *f. R.L.* iii. 130
Clapp'd his glad wings, and sate to view the *f. R.L.* v. 54
Nor fear'd the Chief th' unequal *f.* to try *R.L.* v. 77
That threats a *f.*, and spurns the rising sand *Sp.* 48
And mow'd down armies in the f—s *of Lu R.L.* iii. 62
Heav'n's Swiss, who *f. for any God*, or Man *D.* ii. 358
Let subtle schoolmen teach these friends to *f. E.M.* ii. 81
Passions, like Elements, tho' born to *f. E.M.* ii. 111
For modes of Faith let graceless zealots *f. E.M.* iii. 305
In vain may Heroes *f.*, and Patriots rave *M.E.* iii. 33
There Gladiators *f.* or die in flow'rs *M.E.* iv. 124
A Scot will *f.* for Christ's Kirk o' the Green *S.* v. 40
Like Gods they *f.*, nor dread a mortal wound *R.L.* v. 44

Fights.
Where Folly *f.* for kings, or dives for gain *E.M.* iv. 154
Who drinks, whores, *f.*, and in a duel dies *M.E.* iii. 390

Figure.
Wide as a wind-mill all his *f.* spread *D.* ii. 66
And each bold *f.* just begins to live *E.C.* 491
Show'd Rome her Cato's *f.* drawn in state *P.C.* 30
But diff'ring far in *f.* and in face *R.L.* iv. 26
As want of *f.*, and a small Estate *S.* iii. 68
Kind to my dress, my *f.*, not to Me *S.* iii. 176
Assign'd his *f.* to Bernini's care *S.* v. 381
The Ship itself may make a better *f. S.* vi. 298
In pow'r, wit, *f.*, virtue, fortune, plac'd *S.* vi. 302

FIGUR'D—FINE.

F—s *ill-pair'd, and Similes unlike* D. i. 66
Vet should the Graces all thy *f.* place *E.* iii. 71
The memory's soft *f.* melt away *E.C.* 59
Some *f.* monstrous and mis-shap'd appear *E.C.* 171
Can mark the *f.* on an Indian chest *M.E.* ii. 168
And both the struggling *f.* seem alive *Mi.* ix. 32
Four *f.* rising from the work appear *Sp.* 37

Figur'd.
O'er *f.* worlds now travels with his eye *W.F.* 246
The *f.* streams in waves of silver roll'd *W.F.* 335

Files.
Here *f.* of pins extend their shining rows *R.L.* i. 137

Fill.
Vou've play'd, and lov'd, and eat, and drank your *f.* S. vi. 323
Or serve (like other fools) to *f.* a room *D.* i. 136
Worthy to *f.* Pythagoras's Place *D.* iv. 572
F. my fond heart with God alone, for he *E.A.* 205
And *f.* the gen'ral chorus of mankind *E.C.* 188
That each may *f.* the circle mark'd by Heav'n *E.M.* i. 86
Nor ev'ning Cynthia *f.* her silver horn *M.* 100
F. the capacious Squire, and deep Divine *M.E.* iii. 204
F. half the Land with Imitating-Fools *M.E.* iv. 26
And *f.* with spreading sounds the skies *O.* i. 15
But *f.* their purse, our Poet's work is done *S.* v. 294
How shall we *f.* a Library with Wit *S.* v. 354
And savage howlings *f.* the sacred quires *W.F.* 72
To Thames's banks, which fragrant breezes *f.* *W.F.* 263

Fill'd.
And Delia's name and Doris' *f.* the Grove *A.* 4
F. with the Sense of Age, the Fire of Youth *Ep.* ii. 7
Enough that Virtue *f.* the space between *M.E.* iii. 289
Her hand is *f.*; her bosom with lampoons *R.L.* iv. 30
All the Court *f.* with stranger things than he *S.* viii. 181
Then *f.* the groves, as heav'nly Mira now *W.F.* 298

Fillet.
A belt her waist, a *f.* binds her hair *W.F.* 178
For this with f—s strain'd your tender head *R.L.* iv. 101

Fills.
And with deep murmurs *f.* the sounding shores *A.* 20
Her ample presence *f.* up all the place *D.* i. 261
Joy *f.* his soul, joy innocent of thought *D.* ii. 249
With spirits feeds, with vigour *f.* the whole *E.C.* 77
And *f.* up all the mighty Void of sense *E.C.* 210
Of hearing, from the life that *f.* the Flood *E.M.* i. 215
He *f.*, he bounds, connects, and equals all *E.M.* i. 280
Whatever warms the heart, or *f.* the head *E.M.* ii. 141
It pours the bliss that *f.* up all the mind *E.M.* iv. 344
Whose sacred flow'r with fragrance *f.* the skies *M.* 10
The nymph exulting *f.* with shouts the sky *R.L.* iii. 99
A Vial next she *f.* with fainting fears *R.L.* iv. 85

Films.
He from thick *f.* shall purge the visual ray *M.* 39

Filmy.
Thin glitt'ring textures of the *f.* dew *R.L.* ii. 64

Filth.
Obscene with *f.* the miscreant lies bewray'd *D.* ii. 75
Who flings most *f.*, and wide pollutes around *D.* ii. 279

Filthy.
This *f.* simile, this beastly line *E.S.* ii. 181
Ih *f.* check on all industrious skill *M.E.* iii. 75

Fins.
The bright-ey'd perch with *f.* of Tyrian dye *W.F.* 142

Final.
Make God Man's Image, Man the *f.* Cause *D.* iv. 478

Find.
How random thoughts now meaning chance to *f.* *D.* i. 275
Son, what thou seek'st is in thee! Look, and *f.* *D.* iii. 251
The most recluse, discreetly open'd *f.* *D.* iv. 447
F. Virtue local, all Relation scorn *D.* iv. 479
I tremble too, where'er my own I *f.* *E.A.* 33

I shrink, start up, the same sad prospect *f.* *E.A.* 247
Vet if we look more closely, we shall *f.* *E.C.* 39
For as in bodies, thus in souls, we *f.* *E.C.* 207
Survey the WHOLE, nor seek slight faults to *f.* *E.C.* 235
Something, whose truth convinc'd at sight we *f.* *E.C.* 209
Where'er you *f.* "the cooling western breeze" *E.C.* 350
No pardon vile Obsceenity should *f.* *E.C.* 530
And Vice admir'd to *f.* a flatt'rer there *E.C.* 551
In grave Quintilian's copious work, we *f.* *E.C.* 669
From her own Sex should mercy *f.* to-day *E.Y.S.* 2
Presumptuous Man! the reason wouldst thou *f.* *E.M.* i. 35
The bliss of Man (could Pride that blessing *f.*) *E.M.* i. 189
Nor God alone in the still calm we *f.* *E.M.* ii. 109
Present to grasp, and future still to *f.* *E.M.* ii. 125
All, all alike *f.* Reason on their side *E.M.* iii. 174
To *f.* the means proportion'd to their end *E.M.* iii. 82
Here too all forms of social union *f.* *E.M.* iii. 179
Some sunk to Beasts, *f.* pleasure end in pain *E.M.* iv. 23
There's not a blessing Individuals *f.* *E.M.* iv. 39
Shall *f.*, that pleasure pays not half the pain *E.M.* iv. 48
Know, all the good that individuals *f.* *E.M.* iv. 77
You'll *f.*, if once the monarch acts the monk *E.M.* iv. 201
The whole strange purpose of their lives to *f.* *E.M.* iv. 221
The bad must miss; the good, untaught, will *f.* *E.M.* iv. 330
Are giv'n in vain, but what they seek they *f.* *E.M.* iv. 348
Would he oblige me? let me only *f.* *E.S.* i. 33
You'd quickly *f.* him in Lord *Fanny*'s case *E.S.* i. 50
To *f.* an honest man I beat about *E.S.* ii. 22
F. you the Virtue, and I'll *f.* the Verse *E.S.* ii. 105
Do good by stealth, and blush to *f.* it Fame *E.S.* ii. 136
Now this I'll say; you'll *f.* in me *I.H.* i. 39
Direct my Plough to *f.* a Treasure *I.H.* ii. 20 s
And *f.* his Honour in a Pound *I.H.* ii. 47 s
But these plain Characters we rarely *f.* *M.E.* i. 63
Not always Actions shew the man; we *f.* *M.E.* i. 109
F., if you can, in what you cannot change *M.E.* i. 171
In Men, we various Ruling Passions *f.* *M.E.* i. 207
We *f.* our tenets just the same at last *M.E.* iii. 16
Poor Avarice one torment more would *f.* *M.E.* iii. 59
Or *f.* some Doctor that would save the life *M.E.* iii. 93
That Woman is a Worm, we *f.* *Mi.* iv. 9
Blest, who can unconcern'dly *f.* *O.* iv. 9
A man's true merit 'tis not hard to *f.* *P.S.* 275
Of broken troops an easy conquest *f.* *R.L.* iii. 78
How soon they *f.* fit instruments of ill *R.L.* iii. 126
Clos'd their long glories with a sigh, to *f.* *S.* v. 13
In Palace-yard at nine you'll *f.* me there *S.* vi. 94
Nay tho' at Court (perhaps) it may *f.* grace *S.* vi. 162
Say, can you *f.* out one such lodger there *S.* vi. 223
Talk whate you will of Taste, my friend, you'll *f.* *S.* vi. 268
One whom the mob, when next we *f.* or make *S.* viii. 34
Than mine, to *f.* a subject staid and wise *S.* viii. 168
To *f.* that better way *U.P.* 28
The grave unites; where e'en the great *f.* rest *W.F.* 317

Finding.
How oft review; each *f.* like a friend *E.* iii. 21

Finds.
Now running round the Circle *f.* it square *D.* iv. 34
And *f.* a fairer Rambouillet in you *E.* iv. 76
Love *f.* an altar for forbidden fires *E.A.* 182
Who *f.* not Providence all good and wise *E.M.* i. 205
In him who is, or him who *f.* a friend *E.M.* iv. 64
Our depths who fathoms, or our shallows *f.* *M.E.* i. 23
Alas! 'tis more than Turner *f.* they give *M.E.* ii. 82
F. all her life one warfare upon earth *M.E.* ii. 118
Virtue she *f.* too painful an endeavour *M.E.* iii. 163
He *f.* at last he better likes a Field *M.E.* iv. 88
He *f.* no relish in the sweetest meat *S.* ii. 32
F. envy never conquer'd but by Death *S.* v. 16
Who pants for glory *f.* but short repose *S.* v. 300

Fine.
Could not but think, to pay his *f.* was odd *S.* viii. 17
What the *f.* gentleman wore yesterday *E.C.* 330
The spider's touch how exquisitely *f.* *E.M.* i. 217
That gay Free-thinker, a *f.* talker once *M.E.* i. 162
F. by defect, and delicately weak *M.E.* ii. 43
Or soft Adonis, so perfum'd and *f.* *M.E.* ii. 73
Than his *f.* Wife, alas! or finer Whore *M.E.* iv. 12
His Son's *f.* Taste an op'ner Vista loves *M.E.* iv. 93
Transparent forms, too *f.* for mortal sight *R.L.* ii. 61
Repeat unask'd; lament the Wit's too *f.* *S.* v. 366

FIN'D—FIRST.

Extremely *f*., but what no man will wear *S*. vii. 124
As the fair fields they sold to look so *f*. *S*. viii. 217

Fin'd.
For Right Hereditary tax'd and *f*. *S*. vi. 64

Finer.
Say what the use, were *f*. optics giv'n *E.M.* i. 195
In vain thy Reason *f*. webs shall draw *E.M.* iii. 191
Than his fine Wife, alas ! or *f*. Whore *M.E.* iv. 12

Finger.
She with one *f*. and a thumb subdu'd *R.L.* v. 80
Presents her harp still to his f—s *Mi.* xii. 8
The little engine at his f—s' ends *R.L.* iii. 132

Finish.
Shall *f*. what his short-liv'd Sire begun *M*. 64

Finish'd.
Lo ev'ry *f*. son returns to thee *D*. iv. 500
How *f*. with illustrious toil appears *E*. iii. 39
And *f*. more thro' happiness than pains *E*. iii. 68
And the Monks *f*. what the Goths begun *E.C.* 692
Thus *f*., and corrected to a hair *S*. viii. 248

Finny.
Slight lines of hair surprise the *f*. prey *R.L.* ii. 26
Go drive the Deer, and drag the *f*. prey *S*. iv. 113

Fir.
The spiry *f*. and shapely box adorn *M*. 74

Fire.
The art of Terence, and Menander's *f*. *A*. 8
And 'scape the martyrdom of jakes and *f*. *D*. i. 144
And were my Elasticity and *F*. *D*. i. 186
Not sulphur-dipt emblaze an Ale-house *f*. *D*. i. 235
A *f*., a jig, a battle, and a ball *D*. iii. 239
Illumes their light, and sets their flames on *f*. *D*. iii. 260
Thy stage shall stand, ensure it but from *F*. *D*. iii. 312
And shook from out his pipe the seeds of *f*. *D*. iv. 494
Fresnoy's close Art, and Dryden's native *F*. *E*. iii. 8
Each purer flame inform'd with purer *f*. *E*. iii. 50
Divert her eyes with pictures in the *f*. *E*. v. 19
The gen'rous Critic fann'd the Poet's *f*. *E.C.* 100
Or may some spark of your celestial *f*. *E.C.* 195
Yet judg'd with coolness, tho' he sung with *f*. *E.C.* 659
And bless their Critic with a Poet's *f*. *E.C.* 676
Such rage without betrays the *f*. within *E.g.S.* 17
He asks no Angel's wing, no Seraph's *f*. *M.E.* i. 110
Taught to command the *f*., control the flood *E.M.* iii. 220
Fill'd with the Sense of Age, the *F*. of Youth *Ep*. ii. 7
Hold out some months 'twixt Sun and *F*. *I.H.* i. 18
Adieu, food hope of mutual *f*. *I.H.* iii. 33
Who touch'd Isaiah's hallow'd lips with *f*. *M*. 6
Meat, *F*., and Clothes. What more? Meat, Clothes, and *F*. *M.E.* iii. 80
And Papal piety, and Gothic *f*. *M.E.* v. 14
While solemn airs improve the sacred *f*. *O*. i. 129
A wand'ring, self-consuming *f*. *O*. iii. 20
In winter *f*. *O*. iv. 8
F. in each eye, and papers in each hand *P.S.* 9
And breathes three am'rous sighs to raise the *f*. *R.L.* ii 42
And fierce Thalestris fans the rising *f*. *R.L.* iv. 94
Or nobly wild, with Budgel's and force *S*. i. 27
Lest stiff, and stately, void of *f*. or force *S*. iii. 15
Exact Racine, and Corneille's noble *f*. *S*. v. 274
Some doubt if equal pains, or equal *f*. *S*. v. 282
In spite of witches, devils, dreams, and *f*. *S*. vi. 313
He starves with cold to save them from the *f*. *S*. vii. 72
No kitchens emulate the vestal *f*. *S*. vii. 112
Pursu'd her flight; her flight increas'd his *f*. *W.F.* 184
Her sacred domes involv'd in rolling *f*. *W.F.* 324
Great Cæsar roars, and hisses in the f—s *D*. i. 251
Consent, each emanation of his *f*. *D*. i. 272
Wit shoots in vain its momentary *f*. *D*. iv. 633
Religion blushing veils her sacred *f*. *D*. iv. 649
Warm to the soul, and faithful to its *f*. *E.A.* 54
The jealous God, when we profane his *f*. *E.A.* 81
Love finds an altar for forbidden *f*. *E.A.* 182
Who saw its *f*. here rise, and there descend *E.M.* ii. 37
Forget to thunder, or recall her *f*. *E.M.* iv. 124
Turn, turn to willing hearts your wanton *f*. *I.H.* iii. 8
F. that glow *O*. i. 58
F. that scorch, yet dare not shine *O*. iii. 40
Peace to all such ! but were there One whose *f*. *P.S.* 193

Pale spectres, gaping tombs, and purple *f*. *R.L.* iv. 44
Her weapons blunted, and extinct her *f*. *W.F.* 418
And let the past and future f. thy brain *D*. iii. 66
Why, Nature, dost thou soonest *f*. *O*. iii. 11
Whose raptures *f*. me, and whose visions bless *W.F.* 260

Fir'd.
F. with Ideas of fair Italy *E*. iii. 26
But let heav'n seize it, all at once 'tis *f*. *E.A.* 201
F. at first sight with what the Muse imparts *E.C.* 219
What has not *f*. her bosom or her brain *M.E.* ii. 77
'Twas no Court-badge, great Scriv'ner ! *f*. thy brain *M.E.* iii. 145
F. by the sight, all Reason I disdain *Mi.* ix. 83
Where heav'nly visions Plato *f*. *O*. ii. 3
F. that the House reject him, "'Sdeath, I'll print it *P.S.* 61
With foolish pride my heart was never *f*. *S*. viii. 9

Fires.
Warriors she *f*. with animated sounds *O*. i. 28
When music softens, and when dancing *f*. *R.L.* i. 76

Firm.
F. Impudence, or Stupefaction mild *D*. iv. 530
A pleasing Form ; a *f*., yet cautious Mind *Ep*. ii. 1
So *f*., yet soft; so strong, yet so refus'd *Ep*. vi. 8
Choose a *f*. cloud, before it fall, and in it *M.E.* ii. 19
Asks no *f*. band, and no unerring line *M.E.* ii. 152
A desp'rate *Bulwark*, sturdy, *f*., and fierce *Mi.* ii. 13
To bear too tender, or too *f*. a heart *U.L.* 7

First.
Still Dunce the second reigns like Dunce the *f*. *D*. i. 6
How new-born nonsense *f*. is taught to cry *D*. i. 60
F. in my care, and ever at my heart *D*. i. 164
Then *f*. (if Poets aught of truth declare) *D*. ii. 77
F. Osborne lean'd against his letter'd post *D*. ii. 171
F. be relates, how sinking to the chin *D*. ii. 331
Slept *f*.; the distant nodded to the hum *D*. ii. 402
One circle *f*., and then a second makes *D*. ii. 406
Shall, *f*. recall'd, rush forward to thy mind *D*. iii. 64
Mark *f*. that youth who takes the foremost place *D*. iii. 139
But murder *f*., and mince them all to bits *D*. iv. 120
Each eager to present their *f*. Address *D*. iv. 136
A Poet the *f*. day he dips his quill *D*. iv. 163
The *f*. came forwards, with an easy mien *D*. iv. 279
So he; but pious, whisper'd *f*. his pray'r *D*. iv. 354
The *f*. thus open'd : "Hear thy suppliant's call *D*. iv. 403
F. slave to Words, then vassal to a Name *D*. iv. 501
Her children *f*. of more distinguish'd sort *D*. iv. 567
Born for *F*. Ministers; as Slaves for Kings *D*. iv. 602
St. James's *f*., for leaden G—— preach'd *D*. iv. 608
Relate, who *f*., who last resign'd to rest *D*. iv. 621
Heav'n *f*. taught letters for some wretch's aid *E.A.* 51
Thou know'st how guiltless *f*. I met thy flame *E.A.* 59
Some have at *f*. for Wits, then Poets past *E.C.* 36
F. follow Nature, and your judgment frame *E.C.* 68
By the same laws which *f*. herself ordain'd *E.C.* 91
When *f*. young Maro in his boundless mind *E.C.* 130
Fir'd at *f*. sight with what the Muse imparts *E.C.* 219
So pleas'd at *f*. the tow'ring Alps we try *E.C.* 225
And the *f*. clouds and mountains seem the last *E.C.* 228
Be not the *f*. by whom the new are try'd *E.C.* 335
Which from the *f*. has shone on ages past *E.C.* 402
When *f*. that sun too pow'rful beams displays *E.C.* 470
Be thou the *f*. true merit to befriend *E.C.* 474
The mighty Stagirite *f*. left the shore *E.C.* 645
Of God above, or Man below *E.M.* i. 17
F., if thou canst, the harder reason guess *E.M.* i. 37
No ('tis reply'd) the *f*. Almighty Cause *E.M.* i. 145
To the *f*. good, *f*. perfect, and *f*. fair *E.M.* ii. 24
F. strip off all her equipage of Pride *E.M.* ii. 44
We *f*. endure, then pity, then embrace *E.M.* ii. 220
No creature owns it in the *f*. degree *E.M.* ii. 255
So from the *f*. eternal ORDER ran *E.M.* iii. 113
Our great *f*. father, and that *f*. ador'd *E.M.* iii. 226
Who *f*. taught souls enslav'd, and realms undone *E.M.* iii. 241
Force *f*. made Conquest, and that conquest Law *E.M.* iii. 245
Then *f*. the Flamen tasted living food *E.M.* iii. 265
Self-love forsook the path it *f*. pursu'd *E.M.* iii. 281
ORDER is Heav'n's *f*. law ; and this confest *E.M.* iv. 49

Which meets contempt, or which compassion *f. E.M.* iv. 88
But *f.* consider how those Just agree *E.M.* iv. 134
Friend, parent, neighbour, *f.* it will embrace *E.M* iv. 367
The *f.*, last purpose of the human soul *E.M.* iv. 338
That *F.* was H—vy's, F—'s next, and thee *E.S.* i. 71
Consider, 'tis my *f.* request *J.H.* ii. 7 *s*
Since Harley bid me *f.* attend *J.H.* ii. 85 *s*
That each from other differs, *f.* confess *M.E.* i. 19
Boastful and rough, your *f.* Son is a Squire *M.E.* i. 151
If second qualities for *f.* they take *M.E.* i. 211
Those, only fix'd, they *f.* or last obey *M.E.* ii. 209
They seek the second not to lose the *f. M.E.* ii. 214
When those blue eyes *f.* open'd on the sphere *M.E.* ii. 284
F., for his Son a gay commission buys *M.E.* iii. 389
F. thro' the length of yon hot Terrace sweat *M.E.* iv. 130
F. shade a Country, and then raise a Town *M.E.* iv. 190
F. sought a Poet's Fortune in the Town *Mi.* iii. 2
Trudges to town, and *f.* turns Chambermaid *Mi.* iii. 16
She *f.* convers'd with her own kind *Mi.* iv. 11
F. from a Worm they take their Rise *Mi.* iv. 19
Then *f.* his Passion was in public shown *Mi.* ix. 40
An awkward Thing, when *f.* she came to Town *Mi.* ix. 59
She was my friend ; I taught her *f.* to spread *Mi.* ix. 61
So when the *f.* bold vessel dar'd the Seas *O.* i. 38
For this the tragic Muse *f.* trod the stage *P.C.* 5
With honest scorn the *f.* fam'd Cato view'd *P.C.* 39
His very Minister who spy'd them *f. P.S.* 71
Who *f.* his judgment ask'd, and then a place *P.S.* 238
The *f.* Lampoon Sir *Will* or *Bufo* makes *P.S.* 280
To their *f.* Elements their Souls retire *R.L.* i. 58
Thy eyes *f.* open'd on a Billet-doux *R.L.* i. 118
F., rob'd in white, the Nymph intent adores *R.L.* i. 123
The Sun *f.* rises o'er the purpled main *R.L.* ii. 2
F., Ariel perch'd upon a Matadore *R.L.* iii. 33
Spadillio *f.*, unconquerable Lord *R.L.* iii. 49
The Club's black Tyrant *f.* her victim dy'd *R.L.* iii. 69
He *f.* the snuff-box open'd, then the case *R.L.* iv. 126
Yet am I not the *f.* mistaken maid *R.L.* iv. 151
Behold the *f.* in virtue as in face *R.L.* v. 18
Not Berenice's locks *f.* rose so bright *R.L.* v. 129
F. Health: The Stomach (cramm'd from ev'ry dish *S.* ii. 69
'Tis the *f.* Virtue, Vices to abhor (*rep.*) *S.* iii. 65
Here Wisdom calls : " Seek Virtue *f.*, be bold *S.* iii. 77
E'en take the Counsel which I gave you *f. S.* iv. 131
Ev'n Radcliffe's Doctors travel *f.* to France *S.* v. 183
Glad, like a Boy, to snatch the *f.* good day *S.* vi. 294
In shillings and in pence at *f.* they steal *S.* vii. 83
Piecemeal they win this acre *f.*, then foot *S.* vii. 91
F. turn plain rash, then vanish quite away *S.* viii. 45
So *f.* to preach a white-glov'd Chaplain goes *S.* viii. 250
F. in these fields I try the sylvan strains *Sp.* 1
Nay tell me *f.*, in what more happy fields *Sp.* 89
Ambition *f.* sprung from your blest abodes *U.L.* 13
There the *f.* roses of the year shall blow *U.L.* 66
Thou *F.* Great Cause, least understood *U.P.* 5
Proud Nimrod *f.* the bloody chase began *W.F.* 61
Here his *f.* lays majestic Denham sung *W.F.* 271
What kings *f.* breath'd upon her winding shore *W.F.* 300
F. the fam'd authors of his ancient name *W.F.* 339
F. in these fields I sung the sylvan strains *W.F.* 434
Whether my vessel be f.-rate, or not *S.* vi. 297

Fish.
Beast, bird, *f.*, insect, what no eye can see *E.M.* i. 239
To beasts his pastures, and to *f.* his floods *E.M.* iii. 58
Tastes for his friend of Fowl and *F. J.H.* ii. 199
While *f.* in streams, or birds delight in air *R.L.* iii. 163
Or *f.* deny'd (the river yet unthaw'd) *S.* ii. 14
A tomb of boil'd and roast, and flesh and *f. S.* ii. 70

Fish'd.
Where as he *f.* her nether realms for Wit *D.* ii. 101

Fisher.
The patient *f.* takes his silent stand *W.F.* 137

Fist.
The more thou ticklest, gripes his *f.* the faster *D.* ii. 210

Fit.
Another in a surly *f. J.H.* ii. 55
Such this day's doctrine—in another *f. M.E.* ii. 75

Who give th' hysteric, or poetic *f. R.L.* iv. 60
A *F.* of Vapours clouds this Demi-God *S.* iii. 188
We wake next morning in a raging *f. S.* v. 179
But let the *F.* pass o'er, I'm wise enough *S.* vi. 151
As breathe, or pause, by f—s, the airs divine *D.* iv. 304
The rogue and fool by *f.* is fair and wise (*rep.*) *E.M.* ii. 233
As *F.* give vigour, just when they destroy *M.E.* i. 223
Between the *F.* this Fever of the soul *S.* iii. 58
And blunt the sense, and f. it for a skull *D.* iii. 25
One science only will one genius *f. E.C.* 60
Those strange examples ne'er were made to *f.* ye *E.J.S.* 41
As Jansen, Fleetwood, Cibber shall think *f. D.* iv. 326
Nature to all things fix'd the limits *f. E.C.* 52
Pleas'd with a work where nothing's just or *f. E.C.* 291
Oft leaving what is natural and *f. E.C.* 448
Receiv'd his laws ; and stood convinc'd 'twas *f. E.C.* 651
Still *f.* for use, and ready at command *E.C.* 674
See some *f.* Passion ev'ry age supply *E.M.* ii. 273
How soon they find *f.* instruments of ill *R.L.* iii. 126
In peace provides *f.* arms against a war *S.* ii. 118
What right, what true, what *f.* we justly call *S.* iii. 19
F. to bestow the Laureate's weighty place *S.* v. 379
And knows what's *f.* for ev'ry state to do *S.* viii. 47
Is therefore *f.* to have a Government *S.* viii. 139

Fits.
But only what my Station *f. J.H.* ii. 21 *s*

Fitted.
But still this world (so *f.* for the Knave) *E.M.* iv. 131

Five.
Or let it cost *f.* hundred pound *J.H.* ii. 39 *s*
To *Number f.* direct your doves *J.H.* iii. 9
This man possest *f.* hundred pounds a year *M.E.* iii. 280
As M * * o's was, but not at *f.* per cent. *S.* ii. 122
Than in *f.* acres now of rented land *S.* ii. 130
His servants up, and rise by *f.* o'clock *S.* v. 162

Fix.
Here thy well study'd marbles *f.* our eye *E.* iii. 33
Describe or *f.* one movement of his Mind *E.M.* ii. 36
With choice we *f.*, with sympathy we burn *E.M.* iii. 135
Seek an admirer, or would *f.* a friend *E.M.* iv. 44
Is Virtue's prize : a better would you *f. E.M.* iv. 169
To charm the Mistress, or to *f.* the Friend *J.H.* iii. 14
End all dispute ; and *f.* the year precise *S.* v. 53
To *f.* him graceful on the bounding Steed *S.* v. 383

Fix'd.
At last it *f.*, 'twas on what plant it pleas'd (*rep.*) *D.* iv. 429
Not on the Cross my eyes were *f.*, but you *E.A.* 116
Thy life a long dead calm of *f.* repose *E.A.* 251
Nature to all things *f.* the limits fit *E.C.* 52
F. to one side, yet mod'rate to the rest *Ep.* ii. 4
F., like a plant on his peculiar spot *E.M.* ii. 63
Their Virtue *f.* ; 'tis *f.* as in a frost *E.M.* ii. 102
'Tis thus the Mercury of Man is *f. E.M.* ii. 177
Laws wise as Nature, and as *f.* as Fate *E.M.* iii. 190
Here *f.* the dreadful, there the blest abodes *E.M.* iii. 255
No *f.* spot is Happiness sincere *E.M.* iv. 15
But *f.* his word, his saving pow'r remains *M.* 107
Those, only *f.*, they first or last obey *M.E.* ii. 209
F. Principles, with Fancy ever new *M.E.* ii. 279
But ev'ry eye was *f.* on her alone *R.L.* ii. 6
Or, as Ixion *f.*, the wretch shall feel *R.L.* ii. 133
Not half so *f.* the Trojan could remain *R.L.* v. 5
Let Us be *f.*, and our own masters still *S.* ii. 180

Flag.
(Earth's wide extremes) her sable *f.* display'd *D.* iii. 71
His *F.* inverted trails along the ground *E.S.* i. 154

Flagellation.
As morning pray'r and *f.* end *D.* ii. 270

Flagitious.
Nor fears a dearth in these *f.* times *E.C.* 529
And harder still, *f.*, yet not great *M.E.* i. 205

Flagrant.
And Tutchin, *f.* from the scourge below *D.* ii. 148

Flags.
When fancy *f.*, and sense is at a stand *D.* ii. 230

FLAME—FLEET.

Flame.

The Maid's romantic wish, the Chemist's *f. D.* iii. 11
A Newton's genius, or a Milton's *f. D.* iii. 216
Nor *public F.*, nor private, dares to shine *D.* iv. 651
And met congenial, mingling *f.* with *f. E.* iii. 14
There stern Religion quench'd th' unwilling *f. E.A.* 39
Thou know'st how guiltless first I met thy *f. E.A.* 59
In seas of *f.* my plunging soul is drown'd *E.A.* 275
The vital *f.*, and swells the genial seeds *E.M.* iii. 118
Carleton's calm Sense, and Stanhope's noble *F. E.S.* ii. 80
Touch'd with the *F.* that breaks from Virtue's Shrine *E.S.* ii. 233
Perhaps by its own ruins sav'd from *f. M.E.* v. 15
The Nymph, whose Tail is all on *F. Mi.* iv. 15
And the bright *f.* was shot thro' Marchmont's Soul *Mi.* x. 12
And Arts but soften us to feel thy *f. O.* iii. 4
Vital spark of heav'nly *f. O.* v. 1
The Sprites of fiery Termagants in *F. R.L.* i. 59
Or for a Titled Punk, or foreign *F. S.* iv. 124
These, were my breast inspir'd with equal *f. W.F.* 9
Go, purify'd by *f—s*, ascend the sky *D.* i. 227
Down sink the *f.*, and with a hiss expire *D.* i. 260
There rival *f.* with equal glory rise *D.* iii. 80
Illumes their light, and sets their *f.* on fire *D.* iii. 260
In *f.*, like Semele's, be brought to bed *D.* iii. 315
Their Wit still sparkling, and their *f.* still warm *E.* iv. 72
Here all its frailties, all its *f.* resign *E.A.* 175
Ah hopeless, lasting *f.*, like those that burn *E.A.* 261
Where *f.* refin'd in breasts seraphic glow *E.A.* 320
Secure from *F.*, from Envy's fiercer rage *E.C.* 183
Love's purer *f.* the Gods approve *O.* iii. 13
But Hymen's kinder *f.* unite *O.* iii. 21
And burn in Cupid's *f.*—but burn alive *R.L.* v. 102
The Poet's bell, its tortures, fiends, and *f. S.* viii. 7
On me love's fiercer *f.* for ever prey *Su.* 91
Where clearer *f.* glow round the frozen Pole *W.F.* 390
Or, meteor-like, f. lawless thro' the void *E.M.* ii. 65

Flam'd.

Now *f.* the Dog-star's unpropitious ray *D.* iv. 9
F. forth this rival to its Sire, the Sun *M.E.* iii. 12

Flamen.

The rev'rend *F.* in his lengthen'd dress *D.* ii. 354
Then first the *F.* tasted living food *E.M.* iii. 265

Flames.

Now *f.* the Cid, and now Perolla burns *D.* i. 250
Molière's old stubble in a moment *f. D.* i. 254
His painted wings, and breast that *f.* with gold *W.F.* 118

Flaming.

Or deep with di'monds in the *f.* mine *E.M.* iv. 10
Which *f.* Phlegethon surrounds *O.* i. 50

Flamy.

Whose sars'net skirts are edg'd with *f.* gold *D.* iii. 254

Flanders.

Gave the gilt Coach, and dappled *F.* Mares *E.* iv. 50

Flap.

Yet let me *f.* this bug with gilded wings *P.S.* 309

Flash.

The meteor drops, and in a *f.* expires *D.* iv. 634
And the pale ghosts start at the *f.* of day *R.L.* v. 52

Flash'd.

Then *f.* the living light'ning from her eyes *R.L.* iii. 155

Flat.

With pert *f.* eyes she window'd well its head *D.* ii. 43

Flatter.

Averse alike to *f.*, or offend *E.C.* 743
No Wit to *f.* left of all his store *M.E.* iii. 311
And when I *f.*, let my dirty leaves *S.* v. 415
And much must *f.*, if the whim should bite *S.* vi. 149
Who cannot *f.*, and detest who can *S.* viii. 198

Flatter'd.

Be grac'd thro' Life, and *f.* in his Grave *E.S.* i. 186
Who never *f.* Folks like you *Ep.* xv. 3
And *f.* ev'ry day, and some days eat *P.S.* 240

Flatterer, Flatt'rer.

The *F.* an Earwig grows *Mi.* iv. 21
But as the *F'r* or Dependant paint *D.* iv. 535
And Vice admir'd to find a *F.* there *E.C.* 551
Without a Fiddler, *F.*, or Buffoon *M.E.* iii. 247
But Foes like these—One *F.*'s worse than all *P.S.* 104
Fop at the toilet, *F.* at the board *P.S.* 328
"That's velvet for a king!" the *f.* swears *S.* viii. 218
Dreading ev'n fools, by *F—s* besieg'd *P.S.* 207
F—'—s and Bigots ev'n in Louis' reign *S.* i. 112
You go to church to hear these *F.* preach *S.* vi. 225

Flatt'ring.

What *f.* scenes our wand'ring fancy wrought *E.* iii. 23

Flatters.

She *f.* her good Lady twice a day *Mi.* iii. 18

Flattery, Flatt'ry.

And pleas'd to 'scape from *F.* to Wit *E.* i. 12
And strikes a blush thro' frontless *F. E.* ii. 7
Nor stop at *F.* or Fib *E.* vi. 24
And *f.* to fulsome Dedicators *E.C.* 593
The Priest whose *F.* bedropt the Crowe *E.S.* ii. 164
Bentley his mouth with classic *f*'y opes *D.* ii. 205
Or vest dull *F.* in the sacred gown *D.* iv. 97
Who without *F.* pleas'd the fair and great *E.* iv. 6
Quite turns my stomach. So does *F.* mine *E.S.* ii. 182
Let *F.* sick'ning see the Incense rise *E.S.* ii. 244
When *F.* glares, all hate it in a Queen *M.E.* i. 61
Or simple pride for *f.* makes demands *P.S.* 253
That *F.*, ev'n to Kings, he held a shame *P.S.* 338
With royal Favourites in *f.* vie *S.* viii. 60
Watch'd both by Envy's and by F's eye *D.* iv. 36
Most warp'd to *F.* side; but some, more nice *S.* v. 259

Flaunts.

One *f.* in rags, one flutters in brocade *E.M.* iv. 196
F. and goes down, an unregarded thing *M.E.* ii. 252
His Daughter *f.* a Viscount's tawdry wife *M.E.* iii. 391

Flavia.

"What *well*? what *weapons*?" (*F.* cries) *E.S.* 13
F.'s a Wit, has too much sense to pray *M.E.* ii. 87

Flavio.

At am'rous *F.* is the stocking thrown *S.* iii. 148

Flaw.

Or some frail China jar receive a *f. R.L.* ii. 106
Who lasts a century can have no *f. S.* v. 55

Flea.

When man's whole frame is obvious to a *F. D.* iv. 238
Cages for gnats, and chains to yoke a *f. R.L.* v. 121

Fleckno.

Henley's gilt tub, or *F.'s* Irish throne *D.* ii. 2

Fled.

It *f.*, I follow'd; now in hope, now pain *D.* iv. 427
Extracts his brain; and Principle is *f. D.* iv. 522
See skulking Truth to her old cavern *f. D.* iv. 641
From the false world in early youth they *f. E.A.* 131
And *f.* from monarchs, St. John! dwells with thee *E.M.* iv. 18
Think not, when Woman's transient breath is *f. R.L.* i. 51
Despairing Quacks with curses *f.* the place *M.E.* iii. 273

Fleeces.

In circling *F.* whiten all the ways *D.* ii. 362
Feed fairer flocks, or richer *f.* shear *Su.* 36
Now sleeping flocks on their soft *f.* lie *W.* 5

Fleecy.

And *f.* clouds were streak'd with purple light *A.* 14
As the good shepherd tends his *f.* care *M.* 49
Pour'd o'er the whitening dale their *f.* care *Sp.* 19
If teeming ewes increase my *f.* breed *W.* 82

Fleet.

Thro' Lud's fam'd gates along the well-known *F. D.* ii. 359
While others, timely, to the neighb'ring *F. D.* ii. 427
The Sylvans groan—no matter—for the *F. M.E.* iii. 210
Where, eas'd of *F—s*, the Adriatic main *D.* iv. 309
And the *f.* shades glide o'er the dusky green *A.* 64
Rouse the *f.* hart, and cheer the opening hound *W.F.* 150
To where F.-ditch with disemboguing streams *D.* ii. 271

Fleetwood.
As Jansen, *F*., Cibber shall think fit *D*. iv. 326

Fle'me—*see* Phlegm.

Flesh.
All *F*. is humbled, Westminster's bold race *D*. iv. 145
Attends; all *f*. is nothing in his sight *D*. iv. 550
To see a piece of sailing *f*. and blood *E*.*J*.*S*. 47
A tomb of boil'd and roast, and *f*. and fish *S*. ii. 70
And serve the *f*., the dev'l, and all but gold *S*. vii. 24

Fleshly.
The godly dame, who *f*. failings damns *E*.*J*.*S*. 21

Fletcher.
What can I now? my *F*. cast aside *D*. i. 199
'Twixt Plautus, *F*., Shakespear, and Corneille *D*. i. 285
How Beaumont's judgment check'd what *F*. writ *S*. v. 84
Here lay poor F.'s half-eat scenes, and here D. i. 131

Fleury.
Sejanus, Wolsey, hurt not honest *F*. *E*.*S*. i. 51
Peace is my dear delight—not F.'s more S. i. 75

Flew.
Intrepid then, o'er seas and lands he *f*. *D*. iv. 293
Thus from the world fair Zephalinda *f*. *E*. v. 7
And Arts still follow'd where her Eagles *f*. *E*.*C*. 684
Loose to the wind their airy garments *f*. *R*.*L*. ii. 62
And Ariel weeping from Belinda *f*. *R*.*L*. iv. 12
And Tauots alternate innocently *f*. *S*. v. 250
So *f*. the soul to its congenial place *U*.*L*. 27
As from the god she *f*. with furious pace *W*.*F*. 189

Flies.
What bave I said? where'er my Delia *f*. *A*. 35
Sudden she *f*., and whelms it o'er the pyre *D*. i. 259
On feet and wings, and *f*., and wades, and hops *D*. ii. 64
As, from the blanket, high in air he *f*. *D*. ii. 152
Swift to whose hand a winged volume *f*. *D*. iii. 234
And thro' the Iv'ry Gate of Vision *f*. *D*. iii. 340
Then give one flirt, and all the vision *f*. *E*. v. 38
Spreads his light wings, and in a moment *f*. *E*.*A*. 76
The phantom *f*. me, as unkind as you *E*.*A*. 236
F. o'er th' unbending corn, and skims along the main *E*.*C*. 373
Before his sacred name *f*. ev'ry fault *E*.*C*. 422
Eye Nature's walks, shoot Folly as it *f*. *E*.*M*. i. 13
'Tis but what Virtue *f*. from and disdains *E*.*M*. iv. 90
Expanded *f*., and gathers all its fame *E*.*M*. iv. 384
There *f*. about a strange report *I*.*H*. ii. 109 *s*
See, wild as the winds, o'er the desert he *f*. *O*. i. 110
A constant Vapour o'er the Palace *f*. *R*.*L*. iv. 39
And swift as lightning to the combat *f*. *R*.*L*. v. 38
While thro' the press eorag'd Thalestris *f*. *R*.*L*. v. 57
See, fierce Belinda on the Baron *f*. *R*.*L*. v. 75
The Sylphs behold it kindling as it *f*. *R*.*L*. v. 131
Taste, that eternal wanderer, which *f*. *S*. v. 312
To bim he *f*., and bows, and bows again *S*. viii. 176
While a kind glance at her pursuer *f*. *Sp*. 59
And high in air Britannia's standard *f*. *W*.*F*. 110

Flight.
Instant, when dipt, away they wing their *f*. *D*. iii. 27
One thought of thee puts all the pomp to *f*. *E*.*A*. 273
Gums and Pomatums shall his *f*. restrain *R*.*L*. ii. 129
For gain, not glory, wing'd his roving *f*. *S*. v. 71
F. of Cashiers, or Mobs, he'll never mind *S*. v. 195
Above the vulgar *f*. of low desire *U*.*L*. 12
Pursu'd ber *f*.; ber *f*. increas'd his fire *W*.*F*. 184
Here cease thy *f*., nor with unhallow'd lays *W*.*F*. 423
When to repress, and when indulge our f—s E.*C*. 93
That on weak wings, from far, pursues your *f*. *E*.*C*. 197
Strange graces still, and stranger *f*. she had *M*.*E*. ii. 49
When airs, and *f*., and screams, and scoldings fail *R*.*L*. v. 32

Flimsy.
Proud of a vast extent of *f*. lines *P*.*S*. 94

Flings.
Who *f*. most filth, and wide pollutes around *D*. ii. 279
On others Int'rest her gay liv'ry *f*. *D*. iv. 537
While ev'ry beam new transient colours *f*. *R*.*L*. ii. 67

Flirt.
Then give one *f*., and all the vision flies *E*. v. 38

Flit.
Chang'd to a bird, and sent to *f*. in air *R*.*L*. iii. 123

Flits.
Pregnant with thousands *f*. the Scrap unseen *M*.*E*. iii. 47
Swift on his sooty pinions *f*. the Gnome *R*.*L*. iv. 17

Floating.
The sun-beams trembling on the *f*. tides *R*.*L*. ii. 48
And *f*. forests paint the waves with green *W*.*F*. 216

Floats.
In broken air, trembling, the wild music *f*. *O*. i. 17
Lo! COBHAM comes, and *f*. them with a Lake *M*.*E*.iv.74

Flock.
Nor has one ATTERBURY spoil'd the *f*. *D*. iv. 246
Ah, think at least thy *f*. deserves thy care *E*.*A*. 129
The shepherds cry, "Thy f—s are left a prey" A. 78
I'll fly from shepherds, *f*., and flow'ry plains *A*. 86
Nightly nodding o'er your *F*. *Mi*. vii. 6
Whose *f*. supply him with attire *O*. iv. 6
Soon as the *f*. shook off the nightly dews *Sp*. 17
For see! the gath'ring *f*. to shelter tend *Sp*. 101
Led forth his *f*. along the silver Thame *Su*. 2
The *f*. around a dumb compassion show *Su*. 6
Feed fairer *f*., or richer fleeces shear *Su*. 36
To closer shades the panting *f*. remove *Su*. 87
Now sleeping *f*. on their soft fleeces lie *W*. 5
For her the *f*. refuse their verdant food *W*. 37
Adieu, my *f*., (farewell ye sylvan crew *W*. 93
See Pan with *f*., with fruits Pomona crown'd *W*.*F*. 37
Then gath'ring *f*. on unknown mountains fed *W*.*F*. 87
Where doves in *f*. the leafless trees o'ershade *W*.*F*. 127
In the clear amire gleam the *f*. are seen *W*.*F*. 215
Shall tend the *f*., or reap the bearded graio *W*.*F*. 370
The boys f. round him, and the people stare S. vi. 120
On once a f.-bed, but repair'd with straw M.*E*. iii. 301

Flood.
With deeper sable blots the silver *f*. *D*. ii. 274
Sons of a Day! just buoyant on the *f*. *D*. ii. 307
When lo! a burst of thunder shook the *f*. *D*. ii. 325
Like buoys that never sink into the *f*. *D*. iv. 241
Of hearing, from the life that fills the *F*. *E*.*M*. i. 215
Or wing the sky, or roll along the *f*. *E*.*M*. iii. 120
Taught to command the fire, control the *f*. *E*.*M*. iii. 220
Has crept thro' scoundrels ever since the *f*. *E*.*M*. iv. 212
And break upon thee in a *f*. of day *M*. 98
At length Corruption, like a gen'ral *f*. *M*.*E*. iii. 135
Bid the broad Arch the dang'rous *F*. contain *M*.*E*. iv. 199
Nor thirsty beifers seek the gliding *f*. *W*. 38
Her fate remurmur to the silver *f*. *W*. 64
And purer spirits swell the sprightly *f*. *W*.*F*. 94
Who swell with tributary urns his *f*. *W*.*F*. 338
And sullen Mole, that hides his diving *f*. *W*.*F*. 347
Red Iber's sands, or Ister's foaming *f*. *W*.*F*. 368
And grateful clusters swell with f—s of wine A. 74
Deepens the murmur of the falling *f*. *E*.*A*. 169
To beasts his pastures, and to fish his *f*. *E*.*M*. iii. 58
Be smooth ye rocks, ye rapid *f*. give way *Mi*. 36
What slaughter'd hecatombs, what *f*. of wine *M*.*E*. iii. 203
Now drain'd a distant country of her *F*. *M*.*E*. v. 8
Eurydice the *f*. *O*. i. 116
The winds and trees and *f*. her death deplore *W*. 67
Who claim'd the skies, dispeopled air and *f*. *W*.*F*. 47
Hills, vales, and *f*. appear already cross'd *W*.*F*. 153
And absent trees that tremble in the *W*.*F*. 214
Thou, too, great father of the British *f*. *W*.*F*. 219
And half thy forests rush into thy *f*. *W*.*F*. 386

Floor.
The cat comes bouncing on the *f*. *I*.*H*. ii. 213
Let such, such only, tread this sacred *F*. *Mi*. x. 13
Our shrines irradiate, or emblaze the f—s E.*A*. 136
Grotesco roofs, and Stucco *f*. *I*.*H*. ii. 192
The *f*. of plaister, and the walls of dung *M*.*E*. iii. 300

Flora.
Here blushing *F*. paints th' enamel'd ground *W*.*F*. 38

Florid.
And how did, pray, the *f*. Youth offend *E*.*S*. ii. 166
Whether in *f*. impotence he speaks *P*.*S*. 317

Florio.
When *F*. speaks what virgin could withstand *R*.*L*. i. 97

Florists.
Some Botanists, or *F*. at the least *D*. iv. 573

Flounce.
To change a *F*., or add a Furbelow *R.L.* ii. 100

Flounders.
But gudgeons, *f*., what my Thames affords *S*. ii. 142

Flounder'd.
Yet wrote and *f*. on, in mere despair *D*. i. 120

Flourish.
And all things *f*. where you turn your eyes *Su*. 76
And palms eternal *f*. round his urn *W.F.* 312

Flourish'd.
The stream, and smoking *f*. o'er his head *D*. ii. 180
But Critic-learning *f*. most in France *E.C.* 712
One boundless Green, or *f*. Carpet views *M.E.* iv. 95
With her they *f*., and with her they die *W*. 34

Flow.
In quiet *f*. from Lucrece to Lucrece *E.M.* iv. 208
The Flow'rs of Bubo, and the *F*. of Y—g *E.S.* i. 68
The Feast of Reason, and the *F*. of Soul *S*. i. 127
One ebb and *f*. of follies all my life *S*. iii. 168
F., *Welsted*, *l*. ! *like thine inspirer*, *Beer D*. iii. 269
Thence endless streams of fair Ideas *f. E.* iii. 43
Nor tears for ages taught to *f*. in vain *E.A.* 28
Or moving spirit bade the waters *f. E.A.* 254
As streams roll down, enlarging as they *f. E.C.* 192
But in such lays as neither ebb, nor *f. E.C.* 379
Now sighs steal out, and tears begin to *f. E.C.* 379
That Pow'r who bids the Ocean ebb and *f. M.E.* iii. 164
From the dry rock who bade the waters *f. M.E.* iii. 254
By the streams that ever *f. O*. i. 71
Here tears shall *f*. from a more gen'rous cause *P.C.* 13
Curst be the verse, how well soe'er it *f. P.S.* 283
Smooth *f*. the waves, the Zephyrs gently play *R.L.* ii. 51
He breaks the Vial whence the sorrows *f. R.L.* iv. 142
And sweetly *f*. thro' all the Royal Line *S*. i. 32
Wit grew polite, and Numbers learn'd to *f. S*. v. 266
Fair Thames, *f*. gently from thy sacred spring *Sp*. 3
O'er golden sands let rich Pactolus *f. Sp*. 61
Soft as he mourn'd ; the streams forgot to *f. Su*. 5
As into air the purer spirits *f. U.L.* 5
So sweetly warble, or so smoothly *f. W.* 4
While lasts the mountain, and while Thames shall *f. W.F.* 266
For me the balm shall bleed, and amber *f. W.F.* 393
Unbounded Thames shall *f*. for all mankind *W.F.* 398

Flow'd.
In *f*. at once a gay embroider'd race *D*. iv. 275
And yielding Metal *f*. to human form *S*. v. 148
Thames heard the numbers as he *f*. aloog *W*. 13
There the last numbers *f*. from Cowley's tongue *W.F.* 272

Flow'r.
Die ev'ry *f*., and perish all, but she *A*. 34
A Nest, a Toad, a Fungus, or a *F. D*. iv. 400
Fair from its humble bed I rear'd this *f. D*. iv. 405
The rising game I chas'd from *f*. to *f. D*. iv. 426
Beauty, frail *f*., that ev'ry season fears *E*. iii. 57
Shades ev'ry *f*., and darkens ev'ry green *E.A.* 168
Like some fair *f*. the early spring supplies *E.C.* 498
Suckles each herb, and spreads out ev'ry *f. E.M.* i. 134
This taste the honey, and not wound the *f. E.M.* ii. 90
Whose sacred *f*. with fragrance fills the skies *M*. 10
And justly set the Gem above the *F. M.E.* i. 148
Shrink his thin essence like a riv'd *f. R.L.* ii. 132
And four fair Queens whose hands sustain a *f. R.L.* iii. 39
In *f*. of age you perish for a song *S*. i. 102
Ye f—s that droop, forsaken by the spring A. 27
Let spring attend, and sudden *f*. arise *A*. 36
Or gives to Zembla fruits, to Barca *f. D*. i. 74
In *f*. and pearls by bounteous Kirkall drest *D*. ii. 160
Celestial palms, and ever-blooming *f. E.A.* 318
A Wild, where weeds and *f*. promiscuous shoot *E.M.* i. 7
The *F*. of Bubo, and the Flow of Y—g *E.S.* i. 68
There Gladiators fight or die in *f. M.E.* iv. 124
O'er th' Elysian *f. O*. i. 73
With golden crowns, and wreaths of heav'nly *f. R.L.* i. 34
To draw fresh colours from the vernal *f. R.L.* ii. 95

Close by those meads, for ever crown'd with *f. R.L.* iii. 1
Plain truth, dear MURRAY, needs no *f*. of speech *S*. iv. 3
On Avon's haok, where *f*. eternal blow *S*. v. 119
Now leaves the trees, and *f*. adorn the ground *Sp*. 43
Hush'd are the birds, and clos'd the drooping *f. Sp*. 70
For you the swains the fairest *f*. design *Su*. 55
Where'er you tread the blushing *f*. shall rise *Su*. 75
Yet shall thy grave with rising *f*. be drest *U.L.* 63
Nor morning odours from the *f*. arise *W*. 46
Or from the meads select unfading *f. W*. 74
While plants their shade, or *f*. their odours give *W*. 83
And draws the aromatic souls of *f. W.F.* 244

Flower'd.
Cato's long wig, *f*. gown, and lacquer'd chair *S*. v. 337

Flow'ring.
To leafless shrubs the *f*. palms succeed *M*. 75

Flow'ry.
I'll fly from shepherds, flocks, and *f*. plains *A*. 86
As *f*. hands in wantonness are worn *E*. iv. 65
Pleas'd to the last, he crops the *f*. food *E.M.* i. 83
For him as kindly spread the *f*. lawn *E.M.* iii. 30
And Carmel's *f*. top perfumes the skies *M*. 28
And boys in *f*. bands the tiger lead *M*. 78
All beneath yon *f*. Rocks *Mi*. vii. 8
With thy *f*. Chaplets crown'd *Mi*. vii. 28
Like gentle *Fanny's* was my *f*. theme *P.S.* 149
Thus on Mæander's *f*. margin lies *R.L.* v. 65
And ev'ry *f*. Courtier writ Romance *S*. v. 146
See, where on earth the *f*. glories lie *W*. 33
To paint anew the *f*. sylvan scenes *W.F.* 285
Cole, whose dark streams his *f*. islands lave *W.F.* 343
Paints the green forests and the *f*. plains *W.F.* 428

Flowing.
Why words so *f*., thoughts so free *I.H.* iii. 39
Soft sorrows, melting griefs, and *f*. tears *R.L.* iv. 86
My head and heart thus *f*. thro' my quill *S*. i. 63

Flows.
Lo ! where Mœotis sleeps, and hardly *f. D*. iii. 87
And boasts a Warmth, that from no Passion *f. E*. ii. 4
And the smooth stream in smoother numbers *f. E.C.* 367
Soon *f*. to this in body and in soul *E.M.* ii. 140
But Ease in writing *f*. from Art, not chance *S*. vi. 178
Thence to their images on earth it *f. U.L.* 15
From heav'n itself tho' sev'n-fold Nilus *f. W.F.* 359

Fluent.
How *f*. nonsense trickles from his tongue *D*. iii. 201
And *f*. Shakespear scarce effac'd a line *S*. v. 279

Fluid.
Or swims along the *f*. atmosphere *D*. iv. 423
Their *f*. bodies half dissolv'd in light *R.L.* ii. 62

Flute.
That *f*. is mine which Colin's tuneful breath *Su*. 39

Flutter.
That *f*. for a Day *Mi*. iv. 18
And sport and *f*. in the fields of Air *R.L.* i. 66
And little hearts to *f*. at a Beau *R.L.* i. 90

Flutter'd.
That once so *f*., and that once so writ *D*. ii. 120

Flutt'ring.
In patch-work *f*., and her head aside *D*. iv. 48
F. spread thy purple pinions *Mi*. vii. 1
The *f*. fan be Zephyretta's care *R.L.* ii. 112
Clothe spice, line trunks, or, *f*. in a row *S*. v. 418

Flutters.
One flaunts in rags, one *f*. in brocade *E.M.* iv. 196
F. in blood, and panting beats the ground *W.F.* 114

Fly.
For this plain reason, Man is not a *F. E.M.* i. 194
And Reason giv'n them but to study Flies *D*. iv. 454
I'll *f*. *from shepherds, flocks, and flow'ry plains A*. 86
As, forc'd from wind-guns, lead itself can *f. D*. i. 181
His papers light *f*. diverse, tost in air *D*. ii. 114
As thick as bees o'er vernal blossoms *f. D*. iii. 33
Proceed, great days ! till Learning *f*. the shore *D*. iii. 333

See *Mystery* to *Mathematics f. D*. iv. 647

FLYING—FOLLY.

Together o'er the Alps methinks we *f. E.* iii. 25
The dear Ideas, where I *f.*, pursue *E.A.* 264
No, *f.* me, *f.* me, far as Pole from Pole *E.A.* 289
See from my cheeks the transient roses *f. E.A.* 331
Conceal his force, nay seem sometimes to *f. E.C.* 178
Nay, *f.* to Altars; there they'll talk you dead *E.C.* 624
Let Earth unbalanc'd from her orbit *f. E.M.* i. 252
Taught on the wings of Truth to *f. I.H.* iv. 3
Swift *f.* the years, and rise th' expected morn *M.* 21
Let Fops or Fortune *f.* which way they will *M.E.* ii. 265
That lends Corruption lighter wings to *f. M.E.* iii. 40
Wait but for wings, and in their season *f. M.E.* iii. 170
Forsaken, friendless, shall ye *f. O.* ii. 14
Lend, lend your wings! I mount! I *f. O.* v. 16
All *f.* to TWIT'NAM, and in humble strain *P.S.* 21
Know, then, unnumber'd Spirits round thee *f. R.L.* i. 41
With like confusion diff'rent nations *f. R.L.* iii. 83
To either India see the merchant *f. S.* iii. 69
F. then, on all the wings of wild desire *S.* iv. 67
Back *f.* the scenes, and enter foot and horse *S.* v. 315
Shall *f.*, like Oglethorpe, from pole to pole *S.* vi. 277
Scar'd at the grizly forms, I sweat, I *f. S.* viii. 278
Not half so swift the trembling doves can *f. W.F.* 185
Shine, buzz, and *f.*-blow *in the setting sun M.E.* ii. 28

Flying.

Suck my last breath, and catch my *f.* soul *E.A.* 324
In Man, the judgment shoots at *f.* game *M.E.* ii. 96
Some *f.* stroke alone can hit 'em right *M.E.* ii. 154
To covet *f.*, and regret when lost *M.E.* ii. 234
So quick retires each *f.* course, you'd swear *M.E.* iv. 159
Trembling, hoping, ling'ring *f. O.* v. 3
On wings of winds come *f.* all abroad *P.S.* 218
And earth rolls back beneath the *f.* steed *IV.F.* 158
And with her dart the *f.* deer she wounds *W.F.* 180

Foals.

For their defrauded absent *f.* they make *D.* ii. 249

Foam'd.

There *f.* rebellious Logic, gagg'd and bound *D.* iv. 23

Foaming.

Then *f.* pour along, and rush into the Thames *W.F.* 218
Tho' *f.* Hermus swells with tides of gold *W.F.* 358
Red Iber's sands, or Ister's *f.* flood *W.F.* 368

Foe.

Sworn *f.* to Myst'ry, yet divinely dark *D.* iv. 460
Nor wish to lose a *F.* these Virtues raise *E.* ii. 11
Make use of ev'ry friend—and ev'ry *f. E.C.* 214
Ah let not Learning too commence its *f. E.C.* 509
And gladly praise the merit of a *f. E.C.* 638
And treat this passion more as friend than *f. E.M.* iii. 164
Who, *f.* to Nature, hears the gen'ral groan *E.M.* iii. 163
And he return'd a friend, who came a *f. E.M.* iii. 206
And play'd the God an engine on his *f. E.M.* iii. 268
Mine, as a *F.* profess'd to false Pretence *E.S.* ii. 201
F. to loud Praise, and Friend to learned Ease *Ep.* x. 5
F. to the Dryads of his Father's groves *M.E.* iv. 94
Wept by each friend, forgiv'n by ev'ry *F. Mi.* ix. 47
A tim'rous *f.*, and a suspicious friend *P.S.* 206
That tends to make one worthy man my *f. P.S.* 284
He stood the furious *f.*, the timid friend *P.S.* 343
F. to his pride, but friend to his distress *P.S.* 371
Thrice she look'd back, and thrice the *f.* drew near *R.L.* iii. 138
Who sought no more than on his *f.* to die *R.L.* v. 78
"Boast not my fall" (he cry'd) "insulting *f.*" *R.L.* v. 97
Britain to soft refinements less a *f. S.* v. 205
Against the *f.*, himself, and all mankind *S.* vi. 39
Canst thou endure a *f.*, forgive a friend *S.* vi. 317
On each I judge thy *F. U.P.* 28
This prize is mine; *who tempt it are my f*—*s D.* ii. 54
Embrace, embrace, my sons! be *f.* no more *D.* iii. 177
Nor *f.* nor fortune take this pow'r away *E.A.* 43
From the same *f.*, at last, both felt their doom *E.C.* 685
In the small circle of our *f.* or friends *E.M.* iv. 242
Whose sons shall blush their fathers were thy *f. E.M.* iv. 388
Laugh them at any, but at Fools or *F. E.S.* i. 53
And *f.* to virtue wonder'd how they wept *P.C.* 8
If *f.*, they write, if friends, they read me dead *P.S.* 32
But *f.* like these—One Flatt'rer's worse than all *P.S.* 104
And ridicules beyond a hundred *f. P.S.* 110
To kill those *f.* to Fair ones, Time and Thought *M.E.* ii. 112

Fair to expose myself, my *f.*, my friends *S.* i. 58
My *f.* shall wish my life a longer date *S.* i. 61
F. to all living worth except your own *S.* v. 33

Fogs.

Beholds thro' *f.*, that magnify the scene *D.* i. 80
A veil of *f.* dilates her awful face *D.* i. 262

Fold.

Some *f.* the sleeve, whilst others plait the gown *R.L.* i. 147

Foliage.

A Myrtle *F.* round the Thimble-Case *Mi.* ix. 34

Folio.

That altar crowns; A *f.* Common-place *D.* i. 159

Folks.

Who never flatter'd *F.* like you *Ep.* xv. 3
See but the Fortune of some *f. I.H.* ii. 108 *s*
My Friends above, my *F.* below *I.H.* ii. 135
Sir Balaam now, he lives like other *f. M.E.* iii. 357
No wonder some *f.* bow, and think them kings *S.* viii. 211

Follow.

Swift as it mounts, all *f.* with their eyes *D.* ii. 185
And Jove's own Thunders *f.* Mars's Drums *D.* iv. 68
First *f.* Nature, and your judgment frame *E.C.* 68
Subject, compound them, *f.* her and God *E.M.* ii. 116
'Tis but by parts we *f.* good or ill *E.M.* ii. 235
I *f. Virtue*: where she shines, I praise *E.S.* ii. 95
Absent I *f.* thro' th' extended Dream *I.H.* iii. 42
But what to *f.*, is a task indeed *M.E.* ii. 200
Still *f.* Sense, of ev'ry Art the Soul *M.E.* iv. 65
That task, which as we *f.*, or despise *S.* iii. 43
And then let Virtue *f.*, if she will *S.* iii. 80
Why do, I'll *f.* them with all my heart *S.* iv. 133
To *f.* nature, and regard his end *W.F.* 252

Follow'd.

Stol'n from a Duel, *f.* by a Nun *D.* iv. 237
It fled, I *f.*; now in hope, now pain *D.* iv. 427
And Arts still *f.* where her Eagles flew *E.C.* 684
Thro' life 'tis *f.*, ev'n at life's expense *E.M.* ii. 171
Pensive hast *f.* to the silent tomb *Ep.* vii. 12
Him Basto *f.*, but his fate more hard *R.L.* iii. 53
Lov'd without youth, and *f.* without pow'r *S.* iii. 183

Follower, Follow'r.

Still let me say: No *F.*, but a Friend *E.S.* ii. 93
F—*r* of God or friend of human-kind *E.M.* ii. 234
Or tread the mazy round his *f*—*s* trod *E.M.* ii. 25
By Wealth of *F. f* without one distress *M.E.* ii. 145

Following.

Signs *f.* signs lead on the mighty year *D.* iii. 321
But *f.* wits from that intention stray'd *E.C.* 104
The *f.* licence of a Foreign reign *E.C.* 544
Like *f.* life thro' creatures you dissect *M.E.* i. 29
Years *f.* years, steal something ev'ry day *S.* vi. 72

Follows.

Some dire misfortune *f.* close behind *E.A.* 34
Who sees and *f.* that great scheme the best *E.M.* iv. 95

Folly.

Close to those walls where *F.* holds her throne *D.* i. 29
All that on *F.* Frenzy could beget *D.* i. 125
O born in sin, and forth in *f.* brought *D.* i. 225
F., my son, has still a Friend at Court *D.* i. 300
And all to one lov'd *F.* sacrifice *E.C.* 266
The current *f.* proves the ready wit *E.C.* 449
Pride, Malice, *F.*, against Dryden rose *E.C.* 458
Eye Nature's walks, shoot *F.* as it flies *E.M.* i. 13
That counter-works each *f.* and caprice *E.M.* ii. 239
Where *F.* fights for Kings, or dives for gain *E.M.* iv. 154
The broadest mirth unfeeling *F.* wears *E.M.* iv. 319
To Vice and *F.* to confine the jest *E.S.* i. 37
Sole Dread of *F.*, Vice, and Insolence *E.S.* ii. 213
Thus in a sea of *f.* toss'd *I.H.* i. 125
If *F.* grow romantic, I must paint it *M.E.* ii. 16
For tho' such motives *F.* you may call (*rep.*) *M.E.* iii. 157
And see the *F.* which I cannot shun *Mi.* ix. 70
And Advocates for *F.* dead and gone *S.* v. 34
Sometimes the *F.* benefits Mankind *S.* v. 191
Confess as well your *F.*, as Disease *S.* vi. 215
Whom *F.* pleases, and whose Follies please *S.* vi. 327

FOND—FOOLISH.

And all was hush'd, as F.'s self lay dead *D.* ii. 418
In *F*. Cap, than Wisdom's grave disguise *D.* iv. 240
Poor W** nipt in *f*. broadest bloom *D.* iv. 513
In *F*. cup still laughs the bubble, joy *E.M.* ii. 288
The sober *f*—ies of the wise and great *E.* i. 10
Consistent in our *f*. and our sins *M.E.* i. 226
At last, to *f*. Youth could scarce defend *M.E.* ii. 235
Your Taste of *F*., with our scorn of Fools *M.E.* ii. 276
One ebb and flow of *f*. all my life *S.* iii. 168
When sick of Muse, our *f*. we deplore *S.* v. 177
Whom Folly pleases, and whose *F*. please *S.* vi. 327
Adieu to all the *f*. of the age *S.* viii. 2

Fond.

Or their *f*. parents drest in red and gold *D.* i. 138
And hears the various vows of *f*. mankind *D.* ii. 87
Prompt to impose, and *f*. to dogmatize *D.* iv. 464
F. to forget the statesman in the friend *E.* i. 8
As some *f*. Virgin, whom her Mother's care *E.* v. 1
More *f*. than mistress, make me that to thee *E.A.* 90
Fill my *f*. heart with God alone, for he *R.A.* 205
Most Critics, *f*. of some subservient art *E.C.* 263
Still *f*. and proud of savage liberty *E.C.* 650
Careless of censure, nor too *f*. of fame *E.C.* 741
Adieu, *f*. hope of mutual fire *I.H.* iii. 33
Is he a Churchman? then he's *f*. of pow'r *M.E.* i. 155
Cease, *f*. Nature, cease thy strife *O.* v. 5
Should such a man, too *f*. to rule alone *P.S.* 197
Are, as when women, wondrous *f*. of place *R.L.* iii. 36
F. to spread friendships, but to cover heats *S.* i. 136
Nor *f*. of bleeding, ev'n in BRUNSWICK'S cause *S.* iii. 10
F. of his Friend, and civil to his Wife *S.* vi. 189

Fonder.

Or meets his spouse's *f*. eye *O.* iii. 32

Fondly.

F. we think we honour merit then *E.C.* 454
A wretched Sylph too *f*. interpos'd *R.L.* iii. 150
Yet these are Wights, who *f*. call their own *S.* vi. 244

Food.

Pleas'd to the last, he crops the flow'ry *f*. *E.M.* i. 83
Thy joy, thy pastime, thy attire, thy *f*. *E.M.* iii. 28
To shun their poison, and to choose their *f*. *E.M.* iii. 100
Learn from the birds what *f*. the thickets yield *E.M.* iii. 173
He from the wond'ring furrow call'd the *f*. *E.M.* iii. 219
Then first the Flamen tasted living *f*. *E.M.* iii. 265
For *f*. digested takes another name *S.* vii. 34
For her the flocks refuse their verdant *f*. *W.* 37

Fool.

This arch Absurd, that wit and *f*. delights *D.* i. 221
With *F*. of Quality completes the Quire *D.* i. 298
A *f*., so just a copy of a wit *D.* ii. 48
But *f*. with *f*. is barb'rous civil war *D.* iii. 176
Or give from *f*. to *f*. the Laurel crown *D.* iv. 98
What tho' we let some better sort of *f*. *D.* iv. 235
The Sire is made a Peer, the Son a *F*. *D.* iv. 548
And, to complete her bliss, a *F*. for Mate *E.* iv. 52
As not to stick at *f*. or ass *E.* vi. 23
I tell ye, *f*., there's nothing in't *E.* vi. 96
A *f*. might once himself alone expose *E.C.* 7
Fear most to tax an Honourable *f*. *E.C.* 388
And thanks his stars he was not born a *f*. *E. 9.S.* 8
Then drop into thyself, and he a *f*. *E.M.* ii. 30
The rogue and *f*. by fits is fair and wise *E.M.* ii. 233
The *f*. is happy that he knows no more *E.M.* ii. 264
'Tis this, Tho' Man's a *f*., yet GOD is WISE *E.M.* ii. 294
Has God, thou *f*., work'd solely for thy good *E.M.* iii. 27
O'er-look'd, scen double, by the *f*. and wise *E.M.* iv. 6
Oh *f*.! to think God hates the worthy mind *E.M.* iv. 189
I'll tell you, friend! a wise man and a *F*. *E.M.* iv. 200
Is but the more a *f*., the more a knave *E.M.* iv. 232
A Patriot is a *F*. in ev'ry age *E.S.* i. 41
And charitably comfort Knave and *F*. *E.S.* i. 62
And let, a' God's name, ev'ry *F*. and Knave *E.S.* i. 85
ST. JOHN has ever been a wealthy *F*. *E.S.* ii. 132
The *F*. lies hid in inconsistencies *M.E.* i. 70
And just her wisest monarch made a *f*. *M.E.* i. 94
The *F*. consistent, and the False sincere *M.E.* i. 176
A *F*. with more of Wit than half mankind *M.E.* i. 200
'Twas all for fear the Knaves should call him *F*. *M.E.* i. 207
A *f*. to Pleasure, yet a slave to Fame *M.E.* ii. 62
Woman and *F*. are two hard things to hit *M.E.* ii. 113

The wisest *F*. much Time has ever made *M.E.* ii. 124
Giv'n to the *F*., the Mad, the Vain, the Evil *M.E.* iii. 19
That "ev'ry man in want is Knave or *f*." *M.E.* iii. 102
No *F*. to laugh at, which he valu'd more *M.E.* iii. 312
Heav'n visits with a Taste the wealthy *f*. *M.E.* iv. 17
Yet plays the *f*. before she dies *Mi.* vi. 8
That secret to each *f*., that he's an Ass *P.S.* 80
No creature smarts so little as a *f*. *P.S.* 84
A *f*. quite angry is quite innocent *P.S.* 107
As yet a child, nor yet a *f*. to fame *P.S.* 127
Nut Fortune's worshipper, nor Fashion's *f*. *P.S.* 334
It was a sin to call our neighbour *f*. *P.S.* 383
The eldest is a *f*., the youngest wise *S.* iii. 44
And feel some comfort, not to be a *f*. *S.* iii. 48
And the first Wisdom, to be *F*. no more *S.* iii. 66
The *F*., whose wife elopes some thrice a quarter *S.* iii. 150
Why then, I say, the Public is a *f*. *S.* v. 94
Or damn all Shakespeare, like th' affected *F*. *S.* v. 105
Better (say I) be pleas'd, and play the *f*. *S.* vi. 181
A worthy member, no small *f*., a Lord *S.* vi. 285
I die in charity with *f*. and knave *S.* viii. 3
But, as the *F*. that in reforming days *S.* viii. 15
So when you plague a *f*., 'tis still the curse *S.* viii. 120
Jests like a licens'd *f*., commands like law *S.* viii. 221
Hence the F.'s *paradise, the Statesman's Scheme D.*iii.9
Or which must end me, a *F*. wrath or love *P.S.* 30
Or serve (like other *F*—s) to fill a room *D.* i. 136
And here she plann'd th' Imperial seat of *F*. *D.* i. 272
Serves but to keep *f*. pert, and knaves awake *D.* iv. 442
Made slaves by honour, and made *F*. by shame *E.* iv. 36
And some made coxcombs Nature meant but *f*. *E.C.* 27
All *f*. have still an itching to deride *E.C.* 32
Turn'd Critics next, and prov'd plain *f*. at last *E.C.* 37
Prescribe, apply, and call their masters *f*. *E.C.* 111
Is *Pride*, the never-failing voice of *f*. *E.C.* 204
Concluding all were desp'rate sots and *f*. *E.C.* 271
Her voice is all these tuneful *f*. admire *E.C.* 340
For *f*. admire, but men of sense approve *E.C.* 391
We think our fathers *f*., so wise we grow *E.C.* 438
Which lives as long as *f*. are pleas'd to laugh *E.C.* 451
By *f*. 'tis hated, and hy knaves undone *E.C.* 507
Contending wits become the sport of *f*. *E.C.* 517
For *F*. rush in where Angels fear to tread *E.C.* 625
Wits, just like *F*., at war about a name *E.M.* ii. 85
F. who from hence into the notion fall *E.M.* ii. 211
What can she more than tell us we are *f*. *E.M.* ii. 152
For Forms of Government let *f*. contest *E.M.* iii. 303
But *f*. the Good alone unhappy call *E.M.* iv. 97
Nor own your fathers have been *f*. so long *E.M.* iv. 214
To laugh at *F*. who put their trust in Peter *E.S.* i. 10
Laugh then at any, but at *F*. or Foes *E.S.* i. 53
See, all our *F*. aspiring to be Knaves *E.S.* i. 63
Thus *F*. with Compliments besiege ye *I.H.* i. 29
And not like forty other *F*. *I.H.* ii. 164
When twenty *F*. I never saw *I.H.* ii. 64
Women and *F*. must like him or he dies *M.E.* i. 183
Shines in exposing Knaves, and painting *F*. *M.E.* ii. 119
Your Taste of Follies, with our Scorn of *F*. *M.E.* ii. 276
And Gold but sent to keep the *f*. in play *M.E.* iii. 5
Not of the Wits his foes, but *F*. his friends *Mi.* iii. 14
We thrive at *Westminster* on *F*. like you *Mi.* xi. 11
F. grant what'er Ambition craves *O.* ii. 27
And shame the *f*.—Your Int'rest, Sir, with Lintot *P.S.*62
Dreading ev'n *f*., by Flatterers besieg'd *P.S.* 207
F. rush into my head, and so I write *S.* i. 14
All the mad Trade of *F*. and Slaves for Gold *S.* iv. 13
Not for yourself, but for your *F*. and Knaves *S.* iv. 92
These *f*. demand not pardon, but Applause *S.* v. 118
You'd think no *f*. disgrac'd the former reign *S.* v. 127
Tell me if Congreve's *F*. are *F*. indeed *S.* v. 287
The Zeal of *F*. offends at any time (*rep.*) *S.* v. 406
There's nothing blackens like the ink of *f*. *S.* v. 411
Composing songs for *F*. to get by heart *S.* vi. 126
That helps it both to fools-coats and to *f*. *S.* viii. 221
Of all beau-kind the best proportion'd *f*. *S.* viii. 241
Peace, *f*., or Gonson will for Papists seize you *S.* viii. 256
The gaze of *f*., and pageant of a day *U.L.* 44
That helps it both to fools-coats and to fools *S.* viii. 221
And with her own *f.-colours* gilds them all *D.* i. 84
Mummius o'erheard him, Mummius *f.-renown'd D.*iv.371

Foolish.

From *f*. Greeks to steal them, was as wise *D.* iv. 378
Weak, *f*. man! will Heav'n reward us there *E.M.*iv.173
And wonder with a *f*. face of praise *P.S.* 212

I

FOOT—FOREST.

To stop thy *f.* views, thy long desires *S.* iii. 75
With *f.* pride my heart was never fir'd *S.* viii. 9
Save me alike from *f.* Pride *U.P.* 33

Foot.

On horse, on *f.*, in hacks, in gilded chariots *D.* ii. 24
Leave not a *f.* of verse, a *f.* of stone *D.* iv. 127
When victims at yon altar's *f.* we lay *E.A.* 108
What if the *f.*, ordain'd the dust to tread *E.M.* i. 259
Slopes at its *f.*, the woods its sides embrace *S.* iii. 141
Back fly the scenes, and enter *f.* and horse *S.* v. 315
And learn to crawl upon poetic feet *D.* i. 62
On *f.* and wings, and flies, and wades, and hops *D.* ii. 64
Pours at great Bourbon's *f.* her silken sons *D.* iv. 298
Should at my *f.* the world's great master fall *E.A.* 85
And harmless serpents lick the pilgrim's *f.* *M.* 80
And Sydney's verse halts ill on Roman *f.* *S.* v. 98
How much at variance are her *f.* and eyes *Sp.* 60

Footman.

To see a *f.* kick'd that took his pay *E.S.* ii. 151
She bids her *F.* put it in her head *M.E.* ii. 178
Strong as the *F.*, as the Master sweet *Mi.* ix. 106

Footsteps.

A hundred *f.* scrape the marble Hall *M.E.* iv. 152

Footstool.

Beneath her *f. Science* groans in Chains *D.* iv. 21
My *f.* earth, my canopy the skies *E.M.* i. 140

Fop.

But *F.* shows *F.* superior complaisance *D.* iv. 138
Scatter your Favours on a *F. I.H.* i. 31
A *F.* their Passion, but their Prize a Sot *M.E.* ii. 247
That *F.*, whose pride affects a patron's name *P.S.* 291
F. at the toilet, flatt'rer at the board *P.S.* 328
What further could I wish the *f.* to do *S.* vii. 19
Nature made ev'ry *F.* to plague his brother *S.* viii. 258
Did on the stage my F—s appear confin'd *D.* i. 191
Some positive, persisting *f.* we know *E.C.* 568
No place so sacred from such *f.* is barr'd *E.C.* 622
Of *F.* in learning, and of Knaves in State *Ep.* i. 4
Let *F.* or Fortune fly which way they will *M.E.* ii. 265
The *F.* are painted Butterflies *Mi.* iv. 17
But sick of *f.*, and poetry and prate *P.S.* ii. 298
While the *F.* envy, and the Ladies stare *R.L.* iv. 104

Fopling.

To see those antics, *F.* and Courtin *S.* viii. 237

For.—*Passim.*

Forbear.

Good friend, *f.* ! you deal in dang'rous things *P.S.* 75
No more the streams their murmur shall *f. W.* 57

Forbears.

But Umbriel, hateful Gnome, *f.* not so *R.L.* iv. 141

Forbid.

Good Heav'n *f.*, that I should blast their glory *E.S.* i. 105
F. it Heav'n, a Favour or a Debt *M.E.* ii. 171
Honour *f.* ! at whose unrivall'd shrine *R.L.* iv. 105

Forbidden.

Love finds an altar for *f.* fires *E.A.* 182
Or Garden, tempting with *f.* fruit *E.M.* i. 8

Forbids.

Her Priestless Muse *f.* the Good to die *E.S.* ii. 234

Forbore.

Preserv'd the freedom, and *f.* the vice *S.* v. 260

Force.

Renew'd by Ordure's sympathetic *f. D.* ii. 103
What *f.* have pious vows ! The Queen of Love *D.* ii. 215
Suspend a while your *F.* inertly strong *D.* iv. 7
See how the *f.* of others pray'rs I try *E.A.* 149
Life, *f.*, and beauty, must to all impart *E.C.* 72
Seizes your fame, and puts his laws in *f. E.C.* 168
Conceal his *f.*, nay seem sometimes to fly *E.C.* 178
But the joint *f.* and full result of all *E.C.* 246
Here with degrees of swiftness, there of *f. E.M.* i. 182
Ev'n mean Self-love becomes, by *f.* divine *E.M.* ii. 291

F. first made Conquest, and that conquest, Law *E.M.* iii. 245
If there be *f.* in Virtue, or in Song *P.S.* 387
By *f.* to ravish, or by fraud betray *R.L.* ii. 32
Few ask, if fraud or *f.* attain'd his ends *R.L.* ii. 34
Some dire disaster, or by *f.*, or slight *R.L.* ii. 103
The skilful Nymph reviews her *f.* with care *R.L.* iii. 45
The conqu'ring *f.* of unresisted steel *R.L.* iii. 178
There she collects the *f.* of female lungs *R.L.* iv. 83
Or nobly wild, with Budgel's fire and *f. S.* i. 27
Lest stiff, and stately, void of fire or *f. S.* iii. 15
That wants or *f.*, or light, or weight, or care *S.* vi. 160
Ready, by *f.*, or of your own accord *S.* vi. 250
And I. that sun but on a part to shine *E.C.* 399

Forc'd.

As, *f.* from wind-guns, lead itself can fly *D.* i. 181
F. into Virtue thus by Self-defence *E.M.* iii. 279
(Some say his Queen) was *f.* to speak, or burst *P.S.* 72
As many more Manillio *f.* to yield *R.L.* iii. 51
And *f.* ev'n me to see the damn'd at Court *S.* viii. 191

Fore-cast.

Mem'ry and *f.* just returns engage *E.M.* iii. 143

Foredoom.

Here Britain's statesmen oft the fall *f. R.L.* iii. 5
And hence the egregious wizard shall *f. R.L.* v. 139

Foredoom'd.

A Clerk, *f.* his father's soul to cross *P.S.* 17

Forefather.

As sings thy great *f.* Ogilby *D.* i. 328
Blest Peer ! his great F—s' ev'ry grace *Ep.* i. 11

Forego.

The dumb shall sing, the lame his crutch *f. M.* 43

Forehead.

Cibberian *f.*, and Cibberian brain *D.* i. 218
Cibberian *f.*, or Cimmerian gloom *D.* iv. 532

Foreign.

I know thee, Love ! on *f.* Mountains bred *A.* 89
F. her air, her robe's discordant pride *D.* iv. 47
Some *f.* writers, some our own despise *E.C.* 394
The following license of a *f.* reign *E.C.* 544
But we, brave Britons, *f.* laws despis'd *E.C.* 715
Nothing is *f.* : Parts relate to whole *E.M.* iii. 21
All fame is *f.*, but of true desert *E.M.* iv. 253
Our Youth, all livery'd with *f.* Gold *E.S.* i. 155
For *f.* glory, *f.* joy, they roam *M.E.* ii. 223
Of *f.* Tyrants, and of Nymphs at home *R.L.* iii. 6
Or for a Titled Puck, or *f.* Flame *S.* iv. 124
In ev'ry taste of *f.* Courts improv'd *S.* v. 141
Rich with the treasures of each *f.* tongue *S.* v. 173
By *f.* hands thy dying eyes were clos'd (*rep.*) *U.L.* 51

Foreigner.

What better teach a *F.* the tongue *S.* v. 206

Foremost.

Mark first that youth who takes the *f.* place *D.* iii. 139
All crowd, who *f.* shall be damn'd to fame *D.* iii. 158
But far the *f.*, two, with earnest zeal *D.* iv. 401
And *f.* in the Circle eye a King *S.* iii. 106
Behind the *f.*, and before the last *S.* vi. 303

Fore-right.

He spits *f.* ; his haughty chest before *S.* viii. 264

Fore-runner.

The sure *f.* of her gentle sway *D.* iii. 300

Foresee.

Some War, some Plague, some Famine they *f. M.E.* iii. 113
His Grace's fate sage Cutler could *f. M.E.* iii. 315

Foreseen.

F. by me, but ah ! withheld from mine *D.* iii. 276

Foresees.

Phryne, *f.* a general Excise *M.E.* iii. 120
And in its fellow's fate *f.* its own *R.L.* iv. 172

Forest.

Benighted wanderers, the *f.* o'er *M.E.* iii. 193

FORETOLD—FORMER.

In *f*. planted by a Father's hand *S*. ii. 135
Bleeds in the *F*. like a wounded hart *W.F.* 84
And bathes the *f*. where she rang'd before *W.F.* 208
He gathers health from herbs the *f*. yields *W.F.* 241
But hark! the groves rejoice, the *f*. rings *W.F.* 281
Beyond the f.'s verdant limits stray'd *W.F.* 182
The f—s dance, the rivers upward rise D. iii. 245
See nodding *f*. on the mountains dance *M*. 26
For thee Idume's spicy *f*. blow *M*. 95
Where rising *F*., not for pride or show *M.E.* iv. 187
The wond'ring *f*. soon shall dance again *Su*. 82
Thy *f*., Windsor! and thy green retreats *W.F.* 1
The *f*. wonder'd at th' unusual grain *W.F.* 89
And floating *f*. paint the waves with green *W.F.* 216
No more the *f*. ring, or groves rejoice *W.F.* 278
To crown the *f*. with immortal greens *W.F.* 281
And half thy *f*. rush into the floods *W.F.* 386
Paints the green *f*. and the flow'ry plains *W.F.* 428
And chaste Diana haunts the f.-shade Su. 62
Swarm o'er the lawns, the *f.-walks* surround *W.F.* 149

Foretold.
This, this is he *f*. by ancient rhymes *D*. iii 319
The Saviour comes! by ancient bards *f. M*. 37

Forfeit.
His Life, to *f*. it a thousand ways *M.E.* i. 197
His wealth, yet dearer, *f*. to the crown *M.E.* iii. 400

Forfex.
The Peer now spreads the glitt'ring *F*. wide *R.L.* ii. 147

Forge.
But Pens can *f*., my Friend, that cannot write *E.S.* ii. 188

Forg'd.
Because the Deed he *f*. was not my own *E.S.* iii. 190

Forget.
Prick all their ears up, and *f*. to graze *D*. ii. 262
Fond to *f*. the statesman in the friend *E*. i. 8
Canst thou *f*. that sad, that solemn day *E.A.* 107
Canst thou *f*. what tears that moment fell *E.A.* 109
'Tis sure the hardest science to *f. E.A.* 190
Conceal, disdain,—do all things but *f. E.A.* 200
F., renounce me, hate whate'er was mine *E.A.* 294
F. to thunder, and recall her fires *E.M.* iv. 124
How can I Pult'ney, Chesterfield *f. E.S.* ii. 84
She e'er should cancel—but she may *f. M.E.* ii. 172
This Phoebus promis'd (I *f*. the year) *M.E.* ii. 283
Look on her face, and you'll *f*. 'em all *R.L.* ii. 18
F. her pray'rs, or miss a masquerade *R.L.* ii. 108
And which it much becomes you to *f. S*. iv. 94
F. his Epic, nay Pindaric Art *S*. v. 77
While silent birds *f*. their tuneful lays *W*. 7
Then bow'd and spoke; the winds *f*. to roar *W.F.* 353

Forgets.
Which whoso tastes, *f*. his former friends *D*. iv. 518
Perhaps *f*. that Oxford e'er was great *E*. i. 18
Here grief *f*. to groan, and love to weep *E.A.* 314
Vice is undone, if she *f*. her Birth *E.S.* i. 141

Forgetting.
The world *f*., by the world forgot *E.A.* 208

Forgive.
Some Dæmon stole my pen (*f*. th' offence) *D*. i. 187
To err is human, to *f*. divine *E.C.* 525
Dear Sir, *f*. the Prejudice of Youth *E.S.* i. 63
And till we share your joys, *f*. our grief *Ep*. vii. 18
Offend her, and she knows not to *f. M.E.* ii. 137
Canst thou endure a foe, *f*. a friend *S*. vi. 317
And as for Courts, *f*. me, if I say *S*. viii. 92

Forgiv'n.
Soft as the slumbers of a saint *f. E.A.* 255
One human tear shall drop and be *f. E.A.* 358
All ties dissolv'd, and ev'ry Sin *f. E.S.* i. 94
Wept by each Friend, *f*. by ev'ry Foe *Mi*. ii. 4

Forgiving.
Our sex are still *f*. at their heart *E.J.S.* 12
He draws him gentle, tender, and *f. E.J.S.* 27

Forgot.
Or peaceably *f*., at once be blest *D*. i. 239
I have not yet *f*. myself to stone *E.A.* 24

The world forgetting, by the world *f. E.A.* 208
And things unknown propos'd as things *f. E.C.* 575
Nature in her then err'd not, but *f. M.E.* ii. 158
Alive, ridiculous, and dead, *f. M.E.* ii. 248
What tho' (the use of barb'rous spits *f*.) *M.E.* iii. 179
In all, let Nature never be *f. M.E.* iv. 50
Ev'n copious Dryden wanted, or *f. S*. v. 280
Thoughts, which at Hyde-park-corner I *f. S*. vi. 208
Soft as he mourn'd, the streams *f*. to flow *Su*. 5
The Muse *f*., and thou be lov'd no more *U.L.* 82

Forgotten.
Like Journals, Odes, and such *f*. things *S*. v. 416

Forked.
Proud as Apollo on his *f*. hill *P.S.* 231

Forky.
And with their *f*. tongues shall innocently play *M*. 84
With hoary whiskers, and a *f*. beard *R.L.* iii. 38

Forlorn.
Alike unheard, unpity'd, and *f. A*. 22

Form.
A Poet's *f*. she plac'd before their eyes *D*. ii. 35
Slow rose a *f*. in majesty of Mud *D*. ii. 326
When lo! a Harlot *f*., soft sliding by *D*. iv. 45
Due distance reconciles to *f*. and grace *E.C.* 174
Stones leap'd to *f*., and rocks began to live *E.C.* 702
A pleasing *F*.; a firm, yet cautious Mind *Ep*. ii. 1
Then shall thy *F*. the Marble grace (rep.) *I.H.* iii. 19
His race, his *f*., his name almost unknown *M.E.* iii. 284
Thro' climes and ages bears each *f*. and name *M.E.* v. 32
Her wrinkled *f*. in black and white array'd *R.L.* iv. 28
Venus shall give him *F*., and Anstis Birth *S*. iv. 82
And yielding Metal flow'd to human *f. S*. v. 148
Then from his closing eyes thy *f*. shall part *U.L.* 79
Then ships of uncouth *f*. shall stem the tide *W.F.* 403
Like *f—s in clouds, or visions of the night D*. ii. 112
Thence Beauty, waking all her *f*., supplies *E*. iii. 45
Too much your Sex is by their *f*. confin'd *E*. iv. 31
All *f*. that perish other *f*. supply *E.M.* iii. 17
Here too all *f*. of social union find *E.M.* iii. 179
For *F*. of Government let fools contest *E.M.* iii. 303
Deceiv'd by Shows and *F. Mi*. iv. 2
See, shady *f*. advance *O*. i. 65
Pretty! in amber to observe the *f. P.S.* 169
Transparent *f*., too fine for mortal sight *R.L.* ii. 61
Of bodies chang'd to various *f*. by Spleen *R.L.* iv. 48
The *f*. august, of King, or conqu'ring Chief *S*. v. 391
Scar'd at the grisly *f*., I sweat, I fly *S*. viii. 278
The heroes sit, the vulgar f. *a ring D*. ii. 384
Thence *f*. your judgment, thence your maxims bring *E.C.* 126
F. short Ideas; and offend in arts *E.C.* 287
That Wisdom infinite must *f*. the best *E.M.* i. 44
F. a strong line about the silver bound *R.L.* ii. 121
To *f*., not to admire, but be admir'd *S*. iv. 41

Formal.
Or bound in *f*., or in real chains *E*. iv. 42

Form'd.
Bays, *f*. by nature, Stage and Town to bless *D*. i. 109
She *f*. this image of well-body'd air *D*. ii. 42
My fancy *f*. thee of angelic kind *E*. i. 36
Why *f*. so weak, so little, and so blind *E.M.* i. 36
Why *f*. no weaker, blinder, and no less *E.M.* i. 38
F. but to check, delib'rate, and advise *E.M.* ii. 70
F. and impell'd its neighbour to embrace *E.M.* iii. 12
Thus states were *f*., the name of King unknown *E.M.* iii. 209
And, *f*. like tyrants, tyrants would believe *E.M.* iii. 260
F. by thy converse, happily to steer *E.M.* iv. 379
F. to delight at once and lash the age *Ep*. xi. 4
Yet Chloe sure was *f*. without a spot *M.E.* ii. 157
But of what marble must that breast be *f. Mi*. ix. 75
F. a vast buckle for his widow's gown *R.L.* v. 92
Since 'twas no *f*. design of serving God *S*. viii. 18
Till Fancy colour'd it, and *f*. a dream *S*. viii. 289
And verdant alders *f*. a quiv'ring shade *Su*. 4

Former.
But blind to *f*. as to future fate *D*. iii. 47
Which whoso tastes, forgets his *f*. friends *D*. iv. 518
'Tis but the Fun'ral of the *f*. year *Mi*. v. 10

I 2

I lose all Mem'ry of my *f.* Fears *Mi.* ix. 94
And all the trophies of his *f.* loves *R.L.* ii. 40
You'd think no Fools disgrac'd the *f.* reign *S.* v. 127
Surrey, the Granville of a *f.* age *W.F.* 292

Formidable.
Or seek some Ruin's *f.* shade *E.* iii. 30

Forming.
Heav'n *f.* each on other to depend *E.M.* ii. 249

Forms.
So watchful Bruin *f.*, with plastic care *D.* i. 101
Who knows but he, whose hand the lightning *f. E.M.* i. 157
Who *f.* the phalanx, and who points the way *E.M.* iii. 108
'Tis Education *f.* the common mind *M.E.* i. 149
Its last best work, but *f.* a softer Man *M.E.* ii. 272
Now *f.* my Quincunx, and now ranks my Vines *S.* i. 130
F. the soft bosom with the gentlest art *S.* v. 219
Who *f.* the Genius in the natal hour *S.* vi. 279
He *f.* one tongue, exotic and refin'd *S.* viii. 49

Forsake.
F. mankind, and all the world—but love *A.* 88
For Merit will by turns *f.* them all *E.S.* i. 89
The Court *f.* him, and Sir Balaam hangs *M.E.* iii. 398

Forsaken.
Ye flow'rs that droop, *f.* by the spring *A.* 27
F., friendless, shall ye fly *O.* ii. 14
The Thrush may chant to the *f.* groves *Sp.* 14
Oh deign to visit our *f.* seats *Su.* 71

Forsaking.
The Nymphs, *f.* ev'ry cave and spring *Su.* 51

Forsook.
Sick was the Sun, the Owl *f.* his bow'r *D.* iv. 11
Self-love *f.* the path it first pursu'd *E.M.* iii. 281
At this the blood the virgin's cheek *f. R.L.* iii. 89
And Cynthus' top *f.* for Windsor shade *W.F.* 166

Forswears.
Who starves a Sister, or *f.* a Debt *E.S.* i. 112

Forswore.
Who starv'd a Sister, who *f.* a Debt *E.S.* ii. 20

Fort.
Tore down a Standard, took the *F.* and all *S.* vi. 41

Forth.—*Passim*.

Fortitude.
Fierce champion *F.*, that knows no fears *D.* i. 47
See anger, zeal and *f.* supply *E.M.* ii. 187

Fortune.
Now (shame to *F.*) an ill Run at Play *D.* i. 113
Know, Kings and *F.* cannot make thee more *E.* ii. 9
Nor foes nor *f.* take this pow'r away *E.A.* 43
A Dean, Sir! no ; his *F.* is not made *E.S.* ii. 34
F. her gifts may variously dispose *E.M.* iv. 67
The good or bad the gifts of *F.* gain *E.M.* iv. 83
F. in Men has some small diff'rence made *E.M.* iv. 195
Yet poor with *f.*, and with learning blind *E.M.* iv. 329
O more than *F.*, Friends, or Country lost *Ep.* xiii. 2
See but the *F.* of some folks *I.H.* ii. 108 *s*
Behold ! if *F.* or a Mistress frowns *M.E.* i. 203
Let Fops or *F.* fly which way they will *M.E.* ii. 265
Old Cotta sham'd his *f.* and his birth *M.E.* iii. 177
To balance *F.* by a just expense *M.E.* iii. 223
Where'er he shines, oh *F.*, gild the scene *M.E.* iii. 245
There Victor of his health, of *f.*, friends *M.E.* iii. 313
First sought a Poet's *F.* in the Town *Mi.* iii. 2
As You by Love, so I by *F.* cross'd *Mi.* ix. 11
With ease the smiles of *F.* I resign *Mi.* ix. 14
Each parent sprung—What *f.*, pray ? Their own *P.S.* 390
To friends, to *f.*, to mankind a shame *S.* ii. 107
Who thinks that *F.* cannot change her mind *S.* ii. 123
F. not much of humbling me can boast *S.* ii. 151
Proud *F.*, and look shallow Greatness thro' *S.* iii. 108
Great without Title, without *F.* bless'd *S.* iii. 181
In pow'r, wit, figure, virtue, *f.*, plac'd *S.* vi. 302
Thro' *F.*'s cloud one truly great can see *E.* i. 39
But *F.* gifts if each alike possest *E.M.* iv. 63

Mend *F.* fault, and justify her grace *M.E.* iii. 232
Not *F.* worshipper, nor fashion's fool *P.S.* 334
Estates have wings; and hang in *F.* pow'r *S.* vi. 248
Happier thy f—s ! *like a rolling stone D.* iii. 293
Manners with *F.*, Humours turn with Climes *M.E.* i. 172
Our fates and *f.*, as the winds shall blow *M.E.* iii. 46
More go to ruin *F.*, than to raise *M.E.* iii. 202
Lay *F.*-struck, *a spectacle of Woe Mi.* ii. 3

Fortun'd.
Here *f.* Curl to slide ; loud shout the band *D.* ii. 73

Forty.
And not like *f.* other Fools *I.H.* ii. 16 *s*
The Courtier smooth, who *f.* years had shin'd *M.E.* i. 252
More rough than *f.* Germans when they scold *S.* vii. 62

Forward, Forwards.—*Passim*.
To help who want, to *f.* who excel *S.* i. 137

Foster.
Let modest *F.*, if he will, excel *E.S.* 131

Fought.
What seas you travers'd, and what fields you *f. S.* v. 396

Foul.
The musty wine, *f.* cloth, or greasy glass *S.* ii. 62

Found.
Plung'd for his sense, but *f.* no bottom there *D.* i. 119
None want a place, for all their Centre *f. D.* iv. 77
Lost was the Nation's Sense, nor could be *f. D.* iv. 611
Like friendly colours *f.* them both unite *E.* iii. 15
Nature and Homer were, he *f.*, the same *E.C.* 135
And worlds applaud that must not yet be *f. E.C.* 194
Much fruit of sense beneath is rarely *f. E.C.* 310
Persians and Greeks like turns of nature *f. E.C.* 380
And *f.* the private in the public good *E.M.* iii. 282
'Tis nowhere to be *f.*, or ev'rywhere *E.M.* iv. 16
No matter where the money's *f. I.H.* ii. 40 *s*
A bird of passage ! gone as soon as *f. M.E.* i. 97
Some God or Spirit he has lately *f. M.E.* i. 164
This clue once *f.*, unravels all the rest *M.E.* i. 178
Unhappy Wharton, waking, *f.* at last *M.E.* iii. 84
Why Shylock wants a meal, the cause is *f. M.E.* iii. 115
Ambition sigh'd : she *f.* it vain to trust *M.E.* v. 19
Two Trav'lers *f.* an Oyster in their way *Mi.* xi. 2
This the divine Cecilia *f. O.* i. 124
"I *f.* him close with *Swift*." "Indeed ? no doubt" *P.S.* 275
Amaz'd, confus'd, he *f.* his pow'r expir'd *R.L.* iii. 145
Sunk in Thalestris' arms the nymph he *f. R.L.* iv. 89
No common weapons in their hands are *f. R.L.* v 43
There broken vows and death-bed alms are *f. R.L.* v.117
But on some lucky day (as when they *f. S.* ii. 55
Now, or long since, what diff'rence will be *f. S.* vi. 238
The lands are bought, but where are to be *f. S.* vii. 109
For bad they *f.* a linguist half so good *S.* viii. 84
And by that laugh the willing fair is *f. Sp.* 56
Descending Gods have *f.* Elysium here *Su.* 60

Foundations.
On plain Experience lay *f.* low *D.* iv. 466
Heav'n's whole *f.* to their centre nod *E.M.* i. 255

Founder.
So Rome's great *f.* to the heav'ns withdrew *R.L.* v. 125

Founds.
F. the whole pile, of all his works the base *D.* i. 160
God in the nature of each being *f. E.M.* iii. 109
Builds Life on Death, on Change Duration *f. M.E.* iii. 167

Fount.
The *f.* of Fame or Infamy *E.* vi. 12

Fountain.
Eridanus his humble *f.* scorns *D.* ii. 182
Is there, Pastora, by a *f.* side *M.E.* ii. 8
The next, a *F.*, spouting thro' his Heir *M.E.* iii. 174
With here a *F.*, never to be play'd *M.E.* iv. 121
I'll stake you lamb, that near the *f.* plays *Sp.* 33
Not bubbling f—s to the thirsty swain A. 43
And but from Nature's *f.* scorn'd to draw *E.C.* 133
The mossy *f.*, and the sylvan shades *M.* 3
Tir'd of the scene Parterres and *F.* yield *M.E.* iv. 87
Beside the fall of *f. O.* i. 98

I shun the *f.* which I sought before *Su.* 30
The mossy *f.*, and the green retreats *Su.* 72

Four.

F. guardian Virtues, round, support her throne *D.* i. 46
Ah why, ye Gods, should two and two make *f. D.* ii. 286
October next it will be *f. I.H.* ii. 84 *s*
Then clap *f.* slices of Pilaster on't *M.E.* iv. 33
And in *f.* months a batter'd Harridan *Mi.* iii. 24
Behold, *f.* Kings in majesty rever'd *R.L.* iii. 37
And *f.* fair Queens whose hands sustain a flow'r *R.L.* iii. 39
F. Knaves in garbs succinct, a trusty band *R.L.* iii. 41
Whose place is quarter'd out, three parts in *f. S.* viii. 136
F. figures rising from the work appear *Sp.* 37

Fourscore.

"Pray then, what wants he?" *F.* thousand pounds *S.* iii. 86

Fowl.

And lo! her bird (a monster of a *f. D.* i. 289
Thro' twilight ages hunt th' Athenian *f. D.* iv. 361
Tastes for his Friend of *F.* and Fish *I.H.* ii. 199

Fowler.

With slaught'ring guns th' unwearied *f.* roves *W.F.* 125

Fox.

Soft as the wily *F.* is seen to creep *D.* iv. 351
The *f.* obscene to gaping tombs retires *W.F.* 71
Mad at a F.-chase, wise at a Debate M.E. i. 74

Fragments.

Be sure I give them *F.*, not a Meal *D.* iv. 230
In glitt'ring dust and painted *f.* lie *R.L.* iii. 160

Fragrance.

To Isles of *f.*, lily-silver'd vales *D.* iv. 303
When from the censer clouds of *f.* roll *E.A.* 271
Whose sacred flow'r with *f.* fills the skies *M.* 10

Fragrant.

In cold December *f.* chaplets blow *D.* i. 77
All-bounteous, *f.* Grains and Golden show'rs *D.* ii. 4
With Sappho *f.* at an ev'ning Masque *M.E.* ii. 26
By the *f.* winds that blow *O.* i. 72
As o'er the *f.* steams she bends her head *R.L.* iii. 134
All fresh and *f.*, to the drawing-room *S.* viii. 215
Nor *f.* herbs their native incense yield *W.* 48
And of their *f.* physic spoils the fields *W.F.* 242
To Thames's banks, which *f.* breezes fill *W.F.* 263

Frail.

Beauty, *f.* flow'r that ev'ry season fears *E.* iii. 57
The *F.* one's advocate, the Weak one's friend *M.E.* ii. 30
Or some *f.* China jar receive a flaw *R.L.* ii. 106
But since, alas! *f.* beauty must decay *R.L.* v. 25
Prodigious this! the F.-one of our Play E.f.S. 1

Frailties.

Here all its *f.*, all its flames resign *E.A.* 175
For God, not man, absolves our *f.* here *E.A.* 316
That, happy *f.* to all ranks apply'd *E.M.* ii. 241
Wants, *f.*, passions closer still ally *E.M.* ii. 253
Unthought-of *F.* cheat us in the Wise *M.E.* i. 69

Frame.

All as the vest, appear'd the wearer's *f. D.* iii. 39
See Alaric's stern port! the martial *f. D.* iii. 91
When Man's whole *f.* is obvious to a Flea *D.* iv. 238
Each purer *f.* inform'd with purer fire *E.* iii. 50
Then too, when fate shall thy fair *f.* destroy *E.A.* 337
But of this *f.* the bearings, and the ties *E.M.* i. 29
To be another, in this gen'ral *f. E.M.* i. 264
Great in the earth, as in th' ethereal *f. E.M.* i. 270
As strong or weak, the organs of the *f. E.M.* ii. 130
So, cast and mingled with his very *f. E.M.* ii. 137
Thus God and Nature link'd the gen'ral *f. E.M.* iii. 317
Till Death unfelt that tender *F.* destroy *Mi.* v. 17
Quit, oh quit this mortal *f. O.* v. 2
There stands a structure of majestic *f. R.L.* iii. 3
Various of temper, as of face or *f. S.* vi. 282
First follow Nature, and your judgment f. E.C. 68
Less mad the wildest whimsey we can *f. M.E.* iii. 155

Fram'd.

But as he *f.* a Whole, the Whole to bless *E.M.* iii. 111
And Those, new Heav'ns and Systems *f. I.H.* iv. 12

France.

Small thanks to *F.*, and none to Rome or Greece *D.* i. 283
Whore, Pupil, and lac'd Governor from *F. D.* iv. 272
Others import yet nobler arts from *F. D.* iv. 597
The brightest eyes of *F.* inspir'd his Muse *E.* iv. 77
But Critic-learning flourish'd most in *F. E.C.* 712
Could *F.* or Rome divert our brave designs *M.E.* iii. 51
And *F.* reveng'd of ANNE's and EDWARD's arms *M.E.* iii. 144
He must repair it; takes a bribe from *F. M.E.* iii. 396
The Soldier breath'd the Gallantries of *F. S.* v. 145
Ev'n Radcliff's Doctors travel first to *F. S.* v. 183
We conquer'd *F.*, but felt our Captive's charms *S.* v. 263
Show'd us that *F.* had something to admire *S.* v. 275
Still in thy song should vanquish'd *F.* appear *W.F.* 309

Frank.

Chaste to her Husband, *f.* to all beside *M.E.* ii. 71

Frankness.

Reserve with *F.*, Art with Truth ally'd *M.E.* ii. 277

Frantic.

Poor Cornus sees his *f.* wife elope *P.S.* 25

Fraternal.

To your *f.* care our sleeping friends *D.* iv. 440

Fraud.

O pious *f.* of am'rous charity *E.A.* 150
All crimes shall cease, and ancient *f.* shall fail *M.* 17
By force to ravish, or by *f.* betray *R.L.* ii. 32
Few ask, if *f.* or force attain'd his ends *R.L.* ii. 34

Fraught.

Then, at the last and only couplet *f. E.C.* 354
Like frigates *f.* with spice and cochinel *S.* viii. 227

Fray.

The growing combat, or assist the *f. R.L.* v. 56

Free.

From the strong fate of drams if thou get *f. D.* iii. 145
Some *f.* from rhyme or reason, rule or check *D.* iii. 161
Then thus: from Priest-craft happily set *f. D.* iv. 499
But candid, *f.*, sincere, as you began *E.* ii. 12
Whether thy hand strike out some *f.* design *E.* iii. 3
Paulo's *f.* stroke, and Titian's warmth divine *E.* iii. 38
F. as thy stroke, yet faultless as thy line *E.* iii. 64
Ah quit not the *f.* innocence of life *E.* iv. 45
Love, *f.* as air, at sight of human ties *E.A.* 75
If there be yet another name more *f. E.A.* 89
Then conscience sleeps, and leaving nature *f. E.A.* 227
Where Heav'n's *f.* subjects might their rights dispute *E.C.* 548
Poets, a race long unconfin'd, and *f. E.C.* 649
Not *f.* from faults, nor yet too vain to mend *E.C.* 744
Expatiate *f.* o'er all this scene of Man *E.M.* i. 5
'Tis never to be bought, but always *f. E.M.* iv. 17
Why yes: with *Scripture* you may still be *f. E.S.* i. 37
A gen'rous Faith, from superstition *f. Ep.* ii. 9
But who, living and dying, serene still and *f. Ep.* xvi. 7
A safe Companion, and a *f. I.H.* i. 40
Why words so flowing, thoughts so *f. I.H.* iii. 39
Who sett'st our Entrails *f. Mi.* iv. 34
No place is sacred, not the Church is *f. P.S.* 11
You'll give me, like a friend both sage and *f. S.* i. 9
F. as young Lyttleton, her Cause pursue *S.* iii. 29
At home, tho' exil'd; *f.* yet tho' in the Tow'r *S.* iii. 184
How *f.*, or frugal, I shall pass my days *S.* vi. 289
As in the pox, some give it to get *f. S.* viii. 171
And the *f.* soul looks down to pity Kings *S.* viii. 187
Base Fear becomes the guilty, not the *f. S.* viii. 194
Left *f.* the Human Will *U.P.* 12
What Blessings thy *f.* Bounty gives *U.P.* 17
What could be *f.*, when lawless beasts obey'd *W.F.* 51
Bids his *f.* soul expatiate in the skies *W.F.* 254
The time shall come, when, *f.*, as seas or wind *W.F.* 397
Some, deep F.-masons, join the silent race D. iv. 571
His butchers Henley! his *f.* Moore *P.S.* 98
And ours, my friends, thro' whuse *f.-op'ning* gate *S.* ii. 157
A smart *F.-thinker!* all things in an hour *M.E.* i. 157
That gay *F.*, a fine talker once *M.E.* i. 162

Freed.

For Spirits, *f.* from mortal laws, with ease *R.L.* i. 69
Till the *f.* Indians in their native groves *W.F.* 409

FREEDOM—FRIEND.

Freedom.
'Twere well might critics still this *f.* take *E.C.* 584
Or WYNDHAM, just to *F.* and the Throne *E.S.* ii. 29
Yes, the last Pen for *F.* let me draw *E.S.* ii. 248
F. and Arts together fall *O.* ii. 26
Preserv'd the *f.*, and forbore the vice *S.* v. 260

Freely.
And censure *f.* who have written well *E.C.* 76
Who to a friend his faults can *f.* show *E.C.* 637

Freer.
Those *f.* beauties, ev'n in them, seem faults *E.C.* 170

Frees.
Wraps in her veil, and *f.* from sense of shame *D.* iv. 336

Freeze.
Burn thro' the Tropic, *f.* beneath the Pole *S.* iii. 72

Freezing.
The *f.* Tanais thro' a waste of snows *D.* iii. 88

Freind.
Let *F.* affect to speak as Terence spoke *D.* iv. 223

French.
By the *F.* born, or by the op'ning hound *D.* iv. 278
With *F.* Libation, and Italian Strain *D.* iv. 559
Maul the *F.* Tyrant, or pull down the POPE *Mi.* ii. 18
On *F.* translation, and Italian song *P.C.* 42
Of twelve vast *F.* Romances, neatly gilt *R.L.* ii. 38
From Latian Syrens, *F.* Circean Feasts *S.* iv. 122
His *F.* is pure; his voice too—you shall hear *S.* vi. 7

Frenchman.
A *F.* comes, presents you with his Boy *S.* vi. 3
"How elegant your F—en?" "Mine, d'ye mean *S.* viii. 110

Frenzy.
Ye pow'rs, what pleasing *f.* sooths my mind *A.* 51
All that on Folly *F.* could beget *D.* i. 125

Frequent.
And *f.* cups prolong the rich repast *R.L.* iii. 112
And *f.* herses shall besiege your gates *U.L.* 38
You, Mr. Dean, f. the Great *I.H.* ii. 113 s

Fresco.
A fading *F.* here demands a sigh *E.* iii. 34

Fresh.
And the *f.* vomit run for ever green *D.* ii. 156
F. blooming Hope, gay daughter of the sky *E.A.* 209
The link dissolves, each *f.* seeks a *f.* embrace *E.M.* iii. 129
To draw *f.* colours from the vernal flow'rs *R.L.* ii. 95
Who has not learn'd, *f.* sturgeon and ham-pie *S.* ii. 103
Know there are Rhymes, which *f.* and *f.* apply'd *S.* iii. 59

All *f.* and fragrant to the drawing-room *S.* viii. 215
F. as the morn, and as the season fair *Sp.* 20
All nature laughs, the groves are *f.* and fair *Sp.* 73
More bright than noon, yet *f.* as early day *Sp.* 82
F. rising blushes paint the war'ry glass *Su.* 28
And with *f.* bays her rural shrine adorn *W.* 20
Fields ever *f.*, and groves for ever green *W.* 72

Freshest.
Seeks *f.* pasture and the purest air *M.* 50

Fresnoy.
F.'s close Art, and Dryden's native Fire *E.* iii. 8

Fret.
And at a Peer, or Peeress, shall I *f. E.S.* i. 111
How should I *f.* to mangle ev'ry line *E.S.* ii. 4
Yet then did Dennis rave in furious *f. P.S.* 153

Friar.
The *f.* hooded, and the monarch crown'd *E.M.* iv. 198
And now the Punk applaud; and now the *F. M.E.* i. 191
Could Laureate Dryden Pimp and *F.* engage *S.* i. 113

Friend.
A *f.* to Party thou, and all her race *D.* i. 206
Folly, my son, has still a *F.* at Court *D.* i. 300
A *f.* in glee, ridiculously grim *D.* iii. 154
Hell thou shalt move; for Faustus is our *f. D.* iii. 308
No Cause, no Trust, no Duty, and no *f. D.* iv. 340
Fond to forget the statesman in the *f. E.* i. 8
Absent or dead, still let a *f.* be dear *E.* i. 13
When the last ling'ring *f.* has bid farewell *E.* i. 34
Then scorn to gain a *F.* by servile ways *E.* ii. 10
Asham'd of any *F.*, not ev'n of Me *E.* ii. 15
This Verse be thine, my *f.*, nor thou refuse *E.* iii. 1
How oft review; each finding like a *f.* iii. 21
The tender sister, daughter, *f.*, and wife *E.* iii. 52
His heart, his mistress and his *f.* did share *E.* iv. 9
But, *f.*, take heed whom you attack *E.* vi. 17
Come thou, my father, brother, husband, *f. E.A.* 152
Make use of ev'ry *f.*—and ev'ry foe *E.C.* 214
For each ill Author is as bad a *F. E.C.* 519
Name a new Play, and he's the Poet's *f. E.C.* 620
Who to a *f.* his faults can freely show *E.C.* 637
Will, like a *f.*, familiarly convey *E.C.* 655
Such late was Walsh—the Muse's judge and *f. E.C.* 729
Yet if a *f.*, a night or so, should need her *E.J.S.* 33
A sharp accuser, but a helpless *f. E.M.* ii. 154
And treat this passion more as *f.* than foe *E.M.* ii. 164
A master, or a servant, or a *f. E.M.* ii. 250
And Pride bestow'd on all a common *f. E.M.* ii. 272
To each unthinking being Heav'n, a *f. E.M.* iii. 71
And he return'd a *f.*, who came a foe *E.M.* iii. 206
Follow'r of God or *f.* of human-kind *E.M.* iii. 284
Seek an admirer, or would fix a *f. E.M.* iv. 44
In him who is, or him who finds a *f. E.M.* iv. 60
I'll tell you, *f.* a wise man and a Fool *E.M.* iv. 200
F., parent, neighbour, first it will embrace *E.M.* iv. 367
Come then, my *F.!* my Genius! come along *E.M.* iv. 373
Thou wert my guide, philosopher, and *f. E.M.* iv. 390
His *F.* and Shame, and was a kind of Screen (*rep.*) *E.S.* i. 22
This, this, my *f.*, I cannot, must not bear *E.S.* i. 127
Not yet, my *F.!* to-morrow 'faith it may *E.S.* ii. 2
Still let me say: no Follower, but a *F. E.S.* ii. 93
Dare they to hope a Poet for their *f. E.S.* ii. 115
Has never made a *F.* in private life *E.S.* ii. 134
To break my Windows, if I treat a *F. E.S.* ii. 143
[*In Pow'r a Servant, out of Pow'r a F.*] *E.S.* ii. 161
Whose Speech you took, and gave it to a *F. E.S.* ii. 167
But pens can forge, my *f.*, that cannot write *E.S.* ii. 188
Th' affront is mine, my *f.*, and should be yours *E.S.* ii. 200
Mine, as a *F.* to ev'ry worthy mind *E.S.* ii. 203
Here lies the *F.* most lov'd, the Son most dear *Ep.* iii. 1
Oh let thy once-lov'd *F.* inscribe thy Stone *Ep.* iii. 7
Lover of peace, and *f.* of human kind *Ep.* vi. 3
'Tis all a Father, all a *F.* can give *Ep.* vii. 20
Thy Country's *f.*, but more of human kind *Ep.* ix. 2
Foe to loud Praise, and *F.* to learned Ease *Ep.* x. 5
A safe Companion, and an easy *F. Ep.* xi. 7
Whatever an Heir, or a *F.* in his stead *Ep.* xvi. 3
Our old *F.* Swift will tell his story *I.H.* i. 82
A handsome House to lodge a *F. I.H.* ii. 3 s
Desiring I would stand their *f. I.H.* ii. 66 s
And chose me for an humble *F. I.H.* ii. 86 s
How think you of our *F.* the Dean *I.H.* ii. 103 s
Our *F.*, Dan Prior, told (you know) *I.H.* ii. 153
Yet lov'd his *F.*, and had a Soul *I.H.* ii. 162
But Lord, my *F.*, this savage scene *I.H.* ii. 175
This doctrine, *F.*, I learnt at Court *I.H.* ii. 180
Tastes for his *F.* of Fowl and Fish *I.H.* ii. 190
To charm the Mistress, or to fix the *F. I.H.* iii. 14
A constant Bounty which no *f.* has made *M.E.* i. 198
The Frail one's advocate, the Weak one's *f. M.E.* ii. 30
And when she sees her *F.* in deep despair *M.E.* ii. 169
Young without Lovers, old without a *F. M.E.* ii. 246
Ah! *F.!* to dazzle let the Vain design *M.E.* iii. 249
But lures the Pirate, and corrupts the *F. M.E.* iii. 30
Give Harpax self the blessing of a *f. M.E.* iii. 92
But who, my *f.*, has reason in his rage *M.E.* iii. 152
Banish'd the doctor, and expell'd the *f. M.E.* iii. 330
Statesman, yet *f.* to Truth! a soul sincere *M.E.* v. 67
Who gain'd no title, and who lost no *f. M.E.* v. 70
Wept by each *f.*, forgiv'n by ev'ry foe *Mi.* 4
And be the *Critic's*, *Briton's*, *Old Man's F. Mi.* ii. 24
O learned *F.* of *Abchurch-Lane Mi.* iv. 33
Long Health, long Youth, long Pleasure, and a *F. Mi.* v. 2
Handsome and witty, yet a *F. Mi.* viii. 4
She was my *f.*; I taught her first to spread *Mi.* ix. 61
As son, as father, brother, husband, *f. O.* iii. 28
F. to my life! (which did not you prolong *P.S.* 27

And is not mine, my *f.*, a sorer case *P.S.* 73
Good *f.*, forbear! you deal in dang'rous things *P.S.* 75
No Names!—be calm!—learn prudence of a *f. P.S.* 102
And more abusive, calls himself my *f. P.S.* 112
The Muse but serv'd to ease some *f.*, not Wife *P.S.* 131
A tim'rous foe, and a suspicious *f. P.S.* 206
Sometimes to call a minister my *f. P.S.* 266
Have I no *f.* to serve, no soul to save *P.S.* 274
Who has the vanity to call you *f. P.S.* 295
He stood the furious foe, the timid *f. P.S.* 343
A *f.* in exile, or a father, dead *P.S.* 355
Foe to his pride, but *f.* to his distress *P.S.* 371
O *F.!* may each domestic bliss be thine *P.S.* 406
May Heav'n, to bless those days, preserve my *f. P.S.* 415
Safe from the treach'rous *f.*, the daring spark *R.L.* i. 73
'Twill then be infamy to seem your *f. R.L.* iv. 112
You'll give me, like a *f.*, both sage and free *S.* i. 9
And ev'ry *f.* the less lament my fate *S.* i. 62
To VIRTUE ONLY and HER FRIENDS a *F. S.* i. 121
'I'd never doubt at Court to make a *f. S.* ii. 44
Thus said our *f.*, and what he said I sing *S.* ii. 68
F. Pope! be prudent, let your Muse take breath *S.* iii. 13
Nothing to make Philosophy thy *f. S.* iii. 74
Is this my Guide, Philosopher, and *F. S.* iii. 177
There are, my *F.!* whose philosophic eyes *S.* iv. 7
Great *F.* of LIBERTY! in Kings a Name *S.* v. 25
To cheat a *F.*, or Ward, he leaves to Peter *S.* v. 197
Till *f.* with *f.*, and families at strife *S.* v. 253
A single verse, we quarrel with a *f. S.* v. 365
Dear Col'nel, Cobham's and your Country's *F. S.* vi. 1
Could you complain, my *F.*, he prov'd so bad *S.* vi. 22
Go on, my *F.* (he cry'd), see yonder walls *S.* vi. 46
In one a Mistress drops, in one a *F. S.* vi. 75
Fond of his *F.*, and civil to his Wife *S.* vi. 189
Talk what you will of Taste, my *f.*, you'll find *S.* vi. 268
Canst thou endure a foe, forgive a *f. S.* vi. 317
Or will you think, my *f.*, your business done *S.* vi. 320
T' observe a mean, be to himself a *f. W.F.* 251
There, where no Father's, Brother's, F.'s disgrace E.S. i. 99
No *f.* complaint, no kind domestic tear *U.L.* 49
Gay dies *unpension'd with a hundred* f—s *D.* iii. 330
A hundred head of Aristotle's *f. D.* iv. 192
To your fraternal care our sleeping *f. D.* iv. 440
Which whoso tastes, forgets his former *f. D.* iv. 518
Let subtle schoolmen teach these *f.* to fight *M.E.* ii. 81
In the small circle of our foes or *f. E.M.* iv. 242
Laugh at your *f.*, and if your *F.* are sore *E.S.* i. 55
Rank'd with their *F.*, not number'd with their Train *E.S.* ii. 91
Some in their choice of *F.* (nay, look not grave) *E.S.* ii. 100
O let my Country's *F.* illumine mine *E.S.* ii. 121
I think your *F.* are out, and would be in *E.S.* ii. 123
O more than Fortune, *F.*, or Country lost *Ep.* xiii. 6
My *F.* above, my Folks below *I.H.* ii. 135
Whether we ought to choose our *F. I.H.* ii. 149
Because she's honest, and the best of *F. M.E.* ii. 104
By Spirit robb'd of Pow'r, by Warmth of *F. M.E.* ii. 144
There, Victor of his health, of fortune, *f. M.E.* iii. 313
Not of the Wits his foes, but Fools his *f. Mi.* iii. 14
If foes, they write, if *f.*, they read me dead *P.S.* 32
Obliged by hunger, and request of *f. P.S.* 44
The Play'rs and I are, luckily, no *f. P.S.* 60
And St. *John's* self (great *Dryden's f.* before) *P.S.* 141
And see what *f.*, and read what books I please *P.S.* 264
Laugh'd at the loss of *f.* he never had *P.S.* 346
Fair to expose myself, my foes, my *f. S.* i. 58
Let's talk, my *f.*, but talk before we dine *S.* ii. 4
More pleas'd to keep it till their *f.* could come *S.* ii. 95
To *f.*, to fortune, to mankind a shame *S.* ii. 107
But ancient *f.* (tho' poor, or out of play) *S.* ii. 239
And yours, my *f.*, thro' whose free-op'ning gate *S.* ii. 157
And then such *F.* as cannot fail to last *S.* iv. 80
And promise our best *F.* to rhyme no more *S.* v. 178
In crowds, and courts, law, business, feasts, and *f. S.* vi. 91
Him the damn'd Doctors and his *F.* immur'd *S.* vi. 192
"My *F.*," he cry'd, "p—x take you for your care *S.* vi. 195
What tho' no *f.* in sable weeds appear *U.L.* 55

Friendless.

The poor and *f.* Villain, than the Great *E.S.* ii. 45
Beauties, like Tyrants, old and *f.* grown *M.E.* ii. 227
Forsaken, *f.*, shall ye fly O. ii. 14

Friendly.

Like *f.* colours found them both unite *E.* iii. 15
F. at Hackney, faithless at Whitehall *M.E.* i. 76
There ST. JOHN mingles with my *f.* bowl *S.* i. 127
Oh ever beauteous, ever *f.!* I tell *U.L.* 5

Friendship.

Divides a *f.* long confirm'd by age *D.* iii. 174
All may allow; but seek your friendship too *E.C.* 565
To these we owe true *f.*, love sincere *E.M.* ii. 255
Yet think not, *F.* only prompts my lays *E.S.* ii. 94
No Pow'r the Muse's *F.* can command *E.S.* ii. 118
Who ne'er knew Joy, but *F.* might divide *Ep.* iii. 3
My *F.*, and a Prologue, and ten pound *P.S.* 48
When Love approach'd me under *F.*'s name *E.A.* 60
Yet sacred keep his F—s, and his Ease Ep. i. 10
Fond to spread *f.*, but to cover heats *S.* L 136

Frigates.

Like *f.* fraught with spice and cochineal *S.* viii. 227

Frighted.

F. I quit the room, but leave it so *S.* viii. 272

Frightful.

Vice is a monster of so *f.* mien *E.M.* ii. 217
One would not, sure, be *f.* when one's dead *M.E.* i. 250

Frippery.

The *f.* of crucify'd Molière *D.* i. 132

Fritter.

Break all their nerves, and *f.* all their sense *D.* iv. 56

Fritter'd.

And these to Notes are *f.* quite away *D.* i. 278

Fro.—*Passim.*

Frolics.

A Youth of *F.*, an old Age of Cards *M.E.* ii. 244
In one our *F.*, our Amusements end *S.* vi. 74

From.—*Passim.*

Front.

De Lyra there a dreadful *f.* extends *D.* i. 153
Support his *f.*, and Oaths bring up the rear *D.* i. 308
Bless'd with his father's *f.*, his mother's tongue *D.* ii. 416
Plough'd was his *f.* with many a deep Remark *D.* iv. 204
She glares in Balls, *f.* Boxes, and the Ring *E.* iv. 53
That, lac'd with bits of rustic, makes a *F. M.E.* iv. 34
Brand the bold *f.* of shameless guilty men *S.* L 106
That men may say, when we the f.-box grace R.L. v. 17

Frontless.

And strikes a blush thro' *f.* Flattery *E.* ii. 7

Frost.

Their Virtue fix'd; 'tis fix'd as in a *f. E.M.* ii. 102
Behold the groves that shine with silver *f. W.* 9
When f—s have whiten'd all the naked groves *W.F.* 126

Froth.

Half *f.*, half venom, spits himself abroad *P.S.* 320

Froths.

And tremble at the sea that *f.* below *R.L.* ii. 136

Frown.

Horneck's fierce eye, and Roome's funeral *f. D.* iii. 152
Chloe stepp'd in, and kill'd him with a *f. R.L.* v. 68
Care, if a livery'd Lord or smile or f. *S.* viii. 197

Frown'd.

Or chanc'd to meet a Minister that *f. M.E.* i. 165
Belinda *f.*, Thalestris call'd her Prude *R.L.* v. 36
When the Queen *f.*, or smil'd, he knows; and what *S.* viii. 132

Frowns.

Behold! if Fortune or a Mistress *f. M.E.* i. 103

Frozen.

Ev'n here, where *f.* chastity retires *E.A.* 181
Against the Gothic sons of *f.* verse *Mi.* ii. 14
Straight a short thunder breaks the *f.* sky *W.F.* 170
Where clearer flames glow round the *f.* Pole *W.F.* 390

FRUGAL—FURY.

Frugal.
The common Soul, of Heav'n's more *f.* make *D.* iv. 441
Has what the *f.*, dirty soil affords *E.S.* ii. 174
A *f.* Mouse upon the whole *I.H.* ii. 161
The *f.* Crone, whom praying priests attend *M.E.* i. 242
Till grows more *f.* in his riper days *P.S.* 247
To teach their *f.* Virtues to his Heir *S.* v. 166
How free, or *f.*, I shall pass my days *S.* vi. 289

Frugality.
Lucullus, when *F.* could charm *M.E.* i. 218

Fruit.
Much *f.* of sense beneath is rarely found *E.C.* 310
Or Garden, tempting with forbidden *f.* *E.M.* i. 8
Their early *f.*, and milk-white turtles bring *Su.* 52
Now golden *f.*—s on loaded branches shine *A.* 73
Or gives to Zembla *f.*, to Barca flow'rs *D.* i. 74
F. of dull Heat, and Sooterkins of Wit *D.* i. 126
As *f.*, ungrateful to the planter's care *E.M.* ii. 181
Sell their presented partridges, and *f. S.* ii. 51
Their *f.* to you, confesses you its lord *S.* vi. 233
See Pan with flocks, with *f.* Pomona crown'd *W.F.* 37
Reap their own *f.*, and woo their sable loves *W.F.* 410

Fruitful.
And from the Pleiads *f.* show'rs descend *Sp.* 102
No rich perfumes refresh the *f.* field *W.* 47
And 'midst the desert *f.* fields arise *W.F.* 26
The winding Isis, and the *f.* Tame *W.F.* 340

Fruitless.
Take back my *f.* penitence and pray'rs *E.A.* 286

Frustrate.
The swain with tears his *f.* labour yields *W.F.* 55

Full.
In each she marks her Image *f.* exprest *D.* i. 107
F. in the middle way there stood a lake *D.* ii. 69
F. and eternal privilege of tongue *D.* ii. 378
And thrusts his person *f.* into your face *D.* iii. 140
Heady, not stroog; o'er-flowing, tho' not *f. D.* iii. 172
F. in the midst of Euclid dip at once *D.* iv. 263
All my commands are easy, short, and *f. D.* iv. 581
A Soul as *f.* of Worth, as void of Pride *E.* ii. 1
All then is *f.*, possessing, and possess'd *E.A.* 93
F. in my view set all the bright abode *E.A.* 127
From the *f.* choir when loud Hosannas rise *E.A.* 353
Some lucky License answer to the *f. E.C.* 148
But the joint force and *f.* result of all *E.C.* 246
When mellowing years their *f.* perfection give *E.C.* 490
But rattling nonsense in *f.* volleys breaks *E.C.* 608
Where all must *f.* or not coherent be *E.M.* i. 45
Or in the *f.* creation leave a void *E.M.* i. 243
As *f.*, as perfect, in a hair as heart (*rep.*) *E.M.* i. 276
Have *f.* as oft no meaning, or the same *E.M.* ii. 86
Thine the *f.* harvest of the golden year *E.M.* iii. 39
Say, where *f.* instinct is th' unerring guide *E.M.* iii. 83
From Order, Union, *f.* Consent of things *E.M.* iii. 296
Why, *f.* of days and honours, lives the Sire *E.M.* iv. 106
The last *f.* fairly gives it to the House *E.S.* ii. 180
To set this matter *f.* before ye *I.H.* i. 81
F. sixty years the World has been her Trade *M.E.* ii. 123
Our bolder Talents in *f.* light display'd *M.E.* ii. 201
Whose measure *f.* o'erflows on human race *M.E.* iii. 231
Want with a *f.*, or with an empty purse *M.E.* iii. 320
Then *f.* against his Cornish lands they roar *M.E.* iii. 355
Till all the Demon makes his *f.* descent *M.E.* iii. 371
When the *f.* organ joins the tuneful quire *O.* i. 126
F. ten years slander'd, did he once reply *P.S.* 374
F. o'er their heads the swelling bag he rent *R.L.* iv. 91
Yet hens of Guinea *f.* as good I hold *S.* ii. 19
F. many a Beast goes in, but none come out *S.* iii. 117
And *f.* in Shakespear, fair in Otway shone *S.* v. 277
Bred up at home, *f.* early I begun *S.* vi. 52
Pour the *f.* tide of eloquence along *S.* vi. 171
Heard, noted, answer'd, as in *f.* debate *S.* vi. 187
So was I punish'd, as if *f.* as proud *S.* viii. 19
Tho' in his pictures Lust be *f.* display'd *S.* viii. 94
Here in *f.* light the russet plains extend *W.F.* 23
Sat f.-blown *Bufo*, puff'd by ev'ry quill *P.S.* 232
All as a partridge plump, *f.-fed*, and fair *D.* ii. 41
Their *f.* Heroes, their pacific May'rs *D.* iii. 281
The varying verse, the *f.-resounding* line *S.* v. 268

Fully.
And tho' no Science, *f.* worth the seven *M.E.* iv. 44

Fulsome.
And flattery to *f.* Dedicators *R.C.* 593
Carthusian fasts, and *f.* Bacchanals *S.* vii. 118

Fulvia.
In *F.'s* buckle ease the throbs below *M.E.* iii. 88

Fume.
How did they *f.*, and stamp, and roar, and chafe *P.S.* 191

Fumes.
In *f.* of burning chocolate shall glow *R.L.* ii. 135

Fuming.
Some, as she sipp'd, the *f.* liquor fann'd *R.L.* iii. 114

Functions.
As the mind opens, and the *f.* spread *E.M.* ii. 142
That lock up all the *f.* of my soul *S.* iii. 40

Fund.
Art from that *f.* each just supply provides *E.C.* 74
I trust that sinking *F.*, my Life *I.H.* i. 74

Fundamental.
And here restor'd Wit's *f.* laws *E.C.* 722

Fun'ral.
'Tis but the *F.* of the former year *Mi.* v. 10
And *F.*—s black'ning all the Doors *I.H.* i. 9
While the long *F.* blacken all the way *U.L.* 40

Funereal.
Horneck's fierce eye, and Roome's *f.* frown *D.* iii. 152

Fungoso.
Unlucky, as *F.* in the play *E.C.* 328

Fungus.
A Nest, a Toad, a *F.*, or a Flow'r *D.* iv. 400

Fur.
To want the strength of bulls, the *f.* of bears *E.M.* i. 176
The *f.* that warms a monarch, warm'd a bear *E.M.* iii. 44
Glad chains, warm *f.*—s, broad banners, and broad faces *D.* i. 88
Chicane in *F.*, and *Casuistry* in Lawn *D.* iv. 28

Furbelow.
To change a Flounce, or add a *F. R.L.* ii. 100

Furious.
F. he dives, precipitately dull *D.* ii. 316
Or bid the *f.* Gaul be rude no more *O.* ii. 16
Yet then did *Dennis* rave in *f.* fret *P.S.* 153
He stood the *f.* foe, the timid friend *P.S.* 343
From *f.* Sappho scarce a milder fate *S.* i. 83
Be *f.*, envious, slothful, mad, or drunk *S.* iii. 61
And kings more *f.* and severe than they *W.F.* 46
As from the god she flew with *f.* pace (*rep.*) *W.F.* 189

Furnish.
We only *f.* what he cannot use *D.* iv. 261

Furrow.
He from the wond'ring *f.* call'd the food *E.M.* iii. 219

Furrow'd.
While yon slow oxen turn the *f.* plain *Sp.* 30
Panting with hope, he tries the *f.* grounds *W.F.* 100

Fury.
Restrain his *f.*, than provoke his speed *E.C.* 85
Now his fierce eyes with sparkling *f.* glow *E.C.* 378
They judge with *f.*, but they write with fle'me *E.C.* 662
But well may put some Statesmen in a *f. E.S.* i. 52
So much the *F.* still out-ran the Wit *M.E.* ii. 127
Some religious rage *M.E.* v. 12
The F—ies *sink upon their iron beds O.* i. 69
Now with *F.* surrounded *O.* i. 106
If I dislike it, "*F.*, death and rage!" *P.S.* 57
And all the *F.* issu'd at the vent *R.L.* iv. 92
Lo these were they, whose souls the *F.* steel'd *U.L.* 41
And gasping *F.* thirst for blood in vain *W.F.* 422
The F.-passions *from that blood began E.M.* iii. 167

FUSTIAN—GARBS.

Fustian.
And he, whose *F.*'s so sublimely bad *P.S.* 187

Future.
Much *f.* Ode, and abdicated Play *D.* i. 122
A vast, vamp'd, *f.*, old, reviv'd, new piece *D.* i. 284
Judge of all present, past, or *f.* wit *D.* ii. 376
But blind to former, as to *f.* fate *D.* iii. 47
And let the past and *f.* fire thy brain *D.* iii. 66
To *f.* ages may thy dulness last *D.* iii. 189
Her modest cheek shall warm a *f.* age *E.* iii. 56
And sure, if fate some *f.* bard shall join *E.A.* 359
Oh blindness to the *f.* I kindly giv'n *E.M.* i. 85
What *f.* bliss, he gives not thee to know *E.M.* i. 93
Reason, the *f.*, and the consequence *E.M.* ii. 74
Present to grasp, and *f.* still to find *E.M.* ii. 125
But *f.* views of better, or of worse *E.M.* iv. 72
Shall then this verse to *f.* age pretend *E.M.* iv. 339
Rapt into *f.* times, the Bard begun *M.* 7
The promis'd father of the *f.* age *M.* 56
See *f.* sons, and daughters yet unborn *M.* 88
But *f.* Buildings, *f.* Navies grow *M.E.* v. 188
Then *f.* ages with delight shall see *M.E.* v. 59
And buy a rope, that *f.* times may tell *S.* ii. 109
Life's instant business to a *f.* day *S.* iii. 42
And swell the *f.* harvest of the field *W.* 16
And *f.* navies on thy shores appear *W.F.* 222

G.
St. James's first, for leaden *G*— preach'd *D.* iv. 608

Gad.
Z—ds! damn the lock! 'fore *G.* you must be civil *R.L.* iv. 128

Gage.
To just three millions stinted modest *G. M.E.* iii. 128

Gagg'd.
There foam'd rebellious *Logic, g.* and bound *D.* iv. 23

Gaiety.
Th' engaging Smile, the *G. I.H.* i. 46

Gaily.
That *g.* blooms, but e'vn in blooming dies *E.C.* 499

Gain.
Glory, and *g.*, th' industrious tribe provoke *D.* ii. 33
Where Folly fights for Kings, or dives for *g. E.M.* iv. 154
Nor lordly Luxury, nor City *G. M.E.* iii. 146
And greater *G.* would rise *Mi.* iv. 30
For *g.*, not glory, wing'd his roving flight *S.* v. 71
Constant at Church and Change; his *g—s were sure M.E.* iii. 347
Would ye be blest? despise low Joys, low *g. S.* iv. 60
If perseverance g. the Diver's prize D. ii. 301
Then scorn to *g.* a Friend by servile ways *E.* ii. 10
A thousand movements scarce one purpose *g. E.M.* i. 54
One prospect lost, another still we *g. E.M.* ii. 289
Sure by quick Nature happiness to *g. E.M.* iii. 91
All join to guard what each desires to *g. E.M.* iii. 278
The good or bad the gifts of Fortune *g. E.M.* iv. 83
The joy unequall'd, if its end it *g. E.M.* iv. 315
Since but to wish more Virtue, is to *g. E.M.* iv. 326
What RICH'LIEU wanted, Louis scarce could *g. E.S.* i. 116
To *g.* those Riches he can ne'er enjoy *M.E.* iv. 2
And all we *g.*, some sad Reflection more *Mi.* v. 8
He *g.* his Prince's ear, or lose his own *P.S.* 367
New Stratagems the radiant Lock to *g. R.L.* iii. 120
Unless good sense preserve what beauty *g. R.L.* v. 16
You'll *g.* at least a *Knighthood*, or the *Bays S.* i. 22
Will *g.* a Wife with half as many more *S.* iv. 78
O Love! for Sylvia let me *g.* the prize *Sp.* 49

Gain'd.
Like kings we lose the conquests *g.* before *E.C.* 64
G. but one trump and one Plebeian card *R.L.* iii. 54
Who *g.* no title, and who lost no friend *M.E.* v. 70

Gains.
As on the land while here the ocean *g. E.C.* 54
Which, without passing thro' the judgment, *g. E.C.* 154
Attention, habit and experience *g. E.M.* ii. 79

The strength he *g.* is from th' embrace he gives *E.M.* iii. 323
And one more Pensioner St. Stephen *g. M.E.* iii. 394
He *g.* all points who pleasingly confounds *M.E.* iv. 55

Gale.
Reason the card, but Passion is the *g. E.M.* ii. 108
Spread the thin oar, and catch the driving *g. E.M.* iii. 178
When Nature sicken'd, and each *g.* was death *E.M.* iv. 108
Pursue the triumph, and partake the *g. E.M.* iv. 396
To save the powder from too rude a *g. R.L.* ii. 93
With what a shifting *g.* your course you ply *S.* v. 298
Go, gentle g—s, and bear my sighs away A. 17, &c.
And cease, ye *g.*, to bear my sighs away *A.* 54
As to soft *g.* top-heavy pines bow low *D.* ii. 391
Diffusing languor in the panting *g. D.* iv. 304
The dying *g.* that pant upon the trees *E.A.* 159
Where'er you walk, cool *g.* shall fan the shade *Sn.* 73
But when the tainted *g.* the game betray *W.F.* 101
Led by new stars, and borne by spicy *g. W.F.* 392

Galileo.
When next he looks thro' *G.*'s eyes *R.L.* v. 138

Gallant.
G. and gay, in Cliveden's proud alcove *M.E.* iii. 307

Gallantries.
The Soldier breath'd the *G.* of France *S.* v. 145

Gallants.
Faith, *g.*, board with saints, and bed with sinners *E.J.S.* 24

Gallery, Gall'ry.
While all its throats the *G.* extends *S.* v. 326
Pit, box, and *g'y* in convulsions hurl'd *P.S.* 87

Gallic.
The sturdy Squire to *G.* masters stoop *D.* iv. 595

Gallop.
And never *g.* Pegasus to death *S.* iii. 14

Game.
But that this well-disputed *g.* may end *D.* ii. 245
The rising *g.*, and chas'd from flow'r to flow'r *D.* iv. 426
Whose *g.* is Whisk, whose treat a toast in sack *E.* v. 24
Tell me, which Knave is lawful *G.*, which not *E.S.* ii. 27
In Man, the judgment shoots at flying *g. M.E.* i. 96
In mumbling of the *g.*, they dare not bite *P.S.* 314
Or change complexions at a losing *g. R.L.* iv. 70
And makes his trembling slaves the royal *g. W.F.* 64
But when the tainted gales the *g.* betray *W.F.* 101
By herald Hawkers, high heroic G—s *D.* ii. 18
A gentler exercise to close the *g. D.* ii. 366
To White's be carry'd as to ancient *g. M.E.* iii. 69
His Grace will g.: to White's a bull be led M.E. iii. 67

Gameful.
Now range the hills, the *g.* woods beset *W.F.* 95

Gamester.
Unelbow'd by a *G.*, Pimp, or Play'r *M.E.* iii. 242
Dash the proud *G.* in his gilded Car *S.* i. 107
Teach Oaths to G—s, and to Nobles Wit D. i. 204

Gaming.
G. and Grub-street skulk behind the King *D.* i. 310

Gammer Gurton.
To *G.* if it give the bays *S.* v. 91

Ganges.
Let barb'rous *G.* arm a servile train *W.F.* 365

Gape.
Had he beheld an Audience *g.* so wide *S.* v. 321

Gap'd.
The Convocation *g.*, but could not speak *D.* iv. 610

Gaping.
And *g.* Tritons spew to wash your face *M.E.* iv. 154
Pale spectres, *g.* tombs and purple fires *R.L.* iv. 44
The fox obscene to *g.* tombs retires *W.F.* 71

Garbs.
As several *g.*, with country, town, and court *E.C.* 323
Four Knaves in *g.* succinct, a trusty band *R.L.* iii. 41

Garden.

Or G., tempting with forbidden fruit *E.M.* i. 8
Hang their old Trophies o'er the G. gates *S.* iii. 8
Enjoys his G. and his book in quiet *S.* v. 199
A River at my G.'s end I.H. ii. 4 s
His G—s next your admiration call *M.E.* iv. 113
Turn Arcs of triumph to a G.-gate M.E. iv. 30

Gard'ner.

Spirts in the g.'s eyes who turns the cock *D.* ii. 178

Garland.

His beaver'd brow a birchen g. wears *D.* iv, 141
Bestow a G. only on a Bier *S.* v. 68
And in one g., all their beauties join *Su.* 56
While she with g—s hung the bending boughs (rep.) *A.* 68
For me the vernal g. bloom no more *I.H.* iii. 32
And all her faded g. bloom anew *M.E.* v. 48
Let Nymphs and Sylvans cypress g. bring *W.* 22

Garments.

Loose to the wind their airy g. flew *R.L.* ii. 63

Garret.

Up to her godly g. after sev'n *E.* v. 21
From drawing-rooms, from colleges, from g—s D. ii. 23
Discharge their G., move their beds, and run *S.* iii. 157

Garter.

The George and G. dangling from that bed *M.E.* iii. 303
In silks, and crapes, in G—s and in Rags D. ii. 22
Scarfs, g., gold, amuse his riper stage *E.M.* ii. 279
And G., Stars, and Coronets appear *R.L.* i. 85
There lay three g., half a pair of gloves *R.L.* ii. 39

Garter'd.

Of Lords, and Earls, and Dukes, and g. Knights *E.* v. 36

Garth.

And we too boast our G. and Addison *D.* ii. 140
G. did not write his own Dispensary *E.C.* 619
Well-natur'd G. inflam'd with early praise *P.S.* 137
Accept, O G., the Muse's early lays *Su.* 9

Gasp.

Life's idle business at one g. be o'er *U.L.* 81

Gasping.

And g. Furies thirst for blood in vain *W.F.* 422

Gasps.

G. as they straiten at each end the cord *D.* iv. 29

Gate.

At some sick miser's triple-bolted g. *D.* ii. 248
To some fam'd round-house, ever open g. *D.* ii. 424
And thro' the Iv'ry G. the Vision flies *D.* iii. 340
While the gaunt mastiff growling at the g. *M.E.* iii. 195
Where Age and Want sit smiling at the g. *M.E.* iii. 266
And yours, my friends? thro' whose free-op'ning g. *S.* ii. 157
Where o'er the g—s, by his fam'd father's hand D. i. 31
Lift up your G., ye Princes, see him come *D.* i. 301
Thro' Lud's fam'd g., along the well-known Fleet *D.* ii. 359
Where Brown and Mears unbar the g. of Light *D.* iii. 28
See barb'rous nations at thy g. attend *M.* 91
Hang their old trophies o'er the Garden g. *S.* iii. 8
And frequent herses shall besiege your g. *U.L.* 38

Gather.

So when small humours g. to a gout *E.M.* ii. 159
Glean on, and g. up the whole estate *S.* vii. 92

Gather'd.

And g. ev'ry Vice on Christian ground *D.* iv. 312

Gath'ring.

The g. number as it moves along *D.* iv. 81
For see the g. flocks to shelter tend *Sp.* 101
Then g. flocks on unknown mountains fed *W.F.* 87

Gathers.

Dove-like, she g. to her wings again *D.* iii. 126
Expanded flies, and g. all its fame *E.M.* iv. 384
He g. health from herbs the forest yields *W.F.* 241

Gaudy.

Its g. colours spreads on ev'ry place *E.C.* 312

Gaul.

See the fierce Visigoths on Spain and G. *D.* iii. 94
Or bid the furious G. be rude no more *O.* ii. 16
The G. subdu'd, or Property secur'd *S.* v. 10

Gaunt.

While the g. mastiff growling at the gate *M.E.* iii. 195

Gave.

Wolves g. thee suck, and savage Tigers fed *A.* 90
Fate in their dotage this fair Idiot g. *D.* i. 13
My life g. ampler lessons to mankind *D.* i. 192
And empty words she g., and sounding strain *D.* ii. 45
With that she g. him (piteous of his case *D.* ii. 141
With holy envy g. one layman place *D.* ii. 324
G. him the cassock, surcingle, and vest *D.* ii. 350
Boyer the State, and Law the Stage g. o'er *D.* ii. 413
A new Edition of old Æson g. *D.* iv. 122
There truant WYNDHAM ev'ry Muse gave o'er *D.* iv. 167
G. the gilt Coach, and dappled Flanders Mares *E.* iv. 50
I g. it you to write again *E.* vi. 16
The Faith and Moral, Nature g. before *E.M.* iii. 286
Say was it Virtue, more tho' Heav'n ne'er g. *E.M.* iv. 103
When his lewd father g. the dire disease *E.M.* iv. 120
But when he heard th' Affront the Fellow g. *E.S.* ii. 152
Whose Speech you took, and g. it to a Friend *E.S.* ii. 167
Or g. his Father Grief but when he died *Ep.* iii. 4
'Tis true, my Lord, I g. my word *I.H.* i. 2
Just what you g. me, Competence *I.H.* ii. 24 s
G. alms at Easter, in a Christian trim *M.E.* ii. 57
Asham'd to own their g. delight before *M.E.* ii. 237
And g. you Beauty, but deny'd the Pelf *M.E.* ii. 281
To you g. Sense, Good-humour, and a Poet *M.E.* ii. 292
I'll now give sixpence where I g. a groat *M.E.* ii. 366
And g. the harmless fellow a good word *Mi.* iii. 6
In complaisance I took the Queen he g. *Mi.* ix. 49
And g. him back the fair *O.* l. 86
Well might they rage, I g. them but their due *R.L.* iii. 174
The pow'rs g. ear, and granted half his pray'r *R.L.* ii. 45
Who g. the ball, or paid the visit last *R.L.* ii. 12
Or e'er to costive lap-dog g. disease *R.L.* iv. 75
Once g. new beauties to the snowy neck *R.L.* v. 170
Faith, I shall give the answer Reynard g. *S.* iii. 114
E'en take the Counsel which I g. you first *S.* iv. 131
With Laws, to which you g. your own assent *S.* vi. 30
G. him much praise, and some reward beside *S.* vi. 43
Don't you remember what reply he g. *S.* vi. 49
Whom crimes g. wealth, and wealth g. Impudence *S.* vii. 46
Yet g. me, in this dark Estate *U.P.* 9
Begin; this charge the dying Daphne g. *W.* 17
But see, the man who spacious regions g. *W.F.* 79

Gav'st.

Thou g. that Ripeness, which so soon began *D.* iv. 287

Gay.

Curl stretches after G., but G. is gone *D.* ii. 127
G. dies unpension'd with a hundred friends *D.* iii. 330
G. pats my shoulder, and you vanish quite *E.* v. 47
Striking their pensive bosoms—Here lies G. *Ep.* xi. 12
From Pope, from Parnell, or from G. *I.H.* ii. 94 s
And those they left me; for they left me G. *P.S.* 256
Here g. Description Egypt glads with show'rs D. i. 73
In flow'd at once a g. embroider'd race *D.* iv. 275
Laid this g. Description of the Spring in dust *D.* iv. 416
On others Int'rest her g. liv'ry flings *D.* iv. 537
Soft without weakness, without glaring g. *E.* iii. 66
In these g. thoughts the Loves and Graces shine *E.* iv. 1
Thus wisely careless, innocently g. *E.* iv. 11
And the g. mourn'd, who never mourn'd before *E.* iv. 16
Let mine an innocent, g. farce appear *E.* iv. 25
Fresh blooming Hope, g. daughter of the sky *E.A.* 299
All glares alike, without distinction g. *E.C.* 314
Yet let not each g. Turn thy rapture move *E.C.* 390
Fancy and art in g. Petronius please *E.C.* 667
From grave to g., from lively to severe *E.M.* iv. 380
His Anger moral, and his Wisdom g. *Ep.* i. 6
And the g. Courtier feels the sigh sincere *Ep.* ix. 6
There Youths and Nymphs in concert g. *I.H.* iii. 29
That g. Free-thinker, a fine talker once *M.E.* i. 162
Attracts each light g. meteor of a Spark *M.E.* ii. 22
Gallant and g., in Cliveden's proud alcove *M.E.* iii. 307

GAZE—GENTLE.

Or just as *g.*, at Council, in a ring *M.E.* iii. 309
First, for his Son a *g.* Commission buys *M.E.* iii. 389
And the *g.* Conscience of a life well spent *Mi.* v. 12
Not grave thro' Pride, or *g.* thro' Folly *Mi.* viii. 6
Then *g.* Ideas crowd the vacant brain *R.L.* i. 83
Belinda smil'd, and all the world was *g. R.L.* ii. 52
In hues as *g.*, and odours as divine *S.* viii. 216
No seas so rich, so *g.* no banks appear *W.F.* 225

Gaze.

The *g.* of fools, and pageant of a day *U.L.* 44
On *him*, and crowds turn Coxcombs as they *g. D.* ii. 8
All *g.* with ardour : some a poet's name *D.* ii. 51
In vain ! they *g.*, turn giddy, rave, and die *D.* iv. 648
I bear thee, view thee, *g.* o'er all thy charms *E.A.* 233
It will be then no crime to *g.* on me *E.A.* 330
To *g.* on Basset, and remain unwarm'd *Mi.* ix. 76
Say with what eyes we ought at Courts to *g. S.* iv. 16
And *g.* on Parian charms with learned eyes *S.* iv. 31
To *g.* on Princes, and to talk of Kings *S.* viii. 101

Gaz'd.

Wond'ring he *g.* : When lo ! a Sage appears *D.* iii. 35
Guiltless I *g.* ; heav'n listen'd while you sung *E.A.* 65

Gazer.

More on a Reader's sense, than *G.'s* eye *S.* v. 351
Bright as the sun, her eyes the *g—s* strike *R.L.* ii. 13

Gazette.

Like the last *G.*, or the last Address *E.S.* ii. 227
And talks *G—s* and Post-boys o'er by heart *S.* viii. 155

Gazetteer.

No *G.* more innocent than I *E.S.* i. 84
And see ! thy very *G—s* give o'er *D.* i. 215
These are, —ah no ! these were, the *G. D.* ii. 314

Gazing.

Expos'd thro' crystal to the *g.* eyes *R.L.* iv. 114

Gellius.

What *G.* or Stobæus hash'd before *D.* iv. 231

Gem.

This small, well-polish'd *G.*, the work of years *E.* iii. 40
And justly set the *G.* above the Flow'r *M.E.* i. 148
An honest factor stole a *G.* away *M.E.* iii. 362
False as his *G—s*, and canker'd as his Coins *D.* iv. 349
Court-virtues bear, like *G.*, the highest rate *M.E.* i. 141
Poets heap Virtues, Painters *G.* at will *M.E.* ii. 185
Can they, in *g.* bid pallid Hippia glow *M.E.* iii. 87
Unpolish'd *G.* no ray on Pride bestow *Mi.* x. 5
This casket India's glowing *G.* unlocks *R.L.* i. 133
Paint, Marble, *G.*, and robes of Persian dye *S.* vi. 265

Gen'ral, General.

The prudent *G.* turn'd it to a jest *E.S.* ii. 154
D'ye think me, noble *G.*, such a Sot *S.* vi. 50
Our *G—s* now, retir'd to their Estates *S.* ii. 7
Tho' triumphs were to *g.* only due *E.C.* 512
Till all tun'd equal, send a *g.* hum *D.* ii. 386
And fill the *g.* chorus of mankind *E.C.* 188
Acts not by partial, but by *g.* laws *E.M.* i. 146, and iv. 36
The *g.* ORDER, since the whole began *E.M.* i. 171
To be another in this *g.* frame *E.M.* i. 264
Press to one centre still, the *g.* Good *E.M.* iii. 14
Who, foe to Nature, hears the *g.* groan *E.M.* iii. 163
Thus God and Nature link'd the *g.* frame *E.M.* iii. 317
Come on then, Satire ! *g.*, uncoufin'd *E.S.* ii. 14
Some *g.* maxims, or be right by chance *M.E.* i. 4
His Passion still, to covet *g.* praise *M.E.* i. 196
Blends in exception to all *g.* rules *M.E.* ii. 275
At length Corruption, like a *g.* flood *M.E.* iii. 135
Extremes in Man concur to *g.* use *M.E.* iii. 162
On one nice Trick depends the *g.* fate *R.L.* iii. 94
Phryne foresees a *general* Excise *M.E.* iii. 120

Generation.

Their *g.'s* so equivocal *E.C.* 43

Gen'rous.

The winged courser, like a *g.* horse *E.C.* 86
The *g.* Critic fann'd the Poet's fire *E.C.* 100
The *g.* pleasure to be charm'd with Wit *E.C.* 238
G. converse ; a soul exempt from pride *E.C.* 641

With manners *g.* as his noble blood *E.C.* 726
'Twas then the studious head or *g.* mind *E.M.* iii. 283
Man, like the *g.* vine, supported lives *E.M.* iii. 311
Compar'd, and knew their *g.* End the same *E.S.* ii. 81
A *g.* Faith, from superstition free *Ep.* ii. 9
At half mankind when *g.* Manly raves *M.E.* i. 57
But never, never, reach'd one *g.* Thought *M.E.* ii. 162
The *g.* God, who Wit and Gold refines *M.E.* ii. 289
Oh say, what sums that *g.* hand supply *M.E.* iii. 277
Was there a *g.*, a reflecting mind *Mi.* 5
The mild and *g.* breast *O.* iii. 12
Here tears shall flow from a more *g.* cause *P.C.* 13
I will, or perish in the *g.* cause *S.* i. 117
Is what two souls so *g.* cannot bear *S.* ii. 58
After a life of *g.* Toils endur'd *S.* v. 9
Shall shortly want the *g.* tear he pays *U.L.* 78

Genial.

Till *g.* Jacob, or a warm Third day *D.* i. 57
For me kind Nature wakes her *g.* Pow'r *E.M.* i. 133
The vital flame, and swells the *g.* seeds *E.M.* iii. 118
Is this a dinner ? this a *G.* room *M.E.* iv. 155
In *g.* spring, beneath the quivering shade *W.F.* 135

Genii.

Fays, Fairies, *G.*, Elves, and Dæmons, hear *R.L.* ii. 74

Genius.

Less human *g.* than God gives to ape *D.* i. 282
With me began this *g.*, and shall end *D.* ii. 55
A Newton's *g.* or a Milton's flame *D.* iii. 216
Shrink, and confess the *g.* of the place *D.* iv. 146
And petrify a *G.* to a Dunce *D.* iv. 264
While thro' Poetic scenes the *G.* roves *D.* iv. 489
In Poets as true *g.* is but rare *E.C.* 11
How far your *g.*, taste, and learning go *E.C.* 49
One science only will one *g.* fit *E.C.* 60
Religion, Country, *g.* of his Age *E.C.* 121
Rome's ancient *G.*, o'er its ruins spread *E.C.* 699
Learn each small People's *g.*, policies *E.M.* iii. 183
Come then ! my Friend ! my *G. !* come along *E.M.* iv. 373
Old England's *G.*, rough with many a Scar *E.S.* i. 152
Some rising *G.* sins up to my Song *E.S.* ii. 9
The throne a Bigot keep, a *G.* quit *M.E.* i. 91
Consult the *G.* of the Place in all *M.E.* iv. 57
The feast, his tow'ring *g.* marks *Mi.* xii. 9
To raise the *g.* and to mend the heart *P.C.* 2
True *G.* kindles, and fair Fame inspires *P.S.* 194
Left me to see neglected *G.* bloom *P.S.* 257
No, such a *G.* never can lie still *P.S.* 278
Or tames the *G.* of the stubborn plain *S.* i. 131
A perfect *g.* at an Opera-song *S.* vi. 11
Yours Milton's *g.*, and mine Homer's spirit *S.* vi. 136
Who forms the *G.* in the natal hour *S.* vi. 279

Genseric.

Of *G. !* and Attila's dread name *D.* iii. 92

Gentle.

Ge, *g.* gales, and bear my sighs away *A.* 17, &c.
And *g.* Dulness ever loves a joke *D.* i. 34
Now *g.* touches wanton o'er his face *D.* ii. 201
The pond'rous books two *g.* readers bring *D.* ii. 383
Each *g.* clerk, and mutt'ring seals his eyes *D.* ii. 404
The sure fore-runner of his *g.* sway *D.* iii. 300
Thou wept'st, and with thee wept each *g.* Muse *D.* iv. 44
Some *g. James* to bless the land again *D.* iv. 176
Now to thy *g.* shadow all are shrunk *D.* iv. 509
Strong as their charms, and *g.* as their soul *E.* iii. 74
Till fate scarce felt his *g.* breath suppress *E.* iv. 13
Amid those Lovers, joys his *g.* Ghost *E.* iv. 74
He draws him *g.*, tender, and forgiving *E.J.S.* 27
Is *g.* love, and charms all womankind *E.M.* ii. 190
These may some *g.* ministerial Wig *E.S.* i. 95
Of Manners *g.*, of Affections mild *Ep.* xi. 1
Attend the shade of *g.* Buckingham *E.V.* x. 10
There leaning near a *g.* Brook *I.H.* ii. 129
As in the *g.* Reign of My Queen Anne *I.H.* iii. 4
G. Cupid, o'er my Heart *Mi.* vii. 2
Like *g. Fanny's* was my flow'ry theme *P.S.* 149
Of *g.* blood (part shed in Honour's cause *P.S.* 388
A well-bred Lord to assault a *g.* Belle *R.L.* i. 8
Could make a *g.* Belle reject a Lord *R.L.* i. 10
If *g.* Damon did not squeeze her hand *R.L.* i. 98
Whose *g.* progress makes a calf an ox *S.* vii. 48

Ah *g.* Sir, you Courtiers so cajole us *S.* viii. 90
Me *g.* Delia beckons from the plain *Sp.* 53
Ye *g.* Muses, leave your crystal spring *W.* 21
Her fate is whisper'd by the *g.* breeze *W.* 61
No lake so *g.*, and no spring so clear *W.F.* 226

Gentleman.

What the fine *g.* wore yesterday *E.C.* 330
Whereat the *g.* began to stare *S.* vi. 194
The mob of G—en who wrote with Ease S. v. 108
Yet these were all poor *G.* / I dare *S.* viii. 78

Gentler.

A *g.* exercise to close the games *D.* ii. 366

Gentlest.

With softest manners, *g.* Arts adorn'd *E.* i. 4
Here, WITHERS, rest, thou bravest, *g.* mind *Ep.* ix. 1
Forms the soft bosom with the *g.* art *S.* v. 219

Gently.

Who *g.* drawn, and struggling less and less *D.* iv. 83
Soft is the strain when Zephyr *g.* blows *E.C.* 366
G. steal upon the ear *O.* i. 13
Smooth flow the waves, the Zephyrs *g.* play *R.L.* ii. 51
Fair Thames, flow *g.* from thy sacred spring *Sp.* 3

Genuine.

Thine is the *g.* head of many a house *D.* iv. 243

George.

'Tis G. and LIBERTY that crowns the cup *M.E.* iii. 207
The G. and Garter dangling from that bed *M.E.* iii. 303
No more than thou, great G.! a birth-day song *P.S.* 222
With ARMS, and G., and BRUNSWICK crowd the verse *S.* i. 24
And swear, all shame is lost in G.'s Age S. v. 126

Geraldine.

Fair G., bright object of his vow *W.F.* 297

German.

On G. Crouzaz, and Dutch Burgersdyck *D.* iv. 198
Believe me, many a G. Prince is worse *S.* iv. 83
More rough than forty G—s when they scold S. vii. 62

Get.

How Farce and Epic *g.* a jumbled race *D.* iv. 70
From the strong fate of drams if thou *g.* free *D.* iii. 145
And hew the Block off, and *g.* out the Man *D.* iv. 270
Could not *g.* out as he got in *I.H.* i. 54
I *g.* a whisper, and withdraw *I.H.* ii. 63 s.
To *g.* my Warrant quickly sign'd *I.H.* ii. 76 s.
There London's voice: "G. Money, Money still *S.* iii. 79
G. Place and Wealth, if possible, with grace *S.* iii. 103
Composing songs for Fools to *g.* by heart *S.* vi. 126
These write to Lords, some mean reward to *g. S.* vii. 25
And *g.*, by speaking truth of monarchs dead *S.* viii. 106
Wild to *g.* loose, his Patience I provoke *S.* viii. 116
As in the pox, some give it to *g.* free *S.* viii. 171

Gets.

Now he begs Verse, and what he *g.* commends *Mi.* iii. 13
And *g.* an Act of Parliament to rob *S.* viii. 143

Getting.

Still, still be *g.*, never, never rest *S.* iv. 96
Ascribes his g—s to his parts and merit M.E. iii. 376

Gew-gaws.

Of hollow *g.*, only dress and face *S.* viii. 209

Ghost.

Amid those Lovers, joys his gentle G. *E.* iv. 74
The well-sung woes will soothe my pensive *g. E.A.* 365
Then mix this dust with thine—O spotless G. *Ep.* xiii. 5
And calls her *g. O.* i. 104
What beck'ning *g.* along the moonlight shade *U.L.* 1
Pleas'd thy pale *g.* or grac'd thy mournful bier *U.L.* 50
Still round and round the G—s of Beauty glide M.E. ii. 241
And cries of tortur'd *g.* (*ref.*) *O.* i. 62
And the pale *g.* start at the flash of day *R.L.* v. 52

Giant.

Strong in new arms, lo! G. Handel stands *D.* iv. 65
Far from a LYON, and not a G. quite *S.* iii. 50
And ten-horn'd fiends and G—s rush to war D. iii. 236
And lin'd with G. deadlier than them all *S.* viii. 275

Vice, with such G. strides comes on amain *E.S.* ii. 6
His *g.* limbs in state unwieldy spread *R.L.* iii. 72
One G. Vice, so excellently ill *S.* vii. 4
One of our G. Statutes opes its jaw *S.* viii. 173

Gibson.

While Sherlock, Hare, and G. preach in vain *D.* iii. 204

Giddy.

Thy *g.* dulness still shall lumber on *D.* iii. 294
Stunn'd with his *g.* Larum half the town *D.* iv. 292
In vain! they gaze, turn *g.*, rave, and die *D.* iv. 648
The latent tracts, the *g.* heights explore *E.M.* i. 11
As Eastern priests in *g.* circles run *E.M.* ii. 27
And *g.* Factions hear away their rage *P.S.* i. 35
Arthur, whose *g.* son neglects the Laws *P.S.* 23
Thro' all the *g.* circle they pursue *R.L.* i. 93
The *g.* motion of the whirling Mill *R.L.* ii. 134

Gift.

Be thine, my stationer! this magic *g. D.* ii. 137
Each with some wondrous *g.* approach the Pow'r *D.* iv. 390
Thus with each *g.* of nature and of art *M.E.* i. 192
Good Sense, which only is the *g.* of Heav'n *M.E.* iii. 43
He takes the *g.* with rev'rence, and extends *R.L.* iii. 131
Had once a pretty *g.* of tongues enough *S.* viii. 77
All hail him victor in both g—s of song D. ii. 267
Thus the soft *g.* of Sleep conclude the day *D.* ii. 419
There all thy *g.* and graces we display *D.* iv. 295
But Fortune's *g.* if each alike possess *E.M.* iv. 63
Fortune her *g.* may variously dispense *E.M.* iv. 67
The good or bad the *g.* of Fortune gain *E.M.* iv. 83
The Gnome rejoicing bears her *g.* away *R.L.* iv. 87
The Mob's applauses or the *g.* of Kings *S.* iv. 15
Each am'rous nymph prefers her *g.* in vain *Su.* 53
Here Ceres' *g.* in waving prospect stand *W.F.* 39

Gigantic.

G. Pride, pale Terror, gloomy Care *W.F.* 415

Gild.

No more the rising Sun shall *g.* the Morn *M.* 99
Where'er he shines, oh Fortune, *g.* the scene *M.E.* iii. 245
Attend to *g.* the Ev'ning of my day *S.* i. 94
If Sylvia smiles, new glories *g.* the shore *Sp.* 75

Gilded.

On horse, on foot, in hacks, and *g.* chariots *D.* ii. 24
Bright with the *g.* button tipt its head *D.* iv. 408
Before her *Fancy's g.* clouds decay *D.* iv. 631
Admires the jay the insect's *g.* wings *E.M.* iii. 55
On *g.* clouds in fair expansion lie *M.E.* iv. 147
Yet let me flap this hug with *g.* wings *P.S.* 309
Her joy in *g.* Chariots, when alive *R.L.* i. 55
Amid the circle, on the *g.* mast *R.L.* ii. 69
Dash the proud Gamester in his *g.* Car *S.* i. 107
The *g.* puppets dance and move above *S.* vii. 18

Gilding.

And I not strip the *g.* off a knave *S.* i. 115
G. my Aurelia's brows *Mi.* vii. 22

Gildon.

Where wretched Withers, Ward, and G. rest *D.* i. 296
Ah Dennis! G. ah! what ill-starr'd rage *D.* iii. 173
Yet then did G. draw his venal quill *P.S.* 151

Gilds.

And with her own fools-colours *g.* them all *D.* i. 84
See where the morning *g.* the palmy shore *D.* iii. 95
It *g.* all objects, but it alters none *E.C.* 317
Mean-while opinion *g.* with varying rays *E.M.* ii. 283

Gill-house.

Thee shall each ale-house, thee each *g.* mourn *D.* iii. 147

Gilt.

Healey's *g.* tub, or Fleckno's Irish throne *D.* i. 2
Gave the *g.* Coach, and dappled Flanders mares *E.* iv. 50
Of twelve vast French Romances, neatly *g. R.L.* ii. 38
Where the *g.* Chariot never marks the way *R.L.* iv. 154
Not when a *g.* Buffet's reflected pride *S.* ii. 5

Gin.

And hurls the Thunder of the Laws on G. *E.S.* i. 130
Must never Patriot then declaim at G. *E.S.* ii. 191
And answering g—shops sourer sighs return D. iii. 148

GIRLS—GLADE.

Girls.
All Boys may read, and *G.* may understand *E.S.* i. 76
The Boys and *G.* whom charity maintains *S.* v. 231

Give.
Sleepless themselves, to *g.* their readers sleep *D.* i. 94
And see ! thy very Gazetteers *g.* o'er *D.* i. 215
Let all *g.* way, and Morris may be read *D.* iii. 168
And last to *g.* the whole creation grace *D.* iii. 247
Or *g.* from fool to fool the Laurel crown *D.* iv. 98
G. law to Words, or war with Words alone *D.* iv. 178
Or *g.* up Cicero to C or K *D.* iv. 222
Be sure I *g.* them Fragments, not a Meal *D.* iv. 230
The Goddess smiling seem'd to *g.* consent *D.* iv. 395
Then *g.* one flirt, and all the vision flies *E.* v. 38
Ah, more than share it, *g.* me all thy grief *E.A.* 50
G. all thou canst—and let me dream the rest *E.A.* 124
But you who seek to *g.* and merit fame *E.C.* 46
When mellowing years their full perfection *g. E.C.* 490
And still the more we *g.*, the more required *E.C.* 503
This praise at least a grateful Muse may *g. E.C.* 734
God gives enough, while he has more to *g. E.M.* iv. 164
Then *g.* Humility a coach and six *E.M.* iv. 170
To whom can Riches *g.* Repute, or Trust *E.M.* iv. 185
The Muse may *g.* thee, but the Gods must guide *E.S.* ii. 215
'Tis all a Father, all a Friend can *g. Ep.* vii. 20
You *g.* the things you never care for *I.H.* i. 34
To *g.* me back my Constitution *I.H.* i. 44
G. me, I cry'd (enough for me) *I.H.* i. 69
I have a thousand thanks to *g. I.H.* ii. 208
G. me again my hollow Tree *I.H.* ii. 200
Be smooth ye rocks, ye rapid floods *g.* way *M.* 36
As Fits *g.* vigour just when they destroy *M.E.* i. 223
And—Betty—*g.* this Cheek a little Red *M.E.* i. 251
"I *g.* and I devise" (old Euclio said *M.E.* i. 256
Why—if I must (then wept) I *g.* it Paul *M.E.* i. 259
Nor asks of God, but of her Stars, to *g. M.E.* ii. 89
You purchase Pain with all that Joy can *g. M.E.* ii. 99
Reduc'd to feign it, when they *g.* no more *M.E.* ii. 238
What Riches *g.* us let us then enquire *M.E.* iii. 79
Alas ! 'tis more than Turner finds they *g. M.E.* iii. 82
What can they *g.* ? to dying Hopkins, Heirs *M.E.* iii. 85
G. Harpax' self the blessing of a friend *M.E.* iii. 92
To buy both sides, and *g.* thy Country peace *M.E.* iii. 150
And *g.* th' eternal wheels to know their rounds *M.E.* iii. 168
I'll now *g.* sixpence where I gave a groat *M.E.* iii. 366
Jones and Le Notre have it not to *g. M.E.* iv. 46
And *g.* to Titus old Vespasian's due *M.E.* iv. 18
Nature must *g.* way to Art *Mi.* vii. 4
Like *Cato*, *g.* his little Senate laws *P.S.* 209
G. Virtue scandal, Innocence a fear *P.S.* 285
Now lap-dogs *g.* themselves the rousing shake *R.L.* i. 15
What tho' no credit doubting Wits may *g. R.L.* i. 39
Ye Sylphs and Sylphids, to your chief *g.* ear *R.L.* ii. 73
While nymphs take treats or assignations *g. R.L.* iii. 69
Who *g.* th' hysteric, or poetic fit *R.L.* iv. 60
"*G.* her the hair"—he spoke, and rapped his box *R.L.* iv. 130
You'll *g.* me, like a friend both sage and free *S.* i. 9
Faith, I shall *g.* the answer Reynard gave *S.* iii. 114
But *g.* the Knight (or *g.* his Lady) spleen *S.* iii. 145
Venus shall *g.* him Forio, and Anstis Birth *S.* iv. 82
To do the Honours, and to *g.* the Wine *S.* iv. 100
To Gammer Gurton if it *g.* the bays *S.* v. 91
And Peers *g.* way, exalted as they are *S.* vi. 106
You *g.* all royal Witchcraft to the Devil *S.* vi. 219
If there be truth in Law, and Use can *g. S.* vi. 230
Here a lean Bard, whose wit could never *g. S.* vii. 13
As in the pox, some *g.* it to get free *S.* vii. 171
Our Court may justly to our stage *g.* rules *S.* viii. 220
And *g.* the conquest to thy Sylvia's eyes *Sp.* 88
While plants their shade, or flow'rs their odours *g. W.* 83

Giv'n.
Whate'er he gives, are *g.* for you to hate *D.* iii. 222
And Reason *g.* them but to study *Flies D.* iv. 454
No silver saints by dying misers *g. E.A.* 137
Just precepts thus from great examples *g. E.C.* 98
Oh blindness to the future ! kindly *g. E.M.* i. 85
Yet simple Nature to his hope has *g. E.M.* i. 103
Say what the use, were finer optics *g. E.M.* i. 195
The rich is happy in the plenty *g. E.M.* ii. 265
And not a vanity is *g.* in vain *E.M.* ii. 290
Nay why external for internal *g. E.M.* iv. 161

Are *g.* in vain, but what they seek they find *E.M.* iv. 348
Manners with Candour are to Benson *g. E.S.* ii. 72
And Chiefs or Sages long to Britain *g. Ep.* xiv. 13
You hold the word from Jove to Momus *g. M.E.* iii. 3
G. to the Fool, the Mad, the Vain, the Evil *M.E.* iii. 19
To Worth or Want well-weigh'd, be Bounty *g. M.E.* iii. 229
To bright Cecilia greater pow'rs is *g. O.* i. 132
Whether that blessing be deny'd or *g. P.S.* 418

Gives.
Or *g.* to Zembla fruits, to Barca flow'rs *D.* i. 74
Less human genius than God *g.* an ape *D.* i. 282
Whate'er he *g.*, are giv'n for you to hate *D.* iii. 222
And dies, when Dulness *g.* her Page the word *D.* iv. 30
A drowsy Watchman, that just *g.* a knock *D.* iv. 443
Then *g.* a smacking buss, and cries, "No words !" *E.* v. 26
"Tis Venus, Venus *g.* these arms *E.* vi. 27
She *g.* in large recruits of needful pride *E.C.* 206
That *g.* us back the image of our mind *E.C.* 300
'Tis not enough no harshness *g.* offence *E.C.* 364
With warmth *g.* sentence, yet is always just *E.C.* 678
What future bliss he *g.* not thee to know (*rep.*) *E.M.* i. 93
Say, here he *g.* too little, there too much *E.M.* i. 116
Alike in what it *g.*, and what denies *E.M.* i. 206
G. all the strength and colour of our life *E.M.* ii. 122
Reason itself but *g.* it edge and pow'r *E.M.* ii. 147
Thus Nature *g.* us (let it check our pride) *E.M.* ii. 195
Some livelier plaything *g.* his youth delight *E.M.* ii. 277
Man cares for all : to birds he *g.* his woods *E.M.* iii. 57
G. not the useless knowledge of its end *E.M.* iii. 72
The strength he gains is from th' embrace he *g. E.M.* iii. 312
God *g.* enough, while he has more to give *E.M.* iv. 164
What nothing earthly *g.*, or can destroy *E.M.* iv. 167
Is blest in what it takes, and what it *g. E.M.* iv. 313
G. thee to make thy neighbour's blessing thine *E.M.* iv. 354
When Paxton *g.* him double Pots and Pay *E.S.* ii. 141
The last full fairly *g.* it to the House *E.S.* ii. 180
Contracts, inverts, and *g.* ten thousand dyes *M.E.* i. 16
That, Nature *g.*; and where the lesson taught *M.E.* i. 211
Prescribes, attends, the med'cine makes and *g. M.E.* iii. 270
While Cato *g.* his little Senate laws *P.C.* 23
When each new night-dress *g.* a new disease *R.L.* iv. 38
That single act *g.* half the world the spleen *R.L.* iv. 78
Earth shakes her nodding tow'rs, the ground *g.* way *R.L.* v. 51
Ask'd for a groat, he *g.* a hundred pounds *S.* iv. 86
'Tis he, who *g.* my breast a thousand pains *S.* v. 342
Well may he blush, who *g.* it, or receives *S.* v. 414
To books and study *g.* seven years complete *S.* vi. 117
It *g.* men happiness, or leaves them ease *S.* vi. 183
Between each drop it *g.*, stays half a minute *S.* viii. 127
What Blessings thy free Bounty *g. U.P.* 17
A wealthier tribute than to thine he *g. W.F.* 224

Giving.
Strives to extract from his soft *g.* palm *D.* ii. 208
His g—s rare, save farthings to the poor M.E. iii. 3 8

Glad.
G. chains, warm furs, broad banners, and broad faces *D.* i. 88
Hark ! a *g.* voice the lonely desert cheers *M.* 29
Or makes his Neighbours *g.*, if he increase *M.E.* iv. 182
G. of a quarrel, straight I clap the door *P.S.* 67
Clapp'd his *g.* wings, and sate to view the fight *R.L.* v. 54
G., like a Boy, to snatch the first good day *S.* vi. 294
Say, Daphnis, say in what *g.* soil appears *Sp.* 85
And now the Queen, to g. her sons, proclaims D. ii. 17
A peck of coals a-piece shall *g.* the rest *D.* ii. 282
Nor *g.* vile Poets with true Critics' gore *D.* iii. 198
Hopkins and Sternhold *g.* the heart with Psalms *S.* v. 230

Gladden'd.
Thence to the south extend thy *g.* eyes *D.* iii. 79

Glade.
When falling dews with spangles deck'd the *g. A.* 99
Where'er you walk cool gales shall fan the *g., Su.* 73
Invites my steps ; and points to yonder *g. U.L.* 2
And lonely woodcocks haunt the wat'ry *g. W.F.* 128
Calls in the Country, catches opening g—s M.E. iv. 61

Glitt'ring thro' the gloomy *g. O.* i. 78
There, interspers'd in lawns and op'ning *g. W.F.* 21

Gladiators.
There *G.* fight or die in flow'rs *M.E.* iv. 124

Gladly.
And *g.* praise the merit of a foe *E.C.* 638

Glads.
Now bright Arcturus *g.* the teeming grain *A.* 72
Here gay Description Egypt *g.* with show'rs *D.* i. 73

Glance.
Come, with one *g.* of those deluding eyes *E.A.* 283
Stop, or turn nonsense, at one *g.* of thee *I.H.* iii. 40
The *g.* by day, the whisper in the dark *R.L.* i. 74
A mournful *g.* Sir Fopling upwards cast *R.L.* v. 63
While a kind *g.* at her pursuer flies *Sp.* 59
Or what ill eyes malignant *g—s* dart *A.* 82
G. on the stone where our cold relics lie E.A. 356

Glancing.
And her Parnassus *g.* o'er at once *D.* iii. 137

Glare.
All sudden, Gorgons hiss, and Dragons *g. D.* iii. 235
The few that *g.*, each character must mark *M.E.* i. 121
And screen'd in shades from day's detested g. *R.L.*iv.22

Glares.
She *g.* in Balls, front Boxes, and the Ring *E.* iv. 53
All *g.* alike, without distinction gay *E.C.* 314
When Flatt'ry *g.*, all hate it in a Queen *M.E.* i. 61

Glaring.
Each sire imprest, and *g.* in his son *D.* i. 100
Soft without weakness, without *g.* gay *E.* iii. 66
One *g.* Chaos, and wild heap of wit *E.C.* 292
And unobserv'd the *g.* Orb declines *M.E.* ii. 256
Now *g.* fiends, and snakes on rolling spires *R.L.* iv. 43

Glass.
Prudence, whose *g.* presents th' approaching jail *D.* i. 51
Then thron'd in *g.*, and nam'd it CAROLINE *D.* iv. 409
Kind Self-conceit to some her *g.* applies *D.* iv. 533
You'd write as smooth again on *g. E.* vi. 21
False Eloquence, like the prismatic *g. E.C.* 311
No *g.* can reach from Infinite to thee *E.M.* i. 240
A heav'nly image in the *g.* appears *R.L.* i. 125
In this impartial *g.* my Muse intends *S.* i. 57
The musty wine, foul cloth, and greasy *g. S.* ii. 66
Fresh rising blushes paint the wat'ry *g. Su.* 28
Oft in her *g.* the musing shepherd spies *W.F.* 211

Gleam.
In the clear azure *g.* the flocks are seen *W.F.* 215
His shining horns diffus'd a golden *g. W.F.* 332
And *g—s of glory brighten'd all the day E.A.* 146
And mild as op'ning *g.* of promis'd heav'n *E.A.* 256
Dreadful *g. O.* i. 56

Gleaming.
Nor fields with *g.* steel be cover'd o'er *M.* 59

Gleams.
Or lengthen'd Thought that *g.* thro' many a page *S.* v. 113
Why dimly *g.* the visionary sword *U.L.* 4

Glean.
G. on, and gather up the whole estate *S.* vii. 92

Glebe.
Or o'er the *g.* distil the kindly rain *R.L.* ii. 86

Glee.
Not with more *g.*, by hands pontific crown'd *D.* ii. 13
A friend in *g.*, ridiculously grim *D.* iii. 154

Glib.
And run, on ivory, so *g. E.* vi. 22

Glide.
And the fleet shades *g.* o'er the dusky green *A.* 64
Or softly *g.* by the canal *I.H.* iii. 46
Still round and round the Ghosts of Beauty *g. M.E.* ii. 241
They pierce my thickets, thro' my Grot they *g. P.S.* 8
Soft yielding minds to Water *g.* away *R.L.* i. 61

From silver spouts the grateful liquors *g. R.L.* iii. 109
And the hush'd waves *g.* softly to the shore *W.F.* 354

Glides.
I stretch my empty arms ; it *g.* away *E.A.* 238
But now secure the painted vessel *g. R.L.* ii. 47
In those fair fields where sacred Isis *g. Su.* 25

Gliding.
Nor thirsty heifer seek the *g.* flood *W.* 38

Glimm'ring.
Nature affords at least a *g.* light *E.C.* 21

Glimpse.
Nor *human* Spark is left, nor *G. divine D.* iv. 652

Glitter.
Shall *g.* o'er the pendant green *I.H.* iii. 23
They strike the Soul, and *g.* in the Eye *Mi.* ix. 82
And groves of lances *g.* on the Rhine *W.F.* 364

Glitt'ring.
G. with ice here hoary hills are seen *D.* i. 75
A vain, unquiet, *g.*, wretched Thing *E.* iv. 54
And *g.* thoughts struck out at ev'ry line *E.C.* 290
G. thro' the gloomy shades *O.* i. 78
A youth more *g.* than a Birth-night Beau *R.L.* i. 23
And decks the Goddess with the *g.* spoil *R.L.* i. 132
Thin *g.* textures of the filmy dew *R.L.* ii. 64
The Peer now spreads the *g.* Forfex wide *R.L.* iii. 147
In *g.* dust, and painted fragments lie *R.L.* iii. 160
Behold ! Augusta's *g.* spires increase *W.F.* 377

Glitters.
And steel now *g.* in the Muses' shades *O.* ii. 8

Globe.
And of all monarchs only grasps the *g. R.L.* iii. 74
The pearly shell its lurid *g.* infold *W.F.* 395

Gloom.
Cibberian forehead, and Cimmerian *g. D.* iv. 532
Lost in a convent's solitary *g. E.A.* 38

Gloomy.
" Be that my task " (replies a *g.* Clerk *D.* iv. 459
Her *g.* presence saddens all the scene *E.A.* 167
G. Pluto, King of Terrors *Mi.* vii. 17
Glitt'ring thro' the *g.* shades *O.* i. 78
Repair'd to search the *g.* Cave of Spleen *R.L.* iv. 16
See *g.* clouds obscure the cheerful day *W.* 30
A dreary desert, and *g.* waste *W.F.* 44
Gigantic Pride, pale Terror, *g.* Care *W.F.* 415

Glorious.
Osborne and Curl accept the *g.* strife *D.* ii. 167
Appear more *g.*, as more hack'd and torn *D.* iv. 124
Thence bursting *g.*, all at once let down *D.* iv. 291
This *g.* Youth, and add one Venus more *D.* iv. 330
More *g.* yet, from barb'rous hands to keep *D.* iv. 379
Beholds these *g.* only in thy Fall *E.* i. 90
The Stoic Husband was the *g.* thing *E.J.S.* 38
To man's low passions, or their *g.* ends *E.M.* iv. 376
G. Ambition ! Peter, swell thy store *M.E.* iii. 125
You show us, Rome was *g.*, not profuse *M.E.* iv. 23
Expos'd in *g.* heaps the tempting Bank *Mi.* ix. 78
A conquest how hard and how *g. O.* i. 89
Not a less pleasing, tho' less *g.* care *R.L.* ii. 92
(The victor cry'd) the *g.* Prize is mine *R.L.* iii. 162
The *g.* fault of Angels and of Gods *U.L.* 14
Draw monarchs chain'd, and Cressi's *g.* field *W.F.* 305

Gloriously.
Great wits sometimes may *g.* offend *E.C.* 159
His wealth brave Timon *g.* confounds *S.* iv. 85

Glory.
The field of *g.* is a field for all (*rep.*) *D.* ii. 32
Old scenes of *g.*, times long cast behind *D.* iii. 63
There rival flames with equal *g.* rise *D.* iii. 80
Not with less *g.* mighty Dulness crown'd *D.* iii. 135
But spread, my sons, your *g.* thin or thick *D.* iv. 129
Intrigu'd with *g.*, and with spirit whor'd *D.* iv. 375
For the dull *g.* of a virtuous Wife *E.* iv. 46
And gleams of *g.* brighten'd all the day *E.A.* 146
And burns with *g.*, and then melts with love *E.C.* 377
Ah ne'er so dire a thirst of *g.* boast *E.C.* 522
The *g.* of the Priesthood, and the shame *E.C.* 694

The *g*., jest, and riddle of the world *E.M.* ii. 18
Let pow'r or knowledge, gold or *g*., please *E.M.* ii. 169
The joy, the peace, the *g*. of Mankind *E.M.* ii. 248
Mark by what wretched steps their *g*. grows *E.M.* iv. 291
A Tale, that blends their *g*. with their shame *E.M.* iv. 308
And where's the *G*. ? 'twill be only thought *E.S.* i. 25
Good Heav'n forbid, that I should blast their *g*. *E.S.* i. 105
Or round a Quaker's Beaver cast a *G*. *E.S.* ii. 97
One tide of *g*., one unclouded blaze *M*. 102
For foreign *g*., foreign joy, they roam *M.E.* ii. 223
Without it, proud Versailles ! thy *g*. falls *M.E.* iv. 71
The hero's *g*. or the virgin's love *P.C.* 10
One speaks the *g*. of the British Queen *R.L.* iii. 13
Which adds new *g*. to the shining sphere *R.L.* v. 142
In moderation placing all my *g*. *S*. i. 67
Those Suns of *G*. please not till they set *S*. v. 22
For gain, not *g*., wing'd his roving flight *S*. v. 71
Newmarket's *g*. rose, as Britain's fell *S*. v. 144
Who pants for *g*. finds but short repose *S*. v. 300
Advance and conquer ! go where *g*. calls *S*. vi. 47
Enjoy the *g*. to be great no more *Sp*. 8
The moon, serene in *g*., mounts the sky *W*. 6
Daphne, our grief ! our *g*. now no more *W*. 68
That Thames's *g*. to the stars shall raise *W.F.* 356
Earth's distant ends our *g*. shall behold *W.F.* 401
Enflamed with *g*'s charms *O*. i. 44
Or rob Rome's ancient geese of all their *g*—s *D*. i. 211
Rome's pompous *g*. rising to our thought *E*. iii. 24
From op'ning skies may streaming *g*. shine *E.A.* 34f
Reflect new *g*., and augment the day *E.C.* 473
All pleasures sicken, and all *g*. sink *E.M.* iv. 46
Nor let us say (those English *g*. gone) *Ep*. ix. 11
Touch'd by thy hand again Rome's *g*. shine *M.E.* v. 46
Not with more *g*., in th' etherial plain *R.L.* ii. 1
How vain are all these *g*., all our pains *R.L.* v. 15
Clos'd their long *G*. with a sigh to find *S*. v. 13
If Sylvia smiles, new *g*. gild the shore *Sp*. 75
See, where on earth the flow'ry *g*. lie *W*. 33

Glosses.
Than Civil Codes with all their *G*. are *S*. vii. 96

Glossy.
Ah ! what avail his *g*., varying dyes *W.F.* 115

Gloves.
There lay three garters, half a pair of *g*. *R.L.* ii. 39
White *g*., and linen worthy Lady Mary *S*. iii. 164

Glow.
A waving *G*. the bloomy beds display *M.E.* iv. 83
Strike in the sketch, or in the picture *g*. *E*. iii. 44
And soft Belinda's blush for ever *g*. *E*. iii. 62
Where flames refin'd in breasts seraphic *g*. *E.A.* 320
Now his fierce eyes with sparkling fury *g*. *E.C.* 378
And seeds of gold in Ophir's mountains *g*. *M*. 96
Can they, in gems bid pallid Hippia *g*. *M.E.* iii. 87
G. in thy heart, and smile upon thy face *Mi*. v. 14
Fires that *g*. *O*. i. 58
That ev'n in slumber caus'd her cheeks to *g*. *R.L.* i. 24
In fumes of burning Chocolate shall *g*. *R.L.* ii. 135
So perish all, whose breast ne'er learn'd to *g*. *U.L.* 45
Here the bright crocus and blue vi'let *g*. *Sp*. 31
Where clearer flames *g*. round the frozen Pole *W.F.* 390
The coral redden, and the ruby *g*. *W.F.* 394
Impale a G.-worm, or Virtu profess D. iv. 569
Is aptly term'd a *G*. *Mi*. iv. 16

Glowing.
How *g*. guilt exalts the keen delight *E.A.* 230
This casket India's *g*. gems unlocks *R.L.* i. 133

Glows.
No pulse that riots, and no blood that *g*. *E.A.* 252
G. while he reads, but trembles while he writes *E.C.* 198
G. in the stars, and blossoms in the trees *E.M.* i. 17a
He trembles, he *g*. *O*. i. 108
And in the breasts of Kings and Heroes *g*. *U.L.* 16
Now Cancer *g*. with Phœbus' fiery car *W.F.* 147

Glue.
And round thy phantom *g*. my clasping arms *E.A.* 234

Glutton.
When the tir'd *g*. labours thro' a treat *S*. ii. 31

Gluttony.
Up, up ! cries *G*., 'tis break of day *S*. iv. 112

Gnats.
Cages for *g*., and chains to yoke a flea *R.L.* v. 121

Gnaw'd.
Then *g*. his pen, then dash'd it on the ground *D*. i. 117

Gnaws.
That *g*. them Night and Day *Mi*. iv. 28

Gnome.
The graver Prude sinks downward to a *G*. *R.L.* i. 63
Swift on his sooty pinions flies the *G*. *R.L.* iv. 17
Safe past the *G*. thro' this fantastic band *R.L.* iv. 55
But oh ! if e'er thy *G*. could spoil a grace *R.L.* iv. 67
The *G*. rejoicing bears her gifts away *R.L.* iv. 87
But Umbriel, hateful *G*., forbears not so *R.L.* iv. 141
The G—s direct, to ev'ry atom just R.L. v. 83
For life predestin'd to the G—s' embrace R.L. i. 80

Go.
G., gentle gales, and bear my sighs away *A*. 17 &c.
G., purify'd by flames, ascend the sky *D*. i. 227
Thea, blessing all, "*G*., Children of my care *D*. iv. 579
Alas, no more ! methinks we wand'ring *g*. *E.A.* 241
Thither, where sinners may have rest, I *g*. *E.A.* 319
G. just alike, yet each believes his own *E.C.* 10
How far your genius, taste, and learning *g*. *E.C.* 49
By chance *g*. right, they purposely *g*. wrong (*rep*.) *E.C.* 427
G., wiser thou ! and, in thy scale of sense *E.M.* i. 113
Above, how high, progressive life may *g*. *E.M.* i. 235
G., wondrous creature ! mount where Science guides (*rep*.) *E.M.* ii. 19
G., soar with Plato to th' empyreal sphere *E.M.* ii. 23
G., teach Eternal Wisdom how to rule *E.M.* ii. 29
One must *g*. right, the other may *g*. wrong *E.M.* iii. 94
G., from the Creatures thy instructions take *E.M.* iii. 172
Yet *g*. ! and thus o'er all the creatures sway *E.M.* iii. 195
Shall gravitation cease, if you *g*. by *E.M.* iv. 128
G., like the Indian, in another life *E.M.* iv. 177
G. ! if your ancient, but ignoble blood *E.M.* iv. 211
G. ! and pretend your family is young *E.M.* iv. 213
G. see Sir Robert—See Sir Robert—hum *E.S.* i. 27
The bribing Statesman—Hold, too high you *g*. *E.S.* ii. 24
G. drench a Pick-pocket, and join the Mob *E.S.* ii. 41
If merely to come in, Sir, they *g*. out *E.S.* ii. 124
Lean as you came, Sir, you must *g*. *I.H.* i. 58
Good Mr. Dean, *g*. change your gown *I.H.* ii. 43 s
G. ! fair example of untainted youth *Ep*. vii. 1
G. live ! for Heav'n's eternal year is thine (*rep*.) *Ep*. vii. 9
G. then, where only bliss sincere is known (*rep*.) *Ep*. vii. 15
More *g*. to ruin Fortunes, than to raise *M.E.* iii. 202
G., search it there, where to be born and die *M.E.* iii. 287
Where once I went to Church, I'll now *g*. twice *M.E.* iii. 367
To bawd for others, and *g*. shares with Punk *Mi*. iii. 26
At last he whispers, "Do ; and we *g*. snacks," *P.S.* 66
G. on, obliging creatures, make me see *P.S.* 119
G. work, hunt, exercise ! (he thus began) *S*. ii. 11
"Pray Heav'n it last !" (cries SWIFT !) "as you *g*. on *S*. ii. 161
Not to *g*. back, is somewhat to advance *S*. iii. 14
G. then, and if you can, admire the state *S*. iv. 28
G. drive the deer, and drag the finny prey (*rep*.) *S*. iv. 113
G. dine with Chartres, in each Vice out-do *S*. iv. 120
The reason, when to come, and when to *g*. *S*. v. 360
G. on, my Friend (he cry'd), see yonder walls (*rep*.) *S*. vi. 46
G., lofty Poet ! and in such a crowd *S*. vi. 108
You *g*. to church to hear these Flatt'rers preach *S*. vi. 225
Would *g*. to Mass in jest (as story says) *S*. viii. 16
As men from Jails to execution *g*. *S*. viii. 273
Oh lead me wheresoe'er I *g*. *U.P.* 43

Goad.
And *g*. the Prelate slumb'ring in his Stall *E.S.* ii. 219

Goal.
Touches some wheel, or verges to some *g*. *E.M.* i. 59
Each individual seeks a sev'ral *g*. *E.M.* ii. 237
For him alone Hope leads from *g*. to *g*. *E.M.* iv. 341

God.

This Box my Thunder, this right hand my *G. D.* i. 202
Less human genius than *G.* gives an ape *D.* i. 282
"*G.* save King Cibber!" mounts in ev'ry note (*rep.*) *D.* i. 318
But pious Needham dropt the name of *G. D.* i. 324
And the hoarse nation croak'd, "*G.* save King Log!" *D.* i. 330
Heav'n's Swiss, who fight for any *G.* or Man *D.* ii. 358
As verse, or prose, infuse the drowsy *G. D.* ii. 396
An hundred sons, and ev'ry son a *G. D.* iii. 134
But "Learn, ye DUNCES, not to scorn your *G." D.* iii. 224
So upright Quakers please both Man and *G. D.* iv. 208
A dauntless infant never scar'd with *G. D.* iv. 284
And reason downward, till we doubt of *G. D.* iv. 472
Make *G.* Man's Image, Man the final Cause *D.* iv. 478
Oh hide the *G.* still more! and make us see (*rep.*) *D.* iv. 483
Lost is his *G.,* his Country, ev'rything *D.* iv. 523
The jealous *G.,* when we profane his fires *E.A.* 81
And make my soul quit Abelard for *G. E.A.* 128
Ah wretch! believ'd the spouse of *G.* in vain *E.A.* 177
Fill my fond heart with *G.* alone, for he *E.A.* 205
Thy image steals between my *G.* and me *E.A.* 268
Assist the fiends! and tear me from my *G. E.A.* 288
For *G.,* not man, absolves our frailties here *E.A.* 316
Lest *G.* himself should seem too absolute *E.C.* 549
But vindicate the ways of *G.* to Man (*rep.*) *E.M.* i. 16
Thro' worlds unnumber'd tho' the *G.* be known *E.M.* i. 21
And drawn supports, upheld by *G.,* or thee *E.M.* i. 34
Is only this, if *G.* has plac'd him wrong *E.M.* i. 50
Is now a victim, and now Egypt's *G. E.M.* i. 64
Who sees with equal eye, as *G.* of all *E.M.* i. 87
Wait the great teacher Death; and *G.* adore *E.M.* i. 92
Sees *G.* in clouds, or hears him in the wind *E.M.* i. 100
Yet cry, if Man 's unhappy, *G.* 's unjust *E.M.* i. 118
Re-judge his justice, be the *G.* of *G. E.M.* i. 122
Vast chain of Being! which from *G.* began *E.M.* i. 237
And Nature tremble to the throne of *G. E.M.* i. 256
Whose body Nature is, and *G.* the soul *E.M.* i. 268
Know then thyself, presume not *G.* to scan *E.M.* ii. 1
In doubt to deem himself a *G.* or Beast *E.M.* ii. 8
Or quitting sense call imitating *G. E.M.* ii. 26
Nor *G.* alone in the still calm we find *E.M.* ii. 109
Subject, compound them, follow her and *G. E.M.* ii. 116
What shall divide? The *G.* within the mind *E.M.* ii. 204
'Tis this, tho' Man 's a fool, yet *G.* is WISE *E.M.* ii. 294
Has *G.,* thou fool! work'd solely for thy good *E.M.* iii. 27
In this 'tis *G.* directs, in that 'tis Man *E.M.* iii. 98
G. in the nature of each being founds *E.M.* iii. 109
The state of Nature was the reign of *G. E.M.* iii. 148
All vocal beings hymn'd their equal *G. E.M.* iii. 156
Whom they rever'd as *G.,* to mourn as Man *E.M.* iii. 224
And own'd a Father, when he own'd a *G. E.M.* iii. 234
No ill could fear in *G.;* and understood *E.M.* iii. 237
That was but love of *G.,* and this of Man *E.M.* iii. 240
And play'd the *G.* an engine on his foe *E.M.* iii. 268
Follow'r of *G.* or friend of human-kind *E.M.* iii. 284
And all of *G.,* that bless Mankind or mend *E.M.* iii. 310
Thus *G.* and Nature link'd the gen'ral frame *E.M.* iii. 317
G. in Externals could not place content *E.M.* iv. 66
Or *G.* and Nature meant to mere Mankind *E.M.* iv. 78
G. sends not ill; if rightly understood *E.M.* iv. 113
This cries there is, and that, there is no *G. E.M.* iv. 140
Why is not Man a *G.,* and Earth a Heav'n *E.M.* iv. 162
G. gives enough, while he has more to give *E.M.* iv. 164
Oh fool! to think *G.* hates the worthy mind *E.M.* iv. 189
An honest Man 's the noblest work of *G. E.M.* iv. 248
But looks thro' Nature up to Nature's *G. E.M.* iv. 332
All end in LOVE OF *G.,* and LOVE OF MAN *E.M.* iv. 340
G. loves from Whole to Parts: but human soul *E.M.* iv. 361
Sets half the world, *G.* knows, against the rest *E.S.* i. 58
To tax Directors, who (thank *G.*) have Plums *E.S.* ii. 49
G. knows, I praise a Courtier when I can *E.S.* ii. 63
Because the insult 's not on Man, but *G. E.S.* ii. 196
Men not afraid of *G.,* afraid of me *E.S.* ii. 209
G. said, Let Newton be! and all was Light *Ep.* xii. 2
Trusts in *G.,* that as well as he was, he shall be *Ep.* xvi. 8
May yield, *G.* knows, to strong temptation *J.H.* ii. 181
Prepare the way! a *G.* appears (*rep.*) *M.* 90
Know, *G.* and NATURE only are the same *M.E.* i. 95
Some *G.,* or Spirit he has lately found *M.E.* i. 164

Then turns repentant, and his *G.* adores *M.E.* i. 188
Nor asks of *G.,* but of her Stars, to give *M.E.* ii. 89
To draw the man who loves his *G.,* or King *M.E.* ii. 196
The gen'rous *G.,* who Wit and Gold refines *M.E.* ii. 289
"*G.* cannot love" (says Blunt, with tearless eyes) *M.E.* iii. 103
Who builds a Church to *G.,* and not to Fame *M.E.* iii. 285
And sad Sir Balaam curses *G.,* and dies *M.E.* iii. 402
From soup to sweet-wine, and *G.* bless the King *M.E.* iv. 162
Bid Temples, worthier of the *G.,* ascend *M.E.* iv. 198
Because *G.* made these large, the other less *S.* ii. 24
I wish to *G.* this house had been your own *S.* ii. 162
It is, and it is not, the voice of *G. S.* v. 90
And *G.* the Father turns a School-divine *S.* v. 102
G. knows, may hurt the very ablest head *S.* vi. 103
The Laws of *G.,* as well as of the land *S.* vi. 246
That *G.* of Nature, who, within us still *S.* vi. 280
What is't to me (a passenger *G.* wot) *S.* vi. 296
Takes *G.* to witness he affects your cause *S.* vii. 76
Since 'twas no form'd design of serving *G. S.* viii. 18
He spies me out. I whisper, "Gracious *G. S.* viii. 62
Bear me, some *G.!* oh quickly bear me hence *S.* viii. 184
For *G.* is pay'd when Man receives *U.P.* 19
And serv'd alike his Vassals and his *G. W.F.* 76
As from the *g.* she flew with furious pace (*rep.*) *W.F.* 189
The *g.* appear'd: he turn'd his azure eyes *W.F.* 351
As much at least as any *G.'s* or more *D.* ii. 80
Where mix'd with *G.,* his lov'd Idea lies *E.A.* 12
In *G.,* one single can its end produce *E.M.* i. 55
If not *G.* image, yet his shadow drew *E.M.* iii. 288
Oh blind to truth, and *G.* whole scheme below *E.M.* iv. 93
The good must merit *G.* peculiar care (*rep.*) *E.M.* iv. 135
And let, a' *G.* name, ev'ry Fool and Knave *E.S.* i. 85
Hold, Sir! for *G.* sake where's th' Affront to you *E.S.* ii. 157
For *G.* sake, come, and live with Men *J.H.* ii. 176
Reveal'd, and *G.* eternal day be thine *M.* 104
Should'ring *G.* altar a vile image stands *M.E.* iii. 293
And *G.* good Providence, a lucky Hit *M.E.* iii. 378
Still Sappho—Hold! for *G.* sake—you'll offend *P.S.* 101
Just G—s! shall all things yield returns but love A. 76
Blasphem'd his *G.,* the Dice, and damn'd his Fate *D.* i. 116
Sign'd with that Ichor which from *G.* distils *D.* ii. 10
Ah why, ye *G.,* should two and two make four *D.* ii. 286
He hears loud Oracles, and talks with *G. D.* iii. 8
Streets pav'd with Heroes, Tiber chok'd with *G. D.* iii. 108
A decent priest, where monkeys were the *g. D.* iii. 208
G., imps, and monsters, music, rage, and mirth *D.* iii. 238
Grubstreet! thy fall should men and *G.* conspire *D.* iii. 321
Which Chalcis *G.,* and mortals call an Owl *D.* iv. 362
What Mortal can resist the Yawn of *G. D.* iv. 606
The *G.* to curse Pamela with her pray'rs *E.* iv. 49
Men would be Angels, Angels would be *G. E.M.* i. 126
Be crown'd as Monarchs, or us *G.* ador'd *E.M.* iii. 198
And *G.* of Conqu'rors, Slaves of Subjects made *E.M.* iii. 248
Saw *G.* descend and fiends infernal rise *E.M.* iii. 254
Fear made her Devils, and weak Hope her *G.* (*rep.*) *E.M.* iii. 256
Some swell'd to *G.,* confess ev'n Virtue vain *E.M.* iv. 24
Ye *G.!* shall Cibber's son, without rebuke *E.S.* i. 115
The Muse may give thee, but the *G.* must guide *E.S.* ii. 215
All that makes Saints of Queens, and *G.* of Kings *E.S.* ii. 226
Or *G.* to save them in a trice *I.H.* ii. 215
For Pembroke, Statues, dirty *G.,* and Coins *M.E.* iv. 8
Fanes, which admiring *G.* with pride survey *M.E.* v. 9
G., Emp'rors, Heroes, Sages, Beauties, lie *M.E.* v. 34
Her *G.,* and god-like Heroes rise to view *M.E.* v. 47
Ye *G.!* what justice rules the ball *O.* ii. 25
Love's purer flames the *G.* approve (*rep.*) *O.* iii. 13
Fear the just *G.,* and think of Scylla's Fate *R.L.* iii. 122
Steel could the labour of the *G.* destroy *R.L.* iii. 173
G.! shall the ravisher display your hair *R.L.* iv. 103
Like *G.* they fight, nor dread a mortal wound (*rep.*) *R.L.* v. 44
Cries "Send me, *G.!* a whole Hog barbecu'd!" *S.* ii. 26

GODDESS—GONSON.

Unless the G. bestow'd a proper Muse *S.* v. 234
Descending G. have found Elysium here *Su.* 60
Ye G.! and is there no relief for Love *Su.* 88
The glorious fault of Angels and of G. *U.L.* 14
Tho' G. assembled grace his tow'ring height *W.F.* 34
Where is their blessings all those G. appear *W.F.* 36
From men their cities, and from G. their fanes *W.F.* 66
To grace the mansion of our earthly G. *W.F.* 230
The thoughts of g. let Granville's verse rehearse *W.F.* 425
One g.-like *Monarch all that pride confounds* D. iii. 75
See g. TURENNE prostrate in the dust *E.M.* iv. 100
As toys and empires for a g. mind *E.M.* iv. 180
Her Gods, and g. Heroes rise to view *M.E.* v. 47
What Plato thought, and g. Cato was *P.C.* 18
By g. Poets venerable made *W.F.* 270

Goddess.

Say how the G. bade Britannia sleep *D.* i. 7
For born a G., Dulness never dies *D.* i. 18
The G. then, o'er his anointed head *D.* i. 287
Oft had the G. heard her servants call *D.* ii. 97
To him the G.: "Son! thy grief lay down *D.* ii. 131
The G. then: "Who best can soot on high *D.* ii. 161
"Now turn to diff'rent sports," (the G. cries) *D.* ii. 221
Here stopt the G.; and in pomp proclaims *D.* ii. 365
In peace, great G., ever be ador'd *D.* iii. 119
That lifts one G. to imperial sway *D.* iii. 124
Hung to the G., and coher'd around *D.* iv. 78
Now crowds on crowds around the G. press *D.* iv. 135
"Oh" (cry'd the G.) "for some pedant Reign *D.* iv. 175
Prompt at the call, around the G. roll *D.* iv. 189
And write about it, G., and about it *D.* iv. 252
Grant, gracious G.! grant me still to cheat *D.* iv. 355
Mine, G.! mine is all the horned race *D.* iv. 376
To prove me, G.! clear of all design *D.* iv. 391
The G. smiling seem'd to give consent *D.* iv. 395
I meddle, G.! only in my sphere *D.* iv. 432
Led up the Youth, and call'd the G. *Dame D.* iv. 498
Thy *Magus, G.!* shall perform the rest *D.* iv. 516
But she, good G., sent to ev'ry child *D.* iv. 529
But treat the G. like a modest fair *M.E.* iv. 51
Thus the *Cyprian* G. weeping *Mi.* vii. 9
Say what strange motive, G., could compel *R.L.* i. 7
And decks the G. with the glitt'ring spoil *R.L.* i. 132
The G. with a discontented air *R.L.* iv. 79
Daphne, our G., and our grief no more *W.* 76
To thee, bright g., oft a lamb shall bleed *W.* 81
Fair Liberty, Britannia's G., rears *W.F.* 91
As bright a G., and as chaste a Queen *W.F.* 162
Scarce could the G. from her nymph be known *W.F.* 175
In her chaste current oft the g. laves *W.F.* 209

Goddess.

A g. Regent tremble at a Star *M.E.* i. 90

Godly.

Up to her g. garret after sev'n *E.* v. 21
The g. dame, who fleshly failings damns *E.Y.S.* 21
And send the g. in a pet to pray *R.L.* iv. 64
From wicked Waters ev'n to g. * * *S.* vii. 80

Goes.

Art after *Art* g. out, and all is *Night D.* iv. 640
Not one looks backward, onward still he g. *E.M.* iv. 223
How Trade increases, and the World g. well *M.E.* i. 159
Whisks it about, and down it g. again *M.E.* ii. 122
Flaunts, and g. down, an unregarded thing *M.E.* ii. 252
Next g. his Wool—to clothe our valiant bands *M.E.* iii. 211
Full many a Beast g. in, but none come out *S.* iii. 117
So first to preach a white-glov'd Chaplain g. *S.* viii. 250

Going.

If—where I'm g.—I could serve you, Sir *M.E.* i. 255
Welcome the coming, speed the g. guest *S.* ii. 160
Who live at Court, for g. once that way *S.* viii. 23

Gold.

Where, in nice balance, truth with g. she weighs *D.* i. 53
Or their fond parents drest in red and g. *D.* i. 238
Whose sars'net skirts are edg'd with flamy g. *D.* iii. 254
And bring Saturnian days of lead and g. *D.* iv. 16
Be rich in ancient brass, tho' not in g. *D.* iv. 365
Down his own throat he risk'd the *Grecian* g. *D.* iv. 382
With g. and jewels cover ev'ry part *E.C.* 295
No fiends torment, no Christians thirst for g. *E.M.* i. 108
Let pow'r or knowledge, g. or glory, please *E.M.* ii. 169

Scarfs, garters, g., amuse his riper stage *E.M.* ii. 279
The shrine with gore unstain'd, with g. undrest *E.M.* iii. 157
Judges and Senates have been bought for g. *E.M.* iv. 187
But stain'd with blood, or ill exchang'd for g. *E.M.* iv. 296
Our Youth, all liv'ry'd o'er with foreign G. *E.S.* i. 155
Heav'n, as its purest g., by Tortures try'd *Ep.* vi. 9
And seeds of g. in *Ophir's* mountains glow *M.* 96
The gen'rous God, who Wit and G. refines *M.E.* ii. 289
And G. but sent to keep the fools in play *M.E.* iii. 5
What nature wants, commodious G. bestows *M.E.* iii. 21
If secret G. sap on from knave to knave *M.E.* iii. 34
G., imp'd by thee, can compass hardest things *M.E.* iii. 41
What say you? Say? Why take it, G. and all *M.E.* iii. 78
Wise Peter sees the World's respect for G. *M.E.* iii. 123
Hereditary Realms, and Worlds of G. *M.E.* iii. 130
And little Eagles wave their wings in g. *M.E.* v. 30
And vanquish'd realms supply recording g. *M.E.* v. 56
Would all my g. in one bad *Deal* were gone *Mi.* ix. 15
And eye the Mine without a wish for G. *Mi.* x. 8
Now lakes of liquid g., Elysian scenes *R.L.* iv. 45
Except you eat the feathers green and g. *S.* ii. 20
As G. to Silver, Virtue is to G. *S.* iii. 78
Alike in nothing but one Lust of G. *S.* iii. 124
All the mad trade of Fools and Slaves for G. *S.* iv. 13
For Indian spices, for Peruvian G. *S.* iv. 71
It is the rust we value, not the g. *S.* v. 36
And place, on good Security, his G. *S.* v. 168
Peers, Heralds, Bishops, Ermine, G. and Lawn *S.* v. 317
Had dearly earn'd a little purse of g. *S.* vi. 34
G., Silver, Iv'ry, Vases sculptur'd high *S.* vi. 264
And scorn the flesh, the dev'l, and all but g. *S.* vii. 74
His painted wings, and breast that flames with g. *W.F.* 118
The yellow carp, in scales bedropp'd with g. *W.F.* 144
And on their banks *Augusta* rose in g. *W.F.* 336
Tho' foaming *Hermus* swells with tides of g. *W.F.* 358
And *Phoebus* warm the rip'ning ore to g. *W.F.* 396
And other *Mexicos* be roof'd with g. *W.F.* 412
On whom three hundred g.-capt *youths* await *D.* iv. 117

Golden.

Now g. fruits on loaded branches shine *A.* 73
All-bounteous, fragrant Grains and G. show'rs *D.* ii. 4
The air-built Castle, and the g. Dream *D.* iii. 10
This g. lance shall guard desert *E.* vi. 6
A standish, steel and g. pen *E.* vi. 14
And whisp'ring Angels prompt her g. beams *E.A.* 216
No longer now that g. age appears *E.C.* 478
But see! each Muse, in LEO'S g. days *E.C.* 697
The starving chemist in his g. views *E.M.* ii. 269
Thine the full harvest of the g. year *E.M.* iii. 39
In g. Chains the willing World she draws *E.S.* i. 147
And Angels guard him in the g. Mean *M.E.* iii. 246
Another age shall see the g. Ear *M.E.* iv. 173
But hark! he strikes the g. lyre *O.* i. 63
With g. crowns and wreaths of heav'nly flow'rs *R.L.* i. 34
Now *Jove* suspends his g. scales in air *R.L.* v. 71
Advance thy g. Mountain to the skies *S.* iv. 73
When g. Angels cease to cure the Evil *S.* vi. 228
O'er g. sands let rich *Pactolus* flow *Sp.* 61
And with your g. darts, now useless grown *W.* 25
Th' industrious bees neglect their g. store *W.* 51
Her cheerful head, and loads the g. years *W.F.* 92
But by the crescent and the g. zone *W.F.* 176
His shining horns diffus'd a g. gleam *W.F.* 332
Touch the fair fame of *Albion's* g. days *W.F.* 424

Gone.

Curl stretches after Gay, for Gay is g. *D.* ii. 127
Fast by, like *Niobe* (her children g.) *D.* ii. 311
G. ev'ry blush, and silent all reproach *D.* iv. 563
But thinks his neighbour further g. than he *E.M.* ii. 226
Nor let us say (those English glories g.) *Ep.* xi. 11
Without your help the Cause is g. *I.H.* ii. 72 s
A bird of passage! g. as soon as found *M.E.* i. 97
That I can do, when all I have is g. *M.E.* iii. 118
Would all my gold in one bad *Deal* were g. *Mi.* ix. 15
My lands are sold, my father's house is g. *S.* ii. 155
And advocates for folly dead and g. *S.* v. 34
I wish you joy, Sir, of a Tyrant g. *S.* vi. 305

Gonson.

Peace, fools, or G. will for Papists seize you *S.* viii. 256
A Pedant makes, the storm of G.'s *lungs* *S.* viii. 53

K

Good.

Dulness whose *g.* old cause I yet defend *D.* i. 165
Dulness, *g.* Queen, repeats the jest again *D.* ii. 122
Oh great Restorer of the *g.* old stage *D.* iii. 205
But she, *g.* Goddess, sent to ev'ry child *D.* iv. 529
G. humour only teaches charms to last *E.* iv. 61
So by false learning is *g.* sense defac'd *E.C.* 25
For works may have more wit than does 'em *g. E.C.* 303
Without *G.* Breeding, truth is disapprov'd *E.C.* 576
And to be dull was construd to be *g. E.C.* 690
Such was Roscommon, not more learn'd than *g. F.C.* 725
And sure such kind *g.* creatures may be living *E.J.S.* 28
In all the rest so impudently *g. E.J.S.* 48
Who finds not Providence all *g.* and wise *E.M.* i. 205
All partial Evil, universal *G. E.M.* i. 292
To the first *g.*, first perfect, and first fair *E.M.* ii. 24
Nor this a *g.*, nor that a bad we call *E.M.* ii. 55
Ascribe all *G.*; to their improper, Ill *E.M.* ii. 58
That sees immediate *g.* by present sense *E.M.* ii. 73
Our greatest evil, or our greatest *g. E.M.* ii. 92
'Tis real *g.*, or seeming, moves them all (*rep.*) *E.M.* ii. 94
Th' Eternal Act educing *g.* from ill *E.M.* ii. 175
Reason the bias turns to *g.* from ill *E.M.* ii. 197
'Tis but by parts we follow *g.* or ill *E.M.* ii. 235
Press to one centre still; the gen'ral *G. E.M.* ii. 14
Has God, thou fool! work'd solely for thy *g. E.M.* iii. 27
A sov'reign being but a sov'reign *g. E.M.* iii. 238
And found the private in the public *g. E.M.* iii. 282
G., Pleasure, Ease, Content I whate'er thy name *E.M.* iv. 2
Subsist not in the *g.* of one, but all *E.M.* iv. 38
Nor present *g.* or ill, the joy or curse *E.M.* iv. 71
Know all the *g.* that individuals find *E.M.* iv. 77
The *g.* or bad the gifts of Fortune gain *E.M.* iv. 83
One they must want, which is, to pass for *g. E.M.* iv. 92
But fools the *G.* alone unhappy call *E.M.* iv. 97
Why drew Marseille's *g.* bishop purer breath *E.M.* iv. 107
Or partial Ill is universal *G. E.M.* iv. 114
The *g.* must merit God's peculiar care *E.M.* iv. 135
The *g.* man may be weak, be indolent *E.M.* iv. 155
No—shall the *g.* want Health, the *g.* want Pow'r *E.M.* iv. 158
Content, or Pleasure, but the *G.* and Just *E.M.* iv. 186
Count me those only who were *g.* and great *E.M.* iv. 210
Like *g.* Aurelius let him reign, or bleed *E.M.* iv. 235
And tastes the *g.* without the fall to ill *E.M.* iv. 312
G., from each object, from each place acquir'd *E.M.* iv. 321
The bad must miss; the *g.* untaught will find *E.M.* iv. 330
G. Heav'n forbid, that I should blast their glory *E.S.* i. 105
Do *g.* by stealth, and blush to find it Fame *E.S.* i. 136
Unless, *g.* man ! he has been fairly in *E.S.* ii. 192
The strong Antipathy of *G.* to Bad *E.S.* ii. 198
Her Priestless Muse forbids the *G.* to die *E.S.* ii. 234
Or beam, *g.* DIGBY, from a heart like thine *E.S.* ii. 241
Here rests a woman, *g.* without pretence *Ep.* vi. 1
G. without noise, without pretension great *Ep.* vii. 4
But that the Worthy, and the *G.* shall say *Ep.* xi. 11
Or any *g.* creature shall lay o'er my head *Ep.* xvi. 4
Be mighty ready to do *g. I.H.* i. 36
G. Mr. Dean, go change your gown *I.H.* ii. 43 *s*
What *g.*, what better, we may call *I.H.* ii. 151
To eat so much—but all's so *g. I.H.* ii. 207
As the *g.* shepherd tends his fleecy care *M.* 49
Here Fannia, leering on her own *g.* man *M.E.* ii. 9
And *g.* Simplicius asks of her advice *M.E.* ii. 32
Yet still a sad, *g.* Christian at her heart *M.E.* ii. 68
Last night her Lord was all that's *g.* and great *M.E.* ii. 141
And yet, believe me, *g.* as well as ill *M.E.* ii. 269
But the *g.* Bishop, with a meeker air *M.E.* iii. 105
Extremes in Nature equal *g.* produce *M.E.* iii. 161
Like some lone Chartreux stands the *g.* old Hall *M.E.* iii. 187
A plain *g.* man, and Balaam was his name *M.E.* iii. 342
And long'd to tempt him like *g.* Job of old *M.E.* iii. 350
And God's *g.* Providence a lucky Hit *M.E.* iii. 378
My *g.* old Lady catch'd a cold, and died *M.E.* iii. 384
G. Sense, which only is the gift of Heav'n *M.E.* iv. 43
Lo some are Vellum, and the rest as *g. M.E.* iv. 137
And gave the harmless fellow a *g.* word *Mi.* iii. 6
She flatters her *g.* Lady twice a day *Mi.* iii. 18

An equal Mixture of *g.* Humour *Mi.* viii. 7
Her last *g.* man dejected Rome ador'd *P.C.* 35
Shut, shut the door, *g.* John ! fatigu'd, I said *P.S.* 1
G. friend, forbear ! you deal in dang'rous things *P.S.* 75
The *g.* man walk'd innoxious thro' his age *P.S.* 395
Unless *g.* sense preserve what beauty gains *R.L.* v. 16
Abuse the City's best *g.* men in metre *S.* i. 39
Like *g.* Erasmus in an honest Mean *S.* i. 66
Your Plea is *g. ;* but still I say, beware *S.* i. 143
Yet hens of Guinea full as *g.* I hold *S.* ii. 19
Swears, like Albutius, a *g.* cook away *S.* ii. 64
Why had not I in those *g.* times my birth *S.* ii. 97
The world's *g.* word is better than a song *S.* ii. 102
This new Court jargon, or the *g.* old song *S.* iii. 98
Thus *g.* or bad, to one extreme betray *S.* iv. 24
I hold that Wit a Classic, *g.* in law *S.* v. 56
And place, on *g.* Security, his Gold *S.* v. 168
The *g.* man heaps up nothing but mere metre *S.* v. 198
D'ye think me *g.* for nothing but to rhyme *S.* vi. 32
The better art to know the *g.* from bad *S.* vi. 55
Glad, like a Boy, to snatch the first *g.* day *S.* vi. 294
The *g.* old landlord's hospitable door *S.* vii. 114
These as *g.* works, 'tis true, we all allow *S.* vii. 121
As prone to ill, as negligent of *g. S.* viii. 20
Was velvet in the youth of *g.* Queen Bess *S.* viii. 41
G. common linguists, and so Panurge was *S.* viii. 75
For bad they found a linguist half so *g. S.* viii. 84
You, that too wise for pride, too *g.* for pow'r *Sp.* 7
But thou, false guardian of a charge too *g. U.L.* 29
For others *g.* or melt at others woe *U.L.* 46
To know but this, that Thou art *G. U.P.* 7
To see the *G.* from Ill *U.P.* 10
Attends the duties of the wise and *g. W.F.* 350
Obvious her *g—s, in no extreme they dwell E.M.* iv. 31
How inconsistent greater *g.* with these *E.M.* iv. 273
To you gave Sense, *G.*-humour *and a Poet M.E.* ii. 292
And keep *g.* still whate'er we lose (*rep.*) *R.L.* v. 30
G.-nature and good sense must ever join *E.C.* 524
Why then declare *G.* is her scorn *M.E.* ii. 59
Of mad *G.*, and of mean Self-love *M.E.* iii. 228
Old, and void of all *g. Mi.* vi. 6
We'd be the best *g.-n—'d* things alive *E.J.S.* 14
Good-nature and *g.-sense* must ever join *E.C.* 524

Goode.

Lo sneering *G.*, half malice and half whim *D.* iii. 153
Not half so pleas'd when *G.* prophesy'd *D.* iii. 232

Goodman.

Goodness.

And melts to *G.*, need I SCARB'ROW name *E.S.* ii. 65
With Truth and *G.*, as with Crown and Ball *M.E.* ii. 184
To laugh, were want uf *g.* and of grace *P.S.* 35
Thy *G.* let me bound *U.P.* 22
Or aught thy *G.* lent *U.P.* 36

Goose.

"See man for mine !" replies a pamper'd *g. E.M.* iii. 46
May some choice patron bless each gray *g.* quill *P.S.* 249
Or rob Rome's ancient geese of all their glories *D.* i. 211
Here sighs a Jar, and there a *G.*-pie talks *R.L.* iv. 52

Gore.

Nor glad vile Poets with true Critics' *g. D.* iii. 178
The shrine with *g.* unstain'd, with gold undrest *E.M.* iii. 157
Altars grew marble then, and reek'd with *g. E.M.* iii. 264
Shall cease to blush with strangers' *g. O.* ii. 20
There purple Vengeance hath'd in *g.* retires *W.F.* 417

Gor'd.

G. with unrelenting Tooth *Mi.* vii. 12
'Tis she—but why that bleeding bosom *g. U.L.* 3

Gorgeous.

High on a *g.* seat that far out-shone *D.* ii. 1

Gorgon.

That live-long wig which *G.*'s self might own *M.E.* iii. 295
All sudden, *G—s* hiss, and Dragons glare *D.* iii. 235

Gormogon.

Rose a Gregorian, one a *G. D.* iv. 576

GOSPEL—GRACIOUS. 131

Gospel.
Faith, G., all, seem'd made to be disputed *E.C.* 442
And hers the G. is, and hers the Laws *E.S.* i. 148

Gothic.
A G. Library ! of Greece and Rome *D.* i. 145
And papal piety, and G. fire *M.E.* v. 14
Against the G. Sons of frozen verse *Mi.* ii. 14

Goths.
Great nurse of G., of Alans, and of Huns *D.* iii. 90
And the Monks finish'd what the G. begun *E.C.* 692
Had brav'd the G., and many a *Vandal* slain *Mi.* ii. 4

Got.
G. by fierce whirlwinds, and in thunder born *A.* 92
Could not get out as he g. in *I.H.* i. 54
If I ne'er g. or lost a groat *I.H.* ii. 13 s
Like stunted hide-bound Trees, that just have g. *Mi.* iii. 11
But wonder how the devil they g. there *P.S.* 172
And better g., than *Bestia's* from the throne *P.S.* 391
The sun e'er g., or slimy Nilus bore *S.* viii. 29
Who sins with whom : who g. his Pension rug *S.* viii. 134

Gout.
So when small humours gather to a g. *E.M.* i. 159
See the same man, in vigour, in the g. *M.E.* i. 71
As sober Lanesbro' dancing in the g. *M.E.* i. 231

Goutez.
Ah ça est bon ! Ah g. ça *I.H.* 201

Govern.
The RIGHT DIVINE of Kings to g. wrong *D.* iv. 188
Each works its end, to move or g. all *E.M.* ii. 56

Government.
Of what restrains him, G. and Laws *E.M.* iii. 272
For Forms of G. let fools contest *E.M.* iii. 303
Is therefore fit to have a G. *S.* viii. 139

Governor.
Whore, Pupil, and lac'd G. from France *D.* iv. 272

Gown.
Sneers at another, in toupee or g. *D.* iv. 88
Or vest dull Flatt'ry in the sacred G. *D.* iv. 97
Rosy and rev'rend, tho' without a G. *D.* iv. 496
Justice a Conqu'ror's sword, or Truth a g. *E.M.* iv. 171
How hurt he you ? he only stain'd the G. *E.S.* ii. 165
Good Mr. Dean, go change your g. *I.H.* ii. 43 s
Some fold the sleeve, while others plait the g. *R.L.* i. 147
Wrapt in a g., for sickness, and for show *R.L.* iv. 36
Form'd a vast buckle for his widow's g. *R.L.* v. 92
Cato's long wig, flower'd g., and lacquer'd chair *S.* v. 337
Not more of Simony beneath black g—s S. vii. 81

Gown'd.
The cobbler apron'd, and the parson g. *E.M.* iv. 197

Gownman.
A G., learn'd ; a Bishop, what you will *M.E.* i. 138

Grace.
With that a Tear (portentous sign of G. *D.* i. 243
His Peers shine round him with reflected g. *D.* ii. 9
The plunging Prelate, and his pond'rous G. *D.* ii. 323
And last, to give the whole creation g. *D.* iv. 247
The Cap and Switch be sacred to his G. *D.* iv. 585
Match Raphael's g. with thy lov'd Guido's air *E.* iii. 36
Have Humour, Wit, a native Ease and G. *E.* iv. 27
Not g., or zeal, love only was my call *E.A.* 117
G. shines around her with serenest beams *E.A.* 215
And dawning g. is op'ning on my soul *E.A.* 280
Take back that g., those sorrows, and those tears *E.A.* 285
Oh G. serene ! oh virtue heav'nly fair *E.A.* 297
And snatch a g. beyond the reach of art *E.C.* 153
Due distance reconciles to form and g. *E.C.* 174
The naked nature and the living g. *E.C.* 294
All rang'd in order, and dispos'd with g. *E.C.* 672
And G. and Virtue, Sense and Reason split *E.M.* ii. 83
Or Japhet preached, like his G., a Will *E.S.* i. 120
All his G. preaches, all his Lordship sings *E.S.* ii. 224
DORSET, the G. of Courts, the Muses' Pride *Ep.* i. 1
Blest Peer ! his great Forefathers' ev'ry g. *Ep.* i. 11
There ev'ry G. and Muse shall throng *I.H.* iii. 27
Behold a rev'rend sire, whom want of g. *M.E.* i. 232

Now drinking citron with his G. and Chartres *M.E.* ii. 64
Or her, who laughs at Hell, but (like his G.) *M.E.* ii. 107
No G. of Heav'n, or token of th' Elect *M.E.* iii. 18
His G. will game : to White's a bull he led *M.E.* iii. 67
Mend Fortune's fault, and justify her g. *M.E.* iii. 232
As well his G. reply'd "Like you, Sir John *M.E.* iii. 317
Calm ev'ry thought, inspirit ev'ry g. *Mi.* v. 13
To laugh, were want of goodness and of g. *P.S.* 35
Pitholeon sends to me : "You know his *P.S.* 49
And in soft sounds, Your G. salutes their ear *R.L.* i. 86
Repairs her smiles, awakens ev'ry g. *R.L.* i. 141
Just then Clarissa drew with tempting g. *R.L.* iii. 127
But oh ! if e'er thy Gnome could spoil a g. *R.L.* iv. 67
There my retreat the best Companions g. *S.* i. 125
And, what's more rare, a Poet shall say G. *S.* ii. 150
Get Place and Wealth, if possible, with g. *S.* iii. 103
And all our G. at table is a Song *S.* v. 174
And speak in public with some sort of g. *S.* v. 208
And feels that g. his pray'r besought in vain *S.* v. 238
How Van wants g., who never wanted wit *S.* v. 289
Or choose at least some Minister of G. *S.* v. 378
And then, unwhipp'd, he had the g. to cry *S.* vi. 18
But grant I may relapse for want of g. *S.* vi. 88
Nay tho' at Court (perhaps) it may find g. *S.* vi. 162
Endue a Peer with honour, truth, and g. *S.* vi. 221
My heir may sigh, and think it want of g. *S.* vi. 286
Leave such to trifle with more g. and ease *S.* vi. 326
I hop'd for no commission from his G. *S.* viii. 11
Blest Swains, whose Nymphs in ev'ry g. excel *Sp.* 95
If I am right, thy g. impart *U.P.* 29
He marches off his G.'s Secretary D. ii. 220
His G. fate sage Cutler could foresee *M.E.* iii. 315
There all thy gifts and g—s we display D. iv. 295
New g. yearly like thy works display *E.* iii. 65
Yet should the G. all thy figures place *E.* iii. 71
In these gay thoughts the Loves and G. shine *E.* iv. 1
Are nameless g. which no methods teach *E.C.* 144
Strange g. still, and stranger flights she had *M.E.* ii. 49
Their sev'ral g. in my SHARPER meet *Mi.* ix. 103
But since those g. please thy eyes no more *Su.* 29
Sepulchral Lies, our holy walls to g. D. i. 43
These Fate reserv'd to g. thy reign divine *D.* iii. 275
Crowns were reserv'd to g. the soldiers too *E.C.* 513
Mark how they g. Lord Umbra or Sir Billy *E.M.* iv. 278
Then shall thy Form the Marble g. *I.H.* iii. 63
The rich Buffet well-colour'd Serpents g. *M.E.* iv. 153
Who thou shall g., or who improve the sail *M.E.* iv. 177
The *Equipage* shall g. SMILINDA's side *Mi.* ix. 110
Or the small pillow g. a Lady's bed *R.L.* iii. 166
That men may say, when we the front-box g. *R.L.* v. 17
What tho' no weeping Loves thy ashes g. *U.L.* 59
Eternal beauties g. the shining scene *W.* 71
Tho' Gods assembled g. his tow'ring height *W.F.* 34
To g. the mansion of our earthly Gods *W.F.* 230
The G.-cup serv'd with all decorum I.H. ii. 138

Grac'd.
Be g. thro' Life, and flatter'd in his Grave *E.S.* i. 86
Yet ne'er one sprig of laurels g. those ribalds *P.S.* 163
Then in a bodkin g. her mother's hairs *R.L.* v. 95
G. as thou art with all the Pow'r of Words *S.* iv. 48
Pleas'd thy pale ghost, or g. thy mournful bier *U.L.* 50

Graceful.
But as in g. act, with awful eye *D.* iv. 109
Horace still charms with g. negligence *E.C.* 653
Yet g. ease, and sweetness void of pride *R.L.* ii. 15
Nourish'd two Locks, which g. hung behind *R.L.* ii. 20
Then grave Clarissa g. wav'd her fan *R.L.* v. 7
To fix him g. on the bounding Steed *S.* v. 383
Bold in the lists, and g. in the dance *W.F.* 294

Graceless.
See g. Venus to a virgin turn'd *D.* iii. 111
If, after this, you took the g. lad *S.* vi. 21
For Modes of Faith let g. zealots fight *E.M.* iii. 305

Gracious.
O ! ever g. to perplex'd mankind *D.* i. 173
Grant, g. Goddess ! grant me still to cheat *D.* iv. 355
But errs not Nature from this g. end *E.M.* i. 141
The g. Dew of Pulpit Eloquence *E.S.* i. 69
Consid'ring where a *Prince* was next *E.S.* i. 108
As thus, "Vouchsafe, oh g. Maker *I.H.* ii. 17 s
Thus g. CHANDOS is belov'd at sight *M.E.* i. 54
He spies me out, I whisper, G. God *S.* viii. 62

K 2

Gradation.

Without this just *g.* could they be *E.M.* i. 229
And, if each system in *g.* roll *E.M.* i. 247
G—s *just, has thy pervading soul E.M.* i. 31

Graft.

And *g.* my love immortal on thy fame *E.A.* 344
That *g.* benevolence on charities *E.M.* iii. 138

Grafts.

G. on this Passion our best principle *E.M.* ii. 176

Grain.

Now bright Arcturus glads the teeming *g. A.* 72
The birds of heav'n shall vindicate their *g. E.M.* iii. 38
There's some Peculiar in each leaf and *g. M.E.* i. 15
Indulg'd the day that hous'd their annual *g. S.* v. 243
A *g.* of courage, or a spark of spirit *S.* vi. 227
In vain kind seasons swell'd the teeming *g. W.F.* 53
The forests wonder'd at th' unusual *g. W.F.* 89
Shall tend the flocks, or reap the bearded *g. W.F.* 370
All bounteous, fragrant G—s and Golden show'rs *D.* ii. 4
The pungent *g.* of titillating dust *R.L.* v. 84

Grammar.

Jacob, the scourge of G., mark with awe *D.* iii. 149

Grammarians.

Roman and Greek G. *I* know your Better *D.* iv. 215

Grammar School.

And turn the Council to a G. *D.* iv. 180

Granaries.

Let rising G. and Temples here *S.* vi. 258

Grand.

So proud, so *g.;* of that stupendous air *M.E.* iv. 101
Blackmore himself, for any *g.* effort *S.* vi. 112

Grandame.

Her infant *g.'s* whistle next it grew *R.L.* v. 93
E'er since our G. evil *Mi.* iv. 10

Grandeur.

Blush, G., blush ! proud Courts withdraw your blaze *M.E.* iii. 281

Grandsire.

Her great great *g.* wore about his neck *R.L.* v. 90
As apes our g—s, *in their doublets drest E.C.* 332
Sons, Sires, and G., all will wear the bays *S.* v. 171

Grant.

To him we *g.* our amplest pow'rs to sit *D.* ii. 378
G., gracious Goddess, *g.* me still to cheat *D.* iv. 355
G. that the pow'rful still the weak controul *E.M.* iii. 49
And *g.* the bad what happiness they would *E.M.* iv. 91
But *g.* him Riches, your demand is o'er *E.M.* iv. 157
But *g.* that those can conquer, these can cheat *E.M.* iv. 229
Virtue, I *g.* you, is an empty boast *E.S.* ii. 113
Or *g.* the Bard whose Distich all commend *E.S.* ii. 160
To *g.* me this and t'other Acre *I.H.* ii. 18 s
G. but as many sorts of Mind as Moss *M.E.* i. 18
But *g.* that Actions best discover man *M.E.* i. 119
Has ev'n been prov'd to *g.* a Lover's pray'r *M.E.* ii. 55
One certain Portrait may (I *g.*) be seen *M.E.* ii. 181
But *g.*, in Public Men sometimes are shown *M.E.* ii. 199
Useful, I *g.*, it serves what life requires *M.E.* iii. 27
Fools *g.* whate'er Ambition craves *O.* ii. 27
O *g.* me, thus to live, and thus to die *P.S.* 404
But *g.* I may relapse, for want of grace *S.* vi. 88
I *g.* that Poetry's a crying sin *S.* vii. 7

Granted.

Atossa, curs'd with ev'ry *g.* pray'r *M.E.* ii. 147
The pow'rs gave ear, and *g.* half his pray'r *R.L.* ii. 45
Why yes, 'tis *g.*, these indeed may pass *S.* viii. 74

Grants.

To some indeed, Heav'n *g.* the happier fate *M.E.* iii. 97
Seems to reject him, tho' she *g.* his pray'r *R.L.* iv. 80

Granville.

But why then publish ? G. the polite *P.S.* 135
G. commands; your aid, O Muses, bring (*vcr.*) *W.F.* 5
Are these reviv'd ? or is it G. sings *W.F.* 282

Grave.

Surrey, the G. of a former age *W.F.* 292
And these be sung till G.'s *Mira die E.* iii. 76
With Waller's strains, or G. moving lays *Sp.* 46
The thoughts of gods let G. verse recite *W.F.* 425

Grape.

Annual for me, the *g.*, the rose renew *E.M.* i. 135
And g—s *long ling'ring on my only wall S.* ii. 146

Grasp.

Present, to *g.*, and future still to find *E.M.* ii. 125
G. the whole worlds of Reason, Life, and Sense *E.M.* iv. 357

Grasps.

He *g.* an empty Joseph for a John *D.* ii. 128
One *g.* a Cecrops in ecstatic dreams *M.E.* v. 40
And of all monarchs, only *g.* the globe *R.L.* iii. 74

Grass.

From the green myriads in the peopled *g. E.M.* i. 210
Sooner shall *g.* in Hyde-Park circus grow *R.L.* iv. 117

Grateful.

And *g.* clusters swell with floods of wine *A.* 74
For sure, if Dulness sees a *g.* Day *D.* iv. 181
This praise at least a *g.* Muse may give *E.C.* 734
Sweet to the World, and *g.* to the Skies *E.S.* ii. 245
While thousand *g.* thoughts arise *O.* iii. 32
From silver spouts the *g.* liquors glide *R.L.* iii. 109
And leave on SWIFT this *g.* verse engrav'd *S.* v. 223
And count each birth-day with a *g.* mind *S.* vi. 315
No *g.* dews descend from ev'ning skies *W.* 45

Gratify.

This who can *g.* ? for who can *guess P.S.* 178
At once they *g.* their scent and taste *R.L.* iii. 11

Gratify'd.

No Passion *g.* except her Rage *M.E.* ii. 126

Gratis.

Can *g.* see the country, or the town *S.* viii. 145
Ye shall not beg, like *g.-*given *Bland D.* i. 231

Gratitude.

While pleasure, *g.*, and hope combin'd *E.M.* iii. 145
Nor more a storm her Hate than G. *M.E.* ii. 132
Th' unwilling G. of base mankind *S.* v. 14

Grave.

While Wren with sorrow to the *g.* descends *D.* iii. 329
A Page, a G. that they can call their own *D.* iv. 198
So K.* so B * * sneak'd into the *g. D.* iv. 311
Alas ! how little from the *g.* we claim *E.* iii. 77
May one kind *g.* unite each hapless name *E.A.* 343
Towns to one *g.*, whole nations to the deep *E.M.* i. 144
Lamented DIGBY ! sunk thee to the *g. E.M.* iv. 104
As Justice tears his body from the *g. E.M.* iv. 250
Be grac'd thro' Life, and flatter'd in his G. *E.S.* i. 86
Than such as Anstis casts into the G. *E.S.* ii. 237
Walk to his *g.* without reproach *Mi.* xii. 19
O G. ! where is thy Victory *O.* v. 37
Shall walk the World, in credit, to his *g. S.* i. 120
Send her to Court, you send her to her *g. S.* iii. 119
Secure of peace at least beyond the *g. S.* viii. 4
By foreign hands thy humble *g.* adorn'd *U.L.* 53
Yet shall thy *g.* with rising flow'rs be drest *U.L.* 63
And said ; " Ye shepherds, sing around my *g. W.* 18
A waste for beasts, himself deny'd a *g. W.F.* 80
The *g.* unites ; where ev'n the great find rest *W.F.* 317
Long-sounding aisles, and intermingled g—s *E.A.* 164
Gross as her sire, and as her mother *g. D.* i. 14
'Twas on the day when * " rich and *g. D.* i. 85
Intoxicates the pert, and lulls the *g. D.* ii. 344
G. Mummers ! sleeveless some, and shirtless others *D.* iii. 116
In Folly's Cap, than Wisdom's *g.* disguise *D.* iv. 240
In *g.* Quintilian's copious work we find *E.C.* 669
From *g.* to gay, from lively to severe *E.M.* iv. 380
Immortal S—k, and *g.* De—re *E.S.* i. 92
Chaste Matrons praise her, and *g.* Bishops bless *E.S.* i. 146
Some, in their choice of Friends (nay, look not *g.*) *E.S.* ii. 100
So odd, my Country's Ruin makes me *g. E.S.* ii. 207
The coxcomb bird, so talkative and *g. M.E.* i. 5
Cotius is ever moral, ever *g. M.E.* i. 77

The *g*. Sir Gilbert holds it for a rule *M.E.* iii. 101
Not *g.* thro' Pride, or gay thro' Folly *Mi.* viii. 6
And to be *g.*, exceeds all Pow'r of face *P.S.* 36
Has Life no joys for me ? or (to be *g.*) *P.S.* 273
Then *g.* Clarissa graceful wav'd her fan *R.L.* v. 7
But *g. Epistles*, bringing Vice to light *S.* i. 151
Which Betterton's *g.* action dignify'd *S.* v. 122
Did not some *g.* Examples yet remain *S.* v. 128
G., as when pris'ners shake the head and swear *S.* vii. 69

Grav'd.
G. on his urn appear'd the moon, that guides *W.F.* 333

Gravely.
Or *g.* try to read the lines *I.H.* ii. 91 *s*
As weak, as earnest, and as *g.* out *M.E.* i. 230

Graver.
Let the strict life of *g.* mortals be *E.* iv. 21
The *g.* Prude sinks downward to a Gnome *R.L.* i. 63

Gravitation.
With all the might of *g.* blest *D.* ii. 318
Shall *g.* cease, if you go by *E.M.* iv. 128

Gravity.
And strong impulsive *g.* of Head *D.* iv. 76
Each had a *g.* would make you split *S.* vi. 131

Gray—*see also* Grey.
May some choice patron bless each *g.* goose quill *P.S.* 249

Graze.
Prick all their ears up, and forget to *g. D.* ii. 262
The lambs with wolves shall *g.* the verdant mead *M.* 77

Greasy.
Or Sappho at her toilet's *g.* task *M.E.* ii. 25
The musty wine, foul cloth, and *g.* glass *S.* ii. 66

Great.
I sing. Say you, her instruments the *G. D.* i. 3
G. Cibber's brazen, brainless brothers stand *D.* i. 32
Here swells the shelf with Ogilby the *g. D.* i. 141
Then he : " *G.* Tamer of all human art *D.* i. 163
G. Cæsar roars and hisses in the fire *D.* i. 251
G. in her charms ! as when on Shrieves and May'rs *D.* i. 263
This the *G.* Mother dearer held than all *D.* i. 269
As sings thy *g.* forefather Ogilby *D.* i. 328
G. Cibber sate : The proud Parnassian sneer *D.* ii. 5
Thus the *g.* Father to the greater Son *D.* iii. 42
G. nurse of Goths, of Alms, and of Huns *D.* iii. 90
In peace, *g.* Goddess, ever be ador'd *D.* iii. 119
Oh *g.* Restorer of the good old Stage *D.* iii. 205
Proceed, *g.* days ! till Learning fly the shore *D.* iii. 333
Joy to *g.* Chaos ! let Division reign *D.* iv. 54
Who pay her homage in hers is *g. D.* iv. 92
Author of something yet more *g.* than Letter *D.* iv. 216
Receive, *g.* Empress ! thy accomplish'd Son *D.* iv. 282
Pours at *g.* Bourbon's feet her silken sons *D.* iv. 298
Witness, *g.* Ammon ! by whose horns I swore *D.* iv. 387
G. Queen, and common Mother of us all *D.* iv. 404
G. C**, H**, P**, R**, K*D. iv. 545
Thy hand, *g.* Anarch, lets the curtain fall *D.* iv. 655
The sober follies of the wise and *g. E.* i. 10
Perhaps forgets that Oxford e'er was great *E.* i. 18
Thro' Fortune's cloud one truly *g.* can see *E.* i. 39
Who without flatt'ry pleas'd the fair and *g. E.* iv. 6
Should at my feet the world's *g.* master fall *E.A.* 85
Just precepts thus from *g.* examples giv'n *E.C.* 98
G. wits sometimes may gloriously offend *E.C.* 159
T' avoid *g.* errors, must the less commit *E.C.* 260
That always shows *g.* pride, or little sense *E.C.* 387
A constant Critic at the *g.* man's board *E.C.* 416
Nay should *g.* Homer lift his awful head *E.C.* 464
And is himself that *g.* Sublime he draws *E.C.* 680
At length Erasmus, that *g.* injur'd name *E.C.* 693
Is the *g.* chain, that draws all to agree *E.M.* i. 33
Wait the *g.* teacher Death ; and God adore *E.M.* i. 92
If the *g.* end be human happiness *E.M.* i. 149
Where, one step broken, the *g.* scale 's destroy'd *E.M.* i. 244
The *g.* directing MIND of ALL ordains *E.M.* i. 266
G. in the earth, as in th' ethereal frame *E.M.* i. 270
To him no high, no low, no *g.*, no small *E.M.* i. 279
A Being darkly wise, and rudely *g. E.M.* ii. 4

G. lord of all things, yet a prey to all *E.M.* ii. 16
But when his own *g.* work is but begun *E.M.* ii. 41
But HEAV'N'S *g.* view is One, and that the Whole *E.M.* ii. 238
Let this *g.* truth be present night and day *E.M.* iii. 5
G. standing miracle ! that Heav'n assign'd *E.M.* iii. 77
G. Nature spoke ; observant Man obey'd *E.M.* iii. 199
Our *g.* first father, and that first ador'd *E.M.* iii. 226
Such is the World's *g.* harmony, that springs *E.M.* iii. 295
Where small and *g.*, where weak and mighty, made *E.M.* iii. 297
All must be false that thwart this One *g.* End *E.M.* iii. 309
Who sees and follows that *g.* scheme the best *E.M.* iv. 95
Or Public Spirit its *g.* cure, a Crown *E.M.* iv. 172
Count me those only who were good and *g. E.M.* iv. 210
'Tis phrase absurd to call a Villain *G. E.M.* iv. 230
Like Socrates, that man is *g.* indeed *E.M.* iv. 236
There in the rich, the honour'd, fam'd, and *g. E.M.* iv. 287
That REASON, PASSION, answer one *g.* aim *E.M.* iv. 395
The *G.* man never offer'd you a great *E.S.* i. 26
Must *g.* Offenders, once escap'd the Crown *E.S.* ii. 28
The poor and friendless Villain, than the *G. E.S.* ii. 45
I study'd Shrewsbury, the wise and *g. E.S.* ii. 79
The scourge of Pride, tho' sanctify'd or *g. Ep.* i. 3
Blest Peer ! his *g.* Forefathers' ev'ry grace *Ep.* i. 11
Good without noise, without pretension *g. Ep.* vii. 4
Whate'er was beauteous, or whate'er was *g. Ep.* viii. 4
Living, *g.* Nature fear'd he might outvie *Ep.* viii. 7
Whom Heav'n kept sacred from the proud and *g. Ep.* x. 4
And uncorrupted, ev'n among the *G. Ep.* xi. 6
Harley, the Nation's *g.* support *I.H.* i. 83
G. Ministers ne'er think of these *I.H.* ii. 38 *s*
About some *g.* Affair, at Two *I.H.* ii. 74 *s*
My Lord and he are grown so *g. I.H.* ii. 105 *s*
You, Mr. Dean, frequent the *G. I.H.* ii. 113 *s*
Both small and *g.*, both you and I *I.H.* ii. 178
Yet more ; the difference is as *g.* between *M.E.* i. 31
Pride guides his steps and bids him shun the *g. M.E.* i. 114
Why risk the world's *g.* empire for a Punk *M.E.* i. 131
And, harder still ! flagitious, yet not *g. M.E.* i. 205
But what are these to *g.* Atossa's mind *M.E.* ii. 115
Last night her Lord was all that 's good and *g. M.E.* ii. 141
As hard a science to the Fair as *G. M.E.* ii. 226
Old Cato is as *g.* a rogue as you *M.E.* iii. 38
To spoil the nations last *g.* trade, Quadrille *M.E.* iii. 76
And be what Rome's *g.* Didius was before *M.E.* iii. 126
'Twas no Court-badge, *g.* Scriv'ner ! fir'd thy brain *M.E.* i. 145
For what to shun will no *g.* knowledge need *M.E.* iii. 199
And zeal for the *g.* House which eats him up *M.E.* iii. 208
G. Villiers lies—alas ! how chang'd from him *M.E.* iii. 305
With Fifty Guineas (a *g.* Pen'worth) bought *Mi.* ix. 30
Approach ! *G.* NATURE studiously behold *Mi.* x. 7
I goobly vain, and impotently *g. P.C.* 29
The World's *g.* Victor pass'd unbeeded by *P.C.* 34
Ammon's g. son one shoulder had too high *P.S.* 117
G. Homer died three thousand years ago *P.S.* 124
And *St. John's* self (*g. Dryden's* friends before) *P.S.* 141
No more than thou, *g.* GEORGE ! a birth-day song *P.S.* 222
But still the *G.* have kindness in reserve *P.S.* 247
Blest be the *G.* ! for those they take away *P.S.* 255
I was not born for Courts or *g.* affairs *P.S.* 267
But why insult the poor, affront the *g. P.S.* 360
Here thou, *g.* ANNA ! whom three realms obey *R.L.* iii. 7
Her *g.* grandsire wore about his neck *R.L.* v. 90
So Rome's *g.* founder to the heav'ns withdrew *R.L.* v. 125
Envy must own, I live among the *G. S.* i. 133
What, and how *g.*, the Virtue and the Art *S.* ii. 1
Of carps and mullets why prefer the *g. S.* ii. 21
My wealth unwieldy, and my heap too *g. S.* ii. 114
But to the world no bugbear is so *g. S.* iii. 67
Who counsels best? who whispers, " Be but *g. S.* iii. 101
G. without Title, without Fortune bless'd *S.* iii. 181
And pay the *G.* our homage of Amaze *S.* iv. 17
While you, *g.* Patron of Mankind, sustain *S.* v. 1
The *g.* Alcides, ev'ry Labour past *S.* v. 17
G. Friend of LIBERTY ! in Kings a Name *S.* v. 25

Yet, Sir, reflect, the mischief is not *g.* *S. v.* 189
Alone deserves the favour of the *G. S. v.* 349
Yet think, *g.* Sir! (so many Virtues shown) *S. v.* 376
And *g.* Nassau to Kneller's hand decreed *S. v.* 382
"Prodigious well," his *g.* Commander cry'd *S. vi.* 42
Its name I know not, and it's no *g.* matter *S. vi.* 45
Each individual: His *g.* End the same *S. vi.* 283
Silence or hurt, he libels the *g.* Man *S. viii.* 159
From such alone the *G.* rebukes endure *S. viii.* 282
Enjoy the glory to be *g.* no more *Sp.* 8
Thou *G.* First Cause, least understood *U.P.* 5
Thus (if small things we may with *g.* compare *W.F.* 105
Thou, too, *g.* father of the British floods *W.F.* 219
Such was the life *g.* Scipio once admir'd *W.F.* 257
The grave unites; where ev'n the *g.* find rest *W.F.* 317
At length *g.* Anna said, "Let Discord cease!" *W.F.* 327
The World's *g.* Oracle in times to come *W.F.* 382

Greater.

G. he looks, and more than mortal stares *D. ii.* 329
But sets up one, a *g.*, in their place *E. iv.* 38
'Tis hard to say, if *g.* want of skill *E.C.* 1
The less, or *g.*, set so justly true *E.M. iii.* 291
Some are, and must be, *g.* than the rest *E.M. iv.* 50
How inconsistent *g.* goods with these *E.M. iv.* 273
What *g.* bliss attends their close of life *E.M. iv.* 301
The Folly's *g.* to have none at all *M.E. iii.* 158
And *g.* Gain would rise *Mi. iv.* 30
To bright Cecilia *g.* pow'r is giv'n *O. i.* 132
But let them own that *g.* Faults than we (*rep.*) *S. v.* 95
The labour *g.*, as th' indulgence less *S. v.* 285

Greatest.

Or deeming meanest what we *g.* call *E. i.* 19
Our *g.* evil, or our *g.* good *E.M. ii.* 92
Connects each being, *g.* with the least *E.M. iii.* 23
His *g.* Virtue, and his *g.* Bliss *E.M. iv.* 350
You still may lash the *g.*—in Disgrace *E.S.* i. 88
Enough for half the *G.* of these days *E.S. ii.* 112
The *G.* can but blaze, and pass away *S. iv.* 47
The last and *g.* Art, the Art to blot *S. v.* 281

Greatly.

And *g.* falling with a falling state *P.C.* 22
For those who *g.* think, or bravely die *U.L.* 10
Judicious drank, and g.-daring *din'd D. iv.* 318

Greatness.

Look next on *G.*; say where *G.* lies *E.M. iv.* 217
In each how guilt and *g.* equal ran *E.M. iv.* 293
Let *G.* own her, and she's mean no more *E.S.* i. 144
G., with Timon, dwells in such a draught *M.E. iv.* 103
The whisper, that to *g.* still too near *P.S.* 356
Proud Fortune, and look shallow *G.* thro' *S. iii.* 108

Grecian.

Down his own throat he risk'd the *G.* gold *D. iv.* 382
As e'er could Dennis, of the *G.* stage *E.C.* 270
(Thy *G.* Form) and Chloe lend the Face *I.H. iii.* 20

Greece.

A Gothic Library! of *G.* and Rome *D. i.* 145
Small thanks to France, and none to Rome or *G. D. i.* 283
Hear how learn'd *G.* her useful rules indites *E.C.* 92
To him the wit of *G.* and Rome was known *E.C.* 729
Rome learning Arts from *G.*, whom she subdu'd *P.C.* 40
Tho' justly *G.* her eldest sons admires *S. v.* 43

Greedy.

From shelves to shelves see *g.* Vulcan roll *D. iii.* 81
But *g.* That, its object would devour *E.M. ii.* 89
Some *g.* minion, or imperious wife *E.M. iv.* 302
Prevent the *g.*, and outbid the bold *S. iv.* 72

Greek.

Senates and Courts with *G.* and Latin rule *D. iv.* 179
Roman and *G.* Grammarians! know your Better *D. iv.* 215
I poach in Suidas for unlicens'd *G. D. iv.* 228
Stand emulous of *G.* and Roman fame *M.E. v.* 54
Above all *G.*, above all Roman fame *S. v.* 26
To read in *G.*, the wrath of Peleus' son *S. vi.* 53
From foolish G—s *to steal them was as wise D. iv.* 378
Persians and *G.* like turns of nature found *E.C.* 380

Green.

And the fleet shades glide o'er the dusky *g. A.* 64
There painted Alleys of eternal *g. D. i.* 76

And the fresh vomit run for ever *g. D. ii.* 156
See Coronations rise on ev'ry *g. E. v.* 24
Red, Blue, and *G.*, nay white and black *E. vi.* 19
Shades ev'ry flow'er, and darkens ev'ry *g. E.A.* 168
Still *g.* with bays each ancient altar stands *E.C.* 181
From the *g.* myriads in the peopled grass *E.M.* i. 210
And hound, sagacious on the tainted *g. E.M.* i. 214
Chequer'd with Ribbons blue and *g. I.H. ii.* 49
Shall glitter o'er the pendant *g. I.H. iii.* 23
The *g.* reed trembles, and the bulrush nods *M.* 72
Pleas'd the *g.* lustre of the scales survey *M.* 83
One boundless *G.*, or flourish'd Carpet views *M.E. iv.* 95
This the blue varnish, that the *g.* endears *M.E. v.* 37
The silver token, and the circled *g. R.L.* i. 32
With throngs promiscuous strow the level *g. R.L. iii.* 80
Except you eat the feathers *g.* and gold *S. ii.* 20
The sprightly Sylvia trips along the *g. Sp.* 57
The mossy fountains, and the *g.* retreats *Su.* 72
And the *g.* turf lie lightly on thy breast *U.L.* 64
Fields ever fresh, and groves for ever *g. W.* 72
Thy forests, Windsor! and thy *g.* retreats *W.F.* 1
Live in description, and look *g.* in song *W.F.* 8
The vivid *g.* his shining plumes unfold *W.F.* 117
And floating forests paint the waves with *g. W.F.* 216
Paints the *g.* forests and the flow'ry plains *W.F.* 428
The bow'ry mazes, and surrounding g—s *W.F.* 262
To crown the forests with immortal *g. W.F.* 286

Greenland.

At *G.*, Zembla, or the Lord knows where *E.M. ii.* 224

Greenwich hill.

No place on earth (he cry'd) like *G. S. iii.* 139

Greet.

With annual joy the redd'ning shoots to *g. M.E. iv.* 91

Gregorian.

Rose a *G.*, one a Gormagon *D. iv.* 576

Grew.

The shrines all trembled, and the lamps *g.* pale *E.A.* 112
Learning and Rome alike in empire *g. E.C.* 683
G. by like means, and join'd, thro' love or fear *E.M. iii.* 202
Altars *g.* marble then, and reek'd with gore *E.M. iii.* 264
And men *g.* heroes at the sound *O.* i. 43
Clipp'd from the lovely head where late it *g. R.L. iv.* 136
Her infant grandame's whistle next it *g. R.L. v.* 93
And *g.* Immortal in his own despite *S. v.* 72
Then Peers *g.* proud in Horsemanship t' excel *S. v.* 143
Then Marble, soften'd into life, *g.* warm *S. v.* 147
With growing years the pleasing license *g. S. v.* 249
Wit *g.* polite, and Numbers learn'd to flow *S. v.* 266
Late, very late, correctness *g.* our care *S. v.* 272
Once I was skill'd in ev'ry herb that *g. Su.* 31
Soft show'rs distilled, and suns *g.* warm in vain *W.F.* 54

Grey—*see also* Gray.

A few *g.* hairs his rev'rend temples crown'd *M.E. iii.* 327
Curl'd or uncurl'd, since locks will turn to *g. M.E. iv.* 50
This g.-goose weapon must have made her stand D. i. 198
Her *g.-hair'd* Synods damning books unread *D. iii.* 103

Grief.

To him the Goddess! "Son I thy *g.* lay down *D. ii.* 131
One Trill shall harmonize, joy, *g.*, and rage *D. iv.* 57
Ah, more than share it, give me all thy *g. E.A.* 50
While prostrate here in humble *g.* I lie *E.A.* 277
Here *g.* forgets to groan, and love to weep *E.A.* 314
Hate, Fear, and *G.*, the family of Pain *E.M. ii.* 118
Or gave his Father *G.* but when he died *Ep.* iii. 4
And 'till we share your joys, forgive our *g. Ep.* vii. 18
A mightier *g.* my heavy heart sustains *Mi.* x. 10
Is that the *g.*, which you compare with mine *Mi.* ix. 13
By whose vile arts this heavy *g.* I bear *Mi.* ix. 56
Music the fiercest *g.* can charm *O.* i. 118
Then see! the nymph in beauteous *g.* appears *R.L. iv.* 143
Between revenge, and *g.*, and hunger join'd *S. vi.* 38
Daphne, our *g.!* our glory now no more *W.* 28
Daphne, our Goddess, and our *g.* no more *W.* 76
G—s to thy *g*—s, *and echo sighs to thine E.A.* 42
And wake to all the *g.* I left behind *E.A.* 248
In sad similitude of *g.* to mine *E.A.* 360
Tell, tell your *g.*; attentive will I stay *Mi.* ix. 27
Soft sorrows, melting *g.*, and flowing tears *R.L. iv.* 86

GRIEVANCE—GROVE.

Grievance.
But here a *G.* seems to lie *I.H.* ii. 9 s

Grieve.
I ought to *g.*, but cannot what I ought *E.A.* 183
Whether we joy or *g.*, the same the curse *S.* iv. 22
G. for an hour, perhaps, then mourn a year *U.L.* 36

Griev'd.
Or thy *g.* Country's copper chains unbind *D.* i. 24
Now looking downwards, just as *g.* appears *E.M.* i. 173

Grieves.
"It *g.* me much" (reply'd the Peer again) *R.L.* iv. 131

Grim.
And each ferocious feature *g.* with ooze *D.* ii. 328
A friend in glee, ridiculously *g. D.* iii. 154
Next his *g.* idol, smear'd with human blood *E.M.* iii. 266
And Hell's *g.* Tyrant feels th' eternal wound *M.* 48

Grimace.
He struts Adonis, and affects *g. D.* ii. 202

Grinning.
'Twas chatt'ring, *g.*, mouthing, jabb'ring all *D.* ii. 237
On *g.* dragons thou shalt mount the wind *D.* iii. 268

Grins.
He *g.*, and looks broad nonsense with a stare *D.* ii. 194

Gripes.
The more thou ticklest, *g.* his fist the faster *D.* ii. 210

Gripus.
Look but on *G.*, or on *G.*' wife *E.M.* iv. 280

Grizly.
Scar'd at the *g.* forms, I sweat, I fly *S.* viii. 278

Groan.
Who, foe to Nature, hears the gen'ral *g. E.M.* iii. 163
His death was instant, and without a *g. P.S.* 403
Hollow *g*—s *O.* i. 61
Taught *rocks to weep, and made the mountains* g. *A.* 16
And bids them make mistaken mortals *g. E.A.* 83
Here grief forgets to *g.*, and love to weep *E.A.* 314
The Sylvans *g.*—no matter—for the Fleet *M.E.* iii. 210
How chang'd from him who made the boxes *g. Mi.* ii. 15
Who bears him *g.*, and does not wish to bleed *P.C.* 26

Groan'd.
And the press *g.* with licens'd blasphemies *E.C.* 553
When rock'd the mountains, and when *g.* the ground *E.M.* iii. 250

Groaning.
And here the *g.* shelves Philemon bends *D.* i. 154
Where mix'd with Slaves the *g.* Martyr toil'd *M.E.* v. 6

Groans.
Beneath her footstool, *Science g.* in Chains *D.* iv. 21

Groat.
Betwixt a Guinea and a *G. I.H.* i. 38
If I ne'er got or lost a *g. I.H.* ii. 13 s
The Great Man never offer'd you a *g. E.S.* i. 26
I'll now give sixpence where I gave a *g. M.E.* iii. 366
Ask'd for a *g.*, he gives a hundred pounds *S.* iv. 86
Let him take Castles, who has ne'er a *g. S.* vi. 51
From dreams of millions, and three g—s *to pay D.* ii. 253

Groom-Porter.
At the *G.'s*, batter'd Bullies play *Mi.* ix. 99

Groping.
Or dark dexterity of *g.* well *D.* ii. 278

Gross.
G. as her sire, and as her mother grave *D.* i. 14
Shall only Man be taken in the *g. M.E.* i. 17
Wealth in the *g.* is death, but life diffus'd *M.E.* iii. 233

Grosser.
Or suck the mists in *g.* air below *R.L.* ii. 83

Grossness.
Th' opposing body's *g.* not its own *E.C.* 469

Grosvenor.
All Townshend's turnips, and all *G.'s* mines *S.* vi. 273

Grot.
His kitchen vied in coolness with his *g. M.E.* iii. 180
To swell the Terrace or to sink the *G. M.E.* iv. 49
Approach; but awful! Lo! th' Egerian *G. Mi.* x. 9
They pierce my thickets, thro' my *G.* they glide *P.S.* 8
Meet and rejoin me, in the pensive *G. S.* vi. 209
Ye *g*—s *and caverns shagg'd with horrid thorn E.A.* 20
Ye *g.* that echo to the tinkling rills *E.A.* 158

Grotesco.
G. roofs, and Stucco floors *I.H.* ii. 192

Grotto.
Here in a *g.*, shelter'd close from air *R.L.* iv. 21
Rolls o'er my *G.*, and but soothes my sleep *S.* i. 124
From her black g—s *near the Temple-wall D.* ii. 98
Alas! to *G.* and to Groves we run *S.* vi. 110

Ground.
Then gnaw'd his pen, then dash'd it on the *g. D.* i. 117
Her magic charms o'er all unclassic *g. D.* iii. 258
There, stript, fair *Rhet'ric* languish'd on the *g. D.* iv. 24
Or set on Metaphysic *g.* to prance *D.* iv. 265
And gather'd ev'ry Vice on Christian *g. D.* iv. 312
All Classic learning lost on Classic *g. D.* iv. 321
Who like his Cheops stinks above the *g. D.* iv. 372
Then thick as Locusts black'ning all the *g. D.* iv. 397
Or fetch th' aerial eagle to the *g. E.M.* iii. 222
When rock'd the mountains, and when groan'd the *g. E.M.* iii. 250
His flag inverted trails along the *g. E.S.* i. 154
Praise cannot stoop, like satire, to the *g. E.S.* ii. 110
Now in the Moon perhaps, now under *g. M.E.* i. 98
Come then, the colours and the *g.* prepare *M.E.* ii. 17
Deep hid the shining mischief under *g. M.E.* iii. 10
The whole a labour'd Quarry above *g. M.E.* iv. 110
In his own *g. O.* iv. 4
Thrice rung the bell, the slipper knock'd the *g. R.L.* i. 17
And hew triumphal arches to the *g. R.L.* iii. 176
Earth shakes her nodding tow'rs, the *g.* gives way *R.L.* v. 51
Those ancient woods, that shaded all the *g. S.* ii. 110
Now Serpent-like, in prose he sweeps the *g. S.* v. 100
Now leaves the trees, and flow'rs adorn the *g. Sp.* 43
The *g.* now sacred by thy reliques made *U.L.* 68
Here blushing Flora paints the enamell'd *g. W.F.* 38
Flutters in blood, and panting beats the *g. W.F.* 114
Panting with hope, he tries the furrow'd g—s *W.F.* 100

Grove.
And Delia's name and Doris' fill'd the *G. A.* 4
Now blushing berries paint the yellow *g. A.* 75
Rise in the *g.*, before the altar rise *E.A.* 265
Pleas'd let me own, in *Esher's* peaceful *G. E.S.* ii. 66
His House, embosom'd in the *G. I.H.* iii. 21
G. nods at *g.*, each Alley has a brother *M.E.* ii. 117
Wand'ring in the myrtle *g. O.* i. 80
To hunt for Truth in Maudlin's learned *g. S.* vi. 57
At morn the plains, at noon the shady *g. Sp.* 78
Where stray ye, Muses, in what lawn or *g. Su.* 23
This harmless *g.* no lurking viper hides *Su.* 67
Your praise the birds shall chant in ev'ry *g. Su.* 79
Seek the clear spring, or haunt the pathless *g. W.F.* 168
I hear soft music the unseen *g. W.F.* 268
Next Æson sung, while Windsor *g*—s *admir'd A.* 55
Or wanders wild in Academic *G. D.* iv. 490
But o'er the twilight *g.* and dusky caves *E.A.* 163
Foe to the Dryads of his Father's *g. M.E.* iv. 94
G., where immortal Sages taught *O.* ii. 2
Alas to Grottoes and to *G.* we run *S.* vi. 110
The Thrush may chant to the forsaken *g. Sp.* 14
Celestial Venus haunts Idalian *g. Sp.* 65
All nature laughs, the *g.* are fresh and fair *Sp.* 73
That taught the *g.* my Rosalinda's name *Sp.* 42
Behold the *g.* that shine with silver frost *W.* 9
Fields ever fresh, and *g.* for ever green *W.* 72
Adieu, ye vales, ye mountains, streams, and *g. W.* 89
The *G.* of Eden, vanish'd now so long *W.F.* 7
Here waving *g.* a chequer'd scene display *W.F.* 17
When frosts have whiten'd all the naked *g. W.F.* 126
No more the forests ring, or *g.* rejoice *W.F.* 278
But hark! the *g.* rejoice, the forest rings *W.F.* 281
Then fill'd the *g.*, as heav'nly Mira now *W.F.* 298
And *g.* of lances glitter on the Rhine *W.F.* 364
Till the freed Indians in their native *g. W.F.* 409

Grov'lling.
How Instinct varies in the *g.* swine *E.M.* i. 221

Grow.
Whose honours with increase of ages *g. E.C.* 191
We think our fathers fools, so wise we *g. E.C.* 438
The Poet's bays and Critic's ivy *g. E.C.* 706
But what will *g.* on Pride, or *g.* on Shame *E.M.* ii. 194
Say in what mortal soil thou deign'st to *g. E.M.* iv. 8
You *g.* correct, that once with Rapture writ *E.S.* i. 3
We *g.* more partial for th' Observer's sake *M.E.* i. 12
If Folly *g.* romantic, I must paint it *M.E.* ii. 16
That Charm shall *g.*, while what fatigues the Ring *M.E.* ii. 251
Nature shall join you; Time shall make it *g. M.E.* iv. 69
But future Buildings, future Navies *g. M.E.* iv. 188
I *g.* impatient, and the Tea's too strong *Mi.* ix. 108
Sooner shall grass in Hyde-park Circus *g. R.L.* iv. 117
Indulge my Candor, and *g.* all to all *S.* iii. 32
G. sick, and damn the climate—like a Lord *S.* iii. 160
Authors, like coins, *g.* dear as they *g.* old *S.* v. 35
If I but ask, if any weed can *g. S.* v. 120
There is a time when Poets will *g.* dull *S.* vi. 200
As winter fruits *g.* mild ere they decay *S.* vi. 319
On Cooper's hill eternal wreaths shall *g. W.F.* 265

Growing.
Each *g.* lump, and brings it to a Bear *D.* i. 102
The *g.* labours of the lengthen'd way *E.C.* 230
King, priest, and parent of his *g.* state *E.M.* iii. 216
The *g.* combat, or assist the fray *R.L.* v. 56
With *g.* years the pleasing License grew *S.* v. 249
Where tow'ring oaks their *g.* honours rear *W.F.* 221

Growling.
While the gaunt mastiff *g.* at the gate *M.E.* iii. 195

Grown.
Custom, *g.* blind with Age, must be your guide *E.* iv. 33
Tho' cold like you, unmov'd and silent *g. E.A.* 23
In sounds and jingling syllables *g.* old *E.C.* 605
My Lord and he are *g.* so great *I.H.* ii. 105 s
They stand amaz'd, and think me *g. I.H.* ii. 123 s
G. all to all, from no one vice exempt *M.E.* i. 194
Beauties, like Tyrants, old and friendless *g. M.E.* ii. 227
Ungrateful wretch, with mimic airs *g.* pert *Mi.* ix. 65
Till *g.* more frugal in his riper days *P.S.* 241
And with your golden darts, now useless *g. W.* 25

Grows.
G. with his growth, and strengthens with his strength *E.M.* ii. 136
Strong *g.* the Virtue, with his nature mix'd *E.M.* ii. 178
Till one man's weakness *g.* the strength of all *E.M.* ii. 252
Where *g.*!—where *g.* it not? If vain our toil *E.M.* iv. 13
Mark by what wretched steps their glory *g. E.M.* iv. 291
It *g.* their Age's prudence to pretend *M.E.* ii. 236
He marries, bows at Court, and *g.* polite *M.E.* iii. 386
The Flatterer an Earwig *g. Mi.* iv. 21
Say at what age a Poet *g.* divine *S.* v. 50
The silly hard *g.* fat, or falls away *S.* v. 303

Growth.
Grows with his *g.*, and strengthens with his strength *E.M.* ii. 136
While with the silent *g.* of ten per cent. *S.* iii. 132

Grubs.
Of hairs, or straws, or dirt, or *g.*, or worms *P.S.* 170

Grubstreet.
And New-year Odes, and all the *G.* race *D.* i. 44
Gaming and *G.* skulk behind the King *D.* i. 310
Three wicked imps of her own *G.* choir *D.* ii. 123
Shall take thro' *G.* her triumphant round *D.* iii. 136
G.! thy fall should men and Gods conspire *D.* iii. 311
One from all *G.* will my fame defend *P.S.* 111
Let *Budgel* charge low *G.* on his quill *P.S.* 378

Grumbler.
Shall this a *Pasquin*, that a *G.* write *D.* iii. 182

Guard.
Reason is here no guide, but still a *g. E.M.* ii. 162
Ariel himself shall be the *g.* of Shock *R.L.* ii. 116
Soon as she spreads her hand th' aërial *g. R.L.* iii. 31

G. the sure barrier between that and Sense D. i. 178
Prompt or to *g.* or stab, to saint or damn *D.* ii. 357
G. my Prerogative, assert my Throne *D.* iv. 583
This golden lance shall *g.* Desert *E.* vi. 6
Whose fame with pains we *g.*, but lose with ease *E.C.* 504
All join to *g.* what each desires to gain *E.M.* iii. 278
And Angels *g.* him in the golden Mean *M.E.* iii. 246
What walls can *g.* me, or what shades can hide *P.S.* 7
And *g.* with Arms divine the British Throne *R.L.* ii. 90
And *g.* the wide circumference around *R.L.* ii. 122

Guardian.
This to disclose is all thy *g.* can *R.L.* i. 113
But thou false *g.* of a charge too good *U.L.* 29
Morality, by her false *G.*—s drawn *D.* iv. 27
Lights of the Church, or *G.* of the Laws *S.* i. 110
Four *g.* Virtues, round, support her throne *D.* i. 46
Thus shall mankind his *g.* care engage *M.* 55
Her *g.* SYLPH prolong'd the balmy rest *R.L.* i. 20

Guards.
Truth *g.* the Poet, sanctifies the line *E.S.* ii. 246
What *g.* the purity of melting Maids *R.L.* i. 71

Gudgeons.
But *g.*, flounders, what my Thames affords *S.* ii. 142

Guess.
Maxims are drawn from Notions, these from *G. M.E.* i. 14
To ask, to *g.*, to know, as they commence *D.* iv. 155
First, if thou canst, the harder reason *g. E.M.* i. 37
The KNAVE OF CLUBS thrice lost: Oh, who could *g. Mi.* ix. 19
This who can gratify? for who can *g. P.S.* 178
But in known Images of life, I *g. S.* v. 284
I *g.*; and with their leave, will tell the fault *S.* v. 357
The suit, if by the fashion one might *g. S.* viii. 40

Guest.
Enter each mild, each amicable *g. E.A.* 301
But 'twas my *G.* at whom they threw the dirt *E.S.* ii. 145
Yet, to his *G.* tho' no way sparing *I.H.* ii. 169
How pale each Worshipful and Rev'rend *g. S.* ii. 75
Welcome the coming, speed the going *g. S.* ii. 160
The *G.*—s *withdrawn had left the Treat I.H.* ii. 196
Hard task! to hit the palate of such *g. S.* vi. 86
Not more amazement seiz'd on Circe's *g. S.* viii. 166

Guide.
Take up the Bible, once my better *g. D.* i. 200
None need a *g.*, by sure attraction led *D.* iv. 75
All-seeing in thy mists, we want no *g. D.* iv. 469
Custom, grown blind with Age, must be your *G. E.* iv. 33
(Her *g.* now lost) no more attempts to rise *E.C.* 737
Trace Science then, with Modesty thy *g. E.M.* ii. 43
Reason is here no *g.*, but still a guard *E.M.* ii. 162
Say, where full Instinct is th' unerring *g. E.M.* iii. 83
Zeal then, not charity, became the *g. E.M.* iii. 261
Thou wert my *g.*, philosopher, and friend *E.M.* iv. 390
Bids Bubo build, and sends him such a *G. M.E.* iv. 20
Is this my *G.*, Philosopher, and Friend *S.* iii. 177
Plac'd at the door of Learning, youth to g. D. iv. 153
'Tis more to *g.*, than spur the Muse's steed *E.C.* 84
The Muse may give thee, but the Gods must *g. E.S.* ii. 215
To wither thy Tomb shall *g.* enquiring eyes *Ep.* v. 4
The Sylphs thro' mystic mazes *g.* their way *R.L.* i. 92
Some *g.* the course of wand'ring orbs on high *R.L.* ii. 79
Watch all their ways, and all their actions *g. R.L.* ii. 88

Guides.
Led by some rule, that *g.*, but not constrains *E.* iii. 67
Each motion *g.*, and ev'ry nerve sustains *E.C.* 78
Go, wond'rous creature! mount where Science *g. E.M.* ii. 19
Pride *g.* his steps, and bids him shun the great *M.E.* i. 114
Which *g.* all those who know not what they mean *S.* iii. 344
Grav'd at his urn appear'd the moon, that *g. W.F.* 333

Guido.
Match Raphael's grace with thy lov'd *G.'s* air *E.* iii. 36

Guild.
A moan so loud, that all the *g.* awake *D.* ii. 250

Guildhall.
The club of Quidnuncs, or her own *G. D.* i. 270
Have you not seen, at G.'s narrow pass *S.* vi. 104

Guilt.
Pomps without *g.* of bloodless swords and maces *D.* i. 87
Which nor to *G.* nor Fear, its Caution owes *E.* ii. 3
How glowing *g.* exalts the keen delight *E. A.* 230
That cause of all my *g.*, and all my joy *E. A.* 338
In each how *g.* and greatness equal ran *E.M.* iv. 293
The Lock, obtain'd with *g.*, and kept with pain *R.L.* v. 109

Guiltless.
Thou knew'st how *g.* first I met thy flame *E. A.* 59
G. I gaz'd; heav'n listen'd while you sung *E. A.* 65
In all the Courts of Pindus *g.* quite *E.S.* ii. 187
In vain your *g.* laurels stood *O.* ii. 5
Poor *g.* I! and can I choose but smile *P.S.* 281

Guilty.
Yet none but you by Name the *G.* lash *E.S.* ii. 10
To W—le *g.* of some venial sin *E.S.* ii. 162
Hence *g.* joys, distastes, surmises *O.* iii. 37
Brand the bold front of shameless *g.* men *S.* i. 106
Base Fear becomes the *g.*, not the free *S.* viii. 194

Guinea.
Betwixt a *G.* and a Groat *I.H.* i. 38
From the crack'd bag the dropping *G.* spoke *M.E.* iii. 36
Yet hens of *G.* full as good I hold *S.* ii. 19
His ven'son too, a *g.* makes your own *S.* vi. 215
With Fifty G—s (*a great Pen'worth*) bought *Mi.* ix. 30
G., Half-Guineas, all the shining train *Mi.* ix. 79

Gulfy.
The *g.* Lea his sedgy tresses rears *W. F.* 346

Gulliver.
Dean, Drapier, Bickerstaff, or *G. D.* i. 20

Gums.
G. and Pomatums shall his flight restrain *R.L.* ii. 129

Gun.
Who visits with a *G.*, presents you birds *E.* v. 25
With *G.*, Drum, Trumpet, Blunderbuss, and Thunder *S.* i. 28
Swords, pikes, and g—s, *with everlasting rust S.* i. 74
With slaught'ring *g.* th' unweary'd fowler roves *W.F.* 125

Gush'd.
Tears *g.* again, as from pale Priam's eyes *D.* i. 255
The triumph ceas'd, tears *g.* from ev'ry eye *P.C.* 33

Gushes.
For me, health *g.* from a thousand springs *E.M.* 138

Gushing.
Line after line my *g.* eyes o'erflow *E. A.* 35

Gust.
Destroy all Creatures for thy sport or *g. E.M.* i. 117
What is loose love? a transient *g. O.* iii. 17

Guthry.
Ev'n *G.* saves half Newgate by a Dash *E.S.* ii. 11

H.
Great C * *, H * *, P * *, R * *, K * *, *D.* iv. 545
And W * and H * * both in town *I H.* i. 14
Blunt could *do Bus'ness*, H—ggins *knew the Town E.S.* i. 14
My *H—ley's* periods, or my Blackmore's numbers *D.* ii. 370
That First was *H—vy's*, F.'s next, and then (*rep.*) *E S.* i. 71

Habit.
Attention, *h.* and experience gains *E.M.* ii. 79
Nature its mother, *H.* is its nurse *E.M.* ii. 145
Judge we by Nature? *H.* can efface *M.E.* i. 166
Of various *h.* and of various dye *R.L.* iii. 84
And still new heeds, new helps, new h—s rise *E.M.* iii. 137

Habitual.
These nat'ral love maintain'd, *h.* those *E.M.* iii. 140

Hack.
Meek modern faith to murder, *h.*, and maul *D.* iii. 210
On horse, on foot, in h—s, *and gilded chariots D.* ii. 24

Hack'd.
Appear more glorious as more *h.* and torn *D.* iv. 124

Hackney.
What? shall each spur-gall'd *H.* of the day *E.S.* ii. 140
Friendly at *H.*, faithless at Whitehall *M.E.* i. 76
In some starv'd h. *sonneteer, or me E.C.* 419
A *h.* coach may chance to spoil a thought *S.* vi. 101

Had, Hadst.—*Passim.*

Hæmus.
Hark! *H.* resounds with the Bacchanals' cries *O.* i. 111

Hags.
As *H.* hold Sabbaths, less for joy than spite *M.E.* ii. 239

Hail.
Mid snows of paper, and fierce *h.* of pease *D.* iii. 262
"Perch'd on his crown." All h. | *and* h. *again D.* i. 291
All *h.* him victor in both gifts of song *D.* ii. 267
H., Bards triumphant! born in happier days *E.C.* 189
And *h.* her passage to the Realms of Rest *E.S.* ii. 81
Shall *h.* the rising, close the parting day *I.H.* iii. 30
The Club must *h.* him master of the joke *M.E.* i. 185
Then thus address'd the pow'r "*H.*, wayward Queen *R.L.* iv. 57
And *h.* with music its propitious ray *R.L.* v. 134
H., sacred peace! *h.*, long-expected days *W.F.* 355

Hair.
As full, as perfect, in a *h.* as heart *E.M.* i. 276
In Magdalen's loose *h.*, and lifted eye *M.E.* ii. 12
These set the head, and those divide the *h. R.L.* i. 146
Slight lines of *h.* surprise the finny prey *R.L.* ii. 26
And beauty draws us with a single *h. R.L.* ii. 28
Some thrid the mazy ringlets of her *h. R.L.* ii. 139
She dearly pays for Nisus' injur'd *h. R.L.* iii. 124
A thousand wings, by turns, blow back the *h. R.L.* iii. 136
The meeting points the sacred *h.* dissever *R.L.* iii. 153
As thou, sad Virgin! for thy ravish'd *h. R.L.* iv. 1
Her eyes dejected, and her *h.* unbound *R.L.* iv. 90
Gods! shall the ravisher display your *h. R.L.* iv. 103
"Give her the *h.*"—he spoke, and rapp'd his box *R.L.* iv. 130
Which never more shall join its parted *h.* *R.L.* iv. 134
Weighs the Men's wits against the Lady's *h. R.L.* v. 72
And drew behind a radiant trail of *h. R.L.* v. 128
Then cease, bright Nymph! to mourn thy ravish'd *h. R.L.* v. 141
I pluck out year by year, and *h.* by *h. S.* v. 64
Thus finish'd and corrected to a *h. S.* viii. 248
A belt her waist, a fillet binds her *h. W.F.* 178
Pants on her cheek, and fans her parting *h. W.F.* 196
Sees h—s *and bores, examines bit by bit D.* iv. 234
A few grey *h.* his rev'rend temples crown'd *M.E.* iii. 327
Of *h.*, or straws, or dirt, or grubs, or worms *P.S.* 170
A brighter wash; to curl their waving *h. R.L.* ii. 97
What wonder then, fair nymph! thy *h.* should feel *R.L.* iii. 177
And bids her beau demand the precious *h. R.L.* iv. 122
See the poor remnants of these slighted *h. R.L.* iv. 167
H. less in sight, or any *h.* but these *R.L.* iv. 176
At length the wits mount up, the *h.* subside *R.L.* v. 74
Then in a bodkin gnac'd her mother's *h. R.L.* v. 95
But where no Prelate's lawn with h.-shirt *lin'd S.* iii. 165

Hairy.
With *h.* springes we the birds betray *R.L.* ii. 25

Halberts.
Caps on their heads, and *h.* in their hand *R.L.* iii. 42

Hale.
From honest Mah'met, or plain Parson *H. M.E.* ii. 198
Nor once to Chanc'ry, nor to *H.* apply *S.* iii. 173

Half.

Are *h.* so charming as thy sight to me *A.* 46
Pours forth, and leaves unpeopl'd *h.* the land *D.* ii. 20
Thro' *h.* the heav'ns he pours th' exalted urn *D.* ii. 183
He brings up *h.* the bottom on his head *D.* ii. 321
Lo sneering Goode, *h.* malice and *h.* whim *D.* iii. 153
H. thro' the solid darkness of his soul *D.* iii. 226
Not *h.* so pleas'd when Goodman prophesy'd *D.* iii. 232
As *h.* to shew, *h.* veil, the deep latent *D.* iv. 4
Stunn'd with thy giddy Larum *h.* the town *D.* iv. 292
A Monarch's *h.*, and *h.* a Harlot's slave *D.* iv. 512
Hum *h.* a tune, tell stories to the squire *E.* v. 20
Still rebel nature holds out *h.* my heart *E.A.* 26
For 'tis but *h.* a Judge's task to know *E.C.* 561
Created *h.* to rise, and *h.* to fall *E.M.* ii. 15
Taught *h.* by Reason, *h.* by mere decay *E.M.* ii. 259
Of *h.* that live, the butcher and the tomb *E.M.* iii. 162
Shall find that pleasure pays not *h.* the pain *E.M.* iv. 48
Is hung on high, to poison *h.* mankind *E.M.* iv. 252
Sets *h.* the world, God knows, against the rest *E.S.* i. 58
Ev'n Guthry saves *h.* Newgate by a Dash *E.S.* ii. 11
Enough for *h.* the Greatest of these days *E.S.* ii. 112
A Terrace-walk, and *h.* a Rood *I.H.* ii. 5 s
Shall stretch thy conquests over *h.* the kind *I.H.* iii. 16
When *h.* our knowledge we must snatch, not take *M.E.* i. 40
At *h.* mankind when gen'rous Manly raves *M.E.* i. 57
A Fool, with more of Wit than *h.* mankind *M.E.* i. 200
'Tis to their Changes *h.* their charms we owe *M.E.* ii. 42
Averted *h.* your Parents' simple Pray'r *M.E.* ii. 286
Fill *h.* the land with Imitating-Fools *M.E.* iv. 26
Where *h.* the skill is decently to hide *M.E.* iv. 54
And *h.* the platform just reflects the other *M.E.* iv. 118
Some bury'd marble *h.* preserves a name *M.E.* v. 16
And *h.* unsheath'd the shining blade *O.* i. 46
Who turns a Persian tale for *h.* a crown *P.S.* 180
H. froth, *h.* venom, spits himself abroad *P.S.* 320
The damning critic, *h.* approving wit *P.S.* 344
There lay three garters, *h.* a pair of gloves *R.L.* ii. 39
The pow'rs gave ear, and granted *h.* his pray'r *R.L.* ii. 45
Their fluid bodies *h.* dissolv'd in light *R.L.* ii. 62
Th' embroider'd King who shows but *h.* his face *R.L.* iii. 76
That single act gives *h.* the world the spleen *R.L.* iv. 78
Not *h.* so fix'd the Trojan could remain *R.L.* v. 5
Shall *h.* the new-built Churches round thee fall *S.* ii. 119
Just *h.* the land would buy, and *h.* be sold *S.* iii. 125
You laugh, *h.* Beau, *h.* Sloven if I stand *S.* iii. 161
Is *h.* so incoherent as my Mind *S.* iii. 166
Nay, *h.* in heav'n—except (what's mighty odd) *S.* iii. 187
Will gain a Wife, with *h.* as many more *S.* iv. 78
When Merlin's Cave is *h.* unfurnish'd yet *S.* v. 355
But knottier points we know not *h.* so well *S.* vi. 58
H. that the Dev'l o'erlooks from Lincoln town *S.* vi. 245
For had they found a linguist *h.* so good *S.* viii. 84
Between each drop it gives, stays *h.* a minute *S.* viii. 127
Already *h.* turn'd traitor by surprise *S.* viii. 169
When *h.* his nose is in his Prince's ear *S.* viii. 179
Not *h.* so swift the trembling doves can fly (*rep.*) *W.F.* 185
And *h.* thy forests rush into thy floods *W.F.* 386
And mighty Dukes pack Cards for h.-a-crown *M.E.* iii. 142
See now, *h.*-cur'd, and perfectly well-bred *D.* iv. 323
Her eyes half-languishing, *h.-drown'd* in tears *D.* iv. 144
Here lay poor Fletcher's *h.-east* scenes, and here *D.* i. 131
Maggots *h.-form'd* in rhyme exactly meet *D.* i. 61
As *h.* insects on the banks of Nile *E.C.* 41
Guineas, *H.-Guineas*, all the shining train *Mi.* ix. 79
In the worst inn's worst room, with mat *h.-hung M.E.* iii. 299
Her eyes *h.-languishing*, half-drown'd in tears *M.E.* 144
Those *h.-learn'd* writings, num'rous in our isle *E.C.* 40
One *h.-pint* bottle serves them both to dine *S.* ii. 53
Compar'd, *h.-rear'ning* elephant, with thine *E.M.* i. 222
And see thro' all things with his *h.-shut* eyes *R.L.* iii. 118

Halifax.

Thus Somers once, and *H.* were mine *E.S.* ii. 77

Hall.

Thames wafts it thence to Rufus' roaring *h. D.* ii. 265
Lost, lost too soon in yonder House or *H. D.* iv. 166

Thee catch'd the Schools; the *H.* scarce kept awake *D.* iv. 609
Ye Tradesmen vile, in Army, Court, or *H. E.S.* ii. 17
To Virtue's work provoke most tardy *H. E.S.* ii. 218
No sooner said, but from the *H. I.H.* ii. 210
Like some lone Chartreux stands the good old *H. M.E.* iii. 187
A hundred footsteps scrape the marble *H. M.E.* iv. 152
From morn to night, at Senate, Rolls, and *H. S.* iv. 36
Old-fashion'd b—s, *dull Aunts, and croaking rooks E.* v. 12
The trophy'd arches, story'd *h.* invade *E.M.* iv. 303
More than ten Holinsheds, or *H.*, or Stowes *S.* viii. 131

Hallow'd.

You rais'd these *h.* walls; the desert smil'd *E.A.* 133
The *h.* taper trembling in thy hand *E.A.* 326
Who touch'd Isaiah's *h.* lips with fire *M.* 6
Still tries to save the *h.* taper's end *M.E.* i. 243
Nor *h.* dirge be mutter'd o'er thy tomb *U.L.* 62
In weeping vaults her *h.* earth contains *W.F.* 302

Halts.

And Sidney's verse *h.* ill on Roman feet *S.* v. 98

Hampton.

Which from the neighb'ring *H.* takes its name *R.L.* iii. 4
While H.'s echoes "Wretched maid!" reply'd R.L. iv. 90
If H.-court these eyes had never seen R.L. iv. 150

Hams.

Thy Truffles, Perigord! thy *H.*, Bayonne *D.* iv. 558
Scarsdale his bottle, Darty his H.-pie *S.* i. 46
Who has not learn'd, fresh sturgeon and *h. S.* ii. 103

Hand.

Where o'er the gates by his fam'd father's *h. D.* i. 31
Could Troy be sav'd by any single *h. D.* i. 197
This Box my Thunder, this right *h.* my God *D.* i. 202
And thrice he dropt it from his quiv'ring *h. D.* i. 246
And now the victor stretch'd his eager *h. D.* i. 309
While thus each *h.* promotes the pleasing pain *D.* ii. 211
Of *h.* of Bavius drench'd thee o'er and o'er *D.* iii. 46
Swift to whose *h.* a winged volume flies *D.* iii. 234
By singing Peers up-held on either *h. D.* iv. 49
Withdrew his *h.*, and clos'd the pompous page *D.* iv. 114
Led by my *h.* be saunter'd Europe round *D.* iv. 311
And well-dissembled em'rald on his *h. D.* iv. 348
And Douglas lend his soft obstetric *h. D.* iv. 394
So back to Pollio, *h.* in *h.*, they went *D.* iv. 396
Thy *h.*, great Anarch! lets the curtain fall *D.* iv. 655
Whether thy *h.* strike out some free design *E.* iii. 3
Take at this *h.* celestial arms *E.* vi. 4
O write it not, my *h.*—the name appears *E.A.* 13
Her heart still dictates, and her *h.* obeys *E.A.* 16
Where, where was Eloise? her voice, her *h. E.A.* 101
Plants of thy *h.*, and children of thy pray'r *E.A.* 130
The hallow'd taper trembling in thy *h. E.A.* 326
And ready Nature waits upon his *h. E.C.* 487
But less to please the eye, than arm the *h. E.C.* 673
And licks the *h.* just rais'd to shed his blood *E.M.* i. 84
Snatch from his *h.* the balance and the rod *E.M.* i. 121
Who knows but he, whose *h.* the lightning forms *E.M.* i. 157
Or *h.*, to toil, aspir'd to be the head *E.M.* i. 260
Safe in the *h.* of one disposing Pow'r *E.M.* i. 287
Feeds from his *h.*, and in his bosom warms *M.* 54
And the same *h.* that sow'd, shall reap the field *M.* 66
The smiling infant in his *h.* shall take *M.* 81
His *h.* sustain'd, his uncorrupted heart *M.E.* i. 82
Time, that on all things lays his lenient *h. M.E.* i. 224
Asks no firm *h.*, and no unerring line *M.E.* ii. 152
Oh say, what sums that gen'rous *h.* supply *M.E.* iii. 277
Touch'd by thy *h.*, again Rome's glories shine *M.E.* v. 46
Till some new Tyrant lifts his purple *h. O.* ii. 23
Fire in each eye, and papers in each *h. P.S.* 5
Horace and he went *h.* in *h.* in song *P.S.* 234
If gentle Damon did not squeeze her *h. R.L.* i. 98
Soon as she spreads her *h.*, th' aërial guard *R.L.* iii. 31
Caps on their heads, and halberts in their *h. R.L.* iii. 42
Lurk'd in her *h.* and mourn'd his captive Queen *R.L.* iii. 96
Her *h.* is fill'd, her bosom with lampoons *R.L.* iv. 30
A branch of healing Spleenwort in his *h. R.L.* iv. 56
On that rapacious *h.* for ever blaze *R.L.* iv. 116
This *h.*, which won it, shall for ever wear *R.L.* iv. 138

HANDEL—HAPPY.   139

Thrice from my trembling *h.* the patch-box fell *R.L.* iv. 162
In forests planted by a Father's *h. S.* ii. 135
Whom honour with your *h.* : to make remarks *S.* iv. 103
Behold the *h.* that wrought a Nation's cure *S.* v. 225
And great Nassau to Kneller's *h.* decreed *S.* v. 382
Let not this weak, unknowing *h. U.P.* 25
And nodding tempt the joyful reaper's *h. W.F.* 40
Intent, his angle trembling in his *h. W.F.* 138
Not with more glee by h—s *pontific crown'd D.* ii. 13
So lab'ring on with shoulders, *h.*, and head *D.* ii. 65
And ministers to Jove with purest *h. D.* ii. 94
Thus the small jet which hasty *h.* unlock *D.* ii. 177
And Milo-like surveys his arms and *h. D.* ii. 284
Tuning his voice, and balancing his *h. D.* iii. 200
Like bold Briareus, with a hundred *h. D.* iv. 66
And holds his breeches close with both his *h. D.* iv. 148
More glorious yet from barb'rous *h.* to keep *D.* iv. 379
Above the reach of sacrilegious *h. E.C.* 182
Pleasures are ever in our *h.* and eyes *E.M.* ii. 122
To all but Heav'n-directed *h.* deny'd *E.S.* ii. 214
Belies his features, my extends his *h. M.E.* iii. 294
The vast Parterres a thousand *h.* shall make *M.E.* iv. 73
Proud to accomplish what such *h.* design'd *M.E.* iv. 196
May dunce by dunce be whistled off my *h. P.S.* 254
And four fair Queens whose *h.* sustain a flow'r *R.L.* iii. 39
A wond'rous Bag with both her *h.* she binds *R.L.* iv. 81
" O wretched maid !" she spread her *h.* and cry'd *R.L.* iv. 95
My *h.* shall rend what ev'n thy rapine spares *R.L.* iv. 168
And tempts once more thy sacrilegious *h. R.L.* iv. 174
No common weapons in their *h.* are found *R.L.* v. 43
At this entranc'd, he lifts his *h.* and eyes *S.* viii. 98
By foreign *h.* thy dying eyes were clos'd *U.L.* 51

Handel.
Strong in new arms, lo ! Giant *H.* stands *D.* iv. 65

Handkerchief.
With *h.* and orange at my side *P.S.* 228
Roar'd for the *h.* that caus'd his pain *R.L.* v. 106

Handle.
One bent ; the *h.* this, and that the spout *R.L.* iv. 56

Handmaid.
Ah let thy *h.*, sister, daughter move *E.A.* 153
Then Criticism the Muse's *h.* prov'd *E.C.* 102
'Tis from a *H.* we must take a Helen *M.E.* ii. 194
Two h—s *wait the throne: alike in place R.L.* iv. 25

Handsome.
A *h.* House to lodge a Friend *I.H.* ii. 3 *s*
Knew what was *h.* and would do 't *I.H.* ii. 163
H. and witty, yet a Friend *Mi.* viii. 4

Hang.
For her, the lilies *h.* their heads and die *A.* 26
And *h.* some curious cobweb in its stead *D.* i. 180
A heavy Lord shall *h.* at ev'ry Wit *D.* iv. 132
We *h.* one jingling padlock on the mind *D.* iv. 162
And low-brow'd rocks *h.* nodding o'er the deeps *E.A.* 244
H. the sad verse on CAROLINA'S Urn *E.S.* i. 80
Learn from their Books, to *h.* himself and Wife *E.S.* i. 126
Dragg'd in the dust ! his arms *h.* idly round *E.S.* i. 153
Reverse your Ornaments, and *h.* them all *M.E.* iv. 91
And snakes uncurl'd *h.* list'ning round their heads *O.* i. 70
H. o'er the Box, and hover round the Ring *R.L.* i. 44
Some *h.* upon the pendants of her ear *R.L.* ii. 140
And wretches *h.* that jurymen may dine *R.L.* iii. 22
Practis'd to lisp and *h.* the head aside *R.L.* iv. 33
H. their old Trophies o'er the Garden gates *S.* ii. 8
Yet *h.* your lip, to see a Seam awry *S.* iii. 174
To see their judgments *h.* upon thy voice *S.* iv. 35
Estates have wings, and *h.* in Fortune's pow'r *S.* vi. 248
But now the reeds shall *h.* on yonder tree *Su.* 43
And headlong streams *h.* list'ning in their fall *Su.* 84
H. o'er their coursers' heads with eager speed *W.F.* 157
As Herod's h.-*dogs in old Tapestry S.* viii. 267

Hang'd.
Strike ? why the man was *h.* ten years ago *E.S.* ii. 55
The number may be *h.*, but not be crown'd *E.S.* ii. 111
A man was *h.* for very honest rhymes *S.* i. 146

Hanging.
The shapeless rock, or *h.* precipice *E.C.* 158
For Chartres' head reserve the *h.* wall *E.M.* iv. 130
Now under *h.* mountains *O.* i. 97
Hard words or *h.*, if your Judge be Page *S.* i. 82

Hangs.
He *h.* between ; in doubt to act or rest *E.M.* ii. 7
The Court forsake him, and Sir Balaam *h. M.E.* iii. 398
Uncurl'd it *h.*, the fatal shears demands *R.L.* iv. 173

Hapless.
There *h.* Shakespear, yet of Tibbald sore *D.* i. 133
Whence *h.* Monsieur much complains at Paris *D.* ii. 135
May one kind grave unite each *h.* name *E.A.* 343
The silver swans her *h.* fate bemoan *W.* 39
Still hears the name the *h.* virgin bore *W.F.* 207

Happier.
H. thy fortunes ! like a rolling stone *D.* iii. 293
No *h.* task these faded eyes pursue *E.A.* 47
Hail, Bards triumphant ! born in *h.* days *E.C.* 789
Some *h.* island in the wat'ry waste *E.M.* i. 106
What *h.* natures shrink at with affright *E.M.* iii. 229
That such are *h.*, shocks all common sense *E.M.* iv. 52
H. as kinder, in whate'er degree *E.M.* iv. 359
Seen him I have, but in his *h.* hour *E.S.* i. 29
Which is the *h.*, or the wiser *I.H.* ii. 147
To some indeed Heav'n grants the *h.* fate *M.E.* iii. 97
H. their author, when by these belov'd *P.S.* 144

Happily.
Then thus : "from Priest-craft *h.* set free *D.* iv. 499
Form'd by thy converse, *h.* to steer *E.M.* iv. 379

Happiness.
And finish'd more thro' *h.* than pains *E.* iii. 68
For there's a *h.* as well as care *E.C.* 142
If the great end be human *H. E.M.* i. 149
Each want of *h.* by hope supply'd *E.M.* ii. 285
Sure by quick Nature *h.* to gain *E.M.* iii. 91
On mutual Wants built mutual *H. E.M.* iii. 112
Oh *H.* ! our being's end and aim *E.M.* iv. 1
Fix'd to no spot is *H.* sincere *E.M.* iv. 15
Than this, that *H.* is *H. E.M.* iv. 28
And makes what *H.* we justly call *E.M.* iv. 37
If all are equal in their *H.* (*rep.*) *E.M.* iv. 54
If then to all Men *H.* was meant *E.M.* iv. 65
And grant the bad what *h.* they would *E.M.* iv. 91
See the false scale of *H.* complete *E.M.* iv. 288
Virtue alone is *H.* below *E.M.* iv. 310
No thought of peace or *h.* at home *M.E.* ii. 224 .
It gives men *h.*, or leaves them ease *S.* vi. 183

Happy.
Still *h.* Impudence obtains the prize *D.* ii. 186
Such *h.* arts attention can command *D.* ii. 229
That once was Britain—*H.* ! had she seen *D.* iii. 117
But (*h.* for him as the times went then) *D.* iv. 115
To *h.* Convents, bosom'd deep in vines *D.* iv. 301
See, to my country *h.* I restore *D.* iv. 329
Live *h.* both, and long promote our arts *D.* iv. 348
His easy Art may *h.* Nature seem *E.* iv. 3
Pleas'd while with smiles his *h.* lines you view *E.* iv. 75
Saw others *h.*, and with sighs withdrew *E.* v. 8
Oh ! *h.* state ! when souls each other draw *E.A.* 91
How *h.* is the blameless Vestal's lot *E.A.* 207
Our Author, *h.* in a Judge so nice *E.C.* 273
But let a Lord once own the *h.* lines *E.C.* 420
Such once were Critics ; such the *h.* few *E.C.* 643
Each beast, each insect *h.* in its own *E.M.* i. 185
That, *h.* frailties to all ranks apply'd *E.M.* ii. 241
The learn'd is *h.* nature to explore (*rep.*) *E.M.* ii. 263
And these be *h.* call'd, unhappy those *E.M.* iv. 68
How *h.* ! those to ruin, these betray *E.M.* iv. 290
Was ever such a *h.* Swain *I.H.* ii. 204
Their *h.* Spots the nice admirer take *M.E.* ii. 44
And made a Widow *h.*, for a whim *M.E.* ii. 58
Thrice *h.* man ! enabled to pursue *M.E.* iii. 275
These Honours Peace to *h.* Britain brings *M.E.* iv. 203
By those *h.* souls who dwell *O.* i. 74
H. the man whose wish and care *O.* iv. 1
H. to catch me just at Dinner-time *P.S.* 14
H. my studies, when by these approv'd *P.S.* 143
H. I ah ten times *h.* had I been *R.L.* iv. 149
In South-sea days not *h.*, when surmis'd *S.* ii. 133
To make men *h.*, and to keep them so *S.* iv. 2

140 HARANGUES—HASTE.

Be virtuous, and be *h.* for your pains *S.* iv. 62
Call'd *h.* Dog! the Beggar at his door *S.* iv. 116
Each prais'd within, is *h.* all day long *S.* vi. 156
"Then, *h.* Man who shows the Tombs!" said I *S.* viii. 102
Nay tell me first, in what more *h.* fields *Sp.* 89
H. the man whom this bright court approves *W.F.* 235
H. next him, who to these shades retires *W.F.* 237

Harangues.
The House impeach him, Coningsby *h.* *M.E.* iii. 397

Harbours.
Bid *H.* open, public Ways extend *M.E.* iv. 197

Harcourt.
If Pope must tell, what *H.* cannot speak *Ep.* iii. 6

Hard.
A Soul supreme in each *h.* instance try'd *E.* i. 23
Critics in Wit, or Life, are *h.* to please *E.* iv. 29
'Tis *h.* to say, if greater want of skill *E.C.* 1
The *h.* inhabitant contends it right *E.M.* ii. 230
Woman and Fool are two *h.* things to hit *M.E.* ii. 113
As *h.* a science to the Fair as Great *M.E.* ii. 226
The Lab'rer bears: What his *h.* heart denies *M.E.* iv. 171
'Tis a Virgin, *h.* of Feature *Mi.* vi. 5
And oh! what makes the disappointment *h.* *Mi* ix. 47
A conquest how *h.* and how glorious *O.* i. 89
A man's true merit 'tis not *h.* to find *P.S.* 175
Him Basto follow'd, but his fate more *h.* *R.L.* iii. 53
H. words or hanging, if your Judge be Page *S.* i. 82
H. task to hit the palate of such guests *S.* vi. 86
Why art thou prouder and more *h.* than they *Su.* 18
And strains, from b.-bound brains, eight lines a year *P.S.* 182

Harden.
And right, too rigid, *h.* into wrong *E.M.* iii. 193

Harder.
First, if thou canst, the *h.* reason guess *E.M.* i. 37
And, *h.* still! flagitious, yet not great *M.E.* i. 205
And others (*h.* still) be paid in kind *P.S.* 244

Hardest.
'Tis sure the *h.* science to forget *E.A.* 190
Gold, imp'd by thee, can compass *h.* things *M.E.* iii. 41

Hardly.
Lo! where Mæotis sleeps, and *h.* flows *D.* iii. 87
To make a wash would *h.* stew a child *M.E.* ii. 54
Poor and disarm'd, and *h.* worth your hate *S.* vii. 12
The watch would *h.* let him pass at noon *S.* viii. 32

Hardness.
This polish'd *H.*, that reflects the Peer *D.* i. 220

Hardy.
For thee the *h.* Vet'ran drops a tear *Ep.* ix. 5

Hare.
While Sherlock, *H.*, and Gibson preach in vain *D.* iii. 204
And trace the mazes of the circling *h.* *W.F.* 122
Turns H—s to Larks, and Pigeons into Toads *D.* iv. 554

Hark.
H.! a glad voice the lonely desert cheers *M.* 29
But *h.!* the chiming Clocks to dinner call *M.E.* iv. 151
H.! the numbers soft and clear *O.* i. 12
But *h.!* he strikes the golden lyre *O.* i. 63
H.! Hæmus resounds with the Bacchanal cries *O.* i. 111
H.! they whisper; Angels say *O.* v. 7
Booth enters—*h.!* the Universal peal *S.* v. 334
But *h.!* the groves rejoice, the forest rings *W.F.* 281

Harlequins.
New Eunuchs, *H.*, and Operas *S.* viii. 125

Harley.
Dear to the Muse! to *H.* dear in vain *E.* i. 6
H., the Nation's great support *I.H.* i. 83
Since *H.* bid me first attend *I.H.* ii. 85 s

Harlot.
When lo! a *H.* form, soft sliding by *D.* iv. 45
A Monarch's half, and half a H.'s slave *D.* iv. 512
The smiles of h—s, and the tears of heirs *R.L.* v. 120

Harmless.
I'll list you in the *h.* roll *E.* iv. 31
Come, *h.* Characters, that no one hit *E.S.* i. 65
And *h.* serpents lick the pilgrim's feet *M.* 80
And gave the *h.* fellow a good word *Mi.* iii. 6
But he who hurts a *h.* neighbour's peace *P.S.* 287
That *h.* mother thought no wife a whore *P.S.* 384
This *h.* grove no lurking viper hides *Su.* 67

Harmonic.
H. twang! of leather, horn, and brass *D.* ii. 254

Harmonious.
Cynthia, tune *h.* Numbers *Mi.* vii. 13

Harmoniously.
But, as the world, *h.* confus'd *W.F.* 14

Harmonize.
One Trill shall *h.* joy, grief, and rage *D.* iv. 57
I learn to smooth and *h.* my Mind *S.* vi. 203

Harmony.
The body's *h.*, the beaming soul *D.* iv. 236
Were there all *h.*, all virtue here *E.M.* i. 165
All Discord, *H.* not understood *E.M.* i. 291
Such is the World's great *h.*, that springs *E.M.* iii. 295

Harms.
Diffusing blessings, or averting *h.* *E.M.* iii. 312

Harness.
A Pension, or such *H.* for a slave *S.* iii. 87

Harp.
Presents her *h.* still to his fingers *Mi.* xii. 8
His living *h.*, and lofty Denham sung *W.F.* 280
To sounds of heav'nly h—s she dies away *E.A.* 221
With simp'ring Angels, Palms, and *H.* divine *M.E.* ii. 14

Harpax.
They might (were *H.* not too wise to spend) (rep.) *M.E.* iii. 91
Bond is but one, but *H.* is a score *S.* i. 44

Harpy.
Oldfield, with more than *H.* throat endu'd *S.* ii. 25

Harridan.
And in four months a batter'd *H.* *Mi.* iii. 24

Harries.
Of all our *H.*, all our Edwards talk *S.* viii. 105

Harshness.
'Tis not enough no *h.* gives offence *E.C.* 364

Hart.
Bleeds in the Forest like a wounded *h.* *W.F.* 84
Rouse the fleet *h.*, and cheer the opening hound *W.F.* 150
Like royal H—s, be never more run down *E.S.* ii. 29

Hartshorn.
H., or something that shall close your eyes *S.* i. 20

Harvest.
Thine the full *h.* of the golden year *E.M.* iii. 39
Bids seed-time, *h.*, equal course maintain *M.E.* iii. 165
To lay this *h.* up, and hoard with haste *S.* iii. 21
The *H.* early, but mature the praise *S.* v. 24
And swell the future *h.* of the field *W.* 16
And heavy h—s nod beneath the snow *D.* i. 78
Or reap'd in iron *h.* of the field *E.M.* iv. 12
Deep *H.* bury all his pride has plano'd *M.E.* iv. 175
O'er sandy wilds were yellow *h.* spread *W.F.* 88
And *h.* on a hundred realms bestows *W.F.* 360

Has, Hast.—Passim.

Hash.
The Doctor's Wormwood style, the *H.* of tongues *S.* viii. 52

Hash'd.
What Gellius or Stobæus *h.* before *D.* iv. 231

Haste.
I hurry me in *h.* away *I.H.* ii. 45 s
To lay this harvest up, and hoard with *h.* *S.* iii. 21

HASTES—HEAD.

H. then, ye spirits! to your charge repair *R.L.* ii. 111
Now rise, and *h.* to yonder woodbine bow'rs *Sp.* 97

Hastes.
How quick Ambition *h.* to ridicule *D.* iv. 547
See Nature *h.* her earliest wreaths to bring *M.* 23

Hasty.
How Shadwell *h.*, Wycherley was slow *S.* v. 85

Hat.
His *H.*, which never vail'd to human pride *D.* iv. 205
Walker! our *h.*"—nor more he deign'd to say *D.* iv. 273
With scarlet h—s wide-waving circled round D. ii. 14
Broad *h.*, and hoods, and caps, a sable shoal *D.* iv. 190

Hatch.
To *h.* a new Saturnian age of Lead *D.* i. 28

Hatchet.
His Saws are toothless, and his *H.*'s Lead *E.S.* ii. 149

Hate.
And public faction doubles private *h. E.C.* 457
H., Fear, and Grief, the family of Pain *E.M.* ii. 118
From spleen, from obstinacy, *h.*, or fear *E.M.* ii. 186
As show'd, Vice had his *h.* and pity too *Ep.* i. 8
A love to Peace, and *h.* of Tyranny *Ep.* ii. 10
Nor more a storm her *H.* than Gratitude *M.E.* ii. 132
Much injur'd Blunt! why bears he Britain's *h. M.E.* iii. 133
Oh curs'd effects of civil *h. O.* ii. 29
P—x'd by her love, or libell'd by her *h. S.* i. 84
Poor and disarm'd, and hardly worth your *h. S.* vii. 12
Beheld such scenes of envy, sin, and *h. S.* viii. 193
Whate'er he gives, are giv'n for you to h. D. iii. 222
How often must it love, how often *h. E.A.* 198
Forget, renounce me, *h.* whate'er was mine *E.A.* 294
Sure to *h.* most the men from whom they learn'd *E.C.* 107
I can't—indeed now—I so *h.* a whore *E.J.S.* 6
Who most to shun or *h.* Mankind pretend *E.M.* iv. 43
When Flatt'ry glares, all *h.* it in a Queen *M.E.* i. 61
As when she touch'd the brink of all we *h. M.E.* ii. 52
Love, if it makes her yield, must make her *h. M.E.* ii. 134
Oblige her, and she'll *h.* you while you live *M.E.* ii. 138
Yet *h.* repose, and dread to be alone *M.E.* ii. 228
T' enrich a Bastard, or a Son they *h. M.E.* iii. 98
Each does but *h.* his neighbour as himself *M.E.* iii. 107
And complaisantly help'd to all I *h. M.E.* iv. 164
And *h.* for arts that caus'd himself to rise *P.S.* 200
Ev'n those you touch not, *h.* you. What should ail them *S.* i. 41
Now Whig, now Tory, what we lov'd we *h. S.* v. 157
This Town, I had the sense to *h.* it too *S.* vii. 2

Hated.
By fools 'tis *h.*, and by knaves undone *E.C.* 507
As, to be *h.*, needs but to be seen *E.M.* ii. 218

Hateful.
Nor ardent warriours meet with *h.* eyes *M.* 58
But Umbriel, *h.* Gnome, forbears not so *R.L.* iv. 141
There *h.* Envy her own snakes shall feel *W.F.* 419

Hates.
Oh fool! to think God *h.* the worthy mind *E.M.* iv. 189
And ev'ry child *h.* Shylock, tho' his soul *M.E.* i. 55
Yet is, whate'er she *h.* and ridicules *M.E.* ii. 120
Bond damns the Poor, and *h.* them from his heart *M.E.* iii. 100
At court, who *h.* whate'er he read at school *S.* v. 106

Haughty.
The fawning Servant turns a *h.* Lord *E.* iv. 44
Spite of his *h.* mien and barb'rous pride *R.L.* iii. 70
He spits fore-right; his *h.* chest before *S.* viii. 264
Our *h.* Norman boasts that barb'rous name *W.F.* 63

Haunt.
(*H.* of the Muses) made their safe retreat *D.* ii. 428
Who *h.* Parnassus but to please their ear *E.J.* 111
And *h.* their slumbers in the pompous shade *E.M.* iv. 304
Those Cares that *h.* the Court and Town *I.H.* ii. 132
And *h.* the places where their Honour died *M.E.* ii. 242
And lonely woodcocks *h.* the wat'ry glade *W.F.* 128
Seek the clear spring, or *h.* the pathless grove *W.F.* 168

Haunted.
Dreadful as hermit's dreams in *h.* shades *R.L.* iv. 41

Haunts.
Celestial Venus *h.* Idalia's groves *Sp.* 65
And chaste Diana *h.* the forest-shade *Su.* 62

Hautgout.
The nose of *H.*, and the Tip of Taste *M.E.* ii. 80

Have.—*Passim.*

Hawk.
Or hears the *h.* when Philomela sings *E.M.* iii. 56

Hawkers.
By herald *H.*, high heroic Games *D.* ii. 18
Or smoking forth, a hundred h.' load P.S. 217

Hawthorns.
Now *h.* blossom, now the daisies spring *Sp.* 42

Hays.
Wash Bladen white, and expiate *H.*'s stain *D.* iv. 560

Hazard.
Early at Bus'ness, and at *H.* late *M.E.* i. 73

Hazarded.
Nor dar'd an Oath, nor *h.* a Lie *P.S.* 397

Hazardia.
H. blush'd, and turn'd her Head aside *Mi.* ix. 41

He.—*Passim.*

Head.
Ere Pallas issu'd from the Thund'rer's *h. D.* i. 10
That slipp'd thro' Cracks and Zig-zags of the *h. D.* i. 124
To this one *h.* like bias to the bowl *D.* i. 170
O'er *h.* and ears plunge for the Commonweal *D.* i. 210
Rous'd by the light, old Dulness heav'd the *h. D.* i. 257
The Goddess then, o'er his anointed *h. D.* i. 287
With pert flat eyes she window'd well its *h. D.* ii. 43
So lab'ring on with shoulders, hands, and *h. D.* ii. 65
The stream, and, smoking, flourish'd o'er his *h. D.* ii. 180
Now at his *h.* the dext'rous task commence *D.* ii. 199
He brings up half the bottom on his *h. D.* ii. 321
Hung silent down his never-blushing *h. D.* ii. 427
On Dulness' lap th' Anointed *h.* repos'd *D.* iii. 2
And Bacon trembling for his brazen *h. D.* iii. 104
Break Priscian's *h.*, and Pegasus's neck *D.* iii. 162
A Lumber-house of books in ev'ry *h. D.* iii. 193
His never-blushing *h.* he turn'd aside *D.* iii. 231
While op'ning Hell spouts wild-fire at your *h. D.* iii. 316
She mounts the Throne: her *h.* a cloud conceal'd *D.* iv. 17
Had not her Sister Satire held her *h. D.* iv. 42
In patch-work flutt'ring, and her *h.* aside *D.* iv. 48
And strong impulsive gravity of *H. D.* iv. 76
Withhold the pension, and set up the *h. D.* iv. 96
Thine is the genuine *h.* of many a house *D.* iv. 243
For thee we dim the eyes, and stuff the *h. D.* iv. 249
With nothing but a Solo in his *h. D.* iv. 324
Benigner influence on thy nodding *h. D.* iv. 346
But pour them thickest on the noble *h. D.* iv. 358
Rattling an ancient Sistrum at his *h. D.* iv. 374
Bright with the gilded button tipt its *h. D.* iv. 408
The *h.* that turns at super-lunar things *D.* iv. 451
A trifling *h.*, and a contracted heart *D.* iv. 504
A *Feather*, shooting from another's *h. D.* iv. 521
Knight lifts the *h.*, for what are crowds undone *D.* iv. 561
Mountains of Casuistry heap'd o'er her *h. D.* iv. 642
What the weak *h.* with strongest bias rules *E.C.* 203
Nay should great Homer lift his awful *h. E.C.* 464
With loads of learned lumber in his *h. E.C.* 613
Shakes off the dust, and rears his rev'rend *h. E.C.* 700
The clearest *h.*, and the sincerest heart *E.C.* 732
You might have held the pretty *h.* aside *E.J.S.* 3
Or hand, to toil, aspir'd to be the *h.* (*rep.*) *E.M.* i. 260
Whatever warms the heart, or fills the *h. E.M.* ii. 141
'Twas then the studious *h.* or gen'rous mind *E.M.* iii. 283
Plays round the *h.*, but comes not to the heart *E.M.* iv. 254
Mounts the Tribunal, lifts her scarlet *h. E.S.* i. 149
Or any good creature shall lay o'er my *h. Ep.* xvi. 4
See lofty Lebanon his *h.* advance *M.* 25

Exalt thy tow'ry *h.*, and lift thy eyes *M.* 86
His comprehensive *h.* / all Int'rests weigh'd *M.E.* i. 83
Her *H.'s* untouch'd, that noble Seat of Thought *M.E.* ii. 74
She bids her Footman put it in her *h. M.E.* ii. 178
With spurning heels, and with a butting *h. M.E.* iii. 68
Like a tall bully, lifts the *h.*, and lies *M.E.* iii. 340
With aspect open shall erect his *h. M.E.* v. 65
HAZARDIA blush'd, and turn'd her *H.* aside *Mi.* ix. 41
Melancholy lifts her *h. O.* i. 30
With honest anguish, and an aching *h. P.S.* 38
Just so immortal *Maro* held his *h. P.S.* 122
Ev'n mitred Rochester would nod the *h. P.S.* 140
And a true *Pindar* stood without a *h. P.S.* 236
Can sleep without a Poem in my *h. P.S.* 269
The trifling *h.* or the corrupted heart *P.S.* 327
The distant threats of vengeance on his *h. P.S.* 348
The morning-dream that hover'd o'er her *h. R.L.* i. 22
But all the vision vanish'd from thy *h. R.L.* i. 120
With *h.* uncover'd, the Cosmetic pow'rs *R.L.* i. 124
These set the *h.*, and those divide the hair *R.L.* i. 146
Superior by the *h.*, was Ariel plac'd *R.L.* ii. 70
What boots the regal circle on his *h. R.L.* iii. 71
As o'er the fragrant steams she bends her *h. R.L.* iii. 134
From the fair *h.*, for ever and for ever *R.L.* iii. 154
Pain at her side, and Megrim at her *h. R.L.* iv. 24
Practis'd to lisp, and hang the *h.* aside *R.L.* iv. 33
For this with fillets strain'd your tender *h. R.L.* iv. 101
Clipp'd from the lovely *h.* where late it grew *R.L.* iv. 136
The long-contended honours of her *h. R.L.* iv. 140
On her heav'd bosom hung her drooping *h. R.L.* v. 145
Not all the tresses that fair *h.* can boast *R.L.* v. 143
Fools rush into my *h.*, and so I write *S.* i. 14
My *h.* and heart thus flowing thro' my quill *S.* i. 63
God knows, may hurt the very ablest *h. S.* vi. 103
And shook his *h.* at Murray, as a Wit *S.* vi. 132
Grave, as when pris'ners shake the *h.*, and swear *S.* vii. 69
Those monkey tails that wag behind their *h. S.* viii. 247
Her cheerful *h.*, and leads the golden years *W.F.* 92
Old father Thames advanc'd his rev'rend *h. W.F.* 330
A hundred *h.* of *Aristotle's friends D.* iv. 192
For her, the lilies hang their h—s *and die A.* 26
Ye Critics ! in whose *h.* as equal scales *D.* ii. 367
Their *h.*, and lift them as they cease to blow (*rep.*) *D.* ii. 392
Round and more round, o'er all the *sea of* h. *D.* ii. 410
Which only *h.* refin'd from Reason know *D.* iii. 6
And empty *h.* console with empty sound *D.* iv. 542
Whose *H.* she partly, whose completely, blest *D.* iv. 622
O'er the pale marble they shall join their *h. E.A.* 349
Those *h.*, as stomachs, are not sure the best *E.C.* 388
While their weak *h.*, like towns unfortify'd *E.C.* 434
And turn their *h.* to imitate the Sun *E.M.* ii. 28
All states can reach it, and all *h.* conceive *E.M.* iv. 30
With *h* declin'd, ye cedars, homage pay *M.* 35
And snakes uncurl'd hang list'ning round their *h. O.* i. 70
Caps on their *h.* and halberts in their hand *R.L.* iii. 42
If e'er with airy horns I planted *h. R.L.* iv. 71
Full o'er their *h.* the swelling bag he rent *R.L.* iv. 91
And beastly Skelton *H.* of Houses quote *S.* v. 38
From *h.* to ears, and now from ears to eyes *S.* v. 313
Hang o'er their coursers' *h.* with eager speed *W.F.* 157
Not plagu'd with h.-*aches or the want of rhyme E.*v.42
Or discompos'd the *h.-dress* of a prude *R.L.* iv. 74

Headless.
To *h.* Phœbe his fair bride postpone *D.* iv. 367

Headlong.
Of smell, the *h.* lioness between *E.M.* i. 213
And *h.* streams hang list'ning in their fall *Su.* 84
The *h.* mountains, and the downward skies *W.F.* 212

Heads.
And *h.* the bold Train-bands, and burns a Pope *M.E.* iii. 214

Heady.
H., not strong ; o'erflowing, tho' not full *D.* iii. 172

Heal.
Or *h.*, old Narses, thy obscener ail *M.E.* iii. 89
To cure thy lambs, but not to *h.* thy heart *Su.* 34

Healing.
Still spread a *h.* mist before the mind *D.* i. 174
But Welsted most the Poet's *h.* balm *D.* ii. 207

From pois'nous herbs extracts the *h.* dew *E.M.* i. 220
That Jeffy's rich, this Malmsey's *h. I.H.* ii. 202
The sick and weak the *h.* plant shall aid *M.* 15
A branch of *h.* Spleenwort in his hand *R.L.* iv. 56

Heals.
As Poison *h.*, in just proportion us'd *M.E.* iii. 234
And *h.* with Morals, what it hurts with Wit *S.* v. 262

Health.
For me, *h.* gushes from a thousand springs *E.M.* i. 138
In all the madness of superfluous *h. E.M.* iii. 3
Lie in three words, *H.*, Peace, and Competence (*rep.*) *E.M.* iv. 80
No—shall the good want *H.*, the good want Pow'r (*rep.*) *E.M.* iv. 158
With Splendour, Charity; with Plenty, *H. M.E.* iii. 225
H. to the sick, and solace to the swain *M.E.* iii. 258
There, Victor of his *h.*, of fortune, friends *M.E.* iii. 313
H. to himself, and to his Infants bread *M.E.* iv. 170
Long *H.*, long Youth, long Pleasure, and a Friend *Mi.* v. 2
In *h.* of body, peace of mind *O.* iv. 11
First *H.*: The stomach (cramm'd from ev'ry dish *S.* ii. 69
Ill *h.* some just indulgence may engage *S.* ii. 87
He gathers *h.* from herbs the forest yields *W.F.* 241
Then cheerful h—s (*your Mistress shall have place*) *S.* ii. 149

Healthful.
Whose life is *h.*, and whose conscience clear *E.M.* iv. 191

Healthy.
H. by temp'rance, and by exercise *P.S.* 401

Heap.
Forth from the *h.* she pluck'd her Vot'ry's pray'r *D.* ii. 95
One glaring Chaos and wild *h.* of wit *E.C.* 292
As the last image of that troubled *h. M.E.* i. 45
My wealth unwieldy, and my *h.* too great *S.* ii. 114
Or to thy country let that *h.* be lent *S.* ii. 121
I melt down Ancients like a *h.* of snow *S.* v. 63
Yes, Sir, how small soever be my *h. S.* vi. 284
A *h.* of dust alone remains of thee *U.L.* 73
And buries madmen in the h—s *they raise E.M.* iv. 76
In *h.*, like Ambergrise, a stink it lies *M.E.* iii. 235
Lo, what huge *h.* of littleness around *M.E.* iv. 109
Expos'd in glorious *h.* the tempting Bank *Mi.* ix. 78
In *h.* on *h.* ; one fate o'erwhelms them all *R.L.* iii. 86
O'er *h.* of ruin stalk'd the stately hind *W.F.* 62
Poets *b. Virtues, Painters Gents at will M.E.* ii. 185
For some to *h.*, and some to throw away *M.E.* iii. 6

Heap'd.
Mountains of Casuistry *h.* o'er her head *D.* iv. 642
And *h.* with products of Sabæan springs *M.* 94

Heaps.
The good man *h.* up nothing but mere metre *S.* v. 198

Hear.
H., Jove ! whose name my bards I adore *D.* ii. 79
The first thus open'd: "*H.* thy suppliant's call *D.* iv. 403
But *h.* a Mother, when she recommends *D.* iv. 439
No more, alas ! the voice of Fame they *h. D.* iv. 543
Still *h.* thy Parnell in his living lays *E.* i. 16
And *h.* a spark, yet think no danger nigh *E.* v. 4
I *h.* thee, view thee, gaze o'er all thy charms *E.A.* 233
I wake :—no more I *h.*, no more I view *E.A.* 235
Thy voice I seem in ev'ry hymn to *h. E.A.* 269
H. how learn'd Greece her useful rules indites *E.C.* 92
H., in all tongues consenting Pæans ring *E.C.* 186
H. how Timotheus' vary'd lays surprize *E.C.* 374
So from a sister sinner you shall *h. E.7.S.* 9
Just what you'*h.*, you have, and what's unknown *E.M.* iv. 239
H. her black Trumpet thro' the Land proclaim *E.S.* i. 159
But *h.* me further—Japhet, 'tis agreed *E.S.* ii. 185
Who knew no wish but what the world might *h. Ep.* vii. 6
H. him, ye deaf, and all ye blind, behold *M.* 98
No sigh, no murmur the wide world shall *h. M.* 45
And starts, amidst the thirsty wilds to *h. M.* 69
But none of Chloe's shall you ever *h. M.E.* ii. 174
She, who can love a Sister's charms, or *h. M.E.* ii. 259
H. then the truth : 'Tis Heav'n each Passion sends *M.E.* iii. 159
And now the Chapel's silver bell you *h. M.E.* iv. 141

HEARD—HEART.

H. me pay my dying Vows *Mi.* vii. 24
The Woman's deaf, and does not *h. Mi.* viii. 12
And giddy Factions *h.* away their rage *O.* i. 35
To *h.* the Poet's pray'r *O.* i. 84
And Angels lean from heav'n to *h. O.* i. 130
As Cato's self had not disdain'd to *h. P.C.* 45
Thou unconcern'd canst *h.* the mighty crack *P.S.* 86
H. this, and spare his family, James Moore *P.S.* 385
H. and believe! thy own importance know *R.L.* i. 35
Fays, Fairies, Genii, Elves, and Dæmons *h. R.L.* ii. 74
H. me, and touch Belinda with chagrin *R.L.* iv. 77
Already *h.* the horrid things they say *R.L.* iv. 108
H. this, and tremble I you who 'scape the Laws *S.* i. 118
H. BETHEL's Sermon, one not vers'd in schools *S.* ii. 9
Now *h.* what blessings Temperance can bring *S.* ii. 67
Unworthy he, the voice of Fame to *h. S.* ii. 99
'Tis Reason's voice, which sometimes one can *h. S.* iii. 12
His French is pure; his Voice too—you shall *h. S.* vi. 7
A Poet begs me, I will *h.* him read *S.* vi. 93
You go to Church to *h.* these Flatt'rers preach *S.* vi. 225
H. how the birds, on ev'ry bloomy spray *Sp.* 23
H. what from Love unpractis'd hearts endure *Su.* 11
The moving mountains *h.* the pow'rful call *Su.* 83
A sweeter music than their own to *h. W.* 58
I *h.* soft music die along the grove *W.F.* 268

Heard.

The Classics of an Age that *h.* of none *D.* i. 148
Oft had the Goddess *h.* her Servants call *D.* ii. 97
Now thousand tongues are *h.* in one loud din *D.* ii. 235
She *h.*, and drove him to th' Hibernian shore *D.* iv. 70
Saw ev'ry Court, *h.* ev'ry King declare *D.* iv. 313
And *h.* thy ever-lasting yawn confess *D.* iv. 343
And saints with wonder *h.* the vows I made *E.A.* 114
From yonder shrine I *h.* a hollow sound *E.A.* 308
But when be *h.* th' Affront the Fellow gave *E.S.* ii. 152
The Senate *h.* him, and his Country lov'd *Ep.* xiv. 8
What sounds were *h. O.* i. 53
A lost Bank-bill, or *h.* their Son was drown'd *S.* ii. 56
As Heav'n's own Oracles from Altars *h. S.* v. 28
H., noted, answer'd, as in full debate *S.* vi. 187
Henley himself I've *h.*, and Budget too *S.* viii. 51
Thames *h.* the numbers as he flow'd along *W.* 13
Succeeding monarchs *h.* the subjects' cries *W.F.* 85

Hearing.

Of *h.*, from the life that fills the Flood *E.M.* i. 215

Hearken.

Can *h.* coldly to my SHARPER's Vows *Mi.* ix. 88
Or bush'd with wonder, *h.* from the sprays *W.* 56

Hearkens.

But some way leans and *h.* to the kind *E.M.* iv. 40

Hearne.

Rare monkish Manuscripts for *H.* alone *M.E.* iv. 9

Hears.

And *h.* the various vows of fond mankind *D.* ii. 87
He *h.* loud Oracles, and talks with Gods *D.* iii. 8
I call aloud; it *h.* not what I say *E.A.* 237
Sees God in clouds, or *h.* him in the wind *E.M.* i. 100
Or *h.* the hawk when Philomela sings *E.M.* iii. 36
Who, foe to Nature, *h.* the gen'ral groan *E.M.* iii. 163
Not for himself he sees, or *h.*, or eats *M.E.* iv. 5
Who *h.* him groan, and does not wish to bleed *P.C.* 26
What boy but *h.* the sayings of old Ben *S.* v. 80
Act sins which Prisca's Confessor scarce *h. S.* vii. 40
He *h.*, and as a Still with simples in it *S.* viii. 126
Now close behind, his sounding steps she *h. W.F.* 192

Hearse—*see* Herse.

Heart.

Who lost my *h.* while I preserv'd my sheep *A.* 80
First in my care, and ever at my *h. D.* i. 164
A brain of feathers, and a *h.* of lead *D.* ii. 44
To move, to raise, to ravish ev'ry *h. D.* ii. 223
See what the charms that smite the simple *h. D.* iii. 229
Let her thy *h.*, next Drabs and Dice, engage *D.* iii. 303
There to her *h.* sad Tragedy addrest *D.* iv. 37
A trifling head, and a contracted *h. D.* iv. 504
His *h.*, his mistress and his friend did share *E.* iv. 93
She sighs, and is no Duchess at her *h. E.* iv. 56
The willing *h.*, and only holds it long *E.* iv. 68
This steel shall stab it to the *h. E.* vi. 8
Why feels my *h.* its long-forgotten heat *E.A.* 6

Hide it, my *h.* within that close disguise *E.A.* 11
Her *h.* still dictates, and her hand obeys *E.A.* 16
Still rebel nature holds out half my *h. E.A.* 26
Excuse the blush, and pour out all the *h. E.A.* 56
And each warm wish springs mutual from the *h. E.A.* 96
Pant on thy lip, and to thy *h.* be press'd *E.A.* 123
Fill my fond *h.* with God alone, for he *E.A.* 205
Oppose thyself to heav'n; dispute my *h. E.A.* 282
When this rebellious *h.* shall beat no more *E.A.* 346
The *h.*, and all its end at once attains *E.C.* 155
The clearest head, and the sincerest *h. E.C.* 732
Our sex are still forgiving at their *h. E.J.S.* 12
As full, as perfect, in a hair as *h. E.M.* i. 276
Whatever warms the *h.*, or fills the head *E.M.* ii. 141
Ask your own *h.*, and nothing is so plain *E.M.* ii. 215
Plays round the head, but comes not to the *h. E.M.* iv. 254
Is this too little for the boundless *h. E.M.* iv. 355
From sounds to things, from fancy to the *h. E.M.* iv. 392
No cheek is known to blush, no *h.* to throb *E.S.* i. 103
Secker is decent, *Rundel* has a *h. E.S.* ii. 71
Or beam, good Digby, from a *h.* like thine *E.S.* ii. 241
May Heav'n, dear Father I now have all thy *H. Ep.* xiii. 2
Ends in the milder Merit of the *H. Ep.* xiv. 12
O for the *h.* of Homer's Mice *I.H.* ii. 214
Noble and young, who strikes the *h. I.H.* iii. 11
His hand unstain'd, his uncorrupted *h. M.E.* i. 82
And wanting nothing but an honest *h. M.E.* i. 193
A Tyrant to the wife his *h.* approves *M.E.* i. 202
'Twas thus Calypso once each *h.* alarm'd *M.E.* i. 45
Yet still a sad, good Christian at her *h. M.E.* ii. 68
Say, what can Chloe want? She wants a *H. M.E.* ii. 160
Then never break your *h.* when Chloe dies *M.E.* ii. 180
But ev'ry Woman is at *h.* a Rake *M.E.* ii. 216
To raise the Thought, and touch the *h.* be thine *M.E.* ii. 250
Bond damns the Poor, and hates them from his *h. M.E.* iii. 100
To ease th' oppress'd, and raise the sinking *h. M.E.* iii. 244
The Lab'rer bears: what his hard *H.* denies *M.E.* iv. 171
Glow in thy *h.*, and smile upon thy face *Mi.* v. 14
Gentle *Cupid*, o'er my *H. Mi.* vii. 2
A mightier grief my heavy *h.* sustains *Mi.* ix. 10
The cruel thought, that stabs me to the *h. Mi.* ix. 54
She dares to steal my Fav'rite Lover's *h. Mi.* ix. 66
What more than marble must that *h.* compose *Mi.* ix. 87
My panting *h.* confesses all his charms *Mi.* ix. 95
Who charm the sense, or mend the *h. O.* iii. 35
His *h.* now melts, now leaps, now burns *O.* iii. 35
To raise the genius, and to mend the *h. P.C.* 2
The trifling head, or the corrupted *h. P.S.* 327
No language, but the language of the *h. P.S.* 399
They shift the moving Toyshop of their *h. R.L.* i. 100
Or lose her *h.*, or necklace, at a ball *R.L.* ii. 109
An earthly Lover lurking at her *h. R.L.* iii. 144
My head and *h.* thus flowing thro' my quill *S.* i. 63
Bare the mean *H.* that lurks beneath a *Star S.* i. 108
To live on little with a cheerful *h. S.* ii. 2
But souse the cabbage with a bounteous *h. S.* ii. 60
And ease thy *h.* of all that it admires *S.* iii. 76
Why do, I'll follow them with all my *h. S.* iv. 133
With Pity, and with Terror, tear my *h. S.* iv. 345
But still I love the language of his *H. S.* v. 78
And pours each human Virtue in the *h. S.* v. 220
Hopkins and Sternhold glad the *h.* with Psalms *S.* v. 230
Tho' faith, I fear, 'twill break his Mother's *h. S.* vi. 16
Composing songs for Fools to get by *h. S.* vi. 126
I ask these sober questions of my *h. S.* vi. 211
The *h.* resolves this matter in a trice *S.* vi. 216
Yet still, not heeding what your *h.* can teach *S.* vi. 224
With foolish pride my *h.* was never fir'd *S.* viii. 9
And talks Gazettes and Post-boys o'er by *h. S.* viii. 155
I quaked at *h.*; and still afraid, to see *S.* viii. 180
Thy victim, Love, shall be the shepherd's *h. Sp.* 52
While in thy *h.* eternal winter reigns *Su.* 22
To cure thy lambs, but not to heal thy *h. Su.* 34
To bear too tender, or too firm a *h. U.L.* 7
And the last pang shall tear thee from his *h. U.L.* 80
If I am wrong, oh teach my *h. U.P.* 7
Oh, skill'd in Nature! see the h—s *of Swains A.* 11
Then Churchill's race shall other *h.* surprise *E.* iii. 59
The truest *h.* for Voiture heav'd with sighs *E.* iv. 17
Our *h.* may bear its slender chain a day *E.* iv. 64
In wit, as nature, what affects our *h. E.C.* 243

144　　　　　　　　HEARTY—HEAV'N.

The pow'r of music all our h. allow *E.C.* 382
In h. of Kings, or arms of Queens who lay *E.M.* iv. 289
Turn, turn, to willing h. your wanton fires *I.H.* iii. 8
And little h. to flutter at a Beau *R.L.* i. 90
And mighty h. are held in slender chains *R.L.* ii. 24
With beating h. the dire event they wait *R.L.* i. 141
Clubs, Diamonds, *H*., in wild disorder seen *R.L.* iii. 79
And wins (oh shameful chance!) the Queen of *H. R.L.* iii. 88
An Ace of *H.* steps forth : The King unseen *R.L.* iii. 95
And lovers' h. with ends of riband bound *R.L.* v. 118
Like nets or lime-twigs, for rich Widows' h. *S.* vii. 58
Dear Countess! you have charms all h. to hit *S.* viii. 232
Hear what from Love unpractis'd h. endure *Su.* 11
And curs'd with h. unknowing how to yield *U.L.* 42
Adieu, the h.-expanding bowl *I.H.* iii. 35
The soul's calm sunshine, and the h.-felt joy *E.M.* iv. 168

Hearty.
Whose laughs are h., tho' his jests are coarse *E.* v. 29
And makes her h. meal upon a dunce *M.E.* ii. 86

Heat.
While lab'ring oxen, spent with toil and h. *A.* 61
Fruits of dull *H*., and Sooterkins of Wit *D.* i. 126
Once brightest shin'd this child of *H.* and Air *D.* iv. 424
Why feels my heart its long-forgotten h. *E.A.* 6
From storms a shelter, and from h. a shade *M.* 16
Buy ev'ry stick of wood, that lends them h. *S.* vi. 242
They parch'd with h., and I inflam'd by thee *Su.* 20
But see, the shepherds shun the noonday h. *Su.* 85
When milder autumn summer's h. succeeds *W.F.* 97
Fond to spread friendships, but to cover h—s *S.* i. 136

Heath.
Ev'n the wild h. displays her purple dyes *W.F.* 25
Oft, as in airy rings they skim the h. *W.F.* 131

Heathcote.
H. himself, and such large-acred men *S.* vi. 240

Heathen.
Of arts, but thund'ring against h. love *D.* iii. 102
A very *H.* in the carnal part *M.E.* ii. 67

Heav'd.
Rous'd by the light old Dulness h. the head *D.* i. 257
The truest hearts for Voiture h. with sighs *R.* v. 17
On her h. bosom hung her drooping head *R.L.* iv. 145
H. by the breath th' inspiring bellows blow *S.* vii. 19

Heav'n.
Yet sure had *H.* decreed to save the state (rep.) *D.* i. 195
H. rings with laughter. Of the laughter vain *D.* ii. 121
Puts his last refuge all in h. and pray'r *D.* ii. 214
Hell rises, *H.* descends, and dance on earth *D.* iii. 237
Breaks out refulgent, with a h. its own *D.* iii. 242
Avert it, *H. !* that thou, vil Cibber, e'er *D.* iii. 287
To aid our cause if *H.* thou canst not bend *D.* iii. 307
Philosophy, that lean'd on *H.* before *D.* iv. 643
There starve and pray, for that's the way to h. *E.* v. 22
H. first taught letters for some wretch's aid *E.A.* 51
Guiltless I gaz'd ; h. list'ned while you sung *E.A.* 65
Nor eavy them that h. I lose for thee *E.A.* 72
H. scarce believ'd the Conquest it survey'd *E.A.* 113
Here brib'd the rage of ill-requited h. *E.A.* 138
Assist me, h. ! but whence arose that pray'r *E.A.* 179
Now turn'd to h., I weep my past offence *E.A.* 187
But let h. seize it, all at once 'tis fir'd *E.A.* 201
Tears that delight, and sighs that waft to h. *E.A.* 214
And mild as op'ning gleams of promis'd h. *E.A.* 256
Oppose thyself to h. ; dispute my heart *E.A.* 282
Devotion's self shall steal a thought from *H. E.A.* 357
Both must alike from *H.* derive their light *E.C.* 13
Some, to whom *H.* in wit has been profuse *E.C.* 80
She drew from thence what they deriv'd from *H. E.C.* 99
" Not so, by *H*." (he answers in a rage) *E.C.* 28:
May tell why *H.* has made us what we are *E.M.* i. 28
Then say not Man's imperfect, *H.* in fault *E.M.* i. 69
H. from all creatures hides the book of Fate *E.M.* i. 77
That each may fill the circle mark'd by *H. E.M.* i. 81
Behind the cloud-topt hill, an humbler h. *E.M.* i. 104
Why charge we *H.* to those, in these acquit *E.M.* i. 163
Is *H.* unkind to Man, and Man alone *E.M.* i. 186
T' inspect a mite, not comprehend the h. *E.M.* i. 196
How would he wish that *H.* had left him still *E.M.* i. 203
Of blindness, weakness, *H.* bestows on thee *E.M.* i. 284

H. forming each on other to depend *E.M.* ii. 249
The poor contents him with the care of *H. E.M.* ii. 266
The birds of *H.* shall vindicate their grain *E.M.* iii. 38
To each unthinking being *H.* a friend *E.M.* iii. 71
Great standing miracle ! that *H.* assigned *E.M.* iii. 77
And hell was built on spite, and *H.* on pride *E.M.* iii. 262
H. to mankind impartial we confess *E.M.* iv. 53
H. breathes thro' ev'ry member of the whole *E.M.* iv. 61
H. still with laughter the vain toil surveys *E.M.* iv. 75
Say was it Virtue, more tho' *H.* ne'er gave *E.M.* iv. 103
Lean *H.* a parent to the poor and me *E.M.* iv. 110
We just as wisely might of *H.* complain *E.M.* iv. 117
Why is not Man a God, and Earth a *H. E.M.* iv. 162
Weak, foolish man! will *H.* reward us there *E.M.* iv. 173
See the sole bliss *H.* could on all bestow *E.M.* iv. 327
Joins h. and earth, and mortal and divine *E.M.* iv. 334
And *H.* beholds its image in his breast *E.M.* iv. 372
Silent and soft, as Saints remove to *H. E.S.* i. 93
Good *H.* forbid, that I should blast their glory *E.S.* i. 105
To *Berkeley* ev'ry Virtue under *H. E.S.* ii. 73
H., as it purest gold, by Tortures try'd *Ep.* v. 9
Kneller, by *H.*, and not a Master, taught *Ep.* viii. 1
Whom *H.* kept sacred from the Proud and Great *Ep.* x. 4
Thank'd *H.* that he had liv'd, and that he died *Ep.* x. 10
May *H.*, dear Father ! now have all thy heart *Ep.* xiii. 2
Yes, "SAVE MY COUNTRY, *H. !*"—he said, and died *Ep.* xiii. 8
Pays the last Tribute of a Saint to *H. Ep.* xiv. 14
And white-rob'd Innocence from h. descend *M.* 20
See h. its sparkling portals wide display *M.* 97
"Oh, save my Country, *H. !*" shall be your last *M.E.* i. 265
Forbid it *H.*, a Favour or a Debt *M.E.* ii. 171
Which *H.* has varnish'd out, and made a Queen *M.E.* ii. 182
H., when it strives to polish all it can *M.E.* ii. 271
That Man was made the standing jest of *H. M.E.* iii. 4
And surely, *H.* and I are of a mind *M.E.* iii. 8
Then careful *H.* supply'd two sorts of Men *M.E.* iii. 13
No Grace of *H.* or token of th' Elect *M.E.* iii. 18
To some indeed, *H.* grants the happier fate *M.E.* iii. 97
Hear then the truth: "'Tis *H.* each Passion sends *M.E.* iii. 159
And ease, or emulate, the care of *H. M.E.* iii. 230
H. visits with a Taste the wealthy fool *M.E.* iv. 17
Good Sense, which only is the gift of *H. M.E.* iv. 43
Make the soul dance upon a Jig to *H. M.E.* iv. 144
Oh be thou blest with all that *H.* can send *Mi.* v. 1
May TOM, whom h. sent down to raise *Mi.* xii. 15
And Angels lean from h. to hear *O.* i. 130
Hers lifts the soul to h. *O.* i. 134
H. opens on my eyes ! my ears *O.* v. 14
But what with pleasure *H.* itself surveys *P.C.* 20
May *H.*, to bless those days, preserve my friend *P.S.* 415
Thus far was right, the rest belongs to *H. P.S.* 419
But h. reveals not what, or how, or where *R.L.* i. 111
Propitious *h.*, and ev'ry pow'r ador'd *R.L.* ii. 36
Or whether *H.* has doom'd that Shock must fall *R.L.* ii. 110
Not louder shrieks to pitying h. are cast *R.L.* iii. 157
Jove's thunder roars, h. trembles all around *R.L.* v. 49
So h. decrees ! with h. who can contest *R.L.* v. 112
" Pray h. it last !" (cries Swift !) " as you go on *S.* ii. 161
Nay, half in h., except (what's mighty odd) *S.* iii. 187
Milton's strong pinion now not *H.* can bound *S.* v. 99
And *H.* is won by Violence of Song *S.* v. 240
There are who have not—and thank h. there are *S.* vi. 266
Is it, in h., a crime to love too well *U.L.* 6
That, more than *H.* pursue *U.P.* 16
Let nature change, let h. and earth deplore *W.* 27
Or looks on h. with more than mortal eyes *W.F.* 253
From h. itself tho' sev'nfold Nilus flows *W.F.* 359
H.'s *twinkling sparks draw light, and point their horns D.* ii. 12
H. Swiss, who fight for any God, or Man *D.* ii. 358
The common Soul of *H.* more frugal make *D.* iv. 441
All is not *H.* while Abelard has part *E.A.* 35
Where *H.* free subjects might their rights dispute *E.C.* 548
If Man alone engross not *H.* high care *E.M.* i. 119
If plagues or earthquakes break not *H.* design *E.M.* i. 155
H. whole foundations to their centre nod *E.M.* i. 255
As *H.* blest beam turns vinegar more sour *E.M.* ii. 148

HEAV'NLY—HELL. 145

But *H*. great view is One, and that the Whole *E.M.* ii. 238
H. attribute was Universal Care *E.M.* iii. 159
With *H*. own thunders shook the world below *E.M.* iii. 267
Order is *H*. first law ; and this confest *E.M.* iv. 49
But *H*. great balance Equal will appear *E.M.* iv. 69
One thinks on Calvin *H*. own spirit fell *E.M.* iv. 137
If Calvin feel *H*. blessing, or its rod *E.M.* iv. 139
Let *Envy* howl, while *H*. whole Chorus rings *E.S.* ii. 242
Go live ! for *H*. Eternal Year is thine *Ep.* vii. 9
Born where *H*. influence scarce can penetrate *M.E.* i. 142
As *H*. own Oracles from Altars heard *S.* v. 28
Charge them with *H*. Artill'ry, bold Divine *S.* viii. 281
Thro' half the h—s *he pours th' exalted urn D.* ii. 183
H.! what a pile ! whole ages perish there *D.* iii. 77
H. not his own, and worlds unknown before *E.M.* iii. 106
And Those, new *H*. and Systems fram'd *I.H.* iv. 72
Ye *H.!* from high the dewy Nectar pour *M.* 13
Or helps th' ambitious Hill the *h*. to scale *M.E.* iv. 59
H.! was I born for nothing but to write *P.S.* 272
So Rome's great founder to the *h*. withdrew *R.L.* v. 125
The *h*. bespangling with dishevell'd light *R.L.* v. 130
H., what new wounds ! and how her old have bled *W.F.* 322
Oh h.-born *sisters* ! *source of art O.* ii. 9
To all but *H.-directed* hands deny'd *E.S.* ii. 214
Or wanders, *H*., to the Poor *M.E.* ii. 150
Who taught that *h*. spire to rise *M.E.* iii. 261

Heav'nly.

Each *h*. piece unwearied we compare *E.* iii. 35
To sounds of *h*. harps she dies away *E.A.* 221
Oh Grace serene ! oh virtue *h*. fair *E.A.* 297
Ask for what end the *h*. bodies shine *E.M.* i. 131
To *h*. themes sublimer strains belong *M.* 2
To *Basset's h*. Joys, and pleasing Cares *Mi.* ix. 102
Where *h*. visions Plato fir'd *O.* ii. 3
Vital spark of *h*. flame *O.* v. 1
With golden crowns and wreaths of *h*. flow'rs *R.L.* i. 34
A *h*. image in the glass appears *R.L.* i. 2
And *h*. breasts with human passions rage *R.L.* v. 46
What *h*. particle inspires the clay *S.* ii. 78
Since fate relentless stopp'd their *h*. voice *W.F.* 277
Then fill'd the groves, as *h*. Mira now *W.F.* 298
Where h.-pensive *contemplation dwells E.A.* 2

Heaves.

Who *h*. old Ocean, and who wings the storms *E.M.* i. 158

Heavier.

Which *h*. Reason labours at in vain *E.M.* iii. 92

Heaviness.

I weigh what author's *h*. prevails *D.* ii. 368
Safe in its *h*., shall never stray *D.* iii. 295

Heavy.

Laborious, *h*., busy, bold, and blind *D.* i. 15
And *h*. harvests nod beneath the snow *D.* i. 78
Thro' the long, *h*., painful page drawl on *D.* ii. 388
See Christians, Jews, one *h*. sabbath keep *D.* iii. 99
A *h*. Lord shall hang at ev'ry Wit *D.* iv. 132
See ! still thy own, the *h*. Cannon roll *D.* iv. 247
As *h*. mules are neither horse nor ass *E.C.* 39
A mightier grief my *h*. heart sustains *Mi.* ix. 10
By whose vile arts this *h*. grief I bear *Mi.* ix. 56
Th' impending woe sat *h*. on his breast *R.L.* ii. 54

Hebrus.

Or where *H*. wanders *O.* i. 99

Hecatomb.

A *h*. of pure unsully'd lays *D.* i. 158
No, 'tis a Temple, and a *H. M.E.* iv. 156
What slaughter'd h—s, *what floods of wine M.E.* iii. 203
Some beasts were kill'd, tho' not whole *h. S.* vii. 116

Hectors.

I only wear it in a land of *H. S.* i. 71

Heed.

But, Friend, take *h*. whom you attack *E.* vi. 17
Ben, old and poor, as little seem'd to h. *S.* v. 73
That Bear or Elephant shall *h*. thee more *S.* v. 325
Another, not to *h*. to treasure more *S.* vi. 293

Heeded.

Poems I *h*. (now be-rhym'd so long) *P.S.* 221

Heeding.

Yet still, not *h*. what your heart can teach *S.* vi. 224

Heeds.

Nor *h*. the brown dishonours of his face *D.* ii. 108

Heels.

Than Cæsar with a Senate at his *h. E.M.* iv. 258
With spurning *h*., and with a butting head *M.E.* iii. 68
Bulls aim their horns, and Asses lift their *h. S.* i. 86

Heideggre.

Something betwixt a *H*. and Owl *D.* i. 290

Heifer.

The milky *h*., and deserving steed *M.E.* iv. 186
Nor thirsty h—s *seek the gliding flood W.* 38

Height.

He said, and climbed a lighter's stranded *h. D.* ii. 287
No monstrous *h*., or breadth, or length appear *E.C.* 251
And *h*. of bliss but *h*. of Charity *E.M.* iv. 360
Triumphant Umbriel on a sconce's *h. R.L.* v. 53
To teach their frugal Virtues to his *H. S.* v. 166
H. urges *h*., like wave impelling wave *S.* vi. 253
My *h*. may sigh, and think it want of grace *S.* vi. 286
Out-cant old Esdras, or out-drink his *h. S.* vii. 37
Immortal h—s *of universal praise E.C.* 190
To me and to my *H*. for ever *I.H.* ii. 12 s
What can they give ? to dying Hopkins, *H. M.E.* iii. 85
The smiles of harlots, and the tears of *h. R.L.* v. 120
Not more of bastardy in *h*. to crowns *S.* vii. 82

Heires.

The deeds, and dextrously omits *ses h. S.* vii. 100

Held.

This the Great Mother dearer *h*. than all *D.* i. 269
Fear *h*. them mute. Alone, untaught to fear *D.* ii. 57
But *h*. in ten-fold bonds the *Muses* lie *D.* iv. 35
Had not her Sister Satire *h*. her head *D.* iv. 42
H. forth the virtue of the dreadful wand *D.* iv. 140
H. from afar, aloft, th' immortal prize *E.C.* 96
You might have *h*. the pretty head aside *E.§.S.* 3
For Wit's false mirror *h*. up Nature's light *E.M.* iv. 393
Show there was one who *h*. it in disdain *E.S.* i. 172
Just so immortal *Maro h*. his head *P.S.* 122
While pure Description *h*. the place of Sense *P.S.* 148
That Flat'ry, ev'n to Kings, he *h*. a shame. *P.S.* 338
Yet why ? that Father *h*. it for a rule *P.S.* 382
And mighty hearts are *h*. in slender chains *R.L.* ii. 24
Here living Tea-pots stand, one arm *h*. out *R.L.* iv. 49
Like that where once Ulysses *h*. the winds *R.L.* iv. 82
And children sacred *h*. a Martin's nest *S.* ii. 38

Helen.

With Zeuxis' *H*. thy Bridgewater vie *E.* iii. 75
'Tis from a Handmaid we must take our *H. M.E.* ii. 194

Hell.

So take the hindmost, *H*. (he said) and run *D.* ii. 60
H. rises, Heav'n descends, and dance on Earth *D.* iii. 237
H. thou shalt move ; for Faustus is our friend *D.* iii. 308
While op'ning *H*. spouts wild-fire at your head *D.* iii. 316
And *h*. was built on spite, and heav'n on pride *E.M.* iii. 262
Another deems him instrument of *h. E.M.* iv. 138
Or her, who laughs at *H*., but (like his Grace) *M.E.* ii. 107
Who breaks with her, provokes Revenge from *H. M.E.* ii. 129

L

Who never mentions *H.* to ears polite *M.E.* iv. 150
He sung, and *h.* consented *O.* i. 83
O'er death, and o'er hell *O.* i. 88
His numbers rais'd a shade from *h. O.* i. 133
Yet here ; as ev'n in *H.*, there must be still *S.* vii. 3
Schoolmen in *h.* new tenements must make *S.* vii. 42
The Poet's *h.*, its tortures, fiends, and flames *S.* viii. 7
A Vision hermits can to *H.* transport *S.* viii. 190
This, teach me more than *H.* to shun *U.P.* 15
Exil'd by thee from earth to deepest *h. W.F.* 413
And *H.'s grim Tyrant feel th' eternal wound M.* 48

Helluo.

A salmon's belly, *H.*, was thy fate *M.E.* i. 238
"Mercy !" cries *H.*, "mercy on my soul !" *M.E.* i. 240
As *H.*, late Dictator of the Feast *M.E.* ii. 79

Helm.

Ev'n Palinurus nodded at the *H. D.* iv. 614

Helmsley.

And *H.*, once proud Buckingham's delight *S.* ii. 177

Help.

Without your *h.* the Cause is gone *I.H.* ii. 72 s
The doctor call'd, declares all *h.* too late *M.E.* i. 239
Implore your *h.* in these pathetic strains *S.* v. 232
And still new needs, new h—s, *new habits rise E.M.* iii. 137
False steps but h. *them to renew the race E.C.* 602
Trade it may *h.*, Society extend *M.E.* iii. 29
To *h.* me thro' this long disease, my Life *P.S.* 132
To *h.* who want, to forward who excel *S.* i. 137
If PETER deigns to *h.* you to your own *S.* vii. 66
Nor could Diana *h.* her injur'd maid *W.F.* 198

Help'd.

And complaisantly *h.* to all I hate *M.E.* iv. 164
He *h.* to bury, whom he *h.* to starve *P.S.* 248
And me, the Muses *h.* to undergo it *S.* vi. 66

Helpless.

A sharp accuser, but a *h.* friend *E.M.* ii. 154
A longer care Man's *h.* kind demands *E.M.* iii. 131
Saw *h.* him from whom their life began *E.M.* iii. 142
How shall I, then, your *h.* fame defend *R.L.* iv. 111

Helps.

And *h.*, another creature's wants and woes *E.M.* iii. 52
Or *h.* th' ambitions Hill the heav'ns to scale *M.E.* iv. 59
Who loves a Lie, lame slander *h.* about *P.S.* 289
That *h.* it both to fools-coats and to fools *S.* viii. 221

Hemm'd.

H. by a triple Circle round *I.H.* ii. 48 s

Hen.

Will choose a pheasant still before a *h.* (*rep.*) *S.* ii. 18
All Worldly's h—s, *nay partridge, sold to town S.* vi. 234

Hence.—*Passim.*

Henley.

Ev'n Ralph repents, and *H.* writes no more *D.* i. 216
How *H.* lay inspir'd beside a sink *D.* ii. 425
Embrown'd with native bronze, lo ! *H.* stands *D.* ii. 199
Still break the benches, *H.!* with thy strain *D.* iii. 203
His butchers, *H.!* his free-masons, Moore *P.S.* 98
H. himself I've heard, and Budgel too *S.* viii. 51
H.'s gilt tub, or Flecno's Irish throne D. ii. 2
Come *H.* Oratory, Osborne's Wit *E.S.* i. 66

Henry.

Edward and *H.*, now the Boast of Fame *S.* v. 7
Let softer strains ill-fated *H.* mourn *W.F.* 311

Her, Hers, Herself.—*Passim.*

Heraclitus.

'Twould burst ev'n *H.* with the spleen *S.* viii. 236

Herald.

By *h.* Hawkers, high heroic Games *D.* ii. 18
Peers, H—s, *Bishops, Ermine, Gold and Lawn S.* v. 317

Herb.

Suckles each *h.*, and spreads out ev'ry flow'r *E.M.* i. 134
Once I was skill'd in ev'ry *h.* that grew *Sw.* 31

From pois'nous h—s *extracts the healing dew E.M.* i. 220
Cheap eggs, and *h.*, and olives still we see *S.* ii. 35
Nor fragrant *h.* their native incense yield *W.* 48
He gathers health from *h.* the forest yields *W.F.* 241

Herd.

The vulgar *h.* turn off to roll with Hogs *D.* iv. 525
Of all this servile *h.* the worst is he *E.C.* 414
Drive to St. James's a whole *h.* of swine *M.E.* iii. 74
Whose h—s *with milk, whose fields with bread O.* iv. 5
The lowing *h.* to murm'ring brooks retreat *Su.* 86

Here.—*Passim.*

Hereditary.

H. Realms, and Worlds of Gold *M.E.* iii. 130
For Right *H.* tax'd and fin'd *S.* vi. 64

Hermes.

Then taught by *H.*, and divinely bold *D.* iv. 381
'Gainst Pallas, Mars ; Latona, *H.* arms *R.L.* v. 47
As Argus eyes by *H.*' wand opprest *D.* iv. 637

Hermit.

No cavern'd *H.*, rests self-satisfy'd *E.M.* iv. 42
The veriest *H.* in the Nation *I.H.* ii. 181
And then—a perfect *H.* in his diet *S.* v. 200
Dreadful as h.'s *dreams in haunted shades R.L.* iv. 41
A Vision h—s *can to Hell transport S.* viii. 190

Hermitage.

Nor in an *H.* set Dr. Clarke *M.E.* iv. 78

Hermus.

Tho' foaming *H.* swells with tides of gold *W.F.* 358

Hero.

Swearing and supperless the *H.* sate *D.* i. 115
Pleas'd, she accepts the *H.*, and the Dame *D.* iv. 335
A *h.* perish, or a sparrow fall *E.M.* i. 88
The sot a *h.*, lunatic a king *E.M.* ii. 268
And all that rais'd the *H.*, sunk the Man *E.M.* iv. 294
The plain rough *H.* turn a crafty knave *M.E.* i. 126
As when that *H.*, who in each campaign *Mi.* ii. 1
She smil'd to see the doughty *h.* slain *R.L.* v. 69
The *H.* William, and the Martyr Charles *S.* v. 386
The monk's humility, the h.'s *pride E.M.* ii. 173
By the *h.* armed shades *O.* i. 77
The *h.* glory, or the virgin's love *P.C.* 10
There *H.* wits are kept in pond'rous vases *R.L.* v. 115
Or tread the path by vent'rous H—es *trod D.* i. 201
The *h.* sit, the vulgar form a ring *D.* ii. 384
Streets pav'd with *H.*, Tiber chok'd with Gods *D.* iii. 108
Their full-fed *H.*, their pacific May'rs *D.* iii. 281
And place it here ! here all ye *H.* bow *D.* iii. 318
Where, but among the H, and the wise (rep.) E.M. iv. 218
When statesmen, *h.*, kings in dust repose *E.M.* iv 387
Is mix'd with *H.*, or with Kings thy dust *Ep.* xi. 10
H. and Kings ! your distance keep *Ep.* xv. 1
In vain may *H.* fight, and Patriots rave *M.E.* iii. 43
Gods, Emp'rors, *H.*, Sages, Beauties, lie *M.E.* v. 34
Her Gods, and god-like *H.* rise to view *M.E.* v. 47
And men grew *h.* at the sound *O.* i. 43
Hither the *H.* and the nymphs resort *R.L.* iii. 9
And in the breasts of Kings and *H.* glows *U.L.* 16
Oh wouldst thou sing what *h.* Windsor bore *W.F.* 299
H—s' *and Heroines' shouts confus'dly rise R.L.* v. 41

Herod.

As *H's* hang-dogs in old Tapestry *S.* viii. 267

Heroic.

By herald Hawkers, high *h.* Games *D.* ii. 18
And his this Drum, whose hoarse *h.* bass *D.* ii. 233
One action Conduct ; one, *h.* Love *M.E.* i. 134
One dedicates in high *h.* prose *P.S.* 109
When this H—s *only deigns to praise S.* vi. 82

Heroines.

Heroes' and *H.*' shouts confus'dly rise *R.L.* v. 41

Herses.

And frequent *h.* shall besiege your gates *U.L.* v. 38

Hesitate.

Just hint a fault, and *h.* dislike *P.S.* 204

Hew.
And *h.* the Block off, and get out the Man *D.* iv. 270
And *h.* triumphal arches to the ground *R.L.* iii. 176

Heydegger, *see* Heideggre.

Heywood.
From eldest *H.*, down to Cibber's Age *S.* ii. 88
And sure succession down from H.'s days D. i. 98

Hibernian.
H. Politics, O Swift ! thy fate *D.* iii. 331
She heard, and drove him to th' *H.* shore *D.* iv. 70

Hid.
Nature and Nature's Laws lay *h.* in Night *Ep.* xii. 1
Others so very close, they're *h.* from none *M.E.* i. 52
The Fool lies *h.* in inconsistencies *M.E.* i. 70
Deep *h.* the shining mischief under ground *M.E.* iii. 10
Some Revelation *h.* from you and me *M.E.* iii. 114
Then *h.* in shades, eludes her eager swain *Sp.* 54

Hide.
Oh *h.* the God still more ! and make us see *D.* iv. 483
Which nothing seeks to shew, or needs to *h. E.* ii. 2
H. it, my heart, within that close disguise *E.A.* 11
And *h.* with ornaments their want of art *E.C.* 296
Not Waller's Wreath can *h.* the Nation's Scar *E.S.* ii. 230
And shew their zeal, and *h.* their want of skill *M.E.* ii. 186
Bred to disguise, in Public 'tis you *h. M.E.* ii. 203
To squander These, and Those to *h.* again *M.E.* iii. 13
Ye little Stars ! *h.* your diminish'd rays *M.E.* iii. 282
Where half the skill is decently to *h. M.E.* iv. 54
A Rival's envy (all in vain) to *h. Mi.* ix. 42
What walls can guard me, or what shades can *h. P.S.* 7
Might *h.* her faults, if Belles had faults to *h. R.L.* ii. 16
To *h.* the Fault I see *U.P.* 38
Public too long, ah let me *h.* my Age *S.* iii. 5
Ye weeping Loves, the stream with myrtles *h. W.* 23
Like stunted h.*-bound Trees, that just have got Mi.* iii. 11

Hideous.
And makes night *h.*—Answer him, ye Owls *D.* iii. 166

Hides.
Heav'n from all creatures *h.* the book of Fate *E.M.* i. 77
By Passions ? these Dissimulation *h. M.E.* i. 169
The Slave that digs it, and the Slave that *h. M.E.* iii. 110
This harmless grove no lurking viper *h. Su.* 67
And sullen Mole that *h.* his diving flood *W.F.* 347

High.
But, *h.* above, more solid Learning shone *D.* i. 147
And thrice he lifted *h.* the Birth-day brand *D.* i. 245
So when Jove's block descended from on *h. D.* i. 327
H. on a gorgeous seat, that far out-shone *D.* ii. 1
By herald Hawkers, *h.* heroic games *D.* ii. 18
Earless on *h.*, stood unabash'd De Foe *D.* ii. 147
As from the blanket *h.* in air he flies *D.* ii. 152
The Goddess then: "Who best can send on *h. D.* ii. 161
H. souqd, attemper'd to the vocal nose *D.* ii. 236
Then raptures *h.* the seat of sense o'erflow *D.* iii. 5
We nobly take the *h.* Priori Road *D.* iv. 471
Perhaps more *h.* some daring son may soar *D.* iv. 599
Wave *h.*, and murmur to the hollow wind *E.A.* 156
H. on Parnassus' top her sons she show'd *E.C.* 94
If Man alone engross not Heav'n's *h.* care *E.M.* i. 119
Above, how *h.*, progressive life may go *E.M.* i. 235
To him, no *h.*, no low, no great, no small *E.M.* i. 279
When the loose mountain trembles from on *h. E.M.* iv. 127
Is hung on *h.*, to poison half mankind *E.M.* iv. 252
Virtue may choose the *h.* or low Degree *E.S.* i. 137
The bribing Statesman—Hold, too *h.* you go *E.S.* ii. 25
Ye Heav'ns ! from *h.* the dewy nectar pour *M.* 13
Who would not praise Patritio's *h.* descent *M.E.* i. 81
'Tis from *h.* Life *h.* characters are drawn *M.E.* i. 135
When simple *Macer*, now of *h.* renown *Mi.* iii. 1
'Twas all th' Ambition his *h.* soul could feel *Mi.* iii. 3
Nor swell too *h.*, nor sink too low *O.* i. 23
H. on the stern the Thracian mais'd his strain *O.* i. 39
"Nine years !" cries he, who *h.* in Drury Lane *P.S.* 41
One dedicates in *h.* heroic prose *P.S.* 109
Ammon's great son one shoulder had too *h. P.S.* 117
Now *h.*, now low, now master up, now miss *P.S.* 324
Some guide the course of wand'ring orbs on *h. R.L.* ii. 79
Or when rich china vessels fall'n from *h. R.L.* iii. 159

And the *h.* dome re-echoes to his nose *R.L.* v. 86
Is Vice too *h.*, reserve it for the next *S.* i. 60
From low St. James's up to *h.* St. Paul *S.* iii. 82
In short that reas'ning, *h.*, immortal Thing *S.* iii. 185
For ever sunk too low, or borne too *h. S.* v. 299
At Quin's *h.* plume, or Oldfield's petticoat *S.* v. 331
Gold, Silver, Iv'ry, Vases sculptur'd *h. S.* vi. 264
But see ! where Daphne wond'ring mounts on *h. W.* 69
And *h.* in air Britannia's standard flies *W.F.* 110
Now marks the course of rolling orbs on *h. W.F.* 245
H. in the midst, upon his urn reclin'd *W.F.* 349
And *h.*-born *Howard*, *more majestic sire D.* i. 297
A Switz, a *H.-dutch*, or a Low-dutch Bear *S.* iii. 63
Squeaks like a *h.-stretch'd* lutestring, and replies *S.* viii. 99
Thou triumph'st, Victor of the *h.-wrought* day *D.* ii. 187

Higher.
Who but to sink the deeper, rose the *h. D.* ii. 290
Von stars, yon suns, he rears at pleasure *h. D.* iii. 259
And if yet *h.* the proud List should end *E.S.* ii. 92

Highest.
Court-virtues bear, like Gems, the *h.* rate *M.E.* i. 141

Highly.
But I, who think more *h.* of our kind *M.E.* iii. 7

Hight.
On parchment scraps y-fed, and Wormius *h. D.* iii. 188

Hill.
Ascend this *h.*, whose cloudy point commands *D.* iii. 67
Behind the cloud-topt *h.*, an humbler heav'n *E.M.* i. 104
Or helps th' ambitious *H.* the heav'ns to scale *M.E.* iv. 59
You'll wish your *h.* or shelter'd seat again *M.E.* iv. 76
Proud as Apollo on his forked *h. P.S.* 231
Might change Olympus for a nobler *h. W.F.* 234
Resound, ye h—s, *resound my mournful strain* A. 57&c.
No more, ye *h.*, resound my mournful lay *A.* 96
Glitt'ring with ice here hoary *h.* are seen *D.* i. 75
Thron'd on seven *h.*, the Antichrist of wit *D.* ii. 16
The wand'ring streams that shine between the *h. E.A.* 157
H. peep o'er *h.*, and Alps on Alps arise *E.C.* 232
A God, a God ! the vocal *h.* reply *M.* 31
Join Cotswood *h.* to Saperton's fair dale *S.* vi. 257
In spring the fields, in autumn *h.* I love *Sp.* 77
The *h.* and rocks attend my doleful lay *Su.* 17
Here *h.* and vales, the woodland and the plain *W.F.* 11
There wrapt in clouds the blueish *h.* ascend *W.F.* 24
Now range the *h.*, the gameful woods beset *W.F.* 95
H., vales, and floods appear already cross'd *W.F.* 153

Him, Himself.—*Passim*.

Hind.
O'er heaps of ruin stalk'd the stately *h. W.F.* 70

Hindmost.
So take the *h.* Hell (he said) and run *D.* ii. 60

Hinge.
This Snuff-Box,—on the *H.* see Brilliants shine *Mi.* ix 43

Hint.
Just *h.* a fault, and hesitate dislike *P.S.* 204

Hinted.
Oft have you *h.* to your brother Peer *M.E.* iv. 39

Hints.
How *h.*, like spawn, scarce quick in embryo lie *D.* i. 59
Nay *h.*, 'tis by connivance of the Court *S.* viii. 164

Hippia.
Can they in gems bid pallid *H.* glow *M.E.* iii. 87

Hire.
Who rhym'd for *h.*, and patroniz'd for pride *D.* iv. 102
I'll *h.* another's ; *is not that my own S.* ii. 156
They *h.* their sculler, and when once aboard *S.* iii. 159
Then *h.* a Slave, or (if you will) a Lord *S.* iv. 99

Hireling.
No *h.* she, no prostitute to praise *E.* i. 36
A *h.* scribbler, or a *h.* peer *P.S.* 364

Hires.
But dreadful too, the dark Assassin *h. M.E.* iii. 28

His.—*Passim.*

Hiss.
Down sunk the flames, and with a *h.* expire *D.* i. 260
Of h—es, blows, or want, or loss of ears *D.* i. 48
All sudden, Gorgons h., and Dragons glare *D.* iii. 235
Reduced at last to *h.* in my own dragon *D.* iii. 286

Hiss'd.
In such a cause the Plaintiff will be *h.* *S.* i. 155

Hisses.
Great Cæsar roars, and *h.* in the fires *D.* i. 251

Historians.
But, sage *h.!* 'tis your task to prove *M.E.* i. 133
Or dubb'd *H.*, by express command *S.* v. 372

Historic.
There warriors frowning in *h.* brass *M.E.* v. 58

History, Hist'ry.
But sober *H.* restrained her rage *D.* iv. 39
Of rich and poor makes all the *h.* *M.E.* iii. 288
It is to *H.* he trusts for Praise *S.* i. 36
H.'y her Pot, Divinity her Pipe *D.* iii. 196

Hit.
Never was dash'd out at one lucky *h.* *D.* ii. 47
And God's good Providence, a lucky *H.* *M.E.* iii. 378
Sure never to o'ershoot, but just to *h.* *E.M.* iii. 89
Come harmless Characters, that no one *h.* *E.S.* i. 65
Woman and Fool are two hard things to *h.* *M.E.* ii. 113
The Pleasure miss'd her, and the Scandal *h.* *M.E.* ii. 128
Some flying stroke alone can *h.* 'em right *M.E.* ii. 154
The coxcomb *h.*, or fearing to be *h.* *P.S.* 345
Hence Satire rose, that just the medium *h.* *S.* v. 261
Hard task! to *h.* the palate of such guests *S.* vi. 86
Dear Countess! you have charms all hearts to *h.* *S.* viii. 232

Hitches.
Slides into verse, and *h.* in a rhyme *S.* i. 78

Hither.—*Passim.*

Ho—y.
But *H.* for a period of a mile *S.* viii. 73

Hoard.
To lay this harvest up, and *h.* with haste *S.* iii. 21

Hoarding.
Still *h.* up, most scandalously nice *E.J.S.* 19

Hoarse.
And the *h.* nation croak'd, "God save King Log!" *D.* i. 330
And his this drum, whose *h.* heroic bass *D.* 233
The *h.*, rough verse should like the torrent roar *E.C.* 369
And rapid Severn *h.* applause resounds *M.E.* iii. 252

Hoary.
Glitt'ring with ice here *h.* hills are seen *D.* i. 75
Whether his *h.* sire he spies *O.* iii. 29
With *h.* whiskers and a forky beard *R.L.* iii. 38
The *h.* Majesty of Spades appears *R.L.* iii. 56

Hockley-hole.
This Mess, toss'd up of *H.* and White's *D.* i. 222
And "Coll!" each Butcher roars at *H.* *D.* i. 326
F. loves the Senate, *H.* his brother *S.* i. 49

Hog.
The *h.*, that ploughs not nor obeys thy call *E.M.* iii. 41
As *H.* to *H.* in huts of Westphaly *E.S.* ii. 172
Cries "Send me, Gods! a whole *h.* barbecu'd!" *S.* ii. 26
The vulgar herd turn off to roll with h—s *D.* iv. 525
No, Sir, you'll leave them to the *H.* *I.H.* ii. 28
Had Colepepper's whole wealth been hops and *h.* *M.E.* iii. 65

Hold.
And desp'rate Misery lays *h.* on Dover *S.* iv. 57
Such with their shelves as due proportion *h.* *D.* i. 137
H.—to the Minister I more incline *D.* i. 213
"*H.*!" (cry'd the Queen) "a Cat-call each shall win *D.* ii. 243
In words, as fashions, the same rule will *h.* *E.C.* 333

The bribing Statesman—*H.*, too high you go *E.S.* ii. 24
H., Sir! for God's sake where's th' Affront to you *E.S.* ii. 157
H. out some months 'twixt Sun and Fire *I.H.* i. 18
You *h.* him no Philosopher at all *M.E.* i. 8
The Manor, Sir?"—"the Manor! *h.*," he cry'd *M.E.* i. 260
As Hags *h.* Sabbaths, less for joy than spite *M.E.* ii. 239
You *h.* the word, from Jove to Momus giv'n *M.E.* iii. 3
Still Sappho—*H.*! for God's sake—you'll offend *P.S.* 101
Yet hens of Guinea full as good I *h.* *S.* ii. 19
For I, who *h.* sage Homer's rule the best *S.* iii. 159
Admire me then what Earth's low entrails *h.* *S.* iv. 11
I *h.* that Wit a Classic, good in law *S.* v. 56
To prove, that Luxury could never *h.* *S.* v. 167
'Tis to small purpose that you *h.* your tongue *S.* vi. 155
With terrors round, can Reason *h.* her throne *S.* vi. 310
In love's, in nature's spite, the siege they *h.* *S.* vii. 23
Language which Boreas might to Auster *h.* *S.* vii. 61

Holds.
Close to those walls where Folly *h.* her throne *D.* i. 29
Yet *h.* the eel of Science by the tail *D.* i. 280
And *h.* his breeches close with both his hands *D.* iv. 148
The willing heart, and only *h.* it long *E.* iv. 68
Still rebel nature *h.* out half my heart *E.A.* 26
The chain *h.* on, and where it ends, unknown *E.M.* iii. 26
Who *h.* dragoons and wooden shoes in scorn *Mi.* ii. 20
Or Envy *h.* a whole week's war with Sense *P.S.* 252
The grave Sir Gilbert *h.* it for a rule *M.E.* iii. 101

Hole.
Still sits at squat, and peeps not from its *h.* *M.E.* i. 56
Convicted of that mortal crime, a *h.* *S.* viii. 245
Admire new light thro' h—s yourselves have made *D.* iv. 126

Holiday.
Till Westminster's whole year he *h.* *D.* iii. 336

Holinshed.
More than ten *H*—s., or Halls, or Stowes *S.* viii. 131

Hollow.
Keen *h.* winds howl thro' the bleak recess *D.* i. 35
Wave high, and murmur to the *h.* wind *E.A.* 156
From yonder shrine I heard a *h.* sound *E.A.* 308
Give me again my *h.* Tree *I.H.* ii. 220
H. groans *O.* i. 61
Eurydice the rocks, and *h.* mountains rung *O.* i. 117
Of *h.* gew-gaws, only dress and face *S.* viii. 209
In *h.* caves sweet Echo silent lies *W.* 41
The *h.* winds thro' naked temples roar *W.F.* 68

Hollowing.
Or with his hound comes *h.* from the stable *E.* v. 57

Holy.
Sepulchral Lies, our *h.* walls to grace *D.* i. 43
With *h.* envy gave one Layman place *D.* ii. 324
And damns implicit faith, and *h.* lies *D.* iv. 463
Nor pass these lips in *h.* silence seal'd *E.A.* 10
Ye rugged rocks! which *h.* knees have worn *E.A.* 19
And drove those *h.* Vandals off the stage *E.C.* 696
Not but that we may exceed, some *h.* time *S.* ii. 85
In time to come, may pass for *h.* writ *S.* viii. 287

Homage.
In *h.* to the mother of the sky *D.* iii. 132
Who pay her *h.* in her sons, the Great *D.* iv. 92
And nothing left but *H.* to a King *D.* iv. 524
With heads declin'd, ye cedars, *h.* pay *M.* 35
When universal *h.* Umbra pays *M.E.* i. 59
I sought no *h.* from the Race that write *P.S.* 219
And pay the Great our *h.* of Amaze *S.* iv. 77
To thee the World its present *h.* pays *S.* v. 23

Home.
Well-pleas'd he enter'd, and confess'd his *h.* *D.* i. 266
Replenish, not ingloriously, at *h.* *D.* ii. 166
Crown'd with the Jordan, walks contented *h.* *D.* ii. 170
It still looks *h.*, and short excursions makes *E.C.* 627
The soul, uneasy and confin'd from *h.* *E.M.* i. 97
Yet on plain Pudding deign'd at *h.* to eat *M.E.* ii. 82
No thought of peace or happiness at *h.* *M.E.* ii. 224
Bear *h.* six Whores, and make his Lady weep *M.E.* iii 72
Of foreign Tyrants, and of Nymphs at *h.* *R.L.* iii. 6

HOMELY—HOPE. 149

Oh had I stay'd, and said my prayers at *h.* *R.L.* iv. 160
Than eat the sweetest by themselves at *h.* *S.* ii. 96
At *h.*, tho' exil'd ; free, tho' in the Tow'r *S.* iii. 184
At *h.*, with Morals, Arts, and Laws amend *S.* v. 4
Bred up at *h.*, full early I begun *S.* vi. 52
Survey the region, and confess her *h.* *W.F.* 256
Each h.-*felt joy that life inherits here E.M.* ii. 256
What *h.* raptures move *O.* iii. 34
Whom humbler joys of *h.* quiet please *W.F.* 239

Homely.

Then scorn a *h.* dinner, if you can *S.* ii. 12

Homer.

Nature and *H.* were, he found, the same *E.C.* 135
Nor is it *H.* nods, but we that dream *E.C.* 180
Nay should great *H.* lift his awful head *E.C.* 464
Great *H.* died three thousand years ago *P.S.* 124
So when bold *H.* makes the Gods engage *R.L.* v. 45
But (thanks to *H.*) since I live and thrive *S.* vi. 68
Be H.'s *works your study and delight E.C.* 124
See Dionysius *H.* thoughts refine *E.C.* 663
O for the heart of *H.* Mice *I.H.* ii. 214
A Pipkin there, like *H.* Tripod walks *R.L.* iv. 51
But I who hold sage *H.* rule the best *S.* ii. 159
Yours Milton's genius, and mine *H.* spirit *S.* vi. 136
See other Cæsars, other H—s *rise D.* iv. 360

Honest.

There many an *h.* man may copy Cato *E.J.S.* 43
But *h.* Instinct comes a volunteer *E.M.* iii. 88
An *h.* man's the noblest work of God *E.M.* iv. 248
Sejanus, Wolsey, hurt not *h.* Fleury *E.S.* i. 51
To find an *h.* man I beat about *E.S.* ii. 102
To *Cato, Virgil* pay'd one *h.* line *E.S.* ii. 120
Rev'rent I touch thee, but with *h.* zeal *E.S.* ii. 216
An *h.* Courtier, yet a Patriot too *Ep.* ii. 5
May truly say, Here lies an *h.* Man *Ep.* x. 2
And wanting nothing but an *h.* heart *M.E.* i. 193
Here *h.* Nature ends as she begins *M.E.* i. 227
Because she's *h.*, and the best of Friends *M.E.* ii. 104
From *h.* Mah'met, or plain Parson Hale *M.E.* ii. 198
Rise, *h.* Muse ! and sing the Man of Ross *M.E.* iii. 250
An *h.* factor stole a gem away *M.E.* iii. 362
Here, rising bold, the Patriot's *h.* face *Mi.* ii. 57
Thought wond'rous *h.*, tho' of mean degree *Mi.* iii. 19
With *h.* scorn the first fam'd Cato view'd *P.C.* 39
With *h.* anguish, and an aching head *P.S.* 38
Yet absent, wounds an *h.* author's fame *P.S.* 292
A lash like mine no *h.* man shall dread *P.S.* 303
By Nature *h.*, by Experience wise *P.S.* 400
Like good Erasmus in an *h.* Mean *S.* i. 66
Could pension'd Boileau lash in *h.* strain *S.* i. 111
A man was hang'd for very *h.* rhymes *S.* i. 146
That sweetest music to an *h.* ear *S.* ii. 100
If *h.* S*z take scandal at a Spark *S.* iii. 112
The Captain's *h.*, Sirs, and that's enough *S.* viii. 262

Honesty.

What crops of wit and *h.* appear *E.M.* ii. 185
A Horse-laugh, if you please, at *H.* *E.S.* i. 38

Honey.

This taste the *h.*, and not wound the flow'r *E.M.* ii. 90
The *H.* dropping from Favonio's tongue *E.S.* i. 67

Honour.

The last, not least in *h.* or applause *D.* iv. 577
Made slaves by *h.*, and made Fools by shame *E.* iv. 36
Let wealth, let *h.*, wait the wedded dame *E.A.* 77
Fame, wealth, and *h. !* what are you to Love *E.A.* 80
Why, full of days and *h.*, lives the Sire *E.M.* iv. 106
H. and shame from no Condition rise (*rep.*) *E.M.* iv. 193
Of *H.* blind me, not to maul his Tools *E.S.* ii. 147
Knew one a Man of *H.*, once a Knave *E.S.* ii. 153
Who think a Coxcomb's *H.* like his Sense *E.S.* ii. 202
And bark at *H.* not conferr'd by Kings *E.S.* ii. 243
H. unchang'd, a Principle profest *Ep.* ii. 3
To find his *H.* in a Pound *I.H.* ii. 47 s
"An't please your *H.*," quoth the Peasant *I.H.* ii. 218
And haunt the places where their *H.* died *M.E.* ii. 242
And *H.* linger ere it leaves the land *M.E.* iii. 248
In action faithful, and in *h.* clear *M.E.* v. 68
Yet wants the *h.*, injur'd, to defend *P.S.* 296
Tho' *H.* is the word with Men below *R.L.* i. 78
Or stain her *h.*, or her new brocade *R.L.* ii. 107

So long my *h.*, name, and praise shall live *R.L.* iii. 170
H. forbid ! at whose unrival'd shrine *R.L.* iv. 105
And all your *h.* in a whisper lost *R.L.* iv. 110
True, conscious *H.* is to feel no sin *S.* iii. 93
Something, which for your *H.* they may cheat *S.* iv. 93
To say too much, might do my *h.* wrong *S.* vi. 12
Endue a Peer with *h.*, truth, and grace *S.* vi. 221
Thy name, thy *h.*, and thy praise shall live *W.* 84
His H.'s *meaning Dulness thus exprest D.* ii. 195
A word, pray, in your *H.* ear *I.H.* i. 42
Of gentle blood (part shed in *H.* cause (*rep.*) *P.S.* 388
To the last H—s *of the Butt and Bays D.* i. 168
Mark'd out for *H.*, honour'd for their Birth *D.* iv. 507
Whose *h.* with increase of ages grow *E.C.* 191
Lies crown'd with Princes' *h.*, Poets' lays *Ep.* viii. 5
These are thy *H. !* not that here thy Bust *Ep.* xi. 9
Yet softer *H.*, and less noisy Fame *Ep.* xiv. 9
These *h.* Peace to happy Britain brings *M.E.* iv. 203
Sudden, these *h.* shall be snatch'd away *R.L.* iii. 103
Which never more its *h.* shall renew *R.L.* iv. 135
The long-contended *h.* of her head *R.L.* iv. 140
But Bug and D—l, Their *H.* and so forth *S.* iii. 90
To do the *H.*, and to give the Word *S.* iv. 100
More *h.*, more rewards, attend the brave *S.* vi. 48
Their faded *h.* scatter'd on her bier *W.* 32
Where tow'ring oaks their growing *h.* rear *W.F.* 221
To sing those *h.* you deserve to wear *W.F.* 289
H. a Syrian Prince above his own D. iv. 368
Fondly we think we *h.* merit then *E.C.* 454
Whom *h.* with your hand : to make remarks *S.* iv. 103

Honourable.

Fear most to tax an *H.* fool *E.C.* 588

Honour'd.

Mark'd out for Honours, *h.* from their Birth *D.* iv. 507
Immortal Vida : on whose *h.* brow *E.C.* 705
There in the rich, the *h.*, fam'd, and great *E.M.* iv. 287
Prais'd, wept, and *h.*, by the Muse he lov'd *Ep.* iii. 6
And *h.* Cæsar less than Cato's sword *P.C.* 36
Say why are Beauties prais'd and *h.* most *R.L.* v. 9
Rich ev'n when plunder'd, *h.* while oppress'd *S* iii. 182
So known, so *h.*, at the House of Lords *S.* iv. 49
By strangers *h.*, and by strangers mourn'd *U.L.* 54
How lov'd, how *h.* once, avails thee not *U.L.* 71

Hoods.

Broad hats, and *h.*, and caps, a sable shoal *D.* iv. 190

Hooded.

The Friar *h.*, and the monarch crown'd *E.M.* iv. 198

Hook.

Like slashing Bentley with his desp'rate *h.* *S.* v. 104

Hoop.

Could she behold us tumbling thro' a *h.* *S.* v. 48
Never by tumbler thro' the h—s *was shown D.* iv. 257
Tho' stiff with *h.*, and arm'd with ribs of whale *R.L.* ii. 120

Hope.

It fled, I follow'd ; now in *h.*, now pain *D.* iv. 427
Whose pious *h.* aspires to see the day *D.* iv. 461
Fresh blooming *H.*, gay daughter of the sky *E.A.* 299
But gives that *H.* to be thy blessing now (*rep.*) *E.M.* i. 94
Yet simple Nature to his *h.* has giv'n *E.M.* i. 103
Love, *H.*, and Joy, fair Pleasure's smiling train *E.M.* ii 117
H. travels thro', nor quits us when we die *E.M.* ii. 274
Each want of happiness by *h.* supply'd *E.M.* ii. 285
While pleasure, gratitude, and *h.* combin'd *E.M.* iii. 145
Fear made her Devils, and weak *H.* her Gods *E.M.* iii. 256
In Faith and *H.* the world will disagree *E.M.* iii. 307
While those are plac'd in *H.*, and these in Fear *E.M.* iv. 70
For him alone, *H.* leads from goal to goal *E.M.* iv. 341
H. of known bliss, and Faith in bliss unknown *E.M.* iv. 346
Adieu, fond *H.* of mutual fire *I.H.* iii. 33
Is there no *h.*—Alas—then bring the jowl *M.E.* i. 241
To town he comes, completes the nation's *h.* *M.E.* iii. 213
Stood up to dash each vain Pretender's *h.* *Mi.* ii. 17
With rev'rence, *h.*, and love *O.* iii. 36
Constant faith, fair *h.*, long leisure *O.* iii. 42
Stretch'd on the lawn his second *h.* survey *W.F.* 81
Panting with *h.* he tries the furrow'd grounds *W.F.* 100

So dies her love, and so my h—s *decay A.* 70
Tho' long my Party built on me their *h. D.* iii. 283
Or sadly told how many *h.* lie here *Ep.* xiv. 6
H. after *h.* of pious Papists fail'd *S.* vi. 62
How often, h., *despair, resent, regret E.A.* 199
H. humbly then; with trembling pioions soar *E.M.* i. 91
As while he dreads it, makes him *h.* it too *E.M.* iii. 74
Dare they to *h.* a Poet for their Friend *E.S.* ii. 115
I *h.* it is your Resolution *I.H.* l. 43
I have but one, I *h.* the fellow's clean *S.* viii. 111

Hop'd.
I *h.* for no commission from his Grace *S.* viii. 11

Hopeless.
Ah *h.,* lasting flames! like those that burn *E.A.* 261
While your Alexis pines in *h.* love *Su.* 24

Hopes.
She runs, but *h.* she does not run unseen *Sp.* 58
And therefore *h.* this Nation may be sold *M.E.* iii. 124
With looks unmov'd, be *h.* the scaly breed *W.F.* 139

Hoping.
Trembling, *h.,* ling'ring, flying *O.* v. 3

Hopkins.
What can they give? to dying *H.,* Heirs *M.E.* iii. 85
When *H.* dies, a thousand lights attend *M.E.* iii. 291
H. and Sternhold glad the heart with Psalms *S.* v. 230

Hops.
Had Colepepper's whole wealth been *h.* and hogs *M.E.* iii. 65
On feet and wings, and flies, and wades, and h. *D.* ii. 64

Horace.
Made *H.* dull, and humbled Milton's strains *D.* iv. 212
And Alsop never but like *H.* joke *D.* iv. 224
H. still charms with graceful negligence *E.C.* 653
Nor suffers *H.* more in wrong Translations *E.C.* 663
And Boileau still in right of *H.* sways *E.C.* 714
'Tis all from *H.; H.* long before ye *E.S.* i. 7
But *H.,* Sir, was delicate, was nice *E.S.* i. 11
H. would say, Sir Billy *serv'd the Crown E.S.* i. 13
Let *H.* blush, and Virgil too *Ep.* xv. 4
I cough, like *H.,* and tho' lean, am short *P.S.* 116
H. and he went hand in hand in song *P.S.* 234
Let me be *H.,* and be Ovid you *S.* vi. 144

Horn.
Harmonic twang! of leather, *h.,* and brass *D.* ii. 254
And Pan to Moses lends his pagan *h. D.* iii. 110
By the French *h.,* or by the op'ning hound *D.* iv. 278
Nor ev'ning Cynthia fill her silver *h. M.* 100
Wind the shrill *h.,* or spread the waving net *W.F.* 96
Heav'n's twinkling Sparks draw light, and point their h—s *D.* ii. 12
So (fam'd like thee for turbulence and *h.) D.* ii. 181
With *h.* and trumpets now to madness swell *D.* ii. 227
Witness, great Ammon! by whose *h.* I swore *D.* iv. 387
If e'er with airy *h.* I planted heads *R.L.* iv. 71
Bulls aim their *h.,* and Asses lift their heels *S.* i. 86
With hounds and *h.* go hunt an Appetite *S.* iv. 114
His shining *h.* diffus'd a golden gleam *W.F.* 332
The trumpet sleep, while cheerful *h.* are blown *W.F.* 373

Hornoek.
H.'s fierce eye, and Roome's funereal frown *D.* iii. 152

Horned.
Mine, Goddess! mine is all the *h.* race *D.* iv. 376

Horrid.
Ye grots and caverns shagg'd with *h.* thorn *E.A.* 20
War, *h.* war, your thoughtful walks invades *O.* ii. 7
Already bear the *h.* things they say *R.L.* iv. 108

Horror.
O'er ev'ry vein a shudd'ring *h.* runs *D.* iv. 143
And breathes a browner *h.* on the woods *E.A.* 170
And screams of *h.* rend th' affrighted skies *R.L.* iii. 156
Shaking the h—s *of his sable brows D.* ii. 327
Alas, how chang'd! what sudden *h.* rise *E.A.* 99
On curst, dear *h.* of all-conscious night *E.A.* 229

Hors-d'œuvres.
Try'd all *h.,* all *liqueurs* defin'd *D.* iv. 317

Horse.
On *h.,* on foot, in hacks, and gilded chariots *D.* ii. 24
And loves you best of all things—but his *h. E.* v. 30
As heavy mules are neither *h.* nor ass *E.C.* 39
The winged courser, like a gen'rous *h. E.C.* 86
Paint Angels trembling round his falling *H. S.* i. 28
You limp, like Blackmore on a Lord Mayor's *h. S.* iii. 16
Back fly the scenes, and enter foot and *h. S.* v. 315
To run with H—s, *or to hunt with Dogs D.* iv. 526
A H.-laugh, *if you please, at Honesty E.S.* i. 38
Then by the rule that made the *H.-tail* bare *S.* v. 63

Horsemanship.
Then Peers grew proud in *H.* t' excel *S.* v. 143

Hosannas.
From the full choir when loud *H.* rise *E.A.* 353

Hospitable.
A Country Mouse, right *h. I.H.* ii. 158
The good old landlord's *h.* door *S.* vii. 114

Host.
His warlike Amazon her *h.* invades *R.L.* iii. 67

Hostile.
So shall each *h.* name become our own *D.* ii. 139
Some *h.* fury, some religious rage *M.E.* v. 12

Hot.
First thro' the length of yon *h.* Terrace sweat *M.E.* iv. 130

Hough.
Such as on *H.'s* unsully'd Mitre shine *E.S.* ii. 240

Hound.
By the French horn, or by the op'ning *h. D.* iv. 278
Or with his *h.* comes hollowing from the stable *E.* v. 27
And *h.,* sagacious on the tainted green *E.M.* i. 214
Rouse the fleet hart, and cheer the op'ning *h. W.F.* 150
With h—s *and horn go hunt an Appetite S.* iv. 114

Hounslow-heath.
To *H.* I point and Bansted-down *S.* ii. 143

Hour.
And see, my son! the *h.* is on its way *D.* iii. 123
The moon-struck Prophet felt the madding *h. D.* iv. 12
In vain, in vain—the all-composing *H. D.* iv. 627
This *h.* she's idoliz'd, the next abus'd *E.C.* 433
This *h.* a slave, the next a deity *E.M.* i. 68
Or in the mortal, *h. E.M.* i. 288
The *h.* conceal'd, and so remote the fear *E.M.* iii. 75
One self-approving *h.* whole years outweighs *E.M.* iv. 255
Seen him I have, but in his happier *h. E.S.* i. 29
How pleasing Atterbury's softer *h. E.S.* ii. 82
A smart Free-thinker? all things in an *h. M.E.* i. 157
Ascendant Phœbus watch'd that *h.* with care *M.E.* ii. 285
And I and Malice from this *h.* are friends *Mi.* l. 8
To act consistent with himself an *h. S.* iii. 137
To him commit the *h.,* the day, the year *S.* iv. 9
An *h.,* and not defraud the Public weal *S.* v. 6
Loose on the point of ev'ry waving *h. S.* vi. 249
Who forms the genius in the natal *h. S.* vi. 279
But does no other lord it at this *h. S.* vi. 306
They march to prate their *h.* before the Fair *S.* viii. 249
Grieve for an *h.,* perhaps, then mourn a year *U.L.* 56
To morning-walks, and pray'rs three h—s *a day E.v.* 14
Men in their loose unguarded *h.* they take *E.M.* iv. 227
My choicest *H.* of life are lost *I.H.* ii. 126
H., days, and years slide soft away *O.* iv. 10
In various talk th' instructive *h.* they past *R.L.* iii. 11
And if we will recite nine *h.* io ten *S.* v. 362
Come, lovely nymph, and bless the silent *h. Su.* 63

House.
Lost, lost too soon in yonder *H.* or Hall *D.* iv. 166
Thine is the genuine head of many a *h. D.* iv. 243
And keep his Lares, tho' his *h.* be sold *D.* iv. 366
You'll bring a *H.* (I mean of Peers) *E.* vi. 18
Since the whole *H.* did afterwards the same *E.S.* ii. 170
The last full fairly gives it to the *H., E.S.* ii. 180
Which one belonging to the *H. I.H.* i. 55
A little *H.,* with trees a-row *I.H.* i. 77
A handsome *H.* to lodge a Friend *I.H.* ii. 3 *s*
To a tall *h.* near Lincoln's-Inn *I.H.* ii. 184
His *H.,* embosom'd in the Grove *I.H.* iii. 21

And Zeal for that great *H*. which eats him up *M.E.* iii. 208
The *H*. impeach him; Coningsby harangues *M.E.*iii.397
Fo'rd that the *H*. reject him, "'Sdeath I'll print it *P.S.*61
My lands are sold, my father's *h*. is gone *S.* ii. 155
I wish to God this *h*. had been your own *S.* ii. 162
Takes the whole *H*. upon the Poet's Day *S.* iv. 88
Who, tho' the *H*. was up, delighted state *S.* vi. 186
Or what's in either of the H—s *I.H.* ii. 144
Cutler saw tenants break, and *h*. fall *M.E.* iii. 323
Let lands and *h*. have what Lords they will *S.* ii. 179
And beastly Skelton Heads of *H*. quote *S.* v. 38
And h. *with Montaigne now, and now with Locke S.* iii. 26

House of Lords.

So known, so honour'd, at the *H. S.* iv. 49

Hous'd.

Indulg'd the day that *h*. their annual grain *S.* v. 243

Household.

Mere *h*. trash! of birth-nights, balls, and shows *S.* viii. 130

Housewife.

Who would not scorn what *h*.'s cares produce *R.L.* v. 21

Hover.

Hang o'er the Box, and *h*. round the Ring *R.L.* i. 44
Straight *h*. round the Fair her airy band *R.L.* iii. 113

Hover'd.

The morning-dream that *h*. o'er her head *R.L.* i. 22

Hov'ring.

Morpheus h. o'er my Pillow *Mi.* vii. 23
Till *h*. o'er 'em sweeps the swelling net *W.F.* 104

How, However.—*Passim*.

Howard.

And high-born *H*., more majestic sire *D.* i. 297
Alas! not all the blood of all the H—s *E.M.* iv. 216

Howl.

Keen, hollow winds *h*. thro' the bleak recess *D.* i. 35
Let *Envy h*., while Heav'n's whole Chorus sings *E.S.* ii. 242
H. to the roarings of the Northern deep *S.* v. 329

Howlings.

And savage *h*. fill the sacred quires *W.F.* 72

Howls.

Silence, ye Wolves! while Ralph to Cynthia *h. D.* iii. 165

Hues.

She, tinsell'd o'er with robes of varying *h. D.* i. 81
In *h*. as gay, and odours as divine *S.* viii. 216

Huffing.

For *h*., braggart, puff'd Nobility *S.* viii. 201

Hug.

'Tis a Bear's talent not to kick, but *h. S.* i. 87

Huge.

He left *h*. Lintot, and out-stripp'd the wind *D.* ii. 62
And the *h*. boar is shrunk into an urn *D.* iv. 552
H. bales of British cloth blockade the door *M.E.* iii. 57
Lo what *h*. heaps of littleness around *M.E.* iv. 109
H. Theatres that now unpeopled Woods *M.E.* v. 7
H. moles, whose shadow stretch'd from shore to shore *M.E.* v. 21

Hum.

Till all, tun'd equal, send a gen'ral *h. D.* ii. 386
Slept first; the distant nodded to the *h. D.* ii. 402
Go see Sir Robert—See Sir Robert l—h. *E.S.* i. 27
To the same notes thy sons shall h., *or, snore D.* iv. 59
H. half a tune, tell stories to the squire *E.* v. 20
Look sour, and *h*. a Tune, as you may now *E.* v. 50

Human.

Then he: "Great Tamer of all *h*. art *D.* i. 163
Less *h*. genius than God gives an ape *D.* i. 282
Lo! one vast Egg produces *h*. race *D.* iii. 248
His Hat, which never vail'd to *h*. pride *D.* iv. 205

Their Infamy, still keep the *h*. shape *D.* iv. 528
Nor *h*. Spark is left, nor Glimpse *divine D.* iv. 652
All *h*. race, at sight of *h*. ties *E.A.* 75
One *h*. tear shall drop and be forgiv'n *E.A.* 358
So vast is art, so narrow *h*. wit *E.C.* 61
To err is *h*., to forgive, divine *E.C.* 525
A knowledge both of books and *h*. kind *E.C.* 640
In *h*. works, tho' labour'd on with pain *E.M.* i. 53
Hope springs eternal in the *h*. breast *E.M.* i. 95
If the great end be *h*. happiness *E.M.* i. 149
Natures ethereal, *h*., angel, man *E.M.* i. 238
Or tricks to shew the stretch of *h*. brain *E.M.* ii. 47
Two Principles in *h*. nature reign *E.M.* ii. 53
While still too wide or short is *h*. Wit *E.M.* iii. 90
Next his grim idol smear'd with *h*. blood *E.M.* iii. 266
The only point where *h*. bliss stands still *E.M.* iv. 311
The first, last purpose of the *h*. soul *E.M.* iv. 338
God loves from Whole to parts: but *h*. soul *E.M.* iv. 361
His country next; and next all *h*. race *E.M.* iv. 368
But past the Sense of *h*. Miseries *E.S.* i. 101
Lover of peace, and friend of *h*. kind *Ep.* vii. 8
Thy Country's friend, but more of *h*. kind *Ep.* ix. 4
Who from his study rails at *h*. kind *M.E.* i. 2
On *h*. actions reason tho' you can *M.E.* i. 25
An humble servant to all *h*. kind *M.E.* i. 253
Whose measure full o'erflows on *h*. race *M.E.* iii. 231
Unspotted long with *h*. blood *O.* ii. 6
Virtue confess'd in *h*. shape he draws *P.C.* 17
Others on Earth o'er *h*. race preside *R.L.* ii. 87
And heav'nly breasts with *h*. passions rage *R.L.* v. 46
All *h*. Virtue, to its latest breath *S.* v. 15
And yielding Metal flow'd to *h*. form *S.* v. 148
And pours each *h*. Virtue in the heart *S.* v. 220
Left free the *H*. Will *U.P.* 12
Follow'r of God or Friend of h.-kind *E.M.* iii. 284
The lover and the love of *h. E.M.* iv. 190

Humanity.

O soft *H*., in Age belov'd *Ep.* ix. 4

Humanly.

Modestly bold, and *h*. severe *E.C.* 636

Humble.

Eridanus his *h*. fountain scorns *D.* ii. 182
Fair from its *h*. bed I rear'd this Flow'r *D.* iv. 405
While prostrate here in *h*. grief I lie *E.A.* 277
This *h*. praise, lamented shade I receive *E.C.* 733
Let *h*. ALLEN, with an awkward Shame *E.S.* i. 135
And chose me for an *h*. friend *I.H.* ii. 86 s
Not therefore *h*. he who seeks retreat *M.E.* i. 113
An *h*. servant to all human kind *M.E.* i. 253
We owe to models of an *h*. kind *M.E.* ii. 192
All fly to TWIT'NAM, and in *h*. strain *P.S.* 21
So *h*., he has knock'd at *Tibbald's* door *P.S.* 372
By foreign hands thy *h*. grave adorn'd *U.L.* 53
Than what more *h*. mountains offer here *W.F.* 35
My *h*. Muse, in unambitious strains *W.F.* 427

Humbled.

All flesh is *h*., Westminster's bold race *D.* iv. 145
Made Horace dull, and *h*. Milton's strains *D.* iv. 212
Ambition *h*., mighty Cities storm'd *S.* v. 11

Humbler.

Behind that cloud-topt hill, and *h*. heav'n *E.M.* i. 104
Our *h*. province is to tend the Fair *R.L.* ii. 91
The *h*. Muse of Comedy require *S.* v. 283
Whom *h*. joys of home-felt quiet please *W.F.* 239

Humbling.

Fortune not much of *h*. me can boast *S.* ii. 151

Humbly.

The Sense, they *h*. take upon content *E.C.* 308
Hope *h*., then; with trembling pinions soar *E.M.* i. 91
This, *h*. offers me his Case *I.H.* ii. 67 s
And *h*. live on rabbits, and on roots *S.* ii. 52

Humility.

The monk's *h*., the hero's pride *E.M.* ii. 173
Then give *H*. a coach and six *E.M.* iv. 170

Humming.

Still *h*. on, their drowsy course they keep *E.C.* 600
Like bees, are *h*. in my ears *I.H.* ii. 70 s
The dull may waken to a h.*-bird D.* iv. 446

Humour.

Whose sense instructs us, and whose *h*. charms *A.* 9
Have *H*., Wit, a native Ease and Grace *E.* iv. 27
Good *h.* only teaches charms to last *E.* iv. 61
Each vital *h.* which should feed the whole *E.M.* ii. 139
With native *H.* temp'ring virtuous Rage *Ep.* xi. 3
Yet has her *h.* most, when she obeys *M.E.* ii. 264
An equal mixture of good *H. Mi.* viii. 7
So when small h—s gather to a gout *E.M.* ii. 159
Manners with Fortunes, *H.* turn with Climes *M.E.* i. 172
You h. me when I am sick *I.H.* i. 5

Huns.

Great nurse of Goths, of Alans, and of *H. D.* iii 90
Dennis, who long had warr'd with modern *H. Mi.* ii. 11

Hundred.

Here one poor word an *h*. cleaches makes *D.* i. 63
An *h.* sons, and ev'ry son a God *D.* iii. 134
Behold an *h.* sons, and each a Dunce *D.* iii. 138
Gay dies unpension'd with a *h.* friends *D.* iii. 330
Like bold Briareus with a *h.* hands *D.* iv. 66
On whom three *h.* gold-capt youths await *D.* iv. 117
A *h.* head of Aristotle's friends *D.* iv. 192
An *h.* Souls of Turkeys in a pie *D.* iv. 394
To tell 'em would a *h.* tongues require (*rep.*) *E.C.* 44
Or let it cost five *h.* pound *I.H.* ii. 39 *s*
A *h.* other Men's affairs *I.H.* ii. 69 *s*
He, with a *h.* Arts refin'd *I.H.* iii. 15
A *h.* oxen at your levee roar *M.E.* iii. 58
This man possest—five *h.* pounds a year *M.E.* iii. 280
A *h.* footsteps scrape the marble hall *M.E.* iv. 152
The sacred rust of twice ten *h.* years *M.E.* v. 38
And ridicules beyond a *h.* foes *P.S.* 110
Or smoking forth, a *h.* hawkers' load *P.S.* 217
A *h.* smart in Timon and in Balaam *S.* i. 42
Add one round *h.*, and (if that's not fair) *S.* iv. 75
Ask'd for a groat, he gives a *h.* pounds *S.* iv. 86
Who died, perhaps, an *h.* years ago *S.* v. 52
Sprat, Carew, Sedley, and a *h.* more *S.* v. 109
Bright thro' the rubbish of some *h.* years *S.* vi. 166
When, of a *h.* thorns, you pull out one *S.* vi. 321
And harvests on a *h.* realms bestows *W.F.* 360
In dirt and darkness, h—s stink content *S.* iii. 133

Hung.

While she with garlands *h.* the bending boughs *A.* 68
H. silent down his never-blushing head *D.* ii. 417
H. to the Goddess, and coher'd around *D.* iv. 78
On him, their second Providence, they *h. E.M.* iii. 217
H. o'er with titles, and *h.* round with strings *E.M.* iv. 205
Is *h.* on high, to poison half mankind *E.M.* iv. 252
Tho' wond'ring Senates *h.* on all he spoke *M.E.* i. 184
Who *h.* with woods yon mountain's sultry brow *M.E.* iii. 253
Nourish'd two Locks, which graceful *h.* behind *R.L.* ii. 20
On her heav'd bosom *h.* her graceful head *R.L.* iv. 145
For *h.* with deadly sins I see the wall *S.* viii. 274
Now *h.* with pearls the dropping trees appear *W.* 31
And on his willows *h.* each muse's lyre *W.F.* 276

Hunger.

That very life his learned *h.* craves *E.M.* iii. 63
Oblig'd by *h.*, and request of friends *P.S.* 44
And envy'd Thirst and *H.* to the Poor *S.* iv. 117
Between revenge and grief, and *h.* join'd *S.* vi. 38
Who h., and who thirst for scribbling sake *D.* i. 50

Hungerford.

And *H.* re-echoes bawl for bawl *D.* ii. 266

Hungry.

Yet hence the Poor are cloth'd, the *H.* fed *M.E.* iv. 169
The *h.* Judges soon the sentence sign *R.L.* iii. 21

Hunt.

Thro' twilight ages *h.* th' Athenian fowl *D.* iv. 361
To run with Horses, or to *h.* with Dogs *D.* iv. 526
As beasts of Nature may we *h.* the Squires *M.E.* ii. 31
Go work, *h.*, exercise! (he thus began) *S.* ii. 11
With hounds and horns go *h.* an Appetite *S.* iv. 114
To *h.* for Truth in Maudlin's learned grove *S.* vi. 57

Hunted.

So Proteus, *h.* in a nobler shape *D.* ii. 129

Hunter.

A mighty *h.*, and his prey was man *W.F.* 62

Huntress.

Th' immortal *h.*, and her virgin train *W.F.* 160

Huntsmen.

Six *h.* with a shout precede his chair *D.* ii. 193

Hurl'd.

Atoms or systems into ruin *h. E.M.* i. 89
Let ruling Angels from their spheres be *h. E.M.* i. 253
Sole judge of Truth, in endless Error *h. E.M.* ii. 17
Pit, box, and gall'ry in convulsions *h. P.S.* 87

Hurls.

And *h.* the Thunder of the Laws on Gia *E.S.* i. 130

Hurries.

It *h.* all too fast to mark their way *M.E.* i. 38
And dreads more actions, *h.* from a jail *S.* viii. 183

Hurry.

I *h.* me in haste away *I.H.* ii. 45 *s*

Hurt.

Sejanus, Wolsey, *h. not honest Fleury E.S.* i. 51
You *h.* a man that's rising in the Trade *E.S.* ii. 35
Then wisely plead, to me they meant no *h. E.S.* ii. 144
How *h.* he you? he only stained the Gown *E.S.* ii. 165
Whom have I *h.*? has Poet yet, or Peer *P.S.* 95
Its proper power to *h.*, each creature feels *S.* i. 85
These Madmen never *h.* the Church or State *S.* v. 190
Then too we *h.* ourselves, when to defend *S.* v. 364
God knows, may *h.* the very ablest head *S.* vi. 103
Silence or *h.*, he libels the great Man *S.* viii. 159

Hurts.

These nothing *h.*; they keep their Fashion still *E.S.* i. 43
Scarce *h.* the Lawyer, but undoes the Scribe *E.S.* ii. 47
But he who *h.* a harmless neighbour's peace *P.S.* 287
And heals with Morals, what *h.* with Wit *S.* v. 262
And itch most *h.* when anger'd to a sore *S.* viii. 119

Husband.

Come then, my father, brother, *h.*, friend *E.A.* 152
He has a *h.* that will make amends *E.J.S.* 26
The Stoic *H.* was the glorious thing *E.J.S.* 38
Chaste to her *H.*, frank to all beside *M.E.* ii. 71
She, who ne'er answers till a *H.* cools *M.E.* ii. 261
Oh take the *h.*, or return the wife *O.* i. 82
As soo, as father, brother, *h.*, friend *O.* iii. 28
When h—s, or when lap-dogs breathe their last *R.L.* iii. 158

Hush.

O sing, and *h.* the Nations with thy Song *D.* iv. 626

Hush'd.

Now May'rs and Shrieves all *h.* and satiate lay *D.* i. 91
The clam'rous crowd is *h.* with mugs of Mum *D.* ii. 385
And all was *h.*, as Folly's self lay dead *D.* ii. 418
H. are the birds, and clos'd the drooping flow'rs *Sp.* 70
Or *h.* with wonder, hearken from the sprays *W.* 56
And the *h.* waves glide softly to the shore *W.F.* 354

Huts.

As Hog to Hog in *h.* of Westphaly *E.S.* ii. 172

Huzzas.

Of stupid starers, and of loud *h. E.M.* iv. 256

Hybla.

Diana Cynthus, Ceres *H.* loves (*rep.*) *Sp.* 66

Hyde.

Shall be no more than Tully, or than *H. S.* iv. 53

Hyde-park.

Sooner shall grass in *H.* Circus grow *R.L.* iv. 117
Thoughts which at H.-corner I forget *S.* vi. 208

Hylas.

H. and Ægon sung their rural lays *A.* *u*
H. and Ægon's rural lays I sing *A.* 6
When tuneful *H.* with melodious moan *A.* 15
As *H.* fair was ravish'd long ago *D.* ii. 336

Hymen.

Sacred *H.!* these are thine *O.* iii. 44
Are destin'd *H.*'s willing Victim, too *E.* iv. 58
But *H.* kinder flames unite *O.* iii. 21

Hymenæals.
For her white virgins *H.* sing *E.A.* 220
Hymn.
Thy voice I seem in ev'ry *h.* to hear *E.A.* 263
Hymn'd.
All vocal beings *h.* their equal God *E.M.* iii. 156
Hymning.
Hence *h.* Tyburn's elegiac lines *D.* i. 41
Hyperborean.
Soon as they dawn, from *H.* skies *D.* iii. 85
Hypocrite.
Without the soul, the Muse's *H. D.* iv. 100
Hysteric.
Who give th' *h.*, or poetic fit *R.L.* iv. 60

I.

I.—*Passim.*
Iber.
Red *I.'s* sands, or Ister's foaming flood *W.F.* 368
Iberian.
And He, whose light'ning pierc'd th' *I.* lines *S.* i. 129
Ice.
Glitt'ring with *i.* here hoary hills are seen *D.* i. 75
Ichor.
Sign'd with that *I.* which from Gods distils *D.* ii. 92
Icy.
Tempt *i.* seas, where scarce the waters roll *W.F.* 389
Idalia.
Celestial Venus haunts *I.'s* groves *Sp.* 65
Idea.
Where mix'd with God's his lov'd *I.* lies *E.A.* 12
Blot out each bright *I.* of the skies *E.A.* 284
Some bright *I.* of the master's mind *E.C.* 485
Fir'd with I—s *of fair Italy E.* iii. 26
Thence endless streams of fair *I.* flow *E.* iii. 43
The dear *I.*, where I fly, pursue *E.A.* 264
Long lov'd, ador'd *i.*, all adieu *E.* 296
Form short *I.*; and offend in arts *E.C.* 287
Till Kings call forth th' *I.* of your mind *M.E.* iv. 195
Then gay *I.* crowd the vacant brain *R.L.* i. 83
He watch'd th' *I.* rising in her mind *R.L.* iii. 142
Idiot.
Fate in their dotage this fair *I.* gave *D.* i. 13
Stretch'd to relieve the *I.* and the Poor *S.* v. 226
Idle.
So when your Slave, at some dear *i.* time *E.* v. 41
Here no man prates of *i.* things *I.H.* ii. 141
The world had wanted many an *i.* song *P.S.* 28
I left no calling for this *i.* trade *P.S.* 129
And *i.* Cibber, how he breaks the laws *S.* v. 292
Shall I, in London, act this *i.* part *S.* vi. 125
As vain, as *i.*, and as false as they *S.* viii. 22
The busy, *i.*, blockheads of the ball *S.* viii. 203
Life's *i.* business at one gasp be o'er *U.L.* 81
Idleness.
The Pains and Penalties of *I. D.* iv. 344
Or Learning's Luxury, or *I. E.M.* ii. 46
Idly.
Dragg'd in the dust! his arms hang *i.* round *E.S.* i. 153
Idol.
But senseless, lifeless! *i.* void and vain *D.* ii. 46
Next his grim *i.* smear'd with human blood *E.M.* iii. 266
Idoliz'd.
This hour she's *i.*, the next abus'd *E.C.* 433
Idume.
For thee *I.'s* spicy forests blow *M.* 95

II.—*Passim.*
Ignoble.
Envy, to which th' *i.* mind's a slave *E.M.* ii. 191
Go! if your ancient, but *i.* blood *E.M.* iv. 211
The thriving plants, *i.* broomsticks made *M.E.* iv. 97
Ignobly.
I. vain, and impotently great *P.C.* 29
Ignorance, Ign'rance.
And saving *I.* enthrones by Laws *D.* iii. 98
Alike in *i.*, his reason such *E.M.* ii. 11
If Wit so much from *I'e* undergo *E.C.* 308
Ignorant.
And men, once *i.*, are slaves *O.* ii. 28
Ignorantly.
The bookful blockhead, *i.* read *E.C.* 612
Ilion.
When the last blaze sent *I.* to the skies *D.* i. 236

Ill.
Or what *i.* eyes malignant glances dart *A.* 82
Now (shame to Fortune) an *i.* Run at Play *D.* i. 113
Appear in writing or in judging *i. E.C.* 2
For each *i.* Author is as bad a Friend *E.C.* 519
Ascribe all Good; to their improper, *I. E.M.* ii. 58
Th' Eternal Act educing good from *i. E.M.* ii. 175
Reason the bias turns to good from *i. E.M.* ii. 197
'Tis but by parts we follow good or *i. E.M.* ii. 235
No *i.* could fear in God; and understood *E.M.* ii. 237
Nor present good or *i.*, the joy or curse *E.M.* iv. 71
What makes all physical or moral *i. E.M.* iv. 111
God sends not *i.*; if rightly understood (*rep.*) *E.M.* iv. 113
As that the virtuous son is *i.* at ease *E.M.* iv. 119
But stain'd with blood, or *i.* exchanged for gold *E.M.* iv. 296
And tastes the good without the fall to *i. E.M.* iv. 312
Agrees as *i.* with Rufa studying Locke *M.E.* i. 23
And yet, believe me, good as well as *i. M.E.* ii. 269
And swear no day was ever past so *i. M.E.* iv. 168
By *Cards' I.* Usage, or by *Lovers lost Mi.* ix. 26
She sees, and trembles at th' approaching *i. R.L.* iii. 91
How soon they find fit instruments of *i. R.L.* iii. 126
Whate'er my fate,—or well or *i.* at Court *S.* i. 97
I. health some just indulgence may engage *S.* ii. 87
Careless how *i.* I with myself agree *S.* vii. 175
And Sidney's verse halts *i.* on Roman feet *S.* v. 98
One Giant-Vice, so excellently *i. S.* vii. 4
Excuse for writing, and for writing *i. S.* vii. 28
And says our wars thrive *i.*, because delay'd *S.* viii. 163
As prone to *i.*, as negligent of good *S.* viii. 200
To see the Good from *I. U.P.* 10
For *i*—s *or accidents that chance to all E.M.* iv. 98
By love of Courts to num'rous *i.* betray'd *R.L.* iv. 152
Is by *i.*-colouring but the more disgrac'd *E.C.* 24
Of Social Pleasure, *i.*-exchang'd for Pow'r *E.S.* i. 30
Oh wealth *i.*-fated! which no act of fame *E.M.* iv. 299
Let softer strains *i.* Henry mourn *W.F.* 311
What brought Sir Visto's *i.*-got wealth to waste *M.E.* iv. 15
Then strongly fencing *i.* wealth by law *S.* vii. 93
But Times corrupt, and Nature *i.*-inclin'd *S.* v. 251
Here stood *I.*-nature like an ancient maid *R.L.* iv. 27
Figures *i.*-pair'd, and Similes unlike *D.* i. 66
Here brib'd the rage of *i.*-requited beav'n *E.A.* 138
Ah Dennis! Gildon ah! what *i.*-starr'd rage *D.* iii. 173

Illumes.
I. their light, and sets their flames on fire *D.* iii. 260
Illumine.
O let my Country's Friends *i.* mine *E.S.* ii. 121
Illusion.
And turn this whole *i.* on the town *D.* ii. 132
Ye soft *i*—s, dear deceits, arise *E.A.* 240
Illustrious.
Glory, and gain, th' *i.* tribe provoke *D.* ii. 33
See all her progeny, *i.* sight *D.* iii. 129
How finish'd with *i.* toil appears *E.* iii. 39
Boast the pure blood of an *i.* race *E.M.* iv. 207
And so may'st thou, *i.* Passeran *E.S.* i. 124

Illustriously.
To all the world *i.* are lost *S p.* 10

Image.
In each she marks her *I.* full exprest *D.* i. 107
She form'd this *i.* of well-body'd air *D.* ii. 42
Make God Man's *I.,* Man the final Cause *D.* iv. 478
Or that bright *I.* to our fancy draw *D.* iv. 487
The living *i.* in the painter's breast *E.* iii. 42
Thy *i.* steals between my God and me *E.A.* 268
That gives us back the *i.* of our mind *E.C.* 300
If not God's *i.,* yet his shadow drew *E.M.* iii. 288
And Heav'n beholds its *i.* in his breast *E.M.* iv. 372
As the last *i.* of that troubled heap *M.E.* i. 45
Should'ring God's altar a vile *i.* stands *M.E.* iii. 293
As her dead Father's rev'rend *i.* past *P.C.* 31
A heav'nly *i.* in the glass appears *R.L.* i. 125
There motley i—s *her fancy strike D.* i. 65
While *I.* reflect from art to art *E.* iii. 20
And Art reflected *i.* to Art *M.E.* v. 52
But in known *I.* of life, I guess *S.* v. 281
Thence to their *i.* on earth it flows *U.L.* 15
And i. *charms he must behold no more E.A.* 362

Imaginary.
And builds *i.* Rome anew *E.* iii. 32
Before you pass th' *i.* sights *E.* v. 35

Imagination.
Where beams of warm *i.* play *E.C.* 58
I. plies her dang'rous art *E.M.* ii. 143

Imagine.
Oft, when the world *i.* women stray *R.L.* i. 91

Imbibes.
I. new life, and scours and stinks along *D.* ii. 106

Imitate.
And turn their heads to *i.* the Sun *E.M.* ii. 28
And, as I love, would *i.* the Man *E.M.* ii. 132
No more the birds shall *i.* her lays *W.* 55

Imitating.
And quitting sense call *i.* God *E.M.* ii. 26
Fill half the land with I.-*Fools M.E.* iv. 26

Imitation.
The Vulgar thus thro' *I.* err *E.C.* 424

Immac'late.
Sweeter than Sbaroo, in *i.* trim *S.* viii. 252

Immediate.
That sees *i.* good by present sense *E.M.* ii. 73

Immense.
I. the pow'r, *i.* were the demand *E.M.* iv. 165
Pursues that Chain which links th' *i.* design *E.M.* iv. 333

Immensity.
He who thro' vast *I.* can pierce *E.M.* i. 23

Immortal.
She saw, with joy, the line *i.* run *D.* i. 99
But oh ! with One, *i.* One dispense *D.* iii. 217
I. Rich ¡ how calm he sits at ease *D.* iii. 261
And graft my love *i.* on thy fame *E.A.* 344
Held from afar, aloft, th' *i.* prize *E.C.* 96
A work t' outlast *i.* Rome design'd *E.C.* 131
I. heirs of universal praise *E.C.* 190
I. Vida: on whose honour'd brow *E.C.* 705
Alone made perfect here, *i.* there *E.M.* i. 120
I. S— k, and grave De—re *E.S.* i. 92
And makes *i.,* Verse as mean as mine *E.S.* i. 247
Th' *i.* pow'rs incline their ear *O.* i. 127
Groves, where *i.* sages taught *O.* ii. 2
Just so *i. Maro* held his head *P.S.* 122'
In short that reas'ning, high, *i.* Thing *S.* iii. 185
And grew *I.* in his own despite *S.* v. 72
Th' *i.* huntress, and her virgin train *W.F.* 160
To crown the forest with *i.* greens *W.F.* 286
Tho' Tiber's streams *i.* Rome behold *W.F.* 357
Can touch I—s, *'tis a Soul like thine E.* i. 22

Immortality.
And Faith, our early *i. E.A.* 300

Immortalize.
When British bards begin t' *i. S.* v. 54

Immur'd.
Him the damn'd Doctors and his Friends *i. S.* vi. 192

Imps.
Three wicked *i.* of her own Grub-street choir *D.* ii. 123
Gods, *i.,* and monsters, music, rage, and mirth *D.*iii.238

Impairs.
But let them write for you, each rogue *i. S.* vii. 99

Impale.
I. a Glow-worm, or Virtu profess *D.* iv. 569

Impart.
How oft our slowly-growing works *i. E.* iii. 19
The virgin's wish, without her fears *i. E.A.* 55
Life, force, and beauty, must to all *i. E.C.* 72
T' enjoy them, and the Virtue to *i. M.E.* iii. 220
Oil, though it stink, they drop by drop *i. S.* ii. 59
Or better Precepts if you can *i. S.* iv. 132
No lambs or sheep for victims I'll *i. S p.* 51
If I am right, thy grace *i. U.P.* 29

Imparted.
Those, that *i.,* court a nobler aim *E.M.* ii. 99

Impartial.
Heav'n to mankind *i.* we confess *E.M.* iv. 53
Did not the Sneer of more *i.* men *E.S.* i. 59
I., she shall say who suffers most *Mi.* ix. 25
In this *i.* glass, my Muse intends *S.* i. 57

Imparts.
Fir'd at first sight with what the Muse *i. E.C.* 219
To Man *i.* it ; but with such a view *E.M.* iii. 73

Impatient.
Rush to the world, *i.* for the day *D.* iii. 30
Demanding life, *i.* for the skies *M.* 90
I grow *i.,* and the Tea's too strong *Mi.* ix. 108
Th' *i.* courser pants in ev'ry vein *W.F.* 151

Impeach.
The House *i.* him, Coningsby harangues *M.E.* iii. 397

Imp'd.
Gold, *i.* by thee, can compass hardest things *M.E.* iii. 41

Impell'd.
Why doing, suff'ring, check'd, *i.;* and why *E.M.* i. 67
Form'd and *i.* its neighbour to embrace *E.M.* iii. 12
The same adust complexion has *i. M.E.* i. 107

Impelling.
Heir urges heir, like wave *i.* wave *S.* vi. 253

Impels.
Active its task, it prompts, *i.,* inspires *E.M.* ii. 68
And sev'ral Men *i.* to sev'ral ends *E.M.* ii. 166

Impend.
I saw, alas ! some dread event *i. R.L.* i. 109

Impending.
Th' *i.* woe sat heavy on his breast *R.L.* ii. 54

Impenetrably.
Of solid proof, *i.* dull *D.* iii. 26

Impenitently.
What crowds of these, *i.* bold *E.C.* 604

Imperfect.
Then say not Man's *i.,* Heav'n in fault *E.M.* i. 69

Imperfection.
Call *i.* what thou fancy'st such *E.M.* i. 115
Cease then, nor ORDER *I.* name *E.M.* i. 281

Imperial.
And here she plann'd th' *i.* seat of Fools *D.* i. 272
That lifts our Goddess to *i.* sway *D.* iii. 124
Her seat *i.* Dulness shall transport *D.* iii. 298
Mark how it mounts to Man's *i.* race *E.M.* i. 209
Rise, crown'd with light, *i.* Salem, rise *M.* 85
These are *I.* works, and worthy Kings *M.E.* iv. 204
I. wonders rais'd on Nations spoil'd *M.E.* v. 5

IMPERIOUS—INCREASES.   155

Fair tresses man's *i.* race ensnare *R.L.* ii. 27
Th' *i.* consort of the crown of Spades *R.L.* iii. 68
And strike to dust th' *i.* tow'rs of Troy *R.L.* iii. 174

Imperious.
Some greedy minion, or *i.* wife *E.M.* iv. 302

Impertinence.
And old *i.* expel by new *R.L.* i. 94

Impertinent.
Neatness itself *i.* in him *S.* viii. 253

Impetuous.
Not so from shameless Curl; *i.* spread *D.* ii. 179
Down, down thy larum, with *i.* whirl *D.* iii. 163

Impiety.
Vile worm!—Oh Madness! Pride! *I. E.M.* i. 258

Impious.
Or, *i.*, preach his word without a call *D.* iv. 94
But soon by *i.* arms from Latium chas'd *E.C.* 709
Or *i.* Discontent *U.P.* 24

Implicit.
And damns *i.* faith, and holy lies *D.* iv. 463

Implore.
I. your help in these pathetic strains *S.* v. 232
Behold us kindly, who your name *i. IV.* 75

Implor'd.
For this, ere Phœbus rose, he had *i. R.L.* ii. 35

Import.
Others *i.* yet nobler arts from France *D.* iv. 597

Importance.
Hear and believe! thy own *i.* know *R.L.* i. 35

Important.
Dear BETTY shall th' *i.* point decide *Mi.* ix. 23
We trust th' *i.* charge, the Petticoat *R.L.* ii. 118
Descend, and sit on each *i.* card *R.L.* iii. 32

Imported.
And little sure *i.* to remove *S.* vi. 56

Imports.
'Faith, it *i.* not much from whom it came *E.S.* ii. 168

Impose.
Prompt to *i.*, and fond to dogmatize *D.* iv. 464

Impotence.
As shameful sure as *I.* in love *E.C.* 533
And rhyme with all the rage of *I. E.C.* 609
Say what can cause such *i.* of mind *M.E.* ii. 93
Whether in florid *i.* he speaks *P.S.* 317

Impotently.
Ignobly vain, and *i.* great *P.C.* 29

Imprest.
Each sire *i.*, and glaring in his son *D.* i. 100
What Dulness dropt among her sons *i. D.* ii. 407
On air or sea new motions be *i. E.M.* iv. 125
Which Nature has *i. O.* iii. 10

Imprison'd.
Nor let th' *i.* essences exhale *R.L.* ii. 94

Improper.
Ascribe all Good; to their *i.*, Ill *E.M.* ii. 58

Improve.
I. we these. Three Cat-calls be the bribe *D.* ii. 231
Reflection, Reason, still the ties *i. E.M.* iii. 131
Who then shall grace, or who *i.* the Soil *M.E.* iv. 177
Let day *i.* on day, and year on year *Mi.* v. 15
Our joys below it can *i. O.* i. 122
While solemn airs *i.* the sacred fire *O.* i. 129
If Time *i.* our Wit as well as Wine *S.* v. 49

Improv'd.
Short, and but rare, till Man *i.* it all *E.M.* iv. 116
In ev'ry taste of foreign Courts *i. S.* v. 141

Improves.
Clears and *i.* whate'er it shines upon *E.C.* 316
I. the keenness of the Northern wind *M.E.* iv. 112

Impudence.
Still happy *I.* obtains the prize *D.* ii. 186
Firm *I.*, or Stupefaction mild *D.* iv. 530
The trim of pride, the *i.* of wealth *E.M.* iii. 4
Oh *I.* of wealth! with all thy store *S.* ii. 117
Whom crimes gave wealth, and wealth gave *I. S.* vii. 46

Impudent.
So *i.*, I own myself no knave *E.S.* ii. 206

Impudently.
In all the rest so *i.* good *E.J.S.* 48
Not Fannius' self more *i.* near *S.* viii. 175

Impulsive.
And strong *i.* gravity of Head *D.* iv. 76

Imputed.
And, instant, fancy feels th' *i.* sense *D.* ii. 200
Th' *i.* trash, and dulness not his own *P.S.* 351

Imputes.
I. to me and my damn'd works the cause *P.S.* 24

In.—*Passim.*

Inanimate.
And leave *i.* the naked wall *W.F.* 308

Incense.
Let Flatt'ry sick'ning see the *I.* rise *E.S.* ii. 244
With all the *i.* of the breathing spring *M.* 24
But well-dispers'd, is *I.* to the Skies *M.E.* iii. 236
All Nature's *I.* rise *U.P.* 52
Nor fragrant herbs their native *i.* yield *W.* 48

Incens'd.
Now meet thy fate, *i.* Belinda cry'd *R.L.* v. 87

Incline.
Hold—to the Minister I more *i. D.* i. 213
The very best will variously *i. E.M.* iv. 143
Th' immortal pow'rs *i.* their ear *O.* i. 127

Inclin'd.
Just as the Twig is bent, the Tree's *i. M.E.* i. 150

Inclines.
Now to the Baron fate *i.* the field *R.L.* iii. 66
The Soul subsides, and wickedly *i. S.* ii. 79
I. our action, not constrains our will *S.* vi. 281

Inclose.
T' *i.* the Lock; now joins it to divide *R.L.* iii. 148

Inclos'd.
And once *i.* in Woman's beauteous mould *R.L.* i. 48

Incoherent.
Is half so *i.* as my Mind *S.* iii. 166

Inconsistencies.
The Fool lies hid in *i. M.E.* i. 70

Inconsistent.
How *i.* greater goods with these *E.M.* iv. 273

Incorrect.
The piece, you think, is *i.*? why, take it *P.S.* 45

Increase.
Whose honours with *i.* of ages grow *E.C.* 191
Sprung the rank weed, and thriv'd with large *i. E.C.* 535
Tho' each may feel *i.*—s and decays *E.C.* 404
But mutual wants this Happiness *i. E.M.* iv. 55
I ask not to *i.* my store *I.H.* ii. 8 s
Or makes his Neighbours glad, if he *i. M.E.* iv. 182
If teeming ewes *i.* my fleecy breed *W.* 82
Behold! Augusta's glitt'ring spires *i. W.F.* 377

Increas'd.
Pursu'd her flight; her flight *i.* his fire *W.F.* 184

Increases.
How Trade *i.*: and the World goes well *M.E.* i. 159

Increasing.
Th' *i.* prospect tires our wand'ring eyes *E.C.* 231
Indebted.
I. to no Prince, or Peer alive *S.* vi. 69
Indeed.—*Passim.*
Indentures.
I., Cov'nants, Articles they draw *S.* vii. 94
Independency.
My Bread and *I. I.H.* i. 70
Index-hand.
When lo ! a Spectre rose, whose *i. D.* iv. 139
Index-learning.
How *i.* turns no student pale *D.* i. 279
India.
To either *I.* see the Merchant fly *S.* iii. 69
Let *I.* boast her plants, nor envy we *W.F.* 29
This casket I.'s *glowing gems unlocks R.L.* i. 133
Indian.
Lo the poor *I.* ! whose untutor'd mind *E.M.* i. 99
Go, like the *I.*, in another life *E.M.* iv. 177
Can mark the figures on an *I.* chest *M.E.* ii. 168
Asleep and naked as an *I.* lay *M.E.* iii. 361
Arabian shores, or *I.* seas infold *S.* v. 11
For *I.* spices, for Peruvian gold *S.* iv. 71
And one describes a charming *I.* screen *R.L.* iii. 14
Till the freed I—*s in their native groves W.F.* 409
Indites.
Hear how learn'd Greece her useful rules *i. E.C.* 92
Individual.
Each *i.* seeks a sev'ral goal *E.M.* ii. 237
The Boy and Man an *i.* makes' *E.M.* iv. 175
Must rise from *I.* to the Whole *E.M.* iv. 362
Each *i.* : His great End the same *S.* vi. 283
There's not a blessing I—*s find E.M.* iv. 39
Know, all the good that *i.* find *E.M.* iv. 77
Indolence.
The merchant's toil, the sage's *i. E.M.* ii. 172
Indolent.
Or *i.*, to each extreme they fall *E.M.* iv. 25
The good man may be weak, be *i. E.M.* iv. 155
Indulge.
I., dread Chaos, and eternal Night *D.* iv. 2
When to repress, and when *i.* our flights *E.C.* 93
I. my candour, and grow all to all *S.* iii. 32
Indulg'd.
St. John, whose love *i.* my labours past *S.* iii. 1
I. the day that hous'd their annual grain *S.* v. 243
Indulgence.
Ill health some just *i.* may engage *S.* ii. 87
The labour greater, as th' *i.* less *S.* v. 285
Indulges.
Nor quite *i.*, nor can quite repress *W.F.* 20
Indus.
And waft a sigh from *I.* to the Pole *E.A.* 58
Industrious.
And suck'd all o'er like an *i.* Bug *D.* i. 130
Oh filthy check on all *i.* skill *M.E.* iii. 75
Th' *i.* bees neglect their golden store *W.* 51
The fields are ravish'd from the *i.* swains *W. F.* 65
Industry.
Rich *I.* sits smiling on the plains *W.F.* 41
Inertly.
Suspend a while your Force *i.* strong *D.* iv. 7
Inestimable.
And shall this prize, th' *i.* prize *R.L.* iv. 113
Inexorable.
I. Death shall level all *S.* vi. 262
Infamous.
Or *i.* for plunder'd provinces *E.M.* iv. 298

Infamy.
Their *I.*, still keep the human shape *D.* iv. 528
The Fount of Fame or *I. E.* vi. 12
'Twill then be *i.* to seem your friend *R.L.* iv. 112
Are no rewards for want and *i. S.* ii. 104
With Praise or *I.* leave that to fate *S.* iii. 102
Infant.
O ! pass more innocent, in *i.* state *D.* i. 237
The soil that arts and *i.* letters bore *D.* iii. 96
A dauntless *i. I* never scar'd with God *D.*i v. 284
The smiling *i.* in his hand shall take *M.* 81
If e'er one vision touch'd thy *i.* thought *R.L.* i. 29
Her *i.* grandame's whistle next it grew *R.L.* v. 93
Dropping with I.'s *blood, and Mother's tears D.* iv. 142
As smiling I—*s sport themselves to rest E.* iv. 14
Health to himself, and to his *I.* bread *M.E.* iv. 170
Teach I.-checks *a bidden blush to know R.L.* i. 89
Infected.
All seems *i.* that th' *i.* spy *E.C.* 558
Infection.
I felt th' *i.* slide from him to me *S.* viii. 170
Infer.
I. the motive from the Deed, and shew *M.E.* i. 101
Inferior.
Were we to press, *i.* might on ours *E.M.* i. 242
But an *I.* not dependant ? worse *M.E.* ii. 136
Th' *i.* Priestess at her altar's side *R.L.* i. 127
Infernal.
Saw Gods descend, and fiends *i.* rise *E. M.* iii. 254
And when thro' all th' *i.* bounds *O.* i. 49
Not Dante dreaming all th' *i.* state *S.* viii. 192
Infers.
More rich, more wise ; but who *i.* from hence *E.M.* iv. 51
Infidels.
Which Jews might kiss, and *I.* adore *R.L.* ii. 8
Infinite.
That Wisdom *i.* must form the best *E.M.* i. 44
No glass can reach ; from *I.* to thee *E. M.* i. 240
Inflame.
Others a sword-knot and lac'd suit *i. D.* ii. 52
Hence diff'rent Passions more or less *i. E.M.* ii. 129
Like Citron-waters matrons' cheeks *i. R.L.* iv. 69
Does neither Rage *i.*, nor Fear appal *S.* vi. 308
Inflam'd.
Well-natur'd Garth *i.* with early praise *P.S.* 137
They parch'd with heat, and I *i.* by thee *S*u. 20
Influence.
Oh spread thy *I.*, but restrain thy Rage *D.* iii. 122
Beniger *i.* on thy nodding head *D.* iv. 346
Born where heav'n's *i.* scarce can penetrate *M.E.* . 142
Infold.
Arabian shores or Indian seas *i. S.* iv. 11
The pearly shell its lucid globe *i. W.F.* 395
Inform.
I. us, will the Emp'ror treat *I.H.* ii. 114 *s*
Inform'd.
Each purer frame *i.* with purer fire *E.* iii. 50
Informer.
Nor sly *i.* watch these words to draw *S.* vii. 127
Informing.
In some fair body thus th' *i.* soul *E.C.* 76
Informs.
Breathes in our soul, *i.* our mortal part *E.M.* i. 275
I. you, Sir, 'Twas when he knew no better *P.S.* 52
Infuse.
As verse, or prose, *i.* the drowsy God *D.* ii. 396
Ingenious.
Mere curious pleasure, or *i.* pain *E.M.* ii. 48

Inglorious.
I. triumphs and dishonest scars *W.F.* 326

Ingloriously.
Replenish, not *i.*, at home *D.* ii. 166

Ingratitude.
I.'s the certain Crop *I.H.* i. 32

Inhabitant.
The hard *i.* contends is right *E.M.* ii. 230
Of thousand bright I—*s of air R.L.* i. 28

Inheriting.
Born to no Pride, *i.* no Strife *P.S.* 392

Inherits.
Each home-felt joy that life *i.* here *E.M.* ii. 256

Injur'd.
At length Erasmus, that great *i.* name *E.C.* 693
Equal, the *i.* to defend *I.H.* iii. 13
Much *i.* Blunt! why bears he Britain's hate *M.E.* iii. 133
Yet wants the honour, *i.*, to defend *P.S.* 296
She dearly pays for Nisus' *i.* hair *R.L.* iii. 124
Proud Vice to brand, and *i.* Worth adorn *S.* v. 227
Nor could Diana help her *i.* maid *W.F.* 198

Ink.
Is there, who, lock'd from *i.* and paper, scrawls *P.S.* 19
Dipt me in *i.*, my parents', or my own *P.S.* 126
And call for pen and *i.* to show our Wit *S.* v. 180
There's nothing blackens like the *i.* of fools *S.* v. 411

Inmost.
Why bows the side-box from its *i.* rows *R.L.* v. 14

Inn.
In the worst *i.*'s worst room, with mat half-hung *M.E.* iii. 299
Who study Shakespeare at the I—*s of Court D.* iv. 568

Innocence.
He ceas'd and wept. With *i.* of mien *D.* iv. 419
Ah quit not the free *i.* of life *E.* iv. 45
Now think of thee, and curse my *i. E.A.* 188
And white-rob'd *I.* from Heav'n descend *M.* 20
And *I.*, which most does please *O.* iv. 15
Give Virtue scandal, *I.* a fear *P.S.* 285

Innocent.
O! pass more *i.*, in infant state *D.* i. 237
Joy fills his soul, joy *i.* of thought *D.* iii. 249
Let mine an *i.* gay farce appear *E.* iv. 25
No *Gazetteer* more *i.* than I *E.S.* i. 84
A fool quite angry is quite *i. P.S.* 107
The Fair and *I.* shall still believe *R.L.* i. 40
He's arm'd without that's *i.* within *S.* iii. 94

Innocently.
Thus wisely careless, *i.* gay *E.* iv. 11
And with their forky tongues shall *i.* play *M.* 84
And latent Metals *i.* glow *Mi.* x. 6
And Taunts alternate *i.* flew *S.* v. 250

Innoxious.
The good man walk'd *i.* thro' his age *P.S.* 395

Inquire.
There mighty Nations shall *i.* their doom *W.F.* 381

Inscribe.
Oh let thy once-lov'd Friend *i.* thy Stone *Ep.* iii. 7
And midst the stars *i.* Belinda's name *R.L.* v. 150
I. a verse on this relenting stone *W.* 26

Inscription.
And what? no monument, *i.*, stone *M.E.* iii. 283
Th' *i.* value, but the rust adore *M.E.* v. 36

Insect.
And lo the wretch! whose vile, whose *i.* lust *D.* iv. 415
Each beast, each *i.*, happy in its own *E.M.* i. 185
Beast, bird, fish, *i.*, what no eye can see *E.M.* i. 239
A puny *i.*, shiv'ring at a breeze *M.E.* iv. 108
Admires the jay the i.*'s gilded wings E.M.* iii. 55
As half-form'd i—*s on the banks of Nile E.C.* 41
Ye tinsel *I.!* whom a Court maintains *E.S.* ii. 220
So morning *i.* that in muck begun *M.E.* ii. 27

Inserted.
Riches, like *i.*, when conceal'd they lie *M.E.* iii. 169
Some to the sun their i-*wings unfold R.L.* ii. 59

Inserted.
On savage stocks *i.*, learn to bear *E.M.* ii. 182

Insinuating.
His sly, polite, *i.* style *E.S.* i. 19

Insolence.
Sole Dread of Folly, Vice, and *I. E.S.* ii. 213
To have a Taste is *i.* indeed *S.* ii. 112

Inspect.
T' *i.* a mite, not comprehend a heav'n *E.M.* i. 196

Inspire.
Thou, whom the Nine with Plautus' wit *i. A.* 7
Me Emptiness, and Dulness could *i. D.* i. 185
The last, the meanest of your sons *i. E.C.* 196
His Precepts teach but what his works *i. E.C.* 660
Thee, bold Longinus! all the Nine *i. E.C.* 675
Delight no more—O thou my voice *i. M.* 5
The breathing instruments *i. O.* i. 2
If She *i.*, and He approve my lays *R.L.* i. 6
Assist their blushes, and *i.* their airs *R.L.* ii. 98
O let my Muse, her slender reed *i. Sp.* 11
I. me, Phoebus, in my Delia's praise *Sp.* 45

Inspir'd.
Rehearse, ye Muses, what yourselves *i. A.* 56
I. he seizes; these an altar raise *D.* i. 157
How Henley lay *i.* beside a sink *D.* ii. 423
The brightest eyes of France *i.* his Muse *E.* iv. 77
Not touch'd, but rapt; not waken'd, but *i. E.A.* 202
And Epicurus lay *i. O.* ii. 4
I. when living, and bequeath'd in death *Su.* 40
These, were my breast *i.* with equal flame *W.F.* 9

Inspirer.
Flow, Welsted, flow! like thine *i.*, Beer *D.* iii. 169

Inspires.
That beams on earth, each Virtue he *i. D.* iii. 220
They live, they speak, they breathe what love *i. E.A.* 53
Those restless passions in revenge *i. E.A.* 82
Active its task, it prompts, impels, *i. E.M.* ii. 68
True Genius kindles, and fair Fame *i. P.S.* 194
What heav'nly particle *i.* the clay *S.* ii. 78
Whom Nature charms, and whom the Muse *i. W.F.* 238

Inspiring.
Or wait *i.* Dreams at Maro's urn *E.* iii. 28
Heav'd by the breath th' *i.* bellows blow (*rep.*) *S.* vii. 19

Inspirit.
Calm ev'ry thought, *i.* ev'ry grace *Mi.* v. 13

Instance.
A soul supreme in each hard *i.* try'd *E.* i. 23
Just in one *i.*, be it yet confest *S.* v. 31

Instant.
That *i.*, I declare, he has my Love *E.S.* ii. 75
That *i.* 'tis his Principle no more *M.E.* i. 28
Just in that *i.* anxious Ariel sought *R.L.* iii. 139
And, i., *fancy feels th' imputed sense D.* ii. 200
He buoys up *i.*, and returns to light *D.* ii. 296
I., when dipt, away they wing their flight *D.* iii. 27
Life's *i.* business to a future day *S.* iii. 42
His death was *i.*, and without a groan *P.S.* 403

Instantly.
Churches and Chapels *i.* it reach'd *D.* iv. 607

Instinct.
One *i.* seizes, and transports away *D.* iv. 74
How *I.* varies in the grov'lling swine *E.M.* i. 221
Whether with Reason or with *I.* blest *E.M.* iii. 79
Say, where full *I.* is th' unerring guide *E.M.* iii. 83
But honest *I.* comes a volunteer *E.M.* iii. 88
And Reason raise o'er *I.* as you can *E.M.* iii. 97
There stops the *I.*, and there ends the care *E.M.* iii. 128
To copy *I.* then was Reason's part *E.M.* iii. 169
And for those Arts mere *I.* could afford *E.M.* iii. 197

Instruct.
Ah no! *i.* me other joys to prize *E.A.* 125
But the kind cuckold might *i.* the city *E.J.S.* 42

I. the planets in what orbs to run *E.M.* ii. 21
And hence let Reason, late, *i.* Mankind *E.M.* iii. 180
I. the eyes of young Coquettes to roll *R.L.* i. 68
I. his Family in ev'ry rule *S.* v. 163
Let me for once presume t' *i.* the times *S.* v. 340

Instructed.
I. thus, you bow, embrace, protest *S.* iv. 107

Instructions.
Go, from the Creatures thy *i.* take *E.M.* iii. 172

Instructive.
I. work ! whose wry-mouth'd portraiture *D.* ii. 145
Read these *i.* leaves, in which conspire *E.* iii. 7
In various talk th' *i.* hours they past *R.L.* iii. 11

Instructs.
Whose sense *i.* us, and whose humour charms *A.* 9

Instrument.
Another deems him *i.* of hell *E.M.* iv. 138
I sing. Say you, her *i*—s the Great *D.* i. 3
The breathing *i.* inspire *O.* i. 2
How soon they find fit *i.* of ill *R.L.* iii. 126

Insult.
Because the *i.'s* not on Man, but God *E.S.* ii. 196
But why *i.* the poor, affront the great *P.S.* 360

Insulting.
Boast not my fall (he cry'd) *i.* foe *R.L.* v. 97

Insults.
I. fall'n worth, or Beauty in distress *P.S.* 288

Insuperable.
Yet never pass th' *i.* line *E.M.* i. 228

Insure.
Thy stage shall stand, *i.* it but from fire *D.* iii 312

Intemp'rate.
If our *i.* Youth the vessel drains *S.* ii. 90

Intend.
Since none can compass more than they *i. E.C.* 256
To build, to plant, whatever you *i. M.E.* iv. 47

Intending.
Now breaks, or now directs, th' *i.* lines. *M.E.* iv. 63

Intends.
In this impartial glass, my Muse *i. S.* i. 57

Intent.
As half to shew, half veil, the deep *I. D.* iv. 4
Th' *i.* propos'd, that License is a rule *E.C.* 149
I. to reason, or polite to please E.M. iv. 382
First, rob'd in white, the Nymph *i.* adores *R.L.* i. 123
I., his angle trembling in his hand *W.F.* 138

Intention.
But following wits from that *i.* stray'd *E.C.* 104

Inter nos.
Where all that passes, *i. I.H.* ii. 99 s

Intercourse.
Speed the soft *i.* from soul to soul *E.A.* 57

Int'rest.
On others *I.* her gay liv'ry flings (*rep.*) *D.* iv. 537
Who careless now of *I.*, Fame, or Fate *E.* i. 17
When *I.* calls off all her sneaking train *E.* i. 31
And in one *i.* body acts with mind *E.M.* ii. 180
Which seeks no *i.*, no reward but praise *E.M.* ii. 246
The common *i.*, or endear the tie *E.M.* ii. 254
For some his *I.* prompts him to provide *E.M.* iii. 59
At once extend the *i.* and the love *E.M.* iii. 134
Still spread the *i.*, and preserv'd the kind *E.M.* iii. 146
Till common *i.* plac'd the sway in one *E.M.* iii. 210
That, begs my *i.* for a place *I.H.* ii. 68 s
I. o'ercame, or Policy take place *M.E.* i. 167
And, by my *i.*, *Cosens* made her stays *Mi.* ix. 64
And shame the fools—Your *I.*, Sir, with Lintot *P.S.* 62
Those joys, those loves, those *i*—s to resign *E.M.* ii. 258
Till jarring *i.* of themselves create *E.M.* iii. 293
His comprehensive head ! all *I.* weigh'd *M.E.* i. 83

Intermingled.
Long-sounding aisles, and *i.* graves *E.A.* 164

Internal.
Nay, why external for *i.* giv'n *E.M.* iv. 161
Something as dim to our *i.* view *M.E.* i. 49

Interpose.
Clouds *i.*, waves roar, and winds arise *E.A.* 246

Interpos'd.
A wretched Sylph too fondly *i. R.L.* iii. 150

Interprets.
A third *i.* motions, looks, and eyes *R.L.* iii. 15

Interruption.
And Snip-snap short, and *I.* smart *D.* ii. 240

Interspers'd.
There, *i.* in lawns and op'ning glades *W.F.* 21

Intervene.
No pleasing Intricacies *i. M.E.* iv. 115

Intestine.
I. war no more our Passions wage *O.* i. 34
And all the man is one *i.* war *S.* ii. 72
A dreadful series of *i.* wars *W.F.* 325

Into.—*Passim.*

Intones.
So swells each wind-pipe; Ass *i.* to Ass *D.* ii. 253

Intoxicate.
There shallow draughts *i.* the brain *E.C.* 217

Intoxicates.
I. the pert, and lulls the grave *D.* ii. 344

Intrepid.
I. then, o'er seas and lands he flew *D.* iv. 293
Survey both worlds, *i.* and entire *S.* vi. 312

Intricacies.
No pleasing *I.* intervene *M.E.* iv. 115

Intrigu'd.
I. with glory, and with spirit whor'd *D.* iv. 316

Introduc'd.
I *i.* her to the Park and Plays *Mi.* ix. 63

Intruder.
Love, soft *i.*, enters here *O.* iii. 5

Invade.
But tho' the Ancients thus their rules *i. E.C.* 161
Tho' each by turns the other's bound *i. E.M.* ii. 207
To serve, not suffer, strengthen, not *i. E.M.* iii. 298
The trophy'd arches, story'd halls *i. E.M.* iv. 303

Invades.
War, horrid war, your thoughtful walks *i. O.* ii. 7
His warlike Amazon her host *i. R.L.* iii. 67

Invent.
And own stale nonsense which they ne'er *i. E.C.* 411

Invention.
I. strives to be before in vain *E.S.* ii. 7
Nay oft, in dreams, *i.* we bestow *R.L.* ii. 99
Some drily plain, without i.'s aid E.C. 114

Invert.
And who but wishes to *i.* the laws *E.M.* i. 129
T' *i.* the world, and counter-work its Cause *E.M.* iii. 244

Inverted.
His Flag *i.* trails along the ground *E.S.* i. 154
The suff'ring eye *i.* Nature sees *M.E.* iv. 119

Inverts.
Contracts, *i.*, and gives ten thousand dyes *M.E.* i. 36

Invest.
Whirlpools and storms his circling arm *i. D.* ii. 317
Near, and more near, the closing lines *i. W.F.* 108

Invite.
To rest, the Cushion and soft Dean *i. M.E.* iv. 147
Whether the darken'd room to muse *i. S.* i. 97
I. my lays. Be present, sylvan maids *W.F.* 3

Invited.
See Ward by batter'd Beaux *i.* over *S.* iv. 56

Invites.
No noon-tide bell *i.* the country round *M.E.* iii. 190
Dare you refuse him? Curll *i.* to dine *P.S.* 53
Belinda now, whom thirst of fame *i. R.L.* iii. 25
I. my steps, and points to yonder glade *U.L.* 2

Invoke.
I. the Muses, and resound your praise *Su.* 78

Involuntary.
Involves a vast *i.* throng *D.* iv. 82
Steals down my cheek th' *i.* Tear *I.H.* iii. 38

Involve.
And Metaphysic smokes *i.* the Pole *D.* iv. 248

Involv'd.
Her sacred domes *i.* in rolling fire *W.F.* 324

Involves.
The rolling smoke *i.* the sacrifice *D.* i. 248
I. a vast involuntary throng *D.* iv. 82

Inward.
The young, the old, who feel her *i.* sway *D.* iv. 73

Ire.
Belinda burns with more than mortal *i. R.L.* iv. 93

Ireland.
Let *I.* tell, how Wit upheld her cause *S.* v. 221
And *I.*, mother of sweet singers *Mi.* xii. 7

Irish.
Henley's gilt tub, or Flecknoe's *I.* throne *D.* ii. 2

Irishmen.
Out-usure Jews, or *I.* out-swear *S.* vii. 38

Iron.
Or reap'd in *i.* harvests of the field *E.M.* iv. 12
The Furies sink upon their *i.* beds *O.* i. 69
But as coarse *i.*, sharpen'd, mangles more *S.* viii. 118
Stretch'd o'er the Poor and Church his *i.* rod *W.F.* 75
Let Volga's banks with *i.* squadrons shine *W.F.* 363
For this with tort'ring i—s wreath'd around R.L. iv. 100

Irradiate.
Our shrines *i.*, or emblaze the floors *E.A.* 136

Is.—*Passim.*
Man never *I.*, but always To be blest *E.M.* i. 96

Isaiah.
Who touch'd *I.'s* hallow'd lips with fire *M*, 6

Isis.
May you, may Cam and *I.*, preach it long *D.* iv. 187
Nor wert thou, *I.!* wanting to the day *D.* iv. 193
I. and Cam made DOCTORS of her LAWS *D.* iv. 578
In those fair fields where sacred *I.* glides *Su.* 25
The winding *I.*, and the fruitful Thame *W.F.* 340
Till I.' *Elders reel, their pupil's sport D.* iii. 337
The man, who, stretch'd in *I.* calm retreat *S*, vi. 116

Island.
Some happier *i.* in the wat'ry waste *E.M.* i. 106
Cole, whose dark streams his flowery i—s lave W.F. 343

Isle.
Behold yon *I.*, by Palmers, Pilgrims trod *D.* iii. 113
This fav'rite *I.* long sever'd from her reign *D.* iii. 125
Those half-learn'd witlings, num'rous in our *i. E.C.* 40
Once School-divines this zealous *i.* o'erspread *E.C.* 440
In some lone *i.*, or distant Northern land *R.L.* iv. 154
To i—s *of fragrance, lily-silver'd vales D.* iv. 303
Like verdant *i.* the sable waste adorn *W.F.* 28

Issue.
And, at their second birth, they *i.* mine *D.* iv. 386
Or *i.* Members of an Annual feast *D.* iv. 574

Issu'd.
Ere Pallas *i.* from the Thund'rer's head *D.* i. 10
And all the Furies *i.* at the vent *R.L.* iv. 92

Issuing.
Then, *i.* forth, the rival of his beams *R.L.* ii. 3

Ister.
Red Iber's sands, or *I.*'s foaming flood *W.F.* 368

Isthmus.
Plac'd on this *i.* of a middle state *E.M.* ii. 3

It, Its.—*Passim.*

Italian.
Vain of *I.* Arts, *I.* souls *D.* iv. 300
With French Libation, and *I.* Strain *D.* iv. 559
How this or that *I.* sings *I.H.* ii. 142
On French translation, and *I.* song *P.C.* 42

Italy.
Fir'd with Ideas of fair *I. E.* iii. 26

Itch.
All see 'tis Vice, and *i.* of vulgar praise *M.E.* i. 60
To spread about the *i.* of verse and praise *P.S.* 224
Well, but the Poor—The Poor have the same *i. S.* iii. 154
Now times are chang'd, and none Poetic *I. S.* v. 169
Nor the vain *i.* t' admire and be admir'd *S.* viii. 10
And *i.* hurts most when anger'd to a sore *S.* viii. 119

Itching.
All fools have still an *i.* to deride *E.C.* 32

Ivory, Iv'ry.
And run, on *i.*, so glib *E.* vi. 22
And thro' the *I.-'-y* Gate the Vision flies *D.* iii. 340
With shining ringlets the smooth *i.* neck *R.L.* ii. 22
Gold, Silver, *I.*, Vases sculptur'd high *S.* vi. 264

Ivy.
The creeping, dirty, courtly *I.* join *D.* i. 304
Mix'd the Owl's *i.* with the Poet's bays *D.* iii. 54
Where round some mould'ring tow'r pale *i.* creeps *E.A.* 243
The Poet's bays and Critic's *i.* grow *E.C.* 706
And I this bowl, where wanton *J.* twines *Sp.* 35
That adds this wreath of *I.* to thy Bays *Su.* 10
Round broken columns clasping *i.* twin'd *W.F.* 69

Ixion.
I. rests upon his wheel *O.* i. 67
Or, as *I.* fix'd, the wretch shall feel *R.L.* ii. 133

J.

Jabb'ring.
'Twas chatt'ring, grinning, mouthing, *j.* all *D.* ii. 237

Jacks.
Scream like the winding of ten thousand *j. D.* iii. 160

Jacob.
Till genial *J.* or a warm third day *D.* i. 57
And left-legg'd *J.* seems to emulate *D.* ii. 68
J., the scourge of Grammar, mark with awe *D.* iii. 149

Jade.
By names of Toasts retails each batter'd *j. D.* ii. 134
As, after stumbling, J—s *will mend their pace E.C.* 603

Jail.
Prudence, whose glass presents th' approaching *j. D.* i. 51
Sporus at court, or *Japhet* in a *j. P.S.* 363
And dreads more actions, hurries from a *j. S.* viii. 183
As men from J—s *to execution go S.* viii. 273

Jakes.
And 'scape the martyrdom of *j.* and fire *D.* i. 144

James—*see also Moore.*
Some gentle *J.* to bless the land again *D.* iv. 176
Yet neither Charles nor *J.* be in a rage *S.* i. 114

Jansen.
As *J.*, Fleetwood, Cibber shall think fit *D.* iv. 326
Or when a Duke to *J.* punts at White's *S.* vii. 88

Japan.
On shining Altars of *J.* they raise *R.L.* iii. 107

Japanner.
Prefer a new *J.* to their shoes *S.* iii. 156

Japhet.
Or *J.* pocket, like his Grace, a Will *E.S.* i. 120
But hear me further—*J.*, tis agreed *E.S.* ii. 185
To Chartres, Vigour ; *J.*, Nose and Ears *M.E.* iii. 86
Sporus at court, or *J.* in a jail *P.S.* 363
And shall no egg in J.'s *face be thrown E.S.* ii. 189

Jar.
Or some frail China *j.* receive a flaw *R.L.* ii. 106
Here sighs a *J.*, and there a Goose-pie talks *R.L.* iv. 52
Sir, Spain has sent a thousand j—s *of oil M.E.* iii. 56
Where bile, and wind, and phlegm, and acid j. *S.* ii. 71

Jargon.
This new Court *j.*, or the good old song *S.* iii. 98

Jarring.
Till *j.* int'rests, of themselves create *E.M.* iii. 293

Jaundic'd.
As all looks yellow to the *j.* eye *E.C.* 559

Jaw.
One of our Giant Statutes opes its *j. S.* viii. 173
Just in the j—s *of ruin and Codille R.L.* iii. 92

Jay.
Admires the *j.* the insect's gilded wings *E.M.* iii. 55

Jealous.
The conscious simper, and the *j.* leer *D.* ii. 6
The *j.* God, when we profane his fires *E.A.* 81
And when self-love each *j.* writer rules *E.C.* 516
View him with scornful, yet with *j.* eyes *P.S.* 199
This *j.*, waspish, wrong-head, rhyming race *S.* vi. 148

Jeer.
Tindal and Toland, prompt at priests to *j. D.* ii. 309

Jehovah.
J., Jove, or Lord *U.P.* 4

Jekyl.
A Joke on *J.*, or some odd *Old Whig E.S.* i. 39

Jelly.
Beeves, at his touch, at once to *j.* turn *D.* iv. 551
That *J.'s* rich, this Malmsey healing *I.H.* ii. 202

Jesse.
From *J.'s* root behold a branch arise *M.* 9

Jest.
List'ning delighted to the *j.* unclean *D.* ii. 99
Dulness, good Queen, repeats the *j.* again *D.* ii. 122
The glory, *j.*, and riddle of the world *E.M.* ii. 18
To Vice and Folly to confine the *j. E.S.* i. 57
The prudent Gen'ral turn'd it to a *j. E.S.* ii. 154
Toasts live a scorn, and Queens may die a *j. M.E.*ii.282
That Man was made the standing *j.* of Heav'n *M.E.*iii.4
Plague on't I 'tis past a *j.*—nay prithee, pox *R.L.*iv.129
Prepares a dreadful *j.* for all mankind *S.* iv. 124
Then turn about, and laugh at your own *j. S.* iv. 109
The laugh, the *j.*, attendants on the bowl *S.* v. 247
The Champion too ! and to complete the *j. S.* v. 318
Would go to Mass in *j.* (as story says) *S.* viii. 16
Whose laughs are hearty, tho' his j—s *are coarse E.* v. 29
But sense surviv'd, when merry *j.* were past *E.C.* 460
Patriots there are, who wish you'd j. *no more E.S.* i. 24
Ah Doctor, how you love to *j. I.H.* ii. 117 s

Jests.
J. like a licens'd fool, commands like law *S.* viii. 271

Jesu.
If once he catch you at your *J.* / *J.* / *S.* viii. 257

Jesuit.
A popish plot, shall for a *J.* take *S.* viii. 35

Jet.
Thus the small *j.*, which hasty hands unlock *D.* ii. 177

Jetty.
Vied for his love in *j.* bow'rs below *D.* ii. 335

Jews.
See Christians, *J.*, one heavy sabbath keep *D.* iii. 97
Which *J.* might kiss, and Infidels adore *R.L.* ii. 8
Out-usure *J.*, or Irishmen out-swear *S.* vii. 38

Jewels.
The shining robes, rich *j.*, beds of state *E.* iv. 51
With gold and *j.* cover ev'ry part *E.C.* 295

Jig.
A fire, a *j.*, a battle, and a ball *D.* ii. 239
Make the soul dance upon a *J.* to Heav'n *M.E.* iv. 144
Joys in my j—s, *and dances in my chains D.* iv. 62

Jilts.
J. rul'd the state, and statesmen farces writ *E.C.* 538

Jingled.
The bells she *j.*, and the whistle blew *R.L.* v. 94

Jingling.
We hang one *j.* padlock on the mind *D.* iv. 162
In sounds and *j.* syllables grown old *E.C.* 605
And *j.* down the back-stairs, told the crew *M.E.* iii. 37

Job.
Save when they lose a Question, or a *J. E.S.* i. 104
Or if a Court or Country's made a *j. E.S.* ii. 40
And long'd to tempt him like good *J.* of old *M.E.* iii. 350
Who makes a Trust or Charity a *J. S.* iii. 142
And Judges j., *and Bishops bite the town M.E.* iii. 141

Jockeys.
" Room for my Lord ! " three *j.* in his train *D.* ii. 192

John.
He grasps an empty Joseph for a *J. D.* ii. 128
Shut, shut the door, good *J.* I fatigu'd, I said *P.S.* 1

Johnston.
Milton's on this, on that one *J.'s* name *D.* iv. 112

Join.
Where Dukes and Butchers *j.* to wreathe my crown *D.* i. 223
The creeping, dirty, courtly Ivy *j. D.* i. 304
Pluto with Cato thou for this shalt *j. D.* iii. 309
Some, deep Free-Masons, *j.* the silent race *D.* iv. 571
Yet write, oh write me all, that I may *j. E.A.* 41
O'er the pale marble they shall *j.* their heads *E.A.* 349
And sure, if fate some future bard shall *j. E.A.* 359
While expletives their feeble aid do *j. E.C.* 346
Where Denham's strength, and Waller's sweetness *j. E.C.* 361
Good-nature and good-sense must ever *j. E.C.* 524
'Tis not enough, taste, judgment, learning, *j. E.C.* 562
And Middle natures, how they long to *j. E.M.* i. 227
In Man they *j.* in some mysterious use *E.M.* ii. 206
All *j.* to guard what each desires to gain *E.M.* iii. 278
Go drench a Pick-pocket, and *j.* the Mob *E.S.* ii. 41
J. with Economy, Magnificence *M.E.* iii. 224
Nature shall *j.* you ; Time shall make it grow *M.E.* iv. 69
Straight the three bands prepare in arms to *j. R.L.*iii.29
Which never more shall *j.* its parted hair *R.L.* iv. 134
And figs from standard and espalier *j. S.* ii. 147
In Quibbles Angel and Archangel *j. S.* v. 101
Waller was smooth, but Dryden taught to *j. S.* v. 267
J. Cotswood hills to Saperton's fair dale *S.* vi. 257
And in one garland all their beauties *j. Su.* 56
And seas but *j.* the regions they divide *W.F.* 400

Join'd.
Behold yon pair, in strict embraces *j. D.* iii. 179
So mix'd our studies, and so *j.* our name *E.* iii. 10
In praise so just let ev'ry voice be *j. E.C.* 187
The justest rules, and clearest method *j. E.C.* 670
With Tyranny, then Superstition *j. E.C.* 687
This light and darkness in one chaos *j. E.M.* ii. 203

JOINS—JUDGE.

Grew by like means, and *j.*, thro' love or fear *E.M.* iii. 202
Between revenge, and grief, and hunger *j. S.* vi. 38
Of whose best phrase and courtly accent *j. S.* viii. 48

Joins.

That in proud dulness *j.* with Quality *E.C.* 415
J. heav'n and earth, and mortal and divine *E.M.* iii.334
Congenial souls! whose life one Av'rice *j. M.E.* iii. 131
Leaves the dull Cits, and *j.* (to please the fair) *M.E.* iii. 387
J. willing woods, and varies shades from shades *M.E.* iv. 62
When the full organ *j.*, the tuneful quire *O.* i. 126
T' inclose the Lock; now *j.* it, to divide *R.L.* iii. 148
Then close as Umbra, *j.* the dirty train *S.* viii. 177

Joint.

But the *j.* force and full result of all *E.C.* 246
Man walk'd with beast, *j.* tenant of the shade *E.M.* iii. 152

Jointure.

Or in a *j.*, vanish from the heir *S.* ii. 170

Joke.

And gentle Dulness ever loves a *j. D.* ii. 34
A *J.* on JEKYL, or some odd *Old Whig E.S.* i. 39
The Club must hail him master of the *j. M.E.* i. 185
Enclose whole downs in walls, 'tis all a *j. S.* vi. 261
What, *they admire him for his* j—s *I.H.* ii. 107 s
He takes his chirping pint, and cracks his *j. M.E.* iii.358
And Alsop *never but like Horace* j. *D.* iv. 224

Jones.

J. and Le Nôtre have it not to give *M.E.* iii. 46
J. and Palladio to themselves restore *M.E.* iv. 193
While J.' *and Boyle's united Labours fall D.* iii. 328

Jonson.

With Shakespear's nature or with *J.'s* art *D.* ii. 224
Not one but nods, and talks of *J.* Art *S.V.* 82

Jordan.

This China *J.* let the chief o'ercome *D.* ii. 165
Crown'd with the *J.* walks contented home *D.* ii. 190

Joseph.

He grasps an empty *J.* for a John *D.* ii. 128

Jostle.

To *j.* here among a crowd *I.H.* ii. 54 s

Journal.

He'll write a *J.*, or he'll turn Divine *P.S.* 54
Hence J—s, Medleys, Merc'ries, MAGAZINES *D.* i. 42
The stream, be his the Weekly *J.* bound *D.* ii. 280
And loudly claims the *J.* and the Lead *D.* ii. 322
Like *J.*, Odes, and such forgotten things *S.* v. 416

Journey.

Another Cynthia her new *j.* runs *D.* iii. 243
To the cool ocean where his *j.* ends *Su.* 90

Jove.

Call'd to this work by Dulness, *J.*, and Fate *D.* i. 4
Hear, *J. !* whose name my bards and I adore *D.* ii. 79
Where from Ambrosia, *J.* retires for ease *D.* ii. 84
And ministers to *J.* with purest hands *D.* ii. 94
Till Peter's keys some christen'd *J.* adorn *D.* iii. 109
While, at each change, the son of Libyan *J. E.C.* 376
You hold the word from *J.* to Momus giv'n *M.E.* iii. 3
J., *J.* himself does on the Scissors shine *Mi.* ix. 35
But Fate and *J.* had stopp'd the Baron's ears *R.L.* v. 2
Now *J.* suspends his golden scales in air *R.L.* v. 71
Save but our *Army !* and let *J.* encrust *S.* i. 73
Just less than *J.*, and much above a King *S.* iii. 186
And *J.* consented in a silent shower *Su.* 8
Jehovah, *J.*, or Lord *U.P.* 4
Where *J.*, subdued by mortal Passion still *W.F.* 233
So *when* J.'s *block, descending from on high D.* i. 327
So *J.* bright bow displays his wat'ry round *D.* ii. 173
And *J.* own Thunder outdoes the Mars's Drums *D.* iv. 68
Why *J.* *Satellites* are less than *J. E.M.* i. 42
J. thunder roars, heav'n trembles all around *R.L.* v. 49

Jowl.

Is there no hope?—Alas!—then bring the *j. M.E.* i. 241

Joy.

She saw with *j.* the line immortal run *D.* i. 99
J. fills his soul, *j.* innocent of thought *D.* iii. 249
J. to great Chaos! let Division reign *D.* iv. 54
One Trill shall harmonize *j.*, grief, and rage *D.* iv. 57
Aim not at *J.*, but rest content with Ease *E.* iv. 48
Far other raptures of unholy *j. E.A.* 224
That cause of all my guilt and all my *j. E.A.* 338
Love, Hope, and *J.*, fair Pleasure's smiling train *E.M.* ii. 117
The *j.*, the peace, the glory of Mankind *E.M.* ii. 248
Each home-felt *j.* that life inherits here *E.M.* ii. 256
In Folly's cup still laughs the bubble, *j. E.M.* ii. 288
Thy *j.*, thy pastime, thy food *E.M.* iii. 28
J. tunes his voice, *j.* elevates his wings *E.M.* iii. 32
Nor present good or ill, the *j.* or curse *E.M.* iv. 71
The soul's calm sunshine, and the heart-felt *j. E.M.* iv. 168
No *j.*, or be destructive of the thing *E.M.* iv. 182
And more true *j.* Marcellus exil'd feels *E.M.* iv. 257
The *j.* unequall'd, if its end it gain *E.M.* iv. 315
Who ne'er knew *J.* but Friendship might divide *Ep.*iii.3
Compos'd in suff'rings, and in *j.* sedate *Ep.* vii. 3
Them spend your life in *J.* and Sport *I.H.* ii. 179
You purchase Pain with all that *J.* can give *M.E.* ii. 99
For foreign glory, foreign *j.*, they roam *M.E.* ii. 223
As Hags hold Sabbaths, less for *j.* than spite *M.E.*ii.239
With annual *j.* the redd'ning shoots to greet *M.E.* iv. 91
Some *j.* still lost, as each vain year runs o'er *Mi.* v. 7
Let *J.* or Ease, let Affluence or Content *Mi.* v. 11
In some soft Dream, or Extasy of *j. Mi.* v. 18
United wish, and mutual *J. O.* iii. 26
Who sprung from Kings shall know less *j.* than I *P.S.* 405
Her *j.* in gilded Chariots, when alive *R.L.* i. 55
If in the Pomp of Life consist the *j. S.* iv. 98
The *j.* their wives, their sons, and servants share *S.*v.245
I wish you *j.*, Sir, of a Tyrant gone *S.* vi. 305
Satan himself feels far less *j.* than they *S.* vi. 90
Short is his *j.*; he feels the fiery wound *W.F.* 113
Dim *and remote the* j—s *of saints I see E.A.* 17
Ah no! instruct me other *j.* to prize *E.A.* 125
Those *j.*, those loves, those int'rests to resign *E.M.*ii.258
Reason's whole pleasure, all the *j.* of Sense *E.M.* iv. 79
And till we share your *j.*, forgive our grief *Ep.* vii. 18
To me, alas! those *j.* are o'er *I.H.* iii. 31
To *Basset's* heav'nly *J.*, and pleasing Cares *Mi.* ix. 102
If in her breast tumultuous *j.* arise *O.* i. 24
Our *j.* below it can improve *O.* i. 122
What various *j.* on one attend *O.* iii. 27
Hence guilty *j.*, distastes, surmises *O.* iii. 37
Has Life no *j.* for me? or, (to be grave) *P.S.* 273
Would ye be blest? despise low *J.*, low Gains *S.* iv. 60
Whom humbler *j.* of home-felt quiet please *W.F.* 239
Whether *we* j. *or grieve, the same the curse S.* iv. 22

Joyful.

Then palaces shall rise; the *j.* Son *M.* 63
And nodding tempt the *j.* reaper's hand *W.F.* 40
With *j.* pride survey'st our lofty woods *W.F.* 220

Joyless.

I *j.* make my once ador'd *Alpeu Mi.* ix. 5

Joyous.

With *j.* musick wake the dawning day *Sp.* 24

Joys.

J. in my jigs, and dances in my chains *D.* iv. 62
Amid those Lovers *j.* his gentle Ghost *E.* iv. 74

Judæa.

Beneath her Palm here sad *J.* weeps *M.E.* v. 26

Judge.

J. of all present, past, or future wit *D.* ii. 376
The *J.* to dance his brother Sergeant call *D.* iv. 591
A perfect *J.* will read each work of Wit *E.C.* 233
Our Author, happy in a *j.* so nice *E.C.* 273
An ardent *J.*, who zealous in his trust *E.C.* 677
Such late was Walsh—the Muse's *j.* and friend *E.C.* 729
Sole *j.* of Truth, in endless Error hurl'd *E.M.* ii. 17
Or from a *j.* turn pleader to persuade *E.M.* ii. 355
Without a second, or without a *j. E.M.* iv. 264
Patron of Arts, and *J.* of Nature, died *Ep.* i. 2
A *J.* is just, a Chanc'llor juster still *M.E.* i. 137

M

162   JUDG'D—JUST.

Hard words or hanging, if your *J.* be Page *S.* i. 82
For 'tis but half a J.'s task to know *E.C.* 561
J—s and Senators have been bought for gold *E.M.* iv. 287
And *J.* job, and Bishops bite the town *M.E.* iii. 141
The hungry *J.* soon the sentence sign *R.L.* iii. 21
My Lords the *J.* laugh, and you're dismiss'd *S.* i. 156
Their own strict *J.*, not a word they spare *S.* vi. 159
Those born to *j.*, as well as those to write *E.C.* 14
There are who *j.* still worse than he can write *E.C.* 35
But most by Numbers *j.* a Poet's song *E.C.* 337
Some *j.* of authors' names, not works, and then *E.C.* 412
They *j.* with fury, but they write with fic'me *E.C.* 662
J. we by Nature? Habit can efface *M.E.* i. 166
Seiz'd, and tied down to *j.*, how wretched I *P.S.* 33
From these the world will *j.* of men and books *P.S.* 145
Consider then, and *j.* me in this light *S.* vi. 27
On each I *j.* thy Foe *U.P.* 28

Judg'd.
Yet *j.* with coolness, tho' he sung with fire *E.C.* 659
So well in paint and stone they *j.* of merit *S.* v. 384

Judging.
A Face untaught to feign ; a *j.* Eye *E.* ii. 5
Appear in writing or in *j.* ill *E.C.* 2
Dryden alone escap'd this *j.* eye *P.S.* 246

Judgment.
Whose *j.* sways us, and whose humour charms *A.* 10
The Senior's *j.* all the crowd admire *D.* ii. 289
But are not Critics to their *j.* too *E.C.* 18
Most have the seeds of *j.* in their mind *E.C.* 20
First follow Nature, and your *j.* frame *E.C.* 68
For wit and *j.* often are at strife *E.C.* 82
You then whose *j.* the right course would steer *E.C.* 118
Thence form your *j.*, thence your maxims bring *E.C.* 126
Which, without passing thro' the *j.*, gains *E.C.* 154
Man's erring *j.*, and misguide the mind *E.C.* 202
Thus Critics, of less *j.* than caprice *E.C.* 285
Some ne'er advance a *J.* of their own *E.C.* 408
'Tis not enough, taste, *j.*, learning, join *E.C.* 562
He, who supreme in *j.*, as in wit *E.C.* 657
New-market fame, and *j.* at a Bet *M.E.* i. 86
In Man, the *J.* shoots at flying game *M.E.* i. 96
And for his *j.*, lo a pudden *Mi.* xii. 12
Who first his *j.* ask'd, and then a place *P.S.* 238
How Beaumont's *j.* check'd what Fletcher writ *S.* v. 84
'Tis with our *j*—s as our watches, none *E.C.* 9
To see their *j.* hang upon thy voice *S.* iv. 35

Judicious.
J. drank, and greatly-daring din'd *D.* iv. 318
J. Wits spread wide the Ridicule *E.S.* i. 61

Juice.
The *j.* nectareous, and the balmy dew *E.M.* i. 136
As oil'd with magic j—s for the course *D.* ii. 104

Jumbled.
How Farce and Epic get a *j.* race *D.* i. 70

June.
I would be with you, *J.* the third *I.H.* i. 2

Junia.
And sterner Cassius melts at *J.*'s eyes *O.* iii. 16

Juno.
His be you *J.* of majestic size *D.* ii. 163
See the bird of *J.* stooping *M.* vii. 31

Jurymen.
And wretches hang that *j.* may dine *R.L.* iii. 22

Just.
J. Gods! shall all things yield returns but love *A.* 76
A fool, so *j.* a copy of a wit *D.* ii. 48
Sons of a Day! *j.* buoyant on the flood *D.* ii. 307
A drowsy Watchman, that *j.* gives a knock *D.* iv. 443
Ob *j.* beheld and lost ! admir'd and mourn'd *E.* i. 3
So *j.* thy skill, so regular my rage *E.* iii. 12
J. when she learns to roll a melting eye *E.* v. 3
J. when his fancy points your sprightly eyes *E.* v. 45
Kind, virtuous drops *j.* gath'ring in my eye *E.A.* 278
Snatch me, *j.* mounting, from the blest abode *E.A.* 287
Go *j.* alike, yet each believes his own *E.C.* 10
By her *j.* standard, which is still the same *E.C.* 69
Art from that fund each *j.* supply provides *E.C.* 74
j. precepts thus from great examples giv'n *E.C.* 98
Learn hence for ancient rules a *j.* esteem *E.C.* 139
In praise so *j.* let ev'ry voice be join'd *E.C.* 187
The world's *j.* wonder, and ev'n thine, O Rome *E.C.* 248
And if the means be *j.*, the conduct true *E.C.* 257
Discours'd in terms as *j.*, with looks as sage *E.C.* 269
Pleas'd with a work where nothing's *j.* or fit *E.C.* 291
And 'tis but *j.* to let them live betimes *E.C.* 477
And sweetly melt into *j.* shade and light *E.C.* 489
And each bold figure *j.* begins to live *E.C.* 491
With warmth gives sentence, yet is always *j. E.C.* 678
As a blockhead rubs his thoughtless skull *E.F.S.* 7
Than *J.* to look about us and to die *E.M.* i. 4
Gradations *j.*, has tby pervading soul *E.M.* i. 31
And licks the hand *j.* rais'd to shed his blood *E.M.* i. 84
Now looking downwards, *j.* as griev'd appears *E.M.* i. 175
Without this *j.* gradation, could they be *E.M.* i. 229
J. as absurd for any part to claim (*rep.*) *E.M.* i. 263
Wits, *j.* like Fools, at war about a name *E.M.* ii. 85
And *j.* as short of reason he must fall *E.M.* iii. 47
Sure never to o'er-shoot, but *j.* to hit *E.M.* iii. 89
Mem'ry and fore-cast *j.* returns engage *E.M.* iii. 143
But *j.* disease to luxury succeeds *E.M.* iii. 165
So drives Self-love, thro' *j.* and thro' unjust *E.M.* iii. 269
But Heav'n's *j.* balance equal will appear *E.M.* iv. 69
See FALKLAND dies, the virtuous and the *j. E.M.* iv. 99
We *j.* as wisely might of Heav'n complain *E.M.* iv. 117
A Kingdom of the *J.* then let it be (*rep.*) *E.M.* iv. 133
Content and Pleasure, but the Good and *J. E.M.* iv. 186
J. what you hear, you have, and what's unknown *E.M.* iv. 239
'Tis *j.* alike to Virtue, and to me *E.S.* i. 138
Or WYNDHAM, *j.* to Freedom and the Throne *E.S.* ii. 88
J. to his Prince, and to his Country true *Ep.* ii. 6
J. of thy word, in ev'ry thought sincere *Ep.* vii. 5
J. as a Scotsman does his Plums *I.H.* i. 24
And 'tis but *j.*, I'll tell ye wherefore *I.H.* i. 33
And liv'd—*j.* as you see I do *I.H.* i. 72
J. what you gave me, Competence *I.H.* ii. 241
J. as a Farmer might a Lord *I.H.* ii. 160
On *j.* occasion, coûte qui coûte *I.H.* ii. 164
Save *j.* at dinner—then, prefers, no doubt *M.E.* i. 79
And *J.* her wisest monarch made a fool *M.E.* i. 94
Perhaps the wind *j.* shifted from the east *M.E.* i. 112
A Judge is *j.*, a Chanc'llor juster still *M.E.* i. 137
More wise, more learn'd, more *j.*, more ev'rything *M.E.* i. 140
J. as the Twig is bent, the Tree's inclin'd *M.E.* i. 150
As Fits give vigour, *j.* when they destroy *M.E.* i. 223
J. brought out this, when scarce his tongue could stir *M.E.* i. 254
Was *j.* not ugly, and was *j.* not mad *M.E.* ii. 50
She speaks, behaves, and acts *j.* as she ought *M.E.* ii. 161
We find our tenets *j.* the same at last *M.E.* iii. 16
Yet to be *j.* to these poor men of pelf *M.E.* iii. 107
To *j.* three millions stinted modest Gaze *M.E.* iii. 128
To balance Fortune by a *j.* expense *M.E.* iii. 223
As Poison heals, in *j.* proportion us'd *M.E.* iii. 234
And *j.* as gay, at Council, in a ring *M.E.* iii. 309
Yet shall, my Lord, your *j.*, your noble rules *M.E.* iv. 25
And half the platform *j.* reflects the other *E.M.* iv. 118
J. at his Study-door he'll bless your eyes *M.E.* iv. 132
Let him to night his *j.* assistance lend *Mi.* i. 23
Like stunted hide-bound Trees, that *j.* have got *Mi.* iii. 11
But *j.* endur'd the winter she began *Mi.* iii. 23
Happy to catch me *j.* at Dinner-time *P.S.* 14
J. so immortal Maro held his head *P.S.* 122
Pains, reading, study, are their *j.* pretence *P.S.* 159
J. writes to make his barrenness appear *P.S.* 181
J. hint a fault, and hesitate dislike *P.S.* 204
And *j.* as rich as when he serv'd a QUEEN *P.S.* 417
And sleepless lovers, *j.* at twelve, awake *R.L.* i. 16
Proves the *j.* victim of his royal rage *R.L.* iii. 60
J. in the jaws of ruin and Codille *R.L.* iii. 92
Fear the *J.* Gods, and think of Scylla's Fate *R.L.* iii. 122
J. then Clarissa drew with tempting grace *R.L.* iii. 127
This *j.* behind Belinda's neck he spread *R.L.* iii. 133
In that instant, anxious Ariel sought *R.L.* iii. 139
J. where the breath of life his nostrils drew *R.L.* v. 81
The Gnomes direct, to ev'ry atom *j. R.L.* v. 83
Ill health some *j.* indulgence may engage *S.* ii. 87
My Life's amusements have been *j.* the same *S.* ii. 253
J. half the land would buy, and half be sold *S.* iii. 125
J. less than Jove, and much above a King *S.* iii. 186

JUSTER—KICK.

For mark th' advantage ; *j*. so many score S. iv. 77
J. in one instance, be it yet confest S. v. 31
Hence Satire rose, that *j*. the medium hit S. v. 251
Farewell the stage ! if *j*. as thrives the play S. v. 302
You lose your patience, *j*. like other men S. v. 363
All vast possessions (*j*. the same the case S. vi. 254
One, one man only breeds my *j*. offence S. vii. 45
And all mankind might that *j*. Mean observe S. vii. 119
Stood *j*. a-tilt, the Minister came by S. viii. 175
J. as one Beauty mortifies another S. viii. 259

Juster.
Who durst assert the ancient *j*. cause E.C. 721
A Judge is just, a Chanc'llor *j*. still M.E. i. 137

Justest.
The *j*. rules, and clearest method join'd E.C. 670
Could save a parent's *j*. Pride from fate Ep. xiv. 3

Justice.
Poetic *J*., with her lifted scale D. i. 52
Rejudge his *j*., be the GOD of GOD E.M. i. 122
Entangle *j*. in her net of Law E.M. iii. 192
Ev'n Kings learn'd *j*. and benevolence E.M. iii. 280
J. a Conqu'ror's sword, or Truth a gown E.M. iv. 171
As *J*. tears his body from the grave E.M. iv. 250
Returning *J*. lift aloft her scale M. 18
While Scale in hand Dame *J*. past along Mi. xi. 4
Dame *J*. weighing long the doubtful Right Mi. xi. 7
" There take " (says *J*.) " take ye each a *Shell* Mi. xi. 10
Ye Gods ! what *j*. rules the ball O. ii. 25
Appeal'd to Law, and *J*. lent her arm S. v. 256
And the wise *J*. starting from his chair S. viii. 36
Thus, if Eternal *j*. rules the ball U.L. 35

Justify.
The choice we make, or *j*. it made E.M. ii. 156
Yes, strike that *Wild*, I 'll *j*. the blow E.S. ii. 54
Mend Fortune's faults, and *j*. her grace M.E. iii. 332

Justly.
But as the slightest sketch, if *j*. trac'd E.C. 23
And *j*. bears a Critic's noble name E.C. 47
Thus long succeeding Critics *j*. reign'd E.C. 681
Who *j*. knew to blame or to commend E.C. 730
Part pays, and *j*., the deserving steer E.M. iii. 40
The less, or greater, set so *j*. true E.M. iii. 291
And makes what Happiness we *j*. call E.M. iv. 37
And *j*. set the Gem above the Flow'r M.E. i. 148
Be *j*. warm'd with your own native rage P.C. 44
Sir Plume of amber snuff-box *j*. vain R.L. iv. 123
And *J*. CÆSAR scorns the Poet's lays S. i. 35
What right, what true, what fit we *j*. call S. iii. 19
Tho' *j*. Greece her eldest sons admires S. v. 43
Our Court may *j*. to our stage give rules S. viii. 220

K.

Or give up Cicero to C or *K* D. iv. 222
So *K* * so B * * sneak'd into the grave D. iv. 511
Great C * *, H * *, P * * R * *, *K* * D. iv. 545
K—*t*'s lewd Cargo, or Ty—y's Crew S. iv. 121

Keen.
K. hollow winds howl thro' the bleak recess D. i. 35
How *k*. the war, if dulness draw the sword D. i. 120
How glowing guilt exalts the *k*. delight E.A. 230

Keener.
See, round the Poles where *k*. spangles shine D. iii. 69
And *k*. lightnings quicken in her eyes R.L. i. 144

Keenness.
Improves the *k*. of the Northern wind M.E. iv. 112

Keep.
Ah ! what avails it me, the flocks to *k*. A. 79
While peevish Poets painful vigils *k*. D. i. 93
See Christians, Jews, one heavy sabbath *k*. D. iii. 99
And *k*. them in the pale of Words till death D. iv. 160
And *k*. his Lares, tho' his house be sold D. iv. 366
More glorious yet, from bar'brous hands to *k*. D. iv. 379
Serves but to *k*. fools pert and knaves awake D. iv. 442

Their Infamy, still *k*. their human shape D. iv. 528
And if a Vice dares *k*. the field E. vi. 7
Shrines ! where their vigils pale ey'd virgins *k*. E.A. 21
How shall I lose the sin, yet *k*. the sense E.A. 191
Labour and rest that equal periods *k*. E.A. 211
That shunning faults, one quiet tenour *k*. E.C. 241
Still humming on, their drowsy course they *k*. E.C. 600
Suffice that Reason *k*. to Nature's road E.M. ii. 115
How shall he *k*., what, sleeping or awake E.M. iii. 275
These nothing hurts ; they *k*. their Fashion still E.S. i. 43
To pay their Debts, or *k*. their Faith, like Kings E.S. i. 122
See, now I *k*. the Secret, and not you E.S. ii. 23
Yet sacred *k*. his Friendships, and his Ease Ep. i. 10
Heroes and Kings! your distance *k*. Ep. xv. 1
The throne a Bigot *k*., a Genius quit M.E. i. 91
And Gold but sent to *k*. the fools in play M.E. iii. 5
Ask we what makes one *k*. and one bestow M.E. iii. 163
This year a Reservoir to *k*. and spare M.E. iii. 173
Apply to me, to *k*. them mad or vain P.S. 22
This saving counsel, " *K*. your piece nine years " P.S. 40
K. close to ears, and those Jet asses prick P.S. 77
And *k*. a while one parent from the sky P.S. 413
And *k*. good humour still whate'er we lose R.L. v. 30
Know, all the distant din that world can *k*. S. i. 123
'Tis yet in vain, I own, to *k*. a pother S. ii. 45
More pleas'd to *k*. it till their friends could come S. ii. 95
That *k*. me from myself, and still delay S. iii. 41
To *k*. these limbs, and to preserve these eyes S. iii. 51
Some *k*. Assemblies, and would *k*. the Stews S. iii. 129
To make men happy, and to *k*. them so S. iv. 2
If wealth alone then make and *k*. us blest S. iv. 95
Much do I suffer, much, to *k*. in decency S. vi. 147
And *k*. the equal measure of the Soul S. vi. 205
A part I will enjoy, as well as *k*. S. vi. 285
Like Eastern kings a lazy state they *k*. U.L. 21

Keeps.
But chief her shrine where naked Venus *k*. D. iv. 307
Whate'er of life all-quick'ning æther *k*. E.M. iii. 115
All Nature's diff'rence *k*. all Nature's peace E.M. iv. 56
A narrow orb each crowded conquest *k*. M.E. v. 25
He knows to live, who *k*. the middle state S. ii. 67
His Office *k*. your Parchment fates entire S. vii. 71
Confounds the civil, *k*. the rude in awe S. viii. 270
The silver stream her virgin coldness *k*. W.F. 205

Kennet.
The *K*. swift, for silver eels renown'd W.F. 341

Kent.
Where *K*. and Nature vie for Pelham's love E.S. ii. 67

Kept.
Tho' Christ-church long *k*. prudishly away D. iv. 194
Then catch'd the Schools ; the Hall scarce *k*. awake D. iv. 609
And *k*. unconquer'd, and unciviliz'd E.C. 716
Is *k*. in Nature, and is *k*. in Man E.M. i. 48
Whom Heav'n *k*. sacred from the Proud and Great Ep. x. 4
Have *k*. it—as you do at Court I.H. i. 4
And *k*. you up so oft till one I.H. i. 48
And to be *k*. in my right wits I.H. ii. 221
K. dross for Duchesses, the world shall know it M.E. ii. 291
So *k*. the Di'mond, and the rogue was bit M.E. ii. 364
Tyrants no more their savage nature *k*. P.C. 7
I *k*., like Asian monarchs, from their sight P.S. 220
There *k*. my charms conceal'd from mortal eye R.L. iv. 157
The Lock, obtain'd with guilt, and *k*. with pain R.L. v. 109
There Hero's wits are *k*. in pond'rous vases R.L. v. 115
The Soul stood forth, nor *k*. a thought within S. i. 54
Two Swains, whom Love *k*. wakeful, and the Muse Sp. 18

Keys.
'Till Peter's *k*. some christen'd Jove adorn D. iii. 109

Kick.
And begg'd, he'd take the pains to *k*. the rest E.S. ii. 155
'Tis nothing—Nothing ? if they bite and *k*. P.S. 78
'Tis a Bear's talent not to *k*., but hug S. i. 87

Kick'd.
To see a footman *k.* that took his pay *E.S.* ii. 151
Kill.
To *k.* those foes to Fair-ones, Time and Thought *M.E.* ii. 112
Kill'd.
Chloe stepp'd in, and *k.* him with a frown *R.L.* v. 68
Some beasts were *k.*, tho' not whole hecatombs *S.* vii. 116
Killing.
But ah ! what aggravates the *k.* smart *Mi.* ix. 53
"Those eyes were made so *k.*"—was his last *R.L.* v. 64
Kills.
It is the slaver *k.*, and not the bite *P.S.* 106
Kind.
My fancy form'd thee of angelic *k.* *E.A.* 61
A knowledge both of books and human *k.* *E.C.* 640
Know thy own point; This *k.*, this due degree *E.M.* i. 283
Exalt their *k.*, and take some Virtue's name *E.M.* ii. 100
A longer care Man's helpless *k.* demands *E.M.* iii. 131
Still spread the int'rest, and preserv'd the *k.* *E.M.* iii. 146
But some way leans and hearkens to the *k.* *E.M.* iv. 40
Nature, whose dictates to no other *k.* *E.M.* iv. 347
Take ev'ry creature in, of ev'ry *k.* *E.M.* iv. 370
His Friend and Shame, and was a *k.* of *Screen* *E.S.* i. 22
Spread thy broad wing, and souse on all the *k.* *E.S.* ii. 15
Lover of peace, and friend of human *k.* *Ep.* vii. 8
Thy Country's friend, but more of human *k.* *Ep.* ix. 2
Shall stretch thy conquests over half the *k.* *I.H.* iii. 16
Who from his study rails at human *k.* *M.E.* i. 2
An humble servant to all human *k.* *M.E.* i. 253
We owe to models of an humble *k.* *M.E.* ii. 192
In Women, two almost divide the *k.* *M.E.* ii. 208
But I, who think more highly of our *k.* *M.E.* iii. 7
Nor could Profusion squander all in *k.* *M.E.* iii. 60
She first convers'd with her own *K.* *Mi.* iv. 11
And others (harder still) he paid in *k.* *P.S.* 244
By laws eternal to th' aërial *k.* *R.L.* ii. 76
Do lovers dream, or is my Delia k. *A.* 52
Thro' School and College, thy *k.* cloud o'ercast *D.* iv. 289
K. self-conceit to some her glass applies *D.* iv. 533
And is my Abelard less *k.* than they *E.A.* 44
For thee the fates, severely *k.*, ordain *E.A.* 249
K., virtuous drops just gath'ring in my eye *E.A.* 278
May one *k.* grave unite each hapless name *E.A.* 343
And sure such *k.* good creatures may be living *E.J.S.* 28
But the *k.* cuckold might instruct the city *E.J.S.* 42
For me *k.* Nature wakes her genial Pow'r *E.M.* i. 133
Nature to these, without profusion, *k.* *E.M.* i. 179
And all the *k.* Deceivers of the soul *I.H.* iii. 76
Who does a kindness, is not therefore *k.* *M.E.* i. 110
A Spark too fickle, or a Spouse too *k.* *M.E.* ii. 94
K. Boyle, before his poet lays *Mr.* xii. 5
When *k.* occasion prompts their warm desires *R.L.* i. 75
Satire be *k.*, and let the wretch alone *S.* iii. 135
K. to my dress, my figure, not to Me *S.* iii. 176
And knows no losses while the Muse is *k.* *S.* v. 196
While a *k.* glance at her pursuer flies *Sp.* 59
No friend's complaint, no *k.* domestic tear *U.L.* 49
So may *k.* rains their vital moisture yield *W.* 15
In vain *k.* seasons swell'd the teeming grain *W.F.* 53
Kinder.
Happier as *k.*, in whate'er degree *E.M.* iv. 359
But Hymen's *k.* flames unite *O.* iii. 21
Kindle.
I view my crime, but *k.* at the view *E.A.* 185
The brazen trumpets *k.* rage no more *M.* 60
Kindled.
Re-lum'd her ancient lights, not *k.* new *E.M.* iii. 287
Kindles.
True Genius *k.*, and fair Fame inspires *P.S.* 194
Kindling.
The Sylphs behold it *k.*, as it flies *R.L.* v. 131
Kindly.
Secure us *k.* in our native night *D.* i. 176
Oh blindness to the future ! *k.* giv'n *E.M.* i. 85
Behold the child, by Nature's *k.* law *E.M.* ii. 275

For him as *k.* spread the flow'ry lawn *E.M.* iii. 30
And take it *k.* meant to show *I.H.* ii. 61 s
And in soft silence shed the *k.* show'r *M.* 14
Or o'er the glebe distil the *k.* rain *R.L.* ii. 86
Behold us *k.*, who your name implore *W.* 75
Kindness.
Who does a *k.*, is not therefore kind *M.E.* i. 110
But still the *Great* have *k.* in reserve *P.S.* 247
Kindred.
The *k.* Arts shall in their praise conspire *E.* iii. 69
Amidst their *k.* cobwebs in Duck-lane *E.C.* 445
While Argo saw her *k.* trees *O.* i. 40
And sep'rate from their *k.* dregs below *U.L.* 26
Amid her *k.* stars familiar roam *W.F.* 255
King.
Gaming and Grub-street skulk behind the *K.* *D.* i. 310
"God save *K.* Cibber !" mounts in ev'ry note (*rep.*) *D.* i. 328
The *k.* of dykes ! than whom no sluice of mud *D.* ii. 273
The *K.* descending views th' Elysian shade *D.* iii. 14
Teach but that one, sufficient for a *K.* *D.* iv. 184
Saw ev'ry Court, heard ev'ry *K.* declare *D.* iv. 313
And nothing left but Homage to a *K.* *D.* iv. 524
The sot a hero, lunatic a *K.* *E.M.* ii. 268
Thus States were form'd, the name of *K.* unknown *E.M.* iii. 209
K., priest, and parent of his growing state *E.M.* iii. 216
Beast, Man, or Angel, Servant, Lord, or *K.* *E.M.* iii. 302
Bliss is the same in subject, or in *k.* *E.M.* iv. 58
Why bounded Pow'r? why private? why no *k.* *E.M.* iv. 160
Who cropt our Ears, and sent them to the *K.* *E.S.* i. 18
Receive, and place for ever near a *K.* *E.S.* i. 96
Dwell in a Monk, or light upon a *K.* *E.S.* i. 139
May pinch ev'n there—why lay it on a *K.* *E.S.* ii. 51
Blest Courtier ! who could *K.* and Country please *Ep.* i. 9
Wise, if a Minister; but, if a *K.* *M.E.* i. 139
A Rebel to the very *K.* he loves *M.E.* i. 203
To draw the man who loves his God, or *K.* *M.E.* ii. 196
And silent sells a *K.*, or buys a Queen *M.E.* ii. 48
Of mimic'd Statesmen, and their merry *K.* *M.E.* iii. 310
The Devil and the *K.* divide the prize *M.E.* iii. 401
From soup to sweet-wine, and God bless the *K.* *M.E.* iv. 162
Gloomy Pluto, *K.* of Terrors *Mi.* vii. 17
Midas, a sacred person and a *k.* *P.S.* 70
Th' embroider'd *K.* who shows but half his face *R.L.* iii. 76
An Ace of Hearts stepp'd forth : The *K.* unseen *R.L.* iii. 95
Such as a *K.* might read, a Bishop write *S.* i. 152
Virtue, brave boys ! 'tis Virtue makes a *K.* *S.* iii. 92
And foremost in the Circle eye a *K.* *S.* iii. 106
Well, if a *K.* 's a Lion, at the least *S.* iii. 120
Just less than Jove, and much above a *K.* *S.* iii. 186
Unless he praise some Monster of a *K.* *S.* v. 210
We needs will write Epistles to the *K.* *S.* v. 369
The Forms august, of *K.* or conqu'ring Chief *S.* v. 391
The *K.* would smile on you—at least the Queen *S.* viii. 89
He, ev'ry day, from *K.* to *K.* can walk *S.* viii. 104
"That's velvet for a *K.* !" the flatt'rer swears *S.* viii. 218
All, by the *K.*'s *example, liv'd and lov'd* S. v. 142
Like a *K.* Favourite—or like a King *S.* vii. 78
"What Speech esteem you most?" "The *K.*" said I *S.* viii. 68
The Smithfield Muses to the ear of K—s *D.* i. 2
The RIGHT DIVINE of *K.* to govern wrong *D.* iv. 188
Teach *K.* to fiddle, or make Senates dance *D.* iv. 598
Born for First Ministers, as Slaves for *K.* *D.* iv. 602
Know, *K.*, and Fortune cannot make thee more *E.* ii. 9
Like *k.* we lose the conquests gain'd before *E.C.* 64
As *K.* dispense with laws themselves have made *E.C.* 162
To low ambition, and the pride of *K.* *E.M.* i. 2
To *k.* presumption, and to crowds belief *E.M.* ii. 244
Ev'n *K.* learn'd justice and benevolence *E.M.* iii. 280
Taught Pow'r's due use to People and to *K.* *E.M.* iii. 289
Where Folly fights for *k.*, or dives for gain *E.M.* iv. 154
That thou mayst be by *k.*, or whores of *k.* *E.M.* iv. 206
In hearts of *K.*, or arms of Queens who lay *E.M.* iv. 289
When statesmen, heroes, *k.*, in dust repose *E.M.* iv. 387
As Pride in Slaves, and Avarice in *K.* *E.S.* i. 110

KING JOHN—KNIGHTHOOD.

To pay their Debts, or keep their Faith, like *K*. *E.S.* i. 122
All that makes Saints of Queens, and Gods of *K*. *E.S.* ii. 225
And bark at Honour not conferr'd by *K*. *E.S.* ii. 243
Is mix'd with Heroes, or with *K*. thy dust *Ep*. xi. 10
Heroes and *K*.! your distance keep *Ep*. xv. 1
Can pocket States, can fetch or carry *K*. *M.E.* iii. 42
Till *K*. call forth th' Ideas of your mind *M.E.* iv. 195
These are Imperial Works, and worthy *K*. *M.E.* iv. 204
When *K*., *Queens*, *Knaves*, are set in decent rank *Mi.* ix. 77
I'd never name Queens, Ministers, or *K*. *P.S.* 76
That Flatt'ry, ev'n to *K*., he held a shame *P.S.* 338
Who sprung from *K*. shall know less joy than I *P.S.* 405
Behold, four *k*. in majesty rever'd *R.L.* iii. 37
Ev'n mighty Pam, that *K*. and Queens o'erthrew *R.L.* iii. 61
Not youthful *k*. in battle seiz'd alive *R.L.* iv. 3
The Mob's applauses, or the gifts of *K*. iv. 15
(More silent far) where *K*. and Poets lie *S*. iv. 51.
Great Friend of LIBERTY, in *K*. a Name *S*. v. 25
Wonder of *K*.! like whom, to mortal eyes *S*. v. 29
But *K*. in Wit may want discerning Spirit *S*. v. 385
As Eusden, Philips, Settle, writ of *K*. *S*. v. 417
To gaze on Princes, and to talk of *K*. *S*. viii. 101
And the free soul looks down to pity *K*. *S*. viii. 187
No wonder some folks bow, and think them *K*. *S*.viii.211
And in the breasts of *K*. and Heroes glows *U.L.* 16
Like Eastern *K*. a lazy state they keep *U.L.* 21
And *k*. more furious and severe than they *W.F.* 46
What *K*. first breath'd upon her winding shore *W.F.* 300
There *K*. shall sue, and suppliant nations bend *W.F.* 383
Peru once more a race of *k*. behold *W.F.* 411

King John.
K. in silence modestly expires *D*. i. 252

King Lear.
'Tis true, for ten days hence 'twill be *K*.'s *S*. viii. 219

King Log.
And the hoarse nation croak'd, " God save *K*." *D*. i. 330

Kingdom.
A *k*. of the Just then let it be *E.M.* iv. 133

Kingly.
Low bow'd the rest ; He, *k*., did but nod *D*. iv. 207

Kirkall.
In flow'rs and pearls by bounteous *K*. dress'd *D*. ii. 160

Kiss.
Yet takes one *k*. before she parts for ever *E*. v. 6
Not ancient ladies when refus'd a *k*. *R.L.* iv. 6
And I those k—es he receives enjoy *Su*. 48
And Eloïsa yet must k. the name *E.A.* 8
Which Jews might *k*., and Infidels adore *R.L.* ii. 8

Kiss'd.
As with cold lips I *k*. the sacred veil *E.A.* 111
If wrong, I smil'd ; if right, I *k*. the rod *P.S.* 158

Kitchen.
His *k*. vied in coolness with his grot *M.E.* iii. 180
No k—s emulate the vestal fire *S*. vii. 112

Knack.
For how could equal Colours do the *k*. *M.E.* ii. 155
You think 'tis Nature, and a *k*. to please *S*. vi. 177

Knave.
And makes a patriot as it makes a *k*. *E.M.* ii. 202
But still this world (so fitted for the *k*.) *E.M.* iv. 131
The *k*. deserves it, when he tills the soil (*rep*.) *E.M.* iv. 152
Is but the more a fool, the more a *k*. *E.M.* iv. 232
And charitably comfort *K*. and Fool *E.S.* i. 62
And let, a' God's name, ev'ry Fool and *K*. *E.S.* i. 85
Tell me, which *K*. is lawful Game, which not *E.S.* ii. 27
Have still a secret Bias to a *K*. *E.S.* ii. 101
And LYTTLETON a dark, designing *K*. *E.S.* ii. 131
Knew one a MAN of Honour, one a *K*. *E.S.* ii. 153
So impudent, I own myself no *K*. *E.S.* ii. 206
That from his cage cries, Cuckold, Whore, and *K*. *M.E.* i. 6
Thinks who endures a *k*., is next a *k*. *M.E.* i. 78

The plain rough Hero turn a crafty *K*. *M.E.* i. 126
Will sneaks a Scriv'ner, an exceeding *k*. *M.E.* i. 154
A *K*. this morning, and his Will a Cheat *M.E.* ii. 142
If secret Gold sap on from *k*. to *k*. *M.E.* iii. 34
That " ev'ry man in want is *k*. or fool " *M.E.* iii. 102
The *K*. OF CLUBS thrice lost : Oh ! who could guess *Mi*. ix. 19
Tho' my own secret wish was for the *K*. (*rep*.) *Mi.* ix.50
A *k*.'s a *k*., to me, in ev'ry state *P.S.* 361
The rebel *k*., who dares his prince engage *R.L.* iii. 59
The *K*. of Diamonds tries his wily arts *R.L.* iii. 87
And I not strip the gilding off a *k*. *S*. i. 115
Yes, while I live, no rich or noble *k*. *S*. i. 119
I die in charity with fool and *k*. *S*. viii. 3
Serves but to keep fools pert, and k—s awake *D*. iv. 442
By fools 'tis hated, and by *k*. undone *E.S.* 507
See, all our Fools aspiring to be *K*. *E.S.* i. 164
I only call those *K*. who are so now *E.S.* ii. 127
Of Fops in Learning, and of *K*. in State *Ep*. i. 4
All know 'tis Virtue, for he thinks them *k*. *M.E.* i. 58
'Twas all for fear the *K*. should call him Fool *M.E.* i. 217
Shines in exposing *K*., and painting Fools *M.E.* ii. 11)
When *Kings*, *Queens*, *K*. are set in decent rank *Mi*. ix. 77
Four *k*. in garbs succinct, a trusty band *R.L.* iii. 41
Not for yourself, but for your Fools and *K*. *S*. iv. 92

Knee.
Who, false to Phœbus, how the *k*. to Baal *D*. iv. 93
Next, bidding all draw near on bended k—s *D*. iv. 565
Makes love with nods, and *k*. beneath a table *E*. v. 28
Aw'd, on my bended *k*. I fell *E*. vi. 9
Ye rugged rocks ! which holy *k*. have worn *E.A.* 19
Still to his wench he crawls on knocking *k*. *M.E.* i. 236

Kneller.
K., by Heav'n, and not a Master taught *Ep*. viii. 1
And great Nassau to *K*.'s hand decreed *S*. v. 382

Knew.
And all who *k*. those Dunces to reward *D*. ii. 26
Who *k*. no wish but what the world might hear *E*. vii. 6
Who *k*. most Sentences, was deepest read *E.C.* 441
Athens and Rome in better ages *k*. *E.C.* 644
Of those who less presum'd, and better *k*. *E.C.* 720
Who justly *k*. to blame or to commend *E.C.* 730
They earn'd reflect on what before they *k*. *E.C.* 740
For Nature *k*. no right divine in Men *E.M.* iii. 236
Blunt could *do Bus'ness*, H-ggins *k*. *the Town E.S.* i. 14
I fain would please you, if I *k*. with what *E.S.* ii. 26
Compar'd, and *k*. their gen'rous End the same *E.S.* ii. 81
K. one a Man of Honour, one a Knave *E.S.* ii. 153
Who ne'er *k*. Joy, but Friendship might divide *Ep*. iii. 3
I doubt not if his Lordship *k*. *I.H.* ii. 8
K. what was handsome, and would do't *I.H.* ii. 163
Informs you, Sir, 'twas when he *k*. no better *P.S.* 52
Unlearn'd, he *k*. no schoolman's subtle art *P.S.* 398
But knottier points we *k*. not half so well *S*. vi. 58
Yes ; thank my stars ! as early as I *k*. *S*. vii. 1
Talkers I've learn'd to bear ; Motteux I *k*. *S*. viii. 50

Knight.
The decent *K*. retir'd with sober rage *D*. iv. 113
K. lifts the head, for what are crowds undone *D*. iv. 561
Once on a time, La Mancha's *K*., they say *E.C.* 267
" What ! leave the Combat out ? " exclaims the *K*. *E.C.* 279
Admit your Law to spare the *K*. requires *E.S.* ii. 30
He pledg'd it to the *k*. ; the *k*. had wit *M.E.* iii. 363
A Nymph of Quality admires our *K*. *M.E.* iii. 384
So Ladies in Romance assist their *K*. *R.L.* iii. 129
K. of the post reputed, or a city *K*. *S*. ii. 178
Slides to a Scriv'ner or a city *K*. *S*. iii. 145
But give the *K*. (or give his Lady) spleen *S*. iii. 145
Produc'd his Play, and begg'd the *K*.'s advice *E.C.* 274
Of Lords, and Earls, and Dukes, and garter'd K—s *E*. v. 36
K., squires, and steeds, must enter on the stage *E.C.* 282
What could they more than *K*. and Squires confound *M.E.* iii. 53
Burns to encounter two advent'rous *K*. *R.L.* iii. 26

Knighted.
One *k*. Blackmore, and one pension'd Quarles *S*. v. 387

Knighthood.
You'll gain at least a *K*., or the Bays *S*. i. 22

Knit.
Vex'd to be still in town, I *k*. my brow *E.* v. 49

Knock.
A drowsy Watchman, that just gives a *k*. *D.* iv. 443
As drives the storm, at any door I *k*. *S.* iii. 25
Time was, a sober Englishman would *k*. *S.* v.'161

Knock'd.
By potent Arthur, *k*. his chin and breast *D.* ii. 398
So humble, he has *k*. at *Tibbald's* door *P.S.* 372
Thrice rung the bell, the slipper *k*. the ground *R.L.* i. 17

Knocker.
Tie up the *k*., say I'm sick, I'm dead *P.S.* 2

Knocking.
Still to his wench he crawls on *k*. knees *M.E.* i. 236

Knotted.
Let op'ning roses *k*. oaks adorn *A.* 37

Knottier.
But *k*. points we knew not half so well *S.* vi. 58

Knotty.
A *k*. point! to which we now proceed *M.E.* iii. 337

Know.
I *k*. thee, Love! on foreign Mountains bred *A.* 89
K., Eusden thirsts no more for sack or praise *D.* i. 293
Which only heads refus'd from reason *k. D.* iii. 6
To ask, to guess, to *k*., as they commence *D.* iv. 155
Romans and Greek Grammarians! *k*. your Better *D.* iv.215
K., Kings and Fortune cannot make thee more *E.* ii. 9
Be sure yourself and your own reach to *k. E.C.* 48
K. well each ANCIENT's proper character *E.C.* 119
I *k*. there are, to whose presumptuous thoughts *E.C.* 169
Trust not yourself; but your defects to *k. E.C.* 213
For not to *k*. some trifles, is a praise *E.C.* 262
Leave such to tune their own dull rhymes, and *k. E.C.* 358
For 'tis but half a Judge's task, to *k. E.C.* 561
Some positive, persisting fops we *k. E.C.* 568
Still pleas'd to teach, and not too proud to *k. E.C.* 612
What can we reason, but from what we *k. E.M.* i. 18
When the proud steed shall *k*. why Man restrains *E.M.* i. 61
From brutes what men, from men what spirits *k. E.M.* i. 79
What future bliss, he gives not thee to *k. E.M.* i. 93
K. thy own point: This kind, this due degree *E M*.i.283
K. then thyself, presume not God to scan *E.M.* ii. 1
K., Nature's children all divide her care *E.M.* iii. 43
K., all enjoy that pow'r which suits them best *E.M.* iii. 80
And Anarchy without confusion *k. E.M.* iii. 186
K., all the good that individuals find *E.M.* iv. 77
'Tis but to *k*. how little can be known *E.M.* iv. 261
K. then this truth (enough for Man to *k*.) *E.M.* iv. 309
Which who but feels can taste, but thinks can *k. E.M.* iv. 328
Sees that no Being any bliss can *k. E.M.* iv. 335
And all our knowledge is, OURSELVES TO *K. E.M.* iv. 398
Would you *k*. when? exactly when they fall *E.S.* i. 90
Who *k*. how Whig Ministers to Tory *E.S.* i. 106
Suppose I censure—you *k*. what I mean *E.S.* ii. 32
My Lord, your Favours will I *k. I.H.* i. 21
Let my Lord *k*. you're come to town *I.H.* ii. 44 s
What I desire the World should *k. I.H.* ii. 62 s
Yet some I *k*. with envy swell *I.H.* ii. 101 s
Faith, Sir, you *k*. as much as I *I.H.* ii. 116 s
I *k*. no more than my Lord Mayor *I.H.* ii. 122 s
Our Friend, Dan Prior, told, (you *k*.) *I.H.* ii. 153
All *k*., 'tis Virtue, for he thinks them knaves *M.E.* i. 58
K., GOD and NATURE only are the same *M.E.* i. 95
Would Chloe *k*. if you're alive or dead *M.E.* ii. 177
Kept Dross for Duchesses, the world shall *k*. it *M.E.* ii. 291
And gives th' eternal wheels to *k*. their rounds *M.E.* iii. 168
I *k*. the thing that's most uncommon *Mi.* viii. 1
I *k*. a reasonable woman *Mi.* viii. 3
She all the cares of Love and Play does *k. Mi.* ix. 22
I *k*. the Bite, yet to my Ruin run *Mi.* ix. 69
By Music minds an equal temper *k. O.* i. 22
Pitholeon sends to me: " You *k*. his Grace *P.S.* 49
And when I die, be sure you let me *k. P.S.* 123

The things, we *k*., are neither rich nor rare *P.S.* 171
Nor *k*., if *Dennis* be alive or dead *P.S.* 270
Who sprung from Kings shall *k*. less joy than I *P.S.* 405
Hear and believe! thy own importance *k. R.L.* i. 35
K., then, unnumber'd Spirits round thee fly *R.L.* i. 41
K. further yet; whoever fair and chaste *R.L.* i. 67
'Tis but their Sylph, the wise Celestials *k. R.L.* i. 77
Teach Infant-cheeks a bidden blush to *k. R.L.* i. 89
Ye *k*. the spheres and various tasks assign'd *R.L.* ii. 75
K., all the distant din that world can keep *S.* i. 123
This all who *k*. me, *k*.; who love me, tell *S.* i. 138
K., there are Words and Spells, which can control *S.* iii. 57
K., there are Rhymes, which fresh and fresh apply'd *S.* iii. 59
Who *k*. themselves so little what to do *S.* iii. 123
Which guides all those who *k*. not what they mean *S.* iii. 144
(They *k*. not whither) in a Chaise and one *S.* iii. 158
Not to admire, is all the Art I *k. S.* iv. 1
To *k*. the poet from the Man of rhymes *S.* v. 341
To sing, or cease to sing, we never *k. S.* v. 361
Its name I *k*. not, and it's no great matter *S.* vi. 45
The better art to *k*. the good from bad *S.* vi. 55
To *k*. but this, that Thou art Good *U.P.* 7

Know'st.
Thou *k*., how guiltless first I met thy flame *E.A.* 59
Thou *k*. if best bestow'd or not *U.P.* 47

Knowing.
Curious not *k*., not exact but nice *E.C.* 286
And *k. Walsh*, would tell me I could write *P.S.* 136

Knowledge.
By common sense to common *k*. bred *D.* iv. 467
A *k*. both of books and human kind *E.C.* 640
His *k*. measur'd to his state and place *E.M.* i. 71
With too much *k*. for the Sceptic side *E.M.* ii. 5
Let pow'r or *k*., gold or glory, please *E.M.* ii. 169
Whate'er the Passion, *k*., fame, or pelf *E.M.* ii. 201
These build as fast as *k*. can destroy *E.M.* ii. 287
Gives not the useless *k*. of its end *E.M.* iii. 72
And all our *k*. is, OURSELVES TO KNOW *E.M.* iv. 398
When half our *k*. we must snatch, not take *M.E.* i. 40
For what to shun will no great *k*. need *M.E.* iii. 199

Known.
By his broad shoulders *k*., and length of ears (*rep.*) *D.* iii. 36
A second see, by meeker manners *k. D.* iii. 143
Then thus. " Since Man from beast by Words is *k. D.* iv. 149
To teach vain Wits a science little *k. E.C.* 199
For envy'd Wit, like Sol eclips'd, makes *k. E.C.* 468
To him the wit of Greece and Rome was *k. E.C.* 727
Thro' worlds unnumber'd tho' the God be *k. E.M.* i. 21
The worker from the work distinct was *k. E.M.* iii. 229
'Tis but to know how little can be *k. E.M.* iv. 261
Hope of *k*. bliss, and Faith in bliss unknown *E.M.*iv. 346
No cheek is *k*. to blush, no heart to throb *E.S.* i. 103
Go then, where only bliss sincere is *k. Ep.* vii. 15
The closest mortal ever *k. I.H.* ii. 124 s
True, some are open, and to all men *k. M.E.* i. 51
The Wild are constant, and the Cunning *k. M.E.* i. 175
Nature well *k*., no prodigies remain *M.E.* i. 208
Yet his *k*. Falsehood could no Warning prove *Mi.* ix. 73
Oft have we *k*. that seven-fold fence to fail *R.L.* ii. 119
So *k*., so honour'd, at the House of Lords *S.* iv. 49
But in *k*. Images of life, I guess *S.* v. 284
Ah think, what Poet best may make them *k. S.* v. 377
Is *k*. alone to that Directing Pow'r *S.* vi. 278
Despise the *k*., nor tremble at th' unknown *S.* vi. 311
'Tis such a bounty as was never *k. S.* vii. 65
Scarce could the Goddess from her nymph be *k. W.F.* 175
Make sacred Charles's tomb for ever *k. W.F.* 319

Knows.
Fierce champion Fortitude, that *k*. no fears *D.* i. 47
And " Oh!" (he cry'd) " what street, what lane but *k. D.* ii. 153
What mortal *k*. his pre-existent state (*rep.*) *D.* iii. 48
Blest in one Niger, till he *k*. of two *D.* iv. 370
Unfinish'd things, one *k*. not what to call *E.C.* 42
Who *k*. but he, whose hand the light'ning forms *E.M.* i. 157

At Greenland, Zembla, or the Lord *k.* where *E.M.* ii. 224
The fool is happy that he *k.* no more *E.M.* ii. 264
Nature that Tyrant checks; he only *k. E.M.* iii 51
Best *k.* the blessing, and will most be blest *E.M.* iv. 96
Aod *k.*, where Faith, Law, Morals, all began *E.M.* iv. 339
Sets half the world, God *k.*, against the rest *E.S.* i. 58
Why so! if Satire *k.* its Time and Place *E.S.* i. 87
God *k.*, I praise a Courtier when I can *E.S.* ii. 63
May yield, God *k.*, to strong temptation *I.H.* ii. 182
My Lord alone *k.* how to live *I.H.* ii. 209
Offend her, and she *k.* not to forgive *M.E.* ii. 137
Is there a Lord, who *k.* a cheerful noon *M.E.* iii. 239
And there a Summer-house, that *k.* no shade *M.E.* iv. 122
For all his Lordship *k.*, but they are Wood *M.E.* iv.138
When ev'ry Coxcomb *k.* me by my *Style P.S.* 282
No cheerful breeze this sullen region *k. R.L.* iv. 19
He *k.* to live, who keeps the middle state *S.* ii. 61
And *k.* no losses, while the Muse is kind *S.* v. 196
God *k.*, may hurt the very ablest head *S.* vi. 103
As who *k.* Sappho, smiles at other whores *S.* vii. 6
Catch'd like the Plague, or Love, the Lord *k.* how *S.*vii.9
And *k.* what's fit for ev'ry state to do *S.* viii. 47
When the Queen frown'd, or smil'd, he *k.*; and what *S.* viii. 132
But your Alexis *k.* no sweets but you *Sa.* 70

Kuster.
Are things which *K.*, Burman, Wasse shall see *D.*iv.237

L.

L. — and all about your ears *E.* vi. 20

Laborious.
L., heavy, busy, bold, and blind *D.* i. 15

Labour.
This *l.* past, by Bridewell all descend *D.* ii. 269
There all the Learn'd shall at the *l.* stand *D.* iv. 393
L. and rest, that equal periods keep *E.A.* 211
But when by Man's audacious *l.* won *M.E.* iii. 11
Steel could the *l.* of the Gods destroy *R.L.* iii. 173
How easy ev'ry *l.* it pursues *S.* ii. 83
But wherefore all this *l.*, all this strife *S.* iv. 38
The great Alcides, ev'ry *L.* past *S.* v. 17
Patient of *l.* when the end was rest *S.* v. 242
The *l.* greater, as th' indulgence less *S.* v. 285
The swain with tears his frustrate *l.* yields *W.F.* 55
In ev'ry loom our l—s shall be seen D. ii. 155
Alike their *l.*, and alike their praise *D.* iii. 272
While Jones' and Boyle's united *L.* fail *D.* iii. 328
The growing *l.* of the lengthen'd way *E.C.* 230
Lives on the *l.* of this lord of all *E.M.* iii. 42
And Betty's prais'd for *l.* not her own *R.L.* i. 148
And the long *l.* of the Toilet cease *R.L.* iii. 24
St. John, whose love indulg'd my *l.* past *S.* iii. 1
The young who l., and the old who rest M.E. iii. 268

Labour'd.
It rose, and *l.* to a curve at most *D.* ii. 172
And rules as strict his *l.* work confine *E.C.* 137
Such *l.* nothings, in so strange a style *E.C.* 326
In human works, tho' *l.* on with pain *E.M.* i. 53
The whole, a *l.* Quarry above ground *M.E.* iv. 110
And secret passions *l.* in her breast *R.L.* iv. 2

Lab'rer.
The *L.* bears: what his hard Heart denies *M.E.* iv. 171
Not balmy sleep to l—s faint with pain A. 44

Lab'ring.
While *l.* oxen, spent with toil and heat *A.* 61
So *l.* on, with shoulders, hands, and head *D.* ii. 65
Such as from *l.* lungs, th' Enthusiast blows *D.* ii. 255
The blessing thrills thro' all the *l.* throng *S.* v. 239

Labours.
And *l.* till it clouds itself all o'er *D.* iv. 254
The line too *l.*, and the words move slow *E.C.* 371
Which heavier Reason *l.* at in vain *Ill.* 92
When the tir'd glutton *l.* thro' a treat *S.* ii. 31
For you he sweats and *l.* at the laws *S.* vii. 75

Lab'rinth, Labyrinths.
Pierce the soft *l.* of a Lady's ear *S.* vii. 55
Love in these l—s his slaves detains R.L. ii. 23

Lace.
No, let a charming Chintz, and Brussels *l. M.E.* i. 248

Lac'd.
Others a sword-knot and *l.* suit inflame *D.* ii. 52
Whore, Pupil, and *l.* Governor from France *D.* iv. 272
That, *l.* with bits of rustic, makes a front *M.E.* iv. 31

Lacquer'd.
Cato's long wig, flower'd gown, and *l.* chair *S.* v. 337

Lad.
Who scorn a *L.* should teach his father skill *S.* v. 129
Bows and begins—"This *L.*, Sir, is of Blois *S.* vi. 4
If, after this, you took the graceless *l. S.* vi. 21
Besides, my father taught me from a *l. S.* vi. 54
Shortly no *l.* shall chuck, or lady vole *S.* viii. 146

Lady.
But ev'ry *L.* would be Queen for life *M.E.* ii. 218
Bear home six Whores, and make his *L.* weep *M.E.*iii.72
My good old *L.* catch'd a cold, and died *M.E.* iii. 384
My *L.* falls to play; so bad her chance *M.E.* iii. 395
She flatters her good *L.* twice a day *Mi.* iii. 18
Now trips a *L.*, and now struts a Lord *P.S.* 329
But give the Knight (or give his *L.*) spleen *S.* iii. 145
Shortly no lad shall chuck, or *l.* vole *S.* viii. 146
"*Live like yourself,*" *was soon my* L.'s *word M.E.* iii. 359
Or the small pillow grace a *L.* bed *R.L.* iii. 166
Weighs the Men's wits against the *L.* hair *R.L.* v. 72
Pierce the soft lab'rinth of a *L.* ear *S.* vii. 55
What *L.* face is not a whited wall *S.* viii. 151
That virtuous l—s envy while they rail E.J.S. 16
L., like variegated Tulips, show *M.E.* ii. 41
As *L.* in Romance assist their Knight *R.L.* iii. 129
Not ancient *l.* when refus'd a kiss *R.L.* iv. 6
While the Fops envy and the *L.* stare *R.L.* iv. 104
Or if three *L.* like a luckless Play *S.* iv. 87
Sail in the *L.*; how each pirate eyes *S.* viii. 228
Let but the *L.* smile, and they are blest *S.* viii. 254

Lady Mary.
White gloves, and linen worthy *L. M. S.* iii. 164
Of wrongs from Duchesses and L. M*—ies D.* ii. 136

La-guerre.
Where sprawl the Saints of Verrio or *L. M.E.* iv. 146

Laid.
Fall'n in the plash his wickedness had *l. D.* ii. 76
Walker with rev'rence took, and *l.* aside *D.* iv. 206
L. this gay daughter of the Spring in dust *D.* iv. 416
With thee repose, where Tully once was *l. E.* iii. 49
In some fair ev'ning, on your elbow *l. E.* v. 81
Each silver Vase in mystic order *l. R.L.* i. 122
Thou by some other shalt be *l.* as low *R.L.* v. 98
And all those tresses shall be *l.* as low *R.L.* v. 148
Cities *l.* waste, they storm'd the dens and caves *W.F.*49

Lake.
Full in the middle way there stood a *l. D.* ii. 69
Th' unconscious stream sleeps o'er thee like a *l. D.*ii.304
Behold the wonders of th' oblivious *l. D.* iii. 44
As the small pebble stirs the peaceful *l. E.M.* iv. 364
Lo! *Cobham* comes and floats them with a *L. M.E.*iv. 74
Two Cupids squirt before; a *L.* behind *M.E.* iv. 111
And send up vows from Rosamunda's *l. R.L.* v. 136
No *l.* so gentle, and no spring so clear *W.F.* 226
As what a Dutchman plumps into the l—s D. ii. 405
The *l.* that quiver to the curling breeze *E.A.* 160
Or plung'd in *l.* of bitter washes lie *R.L.* ii. 127
Now *l.* of liquid gold, Elysian scenes *R.L.* iv. 45

La Mancha.
Once on a time, *La M.*'s knight, they say *E.C.* 267

Lamb.
The *l.* thy riot dooms to bleed to-day *E.M.* i. 81
I'll stake you *l.*, that near the fountain plays *Sp.* 33
The bowl to Strephon, and the *l.* to thee *Sp.* 94
To thee, bright goddess, offer a *l.* shall bleed *W.* 81
The tender l—s he raises in his arms M. 53
The *l.* with wolves shall graze the verdant mend *M.* 77

No *l.* or sheep for victims I'll impart *Sp.* 51
Feed here my *l.*, I'll seek no distant field *Sp.* 64
To cure thy *l.*, but not to heal thy heart *Su.* 34

Lambent.
Shone sweetly *l.* with celestial day *E.A.* 64

Lame.
This prose on stilts, that poetry fall'n *D.* i. 190
The dumb shall sing, the *l.* his crutch forego *M.* 43
Who loves a lie, *l.* slander helps about *P.S.* 289

Lament.
I mourn the lover, not *l.* the fault *E.A.* 184
And ev'ry friend the less *l.* my fate *S.* i. 62
Repeat unask'd ; *l.*, the Wit's too fine *S.* v. 366
L. the ceasing of a sweeter breath *W.* 50

Lamented.
This humble praise, *l.* shade I receive *E.C.* 733
L. DIGBY I sunk thee to the grave *E.M.* iv. 104
Unblam'd thro' life, *l.* in thy End *Ep.* xi. 8

Lamp.
I waste the Matin *l.* in sighs for thee *E.A.* 267
The silver *l.* ; the fiery spirits blaze *R.L.* iii. 108
The shrines all trembled and the *l.*—s grew pale *E.A.* 112
Here as I watch'd the dying *l.* around *E.A.* 307
Useless, unseen, as *l.* in sepulchres *U.L.* 20

Lampoon.
The first *L.* Sir Will or Bubo makes *P.S.* 280
Make Satire a *L.*, and Fiction, Lie *P.S.* 302
Her hand is fill'd ; her bosom with l—s *R.L.* iv. 30

Lance.
This golden *l.* shall guard Desert *E.* vi. 6
Matchless his pen, victorious was his *l. W.F.* 293
But useless *l*—s into scythes shall bend *M.* 61
And groves of *l.* glitter on the Rhine *W.F.* 364

Land.
And pour'd her spirit o'er the *l.* and deep *D.* i. 8
Realms shift their place, and Ocean turns to *l. D.* i. 72
Like Cimon, triumph'd both on *l.* and sea *D.* i. 85
Sent with a Pass, and vagrant thro' the *l. D.* i. 232
My son, the promised *l.* expects your reign *D.* i. 292
And suckle armies, and dry-nurse the *L. D.* i. 316
Pours forth, and leaves unpeopled half the *L. D.* ii. 20
And wafting Vapours from the *L.* of dreams *D.* ii. 340
Some gentle JAMES to bless the *l.* again *D.* iv. 176
And MAKE ONE MIGHTY DUNCIAD OF THE *L.! D.* iv. 604
As on the *l.* while here the ocean gains *E.C.* 54
Where slaves once more their native *l.* behold *E.M.* i. 107
Truths would you teach, or save a sinking *l. E.M.* iv. 265
Hear her black Trumpet thro' the *L.* proclaim *E.S.* i. 159
Of *L.*, set out to plant a Wood *I.H.* ii. 6 s
Bu· bribes a Senate, and the *L.*'s betray'd *M.E.* iii. 32
And Honour linger ere it leaves the *L. M.E.* iii. 248
Fill half the *l.* with Imitating-Fools *M.E.* iv. 26
And laughing Ceres re-assume the *l. M.E.* iv. 176
And roll obedient Rivers thro' the *L. M.E.* iv. 202
And civil madness tears them from the *l. O.* ii. 24
They rave, recite, and madden round the *l. P.S.* 6
By *l.*, by water, they renew the charge *P.S.* 9
In some lone isle, or distant Northern *l. R.L.* v. 154
Why deck'd with all that *l.* and sea afford *R.L.* v. 11
I only wear it in a *l.* of Hectors *S.* i. 71
Than in five acres now of rented *l. S.* ii. 136
Just half the *l.* would buy, and half be sold *S.* iii. 125
T' enroll your Triumphs o'er the seas and *l. S.* v. 373
How, when you nodded, o'er the *l.* and deep *S.* v. 400
The Laws of God, as well as of the *l. S.* v. 246
Till, like the Sea, they compass all the *l. S.* vii. 85
And deal damnation round the *l. U.P.* 27
Not thus the *l.* appear'd in ages past *W.F.* 43
Her boundless empire over seas and l—s *D.* iv. 68
Intrepid then, o'er seas and *l.* he flew *D.* iv. 293
To *l.* of singing or of dancing slaves *D.* iv. 305
And drown his *L.* and Manors in a Soupe *D.* iv. 596
And sigh'd) "my *l.* and tenements to Ned" *M.E.* i. 257
Last, for his Country's love, he sells his *L. M.E.* iii. 312
Then full against his Cornish *l.* they roar *M.E.* iii. 355
My *l.* are sold, my father's house is gone *S.* ii. 255
Let *l.* and houses have what Lords they will *S.* ii. 179
The *l.* are bought, but where are to be found *S.* vii. 109
What 'Squire his *l.*, what Citizen his wife *S.* viii. 149

Landlord.
The good old *L.*'s hospitable door *S.* vii. 114

Landscape.
The wat'ry *l.* of the pendant woods *W.F.* 213

Lane.
And "Oh!" (he cry'd) "what street, what *l.* but knows *D.* ii. 153

Lanesb'row.
As sober *L.* dancing in the gout *M.E.* i. 231

Language.
Spoil'd his own *l.*, and acquir'd no more *D.* iv. 320
Others for *L.* all their care express *E.C.* 305
Our sons their fathers' failing *l.* see *E.C.* 482
No *l.* but the *l.* of the heart *P.S.* 399
The modern *l.* of corrupted Peers *S.* iii. 99
One likes no *l.* but the Faery Queen *S.* v. 39
But still I love the *l.* of his Heart *S.* v. 78
And woe in *l.* of the Pleas and Bench (rep.) *S.* vii. 60
This thing has travell'd, speaks each *l.* too *S.* viii. 46

Languid.
With mincing step, small voice, and *l.* eye *D.* iv. 46

Languish.
See the last sparkle *l.* in my eye *E.A.* 332
And let me *l.* into life *O.* v. 6

Languish'd.
There, stript, fair Rhet'ric *l.* on the ground *D.* iv. 21

Languishes.
Faints into airs, and *l.* with pride *R.L.* iv. 34

Languishing.
Say for my comfort, *l.* in bed *P.S.* 121

Languishingly.
What's roundly smooth or *l.* slow *E.C.* 359

Languor.
Diffusing *l.* in the panting gales *D.* iv. 304
Make *L.* smile, and smooth the bed of Death *P.S.* 411

Lap.
On Dulness' *l.* th' Anointed head repos'd *D.* iii. 2
Soft on her *l.* her Laureate son reclines *D.* iv. 20
Some o'er her *l.* their careful plumes display'd *R.L.* iii. 115
Or e'er to costive *l.*-dog gave disease *R.L.* iv. 79
Now *l*—s give themselves the rousing shake *R.L.* i. 15
When husbands, or when *l.* breathe their last *R.L.* iii. 158
Men, monkeys, *l.*, parrots, perish all *R.L.* iv. 120

Lapwings.
The clam'rous *l.* feel the leaden death *W.F.* 132

Lares.
And keep his *L.*, tho' his house be sold *D.* iv. 366

Large.
Rolls the *l.* tribute of dead dogs to Thames *D.* ii. 272
She gives in *l.* recruits of needful pride *E.C.* 206
As things seem *l.* which we thro' mists descry *E.C.* 392
Sprung the rank weed, and thriv'd with *l.* increase *E.C.* 535
His post neglects, or leaves the fair at *l. R.L.* ii. 124
Because God made these *l.*, the other less *S.* ii. 24
In what Commandment's *l.* contents they dwell *S.* vii. 44
L. as the fields themselves, and larger far *S.* vii. 95
Heathcote himself, and such l.-acred men *S.* vi. 240

Largely.
And drinking *l.* sobers us again *E.C.* 218

Larger.
Large as the fields themselves, and *l.* too *S.* vii. 95

Lark.
Is it for thee the *l.* ascends and sings *E.M.* iii. 31
Not show'rs to *l*—s, nor sun-shine to the bee *A.* 45
Turns Hares to *L.*, and Pigeons into Toads *D.* iv. 554
In yonder wild-goose and the *l. Mi.* xii. 10
No more the mounting *l.*, while Daphne sings *W.* 53
Oft, as the mounting *l.* their notes prepare *W.F.* 133

LARUM—LATIUM.

Larum.
Stunn'd with his giddy *l.* half the town *D.* iv. 292
Down, down, they l., *with impetuous whirl D.* iii. 163

Lash.
A *l.* like mine no honest man shall dread *P.S.* 303
But *when loud surges* l. *the sounding shore E.C.* 368
You still may *l.* the greatest—in Disgrace *E.S.* i. 88
Yet none but you by Name the guilty *l. E.S.* ii. 10
Form'd to delight at once, and *l.* the age *Ep.* xi. 4
Could peusion'd Boileau *l.* in honest strain *S.* i. 111

Lash'd.
And *l.* so long, like tops, are *l.* asleep *E.C.* 601
Bubo observes, he *l.* no sort of *Vice E.S.* i. 12
He *l.* him not, but let her be his wife *P.S.* 377

Last.
To the *L* honours of the Butt and Bays *D.* i. 168
When the *l.* blaze sent Ilion to the skies *D.* i. 256
Back to the Devil the *l.* echoes roll *D.* i. 325
Puts his *l.* refuge all in heav'n and pray'r *D.* ii. 214
At *l.* Centlivre felt her voice to fail *D.* ii. 411
But in her Temple's *L* recess enclos'd *D.* ii. 1
And *l.*, to give the whole creation grace *D.* iii. 247
Reduc'd at *l.* to hiss in my own dragon *D.* iii. 286
And carry'd off in some dog's tail at *l. D.* iii. 292
And ev'ry year be duller than the *l. D.* iii. 296
And (*l.* and worst) with all the cant of wit *D.* iv. 99
And what the *l.* ? A very Poet still *D.* iv. 164
And *l.* turn'd *Air*, the Echo of a Sound *D.* iv. 322
At *l.* it fix'd, 'twas on what flow'r it pleas'd *D.* iv. 428
And *l.*, to Nature's Cause thro' Nature led *D.* iv. 468
The *l.*, not least in honour or applause *D.* iv. 577
Relate who first, who *l.* resign'd to rest *D.* iv. 621
When the *l.* ling'ring friend has bid farewell *E.* i. 34
But the *l.* Tyrant ever proves the worst *E.* iv. 40
Why rove my thoughts beyond this *L* retreat *E.A.* 5
Thou, Abelard, the *l.* sad office pay *E.A.* 321
Suck my *l.* breath, and catch my flying soul *E.A.* 324
See the *l.* sparkle languish in my eye *E.A.* 332
Turn'd Critics next, and prov'd plain fools at *l. E.C.* 37
The *l.*, the meanest of your sons inspire *E.C.* 196
And the first clouds and mountains seem the *l. E.C.* 228
Nor yet the *l.* to lay the old aside *E.C.* 336
Then, at the *l.* and only couplet fraught *E.C.* 354
Enlights the present, and shall warm the *l. R.C.* 403
But always think the *L* opinion right *E.C.* 431
For rising merit will buoy up at *l. E.C.* 461
But ev'n those clouds at *l.* adorn its way *E.C.* 472
And make each day a Critic on the *l. E.C.* 571
Strain out the *l.* dull droppings of their sense *E.C.* 608
From the same foes, at *l.*, both felt their doom *E.C.* 685
Pleas'd to the *L*, he crops the flow'ry food *E.M.* i. 83
The *l.* scarce ripen'd into perfect Man *E.M.* iii. 141
The first, *L* purpose of the human soul *E.M.* iv. 338
The *l.* full fairly gives it to the *House E.S.* ii. 180
Like the *l. Gazette*, to *l.* Address *E.S.* ii. 210
Yes, the *l.* Pen for Freedom let me draw *E.S.* ii. 248
Here, *L.* of Britons ! let your Names be read *E.S.* ii. 250
The *l.* true Briton lies beneath this stone *Ep.* ix. 12
Pays the *l* Tribute of a Saint to Heav'n *Ep.* xiv. 14
Tir'd, not determin'd, to the *l.* we yield *M.E.* i. 43
As the *l.* image of that troubled heap *M.E.* i. 225
Yet tames not this ; it sticks to our *l.* sand *M.E.* i. 225
And totter on in bus'ness to the *l. M.E.* i. 247
Were the *l.* words that poor Narcissa spoke *M.E.* i. 247
"Oh, save my Country, Heav'n!" shall be your *l. M.E.* i. 263
L. night her Lord was all that's good and great *M.E.* ii. 141
Those, only fix'd, they first or *l.* obey *M.E.* ii. 209
At *l.*, to follies Youth could scarce defend *M.E.* ii. 235
Its *l.* best work, but forms a softer Man *M.E.* ii. 272
We find our tenets just the same at *l. M.E.* iii. 16
Blest paper-credit ! *l.* and best supply *M.E.* iii. 39
To spoil the nation's *l.* great trade, Quadrille *M.E.* iii. 76
Unhappy Wharton, waking, found at *l. M.E.* iii. 84
L., for his Country's love, he sells his Lands *M.E.* iii. 212
He finds at *l.* he better likes a Field *M.E.* iv. 88
Her *l.* good man dejected Rome ador'd *P.C.* 35
And drop at *l.*, but in unwilling ears *P.S.* 39
At *l.* he whispers, "Do ; and we go snacks" *P.S.* 66
For thee, fair Virtue! welcome ev'n the *l. P.S.* 359
Who gave the ball, or paid the visit *l. R.L.* ii. 12
When husbands, or when lapdogs breath their *l. R.L.* iii. 158

"Those eyes were made so killing"—was his *l. R.L.* v. 64
Matures my present, and shall bound my *l. S.* iii. 2
What ev'ry day will want, and most, the *l. S.* iii. 22
Had still this Monster to subdue at *l. S.* v. 18
The *l.* and greatest Art, the Art to blot *S.* v. 281
At *l.* they steal us from ourselves away *S.* vi. 73
Behind the foremost, and before the *l. S.* vi. 303
Time, that at *l.* matures a clap to pox *S.* vii. 47
And *l.* (which proves him wiser still than all) *S.* viii. 150
Pay their *l.* duty to the Court, and come *S.* viii. 214
And the *l.* pang shall tear thee from his heart *U.L.* 80
There the *L* numbers flow'd from Cowley's toogue *W.F.* 272
To future ages may thy dulness l. *D.* iii. 189
Good humour only teaches charms to *l. E.* iv. 61
And 'twas their point, I ween, to make it *l. S.* ii. 94
"Pray heav'n it *l.!*" (cries Swift !) "as you go on *S.* ii. 161
And then such Friends—as cannot fail to *l. S.* iv. 80
The Muse shall sing, and what she sings shall *l. W.F.* 174

Lasting.
Oh *l.* as those Colours may they shine *E.* iii. 63
Death, only death, can break the *l.* chain *E.A.* 173
Ah hopeless, *l.* flames I like those that burn *E.*. 261
That longer care contracts more *l.* hands *E.M.* iii. 132
Matter too soft a *l.* mark to bear *M.E.* 71
And round the orb in *l.* notes be read *M.E.* v. 66

Lasts.
Thy realm for ever *l.*, thy own MESSIAH reigns *M.* 108
Who *l.* a century can have no flaw *S.* v. 55
While *l.* the mountain, and while Thames shall flow *W.F.* 266

Late.
Where Bentley *l.* 'tempestuous wont to sport *D.* iv. 201
Those Age or Sickness soon or *l.* disarms *E.* iv. 60
Such *l.* was Walsh—the Muse's judge and friend *E.C.* 729
What matter, soon or *l.*, or here or there *E.M.* i. 74
Superior beings, when of *l.* they saw *E.M.* ii. 31
And hence let Reason, *l.*, instruct Mankind *E.M.* iii. 180
When all their Lordships had sat *l. I.H.* ii. 186
On rifted rocks, the Dragon's *l.* abodes *M.* 71
Early at Bus'ness, and at Hazard *l. M.E.* i. 73
To that each Passion turns, or soon or *l. M.E.* i. 133
The doctor call'd, declares all help too *l. M.E.* i. 239
As Helluo, *l.* Dictator of the Feast *M.E.* i. 79
What *l.* he call'd a Blessing, now was Wit *M.E.* iii. 377
L., as I rang'd the crystal wilds of air *R.L.* i. 107
Ah cease, rash youth ! desist ere 'tis tno *l. R.L.* iii. 121
Clipp'd from the lovely head where *l.* it grew *R.L.* iv. 136
In mystic visions, now believ'd too *l. R.L.* iv. 166
The Robin-red-breast till of *l.* had rest *S.* ii. 12
None comes too early, none departs too *l. S.* ii. 158
L. as it is, I put myself to school *S.* iii. 47
Plead much, read more, dine *l.*, or not at all *S.* iv. 37
L., very *l.*, correctness grew our care *S.* v. 272
Charles, to *l.* times to be transmitted fair *S.* v. 380
The Temple *l.* two brother Sergeants saw *S.* vi. 127
Wisdom (curse on it) will come soon or *l. S.* vi. 199

Lately.
Some God, or Spirit he has *l.* found *M.E.* i. 164
The silver flood, so *l.* calm, appears *W.* 65

Latent.
The *l.* tracts, the giddy heights, explore *E.M.* i. 11
And *l.* Metals innocently glow *Mi.* x. 6

Latest.
'Tis hers, the brave man's *l.* steps to trace *E.* i. 29
And you, brave COBHAM, to the *l.* breath *M.E.* i. 262
All human Virtue, to its *l.* breath *S.* v. 15

Latian.
From *L.* Syrens, French Circean Feasts *S.* iv. 122

Latin.
Senates and Courts with Greek and *L.* rule *D.* iv. 179
Dropt the dull lumber of the *L.* store *D.* iv. 319
So *L.*, yet so English all the while *E.S.* i. 74

Latium.
See the bold Ostrogoths on *L.* fall *D.* iii. 93
But soon by impious arms from *L.* chas'd *E.C.* 709

Latona.

'Gainst Pallas, Mars ; L., Hermes arms *R.L.* v. 47

Laugh.

The *l.*, the jest, attendants on the bowl *S.* v. 247
But feigns a *l.*, to see me search around (*rep.*) *Sp.* 55
Whose *l—s are hearty, tho' his jests are coarse E.* v. 29
Or *l.* and shake in Rab*lais' easy chair D.* i. 22
Which lives as long as fools are pleas'd to *l. E.C.* 451
L. where we must, be candid where we can *E.M.* i. 15
To *l.* at Fools who put their trust in Peter *E.S.* i. 10
And never *l.* for all my life to come *E.S.* i. 28
Come, come, at all I *l.*, he laughs no doubt (*rep.*) *E.S.* i. 35
L. then at any, but at Fools or Foes *E.S.* i. 53
L. at your friends, and if your Friends are sore (*rep.*) *E.S.* i. 55
No Fool to *l.* at, which he valu'd more *M.E.* iii. 312
Who but must *L.*, the Master when he sees *M.E.* iv. 107
To *L* were want of goodness and of grace *P.S.* 35
Who but must *l.*, if such a man there be *P.S.* 213
And *l.* at Peers that put their trust in Peter *S.* i. 40
My Lords the Judges *L.*, and you're dismiss'd *S.* i. 156
You *L.*, half Beau, half Sloven, if I stand *S.* iii. 161
You *L.*, if coat and breeches strangely vary *S.* iii. 163
Then turn about, and *l.* at your own jest *S.* iv. 109

Laugh'd.

She tripp'd and *L.*, too pretty much to stand *D.* iv. 50
That *L.* down many a Summer Sun *I.H.* i. 47
L. at the loss of friends he never had *P.S.* 346

Laughing.

And fain would be upon the *l.* side *E.C.* 33
Chatting and *l.* all-a-row *I.H.* ii. 136
And *l.* Ceres re-assume the land *M.E.* iv. 176
With singing, *l.*, ogling, *and all that R.L.* iii. 18

Laughs.

And *L* to think Monroe would take her down *D.* i. 30
In Folly's cup still *l.* the bubble, joy *E.M.* ii. 288
Come, come, at all I laugh, he *l.* no doubt *E.S.* i. 35
Or her, who *l.* at Hell, but (like her Grace) *M.E.* ii. 107
Prudina likes a Man, and *l.* at Show *Mi.* ix. 104
The Man that loves and *l.* must sure do well *S.* iv. 109
All nature *l.*, the groves are fresh and fair *Sp.* 73

Laughter.

Heav'n rings with *l.* Of the *l.* vain *D.* ii. 121
Heav'n still with *l.* the vain toil surveys *E.M.* iv. 75
Let peals of *l.* Codrus ! round thee break *P.S.* 85
With *l.* sure Democritus had died *S.* v. 320

Launch.

L. not beyond your depth, but be discreet *E.C.* 50
And the new world *l.* forth to seek the old *W.F.* 402

Launch'd.

L. on the bosom of the silver Thames *R.L.* ii. 4

Laureate.

Soft on her lap her *L.* son reclines *D.* iv. 20
They scarce can bear their *L.* twice a year *S.* i. 31
Could *L.* Drydeo Pimp and Friar engage *S.* i. 113
Fit to bestow the L.'s weighty place *S.* v. 379

Laurel.

Thou, Cibber ! thou, his *L.* shalt support *D.* i. 299
Or give from fool to fool the *L.* crown *D.* iv. 98
Yet ne'er one sprig of *l.* grac'd those ribalds *P.S.* 163
Weave *l.* Crowns, and take what names we please *S.* vi. 142
Twis*'d with the wreaths Parnassian l—s yield E.M.* iv. 11
Now Europe's *l.* on their brows behold *E.M.* iv. 295
In vain your guiltless *l.* stood *O.* ii. 5

Laurell'd.

Or in fair series *l.* Bards be shown *M.E.* v. 61

Lave.

Cole, whose dark streams his flow'ry islands *l. W.F.* 343

Laves.

In her chaste current oft the goddess *l. W.F.* 209

Lavish.

In *l.* streams to quench a Country's thirst *M.E.* i. 175
I curse such *l.* cost, and little skill *M.E.* iv. 167
And *l.* nature paints the purple year *Sp.* 28

Law.

Shade him from Light, and cover him from *L. D.* i. 314
Boyer the State, and *L.* the Stage give o'er *D.* ii. 413
Nor less revere him, blunderbuss of *L. D.* iii. 150
Give *l.* to Words, or war with Words alone *D.* iv. 178
When love is liberty, and nature *l. E.A.* 92
Perhaps he seem'd above the critic's *l. E.C.* 132
A mortal Man unfold all Nature's *l. E.M.* ii. 32
Behold the child, by Nature's kindly *l. E.M.* ii. 275
Entangle Justice in her net of *L. E.M.* iii. 192
When Love was Liberty, and Nature *L. E.M.* iii. 208
Their *L* his eye, their oracle his tongue *E.M.* iii. 218
Force first made Conquest, and that conquest, *L. E.M.* iii. 245
Order is Heav'n's first *l.*; and this confest *E.M.* iv. 49
And knows, where Faith, *L.*, Morals, all began *E.M.* iv. 339
At Crimes that 'scape, or triumph o'er the *L. E.S.* i. 168
Admit your *L.* to spare the Knight requires *E.S.* ii. 30
When Truth stands trembling on the edge of *L. E.S.* ii. 249
Tells all their names, lays down the *l. I.H.* ii. 200
Whether the nymph shall break Diana's *l. R.L.* ii. 105
I come to Counsel learned in the *L. S.* i. 8
I hold that Wit a Classic, good in *l. S.* v. 56
Appeal'd to *L.*, and Justice lent her arm *S.* v. 256
In crowds, and courts, *l.*, business, feasts, and friends *S.* vi. 91
Who deem'd each other Oracles of *L. S.* vi. 128
'Twas "Sir, your *L.*"—and "Sir, your eloquence" *S.* vi. 133
If there be truth in *L.*, and Use can give *S.* vi. 230
The Thief condemn'd, in *l.* already dead *S.* vii. 15
Then strongly fencing ill-got wealth by *l. S.* vii. 93
Within the reach of Treason, or the *L. S.* vii. 108
Jests like a licens'd fool, commands like *L. S.* viii. 271
And saving Ignorance enthrones by L—d D. iii. 98
Thence a new world to Nature's *l.* unknown *D.* iii. 241
Not those alone who passive own her *l. D.* iv. 85
Or, at one bound, o'er-leaping all his *l. D.* iv. 477
Isis and Cam made Doctors of her *L. D.* iv. 578
Curse on all *l.* but those which Love has made *E.A.* 74
By the same *l.* which first herself ordain'd *E.C.* 91
As Kings dispense with *l.* themselves have made *E.C.* 162
Seizes your fame, and puts his *l.* in force *E.C.* 158
Receiv'd his *l.*; and stood convinc'd 'twas fit *E.C.* 651
Whose own example strengthens all his *l. E.C.* 679
License repress'd, and useful *l.* ordain'd *E.C.* 682
But we, brave Britons, foreign *l.* despis'd *E.C.* 715
And here restor'd Wit's fundamental *l. E.C.* 722
And who but wishes to invert the *l. E.M.* i. 129
Acts not by partial, but by gen'ral *l. E.M.* i. 146, *and E.M.* iv. 36
Acts to one end, but acts by various *l. E.M.* iii. 2
Mark what unvary'd *l.* preserve each state (*rep.*) *E.M.* iii. 189
That proud exception to all Nature's *l. E.M.* iii. 243
Of what restrains him, Government and *L. E.M.* iii. 272
Prone for his fav'rites to reverse his *l. E.M.* iv. 122
And hurls the Thunder of our *L.* on Gin *E.S.* i. 130
And hers the Gospel is, and hers the *L. E.S.* i. 148
Nature and Nature's *L.* lay hid in Night *Ep.* xii. 1
His thankless Country leaves him to her *L. M.E.* iii. 218
Before her death with clamour pleads the *l. Mi.* v. 5
Such Tears as Patriots shed for dying *L. P.C.* 14
While Cato gives his little Senate *l. P.C.* 23
Arthur, whose giddy son neglects the *L. P.S.* 23
Like *Cato,* give his little Senate *l. P.S.* 209
For Spirits, freed from mortal *l.*, with ease *R.L.* i. 69
By *l.* eternal to th' aerial kind *R.L.* ii. 76
Lights of the Church, or Guardians of the *L. S.* i. 110
Hear this, and tremble ! you, who 'scape the *L. S.* i. 118
What saith my Counsel, learned in the *l. S.* i. 142
L. are explain'd by Men—so have a care *S.* i. 144
At home with Morals, Arts, and *L.* amend *S.* v. 4
Or *L.* establish'd, and the world reform'd *S.* v. 12
While if our Elders break all reason's *l. S.* v. 117
Now for Prerogative, and now for *L. S.* v. 159
Her Trade supported, and supply'd her *L. S.* v. 222
And idle Cibber, how he breaks the *L. S.* v. 209
With *L.*, to which you gave your own assent *S.* vi. 30
And certain *L.*, by suff'rers thought unjust *S.* vi. 60
L. of God, as well as of the land *S.* vi. 246
For you he sweats and labours at the *L S.* vii. 75
But having cast his cowl, and left those *l. S.* vii. 107
To savage beasts, and savage *l.* a prey *W.F.* 45

Lawful.
We, wretched subjects, tho' to *l.* sway *E.M.* ii. 149
Tell me, which Knave is *l.* Game, which not *E.S.* ii. 27

Lawless.
Planets and Suns run *l.* thro' the sky *E.M.* i. 252
Or, meteor-like, flame *l.* thro' the void *E.M.* ii. 65
Libels and *Satires* ! *l.* things indeed *S.* i. 150
What could be free, when *l.* beasts obey'd *W.F.* 51

Lawn.
Chicane in Furs, and *Casuistry* in *L. D.* iv. 28
For him as kindly spread the flow'ry *l. E.M.* iii. 30
A Saint in Crape is twice a Saint in *L. M.E.* i. 136
But when no Prelate's *L.* with hair'd-shirt lin'd *S.* iii. 165
Peers, Heralds, Bishops, Ermine, Gold, and *L. S.* v. 317
Where stray ye, Muses, in what *l.* or grove *Su.* 23
Stretch'd on the *l.* his second hope survey *W.F.* 81
Her buskin'd Virgins trac'd the dewy *l. W.F.* 170
Whose ample L—s are not asham'd to feed M.E. iv. 185
There, intersperc'd in *l.* and op'ning glades *W.F.* 21
Swarm o'er the *l.*, the forest walks surround *W.F.* 149

Lawyer.
Scarce hurts the *L.*, but undoes the Scribe *E.S.* ii. 47
Or in a mortgage, prove a L.'s share S. ii. 16)

Lay.
She comes, my Delia comes !—Now cease my *l. A.* 53
Resound ye hills, resound my mournful *l. A.* 65 &c
Nor pensive Cowley's moral *l. I.H.* iv. 8
Yet soft his Nature, tho' severe his *L. Ep.* i. 5
Let CAROLINA smooth the tuneful *l. S.* i. 30
And Albion's cliffs resound the rural *l. Su.* 6
The hills and rocks attend my doleful *l. Su.* 17
Hylas and *Ægon sung their rural l—s A.* 2
Hylas and Ægon's rural *l.* I sing *A.* 6
A hecatomb of pure unsully'd *l. D.* i. 158
Still hear thy Parnell in his living *l. E.* i. 16
But in such *l.* as neither ebb nor flow *E.C.* 239
Hear how Timotheus' vary'd *l.* surprize *E.C.* 374
Yet think not Friendship only prompts my *l. E.S.* ii. 94
Lies crown'd with Princes' honours, Poets' *l. Ep.* viii. 5
And *Congreve* lov'd, and *Swift* endur'd my *l. P.S.* 138
If She inspire, and He approve my *l. R.L.* i. 6
And justly Cæsar scorns the Poets' *l. S.* i. 45
Sharp Satire that, and that Pindaric *l. S.* vi. 83
With Waller's strains, or Granville's moving *l. Sp.* 46
Accept, O GARTH, the Muse's early *l. Su.* 9
But nigh yon mountain let me tune my *l. Su.* 27
Ev'n he, whose soul now melts in mournful *l. U.L.* 77
While silent birds forget their tuneful *l. W.* 7
No more the birds shall imitate her *l. W.* 55
Adieu, ye shepherds' rural *l.* and loves *W.* 90
Invite my *L.* Be present, sylvan maids *W.F.* 3
Nor Po so swells the fabling Poets' *l. W.F.* 227
Here his first *l.* majestic Denham sung *W.F.* 271
Here cease thy flight, nor with unhallow'd *l. W.F.* 423
Now May'rs and Shrieves all hush'd and satiate l. *D.* i. 91
Round him much Embryo, much Abortion *l. D.* ii. 121
Here *l.* poor Fletcher's half-eat scenes, and here *D.* i. 131
To him the *Goddess;* "Son I thy grief *l.* down *D.* ii. 131
And all was hush'd, as Folly's self *l.* dead *D.* ii. 418
And stretch'd on bulks, as usual, Poets *l. D.* ii. 420
How Henley *l.* inspir'd beside a sink *D.* ii. 425
On plain Experience *l.* foundations low *D.* iv. 466
When victims at yon altar's foot we *l. E.A.* 108
Nor yet the last to *l.* the old aside *E.C.* 336
In hearts of Kings, or arms of Queens who *l. E.M.* iv. 289
May pinch ev'n there—why *l.* it on a King *E.S.* ii. 51
Nature and Nature's laws *l.* hid in Night *Ep.* xii. 1
Or any good creature shall *l.* o'er my head *Ep.* xvi. 4
Asleep and naked as an Indian *l. M.E.* iii. 361
L. Fortune-struck, a spectacle of Woe *M.E.* ii. 3
And Epicurus *l.* inspir'd *O.* ii. 9
Seem'd to her ear his winning lips to *l. R.L.* i. 25
There *l.* three garters, half a pair of gloves *R.L.* ii. 39
T'o *l.* this harvest up, and hoard with haste *S.* iii. 21
She said, and melting as in tears she *l. W.F.* 203

Layman.
With holy envy gave one *L.* place *D.* ii. 324

Lays.
Neglect the rules each verbal Critic *l. E.C.* 261

Tells all their names, *l.* down the law *I.H.* ii. 200
Time that on all things *l.* his lenient hand *M.E.* i. 224
Kind Boyle, before his poet, *L. Mi.* xii. 5
And desp'rate Misery *l.* hold on Dover *S.* iv. 57

Lazy.
Then mounts the clerks, and in one *l.* tone *D.* ii. 327
Then look'd, and saw a *l.*, lolling sort *D.* iv. 357
In *l.* Apathy let Stoics boast *E.M.* ii. 101
Like Eastern Kings a *l.* state they keep *U.L.* 21

Lea.
The gulfy *L.* his sedgy tresses rears *W.F.* 346

Lead.
To hatch a new Saturnian age of *l. D.* i. 28
Nonsense precipitate, like running *L. D.* i. 123
As forc'd from wind-guns, *l.* itself can fly *D.* i. 181
A brain of feathers, and a heart of *L. D.* ii. 44
A pig of *l.* to him who dives the best *D.* ii. 281
And loudly claims the Journals and the *L. D.* ii. 322
And bring Saturnian days of *L.* and Gold *D.* iv. 16
His Saws are toothless, and his Hatchet's *L. E.S.* ii. 149
And bravely bore the double loads of *l. R.L.* iv. 102
And then a nodding beam, or pig of *l. S.* vi. 102
And thou l. his Aide-de-camp, L on my sons D. i. 305
Signs following signs *l.* on the mighty year *D.* iii. 321
With Staff and Pumps the Marquis *l.* the race *D.* iv. 586
And boys in flow'ry bands the tiger *l. M.* 78
L. me to the Crystal Mirrors *Mi.* vii. 19
Who *l.* fair Virtue's train along *O.* ii. 11
Oh *l.* me wheresoe'er I go *U.P.* 43

Leaden.
St. James's first, for *l. G—* preach'd *D.* iv. 608
A perjur'd Prince a *l.* Saint revere *M.E.* i. 89
The clam'rous lapwings feel the *l.* death *W.F.* 132

Leaders.
In show like *l.* of the swarthy Moors *R.L.* iii. 48

Lead'st.
And the pleas'd dame, soft smiling, *l.* away *D.* ii. 188

Leads.
For him alone Hope *l.* from goal to goal *E.M.* iv. 341
One who believes as Tindal *l.* the way *S.* iv. 64
Her cheerful head, and *l.* the golden years *W.F.* 92

Leaf.
There's some Peculiar in each *l.* and grain *M.E.* i. 15
A single *l.* shall waft an Army o'er *M.E.* iii. 43
A *L.* like Sibyl's, scatter to and fro *M.E.* iii. 45
Soft on the paper ruff its l—ves I spread D. iv. 407
Read these instructive *l*, in which conspire *E.* iii. 7
Some on the *l.* of ancient authors prey *E.C.* 112
Words are like *l.*; and where they most abound *E.C.* 309
Th' Æthereal spirit o'er its *l.* shall move *M.* 11
And when I flatter, let my dirty *l. S.* v. 415
Now *l.* the trees, and flow'rs adorn the ground *Sp.* 43
Pants on the *l.*, and dies upon the trees *W.* 80

Leafless.
To *l.* shrubs the flow'ring palms succeed *M.* 75
Where doves in flocks the *l.* trees o'ershade *W.F.* 127

Lean.
L. as you came, Sir, you must go *I.H.* i. 58
He brought him Bacon (nothing *l.*) *I.H.* ii. 165
I cough, like *Horace,* and tho' *l.* am short *P.S.* 116
Here a *L.* Bard, whose wit could never give *S.* vii. 13
And Angels l. *from Heaven to hear O.* i. 130

Lean'd.
First Osborne *l.* against his letter'd post *D.* ii. 171
Philosophy, that *l.* on Heav'n before *D.* iv. 643

Leaning.
There, *l.* near a gentle Brook *I.H.* ii. 129
And he, who now to sense, now nonsense *L. P.S.* 185

Leans.
On this he sits, to that he *l.* his ear *D.* ii. 85
But some way *l.* and hearkens to the kind *E.M.* iv. 40
And neither *l.* on this side, nor on that *S.* ii. 62

Leap.
One *l.* from yonder cliff shall end my pains *A.* 95
Here strip, my children ! here at once l. *in D.* ii. 275
And *l.* exulting like the bounding roe *M.* 44

Leap'd.

Stones *l.* to form, and rocks began to live *E.C.* 702
L. up, and wak'd his mistress with his tongue *R.L.* i.116
He *l.* the trenches, scal'd a Castle-wall *S.* vi. 40

Leaps.

Where a new world *l.* out at his command *F.C.* 486
His heart now melts, now *l.*, now burns *O.* iii. 35

Learn.

And *l.* to crawl upon poetic feet *D.* i. 67
And *l.*, my sons, the wond'rous pow'r of Noise *D.* ii. 222
But "*L.*, ye DUNCES ! not to scorn your God" *D* iii.224
O ! if my sons may *l.* one earthly thing *D.* iv. 183
L. but to trifle ; or, who most observe *D.* iv. 457
And pitying saints whose statues *l.* to weep *E.A.* 22
Teach me at once, and *l.* of me to die *E.A.* 328
L. hence for ancient rules a just esteem *E.C.* 139
L. then what MORALS Critics ought to show *E.C.* 560
On savage stocks inserted, *l.* to bear *E.M.* ii. 162
Yet from the same we *l.*, in its decline *E.M.* ii. 257
L. from the birds what food the thickets yield (*rep.*) *E.M.* iii. 173
L. of the mole to plough, the worm to weave (*rep.*) *E.M.* iii. 176
L. each small People's genius, policies *E.M.* iii. 183
From ancient story *l.* to scorn them all *E.M.* iv. 286
L., from this union of the mind Whole *E.M.* iv. 337
L. from their books to hang himself and Wife *E.S.* i.126
And quite a scandal not to *l. I.H.* ii. 146
No Names !—be calm !—*l.* prudence of a friend *P.S.* 102
Where none *l.* Ombre, none e'er taste Bohea *R.L.* iv.156
Or who would *l.* one earthly thing of use *R.L.* v. 22
What will a Child *l.* sooner than a Song *S.* v. 205
I *l.* to smooth and harmonize my Mind *S.* vi. 203
L. to live well, or fairly make your will *S.* vi. 322
None should, by my advice, *l.* Virtue there *S.* viii. 97
And bade his willows *l.* the moving song *W.* 14
And *l.* of man each other to undo *W.F.* 124

Learned, Learn'd, Learnt.

Fatten the Courtier, starve the *l.* band *D.* i. 315
Of sober face, with *l.* dust besprent *D.* iii. 188
The *l.* Baron Butterflies design *D.* iv. 589
Amaze th' unlearn'd, and make the *l.* smile *E.C.* 327
With loads of *l.* lumber in his head *E.C.* 613
That very life his *l.* hunger craves *E.M.* iii. 63
Foe to loud Praise, and Friend to *l.* Ease *Ep.* x. 5
Poor Vadius, long with *l.* spleen devour'd *M.E.* v. 41
O *l.* Friend of Abchurch-lane *Mi.* iv. 33
Some secret truths from *l.* pride conceal'd *R.L.* i. 37
I come to Counsel *l.* in the Law *S.* i. 8
Then, *l.* Sir ! (to cut the matter short) *S.* i. 91
What saith my Counsel, *l.* in the laws *S.* i. 142
And gaze on Parian Charms with *l.* eyes *S.* iv. 31
And *l.* Athens to our art must stoop *S.* v. 47
By *l.* Critics, of the mighty Dead *S.* v. 138
To hunt for Truth in Maudlin's *l.* grove *S.* vi. 57
The vulgar boil, the *l.* roast an egg *S.* vi. 85
See I strew'd with *l.* dust, his night-cap on *S.* vi. 118
Of ancient writ unlocks the *l.* store *W.F.* 247
There all the l.'d shall at the labour stand D. iv. 393
Why all your Toils ? your sons have *l.* to sing *D.* iv. 516
Hear how *l.* Greece her useful rules indites *E.C.* 92
Sure to hate most the men from whom they *l. E.C.* 107
Sex, from each clime the *l.* their incense bring *E.C.* 185
As those move easiest who have *l.* to dance *E.C.* 363 *and S.* vi. 179
As oft the *L.* by being singular *E.C.* 425
Pulpits their sacred satire *l.* to spare *E.C.* 550
Tho' *l.*, well-bred ; and tho' well-bred, sincere *E.C.* 635
Such was Roscommon, not more *l.* than good *E.C.* 725
The *L.* reflect on what before they knew *E.C.* 740
Is emulation in the *L.* or brave *E.M.* ii. 192
The *l.* is happy nature to explore *E.M.* ii. 263
Ev'n Kings *l.* justice and benevolence *E.M.* iii. 280
Ask of the *L.* the way? the *L.* are blind *E.M.* iv. 19
A Gowanian, *l.*; a Bishop, what you will *M.E.* i. 138
More wise, more *l.*, more just, more ev'ry thing *M.E.* i. 140
That name the *l.* with fierce disputes pursue *M.E.* v. 17
The *L.* themselves we Book-worms name *Mi.* iv. 13
The prudent, *l.*, and virtuous breast *O.* iii. 2
Of all mad creatures, if the *l.* are right *P.S.* 105
Who has not *l.*, fresh sturgeon and ham-pie *S.* ii. 103
Chaucer's worst ribaldry is *l.* by rote *S.* v. 37

Nor dare to practise till they've *l.* to dance *S.* v. 184
The Poets *l.* to please, and not to wound *S.* v. 258
Wit grew polite, and Numbers *l.* to flow *S.* v. 266
O'er a *l.* unintelligible place *S.* vii. 102
Talkers I've *l.* to bear, Motteux I knew *S.* viii. 50
So perish all, whose breast ne'er *l.* to glow *U.L.* 45
As, taught by Venus, Paris l.—t the art D. ii. 217
This doctrine, Friend, I *l.* at Court *I.H.* ii. 180

Learning.

But high above more solid *L.* shone *D.* i. 147
And one bright blaze turns *L.* into air *D.* iii. 78
Proceed, great days ! till *L.* fly the shore *D.* iii. 313
Plac'd at the door of *L.*, youth to guide *D.* iv. 153
All Classic *l.* lost on Classic ground *D.* iv. 321
So by false *l.* is good sense defac'd *E.C.* 25
How far your genius, taste, and *l* go *E.C.* 49
These leave the sense, their *l.* to display *E.C.* 116
A *little l.* is a dang'rous thing *E.C.* 215
Ah let not *L.* too commence its foe *E.C.* 500
'Tis not enough, taste, judgment, *l.*, join *E.C.* 562
As without *l.* they can take Degrees *E.C.* 591
The scholar's *l.*, with the courtier's ease *E.C.* 668
L. and Rome alike in Empire grew *E.C.* 683
And the same age saw *L.* fall, and Rome *E.C.* 686
A second deluge *L.* thus o'er run *E.C.* 691
Yet poor with fortune, and with *l.* blind *E.M.* iv. 329
Of Fops in *L.*, and of Knaves in State *Ep.* i. 4
Theirs is the Vanity, the *L.* thine *M.E.* v. 45
Shall one whom Nature, *L.*, Birth, conspir'd *S.* iv. 40
On *L.*'s surface we but lie and nod *D.* iv. 242
Or *L.* Luxury, or Idleness *E.M.* ii. 46
Rome l. arts from Greece, whom she subdu'd P.C. 40

Learns.

Just when she *l.* to roll a melting eye *E.* v. 3
Tho' what he *l.* he speaks, and may advance *M.R.* i. 3
But ent'ring *l.* to be sincere *O.* iii. 6

Least.

As much at *l.* as any God's, or more *D.* ii. 80
Th' embroider'd suit at *l.* he deem'd his prey *D.* ii. 117
Some Botanists, or Florists at the *L D.* iv. 573
The last, not *l.* in honour or applause *D.* iv. 577
Those still at *l.* are left thee to bestow *E.A.* 120
Ah, think at *l.* thy flock deserves thy care *E.A.* 129
Nature affords at *l.* a glimm'ring light *E.C.* 21
And have, at *l.*, their precedent to plead *E.C.* 166
This praise at *l.* a grateful Muse may give *E.C.* 734
The *L* confusion but in one, not all *E.M.* i. 249
Connects each being, greatest with the *l., E.M.* iii. 23
Then might I sing, without the *l.* offence *E.S.* i. 77
And if he lie not, must at *l.* betray *P.S.* 308
You'll gain at *l.* a *Knighthood* or the *Bays S.* i. 24
Will prove at *l.* the medium must be clear *S.* i. 56
Thou hast at *l.* bestow'd one penny well *S.* ii. 110
And men must walk at *l.* before they dance *S.* iii. 54
Well, if a King's a Lion, at the *L S.* iii. 120
Adopt him Son, or Cousin at the *l. S.* iv. 108
Or choose at *l.* some Minister of Grace *S.* v. 378
By sale, at *l.* by death, to change their lord *S.* vi. 251
Secure of peace at *l.* beyond the grave *S.* viii. 4
The King would smile on you—at *l.* the Queen *S.*viii. 89
Thou Great First Cause, *l.* understood *U.P.* 5

Leather.

Harmonic twang ! of *l.*, horn, and brass *D.* ii. 254
The rest is all but *l.* or prunella *E.M.* iv. 204

Leave.

Treated, caress'd, and tir'd, I take my *l. M.E.* iv. 165
I guess, and, with their *L.*, will tell the fault *S.* v. 357
Now l. all memory of sense behind D. i. 276
L. not a foot of verse, a foot of stone *D.* iv. 127
These *l.* the sense, their learning to display *E.C.* 116
"What ! *l.* the Combat out ?" exclaims the Knight *E.C.* 279
L. such to tune their own dull rhymes, and know *E.C.* 358
L. dang'rous truths to unsuccessful Satires *E.C.* 592
Awake, my ST. JOHN ! *l.* all meaner things *E.M.* i. 1
Or in the full creation *l.* a void *E.M.* i. 243
Take Nature's path, and mad Opinion's *l. E.M.* iv. 29
Still *l.* some ancient Virtues to our age *Ep.* ix. 10
No, Sir, you'll *l.* them to the Hogs *I.H.* i. 28

LEAVES—LE NÔTRE

l., me but Liberty and Ease *I.H.* i. 66
Nor *l.* one sigh behind them, when they die *M.E.* ii. 230
And Honour linger ere it *l.* the laod *M.E.* iii. 248
Nor over-dress, nor *l.* her wholly bare *M.E.* iv. 52
Now *l.* complaining, and begin your Tea *Mi.* ix. 112
With Praise or Infamy *l.* that to fate *S.* iii. 102
And *l.* on Swift this grateful verse engrav'd *S.* v. 223
What will it *l.* me, if it snatch my rhyme *S.* vi. 77
I'll e'en *l.* verses to the boys at school *S.* vi. 201
L. such to trifle with more grace and ease *S.* vi. 326
Or, in quotation, shrewd Divines *l.* out *S.* vii. 103
Frighted, I quit the room, but *l.* it so *S.* viii. 272
Ye gentle Muses, *l.* your crystal spring *W.* 21
They fail, and *l.* their little lives in air *W.F.* 134
And *l.* inanimate the naked wall *W.F.* 308
Thy trees, fair Windsor I now shall *l.* their woods *W.F.* 385

Leaves.
Pours forth, and *l.* unpeopled half the land *D.* ii. 20
Swift as a bard a bailiff *l.* behind *D.* ii. 61
In other parts it *l.* wide sandy plains *E.C.* 55
As *l.* them scarce a subject in their Age *M.E.* ii. 222
Admits, and *l.* them, Providence's care *M.E.* iii. 106
His thankless Country *l.* him to her Laws *M.E.* iii. 218
L. the dull City, and joins (to please the fair) *M.E.* iii. 387
His post neglects, or *l.* the fair at large *R.L.* ii. 124
That *l.* the load of yesterday behind *S.* i. 82
To cheat a Friend, or Ward, he *l.* to Peter *S.* v. 297
It gives men happiness, or *l.* them ease *S.* vi. 183

Leaving.
And straight succeeded, *l.* shame no room *D.* iv. 531
Then conscience sleeps, and *l.* nature free *E.A.* 227
Oft, *l.* what is natural and fit *E.C.* 448
All that I dread is *l.* you behind *R.L.* v. 100

Lebanon.
See lofty *L.* his head advance *M.* 25

Lect'ring.
So Philomedé *l.* all mankind *M.E.* ii. 83

Led.
They *l.* him soft; each rev'rend Bard arose *D.* ii. 348
A slip-shod Sibyl *l.* his steps along *D.* iii. 15
None need a guide, by sure attraction *l. D.* iv. 75
l. by my hand, he saunter'd Europe round *D.* iv. 311
And last, to Nature's Cause thro' Nature *l. D.* iv. 408
L. up the Youth, and called the Goddess *Dame D.*iv. 498
L. by some rule that guides, but not constrains *E.* iii. 07
L. thro' a sad variety of woe *E.A.* 36
By thee to mountains, wilds, and deserts *l. E.A.* 132
L. by the light of the Mæonian Star *E.C.* 648
His Grace will game; to White's a bull he *l. M.E.*iii. 67
Love, strong as Death, the Poet *l. O.* i. 51
L. off two captive trumps, and swept the board *R.L.* iii. 50
L. forth his flocks along the silver Thame *Su.* 2
While *l.* along the skies his current strays *W.F.* 228
L. by the sound, I roam from shade to shade *W.F.* 269
When the sad pomp along his banks was *l. W.F.* 274
L. by new stars, and borne by spicy gales *W.F.* 392

Leda.
And there, a naked *L.* with a Swan *M.E.* ii. 10

Lee.
Like *L.* or Budgel, I will rhyme and print *S.* i. 100

Leer.
The conscious simper, and the jealous *l. D.* ii. 6
Damn with faint praise, assent with civil *l. P.S.* 201

Leering.
Here Fannia, *l.* on her own good man *M.E.* ii. 9

Left.
Ye birds that, *l.* by summer, cease to sing *A.* 28
The shepherds cry, "Thy flocks are *l.* a prey" *A.* 78
He *l.* huge Lintot, and out-stripp'd the wind *D.* ii. 62
Motteux himself unfinish'd *l.* his tale *D.* ii. 412
And nothing *l.* but Homage to a King *D.* iv. 524
Nor human Spark is *l.*, nor Glimpse *divine D.* iv. 652
No craving void *l.* aking in the breast *E.A.* 94
Those still at least are *l.* thee to bestow *E.A.* 120
And wake to all the griefs I *l.* behind *E.A.* 248

Were but a Combat in the lists *l.* out *E.C.* 278
The mighty Stagirite first *l.* the shore *E.C.* 645
How would he wish that Heav'n had *l.* him still *E.M.* i. 203
O sacred weapon! *l.* for Truth's defence *E.S.* ii. 212
Whose Chariot's that we *l.* behind *I.H.* ii. 90 *s*
The Guests withdrawn had *l.* the Treat *I.H.* ii. 196
No wit to flatter *l.* of all his store *M.E.* iii. 311
Now nothing *l.*, but wither'd, pale, and shrunk *Mi.*iii. 25
I *l.* no calling for this idle trade *P.S.* 129
Steals much, spends little, yet has nothing *l. P.S.* 184
To *Bufo l.* the whole *Castalian* state *P.S.* 230
And those they *l.* me; for they *l.* me GAV (*rep.*) *P.S.* 256
Thus much is *l.* of old Simplicity *S.* ii. 36
See, Modest Cibber now has *l.* the Stage *S.* iii. 6
Produc'd the point that *l.* the sting behind *S.* v. 252
But having east his cowl, and *l.* those laws *S.* vii. 107
Nor *l.* one virtue to redeem her Race *U.L.* 28
L. free the Human Will *U.P.* 12
And *l.*-legg'd *Jacob seems to emulate D.* ii. 68

Leg.
Puts forth one manly *l.*, to sight reveal'd *R.L.* iii. 56
One likes the Pheasant's wing, and one the *l. S.* v. 84

Leisure.
Constant faith, fair hope, long *l. O.* iii. 42
Verse cheers their *L*, Verse assists their work *S.* v. 235

Leisurely.
Our sons shall see it *l.* decay *S.* viii. 44

Lely.
L. on animated Canvas stole *S.* v. 149

Lend.
So may the fates preserve the ears you *l. D.* iii. 214
And Douglas *l.* his soft obstetric hand *D.* iv. 394
To *l.* a wife, few here would scruple make *E.J.S.* 35
Ah! if she *l.* not arms, as well as rules *E.M.* ii. 151
(Thy Grecian Form) and Chloe *l.* the Face *I.H.* ii. 20
Behold what blessings Wealth to life can *l. M.E.* iii. 297
Let him to night his just assistance *l. Mi.* ii. 23
Bright *Apollo, l.* thy Choir *Mi.* vii. 16
L., *le* your wings! I mount! I fly *O.* v. 16

Lends.
Taylor, their better Charon, *l.* an oar *D.* iii. 19
And Pan to Moses *l.* his pagan horn *D.* iii. 110
That *l.* Corruption lighter wings to fly *M.E.* iii. 40
Buy ev'ry stick of wood, that *l.* them heat *S.* vi. 242

Length.
Yet smiling at his rueful *l.* of face *D.* ii. 142
By his broad shoulders known, and *l.* of ears *D.* iii. 36
No monstrous height, or breadth, or *l.* appears *E C.* 251
That, like a wounded snake, drags its slow *l.* aloog *E*,*C.* 357
Now *l.* of Fame (our second life) is lost *E.C.* 480
At *l.* Erasmus, that great injur'd name *E.C.* 693
The young disease, that must subdue at *l. E.M.* ii. 135
At *l.* enjoys that Liberty he lov'd *Ep.* ii. 12
As *l.* Corruption, like a gen'ral flood *M.E.* iii. 135
First thro' the *L.* of yon hot Terrace sweat *M.E.* iv. 130
On cares like these if *l.* of days attend *P.S.* 414
At *l.* the wits mount up, the hairs subside *R.L.* v. 74
At *l.*, by wholesome dread of statutes bound *S.* v. 257
Dim lights of life that burn a *l.* of years *U.L.* 19
At *l.* great Anna said, "Let Discord cease!" *W.F.* 327
Short views we take, nor see the l—s behind E.C. 222

Lengthen'd.
And the low sun had *l.* ev'ry shade *A.* 100
The rev'rend Flamen in his *l.* dress *D.* ii. 354
The growing labours of the *l.* way *E.C.* 230
Till *l.* on to Faith, and unconfin'd *E.M.* iv. 343
While in more *l.* notes and slow *O.* i. 10
Or *l.* Thought that gleams thro' many a page *S.* v 113
His shadow *l.* by the setting sun *W.F.* 194

Lenient.
Time, that on all things lays his *l.* hand *M.E.* i. 224
With *l.* arts extend a Mother's breath *P.S.* 410

Le Nôtre.
Jones and *Le N.* have it not to give *M.E.* iii. 46

Lent.

Of darkness visible so much be *l. D.* iv. 3
Then shar'd the Tyranny, then *l.* it aid *E M.* iii. 247
L. Heav'n a parent to the poor and me *E.M.* v. 110
Or to thy country let that heap be *l. S.* ii. 121
Appeal'd to Law, and Justice *l.* her arm *S.* v. 256
Or aught thy goodness *l. U.P.* 36

Leo

But see! each Muse, in *L.'s* golden days *E.C.* 697

Lepell.

That rails at dear *L.* and You *Mi.* vi. 10

Less.

How with *l.* reading than makes felons 'scape (*rep.*) *D.* i. 281
Not with *L* glory mighty Dulness crown'd *D.* iii. 135
Nor *l.* revere him, blunderbuss of Law *D.* iii. 150
Who gently drawn, and struggling *l.* and *l. D.* iv. 83
Still with esteem no *l.* convers'd than read *E.* iv. 7
And is my Abelard *l.* kind than they *E.A.* 44
But, of the two, *l.* dang'rous is th' offence *E.C.* 3
T' avoid great errors, must the *l.* commit *E.C.* 260
Thus Critics, of *l.* judgment than caprice *E.C.* 285
But *l.* to please the eye, than arm the hand *E.C.* 673
Of those who *l.* presum'd, and better knew *E.C.* 720
Why form'd no weaker, blinder, and no *l. E.M.* i. 38
Why Jove's *satellites* are *l.* than Jove *E.M.* i. 42
Then Nature deviates; and can Man do *l. E.M.* i. 150
And little *l.* than Angel, would be more *E.M.* i. 174
Hence diff'rent Passions more or *l.* inflame *E.M.* ii. 129
The *l.*, or greater, set so justly true *E.M.* iii. 291
Who thus define it, say they more or *l. E.M.* iv. 27
But these *l.* taste them, as they worse obtain *E.M.* iv. 84
No *l.* alike the Politic and Wise *E.M.* iv. 225
L, pleasing far than Virtue's very tears *E.M.* iv. 320
Much *l.* the 'Prentice who to-morrow may *E.S.* ii. 37
Have you *l.* pity for the needy Cheat *E.S.* ii. 4
Yet softer Honours, and *l.* noisy Fame *Ep.* xiv. 9
To written Wisdom, as another's, *l. M.E.* i. 20
Next, that he varies from himself no *l. M.E.* i. 20
So Darkness strikes the sense no *l.* than Light *M.E.* i. 53
L. Wit than Mimic, more a Wit than wise *M.E.* ii. 48
As Hags hold Sabbaths, *L* for joy than spite *M.E.* ii. 239
L. mad the wildest whimsey we can frame *M.E.* iii. 155
Is it *l.* strange, the prodigal should waste *M.E.* iv. 3
Statues of Men, scarce *l.* alive than they *M.E.* v. 10
And honour'd Cæsar *l.* than Cato's sword *P.C.* 36
Who sprung from Kings shall know *l.* joy than I *P.S.* 405
Some *l.* refin'd, beneath the moon's pale light *R.L.* ii. 81
Not a *l.* pleasing, tho' *l.* glorious care *R.L.* ii. 92
Hairs *l.* in sight, or any hairs but these *R.L.* iv. 176
And ev'ry friend the *L* lament my fate *S.* i. 62
Because God made these large, the other *l. S.* ii. 24
That *l.* admires the Palace than the Park *S.* iii. 113
Just *l.* than Jove, and much above a King *S.* iii. 186
Britain to soft refinements *l.* a foe *S.* v. 265
The labour greater, as th' indulgence *l. S.* v. 285
But I that sail, am neither *l.* nor bigger *S.* vi. 299
Satan himself feels far *l.* joy than they *S.* vii. 90
Are Fathers of the Church for writing *l. S.* vii. 98
Or should one pound of powder *l.* bespread *S.* viii. 246

Less'ning.

Here where the mountains, *l.* as they rise *A.* 59
Quartos, octavos, shape the *l.* pyre *D.* i. 161

Lesser.

Alas! far *l.* losses than I bear *Mi.* ix. 45

Lesson.

That, Nature gives; and where the *l.* taught *M.E.* ii. 211
My life gave ample l—s to mankind *D.* i. 192
No *l.* now are taught the Spartan way *S.* viii. 93

Lest.—*Passim.*

Let, Lets.—*Passim.*

Lethe.

Here in a dusky vale where *L.* rolls *D.* iii. 23
Then tinctur'd as it runs from *L.*'s streams *D.* ii. 339

Letter.

Did the dead *l.* unsuccessful prove *D.* i. 193
When Reason doubtful, like the Samian *l. D.* iv. 151

Author of something yet more great than *l. D.* iv. 216
Pitholeon libell'd me,—"but here's a *l. P.S.* 51
The soil that arts and infant l—s *bore D.* iii. 96
Soon as thy *l.* trembling I unclose *E.A.* 29
Heav'n first taught *l.* for some wretch's aid *E.A.* 51
This prints my *L.*, that expects a bribe *P.S.* 113

Letter'd.

First Osborne lean'd against his *l.* post *D.* ii. 171

Lettuce.

L. and cowslip-wine: *Probatum est S.* i. 18

Levee.

A hundred oxen at your *l.* roar *M.E.* iii. 58
Tell at your *l.*, as the crowds approach *S.* iv. 101
Not thinking it is L.-day *I.H.* ii. 46 s

Level.

We bring to one dead *l.* ev'ry mind *D.* iv. 268
While from the bounded *l.* of our mind *E.C.* 92†
In throngs promiscuous strow the *l.* green *R.L.* iii. 80
Inexorable Death shall *l.* all *S.* vi. 262

Levell'd.

The *l.* towns with weeds lie cover'd o'er *W.F.* 67

Levels.

He lifts the tube, and *l.* with his eye *W.F.* 129

Levity.

This erring mortals *L.* may call *R.L.* i. 103

Lewd.

When his *l.* father gave the dire disease *E.M.* iv. 120
K—l's *l.* Cargo, or Ty—y's Crew *S.* iv. 121
To please a *l.* or unbelieving Court *S.* v. 212

Lewis.

L., the Dean will be of use *I.H.* ii. 35 s

Liar.

The next a Tradesman, meek, and much a *l. M.E.* i. 152

Libation.

With French *L.*, and Italian Strain *D.* iv. 559

Libel.

'Tis all a *L.*—Paxton (Sir) will say *E.S.* ii. 1
Who writes a *L.*, or who copies out *P.S.* 290
See L—s, *Satires—here you have it—read* (*rep.*) *S.* i. 149

Libell'd.

Pitholeon *l.* me,—"but here's a letter *P.S.* 51
The *l.* person, and the pictur'd shape *P.S.* 353
P—x'd by her love, or *l.* by her hate *S.* i. 84

Libels.

Silence or hurt, he *l.* the great Man *S.* viii. 159

Liberty.

When love is *l.*, and nature law *E.A.* 92
Nature, like *L.*, is but restrain'd *E.C.* 90
Still fond and proud of savage *l. E.C.* 650
When love was *l.*, and nature law *E.M.* iii. 208
His safety must his *l.* restrain *E.M.* iii. 277
At length enjoys that *L.* he lov'd *Ep.* ii. 12
Leave me but *L.* and Ease *I.H.* i. 66
A crust of Bread, and *L. I.H.* ii. 221
'Tis GEORGE and *L.* that crowns the cup *M.E.* iii. 207
Great Friend of *L.* ! in *King's* a Name *S.* v. 25
Fair *L.*, Britannia's Goddess, rears *W.F.* 91
Fierce for the l—ies of wit, and bold *E.C.* 717

Library.

A Gothic *L.*! of Greece and Rome *D.* i. 145
His *L.* (where busts of Poets dead *P.S.* 235
How shall we fill a *L.* with Wit *S.* v. 354

Libyan.

While, at each change, the son of *L.* Jove *E.C.* 376

License.

Some lucky *L.* answer to the full (*rep.*) *E.C.* 148
The following *l.* of a Foreign reign *E.C.* 544
L. repress'd, and useful laws ordain'd *E.C.* 682
With growing years the pleasing *l.* grew *S.* v. 249

Licens'd.

From Stage to Stage the *l.* Earl may run *D.* iv. 587

LICK—LIFE.

And the press groan'd with *l.* blasphemies *E.C.* 553
Then as a *l.* spy, whom nothing can *S.* viii. 158
Jests like a *l.* fool, commands like law *S.* viii. 271

Lick.
And *l.* up all the Physic of the Soul *D.* iii. 82
But *l.* up ev'ry blockhead in the way *D.* iii. 293
And harmless serpents *l.* the pilgrim's feet *M.* 80

Lick'd.
When Luxury has *l.* up all thy pelf *S.* ii. 105

Licks.
And *l.* the hand just rais'd to shed his blood *E.M.* i. 84
Wit that can creep, and pride that *l.* the dust *I'.S.* 333

Lie.
That darts severe upon a rising *L. E.* ii. 6
And in the Cunning, Truth itself's a *l. M.E.* i. 63
Who loves a *L.*, lame Slander helps about *P.S.* 289
Make Satire a Lampoon, and Fiction, *L. P.S.* 302
And thought a *L.* in verse or prose the same *P.S.* 339
The tale reviv'd, the *l.* so oft o'erthrown *P.S.* 350
Three thousand suns went down on *Welsted's l. P.S.* 375
Nor dar'd an Oath, nor hazarded a *L. P.S.* 397
Once (and but once) I caught him in a *l. S.* vi. 17
In that nice moment, as another *L. S.* viii. 178
Sepulchral l—s, *our holy walls to grace D.* i. 43
And damns implicit faith, and holy *l. D.* iv. 463
That dares tell neither Truth nor *L. E.* vi. 30
In puns, or politics, or tales, or *l. P.S.* 321
If true, a woeful likeness ; and if *l. S.* v. 412
By little and by little, drops his *l. S.* viii. 129
How hints, like spawn, scarce quick in embryo l. D. i 59
And Alma Mater *l.* dissolv'd in Port *D.* iii. 338
But held in ten-fold bonds the *Muses l. D.* iv. 35
On Learning's surface we but *l.* and nod *D.* iv. 242
Still on that breast enamour'd let me *l. E.A.* 121
While prostrate here in humble grief I *l. E.A.* 277
Glance on the stone where our cold relics *l. E.A.* 356
Reason's at distance, and in prospect *l. E.M.* ii. 72
L. in three words, Health, Peace, and Competence *E.M.* iv. 80
Spirit of *Arnall!* aid me while I *l. E.S.* ii. 129
Or sadly told, how many hopes *l.* here *Ep.* xiv. 6
But here a Grievance seems to *l. I.H.* ii. 9 s
Or do the Prints and Papers *l. I.H.* ii. 115 s
Riches, like insects, when conceal'd they *l. M.E.* iii. 169
On gilded clouds in fair expansion *l. M.E.* iv. 147
Gods, Emp'rors, Heroes, Sages, Beauties *l. M.E.* v. 34
In bright Confusion open *Rouleaux l. Mi.* ix. 81
Tell where I *l. O.* iv. 20
Who can't be silent, and who will not *l. P.S.* 34
The truth once told (and wherefore should we *l.*) *P.S.* 81
No, such a Genius never can *l.* still *P.S.* 278
And, if he *l.* not, must at least betray *P.S.* 298
Or plung'd in lakes of bitter washes *l. R.L.* ii. 127
In glitt'ring dust and painted fragmeots *l. R.L.* iii. 160
Be brib'd as often, and as often *l. S.* i. 118
That very night he longs to *l.* alone *S.* iii. 149
(More silent far) where Kings and Poets *l. S.* iv. 51
But if to Pow'r and Place your passion *l. S.* iv. 97
I, who so oft renounce the Muses *l. S.* v. 175
Th' inspiring bellows *l.* aod pant below *S.* vii. 50
Where twelve fair Signs in beauteous order *l. Sp.* 40
And the green turf *l.* lightly on thy breast *U.L.* 64
Now sleeping flocks on their soft fleeces *l. W.* 5
See, where on earth the flow'ry glories *l. W.* 33
The level'd towns with weeds *l.* cover'd o'er *W.F.* 67
And blended *l.* th' oppressor and th' opprest *W.F.* 318

Liege.
My *L.l* why Writers little claim your thought *S.* v. 356

Lies.
Obscene with filth the miscreant *l.* bewray'd *D.* ii. 75
Then down are roll'd the books ; stretch'd o'er 'em *l. D.* ii. 403
Ah, think not, Mistress ! more true Dulness *l. D.* iv. 239
Where mix'd with God's, his lov'd Idea *l. E.A.* 12
A naked Lover bound and bleeding *l. E.A.* 100
In Pride, in reas'ning Pride, our error *l. E.M.* i. 123
Sedate and quiet the comparing *l. E.M.* ii. 69
Which still so near us, yet beyond us *l. E.M.* iv. 5
Act well your part, there all the honour *l. E.M.* iv. 194
Look next on Greatness ; say where Greatness *l. E.M.* iv. 217

In Parts superior what advantage *l. E.M.* iv. 259
Here *l.* the Friend most lov'd, the Son most dear *Ep.* iii. 2
Beneath a rude and nameless Stone he *l. Ep.* v. 3
L. crown'd with Princes' honours, Poets' lays *Ep.* viii. 5
The last true Briton *l.* beneath this stone *Ep.* ix. 12
May truly say, Here *l.* an honest Man *Ep.* x. 2
Striking their pensive bosoms—Here *l.* GAY *Ep.* xi. 12
L. one who ne'er car'd, and still cares not a pin *Ep.* xvi. 5
The Fool *l.* hid in inconsistencies *M.E.* i. 70
His pride in Reas'ning, not in Acting *l. M.E.* i. 118
In heaps, like Ambergrise, a stink it *l. M.E.* ii. 235
Great Villiers *L.*—Alas ! how chang'd from him *M.E.* iii. 305
Like a tall bully, lifts the head, and *l. M.E.* iii. 340
When press'd by want and weakness *Dennis l. Mi.* ii. 10
Thus on Mæander's flow'ry margin *l. R.L.* v. 65
The pleasure *l.* in you, and not the meat *S.* ii. 16
Between Excess and Famine *l.* a mean *S.* ii. 47
And *l.* to ev'ry Lord in ev'ry thing *S.* vii. 77
In hollow caves sweet Echo silent *l. W.* 41
Couch'd close he *l.*, and meditates the prey *W.F.* 102

Life.
My *l.* gave ampler lessons to mankind *D.* i. 102
Imbibes new *L.*, and scours and stinks along *D.* ii. 106
Bland and familiar as in *l.*, begun *D.* iii. 41
Where *L.* awakes, and dawns at ev'ry line *E.* iii. 4
Bid her be all that cheers or softens *l. E.* iii. 51
Cheerful he play'd the trifle, *L.*, away *E.* iv. 12
Let the strict *l.* of graver mortals be *E.* iv. 21
Critics in Wit, or *L.*, are hard to please *E.* iv. 29
Ah quit not the free innocence of *l. E.* iv. 45
Renounce my love, my *l.*, myself—and you *E.A.* 204
Thy *l.* a long dead calm of fix'd repose *E.A.* 251
L., force, and beauty must to all impart *E.C.* 72
Now length of Fame (our second *l.*) is lost *E.C.* 480
Plu—Plutarch, what's his name that writes his *l. E.J.S.* 31
Let us (since *l.* can little more supply) *E.M.* i. 3
Then, in the scale of reas'ning *l.*, 'tis plain *E.M.* i. 47
Rests, and expatiates in a *l.* to come *E.M.* i. 98
And Passions are the elements of *L. E.M.* i. 170
Of hearing, from the *l.* that fills the Flood *E.M.* i. 215
Above, how high, progressive *l.* may go *E.M.* i. 235
Lives thro' all *l.*, extends thro' all extent *E.M.* i. 273
Gives all the strength and colour of our *l. E.M.* ii. 132
Thro' *l.* 'tis follow'd, ev'n at life's expense *E.M.* ii. 171
Each home-felt joy that *l.* inherits here *E.M.* ii. 256
See Matter next, with various *l.* endu'd *E.M.* iii. 13
See dying vegetables *l.* sustain (*rep.*) *E.M.* iii. 15
That very *l.* his learned hunger craves *E.M.* iii. 63
The creature had his feast of *l.* before *E.M.* iii. 69
Whate'er of *l.* all-quick'ning æther keeps *E.M.* iii. 115
Saw helpless him from whom their *l.* began *E.M.* iii. 142
His can't be wrong whose *l.* is in the right *E.M.* iii. 306
Was this their Virtue, or Contempt of *L. E.M.* iv. 102
Or why so long (in *L* if long can be) *E.M.* iv. 109
Go, like the Indian, in another *l. E.M.* iv. 177
Whose *l.* is healthful, and whose conscience clear *E.M.* iv. 191
What's Fame ? a fancy'd *l.* in others' breath *E.M.* iv. 237
How sometimes *l.* is risk'd, and always ease *E.M.* iv. 274
Is yellow dirt the passion of thy *l. E.M.* iv. 279
What greater bliss attends their close of *l. E.M.* iv. 301
Grasp the whole worlds of Reason, *L.*, and Sense *E.M.* iv. 357
And never laugh for all my *l.* to come *E.S.* i. 28
Be grac'd thro' *L.*, and flatter'd in his Grave *E.S.* i. 86
But shall a Printer, weary of his *l. E.S.* i. 125
Out-do Llandaff in Doctrine,—yea in *L. E.S.* i. 134
Has never made a Friend in private *l. E.S.* ii. 134
Calmly he look'd on either *L.*, and here *Ep.* x. 7
Unblam'd thro' *L.*, lamented in thy End *Ep.* xi. 8
I trust that sinking Fund my *L. I.H.* i. 74
For *l.*, six hundred pounds a year *I.H.* ii. 2 s
My choicest hours of *L.* are lost *I.H.* ii. 54
Name a Town *L.*, and in a trice *I.H.* ii. 155
Then spend your *l.* in Joy and Sport *I.H.* ii. 179
Sacred to social *l.* and social love *I.H.* iii. 22
Demanding *l.*, impatient for the skies *M.* 90
And all Opinion's colours cast on *l. M.E.* i. 27
Like following *l.* thro' creatures you dissect *M.E.* i. 29
'Tis from high *L.* high Characters are drawn *M.E.* i. 135
His *L.*, to forfeit it a thousand ways *M.E.* i. 197
Collects her breath, as ebbing *l.* retires *M.E.* i. 244

LIFELESS—LIGHT.

Or her, whose *l.* the Church and Scandal share *M.E.* ii. 105
Finds all her *l.* one warfare upon earth *M.E.* ii. 118
A Woman's seen in Private *l.* alone *M.E.* ii. 200
But ev'ry Lady would be Queen for *l. M.E.* ii. 218
Useful, I grant, it serves what *l* requires *M.E.* ii. 27
Or find the Doctor that would save the *l. M.E.* iii. 93
Congenial souls ! whose *l.* one Av'rice joins *M.E.* iii. 131
Builds *L.* on Death, on Change Duration founds *M.E.* iii. 167
Wealth in the gross is death, but *L* diffus'd *M.E.* iii. 233
Behold what blessings Wealth to *l.* can lead *M.E.* iii. 297
That *l.* of pleasure, and that soul of whim *M.E.* iii. 306
Thy *l.* more wretched, Cutler, was confess'd *M.E.* iii. 321
Seldom at church ('twas such a busy *l.*) *M.E.* iii. 381
She bears a Coronet and P—x for *l. M.E.* iii. 392
With added years if *L.* bring nothing new *Mi.* v. 5
And the gay Conscience of a *L.* well spent *Mi.* v. 12
And wake to Raptures in a *L.* to come *Mi.* v. 20
Restore, restore Eurydice to *l. O.* i. 82
And let me languish into *l. O.* v. 6
Friend to my *L.* ! (which did not you prolong *P.S.* 27
To help me thro' this long disease, my *L. P.S.* 132
Of all thy blameless *l.* the sole return *P.S.* 259
Has *L.* no joys for me ? or, (to be grave) *P.S.* 273
To please a Mistress one aspers'd his *l. P.S.* 376
His *l.*, tho' long, to sickness past unknown *P.S.* 402
For *l.* predestin'd to the Gnomes' embrace *R.L.* i. 80
Just where the breath of *l.* his nostrils drew *R.L.* v. 81
You could not do a worse thing for your *l. S.* i. 15
My foes shall wish my *L.* a longer date *S.* i. 61
Sacred to Ridicule his whole *l.* long *S.* i. 79
Will club their Testers, now, to take your *l. S.* i. 104
What *l.* in all that ample body, say *S.* ii. 77
And more the sickness of long *l.*, Old age *S.* ii. 88
Why, you'll enjoy it only all your *l. S.* ii. 164
One ebb and flow of follies all my *l. S.* iii. 168
If in the Pomp of *L.* consist the joy *S.* iv. 98
Or if your *l.* be one continu'd Treat *S.* iv. 110
The Cordial Drop of *L.* is Love alone *S.* iv. 127
After a *L.* of gea'rous Toils endur'd *S.* v. 9
The *L.* to come, in ev'ry Poet's Creed *S.* v. 74
Then Marble, soften'd into *l.*, grew warm *S.* v. 147
Triumphant Malice rag'd thro' private *l. S.* v. 246
But in known Images of *l.*, I guess *S.* v. 284
This subtle Thief of *l.*, this paltry Time *S.* vi. 76
Then polish all, with so much *l.* and ease *S.* vi. 176
In all but this, a man of sober *l. S.* vi. 188
Has *l.* no sourness, drawn so near its end *S.* vi. 316
He tells what places strumpets sell for *l. S.* viii. 148
Dim lights of *l.*, that burn a length of years *U.L.* 19
Thro' this day's *L.* or Death *U.P.* 44
Such was the *l.* great Scipio once admir'd *W.F.* 257
Nor will L.'s *stream for Observation stay W.F.* 37
On *l.* vast ocean diversely we sail *E.M.* ii. 107
Thro' life 'tis follow'd, ev'n at *l.* expense *E.M.* ii. 171
Till tir'd he sleeps, and *L.* poor play is o'er *E.M.* ii. 282
Above *l.* weakness, and its comforts too *E.M.* iv. 268
In *L* low vale, the soil the Virtues like *M.E.* i. 143
My *L.* amusements have been just the same *S.* ii. 153
In *L.* cool Ev'ning, satiate of Applause *S.* iii. 9
L. instant business to a future day *S.* iii. 42
L. idle business at one gasp be o'er *U.L.* 82
The whole strange purpose of their l—*ves to find E.M.* iv. 221
They fall, and leave their little *L* in air *W.F.* 134

Lifeless.

But senseless, *L. !* idol void and vain *D.* ii. 46
Wrap my cold limbs, and shade my *l.* face *M.E.* i. 249

Lift.

L. up your gates, ye Princes, see him come *D.* i. 301
Their heads, and *l.* them as they cease to blow *D.* ii. 392
And swelling organs *l.* the rising soul *E.A.* 272
Nay should great Homer *l.* his awful head *E.C.* 464
Returning Justice *l.* aloft her scale *M.* 18
Exalt thy tow'ry head, and *l.* thy eyes *M.* 86
Hers *l.* the soul to heav'n *O.* i. 134
Bolls aim their horns, and Asses *l.* their heels *S.* i. 86
And *l.* her turrets nearer to the skies *W.F.* 288

Lifted.

Poetic Justice, with her *l.* scale *D.* i. 52
And thrice he *l.* high the Birth-day brand *D.* i. 245
Present the Cross before my *l.* eye *E.A.* 327

The modest fan was *l.* up no more *E.C.* 542
In Magdalen's loose hair, and *l.* eye *M.E.* ii. 12

Lifts.

That *l.* our Goddess to imperial sway *D.* iii. 124
But, where each Science *l.* its modern type *D.* iii. 195
Now to pure Space *l.* her ecstatic stare *D.* iv. 33
KNIGHT *l.* the head, for what are crowds undone *D.* iv. 561
Mounts the Tribunal, *l.* her scarlet head *E.S.* i. 119
Like a tall bully, *l.* the head, and lies *M.E.* iii. 340
Melancholy *l.* her head *O.* i. 30
Till some new Tyrant *l.* his purple hand *O.* ii. 23
At this entranc'd, he *l.* his hands and eyes *S.* viii. 98
He *l.* the tube, and levels with his eye *W.F.* 129

Light.

And fleecy clouds were streak'd with purple *l. A.* 14
Farewell, ye woods ! adieu the *l.* of day *A.* 94
The skies set blushing with departing *l. A.* 98
And lest we err by Wit's wild dancing *l. D.* i. 175
Rous'd by the *l.*, old Dulness heav'd the head *D.* i. 257
Shade him from *L.*, and cover him from Law *D.* i. 314
Heav'n's twinkling Sparks draw *L.*, and point their horns *D.* ii. 12
He buoys up Instant, and returns to *l. D.* ii. 296
Where Brown and Mears unbar the gates of *L. D.* iii. 28
Behold, and count them, as they rise to *l. D.* iii. 130
The source of Newton's *L.*, of Bacon's Sense *D.* iii. 218
Illumes their *L.*, and sets their flames on fire *D.* iii. 260
Yet, yet a moment, one dim Ray of *L. D.* iv. 1
To blot out Order, and extinguish *L. D.* iv. 14
Admire new *L.* thro' holes yourselves have made *D.* iv. 126
Such vary'd *l.* in one promiscuous blaze *D.* iv. 412
L. dies before thy uncreating word *D.* iv. 654
And each from each contract new strength and *l. E.* iii. 16
And the dim windows shed a solemn *l. E.A.* 144
Both must alike from Heav'n derive their *l. E.C.* 13
Nature affords at least a glimm'ring *l. E.C.* 21
One clear, unchang'd, and universal *l. E.C.* 71
Which, but proportion'd to their, *l.*, or place *E.C.* 173
As shades more sweetly recommend the *l. E.C.* 301
And sweetly melt into just shade and *l. E.C.* 489
Led by the *L* of the Mæonian Star *E.C.* 648
The *l.* and darkness in one chaos join'd *E.M.* ii. 203
As, in some well-wrought picture, *l.* and shade *E.M.* ii. 208
Ere Wit oblique had broke that steady *l. E.M.* iii. 231
Re-lum'd her ancient *l.*, not kindled new *E.M.* iii. 287
For Wit's false mirror held up Nature's *l. E.M.* iv. 393
GOD said, *Let Newton be !* and all was *L. Ep.* xii. 2
Oh spring to *l.*, auspicious Babe, be born *M.* 22
Rise, crown'd with *l.*, imperial Salem, rise *M.* 85
Walk in thy *l.* and in thy temple bend *M.* 92
O'erflow thy courts : the *l.* himself shall shine *M.* 103
So Darkness strikes the sense no less than *L. M.E.* i. 53
Some wand'ring touches, some reflected *l. M.E.* ii. 153
Our bolder Talents in full *l.* display'd *M.E.* ii. 201
All mild ascends the Moon's more sober *l. M.E.* ii. 254
A *L.*, which in yourself you must perceive *M.E.* iv. 43
And strength of shade contends with strength of *L. M.E.* iv. 82
Chaste as cold Cynthia's virgin *L O.* iii. 23
Why am I ask'd what next shall see the *l. P.S.* 271
Their fluid bodies half dissolv'd in *l. R.L.* ii. 62
Where *l.* disports in ever-mingling dyes *R.L.* ii. 66
Some, less refin'd, beneath the moon's pale *l. R.L.* ii. 81
As ever sully'd the fair face of *l. R.L.* iv. 14
The heav'ns bespangling with dishevell'd *l. R.L.* v. 130
But grave *Epistles*, bringing Vice to *l. S.* i. 151
Consider then, and judge me in this *l. S.* vi. 27
That wants or force, or *l.*, or weight, or care *S.* vi. 160
Here in full *l.* the russet plains extend *W.F.* 23
The Earth's fair *l.* and Empress of the main *W.F.* 164
And bring the scenes of op'ning fate to *l. W.F.* 426
The l—*s and shades, whose well accorded strife E.M.* ii. 121
When Hopkins dies, a thousand *l.* attend *M.E.* iii. 291
L. of the Church, or Guardians of the Laws *S.* i. 210
Dim *l.* of life, that burn a length of years *U.L.* 19
To *l.* the *Dead, and warm the unfruitful urn E.A.* 262
Seas roll to waft me, suns to *l.* me rise *E.M.* i. 139
Dwell in a Monk, or *l.* upon a King *E.M.* i. 139
His papers l. *fly diverse, tost in air D.* ii. 114
Spreads his *l.* wings, and in a moment flies *E.A.* 76

Attracts each *l.* gay meteor of a Spark *M.E.* ii. 22
L. quirks of Music, broken and uneven *M.E.* iv. 143
The *l.* Militia of the lower sky *R.L.* i. 42
The *l.* Coquettes in Sylphs aloft repair *R.L.* i. 65
The temp'rate sleeps, and spirits *l.* as air *S.* ii. 74
O you! whom Vanity's *l.* bark conveys *S.* v. 296
'Tis mine to wash a few *l.* stains, but theirs *S.* viii. 284
L.-arm'd *with Points, Antitheses, and Puns D.* i. 306

Lighter.
He said, and climb'd a *L.'s* stranded height *D.* ii. 287
That lends Corruption l. *wings to fly M.E.* iii. 40

Lightly.
And the green turf lie *l.* on thy breast *U.L.* 64

Lightning.
Wings the red *l.*, and the thunder rolls *D.* iii. 256
Who knows but he, whose haad the *l.* forms *E.M.* i. 157
Then flash'd the living *l.* from her eyes *R.L.* iii. 155
And swift as *l.* to the combat flies *R.L.* v. 38
With more than usual *l.* in her eyes *R.L.* v. 76
And HE, whose *l.* pierc'd th' Iberian lines *S.* i. 129
She midst the l.*'s blaze, and thunder's sound E.M.* iii. 249
And keener l—s *quicken in her eyes R.L.* i. 144

Lights.
Then *l.* the structure with averted eyes *D.* i. 247
With tender Bilet-doux be *l.* the pyre *R.L.* ii. 41

Like.—*Passim.*

Lik'd.
And strangely *l.* for her *Simplicity Mi.* iii. 20

Likeness.
Each monster meets his *l.* in thy mind *D.* iii. 252
If true, a woeful *l.;* and if lies *S.* v. 412

Likes.
For, what one *l.*, if others like as well *E.M.* iii. 273
He finds at last he better *l.* a Field *M.E.* iv. 88
PRUDINA; a Man, and laughs at Show *Mi.* ix. 104
One *l.* no language but the Faëry Queen *S.* v. 39
One *l.* the Pheasant's wing, and one the leg *S.* vi. 84

Lily.
Look'd a white *l.* sunk beneath a show'r *D.* iv. 104
With band of *L.*, and with cheek of Rose *S.* viii. 251
The Thistle springs, to which the *L.* yields *Sp.* 90
For her, the l—*ies hang their heads and die A.* 26
See *l.* spring, and sudden verdure rise *M.* 68
The *l.* blazing on the regal shield *W.F.* 306
To *Isles of fragrance*, l.-silver'd *vales D.* iv. 303

Limb.
Weak tho' I am of *l.*, and short of sight *S.* iii. 49
Wrap my cold l—s, *and shade my lifeless face M.E.* i. 249
His giant *l.*, in state unwieldy spread *R.L.* iii. 72
To keep these *l.*, and to preserve these eyes *S.* iii. 52
See them survey their *l.* by Durer's rules *S.* viii. 240
By foreign hands thy decent *l.* compos'd *U.L.* 52

Limbo.
To the mild *L.* of our Father Tate *D.* i. 238

Limes.
For her, the *l.* their pleasing shades deny *A.* 25

Lime-twigs.
Like nets or *l.*, for rich Widows' hearts *S.* vii. 58

Limits.
Nature to all things fix'd the *l.* fit *E.C.* 52
Now scantier *l.* the proud Arch confine *M.E.* v. 27
Beyond the forest's verdant *l.* stray'd *W.F.* 182

Limp.
You *l.*, like Blackmore on a Lord Mayor's horse *S.* iii. 16

Lincoln.
Lords of fat E'sham, or of *L.* fen *S.* vi. 241
Half that the Dev'l o'erlooks from *L.* town *S.* vi. 245
Here shouts all Drury, there all L.—*'s-inn D.* iii. 270
To a tall house near *L. I.H.* iv. 184

Line.
She saw, with joy, the *l.* immortal run *D.* i. 69
And Eusden eke out Blackmore's endless *l. D.* i. 104

At ev'ry *l.* they stretch, they yawn, they doze *D.* iii. 390
Where spices smoke beneath the burning *l. D.* iii. 70
Or draw to silk Arachne's subtile *l. D.* iii. 590
Where Life awakes, and dawns at ev'ry *l. E.* iii. 4
Caracci's strength, Correggio's softer *l. E.* iii. 37
Free as thy stroke, yet faultless as thy *l. E.* iii. 64
And all the writer lives in ev'ry *l. E.* iv. 2
And *l.* after *l.* my gushing eyes o'erflow *E.A.* 35
As if the Stagirite o'erlook'd each *l. E.C.* 138
And glitt'ring thoughts struck out at ev'ry *l. E.C.* 290
And ten low words oft creep in one dull *l. E.C.* 347
In the next *l.*, it "whispers thro' the trees" *E.C.* 351
And praise the easy vigour of a *l. E.C.* 360
The *l.* too labours, and the words move slow *E.C.* 371
And call new beauties forth from ev'ry *l. E.C.* 666
Feels at each thread, and lives along the *l. E.M.* i. 218
Yet never pass th' insuperable *l. E.M.* i. 228
Sure as Demoivre, without rule or *l. E.M.* iii. 104
How should I fret to mangle ev'ry *l. E.S.* ii. 4
To *Cato, Virgil* paid one honest *l. E.S.* ii. 120
This filthy simile, this beastly *l. E.S.* ii. 181
Truth guards the Poet, sanctifies the *l. E.S.* ii. 246
Fall by the Votes of their degenerate *l. E.S.* ii. 253
And Patriots still, or Poets, deck the *L. E.* i. 74
Asks no firm hand, and no unerring *l. M.E.* ii. 152
Form a strong *l.* about the silver bound *R.L.* ii. 121
And sweetly flow thro' all the Royal *L. S.* i. 31
Yet Time ennobles, or degrades each *L. S.* iv. 44
The varying verse, the full resounding *l. S.* v. 268
And fluent Shakespear scarce effac'd a *l. S.* v. 279
For vulgar eyes, and point out ev'ry *l. S.* v. 367
But show no mercy to an empty *l. S.* v. 175
On all the *l.* a sudden vengeance waits *U.L.* 37
Hence hymning *Tyburn's elegiac* l—s *D.* i. 41
But that for ever in his *l.* they breathe *E.* iv. 20
Pleas'd while with smiles his happier *l.* you view *E.* iv. 75
The *l.*, tho' touch'd but faintly, are drawn right *E.C.* 22
But let a Lord once own the happy *l. E.C.* 420
Or gravely try to read the *l. I.H.* ii. 91 s
Now breaks, or now directs, th' intending *L. M.E.* iv. 63
Proud of a vast extent of flimsy *l. P.S.* 94
And strains, from hard-bound brains, eight *l.* a year *P.S.* 182
Slight *l.* of hair surprise the finny prey *R.L.* ii. 26
The *l.* are weak, another's pleas'd to say *S.* v. 1
And HE, whose light'ning pierc'd th' Iberian *L. S.* i. 129
In the dry desert of a thousand *l. S.* v. 112
Clatt'ring their sticks before ten *l.* are spoke *S.* v. 308
Near, and more near, the closing *l.* invest *W.F.* 108
Clothe spice, l. *trunks, or flutt'ring in a row S.* v. 418

Lin'd.
But when no Prelate's lawn with hair-shirt *l. S.* iii. 165
And *l.* with Giants deadlier than 'em all *S.* viii. 275

Linen.
White gloves, and *l.* worthy Lady Mary *S.* iii. 144

Linger.
And Honour *l.* ere it leaves the land *M.E.* iii. 248

Ling'ring.
When the last *l.* friend has bid farewell *E.* i. 34
Where *l.* drops from min'ral Roofs distill *Mi.* x. 3
Trembling, hoping, *l.* dying *O.* v. 3
And grapes long *l.* on my only wall *S.* ii. 146
Thro' the fair scene roll slow the *l.* streams *W.F.* 217

Linguist.
For had they found a *l.* half so good *S.* viii. 84
Good common l—s, *and so Panurge was S.* viii. 75

Link.
From Nature's chain whatever *l.* you strike *E.M.* i. 245
The *l.* dissolves, each seeks a fresh embrace *E.M.* iii. 129
And l. *the Mourning Bride to Proserpine D.* iii. 310
L. towns to towns with avenues of oak *S.* iv. 260
Of l.-*boys vile, and watermen obscene D.* ii. 100

Link'd.
And creature *l.* to creature, man to man *E.M.* iii. 114
Thus God and Nature *l.* the gen'ral frame *E.M.* iii. 317

Links.
Pursues that Chain which *l.* th' immense design *E.M.* iv. 333

Linnet.
Is it for thee the *l.* pours his throat *E.M.* iii. 33
Why sit we mute, when early l—s sing Sp. 25

Linsey-wolsey.
Peel'd, patch'd, and pyebald, *l.* brothers *D.* iii. 115

Lintot—*see also* Bernard.
But lofty *L.* in the circle rose *D.* ii. 53
He spoke: and who with *L.* shall contend *D.* ii. 56
He left huge *L.*, and out-stripp'd the wind *D.* ii. 62
Re-passes *L.*, vindicates the race *D.* ii. 107
And shame the fools—Your Int'rest, Sir, with *L.* (*rep.*) *P.S.* 62
Of Curl's chaste press, and L.'s rubric post D. i. 40

Lion.
And Cupids ride the *L.* of the Deeps *D.* iv. 328
The steer and *l.* at one crib shall meet *M.* 79
Well, if a King's a *L.*, at the least *S.* iii. 120

Lioness.
Of smell, the headlong *l.* between *E.M.* i. 213

Lip.
Pant on thy *l.*, and to thy heart be press'd *E.A.* 123
'Tis not a *L.*, or eye, we beauty call *E.C.* 245
Yet hang your *l.*, to see a Seam awry *S.* iii. 174
Nor pass these l—s in holy silence seal'd E.A. 10
From *l.* like those, what precept fail'd to move *E.A.* 67
Ev'n thought meets thought, ere from the *l.* it part *E.A.* 95
As with cold *l.* I kiss'd the sacred veil *E.A.* 111
See my *l.* tremble, and my eye-balls roll *E.A.* 323
Who touch'd Isaiah's hallow'd *l.* with fire *M.* 6
Seem'd to her ear his winning *l.* to lay *R.L.* i. 25
See on these ruby *l.* the trembling breath *U.L.* 31

Liqueurs.
Try'd all *hors-d'œuvres*, all *l.* defin'd *D.* iv. 327

Liquid.
And *l.* amber drop from ev'ry thorn *A.* 38
Now lakes of *L* gold, Elysian scenes *R.L.* iv. 45
A sudden Star, it shot thro' *L* air *R.L.* v. 127
Lull with Amelia's *l.* name the Nice *S.* i. 31
When the fierce eagle cleaves the *l.* sky *W.F.* 186

Liquor.
Some, as she sipp'd, the fuming *l.* fann'd *R.L.* iii. 114
From silver spouts the grateful l—s glide R.L. iii. 109

Lisp.
Practis'd to *L.*, and hang the head aside *R.L.* iv. 33

Lisp'd.
I *l.* in numbers; for the numbers came *P.S.* 128

Lisping.
"The MAN of ROSS," each *l.* babe replies *M.E.* iii. 262

List.
Proud to my *l.* to add one Monarch more *D.* iv. 600
And if yet higher the proud *L.* should end *E.S.* ii. 92
I'll l. you in the harmless roll E. vi. 31
L. under Reason, and deserve her care *E.M.* ii. 98

Listen.
How all things *l.*, while thy Muse complains *W.* 77

Listen'd.
Guiltless I gaz'd; heav'n *l.* while you sung *E.A.* 65

List'ning.
L. delighted to the jest unclean *D.* ii. 99
And always *l.* to himself appears *E.C.* 615
And those feign'd sighs which cheat the *l.* Fair *Mi.* ix. 8
L. Envy drops her snakes *O.* i. 33
And snakes uncurl'd hang *l.* round their heads *O.* i. 70
Then might my voice thy *l.* ears employ *Su.* 47
And headlong streams hang *l.* in their fall *Su.* 84
That call'd the *l.* Dryads to the plain *W.* 12
Shall *l.* in mid air suspend their wings *W.* 54
Enough for me that to the *l.* swains *W.F.* 433

Listens.
But, charm'd to silence, *l.* while she sings *Sp.* 15

Lists.
Were but a Combat in the *L.* left out *E.C.* 278
Bold in the *l.*, and graceful in the dance *W.F.* 294

Little.
How *l.*, mark! that portion of the ball *D.* iii. 83
Alas! how *l.* from the grave we claim *E.* iii. 77
A *l. learning* is a dang'rons thing *E.C.* 215
Who still are pleas'd too *l.* or too much *E.C.* 385
That always shows great pride, or *l.* sense *E.C.* 387
Much was believ'd, but *l.* understood *E.C.* 689
Let us (since Life can *l.* more supply *E.M.* i. 5
Why form'd so weak, so *l.*, and so blind *E.M.* i. 36
Say, here he gives too *l.*, there too much *E.M.* i. 116
And *L* less than Angel, would be more *E.M.* i. 174
And—Betty—give this Cheek a *l.* Red *E.M.* i. 251
Whether he thinks too *l.*, or too much *E.M.* ii. 12
Then see how *l.* the remaining sum *E.M.* ii. 51
A *L* louder, but as empty quite *E.M.* ii. 278
Learn of the *L.* Nautilus to sail *E.M.* iii. 177
Here rose one *l.* state, another near *E.M.* iii. 201
'Tis but to know how *l.* can be known *E.M.* iv. 261
Is this too *l.* for the boundless heart *E.M.* iv. 355
Say, shall my *l.* bark attendant sail *E.M.* iv. 385
Is that too *l.?* Come then, I'll comply *E.S.* ii. 128
These *l.* rites, a Stone, a Verse, receive *Ep.* vii. 19
A *l.* House, with trees a-row *I.H.* i. 77
Is this too *l.?* would you more than live *M.E.* iii. 81
Ye *l.* Stars! hide your diminish'd rays *M.E.* iii. 282
I curse such lavish cost, and *l.* skill *M.E.* iv. 167
And *L* Eagles wave their wings in gold *M.E.* v. 30
But has the wit to make the most of *l. M.E.* iii. 10
While Cato gives his *L.* Senate laws *P.C.* 23
No creature smarts so *l.* as a fool *P.S.* 84
Steals much, spends *l.*, yet has nothing left *P.S.* 184
Like *Cato*, gives his *l.* Senate laws *P.S.* 209
In tasks so bold, can *l.* men engage *R.L.* i. 11
And *l.* hearts to flutter at a Beau *R.L.* i. 90
The *l.* engine on his fingers' ends *R.L.* iii. 132
To live on *L* with a cheerful heart *S.* ii. 2
Or blest with *L.*, whose preventing care *S.* ii. 127
Content with *L.*, I can piddle here *S.* ii. 137
Tho' double tax'd, how *L* have I lost *S.* ii. 152
Who know themselves so *l.* what to do *S.* iii. 123
Of *l.* use the Man you may suppose *S.* v. 201
Our rural Ancestors, with *l.* blest *S.* v. 241
My Liege! why Writers *l.* claim your thought *S.* v. 356
Had dearly earn'd a *l.* purse of gold *S.* vi. 34
And *l.* sure imported to remove *S.* vi. 56
And steal so *l.*, few perceive they steal *S.* vii. 84
By *l.* and by *l.*, drops his lies *S.* viii. 129
They fall, and leave their *l.* lives in air *W.F.* 134

Littleness.
Lo, what huge heaps of *l.* around *M.E.* iv. 109

Live.
And bade thee *l.* to crown Britannia's praise *D.* iii. 211
L. happy both, and long promote our arts *D.* iv. 348
Few write to those, and none can *l.* to these *E.* iv. 30
By this he ev'n now they *L*, ev'n now they charm *E.* iv. 71
They *l.*, they speak, they breathe what love inspires *E.A.* 53
And 'tis but just to let them *l.* betimes *E.C.* 477
And each bold figure just begins to *l. E.C.* 702
Stones leap'd to form, and rocks began to *l. E.C.* 702
Of half that *l.* the butcher and the tomb *E.M.* iii. 162
For which we bear to *l.*, or dare to die *E.M.* iv. 4
Go *l. I* for Heav'n's Eternal Year is thine' *Ep.* vii. 9
Let me but *l.* on this side Trent *I.H.* ii. 30
For God's sake, come, and *l.* with Men *I.H.* i. 176
My Lord alone knows how to *l. I.H.* ii. 209
The mighty blessing, "while we *l.* to *l.*" *M.E.* ii. 90
And die of nothing, but a Rage to *l. M.E.* ii. 100
Oblige her, and she'll hate you while you *l. M.E.* ii. 138
Toasts *l.* a scorn, and Queens may die a jest *M.E.* ii. 282
Is this too little? would you more than live *M.E.* iii. 81
To *L.* on Ven'son when it sold so dear *M.E.* iii. 118
And well (he thought) advis'd him, "*L.* like me" *M.E.* iii. 316
"*L.* like yourself," was soon my Lady's word *M.E.* iii. 359
'Twas a fat Oyster—*L.* in peace—Adieu *Mi.* xi. 12
Resign'd to *L.*, prepar'd to die *Mi.* xii. 1
Thus let me *l.*, unseen, unknown *O.* iv. 17
L. o'er each scene; and be what they behold *P.C.* 4

LIV'D—LODGER.

And born to write, converse, and *l* with ease *P.S.* 196
Oh let me *l.* my own, and die so too (*rep.*) *P.S.* 261
O grant me thus to *L*, and thus to die *P.S.* 404
So long my honour, name, and praise shall *l. R.L.*iii.170
Yes, while I *L*, no rich or noble knave *S.* i. 119
Envy must own, I *l.* among the Great *S.* i. 133
To *L*. on little with a cheerful heart *S.* ii. 2
And humbly *L.* on rabbits, and on roots *S.* ii. 52
He knows to *L*, who keeps the middle state *S.* ii. 61
For Song's the word: my dear! we'll *l.* in town *S.* iii. 147
If to *L.* well means nothing but to eat *S.* iv. 111
But thanks to Homer, since I *l.* and thrive *S.* vi. 68
A Property, that's yours on which you *L*. *S.* vi. 231
A man so poor would *l.* without a place *S.* vi. 287
Learn to *l.* well, or fairly make your will *S.* vi. 322
Himself a dinner, makes an Actor *l. S.* vii. 14
Who *l.* like S—tt—n, or who die like Chartres *S.* vii. 36
Who *l.* at Court, for going once that way *S.* viii. 23
Thy name, thy honour, and thy praise shall *l. W.* 84
L. in description, and look green in song *W.F.* 8
Or ev'n to crack *l. Craw-fish recommend S.* ii. 43
That *L*-long *wig which Gorgon's self might own M.E.* iii. 295

Liv'd.

But *l.* in Settle's numbers one day more *D.* i. 90
Thank'd Heav'n that he had *l*, and that he died *Ep.*x.10
Yes, we have *L*—one pang, and then we part *Ep.* xiii. 1
And *l*—just as you see I do *I.H.* i. 72
If Cotta *l.* on pulse, it was no more *M.E.* iii. 183
All, by the King's Example, *l.* and lov'd *S.* v. 142
There *l. in primo Georgii* (they record) *S.* vi. 184

Livelier.

Some *l.* plaything gives his youth delight *E.M.* 277

Lively.

Dulness with transport eyes the *l.* Dunce *D.* i. 111
From grave to gay, from *l.* to severe *E.M.* iv. 380
The sprightly Wit, the *l.* Eye *I.H.* i. 45
Her *l.* looks a sprightly mind disclose *R.L.* ii. 9

Livery, Liv'ry.

Our Birth-day Nobles' splendid *L. S.* iv. 33
On others Int'rest her gay *l.'y* flings *D.* iv. 537

Liv'ry'd.

Our Youth, all *L.* o'er with foreign Gold *E.S.* i. 155
Care, if a *l.* Lord or smile or frown *S.* viii. 197

Lives.

Which as it dies, or *l.*, we fall, or reign *D.* iv. 186
And all the Writer *l.* in ev'ry line *E.* iv. 2
Which *l.* as long as fools are pleas'd to laugh *E.C.* 451
Feels at each thread, and *l.* along the line *E.M.* i. 218
L. thro' all life, extends thro' all extent *E.M.* i. 273
L. on the labours of this lord of all *E.M.* iii. 6
Man, like the gen'rous vine, supported *l. E.M.* iii. 311
Why, full of days and honour, *l.* the sire *E.M.* iv. 106
As S—k, if he *L*, will love the *Prince E.S.* ii. 61
Sir Balaam now, he *L* like other folks *M.E.* iii. 357
Each King-catcher, that *L*. on syllables *P.S.* 166
He, who still wanting, tho' he *L* on theft *P.S.* 183
Consults the dead, and *l.* past ages o'er *W.F.* 248

Livid.

From burning suns when *l.* deaths descend *E.M.* i. 142
A *l.* paleness spreads o'er all her look *R.L.* iii. 90

Living.

Sense, speech, and measure, *l.* tongues and dead *D.* iii. 167
Patrons, who sneak from *l.* worth to dead *D.* iv. 95
I bought them, shrouded in their *l.* shrine *D.* iv. 385
Still hear thy Parnell in his *l.* lays *E.* i. 16
The *l.* image in the painter's breast *E.* iii. 42
And dead, as *l.*, 'tis our Author's pride *E.* iv. 79
The naked nature and the *L* grace *E.C.* 294
And sure such kind good creatures may be *l. E.J.S.* 28
And catch the Manners *l.* as they rise *E.M.* i. 14
Then first the Flamen tasted *l.* food *E.M.* iii. 265
As Eugene *l.*, as a Cæsar dead *E.M.* iv. 244
Are none, none *l.*! let me praise the dead *E.S.* ii. 251
L., great Nature fear'd he might outvie *Ep.* viii. 7
The *L*. Virtue now had shone approv'd *Ep.* xiv. 7
But who, *l.* and dying, serene still and free *Ep.* xvi. 7
The wretch, who *l.* sav'd a candle's end *M.E.* iii. 292

In *l*. medals see her wars enroll'd *M.E.* v. 55
Then flash'd the *l.* lightning from her eyes *R.L.* iii. 155
Here *l.* Tea-pots stand, one arm held out *R.L.* iv. 49
Oh cruel nymph! a *l.* death I bear *R.L.* v. 61
Foes to all *l.* worth except your own *S.* v. 53
What few can of the *l.*, Ease and Bread *S.* viii. 107
Inspir'd when *l.*, and bequeath'd in death *Su.* 40
His *l.* harp, and lofty Denham sung *W.F.* 260

Livy.

Padua, with sighs, beholds her *L*. burn *D.* iii. 105

Llandaff.

Out-do *L*. in Doctrine,—yea in Life *E.S.* i. 134

Lo.—*Passim.*

Load.

The wheels above urg'd by the *L.* below *D.* i. 184
Or smoking forth a hundred hawkers' *l. P.S.* 217
That leaves the *l.* of yesterday behind *S.* i. 82
Sinks the lost Actor in the tawdry *l. S,* v. 333
With *l*—s *of learned lumber in his head E.C.* 613
And bravely bore the double *l.* of lead *R.L.* iv. 102
While by our oaks the precious *l.* are borne *W.F.* 31
We ply the Memory, we l. *the brain D.* iv. 157
L. some vain Church with old Theatric state *M.E.* iv. 29

Loaded.

Now golden fruits on *l.* branches shine *A.* 73

Loads.

The board with specious miracles he *l. D.* iv. 553

Loaf.

He thinks a *L.* will rise to fifty pound *M.E.* iii. 116

Loathsome.

Like a big wife at sight of *l.* meat *S.* viii. 156

Local.

Find Virtue *L.*, all Relation scorn *D.* iv. 479

Lock.

Do thou, Crispissa, tend her fav'rite *L. R.L.* ii. 115
New Stratagems, the radiant *L.* to gain *R.L.* iii. 120
Swift to the *L.* a thousand Sprites repair *R.L.* iii. 135
T' inclose the *L.*; now joins it, to divide *R.L.* iii. 148
Z—ds! damn the *l.!* 'fore Gad, you must be civil *R.L.* iv. 128
But by this *L.*, this sacred *L.* I swear *R.L.* iv. 133
"Restore the *L.*!" she cries; and all around (*rep.*) *R.L.* v. 103
The *L.*, obtain'd with guilt, and kept with pain *R.L.* v. 109
Shall draw such envy as the *L.* you lost *R.L.* v. 144
This *L.*, the Muse shall consecrate to fame *R.L.* v. 149
Nourish'd two L—s, *which graceful hung behind R.L.* ii. 20
Th' advent'rous Baron the bright *l.* admir'd *R.L.* ii. 29
For this your *l.* in paper durance bound *R.L.* iv. 99
Curl'd or uncurl'd, since *L.* will turn to grey *R.L.* v. 26
Not Berenice's *L.* first rose so bright *R.L.* v. 129
Observe his shape how clean! his *l.* how curl'd *S.* vi. 5
That *l.* up all the Functions of my soul *S.* iii. 40

Locke.

'Tis yours a Bacon or a *L.* to blame *D.* iii. 215
Each fierce Logician, still expelling *L. D.* iv. 196
Agrees as ill with Rufa studying *L. M.E.* ii. 23
For *L.* or Milton 'tis in vain to look *M.E.* v. 139
And house with Montaigne now, and now with *L. S.* iii. 26

Look'd.

Is there, who, *l.* from ink and paper, scrawls *P.S.* 19
Your wine *l.* up, your butler stroll'd abroad *S.* ii. 13

Locusts.

Then thick as *L.* black'ning all the ground *D.* iv. 397

Loddon.

The *L.* slow, with verdant alders crown'd *W.F.* 342

Lodge.

A handsome House to *l.* a Friend *I.H.* ii, 3 s

Lodger.

Say, can you find out one such *l.* there *S.* vi. 223

Lodging.

Noah had refus'd it *l.* in his Ark *S.* viii. 26
And wits take !—*s in the sound of Bow R.L.* iv. 118

Lodona.

Thy offspring, Thames ! the fair *L.* nam'd (*rep.*) *W.F.* 172

Lofty.

But *l.* Lintot in the circle rose *D.* ii. 53
In *l.* madness meditating song *D.* iii. 16
Now, they who reach Parnassus' *l.* crown *E.C.* 514
See *l.* Lebanon his head advance *M.* 25
Nor think to die dejects my *l.* mind *R.L.* v. 99
Go, *l.* Poet ! and is such a crowd *S.* vi. 108
With joyful pride survey'st our *l.* woods *W.F.* 220
His living harp, and *l.* Denham sung *W.F.* 280
Make Windsor-hills in *l.* numbers rise *W.F.* 287

Logic.

There foam'd rebellious *L.* gagg'd and bound *D.* iv. 23

Logician.

Each fierce *L.* still expelling Locke *D.* iv. 196

Loit'rers.

Of ever-listless *L.*, that attend *D.* iv. 339

Loit'ring.

Prose swell'd to verse, verse *l.* into prose *D.* i. 274

Lolling.

Then look'd, and saw a lazy, *l.* sort *D.* iv. 337

London.

Again to rhyme, can *L.* be the place *S.* vi. 89
Shall I, in *L.*, act this idle part *S.* vi. 125
Where *L.*'s *column, pointing at the skies M.E.* iii. 339
There, *L.* voice : " Get Money, Money still *S.* iii. 79

Lone.

In these *l.* walls (their days eternal bound) *E.A.* 141
And leave you in *l.* woods, and empty walls *E.* v. 40
Like some *l.* Chartreux stands the good old Hall *M.E.* iii. 187
In some *l.* isle, or distant Northern land *R.L.* iv. 154

Lonely.

Hark ! a glad voice the *l.* desert cheers *M.* 29
The *L* lords of empty wilds and woods *W.F.* 48
And *l.* woodcocks haunt the wat'ry glade *W.F.* 128

Long.

Come, Delia, come ; ah, why this *l.* delay *A.* 48
Hence Bards, like Proteus *l.* in vain tied down *D.* i. 37
A motley mixture ! in *l.* wigs, in bags *D.* ii. 21
L. Chanc'ry-lane retentive rolls the sound *l. D.* ii. 263
Who sings so loudly, and who sings so *l. D.* ii. 268
As Hylas fair was ravish'd *l.* ago *D.* ii. 336
Thro' the *l.*, heavy, painful page drawl on *D.* ii. 388
Who knows how *l.* thy transmigrating soul *D.* iii. 49
Old scenes of glory, times *l.* cast behind *D.* iii. 63
He, whose *l.* wall the wand'ring Tartar bounds *D.* iii. 76
This fav'rite Isle, *l.* sever'd from her reign *D.* iii. 125
Divides a friendship *l.* confirm'd by age *D.* iii. 174
In Lud's old walls tho' *l.* I rul'd, renown'd *D.* iii. 277
Tho' *l.* my Party built on me their hopes *D.* iii. 283
Tho' Christ-church *l.* kept prudishly away *D.* iv. 194
And make a *l.* Posterity thy own *D.* iv. 334
Live happy both, and, *l.* promote our arts *D.* iv. 438
While the *l.* solemn Unison went round *D.* iv. 612
Like them to shine thro' *l.* succeeding age *E.* iii. 11
A *l.*, exact, and serious Comedy *E.* iv. 22
The willing heart, and only holds it *l. E.* iv. 68
Thy life a *l.* dead calm of fix'd repose *E.A.* 251
L. lov'd, ador'd ideas, all adieu *E.A.* 296
Such if there be, who loves so *l.*, so well *E.A.* 363
Which lives as *l.* as fools are pleas'd to laugh *E.C.* 451
For who can rail so *l.* as they can write *E.C.* 599
And lash'd so *l.*, like tops, are lash'd asleep *E.C.* 601
Poets, a race *l.* unconfin'd, and free *E.C.* 649
Thus *l.* succeeding critics justly reign'd *E.C.* 681
And all the question (wrangle ne'er so *l.*) *E.M.* i. 49
This too serves always, Reason never *l. E.M.* iii. 93
Or why so *L* in (life if *l.* can be) *E.M.* iv. 109
Nor own your fathers have been fools so *l. E.M.* iv. 214
'Tis all from Horace ; Horace long before ye *E.S.* i. 17
Names, which I *l.* have lov'd, nor lov'd in vain *E.S.* ii. 90

Not parted *l.*, and now to part no more *Ep.* vii. 14
And Chiefs or Sages *l.* to Britain giv'n *Ep.* xiv. 13
See, a *l.* race thy spacious courts adorn *M.* 87
So *l.* by watchful Ministers withstood *M.E.* iii. 136
Shall call the winds thro' *l.* arcades to roar *M.E.* iv. 35
Poor Vadius, *l.* with learn'd spleen devour'd *M.E.* v. 41
Dennis, who *l.* had warr'd with modern Huns *Mi.* ii. 11
L. Health, *l.* Youth, *l.* Pleasure and a Friend *Mi.* v. 2
Cease your contention, which has been too *l. Mi.* ix. 107
Dame *Justice* weighing *l.* the doubtful Right *Mi.* xi. 7
Unspotted *l.* with human blood *O.* ii. 6
Constant faith, fair hope, *l.* leisure *O.* iii. 42
Your scene precariously subsists too *l. P.C.* 41
To help me thro' this *l.* disease, my Life *P.S.* 132
Poems I heeded (now be-rhym'd so *L*) *P.S.* 227
Fed with soft Dedication all day *l. P.S.* 233
That not in Fancy's maze he wander'd *l. P.S.* 340
Unspotted names, and venerable *l. P.S.* 386
His life, tho' *l.*, to sickness past unknown *P.S.* 402
Me, let the tender office *l.* engage *P.S.* 408
He said ; when Shock, who thought she slept too *l. R.L.* i. 115
Soon to obtain, and *l.* possess the prize *R.L.* ii. 44
And the *l.* labours of the Toilet cease *R.L.* iii. 24
That *l.* behind he trails his pompous robe *R.L.* iii. 73
The walls, the woods, the *l.* canals reply *R.L.* iii. 100
As *l.* as Atalantis shall be read *R.L.* iii. 165
So *l.* my honour, name and praise shall live *R.L.* iii. 170
The doubtful beam *l.* nods from side to side *R.L.* v. 73
Which *l.* she wore, and now Belinda wears *R.L.* v. 96
Sacred to Ridicule his whole life *l. S.* i. 79
Alas, young man ! your days can ne'er be *l. S.* i. 101
And more the sickness of *l.* life, Old age *S.* ii. 88
And grapes *l.* ling'ring on my only wall *S.* ii. 146
Public too *l.*, ah let me hide my Age *S.* iii. 5
L., as to him who works for debt, the day (*rep.*) *S.* iii. 35
To stop thy foolish views, thy *l.* desires *S.* iii. 75
Where MURRAY (*L* enough his Country's pride) *S.* iv. 52
Closed their *l.* glories with a sigh, to find *S.* v. 13
What's *l.* or short, each accent where to place *S.* v. 207
The *l.* majestic March and Energy divine *S.* v. 269
Pageants on Pageants, in *l.* order drawn *S.* v. 316
Cato's *L.* wig, flower'd gown, and lacquer'd chair *S.* v. 337
Each prais'd within, is happy all day *l. S.* vi. 156
Command old words that have *l.* slept, to wake *S.* vi. 167
Now, or *l.* since, what diff'rence will be found *S.* vi. 238
So Luther thought the Paternoster *l. S.* vii. 105
While the *l.* funerals blacken all the way *U.L.* 40
The Groves of Eden, vanish'd now so *l. W.F.* 7
Lodona's fate in *l.* oblivion cast *W.F.* 173
Stretch his *l.* triumphs down thro' ev'ry age *W.F.* 304
Project *l.* shadows o'er the crystal tide *W.F.* 376
And *Middle natures, how they* l. *to join E.M.* l. 227
Or see the stretching branches *l.* to meet *M.E.* iv. 92
Oh ! how I *l.* with you to pass my days *Su.* 77
Such is the shout, the l.-*applauding note S.* v. 330
The *l.*-contended honours of her head *R.L.* iv. 140
As when the *L.*-ear'd milky mothers wait *D.* ii. 247
Hail, sacred peace ! bail *l.*-expected days *W.F.* 355
Why feels my heart its *l.*-forgotten heat *E.A.* 6
L.-sounding aisles, and intermingled graves *E.A.* 164
A cold, *l.*-winded native of the deep *D.* ii. 300

Long'd.

And *l.* to tempt him like good Job of old *M.E.* iii. 350

Longer.

Heav'n had decreed these works a *l.* date *D.* i. 196
Or Tiber, now no *l.* Roman, rolls *D.* iv. 299
No *l.* now that golden age appears *E.C.* 478
A *l.* care Man's helpless kind demands (*rep.*) *E.M.* iii. 131
My foes should wish my Life a *l.* date *S.* i. 61
One sings the Fair ; but songs no *l.* move *S.* vii. 21
Sense, past thro' him, no *l.* is the same *S.* vii. 33

Longs.

Affrights the beggar whom he *l.* to eat *M.E.* iii. 196
That very night he *l.* to lie alone *S.* iii. 149

Longinus.

Thee, bold *L.* ! all the Nine inspire *E.C.* 675

Loo—*see* Lu.

Look.

Mix in his *l.* All eyes direct their rays *D.* ii. 7

LOOK'D—LORD.

Cast on the prostrate Nine a scornful *l. D.* iv. 51
A livid paleness spreads o'er her *l. R.L.* iii. 90
Whose air cries Arm! whose very *l.*'s an oath *S.* viii.261
Come l with thy l—s, thy words, relieve my woe E.A. 119
Fair eyes, and tempting *l.* (which yet I view) *E.A.* 295
Discours'd in terms as just, with *l.* as sage *E.C.* 269
How Plato's, Bacon's, Newton's, *l.* agree *M.E.* v. 60
Such unfeign'd Passion in his *L.* appears *Mi.* ix. 93
Her lively *l.* a sprightly mind disclose *R.L.* ii. 9
A third interprets motions, *l.*, and eyes *R.L.* iii. 15
With *l.* unmov'd, he hopes the scaly breed *W.F.* 139
All l., all sigh, and call on Smedley lost D. ii. 293
Now *l.* thro' Fate! behold the scene she draws *D.* iii. 127
Son, what thou seek'st is in thee! *L.*, and find *D.*iii.251
L. sour, and hum a Tune, as you may now *E.* v. 50
Yet if we *l.* more closely, we shall find *E.C.* 19
Than just to *l.* about us and to die *E.M.* i. 4
L. round our World; behold the chain of Love *E.M.* iii. 7
L. next on Greatness; say where Greatness lies *E.M.* iv. 217
L. but on Gripus, or on Gripus' wife *E.M.* iv. 280
All, all *l.* up, with reverential Awe *E.S.* i. 167
Some, in their choice of Friends (nay, *l.* not grave) *E.S.* ii. 100
Turn then from Wits; and *l.* on Simo's Mate *M.E.* ii. 101
On ev'ry side you *l.*, behold the Wall *M.E.* iv. 114
For Locke or Milton 'tis in vain to *l. M.E.* iv. 139
L. upon Basset, you who Reason boast *Mi.* ix. 85
L. on her face, and you'll forget 'em all *R.L.* ii. 28
Proud Fortune, and *l.* shallow Greatness thro' *S.* iii. 108
L. thro', and trust the Ruler with his skies *S.* v. 8
While you to measure merits, *l.* in Stowe *S.* v. 66
L. in that breast, most dirty D—— I be fair *S.* vi. 222
Pleas'd to *l.* forward, pleas'd to *l.* behind *S.* vi. 314
As the fair fields they sold to *l.* so fine *S.* viii. 217
Has yet a strange ambition to *l.* worse *S.* viii. 269
Live in description, and *l.* green in song *W.F.* 8

Look'd.
The very worsted still *l.* black and blue *D.* ii. 150
And *l.*, and saw a sable Sorcerer rise *D.* iii. 233
L. a white lily sunk beneath a show'r *D.* iv. 104
She *l.*, and saw a lazy, lolling sort *D.* iv. 337
Who ne'er saw naked sword, or *l.* in Plato *E.J.S.* 44
L. thro'? or can a part contain the whole *E.M.* i. 32
Calmly he *l.* on either Life, and here *Ep.* x. 7
Thrice she *l.* back, and thrice the foe drew near *R.L.* iii. 138

Looking.
Now *l.* downwards, just as griev'd appears *E.M.* i. 175
Then, *l.* up from sire to sire, explor'd *E.M.* iii. 225

Looks.
She *l.*, and breathes herself into their airs *D.* i. 264
He grins, and *l.* broad nonsense with a stare *D.* ii. 194
Greater he *l.*, and more than mortal stares *D.* ii. 329
Which no one *l.* in with another's eyes *D.* iv. 534
As all *l.* yellow to the jaundic'd eye *E.C.* 559
It still *l.* home, and short excursions takes *E.C.* 627
Not one *l.* backward, onward still he goes (*rep.*) *E.M.* iv. 223
But *l.* thro' Nature up to Nature's God *E.M.* iv. 332
When next he *l.* thro' Galileo's eyes *R.L.* v. 138
And the free soul *l.* down to pity Kings *S.* viii. 187
Or *l.* on heav'n with more than mortal eyes *W.F.* 253

Loom.
In ev'ry *l.* our labours will be seen *D.* ii. 155

Loose.
In their *l.* traces from the fields retreat *A.* 62
In a dun-night gown of his own *l.* skin *D.* ii. 38
Coach'd, carted, trod upon, now *l.*, now fast *D.* iii. 291
All my *l.* soul unbounded springs to thee *E.A.* 228
Or turns young Ammon *l.* to scourge mankind *E.M.* i. 160
When the *l.* mountain trembles from on high *E.M.*iv.127
Men in their *l.* unguarded hours they take *E.M.* iv. 227
In Magdalen's *l.* hair, and lifted eye *M.E.* ii. 12
What is *l.* love? a transient gust *O.* iii. 7
L. to the wind their airy garments flew *R.L.* ii. 63
L. on the point of ev'ry wav'ring hour *S.* vi. 249
Wild to get *l.*, his Patience I provoke *S.* viii. 116

Loosely.
The stage how *l.* does Astræa tread *S.* v. 290

Lop.
Expunge the whole, or *l.* th' excrescent parts *E.M.* ii.49
Not that I'd *l.* the Beauties from his book *S.* v. 103

Lord—*see also* House of Lords.
" Room for my *L.*!" three jockeys in his train *D.* ii.192
A heavy *L.* shall hang at ev'ry Wit *D.* iv. 132
L. of an Otho, if I vouch it true *D.* iv. 369
The fawning Servant turns a haughty *L. E.* iv. 44
To fetch and carry nonsense for my *L. E.C.* 417
But let a *L.* once own the happy lines *E.C.* 420
Great *L.* of all things, yet a prey to all *E.M.* ii. 16
At Greenland, Zembla, or the *L.* knows where *E.M.* ii. 224
Shares with his *l.* the pleasure and the pride *E.M.* iii. 36
Lives on the labours of his *l.* of all *E.M.* iii. 42
Beast, Man, or Angel, Servant, *L.*, or King *E.M.*iii.302
The same (my *L.*) if Tully's, or your own *E.M.* iv. 240
Swear like a *L.*, or Rich out-whore a Duke *E.S.* i. 116
'Tis true, my *L.*, I gave my word *I.H.* i. 1
My *L.*, your favours well I know *I.H.* i. 21
Let my *L.* know you're come to town *I.H.* ii. 445
The Duke expects my *L.* and you *I.H.* ii. 1055
My *L.* and me as far as Staines *I.H.* ii. 965
My *L.* and he are grown so great *I.H.* ii. 1051
Just as a Farmer might a *L. I.H.* ii. 160
But *L.*, my Friend, this savage scene *I.H.* ii. 175
My *L.* alone knows how to eat *I.H.* ii. 209
Last night her *L.* was all that's good and great *M.E.* ii. 141
Since then, my *L.*, on such a World we fall *M.E.* iii. 77
Is there a *L.*, who knows a cheerful noon *M.E.* iii. 239
And fame, this *L.* of useless thousands ends *M.E.*iii.314
Yet shall, my *L.*, your just, your noble rules *M.E.*iv.25
My *L.* advances with majestic mien *M.E.* iv. 127
In Books, not Authors, curious is my *L. M.E.* iv. 134
Yet to their *L.* owe more than to the soil *M.E.* iv. 184
'Twas my own *L.* that drew the *fatal card Mi.* ix. 48
And has not Colley still his *L.* and whore *P.S.* 97
Now trips a Lady, and now struts a *L. P.S.* 329
A well-bred *L.* at assault a gentle Belle *R.L.* i. 8
Could make a gentle Belle reject a *L. R.L.* i. 10
Spadilio first, unconquerable *L. R.L.* iii. 49
And thus broke out—" My *L.*, why, what the devil *R.L.* iv. 127
But this bold *L.* with manly strength endu'd *R.L.* v. 79
Tho' cut in pieces ere my *L.* can eat *S.* ii. 22
The *L.* of Thousands, than if now *Excis'd S.* ii. 134
Become the portion of a booby *L. S.* ii. 176
Grow sick, and damn the climate—like a *L. S.* iii. 160
Then hire a Slave, or (if you will) a *L. S.* iv. 99
His whole ambition was to serve a *L. S.* vi. 14
L. how we strut thro' Merlin's Cave, to see *S.* vi. 139
A worthy member, no small fool, a *L. S.* vi. 185
Their fruits to you, confesses you its *l. S.* vi. 251
By sale, at least by death, to change their *l. S.* vi. 251
Catch'd like the Plague, or Love, the *L.* knows how *S.* vii. 9
And lies to ev'ry *L.* in ev'ry thing *S.* vii. 77
L., Sir, a mere Mechanic! strangely low *S.* viii. 108
Care, if a livery'd *L.* or smile or frown *S.* viii. 197
Jehovah, Jove, or *L. U.P.* 4
Or think thee *L.* alone of Man *U.P.* 23
Before his *l.* the ready spaniel bounds *W.F.* 99
If one, thro' Nature's Bounty, or his L.'s E.S. ii. 173
An added pudding solemniz'd the *L. M.E.* iii. 346
No *L.* anointed, but a Russian Bear *S.* v. 389
Of L—s, and Earls, and Dukes, and garter'd Knights E. v. 36
Nay wits had pensions, and young *L.* had wit *E.C.* 539
But all our praises why should *L.* engross *M.E.* iii. 249
What mov'd my mind with youthful *l.* to roam *E.C.* 159
My *L.* the Judges laugh, and you're dismissed *S.* i. 156
Let lands and houses have what *L.* they will *S.* ii. 173
Ever the taste of Mohs, but now of *L. S.* v. 311
Before the *L.* at twelve my Cause comes on *S.* vi. 96
L. of fat E'sham, or of Lincoln fen *S.* vi. 241
These write to *L.* some meann reward to get *S.* vii. 25
The lonely *l.* of empty wilds and woods *W.F.* 48
But does no other l. *it at this hour S.* vi. 306
Put my *L.* Bolingbroke *in mind I.H.* ii. 755
Whom all *L. Chamberlains* allow the Stage *E.S.* i. 42

LORDLY—LOVE.

Our Midas sits *L. Chancellor* of Plays *D.* iii. 324
L. Fanny spins a thousand such a day *S.* i. 6
For 'faith, *L. F.*, you are in the wrong *S.* ii. 101
You'd quickly find him in *L. F.*'s case *E.S.* i. 50
Din'd with the MAN OF ROSS, or my *L. May'r E.S.*ii.99
I know no more than my *L. M. I.H.* ii. 122 s
You limp, like Blackmore on a *L. M.*'s horse *S*, iii. 16
Mark how they grace *L, Umbra* or Sir Billy *E.M.*iv.278

Lordly.

Nor *l.* Luxury nor City Gain *M.E.* iii. 146
Well, I could wish, that still in *l.* domes *S.* vii. 115

Lordship.

All his Grace preaches, all his *L.* sings *E.S.* ii. 224
I doubt not, if his *L.* knew *I.H.* ii. 81 s
For all his *L.* knows, but they are Wood *M.E.* iv. 138
"Right," cries his *L.*, "for a rogue in need *S.* i. 111
When all their L—s had sat late I.H. ii. 186

Lore.

Of arts, but thund'ring against heathen *l. D.* iii. 102

Lose.

L. the low vales, and steal into the skies *A.* 60
Nor wish to *l.* a Foe these Virtues raise *E.* ii. 11
Nor envy them that heav'n I *l.* for thee *E.A.* 72
And if I *l.* thy love, I *l.* my all *E.A.* 118
How shall I *l.* the sin, yet keep the sense *E.A.* 191
In search of wit these *l.* their common sense *E.C.* 28
Like kings we *l.* the conquests gain'd before *E.C.* 64
Nor *l.*, for that malignant dull delight *E.C.* 237
Whose fame with pains we guard, but *l.* with ease *E.C.* 504
Or he whose Virtue sigh'd to *l.* a day *E.M.* iv. 148
And if it *l.*, atteoded with no pain *E.M.* iv. 316
Save when they *l.* a Question or a Job *E.S.* i. 104
You *l.* it in the moment you detect *M.E.* i. 30
They seek the second not to *l.* the first *M.E.* ii. 214
And, the next *Pull*, my *Septleva* I *l. Mi.* ix. 52
I *l.* all Mem'ry of my former Fears *Mi.* ix. 94
He gain his Prince's ear, or *l.* his own *P.S.* 367
Or *l.* her heart, or necklace, at a ball *R.L.* ii. 109
And keep good-humour still whate'er we *l. R.L.* v. 30
I *l.* my patience, and I own it too. *S.* v. 115
You *l.* your patience, just like other men *S.* v. 363

Loser.

The Winner's pleasure, and the *L.*'s pain *Mi.* ix. 80

Loses.

Ev'n superstition *l.* ev'ry fear *E.A.* 315

Losing.

Or change complexions at a *l.* game *R.L.* iv. 70

Loss.

Of hisses, blows, or want, or *l.* of ears *D.* i. 48
The mind in Metaphysics at a *l. D.* iv. 449
Disdains all *l.* of Tickets or Codille *M.E.* ii. 266
Laugh'd at the *l.* of friends he never had *P.S.* 346
Alas ! *far lesser l—es than I bear Mi.* ix. 45
And knows no *l.*, while the Muse is kind *S.* v. 196

Lost.

As some sad Turtle his *l.* love deplores *A.* 19
Who *l.* my heart while I preserv'd my sheep *A.* 80
All look, all sigh, and call on Smedley *l. D.* ii. 293
L., *l.* too soon in yonder House or Hall *D.* iv. 166
How many Martials were in PULT'NEY *l. D.* iv. 170
All Classic learning *l.* on Classic ground *D.* iv. 321
L. is his God, his Country, ev'ry thing *D.* iv. 523
L. was the Nation's Sense, nor could be found *D.* iv. 611
Oh just beheld and *l. l* admir'd and mourn'd *E.* i. 3
O more than Fortune, Friends, or Country *l. E.* xlii. 6
In vain *l.* Eloisa weeps and prays *E.A.* 15
L. in a convent's solitary gloom *E.A.* 38
For hearts so touch'd, so pierc'd, so *l.* as mine *E.A.* 196
His praise is *l.*, who stays till all commend *E.C.* 475
Now length of Fame (our second life) is *l. E.C.* 480
But soon the short-liv'd vanity is *l. E.C.* 497
Nor in the Critic let the Man be *l. E.C.* 523
(Her guide now *l.*) no more attempts to rise *E.C.* 737
One prospect *l.*, another still we gain *E.M.* iv. 272
How each for other oft is wholly *l. E.M.* iv. 272
But shall the Dignity of *Vice* be *l. E.S.* i. 114
If I ne'er got or *l.* a groat *I.H.* ii. 13 s

My choicest Hours of life are *l. I.H.* ii. 126
Explores the *l.*, the wand'ring sheep directs *M.* 51
But *l.*, dissolv'd in thy superior rays *M.* 101
One spring of action to ourselves is *l. M.E.* i. 42
To covet flying, and regret when *l. M.E.* ii. 234
Or in proud falls magnificently *l. M.E.* iii. 256
Who gain'd no title, and who *l.* no friend *M.E.* v. 70
For ever, ever, ever *l. O.* i. 105
Some joy still *l.*, as each vain year runs o'er *Mi.* v. 7
One, one bad *Deal*, three *Septlevas* have *l. Mi.* ix. 12
A lover *l.*, is but a common care *Mi.* ix. 17
The KNAVE OF CLUBS thrice *l.*: Oh ! who could guess *Mi.* ix. 19
By *Cards' Ill Usage*, or by *Lovers l. Mi.* ix. 26
And see if Reason must not *there* be *l. Mi.* ix. 86
For such a moment, Prudence well were *l. Mi.* ix. 98
L. the arch'd eye-brow, or Parnassian sneer *P.S.* 96
And all your honour in a whisper *l. R.L.* iv. 110
And chiefs contend till all the prize is *l*, *R.L.* v. 108
Since all things *l.* on earth are treasur'd there *R.L.* v. 114
Shall draw such envy as the Lock you *l. R.L.* v. 144
A *l.* Bank-bill, or heard their Son was drown'd *S.* ii. 56
Tho' double-tax'd, how little have I *l. S.* ii. 152
And swear, all shame is *l.* in George's Age *S.* v. 126
Sinks the *l.* Actor in the tawdry load *S.* v. 333
He slept, poor dog ! and *l.* it to a doit *S.* vi. 36
Who having *l.* his credit, pawn'd his rent *S*, viii. 138
To all the world illustriously are *l. Sp.* 10
Their beauty wither'd, and their verdure *l. W.* 10
And ere he starts, a thousand steps are *l. W.F.* 154
Oh early *l. l* what tears the river shed *W.F.* 273
L. in my fame, as in the sea their streams *W.F.* 362

Lot.

And once the *l.* of Abelard and me *E.A.* 98
How happy is the blameless Vestal's *l. E.A.* 207
This day be Bread and Peace my *L. U.P.* 45

Loth.

L. to enrich me with too quick replies *S.* viii. 128

Loud.

L. thunder to its bottom shook the bog *D.* i. 329
Here fortun'd Curl to slide ; *l.* shout the band *D.* ii. 73
Drowns the *l.* clarion of the braying Ass (*rep.*) *D.* ii. 234
A moan so *l.*, that all the guild awake *D.* ii. 250
He hears *l.* Oracles, and talks with Gods *D.* iii. 8
Far as *l.* Bow's stupendous bells resound *D.* iii. 278
From the full choir when *l.* Hosannas rise *E.A.* 353
But when *l.* surges lash the sounding shore *E.C.* 368
Of stupid starers, and of *l.* huzzas *E.M.* iv. 256
Foe to *l.* Praise, and Friend to learned Ease *Ep.* x. 5
Let the *l.* trumpet sound *O.* i. 7
And all Olympus rings with *l.* alarms *R.L.* v. 48
Not fierce Othello in so *l.* a strain *R.L.* v. 105
L. as the Wolves, on Orcas' stormy steep *S.* v. 328

Louder.

A little *l.*, but as empty quite *E.M.* ii. 278
Now *l.* and yet *l.* rise *O.* i. 74
Not *l.* shrieks to pitying heav'n are cast *R.L.* iii. 57

Loudly.

Who sings so *l.*, and who sings so long *D.* ii. 268
And *l.* claims the Journals and the Lead *D.* ii. 322

Louis.

What RICH'LIEU wanted, *L.* scarce could gain *E.S.* ii. 116
The fate of *L.*, and the fall of Rome *R.L.* v. 140
As once for *L.*, Boileau and Racine *S.* v. 375
Flatt'rers and Bigots ev'n in L.' reign S. i. 112

Love.

This mourn'd a faithless, that an absent *L. A.* 3
As some sad Turtle his lost *L* deplores *A.* 19
So dies her *l.*, and so my hopes decay *A.* 70
Just Gods ! shall all things yield returns but *l. A.* 76
And is there magic but what dwells in *l. A.* 84
Forsake mankind, and all the world—but *l.* (*rep.*) *A.* 88
Two babes of *l.* close clinging to her waist *D.* ii. 158
What force have pious vows ! The Queen of *L. D.* ii. 215
And who the most in *l.* of dirt excel *D.* ii. 277
Vied for his *l.* in jetty bow'rs below *E.* ii. 335
And smit with *l.* of Poesy and Prate *D.* ii. 382
Smit with the *l.* of Sister-Arts we came *E.* iii. 73
L., rais'd on Beauty, will like that decay *E.* iv. 63

LOVE (continued)—LOV'D.

Makes *l*. with nods, and knees beneath a table *E*. v. 28
Now warm in *l*., now with'ring in my bloom *E. A.* 37
There died the best of passions, *L.* and Fame *E. A.* 40
L. but demands what else were shed in pray'r *E. A.* 46
They live, they speak, they breathe what *l.* inspires *E. A.* 53
When *L.* approach'd me under Friendship's name *E. A.* 60
Curse on all laws but those which *l.* has made (*rep.*) *E. A.* 74
Fame, wealth, and honour! what are you to *L. E. A.* 80
Who seek in *l.* for aught but *l.* alone *E. A.* 84
When *l.* is liberty, and nature law *E. A.* 92
Not grace, or zeal, *l.* only was my *l.* (*rep.*) *E. A.* 117
And all those tender names in one, thy *l. E. A.* 154
Confess'd within the slave of *l.* and man *E. A.* 178
L. finds an altar for forbidden fires *E. A.* 182
Or how distinguish penitence from *l. E. A.* 194
Renounce my *l.*, my life, myself—and you *E. A.* 204
And stir within me ev'ry source of *l. E. A.* 232
Here grief forgets to groan, and *l.* to weep *E. A.* 314
And saints embrace thee with a *l.* like mine *E. A.* 342
And graft my *l.* immortal on thy fame *E. A.* 344
(As most in manners) by a *l.* to parts *E. C.* 288
Now burns with glory, and then melts with *l. E. C.* 377
As shameful sure as Impotence in *l. E. C.* 533
When *l.*, was all an easy Monarch's care *E. C.* 536
L., Hope, and Joy, fair Pleasure's smiling train *E. M.* ii. 117
Or (oft more strong than all) the *l.* of ease *E. M.* ii. 170
Is gentle *l.*, and charms all womankind *E. M.* ii. 190
To thee we owe true friendship, *l.* sincere *E. M.* ii. 255
Look round our World; behold the chain of *L. E. M.* iii. 7
Another *l.* succeeds, another race *E. M.* iii. 130
At once extend the int'rest and the *l. E. M.* iii. 134
These nat'ral *l.* maintain'd, habitual those *E. M.* iii. 140
Grew by like means, and join'd thro' *l.* or fear *E. M.* iii 202
Converse and *l.* mankind might strongly draw (*rep.*) *E. M.* iii. 207
L. all the faith, and all th' allegiance then *E. M.* iii. 235
That was but *l.* of God, and this of Man *E. M.* iii. 240
Esteem and *L.* were never to be sold *E. M.* iv. 288
The lover and the *l.* of human-kind *E. M.* iv. 190
All end in *L.* of GOD, and *L.* of MAN *E. M.* iv. 340
That instant, I declare, he has my *l. E. S.* i. 75
But, Sir, I beg you (for the *L.* of Vice) *E. S.* ii. 42
Where *Kent* and Nature vie for PELHAM's *L. E. S.* ii. 67
A *l.* to Peace, and hate of Tyranny *Ep.* ii. 10
Thy Martial spirit, or thy Social *L Ep.* ix. 8
So eager to express your *l. I. H.* ii. 57
Sacred to social life and social *l. I. H.* iii. 22
Perhaps was sick, in *l.*, or had not din'd *M. E.* i. 128
One action, Conduct; one, heroic *L. M. E.* i. 134
She sins with Poets thro' pure *L.* of Wit *M. E.* ii. 76
L., if it makes her yield, must make her hate *M. E.* ii. 134
The *L.* of Pleasure, and the *L.* of Sway *M. E.* ii. 210
Your *l.* of Pleasure, our desire of Rest *M. E.* ii. 274
Last, for his Country's *l.*, he sells his lands *M. E.* iii. 212
The bow'r of wanton Shrewsbury and *l. M. E.* iii. 308
As You by *L.*, so I by Fortune cross'd *Mi.* ix. 11
She all the cares of *L.* and Play does know *Mi.* ix. 22
This *Snuff-box*,—once the pledge of SHARPER's *l. Mi.* ix. 37
Ah! what is warning to a Maid in *L. Mi.* ix. 74
When awful *L.* seems melting in his Eyes *Mi.* ix. 90
L., strong as Death, the Poet led *O.* i. 51
By the youths that died for *L. O.* i. 79
Yet music and *l.* were victorious *O.* i. 92
Oh Tyrant *L.*! hast thou possest *O.* iii. 1
L., soft intruder, enters here *O.* iii. 5
What is loose *l.*? a transient gust *O.* iii. 17
With rev'rence, hope, and *l. O.* iii. 36
The hero's glory, or the virgin's *l.* (*rep.*) *P. C.* 10
Or which must end me, a Fool's wrath or *l. l. P. S.* 30
And show the *sense* of it without the *l. P. S.* 294
And *l.* of Ombre, after death survive *R. L.* i. 56
When offers are disdain'd, and *l.* deny'd *R. L.* i. 82
L. in these labyrinths his slaves detains *R. L.* ii. 23
But chiefly *L.*—to *L.* an Altar built *R. L.* ii. 37
By *l.* of Courts to num'rous ills betray'd *R. L.* iv. 152
P—x'd by her *l.*, or libell'd by her hate *S.* i. 84
St John, whose *l.* indulg'd my labours past *S.* iii. 1
Farewell then Verse, and *L.*, and ev'ry Toy *S.* iii. 17

Long as the Night to her whose *L.*'s away *S.* iii. 36
With wretched Av'rice, or as wretched *L. S.* iii. 56
The Cordial Drop of Life is *L.* alone *S.* iv. 127
No wonder then, when all was *l.* and sport *S.* v. 151
Catch'd like the Plague, or *L.*, the Lord knows how *S.* vii. 9
No rat is rhym'd to death, nor maid to *l.* (*rep.*) *S.* vii. 22
Two Swains, whom *L.* kept wakeful, and the Muse *Sp.* 28
O *L.*! for Sylvia let me gain the prize *Sp.* 49
Thy victim, *L.*, shall be the shepherd's heart *Sp.* 52
Hear what from *L.* unpractis'd hearts endure (*rep.*) *Su.* 11
While your Alexis pines in hopeless *l. Su.* 24
Embrace my *L.*, and bind my brows with bays *Su.* 38
But in my Abelard the serpent *L.* abides *Su.* 68
Ye Gods! and is there no relief for *L. Su.* 88
Fair Daphne's dead, and *l.* is now no more *W.* 28
To the same notes, of *l.*, and soft desire *W. F.* 296
L.'s *victim then, tho' now a sainted maid E. A.* 312
L. purer flames the Gods approve (*rep.*) *O.* iii. 13
Purest *l.* unwasting treasure *O.* iii. 41
On me *l.* fiercer flames for ever prey *Su.* 91
In these gay thoughts the L—s *and Graces shine E.* iv. 1
The Smiles and *L.* had died in Voiture's death *E.* iv. 19
Those joys, those *l.*, those int'rests to resign *E. M.* ii. 258
L. of his own and raptures swell the note *E. M.* iii. 34
There spread round MURRAY all your blooming *l. I. H.* iii. 10
Shall call the smiling *L.*, and young Desires *I. H.* iii. 26
And all the trophies of his former *l. R. L.* ii. 40
What tho' no weeping *L.* thy ashes grace *U. L.* 59
Ye weeping *L.*, the stream with myrtles hide *W.* 23
Adieu, ye shepherds' rural lays and *l. W.* 90
Reap their own fruits, and woo their sable *l. W. F.* 410
Say, is not absence death to those who *l. A.* 30
And streams to murmur, e'er I cease to *l. A.* 42
Yet, yet I *l.*! From Abelard it came *E. A.* 7
Too soon they taught me 'twas no sin to *l. E. A.* 68
No, make me mistress to the man I *l. E. A.* 88
And love th' offender, yet detest th' offence *E. A.* 192
How often must it *l.*, how often hate *E. A.* 198
What dust we dote on, when 'tis man we *l. E. A.* 336
Oh may we never *l.* as these have lov'd *E. A.* 352
And *l.* to praise, with reason on his side *E. C.* 642
They *l.* themselves, a third time in their race *E. M.* iii. 114
As S—k, if he lives, will *l.* the PRINCE *E. S.* ii. 61
And *l.* him, court him, praise him, in or out *E. S.* ii. 103
Go, where to *l.* and to enjoy are one *Ep.* vii. 16
Ah Doctor, how you *l.* to jest *I. H.* ii. 137
As never yet to *l.*, or to be lov'd *M. E.* ii. 166
She, who can *l.* a Sister's charms, or hear *M. E.* ii. 259
"God cannot *l.*" (says Blunt with tearless eyes) *M. E.* iii. 103
Who dare to *l.* their country and be poor *Mi.* x. 14
No crime to *l.* me, no crime to *l. O.* i. 96
I *l.* to pour out all myself, as plain *S.* i. 51
This, all who know me, know; who *l.* me, tell *S.* i. 138
And, as I *l.*, would imitate the Man *S.* ii. 132
But still I *l.* the language of his heart *S.* v. 78
You *l.* a Verse, take such as I can send *S.* vi. 2
In spring the fields, in autumn hills I *l. Sp.* 77
Is it, in heav'n, a crime to *l.* too well *U. L.* 6
L.-whisp'ring *woods, and lute-resounding waves D.* iv. 306
And those *l.-darting* eyes must roll no more *U. L.* 34

Lov'd.

Where mix'd with God's, his *l.* Idea lies *E. A.* 12
Nor wish'd an Angel whom I *l.* a Man *E. A.* 70
Long *l.*, ador'd ideas, all adieu *E. A.* 296
And ev'n my Abelard be *l.* no more *E. A.* 334
Oh may we never love as these have *l. E. A.* 352
Match Raphael's grandeur with thy *l.* Guido's air *E.* iii. 36
And all to one *l.* Folly sacrifice *E. C.* 266
Tells us that Cato dearly *l.* his wife *E. J. S.* 32
And *l.* his country—but what's that to you *E. J. S.* 40
At length enjoys that liberty he *l. Ep.* ii. 12
Here lies the Friend most *l.*, the Son most dear *Ep.* iii. 2
Prais'd, wept, and honour'd, by the Muse he *l. Ep.* ii. 6
Yet ah! how once we *l.*, remember still *Ep.* xiii. 3
The Senate heard him, and his Country *l. Ep.* xiv. 8
Names, which I long have *l.*, nor *l.* in vain *E. S.* ii. 90
Yet *l.* his Friend, and had a Soul *I. H.* ii. 162

LOVELESS—LULLABIES.

As never yet to love, or to be *l. M.E.* ii. 166
And prais'd, unenvy'd, by the Muse he *l. M.E.* v. 72
And *Congreve l.*, and *Swift* endur'd my lays *P.S.* 138
Abuse, on all he *L.*, or *l.* him, spread *P.S.* 354
In them, as certain to be *l.* as seen *S.* i. 53
L. without youth, and follow'd without pow'r *S.* iii. 183
All, by the King's Example, liv'd and *L. S.* v. 142
Now Whig, now Tory, what we *l.* we hate *S.* v. 157
If D * * * *l.* sixpence more than he *S..* vi. 229
You've paid, and *l.*, and eat, and drank your fill *S.* vi. 323
How *l.*, how honour'd once, avails thee not *U.L.* 71
The Muse forgot, and thou be *l.* no more *U.L.* 82
Pan saw and *l.*, and, burning with desire *W.F.* 183

Loveless.
From *l.* youth to unrespected age *M.E.* ii. 125

Lovely.
Were *l.* SHARPER mine, and mine alone *Mi.* ix. 76
Clipp'd from the *l.* head where late it grew *R.L.* iv. 136
Come, *l.* nymph, and bless the silent hours *Su.* 63

Lover.
Some banish'd *l.*, or some captive maid *E.A.* 52
A naked *L.* bound and bleeding lies *E.A.* 100
Sad proof how well a *l.* can obey *E.A.* 172
I mourn the *l.*, not lament the fault *E.A.* 184
Of all affliction taught a *l.* yet *E.A.* 289
The *l.* and the love of human-kind *E.M.* iv. 190
L. of peace, and friend of human kind *Ep.* vii. 8
She, while her *L.* pants upon her breast *M.E.* ii. 167
A *L.* lost, is but a common care *Mi.* ix. 17
Have made a Soldier sigh, a *L.* swear *Mi.* ix. 46
But soon, too soon, the *l.* turns his eyes *O.* i. 93
An earthly *L.* lurking at her heart *R.L.* iii. 144
This the blest *L.* shall for Venus take *R.L.* v. 135
Has ev'n been prov'd to grant a L.'s pray'r M.E. ii. 55
She dares to steal my Fav'rite *L.* heart *Mi.* ix. 66
Pours balm into the bleeding *l.* wounds *O.* i. 29
For when success a *L.* Toil attends *R.L.* ii. 33
To act a *L.* or a Roman's part *U.L.* 8
As some coy nymph her *l.* warm address *W.F.* 19
Do l—s *dream, or is my Delia kind A.* 52
Amid those *L.* joys his gentle Ghost *E.* iv. 74
If ever chance two wand'ring *l.* brings *E.A.* 347
Young without *L.*, old without a Friend *M.E.* ii. 246
On thy Margin *L.* wander *Mi.* vii. 27
By *Cards' Ill Usage*, or by *L.* lost *Mi.* ix. 26
And sleepless *l.*, just at twelve, awake *R.L.* i. 16
Not ardent *L.* robb'd of all their bliss *R.L.* iv. 5
And l.' *hearts with ends of riband bound R.L.* v. 118

Loves.
And gentle Dulness ever *l.* a joke *D.* ii. 34
And *l.* you best of all things—but his horse *E.* v. 30
Ev'n thou art cold—yet Eloïsa *l. E.A.* 260
Such if there be, who *l.* so long, so well *E.A.* 363
Each *l.* itself, but not itself alone *E.M.* iii. 121
God *l.* from Whole to Parts: but human soul *E.M.* iv. 361
A Rebel to the very king he *l. M.E.* i. 203
To draw the man who *l.* his God, or King *M.E.* ii. 196
His Son's fine Taste an op'ner Vista *l. M.E.* v. 93
"He L,"—I whisper to myself, "He l!" *Mi.* ix. 92
Marcus with blushes owns he *l. O.* iii. 7
Who *l.* a lie, lame slander helps about *P.S.* 289
The Man that *l.* and laughs, must sure do well *S.* iv. 129
F. *l.* the Senate, Hockley-hole his brother *S.* i. 50
This, he who *L* me, and who ought to mend *S.* iii. 178
When Oldfield *L*, what Dartineuf detests *S.* vi. 87
Diana Cynthus, Ceres Hybla *l. Sp.* 66
His Sov'reign favours, and his Country *l. W.F.* 236

Low.
Lose the *l.* vales and steal into the skies *A.* 60
And the *l.* sun had lengthen'd ev'ry shade *A.* 100
As to soft gales top-heavy pines bow *l. D.* ii. 391
L. bow'd the rest: He, kingly, did but nod *D.* iv. 207
On plain Experience lay foundations *l. D.* iv. 466
In each *L* wind methinks a Spirit calls *E.A.* 305
Correctly cold, and regularly *l. E.C.* 240
And ten *l.* words oft creep in one dull line *E.C.* 347
But in *l.* numbers short excursions tries *E.C.* 738
To *l.* ambition, and the pride of Kings *M.E.* i. 2
To him no high, no *l.*, no great, no small *E.M.* i. 279
To man's *l.* passions, or their glorious ends *E.M.* iv. 375

Virtue may choose the high or *l.* degree *E.S.* i. 137
The brib'd Elector.—There you stoop too *l. E.S.* ii. 25
Above Temptation, in a *l.* Estate *Ep.* xi. 5
And like its Master, very *l. I.H.* 78
In life's *L* vale, the soil the Virtues like *M.E.* i. 143
Nor swell too high, nor sink too *l. O.* i. 23
Now high, now *L*, now master up, now miss *P.S.* 324
Let *Budgel* charge *l. Grubstreet* on his quill *P.S.* 378
Thou by some other shalt be laid as *L R.L.* v. 98
From *l.* St. James's up to high St. Paul *S.* iii. 82
Admire we then what Earth's *L* entrails hold *S.* iv. 11
Would ye be blest? despise *l.* Joys, *l.* Gains *S.* iv. 60
What part, *l.* dialogue has Farquhar writ *S.* v. 288
For ever sunk too *l.*, or borne too high *S.* v. 299
Lord, Sir, a mere mechanic *l.* strangely *l. S.* viii. 108
Above the vulgar flight of *l.* desire *U.L.* 72
A l.-born, *cell-bred, selfish, servile band D.* ii. 356
Spread like a *l.* mist, and blot the Sun *M.E.* iii. 138
And *l.-brow'd* rocks hang nodding o'er the deep *E.A.* 244
A Swiss, a High-Dutch, o'er a *L.-Dutch* Bear *S.* iii. 63
Divine oblivion of *l.-thoughted* care *E.A.* 298

Lower.
The light Militia of the *l.* sky *R.L.* i. 42

Lowing.
The *l.* herds to murm'ring brooks retreat *Su.* 86

Lowly.
See spicy clouds from *l.* Saron rise *M.* 27

Lu.
And mow'd down armies in the fights of *L*, *R.L.* iii. 62

Lucid.
The *L* squadrons round the sails repair *R.L.* ii. 56
The pearly shell its *l.* globe unfold *W.F.* 395

Luckily.
The Play'rs and I are, *l.*, no friends *P.S.* 60

Luckless.
Or if three Ladies like a *l.* play *S.* iv. 87
Ah *l.* Poet ! stretch thy lungs and roar *S.* v. 324
Tir'd with a tedious march, one *l.* night *S.* vi. 35

Lucky.
Never was dash'd out at one *l.* hit *D.* ii. 47
Some *l.* License answer to the full *E.C.* 148
And two rich ship-wrecks bless the *l.* shore *M.E.* iii. 356
And God's good Providence, a *l.* Hit *M.E.* iii. 378
But on some *l.* day (as when they found *S.* ii. 55

Lucre.
The lust of *L.*, and the dread of Death *E.* i. 26
To one Man's pow'r, ambition, *l.*, lust *E.M.* iii. 270
See Britain sunk in l.'s *sordid charms M.E.* iii. 143
Not *L.* madman, nor Ambition's tool *P.S.* 335

Lucrece.
In quiet flow from *L.* to *L. E.M.* iv. 208

Lucretia.
L.'s dagger, Rosamonda's bowl *M.E.* ii. 92

Lucretius.
Such as *L.* drew, a God like thee *D.* iv. 484

Lucullus.
L., when Frugality could charm *M.E.* i. 218

Lud.
Thro' *L.*'s fam'd gates, along the well-known Fleet *D.* ii. 359
In *L.* old walls tho' long I rul'd, renown'd *D.* iii. 277

Lug.
To *l.* the pond'rous volume off in state *D.* iv. 118

Lull.
Wake the dull Church, and *l.* the ranting stage *D.* iv. 58
To *l.* the sons of Marg'ret and Clare-hall *L. D.* iv. 200
What Charms could Faction, what Ambition *L D.* iv. 623
Or *l.* to rest the visionary maid *E.A.* 162
L. with Amelia's liquid name the Nine *S.* i. 31

Lullabies.
Till Senates nod to *L.* divine *D.* i. 317

Lull'd.

L. with the sweet Nepenthe of a Court *E.S.* i. 98
L. by soft Zephyrs thro' the broken pane *P.S.* 42
One *l.* th' Exchequer, and one stunn'd the Rolls *S.* vi. 130

Lulls.

Intoxicates the pert, and *l.* the grave *D.* ii. 344

Lumber.

Dropt the dull *l.* of the Latin store *D.* iv. 319
With loads of learned *l.* in his head *E.C.* 613
Thy giddy Dulness still shall *l.* on *D.* iii. 294
A l.-house of books in ev'ry head *D.* iii. 193

Lump.

Each growing *l.*, and brings it to a Bear *D.* i. 102

Lunar.

Some thought it mounted to the *L.* sphere *R.L.* v. 113

Lunatic.

The sot a hero, *l.* a king *E.M.* ii. 268

Lungs.

Such as from lab'ring *l.* th' Enthusiast blows *D.* ii. 255
There she collects the force of female *l. R.L.* iv. 83
Ah luckless Poet! stretch thy *l.* and roar *S.* v. 324
A Pedant makes, the storm of Gonson's *l. S.* viii. 53

Lures.

But *l.* the Pirate, and corrupts the Friend *M.E.* iii. 30

Lurk'd.

L. in her hand, and mourn'd his captive Queen *R.L.* iii. 96

Lurking.

Receives the *l.* principle of death *E.M.* ii. 134
An Earthly Lover *l.* at her heart *R.L.* iii. 144
This harmless grove no *l.* viper hides *Su.* 67

Lurks.

Bare the mean Heart that *l.* beneath a Star *S.* i. 108

Luscious.

And when rank Widows purchase *l.* nights *S.* vii. 87

Lust.

And lo the wretch! whose vile, whose insect *l. D.* iv. 415
The *L.* of Lucre, and the dread of Death *E.* i. 26
Are mortals urg'd thro' sacred *l.* of praise *E.C.* 521
L., thro' some certain strainers well refio'd *E.M.* ii. 189
Whose attributes were Rage, Revenge, or *L. E.M.* iii. 258
To one man's pow'r, ambition, lucre, *l. E.M.* iii. 270
Whose ruling Passion was the *L.* of Praise *M.E.* i. 181
In this the *L.*, in that the Avarice *M.E.* i. 214
Extends to Luxury, extends to *L. M.E.* iii. 26
Still, when the *l.* of tyrant pow'r succeeds *O.* ii. 31
Spent in a sudden storm of *l. O.* iii. 18
Who reads, but with a *l.* to misapply *P.S.* 301
Alike in nothing but one *L.* of Gold *S.* iii. 124
Tho' in his pictures *L.* be full display'd *S.* viii. 94

Lustre.

Pleas'd the green *l.* of the scales survey *M.* 83
The Sun's mild *l.* warms the vital air *Sp.* 74
Nor all his stars above a *l.* show *W.F.* 231
And add new *l.* to her silver star *W.F.* 290
The doubling L—s dance as fast as she *S.* i. 48

Lute.

Let the warbling *l.* complain *O.* i. 6
Love-whisp'ring woods, and *l.*-resounding waves *D.* iv. 306

Lutestring.

Squeaks like a high-stretch'd *l.*, and replies *S.* viii. 99

Lutetia.

How young *L.*, softer than the down *D.* ii. 333

Luther.

So *L.* thought the Paternoster long *S.* vii. 105

Luxuriant.

Prune the *l.*, the uncouth refine *S.* vi. 174

Luxury.

The Bishop stow (Pontific *L.*!) *D.* iv. 593

Or Learning's *L.*, or Idleness *E.M.* ii. 46
Th' extensive blessing of his *l. E.M.* iii. 62
But just disease to *l.* succeeds *E.M.* iii. 165
Amidst Corruption, *L.*, and Rage *Ep.* ix. 9
Extends to *L.*, extends to Lust *M.E.* iii. 26
Nor lordly *L.*, nor City Gain *M.E.* iii. 146
When *L.* has lick'd up all thy pelf *S.* ii. 105
Was sheath'd, and *L.* with *Charles* restor'd *S.* v. 140
To prove, that *L.* could never hold *S.* v. 167

Lying.

Nay all that *l.* Travellers can feign *S.* viii. 31

Lynx.

Far from a *L.*, and not a Giant quite *S.* iii. 50
The mole's dim curtain, and the l.'s beam *E.M.* i. 212

Lyre.

One dip the pencil, and one string the *l. E.* iii. 70
Fair *Discretion*, string the *l. Mi.* vii. 14
And sweep the sounding *l. O.* i. 4
But hark! he strikes the golden *l. O.* i. 63
Till in your native shades you tune the *l. Sp.* 12
And on his willows hung each muse's *l. W.F.* 276
In the same shades the Cupids tun'd his *l. W.F.* 295
Thither, the silver-sounding l—s *I.H.* iii. 25

Lyttleton.

Why, answer *L.*, and I'll engage *E.S.* i. 47
And *L.* a dark, designing Knave *E.S.* ii. 131
Free as young *L.*, her Cause pursue *S.* iii. 29

M.

As *M—o's* was, but not at five per cent. *S.* ii. 122

Maces.

Pomps without guilt, of bloodless swords and *m. D.* i. 87

Macedonia.

From *M.'s* madman to the Swede *E.M.* iv. 220

Macer.

When simple *M.*, now of high renown *Mi.* iii. 1

Machines.

And crystal domes and angels in *m. R.L.* iv. 46

Mad.

And all the mighty *M.* in Dennis rage *D.* i. 106
The third *m.* passion of thy doting age *D.* iii. 304
M. Mathesis alone was uoconfin'd (*rep.*) *D.* iv. 31
There are as *m.* abandon'd Critics too *E.C.* 611
Take Nature's path; and *m.* Opinion's leave *E.M.* iv. 29
No Bandit fierce, no Tyrant *m.* with pride *E.M.* iv. 41
With the same trash *m.* mortals wish for here *E.M.* iv. 174
What! always Peter? Peter thinks you *m. 'E.S.* ii. 58
A Monarch's sword when *m.* Vain-glory draws *E.S.* ii. 229
M. at a Fox-chase, wise at a Debate *M.E.* i. 74
Was just not ugly, and was just not *m. M.E.* ii. 50
Giv'n to the Fool, the *M.*, the Vain, the Evil *M.E.* iii. 19
Less *m.* the wildest whimsey we can frame *M.E.* iii. 155
Of *m.* Good-nature and of mean Self-love *M.E.* iii. 228
What but a want, which you perhaps think *m. M.E.* iii. 331
Apply to me, to keep them *m.* or vain *P.S.* 22
Of all *m.* creatures, if the learn'd are right *P.S.* 105
It is not Poetry, but prose run *m. P.S.* 188
The dull, the proud, the wicked, and the *m. P.S.* 347
Be furious, envious, slothful, *m.*, or drunk *S.* iii. 61
All the *m.* trade of Fools and Slaves for Gold *S.* iv. 13
The worst of Madmen is a Saint run *m. S.* iv. 27
On Fame's *m.* voyage by the wind of praise *S.* v. 297
As wild and *m.*: the Avarice of pow'r *S.* vi. 307
And *m.* Ambition shall attend her there *W.F.* 416

Madam.

But, *M.*, if the Fates withstand, and you *E.* iv. 57
Pictures like these, dear *M.*, to design *M.E.* ii. 151
Ah, *M.*, since my SHARPER is untrue *Mi.* ix. 4

Madden.

They rave, recite, and *m.* round the land *P.S.* 6

Maddest.
Admire whate'er the *m.* can admire *S.* iv. 68

Madding.
Bring, bring the *m.* Bay, the drunken Vine *D.* i. 303
The moon-struck Prophet felt the *m.* hour *D.* iv. 12

Made.
Taught rocks to weep, and *m.* the mountains groan *A.* 16
Which, as more pond'rous, *m.* its aim more true *D.* i. 171
This grey-goose weapon must have *m.* her stand *D.* i. 198
(Haunt of the Muses) *m.* their safe retreat *D.* ii. 428
Admire new light thro' holes yourselves have *m. D.* iv. 126
M. Horace dull, and humbled Milton's strains *D.* iv. 212
The Sire is *m.* a Peer, the Son a Fool *D.* iv. 548
Isis and Cam *m.* Doctors of their Laws *D.* iv. 578
In vain to Deserts thy retreat is *m. E.* i. 27
M. Slaves by honour, and *m.* Fools by shame *E.* iv. 36
Curse on all laws but those which love has *m. E.A.* 74
And saints with wonder heard the vows I *m. E.A.* 114
And some *m.* coxcombs Nature meant but fools *E.C.* 27
Write dull receipts how poems may be *m. E.C.* 115
Since rules were *m.* but to promote their end *E.C.* 147
As Kings dispense with laws themselves have *m. E.C.* 162
M. him observe the subject, and the plot *E.C.* 275
Some by old words to fame have *m.* pretence *E.C.* 324
Faith, Gospel, all, seem'd *m.* to be disputed *E.C.* 442
Those strange examples ne'er were *m.* to fit ye *E.Ş.S.* 41
May tell why Heav'n has *m.* us what we are *E.M.* i. 28
Ask of thy mother earth, why oaks are *m. E.M.* i. 39
Alone *m.* perfect here, immortal there *E.M.* i. 120
M. for his use all creatures if he call *E.M.* i. 177
The choice we make, or justify it *m. E.M.* ii. 156
M. Beast in aid of Man, and Man of Beast *E.M.* iii. 24
Who thinks all *m.* for one, not one for all *E.M.* iii. 48
Who *m.* the spider parallels design *E.M.* iii. 103
Cities were built, Societies were *m. E.M.* iii. 200
A Prince the Father of a People *m. E.M.* iii. 214
Th' enormous faith of many *m.* for one *E.M.* iii. 242
Force first *m.* Conquest, and that Conquest, Law *E.M.* iii. 245
And Gods of Conqu'rors, Slaves of Subjects *m. E.M.* iii. 248
Fear *m.* her Devils, and weak Hope her Gods *E.M.* iii. 256
Where small and great, where weak and mighty, *m. E.M.* iii. 297
Tell me, if Virtue *m.* the son expire *E.M.* iv. 105
Was *m.* for Cæsar—but for Titus too *E.M.* iv. 146
Fortune in Men has some small diff'rence *m. E.M.* iv. 195
A Dean, Sir ? no ; his Fortune is not *m. E.S.* ii. 34
Or if a Court, or Country's *m.* a job *E.S.* ii. 40
Has never *m.* a Friend in private life *E.S.* ii. 134
And for that cause which *m.* your Fathers shine *E.S.* ii. 252
A Weasel once *m.* shift to slink *I.H.* i. 51
What *m.* (say Montagne, or more sage Charron !) *M.E.* i. 87
And just her wisest Monarch *m.* a fool *M.E.* i. 94
A constant Bounty which no friend has *m. M.E.* i. 198
When Cæsar *m.* a noble dame a whore *M.E.* i. 213
Has *m.* the father of a nameless race *M.E.* i. 233
And *m.* a Widow happy, for a whim *M.E.* ii. 58
The wisest Fool much Time has ever *m. M.E.* ii. 124
Which Heav'n has varnish'd out, and *m.* a Queen *M.E.* ii. 182
That Man was *m.* the standing jest of Heav'n *M.E.* iii. 4
What *m.* Directors cheat in South-sea year *M.E.* iii. 117
The thriving plants, ignoble broomsticks *m. M.E.* iv. 97
How chang'd from him who *m.* the boxes groan *Mi.* ii. 15
And, by my int'rest, Cozens *m.* her stays *Mi.* ix. 64
If want provok'd, or madness *m.* them print *P.S.* 155
And own'd that nine such Poets *m.* a Tate *P.S.* 190
"Those eyes were *m.* so killing "—was his last *R.L.* v. 64
Because God *m.* these large, the other less *S.* ii. 24
Then by the rule that *m.* the horse-tail bare *S.* v. 63
What shook the stage, and *m.* the People stare *S.* v. 336
What *m.* old Ben, and surly Dennis swear *S.* v. 388
Hath *m.* him an Attorney of an Ass *S.* vii. 50
Affirm, 'twas Travel *m.* them what they were *S.* viii. 79
Obliging Sir, for Courts you sure were *m. S.* viii. 86
Few are the Converts Aretine has *m. S.* viii. 95
Nature *m.* ev'ry Fop to plague his brother *S.* viii. 258

Oh ! were I *m.* by some transforming pow'r *Su.* 45
The ground, now sacred by thy reliques *m. U.L.* 68
By god-like Poets venerable *m. W.F.* 270

Madly.
Who wickedly is wise, or *m.* brave *E.M.* iv. 231
'Tis one thing *m.* to disperse my store *S.* vi. 292

Madman.
From Macedonia's *m.* to the Swede *E.M.* iv. 220
Not Lucre's *m.*, nor Ambition's tool *P.S.* 335
Not quite a *m.*, tho' a pasty fell *S.* vi. 190
And buries *m*—en *in the heaps they raise E.M.* iv. 76
The worst of *m.* is a Saint run mad *S.* iv. 27
These *m.* never hurt the Church or State *S.* v. 190

Madness.
Pleas'd with the *m.* of the mazy dance *D.* i. 68
With horns and trumpets now to *m.* swell *D.* ii. 227
In lofty *m.* meditating song *D.* iii. 16
Vile worm ; Oh *M.!* Pride ! Impiety ! *E.M.* i. 258
In all the *m.* of superfluous health *E.M.* iii. 3
A Neighbour's *M.*, or his Spouse's *I.H.* ii. 143
"All this is *m.*," cries a sober sage *M.E.* iii. 151
And make despair and *m.* please *O.* i. 121
And civil *m.* tears them from the land *O.* ii. 24
If want provok'd, or *m.* made them print *P.S.* 155
You think this *M.* but a common case *S.* iii. 172

Madrigal.
What woful stuff this *m.* would be *E.C.* 418

Mæander.
The wild *M.* wash'd the Artist's face *D.* ii. 176
Melancholy smooth *M. Mi.* vii. 25
Thus on *M.'s flow'ry margin lies R.L.* v. 63
And ductile Dulness new *m*—takes *D.* i. 64
As man's *M.* to the vital spring *D.* iii. 55
Rolling in *M. O.* i. 100

Mæander'd.
With silver-quiv'ring rills *m.* o'er *M.E.* iv. 85

Mæonian.
Led by the light of the *M.* star *E.C.* 648
Oh ! could I mount on the *M.* wing *S.* v. 394

Mæotis.
Lo ! where *M.* sleeps, and hardly flows *D.* iii. 87

Mævius.
If *M.* scribble in Apollo's spite *E.C.* 34

Magazines.
Hence Journals, Medleys, Mer'cries, *M. D.* i. 42
Thus useful arms in *m.* we place *E.C.* 671

Magdalen—*see also* Maudlin.
In *M.'s* loose hair, and lifted eye *M.E.* ii. 12

Maggots.
M. half-form'd in rhyme exactly meet *D.* i. 61
Who *M.* were before *Mi.* iv. 40

Magic.
Pan came, and ask'd, what *m.* caus'd my smart (*rep.*) *A.* 81
As oil'd with *m.* juices for the course *D.* ii. 104
Be thine, my stationer ! this *m.* gift *D.* ii. 137
Her *m.* charms o'er all unclassic ground *D.* iii. 258
Enrage, compose, with more than *m.* Art *S.* v. 344

Magistrates.
Who prouder march'd, with *m.* in state *D.* ii. 423

Magnificence.
Join with Economy, *M. M.E.* iii. 224
That never Coxcomb reach'd *M. M.E.* iv. 22

Magnificently.
Or in proud falls *m.* lost *M.E.* iii. 256

Magnify.
Or praise a Court, or *m.* Mankind *D.* i. 23
Beholds thro' fogs, that *m.* the scene *D.* i. 80
Dulness is ever apt to *m. E.C.* 393

Magus.
Thy *M.*, Goddess ! shall perform the rest *D.* iv. 516

MAHOMET—MAKE.

Mahomet, Mah'met, Mahound.
Nay, *M.!* the Pigeon at thine ear *D.* iv. 364
From honest *M.'t*, or plain Parson Hale *M.E.* ii. 198
The Mosque of *M—d*, or some queer Pagod *S.* viii. 239

Maid.
And modest as the *m.* that sips alone *D.* iii. 144
Each *m.* cry'd, Charming ! and each youth, Divine *D.* iv. 410
No *m.* cries, Charming ! and no youth, Divine *D.* iv. 414
Some banish'd lover, or some captive *m. E.A.* 52
Or lull to rest the visionary *m. E.A.* 162
Love's victim then, tho' now a sainted *m. E.A.* 312
Who could not win the mistress, woo'd the *m. E.C.* 105
Scolds with her *m.*, or with her chaplain crams *E.J.S.* 22
And thou, blest *M.!* attendant on his doom *Ep.* vii. 11
Ah ! what is warning to a *M.* in Love *Mi.* ix. 74
What tender *m.* but must a victim fall *R.L.* i. 95
Warn'd by the Sylph, oh pious *m.* beware *R.L.* i. 112
Here stood Ill-nature like an ancient *m. R.L.* iv. 27
" O wretched *m.!* " she spread her hands, and cry'd (*rep.*) *R.L.* iv. 95
Yet am I not the first mistaken *m. R.L.* iv. 151
And she who scorns a man, must die a *m. R.L.* v. 28
No rat is rhym'd to death, nor *m.* to love *S.* vii. 22
If Windsor-shades delight the matchless *m. Sp.* 67
It chanc'd, as eager of the chase, the *m. W.F.* 181
Nor could Diana help her injur'd *m. W.F.* 198
The M.'s *romantic wish, the Chemist's flame D.* iii. 11
Then sung, how shown him by the Nut-brown m—s *D.* ii. 337
The dreams of Pindus, and th' Aonian *m. M.* 4
Him portion'd *m.*, apprentic'd orphans blest *M.E.* iii. 267
How many *m.* have SHARPER'S vows deceiv'd *M.* ix. 71
To *M.* alone and children are reveal'd *R.L.* i. 38
What guards the purity of melting *M. R.L.* i. 71
Or bright as visions of expiring *m. R.L.* iv. 42
And *m.* turn'd bottles, call aloud for corks *R.L.* iv. 54
Invite my lays. Be present, sylvan *m. W.F.* 3

Maiden.
Unstain'd, untouch'd, and yet in *m.* sheets *D.* i. 229

Main.
Where, eas'd of Fleets, the Adriatic *m. D.* iv. 309
And Navies yawn'd for Orders on the *M. D.* iv. 618
Flies o'er th' unbending corn, and skims along the *m. E.C.* 373
The knave deserves it, when he tempts the *m. E.M.* iv. 153
The Mole projected break the roaring *M. M.E.* iv. 200
Descend from Pelion to the *m. O.* i. 41
Ere to the *m.* this morning sun descend *R.L.* i. 110
The Sun first rises o'er the purpled *m. R.L.* ii. 2
Or brew fierce tempests on the wintry *m. R.L.* ii. 85
Or cross, to plunder provinces, the *M. S.* iii. 127
The balanc'd World, and open all the *M. S.* v. 2
The Earth's fair light, and Empress of the *M. W.F.* 164
From cold Belerium, to the northern *m. W.F.* 316

Maintain.
That which my Priests, and mine alone, *m. D.* iv. 185
Make and *m.* the balance of the mind *E.M.* ii. 120
Their sep'rate cells and properties *m. E.M.* iii. 188
Bids seed-time, harvest, equal course *m. E.M.* iii. 165
M. a Poet's dignity and ease *P.S.* 263
Better be Cibber, I'll m. it still *S.* i. 37

Maintain'd.
These nat'ral love *m.*, habitual those *E.M.* iii. 140

Maintains.
Still makes new conquests, and *m.* the past *E.* iv. 62
Ye tinsel Insects ! whom a Court *m. E.S.* ii. 220
And thousands more in equal mirth *m. R.L.* iv. 66
The boys and girls whom charity *m. S.* v. 231

Majestic.
And high-born Howard, more *m.* sire *D.* i. 297
His be you Juno of *m.* size *D.* ii. 163
My Lord advances with *m.* mien *M.E.* iv. 127
The deep, *m.*, solemn organs blow *O.* i. 17
There stands a structure of *m.* frame *R.L.* iii. 3
The long *M.* march, and Energy divine *S.* v. 269
Here his first lays *m.* Denham sung *W.F.* 271

Majestically.
See Sin in State, *m.* drunk *M.E.* ii. 69

Majesty.
In clouded *M.* here Dulness shone *D.* i. 45
In naked *M.* Oldmixon stands *D.* ii. 283
Slow rose a form, in *m.* of Mud *D.* ii. 326
Behold, four Kings in *m.* rever'd *R.L.* iii. 37
The hoary *M.* of Spades appears *R.L.* iii. 55
Not with such *m.*, such bold relief *S.* v. 390
But Verse, alas ! your *M.* disdains *S.* v. 404

Major.
And *M.*, Minor, and Conclusion quick *D.* ii. 242

Make.
The common Soul, of Heav'n's more frugal *m. D.* iv. 441
Or, *if to Wit a coxcomb* m. *pretence D.* i. 177
Can *m.* a Cibber, Tibbald, or Ozell *D.* i. 286
Which Curl's Corinna chanc'd that morn to *m. D.* ii. 70
For their defrauded absent foals they *m. D.* ii. 249
Ah why, ye Gods, should two and two *m.* four *D.* ii. 286
No noise, no stir, no motion canst thou *m. D.* ii. 303
Attend the trial we propose to *m. D.* ii. 375
Critics like me shall *m.* it Prose again *D.* iv. 214
And *m.* a long Posterity thy own *D.* iv. 334
True, he had wit, to *m.* their value rise *D.* iv. 377
M. Nature still encroach upon his plan *D.* iv. 473
M. God Man's Image, Man the final Cause *D.* iv. 478
Oh hide the God still more ! and *m.* me see *D.* iv. 483
Teach Kings to fiddle, or *m.* Senates dance *D.* iv. 598
And *m.* ONE MIGHTY DUNCIAD OF THE LAND *D.* iv. 604
Know, Kings and Fortune cannot *m.* thee more *E.* ii. 9
And bids them *m.* mistaken mortals groan *E.A.* 83
No, *m.* me mistress to the man I love *E.A.* 88
More food than mistress, *m.* me that to thee *E.A.* 90
And *m.* my soul quit Abelard for God *E.A.* 128
Where awful arches *m.* a noon-day night *E.A.* 143
By vain ambition still to *m.* them more *E.C.* 65
To dress her charms, and *m.* her more belov'd *E.C.* 103
M. use of ev'ry friend—and ev'ry foe *E.C.* 214
Still *m.* the Whole depend upon a Part *E.C.* 264
Amaze th' unlearn'd, and *m.* the learned smile *E.C.* 327
Still *m.* themselves the measure of mankind *E.C.* 451
And *m.* each day a Critic on the last *E.C.* 571
He has a Husband that will *m.* amends *E.J.S.* 27
To lend a wife, few here would scruple *m. E.J.S.* 35
M. and maintain the balance of the mind *E.M.* ii. 120
Wit, Spirit, Faculties, but *m.* it worse *E.M.* ii. 146
The choice we *m.*, or justify it made *E.M.* iii. 156
Thus let the wiser *m.* the rest obey *E.M.* iii. 196
Yet *m.* at once their circle round the Sun *E.M.* iii. 314
Or *m.*, an enemy of all mankind *E.M.* iv. 222
M. fair deductions ; see to what they mount *E.M.* iv. 270
Gives thee to *m.* thy neighbour's blessing thine *E.M.* iv. 354
Could please at Court, and *m.* AUGUSTUS smile *E.S.* i. 20
You *m.* men desp'rate if they once are bad *E.S.* ii. 59
All that may *m.* me none of mine *I.H.* i. 64
Cheese, such as men in Suffolk *m. I.H.* ii. 167
M. but his Riches equal to his Wit *I.H.* iii. 18
To observations which ourselves we *m. M.E.* i. 11
In vain sedate reflections we would *m. M.E.* i. 39
To *m.* a wash, would hardly stew a child *M.E.* ii. 54
And paid a Tradesman once to *m.* him stare *M.E.* ii. 56
Love, if it makes her yield, must *m.* her hate *M.E.* ii. 134
Can *m.* to-morrow cheerful as to-day *M.E.* ii. 258
Picks from each sex, to *m.* the Fav'rite blest *M.E.* ii. 273
Bear home six whores, and *m.* his Lady weep *M.E.* iii. 72
And of one beauty many blunders *m. M.E.* iv. 28
Nature shall join you ; time shall *m.* it grow *M.E.* iv. 69
The vast Parterres a thousand hands shall *m. M.E.* iv. 73
M. the soul loose upon a Jig to Heav'n *M.E.* iv. 144
You too proceed ! *m.* falling Arts your care *M.E.* iv. 191
But has the wit to *m.* the most of little *Mi.* iii. 10
If thou couldst *m.* the Courtier void *Mi.* iv. 31
I joyless *m.* my once ador'd *Alpeu Mi.* ix. 5
And *m.* despair and madness please *O.* i. 121
To *m.* mankind in conscious virtue bold *P.C.* 2
I'm all submission, what you'd have it, *m.* it *P.S.* 46
Go on, obliging creatures, *m.* me see *P.S.* 119
Just writes to *m.* his barrenness appear *P.S.* 181
That tends to *m.* one worthy man my foe *P.S.* 284
M. Satire a Lampoon, and Fiction lie *P.S.* 302

MAKER—MAN.

M. Languor smile, and smooth the bed of Death *P.S.* 411
Could *m.* a gentle Belle reject a Lord *R.L.* i. 10
M. some take physic, others scribble plays *R.L.* iv. 62
I'd never doubt at Court to *m.* a friend *S.* ii. 44
And 'twas their point, I ween, to *m.* it last *S.* ii. 94
M. Quays, build Bridges, or repair Whitehall *S.* ii. 120
Nothing, to *m.* Philosophy thy friend *S.* iii. 74
Should chance to *m.* the well-drest Rabble stare *S.* iii. 111
Who ought to *m.* me (what he can, or none) *S.* iii. 179
To *m.* men happy, and to keep them so *S.* v. 2
Procure her beauty, *m.* that beauty chaste *S.* iv. 79
If Wealth alone then *m.* and keep us blest *S.* iv. 95
Whom honour with your hand : to *m.* remarks *S.* iv. 103
To *m.* poor Pinky eat with vast applause *S.* v. 293
Can *m.* me feel each Passion that he feigns *S.* v. 343
Ah think, what Poet best may *m.* them known *S.* v. 377
The ship itself may *m.* a better figure *S.* vi. 298
Learn to live well, or fairly *m.* your will *S.* vi. 322
Schoolmen new tenements in hell must *m.* *S.* vii. 42
One whom the mob, when next we fiod or *m.* *S.* viii. 34
M. Scots speak treason, cozen subtlest whores *S.* viii. 59
I *m.* no question but the Tow'r had stood *S.* viii. 85
You only *m.* the matter worse and worse *S.* viii. 121
A subtle Minister may *m.* of that *S.* viii. 133
And *m.* my tongue victorious as her eyes *Sp.* 50
M. Windsor-hills in lofty numbers rise *W.F.* 287
M. sacred Charles's tomb for ever known *W.F.* 319

Maker.

To wonder at their *M.*, not to serve *D.* iv. 458
Man, like his *M.*, saw that all was right *E.M.* iii. 232
As thus, "Vouchsafe, oh gracious *M. I.H.* ii. 178
And only vocal with the M.'s *praise E.A.* 140
And to her *M.* praise confin'd the sound *O.* i. 125

Makes.

Here one poor word an hundred clenches *m.* *D.* i. 63
How with less reading than *m.* felons 'scape *D.* i. 281
One circle first, and then a second *m.* *D.* ii. 406
Whose tuneful whistling *m.* the waters pass *D.* iii. 156
And *m.* might hideous—Answer him, ye Owls *D.* iii. 166
Bid her be all that *m.* mankind adore *E.* iii. 53
Still *m.* new conquests, and maintains the past *E.* iv. 62
M. love with nods, and knees beneath a table *E.* v. 28
Now one in verse *m.* many more in prose *E.C.* 8
For envy'd Wit, like Sol eclips'd, *m.* known *E.C.* 468
That only *m.* superior sense belov'd *E.C.* 577
It still looks home, and short excursions *m.* *E.C.* 627
And *m.* a patriot, as it *m.* a knave *E.M.* ii. 202
And, till he ends the being, *m.* it blest *E.M.* iii. 65
As, while he dreads it, *m.* him hope it too *E.M.* iii. 74
And *m.* what Happiness we justly call *E.M.* iv. 37
What *m.* all physical or moral ill *E.M.* iv. 111
The Boy and Man an individual *m.* *E.M.* iv. 175
Worth *m.* the Man, the want of it the fellow *E.M.* iv. 203
That virtue only *m.* our Bliss below *E.M.* iv. 397
So odd, my Country's Ruin *m.* me grave *E.S.* ii. 207
All that *m.* Saints of Queens, and Gods of Kings *E.S.* ii. 225
And *m.* immortal, Verse as mean as mine *E.S.* ii. 247
But *m.* a diff'rence in his thought *I.H.* i. 37
And *m.* her hearty meal upon a dunce *M.E.* ii. 86
Love, if it *m.* her yield, must make her hate *M.E.* ii. 134
Ask we what *m.* one keep, and one bestow *M.E.* iii. 163
Prescribes, attends, the med'cine *m.*, and gives *M.E.* iii. 270
Of rich and poor *m.* all the history *M.E.* iii. 288
Till all the Demon *m.* his full descent *M.E.* iii. 371
That, lac'd with bits of rustic, *m.* a Front *M.E.* iv. 34
Or *m.* his Neighbours glad, if he increase *M.E.* iv. 182
And Oh ! what *m.* the disappointment hard *Mi.* ix. 47
He *m.* his moan *O.* i. 103
Or simple pride for flatt'ry *m.* demands *P.S.* 253
The first Lampoon *Sir Will* or *Bubo m. P.S.* 280
Coffee (which *m.* the politician wise *R.L.* iii. 117
So when bold Homer *m.* the Gods engage *R.L.* v. 45
Virtue, brave boys ! 'tis Virtue *m.* a King *S.* iii. 92
That *m.* three members, this can choose a May'r *S.* iv. 106
His ven'son too, a guinea *m.* your own *S.* vi. 235
Himself a dinner, *m.* an Actor live *S.* vii. 14
Is he who *m.* his meal on other's wit *S.* vii. 30
His rank digestion *m.* it wit no more *S.* vii. 32
Whose gentle progress *m.* a calf an ox *S.* vii. 48

A Pedant *m.*, the storm of Gonson's lungs *S.* viii. 53
Who *m.* a Trust or Charity a Job *S.* viii. 142
And *m.* his trembling slaves the royal game *W.F.* 64

Making.

And tempts by *m.* rich, not *m.* poor *M.E.* iii. 352

Maladies.

The fair ones feel such *m.* as these *R.L.* iv. 37

Male.

Nor Virtue, *m.* or female, can we name *E.M.* ii. 193

Malice.

Lo sneering Goode, half *m.* and half whim *D.* iii. 153
Pride, *M.*, Folly, against Dryden rose *E.C.* 458
Triumphant *M.* rag'd thro' private life *S.* v. 246

Malignant.

Or what ill eyes *m.* glances dart *A.* 82
Nor lose, for that *m.* dull delight *E.C.* 237

Malignly.

Or praise *m.* Arts I cannot reach *S.* v. 339

Mall.

And swiftly shoot along the *M. I.H.* iii. 45
This the Beau-monde shall from the *M.* survey *R.L.* v. 133

Malmsey.

That Jelly's rich, this *M.* healing *I.H.* ii. 202

Mammon.

Who sees pale *M.* pine amidst his store *M.E.* iii. 171

Man.

Heav'n's Swiss, who fight for any God or *M. D.* ii. 358
If there be *m.* who o'er such works can wake *D.* ii. 372
Persist, by all divine in *M.* unaw'd *D.* iii. 223
Then thus. " Since *M.* from beast by Words is known (*rep.*) *D.* iv. 149
And South beheld that Master-piece of *M. D.* iv. 174
So upright Quakers please both *M.* and God *D.* iv. 208
And hew the Block off, and get out the *M. D.* iv. 270
And ceas'd so soon, he ne'er was Boy, nor *M. D.* iv. 288
Then dupe to Party, child and *m.* the same *D.* iv. 502
Proceed,—a Minister but still a *M. E.* ii. 15
From the dear *m.* unwilling she must sever *E.* v. 5
Nor wish'd an Angel, whom I lov'd a *M. E.A.* 70
No, make me mistress to the *m.* I love *E.A.* 88
Confess'd within the slave of love and *m. E.A.* 178
For God, not *m.*, absolves our frailties here *E.A.* 316
What dust we dote on, when 'tis *m.* we love *E.A.* 336
Tho' meant each other's aid, like *m.* and wife *E.C.* 83
Thus Wit, like Faith, by each *m.* is apply'd *E.C.* 396
Nor in the Critic let the *M.* be lost *E.C.* 523
But where's the *m.*, who counsel can bestow *E.C.* 631
The *m.* had courage, was a sage, 'tis true *E.7.S.* 39
There many an honest *m.* may copy Cato *E.7.S.* 53
Expatiate free o'er all this scene of *M. E.M.* i. 5
But vindicate the ways of God to *M.* (*rep.*) *E.M.* i. 16
Of *M.*, what see we but his station here *E.M.* i. 19
Presumptuous *M.* ! the reason wouldst thou find *E.M.* i. 35
There must be, somewhere, such a rank as *M. E.M.* i. 48
Respecting *M.*, whatever wrong we call *E.M.* i. 51
So *M.*, who here seems principal alone *E.M.* i. 57
When the proud steed shall know why *M.* restrains *E.M.* i. 61
Then say not *M.*'s imperfect, Heav'n in fault (*rep.*) *E.M.* i. 69
M. never Is, but always To be blest *E.M.* i. 96
Yet cry, if *M.*'s unhappy, God's unjust (*rep.*) *E.M.* i. 118
And what created perfect ? why then *M. E.M.* i. 148
Then Nature deviates ; and can *M.* do less *E.M.* i. 150
Is kept in Nature, and is kept in *M.* (*rep.*) *E.M.* i. 172
Is Heav'n united to *M.*, and *M.* alone *E.M.* i. 186
The bliss of *M.* (could Pride that blessing find) *E.M.* i. 189
Why has not *M.* a microscopic Eye (*rep.*) *E.M.* i. 193
Natures ethereal, human, angel, *m. E.M.* i. 238
As full, as perfect, in vile *M.* that mourns *E.M.* i. 277
The proper study of Mankind is *M. E.M.* ii. 2
A mortal *M.* unfold all Nature's law *E.M.* ii. 32
M., but for that, no action could attend *E.M.* ii. 61
But what composes *M.*, can *M.* destroy *E.M.* ii. 114

MAN (continued).

As *M.*, perhaps, the moment of his breath *E.M.* ii. 133
The last, scarce ripen'd into perfect *M. E.M.* ii. 141
'Tis thus the Mercury of *M.* is fix'd *E.M.* ii. 177
In *M.* they join in some mysterious use *E.M.* ii. 206
Virtuous and vicious ev'ry *M.* must be *E.M.* ii. 231
'Tis this, Tho' *M.*'s a fool, yet GOD IS WISE *E.M.* ii. 294
Made Beast in aid of *M.*, and *M.* of Beast *E.M.* iii. 24
While *M.* exclaims, "See all things for my use!" (*rep.*) *E.M.* iii. 45
Be *M.* the Wit and Tyrant of the whole *E.M.* iii. 50
M. cares for all; to birds, he gives his woods *E.M.* iii. 57
Than favour'd *M.* by touch ethereal slain *E.M.* iii. 68
To *M.* imparts it; but with such a view *E.M.* iii. 224
In this 'tis God directs, in that 'tis *M. E.M.* iii. 98
And creature link'd to creature, *m.* to *m. E.M.* iii. 114
Not *M.* alone, but all that roam the wood *E.M.* iii. 119
Unloo the bond of all things, and of *M. E.M.* iii. 150
M. walk'd with beast, joint tenant of the shade *E.M.* iii. 152
Ah! how unlike the *m.* of times to come *E.M.* iii. 161
And turn'd on *M.* a fiercer savage, *M. E.M.* iii. 168
Thus then to *M.* the voice of Nature spake *E.M.* iii. 171
Whom they rever'd as God, the mourn as *M. E.M.* iii. 224
M., like his Maker, saw that all was right *E.M.* iii. 232
That was but love of God, and this of *M. E.M.* iii. 240
Beast, *M.*, or Angel, Servant, Lord, or King *E.M.* iii. 302
M., like a gen'rous vine, supported lives *E.M.* iii. 311
Remember, *M.*, "the Universal Cause *E.M.* iv. 35
Short, and but rare, till *M.* improv'd it all *E.M.* iv. 116
The good *m.* may be weak, be indolent *E.M.* iv. 155
Why is not *M.* a God, and Earth a Heav'n *E.M.* iv. 162
Weak, foolish *m.!* will Heav'n reward us there *E.M.* iv. 173
The Boy and *M.* an individual makes *E.M.* iv. 175
Worth makes the *m.*, the want of it the fellow *E.M.* iv. 203
Like Socrates, that *M.* is great indeed *E.M.* iv. 236
An honest *M.*'s the noblest work of God *E.M.* iv. 248
Say, wouldst thou be the *M.* to whom they fall *E.M.* iv. 276
And all that rais'd the Hero, sunk the *M. E.M.* iv. 294
Know then this truth (enough for *M.* to know *E.M.* iv. 310
Never elated, while one *m.*'s oppress'd *E.M.* iv. 323
All end, in LOVE OF GOD, AND LOVE OF *M. E.M.* iv. 340
He sees, why Nature plants in *M.* alone *E.M.* iv. 345
The Great *m.* never offer'd you a groat *E.S.* i. 26
If any ask you, "Who's the *M.* so near *E.S.* i. 45
If Blount despatch'd himself, he play'd the *m. E.S.* i. 123
In Soldier, Churchman, Patriot, *M.* in Pow'r *E.S.* i. 161
You hurt a *m.* that's rising in the Trade *E.S.* i. 35
Strike? why the *m.* was hang'd ten years ago *E.S.* ii. 55
Strange spleen to S—k! Do I wrong the *M. E.S.* ii. 60
But does the Court a worthy *M.* remove *E.S.* ii. 74
To find an honest *m.* I beat about *E.S.* ii. 102
Knew one a *M.* of Honour, one a Knave *E.S.* ii. 153
Unless, good *m.!* he has been fairly in *E.S.* ii. 192
Because the insult's not on *M.*, but God *E.S.* ii. 196
And mine as *M.*, who feel for all mankind *E.S.* ii. 204
And write next winter more *Essays on M. E.S.* ii. 255
Such this *M.* was; who now from earth remov'd *Ep.* v. 11
May truly say, Here lies an honest *M. Ep.* x. 2
In Wit, a *M.*; Simplicity, a Child *Ep.* xi. 2
A wise *m.* always is or should *I.H.* i. 35
'Twas not a *M.*, it was a Mouse *I.H.* i. 57
Here no *m.* prates of idle things *I.H.* ii. 141
A *m.* of Merit, or a Miser *I.H.* ii. 148
I am not now, alas! the *m. I.H.* iii. 3
Yes, you despise the *m.* to Books confin'd *M.E.* i. 1
Shall only *M.* be taken in the gross *M.E.* i. 17
It may be Reason, but it is not *M. M.E.* i. 26
See the same *m.*, in vigour, in the gout *M.E.* i. 71
In *M.*, the judgment shoots at flying game *M.E.* i. 96
Not always actions shew the *m.*; we find *M.E.* i. 109
But grant that Actions best discover *m. M.E.* i. 119
Alas! in truth the *m.* but chang'd his mind *M.E.* i. 127
An angel Tongue, which no *m.* can persuade *M.E.* i. 199
In this one Passion *m.* can strength enjoy *M.E.* i. 222
Here Fannia, leaning on her own good *m. M.E.* ii. 9
But he's a bolder *m.* who dares be well *M.E.* ii. 130
To draw the *m.* who loves his God, or King *M.E.* ii. 196
Its last best work, but forms a softer *M. M.E.* ii. 272
That *M.* was made the standing jest of Heav'n *M.E.* iii. 4
That "ev'ry *m.* in want is knave or fool." *M.E.* iii. 102
Alas! they fear a *m.* will cost a plum *M.E.* iii. 122
Extremes in *M.* concur to gen'ral use *M.E.* iii. 162
Thrice happy *m.!* enabled to pursue *M.E.* iii. 275
This *m.* possest—five hundred pounds a year *M.E.* iii. 280
A plain good *m.*, and Balaam was his name *M.E.* iii. 342
Behold Sir Balaam, now a *m.* of spirit *M.E.* iii. 375
M. is a very Worm by birth *Mi.* iv. 5
PRUDINA likes a *M.*, and laughs at Show *Mi.* ix. 104
Happy the *m.* whose wish and care *O.* iv. 1
A brave *m.* struggling in the storms of fate *P.C.* 21
Her last good *m.* dejected Rome ador'd *P.C.* 35
Then from the Mint walks forth the *M.* of rhyme *P.S.* 13
I wish'd the *m.* a dinner, and sat still *P.S.* 152
Should such a *m.*, too fond to rule alone *P.S.* 197
Who but must laugh, if such a *m.* there be *P.S.* 213
That tends to make one worthy *m.* my foe *P.S.* 284
A lash like mine, no honest *m.* shall dread *P.S.* 303
Sappho can tell you how this *m.* was bit *P.S.* 369
The good *m.* walk'd innoxious thro' his age *P.S.* 395
Beware of all, but most beware of *M. R.L.* i. 114
And she who scorns a *m.*, must die a maid *R.L.* v. 28
And all the *m.* is one intestine war *S.* i. 72
And no *m.* wonders he's not stung by Pug *S.* i. 88
Alas! young *m.!* your days can ne'er be long *S.* i. 101
A *m.* was hang'd for very honest rhymes *S.* i. 146
How dar'st thou let one worthy *m.* be poor *S.* ii. 118
And, as I love, would imitate the *M. S.* ii. 132
The Rhymes or Rattles of the *M.* or Boy *S.* iii. 18
That *M.* divine whom wisdom calls her own *S.* iii. 180
Th' unbalanc'd Mind, and snatch the *M.* away *S.* iv. 25
A *M.* of wealth, is dubb'd a *M.* of worth *S.* iv. 81
The *M.* that loves and laughs must sure do well *S.* iv. 129
All rhyme, and scrawl, and scribble, to a *m. S.* v. 188
The good *m.* heaps up nothing but mere metre *S.* v. 198
Of little use the *M.* you may suppose *S.* v. 201
To know the Poet from the *M.* of rhymes *S.* v. 341
This put the *m.* in such a desp'rate mind *S.* vi. 37
The *M.*, who, stretch'd in Isis' calm retreat *S.* vi. 116
In all but this, of sober life *S.* vi. 188
The wisest *m.* might blush, I must agree *S.* vi. 228
M.! and *for ever?* wretch what would'st thou have *S.* vi. 252
A *m.* so poor would live without a place *S.* vi. 287
One, one *m.* only breeds my just offence *S.* vii. 45
Extremely fine, but what no *m.* will wear *S.* vii. 124
"Then, happy *M.* who shows the Tombs!" said I *S.* viii. 102
Silence or hurt, he libels the great *M. S.* viii. 159
Each *m.* an Askapart, of strength to toss *S.* viii. 276
For God is pay'd when *M.* receives *U.P.* 19
Or think thee Lord alone of *M. U.P.* 23
A mighty hunter, and his prey was *m. W.F.* 62
But see the *m.* who spacious regions gave *W.F.* 79
And learn of *m.* each other to undo *W.F.* 124
Happy the *m.* whom this bright court approves *W.F.* 235
As m.'s *Maeanders* to the vital spring *D.* iii. 55
When *M.* whole frame is obvious to a Flea *D.* iv. 238
Make God *M.* Image, Man the final Cause *D.* iv. 478
'Tis hers, the brave *m.* latest steps to trace *E.* i. 299
And wisely curb'd proud *m.* pretending wit *E.C.* 53
M. erring judgment, and misguide the mind *E.C.* 202
A constant Critic at the great *m.* board *E.C.* 416
Then shall *M.* pride and dulness comprehend *E.M.* i. 65
Mark how it mounts to *M.* imperial race *E.M.* i. 209
Of show'rs and sunshine, as of *M.* desires *E.M.* i. 152
Alas what wonder! *M.* superior part *E.M.* ii. 39
Till one *m.* weakness grows the strength of all *E.M.* ii. 252
A longer care *M.* helpless kind demands *E.M.* iii. 131
And *M.* prerogative to rule, but spare *E.M.* iii. 160
To one *m.* pow'r, ambition, lucre, lust *E.M.* iii. 270
To *M.* low passions, or their glorious ends *E.M.* iv. 376
There died my Father, no *m.* debtor *I.H.* i. 79
Experience, this; by *M.* oppression curst *M.E.* ii. 213
And when by *M.* audacious labour won *M.E.* iii. 11
And the Critic's, Briton's, Old *M.* Friend *Mi.* ii. 24
A *m.* true merit 'tis not hard to find (*rep.*) *P.S.* 175
To one *m.* treat, but for another's ball *R.L.* i. 96
Fair tresses *m.* imperial race insnare *R.L.* ii. 27
The wise *m.* passion and the vain *m.* toast *R.L.* v. 30
The courtier's promises, and sick *m.* pray'rs *R.L.* v. 119
Unplac'd, unpension'd, no *m.* heir or slave *S.* i. 116
Men *bearded, bald, cowl'd, uncowl'd, shod, unshod, D.* iii. 114

MAN OF ROSS—MANNER.

Grubstreet! thy fall should *m.* and Gods conspire *D.* iii. 311
For thee explain a thing till all *m.* doubt it *D.* iv. 251
O! would the Sons of *M.* once think their Eyes *D.* iv. 453
Sure to hate most the *m.* from whom they learn'd *E.C.* 107
As *m.* of breeding, sometimes *m.* of wit *E.C.* 259
And value books, as women *m.*, for dress *E.C.* 306
For fools admire, but *m.* of sense approve *E.C.* 391
Nor praise nor blame the writings, but the *m.* *E.C.* 413
When we but praise ourselves in other *m.* *E.C.* 455
The owner's wife, that other *m.* enjoy *E.C.* 501
M. must be taught, as if you taught them not *E.C.* 574
From brutes what *m.*, from *m.* what spirits know *E.M.* i. 79
M. would be Angels, Angels would be Gods *E.M.* i. 126
Aspiring to be Angels, *M.* rebel *E.M.* i. 128
As *M.* for ever temp'rate, calm and wise *E.M.* i. 154
And sev'ral *M.* impels to sev'ral ends *E.M.* ii. 166
For Nature knew no right divine in *M.* *E.M.* ii. 236
Great Nature spoke; observant *M.* obey'd *E.M.* iii. 199
If then to all *M.* Happiness was meant *E.M.* iv. 65
Fortune in *M.* has some small diff'rence made *E.M.* iv. 195
M. in their loose unguarded hours they take *E.M.* iv. 227
Did not the Sneer of more impartial *m.* *E.S.* i. 59
You make *m.* desp'rate if they once are bad *E.S.* ii. 59
Each widow asks it for *the Best of M.* *E.S.* ii. 108
M. not afraid to God, afraid of me *E.S.* ii. 209
Cheese such as *m.* in Suffolk make *I.H.* ii. 167
For God's sake, come, and live with *M.* (rep.) *I.H.* ii. 176
The Moon was up and *M.* a-bed *I.H.* ii. 194
M. may be read as well as Books, too much *M.E.* i. 10
True, some are open, and to all *m.* known *M.E.* i. 51
But grant, in Public *M.* sometimes are shown *M.E.* ii. 199
In *M.*, we various Ruling Passions find *M.E.* ii. 207
M., some to Bus'ness, some to Pleasure take *M.E.* ii. 215
M., some to Quiet, some to Public Strife *M.E.* ii. 217
Then careful Heav'n supply'd two sorts of *M.* *M.E.* iii. 53
Yet to be just to these poor *m.* of pelf *M.E.* iii. 107
And diff'rent *m.* directs to diff'rent ends *M.E.* iii. 160
And *m.* and dogs shall drink him till they burst *M.E.* iii. 178
Statues of *M.*, scarce less alive than they *M.E.* v. 10
And *m.* grew heroes at the sound *O.* i. 43
And *m.*, once ignorant, are slaves *O.* ii. 28
From these the world will judge of *m.* and books *P.S.* 145
In tasks so bold can little *m.* engage *R.L.* i. 11
Tho' Honour is the word with *M.* below *R.L.* i. 78
And monuments, like *m.*, submit to fate *R.L.* iii. 172
M. prove with child, as pow'rful fancy works *R.L.* iv. 53
M., monkeys, lap-dogs, parrots perish all *R.L.* iv. 120
That *m.* may say, when we the froot-box grace *R.L.* v. 17
Abuse the City's best good *m.* in metre *S.* i. 39
Brand the bold front of shameless guilty *m.* *S.* i. 106
Laws are explain'd by *M.*—so have a care *S.* i. 144
Preach as I please, I doubt our curious *m.* *S.* ii. 17
Perhaps, young *m.!* our fathers had no nose *S.* ii. 92
And *m.* must walk at least before they dance *S.* iii. 54
To make *m.* happy and to keep them so *S.* iii. 2
There all *M.* may be cur'd, whene'er they please *S.* iv. 59
Yet surely, surely, these were famous *m.* *S.* v. 79
He ne'er rebels, nor plots, like other *m.* *S.* v. 194
You lose your patience, just like other *m.* *S.* v. 363
The *m.*, who write such Verse as we can read *S.* vi. 158
It gives *m.* happiness, or leaves them ease *S.* vi. 183
M. only feel the Smart, but not the Vice *S.* vi. 217
Heathcote himself, and such large-acred *m.* *S.* vi. 240
As *m.* from Jails to execution go *S.* viii. 273
From *m.* their cities and from Gods their fanes *W.F.* 66
A hundred other Men's *affairs* *I.H.* ii. 69 s
Ask *m.* opinioes; Scoto now shall tell *M.E.* i. 158
Weighs the *M.* wits against the Lady's hair *R.L.* v. 72

Man of Ross.

Din'd with the *M.*, or my LORD MAY'R *E.S.* ii. 99
Rise, honest Muse! and sing the *M.* *M.E.* iii. 250
"The *M.*," each lisping babe replies *M.E.* iii. 262
The *M.* divides the weekly bread *M.E.* iii. 264
Is any sick? the *M.* relieves *M.E.* iii. 269

Manager.

An artful *M.* that crept between *E.S.* i. 21

Mandevil.

Morgan and *M.* could prate no more *D.* ii. 414

Mangle.

How should I fret to *m.* ev'ry line *E.S.* ii. 4

Mangles.

But as coarse iron, sharpen'd, *m.* more *S.* viii. 118

Manilio.

As many more *M.* forc'd to yield *R.L.* iii. 51

Manilius.

M. or Solinus shall supply *D.* iv. 226

Mankind.

Forsake *m.*, and all the world—but love *A.* 88
Or praise the Court, or magnify *M.* *D.* i. 23
O! ever gracious to perplex'd *m.* *D.* i. 173
My life gave ampler lessons to *m.* *D.* i. 192
And hears the various vows of fond *m.* *D.* ii. 87
Bid her be all that makes *m.* adore *E.* iii. 53
And fill the gen'ral chorus of *m.* *E.C.* 188
Still make themselves the measure of *m.* *E.C.* 453
Or turns young Ammon loose to scourge *m.* *E.M.* i. 160
Is not to act or think beyond *m.* *E.M.* i. 190
The proper study of *M.* is Man *E.M.* ii. 2
The joy, the peace, the glory of *M.* *E.M.* ii. 248
And hence let Reason, late, instruct *M.* *E.M.* iii. 180
Converse and Love *m.* might strongly draw *E.M.* iii. 207
And all of God that bless *M.* or mend *M.* *E.M.* iii. 310
This bids to serve, and that to shun *m.* *E.M.* iv. 20
Who most to shun or hate *M.* pretend *E.M.* iv. 49
Heav'n to *m.* impartial we confess *E.M.* iv. 53
Or God and Nature meant to mere *M.* *E.M.* iv. 78
Or make an enemy of all *m.* *E.M.* iv. 222
Is hung on high to poison half *m.* *E.M.* iv. 252
The wisest, brightest, meanest of *m.* *E.M.* iv. 282
He does not think me what he thinks *m.* *E.S.* i. 34
And mine as Man, who feel for all *m.* *E.S.* ii. 204
Thus shall *m.* his guardian care engage *M.* 55
At half *m.* when gen'rous Manly raves *M.E.* i. 57
A Fool, with more of Wit than half *m.* *M.E.* i. 200
So Philomedé lect'ring all *m.* *M.E.* ii. 83
To make *m.* in conscious virtue bold *P.C.* 3
Rejects *m.*, is by some Sylph embrac'd *R.L.* i. 68
This Nymph, to the destruction of *m.* *R.L.* i. 19
To friends, to fortune, to *m.* a shame *S.* ii. 107
Prepares a dreadful jest for all *m.* *S.* ii. 124
While you, great Patron of *M.!* sustain *S.* v. 1
Th' unwilling Gratitude of base *m.* *S.* v. 14
Sometimes the Folly benefits *M.* *S.* v. 191
Of all *m.*, the creatures most absurd *S.* v. 359
Against the foe, himself, and all *m.* *S.* vi. 39
In vain bad Rhymers all *m.* reject *S.* vi. 153
And all *m.* might that just Mean observe *S.* vii. 119
Unbounded Thames shall flow for all *m.* *W.F.* 398
But all *M.'s concern is Charity E.M.* iii. 308

Manly.

At half mankind when gen'rous *M.* raves *M.E.* i. 57
One on his m. confidence relies D. ii. 169
That, if he pleas'd, he pleas'd by *m.* ways *P.S.* 337
Puts forth one *m.* leg, to sight reveal'd *R.L.* iii. 57
But this bold Lord with *m.* strength endu'd *R.L.* v. 79

Manner.

"Yours, Cowper's *m.*"—and "yours, Talbot's sense" *S.* vi. 134
A second see, by meeker m.—s known D. iii. 143
How like in *m.*, and how like in mind *D.* iii. 180
With softest *m.*, gentlest Arts adorn'd *E.* i. 4
The *m.*, passions, unities; what not *E.C.* 276
(As most in *m.*) by a love to parts *E.C.* 288
With *m.* gen'rous as his noble blood *E.C.* 726
And catch the *M.* living as they rise *E.M.* i. 14
M. with Candour are to *Benson* giv'n *E.S.* ii. 72
Of softest *m.*, unaffected mind *Ep.* vii. 7
Of *M.* gentle, of Affections mild *Ep.* xi. 1
All *M.* take a tincture from our own *M.E.* i. 33
M. with Fortunes, Humours turn with Climes *M.E.* i. 172
Things change their titles as our *m.* turn *M.E.* iii. 379
(In polish'd verse) the *M.* and the Mind *S.* v. 393

Manor.

"The *M.*, Sir?"—"The *M.*! hold," he cry'd *M.E.*i.260
And drown his Lands and M—s in a Soupe *D.* iv. 596

Mansion.
To grace the *m.* of our earthly Gods *W.F.* 230

Manteau.
Not Cynthia when her *m.*'s pinn'd awry *R.L.* iv. 8

Mantle.
His sea-green *m.* waving with the wind *W.F.* 350

Mantling.
And the brain dances to the *m.* howl *S.* ii. 8

Mantua.
As next in place to *M.*, next in fame *E.C.* 708

Mantuan.
Ye *M.* nymphs, your sacred succour bring *A.* 5
And let your comment be the *M.* Muse *E.C.* 129

Manures.
Ploughs, burns, *m.* and toils from sun to sun *S.* vi. 271

Manuscripts.
Rare monkish *M.* for Hearne alone *M.E.* iv. 9

Many.—*Passim.*
The rest his *m.-colour'd* robe conceal'd *R.L.* iii. 58
The People are a *m.-headed* Beast *S.* iii. 121
The *m.* Monster of the Pit *S.* v. 305

Marble.
Then view this *M.*, and be vain no more *E.* iii. 54
O'er the pale *m.* they shall join their heads *E.A.* 349
Altars grew *m.* then, and reek'd with gore *E.M.* iii. 264
This weeping *m.* had not ask'd thy Tear *Ep.* xiv. 5
Under this *M.*, or under this Sill *Ep.* xvi. 1
Then shall thy Form the *M.* grace *I.H.* iii. 19
Will never mark the *m.* with his Name *M.E.* iii. 286
A hundred footsteps scrape the *m.* Hall *M.E.* iv. 152
Some bury'd *m.* half preserves a name *M.E.* v. 16
But of what *m.* must that breast be form'd *Mi.* ix. 75
What more than *m.* must that heart compose *Mi.* ix. 87
The silver Thames reflects its *m.* face *S.* iii. 142
Then *M.*, soften'd into life, grew warm *S.* v. 147
E'er swell'd on *m.*; as in verse have shin'd *S.* v. 392
Paint, *M.*, Gems, and robes of Persian dyes *S.* vi. 265
Nor polish'd *m.* emulate thy face *U.L.* 60
Here o'er the martyr-king the *m.* weeps *W.F.* 313
Here thy well-study'd m—s fix our eye *E.* iii. 33
This modest Stone, what few vain *M.* can *Ep.* x. 1

Marcellus.
And more true joy *M.* exil'd feels *E.M.* iv. 257

March.
The long majestic *M.*, and Energy divine *S.* v. 269
Tir'd with a tedious *m.*, one luckless night *S.* vi. 35
They m., to prate their hour before the Fair *S.* viii. 249

March'd.
Who prouder *m.*, with magistrates in state *D.* ii. 423
There *m.* the bard and blockhead, side by side *D.*iv.101
Before them *m.* that awful Aristarch *D.* iv. 203
And *m.* a victor from the verdant field *R.L.* iii. 52

Marches.
He *m.* off his Grace's Secretary *D.* ii. 220

Marchmont.
And the bright flame was shot thro' *M.'s* Soul *Mi.* x. 12

Marcus.
M. with blushes owns he loves *O.* iii. 7

Mares.
Gave the gilt Coach and dappled Flanders *M. E.* iv. 50

Marg'ret.
To lull the sons of *M.* and Clare-hall *D.* iv. 200

Margin.
On thy *M.* Lovers wander *Mi.* vii. 27
Thus on Mæander's flow'ry *m.* lies *R.L.* v. 65

Maria.
But nobler scenes *M.'s* dreams unfold *M.E.* iii. 129

Mark.
Obliquely waddling to the *m.* in view *D.* i. 172
Matter too soft a lasting *m.* to bear *M.E.* ii. 3
How little, m.! that portion of the ball *D.* iii. 83
M. first that youth who takes the foremost place *D.* iii. 139
Jacob, the scourge of Grammar, *m.* with awe *D.* iii. 149
There, dim in clouds, the poring Scholiasts *m. D.* iii. 191
And *m.* that point where sense and dulness meet *E.C.* 51
M. how it mounts to Man's imperial race *E.M.* i. 209
M. what unvary'd laws preserve each state *E.M.* iii. 189
M. how they grace Lord Umbra, or Sir Billy *E.M.* iv. 278
M. by what wretched steps their glory grows *E.M.* iv. 291
It hurries all too fast to *m.* their way *M.E.* i. 38
The few that glare, each character must *m. M.E.* i. 121
Can *m.* the figures on an Indian chest *M.E.* ii. 168
But *m.* the fate of a whole Sex of Queens *M.E.* ii. 219
Will never *m.* the marble with his Name *M.E.* iii. 286
For, *m.* th' advantage; just so many more *S.* iv. 77
M. where a bold expressive phrase appears *S.* vi. 165

Mark'd.
Thee too, my Paridel! she *m.* thee there *D.* iv. 341
M. out for Honours, honour'd from their Birth *D.*iv.507
That each may fill the circle *m.* by Heav'n *E.M.* i. 86
Not so his Son; he *m.* this oversight *M.E.* iii. 197
Tho' *m.* by none but quick, poetic eyes *R.L.* v. 123

Market-place.
Behold the *M.* with poor o'erspread *M.E.* iii. 263

Marks.
In each she *m.* her Image full exprest *D.* i. 107
The feast, his tow'ring genius *m. Mi.* xii. 9
Where the gilt Chariot never *m.* the way *R.L.* iv. 155
Now *m.* the course of rolling orbs on high *W.F.* 245

Maro.
When first young *M.* in his boundless mind *E.C.* 130
Just so immortal *M.* held his head *P.S.* 122
Or wait inspiring Dreams at *M.'s* Urn *E.* iii. 28

Marquis.
With Staff and Pumps the *M.* lead the Race *D.* iv. 586

Marriage.
M. may all those petty Tyrants chase *E.* iv. 37
How oft, when press'd to *m.*, I have said *E.A.* 73

Marries.
He *m.*, bows at Court, and grows polite *M.E.* iii. 386

Marrying.
Nor *m.* Discord in a noble wife *P.S.* 393

Mars.
See on the Tooth-pick, *M.* and Cupid strive *Mi.* ix. 31
'Gainst Pallas, *M.*; Latona, Hermes arms *R.L.* v. 47
And Jove's own Thunders follow *M.'s* Drums *D.* iv. 68

Marseille.
Why drew *M.'s* good bishop purer breath *E.M.* iv. 107

Martial.
See Alaric's stern port! the *m.* frame *D.* iii. 81
See Sidney bleeds amid the *m.* strife *E.M.* iv. 101
Thy *M.* spirit, or thy Social love *Ep.* ix. 8
How *m.* music ev'ry bosom warms *O.* i. 37
How many M—s were in Pult'ney lost *D.* iv. 170

Martin.
And children sacred held a *M.'s* nest *S.* ii. 38

Martyr.—*See also* Book of Martyrs.
Where mix'd with Slaves the groaning *M.* toil'd *M.E.* v. 6
For matrimonial solace dies a *m. S.* iii. 151
The Hero William, and the *M.* Charles *S.* v. 386
I pass o'er all those Confessors and M—s *S.* vii. 35
Here o'er the m.-king the marble weeps *W.F.* 313

Martyr'd.
Rack'd with Sciatics, *m.* with the Stone *S.* iv. 54

Martyrdom.
And 'scape the *m.* of jakes and fire *D.* i. 144

Mary-Bone.
Some DUKES at *M.* bowl Time away *Mi.* ix. 100

Mask.
And not a *M.* went unimprov'd away *E.C.* 541

Masque.
With Sappho fragrant at an ev'ning *M. M.E.* ii. 26

Masquerade.
Forget her pray'rs or miss a *m. R.L.* ii. 108
In courtly balls, and midnight m—s R.L. i. 72

Mass.
Call forth each *m.*, a Poem or a Play *D.* i. 58
Soon to that *m.* of Nonsense to return *D.* i. 241
Or blend in beauteous tints the colour'd *m. E.* iii. 5
Would go to *M.* in jest (as story says) *S.* viii. 16

Mast.
Amid the circle, on the gilded *m. R.L.* ii. 69

Master.
Stole from the *M.* of the sev'nfold Face *D.* i. 244
Unlucky Welsted! thy unfeeling *m. D.* ii. 209
Should at my feet the world's great *m.* fall *E.A.* 85
And hence one *M.* PASSION in the breast *E.M.* ii. 131
A *m.*, or a servant, or a friend *E.M.* ii. 250
Oh *m.* of the poet, and the song *E.M.* iv. 374
A Fav'rite's Porter with his *M.* vie *E.S.* i. 117
The Scene, the *M.*, op'ning to my view *E.S.* ii. 68
The *M.* of our Passions, and his own *E S.* ii. 89
KNELLER, by Heav'n, and not a *M.* taught *Ep.* viii.
And like its *M.*, very low *I.H.* i. 78
And what comes then is *m.* of the field *M.E.* i. 44
The Club must hail him *m.* of the joke *M.E.* i. 185
Who but must laugh, the *M.* when he sees *M.E.* iv. 107
Strong as the Footman, as the *M.* sweet *Mi.* ix. 106
Now high, now low, now *m.* up, now miss *P.S.* 323
Sworn to no *M.*, of no Sect am I *S.* iii. 24
Some bright Idea of the m.'s mind E.C. 485
The sturdy Squire to Gothic m—s *stoop D.* iv. 595
Prescribe, apply, and call their *m.* fools *E.C.* 111
Let *Us* be fix'd, and our own *m.* still *S.* ii. 180
And what a m.-hand *alone can reach E.C.* 145
And South beheld that *M.-piece* of Man *D.* iv. 174
Nature's chief *M.* is writing well *E.C.* 724

Mastiff.
While the gaunt *m.* growling at the gate *M.E.* iii. 195

Mat.
In the worst inn's worst room, with *m.* half-hung *M.E.* iii. 299

Matadore.
First Ariel perch'd upon a *M. R.L.* iii. 33
Now move to war her sable M—s *R.L.* iii. 47

Match.
M. Raphael's grace with thy lov'd Guido's air *E.* i. 36
How *m.* the bards whom none e'er matched before *S.* vi. 115

Match'd.
How match the bards whom none e'er *m.* before *S.* vi. 115
Dear Cibber! never *m.* one ode of thine *S.* vi. 138

Matchless.
A *m.* youth! his nod these worlds controls *D.* iii. 255
Style the divine, the *m.*, what you will *S.* v. 70
If Windsor-shades delight the *m.* maid *Sp.* 67
M. his pen, victorious was his lance *W.F.* 293

Mate.
And to complete her bliss, a Fool for *M. E.* iv. 52
Turn them from Wits; and look on Simo's *M. M.E.* ii. 101
Softly seeks her silent *M. Mi.* vii. 30

Material.
Too mad for mere *m.* chains to bind *D.* iv. 32

Mathematics.
See *Mystery* to *M.* fly *D.* iv. 647

Mathers.
Behold this *Equipage*, by *M.* wrought *Mi.* ix. 29

Mathesis.
Mad *M.* alone was unconfin'd *D.* iv. 31

Matin.
I waste the *M.* lamp in sighs for thee *E.A.* 267

Matrimonial.
For *m.* solace dies a martyr *S.* iii. 151

Matron.
Shame to the virgin, to the *m.* pride *E.M.* ii. 242
Faith, let the modest M—s *of the town F.J.S.* 49
Chaste *m.* praise her, and grave Bishops bless *E.S.* i. 146
Like Citron-waters m—s' *cheeks inflame R.L.* iv. 69

Matter.
Congenial *m.* in the Cockle-kind *D.* iv. 448
Or bind in *M.*, or diffuse in Space *D.* iv. 476
What *m.*, soon or late, or here or there *E.M.* i. 74
All *m.* quick, and bursting into birth *E.M.* i. 234
See *M.* next, with various life endu'd *E.M.* iii. 13
Like bubbles on the sea of *M.* born *E.M.* iii. 19
The *m.'s* weighty, pray consider twice *E.S.* ii. 43
To set this *m.* full before ye *I.H.* i. 81
No *m.* where the money's found *I.H.* ii. 40
M. too soft a lasting mark to bear *M.E.* ii. 3
Thy Sylvans groan—no *m.*—for the Fleet *M.E.* iii. 210
Explain'd the *m.*, and would win the cause *Mi.* xi. 6
Then, learned Sir! (to cut the *m.* short) *S.* i. 91
Avidien, or his Wife (no *m.* which *S.* ii. 49
Its name I know not, and it's no great *m. S.* vi. 45
The heart resolves this *m.* in a trice *S.* vi. 216
You only make the *m.* worse and worse *S.* viii. 121

Mature.
The Harvest early, but *m.* the praise *S.* v. 24

Matures.
M. my present, and shall bound my last *S.* iii. 2
Time, that at last *m.* a clap to pox *S.* vii. 47

Maudlin.
A *m.* Poetess, a rhyming Peer *P.S.* 16
To hunt for truth in M.'s *learned grove S.* vi. 57

Maul.
Meek modern faith to murder, hack, and *m. D.* iii. 210
Of Honour, bind me not to *m.* his Tools *E.S.* ii. 147
M. the French Tyrant, or pull down the POPE *Mi.* ii. 18

Mawkish.
So sweetly *m.*, and so smoothly dull *D.* iii. 171

Maxims.
Thence form your judgment, thence your *m.* bring *E.C.* 126
Some gen'ral *m.*, or be right by chance *M.E.* i. 4
M. are drawn from Notions, these from Guess *M.E.* i. 14

May, Mayst.—*Passim.*
Sylvia's like autumn ripe, yet mild as *M. Sp.* 81
Where the tall m.-pole *once o'erlooked the Strand D.* ii. 28

May'r.
Appear'd Apollo's *M.* and Aldermen *D.* iv. 116
That makes three members, this can choose a *M. S.* iv. 106
Now M—s *and Shrieves all husk'd and satiate lay D.* i. 91
Great in her charms! as when on Shrieves and *M. D.* i. 263
Their full-fed Heroes, their pacific *M. D.* iii. 281

Maze.
Some are bewilder'd in the *m.* of schools *E.C.* 26
A mighty *m.*! but not without a plan *E.M.* i. 6
That not in Fancy's *m.* he wander'd long *P.S.* 340
The Sylphs thro' mystic m—s *guide their way R.L.* i. 92
And trace the *m.* of the circling hare *W.F.* 122
The bow'ry *m.*, and surrounding greens *W.F.* 262

Maz'd.
Whom with a wig so wild, and mien so *m. M.E.* iii. 63

Mazy.
Pleas'd with the madness of the *m.* dance *D.* i. 68
Or tread the *m.* round his follow'rs trod *E.M.* ii. 25
Some thrid the *m.* ringlets of her hair *R.L.* ii. 139

ME—MEDITATING.

Me.—*Passim.*
Disputes of *M.* or *Te*, of *aut* or at *D.* iv. 220
Asham'd of any Friend, not ev'n of *M. E.* ii. 15
Kind to my dress, my figure, not to *M. S.* iii. 176

Mead.
The lambs with wolves shall graze the verdant *m. M.* 77
And Books for *M.*, and Butterflies for Sloane *M. E.* iv. 10
I'll do what *M.* and Cheselden advise *S.* iii. 51
Where cooliog vapours breathe along the *m. W. F.* 136
In yellow m—s of Asphodel O. i. 75
Close by those *m.*, for ever crown'd with flow'rs *R. L.* i. 1
Or from those *m.* select unfading flow'rs *W.* 74

Meadows.
'Tis (no, 'tisn't) like Miss *M. Mi.* vi. 4

Meagre.
No *m.*, muse-rid mope, adust and thin *D.* ii. 37

Meal.
Be sure I give them Fragments, not a *M. D.* iv. 230
And makes her hearty *m.* upon a dunce *M. E.* ii. 86
Why Shylock wants a *m.*, the cause is found *M. E.* iii. 115
One solid dish his week-day *m.* affords *M. E.* iii. 345
Is he who makes his *m.* on others' wit *S.* vii. 30

Mean.
Blest Satirist! who touch'd the *M.* so true *Ep.* i. 7
And Angels guard him in the golden *M. M. E.* iii. 246
Like good Erasmus in an honest *M. S.* i. 66
Between Excess and Famine lies a *m.* ii. 33 *s*
And all mankind might that just *M.* observe *S.* vii. 119
T' observe a *m.*, be to himself a friend *W. F.* 251
And if the m—s be just, the conduct true E. C. 257
Passions, tho' selfish, if their *m.* be fair *E. M.* ii. 97
To find the *m.* proportioned to their end *M. E.* iii. 82
Grew by like *m.*, and join'd, thro' love or fear *E. M.* iii. 202
Who risk the most, that take wrong *m.*, or right *E. M.* iv. 86
Who noble ends by noble *m.* obtains *E. M.* iv. 233
I must by all *m.* come to town *I. H.* ii. 33 *s*
Were *m.* not ends; Ambition was the vice *M. E.* i. 215
Strange! by the *M.* defeated of the Ends *M. E.* ii. 143
Pow'r all their end, but Beauty all the *m. M. E.* ii. 220
If not, by any *m.* get Wealth and Place *S.* iii. 104
You'll bring a House (I m. of Peers) E. vi. 18
The poisoning Dame—You m.—I don't—You do *E. S.* ii. 23
Suppose I censure—you know what I *m. E. S.* ii. 32
I wonder what some people *m. I. H.* ii. 104 *s*
Who guides all those who know not what they *m. S.* iii. 144
You miss my aim, I *m.* the most acute *S.* viii. 70
"How elegant your Frenchmen?" "Mine, d'ye *m. S.* viii. 110
With *m.* complacence ne'er betray your trust *E. C.* 580
Ev'n *m.* Self-love becomes by force divine *M. E.* ii. 291
Let *Greatness* own her, and she's *m.* no more *E. S.* i. 144
And makes immortal, Verse as *m.* as mine *E. S.* ii. 247
Yet no *m.* motive this profusion draws *M. E.* iii. 205
Of mad Good-nature, and *m.* Self-love *M. E.* iii. 228
Thought wood'rous honest tho' of *m.* degree *Mi.* iii. 19
Bare the *m.* heart that lurks beneath a Star *S.* i. 108
These write to Lords, some *m.* reward to get *S.* vii. 25
Thou *m.* deserter of thy brother's blood *U. L.* 30
M. tho' I am, not wholly so *U. P.* 41

Meaner.
Awake, my St. John! leave all *m.* things *E. M.* i. 1
Each star of *m.* merit fades away *S.* v. 20

Meanest.
Nor past the *m.* unregarded, one *D.* iv. 575
Or deeming *m.* what we greatest call *E.* i. 19
The last, the *m.* of your sons inspire *E. C.* 196
The wisest, brightest, *m.* of mankind *E. M.* iv. 282
He dreads a death-bed like the *m.* slave *M. E.* i. 116
And what is Fame? the *M.* have their Day *S.* iv. 46

Meaning.
How random thoughts now *m.* chance to find *D.* i. 275
His Honour's *m.* Dulness thus exprest *D.* ii. 195
And those explain the *m.* quite away *E. C.* 117
Have full as oft no *m.*, or the same *E. M.* ii. 86

There needs but thinking right, and *m.* well *E. M.* iv. 32
Means not, but blunders round about a *m. P. S.* 186

Meanly.
If Music *m.* borrows aid from sense *D.* iv. 64
M. they seek the blessing to confine *E. C.* 398
Not *m.*, nor ambitiously pursu'd *M. E.* iii. 221

Means.
What *m.* this tumult in a Vestal's veins *E. A.* 4
M. not, but blunders round about a meaning *P. S.* 186
If to live well *m.* nothing but to eat *S.* iv. 111

Meant.
And some made coxcombs Nature *m.* but fools *E. C.* 27
Tho' *m.* each other's aid, like man and wife *E. C.* 83
If then to all Men Happiness was *m. E. M.* iv. 65
Or God and Nature *m.* to mere Mankind *E. M.* iv. 78
Then wisely plead, to me they *m.* no hurt *E. S.* ii. 144
And take it kindly *m.* to show *I. H.* ii. 61 *s*
That what we chanc'd, was what we *m.* to do *M. E.* i. 102
With tape-ty'd curtains, never *m.* to draw *M. E.* iii. 302

Meanwhile.
M. Opinion gilds with varying rays *E. M.* ii. 283
M., declining from the noon of day *R. L.* iii. 19

Mears, *see also* **Brown and Mears.**
M., Warner, Wilkins run: delusive thought *D.* ii. 125

Measure.
Sense, speech, and *m.*, living tongues and dead *D.* iii. 167
Still make themselves the *m.* of mankind *E. C.* 453
Whose *m.* full o'erflows on human race *M. E.* iii. 231
You drink by *m.*, and to minutes eat *M. E.* ii. 158
And keep the equal *m.* of the Soul *S.* vi. 205
Can they direct what m—s to pursue S. iii. 122
Go, m. earth, weigh air, and state the tides E. M. ii. 20
The scale to *m.* others' wants by thine *E. M.* ii. 292
While you to *m.* merits, look in Stowe *S.* v. 66

Measur'd.
His knowledge *m.* to his state and place *E. M.* i. 71

Meat.
Is to refund the Medals with the *m. D.* iv. 390
Critic'd your wine, and analys'd your *m. M. E.* ii. 81
M., Fire and Clothes. What more? *M.*, Clothes and Fire *M. E.* iii. 80
The pleasure lies in you, and not the *m. S.* ii. 16
He finds no relish in the sweetest *m. S.* ii. 32
As needy beggars sing at doors for *m. S.* vii. 26
Like a big wife at sight of loathsome *m. S.* viii. 156
Artists must choose his Pictures, Music, M—s M. E. iv. 6

Mechanic.
Thrust some *M.* Cause into his place *D.* iv. 475
Lord, Sir, a mere *M.!* strangely low *S.* viii. 108

Mechlin.
With eager beats his *M.* Cravat moves *Mi.* ix. 91

Medal.
The *M.*, faithful to its charge of fame *M. E.* v. 31
Is to refund the M—s with the meat D. iv. 390
In living *m.* see her wars enroll'd *M. E.* v. 55

Meddle.
I *m.*, Goddess! only in my sphere *D.* iv. 432

Medea.
An erst *M.* (cruel, so to save!) *D.* iv. 121
As one by one, at dread M.'s strain *D.* iv. 635

Mediation.
'Till earth's extremes your *m.* own *S.* v. 402

Med'cine.
Prescribes, attends, the *m.* makes and gives *M. E.* iii. 270

Meditate.
Read them by day, and *m.* by night *E. C.* 125

Meditates.
Resolv'd to win, be *m.* the way *R. L.* ii. 31
Couch'd close he lies, and *m.* the prey *W. F.* 102

Meditating.
In lofty madness *m.* song *D.* iii. 16

o

Meditation.
No more these scenes my *m.* aid *E.A.* 161
With *m. O.* iv. 16

Medium.
Will prove at least the *m.* must be clear *S.* i. 56
Hence Satire rose, that just the *m.* hit *S. v.* 261

Medleys.
Hence Journals, *M.*, Merc'ries, MAGAZINES *D.* i. 42

Meek.
M. modern faith to murder, hack, and maul *D.* iii. 210
The next a Tradesman, *m.*, and much a liar *M.E.* i. 152
No Ass so *m.*, no Ass so obstinate *M.E.* ii. 102

Meeker.
A second see, by *m.* manners known *D.* iii. 143
But the good Bishop, with a *m.* air *M.E.* iii. 105

Meet.
Maggots half-form'd in rhyme exactly *m. D.* i. 61
And mark that point where sense and dulness *m. E.C.* 51
In town, what objects could I *m. I.H.* i. 7
I'm stopp'd by all the Fools I *m. I.H.* ii. 111
Nor ardent warriors *m.* with hateful eyes *M.* 58
The steer and lion at one crib shall *m. M.* 79
Or chanc'd to *m.* a Minister that frown'd *M.E.* i. 165
Astride his cheese Sir Morgan we might *m. M.E.* iii. 61
His Quincunx darkens, his Espaliers *m. M.E.* iv. 80
Or see the stretching branches long to *m. M.E.* iv. 92
Their sev'ral graces in my SHARPER *m. Mi.* ix. 105
Now *m.* thy fate, incens'd Belinda cry'd *R.L.* v. 87
To run a muck, and tilt at all I *m. S.* i. 70
M., and rejoin me, in the pensive Grot *S.* vi. 209

Meeting.
The *m.* points the sacred hair dissever *R.L.* iii. 153

Meets.
Each monster *m.* his likeness in thy mind *D.* iii. 252
The needy Poet sticks to all he *m. D.* iii. 290
Ev'n thought *m.* thought, ere from the lips it part *E.A.* 95
Which *m.* contempt, or which compassion first *E.M.* iv. 88
Or *m.* his spouse's fonder eye *O.* iii. 31
And raise his mind above the mob he *m. S.* vi. 99

Megrim.
Pain at her side and *M.* at her head *R.L.* iv. 24

Melancholy.
And ever-musing *m.* reigns *E.A.* 3
Black *M.* sits, and round her throws *E.A.* 165
Or teach the *M.* Muse to mourn *E.S.* i. 79
And yet more *M.* Whores *I.H.* i. 10
M. smooth Mæander *Mi.* vii. 25
And sensible soft *M. Mi.* viii. 8
M. lifts her head *O.* i. 30
Be no unpleasing *M.* mine *P.S.* 407
Umbriel, a dusky, *m.* sprite *R.L.* iv. 13

Mellowing.
When *m.* years their full perfection give *E.C.* 490

Melodious.
When tuneful Hylas with *m.* moan *A.* 15

Melody.
M. resigns to Fate *Mi.* vii. 32

Melt.
The memory's soft figures *m.* away *E.C.* 39
And sweetly *m.* into just shade and light *E.C.* 489
Rocks fall to dust, and mountains *m.* away *M.* 106
And *m.* away *O.* i. 20
She said : the pitying audience *m.* in tears *R.L.* v.
I *m.* down Ancients like a heap of snow *S.* v. 65
For others' good, or *m.* at others' woe *U.L.* 46

Melted.
A shapeless shade, it *m.* from his sight *D.* ii. 111
All *m.* down, in Pension, or in Punk *D.* iv. 510
Was there a Chief but *m.* at the Sight *Mi.* ii. 7
In three seal-rings; which after, *m.* down *R.L.* v. 91
Has age but *m.* those rough parts away *S.* vi. 318

Melting.
Just when she learns to roll a *m.* eye *E.* v. 3

When awful Love seems *m.* in his Eyes *Mi.* ix. 90
What guards the purity of *m.* Maids *R.L.* i. 71
While *m.* music steals upon the sky *R.L.* ii. 49
Soft sorrows, *m.* griefs, and flowing tears *R.L.* iv. 85
The sleepy Eye, that spoke the *m.* soul *S.* v. 150
She said, and *m.* as in tears she lay *W.F.* 203

Melts.
And *m.* in visions of eternal day *E.A.* 222
Now burns with glory, and then *m.* with love *E.C.* 377
And *m.* to Goodness, need I SCARB'ROW name *E.S.* ii. 65
And sterner Cassius *m.* at Julia's eyes *O.* iii. 16
His heart now *m.*, now leaps, now burns *O.* iii. 35
Or City-heir in mortgage *m.* away *S.* vii. 89
Ev'n he, whose soul now *m.* in mournful lays *U.L.* 77

Member.
Heav'n breathes thro' ev'ry *m.* of the whole *E.M.* iv. 61
A worthy *m.*, no small fool, a Lord *S.* vi. 185
Nor absent they, no *m*—*s* of her state *D.* iv. 91
Or issue *M.* of an Annual feast *D.* iv. 574
That makes three *m.*, this can choose a May'r *S.* iv. 106

Memory, Mem'ry.
In pleasing *m.*, of all he stole *D.* i. 128
Now leave all *m.* of sense behind *D.* i. 276
We ply the *M.*, we load the brain *D.* iv. 157
Thy oaths I quit, thy *m.* resign *E.A.* 293
Thus in the soul while *m.* prevails *E.C.* 56
M'y and forecast just returns engage *E.M.* iii. 143
I lose all *M.* of my former Fears *Mi.* ix. 94
The *m.'s* soft figures melt away *E.C.* 39
Wits have short *M*—ies, and Dunces none *D.* iv. 620

Menander.
The art of Terence, and *M.'s* fire *A.* 8

Mend.
And rise to faults true Critics dare not *m. E.C.* 160
Not *m.* their minds; as some to Church repair *E.C.* 342
As, after stumbling, Jades will *m.* their pace *E.C.* 603
Nay show'd his faults—but when would Poets *m. E.C.* 621
Not free from faults, nor yet too vain to *m. E.C.* 744
Teach us to mourn our Nature, not to *m. E.M.* ii. 153
And all of God, that bless mankind or *m. E.M.* iii. 310
These you but anger, and you *m.* not those *E.S.* i. 54
M. fortune's fault, and justify her grace *E.M.* iii. 232
Who charm the sense, or *m.* the heart *O.* ii. 10
To raise the genius, and to *m.* the heart *P.C.* 2
This, be who loves me, and who ought to *m. S.* iii. 178

Mended.
And truths divine came *m.* from that tongue *E.A.* 66

Mends.
Or her that owns her faults, but never *m. M.E.* ii. 103

Mental.
Thy *m.* eye, for thou hast much to view *D.* iii. 62
The scale of sensual, *m.* pow'rs ascends *E.M.* i. 208

Mentions.
Who never *m.* Hell to ears polite *M.E.* iv. 150

Merchant.
The *m.* from th' Exchange returns in peace *R.L.* iii. 23
To either India see the *M.* fly *S.* iii. 69
The *m.'s* toil, the sage's indolence *E.M.* ii. 172

Mercury.
'Tis thus the *M.* of Man is fix'd *E.M.* ii. 277
Hence *Journals, Medleys*, M-'-ies, MAGAZINES *D.* i. 42

Mercy.
From her own Sex should *m.* find to-day *E.J.S.* 2
"*M.!*" cries Helluo, "*m.* on my soul !" *M.E.* i. 240
But show no *m.* to an empty line *S.* vi. 175
That *M.* I to others show (*rep.*) *U.P.* 39

Merdamante.
Nigrina black, and *M.* brown *D.* ii. 334

Mere.
Yet wrote and flounder'd on in *m.* despair *D.* i. 120
And to *m.* mortals seem'd a Priest in drink *D.* ii. 426
Too mad for *m.* material chains to bind *D.* iv. 3
Ancients in phrase, *m.* moderns in their sense *E.C.* 325
To serve *m.* engines to the ruling Mind *E.M.* i. 262

MERELY—MIGHT.

M. curious pleasure, or ingenious pain *E.M.* ii. 48
Taught half by Reason, half by *m.* decay *E.M.* ii. 259
And for those Arts *m.* Instinct could afford *E.M.* iii. 197
Or God and Nature meant to *m.* Mankind *E.M.* iv. 78
Who suffer thus, *m.* Charity should own *M.E.* iii. 111
Sporus, that *m.* white curd of ass's milk *P.S.* 306
The good man heaps up nothing but *m.* metre *S.* v. 198
M. wax as yet, you fashion him with ease *S.* vi. 9
But *m.* tuff-taffety what now remain'd *S.* viii. 42
Lord, Sir, a *m.* Mechanic! strangely low *S.* viii. 108
M. household trash! of birth-nights, balls, and shows *S.* viii. 130

Merely.
If *m.* to come in, Sir, they go out *E.S.* ii. 124

Merit.
The rest on Out-side *m.* but presume *D.* i. 135
No *m.* now the dear Nonjuror claims *D.* i. 253
Regardless of our *m.* or default *D.* iv. 486
Fondly we think we honour *m.* then *E.C.* 454
For rising *m.* will buoy up at last *E.C.* 461
Envy will *m.*, as its shade, pursue *E.C.* 466
Be thou the first true *m.* to befriend *E.C.* 474
And gladly praise the *m.* of a foe *E.C.* 638
And ev'ry author's *m.* but his own *E.C.* 728
Where only *M.* constant pay receives *E.M.* iv. 3¹3
For *M.* will by turns forsake them all *E.S.* i. 89
Due to his *M.*, and brave Thirst of praise *Ep.* viii. 6
Ends in the milder *M.* of the Heart *Ep.* xiv. 12
A man of *M.*, or a Miser *I.H.* ii. 148
Whose table, Wit, or modest *M.*, share *M.E.* iii. 241
Ascribes his gettings to his parts and *m. M.E.* iii. 376
A man's true *m.* 'tis not hard to find *P.S.* 175
Who can *your m. selfishly* approve *P.S.* 293
Charms strike the sight, but *m.* wins the soul *R.L.* v. 34
Each star of meaner *m.* fades away *S.* v. 20
So well in paint and stone they judg'd of *m. S.* v. 384
Thus we dispose of all poetic *m. S.* vi. 135
Indeed, could wealth bestow or wit or *m. S.* v. 226
Equal your m—s! *equal is your din D.* ii. 244
Like are their *m.*, like rewards they share *D.* ii. 183
While you to measure *m.*, look in Stowe *S.* v. 66
But you who seek to give and m. *fame E.C.* 46
Those best can bear reproof, who *m.* praise *E.C.* 583
The good must *m.* God's peculiar care *E.M.* iv. 135
That, Vice may *m.*, 'tis the price of toil *E.M.* iv. 151
Not but there are, who *m.* other palms *S.* v. 229
What sin of mine could *m.* such a rod *S.* viii. 63

Merlin.
Did ever Proteus, *M.*, any witch *S.* iii. 152
Extols old Bards, or M.'s *Prophecy S.* v. 132
When *M.* Cave is half unfurnish'd yet *S.* v. 355
Lord! how we strut thro' *M.* Cave, to see *S.* vi. 139

Merry.
But sense surviv'd, when *m.* jests were past *E.C.* 460
So these their *m.*, miserable Night *M.E.* ii. 240
Of mimic'd Statesmen, and their *m.* King *M.E.* iii. 310
And the sad burthen of some *m.* song *S.* i. 80

Mess.
This *m.*, toss'd up of Hockley-hole and White's *D.* i. 222
As pure a *m.* almost as it came in *E.S.* ii. 176

Messiah.
Thy realm for ever lasts, thy own *M.* reigns *M.* 108

Met.
And *m.* congenial, mingling flame with flame *E.* iii. 14
Thou know'st how guiltless first I *m.* thy flame *E.A.* 59
Of old, those *m.* rewards who could excel *E.C.* 510
All that disgrac'd my Betters, *m.* in me *P.S.* 120
He swears the Muses *m.* him at the Devil *S.* v. 42

Metal.
The *M.*, and the Workmanship, divine *Mi.* ix. 36
And yielding *M.* flow'd to human form *S.* v. 148
And latent M—s *innocently flow Mi.* v. 6

Metaphor.
One died in *m.* and one in song *R.L.* v. 60
She sees a Mob of M—s *advance D.* i. 67

Metaphysic.
And *M.* smokes involve the Pole *D.* iv. 248
Or set on *M.* ground to prance *D.* iv. 265

Physic of *M.* begs defence (*rep.*) *D.* iv. 645
The mind in M—s *at a loss D.* iv. 449

Meteor.
The *m.* drops, and in a flash expires *D.* iv. 634
Attracts each light gay *m.* of a Spark *M.E.* ii. 22
Or, m.-like, *flame lawless thro' the void E.M.* ii. 65

Methinks.
Together o'er the Alps *m.* we fly *E.* iii. 25
Alas, no more! *m.* we wand'ring go *E.A.* 241
In each low wind *m.* a Spirit calls *E.A.* 305
M. already I your tears survey *R.L.* iv. 107

Method.
And without *m.* talks us into sense *E.C.* 654
The justest rules, and clearest *m.* join'd *E.C.* 670
Are nameless graces which no m—s *teach E.C.* 144
And taught more pleasant *m.* of salvation *E.C.* 547

Methodiz'd.
Are Nature still, but Nature *m. E.C.* 89

Methought.
And quick to swallow me, *m.* I saw *S.* viii. 172

Metre.
And taught his Romans, in much better *m. E.S.* i. 9
Abuse the City's best good men in *m. S.* i. 39
The good man heaps up nothing but mere *m. S.* v. 198

Metropolitans.
Ten *M.* in preaching well *E.S.* i. 132

Mettle.
Shows most true *m.* when you check his course *E.C.* 87

Mexico's.
And other *M.* be roof'd with gold *W.F.* 412

Microscope.
The critic Eye, that *m.* of Wit *D.* iv. 233

Microsopic.
Why has not man a *m.* eye *E.M.* i. 193

Mid.
But lo! to dark encounter in *m.* air *D.* iii. 265
Shall list'ning in *m.* air suspend their wings *W.* 54
So from the m.-most *the nutation spreads D.* ii. 409

Midas.
Our *M.* sits Lord Chancellor of Plays *D.* iii. 324
The Queen of *M.* slept, and so may I *P.S.* 82
'Tis sung, when M.' *Ears began to spring* (*rep* *P.S.* 69

Middle.
Full in the *m.* way there stood a lake *D.* ii. 69
And *M.* natures, how they long to join *E.M.* i. 22
Plac'd on this isthmus of a *m.* state *E.M.* ii. 3
He knows to live, who keeps the *m.* state *S.* ii. 61

Middleton.
As, tho' the Pride of *M.* and Bland *E.S.* i. 75

Midnight.
In courtly balls, and *m.* masquerades *R.L.* i. 72
To *m.* dances, and the public show *U.L.* 58

Midst.
Full in the *m.* of Euclid dip at once *D.* iv. 263
High in the *m.*, upon his urn reclin'd *W.F.* 349

Mien.
Smit with his *m.* the Mud-nymphs suck'd him in *D.* ii. 332
The first came forwards with as easy *m. D.* iv. 279
He ceas'd and wept. With innocence of *m. D.* iv. 419
Vice is a monster of so frightful *m. E.M.* ii. 217
Whom with a wig so wild, and *m.* so mad'd *M.E.* iii. 63
My Lord advances with majestic *m. M.E.* iv. 127
Spite of his haughty *m.* and barb'rous pride *R.L.* iii. 72
There Affectation, with a sickly *m. R.L.* iv. 31

Might.—*Passim.*
With all the *m.* of gravitation blest *D.* ii. 318
Thus at her felt approach, and secret *m. D.* iv. 639

o 2

Mightier.

A *m.* Pow'r the strong direction sends *E.M.* ii. 165
To Pow'r unseen, and *m.* far than they *E.M.* iii. 252
Arraign no *m.* Thief than wretched *Wild E.S.* ii. 39
A *m.* grief my heavy heart sustains *Mi.* ix. 10
Their Country's wealth our *m.* Misers drain *S.* iii. 126

Mighty.

The *M.* Mother, and her Son, who brings *D.* i. 1
Here pleas'd behold her *m.* wings outspread *D.* i. 27
And all the *m.* Mad in Dennis rage *D.* i. 106
The North by myriads pours her *m.* sons *D.* iii. 89
Not with less glory *m.* Dulness crowd'd *D.* iii. 135
Signs following signs lead on the *m.* year *D.* iii. 321
Thy *m.* Scholiast, whose unweary'd pains *D.* iv. 211
And MAKE ONE *M.* DUNCIAD OF THE LAND *D.* iv. 604
Nations unborn your *m.* names shall sound *E.C.* 193
And fills up all the *m.* Void of sense *E.C.* 210
The *m.* Stagirite first left the shore *E.C.* 645
A *m.* maze ! but not without a plan *E.M.* i. 6
Where small and great, where weak and *m.*, made *E.M.* iii. 297
But let me add, Sir ROBERT'S *m.* dull *E.S.* ii. 133
Be *m.* ready to do good *I.H.* i. 36
Can I retrench ? Yes, *m.* well *I.H.* i. 75
And cry'd " I vow you're *m.* neat *I.H.* ii. 174
I'm quite asham'd—'tis *m.* rude *I.H.* ii. 206
The *m.* blessing, " while we live, to live " *M.E.* ii. 90
And *m.* Dukes pack Cards for half-a-crown *M.E.* ii. 142
Smit with the *m.* pleasure to be seen *M.E.* iv. 128
Thou unconcern'd canst hear the *m.* crack *P.S.* 86
What *m.* contests rise from trivial things *R.L.* i. 2
And in soft bosoms dwells such *m.* Rage *R.L.* i. 12
And *m.* hearts are held in slender chains *R.L.* ii. 24
Ev'n the *m.* Pam, that Kings and Queens o'erthrew *R.L.* iii. 61
Nay, half in heav'n—except (what's *m.* odd) *S.* iii. 187
Ambition humbled, *m.* Cities storm'd *S.* v. 11
By learned Critics, of the *m.* Dead *S.* v. 138
Who to disturb their betters *m.* proud *S.* v. 307
While *m.* WILLIAM'S thund'ring arm prevail'd *S.* vi. 63
A *m.* hunter, and his prey was man *W.F.* 62
There *m.* Nations shall inquire their doom *W.F.* 381

Milbourn.

And *M.* chief, deputed by the rest *D.* ii. 349
New Blackmores and new M—s must arise *E.C.* 463

Mild.

To the *m.* Limbo of our Father Tate *D.* i. 238
And all who since, in *m.* benighted days *D.* iii. 53
From Impudence, or Stupefaction *m.* *D.* iv. 530
The Vapour *m.* o'er each Committee crept *D.* iv. 615
And *m.* as op'ning gleams of promis'd heav'n *E.A.* 256
Enter each *m.*, each amicable guest *E.A.* 301
To failings *m.*, but zealous for desert *E.C.* 731
I shun his Zenith, court his *m.* Decline *E.S.* ii. 76
Of Manners gentle, of Affections *m.* *Ep.* xi. 1
Narcissa's nature, tolerably *m.* *M.E.* ii. 53
All *m.* ascends the Moon's more sober light *M.E.* ii. 254
M. Arcadians, ever blooming *Mi.* vii. 5
The *m.* and gen'rous breast *O.* iii. 12
As winter fruits grow mild ere they decay *S.* vi. 319
The Sun's *m.* lustre warms the vital air *Sp.* 74
Sylvia's like autumn ripe, yet *m.* as May *Sp.* 81

Milder.

Ends in the *m.* Merit of the Heart *Ep.* xiv. 12
From furious Sappho scarce a *m.* fate *S.* i. 83
But soon the sun with *m.* rays descends *Su.* 89
When *m.* autumn summer's heat succeeds *W.F.* 97

Mile.

But Ho—y for a period of a *m.* *S.* viii. 73
Or water all the Quorum ten *m*—s round *M.E.* iii. 54

Militia.

The light *M.* of the lower sky *R.L.* i. 42

Milk.

Whose herds with *m.*, whose fields with bread *O.* iv. 5
Sporus, that mere white curd of Ass's *m.* *P.S.* 306
If then plain bread and *m.* will do the feat *S.* ii. 15
A *m.*-white *bull shall at your altars stand Sp.* 47
Their early fruit, and *m.* turtles bring *Su.* 52

Milky.

As when the long-ear'd *m.* mothers wait *D.* ii. 247
Far as the solar walk, or *m.* way *E.M.* i. 102
The *m.* heifer and deserving steed *M.E.* iv. 186
And chalky Wey, that rolls a *m.* wave *W.F.* 344

Mill.

The giddy motion of the whirling *M. R.L.* ii. 134
The berries crackle, and the *m.* turns round *R.L.* iii. 106
If ev'ry wheel of that unweary'd *M. S.* vi. 78

Millions.

From dreams of *m.*, and three groats to pay *D.* ii. 252
M. and *M.* on these banks he views *D.* iii. 31
See thronging *m.* to the Pagod run *E.S.* i. 157
To just three *m.* stinted modest Gage *M.E.* ii. 128
When, after *m.* slain, yourself shall die *R.L.* v. 146

Milo-like.

And *M.* surveys his arms and hands *D.* ii. 384

Milton.

Tho' daring *M.* sits sublime *I.H.* iv. 5
For Locke or *M.* 'tis in vain to look *M.E.* iv. 139
Our Wives read *M.*, and our Daughters plays *S.* v. 172
A *Newton's genius, or a* M.'s *flame D.* iii. 216
M. on this, on that one Johnston's name *D.* iv. 112
Made Horace dull, and humbled *M.* strains *D.* iv. 212
Preserv'd in *M.* or in *Shakespear's* name *P.S.* 168
M. strong pinion now not Heav'n can bound *S.* v. 99
Yours *M.* genius, and mine Homer's spirit *S.* vi. 136
The Pindars and the M—s of a Curl *D.* iii. 164

Mimic.

Or from the canvas call the *m.* face *E.* iii. 6
Less Wit than *M.*, more a Wit than wise *M.E.* ii. 48
Ungrateful wretch, with *m.* airs grown pert *Mi.* ix. 65
And but so *m.* ancient Wits at best *E.C.* 331

Mimic'd.

Of *m.* Statesmen, and their merry King *M.E.* iii. 310

Mince.

But murder first, and *m.* them all to bits *D.* iv. 120

Mincing.

With *m.* step, small voice, and languid eye *D.* iv. 46

Mind.

Ye pow'rs, what pleasing frenzy sooths my *m. A.* 51
She rul'd, in native Anarchy, the *m. D.* i. 16
Still spread a healing mist before the *m. D.* i. 174
Shall, first recall'd, rush forward to thy *m. D.* iii. 64
How like in manners, and how like in *m. D.* iii. 180
Each monster meets his likeness in thy *m. D.* iii. 252
We hang one jingling padlock on the *m. D.* iv. 162
We bring to one dead level ev'ry *m. D.* iv. 268
The *m.* in Metaphysics at a loss *D.* iv. 449
Some emanation of th' all-beauteous *M. E.A.* 62
Eternal sunshine of the spotless *m. E.A.* 209
Most have the seeds of judgment in their *m. E.C.* 20
When first young Maro in his boundless *m. E.C.* 130
Man's erring judgment, and misguide his *m. E.C.* 202
While from the bounded level of our *m. E.C.* 221
Where nature moves, and rapture warms the *m. E.C.* 236
That gives us back the image of our *m. E.C.* 300
Some valuing those of their own side or *m. E.C.* 452
Some bright Idea of the master's *m. E.C.* 485
Tho' wit and art conspire to move your *m. E.C.* 531
As that the body, this enslav'd the *m. E.C.* 688
Lo the poor Indian ! whose untutor'd *m. E.M.* i. 99
Pours fierce Ambition in a Cæsar's *m. E.M.* i. 159
That never passion discompos'd the *m. E.M.* i. 168
To serve mere engines to the ruling *M. E.M.* i. 262
The great directing *M.* of ALL ordains *E.M.* i. 266
In doubt his *M.* or Body to prefer *E.M.* ii. 9
Describe or fix one movement of his *M. E.M.* ii. 36
But strength of *m.* is Exercise, not Rest *E.M.* ii. 104
Make and maintain the balance of the *m. E.M.* ii. 120
The whole employ of body and of *m. E.M.* ii. 142
As the *m.* opens, and its functions spread *E.M.* ii. 142
And in one interest body acts with *m. E.M.* ii. 180
Envy, to which th' ignoble *m.*'s a slave *E.M.* ii. 191
What shall divide ? The God within the *m. E.M.* ii. 204
And build on wants, and on defects of *m. E.M.* ii. 247
Its only thinking thing this turn of *m. E.M.* iii. 78
'Twas then the studious head or gen'rous *m. E.M.* iii. 283

As toys and empires, for a god-like *m.* *E.M.* iv. 180
Oh fool! to think God hates the worthy *m.* *E.M.* iv. 189
It pours the bliss that fills up all the *m.* *E.M.* iv. 344
Self-love but serves the virtuous *m.* to wake *E.M.* iv. 363
Wide and more wide, th' o'erflowings of the *m.* *E.M.* iv. 369
Mine, as a Friend to ev'ry worthy *m.* *E.S.* ii. 203
A pleasing Form, a firm yet cautious *M.* *Ep.* ii. 1
So unaffected, so compos'd a *m.* *Ep.* vi. 7
Of softest manners, unaffected *m.* *Ep.* vii. 7
Here, Withers, rest! thou bravest, gentlest *m.* *Ep.*ix.1
Put my Lord Bolingbroke in *m.* *I.H.* ii. 75 s
Grant but as many sorts of *M.* as Moss *M.E.* i. 18
Tho' strong the bent, and quick the turns of *m.* *M.E.* i. 64
Alas! in truth the man but chang'd his *m.* *M.E.* i. 127
'Tis Education forms the common *m.* *M.E.* i. 149
Say, what can cause such impotence of *m.* *M.E.* ii. 93
But what are these to Great Atossa's *m.* *M.E.* ii. 115
Th' exactest traits of Body or of *M.* *M.E.* ii. 191
And surely, Heav'n and I are of a *m.* *M.E.* iii. 8
Till Kings call forth th' Ideas of your *m.* *M.E.* iv. 195
Was there a gen'rous, a reflecting *m.* *Mi.* ii. 5
In health of body, peace of *m.* *O.* iv. 11
But each man's secret standard in his *m.* *P.S.* 176
Her lively looks a sprightly *m.* disclose *R.L.* ii. 9
He watch'd th' Ideas rising in her *m.* *R.L.* iii. 142
What mov'd my *m.* with youthful Lords to roam *R.L.* iv. 159
Nor think, to die dejects my lofty *m.* *R.L.* v. 99
On morning wings how active springs the *M.* *S.* ii. 81
Who think that Fortune cannot change her *m.* *S.* ii. 123
His equal *m.* I copy what I can *S.* ii. 131
Is half so incoherent as my *M.* *S.* iii. 166
Th' unbalanc'd *M.*, and snatch the Man away *S.* v. 25
And rarely Av'rice taints the tuneful *m.* *S.* v. 192
(In polish'd verse) the Manners and the *M.* *S.* v. 393
This put the man in such a desp'rate *m.* *S.* vi. 37
He stuck to poverty with peace of *m.* *S.* vi. 65
And raise his *m.* above the mob he meets *S.* vi. 99
I learn to smooth and harmonize my *M.* *S.* vi. 203
My *m.* resumes the thread it dropt before *S.* vi. 207
Two of a face, as soon as of a *m.* *S.* vi. 269
And count each birth-day with a grateful *m.* *S.* vi. 315
The M.'s disease, its Ruling Passion came E.M. ii.138
The case is easier in the *M.* disease *S.* iii. 58
Not mend their m—s: *as some to Church repair E.C.* 342
But if in noble *m.* some dregs remain *E.C.* 526
Quick whirls, and shifting eddies of our *m.* *M.E.* i. 24
By Music, *m.* an equal temper know *O.* i. 22
Soft yielding *m.* to Water glide away *R.L.* i. 61
Flight of Cashiers or Mobs, he'll never m. *S.* v. 195

Mindful.
Much to the *m.* Queen thence recalls *D.* i. 95
For Sylphs, yet *m.* of their ancient race *R.L.* iii. 35

Mine.—*Passim.*
For me, the *m.* a thousand treasures brings *E.M.* i. 137
Or deep with diamonds in the flaming *m.* *E.M.* iv. 10
And eye the *M.* without a wish for Gold *Mi.* x. 8
And ripens Spirits, as he ripens M—s *M.E.* ii. 290
Damn'd to the *M.*, an equal fate betides *M.E.* iii. 109
And one fate buries in th' Asturian *M.* *M.E.* iii. 132
What *m.*, to swell that boundless mine *M.E.* iii. 278
All Townshend's Turnips, and all Grosvenor's *m.* *S.* vi. 273

Min'ral.
Where ling'ring drops from *m.* Roofs distill *Mi.* x. 3
With chymic art exalts the *m.* pow'rs *W.F.* 243

Mingled.
Pours into Thames: and hence the *m.* wave *D.* ii. 343
So, cast and *m.* with my very frame *E.M.* ii. 137
There *m.* farms and pyramids appear *S.* vi. 259

Mingles.
There St. John *m.* with my friendly bowl *S.* i. 127

Mingling.
And met congenial, *m.* flame with flame *E.* iii. 14

Minion.
Some greedy *m.*, or imperious wife *E.M.* iv. 302

Minister.
Hold—to the *M.* I more incline *D.* i. 213
Proceed,—a *M.*, but still a Man *E.* ii. 15
Sure, if I spare the *M.*, no rules *E.S.* ii. 146
Wise, if a *M.*; but, if a King *M.E.* i. 139
Or chanc'd to meet a *M.* that frown'd *M.E.* i. 165
His very *M.* who spy'd them first *P.S.* 71
Sometimes to call a *m.* my friend *P.S.* 266
But touch me, and no *M.* so sore *S.* i. 76
Compar'd to this, a *M.*'s an Ass *S.* iii. 96
Or choose at least some *M.* of Grace *S.* v. 378
A subtle *M.* may make of that *S.* viii. 133
Stood just-a-tilt, the *M.* came by *S.* viii. 175
Born for First M—s *as Slaves for Kings D.* iv. 602
Who know how like Whig *M.* to Tory *E.S.* i. 106
Still better, *M.*; or, if the thing *E.S.* ii. 50
Great *M.* ne'er think of these *I.H.* ii. 38 s
So long by watchful *M.* withstood *M.E.* iii. 136
I'd never name Queens, *M.*, or Kings *P.S.* 76

Ministerial.
These may some gentle *m.* Wing *E.S.* i. 95

Ministers.
And *m.* to Jove with purest hands *D.* ii. 94

Minor.
And Major, *M.*, and Conclusion quick *D.* ii. 242
When the brisk *M.* pants for twenty-one *S.* iii. 38

Mint.
Then from the *M.* walks forth the Man of rhyme *P.S.* 13
I wag'd no war with *Bedlam* or the *M.* *P.S.* 156
In durance, exile, Bedlam, or the *M.* *S.* ii. 99

Minus.
But Tully has it, *Nunquam m. solus* *S.* viii. 91

Minute.
Catch ere she change, the Cynthia of this *m.* *M.E.* ii. 20
Between each drop it gives, stays half a *m.* *S.* viii. 127
You drink by measure, and by m—s *eat M.E.* iv. 158

Mira.
And these be sung till Granville's *M.* die *E.* iii. 76
Then fill'd the groves, as heav'nly *M.* now *W.F.* 298

Miracle.
Great standing *mA* that Heav'n assign'd *E.M.* iii. 77
The board with specious m—s *he loads D.* iv. 553

Mirror.
For Wit's false *m.* held up Nature's light *E.M.* iv. 393
Oft in the clear, still *M.* of Retreat *E.S.* ii. 78
Shines a broad *M.* thro' the shadowy Cave *Mi.* x. 2
In the clear *M.* of thy ruling Star *R.L.* i. 108
Lead me to the crystal M—s *Mi.* vii. 19

Mirth.
Gods, imps, and monsters, music, rage and *m.* *D.* iii. 238
The broadest *m.* unfeeling Folly wears *E.M.* iv. 319
Of *M.* and Opium, Ratafie and Tears *M.E.* ii. 110
And thousands more in equal *m.* maintain *R.L.* iv. 66

Misapply.
Who reads, but with a lust to *m.* *P.S.* 301

Miscall.
Suppress them, or *m.* them Policy *M.E.* i. 124

Miscellanies.
Hence *M.* spring, the weekly boast *D.* i. 39
Like twinkling stars the *M.* o'er *S.* v. 110

Mischief.
Blunt truths more *m.* than nice falsehoods do *E.C.* 573
Deep hid the shining *m.* under ground *M.E.* iii. 10
In search of *m.* still on Earth to roam *R.L.* i. 64
But when to *m.* mortals bend their will *R.L.* iii. 125
Yet, Sir, reflect, the *m.* is not great *S.* v. 189

Miscreant.
Obscene with filth, the *m.* lies bewray'd *D.* ii. 75

Miser.
A man of Merit, or a *M.* *I.H.* ii. 148
'Tis strange the *M.* should his Cares employ *M.E.* iv. 1
At some sick m.'s *triple-bolted gate D.* ii. 248
No silver saints by dying m—s *giv'n E.A.* 137
M. are Muck-worms, Silk-worms Beaus *Mi.* iv. 23
Their Country's wealth our mightier *M.* drain *S.* iii. 126

Miserable.
So these their merry, *m.* Night *M.E.* ii. 240

Misery.
And desp'rate *M.* lays hold on Dover *S.* iv. 57
But past the Sense of human M—ies *E.S.* i. 101

Misfortune.
Some dire *m.* follows close behind *E.A.* 34

Misguide.
Man's erring judgment, and *m.* his mind *E.C.* 202

Mislead.
To tire our patience, than *m.* our sense *E.C.* 4

Miss.
That Edward's *M.* thus perks it in your face *E.J.S.* 46
Now high, now low, now master up, now *m. P.S.* 324
The bad must m. ; the good, untaught, will find *E.M.* iv. 330
Forget her pray'rs, or *m.* a masquerade *R.L.* ii. 108
You *m.* my aim ; I mean the most acute *S.* viii. 70

Miss'd.
The Pleasure *m.* her, and the Scandal hit *M.E.* ii. 128

Mis-shap'd.
Some figures monstrous and *m.* appear *E.C.* 171

Mist.
To Dulness Ridpath is as dear as *M. D.* i. 208
Still spread a healing *m.* before the mind *D.* i. 174
Spread like a low-born *m.*, and blot the Sun *M.E.*iii.138
Thy choicer m—s on this assembly shed *D.* iv. 357
All-seeing in thy *m.*, we want no guide *D.* iv. 469
As things seem large which we thro' *m.* descry *E.C.* 392
Or suck the *m.* in grosser air below *R.L.* ii. 83
Strange phantoms rising as the *m.* arise *R.L.* iv. 40

Mistake.
Will needs *m.* an author into vice *E.C.* 557
'Tis to *m.* them, costs the time and pain *E.M.* ii. 216
Yet, in this search, the wisest may *m. M.E.* i. 210
M. him not ; he envies, not admires *S.* v. 133
M., confound, object at all he spoke *S.* viii. 117

Mistaken.
And bids them make *m.* mortals groan *E.A.* 83
Bold in the practice of *m.* rules *E.C.* 110
Unhappy Wit, like most *m.* things *E.C.* 494
Yet am I not the first *m.* maid *R.L.* iv. 151

Mistakes.
But quite *m.* the scaffold for the pile *M.E.* i. 221
Pity *m.* for some poor tradesman craz'd *M.E.* iii. 64
And then for mine obligiogly *m. P.S.* 279

Mr. Dean.
And, *M.*, one word from you *I.H.* ii. 82 s
You, *M.*, frequent the great *I.H.* ii. 113 s

Mistook.
And then *m.* reverse of wrong for right *M.E.* iii. 198

Mistress.
Lo ! Rome herself, proud *m.* now no more *D.* iii. 101
M. ! dismiss that rabble from your throne *D.* iv. 209
Ah think not, *M.!* more true Dulness lies *D.* iv. 239
His heart, his *m.* and his friend did share *E.* iv. 9
No, make me *m.* to the man I love *E.A.* 88
More fond than *m.*, make me that to thee *E.A.* 90
Who could not win the *m.*, woo'd the maid *E.C.* 105
A Muse by these is like a *m.* us'd *E.C.* 432
To charm the *M.*, or to fix the Friend *I.H.* iii. 14
Behold ! if Fortune or a *M.* frowns *M.E.* i. 103
A teeming *M.*, but a barren Bride *M.E.* ii. 72
And *M.* of herself, tho' China fall *M.E.* ii. 268
A painted *m.*, or a purling stream *P.S.* 150
To please a *M.* one aspers'd his life *P.S.* 376
Leap'd up, and wak'd his *m.* with his tongue *R.L.* i. 116
Then cheerful healths (your *M.* shall have place) *S.*ii.143
In one a *M.* drops, in one a Friend *S.* vi. 75
O my fair *m.* Truth I shall I quit thee *S.* viii. 200
And proud his M.' orders to perform *D.* iii. 263

Mite.
T' inspect a *m.*, not comprehend the heav'n *E.M.* i. 196
A common Soldier, but who clubb'd his *M. Mi.* ii. 8
And 'twere a sin to rob them of their *m. P.S.* 162

Mitre.
Such as on Hough's unsully'd *M.* shine *E.S.* ii. 240

Mitred.
Ev'n *m. Rochester* would nod the head *P.S.* 149

Mix.
M. in his look ; All eyes direct their rays *D.* ii. 7
And wait till 'tis no sin to *m.* with thine *E.A.* 176
And oft so *m.*, the diff'rence is too nice *E.M.* ii. 209
And with a Father's sorrows *m.* his own *Ep.* iii. 8
Then *m.* this dust with thine—O spotless Ghost *Ep.*xiii.5
M. with the World, and battle for the State *S.* iii. 28

Mix'd, Mixt.
M. the Owl's Ivy with the Poet's bays *D.* iii. 54
So *m.* our studies, and so join'd our name *E.* iii. 10
Where *m.* with God's, his lov'd Idea lies *E.A.* 12
Yet, *m.* and soften'd, in his work unite *E.M.* ii. 112
These *m.* with art, and to due bounds confin'd *E.M.* ii. 119
Strong grows the Virtue with his nature *m. E.M.* ii. 178
Is *m.* with Heroes, or with Kings thy dust *Ep.* xi. 10
Where *m.* with Slaves the groaning Martyr toil'd *M.E.* v. 6
Together m—t ; sweet recreation *O.* iv. 14

Mixture.
A motley *m.!* in long wigs, in bags *D.* ii. 21
An equal *M.* of good Humour *Mi.* viii. 7

Moan.
When tuneful Hylas with melodious *m. A.* 15
A *m.* so loud, that all the guild awake *D.* ii. 250
He makes his *m. O.* i. 103
Sullen m—s *O.* i. 60

Moats.
His court with nettles, *m.* with cresses stor'd *M.E.*iii.181

Mob.
She sees a *M.* of Metaphors advance *D.* i. 67
Go drench a Pickpocket, and join the *M. E.S.* ii. 41
Scribblers or Peers, alike are *M.* to me *S.* i. 140
The *M.* of Gentlemen who wrote with Ease *S.* v. 108
And raise his mind above the *m.* he meets *S.* vi. 99
One whom the *m.*, when next we find or make *S.* viii. 34
The *M.*'s applauses, or the gifts of Kings *S.* iv. 15
Flight of Cashiers, or M—s, he'll never mind *S.* v. 195
Ever the taste of *M.*, but now of Lords *S.* v. 311
With *m.*, and duns, and soldiers at their doors *S.* vi. 124

Mockery.
And bear about the *m.* of woe *U.L.* 57

Modes.
What wonder *m.* in Wit should take their turn *E.C.* 147
What *m.* of sight betwixt each wide extreme *E.M.* i. 111
M. of Self-love the Passions we may call *E.M.* ii. 93
For *M.* of Faith let graceless zealots fight *E.M.* iii. 305

Models.
We owe to *m.* of an humble kind *M.E.* ii. 192

Mod'rate.
Fix'd to one side, yet *m.* to the rest *Ep.* ii. 4

Moderation.
In *m.* placing all my glory *S.* i. 67
Back to my native *m.* slide *S.* iii. 33

Modern.
On Codrus' old, or Dunton's *m.* bed *D.* ii. 144
All nonsense thus, of old or *m.* date *D.* iii. 59
But where each Science lifts its *m.* type *D.* iii. 195
Meek *m.* faith to murder, hack, and maul *D.* iii. 210
So *m.* 'Pothecaries, taught the art *E.C.* 108
Short is the date, alas, of *m.* rhymes *E.C.* 476
These shelves admit not any *m.* book *M.E.* iv. 140
Dennis, who long had warr'd with *m. Hans Mi.* ii. 11
The *m.* language of corrupted Peers *S.* iii. 99
At ninety-nine, a *M.* and a Dunce *S.* v. 60
M—s, beware ! or if you must offend *E.C.* 163
Ancients in phrase, mere *m.* in their sense *E.C.* 325
The Ancients only, or the *M.* prize *E.C.* 395

Modest.
And *m.* as the maid that sips alone *D.* iii. 144
Her *m.* check shall warm a future age *E.* iii. 56

So *m*. plainness sets off sprightly wit *E.C.* 302
The *m*. fan was lifted up no more *E.C.* 542
Distrustful sense with *m*. caution speaks *E.C.* 626
Faith, let the *m*. Matrons of the town *E.J.S.* 49
Let *m*. FOSTER, if he will, excel *E.S.* i. 131
Of *m*. wisdom, and pacific truth *Ep.* vii. 2
This *m*. Stone, what few vain marbles can *Ep.* x. 1
If *m*. Youth, with cool Reflection crown'd *Ep.* xiv. 1
To just three millions stinted *m*. Gage *M.E.* iii. 128
Whose table, Wit, or *m*. Merit share *M.E.* iii. 241
But treat the Goddess like a *m*. fair *M.E.* iv. 51
Three things another's *m*. wishes bound *P.S.* 47
All these, my *m*. Satire bade *translate P.S.* 189
See, *M*. Cibber now has left the Stage *S*. iii. 6

Modestly.
King John in silence *m*. expires *D.* i. 252
M. bold, and humanly severe *E.C.* 636

Modesty.
Osborne, thro' perfect *m*. o'ercome *D.* ii. 189
Trace Science then, with *M*. thy guide *E.M.* ii. 43
Who prais'd my *M*. and smil'd *I.H.* i. 68
Serene in Virgin *M*. she shines *M.E.* ii. 255
Courage with Softness, *M*. with Pride *M.E.* ii. 278

Mohair.
Observes how much a Chintz exceeds *M*. *M.E.* ii. 170

Moist.
Nor yet, when *m*. Arcturus clouds the sky *W.F.* 119

Moisture.
So may kind rains their vital *m*. yield *W*. 15

Mole.
Learn of the *m*. to plough, the worm to weave *E.M.* iii. 176
The *M*. projected break the roaring Main *M.E.* iv. 200
And sullen *M*. that hides his diving flood *W.F.* 347
The *m*.'s dim curtain, and the lynx's beam *E.M.* i. 212
Huge m—s, whose shadow stretch'd from shore to shore *M.E.* v. 21

Molest.
Safe, where no Critics damn, no duns *m*. *D.* i. 295

Molière.
The Frippery of crucify'd *M*. *D.* i. 132
M.'s *old stubble in a moment flames D.* i. 254

Moment.
Molière's old stubble in a *m*. flames *D.* i. 254
Yet, yet a *m*., one dim Ray of Light *D.* iv. 1
Spreads his light wings, and in a *m*. flies *E.A.* 76
Canst thou forget what tears that *m*. fell *E.A.* 109
His time a *m*., and a point his space *E.M.* i. 72
As Man, perhaps, the *m*. of his breath *E.M.* ii. 133
Why now, this *m*., don't you see I steal *E.S.* i. 6
You lose it to the *m*. you detect *M.E.* i. 30
How many curs'd the *m*. they believ'd *Mi.* ix. 72
Think of that *m*., you who Prudence boast (rep.) *Mi.* ix. 97
The fair each *m*. rises in her charms *R.L.* i. 140
For, that sad *m*., when the Sylphs withdrew *R.L.* iv. 11
And from the *m*. we oblige the town *S*. v. 370
In that nice *m*., as another Lie *S*. viii. 174
In that blest *m*. from his oozy bed *W.F.* 329
Such in those m—s *as in all the past M.E.* i. 264
So slow th' unprofitable *m*. roll *S*. iii. 39

Momentary.
Sees *m*. monsters rise and fall *D.* i. 83
Wit shoots in vain its *m*. fires *D.* iv. 633

Momentilla.
And, *M*., let the watch be thine *R.L.* ii. 114

Momus.
You hold the word, from Jove to *M*. giv'n *M.E.* iii. 3

Monarch.
O! when shall rise a *M*. all our own *D.* i. 311
One god-like *M*. all that pride confounds *D.* iii. 75
"Enough! enough!" the raptur'd *M*. cries *D.* iii. 339
Proud to my list to add one *M*. more *D.* iv. 600
The fur that warms a *m*., warm'd a bear *E.M.* iii. 44
And these for ever, tho' a *M*. reign *E.M.* iii. 187
The friar hooded, and the *m*. crown'd *E.M.* iv 198

You'll find if once the *m*. acts the monk *E.M.* iv. 201
And just her wisest *m*. made a fool *M.E.* i. 94
How shall the Muse, from such a *M*., steal *S*. v. 5
A *M*.'s *half, and half a Harlot's slave D.* iv. 512
When love was all an easy *M*. care *E.C.* 536
A *M*. sword when mad Vain-glory draws *E.S.* ii. 229
At once the *M*. and the Muse's seats *W.F.* 2
Be crown'd as M—s, or as Gods ador'd E.M. iii. 198
And fled from *m*., ST. JOHN! dwells with thee *E.M.* iv. 18
I kept, like *Asian M*., from their sight *P.S.* 220
And of all *m*., only grasps the globe *R.L.* ii. 74
And get, by speaking truth of *m*. dead *S*. viii. 106
A woondrous Tree that sacred *M*. bears *Sp.* 86
Succeeding *m*. heard their subjects' cries *W.F.* 85
Draw *m*. chain'd, and Cressi's glorious field *W.F.* 305

Monarchy.
And cackling save the *M*. of Tories *D.* i. 212

Monde, *see* Beau.

Money.
No matter where the *m*.'s found *I.H.* ii. 40 s
"Your *m*., Sir;" "My *m*., Sir, what all *M.E.* i. 258
There, London's voice "Get *M*., *M*. still *S*. iii. 79

Mongrel.
Whate'er of *m*. no one class admits *D.* iv. 89

Monk.
You'll find if once the monarch acts the *m*. *E.M.* iv. 201
Dwell in a *M*., or light upon a King *E.S.* i. 139
The *M*.'s *humility, the hero's pride E.M.* ii. 173
How many stages thro' old M—s *she rid D.* iii. 52
And the *M*. finish'd what the Goths begun *E.C.* 692

Monkey.
Those *m*. tails that wag behind their head *S*. viii. 247
A decent priest, where m—s *were the gods D.* iii. 208
Men, *m*., lap-dogs, parrots perish all *R.L.* iv. 120
The *m*.-mimics rush discordant in *D.* ii. 236
Of him, whose chatt'ring shames the *m.-tribe D.* ii. 232

Monkish.
Rare *m*. Manuscripts for Hearne alone *M.E.* iv. 9

Monroe.
And laughs to think *M*. would take her down *D.* i. 30
Sure I should want *the care of ten* M—s *S*. vi. 70

Monsieur.
Whence hapless *M*. much complains at Paris *D.* ii. 135

Monster.
And lo! her bird (a *m*. of a fowl *D.* i. 289
Each *m*. meets his likeness in thy mind *D.* iii. 252
Vice is a *m*. of so frightful mien *E.M.* ii. 217
Had still this *M*. to subdue at last *S*. v. 18
Unless he praise some *M*. of a King *S*. v. 210
The many-headed *m*. of the Pit *S*. v. 305
A verier *m*., than on Afric's shore *S*. viii. 28
Escape in M—s, *and amaze the town D.* i. 38
Sees momentary *m*. rise and fall *D.* i. 83
Gods, imps, and *m*., music, rage, and mirth *D.* iii. 238
These *m*., Critics! with your darts engage *E.C.* 554
Draw forth the *m*. of th' abyss profound *E.M.* iii. 221
But chief in *Boys's* m.-breeding breast *D.* i. 108

Monstrous.
Some figures *m*. and mis-shap'd appear *E.C.* 171
No *m*. height, or breadth, or length appear *E.C.* 251
Why she and Sappho raise that *m*. sum *M.E.* iii. 121

Montaigne.
What made (say *M*. or more sage Charron!) *M.E.* i. 87
As downright SHIPPEN, or as old *M*. *S*, i. 52
And house with *M*. now, and now with Locke *S*. iii. 26

Montalto.
There mov'd *M*. with superior air *D.* iv. 105

Montausier.
And *M*. was only chang'd in name *E*. iv. 70

Months.
Whole years neglected, for some *m*. ador'd *E*. iv. 43
Hold out some *m*. 'twixt Sun and Fire *I.H.* i. 18

To spend six *m.* with Statesmen here *I.H.* ii. 32 *s*
And in four *m.* a batter'd Harridan *Mi.* iii. 24

Monthly.
Their annual trophies, and their *m.* wars *D.* iii. 282

Monument.
With thee on Raphael's *M.* I mourn *E.* iii. 27
And what? no *m.*, inscription, stone *M.E.* iii. 283
And m—s, *like men, submit to fate R.L.* iii. 172

Monumental.
And *m.* brass this record bears *D.* ii. 313

Moon.
The *M.* was up, and Men a-bed *I.H.* iv. 194
Now in the *M.* perhaps, now under ground *M.E.* i. 98
At night, would swear him dropt out of the *M. S.* viii. 33
The *m.*, serene in glory, mounts the sky *W.* 6
Grav'd on his urn appear'd the *m.*, that guides *W.F.* 333
All mild ascends the M.*'s more sober light M.E.* ii. 254
Some, less refin'd, beneath the *m.* pale light *R.L.* ii. 81
Tell how the m.*-beam trembling falls I.H.* ii. 189
The *m.-struck* prophet felt the madding hour *D.* iv. 12

Moonlight.
Of airy Elves by *m.* shadows seen *R.L.* i. 31
What beck'ning ghost, along the *m.* shade *U.L.* 1

Moors.
In show like leaders of the swarthy *M. R.L.* iii. 48

Moore.
A Wit it was, and call'd the phantom *M. D.* ii. 50
How much, egregious *M.*, are we *Mi.* iv. 1
Ah *M.!* thy Skill were well employ'd *Mi.* iv. 29
His butchers Henley? his free-masons *M. P.S.* 98
Has drunk with *Cibber,* nay has rhym'd for *M. P.S.* 373
Hear this, and spare his family, James *M. P.S.* 385

Mope.
No meagre, muse-rid *m.*, adust and thin *D.* ii. 37

Moral.
When *M.* Evidence shall quite decay *D.* iv. 461
In ev'ry scene some *m.* let it teach *E.* iv. 23
Account for *m.*, as for nat'ral things *E.M.* i. 162
The Faith and *M.*, Nature gave before *E.M.* iii. 286
What makes all physical or *m.* ill *E.M.* iv. 111
And are, besides, too *m.* for a Wit *E. S.* i. 4
His Anger *m.*, and his Wisdom gay *Ep.* i. 6
Go, and exalt thy *M.* to divine *Ep.* vii. 10
Nor pensive Cowley's *m.* lay *I.H.* iv. 8
Catius is ever *m.*, ever grave *M.E.* i. 77
M. Truth, and mystic Song *O.* ii. 12
His *M.* pleases, not his pointed wit *S.* v. 76
Learn then what M—s *Critics ought to show E.C.* 560
And knows where Faith, Law, *M.*, all began *E.M.* iv. 339
The *m.* blacken'd, when the writings 'scape *P.S.* 352
At home with *M.*, Arts, and Laws amend *S.* v. 4
And heals with *M.*, what it hurts with Wit *S.* v. 262

Morality.
M., by her false Guardians drawn *D.* iv. 27
And unawares *M.* expires *D.* iv. 650

Moraliz'd.
But stoop'd to Truth, and *m.* his song *P.S.* 341

Mordington.
And may descend to *M.* from STAIR *E.S.* ii. 239

Mors.—*Passim.*

Morgan.
M. and Mandevil could prate no more *D.* ii. 414

Morn.
Which Curl's Corinna chanc'd that *m.* to make *D.* ii. 70
Compute the *m.* and ev'ning to the day *E.M.* iv. 306
Swift fly the years, and rise th' expected *m. M.* 21
No more the rising Sun shall gild the *m. M.* 99
Sick of his civil Pride, from *M.* to Eve *M.E.* iv. 166
From *m.* to night, at Senate, Rolls, and Hall *S.* iv. 36
Fresh as the *m.*, and as the season fair *Sp.* 20
At *m.* the plains, at noon the shady grove *Sp.* 78
Nor plains at *m.*, nor groves at noon delight *Sp.* 80
There shall the *m.* her earliest tears bestow *U.L.* 65

Morning.
As *m.* pray'r and flagellation end *D.* ii. 270
Thick as the stars of night or *m.* dews *D.* iii. 32
See, where the *m.* gilds the palmy shore *D.* iii. 95
Some praise at *m.*, what they blame at night *E.C.* 430
So *m.* insects that in muck began *M.E.* ii. 27
A Knave this *m.*, and his Will a Cheat *M.E.* ii. 142
Ere to the main this *m.* sun descend *R.L.* i. 110
'Twas this the *m.* omens seem'd to tell *R.L.* iv. 161
On *m.* wings how active springs the Mind *S.* ii. 81
We wake next *m.* in a raging fit *S.* v. 179
And ev'ry plant that drinks the *m.* dew *Su.* 32
Nor *m.* odours from the flow'rs arise *W.* 46
A m.'s *pleasure, and at ev'ning torn E.* iv. 66
With store of pray'rs, for m—s, *nights and noons R.L.* iv. 29
The m.*-dream that hover'd o'er her head R.L.* i. 22
To *m.-walks,* and pray'rs three hours a day *E.* v. 14

Morpheus.
M. hov'ring o'er my Pillow *Mi.* vii. 23
M. rouses from his bed *O.* i. 31

Morris.—*See also* Besaleel.
Let all give way, and *M.* may be read *D.* iii. 168

Morrow.—*See* To-morrow.

Mortal.
Greater he looks, and more than *m.* stares *D.* ii. 329
What *m.* knows his pre-existent state *D.* iii. 48
Had reach'd the Work, the All that *m.* can *D.* iv. 173
What *M.* can resist the Yawn of Gods *D.* iv. 606
Breathes in our soul, informs our *m.* part *E.M.* i. 275
Or in the natal, or the *m.* hour *E.M.* i. 288
A *m.* man unfold all Nature's law *E.M.* ii. 32
Say, in what *m.* soil thou deign'st to grow *E.M.* iv. 8
Joins heav'n and earth, and *m.* and divine *E.M.* iv. 334
What they said, or may say, of the *m.* within *Ep.* xvi. 6
The closest *m.* ever known *I.H.* ii. 124 *s*
Quit, oh quit this *m.* frame *O.* v. 2
For spirits, freed from *m.* laws, with ease *R.L.* i. 69
Transparent forms, too fine for *m.* sight *R.L.* ii. 61
Steel could the works of *m.* pride confound *R.L.* iii. 175
Belinda burns with more than *m.* ire *R.L.* iv. 93
There kept my charms conceal'd from *m.* eye *R.L.* iv. 157
Like Gods they fight, nor dread a *m.* wound *R.L.* v. 44
With such a prize no *m.* must be blest *S.* i. 111
Each *m.* has his pleasure: none deny *S.* i. 45
To seem but *m.*, ev'n in sound divines *S.* ii. 80
Will any *m.* let himself alone *S.* iv. 55
Wonder of Kings! like whom, to *m.* eyes *S.* v. 29
Convicted of that *m.* crime, a hole *S.* viii. 243
Where Jove, subdu'd by *m.* Passion still *W.F.* 233
Or looks on heav'n with more than *m.* eyes *W.F.* 253
In eldest time, ere m—s *writ or read D.* i. 9
And to mere *m.* seem'd a Priest in drink *D.* ii. 426
Which Chalcis Gods, and *m.* call an Owl *D.* iv. 362
Let the strict life of graver *m.* be *E.* iv. 21
And bids them make mistaken *m.* groan *E.A.* 83
Are *m.* urg'd thro' sacred lust of praise *E.C.* 521
With the same trash mad *m.* wish for here *E.M.* iv. 174
Why pique all *m.*, yet affect a name *M.E.* ii. 61
Fairest of *m.*, thou distinguish'd care *R.L.* i. 27
This erring *m.* Levity may call *R.L.* i. 103
Oh thoughtless *m.!* ever blind to fate *R.L.* iii. 101
But when to mischief *m.* bend their will *R.L.* iii. 125

Mortality.
Yet take these Tears, *M.*'s relief *Ep.* vii. 17

Mortgage.
Or, in a *m.*, prove a Lawyer's share *S.* ii. 169
Or City-heir in *m.* melts away *S.* vii. 89

Mortifies.
Just as one Beauty *m.* another *S.* viii. 259

Mortify.
There still remains, to *m.* a Wit *S.* v. 304

Mortimer.
Nor fears to tell, that *M.* is he *E.* i. 40

Moses.
And Pan to *M.* lends his pagan horn *D.* iii. 110

Mosque.
The *m.* of Mahound, or some queer Pagod *S.* viii. 239

Moss.
May wander in a wilderness of *M. D.* iv. 450
Grant but as many sorts of Mind as *M. M.E.* i. 18
These m.-grown *domes with spiry turrets crown'd E.A.* 142

Mossy.
The *m.* fountains, and the silvan shades *M.* 3
The *m.* fountains, and the green retreats *Su.* 72

Most.—*Passim.*

Moths.
Nor time nor *m.* e'er spoil'd as much as they *E.C.* 113

Mother.
The Mighty *M.*, and her Son, who brings *D.* i. 1
Gross as her sire, and as her *m.* grave *D.* i. 14
This the Great *M.* dearer held than all *D.* i. 269
In homage to the *m.* of the sky *D.* iii. 132
The *M.* begg'd the blessing of a Rake *D.* iv. 286
Great Queen, and common *M.* of us all *D.* iv. 404
But hear a *M.*, when she recommends *D.* iv. 439
M. of Arrogance, and Source of Pride *D.* iv. 470
Ask of thy *m.* earth, why oaks are made *E.M.* i. 39
Nature its *m.*, Habit is its nurse *E.M.* ii. 145
Each *M.* asks it for her booby Son *E.S.* ii. 107
M. too fierce of dear Desires *I.H.* iii. 7
And Ireland, *m.* of sweet singers *Mt.* xii. 7
His father, *m.*, body, soul, and muse *P.S.* 381
That harmless *M.* thought no wife a whore *P.S.* 384
Bless'd with his father's front, his m.'s tongue *D.* ii. 416
Dropping with Infant's blood, and *M.* tears *D.* iv. 142
As some fond Virgin, whom her *m.* care *E.* v. 1
With lenient arts extend a *M.* breath *P.S.* 410
Then in a bodkin grac'd her *m.* hairs *R.L.* v. 95
Tho' faith, I fear, 'twill break his *m.* heart *S.* vi. 16
As when the *long-ear'd milky* m—*s wait D.* ii. 247
The *m.* nurse it and the sires defend *E.M.* iii. 126

Mother Osborne.
Sits *M.*, stupefy'd to stone *D.* ii. 312

Motion.
As clocks to weight their nimble *m.* owe *D.* i. 183
No noise, no stir, no *m.* canst thou make *D.* ii. 303
Like *m.*, from one circle to the rest *D.* ii. 408
Till ev'ry *m.*, pulse, and breath be o'er *E.A.* 333
Each *m.* guides, and ev'ry nerve sustains *E.C.* 78
Self-love, the spring of *m.*, acts the soul *E.M.* ii. 59
The giddy *m.* of the whirling Mill *R.L.* ii. 134
So two consistent m—s act the soul *E.M.* iii. 315
On air or sea new *m.* be imprest *E.M.* iv. 125
A third interprets *m.*, looks and eyes *R.L.* iii. 15

Motive.
And strongest *m.* to assist the rest *E.M.* iv. 352
Infer the *M.* from the Deed, and shew *M.E.* i. 101
Yet no mean *m.* this profusion draws *M.E.* iii. 205
Say what strange *m.*, Goddess! could impel *R.L.* i. 7
Must act on m—s *pow'rful, tho' unknown M.E.* iii. 112
For tho' such *m.* Folly you may call *M.E.* iii. 157

Motley.
There *m.* images her fancy strike *D.* i. 65
A *m.* mixture! in long wigs, in bags *D.* ii. 21

Motteux.
M. himself unfinish'd left his tale *D.* ii. 412
Talkers I've learn'd to bear; *M.* I knew *S.* viii. 50

Mould.
And once inclos'd in Woman's beauteous *m. R.L.* i. 48
Of dull and venal a new World to *m. D.* iv. 15

Mould'ring.
Where round some *m.* tow'r pale ivy creeps *D.* iv. 243
Some felt the silent stroke of *m.* age *M.E.* v. 11

Mount.
From Scots to Wight, from *M.* to Dover's strand *S.* vii. 86
M. in dark volumes, and descend in snow D. ii. 364
Then *m.* the Clerks, and in one lazy tone *D.* ii. 387
On grinning dragons thou shalt *m.* the wind *D.* iii. 268
Contending Princes *m.* them in their Coach *D.* iv. 5'4
Sudden you *m.*, you beckon from the skies *E.A.* 245
M. o'er the vales, and seem to tread the sky *E.C.* 226
Go, wond'rous creature! *m.* where Science guides *E.M.* ii. 19
Make fair deductions, see to what they *m. E.M.* iv. 270
Lend, lend your wings! I *m.* / I fly *O.* i. 16
M. up, and take a Salamander's name *R.L.* i. 60
At length the wits *m.* up, the hairs subside *R.L.* v. 74
Oh! could I *m.* on the Mæonian wing *S.* v. 394
The gilded puppets dance and *m.* above *S.* vii. 18

Mountain.
When the loose *m.* trembles from on high *E.M.* iv. 127
Advance thy golden *M.* to the skies *S.* iv. 73
Who climb their *m.*, or who taste their spring *S.* v. 353
But when yon *m.* let me tune my lays *Su.* 37
While lasts the *m.*, or|while Thames shall flow *W.F.* 266
Who hung with woods yon m.'s sultry brow *M.E.* iii. 253
The dawn now blushing on the *m.* side *Sp.* 21
Taught rocks to weep, and made the m—s groan *A.* 16
Here where the *m.* less'ning as they rise *A.* 59
I know thee, Love! on foreign *M.* bred *A.* 89
M. of Casuistry heap'd o'er her head *D.* iv. 642
By thee to *m.*, wilds, and deserts led *E.A.* 132
And the first clouds and *m.* seem the last *E.C.* 228
When rock'd the *m.*, and when groan'd the ground *E.M.* iii. 250
By *m.* pil'd on *m.* to the skies *E.M.* iv. 74
See nodding forests on the *m.* dance *M.* 26
Sink down ye *m.*, and ye valleys rise *M.* 34
And seeds of gold in Ophir's *m.* glow *M.* 96
Rocks fall to dust, and *m.* melt away *M.* 106
Or cut wide views thro' *M.* to the Plain *M.E.* iv. 75
Now under hanging *m. O.* i. 97
Eurydice the rocks, and hollow *m.* rung *O.* i. 117
The moving *m.*, hear the pow'rful call *Su.* 83
Adieu, ye vales, ye *m.*, streams, and groves *W.* 89
Than what more humble *m.* offer here *W.F.* 35
Then gath'ring flocks on unknown *m.* fed *W.F.* 87
The headlong *m.* and the downward skies *W.F.* 212

Mounted.
Some thought it *m.* to the Lunar sphere *R.L.* v. 113

Mounting.
All vain petitions to the sky *D.* ii. 89
Snatch me, just *m.*, from the blest abode *E.A.* 287
No more the *m.* larks, while Daphne sings *W.* 53
Oft, as the *m.* larks their notes prepare *W.F.* 133

Mounts.
"God save King Cibber!" *m.* in ev'ry note *D.* i. 318
Swift as it *m.*, all follow with their eyes *D.* ii. 185
And *m.* far off among the Swans of Thames *D.* ii. 298
She *m.* the Throne: her head a Cloud conceal'd *D.* iv. 17
Mark how it *m.* to Man's imperial race *E.M.* i. 209
He *m.* the storm, and walks upon the wind *E.M.* ii. 110
M. the Tribunal, lifts her scarlet head *E.S.* i. 149
Spreads his black wings, and slowly *m.* to day *R.L.* iv. 88
The moon, serene in glory, *m.* the sky *W.* 6
But see! where Daphne wond'ring *m.* on high *W.* 69
And *m.* exulting on triumphant wings *W.F.* 112

Mourn.
Thus, far from *Delia*, to the winds I *m. A.* 21
M. not, my Swift, at aught our Realm acquires *D.* i. 26
And ev'n th' Antipodes Virgilius *m. D.* iii. 106
Thee shall each ale-house, thee each gill-house *m. D.* iii. 147
With thee on Raphael's Monument *E.* iii. 27
I *m.* the lover, not lament the fault *E.A.* 184
Just as absurd to *m.* the tasks or pains *E.M.* i. 265
Teach us to *m.* our Nature, not to mend *E.M.* ii. 153
Whom they rever'd as God, to *m.* as Man *E.M.* iii. 224
And *m.* our various portions as we please *E.M.* iv. 33
Or teach the melancholy Muse to *m. E.S.* i. 79
Un-water'd see the drooping sea-horse *m. M.E.* iv. 125
Then cease, bright Nymph! to *m.* thy ravish'd hair *R.L.* v. 141
To yon I *m.*, nor to the deaf I sing *Su.* 15
Grieve for an hour, perhaps, then *m.* a year *U.L.* 56
Sing, while beside the shaded tomb I *m. W.* 19
Let softer strains ill-fated Henry *m. W.F.* 311
And Persecution *m.* her broken wheel *W.F.* 420

Mourn'd.
This *m.* a faithless, that an absent Love *A.* 3

Oh just beheld and lost! admir'd and *m. E.* i. 3
And the gay *m.* who never *m.* before *E.* iv. 16
M. Adonis, darling Youth *Mi.* vii. 10
Lurk'd in her hand and *m.* his captive Queen *R.L.* iii. 96
Soft as he *m.*, the streams forgot to flow *Su.* 5
By strangers honour'd, and by strangers *m. U.L.* 54

Mournful.

Resound, ye hills, resound my *m.* strain *A.* 57, &c.
With all the *m.* family of Yews *M.E.* iv. 96
M. Cypress, verdant Willow *Mi.* vii. 21
A *m.* glance Sir Fopling upwards cast *R.L.* v. 63
Pleas'd thy pale ghost, or grac'd thy *m.* bier *U.L.* 50
Ev'n he, whose soul now melts in *m.* lays *U.L.* 77
Is not so *m.* as the strains you sing *W.* 2

Mourning Bride.

And link the *M.* to Proserpine *D.* iii. 310

Mourns.

As full, as perfect, in vile Man that *m. E.M.* i. 277
All nature *m.*, the Skies relent in show'rs *Sp.* 69

Mouse.

'Twas not a Man, it was a *M. I.H.* i. 56
A Country *M.*, right hospitable (*rep.*) *I.H.* ii. 158
A frugal *M.* upon the whole *I.H.* ii. 161
He had a story of two Mice I.H. ii. 156
Consider, *M.*, like Men, must die *I.H.* ii. 197
And down the *M.* sate, *tête à tête I.H.* ii. 197
O for the heart of Homer's *M. I.H.* ii. 214

Mouth.

Bentley his *m.* with classic flatt'ry opes *D.* ii. 205
From tail to *m.*, they feast and they carouse *E.S.* ii. 179

Mouth'd.

Nor at Rehearsals, sweat, and *m.*, and cry'd *P.S.* 227

Mouthing.

'Twas chatt'ring, grinning, *m.*, jabb'ring all *D.* ii. 237

Move.

The winds to breathe, the waving woods to *m. A.* 41
What eyes but hers, alas, have pow'r to *m. A.* 83
The brisk Example never fail'd to *m. D.* i. 194
To *m.*, to raise, to ravish ev'ry heart *D.* ii. 223
Hell thou shalt *m.*; for Faustus is our friend *D.* iii. 308
From lips like those what precept fail'd to *m. E.A.* 67
Ah let thy handmaid, sister, daughter, *m. E.A.* 153
As those *m.* easiest who have learn'd to dance *E.C.* 363, and *S.* vi. 179
The line too labours, and the words *m.* slow *E.C.* 371
Yet let not each gay Turn thy rapture *m. E.C.* 390
Tho' wit and art conspire to *m.* your mind *E.C.* 531
Each works its end, to *m.* or govern all *E.M.* ii. 56
Th' Æthereal spirit o'er its leaves shall *m. M.* 11
That secret rare, between th' extremes to *m. M.E.* ii. 227
How wilt thou now the fatal sisters *m. O.* i. 95
What home-felt raptures *m. O.* iii. 34
Our author shuns by vulgar springs to *m. P.C.* 9
Now *m.* to war her sable Matadores *R.L.* iii. 47
For who can *m.* when fair Belinda fails *R.L.* v. 4
Say, does thy blood rebel, thy bosom *m. S.* iii. 55
Discharge their Garrets, *m.* their beds, and run *S.* iii. 157
Thus, as the pipes of some carv'd Orgao *m. S.* vii. 17
One sings the Fair; but songs no longer *m. S.* vii. 21

Mov'd.

There *m.* Montalto with superior air *D.* iv. 105
It stopt, I stopt; it *m.*, I *m.* again *D.* iv. 428
Then sadly say, with mutual pity *m. E.A.* 351
The centre *m.*, a circle straight succeeds *E.M.* iv. 365
And show you have the virtue to be *m. P.C.* 38
What *m.* my mind with youthful lords to roam *R.L.* iv. 159

Movement.

Describe or fix one *m.* of his Mind *E.M.* ii. 36
A thousand *m*—s scarce one purpose gain *E.M.* i. 54

Moves.

The gath'ring number as it *m.* along *D.* iv. 81
Where nature *m.*, and rapture warms the mind *E.C.* 235
'Tis real good, or seeming, *m.* them all *E.M.* ii. 94
With eager beats his Mechlin Cravat *m. Mi.* ix. 91
Not half so swiftly the fierce eagle *m. W.F.* 187

Moving.

Or *m.* spirit bade the waters flow *E.A.* 254
Most strength the *m.* principle requires *E.M.* ii. 67
They shift the *m.* Toy-shop of their heart *R.L.* i. 100
With Waller's strains, or Granville's *m.* lays *Sp.* 46
The *m.* mountains hear the pow'rful call *Su.* 83
And bade his willows learn the *m.* song *W.* 14

Mow'd.

And *m.* down armies in the fights of Lu *R.L.* iii. 62

Much.—*Passim.*

Muck.

So morning insects that in *m.* begun *M.E.* ii. 27
To run a *m.*, and tilt at all I meet *S.* i. 70
Misers are M.-worms, Silk-worms Beaus Mi. iv. 23

Mud.

The king of dykes! than whom no sluice of *m. D.* ii. 273
The quaking *m.*, that clos'd, and op'd no more *D.* ii. 292
Then number'd with the puppies in the *m. D.* ii. 308
Slow rose a form in majesty of *M. D.* ii. 326
Smit with his mien the M.-nymphs suck'd him in D. ii. 332

Mugs.

The clam'rous crowd is hush'd with *m.* of Mum *D.* ii. 385

Mules.

As heavy *m.* are neither horse nor ass *E.C.* 39

Mullets.

Of carps and *m.* why prefer the great *S.* ii. 21

Multiplies.

Or Fancy's beam enlarges, *m. M.E.* i. 35

Mum.

The clam'rous crowd is hush'd with mugs of *M. D.* ii. 385

Mumbling.

In *m.* of the game they dare not bite *P.S.* 314

Mummers.

Grave *M.!* sleeveless some, and shirtless others *D.* iii. 116

Mummies.

There sav'd by spice, like *m.*, many a year *D.* i. 151

Mummius.

M. o'er-heard him, *M.*, Fool-renown'd *D.* iv. 371

Mundungus.

Where vile *M.* trucks for viler rhymes *D.* i. 234

Murder.

No *m.* cloth'd him, and no *m.* fed *E.M.* iii. 154
For, after all the *m*—s *of your eye R.L.* v. 145
Meek modern faith to m., hack, and maul *D.* iii. 210
But *m.* first, and mince them all to bits *D.* iv. 120

Murders.

M. their species, and betrays his own *E.M.* iii. 164

Murmur.

Deepens the *m.* of the falling floods *E.A.* 169
No sigh, no *m.* the wide world shall hear *M.* 45
No more the streams their *m.* shall forbear *W.* 57
And with deep m—s fills the sounding shores A. 90
If crystal streams "with pleasing *m.* creep" *E.C.* 352
And streams to m., ere I cease to love *A.* 42
Wave high, and *m.* to the hollow wind *E.A.* 156
The World beside may *m.* or commend *S.* i. 172
My native shades—there weep, and *m.* there *IV.F.* 202

Murm'ring.

As many quit the streams that *m.* fall *D.* iv. 199
New falls of water *m.* in his ear *M.* 70
The lowing herds to *m.* brooks retreat *Su.* 86
Thyrsis, the music of that *m.* spring *W.* 1

Murmurs.

For ever *m.*, and for ever weeps *W.F.* 206

Murray.

How sweet an Ovid, *M.* was our boast *D.* iv. 169
There spread round *M.* all your blooming Loves *I.H.* iii. 10

MUSCLE—MUTUAL.

Plain truth, dear *M*., needs no flow'rs of speech *S*. iv. 3
Where *M*. (long enough his Country's pride) *S*. iv. 52
And shook his head at *M*., as a Wit *S*. vi. 132

Muscle.
You never change one *m*. of your face *S*. iii. 171

Muse.
With whom my *M*. began, with whom shall end *D*. i. 166
Why should I sing what bards the nightly *M. D.* ii. 421
Thou wept'st, and with thee wept each geotle *M. D.* iv. 44
There truant WYNDHAM ev'ry *M*. gave o'er *D*. iv. 167
Or wed to what he must divorce, a *M. D.* iv. 262
O *M.!* relate (for you can tell alone *D*. iv. 619
Resistless falls; the *M*. obeys the Pow'r *D*. iv. 628
Dear to the *M.!* to Harley dear in vain *E*. i. 6
The *M*. attends thee to thy silent shade *E*. i. 28
This, from no venal or ungrateful *M. E.* iii. 2
M.! at that name thy sacred sorrows shed *E*. iii. 47
His time, the *M*., the witty, and the fair *E*. iv. 10
The brightest eyes of France inspir'd his *M. E.* iv. 77
And let your comment be the Mantuan *M. E.C.* 129
Fir'd at first sight with what the *M*. imparts *E.C.* 219
In the bright *M*. tho' thousand charms conspire *E.C.* 339
A *M*. by these is like a mistress us'd *E.C.* 432
But see! each *M*., is LEO'S golden days *E.C.* 697
Such was the *M*., whose rules and practice tell *E.C.* 723
This praise at least a grateful *M*. can give (*rep.*) *E.C.* 734
Supremely blest, the poet in his *M. E.M.* ii. 270
And while the *M*. now stoops, or now ascends *E.M.* iv. 375
Or teach the melancholy *M*. to mourn *E.S.* i. 79
The *M*. may give thee, but the Gods must guide *E.S.* ii. 215
Her priestless *M*. forbids the Good to die *E.S.* ii. 234
Prais'd, wept, and honour'd, by the *M*. he lov'd *Ep.* iii. 6
There ev'ry Grace and *M*. shall throng *I.H.* iii. 27
Rise, honest *M*., and sing the MAN of Ross *M.E.* iii. 250
And prais'd, unenvy'd, by the *M*. he lov'd *M.E.* v. 72
For this the Tragic *M*. first trod the stage *P.C.* 5
A Virgin Tragedy, an Orphan *M. P.S.* 56
The *M*. but serv'd to ease some friend, not Wife *P.S.* 131
His father, mother, body, soul, and *m. P.S.* 381
I sing.—This verse to CARVL, *M.!* is due *R.L.* i. 3
But trust the *M*.—she saw it upward rise *M.E.* v. 123
This Lock, the *M*. shall consecrate to fame *R.L.* v. 149
In this impartial glass, my *M*. intends *S*. i. 57
How coming to the Poet ev'ry *M. S.* ii. 84
Friend Pope! be prudent, let your *M*. take breath *S*. iii. 13
How shall the *M*., from such a Monarch, steal *S*. v. 5
When sick of *M*., our follies we deplore *S*. v. 177
And knows no losses while the *M*. is kind *S*. v. 196
Unless the Gods bestow'd a proper *M. S.* v. 234
The humbler *M*. of Comedy require *S*. v. 283
Who there his *M*., or self, or soul attends *S*. vi. 90
O let my *M*. her slender reed inspire *Sp*. 11
Two Swains, whom Love kept wakeful, and the *M. Sp.* 18
The *M*. forgot, and thou be lov'd no more *U.L.* 82
How all things listen, while thy *M*. complains *W.F.* 77
The *M*. shall sing, and what she sings shall last *W.F.* 174
Whom Nature charms, and whom the *M*. inspires *W.F.* 238
My humble *M*. in unambitious strains *W.F.* 427
Without the soul, the M.'s *Hypocrite D*. iv. 100
'Tis more to guide, than spur the *M*. steed *E.C.* 84
Then Criticism the *M*. handmaid prov'd *E.C.* 102
Such late was Walsh—the *M*. judge and friend *E.C.* 729
No Pow'r the *M*. Friendship can command *E.S.* ii. 118
The *M*. wing shall brush you all away *E.S.* ii. 223
Then all your *M*. softer art display *S*. i. 29
To ease and silence, ev'ry *M*. son *S*. vi. 111
Accept, O GARTH, the *M*. early lays *Su.* 9
At once the Monarch's and the *M*. seats *W.F.* 2
And on his willows hung each *m*. lyre *W.F.* 276
These now no more shall be the *M*. themes *W.F.* 361
Rehearse, ye M—s, what yourselves inspir'd *A*. 56
The Smithfield *M*. to the ear of Kings *D*. i. 2
(Haunt of the *M*.) made their safe retreat *D*. ii. 428
Some strain in rhyme; the *M*. on their racks *D*. iii. 159
But held in ten-fold bonds the *M*. lie *D*. iv. 35
Yet should the *M*. hid my numbers roll *E*. iii. 73
And trace the *M*. upward to their spring *E.C.* 17
Their ancient hounds the banish'd *M*. pass'd *E.C.* 710

In Spenser native *M*. play *I.H.* iv. 6
He swears the *M*. met him at the Devil *S*. v. 42
The willing *M*. were debauch'd at Court *S*. v. 152
I, who so oft renounce the *M*., lie *S*. v. 175
Or who shall wander where the *M*. sing *S*. v. 352
And me, the *M*. help'd to undergo it *S*. vi. 66
While on thy banks Sicilian *M*. sing *Sp*. 4
Then sing by turns, by turns the *M*. sing *Sp*. 41
Where stray ye, *M*., in what lawn or grove *Su.* 23
Invoke the *M*., and resound your praise *Su.* 78
Ye gentle *M*., leave your crystal spring *W*. 21
GRANVILLE commands; your aid, O *M*., bring (*rep.*) *W.F.* 5
Or where ye *M*. sport on Cooper's Hill *W.F.* 264
And call the *M*. to their ancient seats *W.F.* 284
DORSET, *the Grace of Courts, the* M—*s' Pride Ep.* i. 1
And steel now glitters in the *M*. shades *O*. ii. 8
To *m., and still her solitary tea E.* v. 16
Whether the darken'd room to *m*. invite *S*. i. 97
No meagre, m-rid *mope, adust and thin D.* ii. 37

Mushrooms.
The *m*. shew his wit was sudden *Mi*. xii. 11

Music.
Emblem of *M*. caus'd by Emptiness *D*. i. 36
Gods, imps, and monsters, *m*., rage, and mirth *D*. iii. 238
If *M*. meanly borrows aid from sense *D*. iv. 64
M. resembles Poetry, in each *E.C.* 143
Not for the doctrine, but the *m*. there *E.C.* 343
The pow'r of *M*. all our hearts allow *E.C.* 382
And stunn'd him with the *m*. of the spheres *E.M.* i. 202
Th' according *m*. of a well-mix'd State *E.M.* iii. 294
And bid new *m*. charm th' unfolding ear *M*. 42
Artists must choose his Pictures, *M*., Meats *M.E.* iv. 6
Light quirks of *M*., broken and uneven *M.E.* iv. 143
In broken air, trembling, the wild *m*. floats *O*. i. 17
By *M*., minds an equal temper know *O*. L 22
M. her soft, assuasive voice applies *O*. i. 25
How martial *m*. ev'ry bosom warms *O*. i. 37
Yet *m*. and love were victorious *O*. i. 92
M. the fiercest grief can charm *O*. i. 118
M. can soften pain to ease *O*. i. 120
When *m*. softens, and when dancing fires *R.L.* i. 76
While melting *m*. steals upon the sky *R.L.* ii. 49
And bail with *m*. its propitious ray *R.L.* v. 134
That sweetest *m*. to an honest ear *S*. ii. 100
With joyous *m*. wake the dawning day *Sp*. 24
Thyrsis, the *m*. of that murm'ring spring *W*. 1
A sweeter *m*. than their own to hear *W*. 58
Fair Daphne's dead, and *m*. is no more *W*. 60
I hear soft *m*. die along the grove *W.F.* 263

Musing.
Oft in her glass the *m*. shepherd spies *W.F.* 211

Must.—Passim.

Mustard-bowl.
With Thunder rumbling from the *M. D.* ii. 226

Muster-roll.
Tho' but, perhaps, a *m*. of Names *S*. v. 124

Musty.
The *m*. wine, foul cloth, or greasy glass *S*. ii. 66

Mute.
Fear held them *m*.—Alone, unns'd to fear *D*. ii. 57
Nay, Poll sat *m*., and Shock was most unkind *R.L.* iv. 164
So stiff, so *m*., some statue you would swear *S*. vi. 121
Deaf the prais'd ear, and *m*. the tuneful tongue *U.L.* 76
Why sit we *m*. when early linnets sing *Sp*. 25

Mutter'd
Nor hallow'd dirge be *m*. o'er thy tomb *U.L.* 62

Mutt'ring.
Each gentle clerk, and *m*. seals his eyes *D*. ii. 404

Mutton.
On brocoli and *m*. round the year *S*. ii. 138
Thence comes your *m*., and these chicks my own *S*. ii. 144

Mutual.
And each warm wish springs *m*. from the heart *E.A.* 96
Then sadly say, with *m*. pity mov'd *E.A.* 351

MY—NAM'D

On m. Wants built m. Happiness *E.M.* iii. 112
But m. wants this Happiness increase *E.M.* iv. 55
Adieu, fond hope of m. fire *I.H.* iii. 33
United wish, and m. joy *O.* iii. 26

My, Myself.—*Passim.*

Myriads.

The North by m. pours her mighty sons *D.* iii. 89
From the green m. in the peopled grass *E.M.* i. 210

Myrtle.

Now crown'd with *M*., on th' Elysian coast *E.* iv. 73
And od'rous m. to the noisome weed *M.* 76
Here Amphitrite sails thro' m. bow'rs *M.E.* iv. 123
A *M.* Foliage round the Thimble-Case *Mi.* ix. 34
Wand'ring io the m. grove *O.* i. 80
Ye *weeping Loves, the stream with* m—s *hide W.* 23

Myster.

Right well mine eyes arede the m. wight *D.* iii. 187

Mysterious.

In Man they join in some m. use *E.M.* ii. 206

Mystery, Myst'ry.

See *M.* to Mathematics fly *D.* iv. 647
Sworn foe to *M'y*, yet divinely dark *D.* iv. 460
Ye *Pow'rs, whose* M—ies *restor'd I sing D.* iv. 5

Mystic.

With m. worms, the sacred Opium shed *D.* i. 288
And on its top descends the m. Dove *M.* 12
Moral Truth, and m. Song *O.* ii. 12
The Sylphs thro' m. mazes guide their way *R.L.* i. 92
Each silver Vase in m. order laid *R.L.* i. 122
In m. visions, now believ'd too late *R.L.* iv. 166

N.

Nævius.

Nor lets, like *N*., ev'ry error pass *S.* ii. 65

Naiads.

The *N.* wept in ev'ry wat'ry bow'r *Su.* 7

Naked.

In n. majesty Oldmixon stands *D.* ii. 283
But chief her shrine where n. Venus keeps *D.* iv. 307
I tell the n. fact without disguise *D.* iv. 433
A n. Lover bound and bleeding lies *E.A.* 100
The n. nature, and the living grace *E.C.* 294
Who ne'er saw n. sword, or look'd in Plato *E.J.S.* 44
And there, a n. Leda with a Swan *M.E.* ii. 10
To draw the *N.* is your true delight *M.E.* ii. 188
The woods recede around the n. seat *M.E.* iii. 209
Asleep and n. as an Iodian lay *M.E.* iii. 361
The hollow winds thro' n. temples roar *W.F.* 68
When frosts have whiten'd all the n. groves *W.F.* 126
And leave inanimate the n. wall *W.F.* 308
And n. youths and painted chiefs admire *W.F.* 405

Name.

And Delia's n. and Doris' filled the Grove *A.* 4
Thro' rocks and caves the n. of Delia sounds *A.* 49
But pious Needham dropt the n. of God *D.* i. 324
All gaze with ardour: some a poet's n. *D.* ii. 51
Hear, Jove! whose n. my bards and I adore *D.* ii. 79
So shall each hostile n. become our own *D.* ii. 139
Of Genseric! and Attila's dread n. *D.* iii. 92
Each Songster, Riddler, ev'ry nameless n. *D.* iii. 157
Milton's on this, on that one Johnstoo's n. *D.* iv. 112
Rous'd at his n., up rose the bousy Sire *D.* iv. 493
First slave to Words, then vassal to a *N. D.* iv. 501
So mix'd our studies, and so join'd our n. *E.* iii. 10
Muse! at that *N.* thy sacred sorrows shed *E.* iii. 47
Thou but preserv'st a Name, and I a *N. E.* iii. 78
And Montausier was only chang'd in the *N. E.* iv. 70
And Eloisa yet must kiss the name (*rep.*) *E.A.* 8
O write it not my hand—the n. appears *E.A.* 13
That well-known n. awakens all my woes (*rep.*) *E.A.* 30
When Love approach'd me under Friendship's n. *E.-I.* 60
If there be yet another n. more free *E.A.* 89
May one kind grave unite each hapless n. *E.A.* 313

And justly bear a Critic's noble n. *E.C.* 47
Before his sacred n. flies ev'ry fault *E.C.* 422
At length Erasmus, that great injur'd n. *E.C.* 693
Cremona now shall ever boast thy n. *E.C.* 707
Plu—Plutarch, what's his n. that writes his life *E.J.S.* 31
Wits, just like Fools, at war about a n. *E.M.* ii. 85
Exalt their kind, and take some Virtue's n. *E.M.* ii. 100
Thus States were form'd, the n. of King unknown *E.M.* iii. 209
Good, Pleasure, Ease, Content! whate'er thy n. *E.M.* iv. 2
Fame but from death a villain's n. can save *E.M.* iv. 249
Or ravish'd with the whistling of a *N. E.M.* iv. 283
Oh! while along the stream of Time thy n. *E.M.* iv. 383
And let, a-God's *N*., ev'ry Fool and Knave *E.S.* i. 85
Yet none but you by *N.* the guilty lash *E.S.* ii. 10
Call Verres, Wolsey, any odious n. *E.S.* ii. 137
Why pique all mortals, yet affect a n. *M.E.* ii. 61
His race, his form, his n. almost unknown *M.E.* iii. 284
Will never mark the marble with his *N. M.E.* iii. 266
Virtue! and Wealth! what are ye but a n. *M.E.* iii. 334
A plain good man, and Balaam was his n. *M.E.* iii. 342
Some bury'd marble half preserves a n. (*rep.*) *M.E.* v. 16
Thro' climes and ages bears each form and n. *M.E.* v. 32
She, at whose n. I shed these spiteful tears *Mi.* ix. 57
Preserv'd in *Milton's* or in *Shakespear's* n. *P.S.* 168
What tho' my *N.* stood rubric on the walls *P.S.* 215
That Fop, whose pride affects a patron's n. *P.S.* 291
Mount up, and take a Salamander's n. *R.L.* i. 60
A watchful sprite, and Ariel is my n. *R.L.* i. 106
Which from the neighb'ring Hampton takes its n. *R.L.* iii. 4
So long my honour, n. and praise shall live *R.L.* iii. 170
And midst the stars inscribe Belinda's n. *R.L.* v. 150
Lull with Amelia's liquid n. the Nine *S.* i. 31
Think how posterity will treat thy n. *S.* ii. 108
Whether the n. belong to Pope or Vernon *S.* ii. 166
Renounce our Country, and degrade our *N. S.* iv. 125
And virtuous Alfred, a more sacred *N. S.* v. 8
Great Friend of LIBERTY, in *Kings* a *N. S.* v. 25
Its n. I know not, and it's no great matter *S.* vi. 45
For food digested takes another n. *S.* vii. 34
To crave your sentiments, if ——'s your n. *S.* viii. 67
A Shepherd's Boy (he seeks no better n.) *Su.* 1
That taught the groves my Rosalinda's n. *Su.* 42
So peaceful rests, without a stone, a n. *U.L.* 69
Silent, or only to her n. replies (*rep.*) *W.* 42
Behold us kindly who your n. implore *W.* 75
Thy n., thy honours, and thy praise shall live *W.* 81
Our haughty Norman boasts that barb'rous n. *W.F.* 63
Still bears the n. the hapless virgin bore *W.F.* 207
First the fam'd authors of his ancient n. *W.F.* 339
By n—s *of Toasts retails each batter'd jade D.* ii. 134
Ask ye their n. ? I could as soon disclose (*rep.*) *D.* ii 309
And all those tender n. in one, thy love *E.A.* 154
Nations unborn your mighty n. shall sound *E.C.* 193
Some judge of author's n., not works, and then *E.C.* 412
N., which I long have lov'd, nor lov'd in vain *E.S.* ii. 90
Here, last of Britons, let your *N.* be read *E.S.* ii. 250
Tells all their n., lays down the law *I.H.* ii. 200
No *N.*—be calm!—learn prudence of a friend *P.S.* 102
Unspotted n., and venerable long *P.S.* 386
Tho' but, perhaps, a muster-roll of *N. S.* v. 124
Weave laurel Crowns, and take what *N.* we please *S.* vi. 142
To this were trifles, toys, and empty n. *S.* viii. 8
N. *a new Play, and he's the Poet's friend E.C.* 620
Cease then, nor ORDER Imperfection n. *E.M.* ii. 281
Nor Virtue, male or female, can we n. *E.M.* ii. 193
Ye Rev'rend Atheists—Scandal I n. them! Who *E.S.* ii 18
To save a Bishop, may I n. a Dean *E.S.* ii. 33
And melts to Goodness, need I SCARS'ROW n. *E.S.* ii. 65
N. a Town Life, and in a trice *I.H.* ii. 155
The Learn'd themselves we Book-worms n. *Mi.* iv. 13
I'd never n. Queens, Ministers, or Kings *P.S.* 76
The fewer still you n., you wound the more *S.* i. 43
A thing which Adam had been pos'd to n. *S.* viii. 25

Nam'd.

Then thron'd in glass, and n. it CAROLINE *D.* iv. 409
I never n.; the Town's enquiring yet *E.S.* ii. 21
Ere Cæsar was, or Newton n. *I.H.* iv. 10
Thy offspring, Thames! the fair Lodona n. *W.F.* 172

Nameless.
Where n. Somethings is their causes sleep *D.* i. 56
Each Songster, Riddler, ev'ry n. name *D.* iii. 157
Are n. graces which no methods teach *E.C.* 144
Has made the father of a n. race *M.E.* i. 233
Beneath a rude and n. stone he lies *Ep.* v. 3

Names.
He n. the price for ev'ry office paid *S.* viii. 162

Napkins.
The *N.* white, the Carpet rod *I.H.* ii. 195

Narcissa.
Were the last words that poor *N.* spoke *M.E.* i. 247
N.'s *nature*, tolerably mild *M.E.* ii. 53

Narcissus.
N., prais'd with all a Parson's pow'r *D.* iv. 103

Narrow.
See Nature in some partial n. shape *D.* iv. 455
So vast is art, so n. human wit *E.C.* 61
A n. orb each crowded conquest keeps *M.E.* v. 25
Nor bound thy n. views to things below *R.L.* i. 36
Have you not seen, at Guildhall's n. pass *S.* vi. 104

Narrow'd.
Bounded by Nature, n. still by Art *D.* iv. 503

Narrower.
Points him two ways, the n. is the better *D.* iv. 152

Narses.
Or heal, old *N.*, thy obscener ail *M.E.* iii. 89

Nassau.
And great *N.* to Kneller's hand decreed *S.* v. 382

Natal.
Or in the n., or the mortal hour *E.M.* i. 288
Who forms the genius in the *N.* hour *S.* vi. 279

Nation.
And the hoarse n. croak'd, "God save King Log!" *D.* i. 330
Then unbelieving priests reform'd the n. *E.C.* 546
The rules a n., born to serve, obeys *E.C.* 713
The veriest Hermit in the *N.* *I.H.* 181
No more shall n. against n. rise *M.* 57
And therefore hopes this *N.* may be sold *M.E.* iii. 124
When the tir'd *N.* breath'd from civil war *S.* v. 273
Lost was the N.*'s Sense, nor could be found D.* iv. 611
And all I sung should be the *N.* Sense *E.S.* i. 193
Vice, thus abus'd, demands a *N.* care *E.S.* i. 128
Not Waller's Wreath can hide the *N.* Scar *E.S.* ii. 230
Harley, the *N.* great support *I.H.* i. 83
It raises Armies in a *N.* *M.E.* iii. 31
To spoil the n. last great trade, Quadrille *M.E.* iii. 76
To town he comes, completes the n. hope *M.E.* i. 213
Behold the hand that wrought a n. cure *S.* v. 225
And all the a—s *cover'd in her shade D.* iii. 72
And all the n. summoned to the Throne *D.* iv. 7
O sing, and hush the *N.* with thy Song *D.* iv. 626
N. unborn your mighty names shall sound *E.C.* 193
Towns to one grave, whole n. to the deep *E.M.* i. 144
Who taught the n. of the field and wood *E.M.* iii. 97
See barb'rous n. at thy gates attend *M.* 91
Imperial wonders rais'd on *N.* spoil'd *M.* v. 5
To the pale n. of the dead *O.* i. 52
The spoils of n., and the pomp of wars *P.C.* 28
Of these the chief the care of *N.* own *R.L.* ii. 89
With like confusion diff'rent n. fly *R.L.* iii. 82
And *N.* wonder'd while they dropp'd the sword *S.* v. 399
There mighty *N.* shall inquire their doom *W.F.* 381
Whole n. enter with each swelling tide *W.F.* 399

Native.
She rul'd in n. Anarchy, the mind *D.* i. 16
Secure us kindly in our n. night *D.* i. 176
Ascend and recognise their *N.* Place *D.* i. 268
A cold long-winded n. of the deep *D.* ii. 300
Embrown'd with n. bronze, lo! Henley stands *D.* iii. 199
Fresnoy's close Art, and Dryden's n. Fire *E.* iii. 8
Have Humour, Wit, a n. Ease and Grace *E.* iv. 27
Where slaves once more their n. land behold *E.M.* i. 107
With n. Humour temp'ring virtuous Rage *Ep.* xi. 3
In Spenser n. Muses play *I.H.* iv. 6

Natural, Nat'ral.
Content to breathe his n. air *O.* iv. 3
Be justly warm'd with your own n. rage *P.C.* 44
Back to my n. Moderation slide *S.* iii. 33
Till in your n. shades you tune the lyre *Sp.* 12
Nor fragrant herbs their n. incense yield *W.* 48
My n. shades—there weep, and murmur there *W.F.* 202
Till the freed Indians in their n. groves *W.F.* 409

Natural, Nat'ral.
Oft', leaving what is n. and fit *E.C.* 448
To-Be content's his n. desire *E.M.* i. 109
And brings all n. events to pass *S.* vii. 49
Account for moral as for n.'l things *E.M.* i. 162
These n. love maintain'd, habitual those *E.M.* iii. 140

Nature.
Oh, skill'd in *N.*! see the hearts of Swains *A.* 11
Bays, form'd by *N.*, Stage and Town to bless *D.* i. 109
With Shakespear's n., or with Jonson's art *D.* ii. 224
Not touch'd by *N.*, and not reach'd by Art *D.* iii. 230
See *N.* in some partial narrow shape *D.* iv. 455
And last, to Nature's Cause thro' *N.* led *D.* iv. 468
Make *N.* still encroach upon his plan *D.* iv. 473
That *N.* our Society adores *D.* iv. 491
Bounded by *N.*, narrow'd still by Art *D.* iv. 503
More had she spoke, but yawn'd—All *N.* nods *D.* iv. 605
His easy Art may happy *N.* seem *E.* iv. 3
By *N.* yielding, stubborn but for fame *E.* iv. 35
Still rebel n. holds out half my heart *E.A.* 26
When love is liberty, and n. law *E.A.* 92, *see E.M.* iii. 208
Oh come! oh teach me n. to subdue *E.A.* 203
Then conscience sleeps, and leaving n. free *E.A.* 227
N. stands check'd ; Religion disapproves *E.A.* 259
N. affords at least a glimmering light *E.C.* 21
And some made coxcombs *N.* meant but fools *E.C.* 27
N. to all things fix'd the limits fit *E.C.* 52
First follow *N.*, and your judgment frame *E.C.* 68
Unerring *N.*, still divinely bright *E.C.* 70
Are *N.* still, but *N.* methodis'd (rep.) *E.C.* 89
N. and Homer were, he found, the same *E.C.* 135
To copy n. is to copy them *E.C.* 140
Whatever n. has in worth deny'd *E.C.* 205
Where n. moves, and rapture warms the mind *E.C.* 236
In wit, as n., what affects our hearts *E.C.* 243
The naked n., and the living grace *E.C.* 294
True Wit is *N.* to advantage dress'd *E.C.* 297
The face of *N.* we no more survey *E.C.* 313
Persians and Greeks like turns of n. found *E.C.* 380
And ready *N.* waits upon his hand *E.C.* 487
Who conquer'd *N.*, should preside o'er Wit *E.C.* 652
Yet simple *N.* to his hope has giv'e *E.M.* i. 103
For me kind *N.* wakes her genial Power *E.M.* i. 133
But errs not *N.* from this gracious end *E.M.* i. 141
Then *N.* deviates ; and can Man do less *E.M.* i. 150
Is kept in *N.*, and is kept in Man *E.M.* i. 172
N. to these, without profusion, kind *E.M.* i. 179
But what his n. and his state can bear *E.M.* i. 192
If n. thunder'd in his op'ning ears *E.M.* i. 201
And *N.* tremble to the throne of God *E.M.* i. 256
Whose body *N.* is, and God the soul *E.M.* i. 268
All *N.* is but Art, unknown to thee *E.M.* i. 289
Two Principles in human n. reign *E.M.* ii. 53
N. its mother, Habit is its nurse *E.M.* ii. 145
Teach us to mourn our *N.*, not to mend *E.M.* ii. 153
Strong grows the Virtue with his n. mix'd *E.C.* ii. 178
Thus *N.* gives us (let it check our pride) *E.M.* ii. 195
Extremes in *N.* equal ends produce *E.M.* ii. 205
The learn'd is happy n. to explore *E.M.* ii. 263
See plastic *N.* working to this end *E.M.* iii. 9
N. that Tyrant checks ; he only knows *E.M.* iii. 51
Sure by quick *N.* happiness to gain *E.M.* iii. 91
One in their n., which are two in ours *E.M.* iii. 96
God in the n. of each being founds *E.M.* iii. 109
Or pours profuse on earth, one n. feeds *E.M.* iii. 117
Who, foe to *N.*, bears the gen'ral groan *E.M.* iii. 163
See him from *N.* rising slow to Art *E.M.* iii. 169
Thus then to Man the voice of *N.* spake *E.M.* iii. 171
Laws wise as *N.*, and as fix'd as Fate *E.M.* iii. 190
Great *N.* spoke ; observant Men obey'd *E.M.* iii. 199
When Love was Liberty, and *N.* Law *E.M.* iii. 208, *see E.A.* 92
Till then by *N.* crown'd, each Patriarch sate *E.M.* iii. 215
For *N.* knew no right divine in Men *E.M.* iii. 236
The Faith and Moral, *N.* gave before *E.M.* iii. 286
Thus God and *N.* link'd the gen'ral frame *E.M.* iii. 317

Or God and *N.* meant to mere Mankind *E.M.* iv. 78
There deviates *N.*, and there wanders Will *E.M.* iv. 112
When *N.* sicken'd and each gale was death *E.M.* iv. 108
Or Change admits, or *N.* lets it fall *E.M.* iv. 115
Say, at what part of *n.* will they stand *E.M.* iv. 166
But looks thro' *N.* up to Nature's God *E.M.* iv. 332
He sees, why *N.* plants in Man alone *E.M.* iv. 345
N., whose dictates to no other kind *E.M.* iv. 347
Teach me, like thee, in various *n.* wise *E.M.* iv. 377
As Beasts of *N.* may we hunt the Squires *E.S.* ii. 31
Where Kent and *N.* vie for PELHAM'S Love *E.S.* ii. 67
Patron of Arts, and Judge of *N.* died *Ep.* i. 2
Yet soft his *N.*, tho' severe his lay *Ep.* i. 5
Whose Art was *N.*, and whose Pictures Thought *Ep.* viii. 2
Living, great *N.* fear'd he might outvie *Ep.* viii. 7
N. and Nature's laws lay hid in Night *Ep.* xii. 1
See *N.* hastes her earliest wreaths to bring *M.* 23
Know, GOD and *N.* only are the same *M.E.* i. 95
Judge we by *N.?* Habit can efface *M.E.* i. 166
Thus with each gift of *n.* and of art *M.E.* i. 192
N. well known, no prodigies remain *M.E.* i. 208
Here honest *N.* ends as she begins *M.E.* i. 227
Narcissa's *n.*, tolerably mild *M.E.* ii. 53
N. in her then err'd not, but forgot *M.E.* ii. 158
None see what Parts of *N.* it conceals *M.E.* ii. 190
That, *N.* gives; and where the lesson taught *M.E.* ii. 211
Opine that *N.*, as in duty bound *M.E.* iii. 9
What *n.* wants, commodious Gold bestows *M.E.* iii. 21
What *n.* wants (a phrase I much distrust) *M.E.* iii. 25
Extremes in *N.* equal good produce *M.E.* iii. 161
In all, let *N.* never be forgot *M.E.* iv. 50
N. shall join you; Time shall make it grow *M.E.* iv. 69
The suff'ring eye inverted *N.* sees *M.E.* iv. 119
N. must give way to Art *Mi.* vii. 4
Approach! Great *N.* studiously behold *Mi.* x. 7
Which *N.* has imprest (*rep.*) *O.* iii. 10
Cease, fond *N.*, cease thy strife *O.* v. 5
Tyrants no more their savage *n.* kept *P.C.* 7
Yet soft by *n.*, more a dupe than wit *P.S.* 368
By *N.* honest, by Experience wise *P.S.* 400
Tim'rous by *n.*, of the Rich in awe *S.* i. 7
Shall one whom *N.*, Learning, Birth, conspir'd *S.* iv. 40
Of Shakespear's *N.*, and of Cowley's Wit *S.* v. 83
But Times corrupt, and *N.* ill-inclin'd *S.* v. 251
You think 'tis *N.*, and a knack to please *S.* vi. 177
That God of *N.*, who, within us still *S.* vi. 280
N. made ev'ry Fop to plague his brother *S.* viii. 258
And lavish *n.* paints the purple Year *Sp.* 28
All *n.* mourns, the Skies relent in show'rs *Sp.* 69
All *n.* laughs, the groves are fresh and fair *Sp.* 73
And vanquish'd *n.* seems to charm no more *Sp.* 76
From these perhaps (ere *n.* bade her die) *U.L.* 23
And binding *N.* fast in Fate *U.P.* 11
Let *n.* change, let heav'n and earth display *W.* 27
Ah what avail the beauties *n.* wore *W.* 35
Sharp Boreas blows, and *N.* feels decay *W.* 87
Whom *N.* charms, and whom the Muse inspires *W.F.* 238
To follow *n.*, and regard his end *W.F.* 252
Thence a new world to N.'s *laws unknown D.* iii. 241
Did *N.* pencil ever blend such rays *D.* iv. 411
And last, to *N.* Cause thro' Nature led *D.* iv. 468
And but from *N.* fountains bounden to draw *E.C.* 133
Which out of *n.* common order rise *E.C.* 157
N. chief Master-piece is writing well *E.C.* 724
Eye *N.* walks, shoot Folly as it flies *E.M.* i. 13
From *N.* chain whatever link you strike *E.M.* i. 245
A mortal Man unfold all *N.* law *E.M.* ii. 32
Suffice that reason keep to *N.* road *E.M.* ii. 115
Yes, *N.* road must ever be preferr'd *E.M.* ii. 161
Wild *N.* vigor working at the root *E.M.* ii. 184
Behold the child, by *N.* kindly law *E.M.* ii. 275
Know, *N.* children all divide her care *E.M.* iii. 43
Nor think, in *N.* STATE they blindly trod (*rep.*) *E.M.* iii. 147
That proud exception to all *N.* Laws *E.M.* iii. 243
Take *N.* path, and mad Opinion's leave *E.M.* iv. 29
All *N.* diff'rence keeps all *N.* peace *E.M.* iv. 56
But looks thro' Nature up to *N.* God *E.M.* iv. 332
For Wit's false mirror held up *N.* light *E.M.* iv. 393
If one, thro' *N.* Bounty, to his Lord's *E.S.* ii. 173
From *N.* temp'rate feast rose satisfy'd *Ep.* x. 9
Nature and *N.* Laws were hid in night *Ep.* xii. 1
Add *N.*, Custom's, Reason's, Passion's strife *M.E.* i. 21
In love's, in *n.* spite, the siege they hold *S.* vii. 23
All *N.* Incense rise *U.P.* 52

'Tis done, and *n.* various charms decay *W.* 29
And Middle n—s, *how they long to join E.M.* i. 227
N. ethereal, human, angel, man *E.M.* i. 238
What happier *n.* shrink at with affright *E.M.* ii. 229

Naught.
Of *n.* so certain as our *Reason* still (*rep.*) *D.* iv. 481

Nauseate.
Which *n.* all, and nothing can digest *E.C.* 389
I puke, I *n.*,—yet he thrusts in more *S.* viii. 153

Nautilus.
Learn of the little *N,* to sail *E.M.* iii. 177

Navies.
And *N.* yawn'd for Orders on the Main *D.* iv. 618
But future Buildings, future *N.* grow *M.E.* iv. 188
And future *n.* on thy shores appear *W.F.* 222

Nay.—*Passim.*

Near, Nearer, Nearest.—*Passim.*

Neat.
And cry'd, "I vow you're mighty *n. I.H.* ii. 174
He feeds yon Alms-house, *n.*, but void of state *M.E.* iii. 265

Neatly.
Of twelve vast French Romances, *n.* gilt *R.L.* ii. 38

Neatness.
N. itself impertinent in him *S.* viii. 253

Neck.
Break Priscian's head, and Pegasus's *n. D.* iii. 162
With shining ringlets the smooth iv'ry *n. R.L.* ii. 22
This just behind Belinda's *n.* he spread *R.L.* iii. 133
Once gave new beauties to the snowy *n. R.L.* iv. 170
Her great great grandsire wore about his *n. R.L.* v. 90
Pants on her *n.*, and fans her parting hair *W.F.* 196

Necklace.
Or lose her heart, or *n.*, at a ball *R.L.* ii. 109

Nectar.
Ye Heav'ns! from high the dewy *n.* pour *M.* 13

Nectareous.
The juice *n.*, and the balmy dew *E.M.* i. 136

Ned.
And sigh'd) "my lands and tenements to *N.*" *M.E.* i. 257

Need.
Let it be seldom, and compell'd by *n. E.C.* 165
"Right," cries his Lordship, "for a rogue in *n. S.* ii. 111
And still new n—s, *new helps, new habits rise E.M.* iii. 137
None n. *a guide, by sure attraction led D.* iv. 75
And to excuse it, *n.* but show the Prize *D.* iv. 434
Tears are still mine, and these I *n.* not spare *E.A.* 45
Yet if a friend, a night or so, should *n.* her *E.J.S.* 33
What Pope or Council can they *n.* beside *E.M.* iii. 84
And melts to Goodness, *n.* I Scarb'row name *E.S.* ii. 65
For what to shun will no great knowledge *n. M.* iii. 199
And *n.* no rod but Ripley with a rule *M.E.* iv. 18
Now, in such exigencies not to *n. S.* iv. 89

Needful.
She gives in large recruits of *n.* pride *E.C.* 206
More pow'rful each as *n.* to the rest *E.M.* iii. 299
Something there is more *n.* than Expense *M.E.* iv. 41

Needham.
To *N.'s* quick the voice triumphal rode (*rep.*) *D.* i. 323

Needless.
A *n.* Alexandrine ends the song *E.C.* 356

Needs.
In ancient Sense if any *n.* will deal *D.* iv. 229
Which nothing seeks to shew, or *n.* to hide *E.* ii. 2
Will *n.* mistake an author into vice *E.C.* 557
Who, if once wrong, will *n.* be always so *E.C.* 569
As, to be hated, *n.* but to be seen *E.M.* ii. 218
There *n.* but thinking right, and meaning well *E.M.* iv. 32
Or if you *n.* must write, write CÆSAR'S praise *S.* i. 21

NEEDY—NEW.

Plain truth, dear MURRAY, n. no flow'rs of speech S. iv. 3
We n. will write Epistles to the King S. v. 369

Needy.
The n. Poet sticks to all he meets D. iii. 290
Have you less pity for a n. Cheat E.S. ii. 44
As n. beggars sing at doors for meat S. vii. 26

Neglect.
In rev'rend Bishops note some small N—s E.S. i. 16
For her, the feather'd quires n. their song A. 24
N. the rules each verbal Critic lays E.C. 261
Th' industrious bees n. their golden store W. 51

Neglected.
Whole years n., for some months ador'd E. iv. 43
Left me to see a n. Genius bloom (rep.) P.S. 257

Neglects.
Sighs for an Otho, and n. his bride M.E. v. 44
Arthur, whose giddy son n. the laws P.S. 23
His post n., or leaves the fair at large R.L. ii. 124

Negligence.
Horace still charms with graceful n. E.C. 653

Negligent.
As prone to ill, as n. of good S. viii. 200

Neighbour.
Prop thine, O Empress! like each n. Throne D. iv. 333
Propt on some tomb, a n. of the dead E.A. 304
But thinks his n. further gone than he E.M. ii. 226
Not one will change his n. with himself E.M. ii. 262
Form'd and impell'd its n. to embrace E.M. iii. 10
Friend, parent, n., first it will embrace E.M. iv. 367
Each does but hate his n. as himself M.E. iii. 107
It was a sin to call our n. fool P.S. 383
Her ev'ning cates before his n.'s shop D. ii. 72
Gives thee to make thy n. blessing thine E.M. iv. 354
A N. Madness, or his Spouse's I.H. ii. 143
But be who hurts a harmless n. peace P.S. 287
Or makes his N—s glad, if he increase M.E. iv. 182
Curs'd by thy n., thy trustees, thyself S. ii. 106

Neighb'ring.
While others, timely, to the n. Fleet D. ii. 427
Which from the n. Hampton takes its name R.L. iii. 4

Neither.—Passim.

Nepenthe.
Lull'd with the sweet N. of a Court E.S. i. 98

Neptune.
Blue N. storms, the bellowing deeps resound R.L. v. 50
Not N.'s self from all his streams receives W.F. 223

Nero.
And N. reigns a Titus, if he will E.M. ii. 198
And N.'s terraces desert their walls M.E. iv. 72

Nerve.
Each motion guides, and ev'ry n. sustains E.C. 78
Break all their n—s, and fritter all their sense D. iv. 56

Nerveless.
There sunk Thalia, n., cold, and dead D. iv. 41

Nest.
A N., a Toad, a Fungus, or a Flow'r D. iv. 400
And children sacred held a Martin's n. S. ii. 38

Net.
Entangle Justice in her n. of Law E.M. iii. 192
Wind the shrill horn, or spread the waving n. W.F. 96
Till hov'ring o'er 'em sweeps the swelling n. W.F. 104
Like n—s, or lime-twigs, for rich Widows' hearts S. vii. 58

Nether.
Where as he fish'd her n. realms for Wit D. ii. 101

Nettles.
His court with n., moat with cresses stood M.E. iii. 181

Never.—Passim.
Hung silent down his n.-blushing head D. ii. 417
His n. head he turn'd aside D. iii. 231
Is Pride, the n.-failing voice of fools E.C. 204

New.
To hatch a n. Saturnian age of Lead D. i. 28
And ductile Dulness n. mæanders takes D. i. 64
A vast, vamp'd, future, old, reviv'd, n. piece D. i. 284
N. edge their dulness, and n. bronze their face D. ii. 10
Imbibes n. life, and scours and stinks along D. ii. 106
A second effort brought but n. disgrace D. ii. 175
Demand n. bodies, and in Calf's array D. iii. 29
Old in n. state; another, yet the same D. iii. 40
And a n. Cibber shall the stage adorn D. iii. 142
See under Ripley rise a n. Whitehall D. iii. 237
Thence a n. world to Nature's laws unknown D. iii. 241
Another Cynthia her n. journey runs D. iii. 243
N. wizards rise; I see my Cibber there D. iii. 266
For n. abortions, all ye pregnant fair D. iii. 314
Of dull and venal a n. World to mould D. iv. 15
Strong in n. arms, lo! Giant HANDEL stands D. iv. 65
A n. Edition of old Æson gave D. iv. 122
Admire n. light thro' holes yourselves have made D. iv. 126
And each from each contract n. strength and light E. iii. 16
N. graces yearly like thy works display E. iii. 65
Still makes n. conquests, and maintains the past E.iv.62
Repent old pleasures, and solicit n. E.A. 186
N. distant scenes of endless science rise E.C. 224
Then build a n., or act it in a plain E.C. 284
Alike fantastic, if too n., or old (rep.) E.C. 334
Regard not then if Wit be old or n. E.C. 406
N. Blackmores and n. Milbourns must arise E.C. 463
Reflect n. glories, and augment the day E.C. 473
Where a n. world leaps out at his command E.C. 486
Name a n. Play, and he's the Poet's friend E.C. 620
And call n. beauties forth from ev'ry line E.C. 666
And still n. needs, n. helps, n. habits rise E.M. iii. 137
Relum'd her ancient light, not kindled n. E.M. iii. 287
On air or sea n. motions be imprest E.M. iv. 125
Or, "Have you nothing n. to-day I.H. ii. 93
Again? n. Tumults in my breast I.H. iii. 1
These rais'd n. Empires o'er the Earth (rep.) I.H. iv. 11
And bid n. music charm th' unfolding ear M. 42
N. falls of water murm'ring in his ear M. 70
Shall parts so various aim at nothing n. M.E. i. 186
Fix'd Principles, with Fancy ever n. M.E. ii. 279
Erect n. wonders, and the old repair M.E. iv. 192
With added years if life bring nothing n. Mi. v. 5
To what n. clime, what distant sky O. ii. 13
Till some n. Tyrant lifts his purple hand O. ii. 23
And old impertinence expel by n. R.L. i. 94
While ev'ry beam n. transient colours flings R.L. ii. 67
Or stain her honour, or her n. brocade R.L. ii. 107
N. Stratagems the radiant Lock to gain R.L. iii. 120
When each n. night-dress gives a n. disease R.L. iv. 38
Once gave n. beauties to the snowy neck R.L. iv. 170
Which adds n. glory to the shining sphere R.L. v. 142
This n. Court jargon, or the good old song S. iii. 98
Prefer a n. japanner to their shoes S. iii. 156
But art thou one, whom n. opinions sway S. iv. 63
When works are censur'd, not as bad but n. S. v. 116
What then was n., what had been ancient now S. v. 136
He walks, an object n. beneath the sun S. vi. 119
Or bid the n. be English, ages hence S. vi. 169
Schoolmen to n. tenements in hell must make S. vii. 42
So vast, our n. Divines, we must confess S. vii. 97
Had no n. verses, nor n. suit to show S. viii. 13
He asks, "What News?" I tell him of n. Plays (rep.) S. viii. 124
If Sylvia smiles, n. glories gild the shore Sp. 75
Swell'd with n. passion, and o'erflows with tears W. 66
And add n. lustre to her silver star W.F. 290
Heav'ns, what n. wounds! and how her old have bled W.F. 322
Their ample bow, a n. Whitehall ascend W.F. 380
Led by n. stars, and borne by spicy gales W.F. 392
And the n. world launch forth to seek the old W.F. 402
They change their weekly Barber, weekly N—s. iii. 155
He asks, "What N.?" I tell him of new Plays S.viii.124
No young divine, n.-benefic'd, can be S. vii. 51
How n.-born nonsense first is taught to cry D. i. 60
Shall half the n.-built Churches round thee fall S. ii.119
We see no n. palaces aspire S. vii. 111
Or each n.-pension'd Sycophant, pretend E.S. ii. 142
And in the n.-shorn field the partridge feeds W.F. 98
And n.-year Odes, and all the Grub-street race D. i. 44

Newcastle.
There, stamp'd with arms, *N*. shines complete *D.* i. 142

Newgate.
Ev'n Guthry saves half *N*. by a Dash *E.S.* ii. 11

Newmarket.
N.'s Glory rose, as Britain's fell *S.* v. 144
N.-fame, *and judgment at a Bet M.E.* i. 86

Newton.
And shew'd a *N*. as we show an Ape *E.M.* ii. 34
GOD said, let *N*. be ! and all was Light *Ep.* xii. 2
Ere Cæsar was, or *N*. nam'd *I.H.* iv. 10
A *N*.'s *genius, or a Milton's flame D.* iii. 216
The source of *N*. Light, of Bacon's Sense *D.* iii. 218
How Plato's, Bacon's, *N*. looks agree *M.E.* v. 60

Next.—*Passim.*

Nice.
Where, in *n*. balance, truth with gold she weighs *D.* i. 53
Then his *n*. taste directs our Operas *D.* ii. 204
Our Author, happy in a judge so *n. E.C.* 273
Curious not knowing, not exact but *n. E.C.* 286
Yet shun their fault, who, scandalously *n. E.C.* 556
Blunt truths more mischief than *n.* falsehoods do *E.C.* 573
Still hoarding up, most scandalously *n. E.J.S.* 19
The strong connexions, *n.* dependencies *E.M.* i. 130
In the *n*. bee, what sense so subtly true *E.M.* i. 219
'Twixt that, and Reason, what a *n. barrier E.M.* i. 223
And oft so mix, the diff'rence is too *n. E.M.* ii. 209
But Horace, Sir, was delicate, was *n. E.S.* i. 11
To her, Calista proved her conduct *n. M.E.* ii. 31
Their happy Spots the *n.* admirer take *M.E.* ii. 44
Weakness or Delicacy ; all so *n. M.E.* ii. 205
On one *n*. Trick depends the gen'ral fate *R.L.* iii. 94
And the *n*. conduct of a clouded cane *R.L.* iv. 124
Most warp'd to Flatt'ry's side ; but some, more *n. S.* v. 259
In that *n*. moment, as another Lie *S.* viii. 174

Nicely.
From each she *n.* culls with curious tail *R.L.* i. 131
Thus, others' talents having *n.* shown *S.* viii. 80

Nicer.
Alas few verses touch their *n.* ear *S.* i. 33

Niger.
Blest in one *N*., till he knows of two *D.* iv. 370

Niggards.
Be *n*. of advice on no pretence *E.C.* 578

Nigh.
And hear a spark, yet think no danger *n. E.* v. 4
Self-love still stronger, as its objects *n. E.M.* ii. 71
Dryden alone (what wonder?) came not *n. P.S.* 245
Conspicuous Scene ! another yet is *n. S.* iv. 50
But *n*. you mountain let me tune my lays *Su.* 37

Night.
Thus sung the shepherds till th' approach of *n. A.* 97
Daughter of Chaos, and eternal *N. D.* i. 12
Now *N*. descending, the proud scene was o'er *D.* i. 89
Secure us kindly in our native *n. D.* i. 176
Like forms in clouds, ur visions of the *n. D.* ii. 112
Thick as the stars of *n.*, or morning dews *D.* iii. 32
And makes *n*. hideous—Answer him, ye Owls *D.* iii. 166
Indulge, dread Chaos, and eternal *N. D.* iv. 2
Then rose the Seed of Chaos and of *N. D.* iv. 13
Of *N*. primæval, and of *Chaos* old *D*. iv. 630
Art after Art goes out, and all is *N. D.* iv. 640
Where awful arches make a noon-day *n. E.A.* 143
Oh curst, dear horrors of all-conscious *n. E.C.* 125
Read them by day, and meditate by *n. E.C.* 125
Some praise at morning what they blame at *n. E.C.* 430
Let this great truth be present *n.* and day *E.M.* iii. 5
Yet if a friend, a *n*. or so, should need her *E.J.S.* 33
Nature, and Nature's Laws lay hid in *N. Ep.* xii. 1
'Twas on the *n*. of a Debate *I.H.* ii. 185
By day o'ersees them, and by *n*. protects *M.* 52
Last *n*. her Lord was all that's good and great *M.E.* ii. 141
So these their merry, miserable *N. M.E.* ii. 240
Let him to *n*. his just assistance lend *Mi.* ii. 23

That gnaws them *N*. and Day *Mi.* iv. 28
Sound sleep by *n.;* study and ease *O.* iv. 13
Pursue the stars that shoot athwart the *n. R.L.* ii. 82
But what, or where, the fates have wrapt in *n. R.L.* ii. 104
Oh ! if to dance all *n.*, and dress all day *R.L.* v. 19
I nod in company, I wake at *n. S.* i. 13
Long as the *N*. to her whose Love's away *S.* iii. 36
That very *n*. he longs to lie alone *S.* iii. 149
From morn to *n.*, at Senate, Rolls, and Hall *S.* iv. 36
So Russel did, but could not eat at *n. S.* iv. 115
Tir'd with a tedious march, one luckless *n. S.* vi. 35
At *n.*, would swear he dropt out of the Moon *S.* viii. 33
By *n*. he scorches, as he burns by day *Su.* 92
In twice ten thousand rhyming *n*—*s and days D.* iv. 172
Recall those *n*. that clos'd thy toilsome days *E.* i. 15
Would you enjoy soft *n*. and solid dinners *E.J.S.* 23
O charming Noons ! and *N*. divine *I.H.* ii. 133
Days of ease, and *n*. of pleasure *O.* iii. 43
With store of pray'rs, for mornings, *n.*, and noons *R.L.* iv. 29
Why, if the *n*. are tedious—take a wife *S.* i. 16
And when rank Widows purchase luscious *n. S.* vii. 87
See ! strew'd with learned dust, his *n.*-cap *on S.* vi. 118
When each new *n.-dress* gives a new disease *R.L.* iv. 38
In a dun *n.-gown* of his own loose skin *D.* ii. 38

Nightingale.
So when the *N*. to rest removes *Sp.* 13

Nightly.
Why should I sing what bards the *n*. Muse *D.* ii. 421
The daily Anodyne, and *n*. Draught *M.E.* ii. 111
N. nodding o'er your Flocks *Mi.* vii. 6
Soon as the flocks shook off the *n*. dews *Sp.* 17
When swains from shearing seek their *n*. bow'rs *Su.* 64

Nigrina.
N. black, and Merdamante brown *D.* ii. 334

Nile.
As half-form'd insects on the banks of *N. E.C.* 41
And scarce are seen the prostrate *N*. or Rhine *M.E.* v. 28

Nilus.
The sun e'er got, or slimy *N*. bore *S.* viii. 29
From heav'n itself tho' sev'nfold *N*. flow *W.F.* 359
And swallows roost in *N*.' dusty Urn *M.E.* iv. 126

Nimble.
As clocks to weight their *n*. motion owe *D.* i. 183

Nimblest.
And bade the *n*. racer seize the prize *D.* ii. 36

Nimrod.
Proud *N*. first the bloody chase began *W.F.* 61

Nine.
Thou, whom the *N*. with Plautus' wit inspire *A.* 7
Cast on the prostrate *N*. a scornful look *D.* iv. 51
Thee, bold Longinus ! all the *N*. inspire *E.C.* 675
In rev'rence to the sins of *Thirty n. E.S.* ii. 5
Descend, ye *N*.! descend and sing *O.* i. 1
With Styx *n*. times round her *O.* i. 91
This saving counsel, " Keep your piece *n*. years" (*rep.*) *P.S.* 40
And own'd that *n*. such poets made a *Tate P.S.* 190
Each band the number of the sacred *n. I.H.* ii. 30
Lull with Amelia's liquid name the *N. S.* i. 31
And if we will recite *n*. hours in ten *S.* v. 362
In Palace-yard at *n*. you'll find me there *S.* vi. 94
Call Tibbald Shakespear, and he'll swear the *N. S.* vi. 137
Ye sacred *N*.! that all my soul possess *W.F.* 259

Ninety-nine.
At *n.*, a Modern and a Dunce *S.* v. 60

Niobe.
Fast by, like *N*. her (children gone) *D.* ii. 311

Nisus.
She dearly pays for *N*.' injur'd hair *R.L.* iii. 124

No.—*Passim.*
For true *n.-meaning* puzzles more than wit *M.E.* ii. 114

NOAH—NOSE.   209

Noah.
N. had refus'd it lodging in his Ark *S.* viii. 26

Nobility.
For huffing, braggart, puff'd *N. S.* viii. 201

Noble.
Secure, thro' her, the *n.* prize to carry *D.* ii. 279
Till Birch shall blush with *n.* blood no more *D.* iii. 334
But pour them thickest on the *n.* head *D.* iv. 358
And justly bear a Critic's *n.* name *E.C.* 47
But if in *n.* minds some dregs remain *E.C.* 526
With manners gen'rous as his *n.* blood *E.C.* 726
Who *n.* ends by *n.* means obtains *E.M.* iv. 233
CARLETON's calm Sense, and STANHOPE's *n.* Flame *E.S.* ii. 80
N. and young, who strikes the heart *I.H.* iii. 11
When Cæsar made a *n.* dame a whore *M.E.* i. 213
Her Head's untouch'd, that *n.* Seat of Thought *M.E.* ii. 74
Yet shall, my Lord, your just, your *n.* rules *M.E.* iv. 25
Nor marrying Discord in a *n.* wife *P.S.* 393
Yes, while I live, no rich or *n.* knave *S.* i. 119
In me 'tis *n.*, snits my birth and state *S.* ii. 113
For Fame, for Riches, for a *n.* Wife *S.* iv. 39
A *n.* superfluity it craves *S.* iv. 91
Effects unhappy from a *N.* Cause *S.* v. 160
Exact Racine, and Curneille's *n.* fire *S.* v. 274
D'ye think me, *n.* Gen'ral, such a Sot *S.* vi. 50
Tremble before a *n.* Serving-man *S.* viii. 199
Here *n.* Surrey felt the sacred rage *W.F.* 291
Teach Oaths to Gamesters, and to N—s *Wit D.* i. 204
See, all our *N.* begging to be Slaves *E.S.* i. 163
Who starves by *N.*, or with *N.* eats *M.E.* iii. 237
Aw'd by his *N.*, by his Commons curst *W.F.* 73
Our Birth-day N—s' *splendid Livery S.* iv. 33

Nobler.
So Proteus, hunted in a *n.* shape *D.* ii. 129
But now for Authors *n.* remain *D.* ii. 191
Others import yet *n.* arts from France *D.* iv. 597
Those, that imparted, court a *n.* aim *E.M.* ii. 99
But *n.* scenes Maria's dreams unfold *M.E.* iii. 129
Wilt thou do nothing for a *n.* end *S.* iii. 73
And then a *n.* prize I will resign *Sp.* 91
Not proud Olympus yields a *n.* sight *W.F.* 33
Might change Olympus for a *n.* hill *W.F.* 234

Noblest.
An honest Man's the *n.* work of God *E.M.* iv. 248

Nobly.
We *n.* take the high Priori Road *D.* iv. 471
And *n.* conscious, Princes are but things *D.* iv. 601
And *n.* wishing Party-rage to cease *M.E.* iii. 149
Or *n.* wild, with Budgel's fire and force *S.* i. 27
Where, a.-pensive, ST. JOHN *sate and thought Mi.* x. 10

Nod.
A matchless youth ! his *n.* these worlds controls *D.* iii. 255
This *N.* confirms each Privilege your own *D.* iv. 584
Makes love with n—s, and knees beneath a table E. v. 28
And heavy harvests n. *beneath the snow D.* i. 78
Till Senates *n.* to Lullabies divine *D.* i. 317
And now to this side, now to that they *n. D.* ii. 395
Low bow'd the rest: He, kingly, did but *n. D.* iv. 207
On Learning's surface we but lie and *n. D.* iv. 242
Heav'n's whole foundations to their centre *n. E.M.* i. 255
Embrown the Slope, and *n.* on the Parterre *M.E.* iv. 174
Ev'n mitred *Rochester* would *n.* the head *P.S.* 140
I *n.* in company, I wake at night *S.* i. 13
To whom to *n.*, whom take into your Coach *S.* iv. 102

Nodded.
Slept first ; the distant *n.* to the hum *D.* ii. 402
Ev'n Palinurus *n.* at the Helm *D.* iv. 614
How, when you *n.*, o'er the land and deep *S.* v. 400

Nodding.
Benigner influence on thy *n.* head *D.* iv. 346
And low-brow'd rocks hang *n.* o'er the deeps *E.A.* 244
Or some old temple, *n.* to its fall *E.M.* iv. 129
See *n.* forests on the mountains dance *M.* 26
With *n.* arches, broken temples spread *M.E.* v. 3
Nightly *n.* o'er your Flocks *Mi.* vii. 6
Earth shakes her *n.* tow'rs, the ground gives way *R.L.* v. 51

And then a *n.* beam, or pig of lead *S.* vi. 102
And *n.* tempt the joyful reaper's hand *W.F.* 40

Nods.
Hence from the straw where Bedlam's Prophet *n. D.* iii. 7
And Shadwell *n.* the poppy on his brows *D.* iii. 22
See the Cirque falls, th' unpillar'd Temple *n. D.* iii. 107
More had she spoke, but yawn'd—All Nature *n. D.* iv. 605
Nor is it Homer *n.*, but we that dream *E.C.* 180
The green reed trembles, and the bulrush *n. M.* 72
Grove *n.* at grove, each Alley has a brother *M.E.* iv. 117
The doubtful beam long *n.* from side to side *R.L.* v. 73
Not one but *n.*, and talks of Jonson's Art *S.* i. 82

Noise.
And learn, my sons, the wond'rous pow'r of *N. D.* ii. 222
And *N.* and Norton, Brangling and Breval *D.* ii. 238
No *n.*, no stir, no motion canst thou make *D.* ii. 303
Good without *n.*, without pretention great *Ep.* vii. 4

Noisome.
And od'rous myrtle to the *n.* weed *M.* 76

Noisy.
Yet softer Honours, and less *n.* Fame *Ep.* xiv. 9

None.—*Passim.*

Nonjuror.
No merit now the dear *N.* claims *D.* i. 253

Nonsense.
How new-born *n.* first is taught to cry *D.* i. 60
N. precipitate, like running lead *D.* i. 123
Soon to that mass of *N.* to return *D.* i. 241
He grins, and looks broad *n.* with a stare *D.* ii. 194
All *n.* thus, of old or modern date *D.* iii. 59
How fluent *n.* trickles from his tongue *D.* iii. 201
And own stale *n.* which they ne'er invent *E.C.* 411
To fetch and carry *n.* for my Lord *E.C.* 417
'Twixt sense and *n.* daily change their side *E.C.* 435
But rattling *n.* in full volleys breaks *E.C.* 628
Stop, or turn *n.*, at one glance of thee *I.H.* iii. 40
And He, who now to sense, now *n.* leaning *P.S.* 185

Noon.
Count the slow clock, and dine exact at *n. E.* v. 18
Is there a Lord, who knows a cheerful *n. M.E.* iii. 239
Meanwhile declining from the *n.* of day *R.L.* iii. 19
The watch would hardly let him pass at *n. S.* viii. 32
At morn the plains, at *n.* the shady grove *Sp.* 78
Nor plains at morn, nor groves at *n.* delight *Sp.* 80
More bright than *n.*, yet fresh as early day *Sp.* 82
O charming N—s ! *and Nights divine I.H.* ii. 133
With store of pray'rs for mornings, nights and *n. R.L.* iv. 29
Where awful arches make a n.-day night E.A. 143
But soe, the shepherds shun the *n.* heat *Su.* 85
Alas ! not dazzled with their *n.-tide* ray *E.M.* iv. 305
No *n.* bell invites the country round *M.E.* iii. 190

Nor.—*Passim.*

Norman.
Our haughty *N.* boasts that barb'rous name *W.F.* 63

North.
The *N.* by myriads pours her mighty sons *D.* iii. 89
Ask where's the *N. ?* at York, 'tis on the Tweed *E.M.* ii. 222

Northern.
But ripens spirits in cold *n.* climes *E.C.* 401
Thence Arts o'er all the *n.* world advance *E.C.* 711
Improves the keenness of the *N.* wind *M.E.* iv. 112
In some lone isle, or distant *N.* land *R.L.* iv. 154
Howl to the roarings of the *N.* deep *S.* v. 329
From old Belerium to the *n.* main *W.F.* 316

Norton.
And Noise and *N.*, Brangling and Breval *D.* ii. 238
N. from Daniel and Ostræa sprung *D.* ii. 415

Nose.
High Sound, attemper'd to the vocal *n. D.* ii. 256
Yet ne'er looks forward farther than his *n. E.M.* iv. 224
All eyes may see—a Pimple on her *n. M.E.* ii. 36
The *N.* of Hautgout, and the Tip of Taste *M.E.* ii. 80

P

NOSEGAY—NYMPH.

To Chartres, Vigour; Japhet, *N.* and Ears *M.E.* iii. 86
Such *Ovid's* n—, and "Sir! you have an Eye" *P.S.* 118
And the high dome re-echoes to his *n. R.L.* v. 86
Perhaps, young men! your fathers had no *n. S.* ii. 92
When half his *n.* is in his Prince's ear *S.* viii. 179
Such waxen n—s, *solemn staring things S.* viii. 210

Nosegay.
As on the *n.* in her breast reclin'd *R.L.* iii. 141

Nostrils.
That while my *n.* draw the vital air *R.L.* iv. 137
Just where the breath of life his *n.* drew *R.L.* v. 81

Nostrum.
What *Drop* or *N.* can this plague remove *P.S.* 29

Not.—*Passim.*

Notches.
To him who *n.* sticks at Westminster *S.* iii. 84

Note.
"God save King Cibber!" mounts in ev'ry *n. D.* i. 318
Loves of his own and raptures swell the *n. E.M.* iii. 34
To fifty chosen Sylphs, of special *n. R.L.* ii. 117
On each enervate string they taught the *n. S.* v. 153
Such is the shout, the long-applauding *n. S.* v. 330
That from a Patriot of distinguish'd *n. S.* vi. 196
Begin, the vales shall ev'ry *n.* rebound *Sp.* 44
His drooping swans on ev'ry *n.* expire *W.F.* 275
To Delia's ear the tender n—s *convey A.* 18
And these to *N.* are fritter'd quite away *D.* i. 278
To the same *n.* thy sons shall hum or snore *D.* iv. 59
Such were the *n.* thy once-lov'd Poet sung *E.* i. 1
With sweeter *n.* each rising Temple rung *E.C.* 703
And round the Orb in lasting *n.* be read *M.E.* v. 66
While in more lengthen'd *n.* and slow *O.* i. 10
Exulting in triumph now swell the bold *n. O.* i. 16
Borne on the swelling *n.* our souls aspire *O.* i. 128
In *n.* more sad than when they sing their own *W.* 40
Oft, as the mounting larks their *n.* prepare *W.F.* 133
To the same *n.*, of love, and soft desire *W.F.* 296
In rev'rend Bishops n. *some small Neglects E.S.* i. 16

Noted.
Heard, *n.*, answer'd, as in full debate *S.* vi. 187

Nothing.
Where the tall *N.* stood, or seem'd to stand *D.* ii. 110
With *n.* but a Solo in his head *D.* iv. 324
And *n.* left but Homage to a King *D.* iv. 524
Attends; all flesh is *n.* in his sight *D.* iv. 550
Which *n.* seeks to shew, or needs to hide *E.* ii. 2
I tell ye, fool, there's *n.* in't *E.* iv. 26
Pleas'd with a work where *n.*'s just or fit *E.C.* 291
Which nauseate all, and *n.* can digest *E.C.* 389
N. to add, and *n.* to abate *E.M.* i. 184
Be pleas'd with *n.*, if not bless'd with all *E.M.* i. 188
From these to *N.* On superior pow'rs *E.M.* i. 241
Ask your own heart, and *n.* is so plain *E.M.* ii. 215
N. is foreign: Parts relate to whole *E.M.* iii. 21
All serv'd, all serving: *n.* stands alone *E.M.* iii. 25
What *n.* earthly gives, or can destroy *E.M.* iv. 167
And when it comes, the Court see *n.* in't *E.S.* i. 2
These *n.* hurts; they keep their fashion still *E.S.* i. 43
N. is Sacred now but Villainy *E.S.* i. 170
Saw *n.* to regret, or there to fear *Ep.* x. 8
Or, "Have you *n.* new to-day *I.H.* ii. 93 s
He brought him Bacon (*n.* lean) *I.H.* ii. 165
Shall parts so various aim at *n.* new *M.E.* i. 186
And wanting *n.* but an honest heart *M.E.* ii. 193
N. so true as what you once let fall *M.E.* ii. 1
And die of *n.* but a Rage to live *M.E.* ii. 100
Now *n.* left, but wither'd, pale, and shrunk *Mi.* iii. 25
With added years if Life bring *n.* new *Mi.* v. 5
'Tis *n.*—*N. I* if they bite and kick *P.S.* 78
Steals much, spends little, and has *n.* left *P.S.* 184
Heav'ns! was I born for *n.* but to write *P.S.* 272
Wilt thou do *n.* for a nobler end (*rep.*) *S.* iii. 73
Alike in *n.* but one Lust of Gold *S.* iii. 124
If to live well means *n.* but to eat *S.* iv. 111
The good man heaps up *n.* but mere metre *S.* v. 198
There's *n.* blackens like the ink of fools *S.* v. 411
D'ye think me good for *n.* but to rhyme *S.* vi. 32
Then, as a licens'd spy, whom *n.* can *S.* viii. 158
Such labour'd n—s, *in so strange a style B.C.* 326

Notion.
But catch the spreading *n.* of the Town *E.C.* 409
Fools! who from hence into the *n.* fall *E.M.* ii. 210
They talk of principles, but n—s *prize E.C.* 265
The truest *n.* in the easiest way *E.C.* 656
Maxims are drawn from *N.*, these from Guess *M.E.* i. 14

Nought.—*See also* Naught.
Such wits and beauties are not prais'd for *n. S.* viii. 274

Nourish'd.
N. two Locks, which graceful hung behind *R.L.* ii. 20

Noûs.
And much Divinity without a *N. D.* iv. 244

Now.—*Passim.*

Noxious.
Arise, the pines a *n.* shade diffuse *W.* 86

Number.
The gath'ring *n.*, as it moves along *D.* iv. 81
The *N.* may be hang'd, but not be crown'd *E.S.* ii. 111
To *N. five* direct your Doves *I.H.* iii. 9
Each band the *n.* of the sacred nine *R.L.* iii. 30
But liv'd in Settle's n—s *one day more D.* i. 90
My H—ley's periods, or my Blackmore's *n. D.* ii. 370
Yet should the Muses bid my *n.* roll *E.* iii. 73
Some few in that, but *n.* err in this *E.C.* 5
But most by *N.* judge a Poet's song *E.C.* 337
And the smooth stream in smoother *n.* flows *E.C.* 367
But in low *n.* short excursions tries *E.C.* 738
Yet *n.* feel the want of what he had *M.E.* iii. 332
Cynthia, tune harmonious *N. Mi.* vii. 13
Hark! the *n.* soft and clear *O.* i. 12
His *n.* rais'd a shade from hell *O.* i. 133
I lisp'd in *n.*, for the *n.* came *P.S.* 128
Soft were my *n.* ; who could take offence *P.S.* 147
Wit grew polite, and *N.* learn'd to flow *S.* v. 266
And yet my *n.* please the rural throng *Su.* 49
Thames heard the *n.* as he flow'd along *W.* 13
There the last *n.* flow'd from Cowley's tongue *W.F.* 272
Make Windsor-hills in lofty *n.* rise *W.F.* 287

Number'd.
Then *n.* with the puppies in the mud *D.* ii. 308
Rank'd with their Friends, not *n.* with their Train *E.S.* ii. 91

Num'rous.
Those half-learn'd witlings, *n.* in our isle *E.C.* 40
When *n.* wax lights in bright order blaze *R.L.* iii. 168
By love of Courts to *n.* ills betray'd *R.L.* iv. 152

Nun.
Stol'n from a Duel, follow'd by a *N. D.* iv. 337

Nunquam.
But Tully has it, *N. minus solus S.* viii. 91

Nurse.
Great *n.* of Goths, of Alans, and of Huns *D.* iii. 90
Nature its mother, Habit is its *n. E.M.* ii. 145
Of all the *N.* and all the Priest have taught *R.L.* i. 30
To wholesome Solitude, the *n.* of sense *S.* viii. 185
The mothers n. *it, and the sires defend E.M.* iii. 126

Nurs'd.
Here stood her Opium, here she *n.* her Owls *D.* i. 271

Nursing-mother.
And I, a *N.*, rock the throne *D.* i. 312

Nutation.
So from the mid-most the *n.* spreads *D.* ii. 409

Nut-brown.
Then sung, how shown him by the *N.* maids *D.* ii. 337

Nutrition.
To draw *n.*, propagate, and rot *E.M.* ii. 64

Nuzzles.
Drops to the third, who *n.* close behind *E.S.* ii. 178

Nymph.
How many pictures of one *N.* we view *M.E.* ii. 5
A *N.* of Quality admires our Knight *M.E.* iii. 385

O—OBSERVATION.

The *N.*, whose Tail is all on Flame *Mi.* iv. 15
Rise, pensive *N.*, the *Tattler* waits for you *Mi.* ix. 3
First, rob'd in white, the *N.* intent adores *R.L.* i. 123
This *N.*, to the destruction of mankind *R.L.* ii. 19
Whether the *n.* shall break Diana's law *R.L.* ii. 105
Some, orb in orb, around the *n.* extend *R.L.* ii. 138
The skilful *N.* reviews her force with care *R.L.* iii. 45
The *n.* exulting fills with shouts the sky *R.L.* iii. 99
What wonder then, fair *n.* I thy hairs should feel *R.L.* iii. 177
But anxious cares the pensive *n.* oppress'd *R.L.* iv. 1
A *n.* there is that all thy pow'r disdains *R.L.* iv. 65
Sunk in Thalestris' arms the *n.* he found *R.L.* iv. 89
Then see I the *n.* in beauteous grief appears *R.L.* iv. 143
Silence ensu'd, and thus the *n.* began *R.L.* v. 8
Oh cruel *N.* I a living death I bear *R.L.* v. 61
Then cease, bright *N.* I to mourn thy ravish'd hair *R.L.* v. 141
Each am'rous *n.* prefers her gifts in vain *Su.* 53
Come, lovely *n.*, and bless the silent hours *Su.* 65
As some coy *n.* her lovers warm address *W.F.* 19
Above the rest a rural *n.* was fam'd *W.F.* 171
Scarce could the Goddess from her *n.* be known *W.F.* 175
Now fainting, sinking, pale, the *n.* appears *W.F.* 191
Ye Mantuan n—s, *your sacred succour bring* A. 5
Ye *N.* of Solyma I begin the song *M.* 1
And prudent *N.* against that change prepare *Mi.* ix. 18
There Youths and *N.* in concert gay *I.H.* ii. 29
And sip, with *N.*, their elemental Tea *R.L.* i. 62
Some *n.* there are, too conscious of their face *R.L.* i. 79
Fair *N.*, and well-drest Youths around her shone *R.L.* ii. 5
Of foreign Tyrants and of *N.* at home *R.L.* iii. 6
Hither the heroes and the *n.* resort *R.L.* iii. 9
While *n.* take treats or assignations give *R.L.* iii. 169
Blest Swains, whose *N.* in ev'ry grace excel (*rep.*) *Sp.* 95
The *N.*, forsaking ev'ry cave and spring *Su.* 51
Let *N.* and Sylvans cypress garlands bring *W.* 22

O.

O, Oh.—*Passim.*
To sound or sink in *cano*, *O.* or A *D.* iv. 221

Oak.
Link towns to towns with avenues of *o.* *S.* vi. 260
Let op'ning roses knotted o—s adorn A. 37
Ask of thy mother earth, why *o.* are bald *E.M.* i. 39
While by our *o.* the precious loads are born *W.F.* 31
Where tow'ring *o.* their growing honours rear *W.F.* 221

Oar.
Taylor, their better Charon, lends an *o.* *D.* iii. 19
Spread the thin *o.*, and catch the driving gale *E.M.* iii. 178

Oath.
Nor dar'd an *O.*, nor hazarded a Lie *P.S.* 397
Whose air cries Arm I whose very looks's an *o.* *S.* viii. 261
Teach O—s to Gamesters, and to Nobles Wit D. i. 204
Support his front, and *O.* bring up the rear *D.* i. 308
Thy *o.* I quit, thy memory resign *E.A.* 293

Obedient.
O. slumbers that can wake and weep *E.A.* 212
And roll *o.* Rivers thro' the Land *M.E.* 402
Up starts a Palace ; lo, th' *o.* base *S.* iii. 140

Obey.
Sad proof how well a lover can *o.* *E.A.* 172
In this weak queen some fav'rite still *o.* *E.M.* ii. 150
Thus let the wiser make the rest *o.* *E.M.* iii. 196
Those, only fix'd, they first or last *o.* *M.E.* ii. 209
Here thou, great Anna I whom three realms *o.* *R.L.* iii. 7
T' enjoy is to *o.* *U.P.* 20
Time conquers all, and we must Time *o.* *W.* 88

Obey'd.
With Authors, Stationers *o.* the call *D.* ii. 31
Great Nature spoke ; observant Men *o.* *E.M.* iii. 199
The same which in a Sire the Sons *o.* *M.E.* iii. 213
What could be free, when lawless beasts *o.* *W.F.* 51
She said I the world *o.*, and all was Peace *W.F.* 328

Obeys.
Resistless falls : the Muse *o.* the Pow'r *D.* iv. 628
Her heart still dictates, and her hand *o.* *E.A.* 16
The rules a nation, born to serve, *o.* *E.C.* 713
The hog that ploughs not nor *o.* thy call *E.M.* iii. 41
Yet has her humour most, when she *o.* *M.E.* ii. 264

Object.
Yet by some *o.* ev'ry brain is stirr'd *D.* iv. 445
Call round her Tomb each *o.* of desire *E.* iii. 49
How the dear *o.* from the crime remove *E.A.* 193
But greedy That, its *o.* would devour *E.M.* ii. 89
Good, from each *o.*, from each place acquir'd *E.M.* iv. 321
The optics seeing, as the *o.* seen *M.E.* i. 32
No common *o.* to your sight displays *P.C.* 19
He walks, an *o.* new beneath the sun *S.* vi. 119
Fair Geraldine, bright *o.* of his vow *W.F.* 297
In prospects thus, some o—s please our eyes E.C. 156
It gilds all *o.*, but it alters none *E.C.* 317
Self-love still stronger, as its *o.* nigh *E.M.* ii. 71
On diff'rent senses diff'rent *o.* strike *E.M.* ii. 128
In town, what *O.* could I meet *I.H.* i. 7
Mistake, confound, o. *at all he spoke* S. viii. 117

Oblige.
Would he *o.* me ? let me only find *E.S.* i. 33
Contriving never to *o.* ye *I.H.* i. 30
O. her, and she'll hate you while you live *M.E.* ii. 138
And from the moment we *o.* the town *S.* v. 370

Oblig'd.
And all th' *o.* desert, and all the vain *E.* i. 32
O. by hunger, and request of friends *P.S.* 44
And so obliging, that he ne'er *o.* *P.S.* 208

Obliging.
Go on, *o.* creatures, make me see *P.S.* 119
And so *o.*, that he ne'er oblig'd *P.S.* 208
O. Sir I for courts you sure were made *S.* viii. 25

Obligingly.
And then for mine *o.* mistakes *P.S.* 279

Oblique.
Ere Wit *o.* had broke that steady light *E.M.* iii. 231

Obliquely.
O. waddling to the mark in view *D.* i. 172
The sun *o.* shoots his burning ray *R.L.* iii. 20

Oblivion.
Divine *o.* of low-thoughted care *E.A.* 298
When what t' *o.* better were resign'd *E.M.* iv. 251
And there in sweet *o.* drown *I.H.* ii. 131
Lodona's fate in long *o.* cast *W.F.* 173

Oblivious.
Behold the wonders of th' *o.* Lake *D.* iii. 44

Obscene.
O. with filth the miscreant lies bewray'd *D.* ii. 75
Of link-boys vile, and watermen *o.* *D.* ii. 100
He, from the taste *o.* reclaims our youth *S.* v. 217
The fox *o.* to gaping tombs retires *W.F.* 71

Obscener.
Or heal, old Narses, thy *o.* ail *M.E.* iii. 89

Obscenity.
No pardon vile *O.* should find *E.C.* 530
But Dulness with *O.* must prove *E.C.* 532

Obscure.
O. the place, and uninscrib'd the stone *W.F.* 320
It draws up vapours which o. its rays E.C. 471
See gloomy clouds *o.* the cheerful day *W.* 30

Obsequious.
To where the Seine, *o.* as it rolls *D.* iv. 297

Observant.
Ev'n now, *o.* of the parting Ray *E.* i. 37
Great Nature spoke ; *o.* Men obey'd *E.M.* iii. 199

Observation.
Nor will Life's stream for *O.* stay *M.E.* i. 37
To o—s which ourselves we make M.E. i. 11

Observe.

Learn but to trifle ; or, who most *o. D.* iv. 457
Made him *o.* the subject and the plot *E.C.* 275
O. ! how system into system runs *M.E.* i. 25
But how unequal it bestows, *o. M.E.* iii. 23
Pretty ! in amber to *o.* the forms *P.S.* 169
O. how seldom ev'n the best succeed *S.* v. 286
O. his shape how clean ! his locks how curl'd *S.* vi. 5
And all mankind might that just Mean *o.. S.* vii. 119
T' *o.* a mean, be to himself a friend *W.F.* 251

Observer.

In vain th' *o.* eyes the builder's toil *M.E.* i. 290
We grow more partial for th' *O.'s sake M.E.* i. 12

Observes.

Bubo *o.,* he lash'd no sort of Vice *E.S.* i. 12
Some Wag *o.* me thus perplext *I.H.* ii. 51 s
O. how much a Chintz exceeds Mohair *M.E.* ii. 170

Observing.

O., cry'd, " You 'scape not so *I.H.* i. 57

Obsolete.

Who now that *o.* Example fears *E.S.* ii. 56
Spenser himself affects the *O. S.* v. 97

Obstetric.

And Douglas lends his soft, *o.* hand *D.* iv. 394

Obstinacy.

From spleen, from *o.,* hate, or fear *E.M.* ii. 186

Obstinate.

No Ass so meek, no Ass so *o. M.E.* ii. 102

Obstructed.

'Tis he th' *o.* paths of sound shall clear *M.* 41

Obtain.

Each has his share, and who would more *o. E.M.* iv. 47
In who *o.* defence, and who defend *E.M.* iv. 59
But these less taste them, as they worse *o. E.M.* iv. 84
Soon to *o.,* and long possess the prize *R.L.* iv. 44

Obtain'd.

The Lock, *o.* with guilt, and kept with pain *R.L.* v. 109

Obtains.

Still happy Impudence *o.* the prize *D.* ii. 186
Who noble ends by noble means *o. E.M.* iv. 233
In Britain's Senate he a seat *o. M.E.* ii. 393

Obvious.

O. her goods, in no extreme they dwell *E.M.* iv. 31
When Man's whole frame is *o.* to a *Flea D.* iv. 238

Occasion.

But with th' *o.* and the place comply *E.C.* 177
On just *o., coute qui coute I.H.* ii. 164
When kind *o.* prompts their warm desires *R.L.* i. 75

Ocean.

Realms shift their place, and *O.* turns to land *D.* i. 72
As on the land while here the *o.* gains *E.C.* 54
Who heaves old *O.,* and who wings the storms *E.M.* i. 138
That never air or *o.* felt the wind *E.M.* i. 167
See, thro' this air, this *o.,* and this earth *E.M.* i. 233
On life's vast *o.* diversely we sail *E.M.* ii. 107
That Pow'r who bids the *O.* ebb and flow *M.E.* iii. 164
His pond an *O.,* his parterre a Down *M.E.* iv. 106
To the cool *o.,* where his journey ends *S u.* 90
Rise Alps between us ! and *whole o—s roll E.A.* 290

O'clock.

As " What's *o.* !" And " How's the Wind ?" *I.H.* ii. 89 s
His servants up, and rise by five *o. S.* ii. 162

Octavos.

Quartos, *o.,* shape the less'ning pyre *D.* i. 161

October.

O. next it will be four *I.H.* ii. 84 s

Odd.

A Joke on JEKYLL, or some *o. Old Whig E.S.* i. 39
So *o.,* my Country's Ruin makes me grave *E.S.* ii. 207
Nay, half in heav'n—except (what's mighty *o.) S.* iii. 187

All this may be ; the People's Voice is *o. S.* v. 89
Could not but think to pay his fine was *o. S.* viii. 17
The Presence seems, with things so richly *o. S.* viii. 238

Oddly.

Her Tongue bewitch'd as *o.* as her Eyes *M.E.* ii. 47

Ode.

Much future *O.,* and abdicated Play *D.* i. 122
A twisted Birth-day *O.* completes the spire *D.* i. 162
And all be sleep, as at an *O.* of thine *D.* i. 318
Dear Cibber ! never match'd one *o.* of thine *S.* vi. 138
And New-year O—s, and all the Grubstreet race D. i. 44
Like Journals, *O.,* and such forgotten things *S.* v. 416

Odious.

Call Verres, Wolsey, any *o.* name *E.S.* ii. 137
O. ! in woollen ! 'twould a Saint provoke *M.E.* i. 246
All bath'd in tears—" Oh *o., o.* Trees !" *M.E.* ii. 40

Od'rous.

And *o.* myrtle to the noisome weed *M.* 76

Odours.

In hues as gay, and *o.* as divine *S.* viii. 216
Nor morning *o.* from the flow'rs arise *W.* 46
While plants their shade, or flow'rs their *o.* give *W.* 83

O'er.—*Passim.*

Thro' School and College, thy kind cloud *o.-cast D.* iv. 289
The pomp was darken'd, and the day *o. P.C.* 32
This China Jordan let the chief *o.-come D.* ii. 165
Osborne, thro' perfect modesty *o. D.* ii. 189
Who sate the nearest, by the words *o. D.* ii. 401
Int'rest *o.,* or Policy take place *M.E.* i. 167
Then raptures high the seat of sense *o.-flow D.* iii. 5
Line after line my gushing eyes *o. E.A.* 35
O. thy courts : the light himself shall shine *M.* 103
Heady, not strong ; *o.-flowing,* tho' not full *D.* iii. 172
Wide and more wide, th' *o—s* of the mind *E.M.* iv. 369
Whose measure full *o.-flows* on human race *M.E.* iii. 231
Sudden, with starting tears each eye *o. R.L.* v. 85
Swell'd with new passion, and *o.* with tears *W.* 66
Mummius *o.-heard* him, Mummius Fool-renown'd *D.* iv. 371
Or, at one bound, *o.-leaping* all his laws *D.* iv. 477
(Could you *o.-look* but that) it is to steal *S.* vi. 20
Where the tall may-pole once *o.-look'd* the Strand *D.* ii. 28
As if the Stagirite *o.* each line *E.C.* 138
O., seen double, by the fool and wise *E.M.* iv. 6
And tho' she plays no more, *o.-looks* the cards *R.L.* i. 54
Half that the Dev'l *o.* from Lincoln town *S.* vi. 245
A second deluge Learning thus *o.-run E.C.* 691
By day *o.-sees* them, and by night protects *M.* 52
While angels with their silver wings *o.-shade U.L.* 67
Where doves in flocks the leafless trees *o. W.F.* 127
While the spread fan *o.-shades* the closing eyes *E.* v. 37
Sure never to *o.-shoot,* but just to hit *M.E.* iii. 89
Once School-divines this zealous Isle *o.-spread E.C.* 440
Behold the Market-place with poor *o. M.E.* iii. 263
Shall feel sharp vengeance soon *o.-take* his sins *R.L.* ii. 125
Stands our Digamma, and *o.-tops* them all *D.* iv. 218
Ev'n mighty Pam, that Kings and Queens *o.-threw R.L.* iii. 61
The tale reviv'd, the lie so oft *o.-thrown P.S.* 350
A breath revives him, or a breath *o.-throws S.* v. 301
In heaps on heaps ; one fate *o.-whelms* them all *R.L.* iii. 86

Of, Off.—*Passim.*

Offence.

Some Dæmon stole my pen (forgive th' *o.) D.* i. 187
Now turn'd to heav'n, I weep my past *o. E.A.* 187
And love th' offender, yet detest th' *o. E.A.* 192
But, of the two, less dang'rous is th' *o. E.C.* 3
'Tis not enough no harshness gives *o. E.C.* 364
At ev'ry trifle scorn to take *o. E.C.* 386
Then might I sing, without the least *o. E.S.* i. 77
Soft were my numbers ; who could take *o. P.S.* 147
What dire *o.* from am'rous causes springs *R.L.* i. 1
One, one man only breeds my just *o. S.* vii. 45
Thus much I've said, I trust, without *o. S.* vii. 125

Offend.

Great wits sometimes may gloriously *o. E.C.* 159
Moderns, beware ! or if you must *o. E.C.* 163

OFFENDER—OLIVE.

Form short Ideas: and *o.* in arts *E.C.* 287
Averse alike to flatter, or *o. E.C.* 743
And how did, pray, the florid Youth *o. E.S.* ii. 166
How soft is Silia I fearful to *o. M.E.* ii. 29
O. her, and she knows not to forgive *M.E.* ii. 117
Still Sappho—hold! for God's sake—you'll *o. P.S.* 101

Offender.

And love th' *o.*, yet detest th' offence *E.A.* 102
Must great O—s, once escap'd the Crown E.S. ii. 28

Offends.

Well, if our Author in the Wife *o. E.J.S.* 25
Oft she rejects, but never once *o. R.L.* ii. 12
Whoe'er *o.*, at some unlucky time *S.* i. 77
The Zeal of Fools *o.* at any time *S.* v. 406

Offer.

And *o.* Country, Parent, Wife, or Son *E.S.* i. 158
Than what more humble mountains *o.* here *W.F.* 35

Offer'd.

The Great man never *o.* you a groat *E.S.* i. 26

Off'rings.

Bears Pisa's *o.* to his Arethuse *D.* ii. 342
The various *o.* of the world appear *R.L.* i. 130
With feasts, and *o.*, and a thankful strain *S.* v. 244

Offers.

When *o.* are disdain'd, and love deny'd *R.L.* i. 82
Whose spoils this paper o. to your eye D. iv. 435
This, humbly *o.* me his Case *I.H.* ii. 67 s

Office.

In *o.* here fair Cloacina stands *D.* ii. 93
Unfinish'd Treaties in each *O.* slept *D.* iv. 616
Thou, Abelard! the last sad *o.* pay *E.A.* 321
Me, let the tender *o.* long engage *P.S.* 408
His *O.* keeps your Parchment fates entire *S.* vii. 71
He names the price for ev'ry *o.* paid *S.* viii. 162

Offspring.

As Berecynthia, while her *o.* vie *D.* iii. 131
Thy *o.*, Thames! the fair Lodona nam'd *W.F.* 172

Often, Oft.—*Passim.*

Ogilby.

Here swells the shelf with *O.* the great *D.* i. 141
As sings thy great forefather *O. D.* i. 328

Ogle.

To patch, nay *o.*, might become a saint *R.L.* v. 23

Oglethorpe.

Shall fly, like *O.*, from pole to pole *S.* vi. 277

Ogling.

With singing, laughing, *o. and all that R.L.* iii. 18

Oil.

Sir, Spain has sent a thousand jars of *o. M.E.* iii. 56
O., tho' it stink, they drop by drop impart *S.* ii. 59

Oil'd.

As *o.* with magic juices for the course *D.* ii. 104

Old.

Still her *o.* Empire to restore she tries *D.* i. 17
She saw *o.* Pryn in restless Daniel shine *D.* i. 103
Dulness! whose good *o.* cause I yet defend *D.* i. 165
Molière's *o.* stubble in a moment flames *D.* i. 254
Rous'd by the light, *o.* Dulness heav'd the head *D.* i. 257
A vast, vamp'd, future, *o.*, reviv'd, new piece *D.* i. 284
On Codrus' *o.*, or Dunton's modern bed *D.* ii. 144
O. Bavius sits to dip poetic souls *D.* iii. 24
O., in new state; another, yet the same *D.* iii. 40
How many stages thro' *o.* Monks she rid *D.* iii. 52
All nonsense thus, of *o.* or modern date *D.* iii. 59
O. scenes of glory, times long cast behind *D.* iii. 63
Oh great Restorer of the good *o.* Stage *D.* iii. 205
In Lud's *o.* walls tho' long I rul'd, renown'd *D.* iii. 277
The young, the *o.*, who feel her inward sway *D.* iv. 73
A new edition of *o.* Æson gave *D.* iv. 122
Or chew'd by blind *o.* Scholiasts o'er and o'er *D.* iv. 232
With that a WIZARD *O.* his *cup* extends *D.* iv. 517
Of *Night* primæval and of Chaos *o. D.* iv. 630
See skulking *Truth* to her *o.* cavern fled *D.* iv. 641
Repent *o.* pleasures, and solicit new *E.A.* 186

Those RULES of *o.* discover'd, not devis'd *E.C.* 88
Some by *o.* words to fame have made pretence *E.C.* 324
Alike fantastic, if too new, or *o. E.C.* 334
Nor yet the last to lay the *o.* aside *E.C.* 336
Regard not then if Wit be *o.* or new *E.C.* 406
Of *o.*, those met rewards who could excel *E.C.* 510
Like some fierce Tyrant in *o.* tapestry *E.C.* 587
In sounds and jingling syllables grown *o. E.C.* 603
We still defy'd the Romans, as of *o. E.C.* 718
In days of *o.*, they pardon'd breach of vows *E.J.S.* 29
Who heaves *o.* Ocean, and who wings the storms *E.M.* i. 158
Correct *o.* Time, and regulate the Sun *E.M.* ii. 22,
Or some *o.* temple, nodding to its fall *E.M.* iv. 129
A Joke on JEKYLL or some odd *O. Whig E.S.* i. 39
And wear their strange *o.* Virtue, as they will *E.S.* i. 44
O. England's Genius, rough with many a Scar *E.S.* i. 152
Before her dance: behind her crawl the *O. E.S.* i. 156
Our *o.* Friend Swift will tell his story *I.H.* i. 82
O. Politicians chew on wisdom past *M.E.* i. 228
I give and I devise (*o.* Euclio said *M.E.* i. 256
Beauties, like Tyrants, *o.* and friendless grown *M.E.* ii. 227
A Youth of Frolics, an *o.* Age of Cards *M.E.* ii. 244
Young without Lovers, *o.* without a friend *M.E.* ii. 246
O. Cato is as great a Rogue as you *M.E.* iii. 38
Still, as of *o.*, encumber'd Villainy *M.E.* iii. 50
Or heal, *o.* Narses, thy obscener ail *M.E.* iii. 89
O. Cotta sham'd his fortune, and his birth *M.E.* iii. 177
Like some lone Chartreux stands the good *o.* Hall *M.E.* iii. 187
The young who labour, or the *o.* who rest *M.E.* iii. 268
And long'd to tempt him like good Job of *o. M.E.* iii. 350
My good *o.* Lady catch'd a cold, and died *M.E.* iii. 384
Load some vain Church with *o.* Theatric state *M.E.* iv. 29
Erect new wonders, and the *o.* repair *M.E.* iv. 192
And give to Titus *o.* Vespasian's due *M.E.* v. 18
But pitied Belisarius *o.* and blind *Mi.* ii. 6
And be the *Critic's, Briton's, O. Man's Friend Mi.* ii. 24
O., and void of all good-nature *Mi.* vi. 6
As now your own, our beings were of *o. R.L.* i. 47
And *o.* impertinence expel by new *R.L.* i. 94
Charm'd the small-pox, or chas'd *o.* age away *R.L.* v. 20
As downright SHIPPEN, or as *o.* Montaigne *S.* i. 52
Whether *O.* age, with faint but cheerful ray *S.* i. 93
Thus much is left of *o.* Simplicity *S.* ii. 36
At such a feast, *o.* vinegar to spare *S.* ii. 57
And more the sickness of long life, *o.* age *S.* ii. 88
From yon *o.* walnut-tree a show'r shall fall *S.* ii. 145
Hang their *o.* Trophies o'er the Garden gates *S.* iii. 8
This new Court jargon, or the good *o.* song *S.* iii. 98
Authors, like coins, grow dear as they grow *o. S.* v. 35
Ben, *o.* and poor, as little seem'd to heed *S.* v. 73
What boy but hears the sayings of *o.* Ben *S.* v. 80
Extols *o.* Bards, or Merlin's Prophecy *S.* v. 132
O. Edward's Armour beams on Cibber's breast *S.* v. 319
Which made *o.* Ben, and surly Dennis swear *S.* v. 328
In ANNA's Wars, a Soldier poor and *o. S.* vi. 33
Command *o.* words that have long slept, to wake *S.* vi. 167
Out-cant *o.* Esdras, or out-drink his heir *S.* vii. 37
The good *o.* landlord's hospitable door *S.* vii. 114
Like rich *o.* wardrobes, things extremely rare *S.* vii. 123
As Herod's hang-dogs in *o.* Tapestry *S.* viii. 267
Let *o.* Arcadia boast her ample plain *W.F.* 159
Here too, 'tis sung, of *o.* Diana stray'd *W.F.* 165
Or raise *o.* warriors, whose ador'd remains *W.F.* 301
From *o.* Belerium to the northern main *W.F.* 316
Heav'ns, what new wounds! and how her *o.* have bled *W.F.* 322
O. father Thames advanc'd his rev'rend head *W.F.* 330
And the new world launch forth to seek the *o. W.F.* 402
O.-fashioned *halls, dull Aunts, and croaking rooks E.* v. 12

Oldfield.

O. with more than Harpy throat endu'd *S.* ii. 25
When *O.* loves, what Dartineuf detests *S.* vi. 87
At *Quin's high plume, or O.'s petticoat S.* v. 331

Oldmixon.

In native majesty *O.* stands *D.* ii. 283
And *O.* and Burnet both out-lie *S.* viii. 61
Not from the Burnets, O—s, *and Cookes P.S.* 146

Olive.

Peace o'er the World her *o.* wand extend *M.* 19
Cheap herbs, and eggs, and o—s still we see S. ii. 35
Where Peace descending, bids her *o.* spring *W.F.* 429

Olympus.

And all *O*. rings with loud alarms *R.L.* v. 48
Not proud *O*. yields a nobler sight *W.F.* 33
Might change *O*. for a nobler hill *W.F.* 234

Ombre.

And love of *O*. after death survive *R.L.* i. 56
At *O*. singly to decide their doom *R.L.* iii. 27
Where none learn *O*., none e'er taste Bohea *R.L.* iv. 156

Ombrelia.

This curs'd *O*., this undoing Fair *Mi.* ix. 55
I saw him stand behind O.'s Chair Mi. ix. 6

Omens.

This day black *O*. threat the brightest Fair *R.L.* ii. 101
'Twas this the morning *o*. seem'd to tell *R.L.* iv. 161

Omits.

The deeds, and dextrously *o*., *see heires S.* vii. 100

On.—*Passim*.

Once.

What City Swans *o*. sung within the walls *D.* i. 96
Rememb'ring she herself was Pertness *o. D.* i. 112
And *o*. betray'd me into common sense *D.* i. 188
Take up the Bible, *o*. my better guide *D.* i. 200
At *o*. the Bear and Fiddle of the town *D.* i. 224
Or peaceably forgot, at *o*. be blest *D.* i. 239
Where the tall may-pole *o*. o'er-look'd the Strand *D.* ii. 28
That *o*. so flutter'd, and that *o*. so writ *D.* ii. 120
Here strip, my children ! here at *o*. leap in *D.* ii. 275
" Receive" (he said) " these robes that *o*. were mine *D.* ii. 351
O. swan of Thames, tho' now he sings no more *D.* iii. 20
That *o*. was Britain—Happy ! had she seen *D.* iii. 117
And her Parnassus glancing o'er at *o. D.* iii. 137
Preacher at *o*., and Zany of thy age *D.* iii. 205
Then take at *o*. the Poet and the Song *D.* iv. 8
Full in the midst of Euclid dip at *o. D.* iv. 463
In flow'd at *o*. a gay embroider'd race *D.* iv. 275
O. brightest shin'd this child of Heat and Air *D.* iv. 424
O. I would the Sons of Men *o*. think their Eyes *D.* iv. 453
Beeves, at his touch, at *o*. to jelly turn *D.* iv. 551
With thee repose, where Tully *o*. was laid *E.* iii. 29
And, if it can, at *o*. both please and preach *E.* iv. 24
And *o*. the lot of Abelard and me *E.A.* 98
But let heav'n seize it, all at *o*. 'tis fir'd *E.A.* 201
To dream *o*. more I close my willing eyes *E.A.* 239
Ah, come not, write not, think not *o*. of me *E.A.* 291
O. like thyself, I trembled, wept, and pray'd *E.A.* 311
Teach me at *o*., and learn of me to die *E.A.* 328
A fool might *o*. himself alone expose *E.C.* 7
At *o*. the source, and end, and test of Art *E.C.* 73
Without all these at *o*. before your eyes *E.C.* 122
The heart, and all its end at *o*. attains *E.C.* 155
If *o*. right reason drives that cloud away *E.C.* 211
The Whole at *o*. is bold and regular *E.C.* 252
O. on a time, La Mancha's Knight, they say *E.C.* 267
But let a Lord *o*. own the happy lines *E.C.* 420
O. School-divines this zealous isle o'erspread *E.C.* 440
Might he return, and bless *o*. more our Eyes *E.C.* 462
Who, if *o*. wrong, will needs be always so *E.C.* 569
Such *o*. were Critics ; such the happy few *E.C.* 643
Where slaves *o*. more their native land behold *E.M.* i. 107
At *o*. extend the int'rest, and the love *E.M.* iii. 134
Yet make at *o*. their circle round the Sun *E.M.* iii. 314
You'll find if *o*. the monarch acts the monk *E.M.* iv. 201
At *o*. his own bright prospect to be blest *E.M.* iv. 351
You grow correct, that *o*. with Rapture writ *E.S.* i. 3
The S—te's, and then H—vy's *o*. again *E.S.* i. 72
O. break their rest, or stir them from their Place *E.S.* i. 100
Must great Offenders, *o*. escap'd the Crown *E.S.* ii. 28
You make men desp'rate if they *o*. are bad *E.S.* ii. 59
Thus SOMERS *o*., and HALIFAX were mine *E.S.* ii. 77
It anger'd TURENNE, *o*. upon a day *E.S.* ii. 150
Form'd to delight at *o*. and lash the age *Ep.* xi. 4
Yet ah ! how *o*. we lov'd remember still *Ep.* xiii. 3
A Weasel *o*. made shift to slink *I.H.* i. 51
As *o*. a week we travel down *I.H.* ii. 97
O. on a time (so runs the Fable) *I.H.* ii. 157
Waste sandy valleys, *o*. perplex'd with thorn *M.* 73
His Principle of action *o*. explore *M.E.* i. 27
Must then at *o*. (the character to save) *M.E.* i. 125
That gay Free-thinker, a fine talker *o. M.E.* i. 162
This clue *o*. found, unravels all the rest *M.E.* i. 178
Nothing so true as what you *o*. let fall *M.E.* ii. 1
'Twas thus Calypso *o*. each heart alarm'd *M.E.* ii. 45
And paid a Tradesman *o*. to make him stare *M.E.* ii. 56
Th' Address, the Delicacy—stoops at *o. M.E.* ii. 85
Scarce *o*. herself, by turns all Woman-kind *M.E.* ii. 116
O., we confess, beneath the Patriot's cloak *M.E.* iii. 35
On *o*. a flock-bed, but repair'd with straw *M.E.* iii. 301
Where *o*. I went to Church I'll now go twice *M.E.* iii. 367
And pompous buildings *o*. were things of Use *M.E.* iv. 24
Sufficient sap at *o*. to bear and rot *Mi.* iii. 12
I joyless make my *o*. ador'd *Alpen Mi.* ix. 5
This *Snuff-Box*,—*o*. the pledge of SHARPER's love *Mi.* ix. 37
I yield at *o*., and sink into his arms *Mi.* ix. 96
O. (says an Author ; where, I need not say) *Mi.* xi. 1
And men *o*. ignorant are slaves *O.* ii. 28
The truth *o*. told (and wherefore should we lie ?) *P.S.* 81
Full ten years slander'd, did he *o*. reply *P.S.* 374
And *o*. inclos'd in Woman's beauteous mould *R.L.* i. 48
That all her vanities at *o*. are dead *R.L.* i. 52
Unnumber'd treasures ope at *o*., and here *R.L.* i. 129
Oft she rejects, but never *o*. offends *R.L.* ii. 12
At *o*. they gratify their scent and taste *R.L.* iii. 111
Like that where *o*. Ulysses held the winds *R.L.* iv. 82
O. gave new beauties to the snowy neck *R.L.* iv. 170
And tempts *o*. more thy sacrilegious hands *R.L.* iv. 174
And is at *o*. their vinegar and wine *S.* ii. 54
And Helmsley, *o*. proud Buckingham's delight *S.* ii. 177
Adieu to Virtue, if you're *o*. a Slave *S.* iii. 118
They hire their sculler, and when *o*. aboard *S.* iii. 159
Nor *o*. to Chanc'ry, nor to Hale apply *S.* iii. 173
Or damn to all eternity at *o. S.* v. 59
And, having *o*. been wrong, will be so still *S.* v. 130
Let me for *o*. presume t' instruct the times *S.* v. 340
As *o*. for LOUIS, Boileau and Racine *S.* v. 375
O. (and but *o*.) I caught him in a lie *S.* vi. 17
Who live at Court, for going *o*. that way *S.* viii. 23
Had *o*. a pretty gift of Tongues enough *S.* viii. 77
If *o*. he catch you at your *Jesu! Jesu S.* viii. 257
O. I was skill'd in ev'ry herb that grew *Sw.* 31
Most souls, 'tis true, but peep out *o*. an age *U.L.* 17
What *o*. had beauty, titles, wealth and fame (*rep*.) *U.L.* 70
Her name with pleasure *o*. she taught the shore *W.* 43
At *o*. the Monarch's and the Muse's seats *W.F.* 2
At *o*. the chaser, and at *o*. the prey *W.F.* 82
Such was the life great Scipio *o*. admir'd *W.F.* 257
O. more to bend before a BRITISH QUEEN *W.F.* 384
Peru *o*. more a race of kings behold *W.F.* 411
And, fast beside him, o.-fear'd Edward sleeps W.F. 314
Such were the notes thy *o.-lov'd* Poet sung *E.* i. 1
Ah then, thy *o*. Eloisa see *E.A.* 329
Oh let thy *o*. Friend inscribe thy Stone *Ep.* iii. 7

One.

O. leap from yonder cliff shall end my pains *A.* 95
O. Cell there is conceal'd from vulgar eye *D.* i. 1
Here *o*. poor word an hundred clenches makes *D.* i. 63
But lived in Settle's numbers *o*. day more *D.* i. 90
O. clasp'd in wood, and *o*. in strong cow-hide *D.* i. 150
Never was dash'd out at *o*. lucky hit *D.* i. 47
O. on his manly confidence relies (*rep*.) *D.* ii. 169
Now thousand tongues are heard in *o*. loud din *D.* ii. 235
With holy envy gave *o*. Layman place *D.* ii. 324
Then mount the clerks, and in *o*. lazy tone *D.* ii. 387
O. circle first, and then a second makes *D.* ii. 406
Like motion from *o*. circle to the rest *D.* ii. 408
Such vary'd light in *o*. promiscuous blaze *D.* ii. 412
O. god-like Monarch all that pride confounds *D.* iii. 75
And *o*. bright blaze turns Learning into air *D.* iii. 78
See, Christians, Jews, *o*. heavy sabbath keep *D.* iii. 99
But oh ! with *O*., immortal *O*. dispense *D.* iii. 217
Till *o*. wide conflagration swallows all *D.* iii. 240
Lo ! *o*. vast Egg produces human race *D.* iii. 248
Yet, yet a moment, *o*. dim Ray of Light *D.* iv. 1
O. Trill shall harmonize joy, grief, and rage *D.* iv. 57
O. instinct seizes, and transports away *D.* iv. 74
Whate'er of mongrel no *o*. class admits *D.* iv. 89
Milton's on this, on that *o*. Johnston's name *D.* iv. 112
We hang *o*. jingling padlock on the mind *D.* iv. 162
O ! if my sons may learn *o*. earthly thing (*rep*.) *D.* iv. 183
Nor has *o*. ATTERBURY spoil'd the flock *D.* iv. 246
We bring to *o*. dead level ev'ry mind *D.* iv. 268

ONE (continued).

The Sire saw, o. by o., his virtues wake D. iv. 285
This glorious Youth, and add o. Venus more D. iv. 330
Blest in o. Niger, till he knows of two D. iv. 370
Or at o. bound o'er-leaping all his laws D. iv. 477
Sire, Ancestors, Himself. O. cast his eyes D. iv. 519
Another (for in all what o. can shine) D. iv. 555
To three essential Partridges in o. D. iv. 562
Nor past the meanest unregarded, o. (rep.) D. iv. 575
Proud to my list to add o. Monarch more D. iv. 600
And MAKE O. MIGHTY DUNCIAD OF THE LAND D. iv. 604

As, o. by o., at dread Medea's strain D. iv. 635
Clos'd o. by o. to everlasting rest D. iv. 638
Thro' Fortune's cloud o. truly great can see E. i. 39
O. dip the pencil, and o. string the lyre E. iii. 70
But sets up o., a greater, in their place E. iv. 38
Yet takes o. kiss before she parts for ever E. v. 6
Then give o. flirt, and all the vision flies E. v. 38
And all those tender names in o., thy love E.A. 154
O. thought of thee puts all the pomp to flight E.A. 273
Come, with o. glance of those deluding eyes E.A. 283
Nor share o. pang of all I felt for thee E.A. 292
May o. kind grave unite each hapless name E.A. 343
O. human tear shall drop and be forgiv'n E.A. 358
Ten censure wrong for o. who writes amiss E.C. 6
Now o. in verse makes many more in prose E.C. 8
Unfinish'd things, o. knows not what to call E.C. 45
Or o. vain wit's, that might a hundred tire E.C. 45
O. science only will o. genius fit E.C. 60
O. clear, unchang'd, and universal light E.C. 71
That shunning faults, o. quiet tenour keep E.C. 241
And all to o. lov'd Folly sacrifice E.C. 266
O. glaring Chaos and wild heap of wit E.C. 292
And ten low words oft create in o. dull line E.C. 347
To o. small sect, and all are damn'd beside E.C. 397
See worlds on worlds compose o. universe E.M. i. 24
A thousand movements scarce o. purpose gain (rep.) E.M. i. 54
Towns to o. grave, whole nations to the deep E.M.i.144
Is not thy Reason all these pow'rs in o. E.M. i. 232
Where o. step broken, the great scale's destroy'd E.M. i. 244
The least confusion but in o., not all E.M. i. 249
All are but parts of o. stupendous whole E.M. i. 267
Safe in the hand of o. disposing Pow'r E.M. i. 287
O. truth is clear, WHATEVER IS, IS RIGHT E.M. i. 294
Describe or fix o. movement of his Mind E.M. ii. 36
Self-love and Reason to o. end aspire E.M. ii. 87
And hence o. Master Passion in the breast E.M. ii. 131
And in o. int'rest body acts with mind E.M. ii. 180
But Heav'n's great view is O., and that the Whole E.M. ii. 238
Till o. Man's weakness grows the strength of all E.M. ii. 252
Not o. will change his neighbour with himself E.M. ii. 262
O. prospect lost, another still we gain E.M. ii. 289
See I and confess, o. comfort still must rise E.M. ii. 293
Acts to o. end, but acts by various laws E.M. iii. 2
Press to o. centre still, the gen'ral Good E.M. iii. 14
O. all-extending, all-preserving Soul E.M. iii. 22
Who thinks all made for o., not o. for all E.M. iii. 48
All feed on o. vain Patron, and poison o. E.M. iii. 61
O. must go right, the other may go wrong E.M. iii. 94
O. in their nature, which are two in ours E.M. iii. 96
Or pours profuse on earth, o. nature feeds E.M. iii. 117
Each sex desires alike, till two are o. E.M. iii. 122
Still as o. brood, and as another rose E.M. iii. 139
Here rose o. little state, another near E.M. iii. 201
Till common int'rest plac'd the sway in o. E.M. iii. 210
O. great first father, and that first ador'd E.M. iii. 226
And simple Reason never sought but o. E.M. iii. 230
Th' enormous faith of many made for o. E.M. iii. 242
To o. Man's pow'r, ambition, lucre, lust E.M. iii. 270
For, what o. likes, if others like as well (rep.) E.M. iii. 273
That touching o. must strike the other too E.M. iii. 292
Draw to o. point, and to o. centre bring E.M. iii. 301
All must be false that thwart this O. great End E.M. iii. 309
And o. regards itself, and o. the Whole E.M. iii. 316
Subsist not in the good of o., but all E.M. iv. 38
O. common blessing, as o. common soul E.M. iv. 62
O. they must want, which is, to pass for good E.M.iv.92
O. thinks on Calvin Heav'n's own spirit fell E.M.iv.137
What shocks o. part will edify the rest (rep.) E.M.iv.141

O. flaunts in rags, o. flutters in brocade E.M. iv. 196
Not o. looks backward, onward still he goes E.M.iv.223
O. self-approving hour whole years outweighs E.M. iv. 255
Never elated, while o. mao's oppress'd E.M. iv. 323
In o. close system of Benevolence E.M. iv. 358
That REASON, PASSION, answer o. great aim E.M. iv. 395
Come harmless Characters, that no o. hit E.S. i. 65
Shew there was o. who held it in disdain E.S. i. 172
Ye Statesmen, Priests, of o. Religion all E.S. ii. 16
To Cato, Virgil pay'd o. honest line E.S. ii. 120
Knew o. a Man of Honour, o. a Knave E.S. ii. 153
If o., thro' Nature's Bounty or his Lord's E.S. ii. 173
Fix'd to o. side, yet mod'rate to the rest Ep. ii. 4
Go, where to love and to enjoy are o. Ep. vii. 16
Yes, we have liv'd—o. pang and then we part Ep. xiii. 1
Is there on Earth o. care, o. wish beside Ep. xiii. 7
Or add o. Patriot to the sinking state Ep. xiv. 4
In peace let o. poor Poet sleep Ep. xv. 2
Lies o. who ne'er car'd, and still cares not a pin Ep.xvi.5
And not to ev'ry o. that comes I.H. i. 23
And kept you up so oft till o. I.H. i. 48
Which o. belonging to the House I.H. i. 55
Nor o. that Temperance advance I.H. i. 61
And, Mr. Dean, o. word from you I.H. ii. 82 s
"'Tis o. to me"—"Then tell us, pray I.H. ii. 119?
Stop, or turn nonsense, at o. glance of thee I.H. iii. 40
The steer and lion at o. crib shall meet M. 79
O. tide of glory, o. unclouded blaze M. 102
While o. there is who charms us with his Spleen M.E. i. 62

To ease the Soul of o. oppressive weight M.E. i. 105
O. action Conduct ; o., heroic Love M.E. i. 134
Grown all to all, from no o. vice exempt M.E. i. 194
In this o. Passion man can strength enjoy M.E. i. 222
For o. puff more, and io that puff expires M.E. i. 245
O. would not, sure, be frightful when o.'s dead M.E. i. 250
How many pictures of o. Nymph we view M.E. ii. 5
Let then the Fair o. beautifully cry M.E. ii. 11
Finds all her life o. warfare upon earth M.E. ii. 118
By Wealth of Follow'rs! without o. distress M.E. ii. 145
But never, never, reach'd o. gen'rous Thought M.E. ii. 162
Of all her Dears she never slander'd o. M.E. ii. 175
O. certain Portrait may (I grant) be seen M.E. ii. 181
Nor leave o. sigh behind them when they die M.E. ii. 230
Poor Avarice o. torment more would find M.E. iii. 59
Congenial souls ! whose life o. Av'rice joins (rep.) M.E. iii. 131
Ask we what makes o. keep, and o. bestow M.E. iii. 163
O. solid dish his week-day meal affords M.E. iii. 343
In o. abundant show'r of Cent. per Cent. M.E. iii. 372
There (so the Dev'l ordain'd) o. Christmas-tide M.E. iii. 383
And o. more Pensioner St. Stephen gains M.E. iii. 394
And of o. beauty many blunders make M.E. iv. 28
O. boundless Green, or flourish'd Carpet views M.E. iv. 95
In o. short view subjected to our eye M.E. v. 33
To gain Pescennius o. employs his schemes (rep.) M.E. v. 39
Yes, she has o., I must aver ML viii. 10
O., o. bad Deal, Three Septlevas have lost Mi. ix. 12
Would all my gold in o. bad Deal were gone Mi. ix. 15
With not o. sin, but poetry Mi. xii. 2
And burn for ever o. O. iii. 22
What various joys on o. attend O. iii. 27
Who shames a Scribbler ? break o. cobweb thro' P.S. 89
Does not o. table Bavius still admit (rep.) P.S. 99
But foes like these—O. Flatt'rer's worse than all P.S.104
O. dedicates in high heroic prose P.S. 109
O. from all Grubstreet will my fame defend P.S. 111
Ammon's great son o. shoulder had too high P.S. 117
With open arms receiv'd o. Poet more P.S. 142
Yet ne'er o. sprig of laurel grac'd those ribalds P.S. 161
Peace to all such ! but were there O. whose fires P.S.193
That tends to make o. worthy man my foe P.S. 284
Not proud, nor servile ;—be o. Poet's praise P.S. 336
To please a Mistress o. aspers'd his life P.S. 376
And keep a while o. parent from the sky P.S. 413
If o'er o. vision touch'd thy infant thought R.L. i. 29
O. speaks the glory of the British Queen (rep.) R.L. iii. 13

ONLY—OPINION.

Gain'd but *o.* trump and *o.* Plebeian card *R.L.* iii. 54
Puts forth *o.* manly leg, to sight reveal'd *R.L.* iii. 57
In heaps on heaps ; *o.* fate o'erwhelms them all *R.L.* iii. 86
On *o.* nice Trick depends the gen'ral fate *R.L.* iii. 94
Here living Tea-pots stand, *o.* arm held out *(rep.) R.L.* iv. 49
Or who would learn *o.* earthly thing of use *R.L.* v. 22
O. died in metaphor, and *o.* in song *R.L.* v. 60
She with *o.* finger and a thumb subdu'd *R.L.* v. 80
Bond is but *o.*, but Harpax is a score *S.* i. 44
Like in all else, as *o.* Egg to another *S.* i. 50
Not *o.* but nods, and talks of Jonson's Art *S.* i. 82
But shew me *o.* who has it in his pow'r *S.* i. 136
Hear BETHEL's sermon, *o.* not vers'd in schools *S.* ii. 9
To *o.* that was, or would have been a Peer *S.* ii. 40
About *o.* vice, and fall into the other *S.* ii. 46
O. half-pint bottle serves them both to dine *S.* ii. 53
Nor stops, for *o.* bad cork, his butler's pay *S.* ii. 63
And all the man is *o.* intestine war *S.* ii. 72
Thou hast at least bestow'd *o.* penny well *S.* ii. 110
How dar'st thou let *o.* worthy man be poor *S.* ii. 118
Well, if the use be mine, can it concern *o. S.* ii. 165
'Tis Reason's voice, which sometimes *o.* can hear *S.* iii. 12
Alike in nothing but *o.* Lust of Gold *S.* iii. 124
(They know not whither) in a chaise and *o. S.* iii. 158
O. ebb and flow of follies all my life *S.* iii. 168
You never change *o.* muscle of your face *S.* iii. 171
Thus good or bad, to *o.* extreme betray *S.* iv. 24
Shall *O.*, whom Nature, Learning, Birth conspir'd *S.* iv. 40
But art thou *o.*, whom new opinions sway *(rep.) S.* iv. 63
Add *o.* round hundred, and (if that's not fair) *S.* iv. 75
Or if your life be *o.* continued Treat *S.* iv. 110
Just in *o.* instance, be it yet confest *S.* v. 31
O. likes no language but the Faery Queen *S.* v. 39
O. Simile, that solitary shines *S.* v. 111
O. Tragic sentence if I dare deride *S.* v. 121
Now times are chang'd, and *o.* Poetic Itch *S.* v. 169
O. knighted Blackmore and *o.* pension'd Quarles *S.* v. 387
Tir'd with a tedious march, *o.* luckless night *S.* vi. 35
In *o.* our Frolics, our Amusements end *(rep.) S.* vi. 74
O. likes a Pheasant's wing, and *o.* the leg *S.* vi. 84
There's a Rehearsal, Sir, exact at *o. S.* vi. 97
O. lull'd th' Exchequer, and *o.* stunn'd the Rolls *S.* vi. 130
Dear Cibber ! never match'd *o.* ode of thine *S.* vi. 138
Say, can you find out *o.* such lodger there *S.* vi. 223
Why, of two brothers, rich and restless *o. S.* vi. 270
Why *o.* like Bu—, with pay and scorn content *S.* vi. 274
O., driv'n by strong Benevolence of soul *S.* vi. 287
'Tis *o.* thing madly to disperse my store *S.* vi. 292
When of a hundred thorns, you pull out *o. S.* vi. 321
O. Giant-Vice, so excellently ill *(rep.) S.* vii. 4
O. sings the Fair ; but songs no longer move *S.* vii. 21
O., *o.* man only breeds my just offence *S.* vii. 45
O., whom the mob, when next we find or make *S.* viii. 34
The suit, if by the fashion *o.* might guess *S.* viii. 40
He forms *o.* tongue, exotic and refin'd *S.* viii. 49
And (all those plagues in *o.* the bawling Bar *S.* viii. 55
I have but *o.*, I hope the fellow's clean *S.* viii. 111
As *o.* of Woodward's patients, sick, and sore *S.* viii. 152
O. of our Giant Statutes ope its jaw *S.* viii. 173
Ran out as fast, as *o.* who pays his bail *S.* viii. 282
Or should *o.* pound of powder less bespread *S.* viii. 246
Just as *o.* Beauty mortifies another *S.* viii. 259
And in *o.* garland all their beauties join *Sw.* 56
In whom all beauties are compris'd in *o. Sw.* 58
Nor left *o.* virtue to redeem her Race *U.L.* 28
Life's idle business at *o.* gasp be o'er *U.L.* 81
O. Chorus let all Being raise *U.P.* 51
The Frail *o.*'s *advocate, the Weak o.'s friend M.E.* ii. 30

Only.—*Passim.*

Onslow.
"And perfect *Speaker* ?" "*O.*, past dispute." *S.* viii. 71

Onward.
Not one looks backward, *o.* still he goes *E.M.* iv. 223

Ooze.
And each ferocious feature grim with *o. D.* ii. 328

Oozy.
In that blest moment from his *o.* bed *W.F.* 329

Ope.
Unnumber'd treasures *o.* at once, and here *R.L.* i. 129
One of our Giant Statutes *o.* its jaw *S.* viii. 173

Oped.
The quaking mud, that clos'd, and *o.* no more *D.* ii. 292
And *o.* those eyes that must eclipse the day *R.L.* i. 14

Open.
Tho' oft the ear the *o.* vowels tire *E.C.* 345
Try what the *o.*, what the covert yield *E.M.* i. 10
True, some are *o.*, and to all men known *M.E.* i. 51
Tom struts a Soldier, *o.*, bold, and brave *M.E.* i. 153
With aspect *o.* shall erect his head *M.E.* v. 65
In bright Confusion *o. Rouleaux* lie *Mi.* ix. 81
With *o.* arms receiv'd one Poet more *P.S.* 142
Like batt'ring-rams, beats *o.* ev'ry door *S.* viii. 265
Your virtues o. fairest in the shade M.E. ii. 202
Bid Harbours *o.*, public Ways extend *M.E.* iv. 197
The balanc'd World, and *o.* all the Main *S.* v. 2
Unlock your springs, and *o.* all your shades *W.F.* 4

Open'd.
The first thus *o.*: "Hear thy suppliant's call *D.* iv. 403
The most recluse, discreetly *o.*, find *D.* iv. 447
And Paradise was *o.* in the Wild *E.A.* 134
When those blue eyes first *o.* on the sphere *M.E.* ii. 284
Thy eyes first *o.* on a Billet-doux *R.L.* i. 118
He first the snuff-box *o.*, then the case *R.L.* iv. 126
Smooth'd ev'ry brow, and *o.* ev'ry soul *S.* v. 248

Op'ner.
His Son's fine Taste an *o.* Vista loves *M.E.* iv. 93

Op'ning.
Let *o.* roses knotted oaks adorn *A.* 37
The *o.* clouds disclose each work by turns *D.* i. 249
While *o.* Hell spouts wild-fire at your head *D.* iii. 316
By the French horn, or by the *o.* hound *D.* iv. 278
And mild as *o.* gleams of promis'd heav'n *E.A.* 236
And dawning grace is *o.* on my soul *E.A.* 280
From *o.* skies may streaming glories shine *E.A.* 341
If nature thunder'd in his *o.* ears *E.M.* i. 201
Fair *o.* to some Court's propitious shine *E.M.* v. 9
The Scene, the Master *o.* to my view *E.S.* ii. 68
And ev'ry *o.* Virtue blooming round *Ep.* xiv. 2
Calls in the Country, catches *o.* glades *M.E.* iv. 61
His purple pinions *o.* to the sun *R.L.* ii. 71
While *o.* blooms diffuse their sweets around *Sp.* 100
There, interspers'd in lawns and *o.* glades *W.F.* 21
Rouse the fleet hart, and cheer the *o.* hound *W.F.* 25
And bring the scenes of *o.* fate to light *W.F.* 426

Opens.
As Fancy *o.* the quick springs of Sense *D.* iv. 156
As the mind *o.*, and its functions spread *E.M.* ii. 142
And *o.* still, and *o.* on his soul *E.M.* iv. 342
Heav'n *o.* on my eyes ! my ears *O.* v. 14

Opera, Op'ra.
Already *O.* prepares the way *D.* iii. 299
She went from *O'a*, Park, Assembly, Play *E.* v. 13
Then his nice taste directs our O—s D. ii. 204
New Eunuchs, Harlequins, and *O. S.* viii. 125
His royal Sense of *Op'ras* or the Fair *D.* iv. 314
A perfect genius at an O.-song S. vi. 11

Operates.
Spreads undivided, *o.* unspent *E.M.* i. 274

Operation.
And to their proper *o.* still *E.M.* ii. 57

Opes.
Bentley his mouth with classic flatt'ry *o. D.* ii. 205
And *o.* the Temple of *Eternity E.S.* ii. 235

Ophir.
And seeds of gold in *O.'s* mountains glow *M.* 96

Opiate.
Then all for Death, that *O.* of the soul *M.E.* ii. 91

Opine.
O. that Nature, as in duty bound *M.E.* iii. 9

Opinion.
But always think the last *o.* right *E.C.* 431
Weigh thy *O.* against Providence *E.M.* i. 114

Mean-while *O*. gilds with varying rays *E.M.* ii. 283
When (each *o*. with the next at strife *S.* iii. 167
Take Nature's path and mad O.'s *leave E.M.* iv. 29
And all *O*. colours cast on life *M.E.* i. 22
Ask men's O—s : *Scots now shall tell M.E.* i. 158
O.! they still raise a wider range *M.E.* i. 170
But art thou one, whom new *o*. sway *S.* iv. 63

Opium.
Here stood her *O*., here she nurs'd her Owls *D.* i. 271
With mystic words the sacred *O*. shed *D.* i. 288
Of Mirth and *O*., Ratafie and Tears *M.E.* ii. 110

Oppose.
O. thyself to heav'n ; dispute my heart *E.A.* 282

Oppos'd.
Her poniard had *o*. the dire command *E.A.* 102

Opposing.
Th' *o*. body's grossness, not its own *E.C.* 469

Oppress'd, Opprest.
Never elated, while one man's *o*. *E.M.* iv. 323
To ease th' *o*., and raise the sinking heart *M.E.* iii. 244
But anxious cares the pensive nymph *o*. *R.L.* iv. 1
Rich ev'n when plunder'd, honour'd while *o*. *S.* iii. 182
O. we feel the beam directly beat *S*. v. 21
As Argus' eyes by Hermes' wand *o—t D.* i. 637
All but the Sylph—with careful thoughts *o*. *R.L.* ii. 53
And blended lie th' oppressor and th' *o*. *W.F.* 318

Oppression.
Experience, this ; by Mac's *o*. curst *M.E.* ii. 213

Oppressive.
To ease the Soul of one *o*. weight *M.E.* i. 105

Oppressor.
Th' *O*. rul'd tyrannic where he durst *W.F.* 74
And blended lie th' *o*. and opprest *W.F.* 318

Optics.
Say what the use, were finer *o*. giv'n *E.M.* i. 195
The *o*. seeing, as the object seen *M.E.* i. 32

Or.—*Passim.*

Oracle.
Their law his eye, their *o*. his tongue *E.M.* iii. 218
The World's great *O*. in times to come *W.F.* 384
He hears loud O—s, *and talks with Gods D.* iii. 8
As Heav'n's own *O*. from Altars heard *S.* v. 28
Who deem'd each other *O*. of Law *S.* vi. 128

Orange.
With handkerchief and *o*. at my side *P.S.* 228
Not wrap up O—s, *to pelt your sire D.* i. 236

Orator.
And the puff'd *o*. bursts out in tropes *D.* ii. 206
When thus th' attendant *O*. begun *D.* iv. 281

Oratory.
Come, Henley's *O*., Osborne's Wit *E.S.* i. 65

Orb.
Not closer, *o*. in *o*., conglob'd are seen *D.* iv. 79
And unobserv'd the glaring *O*. declines *M.E.* ii. 256
A narrow *o*. each crowded conquest keeps *M.E.* v. 25
And round the *o*. in lasting notes be read *M.E.* v. 66
Some, *o*. in *o*., around the nymph extend *R.L.* ii. 138
Instruct the planets in what o—s *to run E.M.* ii. 21
Some guide the course of wand'ring *o*. on high *R.L.* ii. 79
Now marks the course of rolling *o*. on high *W.F.* 245

Orbit.
Let Earth unbalanc'd from her *o*. fly *E.M.* i. 251

Orcas.
Loud as the Wolves, on *O*.' stormy steep *S.* v. 328
In Scotland, at the O—des ; *and there E.M.* ii. 223

Ordain.
But now (so ANNE and Piety *o*.) *D.* ii. 29
For thee the fates, severely kind, *o*. *E.A.* 249

Ordain'd.
By the same laws which first herself *o*. *E.C.* 91
License repress'd, and useful laws *o*. *E.C.* 682

What if the foot, *o*. the dust to tread *E.M.* i. 259
There (so the Dev'l *o*.) one Christmas-tide *M.E.* iii. 383
So Time, that changes all things, had *o*. *S.* viii. 43

Ordains.
The great directing MIND of ALL *o*. *E.M.* i. 266

Order.
To blot out *O*., and extinguish Light *D.* iv. 14
Which out of nature's common *o*. rise *E.C.* 157
All rang'd in *o*., and dispos'd with grace *E.C.* 672
Of *O*., sins against th' Eternal Cause *E.M.* i. 130
The gen'ral *O*., since the whole began *E.M.* i. 171
All this dread *O*. break—for whom ? for thee *E.M.* i. 257
Cease then, nor *O*. Imperfection name *E.M.* i. 281
So far the first eternal *O*. ran *E.M.* iii. 113
From *O*., Union, full Consent of things *E.M.* iii. 296
O. is Heav'n's first law ; and this confest *E.M.* iv. 49
Each silver Vase in mystic *o*. laid *R.L.* i. 122
When numerous wax-lights in bright *o*. blaze *R.L.* iii. 168
Pageants on Pageants, in long *o*. drawn *S.* v. 316
Where twelve fair Signs in beauteous *o*. lie *Sp.* 40
Where *o*. in variety we see *W.F.* 15
And proud his Mistress o—s *to perform D.* iii. 263
And Navies yawn'd for *O*. on the Main *D.* iv. 618

Ordure.
Renew'd by *o*.'s sympathetic force *D.* ii. 103

Ore.
On the cast *o*., another Pollio, shine *M.E.* v. 64
And Phœbus warm the rip'ning *o*. to gold *W.F.* 396

Organ.
When the full *o*. joins the tuneful quire *O.* i. 126
Thus, as the pipes of some carv'd *O*. move *S.* vii. 17
The swelling o—s *lift the rising soul E.A.* 272
The proper *o*., proper pow'rs assign'd *E.M.* i. 180
As strong or weak, the *o*. of the frame *E.M.* ii. 130
The deep, majestic, solemn *o*. blow *O.* i. 11

Orient.
And *o*. Science their bright course begun *D.* iii. 74

Orion.
But see, *O*. sheds unwholesome dews *W.* 85

Ornament.
Ev'n in an *o*. its place remark *M.E.* iv. 77
And hide with o—s *their want of art E.C.* 296
Reverse your *O*., and hang them all *M.E.* iv. 31

Orphan.
No weeping *o*. saw his father's stores *E.A.* 135
A Virgin Tragedy, an *O*. Muse *P.S.* 56
Him portion'd maids, apprentic'd o—s *blest M.E.* iii. 267

Orpheus.
Of *O*. now no more let Poets tell *O.* i. 131
But would you sing, and rival O.' *strain Su.* 81

Ortolans.
Cramm'd to the throat with *O. I.H.* i. 62

Osborne.—*See also* Mother Osborne.
O. and Curl accept the glorious strife *D.* ii. 167
First *O*. lean'd against his letter'd post *D.* ii. 171
O., thro' perfect modesty o'ercome *D.* ii. 189
Come, Henley's Oratory, O.'s *Wit E.S.* i. 65

Osiers.
Let vernal airs thro' trembling *o*. play *Sp.* 5

Ostræa.
Norton, from Daniel and *O*. sprung *D.* ii. 415

Ostrogoths.
See the bold *O*. on Latium fall *D.* iii. 93

Othello.
Not fierce *O*. in so loud a strain *R.L.* v. 105

Other, Others.—*Passim.*

Otho.
Lord of an *O*., if I vouch it true *D.* iv. 369
O. a warrior, Cromwell a buffoon *M.E.* i. 88
Sighs for an *O*., and neglects his bride *M.E.* v. 44

Otway.
And full in Shakespear, fair in *O*. shone (*rep.*) *S.* v. 277
And you shall rise up *O*. for your pains *S.* vi. 146

OUGHT—OWN.

Ought.—*Passim.*
Our, Ours, Ourselves.—*Passim.*
Out.—*Passim.*
As weak, as earnest, and as gravely o, *M.E.* i. 230
Prevent the greedy, and o.-bid the *bold S.* iv. 72
O.-cant old Esdras, or out-drink his heir *S.* vii. 37
He dies, sad o.-*cast* of each church and state *M.E.* i. 204
O.-do Llandaff in Doctrine,—yea in Life *E.S.* i. 134
Go dine with Chartres, in each vice *o. S.* iv. 120
Out-cant old Esdras, and *o.-drink* his heir *S.* vii. 37
A work t' o.-*last* immortal Rome design'd *E.C.* 131
And Oldmixon and Burnet both *o.-lie S.* viii. 61
So much the Fury still *o.-ran* the Wit *M.E.* ii. 127
High on a gorgeous seat, that far *o.-shone D.* i. 1
The rest on *O.-side* merit but presume *D.* i. 135
Here pleas'd behold her mighty wings *o.-spread D.* i. 27
He left huge Lintot, and *o.-stripp'd* the wind *D.* ii. 62
O.-usure Jews, or Irishmen *o.-swear S.* vii. 38
Living, great Nature fear'd he might *o.-vie Ep.* viii. 7
One self-approving hour whole years *o.-weighs E.M.* iv. 255
Swear like a Lord, or Rich *o.-whore* a Duke *E.S.* i. 116

Outward.
Pride, Pomp, and State but reach his *o.* part *E.* iv. 55

Over.—*See also* **O'er.**—*Passim.*
Nor *o.-dress*, nor leave her wholly bare *M.E.* iv. 52
Rolls the black troop, and *o.-shades* the street *D.* ii. 360
Not so his Son ; he mark'd this *o.-sight M.E.* iii. 197
'Tis hers to rectify, not *o.-throw E.M.* ii. 163

Ovid.
How sweet an *O.,* MURRAY was our boast *D.* iv. 169
Let me be Horace, and be *O.* you *S.* vi. 144
Such *O.'s* nose, and "*Sir! you have an Eye*" *P.S.* 118

Owe.
As clocks to weight their nimble motion *o. D.* i. 183
To these we *o.* true friendship, love sincere *E.M.* ii. 255
'Tis to their Changes half their charms we *o. M.E.* ii. 42
We *o.* to models of an humble kind *M.E.* ii. 192
Yet to their Lord *o.* more than to the soil *M.E.* iv. 184

Owes.
Which nor to Guilt or Fear, its Caution *o. E.* ii. 3
She *o.* to me the very charms she wears *Mi.* ix. 58

Owl.
Something betwixt a Heideggre and *O. D.* i. 290
Sick was the Sun, the *O.* forsook his Bow'r *D.* iv. 11
Which Chalcis Gods, and mortals call an *O. D.* iv. 362
Mix'd the *O.'s* Ivy *with the Poet's bays D.* iii. 54
Here stood her Opium, here she nurs'd her O—s *D.* i. 291
And makes night hideous—Answer him, ye *O. D.* iii. 166
Wits, who, like *o.,* see only in the dark *D.* iii. 192

Own.
And in her *o.* fools-colours gilds them all *D.* i. 84
And Quarles is sav'd by Beauties not his *o. D.* i. 140
The clubs of Quidnuncs, or her *o.* Guildhall *D.* i. 270
O! when shall rise a Monarch all our *o. D.* i. 311
In a dun night-gown of his *o.* loose skin *D.* ii. 38
Three wicked imps of her *o.* Grub-street choir *D.* ii. 123
So shall each hostile name become our *o. D.* ii. 139
Thus visit not thy *o. I* on this blest age *D.* iii. 121
Breaks out refulgent, with a heav'n its *o. D.* iii. 242
Unknown to thee ? these wonders are thy *o. D.* iii. 274
Tho' my *o.* Aldermen conferr'd the bays *D.* iii. 279
Reduc'd at last to hiss in my *o.* dragon *D.* iii. 286
See, see, our *o.* true Phœbus wears the bays *D.* iii. 323
Another Phœbus, thy *o.* Phœbus, reigns *D.* iv. 61
And Jove's *o.* Thunders follow Mars's Drums *D.* iv. 68
A Page, a Grave, that they can call their *o. D.* iv. 128
See I still thy *o.*, the heavy Canon roll *D.* iv. 247
Spoil'd his *o.* language, and acquir'd no more *D.* iv. 320
And make a long Posterity my *o. D.* iv. 334
Honour a Syrian Prince above his *o. D.* iv. 368
Down his *o.* throat her risk'd the Grecian gold *D.* iv. 382
This Nod confirms each Privilege your *o. D.* iv. 584
I tremble too, where'er my *o.* I find *E.A.* 33
Go just alike, yet each believes his *o. E.C.* 10
And then turn Critics in their *o.* defence *E.C.* 29
Be sure yourself and your *o.* reach to know *E.C.* 48
Against the Poets their *o.* arms they turn'd *E.C.* 106
T' admire superior sense, and doubt their *o. E.C.* 200
Leave such to tune their *o.* dull rhymes, and know *E.C.* 358
Some foreign writers, some our *o.* despise *E.C.* 394
Some ne'er advance a Judgment of their *o. E.C.* 408
Some valuing those of their *o.* side or mind *E.C.* 452
Th' opposing body's grossness, not its *o. E.C.* 469
With his *o.* tongue still edifies his ears *E.C.* 614
Garth did not write his *o.* Dispensary *E.C.* 619
Whose *o.* example strengthens all his laws *E.C.* 679
And ev'ry author's merit, but his *o. E.C.* 728
From her *o.* Sex should mercy find to-day *E.J.S.* 2
'Tis ours to trace him only in our *o. E.M.* i. 22
Each beast, each insect happy in its *o. E.M.* i. 185
Know thy *o.* point : This kind, this due degree *E.M.* i. 283
Explain his *o.* beginning, or his end *E.M.* ii. 38
But when his *o.* great work is but begun *E.M.* ii. 41
And Reason bids us for our *o.* provide *E.M.* ii. 96
Ask your *o.* heart, and nothing is so plain *E.M.* ii. 215
Loves of his *o.* and raptures swell the note *E.M.* iii. 34
Heav'ns not his *o.,* and worlds unknown before *E.M.* iii. 106
Murders their species, and betrays his *o. E.M.* iii. 164
And ev'ry death its *o.* avenger breeds *E.M.* iii. 166
With heav'n's *o.* thunders shook the world below *E.M.* iii. 267
On their *o.* Axis as the Planets run *E.M.* iii. 313
And Peace, oh Virtue! Peace is all thy *o. E.M.* iv. 82
One thinks on Calvin Heav'n's *o.* spirit fell *E.M.* iv. 137
The same (my Lord) if Tully's or your *o. E.M.* iv. 240
To see all others' faults, and feel our *o. E.M.* iv. 262
At once his *o.* bright prospect to be blest *E.M.* iv. 351
The Master of our Passions, and his *o. E.S.* ii. 89
Because the Deed he forg'd was not my *o. E.S.* ii. 190
And with a Father's sorrows mix his *o. Ep.* iii. 8
Convinc'd that Virtue only is our *o. Ep.* vi. 6
For their *o.* Worth, or our *o.* Ends *I.H.* ii. 150
They realm for ever lasts, thy *o.* Messiah reigns *M.* 108
All Manners take a tincture from our *o. M.E.* i. 33
By his *o.* son, that passes by unbless'd *M.E.* i. 235
Here Fannia, leering on her *o.* good man *M.E.* ii. 9
Or are they both, in this their *o.* reward *M.E.* iii. 336
Wife, son, and daughter, Satan ! are thy *o. M.E.* iii. 399
See Rome her *o.* sad Sepulchre appears *M.E.* v. 2
Perhaps by its *o.* ruins sav'd from flame *M.E.* v. 15
And shook the Stage with Thunders all his *o. Mi.* ii. 16
With borrow'd Pins, and Patches not her *o. Mi.* iii. 22
She first convers'd with her *o.* kind *Mi.* iv. 11
'Twas my *o.* Lord that drew the *fatal Card Mi.* ix. 48
Tho' my *o.* secret wish was for the *Knave Mi.* ix. 50
In his *o.* ground *O.* iv. 4
Be justly warm'd with your *o.* native rage *P.C.* 44
Dipt me in ink, my parents', or my *o. P.S.* 126
And sits attentive to his *o.* applause *P.S.* 210
Oh let me live my *o.*, and die so too *P.S.* 261
Th' imputed trash, and dulness not his *o. P.S.* 351
He gain his Prince's ear, or lose his *o. P.S.* 367
Each parent sprung—What fortune, pray?—Their *o. P.S.* 390
Hear and believe! thy *o.* importance know *R.L.* i. 35
As now your *o.,* our beings were of old *R.L.* i. 47
And Betty's prais'd for labours not her *o. R.L.* i. 148
And in its fellow's fate foresees its *o. R.L.* iv. 172
Thence comes your mutton, and these chicks my *o. S.* ii. 144
I'll hire another's ; is not that my *o. S.* ii. 156
I wish to God this house had been your *o. S.* ii. 162
Who cries, "My father's damn'd, and all's my *o.*" *S.* ii. 174
Let Us be fix'd, and our *o.* masters still *S.* ii. 180
Of all these ways, if each pursues his *o. S.* iii. 134
That Man divine whom Wisdom calls her *o. S.* iii. 180
Then turn about, and laugh at your *o.* jest *S.* iv. 109
As Heav'n's *o.* Oracles from Altars heard *S.* v. 28
Foes to all living worth except yours *o. S.* v. 53
And grew Immortal in his *o.* despite *S.* v. 72
And in our *o.* (excuse some Courtly stains) *S.* v. 215
Not but the Tragic spirit was our *o. S.* v. 276
With Laws, to which you gave your *o.* assent *S.* vi. 30
Ev'n to their *o.* S—r—v—nce in a Car *S.* vi. 107
Their *o.* strict Judges, not a word they spare *S.* vi. 159
His Ven'son too, a guinea makes your *o. S.* vi. 235
Yet these are Wights, who fondly call their *o. S.* vi. 244
Ready, by force, or of your *o.* accord *S.* vi. 250
If Peter deigns to help you to your *o. S.* vii. 66
He came by sure transition to his *o. S.* viii. 81
And close confin'd to their *o.* palace sleep *U.L.* 22

OWN'D—PAIN.

In notes more sad than when they sing their *o. W.* 40
A sweeter music than their *o.* to hear *W.* 58
Reap their *o.* fruits, and woo their sable loves *W.F.* 410
There hateful Envy her *o.* snakes shall feel *W.F.* 419
Not those *alone who passive o. her laws D.* iv. 85
And *o.* stale nonsense which they ne'er invent *E.C.* 411
But let a Lord once *o.* the happy lines *E.C.* 420
But you, with pleasure *o.* your errors past *E.C.* 570
Or never feel the rage, or never *o. E.M.* ii. 228
Nor *o.* your fathers have been fools so long *E.M.* iv. 214
And *o.* the Spaniard did a *waggish thing E.S.* i. 17
Let *Greatness o.* her, and she's mean no more *E.S.* i. 144
Pleas'd let me *o.*, in *Esher's* peaceful Grove *E.S.* ii. 66
So impudent, I *o.* myself no Knave *E.S.* ii. 206
I *o.* I'm pleas'd with this rebuke *J.H.* ii. 60 s
Asham'd to *o.* they gave delight before *M.E.* ii. 237
Who suffer thus, mere Charity should *o. M.E.* iii. 111
That live-long wig which Gorgon's self might *o. M.E.* iii. 293
Of these the chief the care of Nations *o. R.L.* ii. 89
Envy must *o.*, I live among the Great *S.* i. 133
'Tis yet in vain, I *o.*, to keep a pother *S.* ii. 45
If, after all, we must with Wilmot *o. S.* iv. 125
But let them *o.*, that greater Faults than we *S.* v. 95
I lose my patience, and I *o.* it too *S.* v. 115

Own'd.

And *o.* a Father when he *o.* a God *E.M.* iii. 234
And *o.* that nine such Poets made a *Tate P.S.* 190

Owner.

The *o.*'s wife, that other men enjoy *E.C.* 501

Owning.

Both fairly *o.*, Riches, in effect *M.E.* iii. 17

Owns.

No creature *o.* it in the first degree *E.M.* ii. 225
Or her, that *o.* her faults, but never mends *M.E.* ii. 103
Marcus with blushes *o.* he loves *O.* iii. 7

Ox.

When the dull *O.*, why now ne breaks the clod *E.M.* i. 63
Whose gentle progress makes a calf an *o. S.* vii. 48
While lab'ring oxen, *spent with toil and heat A.* 61
A hundred *o.* at your levee roar *M.E.* iii. 58
His *o.* perish in his country's cause *M.E.* ii. 206
While yon slow *o.* turn the furrow'd Plain *Sp.* 30
With cow-like udders, and with *o.*-like eyes *D.* ii. 164

Oxford.

Perhaps forgets that *O.* e'er was great *E.* i. 18
Who copies *Your's* or *O.*'s better part *M.E.* iii. 243

Oyster.

Two Trav'lers found an *O.* in their way *Mi.* xi. 2
'Twas a fat *O.*—Live in peace—Adieu *Mi.* xi. 12
Let me extol a Cat, on *o—s fed S.* ii. 41

Ozell.

Can make a Cibber, Tibbald, or *O. D.* i. 286

P.

Great C**, H**, *T**, R**, K* *D.* iv. 545
Or *P—ge* pour'd forth the Torrent of his Wit *E.S.* ii. 159
Lo *P—p—le's* brow, tremendous to the town *D.* iii. 151

Pace.

As, after stumbling, Jades will mend their *p. E.C.* 603
He springs to vengeance with an eager *p. R.L.* iii. 97
As from the god she flew with furious *p. W.F.* 189
Show all his p—s, *not a step advance D.* iv. 266

Pacific.

Their full fed Heroes, their *p.* May'rs *D.* iii. 281
Of modest wisdom, and *p.* truth *Ep.* vii. 2

Pack.

Next plunged a feeble, but a desp'rate *p. D.* ii. 305
And mighty Dukes p. *Cards for half-a-crown M.E.* iii. 142

Packet.

Bless me! a *p.*—"'Tis a stranger sues *P.S.* 55

Pactolus.

O'er golden sands let rich *P.* flow *Sp.* 61

Padlock.

We hang one jingling *p.* on the mind *D.* iv. 162

Padua.

P., with sighs, beholds her Livy burn *D.* iii. 105
Your only wearing is your *P—soy S.* viii. 113

Pæans.

Hear, in all tongues consenting *P.* ring *E.C.* 186

Pagan.

And Pan to Moses lends his *p.* horn *D.* iii. 110

Page.

She saw slow Philips creep like Tate's poor *p. D.* i. 105
Or where the pictures for the *p.* atone *D.* i. 139
Thro' the long, heavy, painful *p.* drawl on *D.* ii. 388
And dies, when Dulness gives her *P.* the word *D.* iv. 30
Withdrew his hand, and clos'd the pompous *p. D.* iv. 114
A *P.*, a Grave, that they can call their own *D.* iv. 198
His sable, subject, scope in ev'ry *p. E.C.* 120
All but the *p.* prescrib'd, their present state *E.M.* i. 78
Hard words or hanging, if your Judge be *P. S.* i. 82
A lengthen'd Thought that gleams thro' many a *p. S.* v. 113
No whiter *p.* than Addison remains *S.* v. 216
With Edward's acts adorn the shining *p. W.F.* 303
And view with scorn two *P*—s and a Chair *R.L.* i. 46
Wicked as *P.*, who in early years *S.* vii. 39

Pageant.

The gaze of fools, and *p.* of a day *U L.* 44
P—s *on p*—s, *in long order drawn S.* v. 316

Pagod.

See thronging Millions to the *P.* run *E.S.* i. 157
The mosque of Mahound, or some queer *P. S.* viii. 239

Paid.—See Pay'd.

Pain.

Not balmy sleep to lab'rers faint with *p. A.* 44
While thus each hand promotes the pleasing *p. D.* ii. 211
It fled, I follow'd; now in hope, now *p. D.* iv. 427
Above all *P.*, all Passion, and all Pride *E.* i. 24
Then share thy *p.*, allow that sad relief *E.A.* 49
The crime was common, common be the *p. E.A.* 104
A cool suspense from pleasure and from *p. E.A.* 250
In human works, tho' labour'd on with *p. E.M.* i. 53
Die of a rose in aromatic *p. E.M.* i. 200
Mere curious pleasure, or ingenious *p. E.M.* ii. 48
P. their aversion, Pleasure their desire *E.M.* ii. 88
Hate, Fear, and Grief, the family of *P. E.M.* ii. 118
'Tis to mistake them, costs the time and *p. E.M.* ii. 216
Which sees no more the stroke, or feels the *p. E.M.* iii. 67
Some sunk to Beasts, find pleasure end in *p. E.M.* iv. 23
Shall find, that pleasure pays not half the *p. E.M.* iv. 48
And if it lose, attended with no *p. E.M.* iv. 316
You purchase *P.* with all that Joy can give *M.E.* ii. 99
Without a *P.*, a Trouble, or a Fear *Mi.* v. 16
BETTY, who oft the *p.* of each has try'd *Mi.* ix. 24
The Winner's pleasure, and the Loser's *p. Mi.* ix. 80
Music can soften *p.* to ease *O.* i. 120
Oh the *p.*, the bliss of dying *O.* v. 4
P. at her side, and Megrim at her head *R.L.* iv. 24
Roar'd for the handkerchief that caus'd his *p. R.L.* v. 106
The Lock, obtain'd with guilt, and kept with *p. R.L.* v. 109
Their artless passions, and their tender p—s *A.* 12
One leap from yonder cliff shall end my *p. A.* 95
And *Wit* dreads Exile, Penalties, and *P. D.* iv. 22
Thy mighty Scholiast, whose unweary'd *p. D.* iv. 211
The *P.* and Penalties of Idleness *D.* iv. 344
And finish'd more thro' happiness than *p. E.* iii. 68
Repentant sighs and voluntary *p. E.A.* 18
Whose fame with *p.* we guard, but lose with ease *E.C.* 504
Employ their *p.* to spurn some other down *E.C.* 515
Just as absurd to mourn the tasks or *p. E.M.* i. 265
And begg'd he'd take the *p.* to kick the rest *E.S.* ii. 15
P., reading, study, are their just pretence *P.S.* 159
How vain are all these glories, all our *p. R.L.* v. 15
See him with *p.* of body, pangs of soul *S.* iii. 71
Be virtuous, and be happy for your *p. S.* iv. 62
Some doubt if equal *p.*, or equal fire *S.* v. 282
'Tis he, who gives my breast a thousand *p. S.* v. 342

PAINFUL—PANG.

And you shall rise up Otway for your *p.* *S.* vi. 146
If such the plague and *p.* to write by rule *S.* vi. 180

Painful.

While pensive Poets *p.* vigils keep *D.* i. 93
Thro' the long, heavy, *p.* page drawl on *D.* ii. 388
P. pre-eminence ! yourself to view *E.M.* iv. 267
Virtue she finds too *p.* an endeavour *M.E.* ii. 163

Paint.

Yet still her charms in breathing *p.* engage *E.* iii. 55
So well in *p.* and stone they judg'd of merit *S.* v. 384
P., Marble, Gems, and robes of Persian dye *S.* vi. 265
Now blushing berries p. *the yellow grove A.* 75
But as the Flatt'rer or Dependant *p. D.* v. 535
He best can *p.* 'em who shall feel 'em most *E.A.* 366
Feign what I will, and *p.* it e'er so strong *E.S.* ii. 8
If Folly grow romantic, I must *p.* it *M.E.* ii. 16
Chameleons who can *p.* in white and black *M.E.* ii. 156
'Tis well—but Artists ! who can *p.* or write *M.E.* ii. 187
Nor could it sure be such a sin to *p. R.L.* v. 24
P. Angels trembling round his falling Horse *S.* i. 28
We build, we *p.*, we sing, we dance as well *S.* v. 46
Fresh rising blushes *p.* the wat'ry glass *Su.* 28
And floating forests *p.* the waves with green *W.F.* 216
To *p.* anew the flow'ry sylvan scenes *W.F.* 285

Painted.

There *p.* valleys of eternal green *D.* i. 76
A Raphael *p.* and a Vida sung *E.C.* 704
Those *p.* clouds that beautify our days *E.M.* ii. 284
For what has Virro *p.* built and planted *M.E.* iv. 13
On *p.* Ceilings you devoutly stare *M.E.* iv. 145
The Fops are *p.* Butterflies *Mi.* iv. 17
A *p.* mistress, or a purling stream *P.S.* 150
This *p.* child of dirt, that stinks and stings *P.S.* 310
But now secure the *p.* vessel glides *R.L.* ii. 47
Or dip their pinions in the *p.* bow *R.L.* ii. 84
In glitt'ring dust and *p.* fragments lie *R.L.* iii. 160
Since *p.* or not *p.* all shall fade *R.L.* v. 27
Such *p.* puppets ! such a varnish'd race *S.* viii. 208
P. for sight, and essenc'd for the smell *S.* viii. 226
His *p.* wings, and breast that flames with gold *W.F.* 118
A *p.* quiver on her shoulder sounds *W.F.* 179
And naked youths and *p.* chiefs admire *W.F.* 405

Painter.

The living image in the *p.*'s breast *E.* iii. 42
Poets like p—s, *thus, unskill'd to trace E.C.* 293
Poets heap Virtues, *P.* Gems at will *M.E.* ii. 185

Painting.

Shines in exposing Knaves, and *p.* Fools *M.E.* ii. 119

Paints.

P. as you plant, and, as you work, designs *M.E.* iv. 64
And lavish Nature *p.* the purple Year *Sp.* 28
Here blushing Flora *p.* th' enamel'd ground *W.F.* 38
P. the green forests and the flow'ry plains *W.F.* 428

Pair.

Behold yon *P.*, in strict embraces join'd *D.* iii. 179
There lay three garters, half a *p.* of gloves *R.L.* ii. 39

Pair'd.

Figures ill-*p.*, and Similes unlike *D.* i. 66
P. with his Fellow-charioteer the Sun *D.* iv. 589

Palace.

The Stews and *P.* equally explor'd *D.* iv. 315
A constant Vapour o'er the *p.* flies *R.L.* iv. 39
That less admires the *P.* than the Park *S.* iii. 113
Up starts a *P.*; lo, th' obedient base *S.* iii. 140
And close confin'd to their own *p.*, sleep *U.L.* 22
Then p—s *shall rise; the joyful Son M.* 63
We see no new-built *p.* aspire *S.* vii. 111
In P.-yard *at nine you'll find me there S.* vi. 94

Palate.

Hard task ! to hit the *p.* of such guests *S.* vi. 86

Pale.

And keep them in the *p.* of Words till death *D.* iv. 160
Tears gush'd again, as from p. Priam's eyes D. i. 255
How Index-learning turns no student *p. D.* i. 279
The *p.* Boy-Senator yet tingling stands *D.* iv. 147
The shrines all trembled and the lamps grew *p. E.A.* 112
Where round some mould'ring tow'r *p.* ivy creeps *E.A.* 243

O'er the *p.* marble they shall join their heads *E.A.* 349
And sees *p.* Virtue carted in her stead *E.S.* i. 150
Who sees *p.* Mammon pine amidst her store *M.E.* iii. 171
With sharpen'd sight *p.* Antiquaries pore *M.E.* v. 35
Now nothing left, but wither'd, *p.*, and shrunk *Mi.* iii. 25
To the *p.* nations of the dead *O.* i. 52
And the *p.* spectres dance *O.* i. 68
Some, less refin'd, beneath the moon's *p.* light *R.L.* ii. 81
P., spectres, gaping tombs, and purple fires *R.L.* iv. 44
And the *p.* ghosts start at the flash of day *R.L.* v. 52
How *p.*, each Worshipful and Rev'rend guest *S.* ii. 75
Scar'd at the spectre of *p.* Poverty *S.* iii. 70
Pleas'd thy *p.* ghost, or grac'd thy mournful bier *U.L.* 50
Now fainting, sinking, *p.*, the nymph appears *W.F.* 191
Gigantic Pride, *p.* Terror, gloomy Care *W.F.* 415
Shrines ! where their vigils p.-ey'd *virgins keep E.A.* 21

Paleness.

A livid *p.* spreads o'er all her look *R.L.* iii. 90

Palinurus.

Ev'n *P.* nodded at the Helm *D.* iv. 614

Palladian.

P. walls, Venetian doors *I.H.* ii. 191
Conscious they act a true *P.* part *M.E.* iv. 37

Palladio.

Jones and *P.* to themselves restore *M.E.* iv. 193

Pallas.

Ere *P.* issu'd from the Thund'rer's head *D.* i. 10
'Gainst *P.*, Mars ; Latona, Hermes arms *R.L.* v. 47

Pallid.

Can they, in gems bid *p.* Hippia glow *M.E.* iii. 87

Palm.

Strives to extract from his soft, giving *p. D.* ii. 208
Beneath her *P.* here sad Judæa weeps *M.E.* v. 26
But now for Authors nobler p—s *remain D.* ii. 191
Celestial *p.*, and ever-blooming flow'rs *E.A.* 318
To leafless shrubs the flow'ring *p.* succeed *M.* 75
With simp'ring Angels, *P.*, and Harps divine *M.E.* ii. 14
Not but there are, who merit other *p. S.* v. 229
And *p.* eternal flourish round his urn *W.F.* 312

Palmers.

Behold yon Isle, by *P.*, Pilgrims trod *D.* iii. 113

Palmy.

See where the morning gilds the *p.* shore *D.* iii. 95

Paltry.

Is it for Bond, or Peter (*p.* things) *E.S.* i. 121
This subtle Thief of life, this *p.* Time *S.* vi. 76
P. and proud, as drabs in Drury-lane *S.* vii. 64

Pam.

Ev'n mighty *P.*, that Kings and Queens o'erthrew *R.L.* iii. 61

Paméla.

The Gods, to curse *P.* with her pray'rs *E.* iv. 49

Pamper'd.

"See man for mine !" replies a *p.* goose *E.M.* iii. 46

Pamphlets.

For writing *P.*, and for roasting Popes *D.* iii. 284

Pan.

P. came, and ask'd, what magic caus'd my smart *A.* 81
And *P.* to Moses lends his pagan horn *D.* iii. 110
Rough Satyrs dance, and *P.* applauds the song *Su.* 50
See *P.* with flocks, with fruits Pomona crown'd *W.F.* 37
P. saw and lov'd, and, burning with desire *W.F.* 183

Pane.

Lull'd by soft Zephyrs thro' the broken *p. P.S.* 42

Panegyric.

And I'm not us'd to *P.* strains *S.* v. 405

Pang.

Nor share one *p.*, of all I felt for thee *E.A.* 292
Yes, we have liv'd—one *p.*, and then we part *Ep.* xiii. 1
And the last *p.* shall tear thee from his heart *U.L.* 80
In trance ecstatic may thy p—s *be drown'd E.A.* 339
See him with pains of body, *p.* of soul *S.* iii. 71

PANT—PART.

Pant.
P. on thy lip, and to thy heart be press'd *E.A.* 123
The dying gales that *p.* upon the trees *E.A.* 159
To *A.*, or tremble thro' an Eunuch's throat *S.* v. 154
Th' inspiring bellows lie and *p.* below *S.* vii. 20

Panting.
Diffusing languor in the *p.* gales *D.* iv. 304
The Fair sate *p.* at a Courtier's play *E.C.* 540
My *p.* heart confesses all his charms *Mi.* ix. 95
To closer shades the *p.* flocks remove *Su.* 87
P. with hope, he tries the furrow'd grounds *W.F.* 100
Flutters in blood, and *p.* beats the ground *W.F.* 114

Pants.
She, while her lover *p.* upon her breast *M.E.* ii. 167
When the brisk Minor *p.* for twenty-one *S.* iii. 38
Who *p.* for glory finds but short repose *S.* v. 300
P. on the leaves, and dies upon the trees *W.* 80
Th' impatient courser *p.* in ev'ry vein *W.F.* 151
P. on her neck, and fans her parting hair *W.F.* 196

Panurge.
Good common linguists, and so P. was *S.* viii. 75

Papal.
And P. piety, and Gothic fire *M.E.* v. 14

Paper.
'Mid snows of *p.*, and fierce hail of pease *D.* iii. 262
On passive *p.*, or on solid brick *D.* iv. 130
Soft on the *p.* ruff its leaves I spread *D.* iv. 407
Whose spoils this *p.* offers to your eye *D.* iv. 435
Is there, who, lock'd from ink and *p.*, scrawls *P.S.* 19
For this your locks in *p.* durance bound *R.L.* iv. 99
To seise his p—s, Curl, was next thy care (*rep.*) *D.* ii.113
Or do the Prints and P. lie *I.H.* ii. 115 *s*
Fire in each eye, and *p.* in each hand *P.S.* 5
Blest p.-credit! last and best supply *M.E.* iii. 39

Papilia.
P., wedded to her am'rous spark *M.E.* ii. 37

Papist.
P. or Protestant, or both between *S.* i. 65
Convict a P. he, and I a Poet *S.* vi. 67
Yet like the P.'s, is the Poet's state *S.* vii. 11
Hopes after hopes of pious P—s fail'd *S.* vi. 62
Peace, fools, or Gonson will for P. seize you *S.* viii. 256

Paraclete.
To P.'s white walls and silver springs *E.A.* 348

Paradise.
Hence the Fool's P., the Statesman's Scheme *D.* iii. 9
And P. was open'd in the Wild *E.A.* 134
And bring all P. before your eye *M.E.* iv. 148

Parallels.
Who made the spider *p.* design *E.M.* iii. 103

Parch'd.
They *p.* with heat, and I inflam'd by thee *Su.* 20

Parchment.
On *p.* scraps y-fed, and Wormius hight *D.* iii. 188
His *Office* keeps your P. fates entire *S.* iii. 71

Pardon.
No *p.* vile Obscenity should find *E.C.* 530
These fools demand not *p.*, but Applause *S.* v. 118
Ev'n those I p., *for whose sinful sake* S. vii. 41

Pardon'd.
In days of old, they *p.* breach of vows *E.J.S.* 29

Parent.
King, priest, and *p.* of his growing state *E.M.* iii. 216
Lent Heav'n a *p.* to the poor and me *E.M.* iv. 110
Friend, *p.*, neighbour, first it will embrace *E.M.* iv. 367
And offer Country, P., Wife, or Son *E.S.* i. 158
Each *p.* sprung—What fortune, pray?—Their own *P.S.* 390
And keep a while one *p.* from the sky *P.S.* 413
P. of vapours and of female wit *R.L.* iv. 59
Could save a P.'s justest Pride from fate *Ep.* xiv. 2
Or their fond p—s drest in red and gold *D.* i. 138
Averted half your P—s' simple pray'r *M.E.* ii. 286
Dipt me in ink, my *p.*, or my own *P.S.* 126

Parian.
Eternal buckle takes in P. stone *M.E.* iii. 276
And gaze on P. charms with learned eyes *S.* iv. 31

Paridel.
Thee too, my P.! she mark'd thee there *D.* iv. 341

Paring.
He ate himself the rind and *p.* *I.H.* ii. 170

Paris.
Whence hapless Monsieur much complains at P. *D.* ii. 135
As, taught by Venus, P. learnt the art *D.* ii. 217

Park.
She went from Op'ra, P., Assembly, Play *E.* v. 13
Rufa, whose eye quick-glancing o'er the P. *M.E.* ii. 21
Sighs for the shades—"How charming is a P.!" (*rep.*) *M.E.* ii. 38
I introduc'd her to the P. and Plays *Mi.* ix. 63
That less admires the Palace than the P. *S.* iii. 113
Whether you call them Villa, P., or Chase *S.* vi. 255

Parliament.
Bows and votes on, in Court and P. *S.* vi. 275
And gets an Act of P. to cheat *S.* viii. 143

Parnassian.
Great Cibber sate: The proud P. sneer *D.* ii. 5
Twin'd with the wreaths P. laurels yield *E.M.* iv. 11
Lost the arch'd eye-brow, or P. sneer *P.S.* 96

Parnassus.
And her P. glancing o'er at once *D.* iii. 137
Who haunt P. but to please their ear *E.C.* 341
All Bedlam, or P., is let out *P.S.* 4
High on P.! top her sons she show'd *E.C.* 94
Now, they who reach P. lofty crown *E.C.* 514

Parnell.
Still hear thy P. in his living lays *E.* i. 16
From Pope, from P., or from Gay *I.H.* ii. 94

Parrots.
Men, monkeys, lap-dogs, *p.* perish all *R.L.* iv. 120

Parson.
The cobbler apron'd, or the *p.* gown'd *E.M.* iv. 197
Or, cobbler-like, the *p.* will be drunk *E.M.* iv. 202
From honest Mah'met, or plain P. Hale *M.E.* ii. 198
Is there a P. much bemus'd in beer *P.S.* 15
Narcissus, prais'd with all a P.'s pow'r *D.* iv. 103
In various shapes of P—s, Critics, Beaus *E.C.* 459

Part.
To touch Achilles' only tender *p.* *D.* ii. 218
Pride, Pomp and State but reach her outward *p.* *E.* iv. 55
All is not Heaven's while Abelard has *p.* *E.A.* 25
By Doctor's bills to play the Doctor's *p.* *E.C.* 109
But when t' examine ev'ry *p.* he came *E.C.* 134
Still make the Whole depend upon a P. *E.C.* 264
With gold and jewels cover ev'ry *p.* *E.C.* 295
And force that sun but on a *p.* to shine *E.C.* 399
Look'd thro'? or can a *p.* contain the whole *E.M.* i. 32
'Tis but a *p.* we see, and not a whole *E.M.* i. 60
Just as absurd for any *p.* to claim *E.M.* i. 263
Breathes in our soul, informs our mortal *p.* *E.M.* i. 275
Alas what wonder! Man's superior *p.* *E.M.* ii. 39
And pours it all upon the peccant *p.* *E.M.* ii. 144
P. pays, and justly, the deserving steer *E.M.* iii. 40
To copy Instinct then, was Reason's *p.* *E.M.* iii. 169
What shocks one *p.* will edify the rest *E.M.* iv. 141
Say, at what *p.* of Nature will they stand *E.M.* iv. 166
Act well your *p.*, there all the honour lies *E.M.* iv. 194
Extend it, let thy enemies have *p.* *E.M.* iv. 356
With ev'ry sprightly, ev'ry decent *p.* *I.H.* iii. 12
A very Heathen in the carnal *p.* *M.E.* ii. 67
With ev'ry pleasing, ev'ry prudent *p.* *M.E.* ii. 159
Perhaps you think the Poor may have their *p.* *M.E.* iii. 99
Who copies Your's or Oxford's better *p.* *M.E.* iii. 243
Conscious they act a true Palladian *p.* *M.E.* iv. 37
The verse and sculpture bore an equal *p.* *M.E.* v. 51
Amphibious thing! that acting either *p.* *P.S.* 326
Of gentle blood (*p.* shed in Honour's cause *P.S.* 388
With varying vanities from ev'ry *p.* *R.L.* i. 99
In all debates where Critics bear a *p.* *S.* i. 81
But not this *p.* of the Poetic State *S.* v. 348

Shall I, in London, act this idle *p. S.* vi. 125
A *p.* I will enjoy, as well as keep *S.* vi. 285
Trims Europe's balance, tops the Statesman's *p. S.* viii. 154
To act a Lover's or a Roman's *p. U.L.* 8
How p—s relate to p—s, or they to whole *D.* iv. 235
"My Sons!" (she answer'd) "both have done your *p. D.* iv. 437
In other *p.* it leaves wide sandy plains *E.C.* 55
But oft in those confin'd to single *p. E.C.* 63
Is not th' exactness of peculiar *p. E.C.* 244
No single *p.* unequally surprize *E.C.* 249
(As most in manners) by a love to *p. E.C.* 288
All are but *p.* of one stupendous whole *E.M.* i. 267
Expunge the whole, or lop th' excrescent *p. E.M.* ii. 49
P. it may ravage, but preserves the whole *E.M.* ii. 106
'Tis but by *p.* we follow good or ill *E.M.* ii. 235
Nothing is foreign: *P.* relate to whole *E.M.* iii. 21
In *P.* superior what advantage lies *E.M.* iv. 259
If *P.* allure thee, think how Bacon shin'd *E.M.* iv. 281
God loves from Whole to *P.*: but human soul *E.M.* iv. 361
Decay of *P.*, alas! we all must feel *E.S.* i. 5
All *P.* perform'd, and *all* her children blest *E.S.* i. 82
Shall *p.* so various aim at nothing new *M.E.* i. 186
None see what *p.* of Nature it conceals *M.E.* ii. 190
Ascribes his gettings to his *p.* and merit *M.E.* iii. 376
P. answ'ring *p.* shall slide into a whole *M.E.* iv. 66
The Wood supports the Plain, the *p.* unite *M.E.* iv. 81
Beauty that shocks you, *p.* that none will trust *P.S.* 332
Has age but melted those rough *p.* away *S.* vi. 318
Or court a Wife, spread out his wily *p. S.* vii. 57
Whose place is quarter'd out, three *p.* in four *S.* viii. 136
To *p. her time 'twixt reading and whole E.* v. 15
Ev'n thought meets thought, ere from the lips it *p. E.A.* 95
From vulgar bounds with brave disorder *p. E.C.* 152
Not parted long, and now to *p.* no more *Ep.* vii. 14
Yes, we have liv'd— one pang and then we *p. Ep.* xiii. 1
Not that—I cannot *p.* with that "—and died *M.E.* i. 261
But, Sir, to you, with what would I not *p. S.* vi. 15
Then from his closing eyes thy form shall *p. U.L.* 79
And p. admit, and p. *exclude* the day *W.F.* 18

Partake.
Calm Temperance, whose blessings those *p. D.* i. 49
Pursue the triumph, and *p.* the gale *E.M.* iv. 386

Parted.
Not *p.* long, and now to part no more *Ep.* vii. 14
Which never more shall join its *p.* hair *R.L.* iv. 134

Parterre.
His pond an Ocean, his *p.* a Down *M.E.* iv. 106
Embrown the Slope, and nod on the *P. M.E.* iv. 174
The vast P—s a thousand hands shall make *M.E.* iv. 73
Tir'd of the scene *P.* and Fountains yield *M.E.* iv. 67

Parthenia.
Or sees the blush of soft *P.* rise *E.* v. 46

Partial.
See Nature in some *p.* narrow shape *D.* iv. 455
With other beauties charm my *p.* eyes *E.A.* 126
Authors are *p.* to their wit, 'tis true *E.C.* 17
Acts not by *p.* but by gen'ral laws *E.M.* i. 146, and *E.M.* iv. 36
All *p.* Evil, universal Good *E.M.* i. 292
Gods *p.* changeful, passionate, unjust *E.M.* iii. 257
Or *p.* Ill is universal Good *E.M.* iv. 114
We grow more *p.* for th' Observer's sake *M.E.* i. 12
Your People, Sir, are *p.* in the rest *S.* v. 32

Particle.
What heav'nly *p.* inspires the clay *S.* ii. 78

Particolour'd.—*See also* Party.
And *p.* troops, a shining train *R.L.* iii. 43

Parting.
Ev'n now, observant of the *p.* Ray *E.* i. 37
Shall hail the rising, close the *p.* day *I.H.* iii. 30
Pants on her neck, and fans her *p.* hair *W.F.* 196

Partitions.
What thin *p.* Sense from Thought divide *E.M.* i. 226

Partly.
Whose Heads she *p.*, whose completely blest *D.* iv. 6:2

Partners.
Ease of their toil, and *p.* of their care *S.* v. 246

Partridge.
All as a *p.* plump, full-fed, and fair *D.* ii. 41
This *P.* soon shall view in cloudless skies *R.L.* v. 137
All Worldly's hens, nay *p.* sold to town *S.* vi. 234
And in the new-shorn field the *p.* feeds *W.F.* 98
To three essential P—s in one *D.* iv. 362
Sell their presented *p.* and fruits *S.* ii. 51

Parts.
Yet takes one kiss before she *p.* for ever *E.* v. 6
Whose Cause-way *p.* the vale with shady rows *M.E:* iii. 259

Party.
Or bidst thou rather *P.* to embrace (*rep.*) *D.* i. 205
Tho' long my *P.* built on me their hopes *D.* iii. 283
Then dupe to *P.*, child and man the same *D.* iv. 502
I'll have a *p.* at the Bedford-head *S.* ii. 42
P—ies in *Wit* attend on those of State *E.C.* 456
All side in *p.*, and begin th' attack *R.L.* v. 39
Int'rest that waves on P.-colour'd *wings D.* iv. 538
And nobly wishing P.-rage to cease *M.E.* iii. 149

Pasquin.
Shall this a *P.*, that a Grumbler write *D.* iii. 182

Pass.
Sent with a *P.*, and vagrant thro' the land *D.* i. 232
Have you not seen at Guildhall's narrow *p. S.* vi. 104
O! *p. more innocent, in infant state D.* i. 237
Whose tuneful whistling makes the waters *p. D.* iii. 156
Before you *p.* th' imaginary rights *E.* v. 35
Nor *p.* these lips in holy silence seal'd *E.A.* 10
Some neither can for Wits nor Critics *p. E.C.* 38
The play may *p.*—but that strange creature, Shore *E.J.S.* 5
Yet never *p.* th' insuperable line *E.M.* i. 228
To welcome death, and calmly *p.* away *E.M.* ii. 260
One they must want, which is, to *p.* for good *E.M.* iv. 92
His word would *p.* for more than he was worth *M.E.* iii. 344
At Timon's Villa let us *p.* a day *M.E.* iv. 99
Out with it, DUNCIAD, let the secret *p. P.S.* 79
Nor lets, like Nævius, ev'ry error *p. S.* ii. 65
The Greatest can but blaze, and *p.* away *S.* iv. 47
But let the Fit *p.* o'er, I'm wise enough *S.* vi. 151
How free, or frugal, I *p.* my days *S.* vi. 269
I *p.* o'er all those Confessors and Martyrs *S.* vii. 35
And brings all natural events to *p. S.* vii. 49
No Commentator can more slily *p. S.* vii. 101
The watch would hardly let him *p.* at noon *S.* viii. 32
Why yes, 'tis granted, these indeed may *p. S.* viii. 74
In time to come may *p.* for holy writ *S.* viii. 287
Oh! how I long with you to *p.* my days *Su.* 77
Thus unlamented *p.* the proud away *U.L.* 43
Ev'n I more sweetly *p.* my careless days *W.F.* 431

Passage.
His rapid waters in their *p.* burn *D.* ii. 184
And smooth my *p.* to the realms of day *E.A.* 322
And hail her *p.* to the Realms of Rest *E.S.* i. 81
A bird of *p.!* gone as soon as found *M.E.* i. 97

Pass'd, Past.
Thro' both he *p.*, and bow'd from side to side *D.* iv. 10
Their ancient bounds the banish'd Muses *p. E.C.* 710
The World's great Victor *p.* unheeded by *P.C.* 34
I ne'er with wits or witlings *p.* my days *P.S.* 223
Beneath yon poplar oft we *p—t* the day *A.* 66
This labour *p.*, by Bridewell all descend *D.* ii. 269
Judge of all present, *p.* or future wit *D.* ii. 376
And let the *p.* and future fire thy brain *D.* ii. 66
As thou preserv'st the dulness of the *p. D.* iii. 190
Safe and unseen the young Æneas *p. D.* iv. 290
Nor *p.* the meanest unregarded, one *D.* iv. 575
Still makes new conquests, and maintains the *p. E.* iv.62
Now turn'd to heav'n, I weep my *p.* offence *E.A.* 187
Some have at first for Wits, then Poets *p. E.C.* 36
Th' eternal snows appear already *p. E.C.* 227
Which from the first has shone on ages *p. E.C.* 402
But sense surviv'd, when merry jests were *p. E.C.* 460
But you with pleasure own your errors *p. E.C.* 570
Which serv'd the *p.*, and must the times to come *E.M.* ii. 52

But *p*. the Sense of human miseries *E.S.* i. 101
Tho' *p*. the recollection of the thought *M.E.* i. 47
Old Politicians chew on Wisdom *p. M.E.* i. 228
Such in those moments as in all the *p. M.E.* i. 264
Like Doctors thus, when much dispute has *p. M.E.* iii.15
Alas! 'tis more than (all his visions *p.*) *M.E.* iii. 83
And swear no Day was ever *p.* so ill *M.E.* iv. 168
As her dead Father's rev'rend image *p. P.C.* 31
The Dog-star rages! nay 'tis *p.* a doubt *P.S.* 3
Welcome for thee, fair Virtue! all the *p. P.S.* 358
His life, tho' long, to sickness *p.* unknown *P.S.* 402
In various talk th' instructive hours they *p. R.L.* iii. 11
Safe *p.* the Gnome thro' this fantastic band *R.L.* iv. 55
Plague on't! 'tis *p.* a jest—nay prithee, pox *R.L.* iv. 129
St. John, whose love indulg'd my labours *p. S.* iii. 1
The great Alcides, ev'ry Labour *p. S.* v. 17
Sense, *p.* thro' him, no longer is the same *S.* vii. 33
"And perfect *Speakers*?" "Onslow, *p.* dispute." *S.*viii.71
He *p.* it o'er; affects an easy smile *S.* vii. 122
Not thus the land appear'd in ages *p. W.F.* 43
Consults the dead, and lives *p.* ages o'er *W.F.* 248

Passenger.
Tho' many a *p.* he rightly call *M.E.* i. 7
What is't to me, (a *p.* God wot) *S.* vi. 296
There p—s shall stand, and pointing say *U.L.* 39

Passeran.
And so may'st thou, illustrious *P. E.S.* i. 124

Passes.
When all that *p., inter nos I.H.* ii. 99 *s*
By his own son, that *p.* by unbless'd *M.E.* i. 231

Passing.
Such skill in *p.* all, and touching none *D.* iv. 258
Which without *p.* thro' the judgment, gains *E.C.* 154

Passion.
The third mad *p.* of thy doting age *D.* iii. 304
Above all Pain, all *P.*, and all Pride *E.* i. 24
And boasts a warmth that from no *P.* flows *E.* ii. 4
Before true *p.* all these views remove *E.A.* 79
Unequal task! a *p.* to resign *E.A.* 195
That never *p.* discompos'd the mind *E.M.* i. 168
Chaos of Thought and *P.*, all confus'd *E.M.* ii. 13
What Reason weaves, by *P.* is undone *E.M.* ii. 42
Reason the card, but *P.* is the gale *E.M.* ii. 108
And hence one MASTER *P.* in the breast *E.M.* ii. 131
The Mind's disease, its RULING *P.* came *E.M.* ii. 138
And treat this *p.* more as friend than foe *E.M.* ii. 164
Grafts on this *P.* our best principle *E.M.* ii. 176
Whate'er the *P.*, knowledge, fame, or pelf *E.M.* ii. 261
See some fit *P.* ev'ry age supply *E.M.* ii. 128
Each Virtue in each *P.* takes its turn *E.M.* iii. 136
Is yellow dirt the *p.* of thy life *E.M.* iv. 279
That REASON, *P.*, answer one great aim *E.M.* iv. 395
There, where no *P.*, Pride, or Shame transport *E.S.*i.97
P. and Pride were to her soul unknown *Ep.* vi. 5
Search then the RULING *P.*: there, alone *M.E.* i. 174
Whose ruling *P.* was the Lust of Praise *M.E.* i. 181
His *P.* still, to covet gen'ral praise *M.E.* i. 196
In this one *P.* man can strength enjoy *M.E.* i. 222
Shall feel your ruling *p.* strong in death *M.E.* i. 263
Yet ne'er so sure our *p.* to create *M.E.* ii. 51
Now Conscience chills her, and now *P.* burns *M.E.* ii. 65
On the soft *P.*, and the Taste refin'd *M.E.* ii. 84
For ever in a *P.*, or a Pray'r *M.E.* ii. 106
No *P.* gratify'd except her Rage *M.E.* ii. 126
To that each *P.* turns, or soon or late *M.E.* ii. 133
A Fop their *P.*, but their Prize a Sot *M.E.* ii. 247
The ruling *P.*, be it what it will (rep.) *M.E.* iii. 153
Than ev'o that *P.*, if it has no Aim *M.E.* iii. 156
Hear thou the truth: "'Tis Heav'n each *P.* sends *M.E.* iii. 159
Not warp'd by *P.*, aw'd by Rumour *Mi.* viii. 5
Then first his *P.* was in public shown *Mi.* ix. 40
Such unfeign'd *P.* in his Looks appears *Mi.* ix. 93
The wise man's *p.*, and the vain man's toast *R.L.* v. 10
Is Wealth thy *p.*! Hence! from Pole to Pole *S.* iv. 69
But if to Pow'r and Place your *p.* lie *S.* iv. 97
Can make me feel each *P.* that he feigns *S.* v. 343
Swell'd with new *p.*, and o'erflows with tears *W.* 66
Where Jove, subdu'd by mortal *P.* still *W.F.* 233
Add Nature's, Custom's, *Reason's*, P.'s strife *M.E.* i.21
Their artless p—s, and their tender pains *A.* 12
There died the best of *p.*, Love and Fame *E.A.* 40

Those restless *p.* in revenge inspires *E.A.* 82
The manners, *p.*, unities; what not *E.C.* 276
And bid alternate *p.* fall and rise *E.C.* 375
And *P.* are the elements of Life *E.M.* i. 170
Modes of Self-love the *P.* we may call *E.M.* ii. 93
P., tho' selfish, if their means be fair *E.M.* ii. 97
P., like Elements, tho' born to fight *E.M.* ii. 111
Hence diff'rent *P.* more or less inflame *E.M.* ii. 129
She but removes weak *p.* for the strong *E.M.* ii. 158
Like varying winds, by other *p.* tost *E.M.* ii. 167
The surest Virtues thus from *P.* shoot *E.M.* ii. 183
Wants, frailties, *p.*, closer still ally *E.M.* ii. 253
To Man's low *p.*, or their glorious ends *E.M.* iv. 376
The Master of our *P.*, and his own *E.S.* ii. 89
Or come discolour'd thro' our *P.* shown *M.E.* i. 34
By *P.*? these dissimulation hides *M.E.* i. 169
In Men, we various ruling *P.* find *M.E.* ii. 207
My *P.* rise, and will not bear the rein *Mi.* i. 84
Intestine war no more our *P.* wage *O.* i. 34
What tender *p.* take their turns *O.* iii. 33
And secret *p.* labour'd in her breast *R.L.* iv. 2
Sighs, sobs, and *p.*, and the war of tongues *R.L.* iv. 84
And heav'nly breasts with human *p.* rage *R.L.* v. 46
But for the *P.*, Southern sure and Rowe *S.* v. 86
And sets the *P.* on the side of Truth *S.* v. 218
His actions', p.', being's, use and end M.E. i. 66
Oft, in the *P.* wild rotation tost *M.E.* i. 41

Passionate.
Gods partial, changeful, *p.*, unjust *E.M.* iii. 257

Passive.
On *p.* paper, or on solid brick *D.* iv. 130
Not those alone who *p.* own her laws *D.* iv. 85

Pastime.
Thy joy, thy *p.*, thy attire, thy food *E.M.* iii. 28

Pastor.
No zealous *P.* blame a failing Spouse *E.S.* ii. 193

Pastora.
Is there, *P.* by a fountain side *M.E.* ii. 8

Pastorals.
The Bard whom pilfer'd *P.* renown *P.S.* 179

Pasture.
Seeks freshest *p.* and the purest air *M.* 50
To beasts his p—s, and to fish his floods E.M. iii. 58

Pasty.
Not quite a madman, tho' a *p.* fell *S.* vi. 190

Patch.
To *p.*, nay ogle, might become a Saint *R.L.* v. 23
With borrow'd pins, and p—es *not her own Mi.* iii. 22
Puffs, Powders, *P.*, Bibles, Billet-doux *R.L.* i. 138
Thrice from my trembling hand the p.-box fell *R.L.* iv. 162
In *p.*-work flutt'ring, and her head aside *D.* iv. 48

Patch'd.
Peel'd, *p.*, and pyebald, linsey-wolsey brothers *D.* iii. 115
On some *p.* dog-hole ek'd with ends of wall *M.E.* iv. 32

Paternal.
Shrink back to my *p.* cell *I.H.* i. 75
A few *p.* acres bound *O.* iv. 2
Depriv'd us soon of our *p.* cell *S.* vi. 59

Pater-noster.
So Luther thought the *P.* long *S.* vii. 105

Path.
Or tread the *p.* by vent'rous Heroes trod *D.* i. 201
The Patriot's plain, but untrod, *p.* pursue *E.* ii. 16
Take Nature's *p.*, and mad Opinion's leave *E.M.* iv. 29
Self-love forsook the *p.* it first pursu'd *E.M.* iii. 281
Back thro' the p—s of pleasing sense I ran E.A. 69
And pointed out those arduous *p.* they trod *E.C.* 95
To Virtue, in the *p.* of Pleasure, trod *E.M.* iii. 233
'Tis he th' obstructed *p.* of sound shall clear *M.* 41

Pathetic
Implore your help in these *p.* strains *S.* v. 232

Pathless.
Seek the clear spring, or haunt the *p.* grove *W.F.* 168

Pathos.
Alike to them, by *P*. or by Pun *S*. v. 295

Patience.
To tire our *p*., than mislead our sense *E.C.* 4
I lose my *p*. and I own it too *S.* v. 115
You lose your *p* just like other men *S*. v. 363
Wild to get loose, his *P*. I provoke *S*. viii. 116

Patient.
All that we ask is but a *p*. Ear *S*. iii. 64
P. of labour when the end was rest *S*. v. 242
The *p*. fisher takes his silent stand *W.F.* 137
As one of Woodward's p—s, sick, and sore S. viii. 152

Patriarch.
Till then, by Nature crown'd, each *P*. sate *E.M.* iii. 215
When P.-wits *surviv'd a thousand years E.C.* 479

Patriot.
Thee shall the *P*., thee the Courtier taste *D.* iii. 297
Beholds himself a *P*., Chief, or Saint *D.* iv. 535
And makes a *p*. as it makes a knave *E.M.* ii. 202
Poet or *P*., rose but to restore *E.M.* iii. 285
A *P.* is a Fool in ev'ry age *E.S.* i. 41
In Soldier, Churchman, *P.*, Man in Pow'r *E.S.* i. 161
Must never *P*. then declaim at Gin *E.S.* ii. 191
An honest Courtier, yet a *P*. too *Ep.* ii. 5
Or add one *P*. to the sinking state *Ep.* xiv. 4
Statesman and *P*. ply alike the Stocks *M.E.* iii. 139
Sometimes a *P*., active in debate *S.* iii. 27
That from a *P*. of distinguish'd note *S*. vi. 196
The P.'s *plain, but untrod, path pursue E.* ii. 16
Once, we confess, beneath the *P.* cloak *M.E.* iii. 35
Here, rising bold, the *P*. honest face *M.E.* v. 57
Courtiers and P—s *in two ranks divide D.* iv. 107
P. there are who wish you'd jest no more *E.S.* i. 24
And *P*. still, or Poets, deck the Line *Ep*. i. 14
In vain may Heroes fight, and *P*. rave *M.E.* iii. 33
Senates degen'rate, *P.* disagree *M.E.* iii. 148
Britain, that pays her *P*. with her Spoils *M.E.* iii. 216
Such tears as *P*. shed for dying Laws *P.C.* 14

Patritio.
Who would not praise *P*.'s high desert *M.E.* i. 81

Patron.
He wins this *P*., who can tickle best *D.* ii. 196
All feed on one vain *P*., and enjoy *E.M.* iii. 61
P. of Arts, and Judge of Nature, died *Ep.* i. 2
I want a *P*.; ask him for a Place *P.S.* 50
May some choice *P*. bless each gray-goose quill *P.S.* 249
Above a *P*., tho' I condescend *P.S.* 265
While you, great *P*. of Mankind! sustain *S*. v. 1
That Fop, whose pride affects a p.'s *name P.S.* 291
P—s, *who sneak from living worth to dead D.* iv. 95

Patroniz'd.
Who rhym'd for hire, and *p*. for pride *D.* iv. 102

Pats.
Gay *p*. my shoulder, and you vanish quite *E.* v. 47

Paul.
Why—if I must—(then wept) I give it *P. M.E.* i. 259
There, all from P.'s *to Aldgate drink and sleep D.* ii. 346
Nor is *P*. church more safe than *P*. churchyard *E.C.* 623

Paulo.
P.'s free stroke, and Titian's warmth divine *E.* iii. 38

Paunch.
(Reply'd soft Annius) "this our *p*. before *D.* iv. 388

Pause.
Snuff, or the fair, supply each *p*. of chat *R.L.* iii. 17
As breathe, or p., *by fits, the airs divine D.* ii. 394

Pav'd.
Streets *p*. with Heroes, Tiber chok'd with Gods *D.* iii. 108

Pawing.
And, *p*., seems to beat the distant plain *W.F.* 152

Pawn'd.
Who having lost his credit, *p*. his rent *S.* viii. 138

Pay.
Where only Merit constant *p*. receives *E.M.* iv. 313
When Paxton gives him double Pots and *P. E.S.* ii. 141
To see a footman kick'd that took his *p. E.S.* ii. 151
When are the troops to have their *p. I.H.* ii. 130 s
Nor stops, for one bad cork, his butler's pay *S.* ii. 63
Why one like Bu—, with *p*. and scorn content *S.* vi. 274
From dreams of millions, and three groats to p. *D.* ii. 252
Who *p*. her homage, in her sons, the Great *D.* iv. 92
Thou, Abelard! the last sad office *p. E.A.* 321
To *p*. their Debts, or keep their Faith, like Kings *E.S.* i. 122
With heads declin'd, ye cedars homage *p. M.* 35
For very want; he could not *p*. a dow'r *M.E.* iii. 326
Awkward and supple each devoir to *p. Mi.* iii. 17
Hear me *p*., my dying Vows *Mi.* vii. 24
There are, who to my person *p*. their court *P.S.* 115
I *p*. my debts, believe, and say my pray'rs *P.S.* 268
And *p*. the Great our homage of Amaze *S.* iv. 17
You *p*. a penny, and he paid a pound *S.* vi. 239
Could not but think to *p*. his fine was odd *S.* viii. 17
As deep in debt, without a thought to *p. S.* viii. 21
P. their last duty to the Court, and come *S.* viii. 214

Pay'd, Paid.
To *Cato, Virgil p*. one honest line *E.S.* ii. 120
For God is *p*. when Man receives *U.P.* 19
And *paid* a Tradesman once to make him stare *M.E.* iii. 56
He *p*. some bards with port, and some with praise *P.S.* 242
And others (harder still) he *p*. in kind *P.S.* 244
Who gave the bail, or *p*. the visit last *M.E.* iii. 12
While visits shall be *p*. on solemn days *R.L.* iii. 167
And *p*. for all my satires, all my rhymes *S.* viii. 6
He names the price for ev'ry office *p. S.* viii. 162

Pays.
Part *p*., and justly, the deserving steer *E.M.* iii. 40
Shall find, that pleasure *p*. not half the pain *E.M.* iv. 48
P. the last Tribute of a Saint to Heav'n *Ep.* xiv. 14
When universal homage Umbra *p. M.E.* i. 59
Britain, that *p*. her Patriots with her Spoils *M.E.* iii. 216
She dearly *p*. for Nisus' injur'd hair *R.L.* iii. 124
To thee the World its present homage *p. S.* v. 23
Ran out as fast, as one who *p*. his bail *S.* viii. 182
Shall shortly want the gen'rous tear he *p. U.L.* 78

Paxton.
'Tis all a Libel—*P*. (Sir) will say *E.S.* ii. 1
When *P*. gives him double Pots and Pay *E.S.* ii. 141

Pea.
'Mid storms of paper, and fierce hail of *p—se D.* iii. 262

Peace.
In *p*., great Goddess, ever be ador'd *D.* iii. 119
Scotists and Thomists, now, in *p*. remain *E.C.* 444
The joy, the *p*., the glory of Mankind *E.M.* ii. 248
All Nature's diff'rence keeps all Nature's *p. E.M.* iv. 56
Lie in three words, Health, *P.*, and Competence *E.M.* iv. 80
And *P.*, oh Virtue! *P*. is all thy own *E.M.* iv. 82
A love to *P.*, and hate of Tyranny *Ep.* ii. 10
Lover of *p*., and friend of human kind *Ep.* vii. 8
Content with Science in the Vale of *P. Ep.* x. 6
In *p*. let one poor Poet sleep *Ep.* xv. 2
P. o'er the World her olive wand extend *M.* 19
No thought of *p*. or happiness at home *M.E.* ii. 224
To buy both sides, and give thy Country *p. M.E.* iii. 150
His Father's Acres who enjoys in *p. M.E.* iii. 181
These Honours *P*. to happy Britain brings *M.E.* iv. 203
'Twas a fat Oyster—Live in *p*.—Adieu *Mi.* xi. 12
In health of body, *p*. of mind *O.* iv. 11
P. to all such! but were there One whose fires *P.S.* 193
But he who hurts a harmless neighbour's *p. P.S.* 287
The merchant from th' Exchange returns in *p. R.L.* iii. 23
P. is my dear delight—not Fleury's more *S.* i. 75
In *p*. provides fit arms against a war *S.* ii. 12
Verse prays for *P.*, or sings down Pope and Turk *S*. v. 236
Your Country's *P*., how oft, how dearly bought *S.* v. 397
P. stole her wing, and wrapt the world in sleep *S*. v. 401
He stuck to poverty with *p*. of mind *S*. vi. 65
Much do I suffer, much, to keep in *p. S.* vi. 147

PEACEABLY—PENITENCE. 225

Secure of *p.* at least beyond the grave *S.* viii. 4
P., fools, or Gonson will for Papists seize you *S.* viii. 256
This day, be Bread and *P.* my Lot *U.P.* 45
And *p.* and plenty tell, a STUART reigns *W.F.* 42
She said! the world obey'd, and all was *P. W.F.* 328
Hail, sacred *p.!* hail, long-expected days *W.F.* 355
And Temples rise, the beauteous works of *P. W.F.* 378
O stretch thy reign, fair *P.!* from shore to shore *W.F.* 407
Where *P.* descending bids her olives spring *W.F.* 429

Peaceably.
Or *p.* forgot, at once be blest *D.* i. 239

Peaceful.
Ere such a soul regains its *p.* state *E.A.* 197
As the small pebble stirs the *p.* lake *E.M.* iv. 364
Pleas'd let me own, in Esher's *p.* grove *E.S.* ii. 66
P. sleep out the Sabbath of the Tomb *Mi.* v. 19
So *p.* rests, without a stone, a name *U.L.* 69
Nor saw displeas'd the *p.* cottage rise *W.F.* 86
Be mine the blessings of a *p.* reign *W.F.* 366

Peal.
Booth enters—hark! the Universal *p. S.* v. 334
Let p—s of laughter, Codrus! round thee break *P.S.* 85

Peal'd.
There, Webster! *p.* thy voice, and Whitfield! thine *D.* ii. 258

Pearls.
In flow'rs and *p.* by bounteous Kirkall dress'd *D.* ii. 160
Now hung with *p.* the dropping trees appear *W.* 31

Pearly.
The *p.* shell its lucid globe unfold *W.F.* 395

Peasant.
"An't please your Honour," quoth the *P. I.II.* ii. 218

Pebble.
As the small *p.* stirs the peaceful lake *E.M.* iv. 364

Peccant.
And pours it all upon the *p.* part *E.M.* ii. 144

Peck.
A *p.* of coals a-piece shall glad the rest *D.* ii. 282

Peculiar.
Sure to charm all was his *p.* fate *E.* iv. 5
Not only bounded to *p.* arts *E.C.* 62
Is not th' exactness of *p.* parts *E.C.* 244
Fix'd like a plant on his *p.* spot *E.M.* ii. 63
The good must merit God's *p.* care *E.M.* iv. 135
There's some *P.* in each leaf and grain *M.E.* i. 15

Pedant.
"Oh" (cry'd the Goddess) "for some *p.* Reign *D.* iv. 175
A *P.* makes, the storm of Gonson's lungs *S.* viii. 53
And titt'ring push'd the P—s off the Place *D.* iv. 276

Pedestal.
Stept from its *p.* to take the air *S.* vi. 122

Pedigree.
Who proud of *P.*, is poor of Purse *S.* iv. 84

Peel'd.
P., patch'd, and pyebald, linsey-wolsey brothers *D.* iii. 115

Peep.
Hills *p.* o'er hills, and Alps on Alps arise *E.C.* 232
Most souls, 'tis true, but *p.* out once an age *U.L.* 17

Peep'd.
P. in your fans, been serious, thus, and cry'd *E.J.S.* 4

Peeps.
Still sits at squat, and *p.* not from its hole *M.E.* i. 56

Peer.
This polish'd Hardness, that reflects the *P. D.* i. 220
The Sire is made a *P.*, the Son a Fool *D.* iv. 548
And at a *P.*, or Peeress, shall I fret *E.S.* i. 111
Blest *P.!* his great Forefathers' ev'ry grace *Ep.* i. 11
From *P.* or Bishop 'tis no easy thing *M.E.* ii. 195
Oft have you hinted to your brother *P. M.E.* iv. 39
A maudlin Poetess, a rhyming *P. P.S.* 16
Whom have I hurt? has Poet yet, or *P. P.S.* 95

A hireling scribbler, or a hireling *p. P.S.* 364
The *P.* now spreads the glitt'ring Forfex wide *R.L.* iii. 147
"It grieves me much" (reply'd the *P.* again) *R.L.* iv. 131
To one that was, or would have been a *P. S.* ii. 51
Indebted to no Prince or *P.* alive *S.* vi. 69
Endue a *P.* with honour, truth, and grace *S.* vi. 221
His P—*s shine round him with reflected grace D.* ii. 9
By singing *P.* upheld on either side *D.* iv. 49
You'll bring a House (I mean of *P.*) *E.* vi. 18
While *P.*, and Dukes, and all their sweeping train *R.L.* i. 84
And laugh at *P.* that put their trust in Peter *S.* i. 40
Scribblers or *P.*, alike are Mob to me *S.* i. 140
The modern language of corrupted *P. S.* iii. 99
Then *P.* grew proud in Horsemanship t' excel *S.* v. 143
P., Heralds, Bishops, Ermine, Gold and Lawn *S.* v. 317
And *P.* give way, exalted as they are *S.* vi. 106

Peeress.
And at a Peer, or *P.* shall I fret *E.S.* i. 111
Proud as a *P.*, prouder as a Punk *M.E.* ii. 70
P. and Butler share alike the Box *M.E.* iii. 140

Peerless.
Fair ev'n in death, this *p. Butterfly D.* iv. 486

Peevishness.
At all my *p.*, and turns his style *S.* viii. 123

Pegasus.
Thus *P.*, a nearer way to take *E.C.* 150
And never gallop *P.* to death *S.* iii. 14
Break Priscian's head, or *P.*'s neck *D.* iii. 162

Peleus.
To read in Greek the wrath of *P.*' son *S.* vi. 53

Pelf.
Whate'er the Passion, knowledge, fame or *p. E.M.* ii. 251
And gave you Beauty, but deny'd the *P. M.E.* ii. 237
Yet to be just to these poor men of *p. M.E.* iii. 107
When Luxury has lick'd up all thy *p. S.* ii. 105

Pelham.
Where *Kent* and Nature vie for *P.*'s Love *E.S.* ii. 67

Pelion.
Descend from *P.* to the main *O.* i. 41

Pelt.
Not wrap up Oranges, to *p.* thy sire *D.* i. 236

Pembroke.
For *P.*, Statues, dirty Gods, and Coins *M.E.* iv. 8

Pen.
Then gnaw'd his *p.* then dash'd it on the ground *D.* i. 117
Some Dæmon stole my *p.* (forgive th' offence) *D.* i. 187
A standish, steel and golden *p. E.* iv. 14
Yes, the last *P.* for Freedom let me draw *E.S.* ii. 248
What? arm'd for Virtue when I point the *p. S.* i. 105
And call for *p.* and ink to show our Wit *S.* v. 180
Allow him but his plaything of a *P. S.* v. 193
Matchless his *p.*, victorious was his lance *W.F.* 293
But P—s can forge, my Friend, that cannot write *E.S.* ii. 188

Penalties.
And *Wit* dreads Exile, *P.*, and Pains *D.* iv. 22
The Pains and *P.* of Idleness *D.* iv. 344

Pence—*see* Penny.

Pencil.
Did Nature's *p.* ever blend such rays *D.* iv. 411
One dip the *p.*, and one string the lyre *E.* iii. 70
So when the faithful *p.* has design'd *E.C.* 484

Pendant.
Shall glitter o'er the *p.* green *I.H.* iii. 23
The wat'ry landscape of the *p.* woods *W.F.* 213
Some hang upon the p—s of her ear *R.L.* ii. 140

Penetrate.
Born where Heav'n's influence scarce can *p. M.E.* i. 142

Penitence.
Or how distinguish *p.* from love *E.A.* 194
Take back my fruitless *p.* and pray'rs *E.A.* 286

Q

PENN'D—PERSECUTE.

Penn'd.
Come with petitions fairly *p. I.H.* ii. 65 s

Penny.
Thou hast at least bestow'd one *p.* well *S.* ii. 110
You pay a *p.*, and he paid a pound *S.* vi. 239
In shillings and in pence as first they steal S. vii. 83
With Fifty Guineas (a great P.-worth) *bought Mi.* ix. 30

Pens.
Who *p.*, a Stanza, when he should *engross P.S.* 18

Pension.
Withhold the *p.*, and set up the head *D.* iv. 96
All melted down, in *P.*, or in Punk *D.* iv. 510
A *P.*, or such Harness for a slave *S.* iii. 87
Strike off his *P.*, by the setting sun *M.E.* i. 160
Expect a place, or *p.* from the Crown *S.* v. 371
Who sins with whom: who got his *P.* rug *S.* viii. 134
Nay wits had p—s, and young Lords had wit E.C. 539

Pension'd.
Could *p.* Boileau lash in honest strain *S.* i. 111
One knighted Blackmore, and one *p.* Quarles *S.* v. 387

Pensioner.
And one more *P.* St. Stephen gains *M.E.* iii. 394

Pensive.
While *p.* Poets painful Vigils keep *D.* i. 93
In *p.* thought recall the fancy'd scene *E.* v. 33
The well-sung woes will soothe my *p.* ghost *E.A.* 365
P. hast follow'd to the silent tomb *Ep.* vii. 12
Striking their *p.* bosoms—*Here* lies GAY *Ep.* xi. 12
Nor *p.* Cowley's moral lay *I.H.* iv. 8
Rise, *p.* Nymph, the *Tatler* waits for you *Mi.* ix. 3
But anxious cares the *p.* nymph oppress'd *R.L.* iv. 1
She sighs for ever on her *p.* bed *R.L.* iv. 23
Meet and rejoin me, in the *p.* Grot *S.* vi. 209

People.
'Twixt Prince and *P.* close the Curtain draw *D.* i. 313
A Prince the Father of a *P.* made *E.M.* iii. 214
Taught Pow'r's due use to *P.*, and to Kings *E.M.* iii. 289
I wonder what some *p.* mean *I.H.* ii. 104 s
The *P.* are a many-headed beast *S.* iii. 121
Your *P.*, Sir, are partial in the rest *S.* v. 32
The *p.*, sure, the *p.* are the sight *S.* v. 323
What shook the stage, and made the *P.* stare *S.* v. 336
The boys flock round him, and the *p.* stare *S.* vi. 120
And feather'd *p.* crowd my wealthy side *W.F.* 404
Learn each small P.'s genius, policies E.M. iii. 183
All this may be; the *P.* voice is odd *S.* v. 89

Peopled.
From the green myriads in the *p.* grass *E.M.* i. 210

Peoples.
What vary'd Being *p.* ev'ry star *E.M.* i. 27

Per.
In one abundant show'r of Cent *p.* Cent *M.E.* iii. 372
As M—o's was, but not at five *p.* cent *S.* ii. 122
While with the silent growth of ten *p.* cent *S.* iii. 132
With rhymes of this *p.* cent, and that *p.* year *S.* vii. 56

Perceive.
A Light, which in yourself you must *p. M.E.* iv. 45
And steal so little, few *p.* they steal *S.* vii. 84

Perch.
The bright-ey'd *p.* with fins of Tyrian dye *W.F.* 142

Perch'd.
P. on his crown. "All hail! and hail again *D.* i. 291
First Ariel *p.* upon a Matadore *R.L.* iii. 33

Perfect.
Osborne, thro' *p.* modesty o'ercome *D.* ii. 189
A *p.* Judge will read each work of Wit *E.C.* 233
Say rather, Man's as *p.* as he ought *E.M.* i. 70
If to be *p.* in a certain sphere *E.M.* i. 73
Alone made *p.* here, immortal there *E.M.* i. 120
And what created *p.*?"—"Why then Man *E.M.* i. 148
As full, as *p.*, in a hair as heart (*vg.*) *E.M.* i. 276
To the first good, first *p.* and first fair *E.M.* i. 24
The last, scarce ripen'd into *p.* Man *E.M.* iii. 141
And then—a *p.* Hermit in his diet *S.* v. 200

A *p.* genius at an Opera-song *S.* vi. 11
"And *p. Speaker!*"—"Onslow, past dispute" *S.* viii. 71

Perfection.
When mellowing years their full *p.* give *E.C.* 490

Perfectly.
See now, half-cur'd, and *p.* well-bred *D.* iv. 323
In short, I'm *p.* content *I.H.* ii. 29 s

Perform.
And proud his Mistress' orders to *p. D.* iii. 263
Thy Magus, Goddess! shall *p.* the rest *D.* iv. 516

Perform'd.
All Parts *p.*, and *all* her children blest *E.S.* i. 82
A solemn Sacrifice, *p.* in state *M.E.* iv. 157

Perfume.
P. to you, to me is Excrement *E.S.* ii. 184
And wings of Seraphs shed divine p—s *E.A.* 218
No rich *p.* refresh the fruitful field *W.* 47

Perfum'd.
Or soft Adonis, so *p.* and fine *M.E.* iii. 73

Perfumes.
And Carmel's flow'ry top *p.* the skies *M.* 28

Perhaps.—*Passim.*

Perigord.
Thy Truffles, *P.!* thy Hams, Bayonne *D.* iv. 558

Period.
But Ho—y for a *p.* of a mile *S.* viii. 73
My H—ley's p—s, or my Blackmore's numbers D. ii. 370
How sweet the *p.*, neither said, nor sung *D.* iii. 202
Labour and rest that equal *p.* keep *E.A.* 211

Perish.
Die ev'ry flow'r, and *p.* all, but she *A.* 34
Heav'ns! what a pile! whole ages *p.* there *D.* iii. 77
As bodies *p.* thro' excess of blood *E.C.* 304
A hero *p.*, or a sparrow fall *E.M.* i. 88
All forms that *p.* other forms supply *E.M.* iii. 17
Thou too must *p.* when thy feast is o'er *E.M.* iii. 70
His oxen *p.* in his country's cause *M.E.* iii. 206
Men, monkeys, lap-dogs, parrots, *p.* all *R.L.* iv. 120
In flow'r of age you *p.* for a song *S.* i. 102
I will, or *p.* in the gen'rous cause *S.* i. 117
So *p.* all, whose breast ne'er learn'd to glow *U.L.* 45

Perish'd.
Their ruins *p.*, and their place no more *M.E.* v. 22
A Beau and Witling *p.* in the throng *R.L.* v. 59

Perishes.
Some Athens *p.*, some Tully bleeds *O.* ii. 32

Periwig.
E'er since Sir Fopling's *P.* was Praise *D.* i. 167

Perjur'd.
Of *p.* Doris, dying I complain *A.* 58
A *p.* Prince a leaden Saint revere *M.E.* i. 89

Perks.
That Edward's Miss thus *p.* it in your face *E.J.S.* 46
When ev'ry coxcomb *p.* them in my face *P.S.* 74

Permit.
"*P.*" (he cries) "no stranger to your fame *S.* viii. 66

Perolla.
Now flames the Cid, and now *P.* burns *D.* i. 250

Perpetuity.
Abhor, a *P.* should stand *S.* vi. 247

Perplex.
No artful wildness to *p.* the scene *M.E.* iv. 116

Perplex'd.
O! ever gracious to *p.* mankind *D.* i. 173
Some Wag observes me thus *p. I.H.* ii. 51 s
Waste sandy valleys, once *p.* with thorn *M.* 73

Persecute.
Plague with Dispute, or *p.* with Rhyme *D.* iv. 260

Persecution.
And *P.* mourn her broken wheel *W.F.* 420

Perseverance.
If *p.* gain the Diver's prize *D.* ii. 301

Persian.
Who turns a *P.* tale for half a crown *P.S.* 180
Paint, Marble, Gems, and robes of *P.* dye *S.* vi. 265
P—s and Greeks like turns of nature found E.C. 380

Persist.
P., by all divine in Man unaw'd *D.* iii. 223

Persisting.
Some positive, *p.* fops we know *E.C.* 568

Person.
And thrusts his *p.* full into your face *D.* iii. 140
Spare then the *P.*, and expose the Vice *E.S.* ii. 12
Midas, a sacred *p.* and a king *P.S.* 70
There are, who to my *p.* pay their court *P.S.* 115
The libell'd *p.*, and the pictur'd shape *P.S.* 353

Personage.
The same, his ancient *p.* to deck *R.L.* v. 89

Persuade.
Or from a judge turn pleader to *p. E.M.* ii. 155
An angel Tongue, which no man can *p. M.E.* i. 199

Pert.
With *p.* flat eyes she window'd well its head *D.* ii. 43
Intoxicates the *p.*, and lulls the grave *D.* ii. 344
Three College Sophs, and three *p.* Templars came *D.* ii. 379
Serves but to keep fools *p.*, and knaves awake *D.* iv. 442
Ungrateful wretch, with mimic airs grown *p. Mi.* ix. 65
More *p.*, more proud, more positive than he *S.* ii. 52
What *p.*, low dialogue has Farquhar writ *S.* v. 286

Pertness.
Rememb'ring she herself was *P.* once *D.* i. 112

Peru.
P. once more a race of kings behold *W.F.* 411

Peruse.
The brightest eyes of Britain now *p. E.* iv. 78
Still with itself compar'd, his text *p. E.C.* 128
Sleep, or *p.* some ancient Book *I.H.* ii. 130

Peruvian.
For Indian spices, for *P.* Gold *S.* iv. 71

Pervading.
Gradations just, has thy *p.* soul *E.M.* i. 31

Pervert.
Let no Court Sycophant *p.* my sense *S.* vii. 126

Pescennius.
To gain *P.* one employs his schemes *M.E.* v. 39

Pet.
And send the godly in a *p.* to pray *R.L.* iv. 64

Peter.
To laugh at Fools who put their trust in *P. E.S.* i. 10
Is it for Bond, or *P.*, (paltry things) *E.S.* i. 121
Ev'n *P.* trembles only for his Ears (*rep.*) *E.S.* ii. 57
Wise *P.* sees the World's respect for Gold *M.E.* iii. 123
Glorious Ambition ! *P.*, swell thy store *M.E.* iii. 125
Scarce to wise *P.* complaisant enough *S.* i. 3
And laugh at Peers that put their trust in *P. S.* i. 40
From you to me, from me to *P.* Walter *S.* ii. 168
To cheat a Friend, or Ward he leaves to *P. S.* v. 197
If *P.* deigns to help you to your own (*rep.*) *S.* vii. 66
For not in Chariots *P.* puts his trust *S.* vii. 74
Till *P.*'s keys some christ'ned Jove adorn *D.* iii. 109

Petitions.
All vain *p.* mounting to the sky *D.* ii. 89
Come with *p.* fairly penn'd *I.H.* ii. 65 *s*

Petrify.
And *p.* a Genius to a Dunce *D.* iv. 264

Petronius.
Fancy and art in gay *P.* please *E.C.* 667

Petticoat.
We trust th' important charge, the *P. R.L.* ii. 18
At Quin's high plume, or Oldfield's *p. S.* v. 331
Or rumpled p—s, or tumbled beds *R.L.* iv. 72

Petty.
Marriage may all those *p.* Tyrants chase *E.* iv. 37

Pews.
The rest, some farm the Poor-box, some the *P. S.* iii. 128
How could Devotion touch the country *p. S.* v. 233

Phalanx.
Who forms the *p.*, and who points the way *E.M.* iii. 108

Phantom.
A Wit it was, and call'd the *p.* Moore *D.* ii. 50
And round thy *p.* glue my clasping arms *E.A.* 234
The *p.* flies me, as unkind as you *E.A.* 236
Strange p—s rising as the mists arise *R.L.* iv. 40

Pheasant.
Will choose a *p.* still before a hen *S.* ii. 18
See! from the brake the whirring *p.* springs *W.F.* 111
One likes the p.'s wing, and one the leg *S.* v. 84

Phidias.
Or *P.* broken, and Apelles burn'd *D.* ii. 112

Philemon.
And here the groaning shelves *P.* bends *D.* i. 154

Philip.
Charles to the Convent, *P.* to the Field *M.E.* i. 108

Philips.—*See also* Ambrose.
She saw slow *P.* creep like Tate's poor page *D.* i. 105
Still to one Bishop *P.* seem a wit *P.S.* 100
As Eusden, *P.*, Settle, writ of Kings *S.* v. 417

Philomede.
So *P.* lect'ring all mankind *M.E.* ii. 83

Philomel.
When warbling *P.* salutes the spring *Sp.* 26

Philomela.
Or hears the hawk when *P.* sings *E.M.* iii. 56
Thus when *P.* drooping *Mi.* vii. 29
Such silence waits on *P.*'s strains *W.* 78

Philosopher.
Thou wert my guide, *p.*, and friend *E.M.* iv. 390
You hold him no *P.* at all *M.E.* i. 8
Is this my Guide, *P.*, and Friend *S.* iii. 177

Philosophic.
There are, my Friend, whose *p.* eyes *S.* iv. 7

Philosophy.
While proud *P.* repines to show *D.* iii. 197
P., that lean'd on Heav'n before *D.* iv. 613
Ev'n av'rice, prudence; sloth, *p. E.M.* ii. 188
Turns you from sound *P.* aside *S.* ii. 6
Nothing to make *P.* thy friend *S.* iii. 74

Phlegethon.
Which flaming *P.* surrounds *O.* i. 50

Phlegm, Fle'me.
Where bile, and wind, and *p.*, and acid jar *S.* ii. 71
They judge with fury, but they write with *f—e E.C.* 662

Phœbe.
To headless *P.* his fair bride postpone *D.* iv. 367

Phœbus.
Now setting *P.* shone serenely bright *A.* 13
A youth unknown to *P.*, in despair *D.* ii. 213
See, see, our own true *P.* wears the bays *D.* iii. 323
Another *P.*, thy own *P.*, reigns *D.* iv. 61
Who, false to *P.*, bow the knee to Baal *D.* iv. 93
This *P.* promis'd (I forget the year) *M.E.* ii. 283
Ascendant *P.* watch'd that hour with care *M.E.* ii. 285
Sheffield approves, consenting *P.* bends *Mi.* i. 7
For this, ere *P.* rose, he had implor'd *R.L.* ii. 35
Inspire me, *P.*, in my Delia's praise *Sp.* 45
And *P.* warm the ripening ore to gold *W.F.* 396
Defence from *P.*, not from Cupid's beams *Su.* 14
Now Cancer glows with *P.* fiery car *W.F.* 147

228 PHOSPHOR—PINION.

Phosphor.
Why sit we sad when *P*. shines so clear *Sp.* 27

Phrase.
For Attic *P*. in Plato let them seek *D.* iv. 227
Ancients in *p*., mere moderns in their sense *E.C.* 325
'Tis *p*. absurd to call a Villain Great *E.M.* iv. 230
What Nature wants (a *p*. I much distrust) *M.E.* iii. 25
Mark where a bold expressive *p*. appears *S.* vi. 165
Of whose best *p*. and courtly accent join'd *S.* viii. 48
And coarse of *p*.—your English all are so *S.* viii. 109

Phryne.
Ask you why *P*. the whole Auction buys (*rep.*) *M.E.* iii. 119

Physic.
And lick up all the *P*. of the Soul *D.* iii. 82
P. of *Metaphysic* begs defence *D.* iv. 645
Learn from the beasts the *p*. of the field *E.M.* iii. 174
Make some take *p*., others scribble plays *R.L.* iv. 62
And of their fragrant *p*. spoils the fields *W.F.* 242

Physical.
What makes all *p*. or moral ill *E.M.* iv. 111

Physicians.
And Death-watches, *P. Mi.* iv. 24

Pick-pocket.
Go drench a *P*., and join the Mob *E.S.* ii. 41

Picks.
P. from each sex, to make the Fav'rite blest *M.E.* ii. 273

Picture.
Strike in the sketch, or in the *p*. glow *E.* iii. 44
As in some well-wrought *p*., light and shade *E.M.* ii. 208
Or where the p—s for the *page atone D.* i. 139
Divert her eyes with *p*. in the fire *E.* v. 19
Whose Art was Nature, and whose *P*. Thought *Ep.*viii.2
How many *p*. of one Nymph we view *M.E.* ii. 5
P. like these, dear Madam, to design *M.E.* ii. 151
Artists must choose his *P*., Music, Meats *M.E.* iv. 6
Much they extoll'd his *p*., much his seat *P.S.* 239
Tho' in his *p*. Lust be full display'd *S.* viii. 91

Pictur'd.
The libell'd person, and the *p*. shape *P.S.* 353

Piddle.
Content with little I can *p*. here *S.* ii. 137

Pidling.
From slashing *Bentley* down to *p. Tibalds P.S.* 164

Pie.
An hundred Souls of Turkeys in a *p. D.* v. 594
Redeem'd from tapers and defrauded p—s *D.* i. 156

Piece.
A vast, vamp'd, future, old, reviv'd, new *p. D.* i. 284
Each heav'nly *p*. unwearied we compare *E.* i. 35
Whoever thinks a faultless *p*. to see *E.C.* 253
To see a *p*. of failing flesh and blood *E.J.S.* 27
A small Euphrates thro' the *p*. is roll'd *M.E.* v. 29
This saving counsel, "Keep your *p*. nine years" *P.S.* 40
The *p*., you think, is incorrect? why, take it *P.S.* 45
Tho' cut in p—s *ere my Lord can eat S.* ii. 22

Piecemeal.
P. they win this acre first, then that *S.* vii. 91

Pierce.
The dagger wont to *p*. the Tyrant's breast *D.* iv. 38
He, who thro' vast immensity can *p*. *E.M.* i. 23
They *p*. my thickets, thro' my Grot they glide *P.S.* 8
P. the soft lab'rinth of a Lady's ear *S.* vii. 55

Pierc'd.
For hearts so touch'd, so *p*., so lost as mine *E.A.* 196
The *p*. battalions disunited fall *R.L.* iii. 85
And He, whose light'ning *p*. th' Iberian lines *S.* i. 129

Pierian.
Drink deep, or taste not the *P*. spring *E.C.* 216

Piety.
But now (so ANNE and *P*. ordain) *D.* ii. 29

But such plain roofs as *P*. could raise *E.A.* 139
Sprung it from *p*., or from despair *E.A.* 180
Faithless thro' *P*., and dup'd thro' Wit *M.E.* i. 92
And Papal *p*., and Gothic fire *M.E.* v. 14

Pig.
A *p*. of lead to him who dives the best *D.* ii. 281
And then a nodding beam, or *p*. of lead *S.* vi. 102

Pigeon.
Nay, Mahomet! the *P*. at thine ear *D.* iv. 364
Turns Hares to Larks, and P—s *into Toads D.* iv. 554

Pikes.
Swords, *p*., and guns, with everlasting rust *S.* i. 74
And *p*., the tyrants of the wat'ry plains *W.F.* 146

Pilaster.
Then clap four slices of *P*. on't *M.E.* iv. 33

Pile.
Founds the whole *p*., of his own works the base *D.* i.160
Heav'ns! what a *p*.! whole ages perish there *D.* iii. 77
But quite mistakes the scaffold for the *p. M.E.* i. 221
Who builds a Bridge that never drove a *p. S.* v. 185
While fancy brings the vanish'd p—s *to view E.* iii. 31

Pil'd.
Dy mountains *p*. on mountains to the skies *E.M.* iv. 74

Pilfer'd.
The Bard whom *p*. Pastorals renown *P.S.* 179

Pilgrim.
And harmless serpents lick the *p*.'s feet *M.* 80
Behold yon Isle, by Palmers, P—s *trod D.* iii. 113

Pillory.
As thick as eggs at Ward in *p. D.* iii. 34
If on a *P*., or near a Throne *P.S.* 366

Pillow.
Morpheus hov'ring o'er my *P. Mi.* vii. 23
Belinda still her downy *p*. prest *R.L.* i. 19
Or the small *p*. grace a Lady's bed *R.L.* iii. 166

Pimp.
Unelbow'd by a Gamester, *P*., or Play'r *M.E.* iii. 242
Could Laureate Dryden *P*. and Friar engage *S.* i. 113
No *P*. of Pleasure, and no Spy of State *S.* i. 134

Pimple.
All eyes may see—a *P*. on her nose *M.E.* ii. 36
Or raise a *p*. on a beauteous face *R.L.* iv. 68

Pin.
Lies one who ne'er car'd, and still cares not a *p. Ep.*xvi.5
With borrow'd P—s, *and Patches not her own Mi.* ii.22
Here files of *p*. extend their shining rows *R.L.* i. 137
Be stopp'd in vials, or transfix'd with *p. R.L.* ii. 126

Pinch.
May *p*. ev'n there—Why lay it on a King *E.S.* ii. 51

Pindar.
And a true *P*. stood without a head *P.S.* 236
The P—s *and the Miltons of a Curl D.* iii. 164

Pindaric.
Forget his Epic, nay *P*. Art *S.* v. 77
Sharp Satire that, and that *P*. lays *S.* vi. 83

Pindus.
In all the Courts of *P*. guiltless quite *E.S.* ii. 187
The dreams of *P*. and th' Aonian maids *M.* 4

Pine.
Who sees pale Mammon *p*. amidst his store *M.E.*iii.171

Pines.
While your Alexis *p*. in hopeless love *Su.* 32
As to soft gales top-heavy p—s *bow low D.* ii. 391
The darksome *p*. that o'er yon rocks reclin'd *E.A.* 155
Arise, the *p*. a noxious shade diffuse *W.* 86

Pinion.
Milton's strong *p*. now not Heav'n can bound *S.* v. 99
Hope humbly then; with trembling p—s *soar E M.*i.91
Flutt'ring spread thy purple *p. Mi.* vii. 1
His purple *p*. op'ning to the sun *R.L.* ii. 71

Or dip their *p.* in the painted bow *R.L.* ii. 84
Swift on his sooty *p.* flies the Gnome *R.L.* iv. 17

Pinion'd.
Some Slave of mine be *p.* to their side *D.* iv. 124

Pinky.
To make poor *P.* eat with vast applause *S.* v. 293

Pinn'd.
Not Cynthia when her manteau's *p.* awry *R.L.* iv. 8

Pint.
He takes his chirping *p.*, and cracks his jokes *M.E.* iii. 358

Pious.
But *p.* Needham dropt the name of God *D.* i. 324
What force have *p.* vows! The Queen of Love *D.* ii. 215
So he, but *p.*, whisper'd first his pray'r *D.* iv. 354
Receiv'd each Demi-God with *p.* care *D.* iv. 383
Whose *p.* hope aspires to see the day *D.* iv. 461
O *p.* fraud of am'rous charity *E.A.* 150
Warned by the Sylph, oh *p.* maid, beware *R.L.* i. 112
Hopes after hopes of *p.* Papists fail'd *S.* vi. 62

Piously.
"The wretch he starves"—and *p.* denies *M.E.* iii. 104

Pipe.
Hist'ry her Pot, Divinity her *P. D.* iii. 196
And shook from out his *P.* the seeds of fire *D.* iv. 494
He said; Alexis take this *p.*, the same *Sn.* 41
Thus, as the p—s of some carv'd Organ move *S.* vii. 17

Pipkin.
A *P.* there, like Homer's Tripod walks *R.L.* iv. 51

Pique.
Why *p.* all mortals, yet affect a name *M.E.* ii. 61

Piqu'd.
The Dev'l was *p.* such saintship to behold *M.E.* iii. 349

Piquet.
He thanks you not, his pride is in *P. M.E.* i. 85

Pirate.
But lures the *P.*, and corrupts the Friend *M.E.* iii. 30
Sail to the Ladies; how each *p.* eyes *S.* viii. 228

Pisa.
Bears *P.'s* off'rings to his Arethuse *D.* ii. 342

Pit.
P., box, and gall'ry in convulsions hurl'd *P.S.* 87
The many-headed Monster of the *P. S.* v. 305
And all the Thunder of the *P.* ascends *S.* v. 327

Piteous.
With that she gave him (*p.* of his case *D.* ii. 141

Pitholeon.
P. sends to me: "You know his Grace *P.S.* 49
P. libell'd me—" but here's a letter *P.S.* 51

Pities.
That all beside, one *p.*, not abhors *S.* vii. 5

Pity.
P.! the charm works only in our wall *D.* iv. 165
She pity'd! but her *P.* only shed *D.* iv. 345
Then sadly say, with mutual *p.* mov'd *E.A.* 351
Have you less *p.* for the needy Cheat *E.S.* ii. 44
As show'd Vice had his hate and *p.* too *Ep.* i. 8
P. mistakes for some poor tradesman craz'd *M.E.* iii. 64
P. ! to build, without a son or wife *S.* ii. 163
With *P.*, and with Terror, tear my heart *S.* iv. 345
P.! you was not Druggerman at Babel *S.* viii. 83
We first endure, then p., then embrace *E.M.* ii. 220
And the free soul looks down to *p.* Kings *S.* viii. 187

Pity'd.
She *p.!* but her Pity only shed *D.* iv. 345
But *p.* Belisarius old and blind *Mi.* ii. 6

Pitying.
And *p.* saints, whose statues learn to weep *E.A.* 22
In *p.* Love, we but our weakness show *P.C.* 11

Not louder shrieks to *p.* heav'n are cast *R.L.* iii. 157
She said: the *p.* audience melt in tears *R.L.* v. 1
Fate snatch'd her early to the *p.* sky *U.L.* 24

Place.
Realms shift their *p.*, and Ocean turns to land *D.* i. 72
Her ample presence fills up all the *p. D.* i. 261
Ascend, and recognize their Native *P. D.* i. 268
A *p.* there is betwixt earth, air, and seas *D.* ii. 83
With holy envy gave one Layman *p. D.* ii. 324
Mark first that youth who takes the foremost *p. D.* iii. 139
None want a *p.*, for all their Centre found *D.* iv. 77
Shrink, and confess the genius of the *p. D.* iv. 146
And titt'ring push'd the Pedants off the *p. D.* iv. 276
Thrust some Mechanic Cause into his *p. D.* iv. 475
Worthy to fill Pythagoras's *p. D.* iv. 572
Tho' not too strictly bound to Time and *P. E.* iv. 28
But sets up one, a greater, in their *p. E.* iv. 38
Thy *p.* is here, sad sister, come away *E.A.* 310
Which, but proportion'd to their light, or *p. E.C.* 173
But with th' occasion and the *p.* comply *E.C.* 177
Its gaudy colours spreads on ev'ry *p. E.C.* 312
No *p.* so sacred from such fops is barr'd *E.C.* 622
As next in *p.* to Mantua, next in fame *E.C.* 708
His knowledge measur'd to his state and *p. E M.* i. 72
Attract, attracted to, the next in *p. E.M.* iii. 11
Good from each object, from each *p.* acquir'd *E.M.* iv. 321
Why so? if Satire knows its Time and *P. E.S.* i. 87
Once break their rest, or stir them from their *P. E.S.* i. 100
And what a dust in ev'ry *p. I.H.* i. 11
That, begs my Int'rest for a *P. I.H.* ii. 68 s
Behold the *p.*, where if a Poet *I.H.* ii. 187
Alone, in company; in *p.*, or out *M.E.* i. 72
Int'rest o'ercome, or Policy take *p. M.E.* i. 167
Cries, "Ah! how charming, if there's no such *p.!*" *M.E.* ii. 108
Despairing Quacks with curses fled the *p. M.E.* iii. 273
Consult the genius of the *P.* in all *M.E.* iv. 57
Ev'n in an ornament its *p.* remark *M.E.* iv. 77
Their ruins perish'd, and their *p.* no more *M.E.* v. 22
No *p.* is sacred, not the Church is free *P.S.* 11
I want a Patron; ask him for a *P. P.S.* 50
While pure Description held the *p.* of Sense *P.S.* 148
Who first his judgment ask'd, and then a *p. P.S.* 238
Are, as when women, wond'rous fond of *p. R.L.* iii. 36
Two handmaids wait the throne: alike in *p. R.L.* iv. 25
In ev'ry *p.* is sought, but sought in vain *R.L.* v. 110
Chiefs out of war, and Statesmen out of *p. S.* i. 126
Then cheerful healths (your Mistress shall have *p.*) *S.* ii. 149
Get *P.* and Wealth, if possible, with grace (*rep.*) *S.* iii. 103
No *p.* on earth (he cry'd) like Greenwich hill *S.* iii. 139
But if to Pow'r and *P.* your passion lie *S.* iv. 97
Expect a *p.*, or pension from the Crown *S.* v. 371
Fit to bestow the Laureate's weighty *p. S.* v. 379
Again to rhyme, can London be the *p. S.* vi. 89
Howe'er unwillingly it quits its *p. S.* vi. 161
When servile Chaplains cry, that birth and *p. S.* vi. 220
A man so poor would live without a *p. S.* vi. 287
O'er a learn'd, unintelligible *p. S.* vii. 102
I bought no benefice, I begg'd no *p. S.* viii. 12
Whose *p.* is quarter'd out, three parts in four *S.* viii. 136
Swears ev'ry *p.* entail'd for years to come *S.* viii. 160
So flew the soul to its congenial *p. U.L.* 27
Obscure the *p.*, and uninscrib'd the stone *W.F.* 320
And haunt the p—s where their Honour died *M. E.* ii. 242
He tells what *p.* strumpets sell for life *S.* viii. 148
And p. it here! here all ye Heroes bow *D.* iii. 318
Yet should the Graces all thy figures *p. E.* iii. 71
Thus useful arms in magazines we *p. E.C.* 673
Some *p.* the bliss in action, some in ease *E.M.* iv. 21
God in externals could not *p.* Content *E.M.* iv. 66
Receive, and *p.* for ever near a King *E.S.* i. 96
And sacred, *p.* by DRYDEN'S awful dust *Ep.* v. 2
And *p.*, on good Security, his Gold *S.* v. 168
What's long or short, each accent where to *p. S.* v. 207

Plac'd.
A Poet's form she *p.* before their eyes *D.* ii. 35
And *p.* it next him, a distinction rare *D.* ii. 96

PLACING—PLAUTUS

See in the circle next, Eliza *p. D.* ii. 157
But fate with butchers *p.* thy priestly stall *D.* iii. 209
P. at the door of Learning, youth to guide *D.* iv. 153
Is only this, if God has *p.* him wrong *E.M.* i. 50
P. on this isthmus of a middle state *E.M.* ii. 3
Till common int'rest *p.* the sway in one *E.M.* iii. 210
While those are *p.* in Hope, and these in Fear *E.M.* iv. 70
Superior by the head, was Ariel *p. R.L.* ii. 70
In pow'r, wit, figure, virtue, fortune *p. S.* vi. 302

Placing.
In moderation *p.* all my glory *S.* i. 67

Plague.
Some War, some *P.*, some Famine they foresee *M.E.* iii. 113
What *Drop* or *Nostrum* can this *p.* remove *P.S.* 29
P. on't ! 'tis past a jest—nay prithee, pox *R.L.* iv. 129
If such the *p.* and pains to write by rule *S.* vi. 180
Catch'd like the *P.*, or Love, the Lord knows how *S.* vii. 9
If p—s and earthquakes break not Heav'n's design *E.M.* i. 155
And (all those *p.* in one) the bawling Bar *S.* viii. 55
P. with Dispute, or persecute with Rhyme D. iv. 260
So when you *p.* a fool, 'tis still the curse *S.* viii. 120
Nature made ev'ry Fop to *p.* his brother *S.* viii. 258
But here's the Captain that will *p.* them both *S.* viii. 260

Plagu'd.
Not *p.* with headaches or the want of rhyme *E.* v. 42

Plain.
The sick'ning stars fade off th' ethereal *p. D.* iv. 636
Then build a new, or act it in a *p. E.C.* 284
Not so, when swift Camilla scours the *p. E.C.* 372
Is thine alone the seed that strews the *p. E.M.* iii. 37
But clear and artless, pouring thro' the *p. M.E.* iii. 257
Or cut wide views thro' Mountains to the *P. M.E.* iv. 75
The Wood supports the *P.*, the parts uaite *M.E.* iv. 81
Not with more glories in th' ethereal *p. R.L.* ii. 1
Draw forth to combat on the velvet *p. R.L.* iii. 44
Or tames the Genius of the stubborn *p. S.* i. 131
While you slow oxen turn the furrow'd *p. Sp.* 30
Me gentle Delia beckons from the *p. Sp.* 53
That call'd the list'ning Dryads to the *p. W.F.* 12
The trembling trees, in ev'ry *p.* and wood *W.F.* 63
Here hills and vales, the woodland and the *p. W.F.* 11
And, pawing, seems to beat the distant *p. W.F.* 152
Let old Arcadia boast her ample *p. W.F.* 159
I'll fly from shepherds, flocks, and flow'ry p—s A. 86
In other parts it leaves wide sandy *p. E.C.* 55
His fiery course, or drives him o'er the *p. E.M.* i. 62
Wat'ring soft Elysian *p.* with. vi. 20
Nor blush to sport on Windsor's blissful *p. Sp.* 2
At morn the *p.*, at noon the shady grove *Sp.* 78
Nor *p.* at morn, nor groves at noon delight *Sp.* 80
The sultry Sirius burns the thirsty *p. Su.* 21
Here in full light the russet *p.* extend *W.F.* 23
Rich Industry sits smiling on the *p. W.F.* 41
To *p.* with well-breath'd beagles we repair *W.F.* 121
And pikes, the tyrants of the wat'ry *p. W.F.* 146
Paints the green forests and the flow'ry *p. W.F.* 428
On *p. Experience lay foundations low D.* iv. 466
But such *p.* roofs as Piety could raise *E.A.* 139
The Patriot's *p.*, but untrod, path pursue *E.* ii. 76
Turn'd Critics next, and prov'd *p.* fools at last *E.C.* 37
Some drily *p.*, without invention's aid *E.C.* 114
So Schismatics the *p.* believers quit *E.C.* 428
Then, in the scale of reas'ning life, 'tis *p. E.M.* i. 47
For this *p.* reason, Man is not a Fly *E.M.* i. 194
Ask your own heart, and nothing is so *p. E.M.* ii. 215
Or *p.* tradition that this All begun *E.M.* iii. 227
Blest with *p.* Reason, and with sober Sense *Ep.* vi. 2
But these *p.* characters we rarely find *M.E.* i. 63
The *p.* rough Hero turn a crafty Knave *M.E.* i. 126
Comets are regular, and Wharton *p. M.E.* i. 209
Yet on *p.* Pudding deign'd at home to eat *M.E.* ii. 82
From honest Mah'met, or *p.* Parson Hale *M.E.* iii. 198
A *p.* good man, and Balaam was his name *M.E.* iii. 342
I love to pour out all myself, as *p. S.* i. 51
If then *p.* bread and milk will do the feat *S.* ii. 15
P., but not sordid; tho' not splendid, clean *S.* ii. 48
P. truth, dear Murray, needs no flow'rs of speech *S.* iv. 3
Well, on the flying *p.* Prose must be my fate *S.* vi. 198
First turn *p.* rash, then vanish quite away *S.* viii. 45
She went to p.-work, and to purling brooks *E.* v. 11

Plainness.
So modest *p.* sets off sprightly wit *E.C.* 302

Plaintiff.
In such a cause the *P.* will be hiss'd *S.* i. 155

Plaister.
The floors of *p.*, and the walls of dung *M.E.* iii. 300

Plaister'd.
With all th' embroid'ry *p.* at thy tail *M.E.* iii. 90
Or *p.* posts, with claps, in capitals *P.S.* 216

Plait.
Some fold the sleeve, whilst others *p.* the gown *R.L.* i. 147

Plan.
Make Nature still encroach upon his *p. D.* iv. 473
A mighty maze ! but not without a *p. E.M.* i. 6
Be call'd to Court to p. *some work divine S.* v. 374

Planets.
And other *p.* circle other suns *D.* iii. 244
What other *p.* circle other suns *E.M.* i. 26
P. and suns run lawless thro' the sky *E.M.* i. 252
Instruct the *p.* in what orbs to run *E.M.* ii. 21
On their own Axis as the *p.* run *E.M.* iii. 313
Or roll the *p.* thro' the boundless sky *R.L.* ii. 80

Plann'd.
And here she *p.* th' Imperial seat of Fools *D.* i. 272
Deep Harvests bury all his pride has *p. M.E.* iv. 175

Plant.
At last it fix'd, 'twas on what *p.* it pleas'd *D.* iv. 429
Fix'd like a *p.* on his peculiar spot *E.M.* ii. 63
P. of celestial seed ! if dropt below *E.M.* iv. 7
The sick and weak the healing *p.* shall aid *M.* 15
And ev'ry *p.* that drinks the morning dew *Su.* 32
P—s of thy hand, and children of thy pray'r E.A. 130
The thriving *p.* ignoble broomsticks made *M.E.* iv. 97
While *p.* their shade, or flow'rs their odours give *W.* 83
Let India boast her *p.*, nor envy we *W.F.* 29
Of Land, set out to p. a Wood I.H. ii. 65
To build, to *p.*, whatever you intend *M.E.* iv. 47
Paints as you *p.*, and, as you work, designs *M.E.* iv. 63
I *p.*, root up ; I build, and then confound *S.* iii. 169

Plantations.
Let his *p.* stretch from down to down *M.E.* iv. 189

Planted.
For what has Virro painted, built, and *p. M.E.* iv. 13
If e'er with airy horns I *p.* heads *R.L.* iv. 71
In forest *p.* by a Father's hand *S.* ii. 135

Planter.
As fruits, ungrateful to the *p.'s* care *E.M.* ii. 181

Plants.
Who *p.* like BATHURST, or who builds like BOYLE *E.M.* iv. 178
He sees why Nature *p.* in Man alone *E.M.* iv. 345

Plash.
Fall'n in the *p.* his wickedness had laid *D.* ii. 76

Plastic.
So watchful Bruin forms with *p.* care *D.* i. 101
See *p.* Nature working to this end *E.M.* iii. 9

Plate.
Not when from *p.* to *p.* your eyeballs roll *S.* ii. 7
Of beaming diamonds, and reflected *p. S.* iv. 29

Platform.
And half the *p.* just reflects the other *E.M.* iv. 118

Plato.
For Attic Phrase in *P.* let them seek *D.* iv. 227
Who ne'er saw naked sword, or look'd in *P. E.J̃.S.* 44
Go, soar with *P.* to th' empyreal sphere *E.M.* ii. 23
Where heav'nly visions *P.* fir'd *O.* ii. 3
What *P.* thought, and godlike Cato was *P.C.* 18
How *P.*'s, Bacon's, Newton's looks agree *M.E.* v. 60

Plautus.
'Twixt *P.*, Fletcher, Shakespear, and Corneille *D.* i. 285
Thou whom the Nine with P.' wit inspire A. 7

Play.

Call forth each mass, a Poem, or a *P. D.* i. 58
Now (shame to Fortune !) an ill Run at *P. D.* i. 113
Much future Ode, and abdicated *P. D.* i. 122
She went from Op'ra, Park, Assembly, *P. E.* v. 13
Produc'd his *P.*, and begg'd the Knight's advice *E.C.* 274
Unlucky, as Fungoso in the *p. E.C.* 326
The Fair sate panting at a Courtier's *p. E.C.* 540
Name a new *P.*, and he's the Poet's friend *E.C.* 620
Prodigious this I the Frail-one of our *P. E.J.S.* 1
The *P.* may pass—but that strange creature, Shore *E.J.S.* 5
Till tir'd he sleeps, and Life's poor *p.* is o'er *E.M.* ii. 282
And Gold but sent to keep the fools in *p. M.E.* iii. 5
My Lady falls to *p.*; so bad her chance *M.E.* iii. 395
And with a borrow'd *P.*, out-did poor *Crown Mi.* iii. 8
She all the cares of *Love* and *P.* does know *Mi.* ix. 22
But ancient friends (tho' poor and out of *p.*) *S.* ii. 139
Or if three Ladies like a luckless *P. S.* iv. 87
But Britain, changeful as a Child at *P. S.* v. 155
Farewell the stage ! if just as thrives the *p. S.* v. 302
The *P.* stands still ; damn action and discourse *S.* v. 314
Our Midas sits Lord Chancellor of P—s *d. D.* iii. 324
I introduc'd her to the Park and *P. Mi.* ix. 63
The price of prologues and of *p. Mi.* xii. 16
Such *P.* alone should win a British ear *P.C.* 45
Make some take physic, others scribble *p. R.L.* iv. 62
Our Wives read Milton, and our Daughters *p. S.* v. 172
He asks, "What News ?" I tell him of new *P. S.*viii.124
Till Thames see *Eton's sons* live for ever p. *D.* iii. 335
Where beams of warm imagination *p. E.C.* 58
By Doctor's bills to *p.* the Doctor's part *E.C.* 109
Had he thy Reason, would he skip and *p. E.M.* i. 82
In Spenser native Muses *p. I.H.* iv. 6
And with their forky tongues shall innocently *p. M.* 84
At the *Groom-Porter's* batter'd Bullies *p. Mi.* ix. 99
Smooth flow the waves, the Zephyrs gently *p. R.L.* ii. 51
Some in the fields of purest Æther *p. R.L.* ii. 77
Better (say I) be pleas'd, and *p.* the fool *S.* vi. 181
Let vernal airs thro' trembling osiers *p. Sp.* 5
Shakespear (whom *you and ev'ry* P.-house bill *S.* v. 69

Play'd.

Cheerful he *p.* the trifle, Life, away *E.* iv. 12
And *p.* the God an engine on his foe *E.M.* iii. 268
If Blount despatch'd himself, he *p.* the man *E.S.* i. 123
With here a Fountain, never to be *p. M.E.* iv. 121
You've *p.*, and lov'd, and eat, and drank your fill *S.* vi. 323
Where dancing sun-beams on the waters *p. Su.* 3

Play'r, Players.

Unelbow'd by a Gamester, Pimp, or *P. M.E.* iii. 242
The P—s *and I are, luckily, no friends P.S.* 60
And why not *p—ers* strut in courtiers' clothes *S.* viii. 222

Plays.

P. round the head, but comes not to the heart *E.M.* iv. 254
Yet *p.* the fool before she dies *Mi.* vi. 8
And tho' she *p.* no more, o'erlooks the cards *R.L.* i. 54
I'll stake yon lamb, that near the fountain *p. Sp.* 33

Plaything.

Some livelier *p.* gives his youth delight *E.M.* ii. 277
Allow him but his *p.* of a Pen *S.* v. 193

Plea.

This is my *p.*, on this I rest my cause *S.* i. 141
Your *P.* is good ; but still I say, beware *S.* i. 143
And woo in language of the P—s *and Bench S.* vii. 60

Plead.

And have, at least, their precedent to *p. E.C.* 166
Then wisely *p.*, to me they meant no hurt *E.S.* ii. 144
P. much, read more, dine late, or not at all *S.* iv. 37

Pleader.

Or from a judge turn *p.* to persuade *E.M.* ii. 155

Pleads.

In vain at Court the Bankrupt *p.* his cause *M.E.* iii. 217
Before her each with clamour *p.* the laws *Mi.* xi. 5

Pleasant.

And taught more *p.* methods of salvation *E.C.* 547
This same Dessert is not so *p. I.H.* ii. 219

Please.

O Thou I whatever title *p.* thine ear *D.* i. 19
So upright Quakers *p.* both Man and God *D.* iv. 208
And, if it can, at once both *p.* and preach *E.* iv. 24
Critics in Wit, or Life, are hard to *p. E.* iv. 29
Nor let false Shows, or empty Titles *p. E.* iv. 47
In prospects thus, some objects *p.* our eyes *E.C.* 156
Who haunt Parnassus but to *p.* their ear *E.C.* 341
Sure some to vex, but never all to *p. E.C.* 505
Such, without wit, are Poets when they *p. E.C.* 590
Fancy and art in gay Petronius *p. E.C.* 667
But less to *p.* the eye, than arm the hand *E.C.* 673
Let pow'r or knowledge, gold or glory, *p. E.M.* ii. 169
And mourn our various portions as we *p. E.M.* iv. 33
Intent to reason, or polite to *p. E.M.* iv. 382
A Horse-laugh, if you *p.*, at *Honesty E.S.* i. 20
I fain would *p.* you, if I knew with what *E.S.* ii. 26
Blest Courtier I who could King and Country *p. Ep.* i. 10
South-sea Subscriptions take who *p. I.H.* i. 65
You may for certain, if you *p. I.H.* ii. 80 s
Each willing to be pleas'd and *p. I.H.* ii. 139
"An't *p.* your Honour," quoth the Peasant *I.H.* ii. 218
They *p.* as beauties, here as wooders strike *M.E.* i. 144
Wise Wretch I with Pleasures too refin'd to *p. M.E.*ii.95
Is but to *p.*, can Pleasure seem a fault *M.E.* ii. 212
Leaves the dull Cits, and joins (to *p.* the fair) *M.E.* iii. 387
And make despair and madness *p. O.* i. 121
And Innocence, which most does *p. O.* iv. 15
Blest with each talent and each art to *p. P.S.* 195
And see what friends, and read what books I *p. P.S.* 264
To *p.* a Mistress one aspers'd his life *P.S.* 376
Assume what sexes and what shapes they *p. R.L.* 70
Preach as I *p.*, I doubt our curious men *S.* ii. 17
There all Men may be cur'd, whene'er they *p. S.* iv. 59
Those Suns of Glory *p.* not till they set *S.* v. 22
To *p.* a lewd or unbelieving Court *S.* v. 212
The Poets learn'd to *p.*, and not to wound *S.* v. 258
Your Barber, Cook, Upholst'rer, what pleases *p. S.* vi. 10
When out of twenty I can *p.* not two *S.* vi. 81
Weave laurel Crowns, and take what names we *p. S.* vi. 142
You think 'tis Nature, and a knack to *p. S.* vi. 177
Whom Folly pleases, and whose Follies *p. S.* vi. 327
But since those graces *p.* thy eyes no more *Su.* 29
And yet my numbers *p.* the rural throng *Su.* 49
Whom bumbler joys of home-felt quiet *p. W.F.* 239

Pleas'd.

Here *p.* behold her mighty wings outspread *D.* i. 27
P. with the madness of the mazy dance *D.* i. 68
Well *p.* he enter'd, and confess'd his home *D.* i. 266
And the *p.* dame, soft smiling, lead'st away *D.* ii. 188
Not half so *p.* when Goodman prophecy'd *D.* iii. 232
P., she accepts the Hero, and the Dame *D.* iv. 335
At last it fix'd, 'twas on what plant it *p. D.* iv. 429
And *p.* to 'scape from Flattery to Wit *E.* i. 12
Who without flatt'ry *p.* the fair and great *E.* iv. 6
P. while with smiles his happy lines you view *E.* iv. 75
So *p.* at first the tow'ring Alps we try *E.C.* 225
P. with a work where nothing's just or fit *E.C.* 291
Who still are *p.* too little or too much *E.C.* 385
Which lives as long as fools are *p.* to laugh *E.C.* 451
Still *p.* to teach, and yet not proud to know *E.C.* 632
Still *p.* to praise, yet not afraid to blame *E.C.* 742
P. to the last, he crops the flow'ry food *E.M.* i. 83
Be *p.* with nothing, if not bless'd with all *E.M.* i. 188
P. with a rattle, tickled with a straw *E.M.* ii. 276
P. with this bauble still, as that before *E.M.* ii. 281
P. let me own, in *Esher's* peaceful Grove *E.S.* ii. 66
I own I'm *p.* with this rebuke *I.H.* ii. 60 s
Each willing to be *p.*, and please *I.H.* ii. 139
Pudding, that might have *p.* a Dean *I.H.* ii. 166
P. the green lustre of the scales survey *M.* 83
P. Vaga echoes thro' her winding bounds *M.E.* iii. 251
Thro' his young Woods how *p.* Sabinus stray'd *M.E.* iv. 89
They *p.* the Fathers of poetic rage *M.E.* v. 50
That, if be *p.*, he *p.* by manly ways *P.S.* 337
And write whate'er he *p.*, except his Will *P.S.* 379
And *p.* pursue its progress thro' the skies *R.L.* v. 132
The lines are weak, another's *p.* to say *S.* i. 5
More *p.* to keep it till their friends could come *S.* ii. 95
If not so *p.*, at Council-board rejoice *S.* iv. 34

PLEASES—PLUNGE.

Next *p.* his Excellence a town to batter *S.* vi. 44
Better (say I) be *p.*, and play the fool *S.* vi. 181
And *p.*, if sordid want be far away *S.* vi. 295
P. to look forward, *p.* to look behind *S.* vi. 314
P. thy pale ghost, or grac'd thy mournful bier *U.L.* 50
P. in the silent shade with empty praise *W.F.* 432

Pleases.

Who now reads Cowley! if he *p.* yet (*rep.*) *S.* v. 75
Whom Folly *p.*, and whose Follies please *S.* vi. 327

Pleasing.

For her, the limes their *p.* shades deny *A.* 25
Ye pow'rs, what *p.* frenzy soothes my mind *A.* 51
In *p.* memory of all he stole *D.* i. 128
While thus each hand promotes the *p.* pain *D.* ii. 311
How oft in *p.* tasks we wear the day *E.* iii. 17
Each *p.* Blount shall endless smiles bestow *E.* iii. 61
Back thro' the paths of *p.* sense I ran *E.A.* 69
If crystal streams "with *p.* murmurs creep" *E.C.* 352
Less *p.* far than Virtue's very tears *E.M.* iv. 320
How *p.* Atterbury's softer hour *E.S.* ii. 82
A *p.* Form; a firm, yet cautious Mind *Ep.* ii. 1
With ev'ry *p.*, ev'ry prudent part *M.E.* ii. 159
No *p.* Intricacies intervene *M.E.* iv. 115
To *Basset's* heav'nly Joys, and *p.* Cares *Mi.* ix. 102
Not a less *p.*, tho' less glorious care *R.L.* ii. 92
With growing years each *p.* license grew *S.* v. 249
The woods and fields their *p.* toils deny *W.F.* 120

Pleasingly.

He gains all points, who *p.* confounds *M.E.* iv. 55

Pleasure.

Yon stars, yon suns, he rears at *p.* higher *D.* iii. 259
Your *p.* is a vice, but not your pride *E.* iv. 34
A morning's *p.*, and at ev'ning torn *E.* iv. 66
A cool suspense from *p.* and from pain *E.A.* 250
The gen'rous *p.* to be charm'd with Wit *E.C.* 238
In the fat age of *p.*, wealth and ease *E.C.* 534
But you, with *p.* own your errors past *E.C.* 570
Mere curious *p.*, or ingenious pain *E.M.* ii. 48
Pain their aversion, *P.* their desire *E.M.* ii. 88
P., or wrong or rightly understood *E.M.* ii. 91
Shares with his lord the *p.* and the pride *E.M.* iii. 36
For more his *p.*, yet for more his pride *E.M.* iii. 60
Nor ends the *p.* with the fierce embrace *E.M.* iii. 123
While *p.*, gratitude, and hope combin'd *E.M.* iii. 145
To Virtue, in the paths of *P.*, trod *E.M.* iii. 233
Good, *P.*, Ease, Content! whate'er thy name *E.M.*iv.22
Those call it *P.*, and Contentment these (*rep.*) *E.M.* iv.
Shall find, that *p.* pays not half the pain *E.M.* iv. 48
Reason's whole *p.*, all the Joys of Sense *E.M.* iv. 79
Content, or *P.*, but the Good and Just *E.M.* iv. 186
Of Social *P.*, ill-exchang'd for Pow'r *E.S.* i. 30
Or if it be thy Will and *P. I.H.* ii. 19
A fool to *P.*, yet a slave to Fame *M.E.* ii. 62
The *P.* miss'd her, and the Scandal hit *M.E.* ii. 128
The Love of *P.*, and the Love of Sway *M.E.* ii. 210
Is but to please, can *P.* seem a fault *M.E.* ii. 212
Men, some to Bus'ness, some to *P.* take *M.E.* ii. 215
P. the sex, as children Birds, pursue *M.E.* ii. 231
Your love of *P.*, our desire of rest *M.E.* ii. 274
That life of *p.*, and that soul of whim *M.E.* iii. 306
Smit with the mighty *p.* to be seen *M.E.* iv. 128
Can taste no *p.* since his Shield was scour'd *M.E.* v. 42
Long Health, long Youth, long *P.*, and a Friend *Mi.* v. 2
The Winner's *p.*, and the Loser's pain *Mi.* ix. 80
Days of ease, and nights of *p. O.* iii. 43
But what with *p.* Heav'n itself surveys *P.C.* 20
Ease, *p.*, virtue, all our sex resign *R.L.* iv. 106
Each mortal has his *p.* : none deny *S.* i. 45
No Pimp of *P.*, and no Spy of State *S.* i. 134
The *p.* lies in you, and not for Church and State *S.* ii. 16
If weak the *p.* that from these can spring *S.* iv. 18
Now all for *P.*, now for Church and State *S.* v. 158
Her name with *p.* once she taught the shore (*rep.*) *W.* 43
Love, Hope, and Joy, fair *P.'s* smiling train *E.M.* ii. 117
Not that their *P*—s caus'd her discontent *E.* v. 9
Repent old *p.*, and solicit new *E.A.* 186
P. are ever in our hands or eyes *E.M.* ii. 123
All *p.* sicken, and all glories sink *E.M.* iv. 46
Wise Wretch! with *P.* too refin'd to please *M.E.* ii. 95
To taste awhile the *p.* of a Court *R.L.* iii. 10

Plebeian.

Gain'd but one trump and one *P.* card *R.L.* iii. 54

Pledge.

This *Snuff-Box*, once the *p.* of SHARPER's love *Mi.*ix.37

Pledg'd.

He *p.* it to the knight; the knight had wit *M.E.* iii. 363

Pleiads.

And from the *P.* fruitful show'rs descend *Sp.* 102

Plenteous.

Our *p.* streams a various race supply *W.F.* 141

Plenty.

The rich is happy in the *p.* giv'n *E.M.* ii. 264
Nor is his claim to *p.*, but content *E.M.* iv. 156
With Splendour, Charity; with *P.*, Health *M.E.* iii. 225
In *p.* starving, tantaliz'd in state *M.E.* iv. 163
And peace and *p.* tell, a STUART reigns *W.F.* 42
Some thoughtless Town, with ease and *p.* blest *W.F.*107

Plies.

Imagination *p.* her dang'rous art *E.M.* ii. 143

Pliny.

For me what Virgil, *P.* may deny *D.* iv. 225

Plot.

Made him observe the subject and the *p. E.C.* 275
A popish *p.*, shall for a Jesuit take *S.* viii. 35

Plots.

He ne'er rebels, nor *p.*, like other men *S.* v. 194

Plough.

Direct my *P.* to find a Treasure *I.H.* ii. 20 s
Learn of the mole to p., the worm to weave *E.M.* iii. 176
And the broad falchion in a p.-share end *M.* 62

Plough'd.

P. was his front with many a deep Remark *D.* iv. 204

Ploughs.

The hog that *p.* not nor obeys thy call *E.M.* iii. 41
P., burns, manures, and toils from sun to sun *S.* vi. 271

Pluck.

I *p.* out year by year, and hair by hair *S.* v. 64

Pluck'd.

Forth from the heap she *p.* her Vot'ry's pray'r *D.* ii. 95

Plum.

Alas! they fear a man will cost a *p. M.E.* iii. 122
To tax Directors, who (thank God) have P—s *E.S.* ii 49
Just as a Scotsman does his *P. I.H.* i. 24
P. and Directors, Shylock and his Wife *S.* i. 103

Plumage.

Smit with her varying *p.*, spare the dove *E.M.* iii. 54

Plume.

At Quin's high *p.*, or Oldfield's petticoat *S.* v. 331
Some o'er her lap their careful p—s display'd *R.L.* iii. 115
The vivid green his shining *p.* unfold *W.F.* 117

Plump.

All as a partridge *p.*, full-fed and fair *D.* ii. 41

Plumps.

As what a Dutchman *p.* into the lakes *D.* ii. 403

Plunder.

Or cross, to *p.* Provinces, the Main *S.* iii. 127

Plunder'd.

How here he sipp'd, how there he *p.* snug *D.* i. 129
Or infamous for *p.* provinces *E.M.* iv. 298
Rich ev'n when *p.*, honour'd while oppress'd *S.* iii. 182

Plunderers.

Suits Tyrants, *P.*, but suits not me *S.* viii. 195

Plunge.

O'er head and ears *p.* for the Commonweal *D.* i. 209
Some *p.* in bus'ness, others shave their crowns *M.E.* i.104
The surge, and *p.* his Father in the deep *M.E.* iii. 354

Plung'd.

P. for his sense, but found no bottom there *D.* i. 119
Shot to the black abyss, and *p.* downright *D.* ii. 288
Next *p.* a feeble, but a desp'rate pack *D.* ii. 305
Or *p.* in lakes of bitter washes lie *R.L.* ii. 127

Plunging.

The *p.* Prelate and his pond'rous Grace *D.* ii. 323
In seas of flame my *p.* soul is drown'd *E.A.* 275

Plutarch.

Plu—*P.*, what's his name that writes his life *E.J.S.* 31

Pluto.

P. with Cato thou for this shalt join *D.* iii. 309
Gloomy *P.*, King of Terrors *Mi.* vii. 17

Ply.

We *p.* the Memory, we load the Brain *D.* iv. 157
Statesman and Patriot *p.* alike the Stocks *M.E.* iii. 139
With what a shifting gale your course you *p.* *S.* v. 298

Ply'd.

The Tempter saw his time; the work he *p.* *M.E.* iii. 369

Po.

And trees weep amber on the banks of *P.* *S*/*. 62
Nor *P.* so swells the fabling Poet's lays *W.F.* 227

Poach.

I *p.* in Suidas for unlicens'd Greek *D.* iv. 228

Pocket.

Or Japhet *p.*, like his Grace, a Will *E.S.* i. 120
Eat some, and *p.* up the rest *I.H.* i. 26
Can *p.* States, can fetch or carry Kings *M.E.* iii. 42

Poem.

Call forth each mass, a *P.*, or a Play *D.* i. 58
Can sleep without a *P.* in my head *P.S.* 269
Write dull receipts how *p*—s may be made *E.C.* 115
P. I heeded (now be-rhym'd so long) *P.S.* 221
Has sanctify'd whole *p.* for an age *S.* v. 114

Poesy.

And smit with love of *P.* and Prate *D.* ii. 382

Poet.

The needy *P.* sticks to all he meets *D.* iii. 290
Then take at once the *P.* and the song *D.* iv. 8
A *P.* the first day he dips his quill (*rep.*) *D.* iv. 163
Such were the notes thy once-lov'd *P.* sung *E.* i. 1
Supremely blest, the *p.* in his Muse *E.M.* ii. 270
P. or Patriot, rose but to restore *E.M.* iii. 285
Oh master of the *p.*, and the song *E.M.* iv. 374
Dare they to hope a *P.* for their Friend *E.S.* ii. 115
Truth guards the *P.*, sanctifies the line *E.S.* ii. 246
A *P.*, blest beyond a Poet's fate *Ep.* x. 3
In peace let one poor *P.* sleep *Ep.* xv. 2
Behold the place, where if a *P.* *I.H.* ii. 187
They had no *P.*, and they died *I.H.* iv. 14
They had no *P.*, and are dead *I.H.* iv. 16
To you gave Sense, Good-humour and a *P.* *M.E.* ii. 292
Kind Boyle, before his *p.*, lays *Mi.* xii. 5
Love, strong as Death, the *P.* led *O.* i. 51
Whom have I hurt? has *P.* yet, or Peer *P.S.* 95
With open arms receiv'd one *P.* more *P.S.* 142
How coming to the *P.* ev'ry Muse *S.* ii. 84
And, what's more rare, a *P.* shall say grace *S.* ii. 150
Say at what age a *P.* grows divine *S.* v. 50
Yet let me show, a *P.'s* of some weight *S.* v. 203
The Rights a Courl attack'd, a *P.* sav'd *S.* v. 224
Ah luckless *P.*! stretch thy lungs and roar *S.* v. 324
To know the *P.* from the man of rhymes *S.* v. 341
Ah think, what *P.* best may have been known *S.* v. 377
Convict a Papist he, and I a *P.* *S.* vi. 67
A *P.* begs me, I will hear him read *S.* vi. 93
Go, lofty *P.*! and in such a crowd *S.* vi. 108
A *P.'s form the plac'd before their eyes D.* ii. 35
All gaze with ardour: some a *p.* name *D.* ii. 51
But Welsted most the *P.* healing balm *D.* ii. 207
And *P.* vision of eternal Fame *D.* iii. 12
Mix'd the Owl's ivy with the *P.* bays *D.* iii. 54
The gen'rous Critic fann'd the *P.* fire *E.C.* 100
But most by Numbers judge a *P.* song *E.C.* 337
Name a new Play, and he's the *P.* friend *E.C.* 620
And bless their Critic with a *P.* fire *E.C.* 676
The *P.* bays and Critic's ivy grow *E.C.* 706

A Poet, blest beyond a *P.* fate *Ep.* x. 3
First sought a *P.* Fortune in the Town *Mi.* ii. 2
To hear the *P.* pray'r *O.* i. 84
Maintain a *P.* dignity and ease *P.S.* 263
Not proud, nor servile;—be one *P.* praise *P.S.* 336
And justly CÆSAR scorns the *P.* lays *S.* i. 35
Takes the whole House upon the *P.* day *S.* iv. 88
The Life to come, in ev'ry *P.* Creed *S.* v. 74
But fill their purse, our *P.* work is done *S.* v. 294
We Poets are (upon a *P.* word) *S.* v. 358
Yet like the Papist's, is the *P.* state *S.* vii. 11
The *P.* hell, its tortures, fiends, and flames *S.* viii. 7
Nor Po so swells the fabling *P.* lays *W.F.* 227
While pensive P—s painful vigils keep *D.* i. 93
Then first (if *P.* aught of truth declare) *D.* ii. 77
And stretch'd on bulks, as usual, *P.* lay *D.* ii. 420
Nor glad vile *P.* with true Critics' gore *D.* iii. 178
In *P.* as true genius is but rare *E.C.* 11
Some have at first for Wits, then *P.* past *E.C.* 36
Against the *P.* their own arms they turn'd *E.C.* 106
P. like painters, thus, unskill'd to trace *E.C.* 293
Such, without wit, are *P.* when they please *E.C.* 590
Still run on *P.* in a raging vein *E.C.* 606
Nay show'd his faults—but when would *P.* mend *E.C.* 621
P., a race long unconfin'd and free *E.C.* 649
And Patriots still, or *P.*, deck the Line *Ep.* i. 14
She sins with *P.* thro' pure Love of Wit *M.E.* ii. 76
P. heap Virtues, Painters Gems at will *M.E.* ii. 185
Of Orpheus now no more let *P.* tell *O.* i. 131
And own'd that nine such *P.* made a *Tate* *P.S.* 190
His Library (where busts of *P.* dead *P.S.* 235
(More silent far) where Kings and *P.* lie *S.* iv. 51
The *P.* learn'd to please, and not to wound *S.* v. 258
We *P.* are (upon a Poet's word) *S.* v. 358
No *P.* there, but Stephen, you, and me *S.* vi. 140
There is a time when *P.* will grow dull *S.* vi. 200
P. themselves must fall, like those they sung *U.L.* 75
By God-like *P.* venerable made *W.F.* 270
On P—s' tombs see Benson's titles writ D. iii. 325
Lies crown'd with Princes' honours, *P.* lays *Ep.* viii. 5

Poetess.

A maudlin *P.*, a rhyming Peer *P.S.* 16

Poetic.

P. Justice with her lifted scale *D.* i. 52
And learn to crawl upon *p.* feet *D.* i. 62
Her tresses staring from *P.* dreams *D.* iii. 17
Old Bavius sits to dip *p.* souls *D.* iii. 24
While thro' *P.* scenes the GENIUS roves *D.* iv. 489
They pleas'd the Fathers of *p.* rage *M.E.* v. 50
Who give th' hysteric or *p.* fit *R.L.* iv. 60
Tho' mark'd by none but quick, *p.* eyes *R.L.* v. 124
Now times are chang'd, and one *P.* Itch *S.* v. 169
But not this part of the *P.* state *S.* v. 348
Thus we dispose of all *p.* merit *S.* vi. 135

Poetry.

The cave of Poverty and *P.* *D.* i. 34
This prose on stilts, that *p.* fall'n lame *D.* i. 190
Music resembles *P.*, in each *E.C.* 143
With not one sin, but *p.* *Mi.* xii. 2
And curses Wit, and *P.* and Pope *P.S.* 26
It is not *P.*, but prose run mad *P.S.* 188
But sick of fops, and *p.*, and prate *P.S.* 229
To rules of *P.* no more confin'd *S.* vi. 202
I grant that *P.'s* a crying sin *S.* vii. 7

Point.

Ascend this hill, whose cloudy *p.* commands *D.* iii. 67
And mark that *p.* where sense and dulness meet *E.C.* 51
His time a moment, and a *p.* his space *E.M.* i. 72
Know thy own *p.*: This kind, this due degree *E.M.* i. 283
Draw to one *p.*, and to one centre bring *E.M.* iii. 301
Heroes are much the same, the *p.'s* agreed *E.M.* iv. 219
The only *p.* where human bliss stands still *E.M.* iv. 311
A knotty *p.*! to which we now proceed *M.E.* ii. 39
Dear BETTY shall th' important *p.* decide *Mi.* ix. 23
Or rather truly, if your *p.* be rest *S.* i. 17
And 'twas their *p.*, I ween, to make it last *S.* ii. 94
Produc'd the *p.* that left a sting behind *S.* v. 252
Loose on the *p.* of ev'ry waving hour *S.* vi. 249
Light-arm'd with P—s, Antitheses, and Puns *D.* i. 306
He gains all *p.*, who pleasingly confounds *M.E.* iv. 55
Commas and *p.* they set exactly right *P.S.* 161
The meeting *p.* the sacred hair dissever *R.L.* iii. 153

But knottier *p.* we knew not half so well *S.* vi. 58
Heav'n's twinkling Sparks draw light, and p. their horns D. ii. 12
P. she to Priest or Elder, Whig or Tory *E.S.* ii. 96
Here *p.* your thunder, and exhaust your rage *E.C.* 555
What? arm'd for Virtue when I *p.* the pen *S.* i. 105
To Hounslow-heath I *p.* and Bansted-down *S.* ii. 143
For vulgar eyes, and *p.* out ev'ry line *S.* v. 367

Pointed.
And *p.* out those arduous pafbs they trod *E.C.* 95
That *p.* back to youth, this on to age *E.M.* iii. 144
And *p.* Crystals break the sparkling Rill *Mi.* x. 4
His Moral pleases, not his *p.* wit *S.* v. 76

Pointing.
Where London's column *p.* at the skies *M.E.* iii. 339
There passengers shall stand, and *p.* say *U.L.* 39

Points.
P. him two ways, the narrower the better *D.* iv. 152
Just when his fancy *p.* your sprightly eyes *E.* v. 45
Who forms the phalanx, and who *p.* the way *E.M.* iii. 108
Invite my steps, and *p.* to yonder glade *U.L.* 2

Poised.
P. with a tail, may steer on Wilkins' wings *D.* iv. 452

Poison.
Still drink delicious *p.* from thy eye *E.A.* 122
To shun their *p.*, and to choose their food *E.M.* iii. 100
As *P.* heals, in just proportion us'd *M.E.* iii. 234
Slander or *P.* dread from Delia's rage *S.* i. 81
Is hung on high, to p. half mankind E.M. iv. 252
They'll never *p.* you, they'll only cheat *S.* i. 90

Pois'ning.
The *p.* Dame—You mean—I don't—You do *E.S.* ii. 22

Pois'nous.
From *p.* herbs extracts the healing dew *E.M.* i. 220

Poitiers
Or what was spoke at CRESSY or *P. S.* lii. 100

Poland.
The Crown of *P.* venal twice an age *M.E.* iii. 127

Pole.
And Metaphysic smokes involve the *P. D.* iv. 248
And waft a sigh from Indus to the *P. E.A.* 58
No, fly me, fly me, far as *P.* from *P. E.A.* 289
And Athens rising near the *p. O.* ii. 22
Burn thro' the Tropic, freeze beneath the *P. S.* iii. 72
Is Wealth thy passion? Hence! from *P.* to *P. S.* iv. 69
Shall fly, like Oglethorpe, from *p.* to *p. S.* vi. 277
Where clearer flames glow round the frozen *P. W.F.* 390
See round the P—s where keener spangles shine D. iii. 69

Polemic.
Each staunch *P.*, stubborn as a rock *D.* iv. 195

Policy.
True faith, and *p.*, united ran *E.M.* iii. 239
The Dull, flat Falsehood serves for *p. M.E.* i. 67
Suppress them, or miscall them *P. M.E.* i. 124
Int'rest o'ercome, or *P.* take place *M.E.* i. 167
Learn each small People's genius, p—ies *E.M.* iii. 183

Polish.
Heav'n when it strives to *p.* all it can *M.E.* ii. 271
But Otway fail'd to *p.* and refine *S.* v. 278
Then *p.* all, with so much life and ease *S.* vi. 176

Polish'd.
This *p.* Hardness, that reflects the Peer *D.* i. 220
(In *p.* verse) the Manners and the Mind *S.* v. 393
Nor *p.* marble emulate thy face *U.L.* 60

Polite.
Equal in wit, and equally *p. D.* iii. 181
Intent to reason, or *p.* to please *E.M.* iv. 382
His sly, *p.*, insinuating style *E.S.* i. 19
He marries, bows at Court, and grows *p. M.E.* iii. 386
Who never mentions Hell to ears *p. M.E.* iv. 150
But why then publish? *Granville* the *p. P.S.* 135
Wit grew *p.*, and Numbers learn'd to flow *S.* v. 266

Politely.
Oh! Sir, *p.* so! nay, let me die *S.* viii. 112

Politic.
No less alike the *P.* and wise *E.M.* iv. 225

Politician.
Coffee (which makes the *p.* wise *R.L.* iii. 117
Old *P—s chew on wisdom past M.E.* i. 228

Politics.
Hibernian *P.*, O Swift! thy fate *D.* iii. 331
In puns, or *p.*, or tales, or lies *P.S.* 321

Poll.
Nay, *P.* sat mute, and Shock was most unkind *R.L.* iv. 164

Pollio.
Came, cramm'd with capon, from where *P.* dines *D.* iv. 350
Bid me with *P.* sup, as well as dine *D.* iv. 392
So back to *P.*, hand in hand, they went *D.* iv. 396
On the cast ore, another *P.*, shine *M.E.* v. 64

Pollutes.
Who flings most filth, and wide *p.* around *D.* ii. 279

Polwarth.
COBHAM's a Coward, *P.* is a Slave *E.S.* ii. 130

Polypheme.
Teach thou the warbling *P.* to roar *D.* iii. 305

Pomatums.
Gums and *P.* shall his flight restrain *R.L.* ii. 129

Pomona.
See Pan with flocks, with fruits *P.* crown'd *W.F.* 37

Pomp.
Here stopt the Goddess; and in *p.* proclaims *D.* ii. 365
Pride, *P.*, and State but reach his outward part *E.* iv. 55
One thought of thee puts all the *p.* to flight *E.A.* 273
And swell the *p.* of dreadful sacrifice *E.A.* 354
Works without show, and without *p.* presides *E.C.* 75
The spoils of nations, and the *p.* of wars *P.C.* 28
The *p.* was darken'd, and the day o'ercast *P.C.* 32
If in the *P.* of Life consist the joy *S.* iv. 98
When the sad *p.* along his banks was led *W.F.* 274
P—s without guilt, of bloodless swords and maces D. i. 87

Pompous.
Withdrew his hand, and clos'd the *p.* page *D.* iv. 114
Rome's *p.* glories rising to our thought *E.* iii. 24
A vile conceit in *p.* words exprest *E.C.* 320
And haunt their slumbers in the *p.* shade *E.M.* iv. 304
And *p.* buildings once were things of Use *M.E.* iv. 24
That long behind he trails his *p.* robe *R.L.* iii. 73
Where Windsor-domes and *p.* turrets rise *W.F.* 352

Pompously.
The bounding steed you *p.* bestride *E.M.* iii. 35

Pond.
His *p.* an Ocean, his parterre a Down *M.E.* iv. 106

Pond'rous.
Which, as more *p.*, made its aim more true *D.* i. 171
And *p.* slugs cut swiftly thro' the sky *D.* i. 182
The plunging Prelate, and his *p.* Grace *D.* ii. 323
The *p.* books two gentle readers bring *D.* ii. 383
To lug the *p.* volume off in state *D.* iv. 118
There Hero's wits are kept in *p.* vases *R.L.* v. 115

Poniard.
Her *p.*, had oppos'd the dire command *E.A.* 102

Pontific.
Not with more glee by hands *p.* crown'd *D.* ii. 13
The Bishop stow (*P.* Luxury!) *D.* iv. 593

Poor.
Here one *p.* word a hundred clenches makes *D.* i. 63
She saw slow Philips creep like Tate's *p.* page *D.* i. 105
Here lay *p.* Fletcher's half-eat scenes, and here *D.* i. 131
P. W** nipt in Folly's broadest bloom *D.* iv. 513
Of those that sing of these *p.* eyes *E.* vi. 32
Lo the *p.* Indian! whose untutor'd mind *E.M.* i. 99

The *p.* contents him with the care of Heav'n *E.M.* ii. 266
Till tir'd he sleeps, and Life's *p.* play is o'er *E.M.* ii. 282
Lent Heav'n a parent to the *p.* and me *E.M.* iv. 110
Yet *p.* with fortune, and with learning blind *E.M.* iv. 329
The *p.* and friendless Villain, than the Great *E.S.* ii. 45
In peace let one *p.* Poet sleep *Ep.* xv. 1
Were the last words that *p.* Narcissa spoke *M.E.* i. 247
Or wanders, Heav'n-directed, to the *P. M.E.* i. 150
P. Avarice one torment more would find *M.E.* iii. 59
Pity mistakes for some *p.* tradesman craz'd *M.E.* iii. 64
Perhaps you think the *P.* might have their part (*rep.*) *M.E.* iii. 99
Yet to be just to these *p.* men of pelf *M.E.* iii. 107
Sees but a backward steward for the *P. M.E.* iii. 172
And who would take the *P.* from Providence *M.E.* iii. 186
Behold the Market-place with *p.* o'erspread *M.E.* iii. 263
And rich aad *p.* makes all the history *M.E.* iii. 288
His givings rare, save farthings to the *p. M.E.* iii. 348
And tempts by making rich, not making *p. M.E.* iii. 352
Yet hence the *P.* are cloth'd, the Hungry fed *M.E.* iv. 169
P. Vadius, long with learned spleen devour'd *M.E.* v. 41
And with a borrow'd Play, out-did *p. Crown Mi.* iii. 8
Who dare to love their Country, and be *p. Mi.* x. 14
P. Cornus sees his frantic wife elope *P.S.* 25
P. guiltless I l and can I choose but smile *P.S.* 281
But why insult the *p.*, affront the great *P.S.* 360
See the *p.* remnants of these slighted hairs *R.L.* iv. 167
And the rich feast concludes extremely *p. S.* ii. 34
How dar'st thou let one worthy man be *p. S.* ii. 118
But ancient friends (tho' *p.*, or out of play) *S.* ii. 139
And which not done, the richest must be *p. S.* iii. 46
Well, but the *P.*—The *P.* have the same itch *S.* iii. 154
Who proud of Pedigree, is *p.* of Purse *S.* iv. 84
And envy'd Thirst and Hunger to the *P. S.* iv. 117
Ben, old and *p.*, as little seem'd to heed *S.* v. 73
Has seiz'd the Court and City, *p.* and rich *S.* v. 170
Ward tried on Puppies, and the *P.*, his Drop *S.* v. 182
Stretch'd to relieve the Idiot and the *P. S.* v. 226
To make *p.* Pinky eat with vast applause *S.* v. 293
In ANNA's wars, a Soldier *p.* and old *S.* vi. 33
He slept, *p.* dog ! and lost it, to a doit *S.* vi. 36
A man so *p.* would live without a place *S.* vi. 287
P. and disarm'd, and hardly worth your hate *S.* vii. 12
Where are those troops of *P.*, that throng'd of yore *S.* vii. 113
Yet these were all *p.* Gentlemen l I dare *S.* viii. 78
And cheats th' unknowing Widow and the *P. S.* viii. 141
Stretch'd o'er the *P.* and Church his iron rod *W.F.* 75
The rest, some farm the *P.*-box, some the Pews *S.* iii. 128

Poorest.
Which done, the *p.* can no wants endure *S.* iii. 45

Pope.
What *P.* or Council can they need beside *E.M.* iii. 84
If *P.* must tell what HARCOURT cannot speak *Ep.* iii. 6
From *P.*, from Parnell, or from Gay *I.H.* ii. 94 s
And heads the bold Train-bands, and burns a *P. M.E.* iii. 214
Maul the French Tyrant, or pull down the *P. Mi.* ii. 18
And curses Wit, and Poetry and *P. P.S.* 26
Whether the name belong to *P.* or Vernon *S.* ii. 166
Friend *P. !* be prudent, let your Muse take breath *S.* iii. 13
Verse prays for Peace, or sings down *P.* and Turk *S.* v. 236
And *P.'s*, ten years to comment and translate *D.* iii. 332
For writing Pamphlets, and for roasting P—s *D.* iii. 286

Pope's Arms.
Down with the Bible, up with the *P. D.* ii. 82

Popish.
A *p.* plot, shall for a Jesuit take *S.* viii. 35

Poplar.
Beneath yon *p.* oft we past the day *A.* 66

Poppy.
And Shadwell nods the *p.* on his brows *D.* iii. 22
Now, Bavius, take the *p.* from thy brow *D.* iii. 317

Popularity.
Or *P. !* or Stars and Strings *S.* iv. 14

Pore.
To smart and agonize at ev'ry *p. E.M.* i. 198

Sees hairs and p—s, examines bit by bit *D.* iv. 234
With sharpen'd sight pale Antiquaries p. *M.E.* v. 35

Poring.
There, dim in clouds, the *p.* Scholiasts mark *D.* iii. 191

Port.
See Alaric's stern *p. !* the martial frame *D.* iii. 91
And Alma Mater lie dissolv'd in *P. D.* iii. 338
In troubled waters, but now sleeps in *P. D.* iv. 202
He paid some bards with *p.*, and some with praise *P.S.* 242
That Spain robs on, and Dunkirk's still a *P. S.* viii. 165

Portals.
See heav'n its sparkling *p.* wide display *M.* 97

Portentous.
With that a Tear (*p.* sign of Grace) *D.* i. 243

Porter.
A Fav'rite's *P.* with his Master vie *E.S.* i. 117

Portia.
Brutus for absent *P.* sighs *O.* iii. 15

Portion.
How little, mark ! that *p.* of the ball *D.* iii. 83
Become the *p.* of a boohy lord *S.* ii. 176
And mourn our various p—s as we please *E.M.* iv. 33

Portion'd.
Him *p.* maids, apprentic'd orphans blest *M.E.* iii. 267

Portrait.
One certain *P.* may (I grant) be seen *M.E.* ii. 181

Portraiture.
Instructive work l whose wry-mouth'd *p. D.* ii. 145

Pos'd.
A thing which Adam had been *p.* to name *S.* viii. 25

Positive.
Some *p.*, persisting fops we know *E.C.* 568
More pert, more proud, more *p.* than he *S.* vii. 52

Possess.
Soon to obtain, and long *p.* the prize *R.L.* ii. 44
Ye sacred Nine l that all my soul *p. W.F.* 259

Possess'd, Possest.
Dulness *p.* o'er all her ancient right *D.* i. 11
All then is full, possessing, and *p. E.A.* 93
But Fortune's gifts if each alike *p—t E.M.* iv. 63
This man *p.* five hundred pounds a year *M.E.* iii. 280
Oh Tyrant Love ! hast thou *p. O.* iii. 1

Possesses.
Sinks deep within him, and *p.* whole *M.E.* iii. 373

Possessing.
All then is full, *p.*, and possess'd *E.A.* 93

Possessions.
All vast *p.* (just the same the case *S.* vi. 254

Possible.
Of Systems *p.*, if 'tis confest *E.M.* i. 43
Get Place and Wealth, if *p.*, with grace *S.* iii. 103

Post.
Of Curl's chaste press, and Lintot's rubric *p. D.* i. 40
First Osborne lean'd against his letter'd *p. D.* ii. 171
Knight of the *p.* corrupt, or of the shire *P.S.* 365
His *p.* neglects, or leaves the fair at large *R.L.* ii. 124
Or plaister'd p—s, with claps, in capitals *P.S.* 216
Deny'd all *p.* of profit or of trust *S.* vi. 61
And talk Gazettes and *P.*-boys o'er by heart *S.* viii. 155

Posterior.
And now bad Fame's *p.* Trumpet blown *D.* iv. 71

Posterity.
And make a long *P.* thy own *D.* iv. 334
Think how *p.* will treat thy name *S.* ii. 108

Postpone.
To headless Phœbe his fair bride *p. D.* iv. 367

Pot.
Hist'ry her *P.*, Divinity her Pipe *D.* iii. 106
When Paxton gives him double P—s and Pay *E.S* ii. 141

Potent.

By *p.* Arthur, knock'd his chin and breast *D.* ii. 398
The silenc'd Preacher yields to *p.* strain *S.* v. 237

'Pothecaries.

So modern *P.*, taught the art *E.C.* 108

Pother.

'Tis yet in vain, I own, to keep a *p. S.* ii. 45

Pound.

Or let it cost five hundred *p., I.H.* ii. 39 *s*
And find his Honour in a *P. I.H.* ii. 47 *s*
He thinks a Loaf will rise to fifty *p. M.E.* iii. 116
'Twas very want that sold them for two *p. M.E.* iii. 328
My Friendship, and a Prologue, and ten *p., P.S.* 48
Sir, he's your slave, for twenty *p.* a year *S.* vi. 8
You pay a penny, and he paid a *p. S.* vi. 239
Or should one *p.* of powder less bespread *S.* viii. 246
Because he wants a thousand p—s a year *E.M.* iv. 192
For life, six hundred *p.* a year *I.H.* ii. 9 *s*
This man possest—five hundred *p.* a year *M.E.* iii. 280
"Pray then, what wants he?" Fourscore thousand *p. S.* iii. 86
Ask'd for a groat, he gives a hundred *p. S.* iv. 86

Pour.

But *p.* them thickest on the noble head *D.* iv. 358
Excuse the blush, and *p.* out all my heart *E.A.* 56
Ye Heav'ns! from high the dewy nectar *p. M.* 13
And on the sightless eye-ball, the day *M.* 40
Stocks and Subscriptions *p.* on ev'ry side *M.E.* iii. 370
I love to *p.* out all my self as plain *S.* i. 51
P. the full tide of eloquence along *S.* vi. 171
Then foaming *p.* along, and rush into the Thames *W.F.* 218

Pour'd.

And *p.* her Spirit o'er the land and deep *D.* i. 8
Or P—ge *p.* forth the Torrent of his Wit *E.S.* ii. 159
P. o'er the whitening vale their fleecy care *Sp.* 19

Pouring.

But clear and artless, *p.* thro' the plain *M.E.* iii. 257

Pours.

Or that where on her Curls the Public *p. D.* ii. 3
P. forth, and leaves unpeopled half the land *D.* ii. 90
Thro' half the heav'ns he *p.* th' exalted urn *D.* ii. 183
P. into Thames: and hence the mingled wave *D.* ii. 343
The North by myriads *p.* her mighty sons *D.* iii. 89
P. at great Bourbon's feet her silken sons *D.* iv. 208
P. fierce Ambition in a Cæsar's mind *E.M.* i. 159
And *p.* it all upon the peccant part *E.M.* ii. 144
Is it for thee the linnet *p.* his throat *E.M.* iii. 33
Or *p.* profuse on earth, one nature feeds *E.M.* iii. 117
It *p.* the bliss that fills up all the mind *E.M.* iv. 344
P. balm into the bleeding lover's wounds *O.* i. 29
The Baron now his Diamonds *p.* apace *R.L.* iii. 75
And *p.* each human Virtue in the heart *S.* v. 220

Poverty.

The Cave of *P.* and Poetry *D.* i. 34
Scar'd at the spectre of pale *P. S.* iii. 70
He stuck to *p.* with peace of mind *S.* vi. 65
And all is splendid *p.* at best *S.* viii. 225

Powder.

Vain is thy Art, thy *P.* vain *Mi.* iv. 35
My wig all *p.*, and all snuff my band *S.* iii. 162
To save the *p.* from too rude a gale *R.L.* ii. 93
Or should one pound of *p.* less bespread *S.* viii. 246
Puffs, P—s, *Patches, Bibles, Billet-doux R.L.* i. 138

Pow'r.

What eyes but hers, alas, have *p.* to move *A.* 83
From thy Bœotia, tho' her *P.* retires *D.* i. 25
And learn, my sons, the wond'rous *p.* of Noise *D.* ii. 222
"What *p.*," he cries, "what *p.* these wonders wrought?" *D.* iii. 250
Roll in her Vortex, and her *p.* confess *D.* iv. 84
Narcissus, prais'd with all a Parson's *p. D.* iv. 103
Each with some wond'rous gift approach'd the *P. D.* iv. 399
Resistless falls: the Muse obeys the *P. D.* iv. 628
The rage of *P.*, the blast of public breath *E.* i. 25
Nor foes nor fortune take this *p.* away *E.A.* 43
The solid *p.* of understanding fails *E.C.* 57
The *p.* of Music all our hearts allow *E.C.* 382
For me kind Nature wakes her genial *P. E.M.* i. 133
Safe in the hand of one disposing *P. E.M.* i. 287
Reason itself but gives it edge and *p. E.M.* ii. 147
Let *p.* or knowledge, gold or glory please *E.M.* ii. 169
A mightier *P.* the strong direction sends *E.M.* ii. 165
Know, all enjoy that *p.* which suits them best *E.M.* iii. 80
To *P.* unseen, and mightier far than they *E.M.* iii. 252
To one Man's *p.*, ambition, lucre, lust *E.M.* iii. 270
No—shall the good want Health, the good want *P.* (*rep.*) *E.M.* iv. 158
Immense the *p.*, immense were the demand *E.M.* iv. 165
Of Social Pleasure, ill-exchang'd for *P. E.S.* i. 30
In Soldier, Churchman, Patriot, Man in *P. E.S.* i. 161
No *P.* the Muse's Friendship can command (*rep.*) *E.S.* ii. 118
[*In P. a Servant, out of P. a Friend*] *E.S.* ii. 161
But fix'd his word, his saving *p.* remains *M.* 107
We prize the stronger effort of his *p. M.E.* i. 147
Is he a Churchman? then he's fond of *P. M.E.* i. 155
By Spirit robb'd of *P.*, by Warmth of Friends *M.E.* ii. 144
P. all their end, but Beauty all the means *M.E.* ii. 220
That *P.* who bids the Ocean ebb and flow *M.E.* iii. 164
What all so wish, but want the *p.* to do *M.E.* iii. 276
His only daughter in a stranger's *p. M.E.* iii. 325
To bright Cecilia greater *p.* is giv'n *O.'l.* 132
Still, when the lust of tyrant *p.* succeeds *O.* ii. 31
And to be grave, exceeds all *P.* of face *P.S.* 36
Propitious heav'n, and ev'ry *p.* ador'd *R.L.* ii. 36
Or Alum styptics with contracting *p. R.L.* ii. 131
Th' expressive emblem of their softer *p. R.L.* iii. 40
Amaz'd, confus'd, he found his *p.* expir'd *R.L.* iii. 145
Then thus address'd the *p.*: "Hail, wayward Queen *R.L.* iv. 57
A nymph there is, that all thy *p.* disdains *R.L.* iv. 65
What then remains but well our *p.* to use *R.L.* v. 29
Its proper *p.* to hurt, each creature feels *S.* i. 85
But shew me one who has it in his *p. S.* iii. 136
Lov'd without youth, and follow'd without *p. S.* iii. 183
Grac'd as thou art, with all the *P.* of Words *S.* iv. 48
But if to *P.* and Place your passion lie *S.* iv. 97
Estates have wings, and hang in Fortune's *p. S.* vi. 248
Is known alone to that Directing *P. S.* vi. 278
In *p.*, wit, figure, virtue, fortune, plac'd *S.* vi. 302
As wild and mad: the Avarice of *p. S.* vi. 307
You, that too wise for pride, too good for *p. Sp.* 7
Oh! were I made by some transforming *p. Su.* 45
Taught P.'s *due use to People and to Kings E.M.* iii. 289
Ye p—s, what *pleasing frenzy sooths my mind A.* 51
To him we grant our amplest *p.* to sit *D.* ii. 375
Ye *P.!* whose mysteries restor'd I sing *D.* iv. 5
His *p.* in equal ranks, and fair array *E.C.* 176
Say what their use, had he the *p.* of all *E.M.* i. 178
The proper organs, proper *p.* assign'd *E.M.* i. 180
No *p.* of body or of soul to share *E.M.* i. 191
The scale of sensual, mental *p.* ascends *E.M.* i. 208
The *p.* of all subdu'd by thee alone (*rep.*) *E.M.* i. 231
From thee to Nothing. On superior *p. E.M.* i. 241
See then the acting and comparing *p. E.M.* iii. 95
Th' immortal *p.* incline their ear *O.* i. 127
With head uncover'd, the Cosmetic *p. R.L.* i. 124
The *p.* gave ear, and granted half his pray'r *R.L.* ii. 45
And his refulgent Queen, with *p.* combin'd *R.L.* iii. 77
And winds shall waft it to the *p.* above *Su.* 80
Why bade ye else, ye *P.!* her soul aspire *U.L.* 11
With chymic art exalts the min'ral *p. W.F.* 243

Pow'r and Glory.

Adds to Christ's pray'r the *P.* clause *S.* vii. 108

Pow'rful.

When first that sun too *p.* beams displays *E.C.* 470
Grant that the *p.* still the weak controul *E.M.* ii. 49
More *p.* each as needful to the rest *E.M.* iii. 299
Must act on motives, *p.* tho' unknown *M.E.* iii. 112
Men prove with child, as *p.* fancy works *R.L.* iv. 53
The moving mountains hear the *p.* call *Su.* 83

Pox.

She bears a Coronet and *P.* for life *M.E.* iii. 392
Plague on 't! 'tis past a jest—nay prithee, *p. R.L.* iv. 129
"My Friends!" he cry'd, "*p.* take you for your care *S.* vi. 195

Time, that at last matures a clap to *p. S.* vii. 47
As in the *p.*, some give it to get free *S.* viii. 171
Now *p.* on those who show a *Court in wax S.* viii. 206

Pox'd.
P. by her love, or libell'd by her hate *S.* i. 84

Practice.
To *P.* now from Theory repair *D.* iv. 580
Bold in the *p.* of mistaken rules *E.C.* 110
Such was the Muse, whose rules and *p.* tell *E.C.* 723

Practise.
Nor dare to *p.* till they've learn'd to dance *S.* v. 184

Practis'd.
P. to lisp, and hang the head aside *R.L.* iv. 33

Praise.
Or solid pudding against empty *p. D.* i. 54
Much she revolves their arts, their ancient *p. D.* i. 97
E'er since Sir Fopling's Periwig was *P. D.* i. 167
Know, Eusden thirsts no more for sack or *p. D.* i. 293
And bade thee live to crown Britannia's *p. D.* iii. 212
Alike their labours, and alike their *p. D.* iii. 272
To me committing their eternal *p. D.* iii. 280
Else sure some Bard, to our eternal *p. E.* i. 171
No hireling she, no prostitute to *p. E.* i. 36
The kindred arts shall in their *p.* conspire *E.* iii. 69
And only vocal with the Maker's *p. E.A.* 140
In *p.* so just let ev'ry voice be join'd *E.C.* 187
Immortal heirs of universal *p. E.C.* 190
For not to know some trifles, is a *p. E.C.* 262
Their *p.* is still—the Style is excellent *E.C.* 307
His *p.* is lost, who stays till all commend *E.C.* 475
In youth alone its empty *p.* we boast *E.C.* 496
Are mortals urg'd thro' sacred lust of *p. E.C.* 521
Those best can bear reproof, who merit *p. E.C.* 583
This humble *p.*, lamented shade! receive *E.C.* 733
Which seeks no int'rest, no reward but *p. E.M.* ii. 246
But random *P.*—the task can ne'er be done *E.S.* ii. 106
P. cannot stoop, like Satire, to the ground *E.S.* ii. 110
To 'scape my Censure, not expect my *P. E.S.* ii. 113
Due to his Merit, and brave Thirst of *p. Ep.* viii. 6
Foe to loud *P.*, and Friend to learned Ease *Ep.* x. 5
All see 'tis Vice, and itch of vulgar *p. M.E.* i. 60
Whose ruling Passion was the Lust of *P. M.E.* i. 181
His Passion still, to covet gen'ral *p. M.E.* i. 196
Had aim'd, like him, by Chastity at *p. M.E.* i. 217
Yet sure, of qualities deserving *p. M.E.* iii. 201
And to her Maker's *p.* confin'd the power of *O.* i. 125
Well-natur'd *Garth* inflam'd with early *p. P.S.* 137
Damn with faint *p.*, assent with civil leer *P.S.* 201
And wonder with a foolish face of *p. P.S.* 212
To spread about the note of verse and *p. P.S.* 224
He paid some bards with port, and some with *p. P.S.* 242
Not proud, nor servile; be one Poet's *p. P.S.* 336
Slight is the subject, but not so the *p. R.L.* i. 5
So long my honour, name, and *p.* shall live *R.L.* iii. 170
Or if you needs must write, write CÆSAR's *p. S.* i. 21
It is to *History* he trusts for *P. S.* i. 36
Now sick alike of Envy and of *P. S.* iii. 4
With *P.* or Infamy leave that to fate *S.* iii. 102
The Harvest early, but mature the *p. S.* v. 24
And yet deny the Careless Husband *p. S.* v. 92
On Fame's mad voyage by the wind of *p. S.* v. 297
That when I aim at *p.*, they say I bite *S.* v. 409
P. undeserv'd is scandal in disguise *S.* v. 413
Gave him much *p.*, and some reward beside *S.* vi. 43
What thanks, what *p.*, if *Peter* but supplies *S.* vii. 67
Inspire me, Phœbus, in my Delia's *p. Sp.* 45
Invoke the Muses, and resound your *p. Su.* 78
Oh sing of Daphne's fate, and Daphne's *p. W.* 8
Thy name, thy honour, and thy *p.* shall live *W.* 84
She scorn'd the *p.* of beauty, and the care *W.F.* 177
Pleas'd in the silent shade with empty *p. W.F.* 432
But all our p—s why should Lords engross *M.E.*iii.249
Or *p. the Court or magnify Mankind D.* i. 23
And *p.* the easy vigour of a line *E.C.* 360
Nor *p.* nor blame the writings, but the men *E.C.* 413
Some *p.* at morning what they blame at night *E.C.* 430
When we but *p.* ourselves in other men *E.C.* 455
Whom, when they *p.*, the world believes no more *E.C.* 594
And gladly *p.* the merit of a foe *E.C.* 628
And love to *p.*, with reason on his side *E.C.* 642
Still pleas'd to *p.*, yet not afraid to blame *E.C.* 742

Chaste Matrons *p.* her, and grave Bishops bless *E.S.* i. 146
God knows, I *p.* a Courtier when I can *E.S.* ii. 63
I follow *Virtue*: where she shines, I *p. E.S.* ii. 95
And love him, court him, *p.* him, in or out *E.S.* ii. 103
But pray, when others *p.* him, do I blame *E.S.* ii. 136
Are none, none living? let me *p.* the Dead *E.S.* ii. 251
Who would not *p.* Patritio's high descent *M.E.* i. 81
When all the World conspires to *p.* her *Mi.* viii. 11
Unless he *p.* some Monster of a King *S.* v. 210
Or *p.* malignly Arts I cannot reach *S.* v. 339
When this Heroics only deigns to *p. S.* vi. 82

Prais'd.
Narcissus, *p.* with all a Parson's pow'r *D.* iv. 103
P., wept, and honour'd by the Muse he lov'd *E.* iv. 6
And such were *p.* who but endeavour'd well *E.C.* 511
Who *p.* my Modesty, and smil'd *I.H.* i. 68
And *p.*, unenvy'd, by the Muse he lov'd *M.E.* v. 72
And Betty's *p.* for labours not her own *R.L.* i. 148
Say why are Beauties *p.* and honour'd most *R.L.* v. 9
Our fathers *p.* rank Ven'son. You suppose *S.* ii. 91
Each *p.* within, is happy all day long *S.* vi. 156
Such wits and beauties are not *p.* for nought *S.* viii. 234
Deaf the *p.* ear, and mute the tuneful tongue *U.L.* 76

Praises.
Who *p.* now? his Chaplain on his Tomb *D.* iv. 514

Prance.
Or set on Metaphysic ground to *p. D.* iv. 265

Prate.
And smit with love of Poesy and *P. D.* ii. 382
But sick of fops, and poetry, and *p. P.S.* 299
Morgan and Mandevil could p. *no more D.* ii. 414
They march, to *p.* their hour before the Fair *S.* viii. 249

Prates.
Here no man *p.* of idle things *I.H.* ii. 141

Prating.
(Cries *p.* Balbus) "something will come out." *P.S.* 276

Pray.
There starve and *p.*, for that's the way to heav'n *E.* v. 22
But *p.*, which of you all would take her back *E.Y.S.* 36
But most be present, if we preach or *p. E.M.* iii. 6
She taught the weak to bend, the proud to *p. E.M.* iii. 251
The matter's weighty, *p.* consider twice *E.S.* ii. 43
But *p.*, when others praise him, do I blame *E.S.* ii. 136
And how did, *p.*, the florid Youth offend *E.S.* ii. 166
Alas! alas! *p.* end what you began *E.S.* ii. 254
P. take them, Sir,—Enough's a Feast *I.H.* i. 25
A word, *p.*, in your Honour's ear *I.H.* i. 42
And if I *p.* by Reason's rules *I.H.* i. 15 s
"'Tis one to me"—"Then tell us, *p. I.H.* ii. 119 s
P., dip your Whiskers and your Tail in *I.H.* ii. 203
Flavia's a Wit, has too much sense to *p. M.E.* ii. 87
Each parent sprung—What fortune, *p.*?—Their own *P.S.* 390
And send the godly in a pet to *p. R.L.* iv. 64
"*P.* heav'n it last!" (cries SWIFT!) "as you go on *S.* ii. 161
"*P.* then, what wants he?" Fourscore thousand pounds *S.* iii. 86

Pray'd.
Once like thyself, I trembled, wept, and *p. E.A.* 311
Faint, breathless, thus she *p.*, nor *p.* in vain *W.F.* 199

Pray'r.
The caitiff Vaticide conceiv'd a *p. D.* ii. 78
Forth from the heap she pluck'd her Vot'ry's *p. D.* ii. 95
Puts his last refuge all in heav'n and *p. D.* ii. 214
As morning *p.* and flagellation end *D.* ii. 270
So he; but pious, whisper'd first his *p. D.* iv. 354
Love but demands what else were shed in *p. E.A.* 46
Plants of thy hand, and children of thy *p. E.A.* 130
Assist me, heav'n! but whence arose that *p. E.A.* 179
Each *p.* accepted, and each wish resign'd *E.A.* 210
Has ev'n been prov'd to grant a lover's *p. M.E.* ii. 55
For ever in a Passion or a *P. M.E.* ii. 106
Atossa, curs'd with ev'ry granted *p. M.E.* ii. 147
Averted half your Parents' simple *P. M.E.* ii. 286
That summons you to all the Pride of *P. M.E.* iv. 142
To hear the Poet's *p. O.* i. 84

238   PRAY'RBOOKS—PRESENCE.

The pow'rs gave ear, and granted half his *p. R.L.* ii. 45
Seems to reject him, tho' she grants his *p. R.L.* iv. 80
And feels that grace his *p.* besought in vain *S.* v. 238
Adds to Christ's *p.*, the *Power and Glory* clause *S.* vii. 108
The Gods, to curse Pamela with her p—s *E.* iv. 49
To morning-walks, and *p.* three hours a day *E.* v. 14
Nor *p.* nor fasts its stubborn pulse restrain *E.A.* 27
See how the force of others' *p.* I try *E.A.* 149
But why should I on others' *p.* depend *E.A.* 151
Take back my fruitless penitence and *p. E.A.* 286
I pay my debts, believe, and say my *p. P.S.* 268
Forget her *p.*, or miss a masquerade *R.L.* ii. 108
With store of *p.*, for mornings, nights, and noons *R.L.* iv. 29
Oh had I stay'd, and said my *p.* at home *R.L.* iv. 160
The courtier's promises, and sick man's *p. R.L.* v. 119

Pray'rbooks.
And beads and *p.* are the toys of age *E.M.* ii. 280

Praying.
While *p.*, trembling, in the dust I roll *E.A.* 279
The frugal Crone, whom *p.* priests attend *M.E.* i. 242

Prays.
In vain lost Eloïsa weeps and *p. E.A.* 15
Verse *p.* for Peace, or sings down Pope and Turk *S.* v. 236

Preach.
While Sherlock, Hare, and Gibson *p.* in vain *D.* iii. 204
Or, impious, *p.* his word without a call *D.* iv. 94
May you, may Cam and Isis, *p.* it long *D.* iv. 187
And, if it can, at once both please and *p. E.* iv. 24
But must be present, if we *p.* or pray *E.M.* iii. 6
P. as I please, I doubt our curious men *S.* ii. 17
You go to church to hear these Flatt'rers *p. S.* vi. 225
So first to *p.* a white-glov'd Chaplain goes *S.* viii. 250

Preach'd.
St. James's first, for leaden G—*p. D.* iv. 608
This, this the saving doctrine *p.* to all *S.* iii. 81

Preacher.
P. at once, and Zany of thy age *D.* iii. 206
The silenc'd *P.* yields to potent strain *S.* v. 237

Preaches.
All his Grace *p.*, all his Lordship sings *E.S.* ii. 224

Preaching.
Ten Metropolitans in *p.* well *E.S.* i. 132

Precariously.
Your scene *p.* subsists too long *P.C.* 41

Precede.
Six huntsmen with a shout *p.* his chair *D.* ii. 193

Precedent.
And have, at least, their *p.* to plead *E.C.* 166
They reason and conclude by *p. E.C.* 410

Precept.
Yet still how faint by *p.* is exprest *E.* iii. 41
From lips like those which *p.* fail'd to move *E.A.* 67
Against the *p.*, ne'er transgress its End *E.C.* 164
Just p—s *thus from great examples giv'n E.C.* 98
Some beauties yet no *p.* can declare *E.C.* 141
His *P.* teach but what his works inspire *E.C.* 660
Or better *P.* if you can impart *S.* iv. 132

Precious.
Tho' Time is *p.*, and I want some Tea *Mi.* ix. 28
And bids her beau demand the *p.* hairs *R.L.* iv. 122
While by our oaks the *p.* loads are born *W.F.* 31

Precipice.
The shapeless rock, or hanging *p. E.C.* 158

Precipitate.
Nonsense *p.*, like running Lead *D.* i. 123

Precipitately.
Furious he dives, *p.* dull *D.* ii. 316

Precise.
End all dispute; and fix the year *p. S.* v. 53

Predestin'd.
For life *p.* to the Gnomes' embrace *R.L.* i. 80

Pre-eminence.
Painful *p.* ! yourself to view *E.M.* iv. 267

Pre-existent.
What mortal knows his *p.* state *D.* iii. 48

Prefaces.
How Prologues into *P.* decay *D.* i. 277

Prefer.
In doubt his Mind or Body to *p. E.M.* ii. 9
Of carps and mullets why *p.* the great *S.* ii. 21
P. a new japanner to their shoes *S.* iii. 156

Preferr'd.
Lo ! Ambrose Philips is *p.* for Wit *D.* iii. 326
Yes, Nature's road must ever be *p. E.M.* ii. 161

Prefers.
Save just at dinner—then *p.*, no doubt *M.E.* i. 79
Each am'rous nymph *p.* her gifts in vain *Su.* 53

Pregnant.
For new abortions, all ye *p.* fair *D.* iii. 314
P. with thousands flits the Scrap unseen *M.E.* iii. 47

Prejudice.
Dear Sir, forgive the *P.* of Youth *E.S.* i. 63

Prelate.
The plunging *P.*, and his pond'rous Grace *D.* ii. 323
And goad the *P.* slumb'ring in his Stall *E.S.* ii. 219
But when no *P.*'s *Lawn with hair-shirt lin'd S.* iii. 165

'Prentice.
Much less the '*P.* who to-morrow may *E.S.* ii. 37

'Prenticeship.
He serv'd a '*P.* who sets up shop *S.* v. 181

Prepare.
Another Æschylus appears ! *p. D.* iii. 313
I come, I come ! *p.* your roseate bow'rs *E.A.* 317
P. the way ! a God, a God appears *M.* 30
Come then, the colours and the ground *p. M.E.* ii. 17
And prudent Nymphs against that change *p. Mi.* ix. 18
Straight the three bands *p.* in arms to join *R.L.* iii. 29
The bodkin, comb, and essence to *p. R.L.* iv. 98
Oft, as the mounting larks their notes *p. W.F.* 133

Prepar'd.
Say for such worth are other worlds *p. M.E.* iii. 335
Resign'd to live, *p.* to die *Mi.* xii. 1

Prepares.
Already Opera *p.* the way *D.* iii. 299
For her the Spouse *p.* the bridal ring *E.A.* 219
P. a dreadful jest for all mankind *S.* ii. 124

Prepossess'd.
Not dully *p.*, nor blindly right *E.C.* 634

Prerogative.
Guard my *P.*, assert my Throne *D.* iv. 583
And Man's *p.* to rule, but spare *E.M.* iii. 160
Now for *P.*, and now for Laws *S.* v. 159

Presbyterian.
A Quaker ? sly : A *P.* ! sour *M.E.* i. 156

Prescient.
P., the tides or tempests to withstand *E.M.* iii. 101

Prescribe.
P., apply, and call their masters fools *E.C.* 111

Prescrib'd.
P. her heights, and prun'd her tender wing *E.C.* 736
All but the page *p.*, their present state *E.M.* i. 78

Prescribes.
P., attends, the med'cine makes and gives *M.E.* iii. 270

Presence.
Her ample *p.* fills up all the place *D.* i. 261
Her gloomy *p.* saddens all the scene *E.A.* 167
The *P.* seems, with things so richly odd *S.* viii. 238

Present.

Wise is her *p.*; she connects in this *E.M.* iv. 349
When rival beauties for the *P.* strove *Mi.* ix. 38
Judge of all p., *past, or future art* D. ii. 376
Enlights the *p.*, and shall warm the last *E.C.* 403
All but the page prescrib'd, their *p.* state *E.M.* i. 78
That sees immediate good by *p.* sense *E.M.* ii. 73
P. to grasp, and future still to find *E.M.* ii. 125
Let this great truth be *p.* night and day (*rep.*) *E.M.* iii. 5
Nor *p.* good or ill, the joy or curse *E.M.* iv. 71
Which not at *p.* having time to do. *E.S.* ii. 156
Publish the *p.* age; but where my text *S.* i. 59
Matures my *p.*, and shall bound my last *S.* iii. 2
To thee, the World its *p.* homage pays *S.* v. 23
Invite my lays. Be *p.*, sylvan maids *W.F.* 3
Each eager to p. *their first Address* D. iv. 136
P. the Cross before my lifted eye *E.A.* 327
P. the spear, and arm him for the fight *R.L.* iii. 130

Presented.

Sell their *p.* partridges, and fruits *S.* ii. 51

Presently.

Then *p.* he falls to tease *I.H.* ii. 79 s

Presents.

Prudence, whose glass *p.* th' approaching jail *D.* i. 51
Who visits with a Gun, *p.* you birds *E.* v. 25
P. her harp still to his fingers *Mi.* xii. 8
A Frenchman comes, *p.* you with his Boy *S.* vi. 3

Preserve.

So may the fates *p.* the ears you lend *D.* iii. 214
Parts it may ravage, but *p.* the whole *E.M.* ii. 106
Mark what unvary'd laws *p.* each state *E.M.* iii. 189
P., Almighty Providence *I.H.* ii. 23 s
May Heav'n, to bless those days, *p.* my friend (*rep.*) *P.S.* 415
Unless good sense *p.* what beauty gains *R.L.* v. 16
To keep these limbs, and to *p.* these eyes *S.* iii. 52

Preserv'd.

Who lost my heart while I *p.* my sheep *A.* 80
Still spread the int'rest, and *p.* the kind *E.M.* iii. 146
And teach the Being you *p.*, to bear *P.S.* 134
P. in *Milton's* or in *Shakespear's* name *P.S.* 168
P. the freedom, and forbore the vice *S.* v. 260

Preserves.

Some bury'd marble half *p.* a name *M.E.* v. 16

Preserv'st.

As thou *p.* the dulness of the past *D.* iii. 193
Thou but *p.* a Face, and I a Name *E.* iii. 78

Preside.

Who conquer'd Nature, should *p.* o'er Wit *E.C.* 652
Others on earth o'er human race *p. R.L.* ii. 87

Presides.

Works without show, and without pomp *p. E.C.* 75

Press.

Of Curl's chaste *p.*, and Lintot's rubric post *D.* i. 40
And the *p.* groan'd with licens'd blasphemies *E.C.* 553
All, all but Truth, drops dead-born from the *P. E.S.* ii. 226
While thro' the *p.* enrag'd Thalestris flies *R.L.* v. 57
Now crowds on crowds around the Goddess p. D. iv. 133
Were we to *p.*, inferior might on ours *E.M.* i. 242
P. to one centre still, the gen'ral Good *E.M.* iii. 14
But rudely *p.* before a Duke *I.H.* ii. 59 s

Press'd, Prest.

How oft, when *p.* to marriage, have I said *E.A.* 73
Pant on thy lip, and to thy heart be *p. E.A.* 123
Shov'd from the wall perhaps, or rudely *p. E.* 234
When *p.* by want and weakness DENNIS lies *Mi.* ii. 10
Or when the soul is *p.* with cares *O.* i. 26
And the *p.* watch return'd a silver sound *R.L.* i. 18
Cares not for service, or but serves when *p—t E.M.* iii. 86
Belinda still her downy pillow *p. R.L.* i. 19

Presume.

The rest on Out-side merit but *p. D.* i. 135
Know thou thyself, *p.* not God to scan *E.M.* ii. 1
Let me for once *p.* t' instruct the times *S.* v. 340
P. thy bolts to throw *U.P.* 26

Presum'd.

Of those who less *p.*, and better knew *E.C.* 720

Presumption.

To kings *p.*, and to crowds belief *E.M.* ii. 244

Presumptuous.

I know there are to whose *p.* thoughts *E.C.* 169
P. Man! the reason wouldst thou find *E.M.* i. 35

Pretence.

Or, if to Wit a coxcomb make *p. D.* i. 177
Some by old words to fame have made *p. E.C.* 324
Be niggards of advice on no *p. E.C.* 578
Mine as a Foe profess'd to false *P. E.S.* ii. 201
Here rests a Woman, good without *p. Ep.* vi. 1
Pains, reading, study, are their just *p. P.S.* 159

Pretend.

Who most to shun or hate Mankind *p. E.M.* iv. 43
Go! and *p.* your family is young *E.M.* iv. 213
Shall then this verse to future age *p. E.M.* iv. 339
Are they not rich? What more can they *p. E.S.* ii. 114
Or each new-pension'd Sycophant *p. E.S.* ii. 142
It grows their Age's prudence to *p. M.E.* ii. 236

Pretender.

Stood up to dash each vain *P.*'s hope *Mi.* ii. 17

Pretending.

And wisely curb'd proud man's *p.* wit *E.C.* 53

Pretension.

Good without noise, without *p.* great *Ep.* vii. 4

Pretty.

She tripp'd and laugh'd, too *p.* much to stand *D.* iv. 50
You might have held the *p.* head aside *E.J.S.* 3
What? rob your Boys? those *p.* rogues *I.H.* i. 27
P. I in amber to observe the forms *P.S.* 169
Beauties in vain their *p.* eyes may roll *R.L.* v. 33
Had once a *p.* gift of Tongues enough *S.* viii. 77

Prevail.

Thus song could *p. O.* i. 87
And trust me, dear! good humour can *p. R.L.* v. 31

Prevail'd.

While mighty WILLIAM's thund'ring arm *p. S.* vi. 63

Prevails.

I weigh what author's heaviness *p. D.* ii. 368
Thus in the soul while memory *p. E.C.* 56

Prevent.

P. the greedy, and out-bid the bold *S.* iv. 72

Preventing.

Or blest with little, whose *p.* care *S.* ii. 127

Previous.

And something *p.* ev'n to Taste—'tis Sense *M.E.* iv. 42

Prey.

The shepherds cry, "Thy flocks are left a *p.*" *A.* 78
Th' embroider'd suit at least he deem'd his *p. D.* ii. 117
Great lord of all things, yet a *p.* to all *E.M.* ii. 16
Slight lines of hair surprise the finny *p. R.L.* ii. 26
Go drive the Deer, and drag the finny *p. S.* iv. 113
To savage beasts, and savage laws a *p. W.F.* 45
A mighty hunter, and his *p.* was man *W.F.* 62
At once the chaser, and at once the *p. W.F.* 81
Couch'd close he lies, and meditates the *p. W.F.* 102
Some on the leaves of ancient authors p. E.C. 112
On me love's fiercer flames for ever *p. Su.* 91

Priam.

Tears gush'd again, as from pale *P.*'s eyes *D.* i. 255

Price.

That, Vice may merit, 'tis the *p.* of toil *E.M.* iv. 151
The *p.* of prologues and of plays *Mi.* xii. 16
Lintot, dull rogue! will think your *p.* too much *P.S.* 63
He names the *p.* for ev'ry office paid *S.* viii. 162

Prick.

P. all their ears up, and forget to graze *D.* ii. 262
Keep close to Ears, and those let asses *p. P.S.* 77

Pride.

One god-like Monarch all that *p.* confounds *D.* iii. 75
Foreign her air, her rube's discordant *p. D.* iv. 47
Who rhym'd for hire, and patroniz'd for *p. D.* iv. 102
His Hat, which never vail'd to human *p. D.* iv. 205
Mother of Arrogance, and Source of *P. D.* iv. 470
Above all Pain, all Passion, and all *P. E.* i. 24
A Soul as full of Worth, as void of *P. E.* ii. 1
Your pleasure is a vice, but not your *p. E.* iv. 34
P., Pomp, and State but reach her outward part *E.* iv. 55
And dead, as living, 'tis our Author's *p. E.* iv. 79
Is *P.*, the never-failing voice of fools *E.C.* 204
She gives in large recruits of needful *p. E.C.* 206
P., where wit fails, steps in to our defence *E.C.* 209
That always shows about *p.*, or little sense *p. Ci.* 87
P., Malice, Folly, against Dryden rose *E.C.* 458
Gen'rous converse; a soul exempt from *p. E.C.* 541
To low ambition, and the *p.* of Kings *E.M.* i. 2
Then shall Man's *p.* and dulcess comprehend *M.E.* i. 65
In *P.*, in reas'ning *P.* our error lies *E.M.* i. 123
P. still is aiming at the blest abodes *E.M.* i. 125
Earth for whose use? *P.* answers "'Tis for mine *E.M.* i. 132
From *p.*, from *p.*, our very reas'ning springs *E.M.* i. 161
The bliss of Man (could *P.* that blessing find) *E.M.* i. 189
Vile worm!—Oh Madness! *P.!* Impiety *E.M.* i. 258
And spite of *P.*, in erring Reason's spite *E.M.* i. 293
With too much weakness for the Stoic's *p. E.M.* ii. 6
First strip off all her equipage of *P. E.M.* ii. 44
The monk's humility, the hero's *p. E.M.* ii. 173
But what will grow on *P.*, or grow on Shame (*rep.*) *E.M.* ii. 194
Shame to the virgin, to the matron *p. E.M.* ii. 242
And *P.* bestow'd on all, a common friend *E.M.* ii. 272
And each vacuity of sense by *P. E.M.* ii. 286
The trim of *p.*, the impudence of wealth *E.M.* iii. 4
Shares with his lord the pleasure and the *p. E.M.* iii. 36
For more his pleasure, yet for more his *p. E.M.* iii. 60
P. then was not; nor Arts, that *P.* to aid *E.M.* iii. 151
And hell was built on spite, and heav'n on *p. E.M.* iii. 262
No Bandit fierce, no Tyrant mad with *p. E.M.* iv. 41
Shew'd erring *P.*, WHATEVER IS, IS RIGHT *E.M.* iv. 394
As, tho' the *P.* of Middleton and Bland *E.S.* i. 75
There, where no Passion, *P.*, or Shame transport *E.S.* i. 97
As *P.* in Slaves, and Avarice in Kings *E.S.* i. 110
DORSET, the Grace of Courts, the Muses' *P. Ep.* i. 1
The scourge of *P.*, tho' sanctify'd or great *Ep.* i. 3
Passion and *P.* were to her soul unknown *Ep.* vi. 5
Could save a Parent's justest *P.* from fate *Ep.* xiv. 3
Nor puff'd by *P.*, nor sunk by Spleen *I.H.* ii. 28 *s*
Vain was the Chief's, the Sage's *p. I.H.* iv. 13
He thanks you not, his *p.* is in Piquet *M.E.* i. 85
P. guides his steps, and bids him shun the great *M.E.* i. 114
His *p.* in Reas'ning, not in Acting lies *M.E.* i. 118
Arcadia's Countess, here, in ermin'd *p. M.E.* ii. 7
There none distinguish 'twixt your Shame or *P. M.E.* ii. 204
Courage with Softness, Modesty with *P. M.E.* ii. 278
See! sportive fate, to punish awkward *p. M.E.* iv. 19
That summons you to all the *P.* of Pray'r *M.E.* iv. 142
Sick of his civil *P.*, from Morn to Eve *M.E.* iv. 166
Deep Harvests bury all his *p.* has plann'd *M.E.* iv. 175
Whose rising Forests, not for *p.* or show *M.E.* iv. 187
Fanes, which admiring Gods with *p.* survey *M.E.* v. 9
Not grave thro' *P.*, or gay thro' Folly *Mi.* viii. 9
Unpolish'd Gems no ray on *P.* bestow *Mi.* x. 5
That Casting-weight *p.* adds to emptiness *P.S.* 177
Or simple *p.* for flatt'ry makes demands *P.S.* 253
That fop, whose *p.* affects a patron's name *P.S.* 291
Wit that can creep, and *p.* that licks the dust *P.S.* 333
Foe to his *p.*, but friend to his distress *P.S.* 371
Born to no *P.*, inheriting no Strife *P.S.* 392
Some secret truths, from learned *p.* conceal'd *R.L.* i. 37
For when the Fair in all their *p.* expire *R.L.* i. 57
These swell their prospects and exalt their *p. R.L.* i. 81
Trembling begins the sacred rites of *P. R.L.* i. 128
Yet graceful ease, and sweetness void of *P. R.L.* ii. 15
Where Thames with *p.* surveys his rising tow'rs *R.L.* ii. 2
Spite of his haughty mien and barb'rous *p. R.L.* iii. 70
Steel could the works of mortal *p.* confound *R.L.* iii. 175
Faints into airs, and languishes with *p. R.L.* iv. 34
Not when a gilt Buffet's reflected *p. S.* ii. 5
Will cure the arrant'st Puppy of his *P. S.* iii. 60
Where *Murray* (long enough his Country's *p.*) *S.* iv. 52
With foolish *p.* my heart was never fir'd *S.* viii. 9
You, that too wise for *p.*, too good for pow'r *Sp.* 7
Save me alike from foolish *P. U.P.* 33
With joyful *p.* survey'st our lofty woods *W.F.* 220
Gigantic *P.*, pale Terror, gloomy Care *W.F.* 415

Priest.

And to mere mortals seem'd a *P.* in drink *D.* ii. 426
A decent *P.*, where monkeys were the gods *D.* iii. 208
On some, a *P.* succinct in amice white *D.* iv. 549
Unbrib'd, unbloody, stood the blameless *p. E.M.* iii. 158
King, *p.*, and parent of his growing state *E.M.* iii. 216
Point she to *P.* or Elder, Whig or Tory *E.S.* ii. 96
The *P.* whose Flattery be-dropt the Crown *E.S.* ii. 164
Of all the Nurse and all the *P.* have taught *R.L.* i. 30
Tindal and Toland prompt at *p——s to jeer D.* iv. 399
That which my *P.*, and mine alone, maintain *D.* iv. 185
P., tapers, temples, swim before my sight *E.A.* 274
Then unbelieving *p.* reform'd the nation *E.C.* 546
As Eastern *p.* in giddy circles run *E.M.* ii. 27
Ye Statesmen, *P.*, of one Religion all *E.S.* ii. 16
P., Princes, Women, no dissemblers here *M.E.* i. 177
The frugal Crone, whom praying *p.* attend *M.E.* i. 242
Then thus: "*from P.-*craft happily set free *D.* iv. 499

Priestess.

Th' inferior *P.*, at her altar's side *R.L.* i. 127

Priesthood.

The glory of the *P.*, and the shame *E.C.* 694
Cry: "By your *P.* tell me what you are" *S.* viii. 37

Priestless.

Her *P.* Muse forbids the Good to die *E.S.* ii. 234

Priestly.

But fate with butchers plac'd thy *p.* stall *D.* iii. 209

Primæval.

Of Night *p.* and of Chaos old *D.* iv. 630

Primo.

There liv'd *in p. Georgii* (they record) *S.* vi. 184
Edwardi sexi. or *prim. et quint. Eliz. S.* i. 148

Prince.

'Twixt *P.* and People close the Curtain draw *D.* i. 313
Honour a Syrian *P.* above his own *D.* iv. 368
A *P.* the Father of a People made *E.M.* iii. 214
Think we, like some weak *P.*, th' Eternal Cause *E.M.* iv. 121
His *P.*, that writes in Verse, and has his ear *E.S.* i. 46
Consid'ring when a *gracious P.* was next *E.S.* i. 108
As S—k, if he lives, will love the *P. E.S.* ii. 67
Just to his *P.*, and to his Country true *Ep.* ii. 6
A perjur'd *P.* a leaden Saint revere *M.E.* i. 89
Rous'd by the *P.* of Air, the whirlwinds sweep *M.E.* iii. 353
The rebel Knave, who dares his *p.* engage *R.L.* iii. 59
Believe me, many a German *P.* is worse *S.* iv. 83
Indebted to no *P.* or Peer alive *S.* vi. 69
He gains his P.'s ear, or lose his own P.S. 367
When half his nose is in his *P.* ear *S.* viii. 179
Lift up your Gates, ye P—s, see him come D. i. 301
Speak'st thou of Syrian *P.*? Traitor base *D.* iv. 375
Contending *P.* mount them in their Coach *D.* iv. 564
And nobly conscious, *P.* are but things *D.* iv. 601
Priests, *P.*, Women, no dissemblers here *M.E.* i. 177
Now calls in *P.*, and now turns away *S.* v. 156
To gaze on *P.*, and to talk of Kings *S.* viii. 101

Principal.

So Man, who here seems *p.* alone *E.M.* i. 57

Principle.

As much Estate, and *P.*, and Wit *D.* iv. 325
Extracts his brain; and *P.* is fled *D.* iv. 522
Most strength the moving *p.* requires *E.M.* ii. 67
Receives the lurking *p.* of death *E.M.* ii. 134
Grafts on this Passion our best *p. E.M.* ii. 176
Who never chang'd his *P.*, or Wig *E.S.* i. 40
Honour unchang'd, a *P.* profest *Ep.* ii. 3
His *P.* of action once explore (*rep.*) *M.E.* ii. 27
Two P—s in human nature reign E.M. ii. 53
They talk of *p.*, but notions prize *E.C.* 265
Tenets with Books, and *P.* with Times *M.E.* i. 173
Fix'd *P.*, with Fancy ever new *M.E.* ii. 279

Print.
In Dryden's Virgil you may see the *p. E.* vi. 28
Not twice a twelve-month you appear in *p. E.S.* i. 1
Or do the P—s and Papers lie *I.H.* ii. 115 *s*
And for that very cause I p. to-day *E.S.* ii. 3
Fir'd that the House reject him, "'Sdeath I'll *p.* it *P.S.* 61
If want provok'd, or madness made them *p. P.S.* 155
Like Lee and Budgel, I will rhyme and *p. S.* i. 100

Printed.
These Aldus *p.*, those Du Sueil has bound *M.E.* iv. 136

Printer.
But shall a *P.*, weary of his life *E.S.* i. 125

Printing.
To court applause by *p.* what I write *S.* vi. 150

Prints.
Rhymes ere he wakes, and *p.* before *Term* ends *P.S.* 43
This *p.* my *Letters*, that expects a bribe *P.S.* 113

Prior—*See also* Dan.
She deck'd like Congreve, Addison, and *P. D.* ii. 124.
Cook shall be *P.*, and Concanen, Swift *D.* ii. 138

Priori.
We nobly take the high *P.* Road *D.* iv. 471

Prisca.
Act sins which *P.'s* Confessor scarce hears *S.* vii. 40

Priscian.
Break *P.'s* head and Pegasus's neck *D.* iii. 162

Prismatic.
False Eloquence, like the *p.* glass *E.C.* 311

Pris'ners.
Grave, as when *p.* shake the head, and swear *S.* vii. 69
Dull sullen *p.* in the body's cage *U.L.* 18

Prithee.
Plague on't! 'tis past a jest—nay *p.*, pox *R.L.* iv. 129

Private.
Nor *public* Flame, nor *p.*, dares to shine *D.* iv. 651
And public faction doubles *p.* hate *E.C.* 457
And found the *p.* in the public good *E.M.* iii. 282
Why bounded Pow'r? why *p.* ? why no king *E.M.* iv. 160
Slave to no sect, who takes no *p.* road *E.M.* iv. 331
Has never made a Friend in *p.* life *E.S.* ii. 134
A Woman's seen in *P.* life alone *M.E.* ii. 200
Who broke no promise, serv'd no *p.* end *M.E.* v. 69
Triumphant Malice rag'd thro' *p.* life *S.* v. 246

Privilege.
Full and eternal *p.* of tongue *D.* ii. 378
This Nod confirms each *P.* your own *D.* iv. 584

Prize.
And bade the nimblest racer seize the *p. D.* ii. 36
This *p.* is mine ; who tempt it are my foes *D.* ii. 54
Still happy Impudence obtains the *p. D.* ii. 186
Secure, thro' her, the noble *p.* to carry *D.* ii. 219
If perseverance gain the Diver's *p. D.* iv. 434
And to excuse it, need but shew the *p. D.* iv. 434
Held from afar, aloft, th' immortal *p. R.L.* C. 96
Is Virtue's *p.* : a better would you fix *E.M.* iv. 169
A Fop their Passion, but their *P.* a Sot *M.E.* ii. 247
The Devil and the King divide the *P. M.E.* iii. 401
This *Snuff-Box* will I stake; the *P.* is mine *Mi.* ix. 44
He saw, he wish'd, and to the *p.* aspir'd *R.L.* ii. 30
Soon to obtain, and long possess the *p. R.L.* ii. 44
(The victor cry'd) the glorious *p.* is mine *R.L.* iii. 162
And shall this *p.*, th' inestimable *p. R.L.* iv. 113
And chiefs contend till all the *p.* is lost *R.L.* v. 108
With such a *p.* no mortal must be blest *R.L.* v. 111
So weak a vessel, and so rich a *p. S.* viii. 229
O Love! for Sylvia let me gain the *p. Sp.* 49
Tell me but this, and I'll disclaim the *p. Sp.* 87
And then a nobler *p.* I will resign *Sp.* 91
Sudden they seize th' amaz'd, defenceless *p. W.F.* 109
Ah no! instruct me other joys to p. E.C. 125
They talk of principles, but notions *p. E.C.* 265
The Ancients only, or the Moderns *p. E.C.* 395
We *p.* the stronger effort of his pow'r *M.E.* i. 147

Priz'd.
If this is *p.* for sweetness, that for stink *S.* ii. 30

Probatum est.
Lettuce and cowslip-wine ; *P. e. S.* i. 18

Proceed.
P., great days! till Learning fly the shore *D.* iii. 333
P.,—a Minister, but still a Man *E.* ii. 15
A knotty point! to which we now *p. M.E.* iii. 337
You too *p.!* make falling Arts your care *M.E.* iv. 191
The Case is alter'd—you may then *p. S.* i. 154
But how severely with themselves *p. S.* vi. 157

Proceeds.
The Critic else *p.* without remorse *E.C.* 167

Proclaim.
Hear her black Trumpet thro' the Land *p. E.S.* i. 159
The rocks *p.* th' approaching Deity *M.* 3*e*

Proclaim'd.
Might be *p.* at Charing Cross *I.H.* ii. 100 *s*

Proclaims.
And now the Queen, to glad her sons, *p. D.* ii. 17
Here stopt the Goddess ; and in pomp *p. D.* ii. 365
Roast beef, tho' old, *p.* him stout *Mi.* xii. 13
Or well-mouth'd Booth with emphasis *p. S.* v. 123

Proculus.
To *P.* alone confess'd in view *R.L.* v. 126

Procure.
P. a Taste to double the surprise *S.* iv. 30
P. her Beauty, make that beauty chaste *S.* iv. 79

Prodigal.
To cram the Rich was *p.* expense *M.E.* iii. 185
Is it less strange, the *P.* should waste *M.E.* iv. 3

Prodigies.
Nature well known, no *p.* remain *M.E.* i. 208

Prodigious.
P. this! the Frail-one of our Play *E.J.S.* 1
"*P.* well;" his great Commander cry'd *S.* vi. 42
P.! how the things *protest, protest S.* viii. 255

Produce.
In God's, one single can its end *p. E.M.* i. 55
Extremes in Nature equal ends *p. E.M.* ii. 205
Extremes in Nature equal good *p. M.E.* iii. 161
Who would not scorn what housewife's cares *p. R.L.* v. 21

Produc'd.
P. his Play, and begg'd the Knight's advice *E.C.* 274
P. the point that left a sting behind *S.* v. 252

Produces.
Lo! one vast Egg *p.* human race *D.* iii. 248
Shakes all together, and *p.* you *M.E.* ii. 280

Productive.
P. as the Sun *O.* iii. 24

Products.
And heap'd with *p.* of Sabæan springs *M.* 94

Profane.
The jealous God, when we *p.* his fires *E.A.* 81

Profess.
Impale a Glow-worm, or Virtu *p. D.* iv. 569
Yet for small Turbots such esteem *p. S.* ii. 23

Profess'd, Profest.
Mine as a Foe *p.* to false Pretence *E.S.* ii. 201
Honour unchang'd, a Principle *p—t Ep.* ii. 3

Profit.
Say, in pursuit of *p.* or delight *E.M.* iv. 85
Deny'd all posts of *p.* or of trust *S.* vi. 61

Profound.
Sinking from thought to thought, a vast *p. D.* i. 118
Draw forth the monsters of th' abyss *p. E.M.* iii. 221
They treat themselves with most *p.* respect *S.* vi. 154

Profuse.
Some, to whom Heav'n in wit has been *p*. *E.C.* 80
Or pours *p*. on earth, one nature feeds *E.M.* iii. 117
You show us, Rome was glorious, not *p*. *M.E.* iv. 23

Profusion.
Nature to these, without *p*., kind *E.M.* i. 179
Nor could P. squander all in kind *M.E.* iii. 60
Yet no mean motive this *p*. draws *M.E.* iii. 205

Progeny.
My better and more Christian *p*. *D.* i. 228
See all her *p*., illustrious sight *D.* iii. 129
Or views his smiling *p*. *O.* ii. 32

Progress.
And pleas'd pursue its *p*. thro' the skies *R.L.* v. 132
Whose gentle *p*. makes a calf an ox *S.* vii. 48

Progressive.
Above, how high, *p*. life may go *E.M.* i. 235

Project.
P. long shadows o'er the crystal tide *W.F.* 376

Projected.
The Mole *p*. break the roaring Main *M.E.* iv. 200

Prologue.
My Friendship, and a *P*., and ten pound *P.S.* 48
How P—s into Prefaces decay *D.* i. 277
The price of *p*. and of plays *Mi.* xii. 16

Prolong.
Friend to my Life! (which did not you *p*. *P.S.* 27
And frequent cups *p*. the rich repast *R.L.* iii. 112

Prolong'd.
Her guardian SYLPH *p*. the balmy rest *R.L.* i. 20

Promiscuous.
Such vary'd light in one *p*. blaze *D.* iv. 412
A Wild, where weeds and flow'rs *p*. shoot *E.M.* i. 7
With throngs *p*. strow the level green *R.L.* iii. 80

Promise.
Who broke no *p*., serv'd no private end *M.E.* v. 69
The courtier's p—s, and sick man's pray'rs *R.L.* v. 119
Than when they p. to give scribbling o'er *E.C.* 595
And *p*. our best Friends to rhyme no more *S.* v. 178

Promis'd.
My son, the *p*. land expects thy reign *D.* i. 292
And *p*. Vengeance on a barb'rous age *D.* iv. 40
And mild as op'ning gleams of *p*. heav'n *E.A.* 256
The *p*. father of the future age *M.* 56
This Phœbus *p*. (I forget the year) *M.E.* ii. 283

Promote.
Live happy both, and long *p*. our arts *D.* iv. 438
Since rules were made but to *p*. their end *E.C.* 147

Promotes.
While thus each hand *p*. the pleasing pain *D.* ii. 211

Prompt.
P., or to guard or stab, to saint or damn *D.* ii. 357
Each *p*. to query, answer, and debate *D.* ii. 381
Tindal and Toland, *p*. at priests to jeer *D.* ii. 399
P. at the call, around the Goddess roll *D.* iv. 189
P. to impose, and fond to dogmatise *D.* iv. 464
And whisp'ring Angels *p*. her golden dreams *E.A.* 216

Prompter.
And as the *p*. breathes, the puppet squeaks *P.S.* 318

Prompts.
Each Art he *p*., each Charm he can create *D.* iii. 221
Active its task, it *p*., impels, inspires *E.M.* ii. 68
For some his Int'rest *p*. him to provide *E.M.* iii. 59
That something still which *p*. th' eternal sigh *E.M.* iv. 3
Yet think not Friendship only *p*. my lays *E.S.* ii. 94
When kind occasion *p*. their warm desires *R.L.* i. 75
So *p*., and saves a rogue who cannot read *S.* vii. 16

Prone.
P. for his fav'rites to reverse his laws *E.M.* iv. 122
As *p*. to ill, as negligent of good *S.* viii. 20

Proof.
Of solid *p*., impenetrably dull *D.* iii. 26
Sad *p*. how well a lover can obey *E.A.* 172

Prop.
P. thine, O Empress! like each neighbour Throne *D.* iv. 333

Propagate.
To draw nutrition, *p*., and rot *E.M.* ii. 64

Proper.
Know well each ANCIENT's *p*. character *E.C.* 119
The *p*. organs, *p*. pow'rs assign'd *E.M.* i. 180
Our *p*. bliss depends on what we blame *E.M.* i. 282
The *p*. study of Mankind is Man *E.M.* ii. 2
And to their *p*. operation still *E.M.* ii. 57
Its *p*. bliss, and sets its *p*. bounds *E.M.* iii. 110
Down to the central earth his *p*. scene *R.L.* iv. 15
Its *p*. pow'r to hurt, each creature feels *S.* i. 85
Unless the Gods bestow'd a *p*. Muse *S.* v. 234

Property.
What's P.! dear Swift! you see it alter *S.* ii. 167
The Gaul subdu'd, or P. secur'd *S.* v. 10
A P., that's yours on which you live *S.* vi. 231
Their sep'rate cells and p—ies maintain *E.M.* iii. 188

Prophecy.
Extols old Bards, or Merlin's *P*. *S.* v. 132

Prophesy'd.
Not half so pleas'd when Goodman *p*. *D.* iii. 232

Prophet.
Hence from the straw where Bedlam's *P*. nods *D.* iii. 7
His conqu'ring tribes th' Arabian *p*. draws *D.* iii. 97
The moon-struck *P*. felt the madding hour *D.* iv. 12

Propitious.
Benlowes, *p*. still to blockheads, bows *D.* iii. 21
Fair op'ning to some Court's *p*. shine *E.M.* iv. 9
P. heav'n, and ev'ry pow'r ador'd *R.L.* ii. 36
And hail with music its *p*. ray *R.L.* v. 134

Proportion.
Such with their shelves as due *p*. hold *D.* i. 137
All in exact *p*. to the state *E.M.* i. 183
And, in *p*. as it blesses, blest *E.M.* iii. 300
As Poison heals, in just *p*. us'd *M.E.* iii. 234

Proportion'd.
Which, but *p*. to their light, or place *E.C.* 173
To find the means *p*. to their end *E.M.* iii. 82
Of all beau-kind the best *p*. fools *S.* viii. 241

Propose.
Attend the trial we *p*. to make *D.* ii. 371

Propos'd.
Th' intent *p*., that License is a rule *E.C.* 149
And things unknown *p*. as things forgot *E.C.* 575

Propp'd, Propt.
P. on their bodkin spears, the Sprites survey *R.L.* v. 55
On two unequal crutches *p*—t he came *D.* iv. 111
P. on some tomb, a neighbour of the dead *E.A.* 304

Prose.
Else all my P. and Verse were much the same (rep.) *D.* i. 189
P. swell'd to verse, verse loit'ring into *p*. *D.* i. 274
As verse, or *p*., infuse the drowsy God *D.* ii. 396
Critics like me shall make it P. again *D.* iv. 214
Now one in verse makes many more in *p*. *E.C.* 8
Something in Verse as true as P. *I.H.* ii. 265
One dedicates in high heroic *p*. *P.S.* 109
It is not Poetry, but *p*. run mad *P.S.* 188
And thought a Lie in verse or *p*. the same *P.S.* 339
Now Serpent-like, in *p*. he sweeps the ground *S.* v. 100
Who says in verse what others say in *p*. *S.* v. 202
Well, on the whole, plain P. must be my fate *S.* vi. 198
Verse-man or P.—man, term me which you will *S.* i. 64

Prosecute.
Faith, in such case, if you should *p*. *S.* vi. 23

Proserpine.
And link the Mourning Bride to *P*. *D.* ii. 310
Stern *P*. relented *O.* i. 85

Prospect.

I shrink, start up, the same sad *p*. find *E.A.* 247
Th' increasing *p*. tires our wand'ring eyes *E.C.* 231
Reason's at distance, and in *p*. lie *E.M.* ii. 72
And when in act they cease, in *p*. rise *E.M.* ii. 124
One *p*. lost, another still we gain *E.M.* ii. 289
At once his own bright *p*. to be blest *E.M.* iv. 351
The *p*. clears, and Wharton stands confest *M.E.* i. 179
Here Ceres' gifts in waving *p*. stand *W.F.* 39
In p—s thus, some objects please our Eyes E.C. 156
These swell their *p*. and exalt their pride *R.L.* i. 81

Prosperity.

Perhaps P. becalm'd his breast *M.E.* i. 111
That spreads and swells in puff'd *p*. *S.* ii. 126

Prosp'rous.

Count all th' advantage *p*. Vice attains *E.M.* iv. 89

Prostitute.

No hireling she, no *p*. to praise *E.* i. 36

Prostrate.

Cast on the *p*. Nine a scornful look *D.* iv. 51
Now *p*.! dead! behold that Caroline *D.* iv. 413
While *p*. here in humble grief I lie *E.A.* 277
See god-like TURENNE *p*. on the dust *E.M.* iv. 100
See thy bright altars throng'd with *p*. kings *M.* 93
And scarce are seen the *p*. Nile or Rhine *M.E.* v. 28
Then *p*. falls, and begs with ardent eyes *R.L.* ii. 43
And falls like thunder on the *p*. Ace *R.L.* iii. 98

Protection.

Of these am I, who thy *p*. claim *R.L.* i. 105

Protects.

By day o'ersees them, and by night *p*. *M.* 52
Whose care, like hers, *p*. the sylvan reign *W.F.* 163

Protest.

"'Tis now no secret"—"I *p*. *I.H.* ii. 118 *s*
Instructed thus you bow, embrace, *p*. *S.* iv. 107
Prodigious! how the things *p*., *p. S.* viii. 255

Protestant.

Papist or *P.*, or both between *S.* i. 65

Proteus.

Hence Bards like *P.* long in vain tied down *D.* i. 37
So *P.* hunted in a nobler shape *D.* ii. 109
Did ever *P.*, Merlin, any witch *S.* iii. 152

Proud.

Now Night descending, the *p*. scene was o'er *D.* i. 89
Great Cibber sate: The *p*. Parnassian sneer *D.* ii. 5
Lo! Rome herself, *p*. mistress now no more *D.* iii. 101
While *p*. Philosophy repines to show *D.* iii. 197
And *p*. his Mistress' orders to perform *D.* iv. 263
My Sons! be *p*., be selfish, and be dull *D.* iv. 582
P. to my list to add one Monarch more *D.* iv. 600
And wisely curb'd *p*. man's pretending wit *E.C.* 53
That in *p*. dulness joins with Quality *E.C.* 415
Still pleas'd to teach, and yet not *p*. to know *E.C.* 632
Still fond and *p*. of savage liberty *E.C.* 650
When the *p*. steed shall know why Man restrains *E.M.* i. 61
His soul, *p*. Science never taught to stray *E.M.* i. 101
P. of an easy conquest all along *E.M.* ii. 157
That *p*. exception to all Nature's laws *E.M.* iii. 243
She taught the weak to bend, the *p*. to pray *E.M.* iii. 251
From dirt and sea-weed as *p*. Venice rose *E.M.* iv. 292
Down, down, *p*. Satire! tho' a Realm be spoil'd *E.S.* ii. 38
And if yet higher the *p*. list should end *E.S.* ii. 92
You're strangely *p*. So *p*. I am no Slave *E.S.* ii. 205
Yes, I am *p*.; I must be *p*. to see *E.S.* ii. 208
Whom Heav'n kept sacred from the *P.* and Great *Ep. x.* 4
I thought the Dean had been too *p*. *I.H.* ii. 53 *s*
P. as a Peeress, prouder as a Punk *M.E.* ii. 70
Or in *p*. falls magnificently lost *M.E.* iii. 256
Blush, Grandeur, blush! *p*. Courts withdraw your blaze *M.E.* iii. 281
Gallant and gay, in Cliveden's *p*. alcove *M.E.* iii. 307
P. to catch cold at a Venetian door *M.E.* iv. 60
Without it, *p*. Versailles! thy glory falls *M.E.* iv. 71
So *p*., so grand; of that stupendous air *M.E.* iv. 100
P. to accomplish what such hands design'd *M.E.* iv. 196

Now scantier limits the *p*. Arch confine *M.E.* v. 27
Ev'n when *p*. Cæsar midst triumphal cars *P.C.* 27
P. of a vast extent of flimsy lines *P.S.* 94
P. as Apollo on his forked hill *P.S.* 231
Not *p*., nor servile;—be one Poet's praise *P.S.* 336
The dull, the *p*., the wicked, and the mad *P.S.* 347
Who cause the *p*., their visits to delay *R.L.* iv. 63
He spoke, and speaking, in *p*. triumph spread *R.L.* iv. 139
Dash the *p*. Gamester in his gilded Car *S.* i. 107
And Helmsley, once *p*. Buckingham's delight *S.* ii. 177
P. Fortune, and look shallow Greatness thro' *S.* iii. 108
Who *p*. of Pedigree, is poor of Purse *S.* iv. 84
Then Peers grew *p*. in Horsemanship t' excel *S.* v. 143
P. Vice to brand, and injur'd Worth adorn *S.* v. 227
Who, to disturb their betters mighty *p*. *S.* v. 307
More pert, more *p*., more positive, than he *S.* vii. 52
Paltry and *p*., as drabs in Drury-lane *S.* vii. 64
So was I punish'd, as if full as *p. S.* viii. 19
Thus unlamented pass the *p*. away *U.L.* 43
'Tis all thou art, and all the *p*. shall be *U.L.* 74
Not *p*. Olympus yields a nobler sight *W.F.* 33
P. Nimrod first the bloody chase began *W.F.* 61

Prouder.

Who *p*. march'd, with magistrates in state *D.* ii. 423
Proud as a Peeress, *p*. as a Punk *M.E.* ii. 70
Why art thou *p*. and more hand than they *Su.* 18

Prove.

Did the dead letter unsuccessful *p*. *D.* i. 193
Here *p*. who best can dash thro' thick and thin *D.* ii. 276
To *p*. me, Goddess! clear of all design *D.* iv. 391
Not Cæsar's empress would I deign to *p*. *E.A.* 87
O Death all-eloquent! you only *p*. *E.A.* 335
But Dulness with Obscenity must *p*. *E.C.* 537
Nor be so civil as to *p*. unjust *E.C.* 581
But, sage historians! 'tis your task to *p*. *M.E.* i. 133
Yet his known Falsehoods could no Warning *p*. *Mi.* ix. 73
Men *p*. with child, as pow'rful fancy works *R.L.* iv. 53
Will *p*. at least the medium must be clear *S.* i. 56
Or, in a mortgage, *p*. a lawyer's share *S.* ii. 169
To *p*., that Luxury could never hold *S.* v. 167
Till I cry'd out: "You *p*. yourself so able *S.* viii. 82

Prov'd.

Turn'd Critics next, and *p*. plain fools at last *E.C.* 37
Then Criticism the Muse's handmaid *p*. *E.C.* 102
To her, Calista *p*. her conduct nice *M.E.* ii. 31
P., by the ends of being, to have been *E.M.* iii. 290
Has ev'n been *p*. to grant a Lover's pray'r *M.E.* ii. 55
Could you complain, my Friend, he *p*. so bad *S.* vi. 22

Proves.

But the last Tyrant ever *p*. the worst *E.* iv. 40
The current folly *p*. the ready wit *E.C.* 449
But like a shadow, *p*. the substance true *E.C.* 467
P. the just victim of his royal rage *R.L.* iii. 60
And last (which *p*. him wiser still than all) *S.* viii. 150

Provide.

And Reason bids us for our own *p*. *E.M.* ii. 96
For some his Int'rest prompts him to *p*. *E.M.* iii. 59

Providence.

Weigh thy Opinion against *P. E.M.* i. 114
Who finds not *P.* all good and wise *E.M.* i. 205
On him, their second *P.*, they hung *E.M.* iii. 217
Preserve, Almighty *P. I.H.* ii. 23 *s*
It was by *P.* they think *I.H.* ii. 216
And who would take the Poor from *P. M.E.* iii. 186
And God's good *P.*, a lucky Hit *M.E.* iii. 378
Admits, and leaves them, P.'s care *M.E.* iii. 106

Provides.

Art from that fund each just supply *p*. *E.C.* 74
In peace *p*. fit arms against a war *S.* ii. 128

Province.

Words are Man's *p*., Words we teach alone *D.* iv. 150
Each might his sev'ral *p*., well command *E.C.* 66
Our humbler *p*. is to tend the Fair *R.L.* i. 91
Or infamous for plunder'd p—s *E.M.* iv. 298
Or cross, to plunder *P.*, the Main *S.* iii. 127

Provocation.

Ask you what *P.* I have had *E.S.* ii. 197

Provoke.
Glory, and gain, th' illustrious tribe *p. D.* ii. 33
Restrain his fury, than *p.* his speed *E.C.* 85
To Virtue's work *p.* the tardy Hall *E.S.* ii. 218
Odious ! in woollen ! 'twould a Saint *p. Al. E.* i. 246
Or whiten'd wall *p.* the skew'r to write *S.* i. 98
Wild to get loose, his Patience I *p. S.* viii. 116

Provok'd.
If want *p.*, or madness made them print *P.S.* 155

Provokes.
Who breaks with her, *p.* Revenge from Hell *M.E.* ii. 129
But when our Country's cause *p.* to Arms *O.* i. 36

Provoking.
P. Dæmons all restraint remove *E.A.* 231
Discharge that rage on more *p.* crimes *E.C.* 528

Prude.
The graver *P.* sinks downward to a Gnome *R.L.* i. 63
Or dis-compos'd the head-dress of a *P. R.L.* iv. 74
Belinda frown'd, Thalestris call'd her *P. R.L.* v. 36

Prudence.
P., whose glass presents th' approaching jail *D.* i. 51
Ev'n av'rice, *p.*; sloth, philosophy *E.M.* ii. 188
It grows their Age's *p.* to pretend *M.E.* ii. 236
Think of that moment, you who *P.* boast (*rep.*) *Mi.* ix. 97
No Names I be calm !—learn *p.* from a friend *P.S.* 102

Prudent.
A *p.* chief not always must display *E.C.* 175
The *p.* Gen'ral turn'd it to a jest *E.S.* ii. 154
Sincere, tho' *p.*; constant, yet resign'd *Ep.* ii. 2
With ev'ry pleasing, ev'ry *p.* part *M.E.* ii. 159
Chloe is *p.*—Would you too be wise *M.E.* ii. 179
And *p.* Nymphs against that change prepare *Mi.* ix. 18
The *p.*, learn'd, and virtuous breast *O.* iii. 2
Friend Pope ! be *p.*, let your Muse take breath *S.* iii. 13

Prudery.
What is *P. !* 'Tis a Beldam *Mi.* vi. 1

Prudina.
P. likes a Man, and laughs at Show *Mi.* ix. 104

Prudishly.
Tho' Christ-church long kept *p.* away *D.* iv. 194

Prune.
P. the luxuriant, the uncouth refine *S.* vi. 174

Prun'd.
Prescrib'd her heights, and *p.* her tender wing *E.C.* 736

Prunella.
The rest is all but leather or *p. E.M.* iv. 204

Prunes.
Where Contemplation *p.* her ruffled wings *S.* viii. 186

Pry.
With eyes that *p.* not, tongue that ne'er repeats *S.* i. 135

Prying.
Walk round and round, now *p.* here, now there *D.* iv. 353

Pryn.
She saw old *P.* in restless Daniel shine *D.* i. 103

Psalms.
Hopkins and Sternhold glad the heart with *P. S.* v. 230

Public.
Or that where on her Curls the *P.* pours *D.* ii. 3
Nor *p.* Flame, nor *private*, dares to shine *D.* iv. 651
The rage of Pow'r, the blast of *p.* breath *E.* i. 25
And *p.* faction doubles private hate *E.C.* 457
And found the private in the *p.* good *E.M.* iii. 282
Or *P.* Spirit its great cure, a Crown *E.M.* v. 98
To rouse the Watchmen of the *p.* Weal *E.S.* ii. 217
When black Ambition stains a *p.* Cause *E.S.* ii. 228
But grant, in *P.* Men sometimes are shown *M.E.* ii. 199
Bred to disguise, in *P.* 'tis you hide *M.E.* ii. 203
Men, some to Quiet, some to *p.* Strife *M.E.* ii. 217
Worn out in *p.*, weary ev'ry eye *M.E.* ii. 229
Bid Harbours open, *p.* Ways extend *M.E.* iv. 197
Then first his Passion was in *p.* shown *Mi.* ix. 40

P. too long, ah let me hide my Age *S.* iii. 5
An hour, and not defraud the *P.* Weal *S.* v. 6
In ev'ry *P.* virtue we excel *S.* v. 45
Why then, I say, the *P.* is a fool *S.* v. 94
And speak in *p.* with some sort of grace *S.* v. 208
To midnight dances and the *p.* show *U.L.* 58

Publish.
But why then *p.! Granville* the polite *P.S.* 135
P, the present age ; but where my text *S.* i. 59

Pudding, Pudden.
Or solid *p.* against Empty praise *D.* i. 54
P., that might have pleas'd a Dean *I.H.* ii. 66
Yet on plain *P.* deign'd at home to eat *M.E.* ii. 82
An added *p.* solemniz'd the Lord's *M.E.* iii. 346
And lo ! two p—s smok'd upon the board *M.E.* iii. 360
And for his judgment, lo a *p—n Mi.* xii. 12

Puff.
For one *p.* more, and in that *p.* expires *M.E.* i. 245
P—s, *Powders, Patches, Bibles, Billet-doux R.L.* i. 138

Puff'd.
And the *p.* orator bursts out in tropes *D.* ii. 206
Nor *p.* by Pride, nor sunk by Spleen *I.H.* ii. 28 s
Sat full-blown Bufo, *p.* by ev'ry quill *P.S.* 232
That spreads and swells in *p.* prosperity *S.* ii. 126
For huffing, braggart, *p.* Nobility *S.* viii. 201

Pug.
And no man wonders he's not stung by *P. S.* i. 88

Puke.
I *p.*, I nauseate,—yet he thrusts in more *S.* viii. 153

Pull.
And, the next *P.*, my *Septleva* I lose *Mi.* ix. 52
Maul *the French Tyrant*, or p. *down the* Pope *Mi.* ii. 18
When, of a hundred thorns, you *p.* out one *S.* vi. 321

Pullet.
Buy ev'ry *p.* they afford to eat *S.* vi. 243

Pulpit.
The gracious Dew of *P.* Eloquence *E.S.* i. 69
Safe from the Bar, the *P.*, and the Throne *E.S.* ii. 210
P—s *their sacred satire learn'd to spare E.C.* 550

Pulse.
Nor pray'rs nor fasts its stubborn *p.* restrain *E.A.* 27
No *p.* that riots, and no blood that glows *E.A.* 252
Till ev'ry motion, *p.*, and breath be o'er *E.A.* 333
If Cotta liv'd on *p.*, it was no more *M.E.* iii. 83

Pult'ney.
How many Martials were in *P.* lost *D.* iv. 170
How can I *P.*, Chesterfield forget *E.S.* ii. 84

Pumps.
With Staff and *P.* the Marquis lead the Race *D.* iv. 586

Pumpings.
Our purgings, *p.*, blanketings, and blows *D.* ii. 154

Pun.
Alike to them, by Pathos or by *P. S.* v. 295
Light-arm'd *with Points, Antitheses, and* P—s *D.* i. 306
Their Quibbles routed, and defy'd their *P. Mi.* ii. 12
In *p.*, or politics, or tales, or lies *P.S.* 321

Punctual.
Religious, *p.*, frugal, and so forth *M.E.* iii. 343

Pungent.
The *p.* grains of titillating dust *R.L.* v. 84

Punish.
Oh *p.* him, or to th' Elysian shades *D.* iv. 417
And what rewards your Virtue, *p.* mine *E.M.* iv. 144
See ! sportive fate, to *p.* awkward pride *M.E.* iv. 19

Punish'd.
And *p.* him that put it in his way *S.* vi. 26
So was I *p.*, as if full as proud *S.* viii. 19

Punk.
All melted down, in Pension, or in *P. D.* iv. 510
Why risk the World's great empire for a *P. M.E.* i. 131

PUNT—PUT. 245

And now the *P.* applaud, and now the Friar *M.E.* i. 191
Proud as a Peeress, prouder as a *P. M.E.* ii. 70
To bawd for others, and go shares with *P. Mi.* iii. 26
Slave to a Wife, or Vassal to a *P. S.* iii. 62
Or for a Titled *P.*, or foreign Flame *S.* iv. 124

Punt.
When WINNALL *tally'd*, I would *p.* no more *Mi.* ix. 68

Punts.
Or when a Duke to *Jansen p.* at White's *S.* vii. 88

Puny.
A *p.* insect, shiv'ring at a breeze *M.E.* iv. 108

Pupil.
Whore, *P.*, and lac'd Governor from France *D.* iv. 272
Till Isis' Elders reel, their P—s' sport *D.* iii. 337

Puppet.
And as the prompter breathes, the *p.* squeaks *P.S.* 318
The gilded p—s dance and mount above *S.* vii. 18
Such painted *p.*, such a varnish'd race *S.* viii. 208

Puppy.
Became, when seiz'd, a *p.*, or an ape *D.* ii. 130
Nor, like a *p.*, daggled thro' the town *P.S.* 225
Will cure the arrant'st *P.* of his Pride *S.* iii. 60
Then number'd with the p—ies in the mud *D.* ii. 308
The names of these blind *p.* as of those *D.* ii. 310
Ward try'd on *P.*, and the Poor, his Drop *S.* v. 182

Purchase.
Vou *p.* Pain with all that Joy can give *M.E.* ii. 99
His wealth, to *p.* what he ne'er can taste *M.E.* iv. 4
You *p.* as you want, and bit by bit *S.* vi. 237
And when rank widows *p.* luscious nights *S.* vii. 87

Purchas'd.
A Park is *p.*, but the Fair he sees *M.E.* ii. 39

Pure.
A hecatomb of *p.* unsully'd lays *D.* j. 158
Now to *p.* Space lifts her ecstatic stare *D.* iv. 33
Boast the *p.* blood of an illustrious race *E.M.* iv. 207
As *p.* a mess almost as it came in *E.S.* ii. 176
She sins with Poets thro' Love of Wit *M.E.* ii. 76
While *p.* Description held the place of Sense *P.S.* 148
Or in *p.* equity (the case not clear) *S.* ii. 171
His French is *p.*; his Voice too—you shall hear *S.* vi. 7
Serenely *p.*, and yet divinely strong *S.* vi. 172

Purer.
Each *p.* frame inform'd with *p.* fire *E.* iii. 50
And there the streams to *p.* rills descend *E.M.* iii. 204
Why drew Marseille's good bishop *p.* breath *E.M.* iv. 107
Love's *p.* flames the Gods approve *O.* iii. 13
Sees by degrees a *p.* blush arise *R.L.* i. 143
As into air the *p.* spirits flow *U.L.* 25
And *p.* spirits swell the sprightly flood *W.F.* 94

Purest.
And ministers to Jove with *p.* hands *D.* ii. 94
Heav'n, as its *p.* gold, by Tortures try'd *Ep.* vi. 9
Seeks freshest pasture and the *p.* air *M.* 50
P. love's unwasting treasure *O.* iii. 41
Some in the fields of *p.* Æther play *R.L.* ii. 77

Purgatory.
I've had my *P.* here betimes *S.* viii. 5

Purge.
He from thick films shall *p.* the visual ray *M.* 39

Purg'd.
Well *p.*, and worthy Settle, Banks and Broome *D.* i. 146
Not yet *p.* off, of spleen and sour disdain *E.C.* 527
They bled, they cupp'd, they *p.*; in short, they cur'd *S.* vi. 193
Have bled and *p.* me to a simple Vote *S.* vi. 197

Purgings.
Our *p.*, pumpings, blanketings and blows *D.* ii. 154

Purify'd.
Go, *p.* by flames, ascend the sky *D.* i. 227

Purity.
What guards the *p.* of melting Maids *R.L.* i. 71

Purling.
She went to plain-work, and to *p.* brooks *E.* v. 11
The whisp'ring Zephyr and the *p.* rill *E.M.* i. 204
A painted mistress, or a *p.* stream *P.S.* 150
Swiftly *p.* in a Round *Mi.* vii. 26

Purple.
And fleecy clouds were streak'd with *p.* light *A.* 14
Where slumber Abbots *p.* as their wines *D.* iv. 302
Is like a clown in regal *p.* dress'd *E.C.* 321
Flutt'ring spread thy *p.* pinions *Mi.* vii. 2
Till some new Tyrant lifts his *p.* hand *O.* ii. 23
His *p.* pinions op'ning to the Sun *R.L.* ii. 71
Pale spectres, gaping tombs, and *p.* fires *R.L.* iv. 44
And lavish nature paints the *p.* Year *Sp.* 28
Ev'n the wild heath displays her *p.* dyes *W.F.* 25
His *p.* crest, and scarlet-circled eyes *W.F.* 116
She saw her sons with *p.* deaths expire *W.F.* 323
There *p.* Vengeance bath'd in gore retires *W.F.* 417

Purpled.
The sun first rises o'er the *p.* main *R.L.* ii. 2

Purpose.
A thousand movements scarce one *p.* gain *E.M.* i. 54
The whole strange *p.* of their lives to find *E.M.* iv. 221
The first, last *p.* of the human soul *E.M.* iv. 338
Fair to no *p.*, artful to no end *M.E.* ii. 245
'Tis to small *p.* that you hold your tongue *S.* vi. 155

Purposely.
By chance go right, they *p.* go wrong *E.C.* 427

Purse.
He chinks his *p.*, and takes his seat of state *D.* ii. 197
Want with a full, or with an empty *p. M.E.* iii. 320
Who proud of Pedigree, is poor of *P. S.* iv. 84
But fill their *p.*, our Poet's work is done *S.* v. 294
Had dearly earn'd a little *p.* of gold *S.* vi. 34

Pursue.
The Patriot's plain, but untrod, path *p. E.* ii. 16
No happier task these faded eyes *p. E.A.* 47
The dear Ideas, where I fly, *p. E.A.* 264
Envy will merit, as its shade, *p. E.C.* 466
P. the triumph, and partake the gale *E.M.* iv. 386
Pleasures the sex, as amusing Birds, *p. M.E.* ii. 231
Thrice happy man I enabled to *p. M.E.* iii. 275
That Name the learn'd with fierce disputes *p. M.E.* v. 17
Thro' all the giddy circle they *p. R.L.* i. 93
P. the stars that shoot athwart the night *R.L.* ii. 82
And pleas'd *p.* its progress thro' the skies *R.L.* v. 132
Free as young Lyttelton, her Cause *p. S.* ii. 29
Can they direct what measures to *p. S.* iii. 122
That, more than Heav'n *p. U.P.* 16
Beasts, urg'd by us, their fellow-beasts *p. W.F.* 123

Pursu'd.
Self-love forsook the path it first *p. E.M.* iii. 281
Her ev'ry turn with Violence *p. M.E.* ii. 137
Not meanly, nor ambitiously *p. M.E.* iii. 221
There sober thought *p.* th' amusing theme *S.* viii. 188
P. her flight; her flight increas'd his fire *W.F.* 184

Pursuer.
While a kind glance at her *p.* flies *Sp.* 59

Pursues.
That on weak wings, from far, *p.* your flights *E.C.* 197
P. that Chain which links th' immense design *E.M.* iv. 333
How easy ev'ry labour it *p. S.* ii. 83
Of all these ways, if each *p.* his own *S.* iii. 134

Pursuit.
Say, in *p.* of profit or delight *E.M.* iv. 85

Push'd.
And titt'ring *p.* the Pedants off the place *D.* iv. 276
Self-love thus *p.* to social, to divine *E.M.* iv. 353

Put.
To laugh at Fools who *p.* their trust in Peter *E.S.* i. 10
But well may *p.* some statesman in a fury *E.S.* i. 52
P. my Lord Bolingbroke in mind *I.H.* ii. 75 *s*
She bids her Footman *p.* it in her head *M.E.* ii. 178
And laugh at Peers who *p.* their trust in Peter *S.* i. 40
Late as it is, I *p.* myself to school *S.* iii. 47

And punish'd him that *p.* it in his way *S.* vi. 26
This *p.* the man in such a desp'rate mind *S.* vi. 37

Puts.
P. his last refuge all in Heav'n and pray'r *D.* ii. 214
One thought of thee *p.* all the pomp to flight *E.A.* 273
Seizes your fame, and *p.* his laws in force *E.C.* 168
The rising tempest *p.* in act the soul *E.M.* ii. 105
Now awful Beauty *p.* on all its arms *R.L.* i. 139
P. forth one manly leg, to sight reveal'd *R.L.* iii. 57
Who fairly *p.* all Characters to bed *S.* v. 291
For not in Chariots Peter *p.* his trust *S.* vii. 74

Puzzles.
For true No-meaning *p.* more than Wit *M.E.* ii. 114

Puzzling.
Or *p.* Contraries confound the whole *M.E.* i. 65

Pyebald.
Peel'd, patch'd, and *p.*, linsey-wolsey brothers *D.* iii. 115

Pyramids.
There mingled farms and *p.* appear *S.* vi. 259

Pyre.
Quartos, octavos, shape the less'ning *p. D.* i. 161
Sudden she flies, and whelms it o'er the *p. D.* i. 259
With tender Billet-doux he lights the *p. R.L.* ii. 41

Pythagoras.
Worthy to fill *P.'s* place *D.* iv. 572

Q.

Quacks.
Despairing *Q.* with curses fled the place *M.E.* iii. 273

Quadrille.
To spoil the nation's last great trade, *Q. M.E.* iii. 76
Than ridicule all Taste, blaspheme *Q. S.* i. 38

Quaint.
Then thus in *q.* Recitative spoke *D.* iv. 52

Quak'd.
I *q.* at heart; and still afraid, to see *S.* viii. 180

Quaker.
A simple *Q.*, or a *Q.'s* Wife *E.S.* i. 133
A *Q.?* sly! A Presbyterian? sour *M.E.* i. 156
Or round a *Q.'s beaver* cast a Glory *E.S.* ii. 97
So upright Q—s *please both Man and God D.* iv. 208

Quaking.
The *q.* mud, that clos'd, and op'd no more *D.* ii. 292

Quality.
With Fool of *Q.* completes the quire *D.* i. 298
That in proud dulness joins with *Q. E.C.* 415
That robe of *Q.* so struts and swells *M.E.* ii. 289
A Nymph of *Q.* admires our Knight *M.E.* iii. 385
If second *q*—ies *for first they take M.E.* i. 211
Yet sure, of *q.* deserving praise *M.E.* iii. 201

Quarles.
And *Q.* is sav'd by Beauties not his own *D.* i. 140
One knighted Blackmore, and one pension'd *Q. S.* v. 387

Quarrel.
Glad of a *q.*, straight I clap the door *P.S.* 67
We shall not q. *for a year or two S.* v. 61
A single verse, we *q.* with a friend *S.* v. 365

Quarry.
The whole, a labour'd *Q.* above ground *M.E.* iv. 110

Quarter.
The Fool, whose Wife elopes some thrice a *q. S.* iii. 150

Quarter'd.
Whose place is *q.* out, three parts in four *S.* viii. 136

Quarto.
Consult the Statute; *quart.* I think it is *S.* i. 147

Quartos.
Q., octavos, shape the less'ning pyre *D.* i. 161

Quays.
Make *Q.*, build Bridges, or repair Whitehall *S.* ii. 120

Queen.
All these and more the cloud-compelling *Q. D.* i. 73
Much to the mindful *Q.* the feast recalls *D.* i. 95
To serve his cause, O *Q.!* is serving thine *D.* i. 214
And now the *Q.*, to glad her sons, proclaims *D.* ii. 17
Dulness, good *Q.*, repeats the jest again *D.* ii. 122
What force have pious vows! The *Q.* of Love *D.* ii. 215
"Hold!" (cry'd the *Q.*) "a Cat-call each shall win *D.* ii. 243
For this our *Q.* unfolds to vision true *D.* iii. 61
The buzzing Bees about their dusky *Q. D.* iv. 80
As if he saw St. James's and the *Q. D.* iv. 280
Great *Q.*, and common Mother of us all *D.* iv. 404
Th' Accus'd stood forth, and thus address'd the *Q. D.* iv. 480
Smiling on all, and smil'd on by a *Q. D.* iv. 506
The *Q.* confers her *Titles* and *Degrees D.* iv. 566
Yes, I beheld th' Athenian *Q. E.* vi. 3
Athenian Q.! and *sober charms E.* vi. 25
In this weak *q.* some fav'rite still obey *E.M.* ii. 150
As in the gentle Reign of My *Q.* Anne *I.H.* iii. 4
When Flatt'ry glares, all hate it in a *Q. M.E.* i. 61
Which Heav'n has varnish'd out, and made a *Q. M.E.* ii. 182
But ev'ry Lady would be *Q.* for life *M.E.* ii. 218
In complaisance, I took the *Q.* he gave *Mi.* ix. 49
(Some say his *Q.*) was forc'd to speak or burst *P.S.* 72
The *Q.* of Midas slept, and so may I *P.S.* 82
And just as rich as when he serv'd a *Q. P.S.* 417
One speaks the glory of the British *Q. R.L.* iii. 13
And his refulgent *Q.*, with pow'rs combin'd *R.L.* iii. 77
And wins (oh shameful chance!) the *Q.* of Hearts *R.L.* iii. 88
Lurk'd in her hand, and mourn'd his captive *Q. R.L.* iii. 96
Then thus address'd the pow'r "Hail, wayward *Q. R.L.* iv. 57
Was velvet in the youth of good *Q. Bess S.* viii. 15
The King would smile on you—at least the *Q. S.* viii. 89
When the *Q.* frown'd or smil'd, he knows; and what *S.* viii. 132
As bright a Goddess, and as chaste a *Q. W.F.* 162
Once more to bend before a BRITISH *Q. W.F.* 384
Upon the bottom shines the Q.'s bright Face *Mi.* ix. 33
In hearts of Kings, or arms of Q—s *who lay E.M.* iv. 269
All that makes Saints of *Q.*, and Gods of Kings *E.S.* ii. 224
But mark the fate of a whole Sex of *Q. M.E.* ii. 219
Toasts live a Scorn, and *Q.* may die a jest *M.E.* ii. 282
When *Kings*, *Q.*, *Knaves* are set in decent rank *Mi.* ix. 77
I'd never name *Q.*, Ministers, or Kings *P.S.* 76
And four fair *Q.* whose hands sustain a flow'r *R.L.* iii. 39
Ev'n mighty Pam, that Kings and *Q.* o'erthrew *R.L.* iii. 61

Queensbury.
If *Q.* to strip there's no compelling *M.E.* ii. 193
My verse, and *Q.* weeping o'er thy urn *P.S.* 260

Queer.
The mosque of Mahound, or some *q.* Pagod *S.* viii. 239

Quench.
In lavish streams to *q.* a Country's thirst *M.E.* i. 177

Quench'd.
There stern Religion *q.* th' unwilling flame *E.A.* 39

Querno.
Rome in her Capitol saw *Q.* sit *D.* ii. 15

Query.
Each prompt to *q.*, answer, and debate *D.* ii. 381

Question.
And all the *q.* (wrangle ne'er so long) *E.M.* i. 49
Save when they lose a *Q.*, or a Job *S.* iii. 104
I make no *q.* but the Tow'r had stood *S.* viii. 85
I ask these sober q—s *of my heart S.* vi. 211
And q. *me of this or that I.H.* ii. 88 s

Quibbles.
Their *q.* routed, and defy'd their Puns *Mi.* ii. 12
In *Q.* Angel and Archangel join *S.* v. 101

QUICK—RABBLE. 247

Quick.
How hints, like spawn, scarce *q.* in embryo lie *D.* i. 59
To Needham's *q.* the voice triumphal rode *D.* i. 323
And *q.* sensations skip from vein to vein *D.* ii. 212
And Major, Minor, and Conclusion *q. D.* ii. 242
As Fancy opens the *q.* springs of Sense *D.* iv. 156
How *q.* Ambition hastes to ridicule *D.* iv. 547
Or *q.* effluvia darting thro' the brain *E.M.* i. 199
All matter *q.*, and bursting into birth *E.M.* i. 234
Sure by *q.* Nature happiness to gain *E.M.* iii. 91
Q. whirls, and shifting eddies of our minds *M.E.* i. 24
Tho' strong the beat, and *q.* the turns of mind *M.E.* i. 64
So *q.* retires each flying course, you'd swear *M.E.* iv. 159
Q. as her eyes, and as unfix'd as those *R.L.* ii. 10
Tho' mark'd by none but *q.* poetic eyes *R.L.* v. 124
Loth to enrich me with too *q.* replies *S.* viii. 128
And *q.* to swallow me, methought I saw *S.* viii. 172
Rufa, whose eye q.*-glancing o'er the Park M.E.* ii. 21

Quicken.
And keener lightnings *q.* in her eyes *R.L.* i. 144

Quicken'd.
Or *q.* a Reversion by a drug *S.* viii. 135
Since *q.* by thy Breath *U.P.* 42

Quickly.
You'd *q.* find him in Lord *Fanny's* case *E.S.* i. 50
To get my Warrant *q.* sign'd *I.H.* ii. 76 s
Almost as *q.* as he conquer'd Spain *S.* i. 132
Bear me, some God! oh *q.* bear me hence *S.* viii. 184

Quickness.
With too much *Q.* ever to be taught *M.E.* ii. 97

Quidnuncs.
The clubs of *Q.*, or her own Guildhall *D.* i. 270

Quiet.
Men, some to *Q.*, some to public Strife *M.E.* ii. 217
Q. by day *O.* iv. 12
Enjoys his Garden and his book in *q. S.* v. 199
Whom humbler joys of home-felt *q.* please *W.F.* 239
Come, if you'll be a q. *soul E.* vi. 29
That shunning faults, one *q.* tenour keep *E.C.* 241
Sedate and *q.* the comparing lies *E.M.* ii. 69
In *q.* flow from Lucrece to Lucrece *H.* iv. 208
Steer'd the same course to the same *q.* shore *Ep.* iv. 13
The Venal q.*, and entrance the Dull D.* iv. 624

Quill.
A Poet the first day he dips his *q. D.* iv. 163
Yet then did *Gildon* draw his venal *q. P.S.* 151
Sat full-blown *Bufo*, puff'd by ev'ry *q. P.S.* 232
May some choice patron bless each gray goose *q. P.S.* 249
Let *Budgel* charge low *Grubstreet* on his *q. P.S.* 378
My head and heart thus flowing thro' my *q. S.* i. 63
With ready Q—s *the Dedicators wait D.* ii. 198
From him whose *q.* stand quiver'd at his ear *S.* iii. 83

Quilt.
On the rich *q.* sinks with becoming woe *R.L.* iv. 35

Quin.
At *Q.*'s high plume, or Oldfield's petticoat *S.* v. 331

Quincunx.
His *Q.* darkens, his Espaliers meet *M.E.* iv. 80
Now forms my *Q.*, and now ranks my Vines *S.* i. 130

Quintilian.
In grave *Q.*'s copious work, we find *E.C.* 669

Quinto.
Edwardi sext. or *prim. et* quint. *Eliz. S.* i. 148

Quire.—*See also* Choir.
With Fool of Quality completes the *q. D.* i. 298
When the full organ joins the tuneful *q. O.* i. 126
For her the feather'd q—s *neglect their song A.* 24
And savage howlings fill the sacred *q. W.F.* 72

Quirks.
Light *Q.* of Music, broken and uneven *M.E.* iv. 143

Quit.
As many *q.* the streams that murm'ring fall *D.* iv. 199
Dext'rous the craving, fawning crowd to *q. E.* i. 11

Ah *q.* not the free innocence of life *E.* iv. 45
And make my soul *q.* Abelard for God *E.A.* 128
Thy oaths I *q.*, thy memory resign *E.A.* 293
So Schismatics the plain believers *q. E.C.* 428
All *q.* their sphere and rush into the skies *E M.* i. 124
The throne a Bigot keep, a Genius *q. M.E.* i. 91
Q., oh *q.* this mortal frame *O.* v. 2
Well, if it be my time to *q.* the stage *S.* viii. 1
O my fair mistress Truth! shall I *q.* thee *S.* viii. 200
Frighted, I *q.* the room, but leave it so *S.* viii. 272
When weary reapers *q.* the sultry field *Su.* 65

Quite.
Or *q.* unravel the reas'ning thread *D.* i. 179
And these to Notes are fritter'd *q.* away *D.* i. 278
When Moral Evidence shall *q.* decay *D.* iv. 462
Gay pats my shoulder, and you vanish *q. E.* v. 47
And those explain the meaning *q.* away *E.C.* 117
A little louder, but as empty *q. E.M.* ii. 278
Q. turns my stomach—So does Flatt'ry mine *E.S.* ii. 182
In all the Courts of Pindus guiltless *q. E.S.* ii. 187
And each Blasphemer *q.* escape the rod *E.S.* ii. 195
And *q.* a scandal not to learn *I.H.* ii. 146
I'm *q.* asham'd—'tis mighty rude *I.H.* ii. 206
Or Affectations *q.* reverse the soul *M.E.* i. 66
But *q.* mistakes the scaffold for the pile *M.E.* i. 221
What is this absorbs me *q. O.* v. 9
A fool *q.* angry is *q.* innocent *P.S.* 107
Far from a Lynx, and not a Giant *q. S.* iii. 50
Not *q.* so well however as he ought *S.* vi. 100
Not *q.* a madman, tho' a pasty fell *S.* vi. 190
First turn plain rash, then vanish *q.* away *S.* viii. 45
Nor *q.* indulges, nor can *q.* repress *W.F.* 20

Quits.
Hope travels thro', nor *q.* us when we die *E.M.* ii. 274
This *q.* an Empire, that embroils a State *M.E.* i. 106
Howe'er unwillingly it *q.* its place *S.* vi. 161

Quitting.
And *q.* sense call imitating God *E.M.* ii. 26

Quiver.
A painted *q.* on her shoulder sounds *W.F.* 179
The lakes that q. *to the curling breeze E.A.* 160

Quiver'd.
For him whose quills stand *q.* at his ear *S.* iii. 83

Quiv'ring.
And thrice he dropt it from his *q.* hand *D.* i. 246
And verdant alders form'd a *q.* shade *Su.* 4
In genial spring, beneath the *q.* shade *W.F.* 135

Quoits.
For *Q.*, both Temple-bar and Charing-cross *S.* viii. 277

Quorum.
Or water all the *Q.* ten miles round *M.E.* iii. 54

Quotation.
Or, in *q.*, shrewd Divines leave out *S.* vii. 103
By Wits, than Critics in as wrong Q—s *E.C.* 664

Quote.
And beastly Skelton Heads of Houses *q. S.* v. 38

Quoth.
"An't please your Honour," *q.* the Peasant *I.H.* ii. 218

R.

Great C**, H**, P**, R**, K* *D.* iv. 545

Rabbins.
Eve's tempter thus the *R.* have exprest *P.S.* 330

Rabbit.
Rank as the ripeness of a *r.*'s tail *S.* ii. 28
And humbly live on r—s *and on roots S.* ii. 52

Rabble.
Mistress! dismiss that *r.* from your throne *D.* iv. 209
Should chance to make the well-drest *R.* stare *S.* iii. 111

Rab'lais.
Or laugh and shake in R.' easy chair *D.* i. 62

Race.
And New-year Odes, and all the Grubstreet *r. D.* i. 44
How Farce and Epic get a jumbled *r. D.* i. 70
A friend to Party thou, and all her *r. D.* i. 206
So Spirits ending their terrestrial *r. D.* i. 267
They summon all her *R.* : an endless band *D.* ii. 19
The *r.* by vigour, not by vaunts is won *D.* ii. 59
Re-passes Lintot, vindicates the *r. D.* ii. 207
Each Cygnet sweet of Bath and Tunbridge *r. D.* iii. 155
Lo ! one vast Egg produces human *r. D.* iii. 248
All Flesh is bumbled, Westminster's bold *r. D.* iv. 145
In flow'd at once a gay embroider'd *r. D.* iv. 275
Mine, Goddess ! mine is all the horned *r. D.* iv. 376
Of all th' enamell'd *r.*, whose silv'ry wing *D.* iv. 421
Some, deep Free-Masons, join the silent *r. D.* iv. 571
With staff and pumps the Marquis leads the *R. D.* iv. 586
Thus Churchill's *r.* shall other hearts surprise *E.* iii. 59
False steps but help them to renew the *r. E.C.* 602
Poets, a *r.* long unconfin'd, and free *E.C.* 649
Mark how it mounts to Man's imperial *r. E.M.* i. 209
They love themselves, a third time, in their *r. E.M.* iii. 124
Another love succeeds, another *r. E.M.* iii. 130
Boast the pure blood of an illustrious *r. E.M.* iv. 207
His country next ; and next all human *r. E.M.* iv. 368
Reflecting, and reflected in his *R. Ep.* i. 12
In whom a *R.*, for Courage fam'd and Art *Ep.* xiv. 11
Their vines a shadow to their *r.* shall yield *M.* 65
See, a long *r.* thy spacious courts adorn *M.* 87
Has made the father of a nameless *r. M.E.* i. 233
Whose measure full o'erflows on human *r. M.E.* iii. 231
And vile Attorneys, now an useless *r. M.E.* iii. 274
His *r.*, his form, his name almost unknown *M.E.* iii. 284
I sought no homage from the *R.* that write *P.S.* 219
Receiv'd of wits an undistinguish'd *r. P.S.* 237
Fair tresses man's imperial *r.* ensnare *R.L.* ii. 27
Others on earth o'er human *r.* preside *R.L.* ii. 87
For Sylphs, yet mindful of their ancient *r. R.L.* iii. 35
This jealous, waspish, wrong-head, rhyming *r. S.* vi. 148
Where all the *R.* of Reptiles might embark *S.* viii. 27
Such painted puppets ! such a varnish'd *r. S.* viii. 208
Nor left one virtue to redeem her *R. U.* i. 28
Our plenteous streams a various *r.* supply *W.F.* 141
Peru once more a *r.* of kings behold *W.F.* 411

Racer.
And bade the nimblest *r.* seize the prize *D.* ii. 36

Racine.
Exact *R.*, and Corneille's noble fire *S.* v. 274
As once for Louis, Boileau and *R. S.* v. 375

Rack.
Stretch'd on the *r.* of n too easy chair *D.* iv. 342
Some strain in rhyme ; the Muses on their *r.*—s *D.* iii. 159
Some Squire, perhaps you take delight to *r. E.* v. 23

Rack'd.
R. with Sciatics, martyr'd with the Stone *S.* iv. 54

Radcliffe.
Ev'n *R.'s* Doctors travel first to France *S.* v. 183

Radiant.
Secure the *r.* weapons yield *E.* vi. 5
New Stratagems, the *r.* Lock to gain *R.L.* iii. 127
And drew behind a *r.* trail of hair *R.L.* v. 128
And what is that, which binds the *r.* sky *SA.* 97

Baffle.
At *Corticelli's* he the *R.* won *Mi.* ix. 39

Rafter'd.
No *r.* roofs with dance and tabor sound *M.E.* iii. 189

Rag.
No *r.*, no scrap, of all the beau, or wit *D.* ii. 119
In silks, in crapes, in Garters, and in R.—s *D.* ii. 22
One flaunts in *r.*, one flutters in brocade *E.M.* iv. 196

Rage.
Oh spread thy Influence, but restrain thy *R. D.* iii. 122
Ah Dennis! Gildon ah ! what ill-starr'd *r. D.* iii. 173
Gods, imps, and monsters, music, *r.*, and mirth *D.* iii. 238

But sober History restrain'd her *r. D.* iv. 39
One will shall harmonise joy, grief, and *r. D.* iv. 37
The decent Knight retir'd with sober *r. D.* iv. 113
The *r.* of Pow'r, the blast of public breath *E.* i. 95
So just thy skill, so regular my *r. E.* iii. 12
I can no more ; by shame, by *r.* suppress'd *E.A.* 105
Here brib'd the *r.* of ill-requited heav'n *E.A.* 138
Secure from Flames, from Envy's fiercer *r. E.C.* 183
"Not so, by Heav'n" (he answers in a *r.*) *E.C.* 281
Discharge that *r.* on more provoking crimes *E.C.* 328
Here point your thunder, and exhaust your *r. E.C.* 555
And rhyme with all the *r.* of Impotence *E.C.* 608
Such *r.* without betrays the fire within *E.J.S.* 17
Or never feel the *r.*, or never own *E.M.* ii. 268
Whose attributes were *R.*, Revenge, or Lust *E.M.* iii. 258

The worthy Youth shall ne'er be in a *r. E.S.* i. 48
Amidst Corruption, Luxury, and *R. Ep.* ix. 9
With native Humour temp'ring virtuous *R. Ep.* xi. 3
The brazen trumpets kindle *r.* no more *M.* 60
And die of nothing but a *R.* to live *M.E.* ii. 102
No Passion gratify'd except her *r. M.E.* ii. 126
In Youth they conquer, with so wild a *r. M.E.* ii. 221
But who, my friend, has reason in his *r. M.E.* iii. 152
Some hostile fury, some religious *r. M.E.* v. 12
They pleas'd the Fathers of poetic *r. M.E.* v. 30
If there's a Critic of distinguish'd *r. M.E.* ii. 21
And giddy Factions bear away their *r. O.* i. 35
And fate's severest *r.* disarm *O.* i. 119
Be justly warm'd with your own native *r. P.C.* 44
If I dislike it, "Furies, death and *r.*!" *P.S.* 37
Stranger to civil and religious *r. P.S.* 394
And in soft bosoms dwells such mighty *R. R.L.* i. 12
Proves the just victim of his royal *r. R.L.* iii. 62
E'er felt such *r.*, resentment, and despair *R.L.* v. 9
Slander or Poison dread from Delia's *r. S.* i. 81
Yet neither Charles nor James be in a *r. S.* i. 124
How will our Fathers rise up in a *r. S.* v. 295
How barb'rous *r.* subsided at your word *S.* v. 398
Does neither *R.* inflame, nor Fear appal *S.* vi. 208
Whose Satire's sacred, and whose *r.* nature *S.* viii. 283
Here noble Surrey felt the sacred *r. W.F.* 291
And all the mighty Mad in Dennis r. *D.* i. 106
Well might they *r.*, I gave them but their own *P.S.* 174
And heav'nly breasts with human passions *r. R.L.* v. 46

Rag'd.
While Anna begg'd and Dido *r.* in vain *R.L.* v. 6
Triumphant Malice *r.* thro' private life *S.* v. 246

Rages.
The Dog-star *r.* ! nay 'tis past a doubt *P.S.* 3

Raging.
Still run on Poets, in a *r.* vein *E.C.* 606
And Fevers *r.* up and down *I.H.* i. 13
She said ; then *r.* to Sir Plume repairs *R.L.* iv. 121
We wake next morning in a *r.* fit *S.* v. 179

Rail.
For who can *r.* so long as they can write *E.C.* 599
That virtuous ladies envy while they *r. E.J.S.* 16
Why *r.* they then, if but a Wreath of mine *E.S.* ii. 138

Raillery.
But let me die, all *r.* apart *E.J.S.* 11

Rails.
Befringe the *r.* of Bedlam and Soho *S.* v. 419
Who from his study r. *at human kind M.E.* i. 2
That *r.* at dear Lepell and Yuu *Mi.* vi. 10

Rain.
Thro' reconcil'd extremes of drought and *r. M.E.* iii. 166
Or o'er the glebe distill the kindly *r. R.L.* ii. 86
For you he walks the streets in *r.* and dust *S.* vii. 73
So may hind *r.*—s their vital moisture yield *IV.* 15

Rainbow.
Dip in the *R.*, trick her off in Air *M.E.* ii. 18
And all its varying R.—*s die away D.* iv. 692
To steal from *r.* e'er they drop in show'rs *R.L.* ii. 96

Raise.
Inspir'd he seizes ; these an altar *r. D.* i. 157
But such a bulk as no twelve bards could *r. D.* ii. 39
To move, to *r.*, to ravish ev'ry heart *D.* ii. 224
Contending Theatres our empire *r. D.* iii. 272

Nor wish to lose a Foe these Virtues *r.* *E.* ii. 11
But such plain roofs as Piety could *r.* *E.A.* 139
Fear not the anger of the wise to *r.* *E.C.* 582
That, Virtue's ends from Vanity can *r.* *E.M.* ii. 245
And Reason *r.* o'er Instinct as you can *E.M.* iii. 97
And buries madmen in the heaps they *r.* *E.M.* iv. 76
To *r.* the Thought, and touch the Heart be thine *M.E.* ii. 250
Why she and Sappho *r.* that monstrous sum *M.E.* iii. 121
More go to ruin Fortunes, than to *r.* *M.E.* iii. 202
To ease the oppress'd, and *r.* the sinking heart *M.E.* iii. 244
First shade a Country, and then *r.* a Town *M.E.* iv. 190
May Tom, whom Heav'n sent down to *r.* *Mi.* xii. 15
To *r.* the genius, and to mend the heart *P.C.* 2
While Wits and Templars ev'ry sentence *r.* *P.S.* 211
And breathes three am'rous sighs to *r.* the fire *R.L.* ii. 42
On shining Altars of Japan they *r.* *R.L.* iii. 107
Or *r.* a pimple on a beauteous face *R.L.* iv. 68
And *r.* his mind above the mob he meets *S.* vi. 99
One Chorus let all Being *r.* *U.P.* 51
Or *r.* old warriors, whose ador'd remains *W.F.* 301
That Thames's glory to the stars shall *r.* *W.F.* 336

Rais'd.

Till *r.* from booths, to Theatre, to Court *D.* iii. 297
Love, *r.* on Beauty, will like that decay *E.* iv. 63
You *r.* these hallow'd walls; the desert smil'd *E.A.* 133
And licks the hand just *r.* to shed his blood *E.M.* i. 84
And all that *r.* the Hero, sunk the Man *E.M.* iv. 294
As when Belinda *r.* my Strain *I.H.* i. 50
These *r.* new Empires o'er the Earth *I.H.* iv. 11
Not sunk by sloth, nor *r.* by servitude *M.E.* iii. 222
Imperial wonders *r.* on Nations spoil'd *M.E.* v. 5
High on the stern the Thracian *r.* his strain *O.* i. 39
His numbers *r.* a shade from hell *O.* i. 133
He *r.* his azure wand, and thus begun *R.L.* ii. 72
Which, with a sigh, she *r.;* and thus she said *R.L.* iv. 146

Raises.

The tender lambs he *r.* in his arms *M.* 53
It *r.* Armies in a Nation's aid *M.E.* iii. 31

Rake.

The Mother begg'd the blessing of a *R.* *D.* iv. 286
But ev'ry Woman is at heart a *R.* *M.E.* ii. 216

Raleigh.

Words that wise Bacon, or brave *R.* spake *S.* vi. 168

Rally.

Yet lest you think I *r.* more than teach *S.* v. 338

Ralph.

Ev'n *R.* repents, and Henley writes no more *D.* i. 216
Silence, ye Wolves! while *R.* to Cynthia howls *D.* iii. 165

Rambouillet.

And finds a fairer *R.* in you *E.* iv. 76

Ran—*see also* Run.

Back thro' the paths of pleasing sense *r.* *E.A.* 69
So from the first, eternal ORDER *r.* *E.M.* iii. 113
True faith, true policy, united *r.* *E.M.* iii. 239
In each how guilt and greatness equal *r.* *E.M.* iv. 293
R. out as fast as one who pays his bail *S.* viii. 182

Random.

How *r.* thoughts now meaning chance to find *D.* i. 275
But *r.* Praise—the task can ne'er be done *E.S.* ii. 106
Who *r.* drawings from your sheets shall take *M.E.* iv. 27

Range.

Far as Creation's ample *r.* extends *E.M.* i. 207
Opinions? they still take a wider *r.* *M.E.* i. 170
Now *r.* *the hills, the gameful woods beset* *W.F.* 95

Rang'd.

All *r.* in order, and dispos'd with grace *E.C.* 672
Late, as I *r.* the crystal wilds of air *R.L.* i. 107
And bathes the forest where she *r.* before *W.F.* 208

Rank.

There must be, somewhere, such a *r.* as Man *E.M.* i. 43
When *Kings, Queens, Knaves,* are set in decent *r.* *All.* ix. 77
Then each, according to the *r.* they bore *R.L.* iii. 34

Courtiers and Patriots in two *r.*—s divide *D.* iv. 107
His pow'rs in equal *r.*, and fair array *E.C.* 176
That, happy frailties to all *r.* apply'd *E.M.* ii. 241
In crowding *r.* on ev'ry side arise *M.* 89
Sprung the *r. weed, and thriv'd with large increase E.C.* 535
R. as the ripeness of a rabbit's tail *S.* ii. 28
Our fathers prais'd *r.* Ven'son—You suppose *S.* ii. 91
His *r.* digestion makes it wit no more *S.* vii. 32
And when *r.* widows purchase luscious nights *S.* vii. 87

Rank'd.

R. with their Friends, not number'd with their Train *E.S.* ii. 91

Ranks.

Now forms my Quincunx, and now *r.* my Vines *S.* i. 130

Ranting.

Wake the dull Church, and lull the *r.* Stage *D.* iv. 58

Rapacious.

On that *r.* hand for ever blaze *R.L.* iv. 116

Raphael.

A *R.* painted, and a Vida sung *E.C.* 704
With thee on *R.*'s *Monument I mourn* *E.* iii. 27
Match *R.* grace with thy lov'd Guido's air *E.* iii. 36

Rapid.

His *r.* waters in their passage burn *D.* ii. 184
To whom Time bears me on his *r.* wing *D.* iv. 6
Could he, whose rules the *r.* Comet bind *E.M.* ii. 35
Be smooth ye rocks, ye *r.* floods give way *M.* 36
And *r.* Severn hoarse applause resounds *M.E.* iii. 252

Rapine.

When Catiline by *r.* swell'd his store *M.E.* i. 212
My hands shall rend what ev'n thy *r.* spares *R.L.* iv. 168

Rapp'd.

" Give her the hair "—he spoke, and *r.* his box *R.L.* iv. 130

Rapt.

Not touch'd, but *r.;* not waken'd, but inspir'd *E.A.* 202
As the *r.* seraph that adores and burns *E.M.* i. 278
R. into future times, the Bard begun *M.* 7

Rapture.

Where nature moves, and *r.* warms the mind *E.C.* 236
Yet let not each gay Turn thy *r.* move *E.C.* 390
You grow correct, that once with *R.* writ *E.S.* i. 3
Then *r.*—s high the seat of sense o'erflow *D.* iii. 5
Far other *r.* of unholy joy *E.A.* 224
Loves of his own and *r.* swell the note *E.M.* iii. 34
And wake to *R.* in a Life to come *Mi.* v. 20
What home-felt *r.* move *O.* iii. 34
Whose *r.* fire me, and whose visions bless *W.F.* 260

Raptur'd.

" Enough! enough! " the *r.* monarch cries *D.* iii. 339
Which Theocles in *r.* vision saw *D.* iv. 488

Rare.

And plac'd it next him, a distinction *r.* *D.* ii. 96
In Poets as true genius is but *r.* *E.C.* 11
Short, and but *r.*, till Man improv'd it all *E.M.* iv. 116
That secret *r.*, between th' extremes to move *M.E.* iii. 227
His givings *r.*, save farthings to the poor *M.E.* iii. 348
R. monkish Manuscripts for Hearne alone *M.E.* iv. 9
The things, we know, are neither rich nor *r.* *P.S.* 171
And, what's more *r.*, a Poet shall say Grace *S.* ii. 150
Like rich old wardrobes, things extremely *r.* *S.* vii. 123

Rarely.

Much fruit of sense beneath is *r.* found *E.C.* 310
But these plain Characters we *r.* find *M.E.* i. 63
And *r.* Av'rice taints the tuneful mind *S.* v. 192

Rascal.

And scorn a *r.* and a coach *Mi.* xii. 20

Rash.

First turn plain *r.*, then vanish quite away *S.* viii. 45
With all the *r. dexterity of wit* *E.M.* ii. 84
Too *r.* for Thought, for Action too refin'd *M.E.* i. 201
Ah cease, *r.* youth! desist ere 'tis too late *R.L.* iii. 121

Rashness.

Fear to the statesman, *r.* to the chief *E.M.* ii. 243

Rat.
A *R.*, a *R.!* clap to the door *I.H.* ii. 212
No *r.* is rhym'd to death, nor maid to love *S.* vii. 22

Ratafie.
Of Mirth and Opium, *R.* and Tears *M.E.* ii. 110

Rate.
Court-virtues bear, like Gems, the highest *r. M.E.* i. 141
But by your *fathers' worth if yours you* r. *E.M.* iv. 209

Rather.—*Passim.*

Rational.
Shall he alone, whom *r.* we call *E.M.* i. 187

Rattle.
Pleas'd with a *r.*, tickled with a straw *E.M.* ii. 276
The Rhymes or R—s *of the Man or Boy S.* iii. 13

Rattling.
R. an ancient Sistrum at his head *D.* iv. 374
But *r.* nonsense in full volleys breaks *E.C.* 628
But who the Bowl, or *r.* Dice compares *Mi.* ix. 101

Ravage.
Parts it may *r.*, but preserves the whole *E.M.* ii. 106

Rave.
In vain! they gaze, turn giddy, *r.*, and die *D.* iv. 648
In vain may Heroes fight, and Patriots *r. M.E.* iii. 33
They *r.*, recite, and madden round the land *P.S.* 6
Yet then did *Dennis r.* in furious fret *P.S.* 153

Raves.
At half mankind when gen'rous Manly *r. E.M.* i. 57
Sudden she storms! she *r.!* You tip the wink *M.E.* ii. 33

Ravish.
To move, to raise, to *r.* ev'ry heart *D.* ii. 223
What War could *r.*, Commerce could bestow *E.M.* iii. 205
By force to *r.*, or by fraud betray *R.L.* ii. 32

Ravish'd.
As Hylas fair was *r.* long ago *D.* ii. 336
Or *r.* with the whistling of a Name *E.M.* iv. 283
As thou, sad Virgin! for thy *r.* Hair *R.L.* iv. 10
Then cease, bright Nymph! to mourn thy *r.* hair *R.L.* v. 141
The fields are *r.* from th' industrious swains *W.F.* 65

Ravisher.
Gods! shall the *r.* display your hair *R.L.* iv. 103

Ray.
Thus he, for then a *r.* of Reason stole *D.* iii. 225
Yet, yet a moment, one dim *R.* of Light *D.* iv. 1
Now flam'd the Dogstar's unpropitious *r. D.* iv. 9
Ev'n more observant of the parting *R. E.* i. 37
Those smiling eyes, attemp'ring ev'ry *r. E.A.* 63
Thy eyes diffus'd a reconciling *r. E.A.* 145
Alas! not dazzled with their noon-tide *r. E.M.* iv. 305
Now shown by Cynthia's silver *r. I.H.* iii. 47
He from thick films that purge the visual *r. M.* 39
Oh! blest with Temper, whose unclouded *r. M.E.* ii. 257
Unpolish'd Gems no *r.* on Pride bestow *Mi.* x. 5
Sol thro' white curtains shot a tim'rous *r. R.L.* i. 13
The sun obliquely shoots his burning *r. R.L.* iii. 20
And hail with music its propitious *r. R.L.* v. 134
Whether Old age, with faint but cheerful *r. S.* i. 93
Then, like the Sun, let Bounty spread her *r. S.* ii. 115
Sure fate of all, beneath whose rising *r. S.* v. 19
And stretch the *R.* to Ages yet unborn *S.* v. 228
Mix in his look; All eyes direct their r—s *D.* ii. 7
Did Nature's pencil ever blend such *r. D.* iv. 411
It draws up vapours which obscure its *r. E.C.* 471
Meanwhile Opinion gilds with varying *r. E.M.* ii. 283
Not so, when diadem'd with *r.* divine *E.S.* ii. 232
But lost, dissolv'd in thy superior *r. M.* 101
Tho' the same sun, with all-diffusive *r. M.E.* i. 145
Ye little Stars! hide your diminish'd *r. M.E.* iii. 282
And Splendour borrows all her *r.* from Sense *M.E.* iv. 180
And heighten'd by the diamond's circling *r. R.L.* iv. 115
But soon the sun with milder *r.* descends *Su.* 89

Reach.
Be sure yourself and your own *r.* to know *E.C.* 48
And snatch a grace beyond the *r.* of art *E.C.* 153

Above the *r.* of sacrilegious hands *E.C.* 182
Above the *r.* of vulgar song *I.H.* iv. 4
Still out of *r.*, but never out of view *M.E.* ii. 232
Within the *r.* of Treason, or of Law *S.* vii. 128
Pride, Pomp, and State but *r. her outward part E.* iv. 55
And which a master-hand alone can *r. E.C.* 145
Now, they who *r.* Parnassus' lofty crown *E.C.* 514
No glass can *r.*; from Infinite to thee *E.M.* i. 240
All states can *r.* it, and all heads conceive *E.M.* iv. 30
Or praise malignly Arts I cannot *r. S.* v. 339
Wants *r.* all states; they beg but better drest *S.* viii. 224

Reach'd.
Not touch'd by Nature, and not *r.* by Art *D.* iii. 230
Had *r.* the work, the All that mortal can *D.* iv. 173
Churches and Chapels instantly it *r. D.* iv. 607
But never, never *r.* one gen'rous Thought *M.E.* ii. 162
That never Coxcomb *r.* Magnificence *M.E.* iv. 22
And in a vapour *r.* the dismal shore *R.L.* iv. 18
And now his shadow *r.* her as she run *W.F.* 193

Read.
R. these instructive leaves, in which conspire *E.* iii. 7
To *r.* and weep is all they now can do *E.A.* 48
R. them by day, and meditate by night *E.C.* 125
A perfect Judge will *r.* each work of Wit *E.C.* 233
All Boys may *r.*, and Girls may understand *E.S.* i. 76
Writ not, and Chartres scarce could write or *r. E.S.* ii. 186
But you may *r.* it; I stop short *I.H.* i. 84
Or gravely try to *r.* the lines *I.H.* ii. 91 s
I sit with sad civility, I *r. P.S.* 37
If foes, they write, if friends, they *r.* me dead *P.S.* 32
And see what friends, and *r.* what books I please *P.S.* 264
See *Libels, Satires*—here you have it—*r. S.* i. 149
Such as a King might *r.*, a Bishop write *S.* i. 152
Plead much, *r.* more, dine late, or not at all *S.* iv. 37
Our Wives *r.* Milton, and our Daughters plays *S.* v. 172
To *r.* in Greek the wrath of Peleus' son *S.* vi. 53
A Poet begs me, I will hear him *r. S.* vi. 93
The men, who write such Verse as we can *r. S.* vi. 158
So prompts, and saves a rogue who cannot *r. S.* vii. 16
In eldest time ere mortals writ or r. *S.* i. 5
Let all give way, and Morris may be *r. D.* iii. 168
For ever reading, never to be *r. D.* iii. 194
With all such reading as was never *r. D.* iv. 250
Still with esteem no less convers'd than *r. E.* iv. 7
Who knew most Sentences, was deepest *r. E.C.* 441
The bookful blockhead, ignorantly *r. R.C.* 612
Here, Last of Britons! let your names be *r. E.S.* ii. 250
Men may be *r.* as well as Books, too much *M.E.* i. 10
And round the orb in lasting notes be *r. M.E.* v. 66
The courtly Talbot, Somers, Sheffield *r. P.S.* 139
Wounds, Charms, and Ardors were no sooner *r. R.L.* i. 119
As long as Atalantis shall be *r. R.L.* iii. 165
At court, who hates whate'er he *r.* at school *S.* v. 106
Or what remain'd, so worthy to be *r. S.* v. 137

Reader.
The *r.*'s threaten'd (not in vain) with "sleep" *E.C.* 353
More on a *R.*'s *sense than Gazers eye S.* v. 351
Sleepless themselves, to give their *r*—s *sleep D.* i. 94
The pond'rous books two gentle *r.* bring *D.* ii. 383

Reading.
How with less *r.* than makes felons 'scape *D.* i. 281
For ever *r.*, never to be read *D.* iii. 194
With all such *r.* as was never read *D.* iv. 250
And *r.* wish, like theirs, our fate and fame *E.* iii. 9
Pains, *r.*, study, are their just pretence *P.S.* 159
To part her time 'twixt *r.* and bohea *E.* v. 15

Reads.
Amus'd he *r.*, then returns the bills *D.* ii. 91
Glows while he *r.*, but trembles as he writes *E.C.* 198
All books he *r.*, and all he *r.* assails *E.C.* 616
Each wight, who *r.* not, and but scans and spells *P.S.* 165
Who *r.*, but with a lust to misapply *P.S.* 301
Who now *r.* Cowley? if he pleases yet *S.* v. 75

Ready.
With *r.* quills the Dedicators wait *D.* ii. 198
The current folly proves the *r.* wit *E.C.* 449

REAL—REBELLIOUS. 251

And r. Nature waits upon his hand *E.C.* 487
Still fit for use, and r. at command *E.C.* 674
Be mighty r. to do good *I.H.* i. 36
Extremely r. to resign *I.H.* i. 63
R., by force, or of your own accord *S.* vi. 250
R. to cast, I yawn, I sigh, and sweat *S.* viii. 157
Before his lord the r. spaniel bounds *W.F.* 99

Real.

Or bound in formal, or in r. chains *E.* iv. 42
'Tis r. good, or seeming, moves them all *E.M.* ii. 94

Realm.

Mourn not, my SWIFT, at aught our *R.* acquires *D.* i. 26
Wide, and more wide, it spread o'er all the r. *D.* iv. 613
The Ant's republic, and the r. of Bees *E.M.* iii. 184
Down, down, proud Satire! tho' a *R.* be spoil'd *E.S.* ii. 38
Thy r. for ever lasts, thy own MESSIAH reigns *M.* 108
R—s *shift their place, and Ocean turns to land D.* i. 72
Where as he fish'd her nether r. for Wit *D.* ii. 101
And smooth my passage to the r. of day *E.A.* 322
Who first taught souls enslav'd, and r. undone *E.M.* iii. 241
And hail her passage to the *R.* of Rest *E.S.* i. 81
Hereditary *R.*, and Worlds of Gold *M.E.* iii. 130
And vanquish'd r. supply recording gold *M.E.* v. 56
Here thou, great Anna! whom three r. obey *R.L.* iii. 7
And r. commanded which those trees adorn *W.F.* 32
And harvests on a hundred r. bestows *W.F.* 360

Reams.

With r. abundant this abode supply *D.* ii. 90

Reap.

And the same hand that sow'd, shall r. the field *M.* 66
Shall tend the flocks, or r. the bearded grain *W.F.* 370
R. their own fruits, and woo their sable loves *W.F.* 410

Reap'd.

Or r. in iron harvests of the field *E.M.* iv. 12

Reaper.

And nodding tempt the joyful r.'s hand *W.F.* 40
When weary r—s quit the sultry field Su. 65

Re-appear.

See! the dull stars roll round and r. *D.* iii. 322

Rear.

Support his front, and Oaths bring up the r. *D.* i. 308
Thus oft they r., and oft the head decline D. ii. 393
To r. the Column, or the Arch to bend *M.E.* iv. 48
Where tow'ring oaks their growing honours r. *W.F.* 221

Rear'd.

Fair from its humble bed I r. this flow'r *D.* iv. 405

Rears.

Yon stars, yon suns, he r. at pleasure higher *D.* iii. 259
Shakes off the dust, and r. his rev'rend head *E.C.* 700
To that she bends, to that her eyes she r. *R.L.* i. 126
Fair Liberty, Britannia's Goddess, r. *W.F.* 91
The gulfy Lee his sedgy tresses r. *W.F.* 346

Reason.

Which only heads refin'd from *R.* know *D.* iii. 6
Some free from rhyme or r., rule or check *D.* iii. 161
Blockheads with r. wicked wits abhor *D.* iii. 175
Thus he, for then a ray of *R.* stole *D.* iii. 225
When *R.* doubtful, like the Samian letter *D.* iv. 151
And *R.* giv'n them but to study *Flies D.* iv. 454
Of naught so certain as our *R.* still *D.* iv. 481
And taught the world with r. to admire *E.C.* 101
If once right r. drives that cloud away *E.C.* 212
And love to praise, with r. on his side *E.C.* 642
Presumptuous Man! the r. wouldst thou find *E.M.* i. 35
First, if thou canst, the harder r. guess *E.M.* i. 37
Had he thy *R.*, would he skip and play *E.M.* i. 82
For this plain r., Man is not a Fly *E.M.* i. 194
'Twixt that and *R.*, what a nice barrier *E.M.* i. 223
Is not thy *R.* all these pow'rs in one *E.M.* i. 232
Alike in ignorance, his r. such *E.M.* ii. 11
What *R.* weaves, by Passion is undone *E.M.* ii. 42
Self-love to urge, and *R.* to restrain *E.M.* ii. 54
R. the future, and the consequence *E.M.* ii. 74
R. still use, to *R.* still attend *E.M.* ii. 78
Each strengthens *R.*, and Self-love restrains *E.M.* ii. 80

And Grace and Virtue, Sense and *R.* split *E.M.* ii. 83
Self-love and *R.* to one end aspire *E.M.* ii. 87
And *R.* bids us for our own provide *E.M.* ii. 96
List under *R.*, and deserve her care *E.M.* ii. 98
R. the card, but Passion is the gale *E.M.* ii. 108
Suffice that *R.* keep to Nature's road *E.M.* ii. 115
R. itself but gives it edge and pow'r *E.M.* ii. 147
R. is here no guide, but still a guard *E.M.* ii. 162
All, all alike, find *R.* on their side *E.M.* ii. 174
R. the bias turns to good from ill *E.M.* ii. 196
Taught half by *R.*, half by mere decay *E.M.* ii. 239
And just as short of r. he must fall *E.M.* iii. 47
Whether with *R.*, or with Instinct blest *E.M.* iii. 79
R., however able, cool at best *E.M.* iii. 85
Which heavier *R.* labours at in vain (*rep.*) *E.M.* iii. 92
And *R.* raise o'er Instinct as you can *E.M.* iii. 97
Reflection, *R.*, still the ties improve *E.M.* iii. 133
And hence let *R.*, late, instruct Mankind *E.M.* iii. 180
In vain thy *R.* finer webs shall draw *E.M.* iii. 191
And simple *R.* never sought but one *E.M.* iii. 210
Grasp the whole worlds of *R.*, Life, and Sense *E.M.* iv. 357
That *R.*, PASSION, answer one great aim *E.M.* iv. 395
Without a staring *R.* on his brows *E.S.* ii. 194
How vain is *R.*, Eloquence how weak *Ep.* iii. 5
Blest with plain *R.*, and with sober Sense *Ep.* vi. 2
It may be *R.*, but it is not Man *M.E.* i. 26
But who, my friend, has r. in his rage *M.E.* iii. 152
The ruling Passion conquers *R.* still *M.E.* iii. 154
Resolve me, *R.*, which of these is worse *M.E.* iii. 319
Fir'd by the sight, all *R.* I disdain *Mi.* ix. 83
Look upon *Basset*, you who *R.* boast (*rep.*) *Mi.* ix. 85
The Feast of *R.*, and the Flow of Soul *S.* i. 128
With terrors round, can *R.* hold her throne *S.* vi. 310
And spite of Pride, in erring R.'s spite E.M. i. 293
R. comparing balance rules the whole *E.M.* ii. 60
R. at distance, and in prospect lie *E.M.* ii. 72
To copy Instinct then was *R.* part *E.M.* iii. 169
R. whole pleasure, all the joys of Sense *E.M.* iv. 79
And if I pray by *R.* rules *I.H.* ii. 15 ‡
Add Nature's, Custom's, *R.*, Passion's strife *M.E.* i. 21
'Tis *R.* voice, which sometimes one can hear *S.* iii. 12
While if our Elders break all r. laws *S.* v. 117
And r. downward till we doubt of God D. iv. 472
They r. and conclude by precedent *E.C.* 410
What can we r., but from what we know *E.M.* i. 18
From which to r., or to which refer *E.M.* i. 20
In both, to r. right is to submit *E.M.* i. 164
Who ask and r. thus, will scarce conceive *E.M.* iv. 163
Intent to r., or polite to please *E.M.* iv. 382
On human actions r. tho' you can *M.E.* i. 25

Reasonable.

So very r., so unmov'd *M.E.* ii. 165
I know a r. Woman *Mi.* viii. 3

Reas'ning.

Or quite unravel all the r. thread *D.* i. 179
Then, in the scale of r. life, 'tis plain *E.M.* i. 47
In Pride, in r. Pride, our error lies *E.M.* i. 123
From pride, from pride, our very r. springs *E.M.* i. 161
Born but to die, and r. but to err *E.M.* ii. 10
His pride in *R.*, not in Acting, lies *M.E.* i. 118
In short, that r., high, immortal Thing *S.* iii. 185

Reasons.

Who r. wisely, is not therefore wise *M.E.* i. 117

Re-assume.

And laughing Ceres r. the land *M.E.* iv. 176

Rebel.

A *R.* to the very king he loves *M.E.* i. 203
Bind r. Wit, and double chain on chain D. iv. 158
Still r. nature holds out half my heart *E.A.* 26
The r. Knave who dares his prince engage *R.L.* iii. 59
But who, weak r—s, more advance her cause D. iv. 86
Aspiring to be Angels, Men r. E.M. i. 128
What serves one will, when many wills r. *E.M.* iii. 274
Say, does thy blood r., thy bosom move *S.* iii. 55

Rebellion.

But soon, ah soon, *R.* will commence *D.* iv. 63
There Faction roar, *R.* bite her chain *W.F.* 421

Rebellious.

There form'd r. *Logic*, gagg'd and bound *D.* iv. 23

To thee the most *r.* things on earth *D.* iv. 508
When this *r.* heart shall beat no more *E.A.* 346

Rebels.
He ne'er *r.*, nor plots, like other men *S.* v. 194

Rebound.
The shrill echoes *r. O.* i. 9
And seas, and rocks, and skies *r. O.* i. 47
Begin, the vales shall ev'ry note *r. Sp.* 44
"Restore the Lock!" the vaulted roofs *r. R.L.* v. 104

Rebounds.
Delia, each cave and echoing rock *r. A.* 30

Rebuke.
Ye Gods! shall Cibber's son, without *r. E.S.* i. 115
I own I'm pleas'd with this *r. I.H.* ii. 60
For such alone the Great r—s *endure S.* viii. 282

Recall.
R. those nights that clos'd thy toilsome days *E.* i. 15
In pensive thought *r.* the fancy'd scene *E.* v. 33
Forget to thunder, and *r.* her fires *E.M.* iv. 124

Recall'd.
Shall, first *r.*, rush forward to thy mind *D.* iii. 64

Recalls.
Much to the mindful Queen the feast *r. D.* i. 95

Recede.
The woods *r.* around the naked seat *M.E.* iii. 209

Recedes.
The world *r.*; it disappears *O.* v. 13

Receipts.
Write dull *r.* how poems may be made *E.C.* 115

Receive.
"*R.*" (he said) "these robes that once were mine *D.* ii. 351
R. great Empress! thy accomplish'd Son *D.* iv. 282
Her too *r.* (for her my soul adores) *D.* iv. 331
R., and wrap me in eternal rest *E.A.* 302
This humble praise, lamented shade! *r. E.C.* 733
Thy arts of building from the bee *r. E.M.* iii. 175
R., and place for ever near a King *E.S.* i. 96
These little rites, a Stone, a Verse, *r. Ep.* vii. 19
Or some frail China jar *r.* a flaw *R.L.* L 106

Receiv'd.
R. each Demi-God, with pious care *D.* iv. 383
R. the weapons of the sky *E.* vi. 10
R. his laws; and stood convinc'd 'twas fit *E.C.* 651
R. a Town Mouse at his Board *I.H.* ii. 159
With open arms *r.* one Poet more *P.S.* 142
R. of wits an undistinguish'd race *P.S.* 237

Receives.
R. the lurking principle of death *E.M.* ii. 134
Where only merit constant pay *r. E.M.* iv. 213
From him the next *r.* it, thick or thin *E.S.* ii. 175
Lo, earth *r.* him from the bending skies *M.* 33
While China's earth *r.* the smoking tide *R.L.* iii. 110
What Time would spare, from Steel *r.* its date *R.L.* iii. 171
Well may he blush who gives it or *r. S.* v. 414
And I those kisses he *r.*, enjoy *Su.* 48
For God is pay'd when Man *r. U.P.* 19
Not Neptune's self from all his streams *r. W.F.* 223

Recess.
Keen, hollow winds howl thro' the bleak *r. D.* i. 35
But in her Temple's last *r.* enclos'd *D.* iii. 1
The close r—es *of the Virgin's thought R.L.* iii. 140

Recitativo.
Then thus in quaint *R.* spoke *D.* iv. 52

Recite.
They rave, *r.*, and madden round the land *P.S.* 6
And if we will *r.* nine hours in ten *S.* v. 362
The thoughts of Gods let Granville's verse *r. W.F.* 425

Reclaim.
Wisdom and wit in vain *r. O.* iii. 3

Reclaims.
He from the taste obscene *r.* our youth *S.* v. 217

Reclin'd.
The darksome pines that o'er yon rocks *r. E.A.* 155
As on the nosegay in her breast *r. R.L.* iii. 141
High in the midst, upon his urn *r. W.F.* 349

Reclines.
Soft on her lap her Laureate son *r. D.* iv. 20

Recluse.
The most *r.*, discreetly open'd, find *D.* iv. 447

Recognize.
Ascend and *r.* their Native Place *D.* i. 268

Recollection.
Tho' past the *r.* of the thought *M.E.* i. 47

Recommend.
As shades more sweetly *r.* the light *E.C.* 301
He'd *r.* her as a special breeder *E.J.S.* 34
Or ev'n to crack live Craw-fish *r. S.* ii. 43

Recommends.
But hear a Mother, when she *r. D.* iv. 439

Reconcil'd.
Thro' *r.* extremes of drought and rain *M.E.* iii. 166

Reconciles.
Due distance *r.* to form and grace *E.C.* 174

Reconciling.
Thy eyes diffus'd a *r.* ray *E.A.* 145

Record.
And Monumental brass this *r.* bears *D.* ii. 313
It stands on *r.*, that in Richard's times *S.* i. 145
There liv'd in primo Georgii (they *r.*) *S.* vi. 184

Recording.
And vanquish'd realms supply'd *r.* gold *M.E.* v. 56

Recreation.
Together mixt; sweet *r. O.* iv. 14

Recruits.
She gives in large *r.* of needful pride *E.C.* 206

Rectify.
'Tis hers to *r.*, not overthrow *E.M.* ii. 163

Red.
Or their fond parents drest in *r.* and gold *D.* i. 138
Wings the *r.* lightning, and the thunder rolls *D.* iii. 256
R., Blue, and Green, nay white and black *E.* vi. 19
The Napkins white, the Carpet *r. I.H.* ii. 195
And—Betty—give this Cheek a little *R. M.E.* i. 251
Where tawdry yellow strove with dirty *r. M.E.* iii. 304
To wear as *r.*, stockings, and to dine with *Steele Mi.* iii. 4
Upon her sallow cheeks, enliv'ning *r. Mi.* ix. 62
And with a face as *r.*, and as awry *S.* viii. 266
R. Iber's sands, or Ister's foaming flood *W.F.* 368

Redden.
The coral *r.*, and the ruby glow *W.F.* 394

Redd'ning.
With annual joy the *r.* shoots to greet *M.E.* iv. 91

Reddens.
But Appius *r.* at each word you speak *E.C.* 585

Redeem.
Nor left one virtue to *r.* her Race *U.L.* 28

Redeem'd.
R. from tapers and defrauded pies *D.* i. 156

Redue'd.
R. at last to hiss in my own dragon *D.* iii. 286
R. to feign it, when they give no more *M.E.* ii. 238

Re-echoes.
And Hungerford *r.* bawl for bawl *D.* ii. 266
And the high dome *r.* to his nose *R.L.* v. 86

Reed.
The green *r.* trembles, and the bulrush nods *M.* 72
O let my Muse her slender *r.* inspire *Sp.* 11

And eyes the dancing cork, and bending *r*. *W.F.* 140
But now the r—s shall hang on yonder tree *Su*. 43
But tell the *r*., and tell the vocal shore *Wi*. 59

Reek'd.
Altars grew marble then, and *r*. with gore *E.M.* iii. 264

Reel.
Till Isis' Elders *r*., their pupils' sport *D*. iii. 337

Refer.
From which to reason, or to which *r*. *E.M.* i. 20

Refine.
See Dionysius Homer's thoughts *r*. *E.C.* 665
But Otway fail'd to polish or *r*. *S*. v. 278
Prune the luxuriant, the uncouth *r*. *S*. vi. 174

Refin'd.
Which only heads *r*. from Reason know *D*. iii. 6
Where flames *r*. in breasts seraphic glow *E.A.* 320
The dross cements what else were too *r*. *E.M.* ii. 179
Lust, thro' some certain strainers well *r*. *E.M.* ii. 189
So firm, yet soft; so strong, yet so *r*. *Ep*. vi. 8
He, with a hundred Arts *r*. *I.H.* iii. 15
Too rash for Thought, for Action too *r*. *M.E.* i. 201
On the soft Passion, and the Taste *r*. *M.E.* ii. 84
Wise Wretch! with Pleasures too *r*. to please *M.E.* ii. 95
Some, less *r*., beneath the moon's pale light *R.L.* ii. 81
He forms one tongue; exotic and *r*. *S*. viii. 49

Refinements.
Britain to soft *r*. less a foe *S*. v. 265

Refines.
How the wit brightens! how the style *r*. *E.C.* 421
The gen'rous God, who Wit and Gold *r*. *M.E.* ii. 289

Reflect.
While Images *r*. from art to art *E*. iii. 20
R. new glories, and augment the day *E.C.* 473
The learn'd *r*. on what before they knew *E.C.* 740
Yet, Sir, *r*., the mischief is not great *S*. v. 189

Reflected.
His Peers shine round him with *r*. grace *D*. ii. 9
Reflecting, and *r*. in his Race *Ep*. i. 12
Some wand'ring touches, some *r*. light *M.E.* ii. 153
And Art *r*. images to Art *M.E.* v. 52
Not when a gilt Buffet's *r*. pride *S*. ii. 5
Of beaming diamonds and *r*. plate *S*. iv. 29

Reflecting.
R., and reflected in his Race *Ep*. i. 12
Was there a gen'rous, a *r*. mind *Mi*. ii. 5

Reflection.
Remembrance and *r*. how ally'd *E.M.* i. 225
R., Reason still the ties improve *E.M.* iii. 133
If modest Youth, with cool *R*. crown'd *Ep*. xiv. 1
And all we gain some sad *R*. more *Mi*. v. 8
In vain sedate r—s we would make *M.E.* i. 39

Reflects.
This polish'd Hardness that *r*. the Peer *D*. i. 220
Where Thames *r*. the visionary scene *I.H.* iii. 24
And half the platform just *r*. the other *M.E.* iv. 118
The silver Thames *r*. its marble face *S*. iii. 142

Reform'd.
Then unbelieving priests *r*. the nation *E.C.* 546
Or Laws establish'd, and the world *r*. *S*. v. 12

Reforming.
But as the Fool that is *r*. days *S*. viii. 15

Refresh.
No rich perfumes *r*. the fruitful field *W*. 47

Refreshes.
Warms in the sun, *r*. in the breeze *E.M.* i. 271

Refuge.
Puts his last *r*. all in heav'n and pray'r *D*. ii. 214

Refulgent.
Breaks out *r*. with a heav'n its own *D*. iii. 242
And his *r*. Queen, with pow'rs combin'd *R.L.* iii. 77

Refund.
Is to *r*. the Medals with the meat *D*. iv. 390

Refuse.
Nor couldst thou, CHESTERFIELD! a tear *r*. *D*. iv. 43
This Verse be thine, my friend, nor thou *r*. *E*. iii. 1
Dare you *r*. him? Curll invites to dine *P.S.* 53
For her the flocks *r*. their verdant food *W*. 37
What Muse for GRANVILLE can *r*. to sing *W.F.* 6

Refus'd.
Not ancient ladies when *r*. a kiss *R.L.* iv. 6
Noah had *r*. it lodging in his Ark *S*. viii. 26

Regains.
Ere such a soul *r*. its peaceful state *E.A.* 197

Regal.
Is like a clown in *r*. purple dress'd *E.C.* 321
What boots the *r*. circle on his head *R.L.* iii. 71
The lilies blazing on the *r*. shield *W.F.* 306

Regard.
Nor blush these studies thy *r*. engage *M.E.* v. 49
Ev'n such small Critics some *r*. may claim *P.S.* 167
In ev'ry work *r*. the writer's End *E.C.* 255
R. not then if Wit be old or new *E.C.* 406
To follow nature, and *r*. his end *W.F.* 252

Regardless.
R. of our merit or default *D*. iv. 486

Regards.
And one *r*. itself, and one the Whole *E.M.* iii. 316
Succeeding vanities she still *r*. *R.L.* i. 53

Regent.
A godless *R*. tremble at a Star *M.E.* i. 90

Region.
No cheerful breeze this sullen *r*. knows *R.L.* iv. 19
Survey the *r*., and confess her home *W.F.* 256
But see, the man who spacious r—s gave *W.F.* 79
To the bright *r*. of the rising day *W.F.* 388
And seas but join the *r*. they divide *W.F.* 400

Regret.
But still the worst with most *r*. commend *E.C.* 518
How often hope, despair, resent, r. *E.A.* 199
Saw nothing to *r*., or there to fear *Ep*. x. 8
To covet flying, and *r*. when lost *M.E.* ii. 234

Regular.
So just thy skill, so *r*. my rage *E*. iii. 12
And more diverting still than *r*. *E*. iv. 26
The Whole at once is bold, and *r*. *E.C.* 252
Comets are *r*., and Wharton plain *M.E.* i. 209
But soft—by *r*. approach—not yet *M.E.* iv. 129

Regularly.
Correctly cold, and *r*. low *E.C.* 340

Regulate.
Correct old Time and *r*. the Sun *E.M.* ii. 22

Rehearsal.
To some a dry *r*. was assigned *P.S.* 243
There's a *R*., Sir, exact at one *S*. vi. 97
Nor at R—s sweat, and mouth'd, and cry'd *P.S.* 227
To Theatres, and to *R*. throng *S*. v. 173

Rehearse.
R., ye Muses, what yourselves inspir'd *A*. 56

Reign.
My son, the promis'd land expects thy *r*. *D*. i. 192
Then stretch thy sight o'er all her rising *r*. *D*. iii. 65
This fav'rite Isle, long sever'd from her *r*. *D*. iii. 125
These Fate reserv'd to grace thy *r*. divine *D*. iii. 275
"Oh" (cry'd the Goddess), "for some pedant *R*. *D*. iv. 175
The following license of a Foreign *r*. *E.C.* 544
The state of Nature was the *r*. of God *E.M.* iii. 148
As in the gentle *R*. of My Queen Anne *I.H.* iii. 4
Flatt'rers and Bigots ev'n in Louis' *r*. *S*. i. 112
You'd think no Fools disgrac'd the former *r*. *S*. v. 127
Were equal crimes in a despotic *r*. *W.F.* 58
Whose care, like hers, protects the sylvan *r*. *W.F.* 163
Be mine the blessings of a peaceful *r*. *W.F.* 366

O stretch thy *r.*, fair Peace! from shore to shore *W.F.* 407
Joy to great Chaos! let Division r. *D.* iv. 54
Which as it dies, or lives, we fail or *r. D.* iv. 186
Two Principles in human nature *r. E.M.* ii. 53
And these for ever, tho' a Monarch *r. E.M.* iii. 187
Like good Aurelius let him *r.*, or bleed *E.M.* iv. 235

Reign'd.
Thus long succeeding Critics justly *r. E.C.* 681

Reigns.
Still Dunce the second *r.* like Dunce the first *D.* i. 6
Another Phœbus, thy own Phœbus, *r. D.* iv. 61
And ever-musing melancholy *r. E.A.* 5
And Nero *r.* a Titus, if he will *E.M.* ii. 198
Thy realm for ever lasts, thy own MESSIAH *r. M.* 108
While in thy heart eternal winter *r. Su.* 22
And peace and plenty tell, a STUART *r. W.F.* 42

Rein.
My Passions rise, and will not bear the *r. Mi.* ix. 84

Reject.
Fir'd that the House *r.* him, "'Sdeath I'll print it *P.S.* 61
Could make a gentle Belle *r.* a Lord *R.L.* i. 10
Seems to *r.* him, tho' she grants his pray'r *R.L.* iv. 80
In vain bad Rhymers all mankind *r. S.* vi. 153

Rejects.
R. mankind, is by some Sylph embrac'd *R.L.* i. 68
Oft she *r.*, but never once offends *R.L.* ii. 12

Rejoice.
If not so pleas'd, at Council-board *r. S.* iv. 34
No more the forests ring, or groves *r. W.F.* 278
But hark! the groves *r.*, the forest rings *W.F.* 281

Rejoicing.
The Gnome *r.* bears her gifts away *R.L.* iv. 87

Rejoin.
Meet and *r.* me, in the pensive Grot *S.* vi. 209

Rejudge.
R. his acts, and dignify disgrace *E.* i. 30
R. his justice, be the GOD of GOD *E.M.* i. 122

Relapse.
But grant I may *r.*, for want of grace *S.* vi. 88

Relate.
How parts *r.* to parts, or they to whole *D.* iv. 235
O Muse! *r.* (for you can tell alone *D.* iv. 619
R., who first, who last resign'd to rest *D.* iv. 621
Nothing is foreign: parts *r.* to whole *E.M.* iii. 21

Related.
To whom *r.*, or by whom begot *U.L.* 72

Relates.
First he *r.*, bow sinking to the chin *D.* ii. 331

Relation.
Find Virtue local, all *R.* scorn *D.* iv. 479
I'm no such Beast, nor his *R. I.H.* i. 60

Relative.
May, must be right, as *r.* to all *E.M.* i. 52

Relent.
All nature mourns, the Skies *r.* in show'rs *Sp.* 69

Relented.
Stern Proserpine *r. O.* i. 85

Relenting.
Amid that scene if some *r.* eye *E.A.* 355
Inscribe a verse on this *r.* stone *W.* 26

Relentless.
R. walls! whose darksome round contains *E.A.* 17
Stern Cato's self was no *r.* spouse *E.J.S.* 30
Since fate *r.* stopp'd their heav'nly voice *W.F.* 277

Relics, Reliques.
Glance on the stone where our cold *r.* lie *E.A.* 366
Thy *r.*, ROWE, to this fair Urn we trust *Ep.* v. 1
The ground, now sacred by thy *r—ques* made *U.L.* 68

Relief.
Then share thy pain, allow that sad *r. E.A.* 49
Yet take these Tears, Mortality's *r. Ep.* vii. 17
Not with such majesty, such bold *r. S.* v. 390
Ye Gods! and is there no *r.* for Love *Su.* 88

Relies.
One on his manly confidence *r. D.* ii. 169

Believe.
Come! with thy looks, thy words, *r.* my woe *E.A.* 319
Oh blameless Bethel! to *r.* thy breast *E.M.* iv. 126
Stretch'd to *r.* the Idiot and the Poor *S.* v. 226

Relieves.
Is any sick? the MAN of Ross *r. M.E.* iii. 269

Religion.
R. blushing veils her sacred fires *D.* iv. 649
There stern *R.* quench'd th' unwilling flame *E.A.* 39
Nature stands check'd; *R.* disapproves *E.A.* 259
R., Country, genius of his Age *E.C.* 121
Ye Statesmen, Priests, of one *R.* all *E.S.* ii. 16
And Atheism and *R.* take their turns *M.E.* ii. 66
Or Virtue, or *R.*, turn to sport *S.* v. 211

Religious.
R., punctual, frugal, and so forth *M.E.* iii. 343
Some hostile fury, some *r.* rage *M.E.* v. 12
Stranger to civil and *r.* rage *P.S.* 394

Relish.
He finds no *r.* in the sweetest meat *S.* ii. 32

Relish'd.
And but more *r.*, as the more distress'd *E.M.* iv. 318

Re-lum'd.
R. her ancient light, not kindled new *E.M.* iii. 287

Rely.
Think of those authors, Sir, who would *r. S.* v. 350

Remain.
What then remains? Ourself. Still, still *r. D.* i. 217
But now for Authors nobler palms *r. D.* ii. 191
And here, ev'n then, shall my cold dust *r. E.A.* 174
Scotists and Thomists, now, in peace *r. E.C.* 444
But if in noble minds some dregs *r. E.C.* 526
And where no wants, no wishes can *r. E.M.* iv. 325
Yet may this Verse (if such a V. *r.*) *E.S.* i. 171
Nature well known, no prodigies *r. M.E.* i. 208
To gaze on Basset, and *r.* unwarm'd *Mi.* ix. 76
Not half so fix'd the Trojan could *r. R.L.* v. 5
Did not some grave Examples yet *r. S.* v. 128
And splay-foot verse, remain'd, and will *r. S.* v. 271
The wanton victims of his sport *r. W.F.* 78

Remain'd.
Oh had I rather unadmir'd *r. R.L.* iv. 153
Or what *r.*, so worthy to be read *S.* v. 137
And splay-foot verse, *r.*, and will remain *S.* v. 271
But mere tuff-taffety what now *r. S.* viii. 42

Remaining.
Then see how little the *r.* sum *E.M.* ii. 51

Remains.
Or raise old warriors, whose ador'd *r. W.F.* 301
What then r.? Ourself. Still, still remain *D.* i. 217
Still in constraint your suff'ring Sex *r. E.* iv. 41
Itself unseen, but in th' effects, *r. E.C.* 79
But fix'd his word, his saving pow'r *r. M.* 107
What then *r.* but well our pow'r to use *R.L.* v. 29
For fainting Age what cordial drop *r. S.* ii. 89
No whiter page than Addison *r. S.* v. 216
There still *r.*, to mortify a Wit *S.* v. 314
A heap of dust alone *r.* of thee *U.L.* 73

Remark.
Plough'd was his front with many a deep *R. D.* iv. 204
Whom honour with your hand: to make r—s *S.* iv. 103
Ev'n in an ornament its place r. *M.E.* iv. 77

Remember.
R., Man, "the Universal Cause *E.M.* iv. 35
Yet ah! how once we lov'd, *r.* still *Ep.* xiii. 3
Don't you *r.* what reply he gave *S.* vi. 49

Rememb'ring.
R. she herself was Partness once *D.* i. 112

Remembers.
R. of the School-boy's simple fare *S.* i. 73

Remembrance.
R. and reflection how ally'd *E.M.* i. 225

Remnants.
See the poor *r.* of these slighted hairs *R.L.* iv. 167

Remorse.
The Critic else proceeds without *r. E.C.* 167

Remote.
Dim and *r.* the joys of saints I see *E.A.* 71
The hour conceal'd, and so *r.* the fear *E.M.* iii. 75
Till, by degrees, *r.* and small *O.* i. 18

Remove.
Ye trees that fade when autumn-heats *r. A.* 29
From shepherds, flocks, and plains, I may *r. A.* 87
Before true passion all these views *r. E.A.* 79
How the dear object from the crime *r. E.A.* 193
Provoking Dæmons all restraint *r. E.A.* 231
Silent and soft, as Saints *r.* to Heav'n *E.S.* i. 93
But does the Court a worthy Man *r. E.S.* ii. 74
Withers, adieu ! yet not with thee *r. Ep.* ix. 7
What *Drop* or *Nostrum* can this plague *r. P.S.* 29
And little sure imported to *r. S.* vi. 56
To closer shades the panting flocks *r. Su.* 87

Remov'd.
Such this Man was ; who now from earth *r. Ep.* ii. 11
R. from all th' Ambitious Scene *I.H.* ii. 27 *s*

Removes.
She but *r.* weak passions for the strong *E.M.* ii. 158
So when the Nightingale to rest *r. Sp.* 13

Remurmur.
Her fate *r.* to the silver flood *W.* 64

Rend.
Sound forth, my Brayers, and the welkin *r. D.* ii. 246
And screams of horror *r.* th' affrighted skies *R.L.* iii. 156
My hands shall *r.* what ev'n thy rapine spares *R.L.* iv. 168
R. with tremendous sound your ears asunder *S.* i. 27

Rending.
She from the *r.* earth and bursting skies *E.M.* iii. 253

Renew.
False steps but help them to *r.* the race *E.C.* 602
Annual for me, the grape, the rose *r. E.M.* i. 135
By land, by water, they *r.* the charge *P.S.* 9
Which never more its honours shall *r. R.L.* iv. 135

Renew'd.
R. by ordure's sympathetic force *D.* ii. 103

Renounce.
R. my love, my life, myself—and you *E.A.* 204
Forget, *r.* me, hate whate'er was mine *E.A.* 294
Yes, or we must *r.* the Stagirite *E.C.* 280
R. our Country, and degrade our Name *S.* iv. 125
I, who so oft *r.* the Muses, lie *S.* v. 175

Renown.
When simple *Macer*, now of high *r. Mi.* iii. 1
The Bard whom *pilfer'd Pastorals* r. *P.S.* 179

Renown'd.
In Lud's old walls tho' long I rul'd, *r. D.* iii. 277
The Kennet swift, for silver eels *r. W.F.* 341

Rent.
So bought an Annual *R.* or two *I.H.* i. 71
Who having lost his credit, pawn'd his *r. S.* viii. 138
The Chanc'ry takes your r—*s for twenty year S.* ii. 172
Dishonest sight ! his breeches r. below *D.* iii. 198
Full o'er their heads the swelling bag he *r. R.L.* iv. 91

Rented.
Than in five acres now of *r.* land *S.* ii. 136

Repair.
To Practice now from Theory *r. D.* iv. 580
Not mend their minds ; as some to Church *r. E.C.* 342
He must *r.* it ; takes a bribe from France *M.E.* iii. 396

Erect new wonders, and the old *r. M.E.* iv. 192
Thence, by a soft transition, we *r. R.L.* i. 49
The light Coquettes in Sylphs aloft *r. R.L.* i. 65
The lucid squadrons round the sails *r. R.L.* ii. 56
Haste, then, ye spirits ! to your charge *r. R.L.* ii. 111
Swift to the Lock a thousand Sprites *r. R.L.* iii. 135
Make Quays, build Bridges, or *r.* Whitehall *S.* ii. 120
To plains with well-breath'd beagles we *r. W.F.* 121
Let me, O let me, to the shades *r. W.F.* 201

Repair'd.
On once a flock-bed, but *r.* with straw *M.E.* iii. 301
R. to search the gloomy Cave of Spleen *R.L.* iv. 16

Repairs.
R. her smiles, awakens ev'ry grace *R.L.* i. 141
She said : then raging to Sir Plume *r. R.L.* iv. 121

Re-passes.
R. Lintot, vindicates the race *D.* ii. 107

Repast.
And frequent cups prolong the rich *r. R.L.* iii. 12
Not so : a Buck was then a week's *r. S.* ii. 93

Repeat.
R. unask'd ; lament, the Wit's too fine *S.* v. 366

Repeats.
Dulness, good Queen, *r.* the jest again *D.* ii. 122
With eyes that pry not, tongue that ne'er *r. S,* i. 135

Repent.
R. old pleasures, and solicit new *E.A.* 186
Alas ! 'tis ten times worse when they *r. P.S.* 108

Repentant.
R. sighs, and voluntary pains *E.A.* 18
Then turns *r.*, and his God adores *M.E.* i. 188

Repents.
Ev'n Ralph *r.*, and Henley writes no more *D.* i. 216

Repin'd.
What if the head, the eye, the ear *r. E.M.* i. 261

Repines.
While proud Philosophy *r.* to show *D.* iii. 197

Replenish'd.
R., not ingloriously, at home *D.* ii. 166
So clouds, *r.* from some bog below *D.* ii. 363

Replied, *see* Reply'd.

Replies.
" God save King Colley ! " Drury-lane *r. D.* i. 320
" Be that my task " (*r.* a gloomy Clerk *D.* iv. 459
" See man for mine ! " *r.* a pamper'd goose *E.M.* iii. 46
" The MAN of ROSS," each lisping babe *r. M.E.* iii. 262
Squeaks like a high-stretch'd lutestring, and *r. S.* viii. 99
Silent, or only to her name *r. W.* 42

Reply.
Don't you remember what *r.* he gave *S.* vi. 49
Loth to enrich me with too quick r—ies *S.* viii. 128
A God, a God, the vocal hills r. *M.* 31
Full ten years slander'd, did he once *r. P.S.* 374
The walls, the woods, and long canals *r. R.L.* iii. 100

Reply'd.
(*R.* soft Annius) " this our paunch before *D.* iv. 388
No, ('tis *r.*) the first Almighty Cause *E.M.* i. 145
As well his Grace *r.*, " Like you, Sir John *M.E.* iii. 317
While Hampton's echoes " Wretched maid ! " *r. R.L.* iv. 96
" It grieves me much." (*r.* the Peer again) *R.L.* iv. 131
Thus Daphnis spoke, and Strephon thus *r. Sp.* 22

Report.
There flies about a strange *r. I.H.* ii. 109 *s*
'Twas then, Belinda, if *r.* say true *R.L.* i. 117

Repose.
A death-like silence, and a dead *r. E.A.* 166
Thy life a long dead calm of fix'd *r. E.A.* 251
Yet hate *r.* and dread to be alone *M.E.* ii. 228
Who pants for glory finds but short *r. S.* v. 300
Your Arms, your Actions, your *r.* to sing *S.* v. 395

Thence to the banks where rev'rend Bards r. *D.* ii. 347
With thee r., where Tully once was laid *E.* iii. 29
When statesmen, heroes, kings, in dust r. *E.M.* iv. 387
Whose Seats the weary Traveller r. *M.E.* iii. 260
If I would scribble, rather than r. *S.* vi. 71

Repos'd.
On Dulness' lap th' Anointed head r. *D.* iii. 2

Reposing.
To rock the cradle of r. Age *P.S.* 409

Repress.
When to r., and when indulge her flights *E.C.* 53
Nor quite indulges, nor can quite r. *W.F.* 20

Repress'd.
License r., and useful laws ordain'd *E.C.* 682

Reproach.
Gone ev'ry blush, and silent all r. *D.* iv. 563
Walk to his grave without r. *Mi.* xii. 19
In vain Thalestris with r. assails *R.L.* v. 3

Reproof.
Those best can bear r., who merit praise *E.C.* 583

Reproves.
And Brutus tenderly r. *O.* iii. 8

Reptile.
A Cherub's face, a r. all the rest *P.S.* 331
Vile, r., weak, and vain *Mi.* iv. 6
Where all the Race of R—s *might embark S.* viii. 27

Republic.
The Ant's r., and the realm of Bees *E.M.* iii. 184

Reputation.
And authors think their r. safe *E.C.* 450
At ev'ry word a r. dies *R.L.* iii. 16

Repute.
To whom can Riches give *R.*, or Trust *E.M.* iv. 185

Request.
Consider, 'tis my first r. *I.H.* ii. 77 5
Oblig'd by hunger, and r. of friends *P.S.* 44

Require.
To tell 'em, would a hundred tongues r. *E.C.* 44
These equal syllables alone r. *E.C.* 344
The humbler Muse of Comedy r. *S.* v. 283

Requir'd.
And still the more we give, the more r. *E.C.* 503

Requires.
As much that end a constant course r. *E.M.* i. 151
Most strength the moving principle r. *E.M.* ii. 67
Shall burning Ætna, if a sage r. *E.M.* iv. 123
Admit your Law to spare the Knight r. *E.S.* ii. 30
Useful, I grant, it serves what life r. *M.E.* iii. 27

Resembles.
Music r. Poetry, in each *E.C.* 143

Resent.
How often hope, despair, r., regret *E.A.* 199

Resentment.
E'er felt such rage, r., and despair *R.L.* iv. 9

Reserve.
Amidst their virtues a r. of vice *E.J.S.* 20
R. with Frankness, Art with Truth ally'd *M.E.* ii. 277
But still the Great have kindness in r. *P.S.* 247
For Chartres' head r. the hanging wall *E.M.* iv. 130
Is Vice too high, r. it for the next *S.* i. 60

Reserv'd.
These Fate r. to grace thy reign divine *D.* iii. 275
Crowns were r. to grace the soldiers too *E.C.* 513
Alike r. to blame or to commend *P.S.* 205

Reservoir.
This year a r. to keep and spare *M.E.* iii. 173

Resign.
Here all its frailties, all its flames r. *E.A.* 175

Unequal task! a passion to r. *E.A.* 195
Thy oaths I quit, thy memory r. *E.A.* 293
Those joys, those loves, those int'rests to r. *E.M.* ii. 258
Extremely ready to r. *I.H.* i. 63
With ease the smiles of Fortune I r. *Mi.* ix. 14
Ease, pleasure, virtue, all our sex r. *R.L.* iv. 106
And then a nobler prize I will r. *Sp.* 91

Resign'd.
Relate who first, who last r. to rest *D.* iv. 621
Each pray'r accepted, and each wish r. *E.A.* 210
When what t' oblivion better were r. *E.M.* iv. 251
Sincere, tho' prudent; constant, yet r. *Ep.* ii. 2
R. to live, prepar'd to die *Mi.* xii. 1
R. to fate, and with a sigh retir'd *R.L.* iii. 146

Resigns.
Melody r. to Fate *Mi.* vii. 32

Resist.
What Mortal can r. the Yawn of Gods *D.* iv. 606

Resistless.
R. falls: the Muse obeys the Pow'r *D.* iv. 628
Trust not too much your now r. charms *E.* iv. 59
Truth breaks upon us with r. day *E.C.* 212
Bursts out, r., with a thund'ring tide *E.C.* 630

Resolution.
I hope it is your *R. I.H.* i. 43

Resolve.
R. me, Reason, which of these is worse *M.E.* iii. 319

Resolv'd.
R. to win, he meditates the way *R.L.* ii. 31

Resolves.
The heart r. this matter in a trice *S.* vi. 216

Resort.
Hither the heroes and the nymphs r. *R.L.* iii. 9

Resound.
R., ye hills, r. my mournful lay *A.* 57 &c.
No more, ye hills, no more r. my strains *A.* 96
Far as loud Bow's stupendous bells r. *D.* ii. 278
Blue Neptune storms, the bellowing deeps r. *R.L.* v. 50
And Albion's cliffs r. the rural lay *Sp.* 6
Invoke the Muses, and r. your praise *Su.* 78

Resounding.
In the same temple, the r. wood *E.M.* iii. 155

Resounds.
"Smedley" in vain r. thro' all the coast *D.* ii. 294
And rapid Severn hoarse applause r. *M.E.* iii. 252
Hark! Hæmus r. with the Bacchanals' cries *O.* i. 111

Respect.
Wise Peter sees the World's r. for Gold *M.E.* iii. 123
Walk with r. behind, while we at ease *S.* vi. 141
They treat themselves with most profound r. *S.* vi. 154

Respecting.
R. Man, whatever wrong we call *E.M.* i. 51

Respire.
And see! the tortur'd ghosts r. *O.* i. 64

Rest.
The r. on Out-side merit but presume *D.* i. 135
In Shadwell's bosom with eternal *R. D.* i. 240
A peck of coals a-piece shall glad the r. *D.* ii. 282
And Milbourn chief, deputed by the r. *D.* ii. 349
Like motion, from one circle to the r. *D.* ii. 408
Low bow'd the r.: He, Kingly, did but nod *D.* iv. 207
And breaks our r. to tell us what's a-clock *D.* iv. 444
Thy *Magus*, Goddess I shall perform the r. *D.* iv. 516
Relate, who first, who last resign'd to r. *D.* iv. 621
Clos'd one by one to everlasting r. *D.* iv. 638
As smiling Infants sport themselves to r. *E.* iv. 14
Let tears, and burning blushes speak the r. *E.A.* 106
Give all thou canst—and let me dream the r. *E.A.* 124
Or lull to r. the visionary maid *E.A.* 162
Labour and r., that equal periods keep *E.A.* 211
Receive, and wrap me in eternal r. *E.A.* 302
Thither, where sinners may have r., I go *E.A.* 319
And urg'd the r. by equal steps to rise *E.C.* 97

In all the *r.*, so impudently good *E. 7.S.* 48
But strength of mind is Exercise, not *R. E.M.* ii. 104
Like Aaron's serpent, swallows up the *r. E.M.* ii. 132
Thus let the wiser make the *r.* obey *E.M.* iii. 196
More pow'rful each as needful to the *r. E.M.* iii. 299
Some are, and must be, greater than the *r. E.M.* iv. 50
What shocks one part will edify the *r. E.M.* iv. 141
The *r.* is all but leather or prunella *E.M.* iv. 204
And strongest motive to assist the *r. E.M.* iv. 352
Sets half the world, God knows, against the *r. E.S.* i. 58
And hail her passage to the Realms of *R. E.S.* i. 81
Once break their *r.*, or stir them from their Place *E.S.* i. 100
And begg'd he'd take the pains to kick the *r. E.S.* i. 155
Fix'd to one side, yet mod'rate to the *r. Ep.* ii. 4
Eat some, and pocket up the *r. I.H.* i. 26
This clue once found, unravels all the *r. M.E.* i. 178
Your love of Pleasure, our desire of *R. M.E.* ii. 274
Lo some are Vellum, and the *r.* as good *M.E.* iv. 137
And without sneering, teach the *r.* to sneer *P.S.* 202
A Cherub's face, a reptile all the *r. P.S.* 331
Thus far was right, the *r.* belongs to Heav'n *P.S.* 419
Her guardian SYLPH proloog'd the balmy *r. R.L.* i. 20
The *r.*, the winds dispers'd in empty air *R.L.* ii. 46
The *r.* his many-colour'd robe conceal'd *R.L.* iii. 58
Or rather truly, if your point be *r. S.* i. 17
The Robin-red-breast till of late had *r. S.* ii. 37
The *r.*, some farm the Poor-box, some the Pews *S.* iii. 128
Your People, Sir, are partial in the *r. S.* v. 32
Patient of labour when the end was *r. S.* v. 242
So when the Nightingale to *r.* removes *Sp.* 13
Above the *r.* a rural nymph was fam'd *W.F.* 171
The grave unites; where ev'n the great find *r. W.F.* 317
Where wretched Withers, Ward, and Gildon *r. D.* i. 296
Aim not at Joy, but *r.* content with Ease *E.* iv. 48
Dear fatal name! *r.* ever unreveal'd *E.A.* 9
He hangs between; in doubt to act or *r. E.M.* ii. 7
Here then we *r.*:—"The Universal Cause *E.M.* iii. 1
Here, WITHERS, *r.!* thou bravest, gentlest mind *Ep.* ix. 1
Ah spare me, Venus! let me, let me *r. I.H.* iii. 2
The young who labour, and the old who *r. M.E.* iii. 268
To *r.*, the Cushion and soft Dean invite *M.E.* iv. 149
This is my plea, on this I *r.* my cause *S.* i. 141
Still, still be printing, never, never *r. S.* iv. 96
There while you *r.* in Amaranthine bow'rs *W.* 73

Restless.
She saw old Pryn in *r.* Daniel shine *D.* i. 103
Those *r.* passions in revenge inspires *E.A.* 82
And Curio, *r.* by the Fair-one's side *M.E.* v. 43
Why, of two brothers, rich and *r.* one *S.* vi. 270

Restore.
Still her old Empire to *r.* she tries *D.* i. 17
See, to my country happy I *r. D.* iv. 329
Poet or Patriot, rose but to *r. E.M.* iii. 285
Jones and Palladio to themselves *r. M.E.* iv. 193
R., *r.* Eurydice to life *O.* i. 81
"*R.* the Lock!" she cries; and all around (*rep.*) *R.L.* v. 103

Restor'd.
Ye Pow'rs! whose Mysteries *r.* I sing *D.* iv. 5
Lo! thy dread Empire, CHAOS! is *r. D.* iv. 653
And here *r.* Wit's fundamental laws *E.C.* 722
Was sheath'd, and *Luxury* with *Charles r. S.* v. 140

Restorer.
Oh great *R.* of the good old Stage *D.* iii. 205

Restores.
Fancy *r.* what vengeance snatch'd away *E.A.* 226

Restrain.
Oh spread thy Influence, but *r.* thy Rage *D.* iii. 122
Nor pray'rs nor fasts its stubborn pulse *r. E.A.* 27
Barbarian, stay! that bloody stroke *r. E.A.* 103
R. his fury, than provoke his speed *E.C.* 85
'Tis best sometimes your censure to *r. E.C.* 596
Self-love to urge, and Reason to *r. E.M.* ii. 54
His safety must his liberty *r. E.M.* iv. 277
Gums and Pomatums shall his flight *r. R.L.* ii. 129

Restrain'd.
But sober History *r.* her rage *D.* iii. 39
Nature, like liberty, is but *r. E.C.* 90

Restrains.
When the proud steed shall know why Man *r. E.M.* i. 61

Each strengthens Reason, and Self-love *r. E.M.* ii. 80
Of what *r.* him, Government and Laws *E.M.* iii. 272

Restraint.
Provoking Dæmons all *r.* remove *E.A.* 231

Rests.
R. and expatiates in a life to come *E.M.* i. 98
No cavern'd Hermit, *r.* self-satisfy'd *E.M.* iv. 42
Here *r.* a Woman, good without pretence *Ep.* vi. 1
Ixion *r.* upon his wheel *O.* i. 67
So peaceful *r.*, without a stone, a name *U.L.* 69

Result.
But the joint force and full *r.* of all *E.C.* 246

Resumes.
My mind *r.* the thread it dropt before *S.* vi. 207

Retails.
By names of Toasts *r.* each batter'd jade *D.* ii. 134

Retain.
The shady empire shall *r.* no trace *W.F.* 371

Retentive.
Long Chanc'ry-lane *r.* rolls the sound *D.* ii. 263

Retire.
Here all his suff'ring brotherhood *r. D.* i. 143
Then southward let your Bard *r. I.H.* i. 17
To their first Elements their Souls *r. R.L.* i. 58

Retir'd.
The decent Knight *r.* with sober rage *D.* i. 113
Resign'd to fate, and with a sigh *r. R.L.* iii. 146
Our Gen'rals oow, *r.* to their Estates *S.* iii. 7
Thus Atticus, and Trumbal thus *r. W.F.* 258

Retires.
From thy Bœotia tho' her Pow'r *r. D.* ii. 5
Where, from Ambrosia, Jove *r.* for ease *D.* ii. 84
Ev'n here, where frozen chastity *r. E.A.* 181
Collects her breath, as ebbing life *r. M.E.* i. 244
So quick *r.* each flying course, you'd swear *M.E.* iv. 159
The fox obscene to gaping tombs *r. W.F.* 71
Happy next him, who to these shades *r. W.F.* 237
There purple Vengeance bath'd in gore *r. W.F.* 417

Retiring.
Contracted all, *r.* to their breast *E.M.* ii. 103

Retouch.
Not, Sir, if you revise it, and *r. P.S.* 64

Retreat.
(Haunt of the Muses) made their safe *r. D.* ii. 428
In vain to Deserts thy *r.* is made *E.* i. 27
Why rove my thoughts beyond this last *r. E.A.* 5
Oft in the clear, still Mirror of *R. E.S.* ii. 78
Not therefore humble he who seeks *r. M.E.* ii. 113
But Wisdom's triumph is well-tim'd *R. M.E.* ii. 225
There, my *r.* the best Companions grace *S.* i. 125
Shades, that to Bacon could *r.* afford *S.* ii. 175
The Man, who stretch'd in Isis' calm *r. S.* vi. 116
A soft *r.* from sudden vernal show'rs *Sp.* 98
The mossy fountains, and the green r.—s. Su. 72
Thy forests, Windsor! and thy green *r. W.F.* 1
'Tis yours, my Lord, to bless our soft *r. W.F.* 283
In their loose traces from the field r. A. 62
Yet always wishing to *r. I.H.* ii. 127
Ask why from Britain Cæsar would *r. M.E.* i. 129
The lowing herds to murm'ring brooks *r. Su.* 86

Retrench.
Can I *r.?* Yes, mighty well *I.H.* i. 75

Retrospective.
In vain the Sage, with *r.* eye *M.E.* i. 99

Return.
Of all thy blameless life the sole *r. P.S.* 259
Just Gods! shall all things yield r—s but love A. 76
With sure *r.* of still expected rhymes *E.C.* 349
Mem'ry and fore-cast just *r.* engage *E.M.* iii. 143
Soon to that mass of Nonsense to r. D. i. 241
And courts to courts *r.* it round and round *D.* ii. 264
And answ'ring gin-shops sourer sighs *r. D.* iii. 148
Might he *r.*, and bless once more our eyes *E.C.* 462
They rise, they break, and to that sea *r. E.M.* iii. 20

Oh take the husband, or *r.* the wife *O.* i. 82
R. well-travell'd, and transform'd to Beasts *S.* iv. 123

Return'd.
But soon the cloud *r.*—and thus the Sire *D.* iii. 227
And he *r.* a friend, who came a foe *E.M.* iii. 206
And the press'd watch *r.* a silver sound *R.L.* i. 18

Returning.
R. Justice lift aloft her scale *M.* 18

Returns.
Amus'd he reads, and then *r.* the bills *D.* ii. 91
He buoys up instant and *r.* to light *D.* ii. 296
Lo! ev'ry finish'd Son *r.* to thee *D.* iv. 500
The merchant from th' Exchange *r.* in peace *R.L.* iii. 23

Reveal.
The fault he has I fairly shall *r. S.* vi. 19

Reveal'd.
In broad Effulgence all below *r. D.* iv. 18
R., and God's eternal day be thine *M.* 104
To Maids alone and Children are *r. R.L.* i. 38
Puts forth one manly leg, to sight *r. R.L.* iii. 57

Reveals.
But heav'n *r.* not what, or how, or where *R.L.* i. 111

Revelation.
Some *R.* hid from you and me *M.E.* iii. 114

Revenge.
Those restless passions in *r.* inspires *E.A.* 82
Whose attributes were Rage, *R.*, or Lust *E.M.* iii. 258
Who breaks with her, provokes *R.* from Hell *M.E.* ii. 129
Between *r.*, and grief, and hunger join'd *S.* vi. 38

Reveng'd.
And France *r.* of ANNE's and EDWARD's arms *M.E.* iii. 144

Revere.
Nor less *r.* him, blunderbuss of Law *D.* iii. 150
A perjur'd Prince a leaden Saint *r. M.E.* i. 89

Rever'd.
Deep in his Entrails—I *r.* them there *D.* iv. 384
Whom they *r.* as God to mourn as Man *E.M.* iii. 224
Behold, four Kings in majesty *r. R.L.* iii. 37
Whose Word is Truth, as sacred and *r. S.* v. 27

Rev'rence.
Walker, with *r.* took, and laid aside *D.* iv. 206
In *r.* to the Sins of Thirty-nine *E.S.* ii. 5
With *r.*, hope, and love *O.* iii. 36
He takes the gift with *r.*, and extends *R.L.* iii. 131

Rev'rend.
Thence to the banks where *r.* Bards repose (*rep.*) *D.* ii. 347
The *r.* Flamen in his lengthen'd dress *D.* ii. 354
Rosy and *r.*, tho' without a Gown *D.* iv. 496
Shakes off the dust, and rears his *r.* head *E.C.* 700
In *r.* Bishops note some *small Neglects E.S.* i. 16
Ye *r.* Atheists—Scandal! name them! Who *E.S.* ii. 18
Behold a *r.* sire, whom want of grace *M.E.* i. 232
A few grey hairs his *r.* temples crown'd *M.E.* iii. 327
As her dead Father's *r.* image past *P.C.* 31
How pale, each Worshipful and *R.* guest *S.* ii. 75
Tho' coarse, was *r.*, and tho' bare, was black *S.* viii. 39
Old father Thames advanc'd his *r.* head *W.F.* 330

Rev'rent.
R. I touch thee! but with honest zeal *E.S.* ii. 216

Reverential.
All, all look up, with *r.* Awe *E.S.* i. 167

Reverse.
And then mistook *r.* of wrong for right *M.E.* iii. 198
Prone for his fav'rites to r. *his laws E.M.* iv. 122
Or Affectations quite *r.* the soul *M.E.* i. 66
R. your Ornaments, and hang them all *M.E.* iv. 31

Reversion.
Or quicken'd a *R.* by a drug *S.* viii. 135
Is there no bright *r.* in the sky *U.L.* 9

Review.
How oft *r.*; each finding like a friend *E.* iii. 21

Reviews.
The skilful Nymph *r.* her force with care *R.L.* iii. 45

Revise.
Not, Sir, if you *r.* it, and retouch *P.S.* 64

Revive.
When Dulcess, smiling—"Thus *r.* the Wits *D.* iv. 119
Then Sculpture and her sister-arts *r. E.C.* 701
In downright charity *r.* the dead *S.* vi. 164

Reviv'd.
A vast, vamp'd, future, old, *r.*, new piece *D.* i. 284
The tale *r.*, the lie so oft o'erthrown *P.S.* 350
But at her smile, the Beau *r.* again *R.L.* v. 70
Are these *r.*? or is it Granville sings *W.F.* 282

Revives.
A breath *r.* him, or a breath o'erthrows *S.* v. 301

Revolves.
Much she *r.* their arts, their ancient praise *D.* i. 97

Reward.
Which seeks no int'rest, no *r.* but praise *E.M.* ii. 246
What then? is the *r.* of Virtue bread *E.M.* iv. 150
Or are they both, in this their own *r. M.E.* iii. 336
Gave him much praise, and some *r.* beside *S.* vi. 43
These write to Lords, some mean *r.* to get *S.* viii. 25
Like are their merits, like r—s *they share D.* iii. 183
Of old, those met *r.* who could excel *E.C.* 510
R., that either would to Virtue bring *E.M.* iv. 181
Are no *r.* for want and infamy *S.* ii. 104
More honours, more *r.*, attend the brave *S.* vi. 48
And all who know those Dunces to r. *D.* ii. 26
Weak, foolish Man! will Heav'n *r.* us there *E.M.* iv. 173
And shall not Britain now *r.* his toils *M.E.* iii. 215

Rewards.
And what *r.* your Virtue, punish mine *E.M.* iv. 144
See how the World its Veterans *r. M.E.* ii. 243

Reynard.
Faith, I shall give the answer *R.* gave *S.* iii. 114

Rhet'ric.
There, stript, fair *R.* languish'd on the ground *D.* iv. 24

Rhine.
Or on the Rubicon, or on the *R. E.M.* iv. 246
And scarce are seen the prostrate Nile or *R. M.E.* v. 28
And groves of lances glitter on the *R. W.F.* 364

Rhodope.
Amidst *R.*'s snows *O.* i. 109

Rhyme.
Maggots half-form'd in *r.* exactly meet *D.* i. 61
Some strain in *r.*; the Muses on their racks *D.* iii. 159
Some free from *r.* or reason, rule or check *D.* iii. 161
Plague with Dispute, or persecute with *R. D.* iv. 260
Then from the Mint walks forth the Man of *r. P.S.* 13
Slides into verse, and hitches in *r. S.* i. 78
Or tir'd in search of Truth, or search of *R. S.* ii. 86
But most of all, the Zeal of Fools in *r. S.* v. 407
What will it leave me, if it snatch my *r. S.* vi. 77
Where vile Mundungus trucks for viler r.—*s D.* i. 234
This, this is he, foretold by ancient *r. D.* iii. 319
Not plagu'd with head-aches, or the want of *r. E.* v. 42
With sure returns of still expected *r. E.C.* 349
Leave such to tune their own dull *r.*, and know *E.C.* 358
Short is the date, alas, of modern *r. E.C.* 476
Or spite, or smut, or *r.*, or blasphemies *P.S.* 322
A man was hang'd for very honest *r. S.* i. 146
The *R.* or Rattles of the Man or Boy *S.* iii. 18
Know, there are *R.*, which fresh and fresh apply'd *S.* iii. 59
To know the Poet from the Man of *r. S.* v. 341
With r. *of this per cent.*, and that *per year S.* vii. 56
And pay'd for all my satires, all my *r. S.* viii. 6
And r. *with all the rage of Impotence E.C.* 609
Like Lee or Budgel, I will *r.* and print *S.* i. 100
And promise our best Friends to *r.* no more *S.* v. 178
All *r.*, and scrawl, and scribble, to a man *S.* v. 188
D'ye think me good for nothing but to *r. S.* vi. 36
Again to *r.*, can London be the place *S.* vi. 89
How shall I *r.* in this eternal roar *S.* vi. 114

Rhym'd.
Who r. for hire, and patroniz'd for pride *D.* iv. 102
Has drunk with *Cibber*, nay has r. for *Moore P.S.* 373
No rat is r. to death, nor maid to love *S.* vii. 22

Rhymers.
In vain bad *R.* all mankind reject *S.* vi. 153

Rhymes.
R. ere he wakes, and prints before *Term* ends *P.S.* 43

Rhyming.
In twice ten thousand r. nights and days *D.* iv. 172
A maudlin Poetess, a r. Peer *P.S.* 16
This jealous, waspish, wrong-head, r., race *S.* vi. 148
Call, if you will, bad r. a disease *S.* vi. 182

Ribs.
Tho' stiff with hoops, and arm'd with r. of whale *R.L.* ii. 120

Ribalds.
Yet ne'er one sprig of laurel grac'd those r. *P.S.* 163

Ribaldry.
Chaucer's worst r. is learn'd by rote *S.* v. 37

Riband, Ribbands, Ribbons.
And lovers' hearts with ends of r. bound *R.L.* v. 118
To sigh for *ribb—s* if thou art so silly *E.M.* iv. 277
Chequer'd with r—*ons* blue and green *I.H.* iv. 49 s

Rich.
Immortal *R.!* how calm he sits at ease *D.* iii. 261
Swear like a Lord, or *R.* out-whore a Duke *E.S.* i. 116
'Twas on the day when * * r. and grave *D.* i. 85
Be r. in ancient brass, tho' not in gold *D.* iv. 365
The shining robes, r. jewels, beds of state *E.* iv. 51
The r. is happy in the plenty giv'n *E,M.* ii. 264
More r., more wise; but who infers from hence *E.M.* iv. 51
There, in the r., the honour'd, fam'd, and great *E.M.* iv. 287
Are they not r.? What more can they pretend *E.S.*ii.114
That Jelly's r., this Malmsey's healing *I.H.* ii. 202
To cram the *R.* was prodigal expense *M.E.* iii. 185
And r. and poor makes all the history *M.E.* iii. 288
And tempts by making r., not making poor *M.E.* iii. 352
And two r. ship-wrecks bless the lucky shore *M.E.* iii. 366
The r. Buffet well-colour'd Serpents grace *M.E.* iv. 153
The things, we know, are neither r. nor rare *P.S.* 171
And just as r. as when he serv'd a QUEEN *P.S.* 417
And frequent cups prolong the r. repast *R.L.* iii. 112
Trembling, and conscious of the r. brocade *R.L.* iii. 116
Or when r. China vessels fall'n from high *R.L.* iii. 159
On the r. quilt sinks with becoming woe *R.L.* iv. 35
Tim'rous by nature, of the r. in awe *S.* i. 7
Yes, while I live, no r. or noble knave *S.* i. 119
And the r. feast concludes extremely poor *S.* ii. 34
Some win r. Widows by their Chine and Brawn *S.*iii.131
Transform themselves so strangely as the *R. S.* iii. 153
R. ev'n when plunder'd, honour'd while oppress'd *S.* iii. 182
Weds the r. Dulness of some Son of earth *S.* iv. 43
Upon my word, you must be r. indeed *S.* iv. 90
Has seiz'd the Court and City, poor and r. *S.* v. 170
R. with the treasures of each foreign tongue *S.* vi. 173
Why, of two brothers, r. and restless one *S.* vi. 270
Like nets or lime-twigs, for r. Widows' hearts *S.* vii. 58
Like r. old wardrobes, things extremely rare *S.* vii. 123
So weak a vessel, and so r. a prize *S.* viii. 229
O'er golden sands let r. Pactolus flow *Sp.* 61
No r. perfumes refresh the fruitful field *W.* 47
R. Industry sits smiling on the plains *W.F.* 41
No seas so r., no banks so duly appear *W.F.* 225

Richard.
It stands on record, that in *R.'s* times *S.* i. 145

Rich'lieu.
What *R.* wanted, *Louis* scarce could gain *E.S.* ii. 116

Richer.
Feed fairer flocks, or r. fleeces shear *Su.* 36

Riches.
But grant him *R.*, your demand is o'er *E.M.* iv. 157
To whom can *R.* give Repute or Trust *E.M.* iv. 185

Make but his *R.* equal to his Wit *I.H.* iii. 18
Both fairly owning, *R.*, in effect *M.E.* iii. 17
What *R.* give us let us then enquire *M.E.* iii. 79
R., like insects, when conceal'd they lie *M.E.* iii. 169
The Sense to value *R.*, with the Art *M.E.* iii. 219
To gain those *R.* he can ne'er enjoy *M.E.* iv. 2
R. that vex, and Vanities that tire *Mi.* v. 4
For Fame, for *R.*, for a noble Wife *S.* iv. 39

Richest.
Dipt in the r. tincture of the skies *R.L.* ii. 65
And which not done, the r. must be poor *S.* iii. 46

Richly.
The Presence seems, with things so r. odd *S.* viii. 238

Rid.
How many stages thro' old Monks she r. *D* iii. 52

Riddle.
The glory, jest, and r. of the world *E.M.* ii. 18

Riddler.
Each Songster, *R.*, ev'ry nameless name *D.* iii. 157

Rids.
And while on Fame's triumphal Car they r. *D.* iv. 133
And Cupids r. the Lion of the Deeps *D.* iv. 308

Rides.
R. in the whirlwind, and directs the storm *D.* iii. 264

Ridicule.
How quick Ambition hastes to r. *D.* iv. 347
Judicious Wits spread wide the *R. E.S.* i. 61
Yet touch'd and sham'd by *R.* alone *E.S.* ii. 211
Sacred to *R.* his whole life long *S.* i. 79
Than r. all Taste, blaspheme Quadrille *S.* i. 38

Ridicules.
Yet is, whate'er she hates and r. *M.E.* ii. 120
And r. beyond a hundred foes *P.S.* 110
A vile Encomium doubly r. *S.* v. 410

Ridiculous.
Alive, r., and dead, forgot *M.E.* ii. 248

Ridiculously.
A friend in glee, r. grim *D.* iii. 154

Ridotta.
R. sips and dances, till she see *S.* i. 47

Ridpath.
To dulness *R.* is as dear as Mist *D.* i. 208
There *R.*, Roper, cudgell'd might ye view *D.* ii. 149

Rifted.
On r. rocks, the dragon's late abodes *M.* 71

Right.
Dulness possess'd o'er all her ancient r. *D.* i. 11
This Box my Thunder, this r. hand my God *D.* i. 202
To cavil, censure, dictate, r. or wrong *D.* i. 377
R. well mine eyes arede the myster wight *D.* iii. 187
The *R.* DIVINE of Kings to govern wrong *D.* iv. 188
Till drown'd was Sense, and Shame, and *R.*, and Wrong *D.* iv. 625
The lines, tho' touch'd but faintly, are drawn r. *E.C.* 22
You then whose judgment the r. course would steer *E.C.* 118
If once r. reason drives that cloud away *E.C.* 211
And smooth or rough, with them is r. or wrong *E.C.* 338
By chance go r., they purposely go wrong *E.C.* 427
But always think the last opinion r. *E.C.* 431
Whose r. it is, uncensur'd, to be dull *E.C.* 589
Not dully prepossess'd, nor blindly r. *E.C.* 634
And Boileau still in r. of Horace sways *E.C.* 714
May, must be r., as relative to all *E.M.* i. 52
In both, to reason r. is to submit *E.M.* i. 164
One truth is clear, WHATEVER IS, IS R. *E.M.* i. 294
The bard inhabitant contends is r. *E.M.* i. 230
One must go r., the other may go wrong *E.M.* iii. 94
And r., too rigid, harden into wrong *E.M.* iii. 193
Man, like his Maker, saw that all was r. *E.M.* iii. 232
For Nature knew no r. divine in Man *E.M.* iii. 236
He can't be wrong whose life is in the r. *E.M.* iii. 305
There needs but thinking r., and meaning well *E.M.* iv.

RIGHTEOUS—RISE.

Who risk the most, that take wrong means, or *r. E.M.*
iv. 86
WHATEVER IS, IS *R.*—This world, 'tis true *E.M.* iv. 145
Shew'd erring Pride, WHATEVER IS, IS *R. E.M.* iv. 394
And to be kept in my *r.* wits *I.H.* ii. 22 s
A Country Mouse, *r.* hospitable *I.H.* ii. 158
Some gen'ral maxims, or be *r.* by chance *M.E.* i. 4
Some flying stroke alone can hit 'em *r. M.E.* ii. 154
And then mistook reverse of wrong for *r. M.E.* iii. 199
Dame *Justice* weighing long the doubtful *R. Mi.* xi. 7
Of all mad creatures if the learn'd are *r. P.S.* 105
If wrong, I smil'd ; if *r.*, I kiss'd the rod *P.S.* 158
Commas and points they set exactly *r. P.S.* 161
Thus far was *r.*, the rest belongs to Heav'n *P.S.* 419
"*R.*," cries his Lordship, "for a rogue in need *S.* ii. 111
What *r.*, what true, what fit we justly call *S.* iii. 19
And shall we deem him Ancient, *r.* and sound *S.* v. 58
For *R.* Hereditary tax'd and fin'd *S.* vi. 64
If I am *r.*, thy grace impart (*rep.*) *U.P.* 29
Where Heav'n's *free subjects might their* r—s *dispute*
E.C. 548
The *R.* a Court attack'd, a Poet sav'd *S.* v. 224

Righteous.

That *r.* Abel was destroy'd by Cain *E.M.* iv. 118
No, 'twas thy *r.* end, asham'd to see *M.E.* iii. 147

Rightly.

Pleasure, or wrong or *r.* understood *E.M.* ii. 91
God sends not ill ; if *r.* understood *E.M.* iv. 113
Tho' many a passenger he *r.* call *M.E.* i. 7

Rigid.

And right, too *r.*, harden into wrong *E.M.* iii. 193

Rill.

The whisp'ring Zephyr and the purling *r. E.M.* i. 204
And pointed Crystals break the sparkling *R. Mi.* x. 4
The grots that echo to the tinkling r—s *E.A.* 158
And there the streams in purer *r.* descend *E.M.* iii. 204
With silver-quiv'ring *r.* mæander'd o'er *M.E.* iv. 83

Rind.

Oft on the *r.* I carv'd her am'rous vows *A.* 67
He ate himself the *r.* and paring *I.H.* ii. 170

Ring.

The heroes sit, the vulgar form a *r. D.* ii. 384
She glares in Balls, front Boxes, and the *R. E.* iv. 53
For her the Spouse prepares the bridal *r. E.A.* 219
That Charm shall grow, while what fatigues the *R. M.E.*
ii. 251
Or just as gay, at Council, in a *r. M.E.* iii. 309
Hang o'er the Box, and hover round the *R. R.L.* i. 44
Oft as in airy r—s *they skim the heath W.F.* 131
Hear, in all tongues consenting Pæans r. *E.C.* 186
While they *r.* round the same unvary'd chimes *E.C.* 348
Tho' with the Stoic Chief our stage may *r. E.J.S.* 37
Between each act the trembling salvers *r. M.E.* iv. 161
With sounds seraphic *r. O.* v. 15
The woods shall answer, and their echo *r. Su.* 16
No more the forests *r.*, or groves rejoice *W.F.* 278

Ringlets.

With shining *r.* the smooth iv'ry neck *R.L.* ii. 22
Some thrid the mazy *r.* of her hair *R.L.* ii. 139
These in two sable *r.* taught to break *R.L.* iv. 169

Rings.

And "Bernard! Bernard!" *r.* thro' all the Strand *D.* ii. 74
Heav'n *r.* with laughter. Of the laughter vain *D.* ii. 121
And all Olympus *r.* with loud alarms *R.L.* v. 48
But hark! the groves rejoice, the forest *r. W.F.* 281

Riot.

The lamb thy *r.* dooms to bleed to-day *E.M.* i. 81
'*Tis thus we* r., *while, who sow it, starve M.E.* iii. 24

Riots.

No pulse that *r.*, and no blood that glows *E.A.* 252

Ripe.

Tho' stale, not *r.*; tho' thin, yet never clear *D.* iii. 170
When the *r.* colours soften and unite *E.C.* 488
Sylvia's like autumn *r.*, yet mild as May *Sp.* 81

Ripen'd.

The last, scarce *r.* into perfect Man *E.M.* iii. 141
And famish'd dies amidst his *r.* fields *W.F.* 56

Ripeness.

Thou gav'st that *R.*, which so soon began *D.* iv. 287
Rank as the *r.* of a rabbit's tail *S.* ii. 28

Rip'ning.

And Phœbus warm the *r.* ore to gold *W.F.* 396

Ripens.

But *r.* spirits in cold northern climes *E.C.* 401
And *r.* Spirits as he *r.* Mines *M.E.* ii. 290

Riper.

Scarfs, garters, gold, amuse his *r.* stage *E.M.* ii. 279
Till grown more frugal in his *r.* days *P.S.* 241

Ripley.

See under *R.* rise a new White-hall *D.* iii. 327
And needs no rod but *R.* with a rule *M.E.* iv. 18
Should *R.* venture, all the world would smile *S.* v. 186

Rise.

First from a Worm they take their *R. Mi.* iv. 19
Here, where the mountains less'ning as they *r. A.* 59
Sees momentary monsters *r.*, and fall *D.* i. 83
O! when shall *r.* a Monarch all our own *D.* i. 311
There rival flames with equal glory *r. D.* iii. 80
Embody'd dark, what clouds of Vandals *r. D.* iii. 86
I look'd, and saw a sable Sorc'rer *r. D.* iii. 233
The forests dance, the rivers upward *r. D.* iii. 245
New wizards *r.*; I see my Cibber there *D.* iii. 260
See under Ripley *r.* a new White-hall *D.* iii. 327
See other Cæsars, other Homers *r. D.* iv. 360
True, he had wit, to make their value *r. D.* iv. 377
And as she turns, the colours fall or *r. D.* iv. 540
See Coronations *r.* on ev'ry green *E.* v. 34
Or sees the blush of soft Parthenia *r. E.* v. 46
Alas, how chang'd! what sudden horrors *r. E.A.* 99
R. in the grove, before the altar *r. E.A.* 265
R. Alps between us! and whole oceans roll *E.A.* 290
From the full choir when in loud Hosannas *r. E.A.* 353
And urg'd the rest by equal steps to *r. E.C.* 97
Which out of nature's common order *r. E.C.* 157
And *r.* to faults true Critics dare not mend *E.C.* 160
New distant scenes of endless science *r. E.C.* 224
And bid alternate passions fall and *r. E.C.* 375
(Her guide now lost) no more attempts to *r. E.C.* 737
And catch the Manners living as they *r. E.M.* i. 14
And all that rises, *r.* in due degree *E.M.* i. 46
Seas roll to waft me, suns to light me *r. E.M.* i. 139
Created half to *r.*, and half to fall *E.M.* ii. 15
Who saw its fires here *r.*, and there descend *E.M.* ii. 37
Uncheck'd may *r.*, and climb from art to art *E.M.* ii. 40
And when in act they cease, in prospect *r. E.M.* ii. 124
See ! and confess, one comfort still must *r. E.M.* ii. 293
They *r.*, they break, and to that sea return *E.M.* iii. 20
And still new needs, new helps, new habits *r. E.M.* iii.
137
Saw Gods descend, and fiends infernal *r. E.M.* iii. 254
Oh sons of earth ! attempt ye still to *r. E.M.* iv. 73
Honour and shame from no Condition *r. E.M.* iv. 193
Must *r.* from Individual to the Whole *E.M.* iv. 362
To fall with dignity, with temper *r. E.M.* iv. 376
Stop ! stop ! Must Satire then nor *r.* nor fall *E.S.* ii. 52
Let *Flatt'ry* sick'ning see the Incense *r. E.S.* ii. 244
Swift fly the years, and *r.* th' expected morn *M.* 21
See spicy clouds from lowly Sarum *r. M.* 27
Sink down ye mountains, and ye valleys *r. M.* 34
No more shall nation against nation *r. M.* 57
Then palaces shall *r.*; the joyful Son *M.* 63
See lilies spring, and sudden verdure *r. M.* 68
R., crown'd with light, imperial Salem, *r. M.* 85
And Temple *r.*—then fall again to dust *M.E.* ii. 140
He thinks a Loaf will *r.* to fifty pound *M.E.* ii. 116
R., honest Muse! and sing the MAN of Ross *M.E.* iii.
250
Who taught that heav'n-directed spire to *r. M.E.* iii. 261
That tells the Waters or to *r.*, or fall *M.E.* iv. 58
Her Gods, and god-like Heroes *r.* to view *M.E.* v. 47
Such, such emotions should in *Britons r. Mi.* ii. 9
And greater Gain would *r. Mi.* iv. 30
R., pensive Nymph, the *Tattler* waits for you *Mi.* ix. 3
My Passions *r.*, and will not hear the rein *Mi.* ix. 84
Then, when he trembles ! when his Blushes *r. Mi.* ix. 89
Now louder, and yet louder *r. O.* i. 14
He bids your breasts with ancient ardour *r. P.C.* 15
And hate for arts that caus'd himself to *r. P.C.* 200
What mighty contests *r.* from trivial things *R.L.* i. 2

Heroes' and Heroines' shouts confus'dly *r. R.L.* v. 41
But trust the Muse—she saw it upward *r. R.L.* v. 123
R. from a Clergy, or a City feast *S.* ii. 76
Self-center'd Sun, and Stars that *r.* and fall *S.* iv 6
On the broad base of fifty thousand *r. S.* iv. 74
None e'er has risen, and none e'er shall *r. S.* v. 30
How will our Fathers *r.* up in a rage *S.* v. 125
His servants up, and *r.* by five o'clock *S.* v. 162
And you shall *r.* up Otway for your pains *S.* vi. 146
Why Turnpikes *r.*, and now no Cit nor clown *S.* viii. 144
Now *r.*, and haste to yonder woodbine bow'rs *Sp.* 97
Where'er you tread, the blushing flow'rs shall *r. Su.* 75
All Nature's Incense *r. U.P.* 52
Nor saw displeas'd the peaceful cottage *r. W.F.* 86
Make Windsor-hills in lofty numbers *r. W.F.* 287
Where Windsor-domes and pompous turrets *r. W.F.* 352
And Temples *r.*, the beauteous works of peace *W.F.* 378

Risen.
None e'er has *r.*, and none e'er shall rise *S.* v. 30

Rises.
Vig'rous he *r.* from th' effluvia strong *D.* ii. 105
A branch of Styx here *r.* from the Shades *D.* ii. 338
Hell *r.*, Heav'n descends, and dance on Earth *D.* iii.237
And all that *r.*, rise in due degree *E.M.* i. 46
The fair each moment *r.* in her charms *R.L.* i. 140
The Sun first *r.* o'er the purple main *R.L.* ii. 2

Rising.
Then stretch thy sight o'er all her *r.* reign *D.* iii. 65
The *r.* game, and chas'd from flow'r to flow'r *D.* iv. 426
That darts severe upon a *r.* Lie *E.* ii. 6
Rome's pompous glories *r.* to our thought *E.* iii. 24
And swelling organs lift the *r.* soul *E.A.* 272
For *r.* merit will buoy up at last *E.C.* 461
With sweeter notes each *r.* Temple rung *E.C.* 703
The *r.* tempest puts in act the soul *E.M.* ii. 105
See him from Nature *r.* slow to Art *E.M.* iii. 169
Learns, from this union of the *r.* Whole *E.M.* iv. 337
Some *r.* Genius sins up to my Song *E.S.* ii. 9
You hurt a man that's *r.* in the Trade *E.S.* ii. 35
Shall hail the *r.*, close the parting day *I.H.* iii. 30
No more the *r.* sun shall gild the morn *M.* 99
Whose *r.* Forests, not for pride or show *M.E.* iv. 187
Here, *r.* bold, the Patriot's honour'd face *M.E.* v. 57
And Athens *r.* near the pole *O.* ii. 32
Where Thames with pride surveys his *r.* tow'rs *R.L.* iii. 2
He watch'd th' Ideas *r.* in her mind *R.L.* iii. 142
Strange phantoms *r.* as the mists arise *R.L.* iv. 40
And fierce Thalestris fans the *r.* fire *R.L.* iv. 93
Sure fate of all, beneath whose *r.* ray *S.* v. 19
Let *r.* Granaries and Temples here *S.* vi. 258
Four figures *r.* from the work appear *Sp.* 37
That threats a fight, and spurns the *r.* sand *Sp.* 48
Fresh *r.* blushes paint the wat'ry glass *Su.* 28
Yet shall thy grave with *r.* flow'rs be drest *U.L.* 63
To the bright regions of the *r.* day *W.F.* 388

Risk.
Who *r.* the most, that take wrong means or right *E.M.* iv. 86
Why *r.* the world's great empire for a Punk *M.E.* i. 131

Risk'd.
Down his own throat he *r.* the Grecian gold *D.* iv. 382
How sometimes life is *r.*, and always ease *E.M.* iv. 274

Rites.
These little *r.*, a Stone, a Verse, receive *Ep.* vii. 19
Trembling begins the sacred *r.* of Pride *R.L.* i. 128
Thy fate unpity'd, and thy *r.* unpaid *U.L.* 48

Rival.
Stood dauntless Curl; "Behold that *r.* here *D.* ii. 58
There *r.* flames with equal glory rise *D.* iii. 80
Ev'n *r.* Wits did Voiture's death deplore *E.* iv. 15
To him each *R.* shall submit *I.H.* iii. 17
Flam'd forth this *r.* to its Sire, the Sun *M.E.* iii. 12
When *r.* beauties for the Present strove *Mi.* ix. 38
Than, issuing forth, the *r.* of his beams *R.L.* ii. 3
Or with a *R*.'s, or an *Eunuch's* spite *E.C.* 31
A *r.* envy (all in vain) to hide *Mi.* ix. 42
Alone can *r.*, can succeed to thee *E.A.* 206
But would you sing, and *r.* Orpheus' strain *Su.* 81

Rival'd.
Shrink his thin essence like a *r.* flow'r *R.L.* ii. 132

River.
A *R.* at my Garden's end *I.H.* ii. 4 s
Or fish deny'd (your *r.* yet unthaw'd) *S.* ii. 14
Oh early lost! what tears the *r.* shed *W.F.* 273
The forests dance, the r.—s upward rise D. iii. 245
And roll obedient *R.* thro' the Land *M.E.* iv. 202
Nor *r.* winding thro' the vales below *W.* 3

Road.
We nobly take the high Priori *R. D.* iv. 471
Suffice that Reason keep to Nature's *r. E.M.* ii. 115
Yes, Nature's *r.* must ever be preferr'd *E.M.* ii. 161
Slave to no sect, who takes no private *r. E.M.* iv. 331

Roam.
Not Man alone, but all that *r.* the wood *E.M.* iii. 119
For foreign glory, foreign joy, they roam *M.E.* ii. 223
In search of mischief still on Earth to *r. R.L.* i. 64
What mov'd my mind with youthful Lords to *r. R.L.* iv. 159
Amid her kindred stars familiar *r. W.F.* 255
Led by the sound I *r.* from shade to shade *W.F.* 269

Roar.
How shall I rhyme in this eternal *r. S.* vi. 115
Teach thou the warbling Polypheme to r. D. iii. 305
Clouds interpose, waves *r.*, and winds arise *E.A.* 246
The hoarse, rough verse should like the torrent *r. E.C.* 369
A hundred oxen at your levee *r. M.E.* iii. 58
Then full against his Cornish lands they *r. M.E.* iii. 355
Shall call the winds thro' long arcades to *r. M.E.* iv. 35
And others *r.* aloud, "Subscribe, subscribe." *P.S.* 114
How did they fume, and stamp, and *r.*, and chafe *P.S.* 191
Ah luckless Poet! stretch thy lungs and *r. S.* v. 324
The hollow winds thro' naked temples *r. W.F.* 68
Then bow'd and spoke; the winds forget to *r. W.F.* 353
There Faction *r.*, Rebellion bite her chain *W.F.* 421

Roar'd.
R. for the handkerchief that caus'd his pain *R.L.* v. 106

Roaring.
Thames wafts it thence to Rufus' *r.* hall *D.* ii. 265
The Mole projected break the *r.* Main *M.E.* iv. 200
Howl to the r—s of the Northern deep S. v. 329

Roars.
Great Cæsar *r.*, and hisses in the fires *D.* i. 251
And "Coll!" each Butcher *r.* at Hockley-hole *D.* i. 326
Jove's thunder *r.*, heav'n trembles all around *R.L.* v. 49
And here, while town, and court, and city *r. S.* vi. 123

Roast.
R. beef, tho' old proclaims him stout *Mi.* xii. 13
A tomb of boil'd and *r.*, and flesh and fish *S.* ii. 70
The vulgar boil, the learned r. an egg S. vi. 85

Roasted.
Had *r.* turnips in the Sabine farm *M.E.* i. 219
For writing Pamphlets, and for *r.* Popes *D.* iii. 284

Rob.
Or *r.* Rome's ancient geese of all their glories *D.* i. 211
What? *r.* your Boys? those pretty rogues *I.H.* 27
And 'twere a sin to *r.* them of their mite *P.S.* 162
And gets an Act of Parliament to *r. S.* viii. 143

Robb'd.
By Spirit *r.* of Pow'r, by Warmth of Friends *M.E.* ii. 144
Not ardent lovers *r.* of all their bliss *R.L.* iv. 5

Robe.
He ceas'd, and spread the *r.*; the crowd confess *D.* ii. 353
That *r.* of Quality so struts and swells *M.E.* ii. 189
The rest his many-colour'd *r.* conceal'd *R.L.* iii. 58
That long behind he trails his pompous *r. R.L.* iii. 73
Foreign her air, her r.'s discordant pride D. iv. 47
She, tinsell'd o'er with r—s of varying hues D. i. 81
"Receive" (he said) "these *r.* that once were mine *D.* ii. 351
And shameless *Billingsgate* her *r.* adorn *D.* iv. 26
The shining *r.*, rich jewels, beds of state *E.* iv. 51
Paint, Marble, Gems and *r.* of Persian dye *S.* vi. 265

Rob'd.
First, *r.* in white, the Nymph intent adores *R.L.* i. 123

Robin-red-breast.
The *R.* till of late had rest *S.* ii. 37

Robs.
That Spain *r.* on, and Dunkirk's still a Port *S.* viii. 165

Rochester.
Ev'n mitred *R.* would nod the head *P.S.* 140

Rock.
Each staunch Polemic, stubborn as a *r. D.* iv. 195
The shapeless *r.*, or hanging precipice *E.C.* 158
From the dry *r.* who bade the waters flow *M.E.* iii. 254
When Ajax strives some *r.*'s vast weight to throw *E.C.* 370
Taught *r*—s *to weep, and made the mountains groan A.* 16
Thro' *r.* and caves the name of Delia sounds (*rep.*) *A.* 49
Ye rugged *r.!* which holy knees have worn *E.A.* 19
The darksome pines that o'er yon *r.* reclin'd *E.A.* 155
And low-brow'd *r.* hang nodding o'er the deeps *E.A.* 244
Stones leap'd to form, and *r.* began to live *E.C.* 702
The *r.* proclaim th' approaching Deity *M.* 32
Be smooth ye *r.*, ye rapid floods give way *M.* 36
On rifted *r.*, the dragon's late abodes *M.* 71
R. fall to dust, and mountains melt away *M.* 106
All beneath yon flow'ry *R. Mi.* vii. 8
And seas, and *r.* and skies rebound *O.* i. 47
Eurydice the *r.*, and holy mountains rung *O.* i. 117
The hills and *r.* attend my doleful lay *Su.* 17
And I, a Nursing-mother *r. the Throne D.* i. 312
To *r.* the cradle of reposing Age *P.S.* 409

Rock'd.
When *r.* the mountains, and when groan'd the ground *E.M.* iii. 250

Rod.
Thine from the birth, and sacred from the *r. D.* iv. 283
Snatch from his hand the balance and the *r. E.M.* i. 121
If Calvin feels Heav'n's blessing, or its *r. E.M.* iv. 139
A Wit's a Feather, and a Chief's a *r. E.M.* iv. 247
And each Blasphemer quite escape the *r. E.S.* ii. 195
And needs no *r.* but Ripley with a rule *M.E.* iv. 18
If wrong, I smil'd ; if right, I kiss'd the *r. P.S.* 158
What sin of mine could merit such a *r. S.* viii. 63
Stretch'd o'er the Poor and Church his iron *r. W.F.* 75

Rode.
To Needham's quick the voice triumphal *r. E.* i. 323

Roe.
And leap exulting like the bounding *r. M.* 44

Rogue.
The *r.* and fool by fits is fair and wise *E.M.* ii. 233
A *R.* with Ven'son to a Saint without *M.E.* i. 80
Old Cato is as great a *R.* as you *M.E.* iii. 38
The Wretch that trusts them, or the *R.* that cheats *M.E.* iii. 238
So kept the Di'mond, and the *r.* was bit *M.E.* iii. 364
Lintot, dull *r.!* will think your price too much *P.S.* 63
"Right," cries his Lordship, " for a *r.* in need " *S.* ii. 111
So prompts, and saves a *r.* who cannot read *S.* vii. 16
But let them write for you, each *r.* impairs *S.* vii. 99
These I could bear ; but not a *r.* so civil *S.* viii. 36
Speak out, and bid me blame no *R*—s *at all E.S.* ii. 53
What ? rob your Boys ? those pretty *r. I.H.* i. 27

Roll.
I'll list you in the harmless *r. E.* vi. 31
Next o'er his Books his eyes began to *r. D.* i. 127
Back to the Devil the last echoes *r. D.* i. 325
Might from Bœotian to Bœotian *r. D.* iii. 50
R. all their tides ; then back the circles bring *D.* iii. 56
From shelves to shelves see greedy Vulcan *r. D.* iii. 81
See ! the dull stars *r.* round and re-appear *D.* iii. 322
R. in her Vortex, and her pow'r confess *D.* iv. 84
Prompt at the call, around the Goddess *r. D.* iv. 189
See ! still thy own, the heavy Canon *r. D.* iv. 247
The vulgar Herd turn off to *r.* with Hogs *D.* iv.
While summer-suns *r.* unperceiv'd away *E.* iii. 18
Yet should the Muses bid my numbers *r. E.* iii. 73
Just when she learns to *r.* a melting eye *E.* v. 3
When from the censer clouds of fragrance *r. E.A.* 271
While praying, trembling, in the dust I *r. E.A.* 279
Rise Alps between us I and whole oceans *r. E.A.* 290
See my lips tremble, and my eye-balls *r. E.A.* 323
As streams *r.* down, enlarging as they flow *E.C.* 192
Seas *r.* to waft me, suns to light me rise *E.M.* i. 139
And, if each system in gradation *r. E.M.* i. 247
Or wing the sky, or *r.* along the flood *E.M.* iii. 120
And *r.* obedient Rivers thro' the Land *M.E.* ii. 202
Instruct the eyes of young Coquettes to *r. R.L.* i. 88
Or *r.* the planets thro' the boundless sky *R.L.* ii. 80
Beauties in vain their pretty eyes may *r. R.L.* v. 33
Not when from plate to plate your eye-balls *r. S.* ii. 7
So slow th' unprofitable moments *r. S.* iii. 39
Where winds can carry, or where waves can *r. S.* iv. 70
Teach ev'ry thought within its bounds to *r. S.* vi. 204
And those never-darting eyes must *r.* no more *U.L.* 34
Thro' the fair scene *r.* slow the ling'ring streams *W.F.* 217
Tempt icy seas, where scarce the waters *r. W.F.* 389

Roll'd.
Then down are *r.* the books ; stretch'd o'er 'em lies *D.* ii. 403
A small Euphrates thro' the piece is *r. M.E.* v. 29
Thou, who since yesterday hast *r.* o'er all *S.* viii. 202
The silver eel in shining volumes *r. W.F.* 143
The figur'd streams in waves of silver *r. W.F.* 335

Rolli.
R. the feather to his ear conveys *D.* ii. 203

Rolling.
The *r.* smoke involves the sacrifice *D.* i. 248
Happier thy fortunes ! like a *r.* stone *D.* iii. 293
And now, on *r.* waters snatch'd away *I.H.* iii. 48
R. in Mæanders *O.* i. 100
Now glaring fiends, and snakes on *r.* spires *R.L.* iv. 43
The various seasons of the *r.* year *SA.* 38
Now marks the course of *r.* orbs on high *W.F.* 245
Her sacred domes involv'd in *r.* fire *W.F.* 324

Rolls.
One lull'd th' Exchequer, and one stunn'd the *R. S.* vi. 130
From morn to night, at Senate, *R.*, and Hall *S.* iv. 36
Long Chanc'ry-lane retentive *r. the sound D.* ii. 263
R. the large tribute of dead dogs to Thames *D.* ii. 272
R. the black troop, and overshades the street *D.* ii. 360
Here in a dusky vale where Lethe *r. D.* iii. 23
Wings the red lightning, and the thunder *r. D.* iii. 256
Or Tiber, now no longer Roman, *r. D.* iv. 299
R. o'er my Grotto, and but soothes my sleep *S.* i. 124
And earth *r.* back beneath the flying steed *W.F.* 158
And chalky Wey, that *r.* a milky wave *W.F.* 344

Roman.
R. and Greek Grammarians ! know your Better *D.* iv. 215
Or Tiber, now no longer *R.*, rolls *D.* iv. 299
While *R.* Spirit charms, and Attic Wit *E.S.* ii. 84
Stand emulous of Greek and *R.* fame *M.E.* v. 54
And calls forth *R.* drops from British eyes *P.C.* 16
And Sydney's verse halts ill on *R.* feet *S.* v. 98
Above all Greek, above all *R.* Fame *S.* v. 26
To act a Lover's or a *R.*'s part *U.L.* 8
We still defy'd the R—s as of old E.C. 718
And taught his *R.* in much better metre *E.S.* i. 9

Romance.
So Ladies in *r.* assist their Knight *R.L.* iii. 129
And ev'ry flow'ry Courtier writ *R. S.* v. 146
Of twelve vast French R—s neatly gilt R.L. ii. 38

Romantic.
The Maid's *r.* wish, the Chemist's flame *D.* iii. 11
Is this the cause of your *R.* strains *Mi.* ix. 9
If Folly grows *r.*, I must paint it *M.E.* ii. 16

Rome.
A Gothic Library ! of Greece and *R. D.* i. 145
Small thanks to France, and none to *R.* or Greece *D.* i. 283
R. in her Capitol saw Querno sit *D.* ii. 15
Lo ! *R.* herself, proud mistress now no more *D.* iii. 101
And builds imaginary *R.* anew *E.* iii. 32
The world's just wonder, and ev'n thine, O *R. E.C.* 248
Athens and *R.* in better ages knew *E.C.* 644

ROOD—ROUTED.

Learning and *R.* alike in Empire grew *E.C.* 683
And the same age saw Learning fall, and *R.* *E.C.* 636
To him the wit of Greece and *R.* was known *E.C.* 727
Could France or *R.* divert our brave designs *M.E.* iii. 51
You show us, *R.* was glorious, not profuse *M.E.* iv. 23
How *R.* her own sad Sepulchre appears *M.E.* v. 2
Show'd *R.* her Cato's figure drawn in state *P.C.* 30
Her last good man dejected *R.* ador'd *P.C.* 35
R. learning arts from Greece, whom she subdu'd *P.C.* 40
The fate of Louis, and the fall of *R.* *R.L.* v. 140
Tho' Tiber's streams immortal *R.* behold *W.F.* 357
Or rob *R.'s ancient geese of all their glories* D. i. 211
R. pompous glories rising to our thought *E.* iii. 24
R. ancient Genius, o'er its ruins spread *E.C.* 699
And be what *R.* great Didius was before *M.E.* iii. 126
Touch'd by thy hand, again *R.* glories shine *M.E.* v. 46
So *R.* great founder to the heav'ns withdrew *R.L.* v. 125

Rood.
A Terrace-walk, and half a *R.* *I.H.* ii. 51

Roofs.
But such plain *r.* as Piety could raise *E.A.* 139
Grotesco *r.*, and Stucco floors *I.H.* ii. 192
No rafter'd *r.* with dance and tabor sound *M.E.* iii. 189
Where ling'ring drops from min'ral *R.* distil *Mi.* x. 3
Till the *r.* all around *O.* i. 8
"Restore the Lock!" the vaulted *r.* rebound *R.L.*v.104
Then, from her *r.* when Verrio's colours fall *W.F.* 307

Roof'd.
And other Mexicos be *r.* with gold *W.F.* 412

Rooks.
Old-fashion'd balls, dull Aunts, and croaking *r.* *E.* v. 12

Room.
Or serve (like other Fools) to fill a *r.* *D.* i. 136
"*R.* for my Lord!" three jockeys in his train *D.* ii. 192
And straight succeeded, leaving shame no *r.* *D.* iv. 531
In the worst inn's worst *r.*, with mat half-hung *M.E.* iii. 299
Is this a Dinner? this a Genial *r.* *M.E.* iv. 155
Whether the darken'd *r.* to muse invite *S.* i. 97
Frighted, I quit the *r.*, but leave it so *S.* viii. 272
What tho' no sacred earth allow thee *r.* *U.L.* 61

Rooms.
Horneck's fierce eye, and *R.'s* funereal frown *D.* iii. 152

Roost.
And swallows *r.* in Nilus' dusty Urn *M.E.* iv. 126

Root.
Wild Nature's vigor working at the *r.* *E.M.* ii. 184
From Jesse's *r.* behold a branch arise *M.* 9
And humbly live on rabbits, and on *r*—s *S.* ii. 52
I plant, *r.* up; I build, and then confound *S.* iii. 163

Rope.
'Tis the same *r.* at diff'rent ends they twist *D.* i. 207
And buy a *r.*, that future times may tell *S.* ii. 109

Roper.
There, Ridpath, *R.*, cudgell'd might ye view *D.* ii. 149

Rosalinda.
That taught the groves my *R.'s* name *Su.* 42

Rosamonda, Rosamunda.
Lucretia's dagger, *R.'s* bowl *M.E.* ii. 92
And send up vows from *R—u—'s* lake *R.L.* v. 136

Roscommon.
Such was *R.*, not more learn'd than good *E.C.* 725
R. only boasts unspotted bays *S.* v. 214

Rose.
R. or Carnation, was below my care *D.* iv. 431
For her th' unfading *r.* of Eden blooms *E.A.* 217
Annual for me, the grape, the *r.* renew *E.M.* i. 135
Die of a *r.* in aromatic pain *E.M.* i. 200
Blush in the *R.*, and in the Di'mond blaze *M.E.* i. 146
With band of Lily, and with cheek of *R.* *S.* viii. 251
Let op'ning *r*—s knotted oaks adorn *A.* 37
See from my cheek the transient *r.* fly *E.A.* 331
Shows in her cheek the *r.* of eighteen *H.* iv. 32
Like *r.*, that in deserts bloom and die *R.L.* iv. 158
Here western winds on breathing *r.* blow *SP.* 32

There the first *r.* of the year shall blow *U.L.* 66
But lofty Lintot in the circle *r.* *D.* ii. 53
It *r.*, and labour'd to a curve at most *D.* ii. 172
Who but to sink the deeper, *r.* the higher *D.* ii. 290
Slow *r.* a form, in majesty of Mud *D.* ii. 326
Then *r.* the seed of Chaos, and of Night *D.* iv. 13
When lo! a Spectre *r.* whose index-hand *D.* iv. 139
Rous'd at his name, up *r.* the bousy Sire *D.* iv. 493
R. a Gregorian, one a Gormogon *D.* iv. 576
From Nature's temp'rate feast *r.* satisfy'd *E.* x. 9
Pride, Malice, Folly, against Dryden *r.* *E.C.* 458
Still as one brood, and as another *r.* *E.M.* iii. 139
Here *r.* one little state, another near *E.M.* iii. 201
Poet or Patriot, *r.* but to restore *E.M.* iii. 285
From dirt and sea-weed as proud Venice *r.* *E.M.* iv. 292
Some scruple *r.*, but thus he eas'd his thought *M.E.* iii. 365
For this, ere Phœbus *r.*, he had implor'd *R.L.* ii. 35
Not Berenice's Locks first *r.* so bright *R.L.* v. 129
Newmarket's Glory *r.*, as Britain's fell *S.* v. 144
Hence Satire *r.*, that just the medium hit *S.* v. 261
And on their banks Augusta *r.* in gold *W.F.* 336

Roseate.
I come, I come! prepare your *r.* bow'rs *E.A.* 317

Ross.—See **Man of Ross.**

Rosy.
R. and rev'rend, though without a Gown *D.* iv. 496
Here bees from blossoms sip the *r.* dew *Su.* 69

Rot.
To draw nutrition, propagate, and *r.* *E.M.* ii. 64
Sufficient sap at once to bear and *r.* *Mi.* iii. 12

Rotation.
Oft, in the Passions' wild *r.* tost *M.E.* i. 41

Rots.
Chaucer's worst ribaldry is learn'd by *r.* *S.* v. 37

Rough.
And smooth or *r.*, with them is right or wrong *E.C.* 338
The hoarse, *r.* verse should like the torrent roar *E.C.* 369
Old England's Genius, *r.* with many a Scar *E.S.* i. 152
The plain *r.* Hero turn a crafty Knave *M.E.* i. 126
Boastful and *r.*, your first Son is a Squire *M.E.* i. 151
And something said of Chartres much too *r.* *S.* i. 4
What! like Sir Richard, rumbling, *r.*, and fierce *S.* i. 23
Has age but melted those *r.* parts away *S.* vi. 318
More *r.* than forty Germans when they scold *S.* vii. 62
Nay troth th' Apostles (tho' perhaps too *r.*) *S.* viii. 76
R. Satyrs dance, and Pan applauds the song *Su.* 50

Rouleaux.
In bright Confusion open *R.* lie *Mi.* ix. 81

Round.—*Passim.*
Relentless walls! whose darksome *r.* contains *E.A.* 17
Or tread the mazy *r.* his followers trod *E.M.* ii. 25
Swiftly purling in a *R.* *Mi.* vii. 26
Turn *r.* to square, and square again to *r.* *S.* iii. 170
And gives th' eternal wheels to know their *r*—s *M.E.* iii. 168
To some fam'd *r.*-house, ever open gate *D.* ii. 424

Roundly.
What's *r.* smooth or languishingly slow *E.C.* 359

Rouse.
To stir, to *r.*, to shake the soul he comes *D.* iv. 67
To *r.* the Watchman of the public Weal *E.S.* ii. 217
R. the fleet hart, and cheer the op'ning hound *W.F.* 150

Rous'd.
R. by the light, old Dulness heav'd the head *D.* i. 257
R. at his name, up rose the bousy Sire *D.* iv. 493
R. by the Prince of Air, the whirlwinds sweep *M.E.* iii. 353

Rouses.
Morpheus *r.* from his bed *O.* i. 31

Rousing.
Now lap-dogs give themselves the *r.* shake *R.L.* i. 15

Routed.
Their Quibbles *r.*, and defy'd their Puns *Mi.* ii. 12
Thus when dispers'd a *r.* army runs *R.L.* iii. 81

Rove.
Why *r.* my thoughts beyond this last retreat *E.A.* 5
Here was she seen o'er airy wastes to *r. W.F.* 167
I seem thro' consecrated walks to *r. W.F.* 267

Rovers.
When Sallee *R.* chas'd him on the deep *D.* iv. 380

Roves.
While thro' Poetic scenes the GENIUS *r. D.* iv. 489
With slaughtering guns th' unweary'd fowler *r. W.F.* 125

Roving.
For gain, not glory, wing'd his *r.* flight *S* v. 71

Row.
Clothe spice, line trunks, or fluttering in a *r. S.* v. 4.8
Whose Causeway parts the vale with shady r—s *M.E.* iii. 259
Here files of pins extend their shining *r. R.L.* i. 137
Why bows the side-box from its inmost *r. R.L.* v. 14

Rowe.
Thy relics, *R.*, to this fair Urn we trust *Ep.* v. 1
But for the Passions, Southern sure and *R. S.* v. 86

Rows.
With arms extended Bernard *r.* his state *D.* ii. 67

Royal.
His *r.* Sense of Op'ras or the Fair *D.* iv. 314
Like *r.* Harts, be never more run down *E.S.* ii. 29
Proves the just victim of his *r.* rage *R.L.* iii. 60
And sweetly flow thro' all the *r.* Line *S.* i. 32
I cannot like, dread Sir, your *R.* Cave *S.* iii. 114
You give all *r.* Witchcraft to the Devil *S.* vi. 219
With *r.* Favourites in flatt'ry vie *S.* viii. 60
He dwells amidst the *r.* Family *S.* viii. 103
And makes his trembling slaves the *r.* game *W.F.* 64

Rubbish.
Bright thro' the *r.* of some hundred years *S.* vi. 166

Rubicon.
Or on the *R.* or on the Rhine *E.M.* iv. 246

Rubric.
Of Curl's chaste press, and Lintot's *r.* post *D.* i. 40
What tho' my name stood *r.* on the walls *P.S.* 215

Rubs.
Just as a blockhead *r.* his thoughtless skull *E.J.S.* 7

Ruby.
See on these *r.* lips the trembling breath *U.L.* 31
The coral redden, and the *r.* glow *W.F.* 394

Ruddier.
Did here the trees with *r.* burdens bend *E.M.* iii. 273

Rude.
Beneath a *r.* and nameless stone he lies *Ep.* v. 3
I'm quite asham'd—'tis mighty *r. I.H.* ii. 206
Or bid the furious Gaul be *r.* no more *O.* ii. 16
To save the powder from too *r.* a gale *R.L.* ii. 93
Or cans'd suspicion when no soul was *r. R.L.* iv. 73
Confounds the civil, keeps the *r.* in awe *S.* viii. 270

Rudely.
A Being darkly wise, and *r.* great *E.M.* ii. 4
But *r.* press before a Duke *I.H.* ii. 59 *s*
Shov'd from the wall perhaps, or *r.* press'd *M.E.* i. 234

Rueful.
Yet smiling at his *r.* length of face *D.* ii. 142

Rufa.
R., whose eye quick-glancing o'er the Park *M.E.* ii. 21
Agrees as ill with *R.* studying Locke *M.E.* ii. 23

Ruff.
Soft on the paper *r*, its leaves I spread *D.* iv. 407

Ruffled.
Where Contemplation prunes her *r.* wings *S.* viii. 186

Rufus.
Lo *R.*, tugging at the deadly dart *W.F.* 83
Thames wafts it thence to R.' roaring hall *D.* ii. 265

Rug [?].
Who sins with whom; who got his Pension *r. S.* viii. 134

Rugged.
Ye *r.* rocks! which holy knees have worn *E.A.* 19

Ruin.
Atoms or systems into *r.* hurl'd *E.M.* i. 89
So odd, my Country's *R.* makes me grave *E.S.* ii. 207
I know the Bite, yet to my *R.* run *Mi.* ix. 69
Just in the jaws of *r.* and Codille *R.L.* iii. 92
O'er heaps of *r.* stalk'd the stately hind *W.F.* 70
Or seek some *R.'s formidable shade E.* iii. 30
Rome's ancient Genius, o'er its r—s spread *E.C.* 699
Perhaps, by its own *r.* sav'd from flame *M.E.* v. 15
Their *r.* perish'd, and their place no more *M.E.* v. 22
How happy! those to r., these betray *E.M.* iv. 290
More go to *r.* Fortunes, than to raise *M.E.* iii. 202

Rule.
Some free from rhyme or reason, *r.* or check *D.* iii. 161
Led by some *r.*, that guides, but not constrains *E.* iii. 67
Th' intent propos'd, that License is a *r. E.C.* 149
All which, exact to *r.*, were brought about *E.C.* 277
In words, as fashions, the same *r.* will hold *E.C.* 333
Sure as Demoivre, without *r.* or line *E.M.* iii. 104
Ask you why Wharton broke thro' ev'ry *r. M.E.* i. 206
The grave Sir Gilbert holds it for a *r. M.E.* iii. 101
And needs no rod but Ripley with a *r. M.E.* iv. 18
You think this cruel? take it for a *r. P.S.* 83
Yet why? that Father held it for a *r. P.S.* 382
For I, who hold sage Homer's *r.* the best *S.* ii. 159
Then by the *r.* that made the horse-tail bare *S.* v. 63
Or say our Fathers never broke a *r. S.* v. 93
Instruct his family in ev'ry *r. S.* v. 163
If such the plague and pains to write by *r. S.* vi. 180
Those *R*—s of old discover'd, not devis'd *E.C.* 88
Hear how learn'd Greece her useful *r.* indites *E.C.* 92
Bold in the practice of mistaken *r. E.C.* 110
And *r.* as strict his labour'd work confine *E.C.* 137
Learn hence for ancient *r.* a just esteem *E.C.* 139
If, where the *r.* not far enough extend (reff.) *E.C.* 146
But tho' the Ancients thus their *r.* invade *E.C.* 161
Neglect the *r.* each verbal Critic lays *E.C.* 261
Who durst depart from Aristotle's *r. E.C.* 272
The justest *r.*, and clearest method join'd *E.C.* 670
The *r.* a nation, born to serve, obeys *E.C.* 723
Such was the Muse, whose *r.* and practice tell *E.C.* 723
Could he, whose *r.* the rapid Comet bind *E.M.* ii. 35
Ah! if she lend not arms, as well as *r. E.M.* ii. 151
Sure, if I spare the Minister, no *r. E.S.* ii. 147
And if I pray by Reason's *r. I.H.* ii. 15 *s*
Blends in exception to all gen'ral *r. M.E.* ii. 275
Yet shall, my Lord, your just, your noble *r. M.E.* iv. 25
And, if they starve, they starve by *r.* of art *M.E.* iv. 38
But strong in sense, and wise without the *r. S.* ii. 70
To *r.* of Poetry no more confin'd *S.* vi. 202
Our Court may justly to our stage give *r. S.* viii. 220
See them survey their limbs by Dürer's *r. S.* viii. 240
Senates and Court with Greek and Latin *r. D.* iv. 179
Go, teach Eternal Wisdom how to *r. E.M.* ii. 29
And Man's prerogative to *r.*, but spare *E.M.* iii. 160
Europe a Woman, Child, or Dotard *r. M.E.* i. 93
Should such a man, too fond to *r.* alone *P.S.* 197
Who *r.* the sex to fifty from fifteen *R.L.* iv. 58

Rul'd.
She *r.*, in native Anarchy, the mind *D.* i. 16
In Lud's old walls tho' long I *r.*, renown'd *D.* iii. 277
Jilts *r.* the state, and statesmen farces writ *E.C.* 538
Th' Oppressor *r.* tyrannic where he durst *W.F.* 74

Ruler.
Look thro', and trust the *R.* with his skies *S.* iv. 8

Rules.
What the weak head with strongest bias *r. E.C.* 203
And while self-love each jealous writer *r. E.C.* 516
Reason's comparing balance *r.* the whole *E.M.* ii. 60
Or, if she *r.* him, never shews she *r. M.E.* ii. 262
Ye Gods I what justice *r.* the ball *O.* ii. 25
Who *r.* in Cornwall, or who *r.* in Berks *S.* iv. 104
Thus, if Eternal justice *r.* the ball *U.L.* 35

Ruling.
Let *r.* Angels from their spheres be hurl'd *E.M.* i. 253
To serve mere engines to the *r.* Mind *E.M.* i. 262
The Mind's disease, its *R.* Passion came *E.M.* ii. 138

Search then the *R.* PASSION: there, alone *M.E.* i. 174
Whose *r.* Passion was the Lust of Praise *M.E.* i. 181
Shall feel your *r.* passion strong in death *M.E.* i. 263
In Men, we various *r.* Passions find *M.E.* ii. 207
The *r.* Passion, be it what it will (*rep.*) *M.E.* iii. 153
In the clear Mirror of thy *r.* Star *R.L.* i. 108

Rumbling.
With Thunder *r.* from the mustard-bowl *D.* ii. 226
What? like Sir Richard, *r.*, rough, and fierce *S.* i. 23

Rumour.
Not warp'd by Passion, aw'd by *R. Mi.* viii. 5

Rumpled.
Or *r.* petticoats, or tumbled beds *R.L.* iv. 72

Run.
Now (shame to Fortune) an ill *R.* at Play *D.* i. 113
She saw, with joy, the line immortal *r. D.* i. 99
So take the hindmost, Hell, (he said) and *r. D.* ii. 60
Mearns, Warner, Wilkins *r.*: delusive thought *D.* ii. 125
And the fresh vomit *r.* for ever green *D.* ii. 156
Thrid ev'ry science, *r.* thro' ev'ry school *D.* iv. 256
To *r.* with Horses, or to hunt with Dogs *D.* iv. 526
From Stage to Stage the licens'd Earl may *r. D.* iv. 587
And *r.*, on ivory, so glib *E.* vi. 22
Still *r.* on Poets, in a raging vein *E.C.* 606
Planets and Suns *r.* lawless thro' the sky *E.M.* i. 252
Instruct the planets in what orbs to *r. E.M.* ii. 21
As Eastern priests in giddy circles *r. E.M.* ii. 27
On their own Axis as the Planets *r. E.M.* iii. 313
See thronging Millions to the Pagod *r. E.S.* i. 157
Like royal Harts, be never more *r.* down *E.S.* ii. 29
I know the Bite, yet to my Ruin *r. Mi.* ix. 69
This day Tom's fair account has *r. Mi.* xii. 3
It is not Poetry, but prose *r.* mad *P.S.* 188
As shallow streams *r.* dimpling all the way *P.S.* 316
To *r.* a muck, and tilt at all I meet *S.* i. 70
Long as the Year's dull circle seems to *r. S.* iii. 37
Discharge their Garrets, move their beds, and *r. S.* iii. 157
The worst of Madmen is a Saint *r.* mad *S.* iv. 27
Alas! to Grottos and to Groves we *r. S.* vi. 110
She runs, but hopes she does not *r.* unseen *Sp.* 58
And now his shadow reach'd her as she *r. W.F.* 193

Rundel.
Secker is decent, *R.* has a Heart *E.S.* ii. 71

Rung.
With sweeter notes each rising Temple *r. E.C.* 703
Eurydice the rocks, and hollow mountains *r. O.* i. 117
Thrice *r.* the bell, the slipper knock'd the ground *R.L.* i. 17

Running.
Nonsense precipitate, like *r.* Lead *D.* i. 123
Now *r.* round the Circle finds it square *D.* iv. 34

Runs.
Then tinctur'd as it *r.* with Lethe's streams *D.* ii. 339
Another Cynthia her new journey *r. D.* iii. 43
O'er ev'ry vein a shudd'ring horror *r. D.* iv. 143
To where the Seine, obsequious as she *r. D.* iv. 297
Observe how system into system *r. E.M.* i. 23
Once on a time (so *r.* the Fable) *J.H.* ii. 157
Some joy still lost, as each vain year *r.* o'er *Mi.* v. 7
Thus when dispers'd a routed army *r. R.L.* iii. 81
She *r.*, but hopes she does not run unseen *Sp.* 58

Rural.
Hylas and Ægon sung their *r.* lays *A.* 2
Hylas and Ægon's *r.* lays I sing *A.* 6
You dream of Triumphs in the *r.* shade *E.* v. 22
Our *r.* Ancestors, with little blest *S.* v. 241
And Albion's cliffs resound the *r.* lay *Sp.* 6
The turf with *r.* dainties shall be crown'd *Sp.* 99
Let other swains attend the *r.* care *Su.* 35
And yet my numbers please the *r.* throng *Su.* 49
And with fresh bays her *r.* shrine adorn *W.* 20
Adieu, ye shepherds' *r.* lays and loves *W.* 90
Above the rest a *r.* nymph was fam'd *W.F.* 171

Rush.
The monkey-mimics *r.* discordant in *D.* ii. 236
R. to the world, impatient for the day *D.* iii. 30
Shall, first recall'd, *r.* forward to thy mind *D.* iii. 64
And ten-horn'd fiends and Giants *r.* to war *D.* iii. 236
Streets, Chairs, and Coxcombs, *r.* upon my sight *E.*v.48
For Fools *r.* in where Angels fear to tread *E.C.* 625
All quit their sphere, and *r.* into the skies *E.M.* i. 124
R. Chaplain, Butler, Dogs and all *J.H.* ii. 211
Fools *r.* into my head, and so I write *S.* i. 14
The youth *r.* eager to the sylvan war *W.F.* 148
R. thro' the thickets, down the valleys sweep *W.F.* 156
Then foaming pour along, and *r.* into the Thames *W.F.* 218
And half thy forests *r.* into thy floods *W.F.* 386

Russel.
So *R.* did, but could not eat at night *S.* iv. 115

Russet.
Here in full light the *r.* plains extend *W.F.* 23

Russian.
No Lord's anointed, but a *R.* Bear *S.* v. 389

Rust.
Th' inscription value, but the *r.* adore *M.E.* v. 36
The sacred *r.* of twice ten hundred years *M.E.* v. 38
Swords, pikes, and guns, with everlasting *r. S.* i. 74
It is the *r.* we value, not the gold *S.* v. 36

Rustic.
That, lac'd with bits of *r.*, makes a Front *M.E.* iv. 31
Tho' still some traces of our *r.* vein *S.* v. 270

Rustle.
Fans clap, silks *r.*, and tough whalebones crack *R.L.*v. 40

S.

Immortal *S—k*, and grave De—re *E.S.* i. 92
As *S—k*, if he lives, will love the PRINCE (*rep.*) *E.S.*ii.61
Against your worship when had *S—k* writ *E.S.* ii. 158
Ev'n to their own *S—r—v—ce* in a Car *S.* vi. 107
The *S—te's*, and then H—vy's once again *E.S.* i. 72
Who live lik *S—tt—n*, or who die lie Chartres *S.* vii. 36
If honest *S*'s take scandal at a Spark *S.* iii. 112

Sabæan.
And heap'd with products of *S.* springs *M.* 94

Sabbath.
See Christians, Jews, one heavy *s.* keep *D.* iii. 99
Peaceful sleep out the *S.* of the Tomb *Mi.* v. 19
Why will you break the *S.* of my days *S.* iii. 3
As Hags hold *S—s, less for joy than spite M.E.* ii. 239
Ev'n Sunday shines no *S.*-day to me *P.S.* 12

Sabine.
Had roasted turnips in the *S.* farm *M.E.* i. 219

Sabinus.
Thro' his young woods how pleas'd *S.* stray'd *M.E.*iv.89

Sable.
With deeper *s.* blots the silver flood *D.* ii. 274
Shaking the horrors of his *s.* brows *D.* ii. 327
Around him wide a *s.* Army stand *D.* ii. 355
(Earth's wide extremes) her *s.* flag display'd *D.* iii. 71
And look'd, and saw a *s.* Sorcerer rise *D.* iii. 233
Broad hats, and hoods, and caps, a *s.* shoal *D.* iv. 190
She comes! she comes! the *s.* Throne behold *D.* iv. 629
And dipt them in the *s.* Well *E.* vi. 11
Now move to war her *s.* Matadores *R.L.* iii. 47
Of Asia's troops and Afric's *s.* sons *R.L.* iii. 82
These in two *s.* ringlets taught to break *R.L.* iv. 69
What tho' no friends in *s.* weeds appear *U.L.* 55
Like verdant isles the *s.* waste adorn *W.F.* 28
Reap their own fruits, and woo their *s.* loves *W.F.* 410

Sabler.
He bears no token of the *s.* streams *D.* ii. 297

Sabre.
With his broad *s.* next, a chief in years *R.L.* iii. 55

Sack.
Know Eusden thirsts no more for *s.* or praise *D.* i. 293
Whose game is Whisk, whose treat a toast in *s. E.* v. 24

Sacred.

Ye Mantuan nymphs, your *s*. succour bring *A*. 5
She bids him wait her to her *s*. Dome *D*. i. 265
With mystic words, the *s*. Opium shed *D*. i. 288
Dulness is *s*. in a sound divine *D*. ii. 352
Thou, yet unborn, hast touch'd this *s*. shore *D*. iii. 45
Or vest dull Flatt'ry in the *s*. Gown *D*. iv. 97
Thine from the birth, and *s*. from the rod *D*. iv. 283
The Cap and Switch be *s*. to his Grace *D*. iv. 585
Religion blushing veils her *s*. fires *D*. iv. 649
August her deed, and *s*. be her fame *E.A*. 78
As with cold lips I kiss'd the *s*. veil *E.A*. 111
Ah no—in *s*. vestments mayst thou stand *E.A*. 325
Muse! at that Name thy *s*. sorrows shed *E*. iii. 47
Before his *s*. name flies ev'ry fault *E.C*. 422
Are mortals urg'd *s*. lust of praise *E.C*. 521
Pulpits their *s*. satire learn'd to spare *E.C*. 550
No place so *s*. from such fops is barr'd *E.C*. 622
Then *s*. seem'd th' ethereal vault no more *E.M*. iii. 263
Nothing is S. now but Villainy *E.S*. i. 170
O *s*. weapon! left for Truth's defence *E.S*. ii. 212
Yet *s*. keep his Friendships and his Ease *Ep*. i. 10
And *s*., place by DRYDEN'S awful dust *Ep*. v. 2
Whom Heav'n kept *s*. from the Proud and Great *Ep*. x. 4
S. to social life and social love *I.H*. iii. 22
Whose *s*. flow'r with fragrance fills the skies *M*. 10
The *s*. rust of twice ten hundred years *M.E*. v. 38
Let such, such only tread this *s*. Floor *Mi*. x. 13
While solemn airs improve the *s*. fire *O*. i. 129
Ye shades, where *s*. truth is sought *O*. i. 1
S. Hymeo! these are thine *O*. iii. 44
No place is *s*., not the Church is free *P.S*. 11
Midas, a *s*. person and a king *P.S*. 70
Trembling begins the *s*. rites of Pride *R.L*. i. 128
Each band the number of the *s*. nine *R.L*. iii. 30
The meeting points the *s*. hair dissever *R.L*. iii. 153
But by this lock, this *s*. lock I swear *R.L*. iv. 133
S. to Ridicule his whole life long *S*. i. 79
And children *s*. held a Martin's nest *S*. ii. 38
And virtuous Alfred, a more *s*. name *S*. v. 8
Whose Word is Truth, as *s*. and reverd *S*. v. 27
Whose Satire's *s*., and whose rage secure *S*. viii. 283
Fair Thames, flow gently from thy *s*. spring *Sp*. 3
A wond'rous Tree that *s*. Monarchs bears *Sp*. 86
In those fair fields where *s*. Isis glides *Su*. 25
What tho' no *s*. earth allow thee room *U.L*. 61
The ground now *s*. by thy reliques made *U.L*. 68
And savage howlings fill the *s*. quires *W.F*. 72
Ye *s*. Nine! that all my soul possess *W.F*. 259
Here noble Surrey felt the *s*. rage *W.F*. 291
Make *s*. Charles's tomb for ever known *W.F*. 319
Her *s*. domes involv'd in rolling fire *W.F*. 324
Hail, *s*. peace! hail, long-expected days *W.F*. 355

Sacrifice.

The rolling smoke involves the *s*. *D*. i. 248
What cannot copious S. atone *D*. iv. 557
And swell the pomp of dreadful *s*. *E.A*. 354
A solemn S., perform'd in state *M.E*. iv. 157
And all to one lov'd Folly s. *E.C*. 266

Sacrilegious.

Above the reach of *s*. hands *E.C*. 182
And tempts, once more, thy *s*. hands *R.L*. iv. 174

Sad.

As some *s*. Turtle his lost love deplores *A*. 19
There to her heart *s*. Tragedy address *D*. iv. 37
But, *s*. example! never to escape *D*. iv. 527
Oh name for ever *s*.! or for ever dear *E.A*. 49
Led thro' a *s*. variety of woe *E.A*. 36
Then share thy pain, allow that *s*. relief *E.A*. 49
Canst thou forget that *s*., that solemn day *E.A*. 107
S. proof how well a lover can obey *E.A*. 172
When at the close of each *s*., sorrowing day *E.A*. 225
I shriek, start up, the same *s*. prospect find *E.A*. 247
See in her cell *s*. Eloïsa spread *E.A*. 303
Thy place is here, *s*. sister, come away *E.A*. 310
Thou, Abelard! the last *s*. office pay *E.A*. 321
In *s*. similitude of griefs to mine *E.A*. 360
Let him our *s*., our tender story tell *E.A*. 364
Hang the *s*. Verse on CAROLINA'S Urn *E.S*. i. 80
To this *s*. shrine, whoe'er thou art I draw near *Ep*. iii. 1
He dies, *s*. outcast of each church and state *M.E*. i. 204
Yet still a *s*. good Christian at her heart *M.E*. ii. 68
And, Sir Balaam curses God and dies *M.E*. iii. 402

How Rome her own *s*. Sepulchre appears *M.E*. v. 2
Beneath her Palm here *s*. Judea weeps *M.E*. v. 26
And all we gain, some *s*. Reflection more *Mi*. v. 8
I sit with *s*. civility, I read *P.S*. 37
S. chance of war'! now destitute of aid *R.L*. iii. 63
As thou, *s*. Virgio! for thy ravish'd Hair (*rep*.) *R.L*. iv. 10
And the *s*. burden of some merry song *S*. i. 80
Why sit we *s*. when Phosphor shines so clear *Sp*. 27
In notes more *s*. than when they sing their own *W*. 40
When the *s*. pomp along his banks was led *W.F*. 274

Saddens.

Her gloomy presence *s*. all the scene *E.A*. 167
Not the black fear of death, that *s*. all *S*. vi. 309

Sadly.

Then *s*. say, with mutual pity mov'd *E.A*. 351
Or *s*. told, how many Hopes lie here *Ep*. xiv. 6
In a s.-*pleasing strain O*. i. 5

Sadness.

'Tis all blank *s*., or continual tears *E.A*. 148

Safe.

S., where no Critics damn, no duns molest *D*. i. 295
(Haunt of the Muses) made their *s*. retreat *D*. ii. 428
S. in its heaviness, shall never stray *D*. iii. 295
S. and unseen the young Æneas past *D*. iv. 290
And authors think their reputation *s*. *E.C*. 450
Nor is Paul's church more *s*. than Paul's churchyard *E.C*. 623
S. in the band of one disposing Pow'r *E.M*. i. 287
S. from the Bar, the Pulpit, and the Throne *E.S*. ii. 210
As *s*. Companion, and an easy Friend *Ep*. xi. 7
As *s*. Companion, and a free *I.H*. i. 4
S. is your Secret still in Chloe's ear *M.E*. ii. 173
And swear not ADDISON himself was *s*. *P.S*. 192
S. from the treach'rous friend, the daring spark *R.L*. i. 73
S. past the Gnome thro' this fantastic band *R.L*. iv. 55
S. on my shore each unmolested swain *W.F*. 369

Safer.

Some *s*. world in depth of woods entranc'd *E.M*. i. 105

Safest.

And who stands *s*.? tell me, is it he *S*. ii. 125

Safety.

His *s*. must his liberty restrain *E.M*. iii. 277

Sagacious.

And hound, *s*. on the tainted green *E.M*. i. 214

Sage.

Wond'ring he gaz'd: When, lo! a S. appears *D*. iii. 35
The man had courage, was a *s*., 'tis true *E.J.S*. 39
Shall burning Ætna, if a *s*. requires *E.M*. iv. 123
In vain the S., with retrospective eye *M.E*. i. 99
"All this is madness," cries a sober *s*. *M.E*. iii. 151
By Saint, by Savage, or by S. *U.P*. 3
The merchant's toil, the s.'*s indolence E.M*. ii. 172
Vain was the Chief's, the S. Pride *I.H*. iv. 13
And Chiefs or S—*s long to Britain giv'n Ep*. xiv. 13
S. and Chiefs long since had birth *I.H*. iv. 9
Than Brahmins, Saints, and S. did before *M.E*. iii. 184
Gods, Emp'rors, Heroes, S., Beauties lie *M.E*. v. 34
Groves, where immortal *s*. taught *O*. ii. 2
As the s. *dame, experienc'd in her trade D*. ii. 133
Discours'd in terms as just, with looks as *s*. *E.C*. 269
What made (say Montagne, or more *s*. Charron!) *M.E*. i. 87
But, *s*. historians! 'tis your task to prove *M.E*. i. 133
His Grace's fate *s*. Cutler could foresee *M.E*. iii. 315
You'll give me, like a friend both *s*. and free *S*. i. 9
A doctrine *s*., but truly none of mine *S*. ii. 3
For I, who hold *s*. Homer's rule the best *S*. ii. 159

Said.

What have I *s*.? where'er my Delia flies *A*. 35
So like, that critics *s*., and courtiers swore *D*. ii. 39
So take the hindmost, Hell, (he *s*.) and run *D*. ii. 60
He *s*., and climb'd a lighter's stranded height *D*. ii. 287
"Receive" (he *s*.) "these robes that once were mine *D*. ii. 351
How sweet the periods, neither *s*., nor sung *D*. iii. 202
Fierce as a startled Adder, swell'd, and *s*. *D*. iv. 373

SAIL—SANCTIFIES.

"And take" (she s., and smil'd serene) *E.* vi. 3
How oft, when press'd to marriage, have I s. *E.A.* 73
Come, sister, come! (it s., or seem'd to say) *E.A.* 309
S. "Tories call'd him Whig, and Whigs a Tory *E.S.* i. 8
Sure, if they cannot cut, it may be s. *E.S.* ii. 148
GOD s., let *Newton* be! and all was Light *Ep.* xii. 2
Yes—SAVE MY COUNTRY, HEAV'N—He s., and died *Ep.* xiii. 8
What they s., or may say of the mortal within *Ep.* xvi. 6
'Twas what I s. to Craggs and Child *I.H.* i. 67
But let it (in a word) be s. *I.H.* ii. 193
No sooner s., but from the Hall *I.H.* ii. 210
"I give and I devise" (old Euclio s.) *M.E.* i. 256
Shut, shut the door, good John! fatigu'd, I s. *P.S.* i.
And thus in whispers s., or seem'd to say *R.L.* i. 26
He s.; when Shock, who thought she slept too long *R.L.* i. 115
Let Spades be trumps! she s., and trumps they were *R.L.* iii. 46
She s., then raging to Sir Plume repairs *R.L.* iv. 121
Which with a sigh, she rais'd; and thus she s. *R.L.* iv. 146
Oh had I stay'd, and s. my pray'rs at home *R.L.* iv. 160
She s.: the pitying audience melt in tears *R.L.* v. 1
And something s. of Chartres much too rough *S.* i. 4
Thus s. our friend, and what he s. I sing *S.* ii. 68
You s. the same, and are you discontent *S.* vi. 29
Thus much I've s., I trust, without offence *S.* vii. 125
What *Speech* esteem you most?" "The *King's*," s. I *S.* viii. 68
"Then happy Man who shows the Tombs!" s. I *S.* viii. 102
He s.; Alexis, take this pipe, the same *Su.* 41
And s.; Ye shepherds, sing around my grave *W.* 18
She s., and melting as in tears she lay *W.F.* 203
At length great Anna s., "Let Discord cease!" (rep.) *W.F.* 327

Sail.

He boarding her, she striking s. to him *S.* viii. 231
Spread all his s—s, and durst the deeps explore E.C. 646
The lucid squadrons round the s. repair *R.L.* ii. 56
He spoke; the spirits from the s. descend *R.L.* ii. 137
Or under southern skies exalt their s. *W.F.* 391
Not s. *with Ward to Ape-and-monkey climes D.* i. 233
On life's vast ocean diversely we s. *E.M.* ii. 107
Learn of the little Nautilus to s. *E.M.* iii. 177
Say, shall my little bark attendant s. *E.M.* iv. 385
But I that s., am neither less nor bigger *S.* vi. 299
S. in the Ladies; how each pirate eyes *S.* viii. 228

Sail'd.

Sir Job s. forth, the ev'ning bright and still *S.* iii. 138

Sails.

Here Amphitrite s. thro' myrtle bow'rs *M.E.* iv. 123

Saint.

Beholds himself a Patriot, Chief, or *S. D.* iv. 536
Soft as the slumbers of a s. forgiv'n *E.A.* 255
The virtues of a s. at twenty-one *E.M.* iv. 184
The *S.* sustain'd it, but the Woman died *Ep.* vi. 10
Pays the last Tribute of a s. to Heav'n *Ep.* xiv. 14
A Rogue with Ven'son to a *S.* without *M.E.* i. 80
A perjur'd Prince a leaden *S.* revere *M.E.* i. 89
A *S.* in Crape is twice a *S.* in Lawn *M.E.* i. 136
Odious! in woollen! 'twould a *S.* provoke *M.E.* i. 246
To patch, nay ogle, might become a *S. R.L.* v. 23
The worst of Madmen is a *S.* run mad *S.* iv. 27
By *S.*, by Savage, and by Sage *U.P.* 3
A *Church* collects the s—s *of Drury-lane D.* ii. 30
And pitying s., whose statues learn to weep *E.A.* 22
Dim and remote the joys of s. I see *E.A.* 71
And s. with wonder heard the vows I made *E.A.* 114
No silver s., by dying misers giv'n *E.A.* 137
And s. embrace thee with a love like mine *E.A.* 342
Faith, gallants, board with s., and bed with sinners *E.S.* 24
Silent and soft, as *S.* remove to Heav'n *E.S.* i. 93
All that makes *S.* of Queens, and Gods of Kings *E.S.* ii. 225
Than Brahmins, *S.*, and Sages did before *M.E.* iii. 284
Where sprawl the *S.* of Verrio or Laguerre *M.E.* iv. 146
Prompt or to guard or stab, to s. or damn D. ii. 357
Whether the Charmer sinner it, or s. it *M.E.* ii. 15

St. James's.

As if he saw *S.* and the Queen *D.* iv. 280
S. first, for leaden G— preach'd *D.* iv. 608
Drive to *S.* a whole herd of swine *M.E.* iii. 74
The well-bred cuckolds in *S.* air *M.E.* iii. 388
From low *S.* up to high St. Paul *S.* iii. 82
If such a doctrine in *S.* air *S.* iii. 110

St. John.

Awake, my *S.*! leave all meaner things *E.M.* i. 1
And fled from monarchs, *S.*! dwells with thee *E.M.* iv. 18
S. has ever been a wealthy Fool *E.S.* ii. 132
Oh All-accomplish'd *S.*! deck thy shrine *E.S.* ii. 139
Where, nobly-pensive, *S.* sate and thought *Mi.* x. 10
There *S.* mingles with my friendly bowl *S.* i. 127
S., whose love indulg'd my labours past *S.* iii. 1
And *S.*'s *self (great Dryden's friends before) P.S.* 141

St. Paul.—*See also* Paul.

Sometimes with Aristippus or *S. S.* iii. 31
From low St. James's up to high *S. S.* iii. 82

St. Stephen.

And one more Pensioner *S.* gains *M.E.* iii. 394

Sainted.

Love's victim then, tho' now a s. maid *E.A.* 312

Saintship.

The Dev'l was piqu'd such s. to behold *M.E.* iii. 349

Saith.

What s. my Counsel, learned in the laws *S.* i. 142

Sake.

Who hunger, and who thirst for scribbling s. *D.* i. 50
Hold, Sir! for God's s. where's th' Affront to you *E.S.* ii. 157
But wish'd it Stilton for his s. *I.H.* ii. 168
For God's s., come and live with Men *I.H.* ii. 176
We grow more partial for th' Observer's s. *M.E.* i. 12
Still Sappho—Hold! for God's s.—you'll offend *P.S.* 101
Ev'n those I pardon, for whose sinful s. *S.* vii. 41

Salads.

With soups unbought, and s. bless'd the board *M.E.* iii. 182

Salamander.

Mount up, and take a *S.*'s Name *R.L.* i. 60

Sale.

By s., at least by death, to change their lord *S.* vi. 251

Salem.

Rise, crown'd with light, imperial *S.*, rise *M.* 85

Salient.

The s. spout far-streaming to the sky *D.* ii. 162

Sallee.

When *S.* Rovers chas'd him on the deep *D.* iv. 380

Sallow.

Upon her s. cheeks, enliv'ning red *Mi.* ix. 62

Salmon.

A s.'s belly, Helluo, was thy fate *M.E.* i. 238

Salutes.

And in soft sounds, Your Grace s. their ear *R.L.* i. 86
When warbling Philomel s. the spring *Sp.* 26

Salvers.

Between each Act the trembling s. ring *M.E.* iv. 161

Same.—*Passim.*

Samian.

When Reason doubtful, like the *S.* letter *D.* iv. 151

Sancho.

S.'s dread Doctor and his Wand were there *M.E.* iv. 160

Sanctifies.

Truth guards the Poet, s. the line *E.S.* ii. 246
'Tis Use alone that s. Expense *M.E.* iv. 179

Sanctify'd.
E'er taught to shine, or s. from shame *E.M.* iv. 300
The scourge of Pride, tho' s. or great *Ep.* i. 3
Has s. whole poems for an age *S.* v. 114

Sand.
Build on the wave, or arch beneath the s. *E.M.* iii. 102
Yet tames not this; it sticks to our last s. *M.E.* i. 225
That threats a fight, and spurns the rising s. *Sp.* 48
O'er golden s—s let rich *Pactolus flow Sp.* 61
Red Iber's s., or Ister's foaming flood *W.F.* 368

Sandy.
In other parts it leaves wide s. plains *E.C.* 55
Waste s. valleys, once perplex'd with thorn *M.* 73
O'er s. wilds were yellow harvests spread *W.F.* 89

Sap.
Sufficient s. at once to bear and rot *Mi.* iii. 12
If secret Gold s. on from knave to knave *M.E.* i. 34

Saperton.
Join Cotswold hills to *S.*'s fair dale *S.* vi. 257

Sappho.
In *S.* touch the *Failings of the Sex E.S.* i. 15
Why she and *S.* raise that monstrous sum *M.E.* iii. 121
Still *S.*—Hold! for God's sake—you'll offend *P.S.* 101
S. can tell you how this man was bit *P.S.* 369
From furious *S.* scarce a milder fate *S.* i. 83
As who knows *S.*, smiles at other whores *S.* vii. 6
As *S.*'s di'monds with her dirty smock (rep.) *M.E.* ii. 24

Saron.
See spicy clouds from lowly *S.* rise *M.* 27

Sare'net.
Whose s. skirts are edg'd with flamy gold *D.* iii. 254

Sat, Sate.
When all their Lordships had s. late *I.H.* ii. 186
Or s. delighted in the thick'ning shade *M.E.* iv. 90
I wish'd the man a dinner, and s. still *P.S.* 152
S. full-blown *Bufo*, puff'd by ev'ry quill *P.S.* 232
Th' impending woe s. heavy on his breast *R.L.* ii. 54
Swearing and supperless the Hero s—e *D.* i. 115
Great Cibber s.: The proud Parnassian sneer *D.* ii. 5
Who s. the nearest, by the words o'ercome *D.* ii. 401
The Fair s. panting at a Courtier's play *E.C.* 540
Till then, by Nature crown'd, each Patriarch s. *E.M.* iii. 215
And down the Mice s. tête-à-tête *I.H.* ii. 197
Where, nobly-pensive, ST. JOHN s. and thought *Mi.* x. 10
Clapp'd his glad wings, and s. to view the fight *R.L.* v. 54
Who, tho' the House was up, delighted s. *S.* vi. 186

Satan.
But *S.* now is wiser than of yore *M.E.* iii. 351
Wife, son, and daughter, *S.*! are thy own *M.E.* iii. 399
S. himself feels far less joy than they *S.* vii. 90

Satéllites.
Why Jove's s. are less than Jove *E.M.* i. 42

Satiate.
Now May'rs and Shrieves all hush'd and s. lay *D.* i. 91
In Life's cool Ev'ning s. of Applause *S.* iii. 9

Satiety.
Without s., tho' e'er so bless'd *E.M.* iv. 317

Satire.
Had not her Sister *S.* held her head *D.* iv. 42
Pulpits their sacred s. learn'd to spare *E.C.* 550
Adieu Distinction, *S.*, Warmth, and Truth *E.S.* i. 64
So—*S.* is no more—I feel it die *E.S.* i. 83
Why so? if *S.* knows its Time and Place *E.S.* i. 87
But let all *S.* in all Changes spare *E.S.* i. 91
Come on then, *S.*, gen'ral, unconfin'd *E.S.* ii. 14
Down, down, proud *S.*! tho' a Realm be spoil'd *E.S.* ii. 38
Stop! stop! Must *S.* then nor rise nor fall *E.S.* ii. 52
Praise cannot stoop, like *S.*, to the ground *E.S.* ii. 110
All these, my modest *S.* bade *translate P.S.* 189
Make *S.* a Lampoon, and Fiction, Lie *P.S.* 302
S. or sense, alas! can Sporus feel *P.S.* 307
There are, to whom my *S.* seems too bold *S.* i. 2
S.'s my weapon, but I'm too discreet *S.* i. 69

S. be kind, and let the wretch alone *S.* iii. 135
Hence *S.* rose, that just the medium hit *S.* v. 261
Sharp *S.* that, and that Pindaric lays *S.* vi. 83
Whose *S.*'s sacred, and whose rage secure *S.* viii. 283
Leave dang'rous truths to unsuccessful *S—s E.C.* 592
See *Libels*, *S.*,—here you have it—read (rep.) *S.* i. 149
And paid for all my s., all my rhymes *S.* viii. 6

Satirist, Sat'rist.
Blest *S.*! who touch'd the Mean so true *Ep.* i. 7
This dreaded *S—t Dennis* will confess *P.S.* 370

Satisfy'd.
Be s., I'll do my best *I.H.* ii. 78 s
From Nature's temp'rate feast rose s. *Ep.* x. 9

Saturnian.
To hatch a new *S.* age of Lead *D.* i. 28
Th' Augustus born to bring *S.* times *D.* iii. 320
And bring *S.* days of Lead and Gold *D.* iv. 16

Satyrs.
Rough *S.* dance, and Pan applauds the song *Su.* 50

Saul.
While tow'ring o'er your Alphabet, like *S.* *D.* iv. 217

Saunter'd.
Led by my hand, he s. Europe round *D.* iv. 311

Savage.
He saves from famine, from the s. saves *E.M.* iii. 64
And turn'd on Man a fiercer s., Mao *E.M.* iii. 168
By Saint, by *S.*, and by Sage *U.P.* 3
Wolves gave thee such, and s. Tigers fed *A.* 90
Still fond and proud of s. liberty *E.C.* 650
On s. stocks inserted, learn to bear *E.M.* ii. 182
But Lord, my Friend, this s. Scene *I.H.* ii. 175
See Arts her s. sons control *O.* ii. 21
Tyrants no more their s. nature kept *P.C.* 7
To s. beasts and s. laws a prey *W.F.* 45
And s. howlings fill the sacred quires *W.F.* 72

Save.
Yet sure had Heav'n decreed to s. the state *D.* i. 195
And cackling s. the Monarchy of Tories *D.* i. 212
"God s. King Cibber!" mounts in ev'ry note (rep.) *D.* i. 318
And the hoarse nation croak'd, "God s. King Log!" *D.* i. 330
As erst Medea (cruel, so to s.!) *D.* iv. 121
The same ambition can destroy or s. *E.M.* ii. 201
Fame but from death a villain's name can s. *E.M.* iv. 249
Truths would you teach, or s. a sinking land *E.M.* iv. 265
To s. a Bishop, may I name a Dean *E.S.* ii. 33
Yes—*S.* MY COUNTRY, HEAV'N—He said, and died *Ep.* xiii. 8
Could s. a Parent's justest Pride from fate *Ep.* xiv. 3
Or Gods to s. them in a trice *I.H.* ii. 215
Must then at once (the character to s.) *M.E.* i. 125
Still tries to s. the hallow'd taper's end *M.E.* i. 243
"Oh, s. my country, Heav'n!" shall be your last *M.E.* i. 265
Or find the Doctor that would s. the life *M.E.* iii 93
Have I no friend to serve, no soul to s. *P.S.* 274
To s. the powder from too rude a gale *R.L.* ii. 93
S. but our *Aruxy*! and let Jove encrust *S.* i. 73
He starves with cold to s. them from the fire *S.* vii. 72
S. me alike from foolish Pride *U.P.* 33
S. when they lose a Question, or a *Job E.S.* i. 104
S. just at dinner—then, prefers, no doubt *M.E.* i. 79
His givings rare, s. farthings to the poor *M.E.* iii. 348

Sav'd.
And Quarles is s. by Beauties not his own *D.* i. 140
There s. by spice, like mummies, many a year *D.* i. 151
Could Troy be s. by any single hand *D.* i. 197
All Europe s., yet Britain not betray'd *M.E.* i. 84
Curse the s. candle, and unop'ning door *M.E.* iii. 194
The wretch, who living s. a candle's end *M.E.* iii. 292
Perhaps, by its own ruins s. from flame *M.E.* v. 15
The Rights a Court attack'd, a Poet s. *S.* v. 224

Saves.
He s. from famine, from the savage s. *E.M.* iii. 64
Ev'n Guthry s. half Newgate by a Dash *E.S.* ii. 11
So prompts, and s. a rogue who cannot read *S.* vii. 16

Saving.

And s. Ignorance enthrones by Laws *D.* iii. 98
But fix'd his word, his s. pow'r remains *M.* 107
This s. counsel, "Keep your piece nine years" *P.S.* 40
This, this the s. doctrine, preach'd to all *S.* iii. 81

Saviour.

The *S.* comes! by ancient bards foretold *M.* 37

Saw.

She s., with joy, the line immortal run *D.* i. 99
She s. old Pryn in restless Daniel shine *D.* i. 103
She s. slow Philips creep like Tate's poor page *D.* i. 105
Rome in her Capitol s. Querno sit *D.* ii. 15
And look'd, and s. a sable Sorc'rer rise *D.* iii. 233
As if he s. St. James's and the Queen *D.* iv. 280
The Sire s., one by one, his virtues wake *D.* iv. 285
Europe he s., and Europe s. him too *D.* iv. 294
S. ev'ry Court, heard ev'ry King declare *D.* iv. 313
Then look'd, and s. a lazy, lolling sort *D.* iv. 337
I s., and started from its vernal bow'r *D.* iv. 425
Which Theocles in raptur'd vision s. *D.* iv. 488
S. others happy, and with sighs withdrew *E.* v. 8
No weeping orphan s. his father's stores *E.A.* 135
And the same age s. Learning fall, and Rome *E.C.* 686
Who ne'er s. naked sword, or look'd in Plato *E.J.S.* 44
Superior beings, where of late they s. *E.M.* ii. 31
Who s. its fires here rise, and there descend *E.M.* ii. 37
S. helpless him from whom their life began *E.M.* iii. 142
Man, like his Maker, s. that all was right *E.M.* iii. 232
S. Gods descend, and fiends infernal rise *E.M.* iii. 254
S. nothing to regret, or there to fear *Ep.* x. 8
When twenty Fools I never s. *I.H.* ii. 64 s
Cutler s. tenants break, and houses fall *M.E.* iii. 323
The Tempter s. his time; the work he ply'd *M.E.* iii. 369
I s. him stand behind OMBRELIA's chair *Mi.* ix. 6
While Argo s. her kindred trees, *O.* i. 40
No Courts he s., no suits would ever try *P.S.* 396
I s., alas! some dread event impend *R.L.* i. 109
He s., he wish'd, and to the prize aspir'd *R.L.* ii. 30
But trust the Muse—she s. it upward rise *R.L.* v. 123
The Temple late two brother Sergeants s. *S.* vi. 127
And quick to swallow me, methought I s. *S.* viii. 172
Nor s. displeas'd the peaceful cottage rise *W.F.* 86
Pan s. and lov'd, and, burning with desire *W.F.* 183
She s. her sons with purple deaths expire *W.F.* 323

Saws.

His s. are toothless, and his Hatchet's lead *E.S.* ii. 149

Say.

S., is not absence death to those who love *A.* 30
I sing. *S.* you, her instruments the Great *D.* i. 3
S. how the Goddess bade Britannia sleep *D.* i.
Walker! our hat"—nor more he deign'd to s. *D.* iv. 273
I call aloud; it hears nor what I s. *E.A.* 237
Come, sister, come! (it said or seem'd to s.) *E.A.* 309
Then sadly s., with mutual pity mov'd *E.A.* 351
'Tis hard to s., if greater want of skill *E.C.* 1
Once on a time, La Mancha's Knight, they s. *E.C.* 267
Ask them the cause; they're wiser still, they s. *E.C.* 436
S. first, of God above, or Man below *E.M.* i. 17
Then s. not Man's imperfect, Heav'n in fault (*rep.*) *E.M.* i. 69
S., here he gives too little, there too much *E.M.* i. 116
S. what their use, had he the pow'rs of all *E.M.* i. 178
S. what the use, were finer optics giv'n *E.M.* i. 195
S., will the falcon, stooping from above *E.M.* iii. 83
S., in what mortal soil thou deign'st to grow *E.M.* iv. 8
Who thus define it, s. they more or less *E.M.* iv. 27
S., in pursuit of profit or delight *E.M.* iv. 85
S., was it Virtue, more tho' Heav'n ne'er gave *E.M.* iv. 103
And which more blest? who chain'd his country, s. *E.M.* iv. 147
S., at what part of nature will they stand *E.M.* iv. 166
Look next on Greatness; s. where Greatness lies *E.M.* iv. 217
S., wouldst thou be the Man to whom they fall *E.M.* iv. 276
S., shall my little bark attendant sail *E.M.* iv. 385
Nor let us s. (those English glories gone) *Ep.* ix. 11
May truly s., Here lies an honest Man *Ep.* x. 2
But that the Worthy, and the Good shall s. *Ep.* xi. 11
What they said, or may s. of the mortal within *Ep.* xvi. 6

Now this I'll s. you'll find in me *I.H.* i. 39
Horace would s., Sir Billy *serv'd the Crown E.S.* i. 13
'Tis all a Libel—Paxton (Sir) will s. *E.S.* ii. 1
Still let me s.: No Follower, but a Friend *E.S.* ii. 93
What made (s. Montagne, or more sage Charron!) *M E.* i. 87
S., what can cause such impotence of mind *M.E.* ii. 93
S., what can Chloe want?"—She wants a Heart *M.E.* ii. 160
What s. you? *S.!* Why take it, Gold and all *M.E.* iii. 78
Oh s., what sums that gen'rous hand supply *M.E.* iii. 277
S., for such worth are other worlds prepar'd *M.E.* iii. 335
Impartial, she shall s. who suffers most *Mi.* ix. 25
Once (says an Author; where, I need not s.) *Mi.* xi. 1
S., will you bless the bleak Atlantic shore *O.* ii. 15
Hark! they whisper; Angels s. *O.* v. 7
Tie up the knocker, s. I'm sick, I'm dead *P.S.* 2
(Some s. his Queen) was forc'd to speak, or burst *P.S.* 72
S. for my comfort, languishing in bed *P.S.* 121
I pay my debts, believe, and s. my pray'rs *P.S.* 268
Who tells whate'er you think, whate'er you s. *P.S.* 297
S. what strange motive, Goddess could impel *R.L.* i. 7
O s. what stranger cause, yet unexplor'd *R.L.* i. 9
And thus in whispers said, or seem'd to s. *R.L.* i. 26
'Twas then, Belinda, if report s. true *R.L.* i. 117
Already hear the horrid things they s. *R.L.* iv. 108
S., why are Beauties prais'd and honour'd most *R.L.* v. 9
That men may s., when we the front-box grace *R.L.* v. 17
The lines are weak, another's pleased to s. *S.* i. 5
Your Plea is good; but still I s. beware *S.* i. 143
What life in all that ample body, s. *S.* ii. 77
And what's more rare, a Poet shall s. Grace *S.* ii. 150
S., does thy blood rebel, thy bosom move *S.* iii. 55
And s., to which shall our applause belong *S.* iii. 97
S. with what eyes we ought at Court to gaze *S.* iv. 16
S. at what age a Poet grows divine *S.* v. 90
Or s. our Fathers never broke a rule (*rep.*) *S.* v. 93
Who says in verse what others s. in prose *S.* v. 202
That when I aim at praise, they s. I bite *S.* v. 409
To s. too much might do my honour wrong *S.* vi. 12
Better (s. I) be pleas'd, and play the fool *S.* vi. 181
S., can you find out one such lodger there *S.* vi. 223
When doom'd to s. his beads and Even-song *S.* vii. 106
And as for Courts, forgive me, if I s. *S.* viii. 90
S., Daphnis, s., in what glad soil appears *Sp.* 85
There passengers shall stand, and pointing s. *U.L.* 39

Sayings.

What boy but hears the s. of old Ben *S.* v. 80

Says.

"God cannot love (s. Blunt with tearless eyes) *M.E.* iii. 103
Has she no faults then (Envy s.) Sir *Mi.* viii. 9
Once (s. an Author; where, I need not say) *Mi.* xi. 1
"There take" (s. Justice) "take ye each a *Shell Mi.* xi. 10
Who s. in verse what others say in prose *S.* v. 202
But sure no statute in his favour s. *S.* vi. 288
Would go to Mass in jest (as story s.) *S.* viii. 16
And s. our wars thrive ill, because delay'd *S.* viii. 163

Saxon.

Whom ev'n the *S.* spar'd and bloody Dane *W.F.* 77

Scaffold.

She waits, or to the s., or the cell *E.* i. 33
But quite mistakes the s. for the pile *M.E.* i. 221
Away, away! take all your s—s down *S.* iii. 146

Scale.

Poetic Justice, with her lifted s. *D.* i. 52
Then, in the s. of reas'ning life 'tis plain *E.M.* i. 47
Go, wiser thou! and in thy s. of sense *E.M.* i. 113
The s. of sensual, mental pow'rs ascends *E.M.* i. 208
Where, one step broken, the great s.'s destroy'd *E.M.* i. 244
The s. to measure others' wants by thine *E.M.* ii. 292
See the false s. of Happiness complete *E.M.* iv. 288
Returning Justice lift aloft her s. *M.* 18
While *S.* in hand Dame *Justice* past along *Mi.* xi. 4
Ye Critics in whose heads as equal s—s *D.* ii. 367
Pleas'd the greco lustre of the s. survey *M.* 83
Now Jove suspends his golden s. in air *R.L.* v. 71
The yellow carp, in s. bedropp'd with gold *W.F.* 144
Or helps th' ambitious Hill the heav'ns to s. *M.E.* iv. 59

Scal'd.
He leap'd the trenches, s. a Castle-wall S. vi. 40

Scaly.
With looks unmov'd, he hopes the s. breed W.F. 139

Scan.
Know then thyself, presume not God to s. E.M. ii. 1

Scandal.
Ye Rev'rend Atheists—S./ name them! Who E.S. ii. 18
And quite a s. not to learn I.H. ii. 146
Or her, whose life the Church and S. share M.E. ii. 105
The Pleasure miss'd her, and the S. hit M.E. ii. 128
Give Virtue s., Innocence a fear P.S. 285
If honest S * s take s. at a Spark S. iii. 112
Praise undeserv'd is s. in disguise S. v. 413

Scandalously.
Yet shun their fault, whn, s. nice E.C. 556
Still bourding up, most s. nice E.J.S. 19

Scans.
Each wight who reads not, and but s. and spells P.S. 165

Scantier.
Now s. limits the proud Arch confine M.E. v. 27

'Scape—see Escape.

Scar.
Old England's Genius, rough with many a S. E.S. i. 152
Not Waller's Wreath can hide the Nation's S. E.S. ii. 230
Inglorious triumphs and dishonest s—s W.F. 326

Scarb'row = Scarborough.
And melts to Goodness, need I S. name E.S. ii. 65

Scarce.
How hints, like spawn, s. quick in embryo lie D. i. 59
Then * essay'd ; s. vanish'd out of sight D. ii. 295
Then catch'd the Schools ; the Hall s. kept awake D. iv. 609
Till fate s. felt his gentle breath supprest E. iv. 13
Heav'n s. believ'd the Conquest it survey'd E.A. 113
A thousand movements s. one purpose gain E.M. i. 54
The last, s. ripen'd into perfect Man E.M. iii. 141
Who ask and reason thus, will s. conceive E.M. iv. 163
And when three Sov'reigns died, could s. be vext E.S. i. 107
S. hurts the Lawyer, but undoes the Scribe E.S. ii. 47
What RICH'LIEU wanted, LOUIS s. could gain E.S. ii. 116
Writ not, and Chartres s. could write or read E.S. ii. 186
Our Courtier s. could touch a bit I.H. ii. 171
Born where Heav'n's influence s. can penetrate M.E. i. 142
Just brought out this, when s. his tongue could stir M.E. i. 254
S. once herself, by turns all Woman-kind M.E. ii. 116
As leaves them s. a subject in their Age M.E. ii. 222
At last, to follies Youth could s. defend M.E. ii. 235
Statues of Men, s. less alive than they M.E. v. 10
And s. are seen the prostrate Nile or Rhine M.E. v. 28
There are, (I s. can think it, but am told) S. i. 2
S. to wise Peter complaisant enough S. i. 3
They s. can bear their Laureate twice a year S. i. 34
From furious Sappho s. a milder fate S. i. 83
I s. can think him such a worthless thing S. v. 209
And fluent Shakespear s. effac'd a line S. v. 279
Act sins which Prisca's Confessor s. hears S. vii. 40
S. was I enter'd, when, behold, there came S. viii. 24
S. could the Goddess from her Nymph be known W.F. 175
Tempt icy seas, where s. the waters roll W.F. 389

Scarecrow.
S. to boys, the breeding woman's curse S. viii. 268

Scar'd.
A dauntless infant ! never s. with God D. iv. 284
S. at the spectre of pale Poverty S. iii. 70
S. at the grizly forms, I sweat, I fly S. viii. 278

Scarfs.
S., garters, gold, amuse his riper stage E.M. ii. 279

Scarlet.
With s. hats wide-waving circled round D. ii. 14

Mounts the Tribunal, lifts her s. head E.S. i. 149
His purple crest, and s.-circled eyes W.F. 116

Scarsdale.
S. his bottle, Darty his Ham-pie S. i. 46

Scatter.
Angel of Dulness, sent to s. round D. iii. 257
S. your Favours on a Fop I.H. i. 31
A leaf, like Sibyl's, s. to and fro M.E. iii. 45

Scatter'd.
Their faded honours s. on her bier W. 32

Scatters.
And s. death around from both her eyes R.L. v. 58
And s. blessings from her dove-like wings W.F. 430

Scene.
Beholds thro' fogs, that magnify the s. D. i. 80
Now Night descending, the proud s. was o'er D. i. 89
Now look thro' Fate ! behold the s. she draws D. iii. 127
In ev'ry s. some Moral let it teach E. iv. 23
In pensive thought recall the fancy'd s. E. v. 33
Her gloomy presence saddens all the s. E.A. 167
Amid that s. if some relenting eye E.A. 355
Expatiate free o'er all this s. of Man E.M. i. 5
The S., the Master, op'ning to my view E.S. ii. 68
Remov'd from all th' Ambitious S. I.H. ii. 275
But Lord, my Friend, this savage s. I.H. ii. 175
Where Thames reflects the visionary s. I.H. iii. 24
Where'er he shines, oh Fortune, gild the s. M.E. iii. 215
Tir'd of the s. Parterres and Fountains yield M.E. iv. 87
No artful wildness to perplex the s. M.E. iv. 116
Live o'er each s., and be what they behold P.C. 4
Your s. precariously subsists too long P.C. 41
Down to the central earth, his proper s. R.L. iv. 15
Conspicuous S./ another yet is nigh S. iv. 50
Eternal beauties grace the shining s. W. 72
Here waving groves a chequer'd s. display W.F. 17
Thro' the fair s. roll slow the ling'ring streams W.F. 217
Here lay poor Fletcher's half-eat s—s, and here D. i. 131
Old s. of glory, times long cast behind D. iii. 63
While thro' Poetic s. the GENIUS roves D. iv. 489
What flatt'ring s. our wand'ring fancy wrought E. iii. 23
No more these s. my meditation aid E.A. 157
What s. appear where'er I turn my view E.A. 263
New distant s. of endless science rise E.C. 224
But nobler s. Maria's dreams unfold M.E. iii. 129
What s. appear'd O. i. 54
Now lakes of liquid gold, Elysian s. R.L. iv. 45
Back fly the s., and enter foot and horse S. v. 315
Beheld such s. of envy, sin, and hate S. viii. 193
See what delights in sylvan s. appear Su. 59
Bear me, O bear me to sequester'd s. W.F. 261
'To paint anew the flow'ry sylvan s. W.F. 285
And bring the s. of op'ning fate to light W.F. 426

Scent.
At once they gratify their s. and taste R.L. iii. 111

Sceptic.
With too much knowledge for the S. side E.M. ii. 5

Sceptres.
Thus vanish s., coronets, and balls E. v. 39

Scheme.
Hence the Fool's Paradise, the Statesman's S. D. iii. 9
Oh blind to truth, and God's whole s. below E.M. iv. 93
Who sees and follows that great s. the best E.M. iv. 95
To gain Pescennius one employs his s—s M.E. v. 39

Schem'd.
In vain they s., in vain they bled I.H. iv. 15

Schismatics.
So S. the plain believers quit E.C. 428

Scholar.
The s.'s learning, with the courtier's ease E.C. 668

Scholiast.
Thy mighty S., whose unweary'd pains D. iv. 211
There, dim in clouds, the poring S—s mark D. iii. 191
Or chew'd by blind old S. o'er and o'er D. iv. 232

School.
Thrid ev'ry science, run thro' ev'ry s. D. iv. 256

Thro' *S.* and College, thy kind cloud o'ercast *D.* iv. 289
Late as it is, I put myself to *s. S.* iii. 47
At court, who hates whate'er he read at *s. S.* v. 106
And orient his Wife to church, his Son to *s. S.* v. 164
I'll e'en leave verses to the boys at *s. S.* vi. 201
Then catch'd the S—s ; *the Hall scarce kept awake D.* iv. 609
Some are bewilder'd in the maze of *s. E.C.* 26
Hear Bethel's sermon, one not vers'd in *s. S.* ii. 9
Remember oft the S.-boy's simple fare S. ii. 73
And God the Father turns a *S.-divine S.* v. 102
Once *S—s* this zealous isle o'er-spread *E.C.* 440

Schoolman.
Unlearn'd, he knew no *s.'s* subtle art *P.S.* 398
Let subtle s.-men teach these friends to fight E.M. ii. 81
S. new tenements in hell must make *S.* vii. 42

Sciatics.
Rack'd with *S.*, martyr'd with the Stone *S.* iv. 54

Science.
Yet holds the eel of *s.* by the tail *D.* i. 280
And orient *S.* their bright course begun *D.* iii. 74
Where, faint at best, the beams of *S.* fall *D.* iii. 84
But where each *S.* lifts its modern type *D.* iii. 195
Beneath her footstool, *S.* groans in Chains *D.* iv. 21
Thrid ev'ry *s.*, run thro' ev'ry school *D.* iv. 256
Blest in each *s.*, blest in ev'ry strain *E.* i. 5
'Tis sure the hardest *s.* to forget *E.A.* 190
One *s.* only will one genius fit *E.C.* 60
To teach vain Wits a *s.* little known *E.C.* 199
New distant scenes of endless *s.* rise *E.C.* 224
His soul, proud *S.* never taught to stray *E.M.* i. 101
Go, wond'rous creature! mount where *S.* guides *E.M.* ii. 19
Trace *S.* then, with Modesty thy Guide *E.M.* ii. 40
Content with *S.* in the Vale of Peace *Ep.* x. 6
As hard a *s.* to the Fair as Great *M.E.* ii. 226
And tho' no *S.*, fully worth the seven *M.E.* iv. 44

Scipio.
Such was the life great *S.* once admir'd *W.F.* 257
That very Cæsar, born in S.'s days M.E. i. 216

Scissors.
Jove, Jove himself does on the *S.* shine *Mi.* ix. 35

Scold.
More rough than forty Germans when they *s. S.* vii. 62

Scolding.
When airs, and flights, and screams, and *s.* fail *R.L.* v. 32

Scolds.
S. with her maid, or with her chaplain crams *E.J.S.* 22

Sconce.
Triumphant Umbriel on a *s.'s* height *R.L.* v. 53

Scoops.
Or *s.* in circling theatres the Vale *M.E.* iv. 60

Scope.
His fable, subject, *s.* in ev'ry page *E.C.* 120

Scorch.
Fires that *s.*, yet dare not shine *O.* iii. 40

Scorches.
By night he *s.*, as he burns by day *Su.* 92

Score.
Bond is but one, but Harpax is a *s. I.* i. 44
For mark th' advantage; just so many *s. S.* iv. 77
A tongue that can cheat widows; cancel—s S. viii. 58

Scorn.
A *S.* of wrangling, yet a Zeal for Truth *Ep.* ii. 8
Wharton, the *s.* and wonder of our days *M.E.* i. 180
Why then declare Good-nature is her *s. M.E.* ii. 59
Your Taste of Follies, with our *S.* of Fools *M.E.* ii. 276
Toasts live a *s.*, and Queens may die a jest *M.E.* ii. 282
Who holds Dragoons and wooden Shoes in *s. Mi.* ii. 20
With honest *s.* the first fam'd Cato view'd *P.C.* 39
Alike my *s.*, if he succeed or fail *P.S.* 362
And view with *s.* two Pages and a Chair *R.L.* i. 46
Why one like Bu—, with pay and *s.* content *S.* vi. 274
But, *"Learn, ye* DUNCES! *not to s. your God" D.* iii. 224

Find Virtue local, all Relation *s. D.* iv. 479
Then *s.* to gain a Friend by servile ways *E.* ii. 10
Himself, his throne, his world, I'd *s.*, 'em all *E.A.* 86
At ev'ry trifle *s.* to take offence *E.C.* 386
So much they *s.* the crowd, that if the throng *E.C.* 426
From ancient story learn to *s.* them all *E.M.* iv. 286
And *s.* a rascal and a coach *Mi.* xii. 20
Who would not *s.* what housewife's cares produce *R.L.* v. 21
Then *s.* a homely dinner, if you can *S.* ii. 12
Who *s.* a Lad should teach his father skill *S.* v. 129
And *s.* the flesh, the dev'l, and all but gold *S.* vii. 24

Scorn'd.
And but from Nature's fountains *s.* to draw *E.C.* 133
She *s.* the praise of beauty and the care *W.F.* 177

Scornful.
Cast on the prostrate Nine a *s.* look *D.* iv. 5
View him with *s.*, yet with jealous eyes *P.S.* 199
Not *s.* virgins who their charms survive *R.L.* iv. 4

Scorning.
Dunce *s.*, Dunce beholds the next advance *D.* iv. 137

Scorns.
Eridanus his humble fountain *s. D.* ii. 182
And she who *s.* a man, must die a maid *R.L.* v. 28
And justly CÆSAR *s.* the Poet's lays *S.* i. 35

Scot.
A *S.* will fight for Christ's Kirk o' the Green *S.* v. 40
From S—s to WIGHT, *from* MOUNT *to* DOVER *strand S.* vii. 86
Make *S.* speak treason, cozen subtlest whores *S.* viii. 59

Scotists.
S. and Thomists now in peace remain *E.C.* 444

Scotland.
In *S.*, at the Orcades; and there *E.M.* ii. 223

Scoto.
Ask Men's Opinions: *S.* now shall tell *M.E.* i. 158

Scotsman.
Just as a *S.* does his Plums *I.H.* i. 24

Scoundrels.
Has crept thro' *S.* ever since the flood *E.M.* iv. 212

Scour'd.
Can taste no pleasure since his Shield was *s. M.E.* v. 42

Scourge.
And Tutchin, flagrant from the *s.* below *D.* ii. 148
Jacob, the *s.* of Grammar, mark with awe *D.* iii. 149
The *s.* of Pride, tho' sanctify'd or great *Ep.* i. 2
Or turns young Ammon loose to *s.* mankind *E.M.* i. 160

Scours.
Imbibes new life, and *s.* and stinks along *D.* ii. 106
Not so, when swift Camilla *s.* the plain *E.C.* 372

Scrap.
No rag, no *s.*, of all the beau, or wit *D.* ii. 119
Pregnant with thousands flits the *s.* unseen *M.E.* iii. 47
On parchment s—s y-fed, and Wormius hight D. iii. 188

Scrape.
A hundred footsteps *s.* the marble Hall *M.E.* iv. 152

Scrawl.
All rhyme, and *s.*, and scribble, to a man *S.* v. 188

Scrawls.
Is there, who, lock'd from ink and paper, *s. P.S.* 19

Scream.
S. like the winding of ten thousand Jacks *D.* iii. 160
And *s.* thyself as none ere scream'd before *D.* iii. 306

Scream'd.
And scream thyself as none ere *s.* before *D.* iii. 306

Screams.
Dismal *s. O.* i. 57
And *s.* of horror rend th' affrighted skies *R.L.* iii. 156
When airs, and flights, and *s.*, and scolding fail *R.L.* v. 32

Screen.

His Friend and Shame, and was a kind of *S*. *E.S.* i. 22
And one describes a charming Indian *s*. *R.L.* iii. 14
Be this thy *S*., and this thy wall of Brass *S*. iii. 95

Screen'd.

And *s*. in shades from day's detested glare *R.L.* iv. 22

Scribble.

If Mævius *s*. in Apollo's spite *E.C.* 34
Make some take physic, others *s*. plays *R.L.* iv. 62
All rhyme, and scrawl, and *s*., to a man *S*. v. 188
If I would *s*., rather than repose *S*. vi. 71
But turn a wit, and *s*. verses too *S*. vii. 54

Scribbler.

Who shames a *S.*? break one cobweb thro' *P.S.* 89
A hireling *s*., or a hireling peer *P.S.* 364
S—s or Peers, alike are Mob to me *S*. i. 140

Scribbling.

Who hunger and who thirst for *s*. sake *D.* i. 50
Than when they promise to give *s*. o'er *E.C.* 595

Scribe.

Scarce hurts the Lawyer, but undoes the *S*. *E.S.* ii. 47

Scripture.

Why yes; with *S*. you may still be free *E.S.* i. 37

Scriv'ner.

Will sneaks a *S*., an exceeding knave *M.E.* i. 154
'Twas no court-badge, great *S.!* fir'd thy brain *M.E.* iii. 145
Slides to a *S*. or a city Knight *S*. ii. 178

Scruple.

To lend a wife, few here would *s*. make *E.J.S.* 35
Some *s*. rose, but thus he eas'd his thought *M.E.* iii. 365

Sculler.

They hire their *s*., and when once aboard *S*. iii. 159

Sculpture.

Then *S*. and her sister-arts revive *E.C.* 701
The verse and *s*. bore an equal part *M.E.* v. 51

Sculptur'd.

Gold, Silver, Iv'ry, Vases *s*. high *S*. vi. 264

Scylla.

Fear the just Gods and think of *S*.'s Fate *R.L.* iii. 122

Scythes.

But useless lances into *s*. shall bend *M*. 61

'Sdeath.

Fir'd that the House reject him, "*S.* I'll print it *P.S.* 61

Sea.

Round and more round o'er all the *s*. *of heads D.* ii. 410
Still as the *s*., ere winds were taught to blow *E.A.* 253
Like bubbles on the *s*. of Matter born (*rep*.) *E.M.* iii. 19
On air or *s*. new motions he imprest *E.M.* iv. 125
Thus in a *s*. of folly tost *I.H.* ii. 125
Back to his bounds their subject *S*. command *M.E.* iv. 201
And tremble at the froths below *R.L.* i. 136
Sooner let earth, air, *s*. to Chaos fall *R.L.* iv. 119
Why deck'd with all that land and *s*. afford *R.L.* v. 11
Till, like the *S*., they compass all the land *S*. vii. 85
Lost in my fame, as in the *s*. their streams *W.F.* 362
A place there is, betwixt earth, air, and s—s *D*. ii. 83
As under *s*. Alpheus' secret sluice *D*. ii. 341
Her boundless empire over *s*. and lands *D*. iii. 68
Intrepid then, o'er *s*. and lands he flew *D*. iv. 293
In *s*. of flame my plunging soul is drown'd *E.A.* 275
S. roll to waft me, suns to light me rise *E.M.* i. 139
The toil, the danger of the *S*. *I.H.* ii. 37
The *s*. shall waste, the skies in smoke decay *M*. 105
So when the first bold vessel dar'd the *s*. *O*. i. 47
And *s*., and rocks, and skies rebound *O*. i. 47
Arabian shores, or Indian *s*. iofold *S*. iv. 11
T' enroll your Triumphs o'er the *s*. and land *S*. v. 373
What *s*. you travers'd, and what fields you fought *S*. v. 396
Whose Altar, Earth, *S*., Skies *U.P.* 50
No *s*. so rich, so gay no banks appear *W.F.* 225
Tempt icy *s*., where scarce the waters roll *W.F.* 389
The time shall come, when, free as *s*. or wind *W.F.* 397
And *s*. but join the regions they divide *W.F.* 400
Around his throne the s.-born *brothers* stood *W.F.* 337
His *s*.-*green* mantle waving with the wind *W.F.* 350
Un-water'd see the drooping *s*.-*horse* mourn *M.E.* iv. 125
From dirt and *s*.-*weed* as proud Venice rose *E.M.* iv. 292

Seal'd.

Nor pass these lips in holy silence *s*. *E.A.* 10

Seal-rings.

In three *s*.; which after, melted down *R.L.* v. 91

Seals.

Each gentle clerk, and mutt'ring *s*. his eye *D*. ii. 404

Seam.

Yet hang your lip, to see a *S*. awry *S*. iii. 174

Search.

In *s*. of wit these lose their common sense *E.C.* 28
Yet, in this *s*., the wisest may mistake *M.E.* i. 210
In *s*. of mischief still on earth to roam *R.L.* i. 64
Or tir'd in *s*. of Truth, or *s*. of Rhyme *S*. ii. 86
S. then the *RULING PASSION: there, alone M.E.* i. 174
Go, *s*. it there, where to be born and die *M.E.* iii. 287
Repair'd to *s*. the gloomy Cave of Spleen *R.L.* iv. 16
But feigns a laugh, to see me *s*. around *Sp*. 55

Season.

Beauty, frail flow'r that ev'ry *s*. fears *E*. iii. 57
Wait but for wings, and in their *s*. fly *M.E.* iii. 170
The *s*., when to come, and when to go *S*. v. 360
Fresh as the morn, and as the *s*. fair *Sp*. 20
The various s—s *of the rolling year Sp*. 28
In vain kind *s*. swell'd the teeming grain *W.F.* 53

Seat.

And here she plann'd th' Imperial *s*. of Fools *D*. i. 272
High on a gorgeous *s*., that far out-shone *D*. ii. 1
Then raptures high the *s*. of sense o'erflow *D*. ii. 5
There in his *s*. two spacious vents appear *D*. ii. 85
He chinks his purse, and takes his *s*. of state *D*. ii. 197
Her *s*. imperial Dulness shall transport *D*. iii. 298
Oh, could I see my Country *S*. *I.H.* ii. 128
Her Head's untouch'd, that noble *S*. of Thought *M.E.* ii. 74
The woods recede around the naked *s*. *M.E.* iii. 209
In Britain's Senate he a *s*. obtains *M.E.* iii. 393
You'll wish your bill or shelter'd *s*. again *M.E.* iv. 76
Much they extoll'd his pictures, much his *s*. *P.S.* 239
And sure if aught below the s—s *divine E*. i. 21
Whose *S*. the weary Traveller repose *M.E.* iii. 260
Oh deign to visit our forsaken *s*. *Su*. 71
At once the Monarch's and the Muse's *s*. *W.F.* 2
And call the Muses to their ancient *s*. *W.F.* 284

Secker.

S. is decent, Rundel has a Heart *E.S.* ii. 71

Second.

Still Dunce the *s*. reigns like Dunce the first *D*. i. 6
A *s*. effort brought but new disgrace *D*. i. 175
One circle first, and then a *s*. makes *D*. ii. 406
A *s*. see, by meeker manners known *D*. iii. 143
And, at their *s*. birth, they issue mine *D*. iv. 386
Shrinks to her *s*. cause, and is no more *D*. iv. 644
Nuw length of Fame (our *s*. life) is lost *E.C.* 480
A *s*. deluge Learning thus o'er-run *E.C.* 691
Perhaps acts *s*. to some sphere unknown *E.M.* i. 58
On him, their *s*. Providence, they hung *E.M.* iii. 217
Without a *s*. or without a judge *E.M.* iv. 264
If *s*. qualities for first they take *M.E.* i. 211
They seek the *s*. not to lose the first *M.E.* ii. 214
Stretch'd on the lawn his *s*. hope survey *W.F.* 81
Yet serves to s. *too some other use E.M.* i. 56
To *s*., Arbuthnot! thy Art and Care *P.S.* 133

Secret.

See, now I keep the *S*., and not you *E.S.* ii. 23
" 'Tis now no *s*."—" I protest *I.H.* ii. 1182
Safe is your *S*. still in Chloe's ear *M.E.* ii. 173
That *s*. rare, between th' extremes to move *M.E.* iii. 227
"Out with it, DUNCIAD! let the *s*. pass (*rep*.) *P.S.* 79
Who in the *s*., deals in Stocks secure *S*. viii. 140
As under seas Alpheus' s. *sluice D*. ii. 341
Thus at his fell approach, and *s*. might *D*. iv. 639
Have still a *s*. Bias to a Knave *E.S.* ii. 101

If *s*. Gold sap on from knave to knave *M.E.* iii. 34
Tho' my own *s*. wish was for the *Knave Mi.* ix. 50
But each man's *s*. standard is his mind *P.S.* 176
Some *s*. truths, from learned pride conceal'd *R.L.* i. 37
And *s*. passions labour'd in her breast *R.L.* iv. 2
And *s*. transport touch'd the conscious swain *W.F.* 90

Secretary.
He marches off his Grace's *S. D.* ii. 220

Sect.
To one small *s*., and all are damn'd beside *E.C.* 397
Slave to no *s*., who takes no private road *E.M.* iv. 331
Sworn to no Master, of no *S*. am I *S.* iii. 24

Secure.
S., thro' her, the noble prize to carry *D.* ii. 219
S. the radiant weapons wield *E.* vi. 5
S. from Flames, from Envy's fiercer rage *E.C.* 183
S. to be as blest as thou canst bear *E.M.* i. 286
But now *s*. the painted vessel glides *R.L.* ii. 47
S. of peace at least beyond the grave *S.* viii 4
Who in the secret, deals in Stocks *s. S.* viii. 140
Whose Satire's sacred, and whose rage *s. S.* viii. 283
S. they trust th' unfaithful field beset *W.F.* 103
S. *us kindly in our native right D.* i. 176

Secur'd.
The Gaul subdu'd, or Property *s. S.* v. 10

Securely.
He steer'd *s*., and discover'd far *E.C.* 647 .

Secures.
Then dubs Director, and *s*. his soul *M.E.* iii. 374

Security.
And place, on good *S*., his Gold *S.* v. 168

Sedate.
S. and quiet the comparing lies *E.M.* ii. 69
Cumpos'd in sufl'rings, and in joy *s. Ep.* vii. 3
In vain *s*. reflections we would make *M.E.* i. 39

Sedgy.
The gulfy Lea his *s*. tresses rears *W.F.* 346

Sedley.
Sprat, Carew, *S*., and a hundred more *S.* v. 109

See.
Oh, skill'd in Nature! *s*. the hearts of swains *A.* 11
And *s*.! thy very gazetteers give o'er *D.* i. 215
Lift up your Gates, ye Princes, *s*. him come *D.* i. 301
S. in the circle next, Eliza plac'd *D.* ii. 157
True to the bottom *s*. Concanen creep *D.* ii. 299
Oh born to *s*. what name can *s*. awake *D.* iii. 43
S., round the Poles where keener spangles shine *D.* iii. 69
From shelves to shelves *s*. greedy Vulcan roll *D.* iii. 81
S. Alaric's stern port *s*. the martial frame *D.* iii. 91
S. the bold Ostrogoths on Latium fall (*rep.*) *D.* iii. 93
S. Christians, Jews, one heavy sabbath keep *D.* iii. 99
S. the Cirque falls, th' unpillar'd Temple nods *D.* iii. 107
S. graceless Venus to a Virgin turn'd *D.* iii. 111
And *s*., my son! the hour is on its way *D.* iii. 123
S. all her progeny, illustrious dirt *D.* iii. 129
A second *s*. by meeker manners known *D.* iii. 143
Wits, who, like owls, *s*. only in the dark *D.* iii. 192
S. now, what Dulness and her sons admire (*rep.*) *D.* iii. 228
New wizards rise ; I *s*. my Cibber there *D.* iii. 266
S.! the dull stars roll round and re-appear (*rep.*) *D.* iii. 322
S. under Ripley rise a new White-hall *D.* iii. 327
Till Thames *s*. Eton's sons for ever play *D.* iii. 335
Are things which Kuster, Burman, Wasse shall *s. D.* iv. 237
S.! still thy own, the heavy Canon roll *D.* iv. 247
But wherefore waste I words? I *s*. advance *D.* iv. 271
S. now, half-cur'd, and perfectly well-bred *D.* iv. 323
S., to my country happy I restore *D.* iv. 329
S. other Cæsars, other Homers rise *D.* iv. 360
Now *s*. an Attys, now a Cecrops clear *D.* iv. 363
S. Nature in some partial narrow shape *D.* iv. 455
Whose pious hope aspires to *s*. the day *D.* iv. 461
S. all in *Self*, and but for self be born *D.* iv. 480
Oh hide the God still more ! and make us *s. D.* iv. 483

S. skulking *Truth* to her old cavern fled *D.* iv. 641
S. Mystery to *Mathematics* fly *D.* iv. 647
Thro' Fortune's cloud one truly great can *s. E.* i. 39
S. Coronations rise on ev'ry green *E.* v. 34
In Dryden's Virgil *s*. the print *E.* vi. 28
Dim and remote the joys of saints I *s. E.A.* 71
S. how the force of others pray'rs I try *E.A.* 149
S. in her cell sad Eloïsa spread *E.A.* 303
S. my lips tremble, and my eye-balls roll *E.A.* 323
Ah then, thy once lov'd Eloïsa *s. E.A.* 329
S. from my cheek the transient roses fly (*rep.*) *E.A.* 331
S. from each clime the learn'd their incense bring *E.C.* 185
Short views we take, nor *s*. the lengths behind *E.C.* 222
Whoever thinks a faultless piece to *s. E.C.* 253
And *s*. now clearer and now darker days *E.C.* 405
Our sons their fathers' failing language *s. E.C.* 482
S. Dionysius Homer's thoughts refine *E.C.* 665
But *s*.! each Muse, in Leo's golden days *E.C.* 697
To *s*. a piece of failing flesh and blood *E.J.S.* 47
Of Man, what *s*. we, but his station here *E.M.* i. 19
S. worlds on worlds compose one universe *E.M.* i. 24
'Tis but a part we *s*., and not a whole *E.M.* i. 60
S., thro' this air, this ocean, and this earth *E.M.* i. 213
Beast, bird, fish, insect, what no eye can *s. E.M.* i. 239
All Chance, Direction, which thou canst not *s. E.M.* i. 294
Then *s*. how little the remaining sum *E.M.* ii. 51
S. anger, zeal and fortitude supply *E.M.* ii. 187
S. the blind beggar dance, the cripple sing *E.M.* ii. 267
S. some strange comfort ev'ry state attend *E.M.* ii. 271
S. some fit Passion ev'ry age supply *E.M.* ii. 273
S.! and confess, one comfort still must rise *E.M.* ii. 293
S. plastic Nature working to this end *E.M.* iii. 9
S. Matter next, with various life endu'd *E.M.* iii. 13
S. dying vegetables life sustain (*rep.*) *E.M.* iii. 15
While Man exclaims, " *S*. all things for my use !" (*rep.*) *E.M.* iii. 45
S. then the acting and comparing pow'rs *E.M.* iii. 95
S. him from Nature rising slow to Art *E.M.* iii. 169
Here subterranean works and cities *s. E.M.* iii. 181
S. FALKLAND dies, the virtuous and the just (*rep.*) *E.M.* iv. 99
To *s*. all other's faults, and feel our own *E.M.* iv. 262
Make fair deductions ; *s*. to what they mount *E.M.* iv. 270
S. Cromwell, damn'd to everlasting fame *E.M.* iv. 284
S. the false scale of Happiness complete *E.M.* iv. 288
Thee *s*. them broke with toils or sunk in ease *E.M.* iv. 297
S. the sole bliss Heav'n could on all bestow *E.M.* iv. 327
And when it comes, the Court *s*. nothing in't *E.S.* i. 2
Why now, this moment, don't I *s*. you steal *E.S.* i. 6
Go *s*. Sir Robert—*S*. Sir Robert!—hum *E.S.* i. 27
S. thronging Millions to the Pagod run *E.S.* i. 157
S., all our Nobles begging to be Slaves (*rep.*) *E.S.* i. 163
S., now I keep the Secret, and not you *E.S.* ii. 23
I sit and dream I *s*. my CRAGGS anew *E.S.* ii. 69
To *s*. a Footman kick'd that took his pay *E.S.* ii. 151
Yes, I am proud ; I must be proud to *s. E.S.* ii. 208
Let Flatt'ry sick'ning *s*. the Incense rise *E.S.* ii. 244
And you shall *s*. the first warm Weather *I.H.* i. 29
And liv'd—just as you *s*. I do *I.H.* i. 72
'Tis (let me *s*.) three years and more *I.H.* ii. 83 *s*
Because they *s*. me us'd so well *I.H.* ii. 102 *s*
S. but the fortune of some folks *I.H.* ii. 108 *s*
Oh, could I *s*. my Country Seat *I.H.* ii. 128
S. Nature hastes her earliest wreaths to bring *M.* 23
S. lilies spring, and sudden verdure rise *M.* 68
S., a long race thy spacious courts adorn *M.* 87
S. barb'rous nations at thy gates attend *M.* 91
S. thy bright altars throng'd with prostrate kings *M.* 93
S. heav'n its sparkling portals wide display *M.* 97
All *s*. 'tis Vice, and itch of vulgar praise *M.E.* i. 60
S. the same man, in vigour, in the gout *M.E.* i. 71
All eyes may *s*. from what the change arose (*rep.*) *M.E.* ii. 35
S. Sin in State, majestically drunk *M.E.* ii. 69
None *s*. what Parts of Nature it conceals *M.E.* ii. 190
S. how the World its Veterans rewards *M.E.* ii. 243
Oh ! that such bulky Bribes as bulk *M.E.* ii. 49
S. Britain sunk in lucre's sordid charms *M.E.* iii. 143
No, 'twas thy righteous end, asham'd to *s. M.E.* iii. 147
And *s*., what comfort it affords our end *M.E.* iii. 298
S.! sportive fate, to punish awkward pride *M.E.* iv. 19
Or *s*. the stretching branches long to meet *M.E.* iv. 92

T

SEE (continued)—SEEMS.

Un-water'd s. the drooping sea-horse mourn *M.E.* iv. 125
Another age shall s. the golden Ear *M.E.* iv. 173
S. the wild waste of all-devouring years *M.E.* v. 1
In living medals s. her wars enroll'd *M.E.* v. 55
Then future ages with delight shall s. *M.E.* v. 59
Whate'er we think, whate'er we s. *Mi.* iv. 2
S. my weary Days consuming *Mi.* vii. 7
S. the Bird of *Juno* stooping *Mi.* vii. 31
S. BETTY LOVET! very à *propos Mi.* ix. 21
S., on the Tooth-pick, Mars and Cupid strive *Mi.* ix. 31
This *Snuff-Box*,—on the Hinge s. Brilliants shine *Mi.* ix. 43
And s. the Folly, which I cannot shun *Mi.* ix. 70
And s. if Reason must not *there* be lost *Mi.* ix. 86
And s. *!* the tortur'd ghosts respire (*rep.*) *O.* i. 64
S., wild as the winds, o'er the desert he flies *O.* i. 110
Ah s., he dies *O.* i. 112
S. Arts her savage sons control *O.* ii. 21
Sir, let me s. you and your works no more *P.S.* 68
Go on, obliging creatures, make me s. *P.S.* 119
Left me to s. neglected Genius bloom *P.S.* 257
And s. what friends, and read what books I please *P.S.* 264
Why am I ask'd what next shall s. the light *P.S.* 271
And s. thro' all things with my half-shut eyes *R.L.* iii. 118
Already s. yon a degraded toast *R.L.* iv. 109
Then s. *!* the nymph in beauteous grief appears *R.L.* iv. 143
S. the poor remnants of these slighted hairs *R.L.* iv. 167
She smil'd to s. the doughty hero slain *R.L.* v. 69
S., fierce Belinda on the Baron flies *R.L.* v. 75
But s. how oft ambitious aims are cross'd *R.L.* v. 107
Ridotta sips and dances, till she s. *S.* i. 47
S. *Libels, Satires*—here you have it—read *S.* i. 149
Cheap Eggs, and herbs, and olives still we s. *S.* ii. 35
What's *Property?* dear Swift! you s. it alter *S.* ii. 167
S., Modest Cibber now has left the Stage *S.* iii. 6
To either India s. the Merchant fly *S.* iii. 69
S. him with pains of body, pangs of soul *S.* iii. 71
Because I s., by all the tracks about *S.* iii. 116
Yet hang your lip, to s. a Seam awry *S.* iii. 174
To s. their Judgments hang upon thy voice *S.* iv. 35
S. Ward by batter'd Beaux invited over *S.* iv. 56
My only son, I'll have him s. the world *S.* vi. 6
S. *!* strew'd with learned dust, his night-cap on *S.* vi. 128
Lord! how we strut thro' Merlin's Cave to s. *S.* vi. 139
We s., no new-built palaces aspire *S.* vii. 111
Our sons shall s. it leisurely decay *S.* viii. 44
Spirits like you, should s. and should be seen *S.* viii. 88
And this yon s. is but my dishabille *S.* viii. 115
Can gratis s. the country or the town *S.* viii. 145
To s. themselves fall end-long into beasts *S.* viii. 167
I quak'd at heart; and still afraid, to s. *S.* viii. 180
And forc'd ev'n me to s. the damn'd at Court *S.* viii. 191
S. *!* where the British youth, engag'd no more *S.* viii. 214
To s. those antics, Fopling and Courtin *S.* viii. 237
S. them survey their limbs by Durer's rules *S.* viii. 240
For hung with deadly sins I s. the wall *S.* viii. 274
But feigns a laugh, to s. me search around *Sp.* 55
For s. *!* the gath'ring flocks to shelter tend *Sp.* 101
S. what delights in sylvan scenes appear *Su.* 59
But s., the shepherds shun the noonday heat *Su.* 85
S. on these ruby lips the trembling breath *U.L.* 31
To s. the Good from ill *U.P.* 10
To hide the Fault I s. *U.P.* 38
S. gloomy clouds obscure the cheerful day *W.* 30
S., where on earth the flow'ry glories lie *W.* 33
But s. *!* where Daphne wond'ring mounts on high *W.* 69
But s., Orion sheds unwholesome dews *W.* 85
Where order in variety we s. *W.F.* 15
S. Pan with flocks, with fruits Pomona crown'd *W.F.* 37
But s., the man who spacious regions gave *W.F.* 79
S. *!* from the brake the whirring pheasant springs *W.F.* 111
S. the bold youth strain up the threat'ning steep *W.F.* 155
I s., I s., where two fair cities bend *W.F.* 379

Seed.

Then rose the *S.* of Chaos and of Night *D.* iv. 13
Is thine alone the s. that strews the plain *E.M.* iii. 37
Plant of celestial s. *!* if dropt below *E.M.* iv. 7
And shook from out his Pipe the s—s *of fire D.* iv. 494
Most have the s. of judgment in their mind *E.C.* 20
The vital flame, and swell'd the genial s. *E.M.* iii. 118
And s. of gold in Ophir's mountains glow *M.* 96
Bids s.-time, *harvest, equal course maintain M.E.* iii. 165

Seeing.

The optics s., as the object seen *M.E.* i. 32

Seek.

For Attic Phrase in Plato let them s. *D.* iv. 227
Or s. some Ruin's formidable shade *E.* iii. 30
Who s. in love for aught but love alone *E.A.* 84
But you who s. to give and merit fame *E.C.* 46
Survey the WHOLE, nor s. slight faults to find *E.C.* 235
Meanly they s. the blessing to confine *E.C.* 398
All may allow; but s. your friendship too *E.C.* 565
S., an admirer, or would fix a friend *E.M.* iv. 44
Are giv'n in vain, but what they s. they find *E.M.* iv. 348
They s. the second not to lose the first *M.E.* ii. 214
Here, Wisdom calls: " *S.* Virtue first, be bold *S.* iii. 77
Feed here my lambs, I'll s. no distant field *Sp.* 64
When swains from shearing s. their nightly bow'rs *Sw.* 64
Nor thirsty heifers s. the gliding flood *W.* 38
S. the clear spring, or haunt the pathless grove *W.F.* 168
And the new world launch forth to s. the old *W.F.* 402

Seek'st.

Son, what thou s. is in thee! Look, and find *D.* iii. 251

Seeks.

Which nothing s. to shew, or needs to hide *E.* ii. 2
Each individual s. a sev'ral goal *E.M.* ii. 237
Which s. no int'rest, no reward but praise *E.M.* ii. 246
The link dissolves, each s. a fresh embrace *E.M.* iii. 129
S. freshest pasture and the purest air *M.* 30
Not therefore humble he who s. retreat *M.E.* i. 113
Softly s. her silent Mate *Mi.* vii. 30
A Shepherd's Boy (he s. no better name) *Su.* 1

Seem.

His easy Art may happy Nature s. *E.* iv. 3
Thy voice I s. in ev'ry hymn to hear *E.A.* 269
Those freer beauties, ev'n in them, s. faults *E.C.* 170
Conceal his force, nay s. sometimes to fly (*rep.*) *E.C.* 1.8
Mount o'er the vales, and s. to tread the sky *E.C.* 226
And the first clouds and mountains s. the last *E.C.* 228
The sound must s. an Echo to the sense *E.C.* 365
As things s. large which we thro' mists descry *E.C.* 392
Lest God himself should s. too absolute *E.C.* 549
He did his best to s. to eat *I.H.* ii. 173
That each may s. a Virtue, or a Vice *M.E.* ii. 206
Is but to please, can Pleasure s. a fault *M.E.* ii. 212
Lean and fretful; would s. wise *Mi.* vi. 7
And both the struggling figures s. alive *Mi.* ix. 32
Still to one Bishop Philips s. a wit *P.S.* 100
'Twill then be infamy to s. your friend *R.L.* iv. 112
Why, if the nights s. tedious,—take a Wife *S.* i. 16
To s. but mortal, ev'n in sound Divines *S.* ii. 80
He, who to s. more deep than you or I *S.* v. 131
Here earth and water s. to strive again *W.F.* 12
I s. thro' consecrated walks to rove *W.F.* 267

Seem'd.

Where the tall Nothing stood, or s. to stand *D.* ii. 110
And to mere mortals s. a Priest in drink *D.* ii. 426
The Goddess smiling s. to give consent *D.* iv. 395
Come, sister, come! (it said, or s. to say) *E.A.* 309
Perhaps he s. above the critic's law *E.C.* 132
Faith, Gospel, all, s. made to be disputed *E.C.* 442
Then sacred s. th' ethereal vault no more *E.M.* iii. 263
S. to her ear his winning lips to lay (*rep.*) *R.L.* i. 25
That s. but Zephyrs to the train beneath *R.L.* ii. 58
'Twas this the morning omens s. to tell *R.L.* iv. 161
Ben, old and poor, as little s. to heed *S.* v. 73

Seeming.

And speak, tho' sure, with s. diffidence *E.C.* 567
Each s. want compensated of course *E.M.* i. 181
'Tis real good, or s., moves them all *E.M.* ii. 94
Death draws still nearer, never s. near *E.M.* iii. 76

Seems.

And left-legg'd Jacob s. to emulate *D.* ii. 68
And, while he s. to study, thinks of you *E.* v. 44
All s. infected, that th' infected spy *E.C.* 558
So Man, who here s. principal alone *E.M.* i. 57
But here a grievance s. to lie *I.H.* ii. 95
When awful Love s. melting in his Eyes *Mi.* ix. 90

SEEN—SENATE. 275

S. to reject him, tho' she grants his pray'r *R.L.* iv. 80
There are, to whom my Satire *s.* too bold *S.* i. 2
Long as a Year's dull circle *s.* to run *S.* iii. 37
The Presence *s.*, with things so richly odd *S.* viii. 238
And vanquish'd nature *s.* to charm no more *Sp.* 76
And, pawing, *s.* to beat the distant plain *W.F.* 152

Seen.

While curling smokes from village-tops are *s. A.* 63
Glitt'ring with ice here hoary hills are *s. D.* i. 75
In ev'ry loom our labours shall be *s. D.* ii. 155
That once was Britain—Happy! had she *s. D.* iii. 117
Not closer, orb in orb, conglob'd are *s. D.* iv. 79
Soft, as the wily Fox is *s.* to creep *M.E.* iv. 352
Thus bred, thus taught, how many have I *s. D.* iv. 505
As, to be hated, needs but to be *s.* (*rep.*) *M.E.* ii. 218
O'er-look'd, *s.* double, by the fool, and wise *E.M.* iv. 6
S. him I have, but in his happier hour *E.S.* i. 29
S. him, uncumber'd with the venal tribe *E.S.* i. 31
Have I, in silent wonder, *s.* such things *E.S.* i. 109
The optics seeing, as the object *s. M.E.* i. 32
One certain Portrait may (I grant) be *s. M.E.* 181
A Woman's *s.* in Private life alone *M.E.* ii. 200
Smit with the mighty pleasure, to be *s. M.E.* iv. 128
And scarce are *s.* the prostrate Nile or Rhine *M.E.* v. 28
That Statesmen have the Worm, are *s. Mi.* iv. 25
Of airy Elves by moonlight shadows *s. R.L.* i. 31
Clubs, Diamonds, Hearts in wild disorder *s. R.L.* iii. 79
Unnumber'd throngs on ev'ry side are *s. R.L.* iv. 47
If Hampton Court these eyes had never *s. R.L.* iv. 150
In them, is certain to be as lov'd as *s. S.* i. 53
Have you not *s.*, at Guildhall's narrow pass *S.* vi. 104
Spirits like you, should see and not be *s. S.* viii. 88
Nor envy, Windsor! since thy shades have *s. W.F.* 161
Here was she *s.* o'er airy wastes to rove *W.F.* 167
In the clear azure gleam the flocks are *s. W.F.*
There Kings shall sue, and suppliant States be *s. W.F.* 383

Seer.

But Annius, crafty *S.*, with ebon wand *D.* iv. 347

Sees.

She *s.* a Mob of Metaphors advance *D.* i. 67
S. momentary monsters rise and fall *D.* i. 83
For sure, if Dulness *s.* a grateful Day *D.* iv. 181
S. hairs and pores, examines bit by bit *D.* iv. 234
Or *s.* the blush of soft Parthenia rise *E.* v. 46
Who *s.* with equal eye, as God of all *E.M.* i. 87
S. God in clouds, or hears him in the wind *E.M.* i. 100
And envies ev'ry sparrow that be *s. E.M.* i. 237
That *s.* immediate good by present sense *E.M.* ii 73
Which *s.* no more the stroke, or feels the pain *E.M.* iii. 67
Who *s.* and follows that great scheme the best *E.M.* iv. 95
S. that no Being any bliss can know *E.M.* iv. 335
He *s.*, why Nature plants in Man alone *M.E.* iv. 345
And *s.* pale Virtue carted in her stead *E.S.* i. 150
A Park is purchas'd, but the Fair he *s. M.E.* ii. 173
And when she *s.* her Friend in deep despair *M.E.* ii. 169
Who *s.* pale Mammon pine amidst his store (*rep.*) *M.E.* iii. 171
Wise Peter *s.* the World's respect for Gold *M.E.* iii. 123
Not for himself he *s.*, or hears, or eats *M.E.* iv. 5
Who but must laugh, the Master when he *s. M.E.* iv.107
The suff'ring eye inverted Nature *s. M.E.* iv. 119
Who *s.* him act, but envies ev'ry deed *P.C.* 25
Poor Cornus *s.* his frantic wife elope *P.S.* 25
And *s.* at Canons what was never there *E.M.* 300
S. by degrees a purer blush arise *R.L.* i. 143
She *s.* and trembles at th' approaching ill *R.L.* iii. 91

See-saw.

His wit all *s.*, between *that* and *this P.S.* 323

Seine.

To where the *S.*, obsequious as she runs *D.* iv. 297

Seize.

And bade the nimblest racer *s.* the prize *D.* ii. 36
To *s.* his papers, Curl, was next thy care *D.* ii. 113
But let heav'n *s.* it, all at once 'tis fir'd *E.A.* 201
Now, now I *s.*, I clasp your charms *I.H.* iii. 43
Oh hadst thou, cruel! been content to *s. R.L.* iv. 175
Peace, fools, or Gonson will for Papists *s.* you *S.*viii.256
Sudden they *s.* th' amaz'd, defenceless prize *W.F.* 109

Seiz'd.

Became, when *s.*, a puppy or an ape *D.* ii. 130
And where it fix'd, the beauteous bird I *s. D.* iv. 430
S. and tied down to judge, how wretched I *P.S.* 33
Not youthful kings in battle *s.* alive *R.L.* iv. 3
Has *s.* the Court and City, poor and rich *S.* v. 170
Not more amazement *s.* on Circe's guests *S.* viii. 166

Seizes.

Inspir'd he *s.*, these an altar raise *D.* i. 157
One instinct *s.*, and transports away *D.* iv. 74
S. your fame, and puts his laws in force *E.C.* 163

Sejanus.

S., Wolsey, hurt not honest Fleury *E.S.* i. 51

Seldom.—*Passim.*

Select.

Or from those meads *s.* unfading flow'rs *W.* 74

Self.—*Passim.*

See all in *S.*, and but for *s.* be born *D.* iv. 480
With s.-applause *her wild creation view D.* i. 82
One *s.-approving* hour whole years outweighs *E.M.* iv. 255
S.-centr'd Sun, and Stars that rise and fall *S.* iv. 6
Kind *S.-conceit* to some her glass applies *D.* iv. 533
A wand'ring, *s.-consuming* fire *O.* iii. 20
Forc'd into Virtue thus by *S.-defence E.M.* iii. 279
And while *s.-love* each jealous writer rules *E.C.* 516
S. to urge, and Reason to restrain *E.M.* ii. 54
S., the spring of motion, acts the soul *E.M.* ii. 59
S. still stronger, as its objects nigh *E.M.* ii. 71
Each strengthens Reason, and *S.* restrains *E.M.* ii. 80
S. and Reason to one end aspire *E.M.* ii. 87
Modes of *S.*, the Passions we may call *E.M.* ii. 93
Ev'n mean *S.*-loveseeking, by force divine *E.M.* ii. 291
S. and Social at her birth began *E.M.* iii. 149
So drives *S.*, thro' just and thro' unjust *E.M.* iii. 26
The same *S.*, in all, becomes the cause *E.M.* iii. 271
S. forsook the path it first pursu'd *E.M.* iii. 281
And bade *S.* and Social be the same *E.M.* iii. 318
S. thus push'd to social, to divine *E.M.* iv. 353
S. but serves the virtuous mind to wake *E.M.* iv. 363
That true *S.* and SOCIAL are the same *E.M.* iv. 396
Of mad Good-nature, and of mean *S. M.E.* iii. 228
He spins the slight, *s.-pleasing* thread anew *P.S.* 90
No cavern'd Hermit, rests *s.-satisfy'd E.M.* iv. 42

Selfish.

A low-born, cell-bred, *s.*, servile band *D.* ii. 356
My Sons! be proud, be *s.*, and be dull *D.* iv. 582
Passions, tho' *s.*, if their means be fair *E.M.* ii. 97

Selfishly.

Who can *your* merit *s.* approve *P.S.* 293

Selfishness.

Sick of herself thro' very *s. M.E.* ii. 146

Sell.

S. their presented partridges and fruits *S.* ii. 51
He tells what places strumpets *s.* for life *S.* viii. 148

Sells.

And silent *s.* a King or buys a Queen *M.E.* iii. 48
Last, for his Country's love, he *s.* his Lands *M.E.*iii. 212

Semele.

In flames, like *S.'s*, be brought to bed *D.* iii. 315

Senate.

Unseen at Church, at *S.*, or at Court *D.* iv. 338
Than Cæsar with a *s.* at his heels *E.M.* iv. 258
And shake alike the *S.* and the Field *E.S.* ii. 87
The *S.* heard him, and his Country lov'd *Ep.* xiv. 8
But bribes a *S.*, and the Land's betray'd *M.E.* iii. 32
In Britain's *S.* he a seat obtains *M.E.* ii. 393
While Cato gives his little *S.* laws *P.C.* 23
Like *Cato*, give his little *S.* laws *P.S.* 209
F—loves the *S.*, Hockley-hole his brother *S.* i. 49
From morn to night, at *S.*, Rolls, and Hall *S.* iv. 36
Till S—s nod to Lullabies divine D. i. 317
S. and Courts with Greek and Latin rule *D.* iv. 179
Teach Kings to fiddle, or make *S.* dance *D.* iv. 598
Judges and *S.* have been bought for gold *E.M.* iv. 187
Tho' wond'ring *S.* hung on all he spoke *M.E.* i. 184

T 2

SENATOR—SENTIMENT

Or ship off *S.* to a distant Shore *M.E.* iii. 44
S. degen'rate, Patriots disagree *M.E.* iii. 148

Senator.
The *S.* at Cricket urge the Ball *D.* iv. 592

Send.
The Goddess then: "Who best can *s.* on high *D.* ii. 161
Till all, tun'd equal, *s.* a gen'ral hum *D.* ii. 386
S. for him up, take no excuse *I.H.* ii. 36 *s*
Oh be thou blest with all that Heav'n can *s. Mi.* v. 1
And *s.* the godly in a pet to pray *R.L.* iv. 64
And *s.* up vows from Rosamunda's lake *R.L.* v. 136
Cries, "*S.* me, Gods! a whole Hog barbecu'd!" *S.* ii. 26
S. her to Court, you *s.* her to her grave *S.* iii. 119
And *s.* his Wife to church, his Son to school *S.* v. 164
You love a Verse, take such as I can *s. S.* vi. 2

Sends.
His sister *s.*, her vot'ress, from above *D.* ii. 216
A mightier Pow'r the strong direction *s. E.M.* ii. 165
God *s.* not ill; if rightly understood *E.M.* iv. 113
Hear than the truth; 'Tis Heav'n each Passion *s. M.E.* iii. 159
Bids Bubo build, and *s.* him such a Guide *E.M.* iv. 20
Pitholeon *s.* to me: "You know his Grace *P.S.* 49
My counsel *s.* to execute a deed *S.* vi. 92
When Albion *s.* her eager sons to war *W.F.* 106

Senior.
If there's a *S.*, who contemns this age *Mi.* ii. 22
The *S.*'s *judgment all the crowd admire D.* ii. 289

Sensations.
And quick *s.* skip from vein to vein *D.* ii. 212

Sense.
Whose *s.* instructs us, and whose humour charms *A.* 9
Plung'd for his *s.*, but found no bottom there *D.* i. 119
Guard the sure barrier between that and *S. D.* i. 178
And once betray'd me into common *s. D.* i. 188
Now leave all memory of *s.* behind *D.* i. 276
And, instant, fancy feels th' imputed *s. D.* ii. 200
When fancy flags, and *s.* is at a stand *D.* ii. 230
Soft creeping, words on words, the *s.* compose *D.* ii. 389
Then raptures high the seat of *s.* o'erflow *D.* iii. 5
And blunt the *s.*, and fit it for a skull *D.* iii. 25
S., speech, and measure, living tongues and dead *D.* iii. 167
The source of Newton's Light, of Bacon's *S. D.* iii. 218
Break all their nerves, and fritter all their *s. D.* iv. 56
If Music meanly borrows aid from *s. D.* iv. 64
As Fancy opens the quick springs of *S. D.* iv. 156
In ancient *S.* if any needs will deal *D.* iv. 229
His royal *S.* of Op'ras or the Fair *D.* iv. 314
Wraps in her veil, and frees from *s.* of shame *D.* iv. 336
By common *s.* to common knowledge bred *D.* iv. 467
Lost was the Nation's *S.*, nor could be found *D.* iv. 611
Till drown'd was *S.*, and Shame, and Right, and Wrong *D.* iv. 625
And *Metaphysic* calls for aid on *S. D.* iv. 646
Back thro' the paths of pleasing *s.* I ran *E.A.* 69
How shall I lose the sin, yet keep the *s. E.A.* 191
To t re our patience, though we mislead our *s. E.C.* 4
So by false learning is good *s.* defac'd *E.C.* 25
In search of wit these lose their common *s. E.C.* 28
And mark that point where *s.* and dulness meet *E.C.* 51
These leave the *s.*, their learning to display *E.C.* 116
T' admire superior *s.*, and doubt their own *E.C.* 200
And fills up all the mighty Void of *s. E.C.* 210
The *S.*, they humbly take upon content *E.C.* 308
Much fruit of *s.* beneath is rarely found *E.C.* 310
Ancients in phrase, mere moderns in their *s. E.C.* 325
The sound must seem an Echo to the *s. E.C.* 365
That always shows great pride, or little *s. E.C.* 387
For fools admire, but men of *s.* approve *E.C.* 391
Twixt *s.* and nonsense daily change their side *E.C.* 435
And none had *s.* enough to be confuted *E.C.* 443
But *s.* surviv'd, when merry jests were past *E.C.* 460
That not alone what to your *s.* is due *E.C.* 564
Be silent always when you doubt your *s. E.C.* 566
That only makes superior *s.* belov'd *E.C.* 577
For the worst avarice is that of *s. E.C.* 579
Strain out the last dull droppings of their *s. E.C.* 608
Distrustful *s.* with modest caution speaks *E.C.* 626
And without method talks us into *s. E.C.* 654
Gn, wiser thou! and in thy scale of *s. E.M.* i. 113

In the nice bee, what *s.* so subtly true *E.M.* i. 219
What thin partitions *S.* from Thought divide *E.M.* i. 226
And quitting *s.* call imitating God *E.M.* ii. 26
That sees immediate good by present *s. E.M.* ii. 73
And Grace and Virtue, *S.* and Reason split *E.M.* ii. 83
And each vacuity of *s.* by Pride *E.M.* ii. 286
Equal is Common *S.*, and Common Ease *E.M.* iv. 34
That such are happier, shocks all common *s. E.M.* iv. 52
Reason's whole pleasure, all the joys of *S. E.M.* iv. 79
Grasp the whole worlds of Reason, Life, and *S*, *E.M.* iv. 357
At *S.* and Virtue, balance all again *E.S.* i. 60
And all the well-whipt Cream of Courtly *S. E.S.* i. 70
And all I sung should be the Nation's *S. E.S.* i. 78
But past the *S.* of human Miseries *E.S.* i. 101
CARLETON's calm *S.*, and STANHOPE's noble Flame *E.S.* ii. 80
Who think a Coxcomb's Honour like his *S. E.S.* ii. 202
Fill'd with the *S.* of Age, the Fire of Youth *Ep.* ii. 7
Blest with plain Reason, and with sober *S.' Ep.* vi. 2
When *S.* subsides, and Fancy sports in sleep *M.E.* i. 46
So Darkness strikes the *s.* no less than Light *M.E.* i. 53
Flavia's a Wit, has too much *s.* to pray *M.E.* ii. 87
To you gave *S.*, Good-humour, and a Poet *M.E.* ii. 292
The *S.* to value Riches, with the Art *M.E.* ii. 219
And something previous ev'n to Taste—'tis *S.* (*rep.*) *M.E.* iv. 42
Still follow *S.*, of ev'ry Art the Soul *M.E.* iv. 65
And Splendour borrows all her rays from *S. M.E.* iv. 280
Who charm the *s.*, or mend the heart *O.* ii. 10
Dare to have *s.* yourselves; assert the stage *P.C.* 43
While pure Description held the place of *S. P.S.* 148
And all they want is spirit, taste, and *s. P.S.* 160
And He, who now to *s.*, now nonsense leaning *P.S.* 185
Or Envy holds a whole week's war with *S., P.S.* 252
And show the *s.* of it without the *love P.S.* 294
Satire or *s.*, alas! can *Sporus* feel *P.S.* 307
Unless good *s.* preserve what beauty gains *R.L.* v. 16
But strong in *s.*, and wise without the rules *S.* ii. 10
Barnard in spirit, *s.*, and truth abounds *S.* iii. 85
More on a Reader's *s.*, than Gazer's eye *S.* v. 351
"Yours, Cowper's manner"—and "yours, Talbot's *s.*" *S.* vi. 134
For Use will father what's begot by *s. S.* vi. 170
This Town, I had the *s.* to hate it too *S.* vii. 2
S., past thro' him, no longer is the same *S.* vii. 33
Let no Court Sycophant pervert my *s. S.* viii. 126
To wholesome Solitude, the nurse of *s. S.* viii. 185
Who all my *S.* confin'd *U.P.* 6
On *different s—s different objects strike E.M.* ii. 206
Steals my *s.*, shuts my sight *O.* v. 10

Senseless.
But *s.*, lifeless! idol void and vain *D.* ii. 46
A *s.*, worthless, and unhonour'd crowd *S.* v. 306

Sensible.
And *s.* soft Melancholy *Mi.* viii. 8

Sensual.
The scale of *s.*, mental pow'rs ascends *E.M.* i. 208

Sent.
S. with a Pass, and vagrant thro' the land *D.* i. 232
When the last blaze a Ilion to the skies *D.* i. 256
Angel of Dulness, *s.* to scatter round *D.* iii. 257
But she, good Goddess, *s.* to ev'ry child *D.* iv. 529
Who cropt our Ears, and *s.* them to the King *E.S.* i. 18
And Gold but *s.* to keep the fools in play *M.E.* iii. 5
Sir, Spain has *s.* a thousand jars of oil *M.E.* iii. 46
Could he himself have *s.* it to the dogs *M.E.* iii. 66
But duly *s.* his family and wife *M.E.* iii. 382
May Tom, whom heav'n *s.* down to raise *Mi.* xii. 15
S. up in vapours to the Baron's brain *R.L.* iii. 119
Chang'd to a bird and *s.* to flit in air *R.L.* iii. 123
Who *s.* the Thief that stole the Cash, away *S.* vi. 25

Sentence.
With warmth gives *s.*, yet is always just *E.C.* 678
While Wits and Templars ev'ry *s.* raise *P.S.* 211
The hungry Judges soon the *s.* sign *R.L.* iii. 21
One Tragic *s.* if I dare deride *S.* v. 121
Who *knew most* S—s, *was deepest read E.C.* 441

Sentiment.
To crave your *s.*, if—'s your name *S.* viii. 67

Sep'rate.
For ever s., yet for ever near E.M. i. 224
Their s. cells and properties maintain E.M. iii. 188
And s. *from their kindred dregs below* U.L. 26

Septleva.
And, the next *Pull, my S.* I lose Mi. ix. 52
One, one bad Deal, *Three* S—s *have lost* Mi. ix. 12

Sepulchral.
S. Lies, our holy walls to grace D. i. 43

Sepulchre.
How Rome her own sad S. appears M.E. v. 2
Useless, unseen, as lamps in s—s U.L. 20

Sequester'd.
Bear me, O bear me to s. scenes W.F. 261

Seraph.
As the rapt S. that adores and burns E.M. i. 278
He asks no Angel's wing, no S.'s *fire* E.M. i. 110
And wings of S—a *shed divine perfumes* E.A. 218

Seraphic.
Where flames refin'd in breasts s. glow E.A. 320
With sounds s. ring O. v. 15

Serene.
"And take" (she said, and smil'd s.) E. vi. 3
Oh Grace s.! oh virtue heav'nly fair E.A. 297
But who, living and dying, s. still and free Ep. xvi. 7
S. in Virgin Modesty she shines M.E. ii. 255
Preserve him social, cheerful, and s. P.S. 416
The moon, s. in glory, mounts the sky W. 6

Serenely.
Now setting Phœbus shone s. bright A. 13
S. pure, and yet divinely strong S. vi. 172

Serenest.
Grace shines around her with s. beams E.A. 215

Sergeant.
The Judge to dance his brother S. call D. iv. 591
The Temple late two brother S—s *saw* S. vi. 127

Series.
Or in fair s. laurell'd bards be shown M.E. v. 61
A dreadful s. of intestine wars W.F. 325

Serious.
Whether thou choose Cervantes' s. air D. i. 21
A long, exact, and s. Comedy E. iv. 22
Peep'd in your fans, been s., thus, and cry'd B.J.S. 4

Serjeant.—*See* Sergeant.

Sermon.
A standing s. at each year's expense M.E. iv. 21
Hear BETHEL's s., one not vers'd in schools S. ii. 9
Till show'rs of S—s, *Characters, Essays* D. ii. 361

Serpent.
Like Aaron's s., swallow up the rest E.M. ii. 132
But in my breast the s. Love abides Su. 68
And harmless s—s *lick the pilgrim's feet* M. 80
The rich Buffet well-colour'd S. grace M.E. ii. 153
Now S.-like, *in prose he sweeps the ground* S. v. 100
Shouldst wag a s.-*tail* in Smithfield fair D. iii. 288

Servant.
The fawning S. turns a haughty Lord E. iv. 44
A master, or a s., or a friend E.M. ii. 250
Beast, Man, or Angel, S., Lord, or King M.E. iii. 302
[*In Pow'r a* S., *out of Pow'r a Friend*] E.S. ii. 161
A humble s. to all human kind M.E. i. 253
Oft had the Goddess heard her s—*s call* D. ii. 97
His s. up, and rise by five o'clock S. v. 162
The joy their wives, their sons, and s. share S. v. 245

Serve.
Or s. (like other Fools) to fill a room D. i. 136
To s. his Cause, O Queen! is serving thine D. i. 214
To wonder at their Maker, not to s. D. iv. 458
The rules a nation, born to s., obeys E.C. i. 7
To s. mere engines to the ruling Mind M.E. i. 262
To s., not suffer, strengthen, not invade M.E. iii. 298
This bids to s., and that to shun mankind E.M. iv. 20

If—where I'm going—I could s. you, Sir M.E. i. 255
Have I no friend to s., no soul to save P.S. 274
His whole ambition was to s. a Lord S. vi. 14

Serv'd.
Which s. the past, and must the times to come E.M. ii. 52
All s., all serving: nothing stands alone E.M. iii. 25
Horace would say, Sir Billy s. *the Crown* E.S. i. 13
The Grace-cup s. with all decorum I.H. ii. 138
Who broke no promise, s. no private end M.E. v. 69
The Muse but s. to ease some friend, not Wife P.S. 131
And just as rich as when he s. a Queen P.S. 417
He s. a 'Prenticeship, who sets up shop S. v. 181
And s. alike his Vassals and his God W.F. 76

Serves.
S. but to keep fools pert, and knaves awake D. iv. 442
Yet s. to second too some other use E.M. i. 56
Cares not for service, or but s. when prest E.M. iii. 86
This too s. always, Reason never long E.M. iii. 93
What s. one will, when many wills rebel E.M. iii. 274
Self-love but s. the virtuous mind to wake E.M. iv. 363
The Dull, flat Falsehood s. for policy M.E. i. 67
Useful, I grant, it s. what life requires M.E. iii. 27
One half-pint bottle s. them both to dine S. ii. 53

Service.
Cares not for s., or but serves when prest E.M. iii. 86
'Tis for the s. of the Crown I.H. ii. 34

Servile.
A low-born, cell-bred, selfish, s. band D. ii. 356
Then scorn to gain a Friend by s. ways E. ii. 10
Of all this s. herd the worst is he E.C. 414
Not proud, nor s.;—be one Poet's praise P.S. 336
When s. Chaplains cry, that birth and place S. vi. 220
Let barb'rous Ganges arm a s. train W.F. 365

Serving.
To serve his cause, O Queen! is s. thine D. i. 214
All serv'd, all s.: nothing stands alone M.E. iii. 25
Since 'twas no form'd design of s. God S. viii. 18
Tremble before a noble S.-*man* S. viii. 199

Servitude.
Nor sunk by sloth, nor rais'd by s. M.E. iii. 222

Ses.
The deeds, and dextr'ously omits s. *heires* S. vii. 100

Set.
Withhold the pension, and s. up the head D. iv. 96
Or s. on Metaphysic ground to prance D. iv. 265
Then thus: "from Priest-craft happily s. free D. iv. 499
Full in my view s. all the bright abode E.A. 127
The less, or greater, s. so justly true E.M. iii. 291
If not the Tradesman who s. up to-day E.S. ii. 36
To s. this matter full before ye I.H. i. 81
Of Land, s. out to plant a Wood I.H. ii. 6 s
The Beans and Bacon s. before 'em I.H. ii. 137
And justly s. the Gem above the Flow'r M.E. i. 148
Nor in an Hermitage s. Dr. Clarke M.E. iv. 78
S. up with these he ventur'd on the Town Mi. ii. 7
When Kings, Queens, Knaves, are s. in decent rank Mi. ix. 77
Commas and points they s. exactly right P.S. 161
These s. the head, and those divide the hair R.L. i. 146
When those fair suns shall s., as s. they must R.L. v. 147
Those Suns of Glory please not till they s. S. v. 22

Sets.
Illumes their light, and s. their flames on fire D. iii. 260
But s. up one, a greater, in their place E. iv. 38
Su modest plainness s. off sprightly wit E.C. 302
Its proper bliss, and s. its proper bounds E.M. iii. 110
S. half the world, God knows, against the rest E.S. i. 58
And, while he bids thee, s. th' Example too S. iii. 109
He serv'd a 'Prenticeship, who s. up shop S. v. 181
And s. the Passions on the side of Truth S. v. 218

Sett'st.
Who s. our Entrails free Mi. iv. 34

Setting.
Now s. Phœbus shone serenely bright A. 13
Strike off his Pension, by the s. sun M.E. i. 169
Shine, buzz, and fly-blow in the s. sun M.E. ii. 28
His shadow lengthen'd by the s. sun W.F. 194

Settle.
Well-purg'd, and worthy S., Banks, and Broome D. i. 146
Known by the band and suit which S. wore D. iii. 37
As Eusden, Philips, S. writ of Kings S. v. 417
But liv'd in S.'s *numbers one day more* D. i. 90

Sève.
Explains the S. and *Verdeur* of the Vine D. iv. 556

Sev'n.
Thron'd on s. hills, the Antichrist of wit D. ii. 16
Up to her godly garret after s. E. v. 21
And tho' no Science, fully worth the s. M.E. iv. 44
To books and study gives s. years complete S. vi. 117
Stole from the Master of the s.-fold Face D. i. 244
Each chief his s. shield display'd O. i. 45
Oft have we known that s. fence to fail R.L. ii. 119
From heav'n itself tho' s. Nilus flows W.F. 359

Sever.
From the dear man unwilling she must s. E. v. 5

Sev'ral.
Each might his s. province well command E.C. 66
As s. garbs with country, town, and court E.C. 323
And s. Men impels to s. ends E.M. ii. 166
Each individual seeks a s. goal E.M. ii. 237
Their s. graces in my SHARPER meet Mi. ix. 105

Severe.
That darts s. upon a rising lie E. ii. 6
S. to all, but most to Womankind E. iv. 32
Modestly bold, and humanly s. E.C. 636
From grave to gay, from lively to s. E.M. iv. 380
Yet soft his Nature, tho' s. his Lay Ep. i. 5
And kings more furious and s. than they W.F. 46

Sever'd.
This fav'rite Isle, long s. from her reign D. iii. 125

Severely.
For thee the fates, s. kind, ordain E.A. 249
But how s. with themselves proceed S. vi. 157

Severest.
And fate's s. rage disarm O. i. 119

Severn.
And rapid S. hoarse applause resounds M.E. iii. 252

Sex.
Too much your S. is by their forms confin'd E. iv. 31
Still in constraint your suff'ring S. remains E. iv. 41
From her own S. should mercy find to-day E.J.S. 2
Our s. are still forgiving at their heart E.J.S. 12
Each s. desires alike, till two are one E.M. iii. 122
In Sappho touch the *Failings of the* S. E.S. i. 15
But mark the fate of a whole S. of Queens M.E. ii. 219
Pleasures the s., as children Birds, pursue M.E. ii. 231
Picks from each s., to make the Fav'rite blest M.E. iv. 273
That buys your s. a Tyrant o'er itself M.E. ii. 288
Who rule the s. to fifty from fifteen R.L. iv. 58
Ease, pleasure, virtue, all our s. resign R.L. iv. 106
Assume what s——es and what shapes they please R.L. i. 70

Sexto.
Edwardi sext. or *prim. et quint.* Eliz. S, i. 148

Shade.
Beneath the s. a spreading beech displays A. 1
And the low sun had lengthen'd ev'ry s. A. 100
A shapeless s., it melted from his sight D. ii. 111
The King descending views th' Elysian s. D. iii. 14
And all the nations cover'd in her s. D. iii. 72
And you, my Critics ! in the chequer'd s. D. iv. 125
'Tis in the s. of Arbitrary Sway D. iv. 182
The Muse attends thee to thy silent s. E. i. 28
Or seek some Ruin's formidable s. E. iii. 30
You dream of Triumphs in the rural s. E. v. 22
Envy will merit, as its s., pursue E.C. 466
And sweetly melt into just s. and light E.C. 489
This humble praise, lamented s. ! receive E.C. 733
As in some well-wrought picture, light and s. E.M. ii. 208
Man walk'd with beast, joint tenant of the s. E.M. iii. 152

To all beside as much an empty s. E.M. iv. 243
And haunt their slumbers in the pompous s. E.M. iv. 304
Till you are dust like me—Dear S. ! I will Ep. xiii. 4
Attend the s. of gentle Buckingham Ep. xiv. 10
From storms a shelter, and from heat a s. M. 16
Your virtues open fairest in the s. M.E. ii. 220
And strength of s. contends with strength of Light M.E. iv. 82
Or sat delighted in the thick'ning s. M.E. iv. 90
And there a Summer-house that knows no s. M.E. iv. 122
His numbers rais'd a s. from hell O. i. 133
Whose trees in summer yield him s. O. iv. 7
To wrap me in the universal s. S. i. 96
Why then for ever bury'd in the s. S. viii. 87
And from the brink his dancing s. surveys S. 34
And verdant alders form a quiv'ring s. Su. 4
Trees, where you sit, shall crowd into a s. Su. 74
What beck'ning ghost, along the moonlight s. U.L. 1
What can atone (oh ever-injur'd s. !) U.L. 47
While plants their s., or flow'rs their odours give W. 63
Arise, the pines a noxious s. diffuse W. 86
In genial spring, beneath the quivering s. W.F. 135
And Cynthus' top forsook for Windsor s. W.F. 166
Led by the sound I roam from s. to s. W.F. 269
Pleas'd in the silent s. with empty praise W.F. 432
For her, the limes their pleasing s——s deny A. 25
And the fleet s. glide o'er the dusky green A. 64
A branch of Styx here rises from the S. D. ii. 338
Oh punish him, or to th' Elysian s. D. iv. 417
As s. more sweetly recommend the light E.C. 301
The lights and s., whose well accorded strife E.M. ii. 121
And let me in these s. compose I.H. ii. 25 s
The mossy fountains, and the sylvan s. M. 3
Sighs for the s.—" How charming is a Park !" M.E. ii. 38
Joins willing woods, and varies s. from s. M.E. iv. 62
By the hero's armed s. O. i. 77
Ye s., where sacred truth is sought O. ii. 1
And steel now glitters in the Muses' s. O. ii. 8
What walls can guard me, or what s. can hide P.S. 7
And screen'd in s. from day's detested glare R.L. iv. 22
Dreadful as hermit's dreams in haunted s. R.L. iv. 41
S., that to Bacon could retreat afford S. ii. 175
Till in your native s. you tune the lyre Sp. 12
Then hid in s., eludes her eager swain Sp. 54
To closer s. the panting flocks remove Su. 87
Unlock your springs, and open all your s. W.F. 4
Thin trees arise that shun each other's s. W.F. 22
Nor envy, Windsor ! since thy s. have seen W.F. 161
Let me, O let me, to the s. repair (rep.) W.F. 201
Happy next him, who to these s. retires W.F. 237
Who now shall charm the s. where Cowley strung W.F. 279
In the same s. the Cupids tun'd his lyre W.F. 295
S. him from Light, and cover him from Law D. i. 314
Taller or stronger than the weeds they s. E.M. i. 40
Wrap my cold limbs, and s. my lifeless face M.E. i. 249
Now sweep those Alleys they were born to s. M.E.iv. 98
First s. a Country ; and then raise a Town M.E. iv. 190

Shaded.
Those ancient woods, that s. all the ground S. vii. 110
Sing, while beside the s. tomb I mourn W. 19

Shadee.
Ev'n now, she s. thy Ev'ning-walk with bays E. i. 35
S. ev'ry flow'r, and darkens ev'ry green E.A. 168

Shadow.
Now to thy gentle s. all are shrunk D. iv. 509
But like a s., proves the substance true E.C. 467
If not God's image, yet his s. true E.M. iii. 288
Their vines a s. to their race shall yield M. 65
Huge moles, whose s. stretch'd from shore to shore M.E. v. 107
And now his s. reach'd her as she run (rep.) W.F. 193
'Tis a fear that starts at s——s Mi. vi. 3
Of airy Elves by moonlight s. seen R.L. i. 31
Project long s. o'er the crystal tide W.F. 376

Shadowy.
Shines a broad Mirror thro' the s. Cave Mi. x. 2

Shadwell.
And S. nods the poppy on his brow D. iii. 22
How S. hasty, Wycherley was slow S. v. 85
In S.'s bosom with eternal Rest D. i. 240

Shady.
Whose Cause-way parts the vale with s. rows M.E. iii. 259
See, s. forms advance O. i. 65
At morn the plains, at noon the s. groves Sp. 78
Ye s. beeches, and ye cooling streams Su. 13
The s. empire shall retain no trace W.F. 371

Shagg'd.
Ye grots and caverns s. with horrid thoro E.A. 20

Shaggy.
A s. Tap'stry, worthy to be spread D. ii. 143

Shake.
Now lap-dogs give themselves the rousing s. R.L. i. 15
Or laugh and s. in Rab'lais' easy chair D. i. 22
Let others aim : 'tis yours to s. the soul D. ii. 225
To stir, to rouse, to s. the soul he comes D. iv. 67
Eton and Wijton s. thro' all their sons D. iv. 144
And s. alike the Senate and the Field E.S. ii. 87
Grave, as when pris'ners s. the head and swear S. vii. 69
And s. all o'er, like a discover'd spy S. viii. 279

Shakes.
S. off the dust, and rears his rev'rend head E.C. 700
S. all together, and produces—You M.E. ii. 280
Earth s. her nodding tow'rs, the ground gives way R.L. v. 51

Shakespear.
There hapless S., yet of Tibbald sore D. i. 133
'Twixt Plautus, Fletcher, S., and Corneille D. i. 285
Who study S. at the Inns of Court D. iv. 368
S. (whom you and ev'ry Play-house bill S. v. 69
Or damn all S., like th' affected Fool S. v. 105
And full in S., fair in Otway shone S. v. 277
And fluent S. scarce effac'd a line S. v. 279
Call Tibbald S., and he'll swear the Nine S. v. 137
With S.'s nature, or with Jonson's art D. ii. 224
Preserved in Milton's or in S. name P.S. 168
Of S. Nature, and of Cowley's Wit S. v. 83

Shaking.
S. the horrors of his sable brows D. ii. 327

Shall, Shalt.—Passim.

Shallow.
So from the Sun's broad beam in s. urns D. ii. 11
There s. draughts intoxicate the brain E.C. 217
As s. streams run dimpling all the way P.S. 316
Proud Fortune, and look s. Greatness thro' S. iii. 108

Shallows.
Our depths who fathoms, or our s. finds M.E. i. 23

Shame.
Now (s. to Fortune !) an ill run at Play D. i. 113
Wraps in her veil, and frees from sense of s. D. iv. 336
And straight succeeded, leaving s. no room D. iv. 531
Till drown'd was Sense, and S., and Right, and Wrong D. iv. 625
Made Slaves by honour, and made Fools by s. E. iv. 36
I can no more ; by s., by rage suppress'd E.A. 105
The glory of the Priesthood, and the s. E.C. 694
But what will grow on Pride, or grow on S. E.M. ii. 194
S. to the virgin, to the matron pride E.M. ii. 242
Honour and s. from no Condition rise E.M. iv. 193
E'er taught to shine, or sanctify'd from s. E.M. iv. 300
A Tale, that blends their glory with their s. E.M. iv. 308
His Friend and S., and was a kind of Screen E.S. i. 22
There, where no Passion, Pride, or S. transport E.S. i. 97
Let humble ALLEN, with an awkward S. E.S. i. 135
That NOT TO BE CORRUPTED IS THE S. E.S. i. 160
There, none distinguish 'twixt your S. or Pride M.E. ii. 204
That Flatt'ry, ev'n to Kings, he held a s. P.S. 338
To friends, to fortune, to mankind a s. S. ii. 107
And swear all s. is lost in George's Age S. v. 126
And s. the fools—Your Int'rest, Sir, with Lintot P.S. 62

Sham'd.
Yet touch'd and s. by Ridicule alone E.S. ii. 211
Old Cotta s. his fortune and his birth M.E. iii. 177

Shameful.
As s. sure as Impotence in love E.C. 533
And wins (oh s. chance !) the Queen of Hearts R.L. iii. 88

Shameless.
Not so from s. Curl ; impetuous spread D. ii. 179
And s. Billingsgate her Robes adorn D. iv. 26
Such s. bards we have ; and yet 'tis true E.C. 610
Brand the bold front of s. guilty men S. i. 106

Shames.
Of him, whose chatt'ring s. the monkey-tribe D. ii. 232
Who s. a Scribbler? break one cobweb thro' P.S. 89

Shape.
So Proteus, hunted in a nobler s. D. ii. 129
See Nature in some partial narrow s. D. iv. 455
Their Infamy, still keep their human s. D. iv. 528
Admir'd such wisdom in an earthly s. E.M. ii. 33
Her S. unfashion'd, and her Face unknown Mi. ix. 60
Virtue confess'd in human s. he draws P.C. 17
The libell'd person, and the pictur'd s. P.S. 353
Observe his s. how clean ! his locks how curl'd S. vi. 5
In various s—s of Parsons, Critics, Beaus E.C. 439
Assume what sexes and what s. they please R.L. i. 70
Quartos, octavos, s. the less'ning pyre D. i. 161

Shapeless.
A s. shade, it melted from his sight D. ii. 111
The s. rock, or hanging precipice E.C. 158

Shapely.
The spiry fir and s. box adorn M. 74

Share.
True Taste as seldom is the Critic's s. E.C. 12
Each has his s.; and who would more obtain E.M. iv. 47
If to her s. some female errors fall R.L. ii. 17
Or, in a mortgage, prove a Lawyer's s. S. ii. 169
To bawd for others, and go s—s with Punk Mi. iii. 26
Like are their merits, like rewards they s. D. iii. 183
His heart. his mistress and his friend did s. E. iv. 9
Then s. thy pain, allow that sad relief (rep.) E.A. 49
Nor s. one pang of all I feel for thee E.A. 292
No pow'rs of body or of soul to s. E.M. i. 191
And till we s. your joys, forgive our grief Ep. vii. 18
Or her whose life the Church and Scandal s. M.E. ii. 105
Peeress and Butler s. alike the Box M.E. iii. 140
Whose table, Wit, or modest Merit s. M.E. iii. 241
The joy their wives, their sons, and servants s. S. v. 245

Shar'd.
Then s. the Tyranny, then lent it aid E.M. iii. 247

Shares.
S. with his lord the pleasure and the pride E.M. iii. 36

Sharon.
Sweeter than S., in immac'late trim S. viii. 252

Sharp.
A s. accuser, but a helpless friend E.M. ii. 154
Shall feel s. vengeance soon o'ertake his sins R.L. ii. 123
S. Satire that, and that Pindaric lays S. vi. 83
S. Boreas blows, and Nature feels decay W. 87

Sharpen'd.
With s. sight pale Antiquaries pore M.E. v. 35
But as coarse iron, s. mangles more S. viii. 118

Sharper.
How, Sir ? not damn the S., but the Dice E.S. ii. 13
Ah, Madam, since my S. is untrue Mi. ix. 4
Were lovely S. mine, and mine alone Mi. ix. 16
Their several graces in my S. meet Mi. ix. 105
This Snuff-Box, once the pledge of S.'s love Mi. ix. 37
How many Maids have S. vows deceiv'd Mi. ix. 71
Can hearken coldly to my S. Vows Mi. ix. 88
Thieves, Supercargoes, S—s and Directors S. i. 72

Shave.
Some plunge in bus'ness, others s. their crowns M.E. i. 104

She.—Passim.

Shear.
Feed fairer flocks, or richer fleeces s. Su. 36

Shearing.
When swains from *s.* seek their nightly bow'rs *Su.* 64

Shears.
Fate urg'd the *s.* and cut the Sylph in twain *R.L.* iii. 151
Uncurl'd it hangs, the fatal *s.* demands *R.L.* iv. 173

Sheath'd.
Was *s.*, and *Luxury* with *Charles* restor'd *S.* v. 140

Shed.
With mystic words, the sacred Opium *s. D.* i. 288
She pity'd ! but her Pity only *s. D.* iv. 345
Thy choicer mists on this assembly *s. D.* iv. 357
Muse ! at that Name thy sacred sorrows *s. E.* iii. 47
Love but demands what else were *s.* in pray'r *E.A.* 46
And the dim windows *s.* a solemn light *E.A.* 144
And wings of Seraphs *s.* divine perfumes *E.A.* 218
And licks the hand just rais'd to *s.* his blood *E.F.* i. 84
And in soft silence *s.* the kindly show'r *M.* 14
She, at whose name I *s.* these spiteful tears *Mi.* ix. 57
Such tears as Patriots *s.* for dying Laws *P.C.* 14
The blow unfelt, the tear he never *s. P.S.* 349
Of gentle blood (part *s.* in Honour's cause *P.S.* 388
Oh early lost ! what tears the river *s. W.F.* 273
Oh fact accurst ! what tears has Albion *s. W.F.* 321

Sheds.
And drink the falling tear each other *s. E.A.* 350
But see, Orion *s.* unwholesome dews *W.* 85

Sheep.
Who lost my heart while I preserv'd my *s. A.* 80
Where bask on sunny banks the simple *s. D.* iv. 352
Explores the lost, the wand'ring *s.* directs *M.* 51
No lambs or *s.* for victims I'll impart *Sp.* 51
The bleating *s.* with my complaints agree *Su.* 19

Sheet.
Then snatch'd a *s.* of Thule from her bed *D.* i. 258
Unstain'd, untouch'd, and yet in maiden—s *D.* i. 229
Who random drawings from your *s.* shall take *M.E.* iv. 27

Sheffield.
S. approves, consenting Phœbus bends *Mi.* i. 7
The courtly *Talbot, Somers, S.* read *P.S.* 139

Shelf.
Here swells the *s.* with Ogilby the great *D.* i. 141
Such with their *s*—ves *as due proportion hold D.* i. 137
And here the groaning *s.* Philemon bends *D.* i. 154
From *s.* to *s.* see greedy Vulcan roll *D.* iii. 81
These *s.* admit not any modern book *M.E.* iv. 140
Or Sloane or Woodward's wondrous *s.* contain *S.* viii. 30

Shell.
"There take" (says *Justice*) "take ye each a *S. Mi.* xi. 10
The pearly *s.* its lucid globe infold *W.F.* 395
A tribe, with weeds and s—s *fantastic crown'd D.* iv. 398

Shelter.
From storms a *s.*, and from heat a shade *M.* 16
For see ! the gath'ring flocks to *s.* tend *Sp.* 101

Shelter'd.
You'll wish your hill or *s.* seat again *M.E.* iv. 76
Here in a grotto, *s.* close from air *R.L.* iv. 21

Shepherd.
As the good *s.* tends his fleecy care *M.* 49
Ah wretch'd *s.*, what avails thy art *Su.* 33
Oft in her glass the musing *s.* spies *W.F.* 211
Thy victim, Love, shall be the s.'s heart Sp. 52
A *S.* Boy (he seeks no better name) *Su.* 1
The s—s cry, " Thy flocks are left a prey" A. 78
I'll fly from *s.*, flocks, and flow'ry plains (*rep.*) *A.* 86
Thus sung the *s.* till th' approach of night *A.* 97
But see, the *s.* shun the noon-day heat *Su.* 85
And said; "Ye *s.*, sing around my grave !" *W.* 18
Adieu, ye s—s' rural lays and loves W. 90

Sheriff.—*See* Shrieves.

Sherlock.
While *S.*, Hare, and Gibson preach in vain *D.* iii. 204

Shew.—*See* Show.

Shield.
Can taste no pleasure since his *S.* was scour'd *M.E.* v. 42
Each chief his sev'nfold *s.* displayed *O.* i. 45
The lilies blazing on the regal *s. W.F.* 306

Shift.
A Weasel once made *s.* to slink *I.H.* i. 51
Realms *s. their place, and Ocean turns to land D.* i. 72
They *s.* the moving Toyshop of their heart *R.L.* i. 100

Shifting.
Quick whirls, and *s.* eddies of our minds *M.E.* i. 24
Perhaps the Virgin just *s.* from the east *M.E.* ii. 112
With what a *s.* gale your course you ply *S.* v. 298

Shillings.
In *s.* and in pence at first they steal *S.* vii. 83

Shine.
Fair op'ning to some Court's propitious *s. E.M.* iv. 9
Now golden fruits on loaded branches s. *A.* 73
She saw old Pryn in restless Daniel *s. D.* i. 103
His Peers *s.* round him with reflected grace *D.* ii. 9
See, round the Poles where keener spangles *s. D.* iii. 69
Another (for in all what one can *s.*) *D.* iv. 555
S. in the dignity of F.R.S. *D.* iv. 570
Nor public Flame, nor private, dares to *s. D.* iv. 651
Like them to *s.* thro' long succeeding age *E.* iii. 11
Oh lasting as those Colours may they *s. E.* iii. 63
In these gay thoughts the Loves and Graces *s. E.* iv. 1
The wand'ring streams that *s.* between the hills *E.A.* 157
From op'ning skies may streaming glories *s. E.A.* 341
And force that sun but on a part to *s. E.C.* 399
In all you speak, let truth and candour *s. E.C.* 563
Ask for what end the heav'nly bodies *s. E.M.* i. 131
Alike or when, or where, they shone, or *s. E.M.* iv. 245
Ere taught to *s.*, or sanctify'd from shame *E.M.* iv. 300
Such as on HOUGH's unsully'd Mitre *s. E.S.* ii. 240
And for that Cause which made your Fathers *s. E.S.* ii. 252
Where other BUCKHURSTS, other DORSETS *s. Ep.* i. 13
O'erflow thy courts : the light himself shall *s. M.* 103
He'll *s.* a Tully and a Wilmot too *M.E.* i. 187
Or drest in smiles of sweet Cecilia *s. M.E.* ii. 13
S., buzz, and fly-blow in the setting sun *M.E.* ii. 28
Touch'd by thy hand, again Rome's glories *s. M.E.* v. 46
On the cast ore, another Pollio, *s. M.E.* v. 64
Jove, Jove himself does on the Scissors *s. Mi.* ix. 36
This *Snuff-Box*,—on the Hinge see Brilliants *s. Mi.* ix. 43
Fires that scorch, yet dare not *s. O.* iii. 40
And, like the sun, they *s.* on all alike *R.L.* ii. 14
And *s.* that superfluity away *S.* ii. 116
Behold the groves that *s.* with silver frost *W.* 9
Let Volga's banks with iron squadrons *s. W.F.* 363

Shin'd.
Once brightest *s.* this child of Heat and Air *D.* iv. 424
If Parts allure thee, think how Bacon *s. E.M.* iv. 281
How *s.* the Soul, unconquer'd in the Tow'r *E.S.* ii. 83
S. in Description, he might show it *I.H.* ii. 188
The Courtier smooth, who forty years had *s. M.E.* i. 252
E'er swell'd on marble ; as in verse have *s. S.* v. 392

Shines.
There, stamp'd with arms, Newcastle *s.* complete *D.* i. 142
That *s.* a Consul, this Commissioner *D.* iii. 184
'Tis thus aspiring Dulness ever *s. D.* iv. 19
Grace *s.* around her with serenest beams *E.A.* 215
Clears and improves whate'er it *s.* upon *E.C.* 316
I follow *Virtue*: where she *s.*, I praise *E.S.* ii. 95
S. in exposing Knaves and painting Fools *M.E.* ii. 119
Serene in Virgin Modesty she *s. M.E.* ii. 255
Where-e'er he *s.*, oh Fortune, gild the scene *M.E.* iii. 245
Upon the bottom *s.* the Queen's bright Face *Mi.* ix. 33
S. a broad Mirror thro' the shadowy Cave *Mi.* x. 2
Ev'n Sunday *s.* no Sabbath-day to me *P.S.* 12
One Simile, that solitary *s. S.* v. 111
Why sit we sad when Phosphor *s.* so clear *Sp.* 27
Ev'n spring displeases, when she *s.* not here *Sp.* 83

Shining.
The *s.* robes, rich jewels, beds of state *E.* iv. 51
Deep hid the *s.* mischief under ground *M.E.* iii. 10

There Warriors *s.* in historic brass *M.E.* v. 58
Guineas, Half-Guineas, all the *s.* train *Mi.* ix. 79
And half unsheath'd the *s.* blade *O.* i. 46
Here files of pins extend their *s.* rows *R.L.* i. 137
With *s.* ringlets the smooth iv'ry neck *R.L.* ii. 22
And particolour'd troops, a *s.* train *R.L.* iii. 43
On *s.* Altars of Japan they raise *R.L.* iii. 107
A two-edg'd weapon from her *s.* case *R.L.* iii. 128
Which adds new glory to the *s.* sphere *R.L.* v. 142
Eternal beauties grace the *s.* scene *W.* 71
The vivid green his *s.* plumes unfold *W.F.* 117
The silver eel, in *s.* volumes roll'd *W.F.* 143
With Edward's acts adorn the *s.* page *W.F.* 303
His *s.* horns diffus'd a golden gleam *W.F.* 332

Ship.
The *S.* itself may make a better figure *S.* vi. 298
Then s—s *of uncouth form shall stem the tide* W.F. 403
Or s. *off Senates to a distant Shore M.E.* iii. 44
And two rich s.-*wrecks bless the lucky shore M.E.*iii.356

Shippen.
As downright *S.*, or as old Montaigne *S.* i. 52

Shire.
Knight of the post corrupt, or of the *s. P.S.* 365

Shirtless.
Grave Mummers! sleeveless some, and *s.* others *D.*iii.116

Shiv'ring.
A puny insect, *s.* at a breeze *M.E.* iv. 108

Shoal.
Broad hats, and hoods, and caps, a sable *s. D.* iv. 190

Shock.
He said; when *S.*, who thought she slept too long *R.L.* i. 115
Or whether Heav'n has doom'd that *S.* must fall *R.L.* ii. 110
Ariel himself, shall be the guard of *S. R.L.* ii. 116
Nay, Poll sat mute, and *S.* was most uukind *R.L.* iv. 164

Shock'd.
And never *s.*, and never turn'd aside *E.C.* 629

Shocks.
That such are happier, *s.* all common sense *E.M.* iv. 52
What *s.* one part will edify the rest *E.M.* iv. 141
Beauty that *s.* you, parts that none will trust *P.S.* 332

Shod.
Men bearded, bald, cowl'd, uncowl'd, *s.*, unshod *D.* iii. 114

Shoes.
Who holds Dragoons and wooden *s.* in scorn *Mi.* ii. 20
Prefer a new Japanner to their *s. S.* iii. 156

Shone.
Now setting Phœbus *s.* serenely bright *A.* 13
In clouded Majesty here Dulness *s. D.* i. 45
But high above more solid Learning *s. D.* i. 147
Thus Voiture's early care still *s.* the same *E.* iv. 69
S. sweetly lambent with celestial day *E.A.* 64
Which from the first has *s.* on ages past *E.C.* 402
Alike or when, or where, they *s.*, or shine *E.M.* iv. 245
The living Virtue now had *s.* approv'd *Ep.* xiv. 7
Fair Nymphs, and well-drest Youths around her *s. R.L.* ii. 5
And full in Shakespear, fair in Otway *s. S.* v. 277

Shook.
Loud thunder to its bottom *s.* the bog *D.* i. 329
When lo! a burst of thunder *s.* the flood *D.* ii. 325
And *s.* from out his Pipe the seeds of fire *D.* iv. 494
With Heav'n's own thunders *s.* the world below *E.M.* iii. 267
And *s.* the Stage with Thunders all his own *Mi.* ii. 16
The tott'ring China *s.* without a wind *R.L.* iv. 163
And *s.* his head at Murray, as a Wit *S.* vi. 132
What *s.* the stage, and made the People stare *S.* v. 336
Soon as the flocks *s.* off the nightly dews *Sp.* 17

Shoot.
A Wild, where weeds and flow'rs promiscuous *s. E.M.* i. 7
Eye Nature's walks, *s.* Folly as it flies *E.M.* i. 13

The surest Virtues thus from Passions *s. E.M.* ii. 183
And swiftly *s.* along the Mall *I.H.* iii. 45
Pursue the stars that *s.* athwart the night *R.L.* ii. 82

Shooting.
A *Feather*, *s.* from another's head *D.* iv. 521

Shoots.
With annual joy the redd'ning *s.* to greet *M.E.* iv. 91
Wit s. *in vain its momentary fires D.* iv. 633
Or breathes thro' air, or *s.* beneath the deeps *E.M.*iii.116
In Man, the judgment *s.* at flying game *M.E.* i. 96
The sun obliquely *s.* his burning ray *R.L.* iii. 20

Shop.
Her ev'ning cates before his neighbour's *s. D.* ii. 70
He serv'd a 'Prenticeship, who sets up *s. S.* v. 181
The s—s *shut up in ev'ry street I.H.* i. 8

Shore.
Thou, yet unborn, hast touch'd this sacred *s. D.* iii. 45
See, where the morning gilds the palmy *s. D.* iii. 95
Proceed, great days! till Learning fly the *s. D.* iii. 333
She heard, and drove him to th' Hibernian *s. D.* iv. 70
But when loud surges lash the sounding *s. E.C.* 368
The mighty Stagirite first left the *s. E.C.* 645
The Play may pass—but that strange creature, *s. E. J.S.* 5
Steer'd the same course to the same quiet *s. Ep.* vii. 13
Or ship off Senates to a distant *S. M.E.* iii. 44
And two rich ship-wrecks bless the lucky *s. M.E.* iii. 356
Huge moles, whose shadow stretch'd from *s.* to *s. M.E.* v. 21
Say, will you bless the bleak Atlantic *s. O.* ii. 15
Perhaps ev'n Britain's utmost *s. O.* ii. 19
A verier monster, than on Afric's *s. S.* viii. 28
If Sylvia smiles, new glories gild the *s. Sp.* 75
Her name with pleasure once she taught the *s. W.* 43
But tell the reeds, and tell the vocal *s. W.* 59
What Kings first breath'd upon her winding *s. W.F.* 300
And the hush'd waves glide softly to the *s. W.F.* 354
Safe on my *s.* each unmolested swain *W.F.* 369
O stretch thy reign, fair Peace! from *s.* to *s. W.F.* 407
And with deep murmurs fills the sounding s—s *A.* 20
Arabian *s.*, or Indian seas infold *S.* iv. 12
Blest Thames's *s.* the brightest beauties yield *Sp.* 63
And future navies on thy *s.* appear *W.F.* 222

Short.
And Snip-snap *s.*, and Interruption smart *D.* ii. 240
All my commands are easy, *s.*, and full *D.* iv. 581
Wits have *s.* Memories, and Dunces none *D.* iv. 620
S. views we take, nor see the lengths behind *E.C.* 222
Form *s.* Ideas; and offend in arts *E.C.* 287
S. is the date, alas, of modern rhymes *E.C.* 476
It stills looks home, and *s.* excursions makes *E.C.* 627
But in low numbers *s.* excursions tries *E.C.* 738
And just as *s.* of reason he must fall *E.M.* iii. 47
While still too wide or *s.* is human Wit *E.M.* iii. 90
S., and but rare, till Man improv'd it all *E.M.* iv. 116
Chang'd it to August, and (in *s.*) *I.H.* i. 3
But you may read it; I stop *s. I.H.* i. 84
In *s.*, I'm perfectly content *I.H.* ii. 29 *s*
In one *s.* view subjected to our eye *M.E.* v. 33
There he stopp'd *s.*, nor since has writ a tittle *Mi.* iii. 9
Some few *s.* years, no more *Mi.* iv. 38
I cough, like *Horace*, and tho' lean, am *s. P.S.* 116
Then, learned Sir! (to cut the matter *s.*) *S.* iii. 5
Weak tho' I am of limb, and *s.* of sight *S.* iii. 49
In *s.*, that reas'ning, high, immortal Thing *S.* iii. 185
What's long or *s.*, each accent where to place *S.* v. 207
Who pants for glory finds but *s.* repose *S.* v. 300
They bled, they cupp'd, they purg'd; in *s.*, they cur'd *S.* vi. 193
S. is his joy; he feels the fiery wound *W.F.* 113
Straight a *s.* thunder breaks the frozen sky *W.F.* 130
But soon the s.-*liv'd vanity is lost E.C.* 497
Shall finish what his *s.* Sire begun *M.* 64

Shorter.
And now his *s.* breath, with sultry air *W.F.* 195

Shortly.
S. no lad shall chuck, or lady vole *S.* viii. 146
Shall *s.* want the gen'rous tear he pays *U.L.* 78

Shot.
That all the *s.* of Dulness now must be *S.* viii. 64
S. to the black abyss, and plung'd downright D. ii. 288

SHOULD—SHRIN'D.

And the bright flame was *s.* thro' MARCHMONT's Soul *Mi.* x. 12
Sol thro' white curtains *s.* a tim'rous ray *R.L.* i. 13
A sudden Star, it *s.* thro' liquid air *R.L.* v. 127

Should, Should'st.—*Passim.*

Shoulder.
Gay pats my *s.*, and you vanish quite *E.* v. 47
Ammon's great son one *s.* had too high *P.S.* 117
A painted quiver on her *s.* sounds *W.F.* 179
So labr'ing on with s—s, hands, and head *D.* ii. 65
By his broad *s.* known, and length of ears *D.* iii. 36

Should'ring.
S. God's altar a vile image stands *M.E.* iii. 293

Shout.
Six huntsmen with a *s.* precede his chair *D.* ii. 193
Such is the *s.*, the long-applauding note *S.* v. 330
The nymph exulting fills with s—s the sky *R.L.* iii. 99
Heroes' and Heroines' *s.* confus'dly rise *R.L.* v. 41
Here fortun'd Curl to slide ; loud *s.* the band *D.* ii. 73

Shouts.
Here *s.* all Drury, there all Lincoln's-inn *D.* iii. 270

Shove.
An·l *s.* him off as far as e'er we can *D.* iv. 474
You ne'er consider whom you *s. I.H.* ii. 58*s*

Shov'd.
S. from the wall, perhaps, or rudely press'd *M.E.* i. 234

Shoves.
Comes titt'ring on, and *s.* you from the stage *S.* vi. 325

Show, Shew.
Works without *s.*, and without pomp presides *E.C.* 75
PRUDINA likes a Man, and laughs at *S. Mi.* ix. 104
In *s.* like leaders of the swarthy Moors *R.L.* iii. 48
Wrapt in a gown, for sickness, and for *s. R.L.* iv. 36
To midnight dances, and the public *s. U.L.* 58
Nor let false S—s, or empty Titles please *E.* iv. 47
Deceiv'd by *S.* and Forms *Mi.* iv. 2
Mere household trash ! of birth-nights, balls, and *s. S.* viii. 130
While proud Philosophy repines to *s. D.* iii. 197
S. all his paces, not a step advance *D.* iv. 266
Learn then what MORALS Critics ought to *s. E.C.* 550
Who to a friend his faults can freely *s. E.C.* 637
And take it kindly meant to *s. I.H.* ii. 61 *s*
Shin'd in Description, he might *s.* it *I.H.* ii. 188
Ladies, like variegated tulips, *s. M.E.* ii. 41
Only to *s.*, how many Tastes he wanted *M.E.* iv. 14
You *s.* us, Rome was glorious, not profuse *M.E.* iv. 23
Whose rising Forests, not for pride or *s. M.E.* iv. 187
In pitying Love, we but our weakness *s. P.C.* 11
And *s.*, you have the virtue to be mov'd *P.C.* 38
And *s.* the sense of it without the love *P.S.* 294
And call for pen and ink to *s.* our Wit *S.* v. 180
Yet let me *s.*, a Poet's of some weight *S.* v. 203
But *s.* no mercy to an empty line *S.* vi. 175
Had no new verses, nor new suit to *s. S.* viii. 13
And tho' the Court *s.* Vice exceeding clear *S.* viii. 96
Now pox on those who *s.* a Court in wax *S.* viii. 206
The flocks around a dumb compassion *s. Su.* 6
That Mercy I to others *s.* (*rep.*) *U.P.* 39
Nor all his stars above a lustre *s. W.F.* 231
As half to *shew*, half veil, the deep Intent *D.* iv. 4
And, to excuse it, need but *s.* the prize *D.* iv. 434
Which nothing seeks to *s.*, or needs to hide *E.* ii. 2
And shew'd a NEWTON as we *s.* an Ape *E.M.* ii. 34
Or tricks to *s.* the stretch of human brain *E.M.* ii. 47
S. there was one who held it in disdain *E.S.* i. 172
Infer the Motive from the Deed, and *s. M.E.* i. 101
Not always Actions *s.* the man : we find *M.E.* i. 109
And *s.* their zeal, and hide their want of skill *M.E.* ii. 186
The mushrooms *s.* his wit was sudden *Mi.* xii. 11
But *s.* me one who has it in his pow'r *S.* iii. 136

Show'd, Shew'd.
High on Parnassus' top her sons she *s. E.C.* 94
Nay *s.* his faults—but when would Poets mend *E.C.* 621
As *s.*, Vice had his hate and pity too *Ep.* i. 8
But *s.* his Breeding and his Wit *I.H.* ii. 172
S'. Rome her Cato's figure drawn in state *P.C.* 30

S. us that France had something to admire *S.* v. 275
And shew'd a NEWTON as we shew an Ape *E.M.* ii. 34
S. erring Pride, WHATEVER IS, IS RIGHT *E.M.* iv. 394

Show'r.
Look'd a white lily sunk beneath a *s. D.* iv. 104
Suckled, and cheer'd, with air, and sun, and *s. D.* iv. 406
And in soft silence shed the kindly *s. M.* 14
In one abundant *s.* of Cent per Cent *M.E.* iii. 372
From yon old walnut-tree a *s.* shall fall *S.* ii. 145
And Jove consented in a silent *s. Su.* 8
Not s—s to larks, nor sun-shine to the bee *A.* 45
Here gay Description Egypt glads with *s. D.* i. 73
All-bounteous, fragrant Grains and Golden *s. D.* ii. 4
Till *s.* of Sermons, Characters, Essays *D.* ii. 361
Of *s.* and sunshine, as of Man's desires *E.M.* i. 152
To steal from rainbows e'er they drop in *s. R.L.* ii. 96
All nature mourns, the Skies relent in *s. Sp.* 69
A soft retreat from sudden vernal *s. Sp.* 98
And from the Pleiads fruitful *s.* descend *Sp.* 102
Soft *s.* distill'd, and suns grew warm in vain *W.F.* 54

Shown.
Then sung, how *s.* him by the Nut-brown maids *D.* ii. 337
Never by tumbler thro' the hoops was *s. D.* iv. 257
Now *s.* by Cynthia's silver ray *I.H.* iii. 47
Or come discolour'd thro' our Passions *s. M.E.* i. 34
But grant, in Public Men sometimes are *s. M.E.* ii. 199
Or in fair series laurell'd Bards be *s. M.E.* v. 61
Then first his Passion was in public *s. Mi.* ix. 40
Yet think, great Sir, (so many Virtues *s.*) *S.* v. 376
Thus, others' talents having nicely *s. S.* viii. 80

Shows, Shews.
S. most true mettle when you check his course *E.C.* 87
That always *s.* great pride, or little sense *E.C.* 387
Th' embroider'd King who *s.* but half his face *R.L.* iii. 76
S. in her cheek the roses of eighteen *R.L.* iv. 32
"Then, happy Man who *s.* the Tombs!" said I *S.* viii. 102
Here to her Chosen all her works she *shews D.* i. 275
But Fop *s.* Fop superior complaisance *D.* iv. 133
Or if she rules him, never *s.* she rules *M.E.* ii. 262

Shrew.
'Tis an ugly envious *S. Mi.* vi. 9

Shrewd.
Or, in quotations, *s.* Divines leave out *S.* vii. 103

Shrewsbury.
I study'd *S.*, the wise and great *E.S.* ii. 79
The bow'r of wanton *S.* and love *M.E.* iii. 308

Shriek.
I *s.*, start up, the same sad prospect find *E.A.* 247

Shrieks.
S. of woe *O.* i. 59
Not louder *s.* to pitying Heav'n are cast *R.L.* iii. 157

Shrieves.
Now May'rs and *S.* all hush'd and satiate lay *D.* i. 91
Great in her charms ! as when on *S.* and May'rs *D.* i. 263

Shrill.
The *s.* echoes rebound *O.* i. 9
Wind the *s.* horn, or spread the waving net *W.F.* 96

Shrine.
But chief her *s.* where naked Venus keeps *D.* iv. 307
I bought them, shrouded in their living *s. D.* iv. 385
From yonder *s.* I heard a hollow sound *E.A.* 308
The *s.* with gore unstain'd, with gold undrest *E.M.* iii. 157
Oh All-accomplish'd ST. JOHN ! deck thy *s. E.S.* ii. 139
Touch'd with the Flame that breaks from *Virtue's S. E.S.* ii. 233
To this sad *s.*, whoe'er thou art ! draw near *Ep.* iii. 1
Honour forbid ! at whose unrivall'd *s. R.L.* iv. 105
And with fresh bays her rural *s.* adorn *W.* 20
S—s where their vigils pale-ey'd virgins keep *E.A.* 21
The *s.* all trembled, and the lamps grew pale *E.A.* 112
Our *s.* irradiate, or emblaze the floors *E.A.* 136

Shrin'd.
Booth in his cloudy tabernacle *s. D.* iii. 267

Shrink.

S., and confess the genius of the place *D*. iv. 146
What happier natures s. at with affright *E.M*. ii. 229
S. back to my Paternal Cell *I.H*. i. 76
And all her triumphs s. into a Coin *M.E*. v. 24
S. his thin essence like a rivel'd flow'r *R.L*. ii. 132

Shrinks.

S. to her second cause, and is no more *D*. iv. 644
Then s. to Earth again *Mi*. iv. 8

Shrivel'd (?).—*See* Rivel'd.

Shrink his thin essence like a s. flow'r *R.L*. ii. 132

Shrouded.

I bought them, s. in their living shrine *D*. iv. 385

Shrouds.

Soft o'er the s. aërial whispers breathe *R.L*. ii. 57

Shrubs.

To leafless s. the flow'ring palms succeed *M*. 75

Shrunk.

Now to thy gentle shadow they are s. *D*. iv. 509
And the huge boar is s. into an urn *D*. iv. 552
Now nothing left, but wither'd, pale, and s. *Mi*. iii. 25

Shudd'ring.

O'er ev'ry vein a s. horror runs *D*. iv. 143

Shun.

Avoid Extremes ; and s. the fault of such *E.C*. 384
'Tis what the vicious fear, the virtuous s. *E.C*. 500
Yet s. their fault, who, scandalously nice *E.C*. 556
To s. their poison, and to choose their food *M.E*. iii. 100
This bids to serve, and that to s. mankind *E.M*. iv. 20
Who most to s. or hate Mankind pretend *E.M*. iv. 43
I s. his Zenith, court his mild Decline *E.M*. ii. 76
Pride guides his steps, and bids him s. the great *M.E*. i. 114
And most contemptible, to s. contempt *M.E*. i. 195
For what to s. will no great knowledge need *M.E*.iii. 199
And see the Folly, which I cannot s. *Mi*. ix. 70
I s. the fountains which I sought before *Su*. 30
But see, the shepherds s. the noonday heat *Sn*. 85
This teach me more than Hell to s. *U.P*. 15
Thin trees arise that s. each other's shades *W.F*. 22

Shunning.

That s. faults, one quiet tenour keep *E.C*. 241

Shuns.

Our author s. by vulgar springs to move *P.C*. 9

Shut.

The shops s. up in ev'ry street *J.H*. i. 8
S., s. the door, good John! fatigu'd, I said *P.S*. 1

Shuts.

Steals my senses, s. my sight *O*. v. 10

Shylock.

And ev'ry child hates S., tho' his soul *M.E*. i. 55
Of wretched S., spite of S.'s wife *M.E*. iii. 94
Why S. wants a meal, the cause is found *M.E*. iii. 115
Plums and Directors, S. and his Wife *M*. i. 103

Sibyl.

A slip-slop S. led his steps along *D*. iii. 15
A leaf, like S.'s, scatter to and fro *M.E*. iii. 45

Sicilian.

While on thy banks S. Muses sing *Sp*. 4

Sick.

At some s. miser's triple-bolted gate *D*. ii. 248
S., was the Sun, the Owl forsook his bow'r *D*. iv. 11
You humour me when I am s. *J.H*. i. 5
The s. and weak the healing plant shall aid *M*. 15
Perhaps was s., in love, or had not din'd *M.E*. i. 128
S. of herself thro' very selfishness *M.E*. ii. 146
Health to the s., and solace to the swain *M.E*. iii. 258
Is any s. ? the MAN of Ross relieves *M.E*. iii. 269
S. of his civil Pride, from Morn to Eve *M.E*. iv. 106
Tie up the knocker, say I'm s., I'm dead *P.S*. 2
But s. of fops, and poetry, and prate *P.S*. 229
The courtier's promises and s. man's pray'rs *R.L*. v. 119
Now s. alike of Envy and of Praise *S*. iii. 4

Sicken.

Grow s., and damn the climate—like a Lord *S*. iii. 160
Whee s. of Muse, our follies we deplore *S*. v. 177
As one of Woodward's patients, s., and sore *S*. viii. 152

Sicken.

All pleasures s., and all glories sink *E.M*. iv. 46

Sicken'd.

When Nature s., and each gale was death *E.M*. iv. 108

Sick'ning.

The s. stars fade off th' ethereal plain *D*. iv. 636
Till drooping, s., dying, they began *E.M*. iii. 223
Let *Flatt'ry* s. see the Incense rise *E.S*. ii. 224

Sickly.

With each a s. bruther at his back *D*. ii. 306
Then Affectation, with a s. mien *R.L*. iv. 31

Sickness.

Those, Age or S., soon or late disarms *E*. iv. 60
His life, tho' long, to s. past unknown *P.S*. 402
Wrapt in a gown, for s., and for show *R.L*. iv. 36
And more the s. of long life, Old age *S*. ii. 88

Side.

There Caxton slept, with Wynkyn at his s. *D*. i. 149
And now to this s., now to that they nod *D*. ii. 395
By singing Peers upheld on either s. *D*. iv. 49
There march'd the bard and blockhead, s. by s. *D*.iv.101
Thro' both he pass'd, and bow'd from s. to s. *D*. iv. 108
Some Slave of mine be pinion'd to their s. *D*. iv. 134
And fain would be upon the laughing s. *E.C*. 33
'Twixt sense and nonsense daily change their s. *E.C*. 435
Some valuing those of their own s. or mind *E.C*. 452
And love to praise, with reason on his s. *E.C*. 642
With too much knowledge for the sceptic s. *E.M*. ii. 5
All, all alike, find Reason on their s. *E.M*. ii. 174
Fix'd to one s., yet mod'rate to the rest *Ep*. ii. 4
Let me but live on this s. Trent *J.H*. ii. 30 s
In crowding ranks on ev'ry s. arise *M*. 89
Is, there, Pastora by a fountain s. *M.E*. ii. 8
Stocks and Subscriptions pour on ev'ry s. *M.E*. iii. 370
On ev'ry s. you look, behold the Wall *M.E*. iv. 114
And Curio, restless by the Fair-one's s. *M.E*. v. 43
The *Equipage* shall grace SMILINDA'S s. *Mi*. ix. 110
With handkerchief and orange at my s. *P.S*. 228
Th' inferior Priestess, at her altar's s. *R.L*. i. 127
Pain at her s. and Megrim at her head *R.L*. iv. 24
Unnumber'd throngs on ev'ry s. are seen *R.L*. iv. 47
The doubtful beam long nods from s. to s. *R.L*. v. 73
And drew a deadly bodkin from her s. *R.L*. v. 88
And neither leans on this s., or on that *S*. ii. 62
And sets the Passions on the s. of Truth *S*. v. 218
Most warp'd to Flatt'ry's s.; but some, more nice *S*. v. 259
The dawn now blushing on the mountain's s. *Sp*. 21
Behold! th' ascending Villas on my s. *W.F*. 375
And feather'd people crowd my wealthy s. *W.F*. 404
To buy both s—s, and give thy Country peace *M.E*. iii. 150
Slopes at its foot, the woods its s. embrace *S*. iii. 141
All s. in parties, and begin th' attack *R.L*. v. 39
Why bows the s.-box from its inmost rows *R.L*. v. 14

Sidney.

See S. bleeds amid the martial strife *E.M*. iv. 101
And S.'s *verse halts ill on Roman feet* *S*. v. 98

Siege.

In love's, in nature's spite, the s. they hold *S*. vii. 23

Sieve.

But, like a S., let ev'ry blessing thro' *Mi*. v. 6

Sigh.

A s. the absent claims, the dead a tear *E*. i. 14
A fading Fresco here claims a s. *E*. iii. 34
And wait a s. from Indus to the Pole *E.A*. 58
That something still which prompts th' eternal s. *E.M*. iv. 3
And the gay Courtier feels the s. sincere *Ep*. ix. 6
No s., no murmur the wide world shall hear *M*. 45
Nor leave one s. behind them when they die *M.E*.ii.230
Resign'd to fate, and with a s. retir'd *R.L*. iii. 146
Which, with a s., she rais'd; and thus she said *R.L*. iv. 146
Clos'd their long Glories with a s., to find *S*. v. 13

SIGH'D—SILL.

Go, gentle gales, and bear my s—s away A. 17, &c.
And cease, ye gales, to bear my s. away A. 54
Padua, with s., beholds her Livy burn D. iii. 105
And ans'wring gin-shops sourer s. return D. iii. 148
The truest hearts for Voiture heav'd with s. E. iv. 17
Saw others happy, and with s. withdrew E. v. 8
Repentant s., and voluntary pains E.A. 18
Still breath'd in s., still usher'd with a tear E.A. 32
Griefs to thy griefs, and echo s. to thine E.A. 42
Tears that delight, and s. that waft to heav'n E.A. 214
I waste the Matin lamp in s. for thee E.A. 267
Now s. steal out, and tears begin to flow E.C. 379
S. for a daughter with unwounded ear M.E. ii. 260
Tenants with s. the smokeless tow'rs survey M.E. iii. 191
And those feigned s. which cheat the list'ning Fair Mi. ix. 8
Where British s. from dying Wyndham stole Mi. x. 11
And breathes three am'rous s. to raise the fire R.L. ii. 42
S., sobs, and passions, and the war of tongues R.L. iv. 84
And told in s. to all the trembling trees W. 6a
All look, all s., all call on Smedley lost D. ii. 293
To s. for ribbands if thou art so silly E.M. iv. 277
Have made a Soldier s., a Lover swear Mi. ix. 46
S., while his Chloe blind to Wit and Worth S. v. 42
My heir may s., and think it want of grace S. vi. 286
Ready to cast, I yawn, I s., I sweat S. viii. 157

Sigh'd.

She s. not that they stay'd, but that she went E. v. 10
Or he whose Virtue s. to lose a day E.M. iv. 147
And s.) "my lands and tenements to Ned" M.E. i. 257
Ambition s.; she found it vain to trust M.E. v. 19

Sigh'st.

Yet s. thou now for apples and for cakes E.M. iv. 176

Sighing.

Then, s., thus, "And am I now threescore D. ii. 285

Sighs.

Sore s. Sir Gilbert, starting at the bray D. ii. 251
She s., and is no Duchess at her heart E. iv. 56
S. for the shades—"How charming is a Park!" M.E. ii. 38
S. for an Otho, and neglects his bride M.E. v. 44
Brutus for absent Portia s. O. iii. 15
She s. for ever on her pensive bed R.L. iv. 23
Here s. a Jar, and there a Goose-pie talks R.L. iv. 52

Sight.

Are half so charming as thy s. to me A. 46
A shapeless shade, it melted from his s. D. ii. 111
Then " essay'd ; scarce vanish'd out of s. D. ii. 295
Then stretch thy s. o'er all her rising reign D. iii. 65
See all her progeny, illustrious s. D. iii. 129
Dishonest s.! his breeches rent below D. iii. 198
Attends; all flesh is nothing in his s. D. iv. 159
Streets, Chairs, and Coxcombs, rush upon my s. E. v. 48
Love, free as air, at s. of human ties E.A. 75
Priests, tapers, temples, swim before my s. E.A. 274
Fir'd at first s. with what the Muse imparts E.C. 219
Something, whose truth convinc'd at s. we find E.C. 299
What modes of s. betwixt each wide extreme E.M. i. 211
Thus gracious Chandos is belov'd at s. M.E. i. 54
So when the Sun's broad beam has tir'd the s. M.E. ii. 253
With sharpen'd s. pale Antiquaries pore M.E. v. 35
Was there a Chief but melted at the S. Mi. ii. 7
Fir'd by the s., all Reason I disdain Mi. ix. 83
Steals my senses, shuts my s. O. v. 10
No common object to your s. displays P.C. 19
I kept, like Asian monarchs, from their s. P.S. 220
Transparent forms, too fine for mortal s. R.L. ii. 61
Puts forth one manly leg, to s. reveal'd R.L. iii. 57
Hairs less in s., or any hairs but these R.L. v. 176
Charms strike the s., but merit wins the soul R.L. v. 34
Weak tho' I am of limb, and short of s. S. iii. 49
The people, sure, the people are the s. S. v. 323
Like a big bride at s. of loathsome meat S. viii. 156
Painted for s., and essenc'd for the smell S. viii. 226
But Delia always; absent from her s. Sp. 79
Not proud Olympus yields a nobler s. W.F. 33
Before you pass th' imaginary s—s E. v. 35

Sightless.

Of all who blindly creep, or s. soar E.M. i. 12
And on the s. eye-ball pour the day M. 40

Sign.

With that, a Tear (portentous s. of Grace) D. i. 243
Sure s. that no spectator shall be drown'd D. ii. 174
S—s following s—s lead on the mighty year D. iii. 321
Writ underneath the Country S. I.H. ii. 92
Where twelve fair S. in beauteous order lie Sp. 40
The hungry Judges soon the sentence s. R.L. iii. 21

Sign'd.

S. with that Ichor which from Gods distils D. ii. 92
To get my warrant quicky s. I.H. ii. 76 s

Silence.

King John in s. modestly expires D. i. 252
S., ye Wolves! while Ralph to Cynthia howls D. iii. 165
Nor pass these lips in holy s. seal'd E.A. 10
A death-like s., and a dead repose E.A. 166
Your s. there is butter than your spite E.C. 598
And in soft s. shed the kindly show'r M. 14
S. without, and Fasts within the wall M.E. iii. 188
Him the Boar, in S. creeping Mi. vii. 11
S. ensu'd, and thus the nymph began R.L. v. 8
To ease and s., ev'ry Muse's son S. vi. 111
But, charm'd to s., listens while she sings Sp. 15
Such s. waits on Philomela's strains W. 78
O Cara! Cara! s. all that train D. iv. 53
S. or hurt, he libels the great man S. viii. 159

Silenc'd.

The s. Preacher yields to potent strain S. v. 237

Silent.

Yet s. bow'd to Christ's No kingdom here D. ii. 400
Hung s. down his never-blushing head D. ii. 417
Gone ev'ry blush, and s. all reproach D. iv. 563
Some, deep Free-Masons, join the s. race D. iv. 571
The Muse attends thee to thy s. shade E. i. 28
Tho' cold like you, unmov'd and s. grown E.A. 23
Re s. always when you doubt your sense E.C. 566
S. and soft, as Saints remove to Heav'n E.S. i. 93
Have I, in s. wonder, seen such things E.S. i. 109
Pensive hast follow'd to the s. tomb Ep. vii. 12
What turns him now a stupid s. dunce M.E. i. 163
And s. sells a King, or buys a Queen M.E. iii. 48
Some felt the s. stroke of mould'ring age M.E. v. 11
Softly seeks her s. Mate Mi. vii. 30
Envy, be s., and attend Mi. viii. 2
Wake into voice each s. string O. i. 3
Who can't be s., and who will not lie P.S. 34
'Twas He had summon'd to her s. bed R.L. i. 21
While with the s. growth of ten per cent. S. ii. 132
(More s. far) where Kings and Poets lie S. iv. 51
And Jove consented in a s. show'r Su. 8
For ever s., since despis'd by thee Su. 44
Come, lovely nymph, and bless the s. hours Su. 63
While s. birds forget their tuneful lays W. 7
In hollow caves sweet echo s. lies W. 41
The balmy Zephyrs, s. since her death W. 49
The patient fisher takes his s. stand W.F. 137
Or wand'ring thoughtful in the s. wood W.F. 249
And s. Darent, stain'd with Danish blood W.F. 348
Pleas'd in the s. shade with empty praise W.F. 432

Silenus.

Where Tindal dictates, and S. snores D. iv. 492

Silia.

How soft is S.! fearful to offend M.E. ii. 29
But spare your censure; S. does not drink M.E. ii. 34

Silk.

Or draw to s. Arachne's subtile line D. iv. 590
Let Sporus tremble. What? that thing of s. P.S. 305
In s—s, in crapes, in Garters, and in Rags D. ii. 22
Fans clap, s. rustle, and tough whalebones crack R.L. v. 40
So spins the s.-worm small its slender store D. iv. 253
Misers are Muck-worms, S—s Beaus Mi. iv. 23

Silken.

Pours at great Bourbon's feet her s. sons D. iv. 298
While clogg'd he beats his s. wings in vain R.L. ii. 130

Sill.

Under this Marble, or under this S. Ep. xvi. 1

Silly.
To sigh for ribbands if thou art so *s*. *E.M.* iv. 277
The *s*. bard grows fat, or falls away *S.* v. 303

Silver.
With deeper sable blots the *s*. flood *D.* ii. 274
No *s*. saints, by dying misers giv'n *E.A.* 137
To Paraclete's white walls and *s*. springs *E.A.* 348
And tips with *S*. all the walls *I.H.* ii. 190
Now shown by Cynthia's ray *I.H.* iii. 47
Which sounds the *s*. Thames along *I.H.* iv. 2
Nor ev'ning Cynthia fill her *s*. horn *M.* 100
And now the Chapel's *s*. bell you hear *M.E.* iv. 141
Who to the *Dean*, and *s. bell* can swear *P.S.* 299
And the press'd watch return'd a *s*. sound *R.L.* i. 18
The *s*. token, and the circled green *R.L.* i. 32
Each *s*. Vase in mystic order laid *R.L.* i. 122
Launch'd on the bosom of the *s*. Thames *R.L.* ii. 4
Form a strong line about the *s*. bound *R.L.* ii. 121
The *s*. lamp; the fiery spirits blaze (*rep.*) *R.L.* iii. 108
As Gold to *S*., Virtue is to Gold *S.* iii. 78
The *s*. Thames reflects its marble face *S.* iii. 142
Gold, *S*., Iv'ry, Vases sculptur'd high *S.* vi. 264
Led forth his flocks along the *s*. Thame *Su.* 2
While Angels with their *s*. wings o'ershade *U.L.* 67
Behold the groves that shine with *s*. frost *W.* 9
The *s*. swans her hapless fate bemoan *W.* 39
Her fate remurmur to the *s*. flood *W.* 64
The *s*. eel, in shining volumes roll'd *W.F.* 143
Here arm'd with *s*. bows, in early dawn *W.F.* 169
In a soft, *s*. stream dissolv'd away (*rep.*) *W.F.* 204
And add new lustre to her *s*. star *W.F.* 290
The figur'd streams in waves of *s*. roll'd *W.F.* 335
The Kennet swift, for *s*. eels renown'd *W.F.* 341
With *s*.-quiv'ring *rills meander'd* o'er *M.E.* iv. 85
Thither, the *s.-sounding* lyres *I.H.* iii. 25

Silv'ry.
Of all th' enamell'd race, whose *s*. wing *D.* iv. 421

Simile.
This filthy *s*., this beastly line *E.S.* ii. 181
One *S*., that solitary shines *S.* v. 111
Figures ill-pair'd, and S—s *unlike D.* i. 66

Similitude.
In sad *s*. of griefs to mine *E.A.* 360

Simo.
Turn then from Wits; and look on *S.'s* Mate *M.E.* ii. 101

Simony.
Not more of *S*. beneath black gowns *S.* vii. 81

Simper.
The conscious *s*., and the jealous leer *D.* ii. 6

Simp'ring.
With *s*. Angels, Palms, and Harps divine *M.E.* ii. 14

Simple.
See what the charms that smite the *s*. heart *D.* iii. 229
Where bask on sunny banks the *s*. sheep *D.* iv. 352
Yet *s*. Nature to his hope has giv'n *E.M.* i. 103
And *s*. Reason never sought but one *E.M.* iii. 280
A *s*. Quaker, or a Quaker's Wife *E.S.* i. 233
Averted half your Parents' *s*. Pray'r *M.E.* ii. 286
When *s. Macer*, now of high renown *Mi.* iii. 1
Or *s*. pride for flatt'ry makes demands *P.S.* 253
Remembers oft the School-boy's *s*. fare *S.* ii. 73
Have bled and purg'd me to a *s*. Vote *S.* vi. 197

Simples.
He hears, and as a Still with *s*. in it *S.* viii. 126

Simplicetta.
Soft *S*. doats upon a Beau *Mi.* ix. 103

Simplicity.
In Wit, a Man; *S*., a Child *Ep.* xi. 2
And strangely lik'd for her *S. Mi.* iii. 20
Thus much is left of old *S. S.* ii. 36

Simplicius.
And good *S*. asks of her advice *M.E.* ii. 32

Sin.
O born in *s*., and forth in folly brought *D.* i. 225

Too soon they taught me 'twas no *s*. to love *E.A.* 68
And wait till 'tis no *s*. to mix with thine *E.A.* 176
How shall I lose the *s*., yet keep the sense *E.A.* 191
All Ties dissolv'd, and ev'ry *S*. forgiv'n *E.S.* i. 94
This calls the Church to deprecate our *S. E.S.* i. 120
What are you thinking? 'Faith the thought's no *s. E.S.* ii. 122
To W—le guilty of some venial *s. E.S.* ii. 162
See *S*. in State, majestically drunk *M.E.* ii. 69
With not one *s*., but poetry *Mi.* xii. 2
Why did I write? what *s*. to me unknown *P.S.* 125
And 'twere a *s*. to rob them of their mite *P.S.* 162
It was a *s*. to call our neighbour fool *P.S.* 383
Nor could it sure be such a *s*. to paint *R.L.* v. 24
True, conscious Honour is to feel no *s. S.* iii. 93
I grant that Poetry's a crying *s. S.* vii. 7
What *s*. of mine could merit such a rod *S.* viii. 63
Beheld such scenes of envy, *s*., and hate *S.* viii. 193
To deluge *s*., and drown a Court in tears *S.* viii. 285
In rev'rence to the S—*s of Thirty-nine E.S.* i. 5
Consistent in our follies and our *s. M.E.* i. 226
Shall feel sharp vengeance soon o'ertake his *s. R.L.* i. 125
Act *s*. which Prisca's Confessor scarce hears *S.* vii. 40
Those venial *s*., an atom, or a straw *S.* viii. 243
For hung with deadly *s*. I see the wall *S.* viii. 274
In some close corner of the soul, they s. E.J.S. 18

Since.—*Passim*.

Sincere.
But candid, free, *s*., as you began *E.* ii. 13
Tho' learn'd, well-bred; and tho' well-bred, *s. E.C.* 635
To these we owe true friendship, love *s. E.M.* ii. 255
Fix'd to no spot is Happiness *s. E.M.* iv. 15
S., tho' prudent; constant, yet resign'd *Ep.* ii. 2
Just of thy Word, in ev'ry thought *s. Ep.* vii. 5
Go then, where only bliss *s*. is known *Ep.* vii. 15
And the gay Courtier feels the sigh *s. Ep.* ix. 6
The Fool consistent, and the False *s. M.E.* i. 176
Statesman, yet friend to Truth! O soul *s. M.E.* v. 67
But ent'ring learns to be *s. O.* iii. 6

Sincerest.
The clearest head, and the *s*. heart *E.C.* 732

Sinful.
Ev'n those I pardon for whose *s*. sake *S.* vii 41
Shall I, the terror of this *s*. town *S.* viii. 196

Sing.
Hylas' and Ægon's rural lays I *s. A.* 6
Ye birds that, left by summer, cease to *s. A.* 28
I *s*. Say you, her instruments the Great *D.* i. 3
Why should I *s*. what bards the nightly Muse *D.* ii. 421
Another Durfey, Ward! shall *s*. in thee *D.* iii. 146
Ye Pow'rs! whose Mysteries restor'd I *s. D.* iv. 5
Why all your Toils; your sons have learn'd to *s. D.* iv. 546
O *s*., and hush the Nations with thy Song *D.* iv. 626
Of those that *s*. of these poor eyes *E.* vi. 32
For her white virgins Hymenæals *s., E.A.* 220
The Muse, whose early voice you taught to *s. E.C.* 735
See the blind beggar dance, the cripple *s. E.M.* ii. 267
Then might I *s*., without the least offence *E.S.* i. 77
The dumb shall *s*., the lame his crutch forego *M.* 43
Rise, honest Muse! and *s*. the Man of Ross *M.E.* iii. 250
Descend, ye Nine! descend and *s. O.* i. 1
I *s*.—This verse to Carvl, Muse! is due *R.L.* i. 3
Thus said our friend, and what he said I *s. S.* ii. 68
Yet ev'ry child another song will *s. S.* iii. 91
For what? to have a Box where Eunuchs *s. S.* iii. 105
We build, we paint, we *s*., we dance as well *S.* v. 46
Or who shall wander where the Muses *s. S.* v. 352
To *s*., or cease to *s*., we never know *S.* v. 361
Your Arms, your Actions, your repose to *s. S.* v. 395
S, thy sonorous verse—but not aloud *S.* vii. 109
As needy beggars *s*. at doors for meat *S.* vii. 26
While on thy banks Sicilian Muses *s. Sp.* 4
Why sit we mute when early linnets *s. Sp.* 25
S. then, and Damon shall attend the strain *Sp.* 29
Then *s*., by turns, by turns the Muses *s. Sp.* 41
The skies to brighten, and the birds to *s. Sp.* 72
Blest Nymphs, whose Swains those graces *s*. so well *Sp.* 96
To you I mourn, nor to the deaf I *s. Su.* 15

But would you s., and rival Orpheus' strain *Su.* 81
Is not so mournful as the strains you s. *W.* 2
Oh s. of Daphne's fate, and Daphne's praise *W.* 8
And said : " Ye shepherds, s. around my grave ! " (*rep.*) *W.* 18
In notes more sad than when they s. their own *W.* 40
What Muse for GRANVILLE can refuse to s. *W.F.* 6
The Muse shall s., and what she sings shall last *W.F.* 174
To s. those honours you deserve to wear *W.F.* 289
Oh wouldst thou s. what heroes Windsor bore *W.F.* 299
To fetch and carry s. *song up and down P.S.* 226

Singers.
And Ireland, mother of sweet s. *Mi.* xii. 7

Singing.
By s. Peers up-held on either side *D.* iv. 49
To lands of s., or of dancing slaves *D.* iv. 305
With s., laughing, ogling *and all that R.L.* iii. 18

Single.
Could Troy be sav'd by any s. hand *D.* i. 197
But oft in those confin'd to s. parts *E.C.* 63
No s. parts unequally surprize *E.C.* 249
In God's, one s. can its ends produce *E.M.* i. 55
The s. atoms each to other tend *M.E.* iii. 10
A s. leaf shall waft an Army o'er *M.E.* iii. 43
And beauty draws us with a s. hair *R.L.* ii. 28
That s. act gives half the world the spleen *R.L.* iv. 78
A s. verse, we quarrel with a friend *S.* v. 365

Singly.
Consider'd s., or beheld too near *E.C.* 172
At Ombre s. to decide their doom *R.L.* iii. 27

Sings.
As s. thy forefather great Ogilby *D.* i. 328
Who s. so loudly, and who s. so long *D.* ii. 268
Once swan of Thames, tho' now he s. no more *D.* iii. 20
Is it for thee the lark ascends and s. *E.M.* iii. 31
Or hears the hawk when Philomela s. *E.M.* iii. 36
All his Grace preaches, all his Lordship s. *E.S.* ii. 224
Let *Envy* howl, while Heav'n's whole Chorus s. *E.S.* ii. 242
How this or that Italian s. *I.H.* ii. 142
Th' expiring Swan, and as he s. he dies *R.L.* v. 66
Verse prays for Peace, or s. down Pope and Turk *S.* v. 236
One sings the Fair ; but songs no longer move *S.* vii. 21
But, charm'd to silence, listens while she s. *Sp.* 15
The captive bird that s. within thy bow'r *Su.* 46
No more the mounting larks, while Daphne s. *W.* 53
The Muse shall sing, and what she s. shall last *W.F.* 174
Are these reviv'd? or is it Granville s. *W.F.* 282

Singular.
As oft the Learn'd by being s. *E.C.* 425

Sink.
Beside s be a s. *D.* ii. 425
Down s. *the flames, and with a kiss expire D.* i. 260
Now s. in sorrows with a tolling bell *D.* ii. 228
Who but to s. the deeper, rose the higher *D.* ii. 290
To sound or s. in *cano*, O or A. *D.* iv. 221
Like buoys that never s. into the flood *D.* iv. 241
All pleasures sicken, and all glories s. *E.M.* iv. 48
S. down ye mountains, and ye valleys rise *M.* 34
To swell the Terrace, or to s. the Grot *M.E.* iv. 49
I yield at once, and s. into his arms *Mi.* ix. 96
Nor swell too high, nor s. too low *O.* i. 23
The Furies s. upon their iron beds *O.* i. 69
Waft on the breeze, or s. in clouds of gold *R.L.* ii. 60

Sinking.
S. from thought to thought, a vast profound *D.* i. 118
First he relates, how s. to the chin *D.* ii. 331
To ease th' oppress'd, and raise the s. heart *E.M.* iii. 244
Truths would you teach, or save a s. land *E.M.* iv. 265
Or add one Patriot to the s. state *Ep.* xiv. 4
I trust that s. Fund, my Life *I.H.* i. 74
Now fainting, s., pale, the nymph appears *W.F.* 191

Sinks.
S. deep within him, and possesses whole *M.E.* iii. 373
When Athens s. by fates unjust *O.* ii. 17
The graver Prude s. downwards to a Gnome *R.L.* i. 63

On the rich Quilt s. with becoming woe *R.L.* iv. 35
S. the lost Actor in the tawdry load *S.* v. 333

Sinner.
So from a sister s. you shall hear *E.J.S.* 9
Thither, where s—s *may have rest, I go E.A.* 319
Faith, gallants, board with saints, and bed with s. *E.J.S.* 24
Whether the Charmer s. it, or saint it *M.E.* ii. 15

Sins.
Of ORDER, s. against th' Eternal Cause *E.M.* i. 130
Some rising Genius s. up to my Song *E.S.* ii. 9
She s. with Poets thro' pure love of Wit *M.E.* ii. 76
Who s. with whom ; who got his pension rug *S.* viii. 134

Sip.
And s., with Nymphs, their elemental Tea *R.L.* i. 62
Here bees from blossoms s. the rosy dew *Su.* 69

Sipp'd.
How here he s., how there he plunder'd snug *D.* i. 129
Some, as she s., the fuming liquor fann'd *R.L.* iii. 114

Sips.
And modest as the maid that s. alone *D.* iii. 144
Ridotta s. and dances, till she see *S.* i. 47

Sir.
But Horace, S., was delicate, was nice *E.S.* i. 11
Dear S., forgive the Prejudice of Youth *E.S.* i. 63
'Tis all a Libel—Paxton (S.) will say *E.S.* ii. 1
How, S.? not damn the Sharper, but the Dice *E.S.* ii. 13
A Dean, S.? no ; his Fortune is not made *E.S.* ii. 34
But, S., I beg you (for the Love of Vice !) *E.S.* ii. 42
If merely to come in, S., they go out *E.S.* ii. 124
Hold, S.! for God's sake where's th' Affront to you *E.S.* ii. 157
Pray take them, S.,—Enough's a Feast *I.H.* i. 25
No, S., you'll leave them to the Hogs *I.H.* i. 48
Lean as you came, S., you must go (*rep.*) *I.H.* i. 58
Faith, S., you know as much as I *I.H.* ii. 116
If—where I'm going, I could serve you, S. *M.E.* i. 255
" Your money, S. ; " " My money, S., what all ? " (*rep.*) *M.E.* i. 258
S., Spain has sent a thousand jars of oil *M.E.* iii. 56
Has she no faults then (Envy says) S. *Mi.* viii. 9
Informs you, S., 'twas when he knew no better *P.S.* 52
And shame the fools—Your Int'rest, S., with Lintot *P.S.* 62
Not, S., if you revise it, and retouch *P.S.* 64
S., let me see you and your works no more *P.S.* 68
Such Ovid's nose, and " S.! you have an Eye." *P.S.* 118
Then, learned S.! (to cut the matter short) *S.* i. 91
I cannot like, dread S., your Royal Cave *S.* iii. 114
Your People, S., are partial in the rest *S.* v. 32
Yet, S., reflect the mischief is not great *S.* v. 189
Think of those Authors, S., who would rely *S.* v. 350
Yet think, great S., (so many Virtues shown) *S.* v. 376
Bows and begins—" This Lad, S., is from Blois *S.* vi. 4
S. he's your slave, for twenty pounds a year *S.* vi. 8
But, S., to you, with what would I not part *S.* vi. 15
At ten for certain, S., in Bloomsb'ry square *S.* vi. 95
There's a Rehearsal, S., exact at one *S.* vi. 97
"'Twas, " S., your law"—and " S., your eloquence." *S.* vi. 133
Yes, S., how small soever be my heap *S.* vi. 284
I wish you joy, S., of a Tyrant gone *S.* vi. 305
" But the best *words* ! " " O, S., the *Dictionary*." *S.* viii. 69
But, S., of writers ? " " Swift, for closer style *S.* viii. 72
Obliging S., for Courts you sure were made *S.* viii. 80
Ah gentle S.! you Courtiers so cajole us *S.* viii. 90
Lord, S., a mere Mechanic ! strangely low *S.* viii. 108
Oh ! S., politely so ! nay, let me die *S.* viii. 112
Not, S., my only, I have better still *S.* viii. 114
The Captain's honest, S—s, *and that's enough S.* viii. 262
S. Balaam *now, he lives like other folks M.E.* iii. 357
Behold S. B., now a man of spirit *M.E.* iii. 375
The Court forsake him, and S. B. hangs *M.E.* iii. 398
And sad S. B. curses God and dies *M.E.* iii. 402
Mark how they grace Lord Umbra or S. Billy *E.M.* iv. 278
Horace would say, S. B. serv'd the Crown *E.S.* i. 13
A mournful glance S. *Fopling* upwards cast *R.L.* v. 63
And " Sweet S. F.! you have so much wit ! " *S.* viii. 233

SIRE—SKULKING.

E'er since *S. F.'s* Periwig was Praise *D.* i. 167
Sore sighs *S. Gilbert*, starting at the bray *D.* ii. 251
The grave *S. G.* holds it for a rule *M.E.* iii. 101
I think *S. Godfrey* should decide the suit *S.* vi. 24
S. Job sail'd forth, the ev'ning bright and still *S.* iii. 138
As well his Grace reply'd, "Like you, *S. John M.E.* iii. 317
Astride his cheese, *S. Morgan* we might meet *M.E.* iii. 61
She said ; then raging to *S. Plume* repairs *R.L.* iv. 121
S. P. of amber snuff-box justly vain *R.L.* i. 123
When bold *S. P.* had drawn Clarissa down *R.L.* v. 67
Go see *S. Robert*—See *S. Robert*!—hum *E.S.* i. 27
But let me add, *S. R.'s* mighty dull *E.S.* ii. 153
Such as *S. R.* would approve—Indeed *S.* i. 153
What, like *S. Richard*, rumbling, rough, and fierce *S.* i. 23
What brought *S. Visto's* ill-got wealth to waste *M.E.* iv. 15
The first lampoon *S. Will* or Bubo makes *P.S.* 280

Sire.
Gross as her *s.*, and as her mother grave *D.* i. 14
Each *s.* imprest, and glaring in his son *D.* i. 100
Not wrap up Oranges, to pelt your *s.*, *D.* L 236
And high-born Howard, more majestic *s. D.* i. 297
But soon the cloud return'd—and thus the *S. D.* iii. 227
The *S.* saw, one by one, his virtues wake *D.* iv. 285
Rous'd at his name, up rose the bousy *S. D.* iv. 493
S., Ancestors, Himself—One casts his eyes *D.* iv. 519
The *S.* is made a Peer, the Son a Fool *D.* iv. 548
The same which in a *S.* the Sons obey'd *E.M.* ii. 213
Then, looking up from *s.* to *s.*, explor'd *E.M.* iii. 225
Convey'd unbroken faith from *s.* to son *E.M.* iii. 228
Why, full of days and honour, lives the *S. E.M.* iv. 106
Shall finish what his short-liv'd *S.* begun *M.* 64
Behold a rev'rend *s.*, whom want of grace *M.E.* i. 232
Flam'd forth this rival to its *S.*, the Suo *M.E.* iii. 12
Whether his hoary *s.* he spies *O.* iii. 29
The mothers nurse it, and the *s*—*s defend E.M.* iii. 126
Why should not We be wiser than our *s. S.* v. 44
And to debase the Sons, exalts the *S. S.* v. 134
Sons, *S.*, and Grandsires, all will wear the bays *S.* v. 171

Sirius.
The sultry *S.* burns the thirsty plains *Su.* 21

Sister.
His *s.* sends, her vot'ress, from above *D.* ii. 216
Had not her *S.* Satire held her head *D.* iv. 42
The tender *s.*, daughter, friend, and wife *E.* iii 52
Ah let thy handmaid, *s.*, daughter, move *E.A.* 153
Come, *s.*, come I (it said, or seem'd to say) (rep.) *E.A.* 309
So from a *s.* sinner you shall hear *E.J.S.* 9
Who starves a *S.*, or forswears a Debt *E.S.* i. 112
Who starv'd a *S.*, who forswore a Debt *E.S.* ii. 20
S. Spirit, come away *O.* v. 8
She, who can love a *S.'s* charms, or hear *M.E.* ii. 259
While all your smutty *s*—*s walk the streets D.* i. 230
Others the Syren *S.* warble round *D.* iv. 541
How wilt thou now the fatal *s.* move *O.* i. 95
Oh heav'n-born *s.!* source of art *O.* ii. 9
Smit with the love of *S.*-Arts we came *E.* iii. 13
Then Sculpture and her *s.* revive *E.C.* 701
The *s.-lock* now sits uncouth, alone *R.L.* iv. 171

Sistrum.
Rattling an ancient *S.* at his head *D.* iv. 374

Sisyphus.
Thy stone, O *S.*, stands still *O.* i. 66

Sit.
Or chair'd at White's amidst the Doctors *s. D.* i. 203
Rome in her Capitol saw Querno *s. D.* ii. 15
To him we grant our amplest pow'rs to *s. D.* ii. 375
The heroes *s.*, the vulgar form a ring *D.* ii. 384
So by each Bard an Alderman shall *s. D.* iv. 131
I *s.* and dream I see my CRAGGS anew *E.S.* ii. 69
Where Age and Want *s.* smiling at the gate *M.E.* iii. 266
I *s.* with sad civility, I read *P.S.* 37
And *s.* attentive to his own applause *P.S.* 210
Descend, and *s.* on each important card *R.L.* iii. 32
Why *s.* we mute when early linnets sing *Sp.* 25
Why *s.* we sad when Phosphor shines so clear *Sp.* 27
Trees, where you *s.*, shall crowd into a shade *Su.* 74

Sits.
On this he *s.*, to that he leans his ear *D.* ii. 86
S. Mother Osborne, stupefy'd to stone *D.* ii. 312
Old Bavius *s.* to dip poetic souls *D.* iii. 24
Immortal Rich ! how calm he *s.* at ease *D.* iii. 261
Our Midas *s.* Lord Chancellor of Plays *D.* iii. 3/4
Black Melancholy *s.*, and round her throws *E.A.* 165
Tho' daring Milton *s.* sublime *I.H.* iv. 5
Still *s.* at squat, and peeps not from its hole *M.E.* i. 56
The sister-lock now *s.* uncouth, alone *R.L.* iv. 171
Rich Industry *s.* smiling on the plains *W.F.* 41

Six.
S. huntsmen with a shout precede his chair *D.* ii. 193
Then give Humility a coach and *s. E.M.* iv. 170
To spend *s.* months with Statesmen here *I.H.* ii. 32
Bear home *s.* Whores, and make his Lady weep *M.E.* iii. 72
Or in a coach and *s.* the British Fair *R.L.* iii. 164
For life, *s.*-hundred *pounds a year I.H.* ii. 2*s*

Sixpence.
I'll now give *s.* where I gave a groat *M.E.* iii. 366
If D * * * lov'd *s.* more than he *S.* vi. 229

Sixty.
How oft by these at *s.* are undone *E.M.* iv. 183
Full *s.* years the World has been her Trade *M.E.* ii. 123

Size.
Of these twelve volumes, twelve of amplest *s. D.*, 155
His be yon Juno of majestic *s. D.* ii. 163
One on his vigour and superior *s. D.* ii. 170

Skelton.
And beastly *S.* Heads of Houses quote *S.* v. 38

Sketch.
But as the slightest *s.* if justly trac'd *E.C.* 23
Strike in the *s.*, or in the picture glow *E.* iii. 44

Skew'r.
Or whiten'd wall provoke the *s.* to write *S.* i. 98

Skilful.
Or whirligigs turn'd round by *s.* swain *D.* iii. 57
The *s.* Nymph reviews her force with care *R.L.* iii. 45

Skill.
Such *s.* in passing all, and touching none *D.* iv. 258
So just thy *s.*, so regular my rage *E.* iii. 12 *s*
'Tis hard to say, if greater want of *s. E.C.* 1
Shall Ward draw Contracts with a Statesman's *s. E.S.* i. 119
And show their zeal, and hide their want of *s. M.E.* ii. 386
Oh filthy check on all industrious *s. M.E.* iii. 75
Where half the *s.* is decently to hide *M.E.* iv. 54
I curse such lavish cost, and little *s. M.E.* iv. 167
Ah *Moore* / thy *S.* were well employ'd *Mi.* iv. 29
Who scorn a Lad should teach his father *s. S.* v. 129

Skill'd.
Oh, *s.* in Nature ! see the hearts of Swains *A.* 11
Once I was *s.* in ev'ry herb that grew *Su.* 31

Skim.
Oft, as in airy rings they *s.* the heath *W.F.* 131

Skims.
Flies o'er th' unbending corn, and *s.* along the main *E.C.* 373

Skin.
In a dun night-gown of his own loose *s. D.* ii. 38
But having amply stuff'd his *s. I.H.* i. 53

Skip.
And quick sensations *s.* from vein to vein *D.* ii. 212
Had be thy Reason, would he *s.* and play *E.M.* i. 82

Skirts.
Whose sars'net *s.* are edg'd with flamy gold *D.* iii. 54

Skulk.
Gaming and Grub-street *s.* behind the King *D.* i. 310

Skulking.
See *s. Truth* to her old cavern fled *D.* iv. 641

Skull.

Not so bold Arnall; with a weight of *s. D.* ii. 315
And blunt the sense, and fit it for a *s. D.* iii. 25
Just as a blockhead rubs his thoughtless *s. E.J.S.* 7

Sky.

And pond'rous slugs cut swiftly thro' the *s. D.* i. 182
Go, purify'd by flames, ascend the *s. D.* i. 227
All vain petitions mounting to the *s. D.* ii. 89
The salient spout far-streaming to the *s. D.* ii. 162
In homage to the mother of the *s. D.* ii. 13a
Receiv'd the weapons of the *s. E.* vi. 10
Fresh blooming Hope, gay daughter of the *s. E.A.* 299
Mount o'er the vales, and seem to tread the *s. E.C.* 226
But thinks, admitted to that equal *s. E.M.* i. 111
Planets and Suns run lawless thro' the *s. E.M.* i. 252
Or wing the *s.*, or roll along the flood *E.M.* iii. 120
To what new clime, what distant *s. O.* ii. 13
And keep awhile one parent from the *s. P.S.* 413
The light Militia of the lower *s. R.L.* i. 42
While melting music steals upon the *s. R.L.* ii. 49
Or roll the planets thro' the boundless *s. R.L.* ii. 80
The nymph exulting fills with shouts the *s. R.L.* iii. 99
And what is that, which binds the radiant *s. Sp.* 39
Is there no bright reversion in the *s. U.L.* 9
Fate snatch'd her early to the pitying *s. U.L.* 24
The moon, serene in glory, mounts the *s. W.* 6
Above the clouds, above the starry *s. W.* 70
Nor yet, when moist Arcturus clouds the *s. W.F.* 129
Straight a short thunder breaks the frozen *s. W.F.* 130
When the fierce eagle cleaves the liquid *s. W.F.* 186
Lose the low vales, and steal into the skies *A.* 60
The *s.* yet blushing with departing light *A.* 98
When the last blaze sent Ilion to the *s. D.* i. 256
Walls, steeples, *s.*, bray back to him again *D.* ii. 260
Soon as they dawn, from Hyperborean *s. D.* iii. 85
Whales sport in woods, and dolphins in the *s. D.* iii. 246
It came from Bertrand's, not the *s. E.* vi. 15
Sudden you mount, you beckon from the *s. E.A.* 245
Blot out each bright Idea of the *s. E.A.* 284
From op'ning *s.* may streaming glories shine *E.A.* 341
Encourag'd thus, Wit's Titans brav'd the *s. E.C.* 552
All quit their sphere, and rush into the *s. E.M.* i. 124
My foot-stool earth, my canopy the *s. E.M.* i. 140
As much eternal springs, and cloudless *s. E.M.* i. 153
She from the rending earth, and bursting *s. E.M.* iii. 253
By mountains pil'd on mountains to the *s. H.* iv. 74
Sweet to the World, and grateful to the *S. E.S.* ii. 245
Whose sacred flow'r with fragrance fills the *s. M.* 10
And Carmel's flow'ry top perfumes the *s. M.* 28
Lo, earth receives him from the bending *s. M.* 33
Demanding life, impatient for the *s. M.* 90
The seas shall waste, the *s.* in smoke decay *M.* 105
But well-dispers'd, is Incense to the *S. M.E.* iii. 236
Not to the *s.* in useless columns tost *M.E.* iii. 255
Where London's column pointing at the *s. M.E.* iii. 339
And fill with spreading sounds the *s. O.* i. 15
And seas, and rocks, and *s.* rebound *O.* i. 47
Dipt in the richest tincture of the *s. R.L.* ii. 65
And screams of horror rend th' affrighted *s. R.L.* iii. 156
And bass, and treble voices strike the *s. R.L.* v. 42
And pleas'd pursue its progress thro' the *s. R.L.* v. 132
This Partridge soon shall view in cloudless *s. R.L.* v. 137
Look thro', and trust the Ruler with his *s. S.* iv. 8
Advance thy golden Mountain to the *s. S.* iv. 73
All nature mourns, the *S.* relent in show'rs *O.* iv. 13
The *s.* to brighten, and the birds to sing *Sp.* 72
Whose Altar, Earth, Seas, *S. U.P.* 50
No grateful dews descend from ev'ning *s. W.* 45
Who claim'd the *s.*, dispeopled air and floods *W.F.* 47
The headlong mountains and the downward *s. W.F.* 212
While led along the *s.* his current strays *W.F.* 228
Bids his free soul expatiate in the *s. W.F.* 254
And lift her turrets nearer to the *s. W.F.* 288
Or under southern *s.* exalt their sails *W.F.* 391

Slack.

Taught nor to *s.*, nor strain its tender strings *E.M.* iii. 290

Slain.

Than favour'd Man by touch ethereal *s. E.M.* iii. 68
Had brav'd the *Goth*, and many a *Vandal s. Mi.* ii. 2
She smil'd to see the doughty hero *s. R.L.* v. 69
When, after millions *s.*, yourself shall die *R.L.* v. 146
What wonder then, a beast or subject *s. W.F.* 57

Slander.

Who loves a Lie, lame *s.* helps about *P.S.* 289
S. or Poison dread from Delia's rage *S.* i. 81

Slander'd.

Of all her Dears she never *s.* one *M.E.* ii. 175
Full ten years *s.*, did he once reply *P.S.* 374

Slashing.

From *s. Bentley* down to pidling *Tibalds P.S.* 164
Like *s. Bentley* with his desp'rate hook *S.* v. 104

Slaughter'd.

What *s.* hecatombs, what floods of wine *M.E.* iii. 203

Slaught'ring.

With *s.* guns th' unweary'd fowler roves *W.F.* 125

Slave.

Some *S.* of mine be pinion'd to their side *D.* iv. 134
First *s.* to Words, then vassal to a Name *D.* iv. 501
A Monarch's half, and half a Harlot's *s. D.* iv. 512
So when your *S.*, at some dear idle time *E.* v. 41
Confess'd within the *s.* of love and man *E.A.* 178
This hour a *s.*, the next a deity *E.M.* i. 68
Envy, to which th' ignoble mind's a *s. E.M.* ii. 191
S. to no sect, who takes no private road *E.M.* iv. 331
COBHAM's a Coward, POLWARTH is a *S. E.S.* ii. 130
You're strangely proud. So proud I am no *S. E.S.* ii. 205
He dreads a death-bed like the meanest *s. M.E.* i. 116
A fool to Pleasure, yet a *s.* to Fame *M.E.* ii. 62
The *S.* that digs it, and the *S.* that hides *M.E.* iii. 110
I a *S.* in thy Dominions *Mi.* vii. 3
Unplac'd, unpension'd, no man's heir or *s. S.* i. 116
S. to a Wife, or Vassal to a Punk *S.* iii. 62
A Pension, or such Harness for a *s. S.* iii. 87
Adieu to Virtue, if you're once a *S. S.* iii. 112
Then hire a *S.*, or (if you will) a Lord *S.* iv. 99
Sir, he's your *s.* for twenty pounds a year *S.* vi. 8
To lands of singing, or of dancing *s—s D.* iv. 305
Born for First Ministers, as *S.* for Kings *D.* iv. 602
Made *S.* by honour, and made Fools by shame *E.* iv. 36
Where *s.* once more their native land behold *E.M.* i. 107
And Gods of Conqu'rors, *S.* of Subjects made *E.M.* iv. 248
What can ennoble sots, or *s.*, or cowards *E.M.* iv. 215
As Pride in *S.*, and Avarice in Kings *E.S.* i. 110
See, all our Nobles begging to be *S. E.S.* i. 163
Where mix'd with *S.* the groaning Martyr toil'd *M.E.* v. 6
And men, once ignorant, are *s. O.* ii. 28
Love in these labyrinths his *s.* detains *R.L.* ii. 3
All the mad trade of Fools and *S.* for Gold *S.* iv. 13
For wiser brutes were backward to be *s. W.F.* 50
And makes his trembling *s.* the royal game *W.F.* 64

Slaver.

It is the *s.* kills, and not the bite *P.S.* 106

Slav'ry.

Till Conquest cease, and *S.* be no more *W.F.* 408

Sleep.

Not balmy *s.* to lab'rers faint with pain *A.* 44
Sleepless themselves, to give their readers *s. D.* i. 94
And all be *s.*, as at an ode of thine *D.* i. 318
Thus the soft gifts of *S.* conclude the day *D.* ii. 419
But all is calm in this eternal *s. E.A.* 313
When Sense subsides, and Fancy sports in *s. M.E.* i. 46
Sound *s.* by night; study and ease *O.* iv. 13
The reader's threaten'd (not in vain) with "*s.*" *E.C.* 353
Rolls o'er my Grotto, and but soothes my *s. S.* i. 124
Peace stole her wing, and wrapp'd the world in *s. S.* v. 401
S.'s all-subduing charms who dares defy *D.* ii. 373
The temp'rate *s—s*, and spirits light as air *S.* ii. 74
Say, how the Goddess bade Britannia *s. D.* i. 7
Where nameless Somethings in their causes *s. D.* i. 56
There, all from Paul's to Aldgate drink and *s. D.* ii. 346
And all the western world believe and *s. D.* iii. 100
Arrest him, Empress, or you *s.* no more *D.* iv. 69
We cannot blame indeed—but we may *s. E.C.* 242
In peace let one poor Poet *s. Ep.* xv. 2
S., or peruse some ancient Book *I.H.* ii. 130
Peaceful *s.* out the Sabbath of the Tomb *Mi.* v. 19
Can *s.* without a Poem in my head *P.S.* 269
And for my soul I cannot *s.* a wink *S.* i. 15
And close confin'd to their own palace, *s. U.L.* 22
The trumpet *s.*, while cheerful horns are blown *W.F.* 373

Sleeping.
To your fraternal care our *s.* friends *D.* iv. 440
How shall he keep, what, *s.* or awake *E.M.* iii. 275
Now *s.* flocks on their soft fleeces lie *W.* 5

Sleepless.
S. themselves, to give their readers sleep *D.* i. 94
And *s.* lovers, just at twelve, awake *R.L.* i. 16

Sleeps.
He *s.* among the dull of ancient days *D.* i. 294
Th' unconscious stream *s.* o'er thee like a lake *D.* ii. 304
Lo! where Mæotis *s.*, and hardly flows *D.* iii. 87
In troubled waters, but now *s.* in Port *D.* iv. 202
Then conscience *s.*, and leaving nature free *E.A.* 227
Till tir'd he *s.*, and Life's poor play is o'er *E.M.* ii. 282
And, fast beside him, once-fear'd Edward *s. W.F.* 314

Sleepy.
The *s.* Eye, that spoke the melting soul *S.* v. 150

Sleeve.
Some fold the *s.*, while others plait the gown *R.L.* i. 147

Sleeveless.
Grave Mummers! *s.* some, and shirtless others *D.* iii. 116

Slender.
So spins the silk-worm small its *s.* store *D.* iv. 253
Our hearts may bear its *s.* chain a day *E.* iv. 64
And mighty hearts are held in *s.* chains *R.L.* ii. 24
O let my Muse her *s.* reed inspire *Sp.* 11

Slept.
There Caxton *s.*, with Wynkyn at his side *D.* i. 149
S. first; the distant nodded to the hum *D.* ii. 402
Unfinish'd Treaties in each Office *s. D.* iv. 616
The Queen of Midas *s.*, and so may I *P.S.* 82
He said; when Sbock, who thought she *s.* too long *R.L.* i. 115
He *s.*, poor dog! and lost it to a dolt *S.* vi. 36
Command old words that long have *s.*, to wake *S.* vi. 167

Slices.
Then clap four *s.* of Plaister on't *M.E.* iv. 33

Slide.
Here fortun'd Curl to *s.*; loud shout the band *D.* ii. 73
Parts answ'ring parts shall *s.* into a whole *M.E.* iv. 66
Hours, days, and years *s.* soft away *O.* iv. 10
Back to my native Moderation *s. S.* iii. 33
I felt th' infection *s.* from him to me *S.* viii. 170

Slides.
S. into verse, and hitches in a rhyme *S.* i. 78
S. to a Scriv'ner or a city Knight *S.* ii. 178

Sliding.
When lo! a Harlot form, soft *s.* by *D.* iv. 45

Slight.
Some dire disaster, or by force, or *s. R.L.* ii. 103
Survey the WHOLE, nor seek s. faults to find E.C. 235
He spins the *s.*, self-pleasing thread anew *P.S.* 90
S. is the subject, but not so the praise *R.L.* i. 5
S. lines of hair surprise the finny prey *R.L.* ii. 26

Slighted.
See the poor remnants of these *s.* hairs *R.L.* iv. 167

Slightest.
But as the *s.* sketch, if justly trac'd *E.C.* 23

Slights.
The other *s.* for women, sports, and wines *S.* vi. 272

Slily.
No Commentator can more *s.* pass *S.* vii. 101

Slimy.
The sun e'er got, or *s.* Nilus hore *S.* viii. 29

Slink.
A Weasel once made shift to *s. I.H.* i. 51

Slipp'd.
That *s.* thro' cracks and zig-zags of the Head *D.* i. 124

Slipper.
Thrice rung the bell, the *s.* knock'd the ground *R.L.* i. 17

Slip-slop.
A *s.* Sibyl led his steps along *D.* iii. 15

Sloane.
And Books for Mead, and Butterflies for *S. M.E.* iv. 10
Or *S.* or Woodward's wondrous shelves contain *S.* viii. 30

Slope.
Embrown the *S.*, and nod on the Parterre *M.E.* iv. 174
And when up ten steep s—s you've dragg'd your thighs M.E. iv. 131

Slopes.
S. at its foot, the woods its sides embrace *S.* iii. 141

Sloth.
Ev'n av'rice, prudence; *s.*, philosophy *E.M.* ii 188
Not sunk by *s.*, nor rais'd by servitude *M R.* vi. 222
S. unfolds her arms and wakes *O.* i. 32

Slothful.
Be furious, envious, *s.*, mad, or drunk *S.* iii. 61

Sloven.
You laugh, half Beau, half *S.* if I stand *S.* iii. 161

Slow.
She saw *s.* Philips creep like Tate's poor page *D.* i. 105
Next Smedley div'd; *s.* circles dimpled o'er *D.* ii. 291
S. rose a form, in majesty of Mud *D.* ii. 326
Let others creep by timid steps, and *s. D.* iv. 465
Count the *s.* clock, and dine exact at noon *E.* v. 18
That, like a wounded snake, drags its *s.* length along *E.C.* 357
What's roundly smooth or languishingly *s. E.C.* 359
The line too labours, and the words move *s. E.C.* 371
See him from Nature rising *s.* to Art *E.M.* iii. 169
All sly *s.* things, with circumspective eyes *E.M.* iv. 226
While in more lengthen'd notes and *s. O.* i. 10
So *s.* th' unprofitable moments roll *S.* iii. 39
How Shadwell hasty, Wycherley was *s. S.* v. 85
While yon *s.* oxen turn the furrow'd Plain *Sp.* 30
Thro' the fair scene roll *s.* the ling'ring streams *W.F.* 217
The Loddon *s.*, with verdant alders crown'd *W.F.* 342
The Blockhead is a S.-worm Mi. iv. 14

Slowly.
Spreads his black wings, and *s.* mounts to day *R.L.* iv. 88
How oft our s.-growing works impart E. iii. 19

Slugs.
And pond'rous *s.* cut swiftly thro' the sky *D.* i. 182

Sluice.
The king of dykes! than whom no *s.* of mud *D.* ii. 273
As under seas Alpheus' secret *s. D.* ii. 341

Slumber.
That ev'n in *s.* caus'd her cheek to glow *R.L.* i. 24
Which most conduce to soothe the soul in —*s D.* ii. 369
Obedient *s.* that can wake and weep *E.A.* 212
Soft as the *s.* of a saint forgiv'n *E.A.* 255
And haunt their *s.* in the pompous shade *E.M.* iv. 304
A Statesman's *s.* how this speech would spoil *M.E.*iii. 55
Soothe my ever-waking *S. Mi.* viii. 15
Where *s. Abbots, purple as their wines D.* iv. 302

Slumb'ring.
Did *s.* visit, and convey to stews *D.* ii. 422
And goad the Prelate *s.* in his Stall *E.S.* ii. 219

Sly.
All *s.* slow things, with circumspective eyes *E.M.*iv. 226
His *s.*, polite, insinuating style *E.S.* i. 19
A Quaker? *s.*: A Presbyterian? sour *M.E.* i. 156
Nor *s.* informer watch these words to draw *S.* vii. 127

Smacking.
Then gives a *s.* buss, and cries, "No words!" *E.* v. 26

Small.
S. thanks to France, and none to Rome or Greece *D.* i. 283
Thus the *s.* jet, which hasty hands unlock *D.* ii. 177
With mincing step, *s.* voice, and languid eye *D.* iv. 46
So spins the silk-worm *s.* its slender store *D.* iv. 253
This *s.*, well-polish'd Gem, the work of years *E.* iii. 40
To one *s.* sect, and all are damn'd beside *E.C.* 397
To him no high, no low, no great, no *s. E.M.* i. 279

u

SMART—SMUT.

So when *s.* humours gather to a gout *E.M.* ii. 159
Learn each *s.* People's genius, policies *E.M.* iii. 183
Where *s.* and great, where weak and mighty, made *E.M.* iii. 297
Fortune in Men has some *s.* diff'rence made *E.M.* iv. 195
In the *s.* circle of our foes or friends *E.M.* iv. 242
As the *s.* pebble stirs the peaceful lake *E.M.* iv. 364
In rev'rend Bishops note some *s. Neglects E.S.* i. 16
Alas! the *s.* Discredit of a Bribe *E.S.* ii. 46
Both *s.* and great, both you and I *I.H.* ii. 178
A *s.* Euphrates thro' the piece is roll'd *M.E.* v. 29
Till, by degrees, remote and *s. O.* i. 18
Ev'n such *s.* Critics some regard may claim *P.S.* 167
Or the *s.* pillow grace a Lady's bed *R.L.* iii. 166
Yet for *s.* Turbots such esteem profess *S.* ii. 23
As want of figure, and a *s.* Estate *S.* iii. 68
'Tis to *s.* purpose that you hold your tongue *S.* vi. 155
A worthy member, no *s.* fool, a Lord *S.* vi. 185
Yes, Sir, how *s.* soever be my heap *S.* vi. 384
Thus (if *s.* things we may with great compare) *W.F.* 105
Spleen, Vapours, or S.-pox, *above them all M.E.* ii. 267
Charm'd the *s.,* or chas'd old-age away *R.L.* v. 20

Smart.

Pan came, and ask'd, what magic caus'd my *s. A.* 81
But ah! what aggravates the killing *s. Mi.* ix. 53
Men only feel the S., but not the Vice *S.* vi. 217
And *Snip-snap short, and Interruption* s. *D.* ii. 240
A *s.* Free-thinker? all things in an hour *M.E.* i. 157
To *s.* and agonize at ev'ry pore *E.M.* i. 198
A hundred *s.* in Timon and in Balaam *S.* i. 42

Smarts.

No creature *s.* so little as a fool *P.S.* 84

Smear'd.

Next his grim idol *s.* with human blood *E.M.* iii. 266

Smedley.

Next S. div'd; slow circles dimpled o'er *D.* ii. 291
All look, all sigh, all call on S. lost (*rep.*) *D.* ii. 293

Smell.

Of *s.,* the headlong lioness between *E.M.* i. 213
Painted for sight, and essenc'd for the *s. S.* viii. 226

Smile.

Th' engaging S., the Gaiety *I.H.* i. 46
But at her *s.,* the Beau reviv'd again *R.L.* v. 70
He past it o'er; affects an easy *s. S.* viii. 122
Each pleasing Blount shall endless s—*s bestow E.* iii. 61
The S. and Loves had died in Voiture's death *E.* iv. 19
Pleas'd while with *s.* his happy lines you view *E.* iv. 75
Or drest in *s.* of sweet Cecilia shine *M.E.* ii. 13
With ease the *s.* of Fortune I resign *Mi.* ix. 14
Eternal *s.* his emptiness betray *P.S.* 315
Repairs her *s.,* awakens ev'ry grace *R.L.* i. 147
Favours to none, to all she *s.* extends *R.L.* ii. 11
The *s.* of harlots, and the tears of heirs *R.L.* v. 120
Amaze th' unlearn'd, and make the learned *s. E.C.* 327
Could please at Court, and make AUGUSTUS *s. E.S.* i. 20
S. without Art, and win without a Bribe *E.S.* i. 32
Glow in the heart, and *s.* upon the face *Mi.* v. 14
Poor guiltless I! and can I choose but *s. P.S.* 281
Make Languor *s.,* and sooth the bed of Death *P.S.* 411
Should Ripley venture, all the world would *s. S.* v. 186
The King would *s.* on you—at least the Queen *S.* viii. 89
Care, if a livery'd Lord or *s.* or frown *S.* viii. 197
Let but the Ladies *s.,* and they are blest *S.* viii. 254
If Delia *s.,* the flow'rs begin to spring *Sp.* 71

Smil'd.

Smiling on all, and *s.* on by a Queen *D.* iv. 506
"And take" (she said, and *s.* serene) *E.* vi. 3
You rais'd these hallow'd walls; the desert *s. E.A.* 133
And Virgins *s,* at what they blush'd before *E.C.* 543
Who rais'd my Modesty, and *s. I.H.* i. 68
If wrong, I *s.;* if right, I kiss'd the rod *P.S.* 158
Belinda *s.,* and all the world was gay *R.L.* ii. 52
She *s.* to see the doughty hero slain *R.L.* v. 69
When the *Queen* frown'd, or *s.,* he knows; and what S. viii. 132

Smiles.

Or falling, *s.* in exile or in chains *E.M.* iv. 234
Earth *s.* around, with boundless bounty blest *E.M.* iv. 371
As who knows Sappho, *s.* at other whores *S.* vii. 6
If Sylvia *s.,* new glories gild the shore *Sp.* 75

Smilinda.

Why stays S. in the Dressing-Room *Mi.* ix. 2
The Equipage shall grace S.'s *side Mi.* ix. 110

Smiling.

Yet *s.* at his rueful length of face *D.* ii. 142
And the pleas'd Dame, soft *s.,* lead'st away *D.* ii. 188
When Dulness, *s.*—" Thus revive the Wits *D.* iv. 119
The Goddess *s.* seem'd to give consent *D.* iv. 395
S. on all, and smil'd on by a Queen *D.* iv. 506
As *s.* Infants sport themselves to rest *E.* iv. 14
Those *s.* eyes, attemp'ring ev'ry ray *E.A.* 63
Love, Hope, and Joy, fair Pleasure's *s.* train *E.M.* ii. 117
And, *s.,* whispers to the next *I.H.* ii. 52?
Shall call the *s.* Loves, and young Desires *I.H.* iii. 26
The *s.* infant in his hand shall take *M.E.* i. 32
Where Age and Want sit *s.* at the gate *M.E.* iii. 266
Or views his *s.* progeny *O.* iii. 32
Rich Industry sits *s.* on the plains *W.F.* 41

Smit.

S. with his mien the Mud-nymphs suck'd him in *D.* ii. 332
And *s.* with love of Poesy and Prate *D.* ii. 382
S. with the love of Sister-Arts we came *E.* iii. 13
S. with her varying plumage, spare the dove *E.M.* iii. 51
S. with the mighty pleasure, to be seen *M.E.* iv. 198

Smite.

See what the charms, that *s.* the simple heart *D.* iii. 229

Smithfield.

The S. Muses to the ear of Kings *D.* i. 2
Shouldst wag a serpent-tail in S. fair *D.* iii. 288

Smock.

As Sappho's di'monds with her dirty *s. M.E.* ii. 24

Smoke.

The rolling *s.* involves the sacrifice *D.* i. 248
The seas shall waste, the skies in *s.* decay *M.* 105
While curling s—*s from village-tops are seen A.* 63
And Metaphysic *s.* involve the Pole *D.* iv. 248
Where spices s. *beneath the burning Line D.* iii. 70

Smok'd.

And lo! two puddings *s.* upon the board *M.E.* i. 360

Smokeless.

Tenants with sighs the *s.* tow'rs survey *M.E.* iii. 191

Smoking.

The stream, and *s.* flourish'd o'er his head *D.* ii. 180
Or *s.* forth, a hundred hawkers' load *P.S.* 217
While China's earth receives the *s.* tide *R.L.* iii. 110

Smooth.

Wafts the *s.* Eunuch, and enamour'd swain *D.* iv. 310
You'd write an *s.* opium on glass *E.* vi. 21
And *s.* or rough, with them is right or wrong *E.C.* 338
What's roundly *s.* or languishingly slow *E.C.* 359
And the *s.* stream in smoother numbers flows *E.C.* 367
Be *s.,* ye rocks, ye rapid floods give way *M.* 36
The Courtier *s.,* who forty years had shin'd *M.E.* i. 252
Melancholy *s. Mæander Mi.* vii. 25
With shining ringlets the *s.* iv'ry neck *R.L.* ii. 22
S. flow the waves, the Zephyrs gently play *R.L.* ii. 51
Waller was *s.;* but Dryden taught to join *S.* v. 267
And s. *my passage to the realms of day E.A.* 322
Make Languor smile, and *s.* the bed of Death *P.S.* 411
Let CAROLINA *s.* the tuneful lay *S.* i. 30
I learn to *s.* and harmonize my Mind *S.* vi. 203

Smooth'd.

S. ev'ry brow, and open'd ev'ry soul *S.* v. 248

Smoother.

And the smooth stream in *s.* numbers flows *E.C.* 367

Smoothly.

So sweetly mawkish, and so *s.* dull *D.* iii. 171
So sweetly warble, or so *s.* flow *W.* 4

Smote.

S. ev'ry Brain, and wither'd ev'ry Bay *D.* iv. 10

Smut.

Or spite, or *s.,* or rhymes, or blasphemies *P.S.* 322

Smutty.
While all your *s.* sisters walk the streets *D.* i. 230

Snacks.
At last he whispers, "Do, and we go *s.*" *P.S.* 66

Snake.
That, like a wounded *s.*, drags its slow length along *E.C.* 357
The crested basilisk, and speckled *s. M.* 82
List'ning Envy drops her *s—s O.* i. 33
And *s.* uncurl'd hang list'ning round their heads *O.* i. 70
Now glaring fiends, and *s.* on rolling spires *R.L.* iv. 43
There hateful Envy her own *s.* shall feel *W.F.* 419

Snapt.
Then *s.* his box, and strok'd his belly down *D.* iv. 495

Snatch.
S. me, just mounting, from the blest abode *E.A.* 287
And *s.* a grace beyond the reach of art *E.C.* 153
S. from his hand the balance and the rod *E.M.* i. 121
When half our knowledge we must *s.*, not take *M.E.* i. 40
Th' unbalanc'd Mind, and *s.* the Man away *S.* iv. 25
Or *s.* me, o'er the earth, or thro' the air *S.* v. 346
What will it leave me, if it *s.* my rhyme *S.* vi. 77
Glad, like a Boy, to *s.* the first good day *S.* vi. 294

Snatch'd.
Then *s.* a sheet of Thule from her bed *D.* i. 258
That suit an unpaid tailor *s.* away *D.* ii. 118
Fancy restores what vengeance *s.* away *E.A.* 226
Now for two ages having *s.* from fate *Ep.* viii. 3
And now, on rolling waters *s.* away *I.H.* iii. 48
Sudden these honours shall be *s.* away *R.L.* iii. 103
Which *s.* my best, my fav'rite curl away *R.L.* iv. 148
Fate *s.* her early to the pitying sky *U.L.* 24

Sneak.
Patrons, who *s.* from living worth to dead *D.* iv. 95

Sneak'd.
So K* so B** *s.* into the grave *D.* iv. 511

Sneaking.
When Int'rest calls off all her *s.* train *E.* i. 31

Sneaks.
Will *s.* a Scriv'ner, an exceeding knave *M.E.* i. 154

Sneer.
Great Cibber sate: The proud Parnassian *s. D.* ii. 5
Did not the *S.* of more impartial men *E.S.* i. 59
Lost the arch'd eye-brow, the Parnassian *s. P.S.* 96
And without sneering, teach the rest to s. P.S. 202

Sneering.
To *s.* Goode, half malice and half whim *D.* iii. 153
And without *s.*, teach the rest to sneer *P.S.* 202

Sneers.
S. at another, in toupee or gown *D.* iv. 88

Snip-snap.
And *S.* short, and Interruption smart *D.* ii. 240

Snore.
To the same notes thy sons shall hum or *s. D.* iv. 59

Snores.
Where Tindal dictates, and Silenus *s. D.* iv. 492

Snow.
And heavy harvests nod beneath the *s. D.* i. 78
Mount in dark volumes, and descend in *s. D.* ii. 364
I melt down Ancients, like a heap of *s. S.* v. 65
The freezing Tanais thro' a waste of s—s D. iii. 83
Mid *s.* of paper, and fierce hail of pease *D.* iii. 262
Th' eternal *s.* appear already past *E.C.* 227
Amidst Rhodope's *s. O.* i. 109

Snowy.
Once gave new beauties to the *s.* neck *R.L.* iv. 170

Snuff.
S., or the fan, supply each pause of chat *R.L.* iii. 17
A charge of *S.* the wily virgin threw *R.L.* v. 82
My wig all powder, and all *s.* my hand *S.* iii. 162
This S-box,—once the pledge of SHARPER's *love Mi.* ix. 37

This *S.*,—on the Hinge see Brilliants shine (*rep.*) *Mi.* ix. 43
The *S.* to CARDELIA I decree *Mi.* ix. 111
Sir Plume of amber *s.* justly vain *R.L.* iv. 123
He first the *s.* open'd, then the case *R.L.* iv. 126
And beau's in s—es and tweezer-cases R.L. v. 116

Snug.
How here he sipp'd, how there he plunder'd *s. D.* i. 129
For "*S.'s* the word; my dear! we'll live in Town" *S.* iii. 147

So, Soever.—*Passim.*

Soar.
Perhaps more high some daring son may *s. D.* iv. 599
Of all who blindly creep, or sightless *s. E.M.* i. 12
Hope humbly then; with trembling pinions *s. E.M.* i. 91
What would this Man? Now upward will he *s. E.M.* i. 173
Go, *s.* with Plato to th' empyreal sphere *E.M.* ii. 23

Sober.
Of *s.* face, with learned dust besprent *D.* iii. 186
But *s.* History restrain'd her rage *D.* iv. 39
The decent Knight retir'd with *s.* rage *D.* iv. 113
He may indeed (if *s.* all this time) *D.* iv. 259
The *s.* follies of the wise and great *E.* i. 10
Descend in all her *s.* charms *E.* vi. 2
Athenian Queen! and *s.* charms *E.* vi. 25
Nor circle *s.* fifty with thy Charms *I.H.* iii. 6
Blest with plain Reason, and with *s.* Sense *Ep.* vi. 2
As *s.* Laneshb'row dancing in the gout *M.E.* i. 231
All mild ascends the Moon's more *s.* light *M.E.* ii. 254
"All this is madness," cries a *s.* sage *M.E.* iii. 151
There dwelt a Citizen, of *s.* fame *M.E.* iii. 341
Did some more *s.* Critic come abroad *P.S.* 157
Time was, a *s.* Eoglishman would knock *S.* v. 161
In all but this, a man of *s.* life *S.* vi. 188
I ask these *s.* questions of my heart *S.* vi. 211
Walk *s.* off; before a sprightlier age *S.* vi. 324
There *s.* thought pursu'd th' amusing theme *S.* viii. 188

Sobers.
And drinking largely *s.* us again *E.C.* 218

Sobs.
Sighs, *s.*, and passions, and the war of tongues *R.L.* iv. 84

Social.
Self-love and *S.* at her birth began *E.M.* iii. 149
Here too all forms of *s.* union find *E.M.* iii. 179
And bade Self-love and *S.* be the same *E.M.* iii. 318
Self-love thus push'd to *s.*, to divine *E.M.* iii. 353
That true SELF-LOVE and *S.* are the same *E.M.* iv. 396
Of *S.* Pleasure, ill-exchang'd for Pow'r *E.S.* i. 30
Thy Martial spirit, or thy *S.* love *Ep.* ix. 8
Sacred to *s.* life, and *s.* love *I.H.* iii. 22
Oh source of ev'ry *s.* tie *O.* iii. 25
Preserve him *s.*, cheerful, and serene *P.S.* 416

Society.
That Nature our *S.* adores *D.* iv. 491
Trade it may help, *S.* extend *M.E.* iii. 29
Cities were built, S—ies were made E.M. iii. 200

Socinus.
Did all the dregs of bold *S.* drain *E.C.* 545

Socrates.
Like *S.*, that Man is great indeed *E.M.* iv. 236

Soft.
And the pleas'd dame, *s.* smiling, lead'st away *D.* ii. 188
Strives to extract from his *s.*, giving palm *D.* ii. 208
They led him *s.*; each rev'rend Bard arose *D.* ii. 348
S. creeping, words on words, the sense compose *D.* ii. 389
As to *s.* gales top-heavy pines bow low *D.* ii. 391
Thus the *s.* gifts of Sleep conclude the day *D.* ii. 419
And *s.* besprinkles with Cimmerian dew *D.* iii. 4
S. on her lap her Laureate son reclines *D.* iv. 20
When lo! a Harlot form, *s.* sliding by *D.* iv. 45
S., as the wily Fox is seen to creep *D.* iv. 351
(Reply'd *s.* Annius) "this our paunch before *D.* iv. 388
And Douglas lend his *s.* obstetric hand *D.* iv. 394
S. on the paper ruff its leaves I spread *D.* iv. 407
And *s.* Belinda's blush for ever glow *E.* iii. 62
S. without weakness, without glaring gay *E.* iii. 66

SOFTEN—SOLID.

Or sees the blush of *s*. Parthenia rise *E.* v. 46
Speed the *s*. intercourse from soul to soul *E.A.* 57
Ye *s*. illusions, dear deceits, arise *E.A*? 240
S. as the slumbers of a saint forgiv'n *E.A.* 255
With ev'ry bead I drop too *s*. a tear *E.A.* 270
The memory's *s*. figures melt away *E.C.* 59
S. is the strain when Zephyr gently blows *E.C.* 366
Would you enjoy *s*. nights and solid dinners *E.J.S.* 23
Silent and *s*., as Saints remove to Heav'n *E.S.* i. 93
Yet *s*. his Nature, tho' severe his Lay *Ep*. i. 5
So firm, yet *s*.; so strong, yet so refin'd *Ep*. vi. 8
O *s*. Humanity, in Age belov'd *Ep*. ix. 4
Ah sound no more thy *s*. alarms *J.H.* iii. 5
And in *s*. silence shed the kindly show'r *M*. 14
Matter too *s*. a lasting mark to bear *M.E.* ii. 3
How *s*. is Silia | fearful to offend *M.E.* ii. 29
On the *s*. Passion, and the Taste refin'd *M.E.* ii. 84
Or *s*. Adonis, so perfum'd and fine *M.E.* iii. 73
S. and Agreeable come never there *M.E.* iv. 102
But *s*.,—by regular approach,—not yet *M.E.* iv. 129
To rest, the Cushion and *s*. Dean invite *M.E.* iv. 149
In some *s*. Dream or Extasy of Joy *Mi*. v. 18
Wat'ring *s*. Elysian Plains *Mi*. vii. 20
And sensible *s*. Melancholy *Mi*. viii. 8
And whisper with that *s*. deluding air *Mi*. ix. 7
S. SIMPLICETTA doats upon a Beau *Mi*. ix. 103
Hark I the numbers *s*. and clear *O*. i. 12
Music her *s*., assuasive voice applies *O*. i. 25
Love, *s*. intruder, enters here *O*. iii. 5
Hours, days, and years slide *s*. away *O*. iv. 10
Lull'd by *s*. Zephyrs thro' the broken pane *P.S.* 42
S. were my numbers; who could take offence *P.S.* 147
Fed with *s*. Dedication all day loug *P.S.* 233
Yet *s*. by nature, more a dupe than wit *P.S.* 368
And in *s*. bosoms dwells such mighty Rage *R.L.* i. 12
Thence, by a *s*. transition, we repair *R.L.* i. 49
S. yielding minds to Water glide away *R.L.* i. 61
And in *s*. sounds, your Grace salutes their ear *R.L.* i. 86
S. o'er the shrouds aërial whispers breathe *R.L.* ii. 57
S. sorrows, melting griefs, and flowing tears *R.L.* iv. 86
Forms the *s*. bosom with the gentlest art *S.* v. 219
Britain to *s*. refinements less a foe *S.* v. 265
Pierce the *s*. lab'rinth of a Lady's ear *S.* vii. 55
A *s*. retreat from sudden vernal show'rs *Sp*. 98
S. as he mourn'd, the streams forgot to flow *Su*. 5
Now sleeping flocks on their *s*. fleeces lie *W.* 5
S. show'rs distill'd, and suns grew warm in vain *W.F.* 54
In a *s*. silver stream dissolv'd away *W.F.* 204
I hear *s*. music die along the grove *W.F.* 268
'Tis yours, my Lord, to bless our *s*. retreats *W.F.* 283
To the same notes, of love, and *s*. desire *W.F.* 296
Or from the *s*.-eyed Virgin steal a tear *P.S.* 286

Soften.

When the ripe colours *s*. and unite *E.C.* 488
If white and black blend, *s*. and unite *E.M.* ii. 213
Music can *s*. pain to ease *O*. i. 120
And Arts but *s*. us to feel thy flame *O*. iii. 4

Soften'd.

Yet, mix'd and *s*., in his work unite *E.M.* ii. 112
And *s*. sounds along the waters die *R.L.* ii. 50
Then Marble, *s*. into life, grew warm *S.* v. 147

Softens.

Bid her be all that cheers or *s*. life *E.* iii. 51
When music *s*., and when dancing fires *R.L.* i. 76

Softer.

How young Lutetia, *s*. than the down *D.* ii. 333
Caracci's strength, Correggio's *s*. line *E.* iii. 37
How pleasing Atterbury's *s*. hour *E.S.* ii. 82
Yet *s*. Honours, and less noisy Fame *Ep*. xiv. 9
Its last best work, but forms a *s*. Man *M.E.* ii. 272
Th' expressive emblem of their *s*. pow'r *R.L.* iii. 40
Then all your Muse's *s*. art display *S.* L 29
Let *s*. strains ill-fated Henry mourn *W.F.* 311

Softest.

With *s*. manners, gentlest Arts adorn'd *E.* i. 4
Of *s*. manners, unaffected mind *Ep*. vii. 7

Softly.

Or *s*. glide by the Canal *J.H.* iii. 46
S. seeks her silent Mate *Mi*. vii. 30
And the hush'd waves glide *s*. to the shore *W.F.* 354

Softness.

Courage with *S*., Modesty with Pride *M.E.* ii. 278

Soho.

Befringe the rails of Bedlam and *S. S.* v. 419

Soil.

The *s*. that arts and infant letters bore *D.* iii. 96
Say, in what mortal *s*. thou deign'st to grow *E.M.* iv. 8
We ought to blame the culture, not the *s. E.M.* iv. 14
The knave deserves it, when he tills the *s. E.M.* iv. 152
Has what the frugal, dirty *s*. affords *E.S.* ii. 174
In life's low vale, the *s*. the Virtues like *M.E.* i. 143
Who then shall grace, or who improve the *S. M.E.* iv. 177
Yet to their Lord owe more than to the *s. M.F.* iv. 184
Say, Daphnis, say, in what glad *s*. appears *Sp*. 85

Sol.

For envy'd Wit, like *S*. eclips'd, makes known *E.C.* 468
S. thro' white curtains shot a tim'rous ray *R.L.* i. 13

Solace.

Health to the sick, and *s*. to the swain *M.E.* iii. 258
For matrimonial *s*. dies a martyr *S.* iii. 151

Solar.

Far as the *s*. walk, or milky way *E.M.* i. 102

Sold.

And keep his Lares, tho' his house be *s. D.* iv. 366
Esteem and Love were never to be *s. E.M.* iv. 188
To live on Ven'son when it *s*. so dear *M.E.* iii. 118
And therefore hopes this Nation may be *s. M.E.* iii. 124
'Twas very want that *s*. them for two pound *M.E.* iii. 328
Till Becca-ficos *s*. so dev'lish dear *S.* ii. 39
My lands are *s*., my father's house is gone *S.* ii. 155
Just half the land would buy, and half he *s. S.* iii. 125
All Worldly's hens, nay partridge, *s*. to town *S.* vi. 234
As the fair fields they *s*. to look so fine *S.* viii. 217

Soldier.

In *S*., Churchman, Patriot, Man in Pow'r *E.S.* i. 161
Tom struts a *S*., open, bold, and brave *M.E.* i. 153
A common *S*., but who clubb'd his Mite *Mi*. ii. 8
Have made a *S*. sigh, a Lover swear *Mi*. ix. 46
The *S*. breath'd the gallantries of France *S.* v. 145
And (tho' no *S*.) useful to the State *S.* v. 204
In ANNA's Wars, a *S*., poor and old *S.* vi. 33
Cronus were reserv'd to grace the s—s too E.C. 513
With mobs, and duns, and *s*. at the door *S.* vi. 124

Sole.

S. judge of Truth, in endless Error hurl'd *E.M.* ii. 17
See the *s*. bliss Heav'n could on all bestow *E.M.* iv. 327
S. dread of Folly, Vice, and Insolence *E.S.* ii. 213
Of all thy blameless life the *s*. return *P.S.* 25
From Love, the *s*. disease thou canst not cure *Su*. 12

Solely.

Has God, thou fool! work'd *s*. for thy good *E.M.* iii. 27

Solemn.

While the long *s*. Unison went round *D.* iv. 612
Canst thou forget that sad, that *s*. day *E.A.* 107
And the dim windows shed a *s*. light *E.A.* 144
A *s*. Sacrifice, perform'd in state *M.E.* iv. 157
The deep, majestic, *s*. organs blow *O*. i. 11
While *s*. airs improve the sacred fire *O*. i. 129
While visits shall be paid on *s*. days *R.L.* iii. 167
And what a *s*. face if he denies *S.* vii. 68
Such waxen noses, *s*. staring things *S.* viii. 210

Solemniz'd.

An added pudding *s*. the Lord's *M.E.* iii. 346

Solemnly.

And tho' I *s*. declare *J.H.* ii. 121 *s*

Solicit.

Repent old pleasures, and *s*. new *E.A.* 186

Solid.

Or *s*. pudding against empty praise *D.* i. 54
But high above more *s*. Learning shone *D.* i. 147
Of *s*. proof, impenetrably dull *D.* iii. 26
Half thro' the *s*. darkness of his soul *D.* iii. 226

SOLINUS—SONG.

On passive paper, or on *s*. brick *D*. iv. 130
The *s*. pow'r of understanding fails *E.C.* 57
Would you enjoy soft nights and *s*. dinners *E.J.S.* 23
One *s*. dish his week-day meal affords *M.E.* iii. 345

Solinus.
Manilius or *S*. shall supply *D*. iv. 226

Solitary.
To muse, and spill her *s*. tea *E*. v. 16
Lost in a convent's *s*. gloom *E.A.* 38
One Simile, that *s*. shines *S*. v. 111

Solitude.
To wholesome *S*., the nurse of sense *S*. viii. 185
In these deep s—s and awful cells *E.A.* 1

Solo.
With nothing but a *S*. in his head *D*. iv. 324

Solus.
But Tully has it, *Nunquam minus s*. *S*. viii. 91

Solyma.
Ye Nymphs of *S.!* begin the song *M*. 1

Some.—*Passim*.

Somers.
Thus *S*. once, and HALIFAX, were mine *E.S.* ii. 77
The courtly *Talbot*, *S*., *Sheffield* read *P.S.* 139

Something.
Author of *s*. yet more great than letter *D*. iv. 216
S. to blame, and *s*. to commend *E*. iii. 22
That *s*. still which prompts th' eternal sigh *E.M.* iv. 3
S. in Verse as true as Prose *I.H.* ii. 261
But *s*. much more our concern *I.H.* ii. 145
S. as dim to our internal view *M.E.* i. 49
S. there is more needful than expense (*rep*.) *M.E.* iv. 41
(Cries prating Balbus) "*s*. will come out" *P.S.* 276
And *s*. said of Chartres much too rough *S*. i. 4
Hartshorn, or *s*. that shall close your eyes *S*. i. 20
He calls for *s*. bitter, *s*. sour *S*. ii. 33
S., which for your Honour they may cheat *S*. iv. 93
Show'd us that France had *s*. to admire *S*. v. 273
Years following years, steal *s*. ev'ry day *S*. vi. 72
Where nameless S—s in their causes sleep *D*. i. 56

Sometimes.—*Passim*.

Somewhat.
Not to go back is *s*. to advance *S*. iii. 53

Son.
The Mighty Mother, and her *S*., who brings *D*. i. 1
Each sire imprest, and glaring in his *s*. *D*. i. 100
My *s*.: the promis'd land expects thy reign *D*. i. 292
Folly, my *s*., has still a Friend at Court *D*. i. 300
To him the Goddess; "*S.!* thy grief lay down *D*. ii. 131
Tho' this his *S*. dissuades, and that his Wife *D*. ii. 168
Thus the great Father to the greater *S*. *D*. iii. 42
And see, my *s.!* the hour is on its way *D*. iii. 103
An hundred sons, and ev'ry *s*. a God *D*. iii. 134
S., what thou seek'st to find in thee! Look, and find *D*. iii. 251
And are these wonders, *S*., to thee unknown *D*. iii. 273
Soft in her lap her Laureate *s*. reclines *D*. iv. 20
Receive, great Empress! thy accomplish'd *S*. *D*. iv. 282
Lo! ev'ry finish'd *S*. returns to thee *D*. iv. 500
The Sire is made a Peer, the *S*. a Fool *D*. iv. 548
Perhaps more high some daring *s*. may soar *D*. iv. 579
While, at each change, the *s*. of Libyan Jove *E.C.* 376
Convey'd unbroken faith from sire to *s*. *E.M.* iii. 228
Tell me, if Virtue made the *s*. expire *E.M.* iv. 103
As that the virtuous *s*. is ill at ease *E.M.* iv. 119
Ye Gods! shall Cibber's *s*., without rebuke *E.S.* i. 115
And offer Country, Parent, Wife, or *S*. *E.S.* i. 158
Each Mother asks it for her booby *S*., *E.S.* ii. 107
Here lies the Friend most lov'd, the *S*. most dear *Ep*. iii. 2
A Virgin shall conceive, a Virgin bear a *S*. *M*. 8
Then palaces shall rise; the joyful *S*. *M*. 63
Boastful and rough, your first *S*. is a Squire *M.E.* i. 151
By his own *s*., that passes by unbless'd *M.E.* i. 235
T' enrich a Bastard, or a *S*. they hate *M.E.* iii. 68
Not so his *S*.; he mark'd this oversight *M.E.* iii. 197
First, for his *S*. a gay commission buys *M.E.* iii. 389

Wife, *s*., and daughter, Satan! are thy own *M.E.* iii. 399
As *s*., as father, brother, husband, friend *O*. iii. 28
Arthur, whose giddy *s*. neglects the Laws *P.S.* 23
Ammon's great *s*. one shoulder had too high *P.S.* 117
A lost Bank-bill, or heard their *S*. was drown'd *S*. ii. 56
Pity! to build, without a *s*. or wife *S*. ii. 163
At best, it falls to some ungracious *s*. *S*. ii. 173
Weds the rich Dulness of some *S*. of earth *S*. iv. 43
Adopt him *S*., or Cousin at the least *S*. iv. 108
And send his Wife to church, his *S*. to school *S*. v. 164
My only *s*., I'd have him see the world *S*. vi. 6
To read in Greek the wrath of Peleus' *s*. *S*. vi. 53
To ease and silence ev'ry Muse's *s*. *S*. vi. 111
His *S*.'s *fine Taste an op'ner Vista loves M.E.* iv. 93
And thou! his Aid-de-camp, lead on my *s*—*s* *D*. i. 305
And now the Queen, to glad her *s*., proclaims *D*. ii. 17
And learn, my *s*., the wond'rous pow'r of Noise *D*. ii. 222
S. of a Day! just buoyant on the flood *D*. ii. 307
What Dulness dropt among her *s*. imprest *D*. ii. 407
The North by myriads pours her mighty *s*. *D*. iii. 89
No fiercer *s*., had Easter never been *D*. iii. 118
An hundred *s*., and ev'ry son a God *D*. iii. 134
Behold an hundred *s*., and each a Dunce *D*. iii. 138
Embrace, embrace, my *s.!* be foes no more *D*. iii. 177
Yet oh, my *s*., a father's words attend *D*. iii. 213
See now, what Dulness and her *s*. admire *D*. iii. 228
Till Thames see Eton's *s*. for ever play *D*. iii. 335
To the same notes thy *s*. shall hum, or snore *D*. iv. 57
Who pay her homage in her *s*., the Great *D*. iv. 92
But spread, my *s*., your glory thin or thick *D*. iv. 129
Eton and Winton shake thro' all their *s*. *D*. iv. 144
O! if my *s*. may learn one earthly thing *D*. iv. 183
To lull the *s*. of Marg'ret and Clare-hall *D*. iv. 202
Pours at great Bourbon's feet her silken *s*. *D*. iv. 298
So may the *s*. of *s*. of *s*. of whores *D*. iv. 332
"My *S.!*" (she answer'd) "both have done your parts *D*. iv. 437
O! would the *S*. of Men once think their Eyes *D*. iv. 453
Why all your Toils? your *s*. have learn'd to sing *D*. iv. 546
My *S.!* be proud, be selfish, and be dull *D*. iv. 582
High on Parnassus' top her *s*. she show'd *E.C.* 94
The last, the meanest of your *s*. inspire *E.C.* 196
Our wiser *s*., no doubt, will think us so *E.C.* 439
Our *s*. their fathers' failing language see *E.C.* 432
The same which in a Sire the *S*. obey'd *E.M.* iii. 213
Whose *s*. shall blush their fathers were thy foes *E.M.* iii. 388
Oh *s*. of earth! attempt ye still to rise *E.M.* iv. 73
See future *s*., and daughters yet unborn *M*. 83
Against the Gothic *S*. of frozen verse *Mi*. ii. 14
Of Asia's troops and Afric's sable *s*. *R.L.* iii. 82
Tho' justly Greece her eldest *S*. admires *S*. v. 43
And to debase the *S*., exalt the Sires *S*. v. 134
S., Sires, and Grandsires, all will wear the bays *S*.v.171
The joy their wives, their *s*., and servants share *S*. v.245
Our *s*. shall see it leisurely decay *S*. viii. 44
When Albion sends her eager *s*. to war *W.F.* 106
She saw her *s*. with purple deaths expire *W.F.* 323
No more thy *s*. shall dye with British blood *W.F.* 367

Song.
For her the feather'd quires neglect their *s*. *A*. 20
The birds shall cease to tune their ev'ning song *A*. 40
All hail him victor in both gifts of *s*, *D*. ii. 267
In lofty madness meditating *s*. *D*. iii. 16
Then take at once the Poet and the *S*. *D*. iv. 8
O sing, and hush the Nations with thy *S*. *D*. iv. 626
But most by Numbers judge a Poet's *s*. *E.C.* 337
A needless Alexandrine ends the *s*. *E.C.* 356
Oh master of the poet, and the *s*. *E.M.* iv. 374
Some rising Genius sins up to my *s*. *E.S.* ii. 9
Exalt the dance, and animate the *s*. *I.H.* iii. 28
Above the reach of vulgar *s*. *I.H.* iv. 4
Ye Nymphs of Solyma! begin the *s*. *M*. 1
Thus *s*. could prevail *O*. i. 87
Moral Truth, or mystic *S*. *O*. ii. 12
On French translation, and Italian *s*. *P.C.* 42
The world had wanted many an idle *s*. *P.S.* 28
No more than thou, great George! a birth-day *s*. *P.S.* 222
Horace and he went hand in hand in *s*. *P.S.* 234
But stoop'd to Truth, and moraliz'd his *s*. *P.S.* 341
If there be force in Virtue, or in *S*. *P.S.* 387
One died in metaphor, and one in *s*. *R.L.* v. 60
And the sad burden of some merry *s*. *S*. i. 80

SONGSTER—SOUL.

In flow'r of age you perish for a *s. S.* i. 102
The world's good word is better than a *s. S.* ii. 102
Yet ev'ry child another *s.* will sing *S.* iii. 91
This new Court jargon, or the good old *s. S.* iii. 98
And all our Grace at table is a *S. S.* v. 174
What will a Child learn sooner than a *s. S.* v. 205
And Heav'n is won by Violence of *S. S.* v. 240
Rough Satyrs dance, and Pan applauds the *s. Sa.* 50
And bade his willows learn the moving *s. W.* 14
Live in description, and look green in *s. W.F.* 8
Still in thy *s.* should vanquish'd France appear *W.F.* 309
S—s, sonnets, epigrams the winds uplift D. ii 115
Composing *s.,* for Fools to get by heart *S.* vi. 126
One sings the Fair ; but *s.* no longer move *S.* vii. 21

Songster.
Each *S.,* Riddler, ev'ry nameless name *D.* iii. 157

Sonica.
The *Knave* won *S.,* which I had chose *Mi.* ix. 51

Sonnets.
Songs, *s.,* epigrams the winds uplift *D.* ii. 115

Sonnetser.
In some starv'd hackney *s.,* or me *E.C.* 419

Sonorous.
But, far o'er all, *s.* Blackmore's strain *D.* ii. 259
Sing thy *s.* verse—but not aloud *S.* vi. 109

Soon, Sooner, Soonest.—*Passim.*

Sooterkins.
Fruits of dull Heat, and *S.* of Wit *D.* i. 126

Sooth.
Which most conduce to *s.* the soul in slumbers *D.* ii. 369
The well-sung woes will *s.* my pensive ghost *E.A.* 365
S. my ever-waking slumbers *Mi.* vii. 15

Sooths.
Ye pow'rs, what pleasing frenzy *s.* my mind *A.* 51
Rolls o'er my Grotto, and but *s.* my sleep *S.* i. 124

Sooty.
Swift on his *s.* pinions flits the Gnome *R.L.* iv. 17

Sophs.
Three College *S.,* and three pert Templars came *D.* ii. 379

Sophistry.
His blunted Arms by *S.* are born *D.* iv. 25
Destroy his fib or *s.,* in vain *P.S.* 91

Sore'rer.
And look'd, and saw a sable *S.* rise *D.* iii. 233

Sordid.
See Britain sunk in lucre's *s.* charms *M.E.* iii. 143
Plain, but not *s.*; tho' not splendid, clean *S.* ii. 48
And pleas'd if *s.* want be far away *S.* vi. 295

Sore.
And itch most hurts when anger'd to a *s. S.* viii. 119
There hapless Shakespear, yet of Tibbald's *D.* i. 133
S. sighs Sir Gilbert, starting at the bray *D.* ii. 251
But 'faith your very Friends will soon be *s. E.S.* i. 23
Laugh at your friends, and if your Friends are *s. E.S.* i. 55
But touch me, and no Minister so *s. S.* i. 76
As one of Woodward's patients; sick, and *s. S.* viii. 152

Sorer.
And is not mine, my friend, a *s.* case *P.S.* 73

Sorrow.
While Wren with *s.* to the grave descends *D.* iii. 329
I never (to my *s.* I declare) *E.S.* ii. 98
Now sink in *s—s with a tolling bell D.* ii. 228
Muse | at that Name thy sacred *s.* shed *E.* iii. 47
Take back that grace, thy love, and those tears *E.A.* 285
And with a Father's *s.* mix his own *Ep.* iii. 8
Soft *s.,* melting griefs, and flowing tears *R.L.* iv. 86
He breaks the Vial whence the *s.* flow *R.L.* iv. 142

Sorrowing.
When at the close of each sad, *s.* day *E.A.* 225

Sort.
What tho' we let some better *s.* of fool *D.* iv. 235
Then look'd, and saw a lazy, lolling *s. D.* iv. 337

Her children first of more distinguish'd *s. D.* iv. 567
Bubo observes, he lash'd no *s.* of *Vice E.S.* i. 12
And speak in public with some *s.* of grace *S.* v. 208
Hast thou, O Sun ! beheld an emptier *s. P.S.* viii. 204
Grant but as many s—s of Mind as Moss M.E. i. 18
Then careful Heav'n supply'd two *s.* of Men *M.E.* iii. 13
For diff'rent styles with diff'rent subjects s. E.C. 322
Take the most strong, and *s.* them as you can *M.E.* i. 120

Sot.
The *s.* a hero, lunatic a king *E.M.* ii. 268
A Fop their Passion, but their Prize a *S. M.E.* ii. 247
D'ye think me, noble Gen'ral, such a *S. S.* vi. 50
Concluding all were desp'rate s—s and fools E.C. 271
What can ennoble *s.,* or slaves, or cowards *E.M.* iv. 215

Sought.
And simple Reason never *s.* but one *E.M.* iii. 230
First *s.* a Poet's Fortune in the Town *Mi.* iii. 2
Ye shades, where sacred truth is *s. O.* ii. 1
I *s.* no homage from the Race that write *P.S.* 219
Just in that instant, anxious Ariel *s. R.L.* iii. 139
Who *s.* no more than on bis foe to die *R.L.* v. 78
In ev'ry place is *s.,* but *s.* in vain *R.L.* v. 110
I shun the fountains which I *s.* before *Su.* 30

Soul.
O thou ! of Bus'ness the directing *s. D.* i. 169
Let others aim : 'tis yours to shake the *s. D.* ii. 225
Which most conduce to sooth the *s.* in slumbers *D.* ii. 369
Who knows how long thro' transmigrating *s. D.* iii. 49
And lick up all the Physic of the *S. D.* iii. 82
Half thro' the solid darkness of his *s. D.* iii. 226
Joy fills his *s.,* joy innocent of thought *D.* iii. 249
To stir, to rouse, to shake the *s.* he comes *D.* iv. 67
Without the *s.,* the Muse's Hypocrite *D.* iv. 100
The body's harmony, the beaming *s. D.* iv. 236
Her too receive (for her my *s.* adores) *D.* iv. 331
Dismiss my *s.,* where no Carnation fades *D.* iv. 418
The common *S.,* of Heav'n's more frugal make *D.* iv. 441
Of naught so doubtful as of *S.* and *Will D.* iv. 482
Can touch Immortals, 'tis a *S.* like thine (*rep.*) *E.* i. 22
A *S.* as full of Worth, as void of Pride *E.* i. 1
Strong as their charms, and gentle as their *s. E.* iii. 74
Come, if you'll be a quiet *s. E.* vi. 29
Warm from the *s.,* and faithful to its fires *E.A.* 54
Speed the soft intercourse from *s.* to *s. E.A.* 57
And make my *s.* quit Abelard for God *E.A.* 128
Ere such a *s.* regains its peaceful state *E.A.* 197
Far other dreams my erring *s.* employ *E.A.* 223
All my loose *s,* unbounded springs to thee *E.A.* 228
Stain all my *s.,* and wanton in my eyes *E.A.* 266
And swelling organs lift the rising *s. E.A.* 272
In seas of flame my plunging *s.* is drown'd *E.A.* 275
And dawning grace is op'ning on my *s. E.A.* 280
Suck my last breath, and catch my flying *s. E.A.* 324
Thus in the *s.* while memory prevails *E.C.* 56
In some fair body thus th' informing *s. E.C.* 76
Gen'rous converse ; a *s.* exempt from pride *E.C.* 641
In some close corner of the *s.,* they sin *E.S.* 18
Gradations just, has thy pervading *s. E.M.* i. 31
The *s.,* uneasy and confin'd from home *E.M.* i. 97
His *s.,* proud Science never taught to stray *E.M.* i. 101
No pow'rs of body or of *s.* to share *E.M.* i. 191
Whose body Nature is, and God the *s. E.M.* i. 268
Breathes in our *s.,* informs the mortal part *E.M.* i. 275
Self-love, the spring of motion, acts the *s. E.M.* ii. 59
The rising tempest puts in act the *s. E.M.* ii. 105
Soon flows to this, in body and in *s. E.M.* ii. 140
The fiery *s.* abhorr'd in Catiline *E.M.* ii. 199
One all-extending, all-preserving *S. E.M.* iii. 22
So two consistent motions act the *S. E.M.* iii. 315
One common blessing, as one common *s. E.M.* iv. 62
The first, last purpose of the human *s. E.M.* iv. 338
And opens still, and opens on his *s. E.M.* iv. 342
God loves from Whole to Parts : but human *s. E.M.* iv. 361
How shin'd the *S.,* unconquer'd in the Tow'r *E.S.* ii. 83
Passion and Pride were to her *s.* unknown *Ep.* vi. 5
Yet lov'd his Friend, and had a *S. I.H.* ii. 162
And all the kind Deceivers of the *s. I.H.* iii. 36
And ev'ry child hates Shylock, tho' his *s. M.E.* i. 55
Or Affectations quite reverse the *s. M.E.* i. 56
To ease the *S.* of one oppressive weight *M.E.* i. 105
" Mercy ! " cries Helluo, " mercy on my *s.*!" *M.E.* i. 240
Then all for Death, that Opiate of the *s. M.E.* ii. 91
That life of pleasure, and that *s.* of whim *M.E.* iii. 306

SOUND—SOW'D.   295

Then dubs Director, and secures his *s. M.E.* iii. 374
Still follow Sense, of ev'ry Art the *S. M.E.* iv. 65
Make the *s.* dance upon a Jig to Heav'n *M.E.* iv. 144
Statesman, yet friend to Truth ! of *s.* sincere *M.E.* v. 67
'Twas all th' Ambition his high *s.* could feel *Mi.* iii. 3
They strike the *S.*, and glitter in the Eye *Mi.* ix. 8a
And the bright flame was shot thro' MARCHMONT's *S. Mi.* x. 12
Or when the *s.* is press'd with cares *O.* i. 26
Hers lifts the *s.* to heav'n *O.* i. 134
Tell me, my *S.*, can this be Death *O.* v. 12
To wake the *s.* by tender strokes of art *P.C.* 1
A Clerk, foredoom'd his father's *s.* to cross *P.S.* 17
Have I no friend to serve, no *s.* to save *P.S.* 274
His father, mother, body, *s.*, and muse *P.S.* 381
'Tis these that early taint the female *s. H.* i. 87
Or caus'd suspicion when no *s.* was rude *R.L.* iv. 73
Charms strike the sight, but merit wins the *s. R.L.* v. 34
And for my *s.* I cannot sleep a wink *S.* i. 12
The *S.* stood forth, nor kept a thought within *S.* i. 54
The Feast of Reason and the Flow of *S. S.* i. 128
The *S.* subsides, and wickedly inclines *S.* ii. 79
That lock up all the Functions of my *s. S.* iii. 40
Between the Fits this Fever of the *s. S.* iii. 58
See him with pains of body, pangs of *s. S.* iii. 71
The sleepy Eye, that spoke the melting *s. S.* v. 150
Smooth'd ev'ry brow, and open'd ev'ry *s. S.* v. 248
Who there his Muse, or self; or *s.* attends *S.* vi. 90
And keep the equal measure of the *S. S.* vi. 205
One driv'n by strong Benevolence of *s. S.* vi. 276
And the free *s.* looks down to pity Kings *S.* viii. 187
But oh ! what terrors must distract the *s. S.* viii. 244
Tho' his *s.*'s bullet, and his body buff *S.* viii. 263
Why bade ye else, ye Pow'rs ! her *s.* aspire *U.L.* 11
So flew the *s.* to its congenial place *U.L.* 27
Ev'n he, whose *s.* now melts in mournful lays *U.L.* 77
Bids his free *s.* expatiate in the skies *W.F.* 254
Ye sacred Nine ! that all my *s.* possess *W.F.* 259
The *s.*'s *calm sunshine, and the heart-felt joy L.M.* iv. 168
Old *Bavius* sits to dip poetic *s—s D.* iii. 24
Vain of Italian Arts, Italian *S. D.* iv. 300
An hundred *s.* of Turkeys in a pie *D.* iv. 594
Oh ! happy state ! when *s.* each other draw *E.A.* 91
For as in bodies, thus in *s.*, we find *E.C.* 207
Who first taught *s.* enslav'd, and realms undone *E.M.* iii. 241
Such as the *s.* of cowards might conceive *E.M.* iii. 259
Congenial *s.*! whose life one Av'rice joins *M.E.* iii. 131
By those happy *s.* who dwell *O.* i. 74
Borne on the swelling notes our *s.* aspire *O.* i. 128
To their first Elements their *S.* retire *R.L.* i. 58
Is what two *s.* so gen'rous cannot bear *S.* i. 48
With equal talents, these congenial *s. S.* v. 129
Most *s.*, 'tis true, but peep out once an age *U.L.* 17
Lo these were they, whose *s.* the Furies steel'd *U.L.* 41
And draws the aromatic *s.* of flow'rs *W.F.* 244

Sound.

High *S.*, attemper'd by the vocal nose *D.* ii. 256
Long Chanc'ry-lane retentive rolls the *S. D.* ii. 263
And last turn'd *Air,* the Echo of a *S. D.* iv. 322
And empty heads console with empty *s. D.* iv. 542
From yonder shrine I heard a hollow *s. E.A.* 308
The *s.* must seem an Echo to the sense *E.C.* 365
And the world's victor stood subdu'd by *S. E C.* 381
She midst the lightning's blaze, and thunder's *s. E.M.* iii. 249
'Tis he th' obstructed paths of *s.* shall clear *M.* 41
And men grew heroes at the *s. O.* i. 43
And to her Maker's praise confin'd the *s. O.* i. 125
And the press'd watch return'd a silver *s. R.L.* i. 18
And wits take lodgings in the *s.* of Bow *R.L.* iv. 118
Rend with tremendous *s.* your ears asunder *S.* i. 27
Led by the *s.* I roam from shade to shade *W.F.* 269
To *s—s* of *heav'nly harps she dies away E.A.* 221
In *s.* and jingling syllables grown old *E.C.* 605
From *s.* to things, from fancy to the heart *E.M.* iv. 392
And fill with spreading *s.* the skies *O.* i. 15
Warriors she fires with animated *s. O.* i. 28
What *s.* were heard *O.* i. 53
With *s.* seraphic ring *O.* v. 15
And in soft *s.*, Your Grace salutes their ear *R.L.* i. 86
And soften'd *s.* along the waters die *R.L.* ii. 50
S., *s.*, ye *Viols; be the Cat-call dumb D.* i. 302
S. forth, my Brayers, and the welkin rend *D.* ii. 245

To *s.* or sink in *cano,* O or A *D.* iv. 221
Nations unborn your mighty names shall *s. E.C.* 193
I can't but think 'twould *s.* more clever *I.H.* ii. 115
Ah *s.* no more thy soft alarms *I.H.* iii. 5
No rafter'd roofs with dance and tabor *s. M.E.* iii. 189
Let the loud trumpet *s. O.* i. 7
Dulness is sacred in a s. divine D. ii. 352
S. sleep by night ; study and ease *O.* iv. 73
Turns you from *s.* Philosophy aside *S.* ii. 6
To seem but mortal ev'n in *s.* divines *S.* ii. 80
And shall we deem him Ancient, right and *s. S.* v. 58

Sounder.

Yet some there were, among the *s.* few *E.C.* 719

Soundest.

And *s.* Casuists, like you and me *M.E.* iii. 7

Sounding.

And with deep murmurs fills the *s.* shores *A.* 20
And empty words she gave, and *s.* strain *D.* ii. 45
But when loud surges lash the *s.* shore *E.C.* 368
And sweep the *s.* lyre *O.* i. 4
Now close behind, his *s.* steps she hears *W.F.* 192

Sounds.

Thro' rocks and caves the name of Delia *s. A.* 49
Which *s.* the silver Thames along *I.H.* iv. 2
A painted quiver on her shoulder *s. W.F.* 179

Soup.

From *s.* to sweet-wine, and God bless the King *M.E.* iv. 162
And drown his lands and Manors in a *S—p D.* iv. 596
With *s—s* unbought, *and salads bless'd his board M.E.* iii. 182

Sour.

Look *s.*, and hum a Tune, as you may now *E.* v. 50
Not yet purg'd off, of spleen and *s.* disdain *E.C.* 527
As Heav'n's blest beam turns vinegar more *s. E.M.* ii. 148
A Quaker? Sly ; A Presbyterian ? *s. M.E.* i. 156
He calls for something bitter, something *s. S.* ii. 33

Source.

The *s.* of Newton's Light, of Bacon's Sense *D.* iii. 213
Mother of Arrogance, and *S.* of Pride *D.* iv. 470
And stir within me ev'ry *s.* of love *E.A.* 232
At once the *s.*, and end, and test of Art *E.C.* 73
Oh heav'n-born sisters ! *s.* of art *O.* i. 9
Oh *s.* of ev'ry social tie *O.* iii. 25

Sourer.

And answ'ring gin-shops *s.* sighs return *D.* iii. 143

Sourness.

Has life no *s.*, drawn so near its end *S.* vi. 316

Souse.

Spread thy broad wing, and *s.* on all the kind *E.S.* ii. 15
But *s.* the cabbage with a bounteous heart *S.* ii. 60

South.

Thence to the *s.* extend they gladden'd eyes *D.* iii. 79
And *S.* beheld that Master-piece of Man *D.* iv. 174
*S.-*sea *Subscriptions take who please I.H.* i. 65
What made Directors cheat in *S.* year *M.E.* iii. 117
In *S.* days not happier, when surmis'd *S.* ii. 133
Oh blast it *S.-winds !* till a stench exhale *S.* ii. 27

Southern.

But for the Passions, *S.* sure and Rowe *S.* v. 86
Which not alone the s. wit sublimes E.C. 400
Or under *s.* skies exalt their sails *W.F.* 391

Southward.

Then *s.* let your Bard retire *I.H.* i. 17

Sov'reign.

A *s.* being, but a *s.* good *E.M.* iii. 238
His *S.* favours, and his Country loves *W.F.* 236
Perhaps, yet vibrates on his S.'s ear P.S. 357
And when three S—s died could scarce be vext E.S. i. 107

Sow.

'Tis thus we riot, while, who *s.* it, starve *M.E.* iii. 24

Sow'd.

And the same hand that *s.*, shall reap the field *M.* 66

Sows.
'Tis thus we eat the bread another *s. M.E.* iii. 22

Space.
Now to pure *S.* lifts his ecstatic stare *D.* iv. 33
Or bind in Matter, or diffuse in *S. D.* iv. 476
His time a moment, and a point his *s. E.M.* i. 72
Enough, that Virtue fill'd the *s.* between *M.E.* iii. 289
To Thee, whose Temple is all *S. U.P.* 49

Spacious.
There in his seat two *s.* vents appear *D.* ii. 85
See, a long race thy *s.* courts adorn *M.* 87
But see, the man who *s.* regions gave *W.F.* 79

Spade.
Falls undistioguish'd by the victor *s. R.L.* iii. 64
Let S—s be trumps! she said, and trumps they were *R.L.* iii. 46
The hoary majesty of *S.* appears *R.L.* iii. 56
Th' imperial consort of the crown of *S. R.L.* iii. 68

Spadillio.
S. first, unconquerable Lord *R.L.* iii. 49

Spain.
See the fierce Visigoths on *S.* and Gaul *D.* iii. 94
Sir, *S.* has sent a thousand jars of oil *M.E.* iii. 56
Almost as quickly as he conquer'd *S. S.* i. 130
That *S.* robs on, and Dunkirk's still a Port *S.* viii. 165

Span.
Yet not to Earth's contracted *S. U.P.* 21

Spangles.
When falling dews with *s.* deck'd the glade *A.* 99
See, round the Poles where keener *S.* shine *D.* iii. 69

Spaniard.
And own the *S.* did a *waggish thing E.S.* i. 17

Spaniel.
Before his lord the ready *s.* bounds *W.F.* 99
So well-bred *s—s civilly delight P.S.* 313

Spake.
Thus then to Man the voice of Nature *s. E.M.* iii. 171
Words that wise Bacon, or brave Raleigh *s. S.* vi. 168

Spare.
Tears are still mine, and these I need not *s. E.A.* 45
Pulpits their sacred satire learn'd to *s. E.C.* 550
Smit with her varying plumage, *s.* the dove *E.M.* iii. 54
And man's prerogative to rule, but *s. E.M.* iii. 160
But let all Satire in all Changes *s. E.S.* i. 91
S., then the Person, and expose the Vice *E.S.* ii. 12
Admit your Law to *s.* the Knight requires *E.S.* ii. 30
Sure, if I *s.* the Minister, no rules *E.S.* ii. 146
Sir, you may *s.* your Application *I.H.* i. 59
Ah *s.* me, Venus! let me, let me rest *I.H.* ii. 2
But *s.* your censure; Silia does not drink *M.E.* ii. 34
This year a Reservoir, to keep and *s. M.E.* iii. 173
Hear this, and *s.* his family, James Moore *P.S.* 385
What time would *s.*, from Steel receives its date *R.L.* iii. 171
At such a feast, old vinegar to *s. S.* ii. 57
Their own strict Judges, not a word they *s. S.* vi. 159
I, who at some times spend, at others *s. S.* vi. 290

Spar'd.
Whom ev'n the Saxon *s.*, and bloody Dane *W.F.* 77

Spares.
My hands shall rend what ev'n thy rapine *s. R.L.* iv. 168

Sparing.
Yet, to his Guest tho' no way *s. I.H.* ii. 169

Spark.
Nor *human S.* is left, nor Glimpse *divine D.* iv. 652
And hear a *s.*, yet think no danger nigh *E.* v. 4
Oh may some *s.* of your celestial fire *E.C.* 195
Attracts each light gay meteor of a *s. M.E.* ii. 22
Papilia, wedded to her am'rous *s. M.E.* ii. 37
A *S.* too fickle, or a Spouse too kind *M.E.* ii. 94
Vital *s.* of heav'nly flame *O.* v. 1
Safe from the treach'rous friend, the daring *s. R.L.* i. 73
If honest S * take scandal at a *S. S.* iii. 212
A grain of courage, or a *s.* of spirit *S.* vi. 227

Sparkle.
Heav'n's twinkling S—s *draw light, and point their horns D.* ii. 12
These *s.* with awkward vanity display *E.C.* 329

Sparkle.
See the last *s.* languish in my eye *E.A.* 332

Sparkling.
Their Wit still *s.*, and their flames still warm *E.* iv. 72
Now his fierce eyes with *s.* fury glow *E.C.* 378
See heav'n its *s.* portals wide display *M.* 97
And pointed Crystals break the *s.* Rill *M.* x. 4
On her white breast a *s.* Cross she bore *R.L.* ii. 7

Sparrow.
A hero perish, or a *s.* fall *E.M.* i. 88
And envies ev'ry *s.* that he sees *M.E.* i. 237

Spartan.
No lessons now are taught the *S.* way *S.* viii. 93

Spawn.
How hints, like *s.*, scarce quick in embryo lie *D.* i. 59

Speak.
Thrice Budgel aim'd to *s.*, but thrice suppresst *D.* ii. 397
Let Freind affect to *s.* as Terence spoke *D.* iv. 223
The Convocation gap'd, but could not *s. D.* iv. 610
They live, they *s.*, they breathe what love inspires *E.A.* 53
Let tears, and burning blushes *s.* the rest *E.A.* 106
In all you *s.*, let truth and candour shine *E.C.* 563
And *s.*, tho' sure, with seeming diffidence *E.C.* 567
But Appius reddens at each word you *s. E.C.* 585
S. out, and bid me blame no Rogues at all *E.S.* ii. 53
If *Pope* must tell what HARCOURT cannot *s. Ep.* iii. 6
(Some say his Queen) was forc'd to *s.*, or burst *P.S.* 72
Who speaks so well should ever *s.* in vain *R.L.* iv. 132
And *s.* in public with some sort of grace *S.* v. 208
Make Scots *s.* treason, cozen subtlest whores *S.* viii. 59

Speaker.
"And perfect *S.?*" "Onslow, past dispute." *S.* viii. 71

Speak'st.
S. thou of Syrian Princes? Traitor base *D.* iv. 375

Speaking.
He spoke, and *s.*, in proud triumph spread *R.L.* iv. 139
And get, by *s.* truth of monarchs dead *S.* viii. 106

Speaks.
Distrustful sense with modest caution *s. E.C.* 626
Tho' what he learns he *s.*, and may advance *M.E.* i. 3
She *s.*, behaves, and acts just as she ought *M.E.* ii. 161
Whether in florid impotence he *s. P.S.* 317
When Florio *s.* what virgin could withstand *R.L.* i. 97
One *s.* the glory of the British Queen *R.L.* iii. 13
Who *s.* so well should ever speak in vain *R.L.* iv. 132
Thus BETHEL spoke, who always *s.* his thought *S.* ii. 129
This thing has travell'd, *s.* each language too *S.* viii. 46

Spear.
Present the *s.*, and arm him for the fight *R.L.* iii. 130
And bleed for ever under Britain's *s. W.F.* 310
Propp'd on their bodkin s—s, *the Sprites survey R.L.* v. 55

Special.
He'd recommend her as a *s.* breeder *F.7.S.* 34
To fifty chosen Sylphs, of *s.* note *R.L.* ii. 117

Species.
Murders their *s.*, and betrays his own *E.M.* iii. 164

Specious.
The board with *s.* miracles he loads *D.* iv. 553

Speckled.
The crested basilisk and *s.* snake *M.* 82
Transform'd to combs the *s.*, and the white *R.L.* i. 136

Spectacle.
Lay Fortune-struck, a *s.* of Woe *Mi.* ii. 3

Spectator.
Sure sign that no *s.* shall be drown'd *D.* ii. 174

Spectre.
When lo! a *S.* rose, whose index-hand *D.* iv. 139

But, stern as Ajax' *s*., strode away *D*. iv. 274
Scar'd at the *s*. of pale Poverty *S*. iii. 70
And the pale s—s dance O. i. 68
Pale *s*., gaping tombs, and purple fires *R.L.* iv. 44

Sped.
A dire dilemma! either way I'm *s. P.S.* 31

Speech.
Sense, *s*., and measure, living tongues and dead *D*. iii. 167
Whose *S*. you took, and gave it to a Friend *E.S.* ii. 167
A Statesman's slumbers how this *s*. would spoil *M.E.* iii. 55
Plain truth, dear *Murray*, needs no flow'rs of *s. S*. iv. 3
"What *S*. esteem you most?" "The King's," said I *S*. viii. 68
Our *s*., our colour, and our strange attire *W.F.* 406

Speed.
Restrain his fury, than provoke his *s. E.C.* 85
Hang o'er their coursers' heads with eager *s. W.F.* 157
S. the soft intercourse from soul to soul E.A. 57
Welcome the coming, *s*. the parting guest *S*. ii. 160

Spells.
Know, there are Words, and *S*., which can control *S*. iii. 57
Each wight, who reads not, and but scans or s. P.S. 165

Spend.
To *s*. six months with Statesmen here *I.H.* ii. 32 *t*
Then *s*. your life in Joy and Sport *I.H.* ii. 179
They might (were Harpax not too wise to *s.) M.E.* iii. 91
I, who at some times *s*., at others spare *S*. vi. 290

Spends.
Steals much, *s*. little, yet has nothing left *P.S.* 184

Spenser.
In *S*. native Muses play *I.H.* iv. 6
S. himself affects the Obsolete *S*. v. 97

Spent.
While lab'ring oxen, *s*. with toil and heat *A*. 61
And the gay Conscience of a life well *s. M.* v. 12
S. in a sudden storm of lust *O*. iii. 18

Spew.
And gaping Tritons *s*. to wash your face *M.E.* iv. 154

Sphere.
I meddle, Goddess! only in my *s. D.* iv. 432
Perhaps acts second to some *s*. unknown *E.M.* i. 58
If to be perfect in a certain *s. E.M.* i. 73
All quit their *s*., and rush into the skies *E.M.* i. 124
Submit—In this, or any other *s. E.M.* i. 285
Go, soar with Plato to th' empyreal *s. E.M.* ii. 23
When those blue eyes first open'd on the *s. M.E.* ii. 284
Some thought it mounted to the Lunar *s. R.L.* v. 113
Which adds new glory to the shining *s. R.L.* v. 142
And stunn'd him with the music of the s—s E.M. i. 202
Let ruling Angels from their *s*. be hurl'd *E.M.* i. 253
Ye know the *s*. and various tasks assign'd *R.L.* ii. 75

Spice.
There sav'd by *s*., like mummies, many a year *D*. i. 151
Clothe *s*., line trunks, or, flutt'ring in a row *S*. v. 418
Like frigates fraught with *s*. and cochineal *S*. viii. 227
Where s—s smoke beneath the burning line D. iii. 70
For Indian *s*., for Peruvian Gold *S*. iv. 71

Spicy.
See *s*. clouds from lowly Saron rise *M*. 27
For thee Idume's *s*. forests blow *M*. 95
Led by new stars, and borne by *s*. gales *W.F.* 392

Spider.
Who made the *s*. parallels design *E.M.* iii. 103
The s.'s touch, how exquisitely fine E.M. i. 217

Spies.
Himself among the story'd chiefs he *s. D.* ii. 151
Whether his hoary sire he *s. O.* iii. 29
He *s*. me out, I whisper "Gracious God *S*. viii. 62
Oft in her glass the musing shepherd *s. W.F.* 211

Spied—*see* Spy'd.

Spill.
To muse, and *s*. her solitary tea *E*. v. 16

Spin.
S. all your Cobwebs o'er the Eye of Day *E.S.* ii. 222

Spins.
So *s*. the silk-worm small its slender store *D*. iv. 253
He *s*. the slight, self-pleasing thread anew *P.S.* 90
Lord Fanny *s*. a thousand such a day *S*. i. 6

Spire.
A twisted Birth-day Ode completes the *s. D.* i. 162
Who taught that heav'n-directed *s*. to rise *M.E.* iii. 261
Now glaring fiends, and snakes on rolling —s *R.L.* iv. 43
Behold! Augusta's glitt'ring *s*. increase *W.F.* 377

Spirit.
Whose judgment sways us, and whose *s*. warms *A*. 10
And pour'd her *S*. o'er the land and deep *D*. i. 8
Intrigu'd with glory, and with *s*. whor'd *D*. iv. 315
Or moving *s*. bade the waters flow *E.A.* 254
In each low wind methinks a *S*. calls *E.A.* 305
With the same *s*. that its author writ *E.C.* 234
Wit, *S*., Faculties, but make it worse *E.M.* ii. 146
One thinks on Calvin heav'n's own *s*. fell *E.M.* iv. 137
Or Public *S*. its great cure, a Crown *E.M.* iv. 172
Correct with' *s*., eloquent with ease *E.M.* iv. 381
While Roman *S*. charms, and Attic Wit *E.S.* ii. 84
S. of *Arnall* I aid me while I lie *E.S.* ii. 129
Thy Martial *s*., or thy Social love *Ep*. ix. 8
Th' Æthereal *s*. o'er its leaves shall move *M*. 11
Some God or *S*. he has lately found *M.E.* i. 164
With the same *s*. that he drinks and whores *M.E.* i. 189
With too much *S*. to be e'er at ease *M.E.* ii. 96
By *S*. robb'd of Pow'r, by Warmth of Friends *M.E.* ii. 144
Behold Sir Balaam, now a man of *s. M.E.* iii. 375
Sister *S*., come away *O*. v. 8
And all they want is *s*., taste, and sense *P.S.* 160
Whatever *s*., careless of his charge *R.L.* ii. 123
Barnard in *s*., sense, and truth abounds *S*. iii. 85
Not but the Tragic *s*. was our own *S*. v. 276
But Kings in Wit may want discerning *S. S*. v. 385
Yours Milton's genius, and mine Homer's *s. S*. vi. 136
A grain of courage, or a spark of *s. S*. vi. 227
That e'er deserv'd a watchful s.'s care R.L. i. 102
So *S*—s *ending their terrestrial race D*. i. 267
With *s*. feeds, with vigour fills the whole *E.C.* 77
What wants in blood and *s*., swell'd with wind *E.C.* 208
But ripens *s*. in cold northern climes *E.C.* 401
From brutes what men, from men what *s*. know *E.M.* i. 79
And ripens *S*. as he ripens Mines *M.E.* ii. 290
Drowns my *s*., draws my breath *O*. v. 11
Know, then, unnumber'd *S*. round thee fly *R.L.* i. 41
For *S*., freed from mortal laws, with ease *R.L.* i. 69
Haste then, ye *s*., to your charge repair *R.L.* ii. 111
He spoke; the *s*. from the sails descend *R.L.* ii. 137
The silver lamp; the fiery *s*. blaze *R.L.* iii. 108
The temp'rate sleeps, and *s*. light as air *S*. ii. 74
S. like you, should see and should be seen *S*. viii. 88
As into air the purer *s*. flow *U.L.* 25
And purer *s*. swell the sprightly flood *W.F.* 94

Spirts.
S. in the gard'ner's eyes who turns the cock *D*. ii. 178

Spiry.
These moss-grown domes with *s*. turrets crown'd *E.A.* 142
The *s*. fir and shapely box adorn *M*. 74

Spite.
Or with a Rival's, or an Eunuch's *s. E.C.* 31
If Mævius scribble in Apollo's *s. E.C.* 34
Applause, in *s*. of trivial faults, is due *E.C.* 258
Your silence there is better than your *s. E.C.* 598
Unbiass'd, or by favour, or by *s. E.C.* 633
And *s*. of Pride, in erring Reason's *s. E.M.* i. 293
And hell was built on *s*., and heav'n on pride *E.M.* iii. 262
As Hags hold Sabbaths, less for joy than *s. M.E.* ii. 230
Of wretched Shylock, *s*. of Shylock's Wife *M.E.* iii. 94
Or *s*., or smut, or rhymes, or blasphemies *P.S.* 322
S. of his haughty mien and barb'rous pride *R.L.* iii. 70

SPITEFUL—SPRAY.

Sudden he view'd, in s. of all her art *R.L.* iii. 143
In s. of witches, devils, dreams, and fire *S.* vi. 313
In love's, in nature's s., the siege they hold *S.* vii. 23

Spiteful.
She, at whose name I shed these s. tears *Mi.* ix. 57

Spits.
What tho' (the use of barb'rous s. forgot) *M.E.* iii. 179
Half froth, half venom, s. himself abroad *P.S.* 320
He s. fore-right; his haughty chest before *S.* viii. 264

Splay-foot.
And s. verse, remain'd, and will remain *S.* v. 279

Spleen.
Not yet purg'd off, of s. and sour disdain *E.C.* 527
From s., from obstinacy, hate, or fear *E.M.* ii. 186
Strange s. to S—k! Do I wrong the Man *E.S.* ii. 62
Nor puff'd by Pride, nor sunk by *S. I.H.* ii. 28 s
While one there is, who charms us with his *S. M.E.* i. 62
S., Vapours, or Small-Pox, above them all *M.E.* ii. 267
Poor Vadius, long with learned s. devour'd *M.E.* v. 41
Repair'd to search the gloomy Cave of *S. R.L.* iv. 16
Of bodies chang'd to various forms by *S. R.L.* iv. 48
That single act gives half the world the s. *R.L.* iv. 78
But give the Knight (or give his Lady) s. *S.* iii. 145
'Twould burst ev'n Heraclitus with the s.! *S.* viii. 236

Spleenwort.
A branch of healing *S.* in his hand *R.L.* iv. 56

Splendid.
Plain, but not sordid; tho' not s., clean *S.* ii. 48
Our Birth-day Nobles' s. Livery *S.* iv. 33
And all is s. poverty at best *S.* viii. 225

Splendour.
With S., Charity; with Plenty, Health *M.E.* iii. 225
And S. borrows all her rays from Sense *M.E.* iv. 180

Splenetic.
Why not when I am s. *I.H.* i. 6

Split.
And Grace and Virtue, Sense and Reason s. *E.M.* ii. 83
Each had a gravity would make you s. *S.* vi. 131

Spoil.
And decks the Goddess with the glitt'ring s. *R.L.* i. 132
Whose s—s this paper offers to your eye *S.* iv. 435
Britain, that pays her Patriots with her *S. M.E.* iii. 216
The s. of nations, and the pomp of wars *P.C.* 28
Sure, if they catch, to s. the Toy at most *M.E.* ii. 233
A Statesman's slumbers how this speech would s. *M.E.* iii. 55
To s. the nation's last great trade, Quadrille *M.E.* iii. 76
But oh! if e'er thy Gnome could s. a grace *R.L.* iv. 67
A hackney coach may chance to s. a thought *S.* vi. 101

Spoil'd.
Nor has one ATTERBURY s. the flock *D.* iv. 246
S. his own language, and acquir'd no more *D.* iv. 320
Nor time nor moths e'er s. so much as they *E.C.* 113
Down, down, proud Satire! tho' a Realm be s. *E.S.* ii. 38
Imperial wonders rais'd on Nations s. *M.E.* v. 5

Spoils.
And of their fragrant physic s. the fields *W.F.* 242

Spoke.
He s.; and who with Lintot shall contend *D.* ii. 56
Then thus in quaint Recitativo s. *D.* iv. 52
Let Freind affect to speak as Terence s. *D.* iv. 223
More had she s., but yawn'd—All Nature nods *D.* iv. 605
Great Nature s.; observant Men obey'd *E.M.* iii. 199
Tho' wond'ring Senates hung on all he s. *M.E.* i. 184
Were the last words that poor Narcissa s. *M.E.* i. 247
From the crack'd bag the dropping guinea s. *M.E.* iii. 36
He s.; the spirits from the sails descend *R.L.* ii. 137
"Give her the hair"—he s., and rapp'd his box *R.L.* iv. 130
He s., and speaking, in proud triumph spread *R.L.* iv. 139
So s. the Dame, but no applause ensu'd *R.L.* v. 35
Thus BETHEL s., who always speaks his thought *S.* ii. 129

Or what was s. at CRESSY and POITIERS *S.* iii. 100
The sleepy Eye, that s. the melting soul *S.* v. 150
Clatt'ring their sticks before ten lines are s. *S.* v. 308
Mistake, confound, object at all he s. *S.* viii. 117
Thus Daphnis s., and Strephon thus reply'd *Sp.* 22
Then bow'd and s.; the winds forget to roar *W.F.* 353

Spoken.
Some would have s., but the voice was drown'd *D.*iv. 277
"But has he s.?" Not a syllable *S.* v. 335

Spontaneous.
S. beauties all around advance *M.E.* iv. 67

Spoon.
Or o'er cold coffee trifle with your s. *E.* v. 17
For lo! the board with cups and s—s is crown'd *R.L.* iii. 105

Sport.
Till Isis' elders reel, their pupils' s. *D.* iii. 337
Contending wits become the s. of fools *E.C.* 517
Destroy all Creatures for thy s. or gust *E.M.* i. 117
Then spend your life in Joy and *S. I.H.* ii. 179
No wonder then, when all was love and s. *S.* v. 151
Or Virtue, or Religion, turn to s. *S.* v. 211
The wanton victims of his s. remain *W.F.* 78
"Now turn to diff'rent s—s," (the Goddess cries) *D.* ii. 221
The other slights for women, s., and wines *S.* vi. 272
Whales s. in woods, and dolphins in the skies *D.* iii. 246
Where Bentley late tempestuous wont to s. *D.* iv. 201
As smiling Infants s. themselves to rest *E.* iv. 14
And s. and flutter in the fields of air *R.L.* i. 66
Nor blush to s. on Windsor's blissful plains *Sp.* 2
Or where ye Muses s. on Cooper's Hill *W.F.* 264

Sportive.
See! s. fate, to punish awkward pride *M.E.* iv. 19
Both doom'd alike, for s. Tyrants bled *W.F.* 59

Sports.
When Sense subsides, and Fancy s. in sleep *M.E.* i. 46

Sporus.
Let S. tremble—What? that thing of silk (rep.) *P.S.* 305
S. at court, or Japhet in a jail *P.S.* 363

Spot.
Fix'd like a plant on his peculiar s. *E.M.* ii. 63
Fix'd to no s. is Happiness sincere *E.M.* iv. 15
Yet Chloe sure was form'd without a s. *M.E.* ii. 157
Their happy S—s the nice admirer take *M.E.* ii. 44
In me what s. (for s. I have) appear *S.* i. 55

Spotless.
Eternal sunshine of the s. mind *E.A.* 209
Then mix this dust with thine—O s. Ghost *Ep.* xiii. 5

Spouse.
Ah wretch! believ'd the s. of God in vain *E.A.* 177
For her the s. prepares the bridal ring *E.A.* 219
Stern Cato's self was no relentless s. *E.J.S.* 30
No zealous Pastor blame a failing *S. E.S.* ii. 193
A Spark too fickle, or a S. too kind *M.E.* ii. 94
A Neighbour's Madness, or his *S.*'s *I.H.* ii. 143
Or meets his s. fonder eye *O.* iii. 31

Spout.
The salient s., far-streaming to the sky *D.* ii. 162
One bent; the handle this, and that the s. *R.L.* iv. 50
From silver s—s the grateful liquors glide *R.L.* iii. 109

Spouting.
The next, a Fountain, s. thro' his Heir *M.E.* iii. 174

Spouts.
While op'ning Hell s. wild-fire at your head *D.* iii. 316

Sprat.
S., Carew, Sedley, and a hundred more *S.* v. 109

Sprawl.
Where s. the Saints of Verrio and Laguerre *M.E.*iv.146

Spray.
Hear how the birds on ev'ry bloomy s. *Sp.* 23
Or hush'd with wonder, hearken from the s—s *W.* 56

Spread.

Still *s.* a healing mist before the mind *D.* i. 174
Wide as a wind-mill all his figure *s. D.* ii. 66
A shaggy Tap'stry, worthy to be *s. D.* ii. 143
Not so from shameless Curl; impetuous *s. D.* ii. 179
He ceas'd, and *s.* the robe; the crowd confess *D.* ii. 353
Oh *s.* thy Influence, but restrain thy Rage *D.* iii. 122
But *s.*, my sons, your glory thin and thick *D.* iv. 129
Soft on the paper ruff its leaves I *s. D.* iv. 407
Wide, and more wide, it *s.* o'er all the realm *D.* iv. 613
While the *s.* fan o'ershades your closing eyes *E.* v. 37
See in her cell sad Eloïsa *s. E.A.* 303
S. all his sails, and durst the deeps explore *E.C.* 646
Rome's ancient Genius, o'er its ruins *s. E.C.* 699
All *s.* their charms, but charm not all alike *E.M.* ii. 127
As the mind opens, and its functions *s. E.M.* ii. 142
For him as kindly *s.* the flow'ry lawn *E.M.* iii. 30
Still *s.* the int'rest, and preserv'd the kind *E.M.* iii. 145
S. the thin oar, and catch the driving gale *E.M.* iii. 178
Judicious Wits *s.* wide the Ridicule *E.S.* i. 61
S. thy broad wing, and souse on all the kind *E.S.* ii. 15
There *s.* round MURRAY all your blooming loves *I.H.* iii. 10
S. like a low-born mist, and blot the Sun *M.E.* iii. 138
With nodding arches, broken temples *s. M.E.* v. 3
Flutt'ring *s.* thy purple pinions *Mi.* vii. 1
The *Basset-Table s.*, the *Tallier* come *Mi.* ix. 1
She was my friend; I taught her first to *s. Mi.* ix. 61
To *s.* about the itch of verse and praise *P.S.* 224
Abuse on all he lov'd, or lov'd him, *s. P.S.* 354
His giant limbs, in state unwieldy *s. R.L.* iii. 72
This just behind Belinda's neck he *s. R.L.* iii. 133
" O wretched maid ! " she *s.* her hands, and cry'd *R.L.* iv. 95
He spoke, and speaking, in proud triumph *s. R.L.* iv. 139
Fond to *s.* friendships, but to cover heats *S.* i. 136
Then, like the Sun, let Bounty, *s.* her ray *S.* ii. 115
Or court a Wife, *s.* out his wily parts *S.* vii. 57
O'er sandy wilds were yellow harvests *s. W.F.* 88
Wind the shrill horn, or *s.* the waving net *W.F.* 96

Spreading.

Beneath the shade a *s.* Beech displays *A.* 1
But catch the *s.* notion of the Town *E.C.* 409
And fill with *s.* sounds the skies *O.* i. 15

Spreads.

So from the mid-most the nutation *s. D.* ii. 409
S. his light wings, and in a moment flies *E.A.* 76
Its gaudy colours *s.* on ev'ry place *E.C.* 312
Suckles each herb, and *s.* out ev'ry flow'r *E.M.* i. 134
S. undivided, operates unspent *E.M.* i. 274
Another still, and still another *s. E.M.* iv. 366
Soon as she *s.* her hand, th' aërial guard *R.L.* iii. 31
A livid paleness *s.* o'er all her look *R.L.* iii. 90
The Peer now *s.* the glitt'ring Forfex wide *R.L.* iii. 147
S. his black wings, and slowly mounts to day *R.L.* iv. 88
That *s.* and swells in puff'd prosperity *S.* ii. 126

Sprig.

Yet ne'er one *s.* of laurel grac'd those ribalds *P.S.* 163

Sprightlier.

Walk sober off; before a *s.* age *S.* vi. 324

Sprightly.

Just when his fancy points your *s.* eyes *E.* v. 45
So modest plainness sets off *s.* wit *E.C.* 302
The *s.* Wit, the lively Eye *I.H.* i. 45
With ev'ry *s.*, ev'ry decent part *I.H.* iii. 12
Her lively looks a *s.* mind disclose *R.L.* ii. 9
The *s.* Sylvia trips along the green *Sp.* 57
And purer spirits swell the *s.* flood *W.F.* 94

Spring.

Ye flow'rs that droop, forsaken by the *s. A.* 27
Let *s.* attend, and sudden flow'rs arise *A.* 36
As man's Mæanders to the vital *s. D.* iii. 55
Laid this gay daughter of the *S.* in dust *D.* iv. 416
Waves to the tepid Zephyrs of the *s. D.* iv. 422
And trace the Muses upward to their *s. E.C.* 127
Drink deep, or taste not the Pierian *s. E.C.* 216
Like some fair flow'r the early *s.* supplies *E.C.* 408
Self-love, the *s.* of motion, acts the soul *E.M.* ii. 59
Our *s.* of action to ourselves is lost *M.E.* i. 42
With all the incense of the breathing *s. M.* 24

Who climb their mountain, or who taste their *s. S.* v. 353
Fair Thames, flow gently from thy sacred *s. Sp.* 3
When warbling Philomel salutes the *s. Sp.* 26
In *s.* the fields, in autumn hills I love *Sp.* 77
Ev'n *s.* displeases, when she shines not here (*rep.*) *Sp.* 83
As in the crystal *s.* I view my face *Su.* 27
The Nymphs, forsaking ev'ry cave and *s. Su.* 51
Thyrsis, the music of that murm'ring *s. W.* 1
Ye gentle Muses, leave your crystal *s. W.* 21
In genial *s.*, beneath the quivering shade *W.F.* 135
Seek the clear *s.*, or haunt the pathless grove *W.F.* 168
No lake so gentle, and no *s.* so clear *W.F.* 226
As *Fancy opens the quick s*—s *of Sense D.* iv. 156
To Paraclete's white walls and silver *s. E.A.* 348
For me, health gushes from a thousand *s. E.M.* i. 138
As much eternal *s.* and cloudless skies *E.M.* i. 153
And heap'd with products of Sabæan *s. M.* 94
Our author shuns by vulgar *s.* to move *P.C.* 9
Unlock your *s.*, and open all your shades *W.F.* 4
Hence *Miscellanies s.*, *the weekly boast D.* i. 39
Oh *s.* to light, auspicious Babe, be born *M.* 22
See illies *s.*, and sudden verdure rise *M.* 68
'Tis sung, when Midas' ears began to *s. P.S.* 69
If weak the pleasure that from these can *s. S.* iv. 18
Now hawthorns blossom, now the daisies *s. Sp.* 42
If Delia smile, the flow'rs begin to *s. Sp.* 71
Where Peace descending bids her olives *s. W.F.* 429

Springes.

With hairy *s.* we the birds betray *R.L.* ii. 25

Springing.

That crown'd with tufted trees and *s.* corn *W.F.* 27

Springs.

And each warm wish *s.* mutual from the heart *E.A.* 96
All my loose soul unbounded *s.* to thee *E.A.* 228
Hope *s.* eternal in the human breast *E.M.* i. 95
From pride, from pride, our very reasoning *s. E.M.* ii. 161
Such is the World's great harmony, that *s. E.M.* iii. 295
What dire offence from am'rous causes *s. R.L.* i. 1
He *s.* to vengeance with an eager pace *R.L.* iii. 97
On morning wings how active *s.* the Mind *S.* ii. 81
The Thistle *s.*, to which the Lily yields *Sp.* 90
See! from the brake the whirring pheasant *s. W.F.* 111

Sprite.

A watchful *s.*, and Ariel is my name *R.L.* i. 106
Umbriel, a dusky, melancholy *s. R.L.* iv. 13
The *S—s of fiery Termagants in Flame R.L.* i. 59
Swift to the Lock a thousand *S.* repair *R.L.* iii. 135
Propp'd on their bodkin spears, the *S.* survey *R.L.* v. 55

Sprung.

Norton, from Daniel and Ostræa *s. D.* ii. 415
S. it from piety, or from despair *E.A.* 180
S. the rank weed, and thriv'd with large increase *E.C.* 535
Each parent *s.*—What fortune, pray?—Their own *P.S.* 390
Who *s.* from Kings shall know less joy than I *P.S.* 405
Ambition first *s.* from your blest abodes *U.L.* 13

Spur.

Came whip and *s.*, and dash'd thro' thin and thick *D.* iv. 197
'Tis more to guide, than *s.* the Muse's steed *E.C.* 84
What! shall each *s.*-gall'd *Hackney of the day E.S.* ii. 140

Spurn.

Employ their pains to *s.* some others down *E.C.* 515
When wild Barbarians *s.* her dust *O.* ii. 18

Spurning.

With *s.* heels, and with a butting head *M.E.* iii. 68

Spurns.

That threats a fight, and *s.* the rising sand *Sp.* 48

Spy.

No Pimp of Pleasure, and no *S.* of State *S.* i. 134
Then as a licens'd *s.*, whom nothing can *S.* viii. 158
And shake all o'er, like a discover'd *s. S.* viii. 279
All seems infected that th' infected s. E.C. 558
Ev'n in a Bishop I can *s.* Desert *E.S.* ii. 70

Spy'd.

Let not each beauty ev'ry where be *s. M.E.* iv. 53
His very Minister who *s.* them first *P.S.* 71

Squadrons.
The lucid s. round the sails repair *R.L.* ii. 56
Let Volga's banks with iron s. shine *W.F.* 363

Squander.
To s. These, and Those to hide again *M.E.* iii. 14
Nor could Profusion s. all in kind *M.E.* iii. 60

Square.
Now running round the Circle find it s. *D.* iv. 31
Turn round to s., and s. again to round *S.* iii. 170
Add fifty more, and bring it to a s. *S.* iv. 76

Squat.
Still sits at s., and peeps not from its hole *M.E.* i. 56

Squeaks.
And, as the prompter breathes, the puppet s. *P.S.* 318
S. like a high-stretch'd lutestring, and replies *S.* viii. 99

Squeeze.
If gentle Damon did not s. her hand *R.L.* i. 98

Squeezings.
Ev'n to the dregs and s. of the brain *E.C.* 607

Squire.
The sturdy S. to Gallic masters stoop *D.* iv. 595
Hum half a tune, tell stories to the s. *E.* v. 20
Some S., perhaps you take delight to rack *E.* v. 23
Boastful and rough, your first Son is a S. *M.E.* i. 151
Fill the capacious S., the deep Divine *M.E.* iii. 204
This brazen Brightness, to the 'S. so dear *D.* i. 219
What 'S. his lands, what Citizen his wife *S.* viii. 149
Knights, s—s, and steeds, must enter on the stage *E.C.* 282
As Beasts of Nature may we hunt the S. *E.S.* ii. 31
What could they more than Knights and S. confound *M.E.* iii. 53

Squirt.
Two Cupids s. before ; a Lake behind *M.E.* iv. 111

Stab.
Prompt or to guard or s., to saint or damn *D.* ii. 357
This steel shall s. it to the heart *E.* vi. 8

Stable.
Or with his hound comes bollowing from the s. *E.* v. 27

Stabs.
The cruel thought that s. me to the heart *Mi.* ix. 54

Staff.
With S. and Pumps the Marquis lead the Race *D.* iv. 586

Stage.
Bays, form'd by Nature S. and Town to bless *D.* i. 109
Did on the s. my Fops appear confin'd *D.* i. 191
Boyer the State, and Law the S. gave o'er *D.* ii. 413
And a new Cibber shall the s. adorn *D.* iii. 142
Oh great Restorer of the good old S. *D.* iii. 205
Thy s. shall stand, ensure it but from Fire *D.* iii. 312
Wake the dull Church, and loll the ranting S. *D.* iv. 58
From S. to S. the licens'd Earl may run *D.* iv. 587
As e'er could Dennis, of the Grecian s. *E.C.* 270
Knights, squires, and steeds, must enter on the s. (*rep.*) *E.C.* 282
And drove those holy Vandals off the s. *E.C.* 696
Tho' with the Stoic Chief our s. may ring *E.J.S.* 37
Scarfs, garters, gold, amuse his riper s. *E.M.* ii. 279
Whom all Lord Chamberlains allow the S. *E.S.* i. 42
And shook the S. with Thunders all his own *Mi.* ii. 16
For this the Tragic Muse first trod the S. *P.C.* 5
Dare to have sense yourselves ; assert the s. *P.C.* 43
If I approve, "Commend it to the S." *P.S.* 58
See, Modest Cibber now has left the S. *S.* iii. 6
These, only these, support the crowded s. *S.* v. 87
The s. how loosely does Astræa tread *S.* v. 290
Farewell the s. ! if just as thrives the play *S.* v. 302
What shook the s., and made the People stare *S.* v. 336
Comes titt'ring on, and shoves you from the s. *S.* vi. 325
Well, if it be my time to quit the s. *S.* viii. 1
Our Court may justly to our s. give rules *S.* viii. 220
How many s—s thro' old Monks she rid *D.* iii. 52

Stagirite.
As if the S. o'erlook'd each line *E.C.* 138
Yes, or we must renounce the S. *E.C.* 280
The mighty S. first left the shore *E.C.* 645

Staid—*see* Stay'd.

Stain.
Wash Bladen white, and expiate Hays's s. *D.* iv. 560
That counts your Beauties only by your S—s *E.S.* ii. 221
And in our own (excuse some Courtly s.) *S.* v. 275
'Tis mine to wash a few light s., but theirs *S.* viii. 284
Swift trouts, diversified with crimson s. *W.F.* 145
S. all my soul, and wanton in my eyes *E.A.* 266
Or s. her honour, or her new brocade *R.L.* ii. 107

Stain'd.
How hurt he you ? he only s. the Gown *E.S.* ii. 165
But s. with blood, or ill exchang'd for gold *E.M.* iv. 296
And silent Darent, s. with Danish blood *W.F.* 348

Staines.
My Lord and me as far as S. *I.H.* ii. 96 s

Stains.
When black Ambition s. a public Cause *E.S.* ii. 228

Stair.
And may descend to Mornington from S. *E.S.* ii. 239

Stake.
I'll s. yon lamb, that near the fountain plays *Sp.* 33
This Snuff-Box will I s.; the Prize is mine *Mi.* ix. 44

Stakes.
Shall then Uxorio, if the s. he sweep *M.E.* iii. 71

Stale.
Tho' s., not ripe ; tho' thin, yet never clear *D.* iii. 170
And own s. nonsense which they ne'er invent *E.C.* 411

Stalk'd.
O'er heaps of ruin s. the stately biod *W.F.* 70

Stall.
But fate with butchers plac'd thy priestly s. *D.* iii. 209
And goad the Prelate slumb'ring in his S. *E.S.* ii. 219

Stamp.
How did they fume, and s., and roar, and chafe *P.S.* 191

Stamp'd.
There, s. with arms, Newcastle shines complete *D.* i. 142

Stand.
Amid that area wide they took their s. *D.* ii. 27
When fancy flags, and sense is at a s. *D.* ii. 230
The patient fisher takes his silent s. *W.F.* 137
Great Cibber's brazen, brainless brothers s. *D.* i. 32
This grey-goose weapon must have made her s. *D.* i. 198
Where the tall Nothing stood, or seem'd to s. *D.* ii. 110
Around him wide a sable Army s. *D.* ii. 355
Thy stage shall s., ensure it but from Fire *D.* iii. 311
She tripp'd and laugh'd, too pretty much to s. *D.* iv. 50
We never suffer it to s. too wide *D.* iv. 154
There all the Learn'd shall at the labour s. *D.* iv. 393
Ah no—in sacred vestments mayst thou s. *E.A.* 325
Say, at what part of nature will they s. *E.M.* iv. 166
Desiring I would s. their friend *I.H.* ii. 66 s
They s. amaz'd, and think me grown *I.H.* 123 s
There, English Bounty yet awhile may s. *M.E.* iii. 247
S. emulous of Greek and Roman fame *M.E.* v. 54
I saw him s. behind OMBRELIA's Chair *Mi.* ix. 6
Here living Tea-pots s., one arm held out *R.L.* iv. 49
From him whose quills s. quiver'd at his ear *S.* iii. 83
You laugh, half Beau, half Sloven if I s. *S.* iii. 161
Abhor, a Perpetuity should s. *S.* vi. 247
A milk-white bull shall at your altars s. *Sp.* 47
There passengers shall s., and pointing say *U.L.* 39
Here Ceres' gifts in waving prospect s. *W.F.* 39

Standard.
By her just s., which is still the same *E.C.* 69
And figs from s. and espalier join *S.* ii. 147
But each man's secret s. in his mind *P.S.* 176
Tore down a S., took the Fort and all *S.* vi. 41
And high in air Britannia's s. flies *W.F.* 110
Let s.-authors, thus like trophies born *D.* iv. 23

Stand'st.
Thou s. unshook amidst a bursting world *P.S.* 88

Standing.
Great s. miracle ! that Heav'n assign'd *E.M.* iii. 77
That Man was made the s. jest of Heav'n *M.E.* iii. 4

STANDISH—STATE.

A *s.* sermon, at each year's expense *M.E.* iv. 21
Before, and after, *S.* Armies came *S.* ii. 154

Standish.
A *s.*, steel and golden pen *E.* vi. 14

Stands.
How Time himself *s.* still at her command *D.* i. 71
In office here fair Cloacina *s. D.* ii. 93
Fair as before her works she *s.* confess'd *D.* ii. 159
In native majesty Oldmixon *s. D.* ii. 283
Embrown'd with native bronze, lo! Henley *s. D.* iii. 199
Strong in new arms, lo! Giant HANDEL *s. D.* iv. 65
The pale Boy-Senator yet tingling *s. D.* iv. 147
S. our Digamma, and o'ertops them all *D.* iv. 218
S. in the streets, abstracted from the crew *E.* v. 43
Nature *s.* check'd; Religion disapproves *E.A.* 259
Still green with bays each ancient Altar *s., E.C.* 181
All serv'd, all serving; nothing *s.* alone *E.M.* iii. 75
The only point where human bliss *s.* still *E.M.* iv. 311
When Truth *s.* trembling on the edge of Law *E.S.* ii. 249
The prospect clears, and Wharton *s.* confest *M.E.* i. 179
Like some lone Chartreux *s.* the good old Hall *M.E.* iii. 187
Should'ring God's altar a vile image *s. M.E.* iii. 293
Tby stone, O Sisyphus, *s.* still *O.* i. 66
And now, unveil'd, the Toilet *s.* display'd *R.L.* i. 121
There *s.* a structure of majestic frame *R.L.* iii. 3
It *s.* on record, that in Richard's times *S.* i. 145
And who *s.* safest? tell me, is it he *S.* ii. 125
The Play *s.* still; damn action and discourse *S.* v. 314
That turn'd ten thousand verses, now *s.* still *S.* vi. 79

Stanhope.
CARLETON'S calm Sense, and *S.'s* noble Flame *E.S.* ii. 80

Stanza.
And each exalted *s.* teems with thought *E.C.* 423
Who pens a *S.*, when he should *engross P.S.* 18

Star.
Up to a *S.*, and like Endymion dies *D.* iv. 520
Led by the light of the Mæonian *S. E.C.* 648
What vary'd Being peoples ev'ry *s. E.M.* i. 27
Nor Boileau turn the Feather to a *S. E.S.* ii. 231
A godless Regent tremble at a *S. M.E.* i. 90
In the clear Mirror of thy ruling *S. R.L.* i. 108
A sudden *S.*, it shot thro' liquid air *R.L.* v. 127
Bare the mean Heart that lurks beneath a *S. S.* i. 108
Each *s.* of meaner merit fades away *S.* v. 20
And add new lustre to her silver *s. W.F.* 290
Thick as the s—s of night, or morning dews D. iii. 32
Yon *s.*, yon suns, he rears at pleasure higher *D.* iii. 259
See! the dull *s.* roll round and re-appear *D.* iii. 322
The sick'ning *s.* fade off th' ethereal plain *D.* iv. 636
And thanks his *s.* he was not born a fool *E.J.S.* 8
Glows in the *s.* and blossoms in the trees *E.M.* i. 272
Far other *S.* than * and * * wear *E.S.* ii. 238
Nor asks of God, but of her *S.*, to give *M.E.* ii. 89
Ye little *S.!* hide your diminish'd rays *M.E.* iii. 282
There (thank my *s.*) my whole Commission ends *P.S.* 59
And Garters, *S.*, and Coronets appear *R.L.* i. 85
Pursue the *s.* that shoot athwart the night *R.L.* ii. 81
And midst the *s.* inscribe Belinda's name *R.L.* v. 150
Self-center'd Sun, and *S.* that rise and fall *S.* iv. 6
Or Popplarity? or *S.* and Strings *S.* iv. 14
Like twinkling *s.* the Miscellanies o'er *S.* v. 170
Yes; thank my *s.!* as early as I knew *S.* vii. 1
Nor all his *s.* above a lustre show *W.F.* 231
Amid her kindred *s.* familiar roam *W.F.* 255
That Thames's glory to the *s.* shall raise *W.F.* 356
Led by new *s.*, and borne by spicy gales *W.F.* 392

Stare.
He grins, and looks broad nonsense with a *s. D.* ii. 194
Now to pure Space lifts her ecstatic *s. D.* iv. 33
Come here in crowds, and s. the strumpet down E.J.S. 50
And paid a Tradesman once to make him *s. M.E.* ii. 56
On painted Ceilings you devoutly *s. M.E.* iv. 145
While the Fops envy and the Ladies *s. E.M.* i. 104
Should chance to make the well-drest Rabble *s. S.* iii. 111
What shook the stage, and made the people *s. S.* v. 336
The boys flock round him, and the people *s. S.* vi. 120
Whereat the gentleman began to *s. S.* vi. 194

Starers.
Of stupid *s.* and of loud huzzas *E.M.* iv. 256

Stares.
Greater he looks, and more than mortal *s. D.* ii. 329
And *s.*, tremendous, with a threat'ning eye *E.C.* 586

Staring.
Her tresses *s.* from Poetic dreams *D.* iii. 17
Without a *s.* Reason on his brows *E.S.* ii. 194
Such waxen noses, solemn *s.* things *S.* viii. 210

Starry.
Above the clouds, above the *s.* sky *W.* 70

Start.
I shriek, *s.* up, the same sad prospect find *E.A.* 247
Zoilus again would *s.* up from the dead *E.C.* 465
S. ev'n from Difficulty, strike from Chance *M.E.* iv. 68
And the pale ghosts *s.* at the flash of day *R.L.* v. 52

Started.
I saw, and *s.* from its vernal bow'r *D.* iv. 424

Starting.
Sore sighs Sir Gilbert *s.* at the bray *D.* ii. 251
Sudden, with *s.* tears each eye o'erflows *R.L.* v. 85
And the wise Justice, *s.* from his chair *S.* viii. 36

Startled.
Fierce as a *s.* Adder, swell'd, and said *D.* iv. 373

Starts.
S. from her trance, and trims her wither'd bays *E.C.* 698
And *s.*, amidst the thirsty wilds to hear *M.* 69
'Tis a fear that *s.* at shadows *Mi.* vi. 3
Up *s.* a Palace; lo, th' obedient base *S.* iii. 140
And ere he *s.*, a thousand steps are lost *W.F.* 154

Starve.
Fatten the Courtier, *s.* the learned band *D.* i. 315
There *s.* and pray, for that's the way to heav'n *E.* v. 22
'Tis thus we riot, while who sow it, *s. M.E.* iii. 24
And, if they *s.*, they *s.* by rules of art *M.E.* iv. 38
He help'd to bury whom he help'd to *s. P.S.* 248
In which none e'er could surfeit, none could *s. S.* vii. 120

Starv'd.
In some *s.* hackney sonneteer, or me *E.C.* 419
Who *s.* a Sister, who forswore a Debt *E.S.* ii. 20
But while the subject *s.*, the beast was fed *W.F.* 60

Starv'ling.
Twelve *s.* bards of these degen'rate days *D.* ii. 40

Starves.
But sometimes Virtue *s.*, while Vice is fed *E.M.* iv. 149
Who *s.* a Sister, or forswears a Debt *E.S.* i. 112
"The wretch he *s.*"—and piously denies *M.E.* iii. 104
Who *s.* by Nobles, or with Nobles eats *M.E.* iii. 237
He *s.* with cold to save them from the fire *S.* vii. 72

Starving.
The *s.* chemist in his golden views *E.M.* ii. 269
In plenty *s.*, tantaliz'd in state *M.E.* iv. 163
But that the cure is *s.*, all allow *S.* vii. 10

State.
Yet sure had Heav'n decreed to save the *s. D.* i. 195
O! pass more innocent, in infant *s. D.* i. 237
With arms expanded Bernard rows his *s. D.* ii. 67
He chinks his purse, and takes his seat of *s. D.* ii. 197
Royer the *S.*, and Law the Stage gave o'er *D.* ii. 413
Who prouder march'd, with magistrates in *s. D.* ii. 423
Old in new *s.*; another, yet the same *D.* iii. 40
What mortal knows his pre-existent *s. D.* iii. 48
Nor absent they, no members of her *s. D.* iv. 91
To lug the pond'rous volume off in *s. D.* iv. 118
For SWIFT and him despis'd the farce of *s. E.* i. 9
The shining robes, rich jewels, beds of *s. E.* iv. 51
Pride, Pomp, and *S.* but reach her outward part *E.* iv. 55
Oh! happy *s.!* when souls each other draw *E.A.* 97
Ere such a soul regains its peaceful *s. E.A.* 197
Parties in Wit attend on those of *S. E.C.* 456
Jilts rul'd the *s.*, and statesmen farces writ *E.C.* 538
His knowledge measur'd to his *s.* and place *E.M.* i. 71
All but the page prescrib'd, their present *s. E.M.* i. 78
All in exact proportion to the *s. E.M.* i. 183
But what his nature and his *s.* can bear *E.M.* i. 192
Plac'd on this isthmus of a middle *s. E.M.* ii. 3
See some strange comfort ev'ry *s.* attend *E.M.* ii. 271

Nor think, in NATURE'S S. they blindly trod (*rep.*) *E.M.*
iii. 147
Mark what unvary'd laws preserve each *s.* *E.M.* iii. 189
Here rose one little *s.*, another near *E.M.* iii. 201
King, priest, and parent of his growing *s. E.M.* iii. 216
Th' according music of a well-mix'd *S. E.M.* i. 294
Of Fops in Learning, and of Knaves in *S. Ep.* i. 4
Or add one Patriot to the sinking *s. Ep.* xiv. 4
This quits an Empire, that embroils a *S. M.E.* i. 106
He dies, sad outcast of each church and *s. M.E.* ii. 204
See Sin in *S.*, majestically drunk *M.E.* ii. 69
He feeds you Alms-house, neat, but void of *s. M.E.* iii. 265
Load some vain Church with old Theatric *s. M.E.* iv. 29
A solemn Sacrifice, perform'd in *s. M.E.* iv. 157
In plenty starving, tantaliz'd in *s. M.E.* iv. 163
In ev'ry age, in ev'ry *s. O.* ii. 30
And greatly falling with a falling *s. P.C.* 22
Show'd Rome her Cato's figure drawn in *s. P.C.* 30
To *Bufo* left the whole *Castalian s. P.S.* 230
A Knave's a knave, to me, in ev'ry *s. P.S.* 361
His giant limbs, in *s.* unwieldy spread *R.L.* iii. 72
And now (as oft in some distemper'd *S.*) *R.L.* iii. 93
No Pimp of Pleasure, and no Spy of *S. S.* i. 134
He knows to live, who keeps the middle *s. S.* ii. 61
In me 'tis noble, suits my birth and *s. S.* ii. 113
Mix with the World, and battle for the *S. S.* iii. 28
Go then, and if you can, admire the *s. S.* iv. 28
Now all for Pleasure, now for Church and *S. S.* v. 158
These Madmen never hurt the Church or *S. S.* v. 190
And (tho' no Soldier) useful to the *S. S.* v. 204
But not this part of the Poetic *s. S.* v. 348
Yet like a Papist's, is the Poet's *s. S.* vii. 11
And knows what's fit for ev'ry *s.* to do *S.* viii. 47
Not Dante dreaming all th' infernal *s. S.* viii. 192
Like Eastern Kings a lazy *s.* they keep *U.L.* 21
ARGYLL, the S.'s *whole thunder born to wield E.S.* ii. 86
Thus S—s *were form'd, the name of King unknown E.M.* iii. 209
All *s.* can reach it, and all heads conceive *R.M.* iv. 30
Can pocket *S.*, can fetch or carry Kings *M.E.* ii. 42
Wants reach all *s.*; they beg but better drest *S.* viii. 224
There Kings shall sue, and suppliant *S.* be seen *W.F.* 383
Go, *measure earth, weigh air, and* s. *the tides E.M.* ii. 20

Stately.

Lest stiff, and *s.*, void of fire or force *S.* iii. 15
O'er heaps of ruin stalk'd the *s.* hind *W.F.* 70

States.

Who calls the council, *s.* the certain day *E.M.* iii. 107

Statesman.

Fond to forget the *s.* in the friend *E.* i. 8
Fear to the *s.*, rashness to the chief *E.M.* ii. 243
The bribing S.—Hold, too high you go *E.S.* ii. 24
S. and Patriot ply alike the Stocks *M.E.* iii. 139
S., yet friend to Truth ! of soul sincere *M.E.* iv. 67
So, when a *S.* wants a day's defence *P.S.* 251
Hence, the Fool's Paradise, the S.'s *Scheme D.* iii. 9
Shall Ward draw Contracts with a *S.* skill *E.S.* i. 119
A *S.* slumbers how this speech would spoil *M.E.* iii. 55
Trims Europe's balance, tops the *s.* part *S.* viii. 154
Tilts rul'd the state, and s—es farces writ E.C. 538
When *s.*, heroes, kings, in dust repose *E.M.* iv. 387
But well may put some *s.* in a fury *E.S.* i. 52
Ye *S.*, Priests, of one Religion all *E.S.* ii. 16
To spend six months with *S.* here *I.H.* ii. 32 *s*
Of mimic'd *S.*, and their merry King *M.E.* iii. 320
That S. have the Worm, is seen *Mi.* iv. 25
Here Britain's *s.* oft the fall foredoom *R.L.* iii. 5
Chiefs out of war, and *S.* out of place *S.* i. 126

Station.

Of Man, what see we but his *s.* here *E.M.* i. 19
But only what my *S.* fits *I.H.* ii. 21 *s*

Stationer.

Be thine, my *S.!* this magic gift *D.* ii. 137
With Authors, S—s *obey'd the call D.* ii. 31

Statue.

So stiff, so mute! some *s.* you would swear *S.* vi. 121
And *pitying saints, whose* s—s *learn to weep E.A.* 22

For Pembroke, *S.*, dirty Gods, and Coins *M.E* iv. 8
Trees cut to *S.*, *S.* thick as trees *M.E.* iv. 120
S. of Men, scarce less alive than they *M.E.* v. 10

Statute.

Consult the *S.*; *quart.* I think, it is *S.* i. 147
But sure no *s.* in his favour says *S.* vi. 288
At length, *by wholesome dread of* s—s *bound S.* v. 257
One of our Giant *S.* ope its jaw *S.* viii. 173

Staunch.

Each *s.* Polemic, stubborn as a rock *D.* iv. 195

Stay.

Curs'd be the fields that cause my Delia's *s. A.* 32
Barbarian, s. ! *that bloody stroke restrain E.A.* 103
Yet here for ever, ever must I *s. E.A.* 171
Nor will Life's stream for Observation *s. M.E.* i. 37
Tell, tell your griefs ; attentive will I *s. Mi.* ix. 27
Still in the right to *s. U.P.* 30

Stay'd.

She sigh'd not that they *s.*, but that she went *E.* v. 10
Oh had I *s.*, and said my pray'rs at home *R.L.* iv. 160
Than mine, to find a subject *s.* and wise *S.* viii. 168

Stays.

And, by my int'rest, Cozens made her *s. Mi.* ix. 64
His praise is lost, who s. *till all commend E.C.* 475
S. till we call, and then not often near *E.M.* iii. 87
Why *s.* SMILINDA in the Dressing-Room *Mi.* ix. 2
Between each drop it gives, *s.* half a minute *S.* viii. 127

Stead.

And hang some curious cobweb in its *s. D.* i. 180
And sees pale Virtue carted in her *s. E.S.* i. 159
Whatever an Heir, or a Friend in his *s. Ep.* xvi. 3
But all such babbling blockheads in his *s. P.S.* 304
Such they'll degrade ; and sometimes, in its *s. S.* vi. 163

Steady.

Ere Wit oblique had broke that *s.* light *E.M.* iii. 231
Or he, who luds thee face with *s.* view *S.* iii. 107

Steal.

Lose the low vales, and *s.* into the skies *A.* 60
From foolish Greeks to *s.* them, was as wise *D.* iv. 378
Devotion's self shall *s.* a thought from Heav'n *E.A.* 357
Now sighs *s.* out, and tears begin to flow *E.C.* 379
With him, most authors *s.* their works, or buy *E.C.* 618
Why now, this moment, don't I see you *s. E.S.* i. 6
She dares to *s.* my Fav'rite Lover's heart *Mi.* ix. 66
Gently *s.* upon the ear *O.* i. 13
S. from the world, and not a stone *O.* iv. 19
Or from the soft-ey'd Virgin *s.* a tear *P.S.* 286
To *s.* from rainbows e'er (*ere*) they drop in show'rs *R.L.* ii. 96
How shall the Muse, from such a Monarch, *s. S.* v. 5
(Could you o'erlook but that) it is to *s. S.* iv. 20
Years following years *s.* something ev'ry day (*rep.*) *S.* vi. 72
And *s.* so little, few perceive they *s. S.* vii. 84

Steals.

Thy image *s.* between my God and me *E.A.* 268
S. down my cheek th' involuntary Tear *I.H.* iii. 38
S. my senses, shuts my sight *O.* v. 10
S. much, spends little, yet has nothing left *P.S.* 184
While melting music *s.* upon the sky *R.L.* ii. 49

Stealth.

Do good by *s.*, and blush to find it Fame *E.S.* i. 136

Steams.

As o'er the fragrant *s.* she bends her head *R.L.* iii. 134

Steed.

'Tis more to guide, than spur the Muse's *s. E.C.* 84
When the proud *s.* shall know why man restrains *E.M.* i. 61
The bounding *s.* you pompously bestride *E.M.* iii. 35
The milky heifer and deserving *s. M.E.* iv. 185
To fix him graceful on the bounding *S. S.* v. 383
And earth rolls back beneath the flying *s. W.F.* 158
Knights, squires, and s—s, *must enter on the stage E.C.* 283
And turn th' unwilling *s.* another way *M.E.* iii. 192

Steel.

This *s.* shall stab it to the heart *E.* vi. 8

A standish, *s.* and golden pen *E.* vi. 14
Nor fields with gleaming *s.* be cover'd o'er *M.* 59
And *s.* now glitters in the Muses' shades *O.* ii. 8
What Time would spare, from *S.* receives its date *R.L.* iii. 171
S. could the labour of the Gods destroy *R.L.* iii. 173
S. could the works of mortal pride confound *R.L.* iii. 175
The conqu'ring force of unresisted *s. R.L.* iii. 178

Steele.
To wear red stockings, and to dine with *S. Mi.* iii. 4

Steel'd.
Lo these were they, whose souls the Furies *s. U.L.* 41

Steep.
Loud as the Wolves, on Orcas' stormy *s. S.* v. 328
See the bold youth strain up the threat'ning *s. W.F.* 155
And when up ten *s.* slopes you've dragg'd your thighs *M.E.* iv. 131

Steeples.
Walls, *s.*, skies, bray back to him again *D.* ii. 260

Steer.
Part pays, and justly, the deserving *s. E.M.* iii. 40
The *s.* and lion at one crib shall meet *M.* 79
Pois'd with a tail, may *s.* on Wilkins' wings *D.* iv. 452
You then whose judgment the right course would *s. E.C.* 118
Form'd by thy converse, happily to *s. E.M.* iv. 379

Steer'd.
He *s.* securely, and discover'd far *E.C.* 647
S. the same course to the same quiet shore *Ep.* vii. 13

Stem.
Then ships of uncouth form shall *s.* the tide *W.F.* 403

Stemm'd.
S. the wild torrent of a barb'rous age *E.C.* 695

Stench.
Oh blast it, South-winds! till a *s.* exhale *S.* ii. 27

Step.
With mincing *s.*, small voice, and languid eye *D.* iv. 46
Show all his paces, not a *s.* advance *D.* iv. 266
Where, one *s.* broken, the great scale's destroy'd *E.M.* i. 244
A slip-slop Sibyl led his *s—s* along *D.* iii. 15 ˙
Let others creep by timid *s.*, and slow *D.* iv. 465
'Tis hers, the brave man's latest *s.* to trace *E.* i. 29
And urg'd the rest by equal *s.* to rise *E.C.* 97
False *s.* but help them to renew the race *E.C.* 602
Mark by what wretched *s.* their glory grows *E.M.* iv. 291
Pride guides his *s.*, and bids him shun the great *M.E.* i. 114
Invites my *s.*, and points to yonder glade *U.L.* 2
And ere he starts, a thousand *s.* are lost *W.F.* 154
Now close behind, his sounding *s.* she hears *W.F.* 192

Stephen.
No Poets there, but *S.*, you, and me *S.* vi. 140

Stepp'd, Stept.
Chloe *s.* in, and kill'd him with a Psalm *R.L.* v. 68
S—t from its pedestal to take the air *S.* vi. 122

Steps.
Pride, where wit fails, *s.* in to our defence *E.C.* 209
An Ace of Hearts *s.* forth: The King unseen *R.L.* iii. 95

Stern.
High on the *s.* the Thracian rais'd his strain *O.* i. 39
See Alaric's *s.* port! the martial frame *D.* iii. 91
But, *s.* as Ajax' spectre, strode away *D.* iv. 274
There *s.* Religion quench'd th' unwilling flame *E.A.* 39
S. Cato's self was no relentless spouse *E.J.S.* 30
S. Proserpine relented *O.* i. 85

Sterner.
And *s.* Cassius melts at Junia's eyes *O.* iii. 16

Sternhold.
Hopkins and *S.* glad the heart with Psalms *S.* v. 230

Stew.
To make a wash would hardly *s.* a child *M.E.* ii. 54

Steward.
Sees but a backward *s.* for the Poor *M.E.* iii. 172

Stews.
Did slumb'ring visit, and convey to *s. D.* ii. 422
The *S.* and Palace equally explor'd *D.* iv. 315
Some keep Assemblies, and would keep the *S. S.* iii. 129
Thro' T'averns, *S.*, and Bagnios take our round *S.* iv. 119

Stick.
Buy ev'ry *s.* of wood that lends them heat *S.* vi. 242
To him who notches *s—s* at Westminster *S.* iii. 84
Clatt'ring their *s.* before ten lines are spoke *S.* v. 308
To *s.* the Doctor's Chair into the Throne *D.* iv. 177
As not to *s.* at fool or ass *E.* vi. 93

Sticks.
The needy Poet *s.* to all he meets *D.* iii. 290
Yet tames not this; it *s.* to our last sand *M.E.* i. 225

Stiff.
Tho' *s.* with hoops, and arm'd with ribs of whale *R.L.* ii. 120
Lest *s.* and stately, void of fire and force *S.* iii. 15
So *s.*, so mute! some statue you would swear *S.* vi. 121

Still.—Passim.
He hears, and as a *S.* with simples in it *S.* viii. 126
The *s.*-believing, *s.*-renew'd desire *I.H.* iii. 34

Stilton.
But wish'd it *S.* for his sake *I.H.* ii. 168

Stilts.
This prose on *s.*, that poetry fall'n lame *D.* i. 190

Sting.
O Death! where is thy *S. O.* v. 18
Produc'd the point that left the *s.* behind *S.* v. 252

Stings.
This painted child of dirt that stinks and *s. P.S.* 310

Stink.
In heaps, like Ambergrise, a *s.* it lies *M.E.* iii. 235
If this is priz'd for sweetness, that for *s. S.* ii. 30
Oil, tho' it *s.*, they drop by drop impart *S.* iii. 59
In dirt and darkness, hundreds *s.* content *S.* iii. 133

Stinks.
Imbibes new life, and scours and *s.* along *D.* ii. 106
Who like his Cheops *s.* above the ground *D.* iv. 372
This painted child of dirt that *s.* and stings *P.S.* 310

Stinted.
To just three millions *s.* modest Gage *M.E.* iii. 128

Stir.
No noise, no *s.*, no motion canst thou make *D.* ii. 303
To *s.*, to rouse, to shake the soul, he comes *D.* iv. 67
And *s.* within me ev'ry source of love *E.A.* 232
Once break their rest, or *s.* them from their Place *E.S.* i. 100
Just brought out this, when scarce his tongue could *s. M.E.* i. 254

Stirr'd.
Yet by some object ev'ry brain is *s. D.* iv. 445

Stirs.
As the small pebble *s.* the peaceful lake *E.M.* iv. 364

Stobæus.
What Gellius or *S.* hash'd before *D.* iv. 231

Stocking.
At am'rous Flavia is the *s.* thrown *S.* iii. 148
To wear red *s—s*, and to dine with Steele *Mi.* iii. 4

Stocks.
On savage *s.* inserted, learn to bear *E.M.* ii. 182
Statesman and Patriot ply alike the *S. M.E.* iii. 139
S. and Subscriptions pour on ev'ry side *M.E.* iii. 370
Who in the secret, deals in *S.* secure *S.* viii. 140

Stoic.
Tho' with the *S.* Chief our stage may ring (rep.) *E.J.S.* 37
With too much weakness for the *S.*'s pride *E.M.* ii. 6
In lazy Apathy let *S—s* boast *E.M.* ii. 101

Stole.
In pleasing memory of all he *s.* *D.* i. 128
Some Dæmon *s.* my pen (forgive th' offence) *D.* i. 187
S. from the Master of the sev'nfold Face *D.* i. 244
Thus he, for then a ray of Reason *s. D.* iii. 225
An honest factor *s.* a Gem worth wearing *M.E.* iii. 362
Where *British* sighs from dying WYNDHAM *s. Mi.* x. 11
Lely on animated Canvas *s. S.* v. 149
Peace *s.* her wing, and wrapt the world in sleep *S.* v. 401
Who sent the Thief that *s.* the Cash, away *S.* vi. 25

Stol'n.
S. from a Duel, follow'd by a Nun *D.* iv. 327

Stomach.
Quite turns my *S.*—So does Flatt'ry mine *E.S.* ii. 182
First Health: The *s.* (cramm'd from ev'ry dish *S.* ii. 69
Those heads, as s—s, *are sure not the best E.C.* 388

Stone.
Sits Mother Osborne, stupefy'd to *s. D.* ii. 312
Happier thy fortunes! like a rolling *s. D.* iii. 293
Leave not a foot of verse, a foot of *s. D.* iv. 127
I have not yet forgot myself to *s. E.A.* 24
Glance on the *s.* where our cold relics lie *E.A.* 356
Oh let thy once-lov'd Friend inscribe thy *S. Ep.* iii. 7
Beneath a rude and nameless *S.* he lies *Ep.* v. 3
These little rites, a *S.*, a verse receive *Ep.* vii. 19
The last true Briton lies beneath this *s. Ep.* ix. 12
This modest *S.*, what few vain Marbles can *Ep.* x. 1
And what? no monument, inscription, *s. M.E.* iii. 283
Eternal buckle takes in Parian *s. M.E.* iii. 296
Thy *s.*, O Sisyphus, stands still *O.* i. 66
Steal from the world, and not a *s. O.* iv. 19
Rack'd with Sciatics, martyr'd with the *S. S.* iv. 54
So well in paint and *s.* they judg'd of merit *S.* v. 384
So peaceful rests, without a *s.*, a name *U.L.* 69
Inscribe a verse on this relenting *s. W.* 26
Obscure the place, and uninscrib'd the *s. W.F.* 320
S—s *leap'd to form, and rocks began to live E.C.* 702
Thinks that but words, and this but brick and *s. S.* iv. 66
And trees, and *s.*, and farms, and farmer fall *S.* vi. 263

Stood.
Here *s.* her Opium, here she nurs'd her Owls *D.* i. 271
S. dauntless Curl; "Behold that rival here *D.* ii. 58
Full in the middle way there *s.* a lake *D.* ii. 69
Where the tall Nothing *s.*, or seem'd to stand *D.* ii. 110
Earless on high, *s.* unabash'd De Foe *D.* ii. 147
Compos'd he *s.*, bold Benson thrust him by *D.* iv. 110
Th' Accus'd *s.* forth, and thus address'd the Queen *D.* iv. 420
And the world's victor *s.* subdu'd by Sound *E.C.* 381
Receiv'd his laws; and *s.* convinc'd 'twas fit *E.C.* 651
Unbrib'd, unbloody, *s.* the blameless priest *E.M.* iii. 158
S. up to dash each vain PRETENDER's hope *Mi.* ii. 17
Transported demi-gods *s.* round *O.* i. 42
In vain your guiltless laurels *s. O.* ii. 5
What tho' my name *s.* rubric on the walls *P.S.* 215
And a true *Pindar s.* without a head *P.S.* 236
He *s.* the furious foe, the timid friend *P.S.* 343
Here *s.* Ill-nature like an ancient maid *R.L.* iv. 27
The Soul *s.* forth, nor kept a thought within *S.* i. 54
I make no question but the Tow'r had *s. S.* viii. 83
S. just a-tilt, the Minister came by *S.* viii. 175
Around his throne the sea-born brothers *s. W.F.* 337

Stoop.
The sturdy Squire to Gallic masters *s. D.* iv. 595
Would all but *s.* to what they understand *E.C.* 67
The brib'd Elector—There you *s.* too low *E.S.* ii. 25
Praise cannot *s.*, like Satire, to the ground *E.S.* ii. 110
And learned Athens to our art must *s. S.* v. 47

Stoop'd.
But *s.* to Truth, and moraliz'd his song *P.S.* 341

Stooping.
Say, will the falcon, *s.* from above *E.M.* iii. 53
See the bird of *Juno s. Mi.* vii. 31

Stoops.
And while the Muse now *s.*, or now ascends *E.M.* iv. 375
And *s.* from Angels to the Dregs of Earth *E.S.* i. 142
Th' Address, the Delicacy, *s.* at once *M.E.* ii. 85

Stop.
Nor *s.* at Flattery or Fib *E.* vi. 24

S.! s.! Must Satire, then, nor rise nor fall *E.S.* ii. 52
But you may read it; I *s.* short *I.H.* i. 84
S., or turn nonsense, at one glance of thee *I.H.* iii. 40
Thou who shalt *s.* where Thames' translucent wave *Mi.* x. 1
They *s.* the chariot, and they board the barge *P.S.* 10
To *s.* thy foolish views, thy long desires *S.* iii. 75
To *s.* my ears to their confounded stuff *S.* vi. 152

Stopp'd, Stopt.
Till Death untimely *s.* his tuneful tongue *E.* i. 2
I'm *s.* by all the Fools I meet *I.H.* iii. 111 *s*
There he *s.* short, nor since has writ a tittle *Mi.* iii. 9
Be *s.* in vials, or transfix'd with pins *R.L.* ii. 126
But Fate and Jove had *s.* the Baron's ears *R.L.* v. 2
Since fate relentless *s.* their heav'nly voice *W.F.* 277
Here *s—t* the Goddess: and in pomp proclaims *D.* ii. 365
It *s.*, I *s.*; it mov'd, I mov'd again *D.* iv. 428

Stops.
There *s.* the Instinct, and there ends the care *E.M.* iii. 128
Nor *s.*, for one bad cork, his butler's pay *S.* ii. 63

Store.
So spins the silk-worm small its slender *s. D.* iv. 253
Dropt the dull lumber of the Latin *s. D.* iv. 319
I ask not to increase my *s. I.H.* ii. 8 *s*
When Catiline by rapine swell'd his *s. M.E.* I. 212
To Heirs unknown descends th' unguarded *s. M.E.* ii. 149
Glorious Ambition! Peter, swell thy *s. M.E.* iii. 125
Who sees pale Mammon pine amidst his *s. M.E.* iii. 171
No Wit to flatter left of all his *s. M.E.* iii. 311
With *s.* of pray'rs for mornings, nights, and noons *R.L.* iv. 29
Oh! Impudence of wealth! with all thy *s. S.* ii. 117
'Tis one thing madly to disperse my *s. S.* vi. 292
Th' industrious bees neglect their golden *s. W.* 51
Of ancient writ unlocks the ancient *s. W.F.* 247
No weeping orphan saw his father's s—s *E.A.* 135

Stor'd.
His courts with nettles, moats with cresses *s. M.E.* iii. 181
His Study! with what Authors is it *s. M.E.* iv. 133

Stork.
Who bid the *s.*, Columbus-like, explore *E.M.* iii. 105

Storm.
Rides in the whirlwind, and directs the *s. D.* iii. 264
He mounts the *s.* and walks upon the wind *E.M.* ii. 110
Nor more a *s.* her Hate than Gratitude *M.E.* ii. 132
Spent in a sudden *s.* of lust *O.* iii. 18
As drives the *s.*, at any door I knock *S.* iii. 25
A Pedant makes, the *s.* of Gonson's lungs *S.* viii. 53
Whirlpools and s—s *his circling arm invest D.* ii. 317
Who heaves old Ocean, and who wings the *s. E.M.* i. 158
From *s.* a shelter, and from heat a shade *M.* 16
A brave man struggling in the *s.* of fate *P.C.* 21

Storm'd.
Ambition humbled, mighty cities *s. S.* v. 11
Cities laid waste, they *s.* the dens and caves *W.F.* 49

Storms.
Sudden she *s.!* she raves! You tip the wink *M.E.* ii. 33
Blue Neptune *s.*, the bellowing deeps resound *R.L.* v. 50

Stormy.
Loud as the Wolves, on Orcas' *s.* steep *S.* v. 328

Story.
Let him our sad, our tender *s.* tell *E.A.* 364
From ancient *s.* learn to scorn them all *E.M.* iv. 286
Our old Friend Swift will tell his *s. I.H.* i. 82
He had a *S.* of two Mice *I.H.* ii. 156
Would go to Mass in jest (as *s.* says) *S.* viii. 16
Hum half a tune, tell s—ies *to the squire E.* v. 20

Story'd.
Himself among the *s.* chiefs he spies *D.* ii. 151
The trophy'd arches, *s.* halls invade *E.M.* iv. 303

Stout.
Roast beef, tho' old, proclaims him *s. Mi.* xii. 13

Stow.
The Bishop *s.* (Pontific Luxury!) *D.* iv. 593

Stowe.

A work to wonder at—perhaps a *S. M.E.* iv. 70
While you to measure merits, look in *S. S.* v. 66
More than ten Holinsheds, or Halls, or S—s *S.* viii. 131

Straight.

And *s.* succeeded, leaving shame no room *D.* iv. 531
The centre mov'd, a circle *s.* succeeds *E.M.* iv. 363
Glad of a quarrel, *s.* I clap the door *P.S.* 67
S. the three-bands prepare in arms to join *R.L.* iii. 29
S. hover round the Fair her airy band *R.L.* iii. 113
S. a short thunder breaks the frozen sky *W.F.* 130

Strain.

Resound, ye hills, resound my mournful *s. A.* 57 &c.
And empty words she gave, and sounding *s. D.* ii. 45
But far o'er all, sonorous Blackmore's *s. D.* iii. 203
Still break the benches, Henley! with thy *s. D.* iii. 203
With French Libation, and Italian *S. D.* iv. 559
As one by one, at dread Medea's *s. D.* iv. 635
Blest in each science, blest in ev'ry *s. E.* i. 5
Soft is the *s.* when Zephyr gently blows *E.C.* 366
As when Belinda rais'd my *S. I.H.* i. 50
In a sadly-pleasing *s. O.* i. 5
High on the stern the Thracian rais'd his *s. O.* i. 39
All fly to TWIT'NAM, and in humble *s. P.S.* 21
Not fierce Othello in so loud a *s. R.L.* v. 105
Could pension'd Boileau lash in honest *s. S.* i. 111
The silenc'd Preacher yields to potent *s. S.* v. 237
With feasts, and off'rings, and a thankful *s. S.* v. 244
Sing then, and Damon shall attend the *s. Sp.* 29
But would you sing, and rival Orpheus' *s. Su.* 81
Here shall I try the sweet Alexis' *s. W.* 11
No more, ye hills, no more resound my s—s *A.* 96
Made Horace dull, and humbled Milton's *s. D.* iv. 212
To heav'nly themes sublimer *s.* belong *M.* 2
Is this the cause of your Romantic *s. Mi.* ix. 9
The *s.* decay *O.* i. 19
Implore your help in these pathetic *s. S.* v. 232
And I'm not us'd to Panegyric *s. S.* v. 405
Or, I'm content, allow me Dryden's *s. S.* vi. 145
First in these fields I try the sylvan *s. Sp.* 1
With Waller's *s.*, or Granville's moving lays *Sp.* 46
Is not so mournful as the *s.* you sing *W.* 2
Such silence waits on Philomela's *s. W.* 78
Let softer *s.* ill-fated Henry mourn *W.F.* 311
My humble Muse, in unambitious *s. W.F.* 427
First in these fields I sung the sylvan *s. W.F.* 434
Some s. *in rhyme; the Muses on their racks D.* iii. 159
S. out the last dull droppings of their sense *E.C.* 608
Taught nor to slack, nor *s.* its tender strings *M.E.* iii. 290
See the bold youth *s.* up the threat'ning steep *W.F.* 155

Strain'd.

For this with fillets *s.* your tender head *R.L.* iv. 101

Strainers.

Lust, thro' some certain *s.* well refin'd *E.M.* i. 289

Straining.

But most when *s.* with too weak a wing *S.* v. 368

Strains.

And *s.*, from hard-bound brains, eight lines a year *P.S.* 182

Strait.

He summons *s.* his Denizens of air *R.L.* ii. 55

Straiten.

Gasps as they *s.* at each end the cord *D.* iv. 29

Strand.

Where the tall may-pole once o'er-look'd the *S. D.* ii. 28
And "Bernard! Bernard!" rings thro' all the *S. D.* ii. 74
From SCOTS to WIGHT, from MOUNT to DOVER *s. S.* vii. 86

Stranded.

He said, and climb'd a lighter's *s.* height *D.* ii. 287

Strange.

But more advanc'd, behold with *s.* surprise *E.C.* 223
Such labour'd nothings, in so *s.* a style *E.C.* 326
The Play may pass—but that *s.* creature, Shore *E.Y.S.* 3
Those *s.* examples ne'er were made to fit ye *E.Y.S.* 41
See some *s.* comfort ev'ry state attend *E.M.* ii. 271

The whole *s.* purpose of their lives to find *E.M.* iv. 221
And wear their *s.* old Virtue, as they will *E.S.* i. 44
S. spleen to S—k! Do I wrong the Man *E.S.* ii. 62
There flies about a *s.* report *I.H.* ii. 109
S. graces still, and stranger flights she had *M.E.* ii. 49
S.! by the Means defeated of the Ends *M.E.* ii. 143
'Tis *s.*, the Miser should his Cares employ *M.E.* iv. 1
Is it less *s.*, the Prodigal should waste *M.E.* iv. 3
Say what *s.* motive, Goddess! could compel *R.L.* i. 7
S. phantoms rising as the mists arise *R.L.* iv. 40
Of whose *s.* crimes no Canonist can tell *S.* vii. 43
Has yet a *s.* ambition to look worse *S.* viii. 269
Our speech, our colour, and our *s.* attire *W.F.* 406

Strangely.

How *s.* you expose yourself, my dear *E.Y.S.* 10
The way they take is *s.* round about *E.S.* ii. 125
You're *s.* proud. So proud I am no Slave *E.S.* ii. 205
And *s.* lik'd for her *Simplicity Mi.* iii. 20
Transform themselves so *s.* as the Rich *S.* iii. 153
You laugh, if coat and breeches *s.* vary *S.* iii. 163
Lord, Sir, a mere Mechanic! *s.* low *S.* viii. 108

Stranger.

Bless me! a packet.—" 'Tis a *s.* sues *P.S.* 55
S. to civil and religious rage *P.S.* 394
"Permit" (he cries) "no *s.* to your fame *S.* viii. 66
By s—s *honour'd, and by* s—s *mourn'd U.L.* 54
Shall cease to blush with s—s *gore O.* ii. 20
Strange graces still, and s. *flights she had M.E.* ii. 49
O say what *s.* cause, yet unexplor'd *R.L.* i. 9
All the Court fill'd with *s.* things than he *S.* viii. 181

Stratagems.

Those oft are *s.* which error seem *E.C.* 179
New *s.*, the radiant Lock to gain *R.L.* iii. 120

Straw.

Hence, from the *s.* where Bedlam's Prophet nods *D.* iii. 7
Like the vile *s.* that's blown about the streets *D.* iii. 289
Pleas'd with a rattle, tickled with a *s. E.M.* ii. 276
On once a flock-bed, but repair'd with *s. M.E.* iii. 301
Those venial sins, an atom, or a *s. S.* viii. 243
Of hairs, or s—s, *or dirt, or grubs, or worms P.S.* 170

Stray.

Safe in its heaviness, shall never *s. D.* iii. 295
His soul, proud Science never taught to *s. E.M.* i. 101
Oft, when the world imagine women *s. R.L.* i. 91
Where *s.* ye, Muses, in what lawn or grove *Su.* 23

Stray'd.

But following wits from that intention *s. E.C.* 104
Thro' his young Woods how pleas'd Sabinus *s. M.E.* iv. 89
In woods bright Venus with Adonis *s. Su.* 61
Here too, 'tis sung, of old Diana *s. W.F.* 165
Beyond the forest's verdant limits *s. W.F.* 182

Strays.

While led along the skies his current *s. W.F.* 228

Streak'd.

And fleecy clouds were *s.* with purple light *A.* 14

Stream.

The *s.*, and smoking flourish'd o'er his head *D.* ii. 180
The *s.*, be his the Weekly Journals bound *D.* ii. 280
Th' unconscious *s.* sleeps o'er thee like a lake *D.* ii. 304
And the smooth *s.* in smoother numbers flows *E.C.* 367
Oh! while along the *s.* of Time thy name *E.M.* iv. 383
Nor will Life's *s.* for Observation stay *M.E.* i. 37
A painted mistress, or a purling *s. P.S.* 150
Ye weeping Loves, the *s.* with myrtles hide *W.* 23
In a soft, silver *s.* dissolv'd away (*ref.*) *W.F.* 204
His tresses dropp'd with dews, and o'er the *s. W.F.* 331
And s—s *to murmur, e'er* (ere) *I cease to love A.* 42
To where Fleet-ditch with disemboguing *s. D.* ii. 271
He bears no token of the sabler *s. D.* ii. 307
Then tinctur'd as it runs with Lethe's *s. D.* ii. 339
And never wash'd, but in Castalia's *s. D.* iii. 18
As many quit the *s.* that murm'ring fall *D.* iv. 199
Thence endless *s.* of fair Ideas flow *E.* iii. 42
The wand'ring *s.* that shine between the hills *E.A.* 157
As *s.* roll down, enlarging as they flow *E.C.* 192
If crystal *s.* "with pleasing murmurs creep" *E.C.* 352
And there the *s.* in purer rills descend *E.M.* iii. 304
In lavish *s.* to quench a Country's thirst *M.E.* iii. 175

By the *s.* that ever flow *O.* i. 71
As shallow *s.* run dimpling all the way *P.S.* 316
While fish in *s.*, or birds delight in air *R.L.* iii. 163
Soft as he mourn'd, the *s.* forgot to flow *Su.* 5
Ye shady beeches, and ye cooling *s. Su.* 13
And headlong *s.* hang listening in their fall *Su.* 84
No more the *s.* their murmur shall forbear *W.* 57
Adieu, ye vales, ye mountains, *s.* and groves *W.* 89
Our plenteous *s.* a various race supply *W.F.* 141
Thro' the fair scene roll slow the ling'ring *s. W.F.* 217
Not Neptune's self from all his *s.* receives *W.F.* 223
The figur'd *s.* in waves of silver roll'd *W.F.* 335
Cole, whose dark *s.* his flowery islands lave *W.F.* 343
Tho' Tiber's *s.* immortal Rome behold *W.F.* 357
Lost in my fame, as in the sea their *s. W.F.* 362
Commanding tears to *s. from ev'ry eye P.C.* 6

Streaming.
From op'ning skies may *s.* glories shine *E.A.* 341

Street.
And "Oh" (he cry'd) "what *s.*, what lane but knows *D.* ii. 153
Rolls the black troop, and overshades the *s. D.* ii. 360
The shops shut up in ev'ry *s. I.H.* i. 8
And catechis'd in ev'ry *s. I.H.* ii. 112 *s*
And Worldly crying coals from *s.* to *s. M.E.* iii. 62
While all your smutty sisters walk the s—s D. i. 230
S, pav'd with Heroes, Tiber chok'd with Gods *D.* iii. 108
Like the vile straw that's blown about the *s. D.* iii. 289
Stands in the *s.*, abstracted from the crew *E.* v. 43
S., Chairs, and Coxcombs, rush upon my sight *E.* v. 48
Oh but a Wit can study in the *s. S.* vi. 98
For you he walks the *s.* in rain and dust *S.* vii. 73

Strength.
And each from each contracts new *s.* and light *E.* iii. 16
Caracci's *s.*, Correggio's softer line *E.* iii. 37
Where Denham's *s.*, and Waller's sweetness join *E.C.* 361
To want the *s.* of bulls, the fur of bears *E.M.* i. 176
Most *s.* the moving principle requires *E.M.* ii. 67
But *s.* of mind is Exercise, not Rest *E.M.* ii. 104
Gives all the *s.* and colour of our life *E.M.* ii. 122
Grows with his growth, and strengthens with his *s. E.M.* ii. 136
Till one Man's weakness grows the *s.* of all *E.M.* ii. 252
The *s.* he gains is from th' embrace he gives *E.M.* iii. 312
In this one Passion man can *s.* enjoy *M.E.* i. 222
And *s.* of Shade contends with *s.* of Light *M.E.* iv. 82
But this bold Lord with manly *s.* endu'd *R.L.* v. 79
Each man an *Askapart*, of *s.* to toss *S.* viii. 276

Strengthen.
To serve, not suffer, *s.*, not invade *E.M.* iii. 298

Strengthens.
Whose own example *s.* all his laws *E.C.* 679
Each *s.* Reason, and Self-love restrains *E.M.* ii. 80
Grows with his growth, and *s.* with his strength *E.M.* ii. 136

Strephon.
Thus Daphnis spoke, and *S.* thus reply'd *Sp.* 22
The bowl to *S.*, and the lamb to thee *Sp.* 94

Stretch.
Or tricks to show the *s.* of human brain *E.M.* ii. 47
At ev'ry line they s., they yawn, they doze D. ii. 390
Then *s.* thy sight o'er all her rising reign *D.* iii. 65
I *s.* my empty arms I it glides away *E.A.* 238
Shall *s.* thy conquests over half the kind *I.H.* iii. 16
Let his plantations *s.* from down to down *M.E.* iv. 189
And *s.* the Ray to Ages yet unborn *S.* v. 228
Ah luckless Poet I *s.* thy lungs and roar *S.* v. 324
S. his long triumphs down thro' ev'ry age *W.F.* 304
O *s.* thy reign, fair Peace I from shore to shore *W.F.* 407

Stretch'd.
And now the victor *s.* his eager hand *D.* ii. 109
Then down are roll'd the books; *s.* o'er 'em lies *D.* ii. 403
And *s.* on bulks, as usual, Poets lay *D.* ii. 420
S. on the rack of a too easy chair *D.* iv. 342
Huge moles, whose shadow *s.* from shore to shore *M.E.* v. 21
S. to relieve the Idiot and the Poor *S.* v. 226
The Man, who, *s.* in Isis' calm retreat *S.* vi. 116

S. o'er the Poor and Church his iron rod *W F.* 75
S. on the lawn his second hope survey *W.F.* 81
His s.-out arm display'd a volume fair D. iv. 106

Stretches.
Curl *s.* after Gay, but Gay is gone *D.* ii. 127

Stretching.
Or see the *s.* branches long to meet *M.E.* iv. 92

Strew.—*See* Strow.

Strew'd.
See l *s.* with learned dust, his night-cap on *S.* vi. 118

Strews.
Is thine alone the seed that *s.* the plain *E.M.* iii. 37

Strict.
Behold yon Pair, in *s.* embraces join'd *D.* iii. 179
Let the *s.* life of graver mortals be *E.* iv. 21
And rules as *s.* his labour'd work confine *E.C.* 137
Bring then these blessings to a *s.* account *E.M.* iv. 269
Their own *s.* Judges, not a word they spare *S.* vi. 159

Strictly.
Tho' not too *s.* bound to Time and Place *E.* iv. 28

Strides.
Vice with such Giant *s.* comes on amain *E.S.* ii. 6

Strife.
Osborne and Curl accept the glorious *s. D.* ii. 167
For wit and judgment often are at *s. E.C.* 82
But ALL subsists by elemental *s. E.M.* i. 169
The lights and shades, whose well accorded *s. E.M.* ii. 121
See SYDNEY bleeds amid the martial *s. E.M.* iv. 101
Add Nature's, Custom's, Reason's, Passion's *s. M.E.* i. 21
Men, some to Quiet, some to public *S. M.E.* ii. 217
Cease, fond Nature, cease thy *s. O.* v. 5
Born to no Pride, inheriting no *S. P.S.* 392
When (each opinion with the next at *s. S.* iii. 167
But wherefore all this labour, all this *s. S.* iv. 38
Till friend with friend, and families at *s. S.* v. 253

Strike.
There motley images her fancy *s. D.* i. 65
Whether thy hand *s.* out some free design *E.* iii. 3
S. in the sketch, or in the picture glow *E.* iii. 44
From Nature's chain whatever link you *s. E.M.* i. 245
On diff'rent senses, diff'rent objects *s. E.M.* ii. 128
That touching one must *s.* the other too *E.M.* iii. 292
Yes, *s.* that *Wild*, I'll justify the blow (*rep.*) *E.S.* ii. 54
They please as beauties, here as wonders *s. M.E.* i. 144
S. off his Pension, by the setting sun *M.E.* i. 160
Start ev'n from Difficulty, *s.* from Chance *M.E.* iv. 68
They *s.* the Soul and glitter in the Eye *M.* ix. 82
Willing to wound, and yet afraid to *s. P.S.* 203
Bright as the sun, her eyes the gazers *s. R.L.* ii. 13
And *s.* to dust th' imperial tow'rs of Troy *R.L.* iii. 174
Charms *s.* the sight, but merit wins the soul *R.L.* v. 34
And bass and treble voices *s.* the skies *R.L.* v. 42

Strikes.
And *s.* a blush thro' frontless Flattery *E.* ii. 7
Noble and young, who *s.* the heart *I.H.* iii. 11
So Darkness *s.* the sense no less than Light *M.E.* i. 53
But hark I he *s.* the golden lyre *O.* i. 63

Striking.
S. their pensive bosoms—*Here* lies GAY *Ep.* xi. 12
He boarding her, she *s.* sail to him *S.* viii. 231

String.
Wake into voice each silent *s. O.* i. 3
On each enervate *s.* they taught the note *S.* v. 153
Taught not to slack, nor strain its tender s—s E.M. i. 290
Stuck o'er with titles, and hung round with *s. E.M.* iv. 205
Or Popularity ! or Stars and *S. S.* iv. 14
One dip the pencil, and one s. the lyre E. iii. 70
Fair Discretion *s.* the lyre *Mi.* vii. 14

Strip.
Here *s.*, my children I here at once leap in *D.* ii. 275
First *s.* off all her equipage of Pride *E.M.* ii. 44

If QUEENSBURY to *s*. there's no compelling *M.E.* ii. 193
And I not *s*. the gilding off a Knave *S.* i. 115
Stript.
There, *s*., fair *Rhetoric* languish'd on the ground *D.*iv. 24
Strive.
See on the Tooth-pick, Mars and Cupid *s. Mi.* ix. 31
Where wigs with wigs, with sword-knots sword-knots *s.*
  R.L. i. 101
Nor *s*. with all the tempest in my teeth *S.* vi. 301
Here earth and water seem to *s*. again *W.F.* 12
Strives.
S. to extract from his soft, giving palm *D.* ii. 208
When Ajax *s*. some rock's vast weight to throw *E.C.* 370
Invention *s*. to be before in vain *E.S.* ii. 7
Heav'n, when it *s*. to polish all it can *M.E.* ii. 271
Strode.
But, stern as Ajax' spectre, *s*. away *D.* iv. 274
Stroke.
Paulo's free *s*., and Titian's warmth divine *E.* iii. 38
Free as thy *s*., yet faultless as thy line *E.* iii. 64
Barbarian, stay ! that bloody *s*. restrain *E.A.* 103
Which sees no more the *s*., or feels the pain *E.M.* iii. 67
This fatal *s*., this unforeseen Distress *Mi.* ix. 20
Some flying *s*. alone can hit 'em right *M.E.* ii. 154
Some felt the sileot *s*. of mould'ring age *M.E.* v. 11
To wake the soul by tender *s—s of art P.C.* 1
Strok'd.
Then soapt his box, and *s*. his belly down *D.* iv. 495
Stroll'd.
Your wine lock'd up, your butler *s*. abroad *S.* ii. 13
Strong.
One clasp'd in wood, and one in *s*. cow-hide *D.* i. 150
Vig'rous he rises from th' effluvia *s. D.* ii. 105
From the *s*. fate of drams if thou get free *D.* iii. 145
Heady, not *s.* ; o'erflowing, tho' not full *D.* iii. 172
Suspend a while your force inertly *s. D.* iv. 7
S. in new arms, lo ! Giant HANDEL stands *D.* iv. 65
And *s*. impulsive gravity of Head *D.* iv. 76
S. as their charms, and gentle as their soul *E.* iii. 74
This binds in ties more easy, yet more *s. E.* iv. 67
The *s*. connexions, nice dependencies *E.M.* i. 30
At best more watchful this, but that more *s. E.M.* ii. 76
As *s*. or weak, the organs of the frame *E.M.* ii. 130
She but removes weak passions for the *s. E.M.* ii. 158
A mightier Pow'r the *s*. direction sends *E.M.* ii. 165
Or (oft more *s.* than all) the love of ease *E.M.* ii. 170
S. grows the Virtue with his nature mix'd *E.M.* ii. 178
Still for the *s*. too weak, the weak too *s. E.M.* iii. 194
Feign what I will, and paint it e'er so *s. E.S.* ii. 8
The *s*. Antipathy of Good to Bad *E.S.* ii. 198
So firm, yet soft ; so *s.*, yet so refin'd *Ep.* vi. 8
May yield, God knows, to *s*. temptation *I.H.* ii. 182
Tho' *s*. the bent, and quick the turns of mind *M.E.* i. 64
Take the most *s.*, and sort them as you can *M.E.* i. 120
Shall feel your ruling passion *s*. in death *M.E.* i. 263
S. as the Footman, as the Master sweet *Mi.* ix. 106
I grow impatient, and the Tea's too *s. Mi.* ix. 108
Love, *s*. as Death, the Poet led *O.* i. 51
Form a *s*. line about the silver bound *R.L.* ii. 121
But *s*. in sense, and wise without the rules *S.* ii. 10
Milton's *s*. pinion now not Heav'n can bound *S.* v. 99
Serenely pure, and yet divinely *s. S.* vi. 172
One, driv'n by *s*. Benevolence of soul *S.* vi. 276
Stronger.
Taller or *s*. than the weeds they shade *E.M.* i. 40
Self-love still *s.*, as its objects nigh *E.M.* ii. 71
The action of the *s*. to suspend *E.M.* ii. 77
A weaker may surprise, a *s*. take *E.M.* iii. 276
We prize the *s*. effort of his pow'r *M.E.* i. 147
Strongest.
What the weak head with *s*. bias rules *E.C.* 203
And *s*. motive to assist the rest *E.M.* iv. 352
Strongly.
Converse and Love mankind might *s*. draw *E.M.* iii. 207
Then *s*. fencing ill-got wealth by law *S.* vii. 93
Strove.
Where tawdry yellow *s*. with dirty red *M.E.* iii. 304
When rival beauties for the Present *s. Mi.* ix. 38

Strow.
In throngs promiscuous *s*. the level green *R.L.* iii. 80
Struck.
And glitt'ring thoughts *s*. out at ev'ry line *E.C.* 290
Be *s*. with bright Brocade, or Tyrian Dye *S.* iv. 32
Structure.
Then lights the *s.*, with averted eyes *D.* i. 247
There stands a *s*. of majestic frame *R.L.* iii. 3
Struggling.
Who gently drawn, and *s*. less and less *D.* iv. 83
And both the *s*. figures seem alive *Mi.* ix. 32
A brave man *s*. in the storms of fate *P.C.* 21
Strumpet.
Come here in crowds, and stare the *s*. down *E.J.S.* 50
He tells what places *s—s sell for life S.* viii. 148
Strung.
Who now shall charm the shades where Cowley *s. W.F.* 279
Strut.
Lord ! how we *s*. thro' Merlin's Cave, to see *S.* vi. 139
I neither *s*. with ev'ry fav'ring breath *S.* vi. 300
And why not players *s*. in courtiers' clothes *S.* viii. 222
Struts.
He *s*. Adonis, and affects grimace *D.* ii. 202
Tom *s*. a Soldier, open, bold, and brave *M.E.* i. 153
That robe of Quality so *s*. and swells *M.E.* ii. 189
Now trips a Lady, and now *s*. a Lord *P.S.* 329
Stuart.
And peace and plenty tell, a *S*. reigns *W.F.* 42
Stubble.
Molière's old *s*. in a moment flames *D.* i. 254
Stubborn.
Each staunch Polemic, *s*. as a rock *D.* iv. 195
By Nature yielding, *s*. but for fame *E.* iv. 35
Nor pray'rs nor fasts its *s*. pulse restrain *E.A.* 27
Or tames the Genius of the *s*. plain *S.* i. 131
Stucco.
Grotesco roofs, and *S*. floors *I.H.* ii. 192
For your damn'd *S*. has no chink *I.H.* ii. 217
Stuck.
S. o'er with titles, and hung round with strings *E.M.* iv. 205
He *s*. to poverty with peace of mind *S.* vi. 65
Student.
How Index-learning turns no *s*. pale *D.* i. 279
Studious.
More *s*. to divide than to unite *E.M.* ii. 82
'Twas then the *s*. head or gen'rous mind *E.M.* iii. 283
Studiously.
Approach ! Great Nature *s*. behold *Mi.* x. 7
Study.
Be Homer's works your *s*. and delight *E.C.* 124
The proper *s*. of Mankind is Man *E.M.* ii. 2
Who from his *s*. rails at human-kind *M.E.* i. 2
His *S.* i with what Authors is it stor'd *M.E.* iv. 133
Sound sleep by night ; *s*. and ease *O.* iv. 13
Pains, reading, *s.*, are their just pretence *P.S.* 159
To books and *s*. gives seven years complete *S.* vi. 117
Successive *s.*, exercise and ease *W.F.* 240
So mix'd our *s—ies, and so join'd our name E.* iii. 10
Nor blush these *s*. thy regard engage *M.E.* v. 49
Happy my *s.*, when by thee approv'd *P.S.* 143
And Reason giv'n them but to *s. Flies D.* iv. 454
Who *s*. Shakespear at the Inns of Court *D.* iv. 568
And while he seems to *s.*, thinks of you *E.* v. 44
Oh but a Wit can *s*. in the streets *S.* vi. 98
Just at his *S*.-door he'll bless your eyes *M.E.* iv. 132
Study'd.
I *s*. SHREWSBURY, the wise and great *E.S.* ii. 79
Studying.
Agrees as ill with Rufa *s*. Locke *M.E.* ii. 23

Stuff.

What woful *s.* this madrigal would be *E.C.* 418
Becomes the *s.* of which our dream is wrought *M.E.* i. 48
To stop my ears to their confounded *s. S.* vi. 152
For thee we dim the eyes, and *s.* the head *D.* iv. 249

Stuff'd.

But having amply *s.* his skin *I.H.* i. 53

Stuffs.

He *s.* and swills, and *s.* again *I.H.* ii. 205

Stumbling.

As, after *s.*, Jades will mend their pace *E.C.* 603

Stung.

And no man wonders he's not *s.* by Pug *S.* i. 88

Stunn'd.

S. with his giddy Larum half the town *D.* iv. 292
And *s.* him with the music of the spheres *E.M.* i. 202
One lull'd th' Exchequer, and one *s.* the Rolls *S.* vi. 130

Stunted.

Like *s.* hide-bound Trees, that just have got *Mi.* iii. 11

Stupefaction.

From Impudence, or *S.* mild *D.* iv. 530

Stupefied.

Sits Mother Osborne, *s.* to stone *D.* ii. 312

Stupendous.

Far as loud Bow's *s.* bells resound *D.* iii. 278
All are but parts of one *s.* whole *E.M.* i. 267
So proud, so grand, of that *s.* air *M.E.* iv. 101

Stupid.

Of *s.* starers, and of loud huzzas *E.M.* iv. 256
What turns him now a *s.* silent dunce *M.E.* i. 163

Sturdy.

The *s.* Squire to Gallic masters stoop *D.* iv. 595
A desp'rate *Bulwark*, *s.*, firm, and fierce *Mi.* ii. 13

Sturgeon.

Who has not learn'd, fresh *s.* and ham-pie *S.* ii. 103

Style.

Their praise is still—the *S.* is excellent *E.C.* 307
Such labour'd nothings in so strange a *s. E.C.* 326
How the wit brightens! how the *s.* refines *E.C.* 421
O come, that easy Ciceronian *s. E.S.* i. 73
His sly, polite, insinuating *s. E.S.* i. 19
When ev'ry Coxcomb knows me by my *s. P.S.* 282
The Doctor's Wormwood *s.*, the flash of tongues *S.* iii. 52
"But, Sir, of writers?" "Swift, for closer *s. S.* viii. 72
At all my peevishness, and turns his *s. S.* viii. 123
For diff'rent *s—s* with diff'rent subjects sort *E.C.* 322
S. the divine, the matchless, what you will S. v. 70

Styptics.

Or Alum *s.* with contracting pow'r *R.L.* ii. 131

Styx.

A branch of *S.* here rises from the shades *D.* ii. 338
With *S.* nine times round her *O.* i. 91

Subdue.

Oh come! oh teach my nature to *s. E.A.* 203
The young disease, that must *s.* at length *E.M.* ii. 135
Had still this Monster to *s.* at last *S.* v. 18

Subdu'd.

And the world's victor stood *s.* by sound *E.C.* 381
The pow'rs of all *s.* by thee alone *E.M.* i. 231
Rome learning arts from Greece, whom she *s. P.C.* 40
She with one finger and a thumb *s. R.L.* v. 80
The Gaul *s.*, or Property secur'd *S.* v. 10
Where Jove, *s.* by mortal Passion still *W.F.* 233

Subject.

His fable, *s.*, scope in ev'ry page *E.C.* 120
Made him observe the *s.*, and the plot *E.C.* 275
As leaves them scarce a *s.* in their Age *M.E.* ii. 222
Slight is the *s.*, but not the praise *R.L.* i. 5
Than mine, to find a *s.* stay'd and wise *S.* viii. 168
What wonder then, a beast or *s.* slain *W.F.* 57
But while the *s.* starv'd, the beast was fed *W.F.* 60
Back to his bounds their *s.* Sea command *M.E.* iv. 201

For diff'rent styles with diff'rent *s—s* sort *E.C.* 322
Where Heav'n's free *s.* might their rights dispute *E.C.* 548
We, wretched *s.*, tho' to lawful sway *E.M.* ii. 149
And Gods of Conqu'rors, Slaves of *S.* made *E.M.* iii. 248
Succeeding monarchs heard the *s—s*' cries *W.F.* 85
S., compound them, follow her and God E.M. ii. 116

Subjected.

S., these to those, and all to thee *E.M.* i. 230
In one short view *s.* to our eye *M.E.* v. 33

Sublime.

And is himself that great *S.* he draws *E.C.* 680
Tho' daring Milton sits *s. I.H.* iv. 5

Sublimely.

And He, whose fustian's so *s.* bad *P.S.* 187

Sublimer.

To heav'nly themes *s.* strains belong *M.* 2

Sublimes.

Which not alone the southern wit *s. E.C.* 400

Submission.

I'm all *s.*, what you'd have it, make it *P.S.* 46

Submit.

In both, to reason right is to *s. E.M.* i. 164
S.—In this, or any other sphere *E.M.* i. 285
To him each Rival shall *s. I.H.* iii. 17
And monuments, like men, *s.* to fate *R.L.* iii. 172

Submitting.

Charms by accepting, by *s.* sways *M.E.* ii. 263

Subscribe.

And others roar aloud, "*S., s.*" *P.S.* 114

Subscriptions.

South-sea *S.* take who please *I.H.* i. 65
Stocks and *S.* pour on ev'ry side *M.E.* iii. 370

Subservient.

Most Critics, fond of some *s.* art *E.C.* 263

Subside.

At length the wits mount up, the hairs *s. R.L.* iv. 74

Subsided.

How barb'rous rage *s.* at your word *S.* v. 398

Subsides.

When Sense *s.*, and Fancy sports in sleep *M.E.* i. 46
The Soul *s.*, and wickedly inclines *S.* ii. 79

Subsist.

S. not in the good of one, but all *E.M.* iv. 38

Subsists.

But ALL *s.* by elemental strife *E.M.* i. 169
Your scene precariously *s.* too long *P.C.* 41

Substance.

But like a shadow, proves the *s.* true *E.C.* 467
But airy *s.* soon unites again *R.L.* iii. 152

Subterranean.

Here *s.* works and cities see *E.M.* iii. 181

Subtile.

Or draw to silk Arachne's *s.* line *D.* iv. 590

Subtle.

Let *s.* schoolmen teach these friends to fight *E.M.* ii. 81
Unlearn'd, he knew no *s.* schoolman's art *P.S.* 398
This *s.* Thief of life, this paltry Time *S.* vi. 76
A *s.* Minister may make of that *S.* viii. 133

Subtlest.

Make Scots speak treason, cozen *s.* whores *S.* viii. 59

Subtly.

In the nice bee, what sense so *s.* true *E.M.* i. 219

Succeed.

Alone can rival, can *s.* to thee *E.A.* 206
To leafless shrubs the flow'ring palms *s. M.* 75
Alike my scorn, if he *s.* or fail *P.S.* 362
Observe how seldom ev'n the best *s. S.* v. 286

Succeeded.
And straight s., leaving shame no room *D.* iv. 531
Succeeding.
Like them to shine thro' long s. age *E.* iii. 11
Thus long s. Critics justly reign'd *E.C.* 681
S. vanities she still regards *R.L.* i. 53
S. monarchs heard the subjects' cries *W.F.* 85
Succeeds.
Another love s., another race *E.M.* iii. 130
But just disease to luxury s. *E.M.* iii. 165
The centre mov'd, a circle straight s. *E.M.* iv. 365
Still, when the lust of tyrant pow'r s. *O.* ii. 31
When milder autumn summer's heat s. *W.F.* 97
Success.
And act, and be, a Coxcomb with s. *D.* i. 110
For when s. a Lover's toil attends *R.L.* ii. 33
Succession.
And sure s. down from Heywood's days *D.* i. 98
In sure s. to the day of doom *S.* viii. 161
Successive.
S. study, exercise, and ease *W.F.* 240
Succinct.
On some, a Priest s. in amice white *D.* iv. 549
Four knaves in garbs s., a trusty band *R.L.* iii. 41
Succour.
Ye Mantuan nymphs, your sacred s. bring *A.* 5
Such.—*Passim.*
Suck.
Wolves gave thee s., and savage tigers fed *A.* 90
S. *the thread in, then yield it out again D.* iii. 58
S. my last breath, and catch my flying soul *E.A.* 324
Or s. the mists in grosser air below *R.L.* ii. 83
Suck'd.
And s. all o'er, like an industrious Bug *D.* i. 130
Smit with his mien the Mud-nymphs s. him in *D.* ii. 332
Suckle.
And s. armies, and dry-nurse the land *D.* i. 316
Suckled.
S., and cheer'd, with air, and sun, and show'r *D.* iv. 406
Suckles.
S. each herb, and spreads out ev'ry flow'r *E.M.* i. 134
Sudden.
Let spring attend, and s. flow'rs arise *A.* 36
S. she flies, and whelms it o'er the pyre *D.* i. 259
All s., Gorgons hiss, and Dragons glare *D.* iii. 235
Alas, how chang'd ! what s. horrors rise *E.A.* 99
S. you mount, you beckon from the skies *E.A.* 245
See lilies spring, and s. verdure rise *M.* 68
S., she storms ! she raves ! You tip the wink *M.E.* ii. 33
The mushrooms shew his wit was s. *Mi.* xii. 11
Spent in a s. storm of lust *O.* ii. 9
S., these honours shall be snatch'd away *R.L.* iii. 103
S. he view'd, in spite of all her art *R.L.* iii. 143
S., with startling tears each eye o'erflows *R.L.* v. 85
A s. Star, it shot thro' liquid air *R.L.* v. 127
A soft retreat from s. vernal show'rs *S‡.* 98
On all the line a s. vengeance waits *U.L.* 37
S. they seize th' amaz'd, defenceless prize *W.F.* 109
Sue.
There Kings shall s., and suppliant States be seen *W.F.* 383
Sues.
Bless me ! a packet.—"'Tis a stranger s. *P.S.* 55
Suffer.
We never s. it to stand too wide *D.* iv. 154
Or who could s. Being here below *E.M.* i. 80
To serve, not s., strengthen, not invade *E.M.* iii. 298
Who s. thus, mere Charity should own *M.E.* iii. 111
Much do I s., much, to keep in peace *S.* vi. 147
Suff'rers.
And certain Laws, by s. thought unjust *S.* vi. 60

Suff'ring.
Here all his s. brotherhood retire *D.* i. 143
Still in constraint your s. sex remains *E.* iv. 41
Why doing, s., check'd, impell'd : and why *E.M.* i. 67
The s. eye inverted Nature sees *M.E.* iv. 119
Suff'rings.
Compos'd in s., and in joy sedate *E‡.* vii. 3
Suffers.
Nor s. Horace more in wrong Translations *E.C.* 663
Impartial, she shall say who s. most *Mi.* ix. 25
Suffice.
S. that Reason keep to Nature's road *E.M.* ii. 115
Sufficient.
Teach but that one, s. for a King *D.* iv. 284
S. sap at once to bear and rot *Mi.* iii. 12
Suffolk.
Cheese, such as men in S. make *I.H.* ii. 167
Suidas.
I poach in S. for unlicens'd Greek *D.* iv. 228
Suit.
Others a sword-knot, and lac'd s. inflame *D.* ii. 52
'Th' embroider'd s. at least he deem'd his prey (*rep.*) *D.* ii. 117
Known by the band and s. which Settle wore (*rep.*) *D.* iii. 37
In a translated S., then tries the Town *Mi.* iii. 21
Or when from Court a birth-day s. bestow'd *S.* v. 332
I think Sir Godfrey should decide the s. *S.* vi. 24
Had no new verses, nor new s. to show *S.* viii. 13
The s., if by the fashion one might guess *S.* viii. 40
No Courts he saw, no s—s would ever try P.S. 396
Thus Worms v. all Conditions Mi. iv. 22
Suitable.
Appears more decent, as more s. *E.C.* 319
Suits.
Know, all enjoy that pow'r which s. them best *E.M.* iii. 80
In me 'tis noble, s. my birth and state *S.* ii. 113
S. Tyrants, Plunderers, but s. not me *S.* viii. 195
Sullen.
S. moans *O.* i. 60
No cheerful breeze this s. region knows *R.L.* iv. 19
Dull s. pris'ners in the body's cage *U.L.* 18
And s. Mole, that hides his diving flood *W.F.* 347
Sully'd.
As ever s. the fair face of light *R.L.* iv. 14
Sulphur-tipt.
Not s. emblaze an Ale-house fire *D.* i. 235
Sultry.
Who hung with woods yon mountain's s. brow *M.E.* iii. 253
The s. Sirius burns the thirsty plains *Su.* 21
When weary reapers quit the s. field *Su.* 65
And now his shorter breath, with s. air *W.F.* 195
Sum.
Then see how little the remaining s. *E.M.* ii. 51
Why she and Sappho raise that monstrous s. *M.E.* iii. 121
Oh say, what s—s that gen'rous hand supply *M.E.* iii. 277
Where all cry out, "What s. are thrown away !" *M.E.* iv. 100
Summer.
Ye birds that, left by s., cease to sing *A.* 28
That laugh'd down many a S. Sun *I.H.* i. 47
Whose trees in s. yield him shade *O.* iv. 7
When milder autumn s.'s heat succeeds W.F. 97
And there a S.-house that knows no shade M.E. iv 122
While s.-*suns* toll unperceiv'd away *E.* iii. 18
Summon.
They s. all her Race : an endless band *D.* ii. 19
Summon'd.
And all the Nations s. to the Throne *D.* iv. 72
'Twas he had s. to her silent bed *R.L.* i. 21

310   SUMMONS—SUPPLY.

Summons.
That *s.* you to all the Pride of Pray'r *M.E.* iv. 142
He *s.* straight his Denizens of air *R.L.* ii. 55

Sun.
And the low *s.* had lengthen'd ev'ry shade *A.* 100
Far eastward cast thine eye, from whence the *S, D.*iii.73
Sick was the *S.,* the Owl forsook his Bow'r *D.* iv. 11
Suckl'd, and cheer'd, with air, and *s.,* and show'r *D.* iv. 406
Turn'd to the *S.,* she casts a thousand dyes *D.* iv. 539
Pair'd with his Fellow-Charioteer the *S. D.* iv. 588
But true expression, like th' unchanging *s. E.C.* 315
And force that *s.* but on a part to shine *E.C.* 399
When first that *s.* too pow'rful beams displays *E.C.* 470
Warms in the *s.,* refreshes in the breeze *E.M.* i. 271
Correct old time and regulate the *s. E.M.* ii. 22
And turn their heads to imitate the *S. E.M.* ii. 28
Yet make at once their circle round the *S. E.M.* iii. 314
Hold out some months 'twixt *S.* and Fire *I.H.* i. 18
That laugh'd down many a Summer *S. I.H.* i. 47
No more the rising *S.* shall gild the morn *M.* 99
Tho' the same *S.* with all-diffusive rays *M.E.* i. 145
Strike off his Pension, by the setting *s. M.E.* i. 160
Flam'd forth this rival to its Sire, the *S. M.E.* iii. 12
Spread like a low-born Mist, and blot the *S. M.E.*iii.138
Productive as the *S. O.* iii. 24
Ere to the main this morning *s.* descend *R.L.* i. 110
The *S.* first rises o'er the purpl'd main *R.L.* ii. 2
Bright as the *s.,* her eyes the gazers strike *R.L.* ii. 13
Some to the *s.* their insect-wings unfold *R.L.* ii. 59
His purple pinions op'ning to the *s. R.L.* ii. 71
The *s.* obliquely shoots his burning ray *R.L.* iii. 20
Then, like the *S.,* let Bounty spread her ray *S.* ii. 115
Self-center'd *S.,* and Stars that rise and fall *S.* vi. 6
He walks, an object new beneath the *s. S.* vi. 119
Ploughs, burns, manures, and toils from *s.* to *s. S.*vi.271
The *s.* e'er got, or slimy Nilus bore *S.* viii. 29
Hast thou, oh *S.!* beheld an emptier sort *S.* viii. 204
But soon the *s.* with milder rays descends *Su.* 89
All else beneath the *S. U.P.* 46
His shadow lengthen'd by the setting *s. W.F.* 194
So from the *S.'s broad beam in shallow urns D.* ii. 11
So when the *S.* broad beam has tir'd the sight *M.E.*ii.253
The *S.* mild lustre warms the vital air *Sp.* 74
And other planets circle other s—s *D.* iii. 244
Yon stars, yon *s.,* he rears at pleasure higher *D.* iii. 259
What other planets circle other *s. E.M.* i. 26
Seas roll to waft me, *s.* to light me rise *E.M.* i. 139
From burning *s.* when livid deaths descend *E.M.* i. 142
Planets and *S.* run lawless thro' the sky *E.M.* i. 252
Three thousand *s.* went down on *Welsted's* lie *P.S.* 375
When those fair *s.* shall set, as set they must *R.L.* v. 147
Those *S.* of Glory please not till they set *S.* v. 22
Soft show'rs distill'd, and *s.* grew warm in vain *W.F.* 54
The s.-beams *trembling on the floating tides R.L.* ii. 48
Where dancing *s.* on the waters play'd *Su.* 3
Eyes the calm *S.-set* of thy various Day *E.* i. 38
Not show'rs to larks, nor *s.-shine* to the bee *A.* 45
Eternal *s.* of thy spotless mind *E.A.* 209
Of show'rs and *s.,* as of Man's desires *E.M.* i. 152
The soul's calm *s.,* and the heart-felt joy *E.M.* iv. 168

Sunday.
Ev'n *S.* shines no Sabbath-day to me *P.S.* 12
His *Counting-house employ'd* the *S.*-morn *M.E.* iii. 380

Sung.
Hylas and Ægon *s.* their rural lays *A.* 2
Next Ægon *s.,* while Windsor groves admir'd *A.* 55
Thus *s.* the shepherds till th' approach of night *A.* 97
What City Swans once *s.* within the walls *D.* ii. 96
Then *s.,* how shown him by the Nut-brown maids *D.* ii. 337
How sweet the periods, neither said, nor *s. D.* iii. 202
Such were the notes thy once-lov'd Poet *s. E.* i. 1
And these be *s.* till Granville's Mira die *E.* iii. 76
Guiltless I gaz'd; heav'n listen'd while you *s. E.C.* 65
Yet judg'd with coolness, tho' he *s.* with fire *E.C.* 639
A Raphael painted, and a Vida *s. E.C.* 704
And all I *s.* should be the *Nation's Sense E.S.* i. 78
He *s.,* and hell consented *O.* i. 83
Yet ev'n in death Eurydice he *s. O.* i. 113
'Tis *s.* when Midas' Ears began to spring *P.S.* 69
Poets themselves must fall, like those they *s. U.L.* 75
Here too, 'tis *s.,* of old Diana stray'd *W.F.* 165

Here his first lays majestic Denham *s. W.F.* 271
His living harp, and lofty Denham *s. W.F.* 280
First in these fields I *s.* the sylvan strain *W.F.* 434

Sunk.
There *s.* Thalia, nerveless, cold, and dead *D.* iv. 41
There *Talbot s.,* and was a Wit no more *D.* iv. 168
Some *s.* to Beasts, find pleasure end in pain *E.M.* iv. 23
Lamented DIGBY ! *s.* thee to thy grave *E.M.* iv. 104
And all that rais'd the Hero, *s.* the Man *E.M.* iv. 294
Then see them broke with toils, or *s.* in ease *E.M.*iv.297
Nor puff'd by Pride, nor *s.* by Spleen *I.H.* ii. 28
See Britain *s.* in lucre's sordid charms *M.E.* iii. 143
Not *s.* by sloth, nor rais'd by servitude *M.E.* iii. 222
S. in Thalestris' arms the nymph he found *R.L.* iv. 89
Cry'd Dapperwit, and *s.* beside his chair *R.L.* iv. 62
For ever *s.* too low, or borne too high *S.* v. 299

Sunny.
Where bask on *s.* banks the simple sheep *D.* iv. 352

Sup.
Bid me with Pollio *s.,* as well as dine *D.* iv. 392
Or when I *s.,* or when I dine *I.H.* ii. 134

Supercargoes.
Thieves, *S.,* Sharpers and Directors *S.* i. 72

Superfluity.
And shine that *s.* away *S.* ii. 116
A noble *s.* it craves *S.* iv. 91

Superfluous.
In all the madness of *s.* health *E.M.* iii. 3

Superior.
One on his vigour and *s.* size *D.* ii. 170
There mov'd Montalto with *s.* air *D.* iv. 105
But Fop shews Fop *s.* complaisance *D.* ii. 138
T' admire *s.* sense, and doubt their own *E.C.* 200
That only makes *s.* sense belov'd *E.C.* 577
From thee to Nothing.—On *s.* pow'rs *E.M.* i. 241
S. beings, when of late they saw *E.M.* ii. 31
Alas what wonder! Man's *s.* part *E.M.* ii. 39
In Parts *s.* what advantage lies *E.M.* iv. 259
But lost, dissolv'd in thy *s.* rays *M.* 101
S. by the head, was Ariel plac'd *R.L.* ii. 70
S—s? *death ! and Equals! what a curse M.E.* ii. 135

Super-lunar.
The head that turns at *s.* things *D.* iv. 451

Superstition.
Ev'n *s.* loses ev'ry fear *E.A.* 315
With Tyranny, then *S.* join'd *E.C.* 687
Till *S.* taught the tyrant awe *E.M.* iii. 246
A gen'rous Faith, from *s.* free *Ep.* ii. 9

Supperless.
Swearing and *s.,* the Hero sate *D.* i. 115

Supple.
Awkward and *s.,* each devoir to pay *Mi.* iii. 17

Suppliant.
There Kings shall sue, and *s.* States be seen *W.F.* 383
The first thus open'd: "Hear thy *s.*'s call *D.* iv. 403

Supplies.
Thence Beauty, waking all her forms, *s. E.* iii. 45
Like some fair flow'r the early spring *s. E.C.* 498
His charitable Vanity *s. M.E.* iv. 172
What thanks, what praise, if *Peter* but *s. S.* vii. 67

Supply.
Art from that fund each just *s.* affords *E.C.* 74
Let Courtly Wits to Wits afford *s. E.S.* ii. 171
Blest paper-credit ! last and best *s. M.E.* iii. 39
With reams abundant this abode s. *D.* ii. 90
Manilius or Solinus shall *s. D.* iv. 226
Let us (since Life can little more *s. E.M.* i. 3
See anger, zeal and fortitude *s. E.M.* ii. 187
See some fit Passion ev'ry age *s. E.M.* ii. 273
All forms that perish other forms *s. E.M.* iii. 17
Oh say, what sums that gen'rous hand *s. M.E.* v. 56
And vanquish'd realms *s.* recording gold *M.E.* v. 56
Whose flocks *s.* him with attire *O.* iv. 6
Snuff, or the fan, *s.* each pause of chat *R.L.* iii. 17
Our plenteous streams a various race *s. W.F.* 141

SUPPLY'D—SURVEY'ST. 311

Supply'd.
Each want of happiness by hope s. *E.M.* ii. 285
Then careful Heav'n s. two sorts of Men *M.E.* iii. 13
Her Trade supported, and s. her Laws *S.* v. 222

Support.
Harley, the Nation's great s. *I.H.* i. 83
Four guardian Virtues, round, s. her throne *D.* i. 46
Thou, Cibber! thou, his Laurel shalt s. *D.* i. 299
S. his front, and Oaths bring up the rear *D.* i. 308
These, only these, s. the crowded stage *S.* v. 87

Supported.
Man, like the gen'rous vine, s. lives *E.M.* iii. 311
Her Trade s., and supply'd her Laws *S.* v. 222

Supports.
And drawn s., upheld by God, or thee *E.M.* i. 34
The Wood s. the Plain, the parts unite *M.E.* iv. 81

Suppose.
S. I censure—you know what I mean *E.S.* ii. 32
Our fathers prais'd rank Ven'son. You s. *S.* ii. 91
S. he wants a year, will you compound *S.* v. 57
Of little use the Man you may s. *S.* v. 201

Suppress.
S. them, or miscall them Policy *M.E.* i. 124

Suppress'd, Supprest.
I can no more; by shame, by rage s. *E.A.* 105
Thrice Budgel aim'd to speak, but thrice s—t *D.* ii. 397
Till fate scarce felt his gentle breath s. *E.* iv. 13

Supreme.
Tyrant s.! shall three Estates command *D.* iv. 603
A Soul s. in each hard instance try'd *E.* i. 23
He, who s. in judgment, as in wit *E.C.* 657

Supremely.
S. blest, the poet in his Muse *E.M.* ii. 270

Surcingle.
Gave him the cassock, s., and vest *D.* ii. 350

Sure.
And s. succession down from Heywood's days *D.* i. 98
Guard the s. barrier between that and Sense *D.* i. 178
Yet s. had Heav'n decreed to save the state *D.* i. 195
S. sign that no spectator shall be drown'd *D.* ii. 174
The s. fore-runner of her gentle sway *D.* iii. 300
None need a guide, by s. attraction led *D.* iv. 75
Else s. some Bard, to our eternal praise *D.* iv. 171
For s., if Dulness sees a grateful Day *D.* iv. 181
Be s. I give them Fragments, not a Meal *D.* iv. 230
With the same CEMENT, ever s. to bind *D.* iv. 267
And s., if aught below the seats divine *E.* i. 21
S. to charm all was his peculiar fate *E.* iv. 5
This s. is bliss (if bliss on earth there be) *E.A.* 97
'Tis s. the hardest science to forget *E.A.* 190
And s., if fate some future bard shall join *E.A.* 359
Be s. yourself and your own reach to know *E.C.* 48
S. to hate most the men from whom they learn'd *E.C.* 107
With s. returns of still expected rhymes *E.C.* 349
S. some to vex, but never all to please *E.C.* 505
As shameful s. as Impotence in love *E.C.* 533
And speak, tho' s., with seeming diffidence *E.C.* 567
And s. such kind good creatures may be living *E.J.S.* 28
S. never to o'er-shoot, but just to hit *E.M.* iii. 89
How much of other each is s. to cost *E.M.* iv. 271
Then better s. it Charity becomes *E.S.* ii. 48
S., if I spare the Minister, no rules *E.S.* ii. 146
S., if they cannot cut, it may be said *E.S.* ii. 148
One would not, s., be frightful when one's dead *M.E.* i. 250
Yet ne'er so s. one passion to create *M.E.* ii. 51
Yet Chloe s. was form'd without a spot *M.E.* ii. 157
S., if they catch, to spoil the Toy at most *M.E.* ii. 233
Yet s., of qualities deserving praise *M.E.* iii. 201
Constant at Church and Change; his gains were s. *M.E.* iii. 347
And when I die, be s. you let me know *P.S.* 123
Nor could it s. be such a sin to paint *R.L.* v. 24
The Man that loves and laughs must s. do well *S.* iv. 129
S. fate of all, beneath whose rising ray *S.* v. 19
But for the Passions, Southern s. and Rowe *S.* v. 86
With laughter s. Democritus had died *S.* v. 320

The people, s., the people are the sight *S.* v. 323
And little s. imported to remove *S.* vi. 56
S. I should want the care of ten Monroes *S.* vi. 70
But s. no statute in his favour says *S.* vi. 288
In s. succession to the day of doom *S.* viii. 161

Surely.
And s. Heav'n and I are of a mind *M.E.* iii. 8
Yet s., s., these were famous men *S.* v. 79

Surest.
The s. Virtues thus from Passions shoot *E.M.* ii. 183

Suretyship.
'Twas only S. that brought 'em there *S.* vii. 70

Surface.
On Learning's s. we but lie and nod *D.* iv. 242

Surfeit.
In which none e'er could s., none could starve *S.* vii. 120

Surge.
The s., and plunge his Father in the deep *M.E.* iii. 354
But when loud s—s lash the sounding shore *E.C.* 368

Surly.
Another in a s. fit *I.H.* ii. 55 s
Which made old Ben, and s. Dennis swear *S.* v. 388

Surmis'd.
In South-sea days not happier, when s. *S.* ii. 133

Surmises.
Hence guilty joys, distastes, s. *O.* iii. 37

Surprise.
But more advanc'd, behold with strange s. *E.C.* 223
The swain in barren deserts with s. *M.* 67
Procure a TASTE to double the s. *S.* iv. 30
Already half turn'd traitor by s. *S.* viii. 169
Dangers, doubts, delays, s—s *O.* iii. 39
Then Churchill's race shall other hearts s. *E.* iii. 59
A weaker may s., a stronger take *E.M.* iii. 276
No single parts unequally s. *E.C.* 249
Hear how Timotheus' vary'd lays s. *E.C.* 374
Slight lines of hair s. the finny prey *R.L.* ii. 26

Surpris'd.
S. at better, or s. at worse *S.* iv. 23

Surprises.
S., varies, and conceals the Bounds *M.E.* iv. 56

Surrey.
Here noble S. felt the sacred rage (rep.) *W.F.* 291

Surround.
The busy Sylphs s. their darling care *R.L.* i. 145
Swarm o'er the lawns, the forest walks s. *W.F.* 149

Surrounded.
Now with Furies s. *O.* i. 106

Surrounding.
The bow'ry mazes, and s. greens *W.F.* 262

Surrounds.
Which flaming Phlegethon s. *O.* i. 50

Survey.
But, those attain'd, we tremble to s. *E.C.* 229
S. the WHOLE, nor seek slight faults to find *E.C.* 235
The face of Nature we oo more s. *E.C.* 313
Pleas'd the green lustre of the scales s. *M.* 83
Tenants with sighs the smokeless tow'rs s. *M.E.* iii. 191
Fanes, which admiring Gods with pride s. *M.E.* v. 9
Methinks already I your tears s. *R.L.* iv. 107
Propp'd on their bodkin spears the Sprites s. *R.L.* v. 55
This the Beau Monde shall from the Mall s. *R.L.* v. 133
S. both worlds, intrepid and entire *S.* vi. 312
See them s. their limbs by Durer's rules *S.* viii. 240
Stretch'd on the lawn his second hope s. *W.F.* 81
S. the region, and confess her home *W.F.* 256

Survey'd.
Heav'n scarce believ'd the conquest it s. *E.A.* 113

Survey'st.
With joyful pride s. our lofty woods *W.F.* 220

Surveys.
And Milo-like *s.* his arms and hands *D.* ii. 284
S. around her, in the blest abode *D.* iii. 233
Heav'n still with laughter the vain toil *s. E.M.* iv. 75
But what with pleasure Heav'n itself *s. P.C.* 20
Where Thames with pride *s.* his rising tow'rs *R.L.* ii. 2
And from the brink his dancing shade *s. Sp.* 34

Survive.
And love of Ombre, after death *s. R.L.* i. 56
Not scornful virgins who their charms *s. R.L.* iv. 4
Rather than so, ah let me still *s. R.L.* v. 101

Surviv'd.
But sense *s.,* when merry jests were past *E.C.* 460
When Patriarch-wits *s.* a thousand years *E.C.* 479

Suspend.
S. a while your Force inertly strong *D.* iv. 7
The action of the stronger to *s. E.M.* ii. 77
Shall list'ning in mid air *s.* their wings *W.* 54

Suspends.
Now Jove *s.* his golden scales in air *R.L.* v. 71

Suspense.
A cool *s.* from pleasure and from pain *E.A.* 250

Suspicion.
Or caus'd *s.* when no soul was rude *R.L.* iv. 73

Suspicious.
A tim'rous foe, and a *s.* friend *P.S.* 206

Sustain.
See dying vegetables life *s. E.M.* ii. 15
And four fair Queens whose hands *s.* a flow'r *R.L.* iii. 39
While you, great Patron of Mankind! *s. S.* v. 1

Sustain'd.
The Saint *s.* it, but the Woman died *Ep.* vi. 10

Sustains.
Each motion guides, and ev'ry nerve *s. E.C.* 78
A mightier grief my heavy heart *s. Mi.* ix. 10

Swain.
Not bubbling fountains to the thirsty *s. A.* 43
Or whirligigs twirl'd round by skilful *s. D.* iii. 57
Wafts the smooth Eunuch, and enamour'd *s. D.* iv. 310
Was ever such a happy *S. I.H.* ii. 204
The *s.* in barren deserts with surprise *M.* 67
Health to the sick, and solace to the *s. M.E.* iii. 258
Then hid in shades, eludes her eager *s. Sp.* 54
The *s.* with tears his frustrate labour yields *W.F.* 55
And secret transport touch'd the conscious *s. W.F.* 90
Safe on my shore each unmolested *s. W.F.* 369
Oh, skill'd in Nature! see the hearts of S—s *A.* 11
Two *S.,* whom Love kept wakeful, and the Muse *Sp.* 18
Blest *S.,* whose Nymphs in ev'ry grace excel (*rep.*) *Sp.* 95
Let other *s.* attend the rural care *Su.* 35
For you the *s.* the fairest flow'rs design *Su.* 55
When *s.* from shearing seek their nightly bow'rs *Su.* 64
The fields are ravish'd from th' industrious *s. W.F.* 65
Ye vig'rous *s.!* while youth ferments your blood *W.F.* 93
Enough for me, that to the list'ning *s. W.F.* 433

Swallow.
And *s—s* roost in Nilus' dusty urn *M.E.* iv. 126
When earth-quakes *s.,* or when tempests sweep *E.M.* i. 143
And quick to *s.* me, methought I saw *S.* viii. 172

Swallows.
And one wide conflagration *s.* all *D.* iii. 240
Like Aaron's serpent *s.* up the rest *E.M.* ii. 112
Takes, opens, *s.* it before their sight *Mi.* xi. 8

Swan.
Once *s.* of Thames, tho' now he sings no more *D.* iii. 20
And there, a naked Leda with a *S. M.E.* ii. 10
Th' expiring *S.,* and as he sings he dies *R.L.* v. 66
What City *S*—*s* once sung within the walls *D.* i. 95
And mounts far off among the *S.* of Thames *D.* ii. 298
The silver *s.* her hapless fate bemoan *W.* 39
His drooping *s.* on ev'ry note expire *W.F.* 275

Swarm.
S. o'er the lawns, the forest walks surround *W.F.* 149

Swarthy.
In show like leaders of the *s.* Moors *R.L.* iii. 48

Sway.
That lifts our Goddess to imperial *s. D.* iii. 124
The sure fore-runner of her gentle *s. D.* iii. 300
The young, the old, who feel her inward *s. D.* iv. 73
'Tis in the shade of Arbitrary *S. D.* iv. 182
We, wretched subjects, tho' to lawful *s. E.M.* ii. 149
Till common int'rest plac'd the *s.* in one *E.M.* iii. 210
The Love of Pleasure, and the Love of *S. M.E.* ii. 210
Yet go! and thus o'er all the creatures *s. E.M.* iii. 195
But art thou one, whom new opinions *s. S.* iv. 63

Sway'd.
And ev'n the elements a tyrant *s. W.F.* 52

Sways.
Whose judgment *s.* us, and whose spirit warms *A.* 10
And Boileau still in right of Horace *s. E.C.* 714
Charms by accepting, by submitting *s. M.E.* ii. 263

Swear.
S. like a Lord, or Rich out-whore a Duke *E.S.* i. 116
So quick retires each flying course, you'd *s. M.E.* iv. 159
And *s.* no Day was ever past so ill *M.E.* iv. 168
Have made a Soldier sigh, a Lover *s. Mi.* ix. 46
And *s.,* not ADDISON himself was safe *P.S.* 192
Who to the Dean, and silver bell can *s. P.S.* 299
But by this Lock, this sacred Lock I *s. R.L.* iv. 133
And *s.,* all shame is lost in George's Age *S.* v. 126
Which made old Ben, and surly Dennis *s. S.* v. 388
So stiff, so mute! some statue you would *s. S.* vi. 121
Call Tibbald Shakespear, and he'll *s.* the Nine *S.* vi. 137
Grave, as when pris'ners shake the head and *s. S.* vii. 67
At night, would *s.* him dropt out of the Moon *S.* viii. 33

Swearing.
S. and supperless, the Hero sate *D.* i. 115

Swears.
S., like Albutius, a good cook away *S.* ii. 64
He *s.* the Muses met him at the Devil *S.* v. 42
S. ev'ry place entail'd for years to come *S.* viii. 160
"That's velvet for a King!" the flatt'rer *s. S.* viii. 218

Sweat.
First thro' the length of yon hot Terrace *s. M.E.* iv. 130
Nor at Rehearsals, *s.,* and mouth'd, and cry'd *P.S.* 227
Ready to cast, I yawn, I sigh, and *s. S.* vii. 157
Scar'd at the grizly forms, I *s.,* I fly *S.* viii. 278

Sweats.
For you he *s.* and labours at the law *S.* vii. 75

Swede.
From Macedonia's madman to the *S. E.M.* iv. 220

Sweep.
When earth-quakes swallow, or when tempests *s. E.M.* i. 143
Shall then Uxorio, if the stakes he *s. M.E.* iii. 71
Rous'd by the Prince of Air the whirlwinds *s. M.E.* iii. 353
Now *s.* those Alleys they were born to shade *M.E.* iv. 98
And *s.* the sounding lyre *O.* i. 4
Rush thro' the thickets, down the valleys *s. W.F.* 156

Sweeping.
While Peers, and Dukes, and all their *s.* train *R.L.* i. 84

Sweeps.
Now Serpent-like, in prose he *s.* the ground *S.* v. 100
Till hov'ring o'er 'em *s.* the swelling net *W.F.* 104

Sweet.
Each cygnet *s.* of Bath and Tunbridge race *D.* iii. 155
How *s.* the periods, neither said, nor sung *D.* iii. 202
How *s.* an Ovid, MURRAY was our boast *D.* iv. 169
Lull'd by the *s.* Nepenthe of a Court *E.S.* i. 98
S. to the World, and grateful to the Skies *E.S.* ii. 245
And there in *s.* Oblivion drown *I.H.* ii. 131
Or drest in smiles of *s.* Cecilia shine *M.E.* ii. 13
Or who in *s.* vicissitude appears *M.E.* ii. 109
Strong as the Footman, as the Master *s. Mi.* ix. 106
And Ireland, mother of *s.* singers *Mi.* xii. 7
Together mixt; *s.* recreation *O.* iv. 14
And, "*S.* Sir Fopling! you have so much wit!" *S.* viii. 233

Here shall I try the *s.* Alexis' strain *W.* 11
In hollow caves *s.* Echo silent lies *W.* 41
From soup to *s.*-wine, *and God bless the King M.E.* iv. 162

Sweeter.

With *s.* notes each rising Temple rung *E.C.* 703
S. than Sharon, in immac'late trim *S.* viii. 252
Lament the ceasing of a *s.* breath *W.* 50
A *s.* music than their own to hear *W.* 58

Sweetest.

He finds no relish in the *s.* meat *S.* ii. 32
Than eat the *s.* by themselves at home *S.* ii. 96
That *s.* music to an honest ear *S.* ii. 100
Oh 'tis the *s.* of all earthly things *S.* viii. 100

Sweetly.

So *s.* mawkish, and so smoothly dull *D.* iii. 171
Shone *s.* lambent with celestial day *E.A.* 64
As shades more *s.* recommend the light *E.C.* 301
And *s.* melt into just shade and light *E.C.* 483
And *s.* flow thro' all the Royal Line *S.* i. 32
So *s.* warble, or so smoothly flow *W.* 4
Ev'n I more *s.* pass my careless days *W.F.* 431

Sweetness.

An Angel's *s.*, or Bridgewater's eyes *E.* iii. 46
Where Denham's strength, and Waller's *s.* join *E.C.* 361
Yet graceful ease, and *s.* void of pride *R.L.* ii. 15
If this is priz'd for *s.*, that for stink *S.* ii. 30
Fair Daphne's dead, and *s.* is no more *W.* 52

Sweets.

While op'ning blooms diffuse their *s.* around *Sp.* 100
But your Alexis knows no *s.* but you *Su.* 70

Swell.

And grateful clusters *s.* with floods of wine *A.* 74
With horns and trumpets now to madness *s. D.* ii. 227
And *s.* the pomp of dreadful sacrifice *E.A.* 354
Loves of his own and raptures *s.* the note *E.M.* iii. 34
Yet some I know with envy *s. I.H.* ii. 101 *s*
Glorious Ambition ! Peter, *s.* thy store *M.E.* iii. 125
What mines to *s.* that boundless charity *M.E.* iii. 278
To *s.* the Terrace, or to sink the Grot *M.E.* iv. 49
Exulting in triumph now *s.* the bold notes *O.* i. 16
Nor *s.* too high, nor sink too low *O.* i. 23
These *s.* their prospects and exalt their pride *R.L.* i. 81
Than such as *s.* this bladder of a court *S.* viii. 205
And *s.* the future harvest of the field *W.* 16
And purer spirits *s.* the sprightly flood *W.F.* 94
Who *s.* with tributary urns his flood *W.F.* 338

Swell'd.

Prose *s.* to verse, verse loit'ring into prose *D.* i. 274
Fierce as a startled Adder, *s.*, and said *D.* iv. 373
What wants in blood and spirits, *s.* with wind *E.C.* 208
Some *s.* to Gods, confess ev'n Virtue vain *E.* iv. 24
When Catiline by rapine *s.* his store *M.E.* i. 212
E'er *s.* on marble ; as in verse have shin'd *S.* v. 392
S. with new passion, and o'erflows with tears *W.* 66
In vain kind seasons *s.* the teeming grain *W.F.* 53

Swelling.

And *s.* organs lift the rising soul *E.A.* 272
Borne on the *s.* notes our souls aspire *O.* i. 128
Full o'er their heads the *s.* bag he rent *R.L.* iv. 91
And *s.* clusters bend the curling vines *Sp.* 36
Till hov'ring o'er 'em sweeps the *s.* net *W.F.* 104
His *s.* waters and alternate tides *W.F.* 334
Whole nations enter with each *s.* tide *W.F.* 399

Swells.

Here *s.* the shelf with Ogilby the great *D.* i. 141
She ceas'd. Then *s.* the Chapel-royal throat *D.* i. 319
So *s.* each wind-pipe ; Ass intones to Ass *D.* ii. 254
The vital flame, and *s.* the genial seeds *E.M.* iii. 118
That robe of Quality so struts and *s. M.E.* ii. 189
And *s.* her breast with conquests yet to come *R.L.* iii. 28
That spreads and *s.* in puff'd prosperity *S.* ii. 126
Nor Po so *s.* the fabling Poet's lays *W.F.* 227
Tho' foaming Hermus *s.* with tides of gold *W.F.* 358

Swept.

Where things destroy'd are *s.* to things unborn *D.* i. 242
Led off two captive trumps, and *s.* the board *R.L.* iii. 50

Swift.

Mourn not, my *S.*, at aught our Realm acquires *D.* i. 26
And whisk 'em back to Evans, Young, and *S. D.* ii. 116
Cook shall be Prior, and Concanen *S. D.* ii. 138
Hibernian Politics, O *S.*! thy fate *D.* iii. 331
For *S.* and him despis'd the farce of state *E.* i. 9
Our old friend *S.* will tell his story *I.H.* i. 82
And *Congreve* lov'd, and *S.* endur'd my lays *P.S.* 138
"I found him close with *S.*"—"Indeed ? no doubt" *P.S.* 275
"Pray heav'n it last !" (cries *S.*) "as you go on *S.* ii. 161
What's *Property ?* dear *S.*! you see it alter *S.* ii. 167
And *S.* cry wisely, "Vive la Bagatelle" *S.* iv. 128
And leave on *S.* this grateful verse engrav'd *S.* v. 223
"But, Sir, us writers ?" "*S.*, for closer style *S.* viii. 72
S. as a bard a bailiff leaves behind D. ii. 61
S. as it mounts, all follow with their eyes *D.* ii. 185
S. to whose hand a winged volume flies *D.* iii. 234
Not so, when *s.* Camilla scours the plain *E.C.* 372
S. fly the years, and rise th' expected morn *M.* 21
S. to the Lock a thousand Sprites repair *R.L.* iii. 135
S. on his sooty pinions flits the Gnome *R.L.* iv. 17
And *s.* as light'ning to the combat flies *R.L.* v. 38
S. trouts, diversified with crimson stains *W.F.* 145
Not half so *s.* the trembling doves can fly *W.F.* 185
The Kennet *s.*, for silver eels renown'd *W.F.* 341

Swiftly.

And pond'rous slugs cut *s.* thro' the sky *D.* i. 182
And *s.* shoot along the Mall *I.H.* iii. 45
S. purling in a Round *Mi.* vii. 26
Not half so *s.* the fierce eagle moves *W.F.* 187

Swiftness.

Here with degrees of *s.*, there of force *E.M.* i. 132

Swills.

He stuffs and *s.*, and stuffs again *I.H.* ii. 205

Swim.

Priests, tapers, temples, *s.* before my sight *E.A.* 274

Swims.

Or *s.* along the fluid atmosphere *D.* iv. 423

Swine.

How Instinct varies in the grov'lling *s. E.M.* ii. 221
Drive to St. James's a whole herd of *s. M.E.* iii. 74

Swiss.—*See also* Switz.

Heav'n's *S.*, who fight for any God, or Man *D.* ii. 358

Switch.

The Cap and *S.* be sacred to his Grace *D.* iv. 585

Switz.

A *S.*, a High-dutch, or a Low-dutch Bear *S.* i. 63

Sword.

How keen the war, if Dulness draw the *s. D.* iii. 120
Who ne'er saw naked *s.*, or look'd in Plato *E.J.S.* 44
Justice a Conqu'ror's *s.*, or Truth a gown *E.M.* iv. 171
A Monarch's *s.*, when mad Vain-glory draws *E.S.* ii. 229
And honour'd Cæsar less than Cato's *s. P.C.* 36
In days of Ease when now the weary *S. S.* v. 139
And Nations wonder'd while they dropp'd with *s. S.* v. 399
Why dimly gleams the visionary *s. U.L.* 4
Pomps without guilt, of bloodless s—s *and maces D.* i. 87
S., pikes, and guns, with everlasting rust *S.* i. 74
Others a *s.*-knot *and lac'd suit inflame D.* ii. 52
Where wigs with wigs, with *s—s s—s* strive *R.L.* i. 101

Swore.

So like, that critics said, and courtiers *s. D.* ii. 49
Witness, great Ammon ! by whose horns I *s. D.* iv. 387
Wretch that I was, how often have I *s. Mi.* ix. 67

Sworn.

S. foe to Myst'ry, yet divinely dark *D.* iv. 460
S. to no Master, of no Sect am I *S.* ii. 24

Sycophant.

Or each new-pension'd *S.*, pretend *E.S.* ii. 142
Let no Court *S.* pervert my sense *S.* vii. 126

Syllable.

"But has he spoken ?" Not a *s. S.* v. 335
These equal s—s *alone require E.C.* 344

In sounds and jingling *s.* grown old *E.C.* 605
Each Word-catcher, that lives on *s. P.S.* 166

Sylph.

Her guardian *S.* prolong'd the balmy rest *R.L.* i. 20
Rejects mankind, is by some *S.* embrac'd *R.L.* i. 68
'Tis but their *S.*, the wise Celestials know *R.L.* i. 77
Warn'd by the *S.*, oh pious maid, beware *R.L.* i. 112
All but the *S.*—with careful thoughts opprest *R.L.* ii. 53
A wretched *S.* too fondly interpos'd (*rep.*) *R.L.* iii. 150
A *S.* too warn'd me of the threats of fate *R.L.* iv. 165
The light Coquettes in S—s aloft repair R.L. i. 65
The *S.* thro' mystic mazes guide their way *R.L.* i. 92
Oh blind to truth! the *S.* contrive it all *R.L.* i. 104
The busy *S.* surround their darling care *R.L.* i. 145
Ye *S.* and Sylphids, to your chief give ear *R.L.* ii. 73
To fifty chosen *S.*, of special note *R.L.* ii. 117
For *S.*, yet mindful of their ancient race *R.L.* iv. 11
For, that sad moment, when the *S.* withdrew *R.L.* iv. 11
The *S.* behold it kindling as it flies *R.L.* v. 131

Sylphids.

Ye Sylphs and *S.*, to your chief give ear *R.L.* ii. 73

Sylvan.

The mossy fountains, and the *s.* shades *M.* 3
First in these fields I try the *s.* strains *Sp.* 1
See what delights in *s.* scenes appear *Su.* 59
Adieu, my flocks, farewell ye *s.* crew *W.* 91
Invite my lays. Be present, *s.* maids *W.F.* 3
The youth rush eager to the *s.* war *W.F.* 148
Whose care, like hers, protects the *s.* reign *W.F.* 163
To paint anew the flow'ry *s.* scenes *W.F.* 285
Of war or blood, but in the *s.* chase *W.F.* 372
First in these fields I sung the *s.* strains *W.F.* 434
The S—s groan—no matter—for the Fleet M.E. iii. 210
Let Nymphs and *S.* cypress garlands bring *W.* 22

Sylvia.

O Love! for *S.* let me gain the prize *Sp.* 49
The sprightly *S.* trips along the green *Sp.* 57
If *S.* smiles, new glories gild the shore *Sp.* 75
S.'s like autumn ripe, yet mild as May *Sp.* 81
For *S.*, charming *S.*, shall be thine *Sp.* 92
And give the conquest to thy *S.*'s eyes *Sp.* 88

Sympathetic.

Renew'd by ordure's *s.* force *D.* ii. 103

Sympathy.

With choice we fix, with *s.* we burn *E.M.* 135

Synods.

Her grey-hair'd *S.* damning books unread *D.* iii. 103

Syren.

Others the *S.* Sisters warble round *D.* iv. 541
From Latian S—s, French Circean Feasts S. iv. 122

Syrian.

Honour a *S.* Prince above his own *D.* iv. 368
Speak'st thou of *S.* Princes? Traitor base *D.* iv. 373

System.

Observe how *s.* into *s.* runs *E.M.* i. 25
And, if each *s.* in gradation roll *E.M.* i. 247
That *s.* only, but the Whole must fall *E.M.* i. 250
Nor with one *s.* can they all be blest *E.M.* iv. 142
In one close *s.* of Benevolence *E.M.* iv. 358
Of *S—s* possible, *if 'tis confest E.M.* i. 43
Atoms or *s.* into ruin hurl'd *E.M.* i. 89
And those new Heav'ns and *S.* fram'd *I.H.* iv. 12

T.

Tabernacle.

Booth in his cloudy *t.* shrin'd *D.* iii. 267

Table.

Makes love with nods, and knees beneath a *t. E.* v. 28
Who for thy *t.* feeds the wanton fawn *E.M.* iii. 29
The name his *t.*, and the same his bed *E.M.* iii. 153
Whose *t.*, Wit, or modest Merit share *M.E.* iii. 241
A *t.*, with a cloth of bays *Mi.* xii. 6
Does not one *t.* Bavius still admit *P.S.* 99
And all our Grace at *t.* is a Song *S.* v. 174

Tabor.

No rafter'd roofs with dance and *t.* sound *M.E.* iii. 189

Tail.

Yet holds the eel of science by the *t. D.* i. 280
And carry'd off in some dog's *t.* at last *D.* iii. 202
Pois'd with a *t.*, may steer on Wilkins' wings *D.* iv. 452
Pray, dip your Whiskers and your *T.* in *I.H.* ii. 203
From *t.* to mouth, they feed and they carouse *E.S.* ii. 179
With all th' embroid'ry plaister'd at thy *t. M.E.* iii. 90
The Nymph, whose *T.* is all on Flame *Mi.* iv. 15
Rank as the ripeness of a rabbit's *t. S.* ii. 28
Those monkey t—s that wag behind their head S. viii. 247

Tailor.

That suit an unpaid *t.* snatch'd away *D.* ii. 118

Taint.

'Tis these that early *t.* the female soul *R.L.* i. 87

Tainted.

And hound, sagacious on the *t.* green *E.M.* i. 214
But when the *t.* gales the game betray *W.F.* 101

Taints.

And rarely Av'rice *t.* the tuneful mind *S.* v. 192

Take.

And laughs to think Munroe would *t.* her down *D.* i. 30
T. up the Bible, once my better guide *D.* i. 200
So *t.* the hindmost Hell (he said) and run *D.* ii. 60
Shall *t.* thro' Grubstreet her triumphant round *D.* iii. 136
Now, Bavius, *t.* the poppy from thy brow *D.* iii. 317
Thea *t.* at once the Poet and the Song *D.* iv. 8
Thea *t.* him to develop, if you can *D.* iv. 269
We nobly *t.* the high Priori Road *D.* iv. 471
Then *t.* them all, ob *t.* them to thy breast *D.* iv. 515
Some Squire, perhaps you *t.* delight to rack *E.* v. 23
"And *t.*" (she said, and smil'd serene) (*rep.*) *E.* vi. 3
But, Friend, *t.* heed whom you attack *E.* vi. 17
Nor foes nor fortune *t.* this pow'r away *E.A.* 43
T. back that grace, those sorrows, and those tears (*rep.*) *E.A.* 285
Thus Pegasus, a nearer way to *t. E.C.* 150
Short views we *t.*, nor see the lengths behind *E.C.* 222
The Sense, they humbly *t.* upon content *E.C.* 308
At ev'ry trifle scorn to *t.* offence *E.C.* 386
What wonder modes in Wit should *t.* their turn *E.C.* 447
'Twere well might critics still this freedom *t. E.C.* 584
As without learning they can *t.* Degrees *E.C.* 591
Our Critics *t.* a contrary extreme *E.C.* 661
But pray, which of you all would *t.* her back *E.J.S.* 36
Exalt their kind, and *t.* some Virtue's name *E.M.* ii. 100
Go, from the Creatures thy instructions *t. E.M.* iii. 172
A weaker may surprise, a stronger *t. E.M.* iii. 294
T. Nature's path, and mad Opinion's leave *E.M.* iv. 29
Who risk the most, that *t.* wrong means, or right *E.M.* iv. 86
Men in their loose unguarded hours they *t. E.M.* iv. 227
T. ev'ry creature in, of ev'ry kind *E.M.* iv. 370
Else might he *t.* to Virtue some years hence *E.S.* ii. 60
The way they *t.* is strangely round about *E.S.* ii. 125
And begg'd he'd *t.* the pains to kick the rest *E.S.* ii. 155
Yet *t.* these Tears, Mortality's relief *Ep.* vii. 17
Pray *t.* them, Sir,—Enough's a Feast *I.H.* i. 25
South-sea Subscriptions *t.* who please *I.H.* i. 65
Send for him up, *t.* no excuse *I.H.* ii. 36 *s*
And *t.* it kindly meant to show *I.H.* ii. 61 *s*
Would *t.* me in his Coach to chat *I.H.* ii. 87 *s*
The smiling infant in his hand shall *t. M.* 81
All Manners take a tincture from our own *M.E.* i. 33
When half our knowledge we must snatch, not *t. M.E.* i. 40
T. the most strong, and sort them as you can *M.E.* i. 120
Int'rest o'ercome, or Policy *t.* place *M.E.* i. 167
Opinions? they still *t.* a wider range *M.E.* i. 170
If second qualities for first they *t. M.E.* i. 211
Their happy Spots the nice admirer *t. M.E.* ii. 44
And Atheism and Religion *t.* their turns *M.E.* ii. 66
'Tis from a Handmaid we must *t.* a Helen *M.E.* ii. 194
Men, some to Bus'ness, some to Pleasure, *t. M.E.* ii. 215
What say you? Say? Why *t.* it, Gold and all *M.E.* iii. 78
And who would *t.* the Poor from Providence *M.E.* iii. 186
Who random drawings from your sheets shall *t. M.E.* iv. 27

TAKEN—TASK.

Treated, caress'd, and tir'd, I *t*. my leave *M.E.* iv. 165
First from a Worm they *t*. their Rise *Mi.* iv. 19
"There *t*." (says Justice) "*t*. ye each a Shell *Mi.* xi. 10
Or *t*. the husband, or return the Wife *O.* i. 82
What tender passions *t*. their turns *O.* iii. 33
The piece you think is incorrect? why, *t*. it *P.S.* 45
You think this cruel? *t*. it for a rule *P.S.* 83
Soft were my numbers ; who could *t*. offence *P.S.* 147
Blest be the Great! for those they *t*. away *P.S.* 255
Mount up, and *t*. a Salamander's name *R.L.* i. 60
Dost sometimes counsel *t*., and sometimes Tea *R.L.* iii. 8
While nymphs *t*. treats or assignations give *R.L.* iii. 169
Make some *t*. physic, others scribble plays *R.L.* iv. 62
And wits *t*. lodgings in the sound of Bow *R.L.* iv. 118
This the blest Lover shall for Venus *t. R.L.* v. 135
Why, if the nights seem tedious,—*t*. a Wife *S.* i. 16
Will club their Testers, now, to *t*. your life *S.* i. 104
Friend Pope! be prudent, let your Muse *t*. breath *S.* iii. 13
If honest S*z *t*. scandal at a Spark *S.* iii. 112
Away, away! *t*. all your scaffolds down *S.* iii. 146
So *t*. it in the very words of Creech *S.* iv. 2
To whom to nod, whom *t*. into your Coach *S.* iv. 102
Thro' Taverns, Stews, and Bagnios *t*. our round *S.* iv. 119
E'en *t*. the Counsel which I gave you first *S.* iv. 131
You love a Verse, *t*. such as I can send *S.* vi. 2
T. him with all his virtues, on my word *S.* vi. 13
Let him *t*. Castles who has ne'er a groat *S.* vi. 51
Stept from its pedestal to *t*. the air *S.* vi. 122
Weave laurel Crowns, and *t*. what names we please *S.* vi. 142
"My Friends!" he cry'd, "p—x *t*. you for your care *S.* vi. 195
A popish plot, shall for a Jesuit *t. S.* viii. 35
He said ; Alexis, *t*. this pipe, the same *Sa.* 41

Taken.
Shall only Man be *t*. in the gross *M.E.* i. 17

Takes.
And ductile Dulness new mæanders *t. D.* i. 64
He chinks his purse, and *t*. his seat of state *D.* ii. 197
Mark first that youth who *t*. the foremost place *D.* iii. 139
Yet *t*. one kiss before she parts for ever *E.* v. 6
Each Virtue in each Passion *t*. its turn *R.M.* iii. 136
Is blest in what it *t*., and what it gives *E.M.* iv. 314
Slave to no sect, who *t*. no private road *E.M.* iv. 331
Eternal buckle *t*. in Parian stone *M.E.* iii. 296
He *t*. his chirping pint, and cracks his jokes *M.E.* iii. 358
He must repair it ; *t*. a bribe from France *M.E.* iii. 396
T., opens, swallows it before their sight *Mi.* xi. 8
Which from the neighb'ring Hampton *t*. its name *R.L.* iii. 4
He *t*. the gift with rev'rence, and extends *R.L.* iii. 131
The Chanc'ry *t*. your rents for twenty year *S.* ii. 172
T. the whole House upon the Poet's day *S.* iv. 88
For food digested *t*. another name *S.* vii. 34
T. God to witness he affects your cause *S.* vii. 76
The patient fisher takes his silent stand *W.F.* 137

Talbot.
There *T*. sunk, and was a Wit no more *D.* iv. 168
The courtly *T*., *Somers, Sheffield* read *P.S.* 139
" *Yours, Cowper's manner*"—and " *yours*, T.'s *sense*" *S.* vi. 134

Tale.
Motteux himself unfinish'd left his *t. D.* ii. 412
There are, 'tis true, who tell another *t. E.*℟*S.* 15
A *T*., that blends their glory with their shame *E.M.* iv. 308
A *T*. extremely à *propos I.H.* ii. 154
But you are tir'd—I'll tell a *t*.—Agreed *M.E.* iii. 338
Who turns a Persian *t*. for half a Crown *P.S.* 180
The *t*. reviv'd, the lie so oft o'erthrown *P.S.* 350
From Dryden's Fables down to Durfey's T—s *E.C.* 617
In puns, or politics, or *t*. or lies *P.S.* 321

Talent.
Blest with each *t*. and each art to please *P.S.* 195
'Tis a Bear's *t*. not to kick, but hug *S.* i. 87
The same their t—s, *and their tastes the same D.* ii. 380
Whate'er the *t*., or howe'er design'd *D.* iv. 161
Our bolder *T*. in full light display'd *M.E.* ii. 201

With equal *t*., these congenial souls *S.* vi. 129
These are the *t*. that adorn them all *S.* vii. 79
Thus, others' *t*. having nicely shown *S.* viii. 80

Talk.
In various *t*. th' instructive hours they past *R.L.* iii. 11
And more than Echoes t. *along the walls E.A.* 306
They *t*. of principles, but notious prize *E.C.* 265
Nay, fly to Altars ; there they'll *t*. you dead *E.C.* 624
But *t*. with Celsus, Celsus will advise *S.* i. 19
Let's *t*., my friends, but *t*. before we dine *S.* ii. 4
T. what you will of Taste, my friend, you'll find *S.* vi. 268
To gaze on Princes, and to *t*. of Kings *S.* viii. 101
Of all our Harries, all our Edwards *t. S.* viii. 105

Talkative.
The coxcomb bird, so *t*. and grave *M.E.* i. 5

Talker.
That gay Free-thinker, a fine *t*. once *M.E.* i. 162
T—s *I've learn'd to bear; Motteux I knew S.* viii. 50

Talks.
He hears loud Oracles, and *t*. with Gods *D.* iii. 8
And without method *t*. us into sense *E.C.* 654
Here sighs a Jar, and there a Goose-pie *t. R.L.* iv. 52
Not one but nods, and *t*. of Jonson's Art *S.* i. 82
And *t*. Gazettes and Post-boys o'er by heart *S.* viii. 155

Tall.
Where the *t*. may-pole once o'er-look'd the Strand *D.* ii. 29
Where the *t*. Nothing stood, or seem'd to stand *D.* ii. 110
To a *t*. house near Lincoln's-Inn *I.H.* ii. 283
Like a *t*. bully, lifts the head and lies *M.E.* iii. 340
I too could write, and I am twice as *t. P.S.* 103
Cæsar and T.-*boy, Charles and Charlemagne M.E.* ii. 78

Taller.
T. or stronger than the weeds they shade *E.M.* i. 40

Tallier.
The *Basset-Table* spread, the *T*. come *Mi.* ix. 1
Rise, pensive Nymph, the *T*. waits for you *Mi.* ix. 3

Tally'd.
When WINNALL *t*., I would *punt* no more *Mi.* ix. 68

Tame.
The winding Isis, and the fruitful *T. W.F.* 340

Tamer.
Then he : "Great *T*. of all human art *D.* i. 163

Tames.
Yet *t*. not this ; it sticks to our last sand *M.E.* i. 225
Or *t*. the Genius of the stubborn plain *S.* i. 131

Tanais.
The freezing *T*. thro' a waste of snows *D.* iii. 83

Tantalized.
In plenty starving, *t*. in state *M.E.* iv. 163

Taper.
The hallow'd *t*. trembling in thy hand *E.A.* 326
Still tries to save the hallow'd t.'*s end M.E.* i. 243
Redeem'd from t—s *and defrauded pies D.* i. 156
Priests, *t*., temples, swim before my sight *E.A.* 274

Tapestry, Tap'stry.
Like some fierce Tyrant in old *t. E.C.* 587
As Herod's hang-dogs in old *t. S.* viii. 267
A shaggy *T'y*, worthy to be spread *D.* ii. 143

Tape-ty'd.
With *t*. curtains, never meant to draw *M.E.* iii. 302

Tardy.
To Virtue's work provoke the *t*. Hall *E.S.* ii. 218

Tartar.
He, whose long wall the wand'ring *T*. hounds *D.* iii. 76

Task.
Now at his head the dext'rous *t*. commence *D.* iv. 199
"Be that my *t*." (replies a gloomy Clerk *D.* iv. 459
No happier *t*. these faded eyes pursue *E.A.* 47
Unequal *t.! a* passion to resign *E.A.* 195

For 'tis but half a judge's *t.*, to know *E.C.* 562
Active its *t.*, it prompts, impels, inspires *E.M.* ii. 68
But random Praise—the *t.* can ne'er be done *E.S.* ii. 106
But, sage historians! 'tis your *t.* to prove *M.E.* i. 133
Or Sappho at her toilet's greasy *t. M.E.* ii. 25
But what to follow, is a *t.* indeed *M.E.* iii. 200
That *t.*, which as we follow, or despise *S.* iii. 43
Hard *t.! t.* to hit the palate of such guests *S.* v. 86
How oft in pleasing t—s *we wear the day E.* iii. 17
Just as absurd to mourn the *t.* or pains *E.M.* i. 265
In *t.* so bold, can little men engage *R.L.* i. 11
Ye know the spheres and various *t.* assign'd *R.L.* ii. 75

Taste.

Then his nice *t.* directs our Operas *D.* ii. 204
True *T.* as seldom is the Critic's share *E.C.* 12
How far your genius, *t.*, and learning go *E.C.* 49
Some to *Conceit* alone their *t.* confine *E.C.* 289
'Tis not enough, *t.*, judgment, learning, join *E.C.* 562
Blest with a *t.* exact, yet unconfin'd *E.C.* 639
The Nose of Hautgout, and the Tip of *T. M.E.* ii. 80
On the soft Passion, and the *T.* refin'd *M.E.* ii. 84
Your *T.* of Follies, with our Scorn of Fools *M.E.* ii. 276
Some dæmon whisper'd "Visto! have a *T.*" (*rep.*) *M.E.* iv. 16
And something previous ev'n to *T.*—'tis Sense *M.E.*iv.42
His Son's fine *T.* an op'ner Vista loves *M.E.* iv. 94
And all they want is spirit, *t.*, and sense *P.S.* 160
At once they gratify their sense and *t. R.L.* iii. 111
Than ridicule all *T.*, blaspheme Quadrille *S.* i. 38
To have a *T.* is insolence indeed *S.* ii. 112
Procure a *T.* to double the surprise *S.* iv. 30
In ev'ry *T.* of foreign Courts improv'd *S.* v. 141
He, from the *t.* obscene reclaims our youth *S.* v. 217
Ever the *t.* of Mobs, but now of Lords (*rep.*) *S.* v. 311
Talk what you will of *T.*, my friend, you'll find *S.*vi.268
The same their talents, and their t—s *the same D.*ii.380
Only to show how many *T.* he wanted *M.E.* iv. 14
Thee shall the Patriot, thee the Courtier t. *D.* iii. 297
Drink deep, or *t.* not the Pierian spring *E.C.* 216
This *t.* the honey, and not wound the flow'r *E.M.* ii. 90
But these less *t.* them, as they worse obtain *E.M.* iv. 84
Which who but feels can *t.*, but thinks can know *E.M.* iv. 328
His wealth, to purchase what he ne'er can *t. M.E.* iv. 4
Can *t.* no pleasure since his shield was scour'd *M.E.*v.42
To *t.* awhile the pleasure of a Court *R.L.* iii. 10
Where none learn Ombre, none e'er *t.* Bohea *R.L.* iv. 156
Who climb their mountain, or who *t.* their spring *S.* v. 353

Tasted.

Then first the Flamen *t.* living food *E.M.* iii. 265

Tastes.

Which whoso *t.*, forgets his former friends *D.* iv. 518
And *t.* the good without the fall to ill *E.M.* iv. 322
T. for his Friend of Fowl and Fish *J.H.* ii. 199
Yet wit ne'er *t.*, and beauty ne'er enjoys *P.S.* 312

Tate.

To the mild Limbo of our Father *T. D.* i. 238
And own'd that nine such Poets made a *T. P.S.* 190
She saw slow Philips creep like T.'s *poor page D.* i. 105

Tattle.

Such *t.* often entertains *J.H.* ii. 95 s

Taught.

T. rocks to weep, and made the mountains groan *A.* 16
How new-born nonsense first is *t.* to cry *D.* i. 60
As, *t.* by Venus, Paris learnt the art *D.* ii. 217
Then *t.* by Hermes, and divinely bold *D.* iv. 381
Thus bred, thus *t.*, how many have I seen *D.* iv. 505
Nor tears for ages *t.* to flow in vain *E.A.* 28
Heav'n first *t.* letters for some wretch's aid *E.A.* 51
Too soon they *t.* me 'twas no sin to love *E.A.* 68
Of all affliction *t.* a lover yet *E.A.* 189
Still as the sea, ere winds were *t.* to blow *E.A.* 253
And *t.* the world with reason to admire *E.C.* 101
So modern 'Pothecaries, *t.* the art *E.C.* 108
And *t.* more pleasant methods of salvation *E.C.* 547
Men must be *t.* as if you *t.* them not *E.C.* 574
The Muse, whose early voice you *t.* to sing *E.C.* 639
His soul, proud Science never *t.* to stray *M.E.* i. 101
T. half by Reason, half by mere decay *E.M.* ii. 259

Who *t.* the nations of the field and wood *E.M.* iii. 99
T. to command the fire, control the flood *E.M.* iii. 220
Who first *t.* souls enslav'd, and realms undone *E.M.* iii. 241
Till Superstition *t.* the tyrant awe *E.M.* iii. 246
She *t.* the weak to bend, the proud to pray *E.M.* iii. 251
T. Pow'r's due use to People and to Kings (*rep.*) *E.M.* iii. 289
E'er *t.* to shine, or sanctify'd from shame *E.M.* iv. 300
And *t.* his Romans, in much better metre *E.S.* i. 9
KNELLER, by Heav'n, and not a Master, *t. Ep.* viii.
T., on the wings of Truth to fly *J.H.* iv. 3
With too much Quickness ever to be *t. M.E.* ii. 97
That, Nature gives; and where the lesson *t. M.E.*ii.211
Who *t.* that heav'n-directed spire to rise *M.E.* iii. 261
She was my friend; I *t.* her first to spread *Mi.* ix. 61
Groves, where immortal Sages *t. O.* ii. 2
Of all the Nurse and all the Priest have *t. R.L.* i. 30
These in two sable ringlets *t.* to break *R.L.* iv. 169
On each enervate string they *t.* the note *S.* v. 153
Waller was smooth; but Dryden *t.* to join *S.* v. 267
Besides, my Father *t.* me from a lad *S.* vi. 54
No lessons now are *t.* the Spartan way *S.* viii. 93
That *t.* the groves my Rosalinda's name *Su.* 42
Her name with pleasure once she *t.* the shore *W.* 43

Taunts.

And *T.* alternate innocently flew *S.* v. 250

Taverns.

Thro' *T.*, Stews and Bagnios take our round *S.* iv. 119

Tawdry.

Where *t.* yellow strove with dirty red *M.E.* iii. 304
His Daughter flaunts a Viscount's *t.* wife *M.E.* iii. 391
Sinks the lost Actor in the *t.* load *S.* v. 333

Taylor.

T., their better Charon, lends an oar *D.* iii. 19
Now deep in *T.* and the Book of Martyrs *M.E.* ii. 63

Tax.

Fear most to *t.* an Honourable fool *E.C.* 588
To *t.* Directors, who (thank God) have Plums *E.S.* ii. 49

Tax'd.

Tho' double *t.*, how little have I lost *S.* ii. 152
For Right Hereditary *t.* and fin'd *S.* vi. 64

Taxes.

Of Debts, and *T.*, Wife and Children clear *M.E.* iii. 279

Te.

Disputes of *Me* and *T.*, of *aut* or *at D.* iv. 220

Tea.

To muse, and spill her solitary *t. E.* v. 16
Tho' Time is precious, and I want some *T. Mi.* ix. 28
I grow impatient, and the *T.*'s too strong *Mi.* ix. 108
Now leave complaining, and begin your *T. Mi.* ix. 112
And sip, with Nymphs, their elemental *T. R.L.* i. 62
Dost sometimes counsel take—and sometimes *T. R.L.* iii. 8
Here living t.-*pots stand, one arm held out R.L.* iv. 49

Teach.

T. Oaths to Gamesters, and to Nobles wit *D.* i. 204
T. thou the warbling Polypheme to roar *D.* iii. 305
Words are Man's province, Words we *t.* alone *D.* iv. 150
T. but that one, sufficient for a King *D.* iv. 184
T. Kings to fiddle, and make Senates dance *D.* iv. 598
In ev'ry scene some Moral let it *t. E.* iv. 23
Oh come! oh *t.* me nature to subdue *E.A.* 203
T. me at once, and learn of me to die *E.A.* 328
Let such *t.* others who themselves excel *E.C.* 15
Are nameless graces which no methods *t. E.C.* 144
To *t.* vain Wits a science little known *E.C.* 199
Still pleas'd to *t.*, and yet not proud to know *E.C.* 632
His Precepts *t.* but what his works inspire *E.C.* 660
Go, *t.* Eternal Wisdom how to rule *E.M.* ii. 29
Let subtle schoolmen *t.* these friends to fight *E.M.* ii. 81
T. us to mourn our Nature, not to mend *E.M.* ii. 153
Truths would you *t.*, or save a sinking land *E.M.*iv.265
T. me, like thee, in various nature wise *E.M.* iv. 377
Or *t.* the melancholy Muse to mourn *E.S.* i. 79
O *t.* us, Bathurst! yet unspoil'd by wealth *M.E.* iii. 226
And *t.* the Being you preserv'd, to bear *P.S.* 134
And without sneering, *t.* the rest to sneer *P.S.* 202

T. infant-cheeks a bidden blush to know *R.L.* i. 89
Who scorn a Lad should *t.* his father skill *S.* v. 129
To *t.* their frugal Virtues to his Heir *S.* v. 166
What better *t.* a Foreigner the tongue *S.* v. 206
Yet lest you think I rally more than *t. S.* v. 338
T. ev'ry thought within its bounds to roll *S.* vi. 204
Yet still, not heeding what your heart can *t. S.* vi. 224
This, *t.* me more than Hell to shun *U.P.* 15
If I am wrong, oh *t.* my heart *U.P.* 31
T. me to feel another's Woe *U.P.* 37

Teacher.
Wait the great *t.* Death ; and God adore *E.M.* i. 92

Teaches.
Good humour only *t.* charms to last *E.* iv. 61

Tear.
With that, a *T.* (portentous sign of Grace !) *D.* i. 243
Nor couldst thou, *Chesterfield !* a *t.* refuse *D.* iv. 43
A sigh the absent claims, the dead a *t. E.* i. 14
Still breath'd in sighs, still usher'd with a *t. E.A.* 32
With ev'ry bead I drop too soft a *t. E.A.* 270
And drink the falling *t.* each other sheds *E.A.* 350
One human *t.* shall drop and be forgiv'n *E.A.* 358
For these the hardy Vet'ran drops a *t. Ep.* ix. 5
This weeping marble had not ask'd thy *T. Ep.* xiv. 5
Steals down my cheek th' involuntary *T. I.H.* iii. 38
From ev'ry face he wipes off ev'ry *t. M.* 46
Or from the soft-ey'd Virgin steal a *t. P.S.* 286
The blow unfelt, the *t.* he never shed *P.S.* 349
No friend's complaint, no kind domestic *t. U.L.* 49
Shall shortly want the gen'rous *t.* he pays *U.L.* 78
T—s gush'd again, as from pale Priam's eyes D. i. 255
Dropping with Infant's blood, and Mother's *t. D.* iv. 142
Those *t.* eternal, that embalm the dead *E.* iii. 38
Already written—wash it out, my *t. E.A.* 1
Nor *t.* for ages taught to flow in vain *E.A.* 28
T. are still mine, and those I need not spare *E.A.* 45
Let *t.*, and burning blushes speak the rest *E.A.* 106
Canst thou forget what *t.* that moment fell *E.A.* 109
'Tis all blank sadness, or continued *t. E.A.* 148
T. that delight, and sighs that waft to heav'n *E.A.* 214
Take back that grace, those sorrows, and those *t. E.A.* 285
Now sighs steal out, and *t.* begin to flow *E.C.* 379
Less pleasing far than Virtue's very *t. E.M.* iv. 320
All *t.* are wip'd for ever from all eyes *E.S.* i. 102
Yet take these *T.*, Mortality's relief *Ep.* vii. 17
All bath'd in *t.—"* Oh odious, odious Trees !" *M.E.* ii. 40
Of Mirth and Opium, Ratafie and *T. M.E.* ii. 110
She, at whose name I shed these spiteful *t. Mi.* ix. 57
Hence false *t.*, deceits, disguises *O.* iii. 38
Commanding *t.* to stream thro' ev'ry age *P.C.* 6
Here *t.* shall flow from a more gen'rous cause (*rep.*) *P.C.* 13
The triumph ceas'd, *t.* gush'd from ev'ry eye *P.C.* 33
Which not the *t.* of brightest eyes could ease *R.L.* iv. 76
Soft sorrows, melting griefs, and flowing *t. R.L.* iv. 86
Methinks already I your "survey *R.L.* iv. 107
Her eyes half-languishing, half-drown'd in *t. R.L.* iv. 144
She said : the pitying audience melt in *t. R.L.* v. 1
Sudden with starting *t.* each eye o'erflows *R.L.* v. 85
The smiles of harlots, and the *t.* of heirs *R.L.* v. 120
To deluge sin, and drown a Court in *t. S.* viii. 285
There shall the morn her earliest *t.* bestow *U.L.* 65
Swell'd with new passion, and o'erflows with *t. W.* 66
The swain with *t.* his frustrate labour yields *W.F.* 55
She said, and melting as in *t.* she lay *W.F.* 203
And with celestial *t.* augments the waves *W.F.* 210
Oh early lost ! what *t.* the river shed *W.F.* 273
Oh fact accurst ! what *t.* has Albion shed *W.F.* 321
Assist the fiends, and t. me from my God E.A. 288
With Pity, and with Terror, *t.* my heart *S.* iv. 345
And the last pang shall *t.* thee from his heart *U.L.* 80

Tearless.
God cannot love (says Blunt with *t.* eyes) *M.E.* iii. 103

Tears.
As Justice *t.* his body from the grave *E.M.* iv. 250
And civil madness *t.* them from the land *O.* ii. 24

Tease.
Then presently he falls to *t. I.H.* ii. 79 s

Tedious.
Why, if the nights seem *t.*,—take a Wife *S.* i. 16
Tir'd with a *t.* march, one luckless night *S.* vi. 35

Teeming.
Now bright Arcturus glads the *t.* grain *A.* 72
A *t.* Mistress, but a barren Bride *M.E.* ii. 72
If *t.* ewes increase my fleecy breed *W.* 82
In vain kind seasons swell'd the *t.* grain *W.F.* 53

Teems.
And each exalted stanza *t.* with thought *E.C.* 423

Teeth.—*See* Tooth.

Tell.
I *t.* the naked fact without disguise *D.* iv. 433
And breaks our rest to *t.* us what's a-clock *D.* iv. 444
O Muse ! relate (for you can *t.* alone *D.* iv. 619
Nor fears to *t.*, that MORTIMER is he *E.* i. 40
Hum half a tune, *t.* stories to the squire *E.* v. 20
I *t.* ye, fool, there's nothing in't *E.* vi. 26
That dares *t.* neither Truth nor Lies *E.* vi. 30
Let him our sad, our tender story, *t. E.A.* 364
To *t.* 'em, would a hundred tongues require *E.C.* 44
Such was the Muse, whose rules and practice *t. E.C* 723
There are, 'tis true, who *t.* another tale *E.J.S.* 15
May *t.* why Heav'n has made us what we are *E.M.* i. 28
What can she more than *t.* us we are fools *E.M.* ii. 152
T. me, if Virtue made the son expire *E.M.* iv. 105
But who, but God, can *t.* us who they are *E.M.* iv. 136
I'll *t.* you, friend ! a wise man and a fool *E.M.* iv. 200
T. (for You can) what is it to be wise *E.M.* iv. 260
T. me, which Knave is lawful Game, which not *E.S.* ii. 27
If *Pope* must *t.* what HARCOURT cannot speak *Ep.* iii. 6
And 'tis but just, I'll *t.* you wherefore *I.H.* i. 33
Our old friend Swift will *t.* his story *I.H.* i. 82
'Tis one to me"—" Then *t.* us, pray *I.H.* ii. 119 s
T. how the Moon-beam trembling falls *I.H.* ii. 189
But why? ah *t.* me, ah too dear *I.H.* iii. 37
Ask men's Opinions : Scoto now shall *t. M.E.* i. 158
Arise and *t.* me, was thy death more bless'd *M.E.* iii. 322
But you are tir'd—I'll *t.* a tale—Agreed *M.E.* iii. 338
T., t. your griefs ; attentive will I stay *Mi.* ix. 27
Of Orpheus now no more let Poets *t. O.* i. 131
T. where I lie *O.* iv. 20
T. me, my Soul, can this be Death *O.* v. 12
And knowing *Walsh*, would *t.* me I could write *P.S.* 136
Neglected die, and *t.* it on his tomb *P.S.* 258
Sappho can *t.* you how this man was bit *P.S.* 369
'Twas this the morning omens seem'd to *t. R.L.* iv. 161
This, all who know me, know ; who love me, *t. S.* i. 138
And buy a rope, that future times may *t. S.* ii. 109
And who stands safest ? *t.* me, is it he *S.* ii. 125
T. at your levee, as the Crowds approach *S.* iv. 101
Let Ireland *t.*, how Wit upheld her cause *S.* v. 221
T. me if Congreve's Fools are Fools indeed *S.* v. 287
I guess ; and, with their leave, will *t.* the fault *S.* v. 357
You *t.* the Doctor ; when the more you have *S.* vi. 213
Of whose strange crimes no Canonist can *t. S.* vii. 43
Cry: "By your Priesthood *t.* me what you are !" *S.* viii. 37
He asks "What News?" I *t.* him of new Plays *S.* viii. 124
T. me but this, and I'll disclaim the Prize *Sp.* 87
Nay *t.* me first, in what more happy fields *Sp.* 89
Oh ever beauteous, ever friendly ! *t. U.L.* 5
But *t.* the reeds, and *t.* the vocal shore *W.* 59
And Peace and Plenty *t.*, a STUART reigns *W.F.* 42

Tells.
T. us that Cato dearly lov'd his wife *E.J.S.* 32
T. me I have more Zeal than Wit *I.H.* ii. 56 s
T. all their names, lays down the law *I.H.* ii. 200
That *t.* the Waters or to rise, or fall *M.E.* iv. 58
Who *t.* whate'er you think, whate'er you say *P.S.* 297
Not —'s self e'er *t.* more *Fibs* than I *S.* v. 176
He *t.* what strumpet places sells for life *S.* viii. 148

Temper.
To fall with dignity, with *t.* rise *E.M.* iv. 378
Oh ! blest with *T.*, whose unclouded ray *M.E.* ii. 257
By Music, minds an equal *t.* know *O.* i. 22
Various of *t.*, as of face or frame *S.* vi. 282
On various t—s act by various ways R.L. iv. 61
Those 'tis enough to t. and employ E.M. ii. 113

Temperance, Temp'rance.
Calm *T*., whose blessings those partake *D*. i. 49
But Health consists with *T*. alone *E.M*. iv. 81
Nor one that *T*. advance *I.H*. i. 61
Now hear what blessings *T*. can bring *S*. ii. 67
Healthy by *t.—'—e* and by exercise *P.S*. 401

Temp'rate.
As men for ever *t*., calm, and wise *E.M*. i. 154
From Nature's *t*. feast rose satisfy'd *Ep*. x. 9
The *t*. sleeps, and spirits light as air *S*. ii. 74

Temp'ring.
With native Humour *t*. virtuous Rage *Ep*. xi. 3

Tempest.
The rising *t*. puts in act the soul *E.M*. ii. 105
Nor strove with all the *t*. in my teeth *S*. vi. 301
When earth-quakes swallow, or when t—s *sweep E.M.* i. 143
Prescient, the tides or *t*. to withstand *E.M*. iii. 101
Or brew fierce *t*. on the wintry main *R.L*. ii. 85

Tempestuous.
Where Bentley late *t*. wont to sport *D*. iv. 201

Templars.
Three College Sophs, and three pert *T*. came *D*. ii. 379
While Wits and *T*. ev'ry sentence raise *P.S*. 211

Temple.
Here brisker vapours o'er the *T*. creep *D*. ii. 345
See the Cirque falls, th' unpillar'd *T*. nods *D*. iii. 107
With sweeter notes each rising *T*. rung *E.C*. 703
In the same *t*., the resounding wood *E.M*. iii. 155
Or some old *t*. nodding to its fall *E.M*. iv. 129
And opes the *T*. of *Eternity E.S*. ii. 235
Walk in thy light, and in thy *t*. bend *M*. 92
And *T*. rise—then fall again to dust *M.E*. ii. 140
No, 'tis a *T*., and a Hecatomb *M.E*. iii. 156
The *T*. late two brother Sergeants saw *S*. vi. 127
To Thee whose *T*. is all Space *U.P*. 49
But in her T.*'s last recess enclosed D.* iii. 1
Priests, tapers, t—s, *swim before my sight E.A*. 274
A few grey hairs his rev'rend *t*. crown'd *M.E*. iii. 327
Bid *T*., worthier of the God, ascend *M.E*. iv. 198
With nodding arches, broken *t*. spread *M.E*. v. 3
Let wreaths of triumph now my *t*. twine *R.L*. i. 161
Let rising Granaries and *T*. here *S*. vi. 258
The hollow winds thro' naked *t*. roar *W.F*. 68
And *T*. rise, the beauteous works of Peace *W.F*. 378
For Quoits, both T.-*bar and Charing-cross S*. viii. 277
From her black grottos near the *T.-wall D*. ii. 98

Tempt.
This prize is mine; who *t*. it are my foes *D*. ii. 54
In fearless youth we *t*. the heights of Arts *E.C*. 220
And long'd to *t*. him like good Job of old *M.E*. iii. 350
And nodding *t*. the joyful reaper's hand *W.F*. 40
T. icy seas, where scarce the waters roll *W.F*. 389

Temptation.
Above *T*., in a low Estate *Ep*. xi. 5
May yield, God knows, to strong *t. I.H*. ii. 182
Thicker than arguments t—s *throng E.M*. ii. 75

Tempter.
The *T*. saw his time; the work he ply'd *M.E*. iii 369
Eve's *t*. thus the Rabbies have exprest *P.S*. 330

Tempting.
Fair eyes, and *t*. locks (which yet I view!) *E.A*. 295
Or Garden, *t*. with forbidden fruit *E.M*. i. 8
Expos'd in glorious heaps the *t*. Bank *Mi*. ix. 78
Just then Clarissa drew with *t*. grace *R.L*. iii. 127

Tempts.
The knave deserves it, when he *t*. the main *E.M*. iv. 153
And *t*. by making rich, not making poor *M.E*. iii. 352
And *t*. once more thy sacrilegious hands *R.L*. iv. 174

Ten.
Scream like the winding of *t*. thousand jacks *D*. iii. 160
And Pope's, *t*. years to comment and translate *D*. iii. 332
In twice *t*. thousand rhyming nights and days *D*. iv. 172
T. censure wrong for one who writes amiss *E.C*. 6
And *t*. low words oft creep in one dull line *E.C*. 347
Tenth, or *t*. thousandth, breaks the chain alike *M.E*. i. 246
Are what *t*. thousand envy and adore *E.S*. i. 166
Strike? why the man was hang'd *t*. years ago *E.S*. ii. 55
T. Metropolitans in preaching well *E.S*. i. 132
Contracts, inverts, and gives *t*. thousand dyes *M.E*. i. 36
Or water all the Quorum *t*. miles round *M.E*. iii. 54
Behold Villario's *t*. years' toil complete *M.E*. iv. 79
And when up *t*. steep slopes you've dragg'd your thighs *M.E*. iv. 131
The sacred rust of twice *t*. hundred years *M.E*. v. 38
My Friendship, and a Prologue, and *t*. pound *P.S*. 48
Alas! 'tis *t*. times worse when they *repent P.S*. 108
Full *t*. years slander'd did he once reply *P.S*. 374
Happy! ah *t*. times happy had I been *R.L*. iv. 149
While with the silent growth of *t*. per cent. *S*. iii. 132
Clatt'ring their sticks before *t*. lines are spoke *S*. v. 308
And if we will recite nine hours in *t. S*. v. 362
Sure I should want the care of *t*. Monroes *S*. vi. 70
That turn'd *t*. thousand verses, now stands still *S*. vi. 79
At *t*. for certain, Sir, in Bloomsb'ry square *S*. vi. 95
More than *t*. Holinsheds, or Halls, or Stowes *S*. viii. 131
'Tis true, for *t*. days hence 'twill be King Lear's *S*. viii. 219
But held in t.*-fold bonds the Muses lie D*. iv. 35
And *t.-horn'd* fiends and Giants rush to war *D*. iii. 236

Tenant.
Man walk'd with beast, joint *t*. of the shade *E.M*. iii. 152
T—s *with sighs the smokeless tow'rs survey M.E*. iii. 191
Cutler saw *t*. break, and houses fall *M.E*. iii. 323
Whose cheerful *T*. bless their yearly toil *M.E*. iv. 183

Tend.
The single atoms each to other *t. E.M*. iii. 10
To bliss alike by that direction *t. E.M*. iii. 81
Our humbler province is to *t*. the Fair *R.L*. ii. 91
Do thou, Crispissa, *t*. her fav'rite Lock *R.L*. ii. 115
For see! the gath'ring flocks to shelter *t. SA*. 101
Shall *t*. the flocks, or reap the bearded grain *W.F*. 370

Tender.
Their artless passions, and their *t*. pains *A*. 12
To Delia's ear the *t*. notes convey *A*. 18
To touch Achilles' only *t*. part *D*. ii. 218
The *t*. sister, daughter, friend, and wife *E*. iii. 52
And all those *t*. names in one, thy love *E.A*. 154
Let him our sad, our *t*. story tell *E.A*. 364
Prescrib'd her heights, and prun'd her *t*. wing *E.C*. 736
He draws him gentle, *t*. and forgiving *E.J.S*. 27
Taught nor to slack, nor strain its *t*. strings *E.M*. iii. 290
Its *t*. lambs he raises in his arms *M*. 53
Till Death unfelt that *t*. frame destroy *Mi*. v. 17
What *t*. passions take their turns *O*. iii. 33
To wake the soul by *t*. strokes of art *P.C*. 1
Me, let the *t*. office long engage *P.S*. 408
What *t*. maid but must a victim fall *R.L*. i. 95
With *t*. Billet-doux he lights the pyre *R.L*. ii. 41
For this with fillets strain'd your *t*. head *R.L*. iv. 101
To bear too *t*., or too firm a heart *U.L*. 7

Tenderly.
And Brutus *t*. reproves *O*. iii. 8

Tends.
As the good shepherd *t*. his fleecy care *M*. 49
That *t*. to make one worthy man my foe *P.S*. 284

Tenements.
And sigh'd) "my lands and *t*. to Ned" *M.E*. i. 257
Schoolmen new *t*. in hell must make *S*. vii. 42

Tenets.
T. with Books, and Principles with Times *M.E*. i. 173
We find our *t*. just the same at last *M.E*. iii. 16

Tenour.
That shunning faults, one quiet *t*. keep *E.C*. 241

Tenth.
T., or ten thousandth, breaks the chain alike *E.M*. i. 246

Tepid.
Waves to the *t*. Zephyrs of the spring *D*. iv. 422

Terence.
The art of *T*., and Menander's fire *A*. 8
Let Freind affect to speak as *T*. spoke *D*. iv. 223

Term.
Rhymes ere he wakes, and prints before *T.* ends *P.S.* 43
Discours'd in t—s *as just, with looks as sage E.C.* 269
The whole Artill'ry of the *t.* of War *S.* viii. 54
Verse-man or Prose-man, t. *me which you will S.* i. 64

Termagants.
The Sprites of fiery *T.* in Flame *R.L.* i. 59

Term'd.
Is aptly *t.* a Glow-worm *M.* iv. 16

Terrace.
To swell the *T.,* or to sink the Grot *M.E.* iv. 49
First thro' the length of yon hot *T.* sweat *M.E.* iv. 130
And Nero's T—s *desert their walls M.E.* iv. 72
A T.-walk, *and half a Rood I.H.* ii. 5 s

Terrestrial.
So Spirits, ending their *t.* race *D.* i. 267

Terror.
With Pity, and with *T.,* tear my heart *S.* v. 345
Shall I, the *T.* of this sinful town *S.* viii. 196
Gigantic Pride, pale *T.,* gloomy Care *W.F.* 415
Gloomy Pluto, King of T—s *Mi.* vii. 17
With *t.* round, can Reason hold her throne *S.* vi. 310
But oh ! what *t.* must distract my soul *S.* viii. 244

Test.
At once the source, and end, and *t.* of Art *E.C.* 73

Testers.
Will club their *T.,* now, to take your life *S.* i. 104

Tête-à-tête.
Always together, *t. I.H.* ii. 106 s
And down the Mice sate *t. I.H.* ii. 197

Text.
Still with itself compar'd, his *t.* peruse *E.C.* 128
Publish the present age : but where my *t. S.* i. 59

Textures.
Thin glitt'ring *t.* of the filmy dew *R.L.* ii. 64

Thalestris.
And fierce *T.* fans the rising fire *R.L.* iv. 94
In vain *T.* with reproach assails *R.L.* v. 3
Belinda frown'd, *T.* called her prude *R.L.* v. 36
While thro' the press enrag'd *T.* flies *R.L.* v. 57
Sunk in T.' *arms the nymph he found R.L.* iv. 89

Thalia.
There sunk *T.,* nerveless, cold, and dead *D.* iv. 41

Thame, Thames.
Led forth his flocks along the silver T—e *Su.* 2
T—s wafts it thence to Rufus' roaring hall *D.* ii. 265
Rolls the large tribute of dead dogs to *T. D.* ii. 272
And mounts far off among the Swans of *T. D.* ii. 248
Pours into *T.;* and hence the mingled wave *D.* ii. 343
Once swan of *T.,* tho' now he sings no more *D.* iii. 20
Till *T.* see Eton's sons for ever play *D.* iii. 335
Where *T.* reflects the visionary scene *I.H.* ii. 24
Which sounds the silver *T.* along *I.H.* iv. 2
Launch'd on the bosom of the silver *T. R.L.* ii. 4
Where *T.* with pride surveys his rising tow'rs *R.L.* iii. 2
But gudgeons, flounders, what my *T.* affords *S.* ii. 142
The silver *T.* reflects its marble face *S.* iii. 142
.. Fair *T.,* flow gently from thy sacred spring *Sp.* 3
T. heard the numbers as he flow'd along *W.* 13
Thy offspring, *T.!* the fair Lodona nam'd *W.F.* 172
In vain on father *T.* she calls for aid *W.F.* 197
Then foaming pour along, and rush into the *T. W.F.* 218
While lasts the mountain, or while *T.* shall flow *W.F.* 266
Old father *T.* advanc'd his reverend head *W.F.* 330
Unbounded *T.* shall flow for all mankind *W.F.* 398
Thou who shalt stop where T—s' *translucent wave Mi.* x. 1
Blest T—s's *shores the brightest beauties yield Sp.* 63
To *T.* banks, which fragrant breezes fill *W.F.* 263
That *T.* glory to the stars shall raise *W.F.* 356

Than.—*Passim.*

Thank.
To tax Directors, who (*t.* God) have Plums *E.S.* ii. 49

There (*t.* my stars) my whole Commission ends *P.S.* 59
There are who have not—and *t.* heav'n there are *S.* vi. 266
Yes ; *t.* my stars ! as early as I knew *S.* vii. 1

Thank'd.
T. Heav'n that he had liv'd, and that he died *Ep.* x. 10

Thankful.
With feasts, and off'rings, and a *t.* strain *S.* v. 244

Thankless.
His *t.* Country leaves him to her Laws *M.E.* iii. 218

Thanks.
Small *t.* to France, and none to Rome or Greece *D.* i. 283
I have a thousand *t.* to give *I.H.* ii. 208
But *t.* to Homer, since I live and thrive *S.* vi. 68
What *t.,* what praise, if *Peter* but supplies *S.* vii. 67
And crown'd with corn their *t.* to Ceres yield *Su.* 66
And t. *his stars he was not born a fool E.J.S.* 8
He *t.* you not, his pride is in Piquet *M.E.* i. 85

That, Those.—*Passim.*
With singing, laughing, ogling, *and all t. R.L.* iii. 18

The.—*Passim.*

Theatre.
Till rais'd from booths, to *T.,* to Court *D.* iii. 299
Contending T—s *our empire raise D.* iii. 271
Or scoops in circling *t.* the Vale *M.E.* iv. 60
Huge *T.,* that now unpeopled Woods *M.E.* v. 7
To *T.,* and to Rehearsals throng *S.* v. 173

Theatric.
Load some vain Church with old *T.* state *M.E.* iv. 29

Thebes.
To *T.,* to Athens, when he will, and where *S.* v. 347

Theft.
He, who still wanting, tho' he lives on *t. P.S.* 183

Them.—*Passim. See also* 'Em.

Theme.
Like gentle *Fanny's* was my flow'ry *t. P.S.* 149
There sober thought pursu'd th' amusing *t. S.* viii. 188
To heav'nly t—s *sublimer strains belong M.* 2
These now no more shall be the Muse's *t. W.F.* 361

Then, Thence.—*Passim.*

Theobald.—*See* Tibald.

Theocles.
Which *T.* in raptur'd vision saw *D.* iv. 488

Theory.
To Practice now from *T.* repair *D.* iv. 580

There, Therefore.—*Passim.*

Theses.
And Demonstration thin, and *T.* thick *D.* ii. 241

Them, They.—*Passim.*

Thick.
And Demonstration thin, and Theses *t. D.* ii. 241
Here prove who best can dash thro' *t.* and thin *D.* ii. 276
T. as the stars of night, or morning dews (*ref.*) *D.* iii. 32
But spread, my sons, your glory thin or *t. D.* iv. 129
T. and more *t.* the black blockade extends *D.* iv. 191
Came whip and spur, and dash'd thro' thin and *t. D.* iv. 197
Then *t.* as Locusts black'ning all the ground *D.* iv. 397
From him the next receives it, *t.* or thin *E.S.* ii. 175
Away they come, thro' *t.* and thin *I.H.* ii. 183
He from *t.* films shall purge the visual ray *M.* 39
Trees cut to Statues, Statues *t.* as trees *M.E.* iv. 120

Thick'ning.
Or sat delighted in the *t.* shade *M.E.* iv. 90

Thicker.
T. than arguments, temptations throng *E.M.* ii. 75

Thickest.
But pour them *t.* on the noble head *D.* iv. 358

Thickets.
Learn from the birds what food the *t.* yield *E.M.* iii. 173
They pierce my *t.*, thro' my Grot they glide *P.S.* 8
Rush thro' the *t.*, down the valleys sweep *W.F.* 156

Thief.
Arraign no mightier *T.* than wretched Wild *E.S.* ii. 39
Who sent the *T.* that stole the Cash away *S.* vi. 25
This subtle *T.* of life, this paltry Time *S.* vi. 76
The *T.* condemn'd, in law already dead *S.* vii. 15
T—ves, *Supercargoes, Sharpers, and Directors S.* i. 72

Thighs.
And when up ten steep slopes you've dragg'd your *t.* *M.E.* iv. 131

Thimble-Case.
A Myrtle Foliage round the *T. Mi.* ix. 34

Thin.
Blank'd his bold visage, and a *t.* Third day *D.* i. 114
No meagre, muse-rid mope, adust and *t. D.* ii. 37
And Demonstration *t.*, and Theses thick *D.* ii. 241
Here prove who best can dash thro' thick and *t. D.*ii.276
Tho' stale, not ripe; tho' *t.*, yet never clear *D.* iii. 170
But spread, my sons, your glory *t.* or thick *D.* iv. 129
Came whip and spur, and dash'd thro' *t.* and thick *D.*iv. 197
What *t.* partitions Sense from Thought divide *E.M.* i. 226
Spread the *t.* oar, and catch the driving gale *E.M.* iii. 178
From him the next receives it, thick or *t. E.S.* ii. 175
And a *t.* Court that wants your Face *I.H.* i. 12
Away they come thro' thick and *t. I.H.* ii. 183
Thron'd in the centre of his *t.* designs *P.S.* 93
T. glitt'ring textures of the filmy dew *R.L.* ii. 64
Shrink his *t.* essence like a rivel'd flow'r *R.L.* ii. 132
T. trees arise that shun each other's shades *W.F.* 22

Thing.
O! if my sons may learn one earthly *t. D.* iv. 183
For thee explain a *t.* till all men doubt it *D.* iv. 251
Lost is his God, his Country, ev'ry *t. D.* iv. 523
A vain, unquiet, glitt'ring, wretched *T, E.* iv. 54
A *little learning* is a dang'rous *t. E.C.* 215
With some unmeaning *t.* they call a thought *E.C.* 355
The Stoic Husband was the glorious *t. E.J.S.* 38
Its only thinking *t.* this turn of mind *E.M.* iii. 78
To trust in ev'ry *t.*, or doubt of all *E.M.* iv. 26
Condition, circumstance, is not the *t. E.M.* iv. 57
Add Health, and Pow'r, and ev'ry earthly *t. E.M.* iv. 159
No joy, or be destructive of the *t. E.M.* iv. 182
A *t.* beyond us, ev'n before our death *E.M.* iv. 238
And own the Spaniard did a *waggish t. E.S.* i. 17
She's still the same belov'd, contented *t. E.S.* i. 140
Why that's the *t.* you bid me not to do *E.S.* ii. 19
Still better, Ministers, or, if the *t. E.S.* ii. 50
For Peer or Bishop 'tis no easy *t. M.E.* ii. 195
Flaunts and goes down, an unregarded *t. M.E.* ii. 252
I know the *t.* that's most uncommon *Mi.* viii. 1
An awkward *T.*, when first she came to Town *Mi.* ix. 59
Let *Sporus* tremble—What? that *t.* of silk *P.S.* 305
Amphibious *t.!* during either part *P.S.* 326
Or who would learn one earthly *t.* of use *R.L.* v. 22
You could not do a worse *t.* for your life *S.* i. 15
And always thinks the very *t.* he ought *S.* ii. 130
In short that reas'ning, high, immortal *T. S.* iii. 185
The fear to want them is as weak a *t. S.* iv. 19
I scarce can think him such a worthless *t. S.* v. 209
'Tis one *t.* madly to disperse my store *S.* vi. 392
And lies to ev'ry Lord in ev'ry *t. S.* vii. 77
A *t.* which Adam had been posed to name *S.* viii. 25
This *t.* has travell'd, speaks each language too *S.* viii. 46
Just Gods! shall all t—s *yield returns but love A.* 76
Where *t.* destroy'd are swept to *t.* unborn *D.* i. 242
Are *t.* which Kuster, Burman, Wasse shall see *D.*iv.237
To thee the most rebellious *t.* on earth *D.* iv. 508
And nobly conscious, Princes are but *t. D.* iv. 601
And loves you best of all *t.*—but his horse *E.* v. 30
Conceal, disdain—do all *t.* but forget *E.A.* 200
Unfinished *t.*, one knows not what to call *E.C.* 42
Nature to all *t.* fix'd the limits fit *R.C.* 52

As *t.* seem large which we thro' mists descry *E.C.* 392
Unhappy Wit, like most mistaken *t. E.C.* 494
And *t.* unknown propos'd as *t.* forgot *E.C.* 575
We'd be the best good-natur'd *t.* alive *E.J.S.* 74
Awake, my ST. JOHN! leave all earthly *t. E.M.* i. 1
Account for moral *t.*, as for nat'ral *t. E.M.* i. 162
Great lord of all *t.*, yet a prey to all *E.M.* ii. 16
While Mae exclaims, "See all *t.* for my use!" *E.M.* iii. 45
Union the bond of all *t.*, and of Man *E.M.* iii. 150
To Order, Union, full Consent of *t. E.M.* iii. 296
All sly slow *t.*, with circumspective eyes *E.M.* iv. 226
Think, and if still the *t.* thy envy call *E.M.* iv. 275
From sounds to *t.*, from fancy to the heart *E.M.* iv. 392
Have I, in silent wonder, seen such *t. E.S.* i. 109
Is it for Bond, or Peter, (paltry *t.) E.S.* i. 121
You give the *t.* you never care for *I.H.* i. 34
Here no man prates of idle *t. I.H.* ii. 141
A smart Free-thinker? all *t.* in an hour *M.E.* i. 157
Time, that on all *t.* lays his lenient hand *M.E.* i. 224
Woman and Fool are two hard *t.* to hit *M.E.* ii. 113
Gold, imp'd by thee, can compass hardest *t. M.E.* iii. 41
T. change their titles, as our manners turn *M.E.* iii. 379
And pompous buildings once were *t.* of Use *M.E.* iv. 24
Three *t.* another's modest wishes bound *P.S.* 47
Good friend, forbear! you deal in dang'rous *t. P.S.* 75
The *t.*, we know, are neither rich nor rare *P.S.* 171
What mighty contests rise from trivial *t. R.L.* i. 2
Nor bound thy narrow views to *t.* below *R.L.* i. 36
And see thro' all *t.* with his half-shut eyes *R.L.* iii. 118
Already hear the horrid *t.* they say *R.L.* iv. 108
Since all *t.* lost on earth are treasur'd there *R.L.* v. 114
Libels and *Satires! lawless t.* indeed *S.* i. 150
Like Journals, Odes, and such forgotten *t. S.* v. 416
Like rich old wardrobes, *t.* extremely rare *S.* vii. 123
As Time, that changes all *t.*, had ordain'd *S.* viii. 43
Oh 'tis the sweetest of all earthly *t. S.* viii. 100
All the Court fill'd with stranger *t.* than he *S.* viii. 181
Such waxen noses, solemn staring *t. S.* viii. 210
The Presence seems, with *t.* so richly odd *S.* viii. 238
Prodigious! how the *t. protest, protest S.* viii. 255
And all *t.* flourish where you turn your eyes *Sa.* 76
How all *t.* listen, while thy Muse complains *W.* 77
And where, tho' all *t.* differ, all agree *W.F.* 16
Thus (if small *t.* we may with great compare) *W.F.* 105

Think.
And laughs to *t.* Monroe would take her down *D.* i. 30
Ah, *t.* not, Mistress! more true Dulness lies *D.* iv. 239
As Jansen, Fleetwood, Cibber shall *t.* fit *D.* iv. 326
O! would the Sons of Men once *t.* their Eyes *D.* iv. 453
And hear a spark, yet *t.* no danger nigh *E.* v. 4
Ah, *t.* at least thy flock deserves thy care *E.A.* 129
Now *t.* of thee, and curse my innocence *E.A.* 189
Ah, come not, write not, *t.* not once of me *E.A.* 291
But always *t.* the last opinion right *E.C.* 431
We *t.* our fathers fools, so wise we grow (*rep.*) *E.C.* 438
And authors *t.* their reputation safe *E.C.* 450
Fondly we *t.* we honour merit then *E.C.* 454
If, after all, you *t.* it a disgrace *E.J.S.* 45
Is not to act or *t.* beyond mankind *E.M.* i. 190
Nor *t.*, in NATURE'S STATE they blindly trod *E.M.* iii. 147
Abstract what others feel, what others *t. E.M.* iv. 45
T. we, like some weak Prince, th' Eternal Cause *E.M.* iv. 121
Oh fool! to *t.* God hates the worthy mind *E.M.* iv. 189
T., and if still the things thy envy call *E.M.* iv. 275
If parts allure thee, *t.* how Bacon shin'd *E.M.* iv. 281
He does not *t.* me what he thinks mankind *E.S.* i. 34
Yet *t.* not Friendship only prompts my lays *E.S.* ii. 94
I *t.* your Friends are out, and would be in *E.S.* ii. 123
Who *t.* a Coxcomb's Honour like his Sense *E.S.* ii. 202
I can't but *t.* 'twould sound more clever *I.H.* ii. 11 *s*
Great Ministers ne'er *t.* of these *I.H.* 38 *s*
How *t.* you of our Friend the Dean *I.H.* ii. 103 *s*
They stand amaz'd, and *t.* me grown *I.H.* ii. 123 *s*
It was by Providence they *t. I.H.* ii. 216
Lest you should *t.* that verse shall die *I.H.* iv. 1
But I, who *t.* more highly of our kind *M.E.* ii. 281
Perhaps you *t.* the Poor might have their part *M.E.* iii. 99
What but a want, which you perhaps *t.* mad *M.E.* iii.331
T. we all these are for himself? no more *M.E.* iv. 11
Whate'er we *t.*, whate'er we see *Mi.* iv. 3
T. of that moment, you who Prudence boast *Mi.* ix. 97

THINKING—THOUGHT.

The piece, you *t.*, is incorrect? why, take it *P.S.* 45
Lintot, dull rogue! will *t.* your price too much *P.S.* 63
You *t.* this cruel? take it for a rule *P.S.* 83
Who tells whate'er you *t.*, whate'er you say *P.S.* 297
T. what an equipage thou hast in Air *R.L.* i. 45
T. not, when Woman's transient breath is fled *R.L.* i. 51
Fear the just Gods, and *t.* of Scylla's Fate *R.L.* iii. 122
Nor *t.*, to die dejects my lofty mind *R.L.* v. 99
There are, (I scarce can *t.* it, but am told) *S.* i. 2
I'd write no more. Not write? but then I *t.* *S.* i. 11
Consult the Statute: *quart.* I *t.*, it is *S.* i. 147
By what Criterion do ye eat, d'ye *t.* *S.* ii. 29
T. how posterity will treat thy name *S.* ii. 108
You *t.* this Madness but a common case *S.* iii. 172
T. that but words, and this but brick and stones *S.* iv. 66
You'd *t.* no Fools disgrac'd the former reign *S.* v. 127
I scarce can *t.* him such a worthless thing *S.* v. 209
Yet lest you *t.* I rally more than teach *S.* v. 338
T. of those Authors, Sir, who would rely *S.* v. 350
Yet *t.*, great Sir! so many Virtues shown (*rep.*) *S.* v. 376
I *t.* Sir Geoffrey should decide the suit *S.* vi. 24
D'ye *t.* me good for nothing but to rhyme *S.* vi. 32
D'ye *t.* me, noble Gen'ral, such a Sot *S.* vi. 50
You *t.* 'tis Nature, and a knack to please *S.* vi. 177
My heir may sigh, and *t.* it want of grace *S.* vi. 267
Or will you *t.*, my friend, your business done *S.* vi. 326
Could not but *t.*, to pay his fine was odd *S.* viii. 17
No wonder some folks bow, and *t.* them Kings *S.* viii. 211
For those who greatly *t.*, or bravely die *U.L.* 10
Or *t.* Thee Lord alone of Man *U.P.* 23

Thinking.

Its only *t.* thing this turn of mind *E.M.* iii. 78
There needs but *t.* right, and meaning well *E.M.* iv. 32
What are you *t.*? 'Faith the thought's no sin *E.S.* ii. 122
Not *t.* it is Levee day *I.H.* ii. 465
With too much *T.* to have common Thought *M.E.* ii. 98

Thinks.

And while he seems to study, *t.* of you *E.* v. 44
Whoever *t.* a faultless piece to see *E.C.* 253
But *t.*, admitted to that equal sky *E.M.* i. 112
Whether he *t.* too little, or too much *E.M.* ii. 12
But *t.* his neighbour farther gone than he *E.M.* ii. 226
Who *t.* all made for one, not one for all *E.M.* iii. 48
One *t.* on Calvin Heav'n's own spirit fell *E.M.* iv. 137
Which who but feels can taste, but *t.* can know *E.M.* iv. 328
He does not think me what he *t.* mankind *E.S.* i. 34
What! always Peter? Peter *t.* you mad *E.S.* ii. 58
All know 'tis Virtue, for he *t.* them knaves *M.E.* i. 58
T. who endures a knave, is next a knave *M.E.* i. 78
He *t.* a Loaf will rise to fifty pound *M.E.* iii. 116
Who *t.* that Fortune cannot change her mind *S.* ii. 123
And always *t.* the very thing he ought *S.* ii. 130

Third.

Till genial Jacob, or a warm *T.* day *D.* i. 57
Black'd his bold visage, and a thin *T.* day *D.* i. 114
The *t.* mad passion of thy doting age *D.* iii. 304
They love themselves, a *t.* time, in their race *E.M.* iii. 124
Drops to the *t.*, who nuzzles close behind *E.S.* ii. 178
I would be with you June the *t.* *I.H.* i. 2
A *t.* interprets motions, looks and eyes *R.L.* iii. 15

Thirst.

Ah ne'er so dire a *t.* of glory boast *E.C.* 522
Due to his Merit, and brave *T.* of praise *Ep.* viii. 6
In lavish streams to quench a Country's *t.* *M.E.* iii. 177
Belinda now, whom *t.* of fame invites *R.L.* ii. 25
And envy'd *T.* and Hunger to the Poor *S.* iv. 117
Who hunger, and who *t.* for scribbling sake *D.* i. 50
No fiends torment, no Christians *t.* for gold *E.M.* i. 108
And gasping Furies *t.* for blood in vain *W.F.* 422

Thirsts.

Know, Eusden *t.* no more for sack or praise *D.* i. 273

Thirsty.

Not bubbling fountains to the *t.* swain *A.* 43
And starts amidst the *t.* wilds to hear *M.* 69
The sultry Sirius burns the *t.* plains *Su.* 21
Nor *t.* heifers seek the gliding flood *W.* 38

Thirty.

In rev'rence to the sins of *T.* nine *S.* ii. 5
Digest his *t.* thousandth dinner *Mi.* xii. 18

This, These.—*Passim.*

Thistle.

The *T.* springs, to which the Lily yields *Sp.* 90

Thither.—*Passim.*

Thomists.

Scotists and *T.*, now, in peace remain *E.C.* 444

Thorn.

And liquid amber drop from ev'ry *t.* *A.* 38
Ye grots, and caverns shagg'd with horrid *t.* *E.A.* 20
Waste sandy valleys, once perplex'd with *t.* *M.* 73
When, of a hundred *t*—s, *you pull out one* *S.* vi. 321

Thou, Thee, Thine, Thy—*Passim.*

Tho'.—*Passim.*

Thought.

Sinking from *t.* to *t.*, a vast profound *D.* i. 118
Mears, Warner, Wilkins run: delusive *t.* *D.* ii. 125
Joy fills his soul, joy innocent of *t.* *D.* iii. 249
Confine the *t.*, to exercise the breath *D.* iv. 159
Wrapt up in Self, a God without a *T.* *D.* iv. 485
Rome's pompous glories rising to our *t.* *E.* iii. 24
In pensive *t.* recall the fancy'd scene *E.* v. 33
Ev'n *t.* meets *t.*, ere from the lips it part *E.A.* 95
One *t.* of thee puts all the pomp to flight *E.A.* 273
Devotion's self shall steal a *t.* from Heav'n *E.A.* 357
Expression is the dress of *t.*, and still *E.C.* 318
With some unmeaning thing they call a *t.* *E.C.* 355
And each exalted stanza teems with *t.* *E.C.* 423
What thin partitions Sense from *T.* divide *E.M.* i. 226
What are you thinking? 'Faith the *t.*'s no sin *E.S.* ii. 122
Just of thy Word, in ev'ry *t.* sincere *Ep.* vii. 5
Whose Art was Nature, and whose Pictures *T.* *Ep.* viii. 2
But makes a diff'rence in his *t.* *I.H.* i. 37
Tho' past the recollection of the *t.* *M.E.* i. 47
Too rash for *T.*, for Action too refin'd *M.E.* i. 201
Her Head's untouch'd, that noble Seat of *T.* *M.E.* ii. 74
With too much Thinking to have common *T.* *M.E.* ii. 98
To kill those foes to Fair ones, Time and *T.* *M.E.* ii. 112
No *T.* advances, but her Eddy Brain *M.E.* ii. 121
But never, never, reach'd one gen'rous *T.* *M.E.* ii. 162
No *t.* of peace or happiness at home *M.E.* ii. 247
To raise the *T.*, and touch the Heart be thine *M.E.* ii. 250
Some scruple rose, but thus he eas'd his *t.* *M.E.* iii. 365
As brings all Brobdignag before your *t.* *M.E.* iv. 104
Calm ev'ry *t.*, inspirit ev'ry grace *Mi.* v. 13
The cruel *t.* that stabs me to the heart *Mi.* ix. 54
Explore the *t.*, explain the asking eye *P.S.* 412
If e'er one vision touch'd thy infant *t.* *R.L.* i. 29
The close recesses of the virgin's *t.* *R.L.* iii. 140
The Soul stood forth nor kept a *t.* within *S.* i. 54
Thus BETHEL spoke, who always speaks his *t.* *S.* ii. 129
Or lengthen'd *T.* that gleams thro' many a page *S.* v. 113
My Liege! why Writers little claim your *t.* *S.* v. 356
A hackney coach may chance to spoil a *t.* *S.* vi. 101
Teach ev'ry *t.* within its bounds to roll *S.* vi. 204
As deep in debt, without a *t.* to pay *S.* viii. 17
There sober *t.* pursu'd th' amusing theme *S.* viii. 188
How random *t*—s now meaning chance to find *D.* i. 275
In these gay *t.* the Loves and Graces shine *E.* iv. 1
Why rove my *t.* beyond this last retreat *E.A.* 5
I know there are, to whose presumptuous *t.* *E.C.* 269
And glitt'ring *t.* struck out at ev'ry line *E.C.* 290
See Dionysius Homer's *t.* refine *E.C.* 665
Why words so flowing, *t.* so free *I.H.* iii. 39
While thousand grateful *t.* arise *O.* iii. 30
All but the Sylph—with careful *t.* opprest *R.L.* ii. 53
T., which at Hyde-park-corner I forgot *S.* vi. 208
The *t.* of gods let Granville's verse recite *W.F.* 425
What oft was *t.*, but ne'er so well express'd *E.C.* 298
And where's the Glory? 'twill be only *t.* *E.S.* i. 25
I *t.* the Dean had been too proud *I.H.* ii. 533
And well (he *t.*) advis'd him, "Live like me." *M.E.* iii. 316
T. wond'rous honest, tho' of mean degree *Mi.* iii. 19
Where, nobly-pensive, ST. JOHN sate and *t.* *Mi.* x. 10
What Plato *t.*, and godlike Cato was *P.C.* 18
And *t.* a Lie in verse or prose the same *P.S.* 339
That harmless Mother *t.* no wife a whore *P.S.* 385
He said; when Shock, who *t.* she slept too long *R.L.* i. 115

V

Some *t.* it mounted to the Lunar sphere *R.L.* v. 113
And certain Laws, by suff'rers *t.* unjust *S.* vi. 60
So Luther *t.* the Pater-noster long *S.* vii. 105

Thoughtful.
War, horrid war, your *t.* walks invades *O.* ii. 7
Or wand'ring *t.* in the silent wood *W.F.* 249

Thoughtless.
Just as a blockhead rubs his *t.* skull *E.J.S.* 7
Oh *t.* mortals! ever blind to fate *R.L.* iii. 101
Some *t.* Town, with ease and plenty blest *W.F.* 107

Thousand.
Now *t.* tongues are heard in one loud din *D.* ii. 235
Scream like the winding of ten *t.* jacks *D.* iii. 160
In twice ten *t.* rhyming nights and days *D.* iv. 172
Turn'd to the Sun, she casts a *t.* dyes *D.* iv. 539
Blooms in thy colours for a *t.* years *E.* iii. 58
In the bright Muse tho' *t.* charms conspire *E.C.* 339
When Patriarch-wits surviv'd a *t.* years *E.C.* 479
A *t.* movements scarce one purpose gain *E.M.* i. 54
As who began a *t.* years ago *E.M.* i. 75
For me, the mine a *t.* treasures brings (*rep.*) *E.M.* i. 137
A *t.* ways, is there no black or white *E.M.* ii. 214
Because he wants a *t.* pounds a year *E.M.* iv. 192
Are what ten *t.* envy and adore *E.S.* i. 166
I have a *t.* thanks to give *I.H.* ii. 208
Contracts, inverts, and gives ten *t.* dyes *M.E.* i. 36
His Life, to forfeit it a *t.* ways *M.E.* i. 197
But cares not if a *t.* are undone *M.E.* ii. 176
Sir, Spain has sent a *t.* jars of oil *M.E.* iii. 56
When Hopkins dies, a *t.* lights attend *M.E.* iii. 291
The vast Parterres a *t.* hands shall make *M.E.* iv. 73
While *t.* grateful thoughts arise *O.* iii. 30
Great *Homer* died three *t.* years ago *P.S.* 124
Three *t.* suns went down on *Welsted's* lie *P.S.* 375
Of *t.* bright inhabitants of air *R.L.* i. 28
Swift to the Lock a *t.* Sprites repair (*rep.*) *R.L.* iii. 135
Lord Fanny spins a *t.* such a day *S.* i. 6
"Pray then, what wants he?" Fourscore *t.* pounds *S.* iii. 86
On the broad base of fifty *t.* rise *S.* iv. 74
In the dry desert of a *t.* lines *S.* v. 112
'Tis he, who gives my breast a *t.* pains *S.* v. 342
That turn'd ten *t.* verses, now stands still *S.* vi. 79
When *t.* worlds are round *U.P.* 24
And ere he starts, a *t.* steps are lost *W.F.* 154
Pregnant with t—s fits the Scrap unseen M.E. iii. 47
But *t.* die, without or this or that *M.E.* iii. 95
And fame, this lord of useless *t.* ends *M.E.* iii. 314
And *t.* more in equal mirth maintains *R.L.* iv. 66
The lord of *t.*, than if now *Excis'd S.* ii. 134
He bought at *t.*, what with better wit *S.* vi. 236

Thousandth.
Tenth, or ten *t.*, breaks the chain alike *E.M.* i. 246
Digest his chitty *t.* dinner *Mi.* xii. 18

Thracian.
High on the stern the *T.* rais'd his strain *O.* i. 39

Thread, Thrid.
Or quite unravel all the reas'ning *t. D.* i. 179
Suck the *t.* in, then yield it out again *D.* iii. 58
Feels at each *t.*, and lives along the line *E.M.* i. 228
He spins the slight, self-pleasing *t.* anew *P.S.* 90
My mind resumes the *t.* it dropt before *S.* vi. 207
How many Dutchmen she vouchsaf'd to thrid *D.* iii. 51
T. ev'ry science, run thro' ev'ry school *D.* iv. 256
Some *t.* the mazy ringlets of her hair *R.L.* ii. 139

Threat.
This day black Omens *t.* the brightest Fair *R.L.* ii. 101

Threaten'd.
The reader's *t.* (not in vain) with sleep *E.C.* 353

Threat'ning.
And stares, tremendous, with a *t.* eye *E.C.* 586
See the bold youth strain up the *t.* steep *W.F.* 155

Threats.
A Sylph too warn'd me of the *t.* of fate *R.L.* iv. 165
The distant *t.* of vengeance on his head *P.S.* 348
That t. a fight, and spurns the rising sand Sp. 48

Three.
T. wicked imps of her own Grubstreet choir *D.* ii. 123
"Room for my Lord!" *t.* jockeys in his train *D.* ii. 192
Improve we these. *T.* Cat-calls be the bribe *D.* ii. 231
From dreams of millions, and *t.* groats to pay *D.* ii. 252
T. College Sophs, and *t.* pert Templars came *D.* ii. 379
(His only suit) for twice *t.* years before *D.* iii. 38
On whom *t.* hundred gold-capt youths await *D.* iv. 117
To *t.* essential Partridges in one *D.* iv. 562
Tyrant supreme! shall *t.* Estates command *D.* iv. 603
To morning-walks, and pray're *t.* hours a day *E.* v. 14
Lie in *t.* words, Health, Peace, and Competence *E.M.* iv. 80
And when *t.* Sov'reigns died, could scarce be vext *E.S.* i. 107
'Tis (let me see) *t.* years and more *I.H.* ii. 83 s
To just *t.* millions stinted modest Gage *M.E.* iii. 128
One, one bad *Deal, T. Septlevas* have lost *Mi.* ix. 12
T. things another's modest wishes bound *P.S.* 47
Great Homer died *t.* thousand years ago *P.S.* 124
T. thousand suns went down on Welsted's lie *P.S.* 375
There lay *t.* garters, half a pair of gloves *R.L.* ii. 39
And breathes *t.* am'rous sighs to raise the fire *R.L.* ii. 42
Here thou, great Anna! whom *t.* realms obey *R.L.* iii. 7
Straight the *t.* bands prepare in arms to join *R.L.* iii. 29
In *t.* seal-rings; which after, melted down *R.L.* v. 91
Or if *t.* Ladies like a luckless Play *S.* iv. 87
That makes *t.* members, this can choose a May'r *S.* iv. 106
Whose place is quarter'd out, *t.* parts in four *S.* viii. 136
Then, sighing, thus, "*And am I now t.-score D.* ii. 285
And bare *t.* is all ev'n that can boast *E.C.* 481

Threw.
But 'twas my Guest at whom they *t.* the dirt *E.S.* ii. 145
A charge of Snuff the wily virgin *t. R.L.* v. 82

Thrice.
And *t.* he lifted high the Birth-day brand (*rep.*) *D.* i. 245
T. Budgel aim'd to speak, but *t.* suppress'd *D.* ii. 397
T. happy man! enabled to pursue *M.E.* iii. 275
The KNAVE OF CLUBS *t.* lost: Oh! who could guess *Mi.* ix. 19
T. rung the bell, the slipper knock'd the ground *R.L.* i. 17
And *t.* they twitch'd the diamond in her ear (*rep.*) *R.L.* iii. 137
T. from my trembling hand the patch-box fell *R.L.* iv. 162
The Fool, whose Wife elopes some *t.* a quarter *S.* iii. 150

Thrills.
The blessing *t.* thro' all the lab'ring throng *S.* v. 239

Thrive.
We *t.* at *Westminster* on Fools like you *Mi.* xi. 11
But thanks to Homer, since I live and *t. S.* v. 68
And says our wars *t.* ill, because delay'd *S.* viii. 163

Thriv'd.
Sprung the rank weed, and *t.* with large increase *E.C.* 535

Thrives.
Farewell the stage! if just as *t.* the play *S.* v. 302

Thriving.
The *t.* plants, ignoble broomsticks made *M.E.* iv. 97

Throat.
She ceas'd—Then swells the Chapel-royal *t. D.* i. 319
Down his own *t.* he risk'd the Grecian gold *D.* iv. 382
Is it for thee the linnet pours his *t. E.M.* iii. 33
Cramm'd to the *t.* with Ortolans *I.H.* i. 62
Oldfield with more than Harpy *t.* endu'd *S.* ii. 25
To pant and tremble thro' an Eunuch's *t. S.* v. 154
While all its t—s the Gallery extends S. v. 236

Throb.
No cheek is known to blush, no heart to *t. E.S.* i. 103
In Fulvia's buckle heal the t—s below M.E. iii. 88

Throne.
Close to those walls where Folly holds her *t. D.* i. 29
Four guardian Virtues, round, support her *t. D.* i. 46
And I, a Nursing-mother, rock the *t. D.* i. 312
Henley's gilt tub, or Fleckno's Irish *t. D.* ii. 2
She mounts the *T.*: her head a cloud conceal'd *D.* ii. 17

THRON'D—TIE. 323

And all the Nations summon'd to the *T. D.* iv. 72
To stick the Doctor's Chair into the *T. D.* iv. 177
Mistress I dismiss that rabble from your *t. D.* iv. 209
Prop thine, O Empress I like each neighbour *T. D.* iv. 333
And aspect ardent to the *T.* appeal *D.* iv. 402
Bland and familiar to the *t.* he came *D.* iv. 497
Guard my Prerogative, assert my *T. D.* iv. 583
She comes! she comes! the sable *T.* behold *D.* iv. 629
Himself, his *t.*, his world, I'd scorn 'em all *E.A.* 86
And Nature tremble to the *t.* of God *E.M.* i. 256
Or Wyndham, just to Freedom and the *T. E.S.* ii. 90
Safe from the Bar, the Pulpit, and the *T. E.S.* ii. 210
The *T.* a Bigot keep, a Genius quit *M.E.* i. 91
Bear, like the Turk, no brother near the *t. P.S.* 198
If on a Pillory, or near a *T. P.S.* 365
And better got than *Bestia's* from the *T. P.S.* 391
And guard with Arms divine the British *T. R.L.* ii. 90
Two handmaids wait the *t.*: alike in place *R.L.* iv. 25
And Asia's Tyrants tremble at your *T. S.* v. 403
With terrors round, can Reason hold her *t. S.* vi. 310
Around his *t.* the sea-born brothers stood *W.F.* 337

Thron'd.

T. on seven hills, the Antichrist of wit *D.* ii. 16
Then *t.* in glass, and nam'd it CAROLINE *D.* iv. 409
T. in the centre of his thin designs *P.S.* 93

Throng.

Involves a vast involuntary *t. D.* iv. 82
So vast a *t.* the stage can ne'er contain *E.C.* 283
So much they scorn the crowd, that if the *t. E.C.* 426
A Beau and Witling perish'd in the *t. R.L.* v. 59
The blessing thrills thro' all the lab'ring *t. S.* v. 239
And yet my numbers please the rural *t. Su.* 49
With t—s *promiscuous strow the level green R.L.* iii.80
Unnumber'd *t.* on ev'ry side are seen *R.L.* iv. 47
Thicker than arguments, temptations *t. E.M.* ii. 75
There ev'ry Grace and Muse shall *t. I.H.* iii. 27
To Theatres, and to Rehearsals *t. S.* v. 173

Throng'd.

See thy bright altars *t.* with prostrate Kings *M.* 93
Where are those troops of Poor, that *t.* of yore *S.*v.i.113

Thronging.

See *t.* Millions to the Pagod run *E.S.* i. 157

Through, Throughout.—*Passim.*

Throw.

When Ajax strives some rock's vast weight to *t. E.C.*370
For some to heap, and some to *t.* away *M.E.* iii. 6
Presume thy bolts to *t. U.P.* 26

Thrown.

And shall no Egg in Japhet's face be *t. E.S.* ii. 189
Where all cry out, "What sums are *t.* away!" *M.E.* iv. 100
At am'rous Flavio is the stocking *t. S.* iii. 148

Throws.

Black Melancholy sits, and round her *t. E.A.* 165

Thrush.

The *T.* may chant to the forsaken groves *Sp.* 14

Thrust.

Compos'd he stood, bold Benson *t.* him by *D.* iv. 110
T. some Mechanic Cause into his place *D.* iv. 475
How should I *t.* myself between *I.H.* ii. 50 s

Thrusts.

And *t.* his person full into your face *D.* iii. 140
I puke, I nauseate,—yet he *t.* in more *S.* viii. 153

Thuis.

Then snatch'd a sheet of *T.* from her bed *D.* i. 258

Thumb.

She with one finger and a *t.* subdu'd *R.L.* v. 80

Thunder.

Got by fierce whirlwinds, and in *t.* born *A.* 99
This Box my *T.*, this right hand my God *D.* i. 202
Loud *t.* to its bottom shook the bog *D.* i. 329
With *t.* rumbling from the mustard-bowl *D.* ii. 226
When lo! a burst of *t.* shook the flood *D.* ii. 325
Wings the red lightning, and the *t.* rolls *D.* iii. 256

Here point your *t.*, and exhaust your rage *E.C.* 555
And hurls the *T.* of our Laws on *Gin E.S.* i. 130
ARGYLL, the State's whole *T.* born to wield *E.S.* ii. 86
And falls like *t.* on the prostrate Ace *R.L.* iii. 98
Jove's *t.* roars, heav'n trembles all around *R.L.* v. 49
With Gun, Drum, Trumpet, Blunderbuss, and *T. S.* i. 28
And ell the *T.* of the Pit ascends *S.* v. 327
Straight a short *t.* breaks the frozen sky *W.F.* 130
Bear Britain's *t.*, and her Cross display *W.F.* 387
She midst the lightning's blaze, and *t.'s* sound *E.M.* iii. 249
And *Jove's own* T—*s follow Mars's Drums D.* iv. 68
With Heav'n's own *t.* shook the world below *E.M.* iii. 267
And shook the Stage with *t.* all his own *Mi.* ii. 16
Forget to *t.*, and recall her *fires E.M.* iv. 124

Thunder'd.

If nature *t.* in his op'ning ears *E.M.* i. 201

Thund'rer.

Ere Pallas issu'd from the *T.'s* head *D.* i. 10

Thund'ring.

Of arts, but *t.* against heathen lore *D.* iii. 102
Bursts out, resistless, with a *t.* tide *E.C.* 630
While mighty WILLIAM'S *t.* arm prevail'd *S.* vi. 63

Thus.—*Passim.*

Thwart.

All must be false that *t.* this One great End *E.M.*iii.309

Thyrsis.

T., the music of that murm'ring spring *W.* 1

Tibbald, Tibalds.

There hapless Shakespear, yet of *T.* sore *D.* i. 133
Can make a Cibber, *T.*, or Ozell *D.* i. 286
Call *T.* Shakespear, and he'll swear the Nine *S.* vi. 137
So humble, he has knock'd at *T.'s* door *P.S.* 372
From slashing Bentley down to *pidling* Tibalds *P.S.* 164

Tiber.

Streets pav'd with Heroes, *T.* chok'd with Gods *D.* iii. 108
Or *T.*, now no longer Roman, rolls *D.* iv. 299
Tho' *T.'s* streams immortal Rome behold *W.F.* 357

Tibullus.

"My dear *T.!*" if that will not do *S.* vi. 143

Tickets.

Disdains all loss of *T.* or Codille *M.E.* ii. 266

Tickle.

He wins this Patron, who can *t.* best *D.* ii. 195

Tickled.

Pleas'd with a rattle, *t.* with a straw *E.M.* ii. 276

Ticklest.

The more thou *t.*, gripes his fist the faster *D.* ii. 210

Tide.

Bursts out, resistless, with a thund'ring *t. E.C.* 630
One *t.* of glory, one unclouded blaze *M.* 102
While China's earth receives the smoking *t. R.L.* iii. 110
And win my way by yielding to the *t. S.* iii. 34
Pour the full *t.* of eloquence along *S.* vi. 171
Project long shadows o'er the crystal *t. W.F.* 376
Whole nations enter with each swelling *t. W.F.* 399
Then ships of uncouth form shall stem the *t. W.F.* 403
Roll all the t—s; then back their circles bring *D.* iii. 56
Go, measure earth, weigh air, and state the *t. E.M.* ii. 20
Prescient, the *t.* or tempests to withstand *E.M.* iii. 101
The sunbeams trembling on the floating *t. R.L.* ii. 48
His wealthy waters and alternate *t. W.F.* 334
Tho' foaming Hermus swells with *t.* of gold *W.F.* 358

Tie.

The common int'rest, or endear the *t. E.M.* ii. 254
Oh source of ev'ry social *t. O.* iii. 25
This binds in *t.* more easy, yet more strong *E.* iv. 67
Love, free as air, at sight of human *t. E.A.* 75
But of this frame, the bearings, and the *t. E.M.* i. 29

Reflection, Reason, still the *t.* improve *E.M.* i. 133
All *T.* dissolv'd, and ev'ry Sin forgiv'n *E.S.* i. 94
T. up the knocker, say I'm sick, I'm dead P.S. a

Tied.
Hence Bards, like Proteus long in vain *t.* down *D.* i. 37
Seiz'd and *t.* down to judge, how wretched I. *P.S.* 33

Tiger.
And boys in flow'ry bands the *t.* lead *M.* 78
Wolves gave thee suck, and savage T—s *fed A.* 90

Till.—*Passim.*

Tills.
The knave deserves it, when he *t.* the soil *E.M.* iv. 152

Tilt.
To run a muck, and *t.* at all I meet *S.* i. 70

Time.
In eldest *t.*, ere mortals writ or read *D.* i. 9
How *T.* himself stands still at her command *D.* i. 71
To whom *T.* bears me on his rapid wing *D.* iv. 6
He may indeed (if sober all this *t.*) *D.* iv. 259
His *t.*, the Muse, the witty, and the fair *E.* iv. 10
Tho' not too strictly bound to *T.* and place *E.* iv. 28
To part her *t.* 'twixt reading and bohea *E.* v. 15
So when your Slave, at some dear idle *t. E.* v. 41
Nor *t.* nor moths e'er spoil'd so much as they *E.C.* 113
Once on a *t.*, La Mancha's Knight, they say *E.C.* 267
His *t.* a moment, and a point his space *E.M.* i. 72
Correct old *T.*, and regulate the Sun *E.M.* ii. 22
'Tis to mistake them, costs the *t.* and pain *E.M.* ii. 216
They love themselves, a third *t.*, in their race *E.M.* iii. 124
Oh! while along the stream of *T.* thy name *E.M.* iv. 383
Why so! if Satire knows its *T.* and Place *E.S.* i. 87
Once on a *t.* (so runs the Fable) *I.H.* ii. 157
Nor yet shall Waller yield to *t. I.H.* iv. 7
T., that on all things lays his lenient hand *M.E.* i. 224
To kill those foes to Fair ones, *T.* and Thought *M.E.* ii. 112
The wisest Fool much *T.* has ever made *M.E.* ii. 124
The Tempter saw his *t.*; the work he ply'd *M.E.* iii. 369
Nature shall join you; *T.* shall make it grow *M.E.* iv. 69
Tho' *T.* is precious, and I want some tea *Mi.* ix. 28
Some Dukes at *Mary-Bone* bowl *T.* away *Mi.* ix. 100
What *T.* would spare, from Steel receives its date *R.L.* iii. 171
Whoe'er offends, at some unlucky *t. S.* i. 77
Not but we may exceed, some holy *t. S.* ii. 85
Yet *T.* ennobles, or degrades each Line *S.* iv. 44
If *T.* improve our Wit as well as Wine *S.* v. 49
T. was, a sober Englishman would knock *S.* v. 161
The Zeal of Fools offends at any *t. S.* v. 406
Nay worse, to ask for Verse at such a *t. S.* vi. 31
This subtle Thief of life, this paltry *T. S.* vi. 77
There is a *t.* when Poets will grow dull *S.* vi. 200
T., that at last matures a clap to pox *S.* vii. 47
Well, if it be my *t.* to quit the stage *S.* viii. 1
So *T.*, that changes all things, had ordain'd *S.* viii. 43
In *t.* to come, may pass for holy writ *S.* viii. 287
T. conquers all, and we must *T.* obey *W.* 88
The *t.* shall come, when, free as seas or wind *W.F.* 397
Old scenes of glory, t—s long cast behind *D.* iii. 63
Th' Augustus born to bring Saturnian *t. D.* iii. 320
But (happy for him as the *t.* went then) *D.* iv. 115
Nor fear a dearth in these flagitious *t. E.C.* 529
Which serv'd the past, and must the *t.* to come *E.M.* ii. 52
Ah! how unlike the man of *t.* to come *E.M.* iii. 161
Rapt into future *t.*, the Bard begun *M.* 7
Tenets with Books, and Principles with *T. M.E.* i. 173
With Styx nine *t.* round her *O.* i. 91
Alas! 'tis ten *t.* worse when they *repent F.S.* 108
Happy! ah ten *t.* happy had I been *R.L.* iv. 149
It stands on record, that in Richard's *t. S.* i. 145
Why had not I in those good *t.* my birth *S.* ii. 97
And buy a rope, that future *t.* may tell *S.* ii. 109
Had ancient *t.* conspir'd to disallow *S.* v. 135
Now *t.* are chang'd, and one Poetic Itch *S.* v. 169
But *T.* corrupt, and Nature, ill-inclin'd *S.* v. 291
Let me for once presume t' instruct the *t. S.* v. 340
Charles, to late *t.* be transmitted fair *S.* v. 380
I, who at some *t.* spend, at others spare *S.* vi. 290
The World's great Oracle in *t.* to come *W.F.* 382

Timely.
While others, *t.*, to the neighb'ring Fleet *D.* ii. 427

Timid.
Let others creep by *t.* steps, and slow *D.* iv. 465
He stood the furious foe, the *t.* friend *I'.S.* 343

Timon.
Greatness, with *T.*, dwells in such a draught *M.E.* iv. 103
A hundred smart in *T.* and in Balaam *S.* i. 41
His Wealth brave *T.* gloriously confounds *S.* iv. 85
At *T.*'s *Villa let us pass a day M.E.* iv. 99

Tim'rous.
A *t.* foe, and a suspicious friend *P.S.* 206
Sol thro' white curtains shot a *t.* ray *R.L.* i. 13
T. by nature, of the Rich in awe *S.* i. 7

Timotheus.
And what *T.* was, is Dryden now *E.C.* 383
Hear how T.' vary'd lays surprise *E.C.* 374

Tincture.
All Manners take a *t.* from our own *M.E.* i. 33
Dipt in the richest *t.* of the skies *R.L.* ii. 65

Tinctur'd.
Then *t.* as it runs with Lethe's streams *D.* ii. 339

Tindal.
T. and Toland, prompt at priests to jeer *D.* ii. 399
Where *T.* dictates, and Silenus snores *D.* iv. 492
One who believes as *T.* leads the way *S.* iv. 64
In Toland's, T.'s, and in Woolston's days *D.* iii. 213

Tingling.
The pale Boy-Senator yet *t.* stands *D.* iv. 147

Tinkling.
The grots that echo to the *t.* rills *E.A.* 158

Tinsel.
Ye *t.* Insects! whom a Court maintains *E.S.* ii. 220

Tinsell'd.
She, *t.* o'er with robes of varying hues *D.* i. 81

Tints.
Or blend in beauteous *t.* the colour'd mass *E.* iii. 5

Tip.
The Nose of Hautgout, and the *T.* of Taste *M.E.* ii. 80
Sudden, she storms! she raves! You t. the wink M.E. ii. 33

Tips.
And *t.* with Silver all the walls *I.H.* ii. 190

Tipt.
Bright with the gilded button *t.* its head *D.* iv. 408

Tire.
To *t.* our patience, than mislead our sense *E.C.* 4
Or one vain wit's, that might a hundred *t. E.C.* 45
Tho' oft the ear the open vowels *t. E.C.* 345
Riches that vex, and Vanities that *t. Mi.* v. 4

Tir'd.
Till *t.* he sleeps, and Life's poor play is o'er *E.M.* ii. 282
For ever exercis'd, yet never *t. E.M.* iv. 322
T., not determin'd, to the last we yield *M.E.* i. 43
So when the Sun's broad beam has *t.* the sight *M.E.* ii. 253
But you are *t.*—I'll tell a tale—Agreed *M.E.* iii. 338
T. of the scene Parterres and Fountains yield *M.E.* iv. 87
Treated, caress'd, and *t.*, I take my leave *M.E.* iv. 165
When the *t.* glutton labours thro' a treat *S.* ii. 31
Or *t.* in search of Truth, or search of Rhyme *S.* ii. 86
When the *t.* Nation breath'd from civil war *S.* v. 273
T. with a tedious march, one luckless night *S.* vi. 35

Tires.
Th' increasing prospect *t.* our wand'ring eyes *E.C.* 231

'Tis.—*Passim.*

Titans.
Encourag'd thus, Wit's *T.* brav'd the skies *E.C.* 552

Titian.
Paulo's free stroke, and *T.'s* warmth divine *E.* iii. 38.

Titillating.
The pungent grains of *t.* dust *R.L.* v. 84.

Title.
O Thou! whatever *t.* please thine ear *D.* i. 19.
Who gain'd no *t.*, and who lost no friend *M.E.* v. 70
Great without *T.*, without Fortune bless'd *S.* iii. 181
On Poets' tombs see Benson's t—s *writ D.* iii. 327
The Queen confers her *T.* and *Degrees D.* iv. 566
Nor let false Shows, or empty *T.* please *E.* iv. 47
Stuck o'er with *t.* and hung round with strings *E.M.* iv. 205
Things change their *t.* as our manners turn *M.E.* iii. 379
What once had beauty, *t.*, wealth and fame *U.L.* 70

Titled.
Or for a *T.* Punk, or foreign Flame *S.* iv. 124

Titt'ring.
And *t.* push'd the Pedants off the place *D.* iv. 276
Comes *t.* on, and shoves you from the stage *S.* vi. 325

Tittle.
There he stopp'd short, nor since has writ a *t. Mi.* iii. 9

Titus.
And Nero reigns a *T.*, if he will *E.M.* ii. 198
Was made for Caesar—but for *T.* too *E.M.* iv. 146
And give to *T.* old Vespasian's due *M.E.* v. 18

To.—*Passim*.

To-be.
Man never Is, but always *T.* blest *E.M.* i. 96
T. contents his natural desire *E.M.* i. 109

To-day.
And still to-morrow's wiser than *t. E.C.* 437
From her own Sex should mercy find *t. E.Y.S:* 2
The blest *t.* is as completely so *E.M.* i. 75
The lamb thy riot dooms to bleed *t. E.M.* i. 81
And for that very cause I print *t. E.S.* ii. 3
If not the Tradesman who set up *t. E.S.* ii. 36
Or, "Have you nothing new *t. I.H.* ii. 93.
Can make to-morrow cheerful as *t. M.E.* ii. 258

To-morrow.
And still *t.*'s wiser than to-day *E.C.* 437
Not yet, my Friend! *t.* 'faith it may *E.S.* ii. 2
Much less the 'Prentice who *t.* may *E.S.* ii. 37
T. my Appeal comes on *I.H.* ii. 71 s
Can make *t.* cheerful as to-day *M.E.* ii. 258

Toad.
A Nest, a *T.*, a Fungus, or a Flow'r *D.* iv. 400
Or at the ear of Eve, familiar *T. P.S.* 319
Turns Hares to Larks, and Pigeons into T—s *D.* iv. 554

Toast.
Whose game is Whisk, whose treat a *t.* in sack *E.* v. 24
Already see you a degraded *t. R.L.* iv. 109
The wise man's passion, and the vain man's *t. R.L.* v. 10
By names of T—s *retails each batter'd jade D.* ii. 134
T. live a scorn, and Queens may die a jest *M.E.* ii. 282
To *T.* our wants and wishes, is her way *M.E.* ii. 88

Together.—*Passim*.

Toil.
While lab'ring oxen, spent with *t.* and beat *A.* 61
Turn what they will to Verse, theirs *t.* is vain *D.* iv. 213
How finish'd with illustrious *t.* appears *E.* iii. 39
The merchant's *t.*, the sage's indolence *E.M.* ii. 172
Where grows?—where grows it not? If vain our *t. E.M.* iv. 13
Heav'n still with laughter the vain *t.* surveys *E.M.* iv. 75
That, vice may merit, 'tis the price of *t. E.M.* iv. 151
The *t.*, the danger of the Seas *I.H.* ii. 71 s
In vain th' observer eyes the builder's *t. M.E.* i. 220
Behold Villario's ten years' *t.* complete *M.E.* iv. 79
Whose cheerful tenants bless their yearly *t. M.E.* iv. 183
From each she nicely culls with curious *t. R.L.* i. 131
For when success a Lover's *t.* attends *R.L.* ii. 33
Ease of their *t.*, and partners of their care *S.* v. 246
Why all your t—s? *your sons have learn'd to sing D.* iv. 546

Then see them broke with *t.*, or sunk in ease *E.M.* iv. 297
And shall not Britain now reward his *t. M.E.* iii. 215
After a life of gen'rous *T.* endur'd *S.* v. 9
The woods and fields their pleasing *t.* deny *W.F.* 120
Or hand, to t., *aspir'd to be the head.E.M.* i. 260

Toil'd.
Where mix'd with Slaves the groaning Martyr *t. M.E.* v. 6

Toilet.
Fop at the *t.*, flatt'rer at the board *P.S.* 328
And now, unveil'd, the *T.* stands display'd *R.L.* i. 121
And the long labours of the *T.* cease *R.L.* iii. 24
Or Sappho at her *t.*'s greasy task *M.E.* ii. 25

Toils.
Ploughs, burns, manures, and *t.* from sun to sun *S.* vi. 271

Toilsome.
Recall those nights that clos'd thy *t.* days *E.* i. 15

Token.
He bears no *t.* of the sabler streams *D.* ii. 297
No Grace of Heav'n or *t.* of th' Elect *M.E.* iii. 18
The silver *t.*, and the circled green *R.L.* i. 32

Toland.
Tindal and *T.* prompt at priests to jeer *D.* ii. 399
In T.'s, *Tindal's, and in Woolston's days D.* iii. 212

Told.
Or sadly *t.*, how many Hopes lie here *Ep.* xiv. 6
Our Friend Dan Prior, *t.*, (you know) *I.H.* ii. 153
And jingling down the back-stairs, *t.* the crew *M.E.* iii. 37
A wizard *t.* him in these words our fate *M.E.* iii. 114
The truth once *t.* (and wherefore should we lie?) *P.S.* 81
There are, (I scarce can think it, but am *t.*,) *S.* i. 1
I *t.* you when I went, I could not write *S.* vi. 1
And *t.* in sighs to all the trembling trees *W.* 62

Tolerably.
Narcissa's nature, *t.* mild *M.E.* ii. 53

Toll.
But some excising Courtier will have *t. S.* viii. 147

Tolling.
Now sink in sorrows with a *t.* bell *D.* ii. 228

Tom.
T. struts a Soldier, open, bold, and brave *M.E.* i. 153
May *T.*, whom heav'n sent down to raise *Mi.* xii. 15
This day T.'s *fair account has run Mi.* xii. 3

Tomb.
Who praises now? his Chaplain on his *T. D.* iv. 514
Call round her *T.* each object of desire *E.* iii. 49
Propt on some *t.*, a neighbour of the dead *E.A.* 304
Of half that live the butcher and the *t. E.M.* iii. 162
To which thy *T.* shall guide enquiring eyes *Ep.* v. 4
Pensive hast follow'd to the silent *t. Ep.* vii. 12
Peaceful sleep out the Sabbath of the *T. Mi.* v. 19
Neglected die, and toll it on his *t. P.S.* 258
A *t.* of boil'd and roast, and flesh and fish *S.* ii. 70
Nor hallow'd dirge be mutter'd o'er thy *t. U.L.* 62
Sing, while beside the shaded *t.* I mourn *W.* 19
Make sacred Charles's *t.* for ever known *W.F.* 319
On Poets' T—s *see Benson's titles writ D.* iii. 235
Pale Spectres, gaping *t.*, and purple fires *R.L.* iv. 44
The very *T.* now vanish'd like their dead *M.E.* v. 4
"Then, happy Man who shows the *T.!*" said I *S.* viii. 102
The fox obscene to gaping *t.* retires *W.F.* 71

Tomes.
Dry'd butterflies, and *t.* of casuistry *R.L.* v. 122

Tone.
Then mount the clerks and in one lazy *t. D.* ii. 387

Tongue.
Full and eternal privilege of *t. D.* ii. 378
Bless'd with his father's front, his mother's *t. D.* ii. 416
How fluent nonsense trickles from his *t. D.* iii. 201
Till Death untimely stopp'd his tuneful *t. E.* i. 2
And truths divine came mended from that *t. E.A.* 66

With his own *t.* still edifies his ears *E.C.* 614
Their law his eye, their oracle his *t. E.M.* iii. 218
The Honey dropping from Favonio's *t. E.S.* i. 67
Eurydice still trembled on his *t. O.* i. 114
An angel *T.*, which no man can persuade *M.E.* i. 199
Just brought out this, when scarce his *t.* could stir *M.E.* i. 254
Her *T.* bewitch'd as oddly as her Eyes *M.E.* ii. 47
Leap'd up, and wak'd his mistress with his *t. R.L.* i. 116
With eyes that pry not, *t.* that ne'er repeats *S.* i. 135
What better teach a Foreigner the *t. S.* v. 206
'Tis to small purpose that you hold your *t. S.* vi. 155
Rich with the treasures of each foreign *t. S.* vi. 173
He forms one *t.*, exotic and refin'd *S.* viii. 49
Whose *t.* will compliment you to the devil (*rep.*) *S.* viii. 57
And make my *t.* victorious as her eyes *Sp.* 50
Deaf the prais'd ear, and mute the tuneful *t. U.L.* 76
There the last numbers flow'd from Cowley's *t. W.F.* 272
Now thousand *t—s are heard in one loud din D.* ii. 235
Sense, speech, and measure, living *t.* and dead *D.* iii. 167
To tell 'em, would a hundred *t.* require *E.C.* 44
Hear, in all *t.* consenting Pæans ring *E.C.* 186
And with their forky *t.* shall innocently play *M.* 84
Sighs, sobs, and passions, and the war of *t. R.L.* iv. 84
The Doctor's Wormwood style, the Hash of *t. S.* viii. 52
Had once a pretty gift of *T.* enough *S.* viii. 77

Too.—*Passim.*

Tool.
Not Lucre's madman, nor Ambition's *t. P.S.* 335
Of Honour, bind me not to maul his T—s E.S. ii. 147

Took.
Amid that area wide they *t.* their stand *D.* ii. 27
Walker with rev'rence *t.*, and laid aside *D.* ii. 106
To see a footman kick'd that *t.* his pay *E.S.* ii. 151
Whose Speech you *t.*, and gave it to a Friend *E.S.* ii. 177
In complaisance, I *t.* the *Queen* he gave *Mi.* ix. 49
Was it for this you *t.* such constant care *R.L.* iv. 97
Who felt the wrong, or fear'd it, *t.* th' alarm *S.* v. 255
If, after this, you *t.* the graceless lad *S.* vi. 21
Tore down a Standard, *t.* the Fort and all *S.* vi. 41

Tooth.
Gor'd with unrelenting *T. Mi.* vii. 12
Nor strive with all the tempest in my teeth S. vi. 301
See on the T.-pick, Mars and Cupid strive Mi. ix. 31

Toothless.
His saws are *t.*, and his Hatchet's Lead *E.S.* ii. 149

Tooting.
Would drink and doze at *T.* or Earls-Court *S.* vi. 113

Top.
High on Parnassus' *t.* her sons she show'd *E.C.* 94
And on its *t.* descends the mystic dove *M.* 12
And Carmel's flow'ry *t.* perfumes the skies *M.* 28
And Cynthus' *t.* forsook for Windsor shades *W.F.* 166
And lash'd so long, like t—s, are lash'd asleep E.C. 601
T.-gallant *he, and she in all her trim S.* viii. 230
As to soft gales *t.-heavy* pines bow low *D.* ii. 391

Topham.
He buys for *T.*, Drawings and Designs *M.E.* iv. 7

Tops.
Trims Europe's balance, *t.* the statesman's part *S.* viii. 154

Torch.
The *t.* of Venus burns not for the dead *E.A.* 258

Tore.
T. down a Standard, took the Fort and all *S.* vi. 41

Torment.
Poor Avarice one *t.* more would find *M.E.* iii. 59
No fiends t., no Christians thirst for gold E.M. i. 108

Torn.
Thou wert from Ætna's burning entrails *t. A.* 91
Appear more glorious, as more hack'd and *t. D.* iv. 124
A morning's pleasure, and at ev'ning *t. E.* iv. 66

Torrent.
The hoarse, rough verse should like the *t.* roar *E.C.* 369
Stemm'd the wild *t.* of a barb'rous age *E.C.* 695
Or P—ge pour'd forth the *T.* of his Wit *E.S.* ii. 159

Tortoise.
The *T.* here, and Elephant unite *R.L.* i. 135

Tortur'd.
And cries of *t.* ghosts (*rep.*) *O.* i. 62

Tortures.
Chromatic *t.* soon shall drive them hence *D.* iv. 55
Heav'n, as its purest Gold, by *T.* try'd *Ep.* vi. 9
The Poet's hell, its *t.*, fiends, and flames *S.* viii. 7

Tort'ring.
For this with *t.* irons wreath'd around *R.L.* iv. 100

Tory.
Said, "Tories call'd him Whig, and Whigs a *T.*;" *E.S.* i. 8
Who know how like Whig Ministers to *T. E.S.* i. 106
Point abo to Priest or Elder, Whig or *T. E.S.* ii. 96
While Tories call me Whig, and Whigs a *T. S.* i. 68
Now Whig, now *T.*, what we lov'd we hate *S.* v. 157
And cackling save the Monarchy of T—ies D. i. 212

Toss.
Each man an Askapart, of strength to *t. S.* viii. 276

Toss'd, Tost.
This Mess, *t.* up of Hockley-hole and White's *D.* i. 222
Thus in a sea of folly *t. I.H.* ii. 125
His papers light fly diverse, *t—t* in air *D.* ii. 114
Oft, in the Passions' wild rotation *t. M.E.* i. 41
Not to the skies in useless columns *t. M.E.* iii. 255

Tot'nham = Tottenham.
In *T.* fields the brethren with amaze *D.* ii. 261

Totter.
And *t.* on in bus'ness to the last *M.E.* i. 129

Tott'ring.
The *t.* China shook without a wind *R.L.* iv. 163

Touch.
Beeves, at his *t.*, at once to jelly turn *D.* iv. 551
Or *t.*, if tremblingly alive all o'er *M.* i. 197
The spider's *t.*, how exquisitely fine *E.M.* i. 217
Than favour'd Man by *t.* ethereal slain *E.M.* iii. 68
Now gentle t—es wanton o'er his face D. ii. 201
Some wand'ring *t.*, some reflected light *M.E.* ii. 153
To t. Achilles' only tender part D. ii. 218
Can *t.* Immortals, 'tis a Soul like thine *E.* i. 22
In Sappho *t.* the *Failings of the Sex E.S.* i. 15
Reverent *t.* thee ! but with honest zeal *E.S.* ii. 216
Our Courtier scarce could *t.* a bit *I.H.* ii. 171
To raise the Thought, and *t.* the Heart be thine *M.E.* ii. 250
Hear me, and *t.* Belinda with chagrin *R.L.* iv. 77
Alas ! few verses *t.* their nicer ear *S.* i. 33
Ev'n those you *t.* not, hate you. What should ail them ? *S.* i. 41
But *t.* me, and no Minister so sore *S.* i. 76
That *t.* my bell, I cannot run away *S.* ii. 12
How could Devotion *t.* the country pews *S.* v. 233
T. the fair fame of Albion's golden days *W.F.* 424

Touch'd.
Thou, yet unborn, hast *t.* this sacred shore *D.* iii. 45
Not *t.* by Nature, and not reach'd by Art *D.* iii. 230
For hearts so *t.*, so pierc'd, so lost as mine *E.A.* 196
Not *t.*, but rapt ; not waken'd, but inspir'd *E.A.* 202
The lines, tho' *t.* but faintly, are drawn right *E.C.* 22
Yet *t.* and sham'd by Ridicule alone *E.S.* ii. 211
T. with the Flame that breaks from *Virtue's Shrine E.S.* ii. 233
Blest Satirist ! who *t.* the mean so true *Ep.* i. 7
Who *t.* Isaiah's hallow'd lips with fire *M.* 6
As when she *t.* the brink of all we hate *M.E.* ii. 42
T. by thy hand, again Rome's glories shine *M.E.* v. 46
If e'er one vision *t.* thy infant thought *R.L.* i. 29
And secret transport *t.* the conscious swain *W.F.* 90

Touches.
T. some wheel, or verges to some goal *E.M.* i. 59
But *t.* some above, and some below *E.M.* iv. 336

Touching.
Such skill in passing all, and *t.* none *D.* iv. 258
That *t.* one must strike the other too *E.M.* iii. 292

TOUGH—TRAITOR.

Tough.
Fans clap, silks rustle, and *t.* whalebones crack *R.L.* v. 40

Toupee.
Sneers at another, in *t.* or gown *D.* iv. 88

Tow'r.
Where round some mould'ring *t.* pale ivy creeps *E.A.*243
How shin'd the Soul, unconquer'd in the *T. E.S.* ii. 83
At home, tho' exil'd; free, tho' in the *T. S.* iii. 184
I make no question but the *T.* had stood *S.* viii. 85
Tenants with sighs the smokeless t—s survey M.E. iii. 191
Where Thames with pride surveys his rising *t. R.L.* iii. 2
And strikes to dust th' imperial *t.* of Troy *R.L.* iii. 174
Earth shakes her nodding *t.*, the ground gives way *R.L.* v. 51

Tow'ring.
While *t.* o'er the Alphabet, like Saul *D.* iv. 217
So pleas'd at first the *t.* Alps we try *E.C.* 225
The feast his *t.* genius marks *Mi.* xii. 9
Tho' Gods assembled grace his *t.* height *W.F.* 34
Where *t.* oaks their growing honours rear *W.F.* 221

Tow'ry.
Exalt thy *t.* head, and lift thy eyes *M.* 86

Town.
Escape in Monsters, and amaze the *t. D.* i. 38
Bays, form'd by Nature Stage and *T.* to bless *D.* i. 109
At once the Bear and Fiddle of the *t. D.* ii. 224
And turn this whole illusion on the *t. D.* ii. 132
Lo P—p—le's brow, tremendous to the *T. D.* iii. 151
Whate'er of dunce in College or in *T. D.* iv. 87
Stunn'd with his giddy Larum half the *t. D.* iv. 292
Drags from the *T.* to wholesome Country air *E.* v. 2
Vext to be still in *t.*, I knit my brow *E.* v. 49
As sev'ral garbs with country, *t.*, and court *E.C.* 323
But catch the spreading notion of the *t. E.C.* 409
Faith, let the modest Matrons of the *t. E.J.S.* 49
Blunt could *do Bus'ness*, H—ggins *knew the T. E.S.*i.14
I never nam'd; the *T.*'s enquiring yet *E.S.* ii. 21
In *t.*, what Objects could I meet *I.H.* i. 7
And W* and H** both in *t. I.H.* i. 14
I must by all means come to *t. I.H.* ii. 33 s
Let my Lord know you're come to *t. I.H.* ii. 44 s
To Windsor and again to *T. I.H.* ii. 98 s
Those Cares that haunt the Court and *T. I.H.* ii. 132
Name a *T.* Life, and in a trice *I.H.* ii. 155
Receiv'd a *T.* Mouse at his Board *I.H.* ii. 159
And Judges job, and Bishops bite the *t. M.E.* iii. 141
To *t.* he comes, completes the nation's hope *M.E.* iii. 213
To compass this, his building is a *T. M.E.* iv. 105
First shade a Country, and then raise a *T. M.E.* iv. 190
First suppl'd a Poet's Fortune in the *T. Mi.* iii. 2
Set up with these he ventur'd on the *T. Mi.* iii. 7
Trudges to *t.*, and first turns Chambermaid *Mi.* iii. 16
In a translated Suit, then tries the *T. Mi.* iii. 21
An awkward Thing, when first she came to *T. Mi.* ix. 59
Nor, like a puppy, daggled thro' the *t. P.S.* 225
Let the two *Curlls* of *T.* and Court, abuse *P.S.* 380
For Snug's the Word: my dear! we'll live in *t. S.* iii. 147
And from the moment we oblige the *t. S.* v. 370
Next pleas'd his Excellence a *t.* to batter *S.* vi. 44
And here, while *t.*, and court, and city roars *S.* vi. 123
All Worldly's hens, nay partridge, sold to *t. S.* vi. 234
Half that the Dev'l o'erlooks from Lincoln *S.* vi. 245
This *T.*, I had the sense to hate is too *S.* vii. 2
Can gratis see the country, or the *t. S.* viii. 145
Shall I, the Terror of this sinful *t. S.* viii. 196
Some thoughtless *T.*, with ease and plenty blest *W.F.*107
While their weak heads, like t—s unfortify'd E.C. 434
T. to one grave, whole nations to the deep *E.M.* i. 144
There *t.* aerial on the waving tree *E.M.* iii. 182
Link *t.* to *t.* with avenues of oak *S.* vi. 260
The levell'd *t.* with weeds lie cover'd o'er *W.F.* 67

Townshend.
All *T.*'s Turnips, and all Grosvenor's mines *S.* vi. 223

Toy.
Sure, if they catch, to spoil the *T.* at most *M.E.* ii. 233
Farewell then Verse, and Love, and ev'ry *T. S.* iii. 17
And beads and pray'r-books are the t—s of age E.M. ii. 280
As *t.* and empires, for a god-like mind *E.M.* iv. 180

Not with those *T.* the female world admire *Mi.* v. 3
To this were trifles, *t.*, and empty names *S.* viii. 8

Toyshop.
They shift the moving *T.* of their heart *R.L.* i. 100

Trace.
The shady empire shall retain no *t. W.F.* 371
In their loose t—s from the fields retreat A. 62
Tho' still some *t.* of our rustic vein *S.* v. 270
'Tis hers, the brave man's latest steps to *t. E.* i. 29
And *t.* the Muses upward to their spring *E.C.* 127
Poets, like painters, thus unskill'd to *t. E.C.* 293
'Tis ours to *t.* him only in our own *E.M.* i. 22
T. Science then, with Modesty thy guide *E.M.* ii. 43
And *t.* the mazes of the circling hare *W.F.* 122

Trac'd.
But as the slightest sketch, if justly *t. E.C.* 23
Her buskin'd Virgins *t.* the dewy lawn *W.F.* 170

Track.
May boldly deviate from the common *t. E.C.* 151
Because I see, by all the t—s about S. iii. 116

Tracts.
The latent *t.*, the giddy heights, explore *E.M.* i. 11

Trade.
As the sage dame, experienc'd in her *t. D.* ii. 133
You hurt a man that's rising in the *T. E.S.* ii. 35
How *T.* increases, and the World goes well *M.E.* i. 159
Full sixty years the World has been her *T. M.E.* ii. 123
T. it may help, Society extend *M.E.* iii. 29
To spoil the nation's last great *t.*, Quadrille *M.E.* iii. 76
I left no calling for this idle *t. P.S.* 129
All the mad *T.* of Fools and Slaves for Gold *S.* iv. 13
Her *T.* supported, and supply'd her Laws *S.* v. 222

Tradesman.
If not the *T.* who set up to-day *E.S.* ii. 36
The next a *T.*, meek, and much a liar *M.E.* i. 152
And paid a *T.* once to make him stare *M.E.* ii. 56
Pity mistakes for some poor *t.* craz'd *M E.* iii. 64
I'e T—an *vile, in Army, Court, or Hall E.S.* ii. 17

Tradition.
Or plain *T.* that this All begun *E.M.* iii. 227

Tragedy.
How *T.* and Comedy embrace *D.* i. 69
There to her heart sad *T.* address *D.* iv. 37
A Virgin *T.*, an Orphan Muse *P.S.* 56

Tragic.
For this the *T.* Muse first trod the stage *P.C.* 5
One *T.* sentence if I dare deride *S.* v. 121
Not but the *T.* spirit was our own *S.* v. 276

Trail.
And drew behind a radiant *t.* of hair *R.L.* v. 128

Trails.
His Flag inverted *t.* along the ground *E.S.* i. 154
That long behind he *t.* his pompous robe *R.L.* iii. 73

Train.
"Room for my Lord!" three jockeys in his *t. D.* ii. 192
O *Cara! Cara!* silence all that *t. D.* iv. 53
When Int'rest calls off all her sneaking *t. E.* i. 31
Love, Hope, and Joy, fair Pleasure's smiling *t. E.M.* ii. 117
Rank'd with their Friends, not number'd in their *T. E.S.* ii. 91
Guineas, Half-Guineas, all the shining *t. Mi.* ix. 79
Who lead fair Virtue's *t.* along *O.* ii. 11
While Peers, and Dukes, and all their sweeping *t. R.L.* i. 84
That seam'd but Zephyrs to the *t. R.L.* ii. 58
And parti-colour'd troops, a shining *t. R.L.* iii. 43
Then, close as Umbra, joins the dirty *t. S.* viii. 177
Th' immortal huntress, and her virgin *t. W.F.* 200
Ah, Cynthia! ah—tho' banish'd from thy *t. W.F.* 200
Let barb'rous Ganges arm a servile *t. W.F.* 365
And heads the bold T.-bands, and burns a Pope M.E. iii. 214

Traitor.
Speak'st thou of Syrian Princes? *T.* base *D.* iv. 375
Already half turn'd *T.* by surprise *S.* viii. 169

Traits.
Th' exactest *t.* of Body or of Mind *M.E.* ii. 191

Trance.
In *t.* ecstatic may thy pangs be drown'd *E.A.* 3T9
Starts from her *t.*, and trims her wither'd bays *E.C.* 698

Transfix'd.
Be stopp'd in vials, or *t.* with pins *R.L.* ii. 126

Transform.
T. themselves so strangely as the Rich *S.* iii. 153

Transform'd.
T. to combs, the speckled and the white *R.L.* i. 136
Return well travell'd; and *t.* to Beasts *S.* iv. 193

Transforming.
Oh ! were I made by some *t.* pow'r *Su.* 45

Transgress.
Against the precept, ne'er *t.* its End *E.C.* 164

Transient.
See from my cheek the *t.* roses fly *E.A.* 331
What is loose love? a *t.* gust *O.* iii. 17
Think not, when Woman's *t.* breath is fled *R.L.* i. 51
While ev'ry beam new *t.* colours flings *R.L.* ii. 67

Transition.
Thence, by a soft *t.*, we repair *R.L.* i. 49
He came by sure *t.* to his own *S.* viii. 81

Translate.
And Pope's, ten years to comment and *t. D.* iii. 332
All these, my modest Satire bade *t. P.S.* 189

Translated.
In a *t.* Suit, then tries the Town *Mi.* iii. 27

Translation.
On French *t.*, and Italian song *P.C.* 42
Nor suffers Horace more in wrong T—s E.C. 663

Translucent.
Thou who shalt stop at *Thames' t.* wave *Mi.* x. 1

Transmigrating.
Who knows how long thy *t.* soul *D.* iii. 49

Transmitted.
Charles, to late times to be *t.* fair *S.* v. 380

Transparent.
T. forms, too fine for mortal sight *R.L.* ii. 61
The blue, *t. Vandalis* appears *W.F.* 345

Transport.
Dulness with *t.* eyes the lively Dunce *D.* i. 111
And secret *t.* touch'd the conscious swain *W.F.* 90
Her seat imperial Dulness shall t. D. iii. 298
There, where no Passion, Pride, or Shame *t. E.S.* i. 97
A Vision hermits can to Hell *t. S.* viii. 190

Transported.
T. demi-gods stood round *O.* i. 42

Transports.
One instinct seizes, and *t.* away *D.* iv. 74

Trash.
With the same *t.* mad mortals wish for here *E.M.* iv. 374
Th' imputed *t.*, and dulness not his own *P.S.* 35t
Mere household *t.!* of birth-nights, balls, and shows *S.* viii. 130

Travel.
Affirm, 'twas *T.* made them what they were *S.* viii. 79
As once a week we t. down I.H. ii. 97 s
Ev'n Radcliff's Doctors *t.* first to France *S.* v. 183

Travell'd.
Return well *t.*, and transform'd to Beasts *S.* iv. 193
This thing has *t.*, speaks each language too *S.* viii. 46

Traveller, Trav'llers.
Whose Seats the weary *T.* repose *M.E.* iii. 260
Nay all that lying T—s can feign S. viii. 31
Two *T—'—s* found an Oyster in their way *Mi.* xi. 2

Travels.
Hope *t.* thro', nor quits us when we die *E.M.* ii. 274
O'er figur'd worlds now *t.* with his eye *W.F.* 246

Travers'd.
What seas you *t.*, and what fields you fought *S.* v. 396

Treach'rous.
The *t.* colours the fair art betray *E.C.* 492
Safe from the *t.* friend, the daring spark *R.L.* i. 73

Tread.
Or *t.* the path by vent'rous Heroes trod *D.* i. 201
Mount o'er the vales, and seem to *t.* the sky *E.C.* 226
For Fools rush in where Angels fear to *t. E.C.* 625
What if the foot, ordain'd the dust to *t. E.M.* i. 259
Or *t.* the mazy round his follow'rs trod *E.M.* i. 25
Let such, such only, *t.* this sacred Floor *Mi.* x. 13
The stage how loosely does Astræa *t. S.* v. 290
Where'er you *t.*, the blushing flow'rs shall rise *Su.* 75

Treason.
Within the reach of *T.*, or of Law *S.* vii. 128
Make Scots speak *t.*, cozen subtlest whores *S.* viii. 59

Treasure.
Direct my Plough to find a *T. I.H.* ii. 201
Purest love's unwasting *t. O.* iii. 41
For me, the mine a thousand *t—s* brings *E.M.* i. 137
Unnumber'd *t.* ope at once, and here *R.L.* i. 129
Rich with the *t.* of each foreign tongue *S.* vi. 173
Another, not to heed to *t.* more *S.* vi. 293

Treasur'd.
Since all things lost on earth are *t.* there *R.L.* v. 114

Treat.
Whose game is Whisk, whose *t.* a toast in sack *E.* v. 94
The Guests withdrawn had left the *T. I.H.* ii. 196
To one man's *t.*, but for another's ball *R.L.* i. 96
When the tir'd glutton labours thro' a *t. S.* ii. 31
Or if your life be one continu'd *T. S.* iv. 110
While nymphs take *t—s*, or assignations give *R.L.* iii. 169
And *t.* this passion more as friend than foe *E.M.* ii 164
To break my windows, if I *t.* a Friend *E.S.* ii. 143
Inform us, will the Emp'ror *t. I.H.* ii. 1145
But *t.* the Goddess like a modest fair *M.E.* iv. 51
Think how posterity will *t.* thy name *S.* ii. 208
They *t.* themselves with most profound respect *S.* vi. 154

Treated.
T., caress'd, and tir'd, I take my leave *M.E.* iv. 165

Treaties.
Unfinish'd *T.* in each Office slept *D.* iv. 616

Treble.
And bass, and *t.* voices strike the skies *R.L.* v. 42

Tree.
Fade ev'ry blossom, wither ev'ry *t. A.* 33
There towns aërial on the waving *t. E.M.* iii. 182
Give me again my hollow *T. I.H.* ii. 220
Just as the Twig is bent, the *T.*'s inclin'd *M.E.* i. 150
A wondrous *T.* that sacred Monarchs bears *Sp.* 86
But now the reeds shall hang on yonder *t. Su.* 43
The weeping amber or the balmy *t. W.F.* 30
Ye t—s that fade when autumn-heats remove A. 29
The dying gales that pant upon the *t. E.A.* 159
In the next line, it "whispers thro' the *t. :" E.C.* 351
Glows in the stars, and blossoms in the *t. E.M.* i. 272
Did here the *t.* with ruddier burdens bend *E.M.* iii. 203
A little House, with *t.* a-row *I.H.* i. 77
All bath'd in tears—"Oh odious, odious *T. !" M.E.* ii. 40
T. cut to Statues, Statues thick as *t. M.E.* iv. 120
Like stunted hide-bound *T.*, that just have got *Mi.* iii. 11
While Argo saw her kindred *t. O.* i. 40
Whose *t.* in summer yield him shade *O.* iv. 7
And *t.*, and stones, and farms, and farmer fall *S.* vi. 263
Now leaves the *t.*, and flow'rs adorn the ground *Sp.* 43
And *t.* weep amber on the banks of Po *Sp.* 62
T., where you sit, shall crowd into a shade *Su.* 74
Now hung with pearls the dropping *t.* appear *W.* 31
And told in sighs to all the trembling *t. W.* 62
The winds and *t.* and floods her death deplore *W.* 67
Pants on the leaves, and dies upon the *t. W.* 80
Thin *t.* arise that shun each other's shades *W.F.* 22

That crown'd with tufted *t.* and springing corn *W.F.* 27
And realms commanded which those *t.* adorn *W.F.* 32
Where doves in flocks the leafless *t.* o'ershade *W.F.* 127
And absent *t.* that tremble in the floods *W.F.* 214
Thy *t.*, fair Windsor | now shall leave their woods *W.F.* 385

Tremble.
I *t.* too, where'er my own I find *E.A.* 33
While Altars blaze, and Angels *t.* round *E.A.* 276
See my lips *t.*, and my eye-balls roll *E.A.* 323
But, those attain'd, we *t.* to survey *E.C.* 229
A godless Regent *t.* at a Star *M.E.* i. 90
Let *Sporus t.*—What? that thing of silk *P.S.* 305
And *t.* at the sea that froths below *R.L.* ii. 136
Hear this, and *t. /* you, who 'scape the Laws *S.* i. 118
To pant, or *t.* thro' an Eunuch's throat *S.* v. 154
And Asia's Tyrants *t.* at your Throne *S.* v. 403
Despise the known, nor *t.* at th' unknown *S.* vi. 311
T. before a noble Serving-man *S.* viii. 199
And absent trees that *t.* in the floods *W.F.* 214

Trembled.
The shrines all *t.* and the lamps grew dim *E.A.* 112
Once like thyself, I *t.*, wept and pray'd *E.A.* 311
Eurydice still *t.* on his tongue *O.* i. 114

Trembles.
Glows while he reads, but *t.* while he writes *E.C.* 198
And Nature *t.* to the throne of God. *E.M.* i. 256
When the loose mountain *t.* from on high *E.M.* iv. 127
Ev'n Peter *t.* only for his Ears *E.S.* ii. 57
The green reed *t.*, and the bulrush nods *M.* 79
Then, when he *t. /* when his Blushes rise *Mi.* ix. 89
He *t.*, he glows *O.* i. 108
She sees, and *t.* at th' approaching ill *R.L.* iii. 91
Jove's thunder roars, heav'n *t.* all around *R.L.* v. 49

Trembling.
And Bacon *t.* for his brazen head *D.* iii. 104
Soon as thy letters *t.* I unclose *E.A.* 29
While praying, *t.*, in the dust I roll *E.A.* 279
The hallow'd taper *t.* in thy hand *E.A.* 326
Hope humbly then; with *t.* pinions soar *E.M.* i. 91
When Truth stands *t.* on the edge of Law *E.S.* ii. 249
Tell how the Moon-beam *t.* falls *I.H.* ii. 189
Between each Act the *t.* salvers ring *O.* iv. 161
In broken air, *t.*, the wild music floats *O.* i. 17
T., hoping, ling'ring, flying *O.* v. 3
T. begins the sacred rites of Pride *R.L.* i. 128
The sun-beams *t.* on the floating tides *R.L.* ii. 48
Anxious, and *t.* for the birth of Fate *R.L.* ii. 142
T., and conscious of the rich brocade *R.L.* ii. 116
Thrice from my *t.* hand the patch-box fell *R.L.* iv. 162
Paint Angels *t.* round his falling Horse *S.* i. 28
Let vernal airs thro' *t.* osiers play *Sp.* 5
See on these ruby lips the *t.* breath *U.L.* 31
And told in sighs to all the *t.* trees (*rep.*) *W.* 62
And makes his *t.* slaves the royal game *W.F.* 64
Intent, his angle *t.* in his hand *W.F.* 138
Not half so swift the *t.* doves can fly *W.F.* 185

Tremblingly.
Or touch, if *t.* alive all o'er *E.M.* i. 197

Tremendous.
Lo P—p—le's brow, *t.* to the town *D.* iii. 151
And stares, *t.*, with a threat'ning eye *E.C.* 586
Rend with *t.* sound your ears asunder *S.* i. 27

Trenches.
He leap'd the *t.*, scal'd a Castle-wall *S.* vi. 40

Trent.
Let me but live on this side *T. I.H.* ii. 305

Tresses.
Her *t.* staring from Poetic dreams *D.* iii. 17
Fair *t.* man's imperial race ensnare *R.L.* ii. 27
Not all the *t.* that fair head can boast *R.L.* v. 143
And all those *t.* shall be laid in dust *R.L.* v. 148
His *t.* dropp'd with dews, and o'er the stream *W.F.* 331
The gulfy Lea his sedgy *t.* rears *W.F.* 346

Trial.
Attend the *t.* we propose to make *D.* ii. 371

Tribe.
Glory, and gain, th' illustrious *t.* provoke *D.* ii. 33

A *t.*, with weeds and shells fantastic crown'd *D.* iv. 398
Seen him, uncumber'd with the venal *t. E.S.* i. 31
His conqu'ring *t—s* th' Arabian prophet draws *D.* iii. 97

Tribunal.
Mounts the *T.*, lifts her scarlet head *E.S.* i. 149

Tributary.
Who swell with *t.* urns his flood *W.F.* 338

Tribute.
Rolls the large *t.* of dead dogs to Thames *D.* ii. 272
Pays the last *T.* of a Saint to Heav'n *Ep.* xiv. 14
A wealthier *t.* than to thine he gives *W.F.* 224

Trice.
Name a Town Life, and in a *t. I.H.* ii. 155
Or Gods to save them in a *t. I.H.* ii. 215
The heart resolves this matter in a *t. S.* vi. 216

Trick.
By any *T.*, or any Fault *I.H.* ii. 143
On one nice *T.* depends the gen'ral fate *R.L.* iii. 94
Or *t—s* to shew the stretch of human brain *E.M.* ii. 47
Dip in the Rainbow, *t.* her off in Air *M.E.* ii. 18

Trickles.
How fluent nonsense *t.* from his tongue *D.* iii. 201

Trickling.
The balm of Dulness *t.* in their ear *D:* iv. 544

Tries.
Still her old Empire to restore she *t. D.* i. 17
But in low numbers short excursions *t. E.C.* 738
Still *t.* to save the hallow'd taper's end *M.E.* i. 243
In a translated Suit, then *t.* the Town *Mi.* iii. 21
The Knave of Diamonds *t.* his wily arts *R.L.* iii. 87
Panting with hope, he *t.* the furrow'd grounds *W.F.* 100

Trifle.
Cheerful he play'd the *t.*, Life, away *E.* iv. 12
At ev'ry *t.* scorn to take offence *E.C.* 386
T—s themselves are elegant in him E. iv. 4
For not to know some *t.*, is a praise *E.C.* 262
As well as dream such *t.* are assign'd *E.M.* iv. 179
To this were *t.*, toys, and empty names *S.* viii. 8
Learn but to t. ; *or, whom most observe D.* iv. 457
Or o'er cold coffee *t.* with the spoon *E.* v. 17
Leave such to *t.* with more grace and ease *S.* vi. 326

Trifling.
A *t.* head, and a contracted heart *D.* iv. 504
The *t.* head, or the corrupted heart *P.S.* 327

Trill.
One *T.* shall harmonize joy, grief, and rage *D.* iv. 57

Trim.
The *t.* of pride, the impudence of wealth *E.M.* iii. 4
Gave alms at Easter, in a Christian *t. M.E.* ii. 57
Top-gallant he, and she in all her *t. S.* viii. 230
Sweeter than Sharon, in immac'late *t. S.* viii. 252

Trims.
Starts from her trance, and *t.* her wither'd bays *E.C.* 698
T. Europe's balance, tops the statesman's part *S.* viii. 154

Triple.
Hemm'd by a *t.* circle round *I.H.* ii. 48 *s*
At some sick miser's *t.* bolted gate *D.* ii. 248

Tripod.
A Pipkin there, like Homer's *T.* walks *R.L.* iv. 51

Tripp'd.
She *t.* and laugh'd, too pretty much to stand *D.* iv. 50

Trips.
Now *t.* a Lady, and now struts a Lord *P.S.* 329
The sprightly Sylvia *t.* along the green *Sp.* 57

Tritons.
And gaping *T.* spew to wash your face *M.E.* iv. 154

Triumph.
Pursue the *t.*, and partake the gale *E.M.* iv. 396
But Wisdom's *t.* is well-tim'd Retreat *M.E.* ii. 225
Turn Arcs of *t.* to a Garden-gate *M.E.* iv. 30

TRIUMPHAL—TRUFFLES.

Exulting in *t.* now swell the bold notes *O.* i. 16
The *T.* ceas'd, tears gush'd from ev'ry eye *P.C.* 33
Let wreaths of *t.* now my temples twine *R.L.* iii. 161
He spoke, and speaking, in proud *t.* spread *R.L.* iv. 139
You dream of T—s in the rural shade *E.* v. 22
Tho' *t.* were to gen'rals only due *E.C.* 512
And all her *t.* shrink into a Coin *M.E.* v. 24
T' enroll your *T.* o'er the seas and land *S.* v. 373
Stretch his long *t.* down thro' ev'ry age *W.F.* 304
Inglorious *t.* and dishonest scars *W.F.* 326
At Crimes that 'scape, or *t.* o'er the Law *E.S.* i. 168

Triumphal.
To Needham's quick the voice *t.* rode *D.* i. 323
And while on Fame's *t.* Car they ride *D.* iv. 133
Lo! at the wheels of her *T.* Car *E.S.* i. 151
Ev'n when proud Cæsar midst *t.* cars *P.C.* 27
And hew *t.* arches to the ground *R.L.* iii. 176

Triumphant.
Shall take thrice Grubstreet her *t.* round *D.* iii. 136
Hail, Bards *t.* ! born in happier days *E.C.* 189
T. Umbriel on a seance's height *R.L.* v. 53
T. Malice rag'd thro' private life *S.* v. 246
And mounts exulting on *t.* wings *W.F.* 112

Triumph'd.
Like Cimon, *t.* both on land and wave *D.* i. 85
Her Arts victorious *t.* o'er our Arms *S.* v. 264

Triumph'st.
Thou *t.*, Victor of the high-wrought day *D.* ii. 187

Trivial.
Applause, in spight of *t.* faults, is due *E.C.* 258
What mighty contests rise from *t.* things *R.L.* i. 2

Trod.
Or tread the path by vent'rous Heroes *t. D.* i. 201
Behold yon Isle, by Palmers, Pilgrims *t. D.* iii. 113
Coach'd, carted, *t.* upon, now loose, now fast *D.* iii. 291
And pointed out those arduous paths they *t. E.C.* 95
Or *t.* the mazy round his follow'rs *t. E.M.* ii. 25
Nor think, in NATURE'S STATE they blindly *t. E.M.* iii. 147
To Virtue, in the paths of Pleasure, *t. E.M.* iii. 233
For this the Tragic Muse first *t.* the stage *P.C.* 5

Trojan.
Not half so fix'd the *T.* could remain *R.L.* v. 5

Troop.
Rolls the black *t.*, and overshades the street *D.* ii. 360
When are the t—s to have their pay *I.H.* ii. 120 s
And particolour'd *t.*, a shining train *R.L.* iii. 43
Of broken *t.*, an easy conquest find *R.L.* iii. 78
Of Asia's *t.*, and Afric's sable sons *R.L.* iii. 82
Where are those *t.* of poor, that throng'd of yore *S.* vii. 113

Tropes.
And the puff'd orator bursts out in *t. D.* ii. 206

Trophies.
Their annual *t.*, and their monthly wars *D.* iii. 281
Let standard-authors, thus, like *t.* born *D.* iv. 193
There, other *T.* deck the truly brave *E.S.* ii. 236
And all the *t.* of his former loves *R.L.* ii. 40
Hang their old *T.* o'er the Garden gates *S.* iii. 8

Trophy'd.
The *t.* arches, story'd halls invade *E.M.* iv. 303

Tropic.
Burn thro' the *T.*, freeze beneath the Pole *S.* iii. 72

Troth.
Nay *t.* th' Apostles (tho' perhaps too rough) *S.* viii. 76

Trouble.
Then most our *t.* still when most admir'd *E.C.* 502
Without a Pain, a *T.*, or a Fear *Mi.* v. 16

Troubled.
In *t.* waters, but now sleeps in Port *D.* iv. 209
As the last image of that *t.* heap *M.E.* i. 45

Troublesome.
This may be *t.*, is near the Chair *S.* iv. 105

Trouts.
Swift *t.*, diversified with crimson stains *W.F.* 145

Troy.
Could *T.* be sav'd by any single hand *D.* i. 197
And strike to dust th' imperial tow'rs of *T. R.L.* iii. 171

Truant.
There *t.* WYNDHAM ev'ry Muse gave o'er *D.* iv. 167

Trucks.
Where vile Mundungus *t.* for viler rhymes *D.* i. 234

Trudges.
T. to town, and first turns Chambermaid *Mi.* iii. 16

True.
Which, as more pond'rous, made its aim more *t. D.* i. 171
All who *t.* Dunces in her cause appear'd *D.* ii. 25
T. to the bottom see Concanen creep *D.* ii. 299
For this our Queen unfolds to vision *t. D.* iii. 62
Nor glad vile Poets with *t.* Critics' gore *D.* iii. 178
See, see, our own *t.* Phœbus wears the bays *D.* iii. 323
'Tis *t.*, on Words is still our whole debate *D.* iv. 219
Ah, think not, Mistress! more *t.* Dulness lies *D.* iv. 239
Lord of an Otho, if I vouch it *t. D.* iv. 369
T., he had wit, to make their value rise *D.* iv. 377
Before *t.* passion all these views remove *E.A.* 79
In Poets as *t.* genius is but rare (rep.) *E.C.* 11
Authors are partial to their wit, 'tis *t. E.C.* 17
Shows most *t.* mettle when you check his course *E.C.* 87
And rise to faults *t.* Critics dare not mend *E.C.* 160
And if the means be just, the conduct *t. E.C.* 257
T. Wit is Nature to advantage dress'd *E.C.* 297
But *t.* expression, like th' unchanging Sun *E.C.* 315
T. ease in writing comes from art, not chance *E.C.* 362
But blame the false, and value still the *t. E.C.* 407
But like a shadow, proves the substance *t. E.C.* 467
Be thou the first *t.* merit to befriend *E.C.* 474
'Tis not enough, your counsel still be *t. E.C.* 572
Such shameless Bards we have; and yet 'tis *t. E.C.* 610
There are, 'tis *t.*, who tell another tale *E.J.S.* 15
The man had courage, was a sage, 'tis *t. E.J.S.* 39
In the nice bee, what sense so subtly *t. E.M.* i. 219
To these we owe *t.* friendship, love sincere *E.M.* ii. 255
T. faith, *t.* policy, united ran *E.M.* iii. 239
The less or greater, set so justly *t. E.M.* iii. 291
WHATEVER IS, IS RIGHT. This world, 'tis *t. E.M.* iv. 145
All foreign, but of *t.* desert *E.M.* iv. 253
And more *t.* joy Marcellus exil'd feels *E.M.* iv. 257
That *t.* SELF-LOVE and SOCIAL are the same *E.M.* iv. 396
Blest Satirist! who touch'd the Mean so *t. Ep.* i. 7
Just to his Prince, and to his Country *t. Ep.* ii. 6
The last *t.* Briton lies beneath this stone *Ep.* ix. 12
'Tis *t.*, my Lord, I gave my word *I.H.* i. 1
'Tis *t.*, but Winter comes apace *I.H.* i. 16
Something in Verse as *t.* as Prose *I.H.* ii. 262
T., some are open, and to all men known *M.E.* i. 51
Nothing so *t.* as what you once let fall *M.E.* ii. 1
All how unlike each other, all how *t. M.E.* ii. 6
For *t.* No-meaning puzzles more than Wit *M.E.* ii. 114
To dare the Naked is your *t.* delight *M.E.* ii. 188
Conscious they act a *t.* Palladian part *M.E.* iv. 37
If there's a *Briton* then, *t.* bred and born *Mi.* ii. 19
A man's *t.* merit 'tis not hard to find *P.S.* 175
T. Genius kindles, and fair Fame inspires *P.S.* 194
And a *t. Pindar* stood without a head *P.S.* 236
'Twas then, Belinda, if report say *t. R.L.* i. 117
'Tis *t.*, no Turbots dignify my boards *S.* ii. 141
What right, what *t.*, what fit we justly call *S.* iii. 19
Still *t.* to Virtue, and as warm as *t. S.* iii. 30
T., conscious Honour is to feel no sin *S.* iii. 93
And each *t.* Briton is to Ben so civil *S.* v. 41
If *t.*, a woeful likeness; and if lies *S.* v. 412
These as good works, 'tis *t.*, we all allow *S.* vii. 121
'Tis *t.*, for ten days hence 'twill be King Lear's *S.* viii. 219
Most souls, 'tis *t.*, but peep out once an age *U.L.* 17

Truest.
The *t.* hearts for Voiture heav'd with sighs *E.* iv. 17
The *t.* notions in the easiest way *E.C.* 656

Truffles.
Thy *T.*, Perigord! thy Hams, Bayonne *D.* iv. 558

Truly.

Thro' Fortune's cloud one *t.* great can see *E.* i. 39
There, other Trophies deck the *t.* brave *E.S.* ii. 236
May *t.* say, Here lies an honest Man *W.F.* x. 2
Or rather *t.*, if your point be rest *S.* i. 17
A doctrine sage, but *t.* none of mine *S.* ii. 3

Trumbal.

Thus Atticus, and *T.* thus retir'd *W.F.* 258

Trump.

Gain'd but one *t.*, and one Plebeian card *R.L.* iii. 54
Let Spades be t—s! she said, and t—s they were R.L.
iii. 46
Led off two captive *t.*, and swept the board *R.L.* iii. 50

Trumpet.

And now bad Fame's posterior *T.* blown *D.* iv. 71
Hear her black *T.* thro' the Land proclaim *E.S.* i. 159
Let the loud *t.* sound *O.* i. 7
With Gun, Drum, *T.*, Blunderbuss, and Thunder *S.* i. 28
The *t.* sleep, while cheerful horns are blown *W.F.* 373
With horns and t—s now to madness swell D. ii. 227
The brazen *t.* kindle rage no more *M.* 60

Trunks.

Clothe spice, line *t.*, or, flutt'ring in a row *S.* v. 418

Trust.

No Cause, no *T.*, no Duty, and no Friend *D.* iv. 340
With mean complacence ne'er betray your *t. E.C.* 580
An ardent Judge, who zealous in his *t. E.C.* 677
To whom can Riches give Repute or *T. E.M.* iv. 285
To laugh at Fools who put their *t.* in Peter *E.S.* i. 10
And laugh at Peers that put their *t.* in Peter *S.* i. 40
Deny'd all posts of profit or of *t. S.* vi. 61
For not in Chariots *Peter* puts his *t. S.* vii. 74
Who makes a *T.* or Charity a Job *S.* viii. 140
T. not too much your now resistless charms E. iv. 59
T. not yourself; but your defects to honour *E.C.* 213
To *t.* in ev'ry thing, or doubt of all *E.M.* iv. 26
Ambition sigh'd: she found it vain to *t. E.* iv. 39
Thy relics, Rowe, to this fair Urn we *t. Ep.* v. 1
I *t.* that sinking Fund, my Life *I.H.* i. 74
Beauty that shocks you, parts that none will *t. P.S.* 332
We *t.* th' important charge, the Petticoat *R.L.* ii. 118
And *t.* me, dear! good-humour can prevail *R.L.* v. 31
But *t.* the Muse—she saw it upward rise *W.F.* v. 123
Look thro', and *t.* the Ruler with his skies *S.* iv. 8
Thus much I've said, I *t.*, without offence *S.* vii. 125
Secure they *t.* th' unfaithful field beset *W.F.* 103

Trustees.

Curs'd by thy neighbours, thy *t.*, thyself *S.* ii. 106

Trusts.

T. in God, that as well as he was, he shall be *Ep.* xvi. 8
The Wretch that *t.* them, or the Rogue that cheats *M.E.*
iii. 238
It is to *History* he *t.* for Praise *S.* i. 36

Trusty.

Four Knaves in garbs succinct, a *t.* band *R.L.* iii. 41

Truth.

Where, in nice balance, *t.* with gold she weighs *D.* i. 53
Then first (if Poets aught of *t.* declare) *D.* ii. 77
See skulking *T.* to her old cavern fled *D.* iv. 641
That dares tell neither *T.* nor Lies *E.* vi. 30
T. breaks upon us with resistless day *E.C.* 212
Something, whose *t.* convinc'd at sight we find *E.C.* 299
In all you speak, let *t.* and candour shine *E.C.* 563
Without Good Breeding, *t.* is disapprov'd *E.C.* 576
One *t.* is clear, WHATEVER IS, IS RIGHT *E.M.* i. 294
Sole judge of *T.*, in endless Error hurl'd *E.M.* ii. 17
Let this great *t.* be present night and day *E.M.* iii. 5
Oh blind to *t.*, and God's whole scheme below *E.M.* iv.93
Justice a Conqu'ror's sword, or *T.* a gown *E.M.* iv. 171
Know then this *t.* (enough for Man to know) *E.M.*iv.309
Adieu Distinction, Satire, Warmth, and *T. E.S.* i. 64
While *T.*, Worth, Wisdom, daily they decry *E.S.* i. 169
When *T.* or Virtue an Affront endures *E.S.* ii. 199
All, all but *T.* drops dead-born from the Press *E.S.* ii. 226
T. guards the Poet, sanctifies the line *E.S.* ii. 246
When *T.* stands trembling on the edge of Law *E.S.* ii.
249
A Scorn of wrangling, yet a Zeal for *T. Ep.* ii. 8

Of modest wisdom, and pacific *t. Ep.* vii. 2
Taught, on the wings of *T.* to fly *I.H.* v. 3
And in the Cunning, *T.* itself's a lie *M.E.* i. 68
Alas I in *t.* the man but chang'd his mind *M.E.* i. 127
With *T.* and Goodness, as with Crown and Ball *M.E.* ii.
184
Reserve with Frankness, Art with *T.* ally'd *M.E.* ii. 277
Hear then the *T.*: "'Tis Heav'n each Passion sends
M.E. iii. 159
A certain *t.*, which many bay too dear *M.E.* iv. 40
Statesman, yet friend to *T.* / of soul sincere *M.E.* v. 67
Ye shades, where sacred *t.* is taught *O.* ii. 1
Moral *T.*, and mystic Song *O.* ii. 12
The *t.* once told (and wherefore should we lie?) *P.S.* 81
But stoop'd to *T.*, and moraliz'd his song *P.S.* 341
Oh blind to *t.* the Sylphs contrive it all *R.L.* i. 104
Or tir'd in search of *T.*, or search of Rhyme *S.* ii. 86
Barnard in spirit, sense, and *t.* abounds *S.* iii. 85
Plain *t.*, dear MURRAY, needs no flow'rs of speech *S.* iv.3
Whose Word is *T.*, as sacred and rever'd *S.* v. 27
And sets the Passions on the side of *T. S.* v. 218
To hunt for *T.* in Maudlin's learned grove *S.* vi. 57
If there be *t.* in Law, and Use can give *S.* vi. 230
And get, by speaking *t.* of Monarchs dead *S.* viii. 106
O my fair mistress *T.* / shall I quit thee *S.* viii. 200
O *sacred weapon! left for T.'s defence E.S.* ii. 212
*And t—s divine came moulded from that tongue E.A.*66
Blunt *t.* more mischief than nice falsehoods do *E.C.* 573
Leave dang'rous *t.* to unsuccessful Satires *E.C.* 592
T. would you teach, or save a sinking land *E.M.* iv. 265
Some secret *t.*, from learned pride conceal'd *R.L.* i. 37

Try.

See how the force of others' pray'rs I *t. E.A.* 149
So pleas'd at first the tow'ring Alps we *t. E.C.* 225
T. what the open, what the covert yield *E.M.* i. 10
Or gravely *t.* to read the lines *I.H.* ii. 91 ?
No Courts he saw, no suits would ever *t. P.S.* 396
Nor fear'd the Chief th' unequal fight to *t. R.L.* v. 77
First in these fields I *t.* the sylvan strains *Sp.* 2
Here shall I *t.* the sweet Alexis' strain *W.* 11

Try'd.

T. all *hors-d'œuvres*, all *liqueurs* defin'd *D.* iv. 317
A Soul supreme in each hard instance *t. Ep.* vi. 9
BETTY, who oft the pain of each has *t. Mi.* ix. 24
Ward *t.* on Puppies, and the Poor, his Drop *S.* v. 182

Tub.

Henley's gilt *t.*, or Fleckno's Irish throne *D.* ii. 2

Tube.

He lifts the *t.*, and levels with his eye *W.F.* 129

Tuff-taffety.

But mere *t.* what now remain'd *S.* viii. 42

Tufted.

That crown'd with *t.* trees and springing corn *W.F.* 27

Tugging.

Lo Rufus, *t.* at the deadly dart *W.F.* 83

Tulips.

Ladies, like variegated *t.*, show *M.E.* ii. 41

Tully.

With thee repose, where *T.* once was laid *E.* iii. 29
He'll shine a *T.* and a Wilmot too *M.E.* i. 187
Some Athens perishes, some *T.* bleeds *O.* ii. 32
Shall be no more than *T.*, or than HYDE *S.* iv. 53
But *T.* has it, *Nusquam minus solus S.* viii. 91
The same (my Lord) if T.'s, or your own E.M. iv. 240

Tumbled.

Or rumpled petticoats, or *t.* beds *R.L.* iv. 72

Tumbler.

Never by *t.* thro' the hoops was shown *D.* iv. 257

Tumbling.

Could she behold us *t.* thro' a hoop *S.* v. 48

Tumult.

What means this *t.* in a Vestal's veins *E.A.* 4
Again I new T—s in my breast I.H. iii. 1

Tumultuous.

If in the breast *t.* joys arise *O.* i. 24

Tunbridge.
Each cygnet sweet, of Bath and *T.* race *D.* iii. 255

Tune.
Hum half a *t.*, tell stories to the squire *E.* v. 20
Look sour, and hum a *T.*, as you may now *E.* v. 50
The birds shall cease to *t.* their ev'ning song *A.* 40
Leave such *to t.* their own dull rhymes, and know *E.C.* 358
Cynthia, t. harmonious Numbers *Mi.* vii. 13
Till in your native shades you *t.* the lyre *Sp.* 12
But nigh yon mountain let me *t.* my lays *Su.* 37

Tun'd.
Till all, *t.* equal, send a gen'ral hum. *D.* ii. 386
In the same shades the Cupids *t.* his lyre *W.F.* 295

Tuneful.
When *t.* Hylas with melodious moan *A.* 15
Whose *t.* whistling makes the waters pass *D.* iii. 156
Till Death untimely stopp'd his *t.* tongue *E.* i. 2
Her voice is all these *t.* fools admire *E.C.* 340
That urg'd by thee, I turn'd the *t.* art *E.M.* iv. 391
When the full organ joins the *t.* quire *O.* i. 126
Let CAROLINA smooth the *t.* lay *S.* i. 30
And rarely Av'rice taunts the *t.* mind *S.* v. 192
That flute is mine which Colin's *t.* breath *Su.* 39
Deaf the prais'd ear, and mute the *t.* tongue *U.L.* 76
While silent birds forget their *t.* lays *W.* 7

Tunes.
Joy *t.* his voice, joy elevates his wings *E.M.* iii. 32

Tuning.
T. his voice, and balancing his hands *D.* iii. 200

Turbots.
Yet for small *T.* such esteem profess *S.* ii. 73
'Tis true, no *T.* dignify my boards *S.* ii. 141

Turbulence.
So (fam'd like thee for *t.* and horns) *D.* ii. 181

Turenne.
See godlike *T.* prostrate on the dust *E.M.* iv. 100
It anger'd *T.*, once upon a day *E.S.* ii. 150

Turf.
Or under this *T.*, or e'en what they will *Ep.* xvi. 2
The *t.* with rural dainties shall be crown'd *Sp.* 99
And the green *t.* lie lightly on thy breast *U.L.* 64

Turk.
Bear, like the *T.*, no brother near the throne *P.S.* 198
Verse prays for Peace, or sings down Pope and *T. S.* v. 236

Turkeys.
An hundred Souls of *T.* in a pie. *D.* iv. 294

Turn.
Yet let not each gay *T.* thy rapture move *E.C.* 390
What wonder modes in Wit should take their *t. E.C.* 447
Its only thinking thing this *t.* of mind *E.M.* iii. 78
Each Virtue in each Passion takes its *t. E.M.* iii. 136
Her ev'ry *t.* with Violence pursu'd *M.E.* ii. 131
The op'ning clouds disclose each work by *t*—s *D.* i. 249
Persians and Greeks like *t.* of nature found *E.C.* 380
Tho' each by *t.* the other's bound invade *E.M.* ii. 207
By *t.* we catch the vital breath and die *E.M.* iii. 18
For Merit will by *t.* forsake them all *E.S.* i. 89
Tho' strong the bent, and quick the *t.* of mind *M.E.* i. 64
And Atheism and Religion take their *t. M.E.* ii. 66
Scarce once herself, by *t.* all Woman-kind *M.E.* ii. 116
What tender passions take their *t. O.* iii. 33
A thousand wings, by *t.*, blow back the hair *R.L.* iii. 136
Then sing by *t.*, by *t.* the Muses sing *Sp.* 41
On him, and crowds *t.* Coxcombs as they gave *D.* ii. 8
And *t.* this whole illusion on the town *D.* ii. 132
" Now *t.* to diff'rent sports," (the Goddess cries) *D.* ii. 221
And *t.* the Council to a Grammar School *D.* iv. 180
T. what they will to Verse, their toil is vain. *D.* iv. 263
The vulgar herd *t.* of to roll with Hogs *D.* iv. 525
Beeves, at his touch, at once to jelly *t. D.* iv. 551
In vain ! they gaze, *t.* giddy, rave, and die *D.* iv. 648
What scenes appear where'er I *t.* my view *E.A.* 263
And then *t.* Critics in their own defence *E.C.* 29
Want as much more, to *t.* it to its use *E.C.* 81

And *t.* their heads to imitate the Sun *E.M.* ii. 28
Or from a judge *t.* pleader to persuade *E.M.* ii. 155
Nor Boileau *t.* the Feather to a Star *E.S.* ii. 231
T., *t.* to willing hearts your wanton fires *I.H.* iii. 8
Stop, or *t.* nonsense, at one glance of thee *I.H.* iii. 40
The plain rough Hero *t.* a crafty Knave *M.E.* i. 126
Manners with Fortunes, Humours *t.* with Climes *M.E.* i. 172
T. then from Wits ;. and look on Simo's Mate *M.E.* ii. 101
And *t.* th' unwilling steeds another way *M.E.* iii. 192
Things change their titles as our manners *t. M.E.* iii. 379
T. Arcs of Triumph to a Garden-gate *M.E.* iv. 30
He'll write a *Journal*, or he'll *t.* Divine *P.S.* 54
Curl'd or uncurl'd, since Locks will *t.* to grey *R.L.* v. 26
That touch my bell, I cannot *t.* away *S.* ii. 140
T. round to square, and square again to round *S.* iii. 170
Then *t.* about, and laugh at your own jest *S.* iv: 109
Or Virtue, or Religion, *t.* to sport *S.* v. 211
But *t.* a wit, and scribble verses too *S.* vii. 54
First *t.* plain rash, then vanish quite away *S.* viii. 45
While yon slow oxen *t.* the furrow'd plain *Sp.* 30
And all things flourish where you *t.* your eyes *Su.* 76

Turn'd.
See, graceless Venus to a Virgin *t. D.* iii. 111
His never-blushing head he *t.* aside *D.* iii. 231
And last *t.* Air, the Echo of a Sound *D.* iv. 322
T. to the Sun, she casts a thousand dyes *D.* iv. 519
Now *t.* to heav'n, I weep my past offence *E.A.* 287
T. Critics next, and prov'd plain fools at last *E.C.* 37
Against the Poets their own arms they *t. E.C.* 106
And never shock'd, and never *t.* aside *E.C.* 629
And *t.* on Man a fiercer savage, Man *E.M.* iii. 168
That urg'd by thee, I *t.* the tuneful art *E.M.* iv. 391
The prudent Gen'ral *t.* it to a jest *E.S.* ii. 152
HAZARDIA blush'd, and *t.* her Head aside *Mi.* ix. 41
And maids *t.* bottles, call aloud for corks *R.L.* iv. 54
That *t.* ten thousand verses, now stands still *S.* vi. 79
Already half *t.* traitor by surprise *S.* viii. 169
The god appear'd : he *t.* his azure eyes *W.F.* 351

Turner.
Alas ! 'tis more than *T.* finds they give *M.E.* iii. 82

Turnips.
Had roasted *t.* in the Sabine farm *M.E.* i. 219
All Townshend's *T.*, and all Grosvenor's mines *S.* vi. 273

Turnpikes.
Why *t.* rose, and now no Cit nor clown *S.* viii. 144

Turns.
Realms shift their place, and Ocean *t.* to land *D.* i. 72
How Index-learning *t.* no student pale *D.* i. 279
Spirits in the gard'ner's eyes who *t.* the cock *D.* ii. 178
And one bright blaze *t.* Learning into air *D.* iii. 78
The head that *t.* at super-lunar things *D.* iv. 451
And as she *t.*, the colours fall or rise *D.* iv. 540
T. Hares to Larks, and Pigeons into Toads *D.* iv. 564
The fawning Servant *t.* a haughty Lord *E.* iv. 44
Or *t.* young Ammon loose to scourge mankind *E.M.* i. 160
As Heav'n's blest beam *t.* vinegar more sour *E.M.* ii. 148
Reason the bias *t.* to good from ill *E.M.* ii. 197
Quite *t.* my stomach—So does Flatt'ry mine *E.S.* ii. 182
What *t.* him now a stupid silent dunce *M.E.* i. 163
Then *t.* repentant, and his God adores *M.E.* i. 188
To each that Passion *t.*, or soon or late *M.E.* ii. 133
To all their dated Backs he *t.* you round *M.E.* iv. 135
Trudges to Court, and first *t.* Chambermaid *Mi.* iii. 10
But soon, too soon, the lover *t.* his eyes *O.* i. 93
Who *t.* a Persian tale for half a Crown *P.S.* 180
The berries crackle and the mill *t.* round *R.L.* iii. 106
T. you from sound Philosophy aside. *S.* ii. 6
And God the Father *t.* a School-divine *S.* v. 102
Now calls in Princes, and now *t.* away *S.* v. 156
At all my peevishness, and *t.* his style *S.* viii. 123

Turrets.
These moss-grown domes with spiry *t.* crown'd *E.A.* 142
And lift her *t.* nearer to the skies *W.F.* 288
Where Windsor-domes and pompous *t.* rise *W.F.* 352

Turtle.
As some sad *T.* his lost love deplores *A.* 19
Their early *fruit, and milk-white t*—s bring *Su.* 52

TUTCHIN—TYRANT.   333

Tutchin.
And *T*., flagrant from the scourge below *D*. ii. 143

Twain.
Fate urg'd the shears and cut the Sylph in *t. R.L*. iii. 151

Twang.
Harmonic *t*. / of leather, horn, and brass *D*. ii. 254

Tweed.
Ask where's the North? at York, 'tis on the *T. E.M*. ii. 222

Tweezer-cases.
And bean's in snuff-boxes and *t. R.L*. v. 116

Twelve.
But such a bulk as no *t*. bards could raise (*rep*.) *D*. ii. 39
Of these *t*. volumes, *t*. of amplest size *D*. i. 155
And sleepless lovers, just at *t*. awake *R.L*. i. 16
Of *t*. vast French Romances, neatly gilt *R.L*. ii. 38
Before the Lords at *t*. my Cause comes on *S*. vi. 96
Where *t*. fair Signs in beauteous order lie *Sp*. 40
Not twice a t.-month you appear in print E.S. i. 2

Twenty.
When *t*. Fools I never saw *I.H*. ii. 64 *s*
The Chanc'ry takes your rents for *t*. year *S*. ii. 170
Sir, he's your slave, for *t*. pound a year *S*. vi. 8
When out of *t*. I can please not two *S*. vi. 81
The virtues of a saint at t.-one E.M. iv. 84
When the brisk Minor pants for *t. S*. iii. 38

Twice.
(His only suit) for *t*. three years before *D*. iii. 38
In *t*. ten thousand rhyming nights and days *D*. iv. 172
Not *t*. a twelve-month you appear in Print *E.S*. i. 1
The matter's weighty, pray consider *t. E.S*. ii. 43
Nor cross the Channel *t*. a year *I.H*. ii. 31 *s*
A Saint in Crape is *t*. a Saint in Lawn *M.E*. i. 136
The Crown of Poland, vocal *t*. an age *M.E*. iii. 127
Where once I went to Church, I'll now go *t. M.E*. iii. 367
The sacred rust of *t*. ten hundred years *M.E*. v. 38
She flatters her good Lady *t*. a day *Mi*. iii. 18
I too could write, and I am *t*. as tall *P.S*. 103
They scarce can bear their *Laureate t*. a year *S*. i. 34

Twig.
Just as the *T*. is bent, the Tree's inclin'd *M.E*. i. 150

Twilight.
Thro' *t*. ages hunt th' Athenian fowl *D*. iv. 361
But o'er the *t*. groves and dusky caves *E.A*. 163

Twine.
Let wreaths of triumph now my temples *t. R.L*. iii. 161

Twin'd.
T. with the wreaths Parnassian laurels yield *E.M*. iv. 11
Round broken columns clasping ivy *t. W.F*. 69

Twines.
And I this bowl, where wanton ivy *t. Sp*. 35

Twinkling.
Heav'n's *t*. Sparks draw light, and point their horns *D*. ii. 12
Like *t*. stars the Miscellanies o'er *S*. v. 110

Twirl'd.
Or whirligigs *t*. round by skilful swain *D*. iii. 57

Twist.
'Tis the same rope at diff'rent ends they *t. D*. i. 207

Twisted.
A *t*. Birth-day Ode completes the spire *D*. i. 162

Twitch'd.
And thrice they *t*. the diamond in her ear *R.L*. iii. 137

Twit'nam = Twickenham.
All fly to *T*., and in humble strain *P.S*. 21

Two.
There in his seat *t*. spacious vents appear *D*. ii. 85
T. babes of love close clinging to her waist *D*. ii. 158
Ah why, ye Gods, should *t*. and *t*. make four *D*. ii. 286
The pond'rous books *t*. gentle readers bring *D*. ii. 382
Courtiers and Patriots in *t*. ranks divide *D*. iv. 207

On *t*. unequal crutches propt he came *D*. iv. 111
Points him *t*. ways, the narrower is the better *D*. iv. 152
Blest in one Niger, till he knows of *t. D*. iv. 370
But far the foremost, *t*., with earnest zeal *D*. iv. 401
If ever chance *t*. wand'ring lovers brings *E.A*. 347
But, of the *t*., less dang'rous is th' offence *E.C*. 3
T. Principles in human nature reign *E.M*. ii. 53
One in their nature, which are *t*. in ours *E.M*. iii. 96
Each sex desires alike, till *t*. are one *E.M*. iii. 122
So *t*. consistent motions act the Soul *E.M*. iii. 315
Now for *t*. ages having snatched from fate *Ep*. viii. 3
So bought an Annual Rent or *t. I.H*. i. 17
About some great Affair, at *T. I.H*. ii. 74 *s*
He had a Story of *t*. Mice *I.H*. ii. 156
Woman and Fool are *t*. hard things to hit *M.E*. ii. 113
In Women, *t*. almost divide the kind *M.E*. ii. 208
Then careful Heav'n supply'd *t*. sorts of Men *M.E*. iii. 13
'Twas very want that sold them for *t*. pound *M.E*. iii. 328
And *t*. rich ship-wrecks bless the lucky shore *M.E*. iii. 356
And lo! *t*. puddings smoke upon the board *M.E*. iii. 360
T. Cupids squirt before, a Lake behind *M.E*. iv. 111
T. Trav'lers found an Oyster in their way *Mi*. xi. 2
Let the *t. Curlls* of Town and Court, abuse *P.S*. 380
And view with scorn *t*. pages and a chair *R.L*. i. 46
Nourish'd *t*. Locks, which graceful hung behind *R.L*. ii. 20
Burns to encounter *t*. advent'rous Knights *R.L*. iii. 26
Led off *t*. captive trumps, and swept the board *R.L*. iii. 50
T. handmaids wait the throne: alike in place *R.L*. iv. 25
These in *t*. sable ringlets taught to break *R.L*. iv. 169
Is what *t*. souls so gen'rous cannot bear *S*. ii. 58
We shall not quarrel for a year or *t. S*. v. 61
When out of twenty I can please not *t. S*. vi. 81
T. Aldermen dispute it with an Ass *S*. vi. 105
The Temple late *t*. brother Sergeants saw *S*. vi. 127
T. of a face, as soon as of a mind (*rep*.) *S*. v. 269
T. Swains, whom Love kept wakeful, and the Muse *Sp*. 18
I see, I see, where *t*. fair cities bend *W.F*. 379
A *t*.-edg'd *weapon from her shining case R.L*. iii. 128

Ty—y.
K—l's lewd Cargo, or *T*.'s Crew *S*. iv. 121

Tyburn.
Hence hymning *T*.'s elegiac lines *D*. i. 41

Type.
But where each Science lifts its modern *t. D*. iii. 195

Tyrannic.
Th' Oppressor rul'd *t*. where he durst *W.F*. 74

Tyranny.
With *T*., then Superstition join'd *E.C*. 687
Then shar'd the *T*., then lent it aid *E.M*. iii. 247
A love to Peace, and hate of *T. Ep*. ii. 10

Tyrant.
T. supreme! shall three Estates command *D*. iv. 603
But the last *T*. ever proves the worst *E*. iv. 40
Like some fierce *T*. in old Tapestry *E.C*. 587
Be Man the Wit and *T*. of the whole (*rep*.) *E.M*. iii. 50
Till Superstition taught the *t*. awe *E.M*. iii. 246
No Bandit fierce, no *T*. mad with Pride *E.M*. iv. 41
And was, besides, a *T*. to his Wife *E.S*. ii. 135
And Hell's grim *T*. feel th' eternal wound *M*. 48
A *T*. to the wife his heart approves *M.E*. ii. 207
That buys your sex a *T*. o'er itself *M.E*. ii. 288
Maul the French *T*., or pull down the Pope *Mi*. ii. 18
Till some new *T*. lifts his purple hand *O*. ii. 23
Still, when the lust of *t*. pow'r succeeds *O*. ii. 31
Oh *T*. Love! hast thou possest *O*. iii. 1
The Club's black *T*. first her Victim dy'd (sic) *R.L*. iii. 69
I wish you joy, Sir, of a *T*. gone *S*. vi. 305
And ev'n the elements a *t*. sway'd *W.F*. 52
The dagger went to pierce the T.'s *breast D*. iv. 38
Marriage may all these petty T—s *chase E*. iv. 37
And, form'd like *t*., *t*. would believe *E.M*. iii. 60
Beauties, like *T*., old and friendless grown *M.E*. ii. 227
T. no more their savage nature kept *P.C*. 7
Of foreign *T*. and of Nymphs at home *R.L*. iii. 6
Not *t*. fierce that unrepenting die *R.L*. iv. 7
And Asia's *T*. tremble at your Throne *S*. v. 403
Suits *T*., Plunderers, but suits not me *S*. viii. 195
Both doom'd alike, for sportive *T*. bled *W.F*. 59
And pikes, the *t*. of the wat'ry plains *W.F*. 146

U.

Tyrian.
Be struck with bright Brocade, or *T.* Dye *S.* iv. 32
The bright-ey'd perch with fins of *T.* dye *W.F.* 142

Uddera.
With cow-like *u.*, and with ox-like eyes *D.* ii. 164

Ugly.
'Tis an *u.* envious Shrew *Mi.* vi. 9
Was just not *u.*, and was just not mad *M.E.* ii. 50

Ulysses.
Like that where once *U.* held the winds *R.L.* iv. 182
And boasts U.' ear, with Argus' eye *D.* ii. 374

Umbra.
When universal homage *U.* pays *M.E.* i. 59
Then, close as *U.*, join the dirty train *S.* viii. 177

Umbriel.
U., a dusky, melancholy sprite *R.L.* iv. 13
But *U.*, hateful Gnome ! forbears not so *R.L.* iv. 145
Triumphant *U.* on a sconce's height *R.L.* v. 53

Unabash'd.
Earless on high, stood *u.* De Foe *D.* ii. 147

Unadmir'd.
Oh had I rather *u.* remain'd *R.L.* iv. 153

Unaffected.
So *u.*, so compos'd a mind *Ep.* vi. 7
Of softest manners, *u.* mind *Ep.* vii. 7

Unambitious.
My humble Muse, in *u.* strains *W.F.* 427

Unask'd.
Repeat *u.* ; lament, the Wit's too fine *S.* v. 366

Unawares.
And *u.* Morality expires *D.* iv. 650

Unaw'd.
Persist, by all divine in Man *u. D.* iii. 223

Unbalanc'd.
Let Earth *u.* from her orbit fly *E.M.* i. 251
Th' *u.* Mind, and snatch the Man away *S.* iv. 25

Unbar.
Where Brown and Mears *u.* the gates of light *D.* iii. 28

Unbelieving.
Then *u.* priests reform'd the nation *E.C.* 546
To please a lewd or *u.* Court *S.* v. 212

Unbending.
Flies o'er th' *u.* core, and skims along the main *E.C.* 373

Unbiass'd.
U. or by favour, or by spite *E.C.* 633

Unbind.
Or thy griev'd Country's copper chains *u. D.* i. 24

Unblam'd.
U. thro' Life, lamented in thy End *Ep.* xi. 8

Unbless'd, Unblest.
By his own son, that passes by *u. M.E.* i. 235
Be this a Woman's Fame : with this *u—t M.E.* ii. 281

Unbloody.
Unbrib'd, *u.*, stood the blameless priest *E.M.* iii. 158

Unborn.
Where things destroy'd are swept to things *u. D.* i. 242
Thou, yet *u.*, hast touch'd this sacred shore *D.* iii. 45
Nations *u.* your mighty names shall sound *E.C.* 193
See future sons, and daughters yet *u. M.* 88
And stretch the Ray to Ages yet *u. S.* v. 228

Unbought.
With soups *u.*, and salads bless'd his board *M.E.* iii. 182

Unbound.
Her eyes dejected, and her hair *u. R.L.* iv. 90

Unbounded.
All my loose soul *u.* springs to thee *E.A.* 228
U. Thames shall flow for all mankind *W.F.* 398

Unbrib'd.
U., unbloody, stood the blameless priest *E.M.* iii. 158

Unbroken.
Convey'd *u.* faith from sire to son *E.M.* iii. 228

Uncensur'd.
Whose right it is, *u.*, to be dull *E.C.* 589

Uncertainty.
By Actions ? those *U.* divides *M.E.* i. 168

Unchang'd.
One clear, *u.*, and universal light *E.C.* 71
Honour *u.*, a Principle profest *Ep.* ii. 3

Unchanging.
But true expression, like th' *u.* Sun *E.C.* 315

Uncheek'd.
U. may rise, and climb from art to art *E.M.* ii. 40

Unciviliz'd.
And kept unconquer'd, and *u. E.C.* 716

Unclassic.
Her magic charms o'er all *u.* ground *D.* iii. 258

Unclean.
List'ning delighted to the jest *u. D.* ii. 99

Unclose.
Soon as thy letters trembling I *u. E.A.* 29

Unclouded.
Oh ! blest with Temper, whose *u.* ray *M.E.* ii. 257
One tide of glory, one *u.* blaze *M.* 102

Uncommon.
I know the thing that's most *u. Mi.* viii. 1

Unconcern'd.
Thou *u.* canst hear the mighty crack *P.S.* 86

Unconcern'dly.
Blest, who can *u.* find *O.* iv. 9

Unconfin'd.
Mad *Matheris* alone was *u. D.* iv. 31
Blest with a taste exact, yet *u. E.C.* 639
Poets, a race long *u.*, and free *E.C.* 649
Till lengthen'd on to Faith, and *u. E.M.* iv. 343
Come on then, Satire ! gen'ral, *u. E.S.* ii. 14

Unconquerable.
Spadillio first, *u.* Lord *R.L.* iii. 49

Unconquer'd.
And kept *u.*, and unciviliz'd *E.C.* 716
How shin'd the Soul, *u.* in the Tow'r *E.S.* ii. 83

Unconscious.
Th' *u.* stream sleeps o'er thee like a lake *D.* ii. 304

Uncorrupted.
And *u.* ev'n among the Great *Ep.* xi. 6
His hand unstain'd, his *u.* heart *M.E.* i. 82

Uncouth.
The sister-lock now sits *u.*, alone *R.L.* iv. 171
Prune the luxuriant, the *u.* refine *S.* vi. 174
Then ships of *u.* form shall stem the tide *W.F.* 403

Uncover'd.
With head *u.*, the Cosmetic pow'rs *R.L.* i. 124

Uncowl'd.
Men hearded, bald, cowl'd, *u.*, shod, unshod *D.* iii. 114

Uncreating.
Light dies before thy *u.* word *D.* iv. 654

Uncumber'd.
Seen him, *u.* with the venal tribe *E.S.* i. 31

UNCURL'D—UNHOLY. 335

Uncurl'd.
And snakes *u.* hung list'ning round their heads *O.* i. 70
U. it hangs, the fatal shears demands *R L.* iv. 173
Curl'd or *u.*, since Locks will turn to grey *R.L.* v. 26

Under.—*Passim.*

Undergo.
If Wit so much from Ign'rance *u. E.C.* 508
And me the Muses help'd to *u.* it *S.* vi. 66

Underneath.
Writ *u.* the Country Signs *I.H.* ii. 92 *s*

Understand.
Would all but stoop to what they *u. E.C.* 67
All fear, none aid you, and few *u. E.M.* iv. 266
All Boys may read, and Girls may *u. E.S.* i. 76

Understanding.
The solid pow'r of *u.* fails *E.C.* 57

Understood.
Much was believ'd, but little *u. E.C.* 689
All Discord, Harmony not *u. E.M.* i. 291
Pleasure, or wrong or rightly *u. E.M.* ii. 91
No ill could fear in God: and *u. E.M.* iii. 237
God sends not ill; if rightly *u. E.M.* iv. 113
Thou Great First Cause, least *u. U.P.* 5

Undeserv'd.
Praise *u.* is scandal in disguise *S.* v. 413

Undistinguish'd.
Receiv'd of wits an *u.* race *P.S.* 237
Falls *u.* by the victor spade *R.L.* iii. 64

Undivided.
Spreads *u.*, operates unspent *E.M.* i. 274

Undo.
And learn of man each other to *u. W.F.* 124

Undoes.
Scarce hurts the Lawyer, but *u.* the Scribe *E.S.* ii. 47

Undoing.
This curs'd OMBRELLA, this *u.* Fair *Mi.* ix. 55

Undone.
And, if a Borough choose him not, *u. D.* iv. 328
KNIGHT lifts the head, for what are crowds *u. D.* iv. 561
By fools 'tis hated, and by knaves *u. E.C.* 507
What Reason weaves, by Passion is *u. E.M.* ii. 42
Who first taught souls enslav'd and realms *u. E.M.* iii. 241
How oft by these at sixty are *u. E.M.* iv. 183
Vice is *u.*, if she forgets her Birth *E.S.* i. 141
And Britain, if not Europe, is *u. M.E.* i. 161
But cares not if a thousand are *u. M.E.* ii. 176

Undrest.
The shrine with gore unstain'd, with gold *u. E.M.* iii. 157

Uneasy.
The soul, *u.* and confin'd from home *E.M.* i. 97

Unelbow'd.
U. by a Gamester, Pimp, or Play'r *M.E.* iii. 247

Unenvy'd.
And prais'd, *u.*, by the Muse he lov'd *M.E.* v. 72

Unequal.
On two *u.* crutches propt he came *D.* iv. 111
U. task! a passion to resign *E.A.* 195
But how *u.* it bestows, observe *M.E.* iii. 23
Nor fear'd the Chief th' *u.* fight to try *R.L.* v. 77

Unequall'd.
The joy *u.*, if its end it gain *E.M.* iv. 315

Unequally.
No single parts *u.* surprize *E.C.* 249

Unerring.
U. NATURE, still divinely bright *E.C.* 70
Say, where full Instinct is th' *u.* guide *E.M.* iii. 83
Asks no firm hand, and no *u.* line *M.E.* ii. 152

Uneven.
Light quirks of Music, broken and *u. M.E.* iv. 143

Unexplor'd.
O say what stranger cause, yet *u. R.L.* i. 9

Unfading.
For her th' *u.* rose of Eden blooms *E.A.* 217
Or from those meads select *u.* flow'rs *IV.* 74

Unfaithful.
Secure they trust th' *u.* field beset *W.F.* 103

Unfashion'd.
Her shape *u.*, and her Face unknown *Mi.* ix. 60

Unfeeling.
Unlucky Welsted! thy *u.* master *D.* ii. 209
The broadest mirth *u.* Folly wears *E.M.* iv. 319

Unfeign'd.
Such *u.* Passion in his Looks appears *Mi.* ix. 93

Unfelt.
Till Death *u.* that tender frame destroy *Mi.* v. 17
The blow *u.*, the tear he never shed *P.S.* 349

Unfinish'd.
Motteux himself *u.* left his tale *D.* ii. 412
U. Treaties in each Office slept *D.* iv. 616
U. things, one knows not what to call *E.C.* 42

Unfix'd.
Quick as her eyes, and as *u.* as those *R.L.* ii. 10

Unfold.
A mortal Man *u.* all Nature's law *E.M.* ii. 32
But nobler scenes Maria's dreams *u. M.E.* iii. 129
Some to the sun their insect wings *u. R.L.* ii. 59
The vivid green his shining plumes *u. W.F.* 117

Unfolding.
And bid new music charm th' *u.* ear *M.* 42

Unfolds.
For this our Queen *u.* to vision true *D.* iii. 61
Sloth *u.* her arms and wakes *O.* i. 32

Unforeseen.
This fatal stroke, this *u.* Distress *Mi.* ix. 20

Unfortify'd.
While their weak heads like towns *u. E.C.* 434

Unfruitful.
To light the dead, and warm th' *u.* urn *E.A.* 262

Unfurnish'd.
When Merlin's Cave is half *u.* yet *S.* v. 355

Ungracious.
At best it falls to some *u.* son *S.* ii. 173

Ungrateful.
This from no venal or *u.* Muse *E.* iii. 2
As fruits, *u.* to the planter's care *E.M.* ii. 181
U. wretch, with mimic airs grown pert *Mi.* ix. 65

Unguarded.
Men in their loose *u.* hours they take *E.M.* iv. 227
To Heirs unknown descends th' *u.* store *M.E.* ii. 149

Unhallow'd.
Here cease thy flight, nor with *u.* lays *W.F.* 423

Unhappy.
U. Wit, like most mistaken things *E.C.* 494
Yet cry, if Man's *u.*, God's unjust *E.M.* i. 118
And these be happy call'd, *u.* those *E.M.* iv. 68
But fools the Good alone *u.* call *E.M.* iv. 97
U. Wharton, waking, found at last *M.E.* iii. 84
Effects *u.* from a Noble Cause *S.* v. 160
U. Dryden! In all Charles's days *S.* v. 213

Unheard.
Alike *u.*, unpity'd, and forlorn *A.* 22
U., unknown *O.* i. 102

Unheeded.
The World's great Victor pass'd *u.* by *I'.C.* 34

Unholy.
Far other raptures of *u.* joy *E.A.* 224

Unhonour'd.
A senseless, worthless, and *u.* crowd *S.* v. 306

Unimprov'd,
And not a Mask went *u.* away *E.C.* 541

Uninscrib'd,
Obscure the place, and *u.* the stone *W.F.* 320

Unintelligible.
O'er a learn'd, *u.* place *S.* vii. 102

Union.
U. the bond of all things, and of Man *E.M.* iii. 150
Here too all forms of social *u.* find *E.M.* iii. 179
From Order, *U.*, full Consent of things *E.M.* iii. 296
Learns, from this *u.* of the rising Whole *E.M.* iv. 337

Unison.
While the long solemn *U.* went round *D.* iv. 612

Unite.
Like friendly colours found them both *u. E.* iii. 15
May one kind grave *u.* each hapless name *E.A.* 343
When the ripe colours soften and *u. E.C.* 488
More studious to divide than to *u. E.M.* ii. 82
Yet, mix'd and soften'd, in his work *u. E.M.* ii. 112
If white and black blend, soften, and *u. E.M.* ii. 213
The Wood supports the Plain, the parts *u. M.E.* iv. 81
But Hymen's kinder flames *u. O.* iii. 21
The Tortoise here and Elephant *u. R.L.* i. 135

United,
While Jones' and Boyle's *u.* Labours fall *D.* iii. 328
All comes *u.* to th' admiring eyes *E.C.* 250
True faith, true policy, *u.* ran *E.M.* iii. 239
If all, *u.*, thy ambition call *E.M.* iv. 285
U. wish, and mutual joy *O.* iii. 26

Unites.
But airy substance soon *u.* again *R.L.* iii. 152
The grave *u.;* where ev'n the great find rest *W.F.* 317

Unities.
The manners, passions, *u.;* what not *E.C.* 276

Universal.
And *u.* Darkness buries All *D.* iv. 656
One clear, unchang'd, and *u.* light *E.C.* 71
Immortal heirs of *u.* praise *E.C.* 190
All partial Evil, *u.* Good. *E.M.* i. 292
Here then we rest: "The *U.* Cause *E.M.* iii. 6
Heav'n's attribute was *u.* Care *E.M.* iii. 159
Remember, Man, "the *U.* Cause *E.M.* iv. 35
Or partial Ill is *u.* Good *E.M.* iv. 114
When *u.* homage Umbra pays *M.E.* i. 59
To wrap me in the *u.* shade *S.* i. 96
Booth enters—hark! the *u.* peal *S.* v. 334

Universe.
See worlds on worlds compose our *u. E.M.* i. 24

Unjust.
Nor be so civil as to prove *u. E.C.* 581
Yet cry, if Man's unhappy, God's *u. E.M.* i. 118
Gods partial, changeful, passionate, *u. E.M.* iii. 257
So drives Self-love, thro' just and thro' *u. E.M.* iii. 269
When Athens sinks by fates *u. O.* ii. 17
And certain Laws, by suff'rers thought *u. S.* vi. 60

Unkind.
The phantom flies me, as *u.* as you *E.A.* 236
Is Heav'n *u.* to Man and Man alone *E.M.* i. 186
Nay, Poll sat mute, and Shock was most *u. R.L.* iv. 164

Unknowing.
And cheats th' *u.* Widow and the Poor *S.* viii. 141
And curs'd with hearts *u.* how to yield *U.L.* 42
Let not this weak, *u.* hand *U.P.* 25

Unknown.
A youth *u.* to Phœbus, in despair *D.* ii. 213
Thence a new world to Nature's laws *u. D.* iii. 241
And are these wonders, Son, to thee *u.* (*rep.*) *D.* iii. 273
Avaunt—is Aristarchus yet *u. D.* iv. 210
And things *u.* propos'd as things forgot *E.C.* 575
Perhaps acts second to some sphere *u. E.M.* i. 58
All Nature is but Art, *u.* to thee *E.M.* i. 289
The chain holds on, and where it ends, *u. E.M.* iii. 26

Heav'ns not his own, and worlds *u.* before *E.M.* iii. 106
Thus States were form'd, the name of King *u. E.M.* iii. 209
Just what you hear, you have, and what's *u. E.M.* iv. 239
Hope of known bliss, and Faith in bliss *u. E.M.* iv. 346
Passion and Pride were to her soul *u. Ep.* vi. 5
To Heirs *u.* descends th' unguarded store *M.E.* ii. 149
Must act un motives pow'rful, tho' *u. M.E.* iii. 112
His race, his form, his name almost *u. M.E.* iii. 284
Her Shape unfashion'd, and her Face *u. Mi.* ix. 60
Thus let me live unseen, *u. O.* i. 102
Unheard, *u. O.* iv. 17
Why did I write? what sin to me *u. P.S.* 125
His life, tho' long, to sickness past *u. P.S.* 402
And who *u.* defame me, let them be *S.* i. 139
Despise the known, nor tremble at th' *u. S.* vi. 311
Then gath'ring flocks on *u.* mountains fed *W.F.* 87

Unlamented.
Thus *u.* let me die *O.* iv. 18
Thus *u.* pass the proud away *U.L.* 43

Unlearn'd.
Amaze th' *u.*, and make the learned smile *E.C.* 327
Content, if hence th' *u.* their wants may view *E.C.* 732
U., he knew no schoolman's subtle art *P.S.* 398

Unless.—*Passim.*

Unlicens'd.
I poach in Suidas for *u.* Greek *D.* iv. 228

Unlike.
Figures ill pair'd and Similes *u. D.* i. 66
Ah ! how *u.* the man of times to come *E.M.* iii. 161
All how *u.* each other, all how true *M.E.* ii. 6

Unlock.
Thus the small jet, which hasty hands *u. D.* ii. 177
U. your springs, and open all your shades *W.F.* 4

Unlocks.
This casket India's glowing gems *u. R.L.* i 133
Of ancient writ *u.* the learned store *W.F.* 247

Unlucky.
U. Welsted! thy unfeeling master *D.* ii. 209
U., as Fungoso in the play *E.C.* 328
Whoe'er offends, at some *u.* time *S.* i. 77

Unmark'd.
Some *u.* fibre, or some varying vein *M.E.* i. 26

Unmeaning.
With some *u.* thing they call a thought *E.C.* 355

Unmolested.
Safe on my shore each *u.* swain *W.F.* 369

Unmov'd.
Tho' cold like you, *u.* and silent grown *E.A.* 23
So very reasonable, so *u. M.E.* ii. 165
With looks *u.*, he hopes the scaly breed *W.F.* 139

Unnumber'd.
Thro' worlds *u.* tho' the God be known *E.M.* i. 21
Know, then, *u.* Spirits round thee fly *R.L.* i. 41
U. treasures ope at once, and here *R.L.* i. 129
U. throngs on ev'ry side are seen *R.L.* iv. 47

Unobserv'd.
And *u.* the glaring Orb declines *M.E.* ii. 256

Unop'ning.
Curse the sav'd candle and *u.* door *M.E.* iii. 19

Unpaid.
That suit an *u.* tailor snatch'd away *D.* ii. 118
Thy fate unpity'd, and thy rites *u. U.L.* 48

Unpension'd.
Gay dies *u.* with a hundred friends *D.* iii. 330
Unplac'd, *u.*, no man's heir or slave *S.* i. 116

Unpeopled.
Pours forth, and leaves *u.* half the land *D.* ii. 20
Huge Theatres that now *u.* Woods *M.E.* v. 7

Unperceiv'd.
While summer-suns roll *u.* away *E.* iii. 18

Unpillar'd.
See the Cirque falls, th' *u*. Temple nods *D.* iii. 107

Unpity'd.
Alike unheard, *u*., and forlorn *A.* 22
Thy fate *u*., and thy rites unpaid *U.L.* 48

Unplac'd.
U., unpension'd, no man's heir or slave *S.* i. 116

Unpleasing.
Be no *u*. Melancholy mine *P.S.* 407

Unpolish'd.
U. Gems no ray on Pride bestow *Mi.* x. 5

Unpractis'd.
Hear what from Love *u*. hearts endure *Su.* 11

Unprofitable.
So slow th' *u*. moments roll *S.* iii. 39

Unpropitious.
Now flam'd the Dog-star's *u*. ray *D.* iv. 9

Unquiet.
A vain, *u*., glitt'ring, wretched Thing *E.* iv. 54

Unravel.
Or quite *u*. all the reas'ning thread *D.* i. 179

Unravels.
This clue once found, *u*. all the rest *M.E.* i. 178

Unread.
Her grey-hair'd Synods damning books *u*. *D.* iii. 103

Unregarded.
Nor past the meanest *u*., one *D.* iv. 515
Flaunts and goes down, an *u*. thing *M.E.* ii. 252

Unrelenting.
Gor'd with *u*. Tooth *Mi.* vii. 12

Unrepenting.
Not tyrants fierce that *u*. die *R.L.* iv. 7

Unresisted.
The conqu'ring force of *u*. steel *R.L.* iii. 178

Unrespected.
From loveless youth to *u*. age *M.E.* ii. 125

Unreveal'd.
Dear fatal name I rest ever *u*. *E.A.* 9

Unrivall'd.
Honour forbid I at whose *u*. shrine *R.L.* iv. 105

Unseen.
Safe and *u*. the young Æneas past *D.* iv. 290
U. at Church, at Senate, or at Court *D.* iv. 338
Itself *u*., but in th' effects, remains *E.C.* 79
To Pow'r *u*., and mightier far than they *E.M.* iii. 252
Pregnant with thousands flits the Scrap *u*. *M.E.* iii. 47
Thus let me live, *u*., unknown *O.* iv. 17
These, tho' *u*., are ever on the wing *R.L.* i. 43
An Ace of Hearts steps forth: the King *u*. *R.L.* iii. 95
She rues, but hopes she does not rue *u*. *Sp.* 58
Useless, *u*., as lamps in sepulchres *U.L.* 20

Unsheath'd.
And half *u*. the shining blade *O.* i. 46

Unshod.
Men bearded, bald, cowl'd, uncowl'd, shod, *u*. *D.* iii. 114

Unshook.
Thou stand'st *u*. amidst a bursting world *P.S.* 88

Unskill'd.
Poets like painters, thus, *u*. to trace *E.C.* 293

Unspent.
Spreads undivided, operates *u*. *E.M.* i. 274

Unspoil'd.
O teach us, Bathurst! yet *u*. by wealth *M.E.* iii. 226

Unspotted.
U. long with human blood *O.* ii. 6

U. names, and venerable long *P.S.* 386
Roscommon only boasts *u*. bays *S.* v. 214

Unstain'd.
U., untouch'd, and yet in maiden sheets *D.* i. 229
The shrine with gore *u*., with gold undrest *E.M.* iii. 157
His hand *u*., his uncorrupted heart *M.E.* i. 82

Unsuccessful.
Did the dead letter *u*. prove *D.* i. 193
Leave dang'rous truths to *u*. Satires *E.C.* 592

Unsully'd.
A hecatomb of pure *u*. lays *D.* i. 158
Such as on Hough's *u*. Mitre shine *E.S.* ii. 240

Untainted.
Go, fair example of *u*. youth *Ep.* vii. 1

Untaught.
Fear held them mute. Alone, *u*. to fear *D.* ii. 57
A Face *u*. to feign; a judging Eye *E.* ii. 5
The bad must miss; the good, *u*., will find *E.M.* iv. 330

Unthaw'd.
Or fish deny'd (the river yet *u*.) *S.* ii. 14

Unthinking.
To each *u*. being Heav'n, a friend *E.M.* iii. 71
With earnest eyes, and round *u*. face *R.L.* iv. 125

Unthought-of.
U. Frailties cheat us in the Wise *M.E.* i. 69

Untimely.
Till Death *u*. stopp'd his tuneful tongue *E.* i. 4

Untouch'd.
Unstain'd, *u*., and yet in maiden sheets *D.* i. 229
Her Head's *u*., that noble Seat of Thought *M.E.* ii. 74

Untrod.
The Patriot's plain, but *u*., path pursue *E.* ii. 16

Untrue.
Ah, Madam, since my Sharper is *u*. *Mi.* ix. 4

Untutor'd.
Lo the poor Indian! whose *u*. mind *E.M.* i. 99

Unusual.
The forests wonder'd at th' *u*. grain *W.F.* 89

Unvary'd.
While they ring round the same *u*. chimes *E.C.* 348
Mark what *u*. laws preserve each state *E.M.* iii. 189

Unveil'd.
And now, *u*., the Toilet stands display'd *R.L.* i. 121

Unwarm'd.
To gaze on *Basset*, and remain *u*. *Mi.* ix. 76

Unwasting.
Purest love's *u*. treasure *O.* iii. 41

Unwater'd.
U. see the drooping sea-horse mourn *M.E.* iv. 125

Unweary'd.
Thy mighty Scholiast, whose *u*. pains *D.* iv. 211
Each heav'nly piece *u*. we compare *E.* iii. 35
Of ev'ry wheel of that *u*. Mill *S.* vi. 78
With slaught'ring guns th' *u*. fowler roves *W.F.* 125

Unwhipp'd.
And then, *u*., he had the grace to cry *S.* vi. 18

Unwholesome.
But see, Orion sheds *u*. dews *W.* 85

Unwieldy.
His giant limbs, in state *u*. spread *R.L.* iii. 72
My wealth *u*., and my heap too great *S.* ii. 114

Unwilling.
From the dear man *u*. she must sever *E.* v. 5
There stern Religion quench'd th' *u*. flame *E.A.* 39
And turn th' *u*. steeds another way *M.E.* iii. 192

z

And drop at last, but in *u.* ears *P.S.* 39
Th' *u.* Gratitude of base mankind *S.* v. 14

Unwillingly.
Howe'er *u.* it quits its place *S.* vi. 161

Unworthy.
U. he, the voice of Fame to hear *S.* ii. 99

Unwounded.
Sighs for a daughter with *u.* ear *M.E.* ii. 260

Up.—*Passim.*

Upheld.
By singing Peers *u.* on either side *D.* iv. 49
And drawn supports, *u.* by God, or thee *E.M.* i. 34
Let Ireland tell, how Wit *u.* her Cause *S.* v. 221

Upholst'rer.
Your Barber, Cook, *U.,* what you please *S.* vi. 10

Uplift.
Songs, sonnets, epigrams the winds *u. D.* ii. 115

Upon.—*Passim.*

Upright.
So *u.* Quakers please both Man and God *D.* iv. 208

Upward.—*Passim.*

Urge.
The Senator at Cricket *u.* the Ball *D.* iv. 592
Self-love to *u.,* and Reason to restrain *E.M.* ii. 54

Urg'd.
The wheels above *u.* by the load below *D.* i. 184
And *u.* the rest by equal steps to rise *E.C.* 97
Are mortals *u.* thro' sacred lust of praise *E.C.* 521
That *u.* by thee, I turn'd the tuneful art *E.M.* iv. 391
Fate *u.* the shears, and cut the Sylph in twain *R.L.* iii. 151
Beasts, *u.* by us, their fellow-beasts pursue *W.F.* 123
Or as the God, more furious, *u.* the chase *W.F.* 190

Urges.
Heir *u.* heir, like wave impelling wave *S.* vi. 253

Urn.
Thro' half the heav'ns he pours th' exalted *u. D.* ii. 283
And the huge boar is shrunk into an *u. D.* iv. 552
Or wait inspiring Dreams at Maro's *U. E.* iii. 28
To light the dead, and warm th' unfruitful *u. E.A.* 262
Hang the sad verse on CAROLINA's *U. E.S.* i. 80
Thy relics, ROWE, to this fair *U.* we trust *Ep.* v. 1
And swallows roost in Nilus' dusty *U. M.E.* iv. 126
My Verse, and Queensb'ry weeping o'er thy *u. P.S.* 260
And palms eternal flourish round his *u. W.F.* 312
Grav'd on his *u.* appear'd the moon, that guides *W.F.* 333
High in the midst, upon his *u.* reclin'd *W.F.* 349
So from the Sun's broad beam in shallow *u—s D.* ii. 11
Who swell with tributary *u.* his flood *W.F.* 338

Us.—*Passim.*

Usage.
By *Cards' Ill U.,* or by *Lovers Lost Mi.* ix. 26

Use.
Want as much more, to turn it to its *u. E.C.* 81
Make *u.* of ev'ry friend—and ev'ry foe *E.C.* 214
Still fit for *u.,* and ready at command *E.C.* 674
Yet serves to second too some other *u. E.M.* i. 56
His actions', passions', beings', *u.* and end *E.M.* i. 66
Earth for whose *u.?* Pride answers "'Tis for mine *E.M.* i. 132
Made for his *u.* all creatures if he call (*rep.*) *E.M.* i. 177
Say what the *u.,* were finer optics giv'n *E.M.* i. 195
In Man they join in some mysterious *u. E.M.* ii. 206
While Man exclaims, "See all things for my *u.!" E.M.* iii. 45
Taught Pow'r's due *u.* to People and to Kings *E.M.* iii. 269
Lewis, the Dean will be of *u. I.H.* ii. 35 *s*
Extremes in Man concur to gen'ral *u. M.E.* iii. 162
What tho' (the *u.* of barb'rous spits forgot) *M.E.* iii. 179

And pompous buildings once were things of *U. M.E.* iv. 24
'Tis *U.* alone that sanctifies Expense *M.E.* iv. 179
Or who would learn one earthly thing of *u. R.L.* v. 22
Well, if tbe *u.* be mine, can it concern one *S.* ii. 165
Of little *u.* the Man you may suppose *S.* v. 201
For *U.,* will father what's begot by Sense *S.* vi. 170
If there be Truth in Law, and *U.* can give *S.* vi. 230
We only furnish what he cannot u. D. iv. 261
Reason still *u.,* to Reason still attend *E.M.* ii. 78
What then remains but well our pow'r to *u. R.L.* v. 29
Advice; and (as you *u.*) without a Fee *S.* i. 10

Us'd.
A Muse by these is like a mistress *u. E.C.* 432
Because they see me *u.* so well *I.H.* ii. 102 *s*
As Poison heals, in just Proportion *u. M.E.* iii. 234
And I'm not *u.* to Panegyric strains *S.* v. 405

Useful.
Hear how learn'd Greece her *u.* rules indites *E.C.* 92
Thus *u.* arms in magazines we place *E.C.* 671
License repress'd, and *u.* laws ordain'd *E.C.* 682
U., I grant, it serves what life requires *M.E.* ii. 27
And (tho' no Soldier) *u.* to the State *S.* v. 204

Useless.
Gives not the *u.* knowledge of its end *E.M.* iii. 72
But *u.* lances into scythes shall bend *M.* 61
Not to the skies in *u.* columns tost *M.E.* iii. 255
And vile Attorneys, now an *u.* race *M.E.* iii. 274
And fame, this lord of *u.* thousands ends *M.E.* iii. 314
U., unseen, as lamps in sepulchres *U.L.* 20
And with your golden darts, now *u.* grown *W.* 25

Usher'd.
Still breath'd in sighs, still *u.* with a tear *E.A.* 32

Usual.
And stretch'd on bulks, as *u.,* Poets lay *D.* ii. 420
With more than *u.* light'ning in her eyes *R.L.* v. 76

Utmost.
Perhaps ev'n Britain's *u.* shore *O.* ii. 19

Uxorio.
Shall then *U.,* if the stakes he sweep *M.E.* iii. 1

V.

Vacant.
Then gay Ideas crowd the *v.* brain *R.L.* i. 83

Vacuity.
And each *v.* of sense by Pride *E.M.* ii. 286

Vadius.
Poor *V.,* long with learned spleen devour'd *M.E.* v. 41

Vaga.
Pleas'd *V.* echoes thro' her winding bounds *M.E.* iii. 251

Vagrant.
Sent with a Pass, and *v.* thro' the land *D.* i. 232

Vail'd.
His Hat, which never *v.* to human pride *D.* iv. 205

Vain.
You by whose care, in *v.* decry'd and curst *D.* i. 5
Hence Bards, like Proteus long in *v.* tied down *D.* i. 37
But senseless, lifeless! idol void and *v. D.* ii. 46
All *v.* petitions mounting to the sky *D.* ii. 89
Heav'n rings with laughter. Of the laughter *v. D.* ii. 121
"Smedley" in *v.* resounds thro' all the coast *D.* ii. 294
While Sherlock, Hare, and Gibson, preach in *v. D.* ii. 204
Turn what they will to Verse, their toil is *v. D.* iv. 213
V., of Italian Arts, Italian Souls *D.* iv. 300
In *v.,* in *v.*—the all-composing Hour *D.* iv. 627
Wit shoots in *v.* its momentary fires *D.* iv. 633
In *v.!* they gaze, turn giddy, rave, and die *D.* iv. 648
Dear to the Muse! to HARLEY dear in *v. E.* i. 6
In *v.* to Deserts thy retreat is made *E.* i. 27

VALE—VAPOUR.   339

And all th' oblig'd desert, and all the v. *E.* i. 32
Then view this Marble, and be v. no more *E.* iii. 54
A v., unquiet, glitt'ring, wretched Thing *E.* iv. 54
In v. lost Eloïsa weeps and prays *E.A.* 15
Nor tears for ages taught to flow in v. *E.A.* 28
Ah wretch! believ'd the spouse of God in v. *E.A.* 177
Or one v. wit's, that might a hundred tire *E.C.* 45
By v. ambition still to make them more *E.C.* 65
To teach v. Wits a science little known *E.C.* 199
The reader's threaten'd (not in v.) with sleep *E.C.* 353
And charitably let the dull be v. *E.C.* 597
Not free from faults, nor yet too v. to mend *E.C.* 744
And not a vanity is giv'n in v. *E.M.* ii. 290
All feed on one v. Patron, and enjoy *E.M.* iii. 61
Which heavier Reason labours at in v. *E.M.* iii. 92
In v. thy Reason finer webs shall draw *E.M.* iii. 191
Where grows?—where grows it not? If v. our toil *E.M.* iv. 13
Some swell'd to Gods, confess ev'n Virtue v. *E.M.* iv. 24
Heav'n still with laughter the v. toil surveys *E.M.* iv. 75
Are giv'n in v., but what they seek they find *E.M.* iv. 348
Invention strives to be before in v. *E.S.* ii. 7
Names, which I long have lov'd, nor lov'd in v. *E.S.* ii. 90
And what young AMMON wish'd, but wish'd in v. *E.S.* ii. 117
How v. is Reason, Eloquence how weak *Ep.* iii. 5
This modest Stone, what few v. Marbles can *Ep.* x. 1
V. was the Chief's, the Sage's pride *I.H.* iv. 13
In v. they schem'd, in v. they bled *I.H.* iv. 15
In v. sedate reflections we would make *M.E.* i. 39
In v. the Sage, with retrospective eye *M.E.* i. 99
In v. th' observer eyes the builder's toil *M.E.* i. 220
Ah! Friend! to dazzle let the V. design *M.E.* ii. 249
Giv'n to the Fool, the Mad, the V. the Evil *M.E.* iii. 19
In v. may Heroes fight, and Patriots rave *M.E.* iii. 33
In v. at Court the Bankrupt pleads his cause *M.E.* iii. 217
Load some v. Church with old Theatric state *M.E.* iv. 29
For Locke or Milton 'tis in v. to look *M.E.* iv. 139
Ambition sigh'd: she found it v. to trust *M.E.* v. 19
Stood up to dash each v. PRETENDER'S hope *Mi.* ii. 17
Vile, reptile, weak, and v. *Mi.* iv. 6
V. is thy Art, thy Powder v. *Mi.* iv. 35
Some joy still lost, as each v. year runs o'er *Mi.* v. 7
A Rival's envy (all in v.) to hide *Mi.* ix. 42
In v. your guiltless laurels stood *O.* ii. 5
Wisdom and wit in v. reclaim *O.* iii. 3
Ignobly v. and impotently great *P.C.* 7
Apply to me, to keep them mad or v. *P.S.* 22
Destroy his fib or sophistry, in v. *P.S.* 91
'Tis all in v., deny it as I will *P.S.* 277
While clogg'd he beats his silken wings in v. *R.L.* ii. 130
Sir Plume of amber snuff-box justly v. *R.L.* iv. 123
Who speaks so well should ever speak in v. *R.L.* iv. 132
In v. Thalestris with reproach assails *R.L.* v. 3
While Anna begg'd, and Dido rag'd in v. *R.L.* v. 6
The wise man's passion, and the v. man's toast *R.L.* v. 10
How v. are all these glories, all our pains *R.L.* v. 15
Beauties in v. their pretty eyes may roll *R.L.* v. 33
In ev'ry place is sought, but sought in v. *R.L.* v. 110
'Tis yet in v., I own, to keep a pother *S.* ii. 45
And feels that grace his pray'r besought in v. *S.* v. 238
In v. bad Rhymers all the world reject *S.* vi. 153
Curs'd be the wretch, so venal and so v. *S.* vii. 63
Nor the v. itch t' admire, and be admir'd *S.* viii. 10
As v., as idle, and as false, as they *S.* viii. 10
Each am'rous nymph prefers her gifts in v. *Su.* 53
In v. kind seasons swell'd the teeming grain (rep.) *W.F.* 53
In v. on father Thames she calls for aid *W.F.* 197
Faint, breathless, thus she pray'd, nor pray'd in v. *W.F.* 199
And gasping Furies thirst for blood in v. *W.F.* 422
A *Monarch's sword when mad* V.-glory *draws E.S.* ii. 229

Vale.

Here in a dusky v. where Lethe rolls *D.* iii. 23
Content with Science in the V. of Peace *Ep.* x. 6
In life's low v., the soil the Virtues like *M.E.* i. 143
Whose Cause-way parts the v. with shady rows *M.E.* iii. 259
Or scoops in circling theatres the V. *M.E.* iv. 60

Pour'd o'er the whitening v. their fleecy care *Sp.* 19
Lose the low v—s, *and steal into the skies A.* 60
To Isles of fragrance, lily-silver'd v. *D.* iv. 303
Mount o'er the v., and seem to tread the sky *E.C.* 226
Begin, the v. shall ev'ry note rebound *Sp.* 44
Or else where Cam his winding v. divides *Su.* 26
Nor rivers winding thro' the v. below *W.* 3
Adieu, ye v., ye mountains *W.* 89
Here hills and v., the woodland and the plain *W.F.* 11
Hills, v., and floods appear already cross'd *W.F.* 153

Valiant.

Next goes his Wool—to clothe our v. bands *M.E.* iii. 211

Valleys.

There painted v. of eternal green *D.* i. 76
Sink down ye mountains, and ye v. rise *M.* 34
Waste sandy v., once perplex'd with thorn *M.* 73
Rush thro' the thickets, down the v. sweep *W.F.* 156

Value.

True, he had wit, to make their v. rise *D.* iv. 377
And v. *books, as women men, for dress E.C.* 306
But blame the false, and v. still the true *E.C.* 407
The Sense to v. Riches with the Art *M.E.* iii. 219
Th' inscription v., but the rust adore *M.E.* v. 36
It is the rust we v., not the gold *S.* v. 36

Valu'd.

No Fool to laugh at, which he v. more *M.E.* iii. 312

Valuing.

Some v. those of their own side or mind *E.C.* 452

Vamp'd.

A vast, v., future, old, reviv'd, new piece *D.* i. 284

Van=Vanbrugh.

How V. wants grace, who never wanted wit *S.* v. 289

Vandal.

Had brav'd the *Goth*, and many a V. slain *Mi.* ii. 2
Embody'd dark, what clouds of V—s *rise D.* iii. 86
And drove those holy V. off the stage *E.C.* 696

Vandalis.

The blue, transparent V. appears *W.F.* 345

Vanish.

Thus v. sceptres, coronets, and balls *E.* v. 39
Gay pats my shoulder, and you v. quite *E.* v. 47
Or, in a jointure, v. from the heir *S.* ii. 170
First turn plain rash, then v. quite away *S.* viii. 45

Vanish'd.

Then * essay'd; scarce v. out of sight *D.* ii. 295
While fancy brings the v. piles to view *E.* iii. 31
The very Tombs now v. like their dead *M.E.* v. 4
But all the Vision v. from thy head *R.L.* i. 120
The Groves of Eden, v. now so long *W.F.* 7

Vanity.

These sparks with awkward v. display *E.C.* 329
But soon the short-liv'd v. is lost *E.C.* 497
Deduct what is but V., or Dress *E.M.* ii. 45
That Virtue's ends from V. can raise *E.M.* ii. 245
And not a v. is giv'n in vain *E.M.* ii. 290
His charitable V. supplies *M.E.* iv. 172
Theirs is the V., the Learning thine *M.E.* v. 45
Who has the v. to call you friend *P.S.* 295
O you! whom V.'s *light bark conveys S.* v. 296
Riches that vex, and V—ies *that tire Mi.* v. 4
That all her v. at once are dead (rep.) *R.L.* i. 52
With varying v., from ev'ry part *R.L.* i. 99

Vanquish'd.

And v. realms supply recording gold *M.E.* v. 56
And v. nature seems to charm no more *Sp.* 76
Still in thy song should v. France appear *W.F.* 309

Vapour.

The V. mild o'er each Committee crept *D.* iv. 615
A v. fed from wild desire *D.* iii. 19
And in a v. reach'd the dismal dome *R.L.* iv. 18
A constant V. o'er the palace flics *R.L.* iv. 39
And wafting V—s *from the Land of dreams D.* ii. 340
Here brisker v. o'er the TEMPLE creep *D.* ii. 345
Him close she curtains round with V. blue *D.* iii. 3

z 2

It draws up *v.* which obscure its rays *E.C.* 471
Spleen, *V.*, or Small-pox, above them all *M.E.* ii. 267
Sent up in *v.* to the Baron's brain *R.L.* iii. 119
Parent of *v.* and of female wit *R.L.* iv. 59
A Fit of *V.* clouds this Demi-God *S.* iii. 188
Where cooling *v.* breathe along the mead *W.F.* 136

Variance.
Is there a *v.?* enter but his door *M.E.* iii. 271
How much at *v.* are her feet and eyes *Sp.* 60

Variegated.
Ladies, like *v.* tulips, show *M.E.* ii. 41

Varies.
How instinct *v.* in the grov'lling swine *E.M.* i. 221
Next, that he *v.* from himself no less *M.E.* i. 20
Surprises, *v.*, and conceals the Bounds *M.E.* iv. 56
Joins willing woods, and *v.* shades from shades *M.E.* iv. 62

Variety.
Led thro' a sad *v.* of woe *E.A.* 36
Where order in *v.* we see *W.F.* 15

Various.
And hears the *v.* vows of fond mankind *D.* ii. 87
Eyes the calm Sun-set of thy *v.* Day *E.* i. 38
In *v.* shapes of Parsons, Critics, Beaux *E.C.* 459
Acts to one end, but acts by *v.* laws *E.M.* iii. 2
See Matter next, with *v.* life endu'd *E.M.* iii. 13
And mourn our *v.* portions as we please *E.M.* iv. 33
Teach me, like thee, in *v.* nature wise *E.M.* iv. 377
Shall parts so *v.* aim at nothing new *M.E.* i. 286
In Men, we *v.* Ruling Passions find *M.E.* ii. 207
What *v.* joys on one attend *O.* iii. 27
The *v.* off'rings of the world appear *R.L.* i. 130
Ye know the spheres and *v.* tasks assign'd *R.L.* ii. 75
In *v.* talk th' instructive hours they past *R.L.* iii. 11
Of *v.* habit and of *v.* dye *R.L.* iii. 84
Of bodies chang'd to *v.* forms by Spleen *R.L.* iv. 48
On *v.* tempers act by *v.* ways *R.L.* iv. 61
V. of temper, as of face or frame *S.* vi. 282
The *v.* seasons of the rolling year *Sp.* 38
'Tis done, and nature's *v.* charms decay *W.* 29
Our plenteous streams a *v.* race supply *W.F.* 141

Variously.
Fortune her gifts may *v.* dispose *E.M.* iv. 67
The very best will *v.* incline *E.M.* iv. 143

Varlets.
Breval, Bond, Besaleel, the *v.* caught *D.* ii. 126

Varnish.
This the blue *v.*, that the green endears *M.E.* v. 37

Varnish'd.
Which Heav'n has *v.* out, and made a Queen *M.E.* ii. 182
Such painted puppets! such a *v.* race *S.* viii. 208

Vary.
You laugh, if coat and breeches strangely *v. S.* iii. 163

Vary'd.
Such *v.* light in one promiscuous blaze *D.* iv. 412
Hear how Timotheus' *v.* lays surprize *E.C.* 374
What *v.* Being peoples ev'ry star *E.M.* i. 27

Varying.
She tinsell'd o'er with robes of *v.* hues *D.* i. 81
And all its *v.* Rainbows die away *D.* iv. 637
Like *v.* winds, by other passions tost *E.M.* ii. 167
Mean-while Opinion gilds with *v.* rays *E.M.* ii. 233
Smit with her *v.* plumage, spare the dove *E.M.* iii. 54
Some unmark'd fibre, or some *v.* vein *M.E.* i. 16
With *v.* vanities from ev'ry part *R.L.* i. 99
The *v.* verse, the full-resounding line *S.* v. 268
Ah! what avail his glossy, *v.* dyes *W.F.* 115

Vase.
Each silver *V.* in mystic order laid *R.L.* i. 122
Fair Coursers, *V—s*, and alluring Dames *M.E.* iii. 70
There Hero's wits are kept in pond'rous *v. R.L.* v. 115
Gold, Silver, Iv'ry, *V.* sculptur'd high *S.* vi. 264

Vassal.
First slave to Words, then *V.* to a Name *D.* ix. 501

Slave to a Wife, or *V.* to a Punk *S.* iii. 62
And serv'd alike his *V—s* and his God *W.F.* 76

Vast.
Sinking from thought to thought, a *v.* profound *D.* i. 118
A *v.*, vamp'd, future, old, reviv'd, new piece *D.* i. 284
Lo! one *v.* extent of flimsy lines *P.S.* 94
One *v.* Egg produces human race *D.* iii. 248
Involves a *v.* involuntary throng *D.* iv. 82
So *v.* is art, so narrow human wit *E.C.* 61
So *v.* a throng the stage can ne'er contain *E.C.* 283
When Ajax strives some rock's *v.* weight to throw *E.C.* 370
He, who thro' *v.* immensity can pierce *E.M.* i. 23
V. chain of Being! which from God began *E.M.* i. 237
On life's *v.* ocean diversely we sail *E.M.* ii. 107
The *v.* Parterres a thousand hands shall make *M.E.* iv. 73
Convinc'd she now contracts her *v.* designs *M.E.* v. 23
Proud of a *v.* extent of flimsy lines *P.S.* 94
Of twelve *v.* French Romances, neatly gilt *R.L.* ii. 38
Form'd a *v.* buckle for his widow's gown *R.L.* v. 92
To make poor Pinky eat with *v.* applause *S.* v. 293
All *v.* possessions (just the same the case *S.* vi. 254
So *v.*, our new Divines, we must confess *S.* vii. 97

Vaticide.
The caitiff *V.* conceiv'd a pray'r *D.* ii. 78

Vault.
Then sacred seem'd th' ethereal *v.* no more *E.M.* iii. 263
This *V.* of Air, this congregated Ball *S.* iv. 5
In weeping *v—s* her hallow'd earth contains *W.F.* 302

Vaulted.
"Restore the Lock!" the *v.* roofs rebound *R.L.* v. 104

Vaunts.
The race by vigour not by *v.* is won *D.* ii. 59

Vegetables.
See dying *v.* life sustain *E.M.* iii. 15

Vegetate.
See life dissolving *v.* again *E.M.* iii. 16

Vehicles.
From earthly *V.* to these of air *R.L.* i. 50

Veil.
A *v.* of fogs dilates her awful face *D.* i. 262
Wraps in her *v.*, and frees from sense of shame *D.* iv. 336
As with cold lips I kiss'd the sacred *v. E.A.* 111
As half to shew, half *v.*, the deep intent *D.* iv. 4

Veils.
Religion blushing *v.* her sacred fires *D.* iv. 649

Vein.
And quick sensations skip from *v.* to *v. D.* ii. 212
O'er ev'ry *v.* a shudd'ring horror runs *D.* iv. 143
Still run on Poets, in a raging *v. E.C.* 606
Some unmark'd fibre, or some varying *v. M.E.* i. 16
And all that voluntary *V. I.H.* i. 49
Tho' still some traces of our rustic *v. S.* v. 20
Th' impatient courser pants in ev'ry *v. W.F.* 151
What means this tumult in a Vestal's *v—s E.A.* 4

Vellum.
Lo some are *V.*, and the rest as good *M.E.* iv. 137

Velvet.
Draw forth to combat on the *v.* plain *R.L.* iii. 44
Was *v.* in the youth of good Queen Bess *S.* viii. 41
"That's *v.* for a King!" the flatt'rer swears *S.* viii. 218

Venal.
Of dull and *v.* a new world to mould *D.* iv. 15
The *V.* quiet, and entrance the Dull *D.* iv. 624
This, from no *v.* or ungrateful Muse *E.* iii. 2
Seen him, uncumber'd by the *v.* tribe *E.S.* i. 27
The Crown of Poland, *v.* twice an age *M.E.* iii. 127
Yet then did Gildon draw his *v.* quill *P.S.* 151
Curs'd be the wretch, so *v.* and so vain *S.* vii. 63

Venerable.
Unspotted names, and *v.* long *P.S.* 386
By god-like Poets *v.* made *W.F.* 270

Venetian.
Palladian walls, *V.* doors *I.H.* ii. 191
Proud to catch cold at a *V.* door *M.E.* iv. 36

Vengeance.
And promis'd *V.* on a barb'rous age *D.* iv. 40
Fancy restores what *v.* snatch'd away *E.A.* 226
The distant threats of *v.* on his head *P.S.* 348
Shall feel sharp *v.* soon o'ertake his sins *R.L.* ii. 125
He springs to *v.* with an eager pace *R.L.* iii. 97
On all the line a sudden *v.* waits *U.L.* 37
There purple *V.* bath'd in gore retires *W.F.* 417

Venial.
To W—le guilty of some *v.* sin *E.S.* ii. 162
Those *v.* sins, an atom, or a straw *S.* viii. 243

Venice.
From dirt and sea-weed as proud *V.* rose *E.M.* iv. 292

Ven'son.
A rogue with *V.* to a Saint without *M.E.* i. 80
To live on *V.* when it sold so dear *M.E.* iii. 118
Our fathers prais'd rank *V.* You suppose *S.* ii. 91
His *V.* too, a guinea makes your own *S.* v. 235

Venom.
Half froth, half *v.*, spits himself abroad *P.S.* 320

Vent.
And all the Furies issu'd at the *v.* *R.L.* iv. 92
There in his seat two spacious v—s appear D. ii. 85
And all your courtly Civet-cats can v. E.S. ii. 183

Venture.
Should Ripley *v.*, all the world would smile *S.* v. 186

Ventur'd.
Set up with these he *v.* on the Town *Mi.* iii. 7

Vent'rous.
Or tread the path by *v.* Heroes trod *D.* i. 201

Venus.
As, taught by *V.*, Paris learnt the art *D.* ii. 217
See graceless *V.* to a Virgin turn'd *D.* iii. 111
But chief her shrine where naked *V.* keeps *D.* iv. 307
This glorious Youth, and add one *V.* more *D.* iv. 330
Tis *V.*, *V.*, gives these arms *E.* vi. 27
The torch of *V.* burns not for the dead *E.A.* 258
Ah spare me, *V.!* let me, let me rest *I.H.* iii. 2
This the blest Lover shall for *V.* take *R.L.* v. 135
V. shall give him Form, and Anstis Birth *S.* iv. 82
Celestial *V.* haunts Idalia's groves *Sp.* 65
In woods bright *V.* with Adonis stray'd *Su.* 61

Verbal.
Neglect the rules each *v.* Critic lays *E.C.* 261

Verdant.
And lambs with wolves shall graze the *v.* mead *M.* 77
Mournful Cypress, *v.* Willow *Mi.* vii. 21
And march'd a victor from the *v.* field *R.L.* iii. 52
And *v.* alders form'd a quiv'ring shade *Su.* 4
For her the flocks refuse their *v.* food *W.* 37
Like *v.* isles the sable waste adorn *W.F.* 37
Beyond the forest's *v.* limits stray'd *W.F.* 182
The Loddon slow, with *v.* alders crown'd *W.F.* 342

Verdeur.
Explains the *Seve* and *V.* of the Vine *D.* iv. 556

Verdure.
See lilies spring, and sudden *v.* rise *M.* 68
Their beauty wither'd, and their *v.* lost *W.* 10

Verges.
Touches some wheel or *v.* to some goal. *E.M.* i. 59

Verier.
A *v.* monster, than on Afric's shore *S.* viii. 28

Veriest.
The *v.* Hermit in the Nation *I.H.* ii. 181

Vernal.
As thick as bees o'er *v.* blossoms fly *D.* iii. 33
I saw, and started from its *v.* bow'r *D.* iv. 424
To that which warbles thro' the *v.* wood *E.M.* i. 216

For me, the *v.* garlands bloom no more *I.H.* iii. 32
To draw fresh colours from the *v.* flow'rs *R.L.* ii. 95
Let *v.* airs thro' trembling osiers play *Sp.* 5
A soft retreat from sudden *v.* show'rs *Sp.* 98

Vernon.
Whether the name belong to Pope or *V. S.* ii. 166

Verres.
Cal *V.*, Wolsey, any odious name *E.S.* ii. 137

Verrio.
Where sprawl the Saints of *V.* or Laguerre *M.E.* iv. 145
Then, from her roofs when V.'s colours fall W.F. 307

Versailles.
Without it, proud *V.!* thy glory falls *M.E.* iv. 71

Verse.
Else all my Prose and *V.* were much the same *D.* i. 189
Prose swell'd to *v.*, *v.* loit'ring into prose *D.* i. 274
As *v.*, or prose, infuse the drowsy God *D.* ii. 396
Leave not a foot of *v.*, a foot of stone *D.* iv. 127
Turn what they will to *V.*, their toil is vain *D.* iv. 213
This *V.* be thine, my friend, nor thou refuse *E.* iii. 1
Now one in *v.* makes many more in prose *E.C.* 8
The hoarse, rough *v.* should like the torrent roar *E.C.* 369
Shall then this *v.* to future age pretend *E.M.* iv. 389
His Prince, that writes in *V.*, and has his ear *E.S.* i. 46
Hang the sad *V.* on CAROLINA's Urn *E.S.* i. 80
Yet may this *V.* (if such a *V.* remain) *E.S.* i. 171
Find you the Virtue, and I'll find the *V. E.S.* ii. 105
And makes immortal, *V.* as mean as mine *E.S.* ii. 247
These little rites, a Stone, a *V.*, receive *Ep.* vii. 19
Something in *V.* as true as Prose *I.H.* ii. 26
Lest you should think that *v.* shall die *I.H.* iv. 1
The *v.* and sculpture bore an equal part *M. E.* v. 51
Let Crowds of Critics now my *v.* assail *Mi.* i. 3
Against the *Gothic* Sons of frozen *V. Mi.* ii. 14
Some ends of *v.* his Betters might afford *Mi.* iii. 5
Now he begs *V.*, and what he gets commends *Mi.* iii. 13
To spread about the itch of *v.* and praise *P.S.* 224
My *V.*, and QUEENS'RY weeping o'er thy urn *P.S.* 260
Curst be the *v.*, how well soe'er it flow *P.S.* 283
And thought a Lie in *v.* or prose the same *P.S.* 339
I sing—This *v.* to CARYL, Muse is due *R.L.* i. 3
With ARMS, and GEORGE, and BRUNSWICK crowd the *v.. S.* i. 24
Slides into *v.*, and hitches in a rhyme *S.* i. 78
Farewell then *V.*, and Love, and ev'ry Toy *S.* iii. 17
And Sidney's *v.* halts ill on Roman feet *S.* v. 98
Who says in *v.* what others say in prose *S.* v. 202
And leave on SWIFT this grateful *v.* engrav'd *S.* v. 223
V. cheers their leisure, *V.* assists their work (*rep.*) *S.* v. 235
The varying *v.*, the full-resounding line *S.* v. 268
And splay-foot *v.*, remain'd, and will remain *S.* v. 271
A single *v.*, we quarrel with a friend *S.* v. 365
E'er swell'd on marble; as in *v.* have shin'd (*rep.*) *S.* v. 392
But *V.*, alas! your Majesty disdains *S.* v. 404
You love a *V.*, take such as I can send *S.* vi. 2
Nay worse, to ask for *V.* at such a time *S.* vi. 31
Sing thy sonorous *v.*—but not aloud *S.* vi. 109
The men who wrote such *v.* as we can read *S.* vi. 158
Inscribe a *v.* on this relenting stone *W.* 26
The thoughts of gods let Granville's *v.* recite *W.F.* 425
But were his V—s vile, his Whisper base E.S. ii. 49
Alas! few *v.* touch their nicer ear *S.* i. 33
That turn'd ten thousand *v.* now stands still *S.* vi. 79
I'll e'en leave *v.* to the boys at school *S.* vi. 201
But turn a wit, and scribble *v.* too *S.* vii. 54
Had no new *v.*, nor new suit to show *S.* viii. 13
V.-man *or Prose-man, term me which you will S.* i. 64

Vers'd.
Hear BETHEL's sermon, one not *v.* in schools *S.* ii. 9

Very.—*Passim.*

Vespasian.
And give to Titus old *V.*'s due *M.F.* v. 18

Vessel.
So when the first bold *v.* dar'd the seas *O.* i. 38
But now secure the painted *v.* glides *R.L.* ii. 47

VEST—VIEW.

If our intemp'rate Youth the *v.* drains *S.* fi. 90
Whether my *v.* be first-rate or not *S.* vi. 297
So weak a *v.*, and so rich a prize *S.* viii. 229
Or when rich China *v—s fall'n from high R.L.* iii. 159

Vest.
Gave him the cassock, surcingle, and *v. D.* ii. 350
All as the *v.*, appear'd the wearer's frame *D.* iii. 39
Or *v. dull Flatt'ry in the sacred Gown D.* iv. 97

Vestal.
No kitchens emulate the *v.* fire *S.* vii. 112
What means this tumult in a V.'s veins E.A. 4
How happy is the blameless *V.* lot *E.A.* 207

Vestments.
Ah no—in sacred *v.* mayst thou stand *E.A.* 325

Vet'ran, Veterans.
For thee the hardy *V.* drops a tear *Ep.* ix. 5
See how the World its *V—s* rewards *M.E.* ii. 243

Vex.
Sure some to *v.*, but never all to please *E.C.* 505
Riches that *v.*, and Vanities that tire *Mi.* v. 4

Vex'd, Vext.
V. to he still in town, I knit my brow *E.* v. 49
And when three Sov'reigns died, could scarce be *v—t E.S.* i. 107

Vial.
A *V.* next she fills with fainting fears *R.L.* iv. 85
He breaks the *V.* whence the sorrows flow *R.L.* iv. 142
Be stopp'd in v—s, or transfix'd with pins R.L. ii. 126

Vibrates.
Perhaps, yet *v.* on his Sov'REIGN's ear *P.S.* 357

Vice.
And gather'd ev'ry *V.* on Christian ground *D.* iv. 312
Your pleasure is a *v.*, but not your pride *E.* iv. 34
And if a *V.* dares keep the field *E.* vi. 7
And *V.* admir'd to find a flatt'rer there *E.C.* 551
Will needs mistake an author into *v. E.C.* 557
Amidst their virtues a reserve of *v. E.F.S.* 20
The virtue nearest to our *v.* ally'd *E.M.* ii. 196
Where ends the Virtue, or begins the *V. E.M.* ii. 210
That *V.* or Virtue there is none at all *E.M.* ii. 212
V. is a monster of so frightful mien *E.M.* ii. 217
But where th' Extreme of *V.*, was ne'er agreed *E.M.* ii. 221
For, *V.* or Virtue, Self directs it still *E.M.* ii. 236
That disappoints th' effect of ev'ry *v. E.M.* ii. 240
Of *V.* or Virtue, whether blest or curst *E.M.* iv. 87
Count all th' advantage prosp'rous *v.* attains *E.M.* iv. 89
Who fancy Bliss to *V.*, to Virtue Woe *E.M.* iv. 94
But sometimes Virtue starves, while *V.* is fed *E.M.* iv. 149
That, *V.* may merit, 'tis the price of toil *E.M.* iv. 151
Bubo observes, he lash'd no sort of *V. E.S.* i. 12
To *V.* and Folly to confine the jest *E.S.* i. 57
But shall the Dignity of *V.* be lost *E.S.* i. 114
V., thus abus'd, demands a Nation's care *E.S.* i. 128
V. is undone, if she forgets her Birth *E.S.* i. 141
V. with such Giant strides comes on amain *E.S.* ii. 6
Spare then the Person, and expose the *V. E.S.* ii. 12
But, Sir, I beg you (for the Love of *V.*) *E.S.* ii. 42
Sole Dread of Folly, *V.*, and Insolence *E.S.* ii. 213
As show'd, *V.* had his hate and pity too *Ep.* i. 8
All see 'tis *V.*, and itch of vulgar praise *M.E.* i. 60
Grown all to all, from no one *v.* exempt *M.E.* i. 191
Were means not ends; Ambition was the *v. M.E.* i. 215
That each may seem a Virtue, or a *V. M.E.* ii. 206
And am so clear too of all other *v. M.E.* iii. 368
Is *V.* too high, reserve it for the next *S.* i. 60
But grave *Epistles*, bringing *V.* to light *S.* i. 151
About one *v.*, and fall into the other *S.* ii. 46
Go dine with Chartres, in each *V.* out-do *S.* iv. 120
Proud *V.* to brand, and injur'd Worth adorn *S.* v. 227
Preserv'd the freedom, and forbore the *v. S.* v. 260
Men only feel the Smart, but not the *V. S.* vi. 217
One Giant *V.*, so excellently ill *S.* vii. 4
And tho' the Court show *V.* exceeding clear *S.* viii. 96
Of all our V—s have created Arts E.M. ii. 50
'Tis the first Virtue, *V.* to abhor *S.* iii. 65

Vicious.
'Tis what the *v.* fear, the virtuous shun *R.C.* 506
Virtuous and *v.* ev'ry Man must be *E.M.* ii. 231

Vicissitude.
Or who in sweet *v.* appears *M.E.* ii. 109

Victim.
Are destin'd Hymen's willing *v.* too *E.* iv. 58
Love's *v.* then, tho' now a sainted maid *E.A.* 312
Is now a *v.*, and now Egypt's God *E.M.* i. 64
What tender maid but must a *v.* fall *R.L.* i. 95
Proves the just *v.* of his royal rage *R.L.* iii. 60
The Club's black Tyrant first her *v.* dy'd *R.L.* iii. 69
When v—s at yon altar's foot we lay E.A. 108
No lambs or sheep for *v.* I'll impart (*rep.*) *Sp.* 51
The wanton *v.* of his sport remain *W.F.* 78

Victor.
And now the *v.* stretch'd his eager hand *D.* ii. 109
Thou triumph'st, *V.* of the high-wrought day *D.* ii. 187
All hail him *v.* in both gifts of song *D.* ii. 267
And the world's *v.* stood subdu'd by sound *E.C.* 381
There, *V.* of his health, of fortune, friends *M.E.* iii. 313
The World's great *V.* pass'd unheeded by *P.C.* 34
And march'd a *v.* from the verdant field *R.L.* iii. 52
Falls undistinguish'd by the *v.* spade *R.L.* iii. 64
(The *v.* cry'd) the glorious Prize is mine *R.L.* iii. 162

Victorious.
Yet music and love were *v. O.* i. 92
And curs'd for ever this *v.* day *R.L.* iii. 104
Her Arts *v.* triumph'd o'er our Arms *S.* v. 264
And make my tongue *v.* as her eyes *Sp.* 50
Matchless his pen, *v.* was his lance *W.F.* 293

Victory.
O Grave! where is thy *V. O.* v. 17

Vida.
A Raphael painted, and a *V.* sung (*rep.*) *E.C.* 704

Vie.
As Berecynthia while her offspring *v. D.* iii. 131
With Zeuxis' Helen thy Bridgewater *v. E.* ii. 75
A Fav'rite's Porter with his Master *v. E.S.* i. 117
Where *Kent* and Nature *v.* for PELHAM's Love *E.S.* ii. 67
With royal Favourites in flatt'ry *v. S.* viii. 60

Vied.
V. for his love in jetty bow'rs below *D.* ii. 335
His kitchen *v.* in coolness with his grot *M.E.* iii. 180

View.
Obliquely waddling to the mark in *v. D.* i. 172
While fancy brings the vanish'd piles to *v. E.* iii. 31
Full in my *v.* set all the bright abode *E.A.* 127
I view my crime, but tremble at the *v. E.A.* 185
What scenes appear where'er I turn my *v. E.A.* 263
But HEAV'N's great *v.* is One, and that the Whole *E.M.* ii. 238
To Man imparts it; but with such a *v. E.M.* iii. 73
The Scene, the Actor, op'ning to my *v. E.S.* ii. 68
Something as dim to our internal *v. M.E.* i. 49
Still out of reach, but never out of *v. M.E.* ii. 232
In one short *v.* subjected to our eye *M.E.* v. 33
Her Gods, and god-like Heroes rise to *v. M.E.* v. 47
To Proculus alone confess'd to *v. R.L.* v. 126
Or he, who bids thee face with steady *v. S.* iii. 107
Before true passion all these v—s remove E.A. 79
Short *v.* we take, nor see the lengths behind *E.C.* 222
The starving chemist in his golden *v. E.M.* ii. 269
But future *v.* of better, or of worse *E.M.* iv. 72
Or cut wide *v.* thro' Mountains to the Plain *M.E.* iv. 75
Nor bound thy narrow *v.* to things below *R.L.* i. 36
To stop thy foolish *v.*, thy long desires *S.* iii. 75
There Ridpath, Roper, cudgell'd might ye v. *D.* ii. 149
Thy mental eye, for thou hast much to *v. D.* iii. 62
Then *v.* this Marble, and be vain no more *E.* iii. 54
Pleas'd while with smiles his happy lines you *v. E.* iv. 75
I *v.* my crime, but tremble at the view *E.A.* 185
I hear thee, *v.* thee, gaze on all thy charms *E.A.* 233
I wake; —no more I hear, no more I *v. E.A.* 235
Fair eyes, and tempting looks (which yet I *v.*) *E.A.* 295
Thus when we *v.* some well-proportion'd dome *E.C.* 247

VIEW'D—VIRTUE. 343

Content, if hence th' unlearn'd their wants may v. *E.C.* 739
Painful pre-eminence! yourself to v. *E.M.* iv. 267
How many pictures of one Nymph we v. *M.E.* ii. 5
V. him with scornful, yet with jealous eyes *P.S.* 199
This, ev'n Belinda may vouchsafe to v. *R.L.* i. 4
And v. with scorn two Pages and a Chair *R.L.* i. 46
Clapp'd his glad wings, and sate to v. the fight *R.L.* v. 54
This Partridge soon shall v. in cloudless skies *R.L.* v.137
And v. this dreadful All without a fear *S.* iv. 10
As in the crystal spring I v. my face *Su.* 27

View'd.
With honest scorn the first fam'd Cato v. *P.C.* 39
Sudden he v. in spite of all her art *R.L.* iii. 143

Views.
With self-applause her wild creation v. *D.* i. 82
The King descending v. th' Elysian Shade *D.* iii. 14
Millions and millions on these banks he v. *D.* iii. 31
One boundless Green, one flourish'd Carpet v. *M.E.* iv. 95
Or v. his smiling progeny *O.* iii. 32

Vigils.
While pensive Poets painful v. keep *D.* i. 93
Shrines! where their v. pale-eyed virgins keep *E.A.* 21

Vig'rous.
V. he rises, from th' effluvia strong *D.* ii. 105
Ye v. swains! while youth ferments your blood *W.F.* 93

Vigour.
The race by v., not by vaunts is won *D.* ii. 59
One on his v. and superior size *D.* ii. 170
With spirits feeds, with v. fills the whole *E.C.* 77
And praise the easy v. of a line *E.C.* 360
Wild Nature's v. working at the root *E.M.* ii. 184
See the same man, in v., in the gout *M.E.* i. 71
As Fits give v., just when they destroy *M.E.* i. 223
To Chartres V., Japhet, Nose and Ears *M.E.* iii. 86

Vile.
Where v. Mundungus trucks for viler rhymes *D.* i. 234
Of link-boys v., and watermen obscene *D.* ii. 100
Nor glad v. Poets with true Critics' gere *D.* iii. 178
Like the v. straw that's blown about the streets *D.*iii.289
And lo the wretch! whose v., whose insect lust *D.*iv.415
A v. conceit in pompous words express'd *E.C.* 320
No pardon v. Obscenity should find *E.C.* 530
V. worm!—Oh Madness! Pride! Impiety *E.M.* i. 258
As full, as perfect, in v. Man that mourns *E.M.* i. 277
But were his Verses v., his Whisper base *E.S.* i. 49
Ye Tradesmen v., in Army, Court, or Hall *E.S.* ii. 17
And v. Attorneys, now an useless race *M.E.* iii. 274
Should'ring God's altar a v. image stands *M.E.* iii. 293
V., reptile, weak, and vain *Mi.* iv. 6
By whose v. arts this heavy grief I bear *Mi.* ix. 36
And he himself one v. Antithesis *P.S.* 325
A v. Encomium doubly ridicules *S.* v. 410

Villa.
At Timon's V. let us pass a day *M.E.* iv. 99
Whether you call them V., Park, or Chase *S.* vi. 255
Behold! th' ascending V—s on my side *W.F.* 375

Village-tops.
While curling smokes from v. are seen *A.* 63

Villain.
'Tis phrase absurd to call a V. Great *E.M.* iv. 230
The poor and friendless V. than the Great *E.S.* ii. 45
Fame but from death a V.'s name can save *E.M.*iv.249

Villainy.
Nothing is Sacred now but V. *E.S.* i. 170
Still, as of old, encumber'd V. *M.E.* iv. 50

Villario.
Enjoy them, you! V. can no more *M.E.* iv. 86
Behold V.'s ten years' toil complete *M.E.* iv. 79

Villiers.
Great V. lies—alas! how chang'd from him *M.E.* iii. 305

Vindicate.
But v. the ways of God to Man *E.M.* i. 16
The birds of heav'n shall v. their grain *E.M.* iii. 38

Vindicates.
Re-passes Lintot, v. the race *D.* ii. 107

Vine.
Bring, bring the madding Bay, the drunken V. *D.* i. 303
Explains the *Stu* and *Verdeur* of the V. *D.* iv. 556
Man, like the gen'rous v., supported lives *E.M.* iii. 311
To happy Convents, bosom'd deep in v—s *D.* iv. 301
Their v. a shadow to their race shall yield *M.* 65
Now forms my Quincunx, and now ranks my V. *S.* i.130
And swelling clusters bend the curling v. *Sp.* 36

Vinegar.
As Heav'ns blest beam turns v. more sour *E.M.* ii. 148
And is at once their v. and wine *S.* ii. 54
At such a feast, old v. to spare *S.* ii. 57

Viols.
Sound, sound, ye V.; be the Cat-call dumb *D.* i. 302

Violence.
Her ev'ry turn with V. pursu'd *M.E.* ii. 131
And Heav'n is won by V. of Song *S.* v. 240

Vi'let.
Here the bright crocus and blue v. glow *Sp.* 31

Viper.
This harmless grove no lurking V. hides *Su.* 67

Virago.
"To arms, to arms!" the fierce V. cries *R.L.* v. 37

Virgil, Virgilius.
For me what V., Pliny may deny *D.* iv. 225
In Dryden's V. see the print *E.* vi. 28
To *Cato*, V. pay'd one honest line *E.S.* ii. 120
Let Horace blush, and V. too *Ep.* xv. 4
A V. there, and here an Addison *M.E.* v. 62
And ev'n th' Antipodes V—ius mourn *D.* iii. 106

Virgin.
See, graceless Venus to a V. turn'd *D.* iii. 117
As some fond V., whom her mother's care *E.* v. 1
Shame to the v., to the matron pride *E.M.* ii. 242
A V. shall conceive, a V. bear a Son *M.* 8
Serene in V. Modesty she shines *M.E.* ii. 255
'Tis a V. hard of Feature *Mi.* vi. 5
Chaste as cold Cynthia's v. light *O.* iii. 23
A V. Tragedy, an orphan Muse *P.S.* 56
Or from the soft-ey'd V. steal a tear *P.S.* 286
When Florio speaks what v. could withstand *R.L.* i. 97
As thou, sad V.! for thy ravish'd Hair *R.L.* iv. 10
A charge of Snuff the wily v. threw *R.L.* v. 82
Th' immortal huntress, and her v. train *W.F.* 160
The silver stream her v. coldness keeps *W.F.* 205
Still bears the name the hapless v. bore *W.F.* 207
The v.'s *wish without her fears impart E.A.* 55
The hero's glory, or the v. love *P.C.* 10
At this, the blood the v. cheek forsook *R.L.* iii. 89
The close recesses of the V. thought *R.L.* iii. 140
Shrines! where their vigils pale-ey'd v—s keep *E.A.* 21
For her white v. Hymenæals sing *E.A.* 220
And V. smil'd at what they blush'd before *E.C.* 543
Or v. visited by Angel-pow'rs *R.L.* i. 33
Not scornful v. who their charms survive *R.L.* iv. 4
Her buskin'd V. trac'd the dewy lawn *W.F.* 170

Virro.
For what has V. painted, built, and planted *M.E.* iv. 13

Virtu.
Impale a Glow-worm or V. profess *D.* iv. 569

Virtue.
That beams on earth, each V. he inspires *D.* iii. 220
Held forth the v. of the dreadful wand *D.* iv. 140
Find V. local, all Relation scorn *D.* iv. 479
And ev'ry op'ning V. blooming round *E.* xiv. 2
Oh Grace serene! oh V. heav'nly fair *E.A.* 297
Were there all harmony, all v. here *E.M.* i. 166
And Grace and V., Sense and Reason split *E.M.* ii. 83
Their V. fix'd; 'tis fix'd as in a frost *E.M.* ii. 102
Strong grows the V. with his nature mix'd *E.M.* ii. 178
Nor V., male or female, can we name *E.M.* ii. 193
The v. nearest to our vice ally'd *E.M.* ii. 196
Where ends the V. or begins the Vice *E.M.* ii. 210
That Vice or V. there is none at all *E.M.* ii. 212

VIRTUE—VITAL.

For, Vice or *V.*, *Self* directs it still *E.M.* ii. 236
Each *V.* in each Passion takes its turn *E.M.* iii. 136
'Twas *V.* ONLY (or in arts or arms *E.M.* iii. 211
To *V.*, in the paths of Pleasure, trod *E.M.* iii. 233
Forc'd into *v.* thus by Self-defence *E.M.* iii. 279
Some swell'd to Gods, confess ev'n *V.* vain *E.M.* iv. 24
And Peace, oh *V.!* Peace is all thy own *E.M.* iv. 82
Of Vice or *V.*, whether blest or curst *E.M.* iv. 87
'Tis but what *V.* flies from and disdains *E.M.* iv. 90
Who fancy Bliss to Vice, to *V.* woe *E.M.* iv. 94
Was this their *V.*, or Contempt of Life (*rep.*) *E.M.* iv. 102
Tell me, if *V.* made the son expire *E.M.* iv. 105
And what rewards your *V.*, punish mine *E.M.* iv. 144
Or he whose *V.* sigh'd to lose a day (*rep.*) *E.M.* iv. 148
Rewards, that either would to *V.* bring *E.M.* iv. 181
V. alone is Happiness below *E.M.* iv. 310
Since but to wish more *V.*, is to gain *E.M.* iv. 326
His greatest *V.*, and his greatest Bliss *E.M.* iv. 350
That *V.* only makes our Bliss below *E.M.* iv. 397
And wear their strange old *V.*, as they will *E.S.* i. 44
At Sense and *V.*, balance all again *E.S.* i. 60
V., I grant you, is an empty boast *E.S.* i. 113
V. may choose the high or low Degree (*rep.*) *E.S.* i. 137
And sees pale *V.* carted in her stead *E.S.* i. 150
Else might he take to *V.* some years hence *E.S.* ii. 60
To *Berkeley* ev'ry *V.* under Heav'n *E.S.* ii. 73
I follow *V.*: where she shines, I praise *E.S.* ii. 95
Find you the *V.*, and I'll find the Verse *E.S.* ii. 105
No Pow'r, when *V.* claims it, can withstand *E.S.* ii. 119
When Truth or *V.* an affront endures *E.S.* ii. 299
Convinc'd that *V.* only is our own *Ep.* vi. 6
The living *V.* now had shone approv'd *Ep.* xiv. 7
All know 'tis *V.*, for he thinks them knaves *M.E.* ii. 58
Aw'd without *V.*, without Beauty charm'd *M.E.* ii. 46
V. she finds too painful an endeavour *M.E.* ii. 163
That each may seem a *V.*, or a Vice *M.E.* ii. 206
T' enjoy them, and the *V.* to impart *M.E.* iii. 220
Enough, that *V.* fill'd the space between *M.E.* iii. 289
V.! and Wealth! what are ye but a name *M.E.* iii. 334
Why, *V.*, dost thou blame desire *O.* iii. 9
To make mankind in conscious *v.* bold *P.C.* 3
And foes to *v.* wonder'd how they wept *P.C.* 8
V. confess'd in human shape he draws *P.C.* 17
And show, you have the *v.* to be mov'd *P.C.* 38
Give *V.* scandal, Innocence a fear *P.S.* 285
Welcome for these, fair *V.!* all the past (*rep.*) *P.S.* 358
If there be force in *V.*, or in Song *P.S.* 387
Ease, pleasure, *v.*, all our sex resign *R.L.* iv. 106
Behold the first is *v.* as in face *R.L.* v. 18
What? arm'd for *V.* when I point the pen *S.* i. 105
To *V.* ONLY and HER FRIENDS A FRIEND *S.* i. 121
What, and how great, the *V.* and the Art *S.* ii. 1
Still true to *V.*, and as warm as true *S.* iii. 30
'Tis the first *V.*, Vices to abhor *S.* iii. 65
Here, Wisdom calls: "Seek *V.* first, be bold (*rep.*) *S.* iii. 77
And then let *V.* follow, if she will *S.* iii. 80
V., brave boys! 'tis *V.* makes a King *S.* iii. 92
Adieu to *V.*, if you're once a Slave *S.* iii. 118
Who *V.* and a Church alike disowns *S.* iv. 65
All human *V.*, to its latest breath *S.* v. 15
In ev'ry Public *V.* we excel *S.* v. 45
Or *V.*, or Religion, turn to sport *S.* v. 211
And pours each human *V.* in the heart *S.* v. 220
In pow'r, wit, figure, *v.*, fortune, plac'd *S.* vi. 302
None should, by my advice, learn *V.* there *S.* viii. 97
Nor left one *V.* to redeem her Race *U.L.* 28
Exalt their kind, and take some V.'s name E.M. ii. 80
That, *V.* ends from Vanity can raise *E.M.* iv. 245
Is *V.* prize: a better would you fix *E.M.* iv. 169
Less pleasing far than *V.* very tears *E.M.* iv. 320
To *V.* work provoke the tardy Hall *E.S.* ii. 218
Touch'd with the Flame that breaks from *V.* Shrine *E.S.* ii. 233
Who lead fair *V.* train along *O.* ii. 11
That not for Fame, but *V.* better end *P.S.* 342
For *V.* self may too much zeal be had *S.* iv. 26
Four guardian V—s, round, support her throne D. i. 46
With all thy Father's *v.* blest, be born *D.* iii. 141
The Sire saw, one by one, his *v.* wake *D.* iv. 285
Nor wish to lose a Foe these *V.* raise *E.* ii. 11
Amidst their *v.* a reserve of vice *E.J.S.* 20
The surest *V.* thus from Passions shoot *M.E.* ii. 183
The *v.* of a Saint at twenty-one *E.M.* iv. 184
Still leave some ancient *V.* to our age *Ep.* ix. 10

In life's low vale, the soil the *V.* like *M.E.* i. 143
Poets heap *V.*, Painters Gems at will *M.E.* ii. 185
Your *v.* open fairest in the shade *M.E.* ii. 202
They had, and greater *V.*, I'll agree *S.* v. 96
To teach their frugal *V.* to his Heir *S.* v. 166
Yet think, great Sir, (so many *V.* shown) *S.* v. 376
Take him with all his *v.*, on my word *S.* vi. 13

Virtuous.

For the dull glory of a *v.* Wife *E.* iv. 46
Kind, *v.* drops just gath'ring in my eye *E.A.* 278
"Tis what the vicious fear, the *v.* shun *E.C.* 506
That *v.* ladies envy while they rail *E.J.S.* 16
And vicious ev'ry man must be *E.M.* ii. 231
See FALKLAND dies, the *v.* and the just *E.M.* iv. 99
As that the *v.* son is ill at ease *E.M.* iv. 119
Self-love but serves the *v.* mind to wake *E.M.* iv. 363
With native Humour temp'ring *v.* Rage *E.A.* xi. 3
The prudent, learn'd, and *v.* breast *O.* iii. 2
Be *v.*, and be happy for your pains *S.* iv. 62
And *v.* Alfred, a more sacred Name *S.* v. 8

Visage.

Blank'd his bold *v.*, and a this Third day *D.* i. 114

Viscount.

His Daughter flaunts a *V.*'s tawdry wife *M.E.* iii. 391

Visible.

Of darkness *v.* so much be lent *D.* iv. 3

Visigoths.

See the fierce *V.* on Spain and Gaul *D.* iii. 94

Vision.

And Poet's *v.* of eternal Fame *D.* iii. 12
For this our Queen unfolds to *v.* true *D.* iii. 61
And thro' the Iv'ry Gate the *V.* flies *D.* iii. 340
Which Theocles in raptur'd *v.* saw *E.* iv. 488
Then give one flirt, and all the *v.* flies *E.* v. 38
If e'er one *v.* touch'd thy infant thought *R.L.* i. 29
But all the *V.* vanish'd from thy head *R.L.* i. 120
A *V.* hermits can to Hell transport *S.* viii. 190
Like forms in clouds, or v—s of the night D. ii. 112
And melts in *v.* of eternal day *E.A.* 222
Alas! 'tis more than (all his *V.* past) *M.E.* ii. 83
Where heav'nly *v.* Plato fir'd *O.* ii. 3
Or bright, as *v.* of expiring maids *R.L.* iv. 42
In mystic *v.*, now believ'd too late *R.L.* iv. 166
Whose raptures fire me, and whose *v.* bless *W.F.* 260

Visionary.

Or lull to rest the *v.* maid *E.A.* 162
Where Thames reflects the *v.* scene *I.H.* iii. 24
Why dimly gleams the *v.* sword *U.L.* 4

Visit.

Who gave the ball, or paid the *v.* last *R.L.* iii. 12
While v—s shall be paid on solemn days R.L. iii. 167
Who cause the proud their *v.* to delay *R.L.* v. 63
Did stumb'ring v., and convey to stews D. ii. 422
Thus *v.* not thy own! on this blest age *D.* iii. 121
Oh deign to *v.* our forsaken seats *Su.* 71

Visited.

Or virgins *v.* by Angel-pow'rs *R.L.* i. 33

Visits.

Who *v.* with a gun, presents you birds *E.* v. 25
Heav'n *v.* with a Taste the wealthy fool *M.E.* iv. 17
As thine, which *v.* Windsor's fam'd abodes *W.F.* 229

Vista.

His Son's fine Taste an op'ning *V.* loves *M.E.* iv. 93

Visto.—*See also* Sir Visto.

Some Dæmon whisper'd, "*V.*, have a Taste" *M.E.* iv. 16

Visual.

He from thick films shall purge the *v.* ray *M.* 39

Vital.

As man's Mæanders to the *v.* spring *D.* iii. 55
Each *v.* humour which shall feed the whole *E.M.* ii. 139
By turns we catch the *v.* breath, and die *E.M.* iii. 18
The *v.* flame, and swells the genial seeds *E.M.* iii. 118
V. spark of heav'nly flame *O.* v. 1
That while my nostrils draw the *v.* air *R.L.* iv. 137

The Sun's mild lustre warms the *v.* air *Sp.* 74
So may kind rains their *v.* moisture yield *W.* 15
Vitruvius.
And be whate'er *V.* was before *M.E.* iv. 194
Vive la Bagatelle.
And Swift cry wisely, " *V.*" *S.* iv. 128
Vivid.
The *v.* green his shining plumes unfold *W.F.* 117
Vocal.
High Sound, attemper'd to the *v.* nose *D.* ii. 256
And only *v.* with the Maker's praise *E.A.* 140
All *v.* beings hymn'd their equal God *E.M.* iii. 156
A God, a God! the *v.* hills reply *M.* 31
But tell the reeds, and tell the *v.* shore *W.* 59
Voice.
To Needham's quick the *v.* triumphal rode *D.* i. 323
There, Webster! peal'd thy *v.*, and Whitfield ! thine *D.* ii. 258
At last Centlivre felt her *v.* to fail *D.* ii. 411
Tuning his *v.*, and balancing his hands *D.* iii. 200
With mincing step, small *v.*, and languid eye *D.* iv. 46
Some would have spoken, but the *V.* was drown'd *D.* iv. 217
No more, alas! the *v.* of Fame they hear *D.* iv. 543
Where, where was Eloïse? her *v.*, her hand *E.A.* 101
Thy *v.* I seem in ev'ry hymn to hear *E.A.* 269
In praise so just let ev'ry *v.* be join'd *E.C.* 187
Is *Pride*, the never-failing *v.* of fools *E.C.* 204
Her *v.* is all these tuneful fools admire *E.C.* 340
The Muse, whose early *v.* you taught to sing *E.C.* 735
Joy tunes his *v.*, joy elevates his wings *E.M.* iii. 32
Thus then to Man the *v.* of Nature spake *E.M.* iii. 171
Delight no more—O thou my *v.* inspire *M.* 4
Hark ! a glad *v.* the lonely desert cheers *M.* 29
Wake into *v.* each silent string *O.* i. 3
Music her soft, assuasive *v.* applies *O.* i. 25
Unworthy he, the *v.* of Fame to hear *S.* ii. 99
A *V.* there is, that whispers in my ear (*rep.*) *S.* iii. 11
There, London's *v.*: " Get Money, Money still *S.* iii. 79
To see their judgments hang upon thy *v. S.* iv. 35
All this may be ; the People's *V.* is odd (*rep.*) *S.* v. 89
His French is pure ; his *V.* too—you shall hear *S.* vi. 7
Then might my *v.* thy list'ning ears employ *Su.* 47
Since fate relentless stopp'd their heavenly *v. W.F.* 277
And bass, and treble v—s strike the skies *R.L.* v. 42
Void.
But senseless, lifeless! idol *v.* and vain *D.* ii. 46
A soul as full of Worth, as *v.* of Pride *E.* ii. 1
No craving *v.* left aking in the breast *E.A.* 94
And fills up all the mighty *V.* of sense *E.C.* 210
Or in the full creation leave a *v. E.M.* i. 243
Or, meteor-like, flame lawless thro' the *v. E.M.* ii. 65
Yet was not Cotta *v.* of wit or worth *M.E.* iii. 178
He feeds yon Alms-house, neat, but *v.* of state *M.E.* iii. 265
Old and *v.* of all good-nature *Mi.* vi. 6
Yet graceful ease, and sweetness *v.* of pride *R.L.* ii. 15
Lent stiff, and stately, *v.* of fire or force *S.* iii. 15
If thou couldst make the Courtier v. *Mi.* iv. 31
Voiture.
The truest hearts for *V.* heav'd with sighs (*rep.*) *E.* iv. 17
Ev'n rival Wits did V.'s *death deplore E.* iv. 15
Thus *V.* early care still shone the same *E.* iv. 69
Vole.
Shortly no lad shall chuck, or lady *v. S.* viii. 146
Volga.
Let *V.'s* banks with iron squadrons shine *W.F.* 363.
Volleys.
But rattling nonsense in full *v.* breaks *E.C.* 608
Volume.
Swift to whose hand a winged *v.* flies *D.* iii. 234
His stretch'd-out arm display'd a *v.* fair *D.* iv. 106
To lug the pond'rous *v.* off in state *D.* iv. 118
Of these twelve v—s, *twelve of amplest size D.* i. 155
Mount in dark *v.*, and descend in snow *D.* ii. 364
The silver eel, in shining *v.* roll'd *W.F.* 143.

Voluntary.
Repentant sighs, and *v.* pains *E.A.* 18
And all that *v.* Vein *I.H.* i. 49
Volunteer.
But honest Instinct comes a *v. E.M.* iii. 88
Vomit.
And the fresh *v.* run for ever green *D.* ii. 156
Vortex.
Roll in her *V.*, and her pow'r confess *D.* iv. 84
Vot'ress.
His sister sends, her *v.*, from above *D.* ii. 216
Vot'ry.
Forth from the heap she pluck'd her *V.'s* pray'r *D.* ii. 93
Vote.
Have bled and purg'd me to a simple *V. S.* vi. 197
Fall by the V—s *of their degen'rate Line E.S.* ii. 253
Votos.
Bows and *v.* on, in Court and Parliament *S.* vi. 275
Vouch.
Lord of an Otho, if I *v.* it true *D.* iv. 369
Vouchsafe.
As thus, " *V.*, oh gracious Maker *I.H.* ii. 17 s
This, ev'n Belinda may *v.* to view *R.L.* i. 4
Vouchsaf'd.
How many Dutchmen she *v.* to thrid *D.* iii. 51
Vow.
Fair Geraldine, bright object of his *v. W.F.* 297
Oft on the rind I carv'd her am'rous v—s *A.* 67
The garlands fade, the *v.* are worn away *A.* 69
And hears the various *v.* of fond mankind *D.* ii. 87
What force have pious *v.!* The Queen of Love *D.* ii. 215
And saints with wonder heard the *v.* I made *E.A.* 114
In days of old, they pardon'd breach of *v. E.J.S.* 29
How many Maids have SHARPER'S *v.* deceiv'd *Mi.* ix. 71
Can hearken coldly to my SHARPER'S *v. Mi.* ix. 88
There broken *v.* and death-bed alms are pour'd *R.L.* v. 117
And send up *v.* from Rosamunda's lake *R.L.* v. 136
And cry'd " I v. *you're mighty neat I.H.* ii. 174
Vowels.
Tho' oft the ear the open *v.* tire *E.C.* 345
Voyage.
On Fame's mad *v.* by the wind of praise *S.* v. 297
Vulcan.
From shelves to shelves see greedy *V.* roll *D.* iii. 81
Vulgar.
One Cell there is, conceal'd from *v.* eye *D.* i. 33
The heroes sit, the *v.* form a ring *D.* ii. 384
The *v.* herd turn off to roll with Hogs *D.* iv. 525
From *v.* bounds with brave disorder part *E.C.* 152
The *V.* thus thro' Imitation err *E.C.* 424
Above the reach of *v.* song *I.H.* iv. 4
All see 'tis Vice, and itch of *v.* praise *M.E.* i. 60
Our author shuns by *v.* springs to move *P.C.* 9.
For *v.* eyes, and point out ev'ry line *S.* v. 357
The *v.* boil, the learned roast an egg *S.* vi. 85
Above the *v.* flight of low desire *U.L.* 12

W.

Poor *W*** nipt in folly's broadest bloom *D.* iv. 513
And *W*** and *H*** both in town *I.H.* i. 14
To *W—le* guilty of some venial sin *E.S.* ii. 162
Waddles.
As when a dab-chick *w.* thro' the copse *D.* ii. 63
Waddling.
Obliquely *w.* to the mark in view *D.* i. 172

Wades
On feet and wings, and flies, and *w.*, and hops *D.* ii. 64

Waft
And *w.* a sigh from Indus to the Pole *E.A.* 58
Tears that delight, and sighs that *w.* to heav'n *E.A.* 214
Seas roll to *w.* me, suns to light me rise *E.M.* i. 139
A single leaf shall *w.* an army o'er *M.E.* iii. 43
W. on the breeze, or sink in clouds of gold *R.L.* ii. 60
And winds shall *w.* it to the pow'rs above *Su.* 80

Wafting
And *w.* Vapours from the Land of dreams *D.* ii. 340

Wafts
Thames *w.* it thence to Rufus' roaring hall *D.* ii. 265
W. the smooth Eunuch, and enamour'd swain *D.* iv. 310

Wag
Some *w.* observes me thus perplext *I.H.* ii. 51 s
Shouldst *w. a serpent-tail in Smithfield fair D.* iii. 288
Those monkey tails that *w.* behind their head *S.* viii. 247

Wage
Intestine war no more our Passions *w. O.* i. 34

Wag'd
I *w.* no war with *Bedlam* or the *Mint P.S.* 156

Waggish
And own the Spaniard did a *w. thing E.S.* i. 17

Waist
Two babes of love close clinging to her *w. D.* ii. 158
A belt her *w.*, a fillet binds her hair *W.F.* 178

Wait
She bids him *w.* her to her sacred Dome *D.* i. 265
With ready quills the Dedicators *w. D.* ii. 194
As when the long-ear'd milky mothers *w. D.* ii. 247
Or *w.* inspiring Dreams at Maro's Urn *E.* iii. 28
Let wealth, let honour, *w.* the wedded dame *E.A.* 77
And *w.* till 'tis no sin to mix with thine *E.A.* 176
W. the great teacher Death ; and God adore *E.M.* i. 92
W. but for wings, and in their season fly *M.E.* iii. 170
With beating hearts the dire event they *w. R.L.* ii. 141
Two handmaids *w.* the throne ; alike in place *R.L.* iv. 25

Waits
She *w.*, or to the scaffold, or the cell *E.* i. 33
And ready Nature *w.* upon his hand *E.C.* 487
Rise, pensive Nymph, the *Tatler w.* for you *Mi.* ix. 3
On all the line a sudden vengeance *w. U.L.* 37
Such silence *w.* on Philomela's strains *W.* 78

Wake
If there be man, who o'er such works can *w. D.* ii. 372
W. the dull Church, and lull the ranting Stage *D.* iv. 58
The Sire saw, one by one, his virtues *w. D.* iv. 285
Obedient slumbers that can *w.* and weep *E.A.* 212
I *w.*: no more I hear, no more I view *E.A.* 235
And *w.* to all the griefs I left behind *E.A.* 248
Self-love but serves the virtuous mind to *w. E.M.* iv. 363
And *w.* to Raptures in a Life to come *Mi.* v. 20
W. into voice each silent string *O.* i. 3
To *w.* the soul by tender strokes of art *P.C.* 1
I nod in company, I *w.* at night *S.* i. 13
We *w.* next morning in a ragged fit *S.* v. 179
Command old words that have long slept, to *w. S.* vi. 167
With joyous musick *w.* the dawning day *Sp.* 24

Wak'd
Leap'd up, and *w.* his mistress with his tongue *R.L.* i. 116

Wakeful
Two Swains, whom Love kept *w.*, and the Muse *Sp.* 18

Waken
The dull may *w.* to a humming-bird *D.* iv. 446

Waken'd
Not touch'd, but rapt ; not *w.*, but inspir'd *E.A.* 202

Wakes
For me kind Nature *w.* her genial Pow'r *E.M.* i. 133
Sloth unfolds her arms and *w. O.* i. 32
Rhymes ere he *w.*, and prints before *Term* ends *P.S.* 43

Waking
Thence Beauty, *w.* all her forms, supplies *E.* iii. 45
Unhappy Wharton, *w.*, found at last *M.E.* iii. 84

Walk
Far as the solar *w.*, or milky way *E.M.* i. 102
Eye Nature's *w—s, shoot Folly as it flies E.M.* i. 13
War, horrid war, your thoughtful *w.* invades *O.* ii. 7
Swarm o'er the lawns, the forest *w.* surround *W.F.* 149
I seem thro' consecrated *w.* to rove *W.F.* 267
While all your smutty sisters w. the streets D. i. 230
W. round and round, now prying here, now there *D.* iv. 353
W. in thy light, and in thy temple bend *M.* 92
W. to his grave without reproach *Mi.* xii. 19
Shall *w.* the World, in credit, to his grave *S.* i. 120
And men must *w.* at least before they dance *S.* iii. 54
W. with respect behind, while we at ease *S.* vi. 141
And much too wise to *w.* into a well *S.* vi. 191
W. sober off ; before a sprightlier age *S.* vi. 324
He, ev'ry day from King to King can *w. S.* viii. 104
Where'er you *w.*, cool gales shall fan the glade *Su.* 73

Walk'd
Man *w.* with beast, joint tenant of the shade *E.M.* iii. 152
The good man *w.* innoxious thro' his age *P.S.* 395

Walker
W. with rev'rence took, and laid aside *D.* iv. 206
W.! our hat "—nor more he deign'd to say *D.* iv. 273

Walks
Crown'd with the Jordan, *w.* contented home *D.* ii. 190
He mounts the storm, and *w.* upon the wind *E.M.* ii. 110
Our Courtier *w.* from dish to dish *I.H.* iv. 198
Then from the Mint *w.* forth the Man of rhyme *P.S.* 13
A Pipkin there, like Homer's Tripod *w. R.L.* iv. 51
He *w.*, an object new beneath the sun *S.* vi. 119
For you he *w.* the streets in rain and dust *S.* vii. 73

Wall
He, whose long *w.* the wand'ring Tartar bounds *D.* iii. 76
Pity ! the charm works only in our *w. D.* iv. 165
For Chartres' head reserve the hanging *w. E.M.* iv. 130
Shov'd from the *w.* perhaps, or rudely press'd *M.E.* i. 234
Silence without, and Fasts within the *w. M.E.* iii. 188
For very want ; he could not build a *w. M.E.* iii. 324
On some patch'd dog-hole ek'd with ends of *w. M.E.* iv. 32
On ev'ry side you look, behold the *W. M.E.* iv. 114
Or whiten'd *w.* provoke the skew'r to write *S.* i. 98
And grapes long ling'ring on my only *w. S.* ii. 146
Be this thy Screen, and this thy *w.* of Brass *S.* iii. 95
What Lady's face is not a whited *w. S.* viii. 151
For hung with deadly sins I see the *w. S.* viii. 274
And leave inanimate the naked *w. W.F.* 308
Close to those w—s where Folly holds her throne D. i. 29
Sepulchral Lies, our holy *w.* to grace *D.* i. 43
What City Swans once sung within the *w. D.* i. 96
W., steeples, skies, bray back to him again *D.* ii. 260
In Lud's old *w.* tho' long I rul'd, renown'd *D.* iii. 277
And leave you in lone woods, or empty *w. E.* v. 40
Relentless *w.!* whose darksome round contains *E.A.* 17
You rais'd these hallow'd *w.* ; the desert smil'd *E.A.* 133
In these lone *w.* (their days eternal bound) *E.A.* 141
And more than Echoes talk along the *w. E.A.* 306
To Paraclete's white *w.*, and silver springs *E.A.* 348
And tips with Silver all the *w. I.H.* 190
The floors of plaister, and the *w.* of dung *M.E.* iii. 300
And Nero's terraces desert their *w. M.E.* iv. 72
What *w.* can guard me, or what shades can hide *P.S.* 7
With desp'rate charcoal round his darken'd *w. P.S.* 20
What tho' my name stood rubric on the *w. P.S.* 215
The *w.*, the woods, and long cannis reply *R.L.* iii. 100
Go on, my Friend (he cry'd), see yonder *w. S.* vi. 46
Enclose whole downs in *w.*, 'tis all a joke *S.* vi. 261
That both extremes were banish'd from their *w. S.* vii. 117

Waller
Nor yet shall *W.* yield to time *I.H.* iv. 7
W. was smooth, but Dryden taught to join *S.* v. 267
Where Denham's strength, and W.'s sweetness join E.C. 361

Not *W.* Wreath can hide the Nation's Scar *E.S.* ii. 230
With *W.* strains, or Granville's moving lays *Sp.* 46

Walnut-tree.
From yon old *w.* a show'r shall fall *S.* ii. 145

Walsh.
Such late was *W.*—the Muse's judge and friend *E.C.* 729
And knowing *W.*, would tell me I could write *P.S.* 136

Walter—*see* Peter.

Walters.
So drink with *W.*, or with Chartres eat *S.* i. 89

Wand.
Held forth the virtue of the dreadful *w. D.* iv. 140
But Annius, crafty Seer, with ebon *w. D.* iv. 347
As Argus' eyes by Hermes' *w.* opprest *D.* iv. 637
Peace o'er the World her olive *w.* extend *M.* 19
Sancho's dread Doctor and his *W.* were there *M.E.* iv. 160
He rais'd his azure *w.*, and thus begun *R.L.* ii. 72

Wander.
May *w.* in a wilderness of Moss *D.* iv. 450
The young dismiss'd to *w.* earth or air *E.M.* iii. 127
On thy Margin Lovers *w. Mi.* vii. 27
Or who shall *w.* where the Muses sing *S.* v. 352

Wander'd.
That not in Fancy's maze he *w.* long *P.S.* 340

Wanderer.
Taste, that eternal *w.*, who flies *S.* v. 312
Benighted *w—s, the forest* o'er *M.E.* iii. 193

Wand'ring.
He whose long wall the *w.* Tartar bounds *D.* iii. 76
What flatt'ring scenes our *w.* fancy wrought *E.* iii. 23
The *w.* streams that shine between the hills *E.A.* 157
Alas, no more! methinks we *w.* go *E.A.* 241
If ever chance two *w.* lovers brings *E.A.* 347
Th' increasing prospect tires our *w.* eyes *E.C.* 231
Explores the lost, the *w.* sheep directs *M.* 51
Some *w.* touches, some reflected light *M.E.* ii. 253
W. in the myrtle grove *O.* i. 80
A *w.*, self-consuming fire *O.* iii. 20
Some guide the course of *w.* orbs on high *R.L.* ii. 79
Or *w.* thoughtful in the silent wood *W.F.* 249

Wanders.
Or *w.* wild in Academic groves *D.* iv. 490
There deviates Nature, and here *w.* Will *E.M.* iv. 112
Or *w.*, Heav'n-directed, to the Poor *M.E.* ii. 150
Or where Hebrus *w. O.* i. 99

Want.
Of hisses, blows, or *w.*, or loss of ears *D.* i. 48
Not plagu'd with head-aches, or the *w.* of rhyme *E.v.* 42
'Tis hard to say, if greater *w.* of skill *E.C.* 1
And hide with ornaments their *w.* of art *E.C.* 296
Each seeming *w.* compensated of course *E.M.* i. 181
Each *w.* of happiness by hope supply'd *E.M.* ii. 285
Worth makes the man, the *w.* of it the fellow *E.M.* iv. 203
Behold a rev'rend sire, whom *w.* of grace *M.E.* i. 232
And shew their zeal, and hide their *w.* of skill *M.E.* ii. 186
That "ev'ry man in *w.* is knave or fool:" *M.E.* iii. 102
To Worth or *W.* well-weigh'd, be Bounty giv'n *M.E.* iii. 229
Where Age and *W.* sit smiling at the gate *M.E.* iii. 266
W. with a full, or with an empty purse *M.E.* iii. 320
For very *w.*; he could not pay a dow'r *M.E.* iii. 326
'Twas very *w.* that sold them for two pound *M.E.* iii. 328
What but a *w.*, which you perhaps think mad (*rep.*) *M.E.* iii. 331
When press'd by *w.* and weakness DENNIS lies *Mi.* ii. 10
To laugh were *w.* of goodness and of grace *P.S.* 35
If *w.* pruvok'd, or madness made them print *P.S.* 155
Are no rewards for *w.*, and infamy *S.* ii. 104
As *w.* of figure, and a small Estate *S.* iii. 68
But grant I may relapse, for *w.* of grace *S.* vi. 88
My heir may sigh, and think it *w.* of grace *S.* vi. 286
And pleas'd, if sordid *w.* be far away *S.* vi. 295

Content, *if hence th' unlearn'd their w - s may view E.C.* 739
And build on *w.*, and on defects of mind *E.M.* ii. 247
W., frailties, passions, closer still ally *E.M.* ii. 253
The scale to measure others' *w.* by thine *E.M.* ii. 292
And helps, another creature's *w.* and woes *E.M.* iii. 52
On mutual *W.* build mutual Happiness *E.M.* iii. 112
But mutual *w.* this Happiness increase *E.M.* iv. 55
And where no *w.*, no wishes can remain *E.M.* iv. 325
To toast our *w.* and wishes, is her way *M.E.* ii. 88
Which done, the poorest can no *w.* endure *S.* iii. 45
W. reach all states; they beg but better drest *S.* viii. 224
None *w. a place, for all their Centre found D.* iv. 77
All-seeing in thy mists, we *w.* no guide *D.* iv. 469
W. as much more, to turn it to its use *E.C.* 81
To *w.* the strength of bulls, the fur of bears *E.M.* i. 176
One they must *w.*, which is, to pass for good *E.M.* iv. 92
No—shall the good *w.* Health, the good *w.* Pow'r *E.M.* iv. 158
Say, what can Chloe *w.?*" She wants a Heart *M.E.* ii. 160
What all so wish, but *w.* the pow'r to do *M.E.* iii. 276
Tho' Time is precious, and I *w.* some Tea *Mi.* ix. 28
I *w.* a Patron; ask him for a Place *P.S.* 50
And all they *w.* is spirit, taste, and sense *P.S.* 160
To help who *w.*, to forward who excel *S.* i. 137
What ev'ry day will *w.*, and most, the last *S.* iii. 22
The fear to *w.* them is as weak a thing *S.* iv. 19
But Kings in Wit may *w.* discerning Spirit *S.* v. 385
Sure I should *w.* the care of ten Monroes *S.* v. 70
The more you *w.*; why not with equal ease *S.* vi. 214
You purchase as you *w.*, and bit by bit *S.* vi. 237
Shall shortly *w.* the gen'rous tear he pays *U.L.* 78

Wanted.
What RICH'LIEU *w.*, Louis scarce could gain *E.S.* ii. 116
Only to show how many Tastes he *w. M.E.* iv. 14
The world had *w.* many an idle song *P.S.* 28
Ev'n copious Dryden *w.*, or forgot *S.* v. 280
How Van wants grace, who never *w.* wit *S.* v. 289

Wanting.
Nor wert thou, Isis! *w.* to the day *D.* iv. 193
And *w.* nothing but an honest heart *M.E.* i. 193
He, who still *w.*, tho' he lives on theft *P.S.* 183
Can there be *w.*, to defend Her cause *S.* i. 109

Wanton.
Who for thy table feeds the *w.* fawn *E.M.* iii. 29
Turn, turn to willing hearts your *w.* fires *I.H.* iii. 8
The bow'r of *w.* Shrewsbury and love *M.E.* iii. 308
And I this bowl, where *w.* Ivy twines *Sp.* 35
The *w.* victims of his sport remain *W.F.* 78
Now gentle touches *w.* o'er his face *D.* ii. 201
Stain all my soul, and *w.* in my eyes *E.A.* 266

Wantonness.
As flow'ry bands in *w.* are worn *E.* iv. 65

Wants.
What *w.* in blood and spirits, swell'd with wind *E.C.* 208
Because he *w.* a thousand pounds a year *E.M.* iv. 192
And a thin Court that *w.* your Face *I.H.* i. 12
Childless with all her Children, *w.* an Heir *M.E.* ii. 148
Say what can Chloe want?" She *w.* a Heart *M.E.* ii. 160
What Nature *w.*, commodious Gold bestows *M.E.* iii. 21
What Nature *w.*, (a phrase I much distrust) *M.E.* iii. 25
Why Shylock *w.* a meal, the cause is found *M.E.* iii. 115
So, when a Statesman *w.* a day's defence *P.S.* 251
Yet *w.* the honour, injur'd, to defend *P.S.* 296
"Pray then, what *w.* he?" Fourscore thousand pounds *S.* iii. 86
Suppose he *w.* a year, will you compound *S.* v. 51
How Van *w.* grace, who never wanted wit *S.* v. 289
That *w.* or force, or light, or weight, or care *S.* vi. 160

War.
How keen the *w.*, if Dulness draw the sword *D.* iii. 120
But fool with fool is barb'rous civil *w. D.* iii. 176
And ten horn'd fiends and Giants rush to *w. D.* iii. 236
Destructive *W.*, and all-involving Age *E.C.* 184
Seldom at council, never in a *w. E.C.* 537
Wits, just like Fools, at *w.* about a name *E.M.* ii. 85
What *W.* could ravish, Commerce could bestow *E.M.* iii. 205

Some *W.*, some Plague, some Famine they foresee *M.E.* iii. 113
Intestine *w.* no more our Passions wage *O.* i. 34
W., horrid *w.*, your thoughtful walks invades *O.* ii. 7
I wag'd no *w.* with *Bedlam* or the *Mint P.S.* 156
Or Envy holds a whole week's *w.* with Sense *P.S.* 252
Now move to *w.*, her sable Matadores *R.L.* iii. 47
Sad chance of *w.*, now destitute of aid *R.L.* iii. 63
Sighs, sobs, and passions, and the *w.* of tongues *R.L.* iv. 84
Chiefs out of *w.*, and Statesmen out of place *S.* i. 126
And all the man is one intestine *w. S.* ii. 72
In peace provides fit arms against a *w. S.* ii. 128
When the tir'd Nation breath'd from civil *w. S.* v. 273
The whole Artill'ry of the terms of *W. S.* viii. 54
When Albion sends her eager sons to *w. W.F.* 106
The youth rush eager to the sylvan *w. W.F.* 148
Of *w.* or blood, but in the sylvan chase *W.F.* 372
Their annual trophies, and their monthly w—s *D.* iii. 282
In living medals see her *w.* enroll'd *M.E.* v. 55
The spoils of nations, and the pomp of *w. P.C.* 28
In ANNA's *w.*, a Soldier poor and old *S.* vi. 33
And says our *w.* thrive ill, because delay'd *S.* viii. 163
A dreadful series of intestine *w. W.F.* 305
Give law to Words, or w. with Words alone D. iv. 178

Warble.
Others the Syren Sisters *w.* round *D.* iv. 541
So sweetly *w.*, or so smoothly flow *W.* 4

Warbles.
To that which *w.* thro' the vernal wood *E.M.* i. 216

Warbling.
Teach thou the *w.* Polypheme to roar *D.* iii. 305
Let the *w.* lute complain *O.* i. 6
When *w.* Philomel salutes the spring *Sp.* 26

Ward.
Not sail with *W.* to Ape-and-monkey climes *D.* i. 233
Where wretched Withers, *W.*, and Gildon rest *D.* i. 296
As thick as eggs at *W.* in pillory *D.* iii. 34
Another Durfey, *W.I* shall sing in thee *D.* iii. 146
To *W.*, to Waters, Chartres, and the Devil *M.E.* iii. 20
Shall *W.* draw Contracts with a Statesman's skill *S.* i. 119
See *W.* by batter'd Beaux invited over *S.* iv. 56
W. try'd on Puppies, and the Poor, his Drop *S.* v. 182
To cheat a Friend, or *W.*, he leaves to Peter *S.* v. 197

Wardrobes.
Like rich old *w.*, things extremely rare *S.* vii. 123

Warfare.
Finds all her life one *w.* upon earth *M.E.* ii. 118

Warlike.
His *w.* Amazon, her host invades *R.L.* iii. 67

Warm.
Till genial Jacob, or a *w.* Third day *D.* i. 57
Glad chains, *w.* furs, broad banners, and broad faces *D.* i. 88
Their wit still sparkling, and their flames still *w. E.* iv. 72
Now *w.* in love, now with'ring in my bloom *E.A.* 37
W. from the soul, and faithful to its fires *E.A.* 54
And each *w.* wish springs mutual from the heart *E.A.* 96
When, *w.* in youth, I bade the world farewell *E.A.* 110
Where beams of *w.* imagination play *E.C.* 58
And you shall see the first *w.* Weather *I.H.* i. 19
Still true to Virtue, and as *w.* as true *S.* iii. 30
Then Marble, soften'd into life, grew *w. S.* v. 147
When kind occasion prompts their *w.* desires *R.L.* i. 75
As some coy nymph her luver's *w.* address *W.F.* 19
Soft show'rs distill'd, and suns grew *w.* in vain *W.F.* 54
Her modest cheek shall w. *a future age E.* iii. 56
To light the dead, and *w.* th' unfruitful urn *E.A.* 262
Enlights the present, and shall *w.* the last *E.C.* 403
And Phoebus *w.* the rip'ning ore to gold *W.F.* 396

Warm'd.
The fur that warms a monarch, *w.* a bear *E.M.* iii. 44
Be justly *w.* with your own native rage *P.C.* 44
Cold is that breast which *w.* the world before *U.L.* 33

Warms.
Whose judgment sways us, and whose spirit *w. A.* 10

And him and his if more devotion *w. D.* ii. 81
Where nature moves, and rapture *w.* the mind *E.C.* 236
W. in the sun, refreshes in the breeze *E.M.* i. 271
Whatever *w.* the heart, or fills the head *E.M.* ii. 141
The fur that *w.* a monarch, warm'd a bear *E.M.* iii. 44
Feeds from his hand, and in his bosom *w. M.* 54
How martial music ev'ry bosom *w. O.* i. 37
The Sun's mild lustre *w.* the vital air *Sp.* 74

Warmth.
And boasts a *W.* that from no Passion flows *E.* ii. 4
Paulo's free stroke, and Titian's *w.* divine *E.* ii. 38
With *w.* gives sentence, yet is always just *E.C.* 678
Adieu Distinction, Satire, *W.*, and Truth *E.S.* i. 64
By Spirit robb'd of Friends, by *W.* of Pow'r *M.E.* ii. 144

Warn'd.
W. by the Sylph, oh pious maid, beware *R.L.* i. 112
A Sylph too *w.* me of the threats of fate *R.L.* iv. 165

Warner.
Mears, *W.*, Wilkins run; delusive thought *D.* ii. 225

Warning.
Yet his known Falsehoods could no *w.* prove (*rep.*) *Mi.* ix. 73

Warns.
Or *w.* me not to do *U.P.* 14

Warp'd.
Not *w.* by Passion, aw'd by Rumour *Mi.* viii. 5
Must *w.* to Flatt'ry's side; but some, more nice *S.* v. 259

Warrant.
To get my *W.* quickly sign'd *I.H.* ii. 76 *s*

Warr'd.
Dennis, who long had *w.* with modern Huns *Mi.* ii. 11

Warrior.
Otho a *w.*, Cromwell a buffoon *M.E.* i. 88
Nor ardent w—s *meet with hateful eyes M.* 58
There *w.* shining in historic brass *M.E.* v. 58
W. she fires with animated sounds *O.* i. 28
Or raise old *w.*, whose ador'd remains *W.F.* 301

Was, Wast, Were.—*Passim.*
Pity! you *was* not Druggerman at Babel *S.* viii. 83

Wash.
To make a *w.* would hardly stew a child *M.E.* ii. 54
A brighter *w.* ; to curl their waving hairs *R.L.* ii. 97
Or plung'd in lakes of bitter w—es *lie R.L.* ii. 127
W. Bladen white, and expiate Hays's stain D. iv. 560
Already written—*w.* it out, my tears *E.A.* 14
And gaping Tritons spew to *w.* your face *M.E.* iv. 154
'Tis mine to a few light stains, but theirs *S.* viii. 284

Wash'd.
The wild Mæander *w.* the Artist's face *D.* ii. 176
And never *w.*, but in Castalia's streams *D.* iii. 18

Waspish.
This jealous, *w.*, wrong-head, rhyming race *S.* vi. 148

Wasse.
Are things which Kuster, Burman, *W.* shall see. *D.* iv. 237

Waste.
The freezing Tanais thro' a *w.* of snows *D.* iii. 88
Some happier island in the wat'ry *w. E.M.* i. 106
What brought Sir Visto's ill-got wealth to *w. M.E.* iv. 15
See the wild *w.* of all-devouring years *M.E.* v. 1
Like verdant isles the sable *w.* adorn *W.F.* 28
A dreary desert, and a gloomy *w. W.F.* 44
A *w.* for beasts, himself deny'd a grave *W.F.* 80
Thro' dreary w—s, *and weep each other's woe E.A.* 242
Here was she seen o'er airy *w.* to rove *W.F.* 167
But wherefore w. *I words*! *I see advance D.* iv. 271
I *w.* the Matin lamp in sighs for thee *E.A.* 267
The seas shall *w.*, the skies in smoke decay *M.* 105
Is it less strange the Prodigal should *w. M.E.* iv. 3
W. sandy valleys, once perplex'd with thorn M. 73
Cities laid *w.*, they storm'd the dens and caves *W.F.* 49

Watch.
And the press'd *w.* return'd a silver sound *R.L.* i. 18
And, Momentilla, let the *w.* be thine *R.L.* ii. 114

WATCH'D—WEAK. 349

The *w.* would hardly let him pass at noon *S.* viii. 32
'Tis with our judgments as our w—es, none *E.C.* 9
Bright clouds descend, and Angels *w.* thee round *E.A.* 340
W. all their ways, and all their actions guide *R.L.* ii. 88
Nor sly informer *w.* these words to draw *S.* vii. 127

Watch'd.

W. both by Envy's and by Flatt'ry's eye *D.* iv. 36
Here, as I *w.* the dying lamps around *E.A.* 307
Ascendant Phœbus *w.* that hour with care *M.E.* ii. 285
He *w.* th' Ideas rising in her mind *R.L.* iii. 142

Watchful.

So *w.* Bruin forms, with plastic care *D.* i. 101
At best more *w.* this, but that more strong *E.M.* ii. 76
So long by *w.* Ministers withstood *M.E.* iii. 136
A *w.* sprite, and Ariel is my name *R.L.* i. 106
That e'er deserv'd a *w.* spirit's care *R.L.* ii. 102

Watchman.

A drowsy *W.*, that just gives a knock *D.* iv. 443
To rouse the W—men *of the public weal E.S.* ii. 217

Water.

New falls of *w.* murm'ring in his ear *M.* 70
By land, by *w.*, they renew the charge *P.S.* 9
Soft yielding minds to *W.* glide away *R.L.* i. 61
Here earth and *w.* seem to strive again *W.F.* 12
Whose tuneful whistling makes the w—s pass *D.* iii. 156
His rapid *w.* in their passage burn *D.* iii. 184
In troubled *w.*, but now sleeps in Port *D.* iv. 202
Or moving spirit bade the *w.* flow *E.A.* 254
And now, on rolling *w.* snatch'd away *I.H.* iii. 48
To Ward, to *W.*, Chartres, and the Dev'l *M.E.* iii. 20
From the dry rock who bade the *w.* flow *M.E.* iii. 254
That tells the *W.* or to rise or fall *M.E.* iv. 58
And soften'd sounds along the *w.* die *R.L.* ii. 50
From wicked *W.* ev'n to godly " *S.* vii. 80
Where dancing sun-beams on the *w.* play'd *Sw.* 3
His swelling *w.* and alternate tides *W.F.* 334
Tempt icy seas, where scarce the *w.* roll *W.F.* 389
Or *w. all the Quorum ten miles round M.E.* iii. 54

Wat'ring.

W. soft Elysian Plains *Mi.* vii. 20

Watermen.

Of link-boys vile, and *w.* obscene *D.* ii. 100

Wat'ry.

So Jove's bright bow displays its *w.* round *D.* ii. 173
Some happier island in the *w.* waste *E.M.* i. 106
The Naiads wept in ev'ry *w.* bow'r *Sw.* 7
Fresh rising blushes paint the *w.* glass *Sw.* 28
And lonely woodcocks haunt the *w.* glade *W.F.* 128
And pikes, the tyrants of the *w.* plains *W.F.* 146
The *w.* landscape of the pendant woods *W.F.* 213

Wave.

Like Cimon, triumph'd both on land and *w. D.* i. 85
Pours into Thames: and hence the mingled *w. D.* ii. 343
Build on the *w.*, or arch beneath the sand *E.M.* iii. 102
Thou who shalt stop where Thames' translucent *w. Mi.* x. 1
Heir urges heir, like *w.* impelling *w. S.* vi. 253
And chalky Wey, that rolls a milky *w. W.F.* 344
Love-whispering woods, and lute-resounding w—s *D.* iv. 306
Clouds interpose, *w.* roar, and winds arise *E.A.* 246
Smooth flow the *w.*, the Zephyrs gently play *R.L.* ii. 51
Where winds can carry, or where *w.* can roll *S.* iv. 70
And with celestial tears augments the *w. W.F.* 210
And floating forests paint the *w.* with green *W.F.* 216
The figur'd streams in *w.* of silver roll'd *W.F.* 335
And the hush'd *w.* glide softly to the shore *W.F.* 354
W. high, and murmur to the hollow wind *E.A.* 136
And little Eagles *w.* their wings in gold *M.E.* v. 30
Colours that change whene'er they *w.* their wings *R.L.* ii. 68

Wav'd.

Then grave Clarissa graceful *w.* her fan *R.L.* v. 7

Wav'ring.

Loose on the point of ev'ry *w.* hour *S.* vi. 249

Waves.

W. to the tepid Zephyrs of the spring *D.* iv. 422
Int'rest that *w.* on Party-colour'd wings *D.* iv. 538

Waving.

The winds to breathe, the *w.* woods to move *A.* 41
There towns aërial on the *w.* tree *E.M.* iii. 182
A *w.* Glow the bloomy beds display *M.E.* iv. 83
A brighter wash ; to curl their *w.* hairs *R.L.* ii. 97
Here *w.* groves a chequer'd scene display *W.F.* 17
Here Ceres' gifts in *w.* prospect stand *W.F.* 39
Wind the shrill horn, or spread the *w.* net *W.F.* 96
His sea-green mantle *w.* with the wind *W.F.* 350

Way.

Full in the middle *w.* there stood a lake *D.* ii. 69
And see, my son! the hour is on its *w. D.* iii. 123
Let all give *w.*, and Morris may be read *D.* iii. 168
Already Opera prepares the *w. D.* iii. 294
But lick up ev'ry blockhead in the *w. D.* iii. 299
Thou, only thou, directing all our *w. D.* iv. 296
There starve and pray, for that's the *w.* to heav'n *E.* v. 22
Thus Pegasus, a nearer *w.* to take *E.C.* 150
The growing labours of the lengthen'd *w. E.C.* 230
A certain bard encoutr'ring on the *w. E.C.* 268
But ev'n those clouds at last adorn its *w. E.C.* 472
The truest notions in the easiest *w. E.C.* 656
Far as the solar walk, or milky *w. E.M.* i. 102
Who forms the phalanx, and who points the *w. E.M.* iii. 108
Ask of the Learn'd the *w.*? The Learn'd are blind *E.M.* iv. 19
But some *w.* leans and hearkens to the kind *E.M.* iv. 40
The *w.* they take is strangely round about *E.S.* ii. 125
Yet, to his Guest tho' no *w.* sparing *I.H.* ii. 169
Prepare the *w.!* a God, a God appears *M.* 30
Be smooth ye rocks, ye rapid floods give *w. M.* 36
It hurries all too fast to mark their *w. M.E.* i. 38
To toast our wants and wishes is her *w. M.E.* ii. 88
Let Fops or Fortune fly which *w.* they will *M.E.* ii. 265
And turn th' unwilling steeds another *w. M.E.* iii. 192
Nature must give *W.* to Art *Mi.* vii. 4
Two trav'lers found an Oyster in their *w. Mi.* xi. 2
A dire dilemma ! either *w.* I'm sped *P.S.* 34
As shallow streams run dimpling all the *w. P.S.* 316
The Sylphs thro' mystic mazes guide their *w. R.L.* i. 92
Resolv'd to win, he meditates the *w. R.L.* ii. 31
Where the gilt Chariot never marks the *w. R.L.* iv. 155
And win my *w.* by yielding to the tide *S.* iii. 34
One who believes as Tindal leads the *w. S.* iv. 64
And punish'd him that put it in his *w. S.* vi. 26
And Peers give *w.*, exalted as they are *S.* vi. 106
Who live at Court, for going once that *w. S.* viii. 23
No lessons now are taught the Spartan *w. S.* viii. 93
While the long fun'rals blacken all the *w. U.L.* 40
To find that better *w. U.P.* 32
In circling fleeces whiten all the w—s *D.* ii. 362
Points him two *w.*, the narrower is the better *D.* iv. 152
Then soon to gain a Friend by servile *w. E.* iv. 110
To what base ends, and by what abject *w. E.C.* 520
But vindicate the *w.* of God to Man *E.M.* i. 16
A thousand *w.*, is there no black or white *E.M.* i. 214
His Life, to forfeit it a thousand *w. M.E.* i. 197
Bid Harbours open, public *W.* extend *M.E.* iv. 197
That, if he pleas'd, he pleas'd by manly *w. P.S.* 337
Watch all their *w.* and all their actions guide *R.L.* ii. 88
On various tempers act by various *w. R.L.* iv. 61
Of all these *w.*, if each pursues his own *S.* iii. 134

Wayward.

Then thus address'd the pow'r " Hail, *w.* Queen *R.L.* iv. 57

Wax.

Mere *w.* as yet, you fashion him with ease *S.* vi. 9
Now pox on those who show a *Court in w. S.* viii. 206
When num'rous *w.*-lights in bright order blaze *R.L.* iii. 168

Waxen.

Such *w.* noses, stately staring things *S.* viii. 210

We.—*Passim.*

Weak.

But who, *w.* rebels, more advance her cause *D.* v. 86

That on w. wings, from far, pursues your flights *E.C.* 197
What the w. head with strongest bias rules *E.C.* 203
While their w. heads like towns unfortify'd *E.C.* 434
Why form'd so w., so little, and so blind *E.M.* i. 36
As strong or w., the organs of the frame *E.M.* ii. 130
In this w. queen some fav'rite still obey *E.M.* ii. 150
She but removes w. passions for the strong *E.M.* ii. 158
Grant that the pow'rful still the w. controul *E.M.* iii. 49
Still for the strong too w., the w. too strong *E.M.* iii. 194
She taught the w. to bend, the proud to pray *E.M.* iii. 251
Fear made her Devils, and w. Hope her Gods *E.M.* iii. 256
Where small and great, where w. and mighty, made *E.M.* iii. 297
Think we, like some w. Prince, th' Eternal Cause *E.M.* iv. 121
The good man may be w., be indolent *E.M.* iv. 155
W., foolish man! will Heav'n reward us there *E.M.* iv. 173
Not that themselves are wise, but others w. *E.M.* iv. 228
How vain is Reason, Eloquence how w. *Ep.* iii. 5
The sick and w. the healing plant shall aid *M.* 15
As w., as earnest, and as gravely out *M.E.* i. 230
The Frail one's advocate, the W. one's friend *M.E.* ii. 30
Fine by defect, and delicately w. *M.E.* ii. 43
Vile, reptile, w., and vain *Mi.* iv. 6
The lines are w., another's pleas'd to say *S.* i. 5
W. tho' I am of limb, and short of sight *S.* iii. 49
If w. the pleasure that from these can spring (*rep.*) *S.* iv. 18
But most, when straining with too w. a wing *S.* v. 368
So w. a vessel, and so rich a prize *S.* viii. 229
Courts are too much for wits so w. as mine *S.* viii. 280
Let not this w., unknowing hand *U.P.* 25

Weaker.
Why form'd no w., blinder, and no less *E.M.* i. 38
A w. may surprise, a stronger take *E.M.* iii. 276

Weakness.
Soft without w., without glaring gay *E.* iii. 66
Of blindness, w., Heav'n bestows on thee *E.M.* i. 284
With too much w. for the Stoic's pride *E.M.* ii. 6
Till one Man's w. grows the strength of all *E.M.* ii. 252
Above life's w., and its comforts too *E.M.* iv. 268
W. or Delicacy; all so nice *M.E.* ii. 205
When press'd by want and w. DENNIS lies *Mi.* ii. 10
In pitying Love, we but our w. show *P.C.* 11

Weal.
To rouse the Watchmen of the public *W. E.S.* ii. 217
An hour, and not defraud the Public *W. S.* v. 6

Wealth.
Let w., let honour, wait the wedded dame *E.A.* 77
Fame, w. and honour! what are you to Love *E.A.* 80
In the fat age of pleasure, w., and ease *E.C.* 534
The trim of pride, the impudence of w. *E.M.* iii. 4
How those in common all their w. bestow *E.M.* iii. 185
Oh w. ill-fated! which no act of fame *E.M.* iv. 299
By *W.* of Follow'rs without one distress *M.E.* ii. 145
Had Colepepper's whole w. been hops and hogs *M.E.* iii. 65
O teach us, Bathurst! yet unspoil'd by w. *M.E.* iii. 226
W. in the gross is death, but life indeed *M.E.* iii. 233
Behold what blessings *W.* to life can lend *M.E.* iii. 297
Virtue! and *W.!* what are but a name *M.E.* iii. 334
His w., yet dearer, forfeit to the Crowe *M.E.* iii. 400
His w. to purchase what he ne'er can taste *M.E.* iv. 4
What brought Sir Visto's ill-got w. to waste *M.E.* iv. 15
My w. unwieldy, and my heap too great *S.* ii. 14
Oh Impudence of w.! with all thy store *S.* ii. 117
Get Place and *W.*, if possible, with grace (*rep.*) *S.* iii. 103
Their Country's w. our mightier Misers drain *S.* iii. 126
Is *W.* thy passion? Hence! from Pole to Pole *S.* iv. 69
A Man of w. is dubb'd a Man of worth *S.* iv. 81
His *W.* brave Timon gloriously confounds *S.* iv. 85
If *W.* alone can make and keep us blest *S.* iv. 95
Indeed, could w. bestow or wit or merit *S.* v. 226
Whom crimes gave w., and w. gave Impudence *S.* vii. 46
Then strongly fencing ill-got w. by law *S.* vii. 93
What once had beauty, titles, w. and fame *U.L.* 70

Wealthier.
A w. tribute then to thine he gives *W.F.* 224

Wealthy.
ST. JOHN has ever been a w. fool *E.S.* ii. 122
Heav'n visits with a Taste the w. fool *E.M.* iv. 17
And feather'd people crowd my w. side *W.F.* 404

Weapon.
This grey-goose w. must have made her stand *D.* i. 198
O sacred w.! left for Truth's defence *E.S.* i. 212
A two-edg'd w. from her shining case *R.L.* iii. 128
Satire's my w., but I'm too discreet *S.* i. 69
Secure the *radiant* w—s *wield* *E.* vi. 5
Receiv'd the w. of the sky *E.* vi. 10
What *well?* what w.? (Flavia cries) *E.* vi. 13
No common w. in your hands are found *R.L.* v. 43
Her w. blunted, and extinct her fires *W.F.* 418

Wear.
How oft in pleasing tasks we w. the day *E.* iii. 17
And w. their strange old virtue, as they will *E.S.* i. 44
To w. red stockings, and to dine with *Steele Mi.* iii. 4
This hand, which won it, shall for ever w. *D.* iv. 138
I only w. it in a land of Hectors *S.* i. 71
Sons, Sires, and Grandsires, all will w. the bays *S.* v. 171
Extremely fine, but what no man will w. *S.* vii. 124
To sing those honours you deserve to w. *W.F.* 289

Wearer.
All as the vest, appear'd the w.'s frame *D.* iii. 39

Wearing.
Your only w. is your Paduasoy *S.* viii. 113

Wears.
See, see, our own true Phœbus w. the bays *D.* iii. 323
His beaver'd brow a birchen garland w. *D.* iv. 141
But now no face divine contentment w. *E.A.* 147
The broadest mirth unfeeling Folly w. *E.M.* iv. 319
She owes to me the very charms she w. *Mi.* ix. 58
Which long she wore, and now Belinda w. *R.L.* v. 96

Weary.
But shall a Printer, w. of his life *E.S.* i. 125
Whose Seats the w. Traveller repose *M.E.* iii. 260
See my w. Days consuming *Mi.* vii. 7
In Days of Ease, when now the w. Sword *S.* v. 139
When w. reapers quit the sultry field *Su.* 65
Worn out in *public*, w. ev'ry eye *M.E.* ii. 229

Weasel.
A *W.* once made shift to slink *I.H.* i. 51

Weather.
And you shall see, the first warm *W. I.H.* i. 19

Weave.
Learn of the mole to plough, the worm to w. *E.M.* iii. 176
W. laurel Crowns, and take what names we please *S.* vi. 142

Weaves.
What Reason w., by Passion is undone *E.M.* ii. 42

Webs.
In vain thy Reason finer w. shall draw *E.M.* iii. 191

Webster.
There, *W.!* peal'd thy voice, and Whitfield! thine *D.* ii. 258

Wed.
Or w. to what he must divorce, a Muse *D.* iv. 262

Wedded.
Let wealth, let honour wait the w. dame *E.A.* 77
Papilia, w. to her am'rous spark *M.E.* ii. 37

Wedg'd.
Or w. whole ages in a bodkin's eye *R.L.* ii. 128

Weds.
For him she weeps, for him she w. again *E.S.* ii. 109
W. the rich Dulness of some Son of earth *S.* iv. 43

Weed.
Sprung the rank w., and thriv'd with large increase *E.C.* 535

And od'rous myrtle to the noisome *w.* *M.* 76
If I but ask, if any *w.* can grow *S.* v. 120
A tribe, with w—s and shells fantastic crown'd d. iv. 308
A Wild, where *w.* and flow'rs promiscuous shoot *E.M.* i. 7
Taller or stronger than the *w.* they shade *E.M.* i. 40
What tho' no friends in sable *w.* appear *U.L.* 55
The level'd towns with *w.* lie cover'd o'er *W.F.* 67

Week.
As once a *w.* we travel down *I.H.* ii. 97 *s*
Or Envy holds a whole w.'s war with Sense P.S. 252
Not so : a Buck was then a *w.* repast *S.* ii. 93
One solid dish his w.-day meal affords M.E. iii. 345

Weekly.
Hence Miscellanies spring, the *w.* boast *D.* i. 39
The stream, be his the *W.* Journals bound *D.* ii. 280
The MAN of Ross divides the *w.* bread *M.E.* iii. 264
They change their *w.* Barber, the News *S.* iii. 155

Ween.
And 'twas their point, I *w.*, to make it last *S.* ii. 94

Weep.
Taught rocks to *w.*, and made the mountains groan *A.* 16
And pitying saints, whose statues learn to *w.* *E.A.* 22
To read and *w.* is all they now can do *E.A.* 48
Now turn'd to heav'n, I *w.* my past offence *E.A.* 187
Obedient slumbers that can wake and *w.* *E.A.* 212
Thro' dreary wastes, and *w.* each other's woe *E.A.* 242
Here grief forgets to groan, and love to *w.* *E.A.* 314
Bear home six Whores, and make his Lady *w.* *M.E.* iii. 72
Who would not *w.*, if ATTICUS were he *P.S.* 214
And trees *w.* amber on the banks of Po *Sp.* 62
My native shades—there *w.*, and murmur there *W.F.* 202

Weeping.
No *w.* orphan saw his father's stores *E.A.* 135
This *w.* marble bad not ask'd thy Tear *Ep.* xiv. 5
Thus the *Cyprian* Goddess *w.* *Mi.* vii. 9
My Verse, and *Queensb'ry w.* o'er thy urn *P.S.* 260
And Ariel *w.* from Belinda flew *R.L.* iv. 12
What tho' no *w.* Loves thy ashes grace *U.L.* 59
Ye *w.* Loves, the stream with myrtles hide *W.* 23
The *w.* amber or the balmy tree *W.F.* 30
In *w.* vaults her hallow'd earth contains *W.F.* 302

Weeps.
In vain lost Eloïsa *w.* and prays *E.A.* 15
For him she *w.*, for him she weds again *E.S.* ii. 109
Beneath her Palm here sad Judæa *w.* *M.E.* v. 26
For ever murmurs and for ever *w.* *W.F.* 206
Here o'er the martyr-king the marble *w.* *W.F.* 313

Weigh.
I *w.* what author's heaviness prevails *D.* ii. 368
W. thy opinion against Providence *E.M.* i. 114
Go, measure Earth, *w.* air, and state the tides *E.M.* ii. 20

Weigh'd.
His comprehensive head I all Int'rests *w.* *M.E.* i. 83

Weighing.
Dame *Justice w.* long the doubtful Right *Mi.* xi. 7

Weighs.
Where, in nice balance, truth with gold she *w.* *D.* i. 53
W. the Men's wits against the Lady's hair *R.L.* v. 72

Weight.
As clocks to *w.* their nimble motion owe *D.* i. 183
Not so bold Arnall ; with a *w.* of skull *D.* ii. 315
When Ajax strives some rock's vast *w.* to throw *E.C.* 370
To ease the Soul of some oppressive *w.* *M.E.* i. 105
Yet let me show, a Poet's of some *w.* *S.* v. 203
That wants or force, or light, or *w.*, or care *S.* vi. 160

Weighty.
The matter's *w.*, pray consider twice *E.S.* ii. 43
Fit to bestow the Laureate's *w.* place *S.* v. 379

Welcome.
To *w.* death, and calmly pass away *E.M.* ii. 260

W. for thee, fair *Virtue* ! all the past (*rep.*) *P.S.* 358
W. the coming, speed the going guest *S.* ii. 160

Welkin.
Sound forth, my Brayers, and the *w.* rend *D.* ii. 246

Well.—*Passim.*
And dipt them in the sable *W.* *E.* vi. 11
"What *w.* ? what weapons?" (Flavia cries) *E.* vi. 13
And much too wise to walk into a *w.* *S.* vi. 191
She form'd this image of w.-body'd air D. ii. 42
To plains with *w.-breath'd* beagles we repair *W.F.* 121
See now, half-cur'd, and perfectly *w.-bred D.* v. 323
With wit well-natur'd, and with books *w.* *E.* iv. 8
Tho' learn'd, *w.*; and tho' *w.*, sincere *E.C.* 635
The *w.* cuckolds in St. James's air *M.E.* iii. 388
So *w.* spaniels civilly delight *P.S.* 313
A *w.* Lord t' assault a gentle Belle *R.L.* i. 8
The rich Buffet *w.-colour'd* Serpents grace *M.E.* iv. 153
But *w.-dispers'd* is Incense to the Skies *M.E.* iii. 236
But that this *w.-disputed* game may end *D.* ii. 245
And *w.-dissembled* em'rald on his hand *D.* iv. 348
Fair Nymphs and *w.-drest* Youths around her shone *R.L.* ii. 5
Should chance to make the *w.* rabble stare *S.* iii. 111
Thro' Lud's fam'd gates along the *w.-known* Fleet *D.* ii. 359
That *w.* name awakens all my woes *E.A.* 30
Th' according music of a *w.-mix'd* State *M.E.* iii. 294
Or *w.-mouthed* Booth with emphasis proclaims *S.* v. 123
With wit *w.-natur'd*, and with books well-bred *E.* iv. 8
W. Garth inflam'd with early praise *P.S.* 137
This small *w.-polish'd* Gem, the work of years *E.* iii. 40
Thus when we view some *w.-proportion'd* dome *E.C.* 247
Here thy *w.-study'd* marbles fix our eye *E.* iii. 33
The *w.-sung* woes will soothe her pensive ghost *E.* i. 365
But Wisdom's triumph is *w.-tim'd* Retreat *M.E.* ii. 225
To Worth or Want *w.-weigh'd*, be Bounty giv'n *M.E.* iii. 229
And all the *w.-whipt* Cream of Courtly Sense *E.S.* i. 70
As in some *w.-wrought* picture, light and shade *E.M.* ii. 208

Welsted.
But *W.* most the Poet's healing balm *D.* ii. 207
Unlucky *W.*! thy unfeeling master *D.* ii. 209
Flow, *W.* flow ! like thine inspirer, Beer *D.* iii. 169
Three thousand suns went down on W.'s *tie P.S.* 375

Wench.
Still to his *w.* he crawls on knocking knees *M.E.* i. 236
So some coarse Country *W.*, almost decay'd *Mi.* iii. 5
Call himself Barrister to ev'ry *w.* *S.* vii. 39

Went.
But (happy for him as the times *w.* then) *D.* iv. 115
So back to Pollio, hand in hand, they *w.* *D.* iv. 396
While the long solemn Unison *w.* round *D.* iv. 612
She sigh'd not that they stay'd, but that she *w.* (*rep.*) *E.* v. 10
She *w.* from Op'ra, Park, Assembly, Play *E.* v. 13
And not a mask *w.* unimprov'd away *E.C.* 541
Where once I *w.* to Church, I'll now go twice *M.E.* iii. 367
Horace and he *w.* hand in hand in song *P.S.* 234
Three thousand suns *w.* down on *Welsted's* lie *P.S.* 375
I told you, when I *w.*, I could not write *S.* vi. 28
Yet *w.* to Court !—the Dev'l would have it so *S.* viii. 14

Wept.
Thou wept'st, and with thee *w.* each gentle Muse *D.* iv. 44
He ceas'd and *w.* With innocence of mien *D.* iv. 419
Voiture was *w.* by all the brightest Eyes *E.* iv. 18
Once like thyself, I trembled, *w.*, and pray'd *E.A.* 311
Prais'd, *w.*, and honour'd by the Muse he lov'd *Ep.* iii. 6
Why—if I must (then *w.*) I give it Paul *M.E.* i. 259
W. by each Friend, forgiv'n by ev'ry Foe *Mi.* ii. 4
And foes to virtue wonder'd how they *w.* *P.C.* 8
The Naiads *w.* in ev'ry wat'ry bow'r *Su.* 7

Wept'st.
Thou *w.*, and with thee wept each gentle Muse *D* iv. 44

Wert.
Nor *w.* thou, Isis ! wanting to the day *D.* iv. 193
All this thou *w.*, and being this before *E.* ii. 8

Western.
Some beg an eastern, some a *w.* wind *D.* ii. 88
And all the *w.* world believe and sleep *D.* iii. 100
Where'er you find "the cooling *w.* breeze," *E.C.* 350
Here *w.* winds on breathing roses blow *Sp.* 32

Westminster.
We thrive at *W.* on Fools like you *Mi.* xi. 11
To him who notches sticks at *W. S.* iii. 84
Till *W.*'s *whole year be holiday D.* iii. 336
All Flesh is humbled, *W.* bold race *D.* iv. 145

Westphaly.
As Hog to Hog in plains of *W. E.S.* ii. 172

Wey.
And chalky *W.*, that rolls a milky wave *W.F.* 344

What, Whatever.—*Passim.*
Would from th' apparent *W.* conclude the Why *M.E.* i. 100

Whale.
Tho' stiff with hoops and arm'd with ribs of *w. R.L.* ii. 120
W—s *sport in woods, and dolphins in the skies D.* iii. 246

Whalebones.
Fans clap, silks rustle, and tough *w.* crack *R.L.* v. 40

Wharton.
The prospect clears, and *W.* stands confest (*rep.*) *M.E.* i. 179
Ask you why *W.* broke thro' ev'ry rule *M.E.* i. 206
Comets are regular, and *W.* plain *M.E.* i. 209
Unhappy *W.*, waking, found at last *M.E.* iii. 84

Wheel.
Touches some *w.*, or verges to some goal *E.M.* i. 59
Ixion rests upon his *w. O.* i. 67
Who breaks a butterfly upon a *w. P.S.* 308
If ev'ry *w.* of that unweary'd Mill *S.* vi. 78
And Persecution mourns her broken *w. W.F.* 420
The *w*—s *above urg'd by the load below* D. i. 184
Lo! at the *w.* of her triumphal Car *E.S.* i. 151
And gives th' eternal *w.* to know their rounds *M.E.* iii. 168

Whelms.
Sudden she flies, and *w.* it o'er the pyre *D.* i. 259

When, Whenever, Whence.—*Passim.*

Where, Wherever, Wherefore, Wherein.—*Passim.*

Whereat.
W. the gentleman began to stare *S.* vi. 194

Whether.—*Passim.*

Which.—*Passim.*

Whig.
Said "Tories call'd him *W.*, and *W*—s a Tory *E.S.* i. 8
A Joke on *Jekyll*, or some odd Old *W. E.S.* i. 39
Who know how like *W.* Ministers to Tory *E.S.* i. 106
Point she to Priest or Elder, *W.* or Tory *E.S.* i. 96
While Tories call me *W.*, and *W*—s a Tory *S.* i. 68

While.—*Passim.*
Suspend a *w.* your Force inertly strong *D.* iv. 7
A *W.* he crawls upon the Earth *Mi.* iv. 7
And keep a *w.* one parent from the sky *P.S.* 413

Whim.
To sneering Goode, half malice and half *w. D.* iii. 153
And made a Widow happy, for a *w. M.E.* ii. 58
That life of pleasure, and that soul of *w. M.E.* iii. 306
And much must flatter, if the *w.* should bite *S.* vi. 149

Whimsey.
Less mad the wildest *w.* we can frame *M.E.* iii. 155
Now let some *w.*, or that Dev'l within *S.* iii. 143

Whip.
Came *w.* and spur, and dash'd thro' thin and thick *D.* iv. 197

Whirl.
Down, down they larum with impetuous *w. D.* iii. 163
Quick *w*—s, *and shifting eddies, of our minds M.E.* i. 24

Whirligigs.
Or *w.* turn'd round by skilful swain *D.* iii. 57

Whirling.
The giddy motion of the *w.* Mill *R.L.* ii. 134

Whirlpools.
W. and storms his circling arm invest *D.* iii. 317

Whirlwind.
Rides in the *w.*, and directs the storm *D.* iii. 264
Got by fierce w—s, *and in thunder born A.* 92
Rous'd by the Prince of Air, the *w.* sweep *M.E.* iii. 353

Whirring.
See! from the brake the *w.* pheasant springs *W.F.* 111

Whisk.
Whose game is *W.*, whose treat a toast in sack *E.* v. 24
And *w.* them back to Evans, Young, and Swift *D.* ii. 116

Whiskers.
Pray, dip your *W.* and your Tail in *I.H.* ii. 203
With hoary *w.* and a forky beard *R.L.* iii. 38

Whisks.
W. it about, and down it goes again *M.E.* ii. 122

Whisper.
But were his Verses vile, his *W.* base *E.S.* i. 49
I get a *w.*, and withdraw *I.H.* ii. 63 s
The *w.*, that to greatness still too near *P.S.* 356
The glance by day, the *w.* in the dark *R.L.* i. 74
And all your honour in a *w.* lost *R.L.* iv. 110
And thus in w—s *said, or seem'd to say R.L.* i. 26
Soft o'er the shrouds aërial *w.* breathe *R.L.* ii. 57
Cæsar himself might w. he was beat M.E. i. 130
And *w.* with that soft, deluding air *Mi.* ix. 7
"*He Loves*,"—I *w.* to myself, "*He Loves!*" *Mi.* ix. 92
Hark! they *w.*; Angels say *O.* v. 7
He spies me out, I *w.*, "Gracious God *S.* viii. 62

Whisper'd.
So he, but pious, *w.* first his pray'r *D.* iv. 354
Some dæmon *w.* "Visto! have a Taste." *M.E.* iv. 16
Her fate is *w.* by the gentle breeze *W.* 61

Whisp'ring.
And *w.* Angels prompt her golden dreams *E.A.* 216
The *w.* Zephyr and the purling rill *E.M.* i. 204
In some still ev'ning, when the *w.* breeze *W.* 79

Whispers.
In the next line, it "*w.* thro' the trees:" *E.C.* 351
And smiling, *w.* to the next *I.H.* ii. 52 s
At last he *w.*, "Do; and we go snacks." *P.S.* 66
A voice there is, that *w.* in my ear *S.* iii. 11
Who counsels best? who *w.*, "Be but great *S.* iii. 101

Whist.—*See* Whisk.

Whistle.
Her infant grandame's *w.* next it grew (*rep.*) *R.L.* v. 93

Whistled.
May dunce by dunce be *w.* off my hands *P.S.* 254

Whistling.
Whose tuneful *w.* makes the waters pass *D.* iii. 156
Or ravish'd with the *w.* of a Name *E.M.* iv. 283

White.
Look'd a *w.* lily sunk beneath a show'r *D.* iv. 104
On some, a Priest succinct in amice *w. D.* iv. 549
Wash Bladen *w.*, or expiate Hays's stain *D.* iv. 560
Red, Blue, and Green, nay *w.* and black *E.* vi. 19
For her *w.* virgins Hymenæals sing *E.A.* 220
To Paraclete's *w.* walls and silver springs *E.A.* 348
If *w.* and black blend, soften, and unite (*rep.*) *E.M.* ii. 213
The Napkins *w.*, the Carpet red *I.H.* ii. 195
Chameleons who can paint in *w.* and black *M.E.* ii. 156
Sporus, that mere *w.* curd of Ass's milk *P.S.* 306
Sol thro' *w.* curtains shot a tim'rous ray *R.L.* i. 204
First, rob'd in *w.*, the Nymph intent adores *R.L.* i. 123
Transform'd to combs, the speckled, and the *w. R.L.* i. 136
On her *w.* breast a sparkling cross she bore *R.L.* ii. 7

Her wrinkled form in black and w. array'd *R.L.* iv. 28
W. gloves, and linen worthy Lady Mary *S.* iii. 164
Let Bear and Elephant be e'er so w. *S.* v. 322
Why round our coaches crowd the w.-glov'd *Beaux R.L.* v. 13
So first to preach a w. Chaplain goes *S.* viii. 250
And w.-rob'd Innocence from Heav'n descend *M.* 20

White's.

Or chair'd at *W.* amidst the Doctors sit *D.* i. 203
This Mess, toss'd up from Hockley-hole and *W. D.*i.222
Familiar *W.*, "God save King Colley!" cries *D.* i. 319
His Grace will game : to *W.* a bull be led *M.E.* iii. 67
To *W.* be carry'd as to ancient games *M.E.* iii. 69
Or when a Duke to Jansen punts at *W. S.* vii. 88
At Fig's, at *W.*, with feloes, or a whore *S.* viii. 213

Whited.

What Lady's face is not a w. wall *S.* viii. 151

Whitehall.

See under Ripley rise a new *W. D.* iii. 237
Friendly at Hackney, faithless at *W. M.E.* i. 76
Make Quays, build Bridges, or repair *W. S.* ii. 120
Their ample bow, a new *W.* ascend *W.F.* 380

Whiten.

In circling fleeces w. all the ways *D.* ii. 362
And bask and w. in the blaze of day *R.L.* ii. 78

Whiten'd.

Or w. wall provoke the skew'r to write *S.* i. 98
When frosts have w. all the naked groves *W.F.* 126

Whitening.

Pour'd o'er the w. vale their fleecy care *Sp.* 19

Whiter.

No w. page than Addison's remains *S.* v. 216

Whitfield.

There, Webster! peal'd thy voice, and *W.!* thine *D.* ii. 258

Whither.—*Passim.*

Who, &c., Whoever, Whoso.—*Passim.*

Whole.

Founds the w. pile, of all his works the base *D.* i. 160
And turn this w. illusion on the town *D.* ii. 139
Heav'ns! what a pile! w. ages perish there *D.* iii. 77
And last, to give the w. creation grace *D.* iii. 247
Till Westminster's w. year be holiday *D.* iii. 396
'Tis true, on Words is still our w. debate *D.* iv. 219
How parts relate to parts, or they to w. *D.* iv. 235
When Man's w. frame is obvious to a Flea *D.* iv. 238
And let the Author of the *W.* escape *D.* iv. 456
W. years neglected, for some months ador'd *E.* iv. 43
Rise Alps between us! and w. oceans roll *E.A.* 290
With spirits feeds, with vigour fills the w. *E.C.* 27
Survey the *W.*, nor seek slight faults to find *E.C.* 235
The *W.* at once is bold, and yet regular *E.C.* 252
Still make the *W.* depend upon a Part *E.C.* 264
Looked thro'? or can a part contain the w. *E.M.* i. 32
'Tis but a part we see, and not a w. *E.M.* i. 60
Alike essential to th' amazing w. *E.M.* i. 248
That system only, but the *W.* must fall *E.M.* i. 250
Heav'n's w. foundations to their centre nod *E.M.* i. 255
All are but parts of one stupendous w. *E.M.* i. 267
Expunge the w., or lop th' excrescent parts *E.M.* ii. 49
Reason's comparing balance rules the w. *E.M.* ii. 60
Parts it may ravage, but preserves the w. *E.M.* ii. 106
The w. employ of body and of mind *E.M.* ii. 126
Each vital humour which should feed the w. *E.M.* ii. 139
But Heav'n's great view is One, and that the *W. E.M.* ii. 238
Nothing is foreign : Parts relate to w. *E.M.* iii. 21
Be Man the Wit and Tyrant of the w. *E.M.* iii. 50
But as he form'd a *W.*, the *W.* to bless *E.M.* iii. 111
And one regards itself, and one the *W. E.M.* iii. 316
Heav'n breathes thro' ev'ry member of the w. *E.M.* iv. 61
Reason's w. pleasure, all the joys of Sense *E.M.* iv. 79
Oh blind to truth and God's w. scheme below *E.M.* iv. 93
The w. strange purpose of their lives to find *E.M.*iv.221

One self-approving hour w. years outweighs *E.M.* iv 255
The w. amount of that enormous fame *E.M.* iv. 327
Learns, from this union of the rising *W. E.M.* iv. 337
Grasp the w. worlds of Reason, Life, and Sense *E.M.* iv. 357
God loves from *W.* to Parts : but human soul (*rep.*) *E.M.* iv. 361
ARGYLL, the State's w. Thunder born to wield *E.S.* ii. 86
Since the w. House did afterwards the same *E.S.* ii. 170
Let *Envy* howl, while Heav'n's w. Chorus sings *E.S.* ii. 242
A frugal Mouse upon the w. *I.H.* ii. 161
Or puzzling Contraries confound the w. *M.E.* i. 65
But mark the fate of a w. Sex of Queens *M.E.* ii. 219
Had Colepepper's w. wealth been hops and hogs *M.E.* iii. 65
Drive to St. James's a w. herd of swine *M.E.* iii. 74
Ask you why Phryne the w. Auction buys *M.E.* iii. 119
Sinks deep within him, and possesses w. *M.E.* iii. 373
Parts answ'ring parts shall slide into a w. *M.E.* iv. 66
The w., a labour'd Quarry above ground *M.E.* iv. 110
There (thank my stars) my w. Commission ends *P.S.* 59
To *Bufo* left the w. *Castalian* state *P.S.* 230
Or Envy holds a w. week's war with Sense *P.S.* 252
Or wedg'd w. ages in a bodkin's eye *R.L.* ii. 128
Sacred to Ridicule his w. life long *S.* i. 79
Cries "Send me, Gods! a w. Hog barbecu'd!" *S.* ii. 26
Takes the w. House upon the Poet's Day *S.* iv. 88
Has sanctify'd w. poems for an age *S.* v. 114
His w. ambition was to serve a Lord *S.* vi. 14
Well, on the w., plain Prose must be my fate *S.* vi. 198
Enclose w. downs in walls, 'tis all a joke *S.* vi. 261
Glean on, and gather up the w. estate *S.* vii. 22
Some beasts were kill'd, tho' not w. hecatombs *S.* vii. 116
The w. Artill'ry of the terms of War *S.* viii. 54
W. nations enter with each swelling tide *W.F.* 399

Wholesome.

Drags from the Town to w. Country air *E.* v. 2
At length, by w. dread of statutes bound *S.* v. 257
To w. Solitude, the nurse of sense *S.* viii. 185

Wholly.—*Passim.*

Whore.

W., Pupil, and lac'd Governor from France *D.* iv. 272
I can't—indeed now—I so hate a w. *E.J.S.* 6
But 'tis the Fall degrades her to a *W. E.S.* i. 143
The Wit of Cheats, the Courage of a *W. E.S.* i. 165
That from his cage cries, Cuckold, *W.*, and Knave *M.E.* i. 6
When Cæsar made a noble dame a w. *M.E.* i. 213
Than his fine Wife, alas! or finer *W. M.E.* iv. 12
And has not Colley still his Lord and w. *P.S.* 97
That harmless Mother thought no wife a w. *P.S.* 384
And whether to a Bishop, or a *W. S.* viii. 137
At Fig's, at White's, with felons, or a w. *S.* viii. 213
So may the sons of sons of sons of w—*S. D.* iv. 332
That thou may'st be by kings, or w. of kings *E.M.* iv. 206
And yet more melancholy *W. I.H.* i. 10
Bear home six *W.*, and make his Lady weep *M.E.* iii. 72
As who knows Sappho, smiles at other w. *S.* vii. 6
Make Scots speak treason, cozen subtlest w. *S.* viii. 59

Whor'd.

Intrigu'd with glory, and with spirit w. *D.* iv. 315

Whores.

With the same spirit that he drinks and w. *M.E.* i. 189
Who drinks, w., fights, and in a duel dies *M.E.* iii. 390

Why.—*Passim.*

Would from th' apparent What conclude the *W. M.E.* i. 100

Wicked.

Three w. imps of her own Grubstreet choir *D.* ii. 123
Blockheads with reason w. wits abhor *D.* iii. 175
And did not w. custom so contrive *E.J.S.* 13
The dull, the proud, the w. and mad *P.S.* 347
W. as Pages, who in early years *S.* vii. 39
From w. Waters ev'n to godly * *S.* vii. 80

Wickedly.

Who w. is wise, or madly brave *E.M.* iv. 231
The Soul subsides, and w. inclines *S.* ii. 79

Wickedness.
Fall'n in the plash his *w.* had laid *D.* ii. 76

Wide.
Amid that area *w.* they took their stand *D.* ii. 27
W. as a wind-mill all his figure spread *D.* ii. 66
Who flings most filth, and *w.* pollutes around *D.* ii. 279
Around him *w.* a sable Army stand *D.* ii. 355
(Earth's *w.* extremes) her sable flag display'd *D.* iii. 71
Till one *w.* conflagration swallows all *D.* iii. 240
We never suffer it to stand too *w. D.* iv. 154
W., and more *w.*, it spread o'er all the realm *D.* iv. 613
In other parts it leaves *w.* sandy plains *E.C.* 55
What modes of sight betwixt each *w.* extreme *E.M.* i. 211
Around, how *w.!* how deep extend below *E.M.* i. 236
While still too *w.* or short is human Wit *E.M.* iii. 90
W. and more *w.*, th' o'erflowings of the mind *E.M.* iv. 369
Judicious Wits spread *w.* the Ridicule *E.S.* i. 61
No sigh, no murmur the *w.* world shall hear *M.* 45
See heav'n its sparkling portals *w.* display *M.* 97
Or cut *w.* views thro' Mountains to the Plain *M.E.* iv. 75
And guard the *w.* circumference around *R.L.* ii. 122
The Peer now spreads the glitt'ring Forfex *w. R.L.* iii. 147
Had he beheld an Audience gape so *w. S.* v. 321
With scarlet hats w.-waving circled round D. ii. 14

Wider.
Opinions? they still take a *w.* range *M.E.* i. 170

Widow.
Each *W.* asks it for *the Best of Men E.S.* ii. 108
And made a *W.* happy, for a Whim *M.E.* ii. 58
And cheats th' unknowing *W.* and the Poor *S.* viii. 141
Form'd a vast buckle for his w.'s gown R.L. v. 92
Some win rich W—s by their Chine and Brawn S. iii. 131
And when rank *W.* purchase luscious nights *S.* vii. 87
A tongue that can cheat *w.*, cancel scores *S.* viii. 58
Like nets or lime-twigs, for rich w—s' hearts S. vii. 58

Wield.
Secure the radiant weapons *w. E.* vi. 5
ARGYLL, the State's whole Thunder born to *w. E.S.* ii. 86

Wife.
Tho' this his Son dissuades, and that his *W. D.* ii. 168
The tender sister, daughter, friend, and *w. E.* iii. 52
For the dull glory of a virtuous *w. E.* iv. 46
Tho' meant each other's aid, like man and *w. E.C.* 83
The owner's *w.*, that other men enjoy *E.C.* 501
Well, if our Author in the *W.* offends *E.J.S.* 25
Tells us that Cato dearly lov'd his *w. E.J.S.* 32
To lend a *w.*, few here would scruple make *E.J.S.* 35
Expect thy dog, thy bottle, and thy *w. E.M.* iv. 178
Look but on Gripus, or on Gripus' *w. E.M.* iv. 280
Some greedy minion, or imperious *w. E.M.* iv. 302
Learn from their Books, to hang himself and *W. E.S.* i. 126
A simple Quaker, or a Quaker's *W. E.S.* i. 133
And offer Country, Parent, *W.*, or Son *E.S.* i. 158
And was, besides, a Tyrant to his *W. E.S.* ii. 135
Near fifty, and without a *W. I.H.* i. 73
A Tyrant to the *w.* his heart approves *M.E.* i. 202
Of wretched Shylock, spite of Shylock's *W. M.E.* iii. 94
Of Debts, and Taxes, *W.* and Children clear *M.E.* iii. 279
But duly sent his family and *w. M.E.* iii. 382
His Daughter flaunts a Viscount's tawdry *w. M.E.* iii. 391
W., son, and daughter, Satan! are thy own *M.E.* iii. 399
Than his fine *W.*, alas! or finer Whore *M.E.* iv. 12
Oh take the husband, or return the *w. O.* i. 82
Poor Cornus sees his frantic *w.* elope *P S.* 25
The Muse but serv'd to ease some friend, not *W. P.S.* 131
He lash'd him not, but let her be his *w. P.S.* 377
That harmless Mother thought no *w.* a whore *P.S.* 384
Nor marrying Discord in a noble *w. P.S.* 393
Why, if the nights seem tedious,—take a *W. S.* i. 16
Plums and Directors, Shylock and his *W. S.* i. 103
Avidien, or his *W.* (no matter which *S.* ii. 49
Pity! to build, without a son or *w. S.* ii. 163
Slave to a *W.*, or Vassal to a Punk *S.* iii. 62

The Fool, whose *W.* elopes three times a quarter *S.* iii. 150
For Fame, for Riches, for a noble *W. S.* iv. 39
Will gain a *W.* with half as many more *S.* iv. 78
And send his *W.* to church, his Son to school *S.* v. 164
Fond of his Friend, and civil to his *W. S.* vi. 189
Or court a *W.*, spread out his wily parts *S.* vii. 57
What 'Squire his lands, what Citizen his *w. S.* viii. 149
Like a big *w.* at sight of loathsome meat *S.* viii. 156
Our Wives read Milton, and our Daughters Plays S. v. 172
The joy, their *w.*, their sons, and servants share *S.v.*245
Thus shall your *w.*, and thus your children fall *U.L.* 36

Wig.
Who never chang'd his Principle or *W. E.S.* i. 40
Whom with a *w.* so wild, and mien so maz'd *M.E.*iii. 63
That live-long *w.* which Gorgon's self might own *M.E.* iii. 295
My *w.* all powder, and all snuff my band *S.* iii. 162
Cato's long *w.*, flower'd gown, and lacquer'd chair *S.* v. 337
A motley mixture! in long w—s, in bags D. ii. 21
Where *w.* with *w.*, with sword-knots sword-knots strive *R.L.* i. 101

Wight.
Right well mine eyes arede the myster *w. D.* iii. 187
Each *w.*, who reads not, and but scans and spells *P.S.* 165
From *Scots* to *W.*, from *Mount* to *Dover* strand *S.* vii. 86
Such was the *w.;* th' apparel on his back *S.* viii. 38
*Yet there are W—s, who fondly call their own S.*vi.244

Wild.
Arraign no mightier Thief than wretch'd *W. E.S.* ii. 39
Yes, strike that *W.*, I'll justify the blow *E.S.* ii. 54
With self-applause her w. creation views D. i. 82
And, lest we err by Wit's *w.* dancing light *D.* i. 175
The *w.* Mæander wash'd the Artist's face *D.* ii. 176
Or wanders *w.* in Academic Groves *D.* iv. 490
And Paradise was open'd in the *W. E.A.* 134
One glaring Chaos and *w.* heap of wit *E.C.* 292
Stemm'd the *w.* torrent of a barb'rous age *E.C.* 695
A *W.* where weeds and flow'rs promiscuous shoot *E.M.* L 7
W. Nature's vigour working at the root *E.M.* ii. 184
Oft in the Passions' *w.* rotation tost *M.E.* i. 41
The *W.* are constant, and the Cunning known *M.E.* i. 175
In Youth they conquer, with so *w.* a rage *M.E.* ii. 221
Whom with a wig so *w.*, and mien so maz'd *M.E.* iii. 63
See the *w.* waste of all-devouring years *M.E.* v. 1
In broken air, trembling, the *w.* music floats *O.* i. 17
See, *w.* as the winds, o'er the desert he flies *O.* i. 110
When *w.* Barbarians spurn her dust *O.* ii. 18
A vapour fed from *w.* desire *O.* iii. 19
And *w.* Ambition well deserves its woe *P.C.* 12
Clubs, Diamonds, Hearts, in *w.* disorder seen *R.L.* iii. 79
Or nobly *w.*, with Budgel's fire and force *S.* i. 27
Fly then, on all the wings of *w.* desire *S.* iv. 67
As *w.* and mad: the Avarice of pow'r *S.* vi. 307
W. to get loose, his Patience I provoke *S.* viii. 116
Ev'n the *w.* heath displays her purple dyes *W.F.* 25
By thee to mountains, w—s, and deserts led E.A. 132
And starts amidst the thirsty *w.* to hear *M.* 69
Late, as I rang'd the crystal *w.* of air *R.L.* i. 107
The lonely lords of empty *w.* and woods *W.F.* 48
O'er sandy *w.* were yellow harvests spread *W.F.* 88
While op'ning Hell spits w.-fire at your head D. iii. 316
In yonder *w.-goose* and the larks *Mi.* xii. 12

Wilderness.
May wander in a *w.* of Moss *D.* iv. 450

Wildest.
Less mad the *w.* whimsey we can frame *M.E.* fl. 155

Wildness.
No artful *w.* to perplex the scene *M.E.* iv. 116

Wilkins.
Mears, Warner, *W.* run: delusive thought *D.* ii. 125
Pois'd with a tail may steer on W.' wings D. iv. 452

Will.—*Passim.*

Of naught so doubtful as of *Soul* and *W. D.* iv. 482
What serves one *w.*, when many wills rebel *E.M.* iii. 274
There deviates Nature, and here wanders *W. E.M.* iv. 112
Or if it be thy *W.* and Pleasure *I.H.* ii. 19 *s*
Or Japhet pocket, like his Grace, a *W. E.S.* i. 120
W. sneaks a Scriv'ner, an exceeding knave *M.E.* i. 154
A Knave this morning, and his *W.* a cheat *M.E.* ii. 142
Poets heap Virtues, Painters Gems at *w. M.E.* ii. 185
And write whate'er he pleas'd, except his *W. P.S.* 379
But when to mischief mortals bend their *w. R.L.* iii. 125
Inclines our action, not constrains our *w. S.* vi. 281
Learn to live well, or fairly make your *w. S.* vi. 322
Left free the Human *W. U.P.* 12
And let Thy *W.* be done *U.P.* 48
What serves one will when many w—s rebel E.M. iii. 274

William.

The Hero *W.*, and the Martyr Charles *S.* v. 386
While mighty W.'s *thund'ring arm prevail'd S.* vi. 63

Willing.

Are destin'd Hymen's *w.* victim too *E.* iv. 58
The *w.* heart, and only holds it long *E.* iv. 68
To dream once more I close my *w.* eyes *E.A.* 239
In golden Chains the *w.* World she draws *E.S.* i. 147
Each *w.* to be pleas'd, and please *I.H.* ii. 139
Turn, turn to *w.* hearts your wanton fires *I.H.* iii. 8
Joins *w.* woods, and varies shades from shades *M.E.* iv. 62
W. to wound, and yet afraid to strike *P.S.* 203
The *w.* Muses were debauch'd at Court *S.* v. 152
And by that laugh the *w.* fair is found *S.* 56

Willow.

Mournful Cypress, verdant *W. Mi.* vii. 21
And bade his w—s learn the moving song W. 14
And on bis *w.* hung each muse's lyre *W.F.* 276

Wilmot.

He'll shine a Tulfy and a *W.* too *M.E.* i. 187
If, after all, we must a *W.* own *S.* iv. 126

Wily.

Soft, as the *w.* Fox is seen to creep *D.* iv. 351
The Knave of Diamonds tries his *w.* arts *R.L.* iii. 87
A charge of Smiff the *w.* virgin threw *R.L.* v. 82
Or court a Wife, spread out his *w.* parts *S.* vii. 57

Win.

"Hold!" (cry'd the Queen) "a Cat-call each shall *w. D.* ii. 243
Who could nut *w.* the mistress, woo'd the maid *E.C.* 105
Smile without Art, and *w.* without a Bribe *E.S.* i. 32
Born with whate'er could *w.* it from the Wise *M.E.* ii. 182
Explain'd the matter, and would *w.* the cause *Mi.* xi. 6
Such plays alone should *w.* a British ear *P.C.* 45
Resolv'd to *w.*, he meditates the Way *R.L.* ii. 31
And *w.* my way by yielding to the tide *S.* iii. 34
Some *w.* rich Widows by their Chine and Brawn *S.* iii. 131
Piecemeal they *w.* this acre first, then that *S.* vii. 91

Wind.

He left huge Lintot, and out-stripp'd the *w. D.* ii. 62
Some beg an eastern, some a western *w. D.* ii. 88
On grinning dragons thou shalt mount the *w. D.* iii. 268
Wave high, and murmur to the hollow *w. E.A.* 156
In each low *w.* methinks a Spirit calls *E.A.* 305
What wants in blood and spirits, swell'd with *w. E.C.* 308
Sees God in clouds, or hears him in the *w. E.M.* i. 100
That never air or ocean felt the *w. E.M.* i. 167
He mounts the storm, and walks upon the *w. E.M.* ii. 110
As, "What's o'clock?" and "How's the *W.*!" *I.H.* ii. 89 *s*
Perhaps the *W.* just shifted from the east *M.E.* i. 112
Improves the keenness of the Northern *w. M.E.* iv. 112
Loose to the *w.* their airy garments flew *R.L.* ii. 63
The dreaded East is all the *w.* that blows *R.L.* iv. 20
The tott'ring China shook without a *w. R.L.* iv. 163
Where bile, and *w.*, and phlegm, and acid jar *S.* ii. 71
On Fame's mad voyage by the *w.* of praise *S.* v. 297
His sea-green mantle waving with the *w. W.F.* 350

The time shall come, when, free as seas or *w. W.F.* 397
Thus, far from Delia, to the w—s I mourn A. 21
The *w.* to breathe, the waving woods to move *A.* 41
Keen hollow *w.* howl thro' the bleak recess *D.* i. 35
Songs, sonnets, epigrams, the *w.* uplift *D.* ii. 115
Clouds interpose, waves roar, and *w.* arise *E.A.* 246
Still as the sea, ere *w.* were taught to blow *E.A.* 253
Like varying *w.* by other passions tost *E.M.* ii. 167
Our fates and fortunes, as the *w.* shall blow *M.E.* iii. 46
Shall call the *w.* thro' long arcades to roar *M.E.* iv. 35
By the fragrant *w.* that blow *O.* i. 72
See, wild as the *w.*, o'er the deserts he flies *O.* i. 110
On wings of *w.* came flying all abroad *P.S.* 218
The rest, the *w.* dispers'd in empty air *R.L.* ii. 46
Like that where once Ulysses held the *w. R.L.* iv. 82
Where *w.* can carry, or where waves can roll *S.* iv. 70
Here western *w.* on breathing roses blow *Sp.* 32
And *w.* shall waft it to the pow'rs above *Su.* 80
The *w.* and trees and floods her death deplore *W.* 67
The hollow *w.* thro' naked temples roar *W.F.* 68
Then bow'd and spoke ; the *w.* forget to roar *W.F.* 353
W. the shrill horn, or spread the waving net W.F. 96
As forc'd from w.-guns lead itself can fly D. i. 181
Wide as a *w.-mill* all his figure spread *D.* ii. 166
So swells each *w.-pipe* ; Ass intones to Ass *D.* ii. 253

Winding.

Scream like the *w.* of ten thousand jacks *D.* iii. 160
Pleas'd Vaga echoes thro' her *w.* bounds *M.E.* iii. 251
By all their *w.* Play *Mi.* iv. 26
Or else where Cam his *w.* vales divides *Su.* 26
Nor rivers *w.* thro' the vales below *W.* 3
What Kings first breath'd upon her *w.* shore *W.F.* 300
The *w.* Isis, and the fruitful Tame *W.F.* 340

Windows.

And the dim *w.* shed a solemn light *E.A.* 144
To break my *W.*, if I treat a Friend *E.S.* ii. 143

Window'd.

With pert flat eyes she *w.* well his head *D.* ii. 43

Windsor.

Next Ægon sung, while *W.* groves admir'd *A.* 55
To *W.* and again to Town *I.H.* ii. 98 *s*
Thy forests, *W.!* and thy green retreats *W.F.* 1
Nor envy, *W.!* since thy shades have seen *W.F.* 161
And Cynthus' top forsook for *W.* shade *W.F.* 166
Oh wouldst thou sing what heroes *W.* bore *W.F.* 299
Thy trees, fair *W.!* now shall leave their woods *W.F.* 385
Nor blush to sport on W.'s *blissful plains Sp.* 2
As thine, which visits *W.* fam'd abodes *W.F.* 229
Where *W.*-domes *and pompous turrets rise W.F.* 352
Make *W.-hills* in lofty numbers rise *W.F.* 287
If *W.-shades* delight the matchless maid (*rep.*) *Sp.* 67

Wine.

And grateful clusters swell with floods of *w. A.* 74
Critic'd your *w.*, and analys'd your meat *M.E.* ii. 81
What slaughter'd hecatombs, what floods of *w. M.E.* iii. 203
Your *w.* lock'd up, your butler stroll'd abroad *S.* ii. 13
If Time improve our Wit as well as *W. S.* ii. 49
And is at once their vinegar and *w. S.* ii. 54
The musty *w.*, foul cloth, or greasy glass *S.* ii. 66
Where slumber Abbots, purple as their w—s D. iv. 302
With all their brandies, or with all their *w. M.E.* iii. 52
The other slights for women, sports and *w. S.* vi. 274

Wing.

And under his, and under Archer's *w. D.* i. 309
And now on Fancy's easy *w.* convey'd *D.* iii. 13
To whom Time bears me on his rapid *w. D.* iv. 6
Of all th' enamell'd race, whose silv'ry *w. D.* iv. 421
Prescrib'd her heights, and prun'd her tender *w. E.C.* 736
He asks no Angel's *w.*, no Seraph's fire *E.M.* i. 110
These may some gentle ministerial *W. E.S.* i. 95
Spread thy broad *w.*, and souse on all the kind *E.S.* ii. 15
The Muse's *w.* shall brush you all away *E.S.* ii. 223
These, tho' unseen, are ever on the *w. R.L.* i. 43
Or Death's black *w.* already be display'd *S.* i. 95
But most, when straining with too weak a *w. S.* v. 368
Oh ! could I mount on the Mæonian *w. S.* v. 394
Peace stole her *w.*, and wrapt the world in sleep *S.* v. 401
One likes the Pheasant's *w.*, and one the leg *S.* vi. 84

356   WINGED—WISER.

And scatters blessings from her dovelike w. *W.F.* 430
Here pleas'd behold her mighty w—s outspread *D.* i. 27
On feet and w., and flies, and wades, and hops *D.* ii. 64
Dove-like, she gathers to her w. again *D.* iii. 126
Pois'd with a tail, may steer on Wilkins' w. *D.* iv. 452
Int'rest that waves on Party-colour'd w. *D.* iv. 538
Spreads his light w., and in a moment flies *E.A.* 76
And w. of Seraphs shed divine perfumes *E.A.* 218
That on weak w., from far, pursues your flight *E.C.* 197
Joy tunes his voice, joy elevates his w. *E.M.* iii. 32
Admires the jay the insect's gilded w. *E.M.* iii. 55
Taught on the w. of Truth to fly *I.H.* iv. 3
That lends Corruption lighter w. to fly *M.E.* iii. 40
Wait but for w., and in their season fly *M.E.* iii. 170
And little Eagles wave their w. in gold *M.E.* v. 30
Lend, lend your w.! I mount! I fly *O.* v. 16
On w. of winds came flying all abroad *P.S.* 218
Yet let me flap this bug with gilded w. *P.S.* 309
Colours that change whene'er they wave their w. *R.L.* ii. 68
While clogg'd he beats his silken w. in vain *R.L.* ii. 130
A thousand w., by turns, blow back the hair *R.L.* iii. 136
Spreads his black w., and slowly mounts to day *R.L.* iv. 88
Clapp'd his glad w., and sate to view the fight *R.L.* v. 54
On morning w. how active springs the Mind *S.* ii. 81
Fly then, on all the w. of wild desire *S.* iv. 67
Estates have w., and hang in Fortune's pow'r *S.* vi. 248
Where Contemplation prunes her ruffled w. *S.* viii. 166
And all th' aërial audience clap their w. *Sp.* 16
While Angels with their silver w. o'ershade *U.L.* 67
Shall list'ning in mid air suspend their w. *W.* 54
And mounts exulting on triumphant w. *W.F.* 112
His painted w., and breast that flames with gold *W.F.* 118
Instant, when dipt, away they w. their flight *D.* iii. 27
Or w. the sky, or roll along the flood *E.M.* iii. 120

Winged, Wing'd.
Swift to whose hand a w. volume flies *D.* iii. 234
The w. courser, like a gen'rous horse *E.C.* 86
For gain, not glory, w—'d his roving flight *S.* v. 71

Wings.
W. the red light'ning, and the thunder rolls *D.* iii. 236
Who heaves old Ocean, and who w. the storms *E.M.* i. 158

Wink.
Sudden, she storms! she raves! you tip the w. *M.E.* ii. 33
And for my soul I cannot sleep a w. *S.* i. 12

Winnall.
When W. tally'd, I would punt no more *Mi.* ix. 68

Winner.
Be ev'ry birth-day more a w. *Mi.* xii. 17
The W.'s pleasure, and the Loser's pain *Mi.* ix. 80

Winning.
Seem'd to her ear his w. lips to lay *R.L.* i. 25

Wins.
He w. this Patron, who can tickle best *D* ii. 195
And w. (oh shameful chance) the Queen of Hearts *R.L.* iii. 68
Charms strike the sight, but merit w. the soul *R.L.* v. 34

Winter.
And write next w. more *Essays on Man E.S.* ii. 255
'Tis true; but W. comes apace *I.H.* i. 16
But just endur'd the w. she began *Mi.* iii. 23
In w. fire *O.* iv. 8
While in thy heart eternal w. reigns *Su.* 22
As w. fruits grow mild ere they decay *S.* vi. 319

Winton.
Eton and W. shake thro' all their sons *D.* iv. 144

Wintry.
Or brew fierce tempests in the w. main *R.L.* ii. 85

Wip'd.
All Tears are w. for ever from all eyes *E.S.* i. 102

Wipes.
From ev'ry face he w. off ev'ry tear *M.* 46

Wisdom.
That W. infinite must form the best *E.M.* i. 44
Go, teach Eternal W. how to rule *E.M.* ii. 29
Admir'd such w. in an earthly shape *E.M.* ii. 33
While Truth, Worth, W., daily they decry *E.S.* i. 169
His Anger moral, and his W. gay *Ep.* i. 6
Of modest w., and pacific truth *Ep.* vii. 2
To written W., as another's, less *M.E.* i. 13
Old Politicians chew on w. past *M.E.* i. 228
W. and Wit in vain reclaim *O.* iii. 3
And the first W., to be Fool no more *S.* iii. 66
Here, W. calls: "Seek Virtue first, be bold *S.* iii. 77
That Man divine whom W. calls her own *S.* iii. 180
W. (curse on it) will come soon or late *S.* iv. 199
At aught thy W. has deny'd *U.P.* 35
In Folly's Cap, than W.'s grave disguise *D.* iv. 240
But W. triumph is well-tim'd Retreat *M.E.* ii. 225

Wise.
Oh worthy thou of Ægypt's w. abodes *D.* iii. 207
From foolish Greeks to steal them, was as w. *D.* iv. 378
The sober follies of the w. and great *E.* i. 10
We think our fathers fools, so w. we grow *E.C.* 438
Fear not the anger of the w. to raise *E.C.* 582
As Men for ever temp'rate, calm, and w. *E.M.* i. 154
Who finds not Providence all good and w. *E.M.* i. 205
A Being darkly w., and rudely great *E.M.* ii. 4
The rogue and fool by fits is fair and w. *E.M.* ii. 233
'Tis this, Tho' Man's a fool, yet GOD IS W. *E.M.* ii. 294
Laws w. as Nature, and as fix'd as Fate *E.M.* iii. 190
O'erlook'd, seen double, by the fool, and w. *E.M.* iv. 6
More rich, more w.; but who infers from hence *E.M.* iv. 51
I'll tell you, friend! a w. man and a Fool *E.M.* iv. 200
Where not among the Heroes and the w. *E.M.* iv. 218
No less alike the Politic and W. *E.M.* iv. 225
Not that themselves are w., but others weak *E.M.* iv. 228
Who wickedly is w., or madly brave *E.M.* iv. 231
Tell (for You can) what is it to be w. *E.M.* iv. 260
W. is her present; she connects in this *E.M.* iv. 349
Teach me, like thee, in various nature w. *E.M.* iv. 377
I study'd Shrewsbury, the w. and great *E.S.* ii. 79
A w. man always is or should *I.H.* i. 35
Unthought-of Frailties cheat us in the W. *M.E.* i. 69
Mad at a Fox-chase, w. at a Debate *M.E.* i. 74
Who reasons wisely is not therefore w. *M.E.* i. 117
W., if a Minister; but, if a King (rep.) *M.E.* i. 129
Born with whate'er could win it from the W. *M.E.* i. 182
Less Wit than Mimic, more a Wit than w. *M.E.* ii. 48
W. Wretch! with Pleasures too refin'd to please *M.E.* ii. 95
Chloe is prudent—Would you too be w. *M.E.* ii. 179
They might (were Harpax not too w. to spend) *M.E.* iii. 91
W. Peter sees the World's respect for Gold *M.E.* iii. 123
By Nature honest, by Experience w. *P.S.* 400
'Tis but their Sylph, the w. Celestials know *R.L.* i. 77
Coffee (which makes the politician w. *R.L.* iii. 117
The w. man's passion, and the vain man's toast *R.L.* v. 10
Scarce to w. Peter complaisant enough *S.* i. 3
But strong in sense, and w. without the rules *S.* ii. 10
The eldest is a fool, the youngest w. *S.* iii. 44
But let the Fit pass o'er, I'm w. enough *S.* vi. 151
Words that w. Bacon, or brave Raleigh spake *S.* vi. 168
And much too w. to walk into a well *S.* vi. 191
And the w. Justice starting from his chair *S.* viii. 36
Than mine to find a subject staid and w. *S.* viii. 168
You, that too w. for pride, too good for pow'r *Sp.* 7
Attends the duties of the w. and good *W.F.* 250

Wisely.
Thus w. careless, innocently gay *E.* iv. 11
And w. curb'd proud man's pretending wit *E.C.* 53
We just as w. might of Heav'n complain *E.M.* iv. 117
Then w. plead, to me they meant no hurt *E.S.* ii. 144
Who reasons w. is not therefore wise *M.E.* i. 117
And SWIFT cry w., "Vive la Bagatelle!" *S.* iv. 128

Wiser.
Ask them the cause; they're w. still they say (rep.) *E.C.* 436
Our w. sons, no doubt, will think us so *E.C.* 439
Go, w. thou! and in thy scale of sense *E.M.* i. 113
Thus let the w. make the rest obey *E.M.* iii. 196
Which is the happier, or the w. *I.H.* ii. 147

But Satan now is *w*. than of yore *M.E.* iii. 351
Why should not we be *w*. than our sires *S*. v. 44
And last (which proves him *w*. still than all) *S*. viii. 150
For *w*. brutes were backward to be slaves *W.F.* 50

Wisest.

The *w*., brightest, meanest of mankind *E.M.* iv. 282
And just her *w*. monarch made a fool *M.E.* i. 94
Yet, in this search, the *w*. may mistake *M.E.* i. 210
The *w*. Fool much Time has ever made *M.E.* ii. 124
The *w*. man might blush, I must agree *S*. vi. 228

Wish.

The Maid's romantic *w*., the Chemist's flame *D*. iii. 11
The virgin's *w*. without her fears impart *E.A.* 55
And each warm *w*. springs mutual from the heart *E.A.* 96
Each pray'r accepted, and each *w*. resign'd *E.A.* 210
Who knew no *w*. but what the world might hear *Ep*. vii. 6
Is there on Earth one care, one *w*. beside *Ep*. xiii. 7
Tho' my own secret *w*. was for the *Knave Mi*. ix. 50
And eye the Mine without a *w*. for Gold *Mi*. x. 8
United *w*., and mutual joy *O*. iii. 26
And where no wants, no w—es can remain E.M. iv.325
To toast our wants and *w*. is her way *M.E.* ii. 88
Three things another's modest *w*. bound *P.S.* 47
Nor *w*. *to lose a Foe these virtues raise* E. ii. 11
And reading *w*., like these, our fate and fame *E*. iii. 9
Well might you *w*. for change by those accurst *E*. iv. 39
How would he *w*. that Heav'n had left him still *E.M.* i. 203
With the same trash mad mortals *w*. for here *E.M.*iv.174
Since but to *w*. more Virtue, is to gain *E.M.* iv. 326
Patriots there are, who *w*. you'd jest no more *E.S.* i. 24
What all so *w*., but want the pow'r to do *M.E.* iii. 276
You'll *w*. your hill or shelter'd seat again *M.E.* iv. 76
Happy the man whose *w*. and care *O*. v. 1
Who hears him groan, and does not *w*. to bleed *P.C.* 26
My foes shall *w*. my Life a longer date *S*. i. 61
I *w*. to God this house had been your own *S*. ii. 162
I *w*. you joy, Sir, of a Tyrant gone *S*. vi. 305
What further could I *w*. the fop to do *S*. vii. 53
Well, I could *w*., that still in lordly domes *S*. vii. 115

Wish'd.

W. he had blotted for himself before *D*. i. 134
Nor *w*. an Angel whom I lov'd a Man *E.A.* 70
And what young AMMON *w*., but *w*. in vain *E.S.* ii. 117
I've often *w*. that I had clear *I.H.* i. 11
But *w*. it Stilton for his sake *I.H.* ii. 168
I *w*. the man a dinner, and sat still *P.S.* 152
He saw, he *w*., and to the prize aspir'd *R.L.* ii. 30

Wishes.

And who but *w*. to invert the laws *E.M.* i. 129

Wishing.

Yet always *w*. to retreat *I.H.* ii. 127
And nobly *w*. Party-rage to cease *M.E.* iii. 149

Wit.

Thou whom the Nine with Plautus' *w*. inspire *A*. 7
Fruits of dull Heat, and Sooterkins of *W*. *D*. i. 126
Or, if to *W*. a coxcomb make pretence *D*. i. 177
Teach Oaths to Gamesters and to Nobles *W*. *D*. i. 204
This arch Absurd, that *w*. and fool delights *D*. i. 221
Thron'd on seven hills, the Antichrist of *w*. *D*. ii. 16
A fool so just a copy of a *w*. *D*. ii. 48
A *W*. it was, and call'd the phantom Moore *D*. ii. 50
Where as he fish'd her nether realms for *W*. *D*. ii. 101
No rag, no scrap, of all the beau, or *w*. *D*. ii. 119
Judge of all present, past, ur future *w*. *D*. ii. 376
Equal in *w*. and equally polite *D*. iii. 181
Lo! Ambrose Philips is preferr'd for *W*. *D*. iii. 326
And *W*. dreads Exile, Penalties, and Pains *D*. iv. 22
A *w*. with dunces, and a dunce with wits *D*. iv. 90
And (last and worst) with all the cant of *w*. *D*. iv. 99
A heavy Lord shall hang at ev'ry *W*. *D*. iv. 132
Bind rebel *W*., and double chain on chain *D*. iv. 158
There TALBOT sunk, and was a *W*. no more *D*. iv. 168
The critic Eye, that Microscope of *W*. *D*. iv. 233
As much Estate, and Principle, and *W*. *D*. iv. 325
True, he had *w*., to make the value rise *D*. iv. 377
W. shoots in vain its momentary fires *D*. iv. 633
And pleas'd to 'scape from Flattery to *W*. *E*. i. 12
With *w*. well-natur'd, and with books well-bred *E*. iv. 8

Have Humour, *W*., a native Ease and Grace *E*. iv. 27
Critics in *W*., or Life, are hard to please *E*. iv. 29
Their *W*. still sparkling, and their flames still warm *E*. iv. 72
Authors are partial to their *w*., 'tis true *E.C.* 17
In search of *w*. these lose their common sense *E.C.* 28
And wisely curb'd proud man's pretending *w*. *E.C.* 53
So vast is art, so narrow human *w*. *E.C.* 61
Some, to whom Heav'n in *w*. has been profuse *E.C.* 80
For *w*. and judgment often are at strife *E.C.* 82
Pride, where *w*. fails, steps in to our defence *E.C.* 209
A perfect Judge will read each work of *W*. *E.C.* 233
The gen'rous pleasure to be charm'd with *W*. *E.C.* 238
In *w*., as nature, what affects our hearts *E.C.* 243
As men of breeding, sometimes men of *w*. *E.C.* 259
One glaring Chaos, and wild heap of *w*. *E.C.* 292
True *W*. is Nature to advantage dress'd *E.C.* 297
So modest plainness sets off sprightly *w*. (*rep*.) *E.C.* 302
Thus *W*., like Faith, by each man is apply'd *E.C.* 396
Which not alone the southern *w*. sublimes *E.C.* 400
Regard not then if *W*. be old or new *E.C.* 406
How the *w*. brightens! how the style refines *E.C.* 421
And are but damn'd for having too much *w*. *E.C.* 429
What wonder modes in *W*. should take their turn *E.C.* 447
The current folly proves the ready *w*. *E.C.* 449
Parties in *W*. attend on those of State *E.C.* 456
For envy'd *W*., like Sol eclips'd, makes known *E.C.* 468
Unhappy *W*., like most mistaken things *E.C.* 494
What is this *W*., which must our cares employ *E.C.* 500
If *W*. so much from Ign'rance undergo *E.C.* 528
Tho' *w*. and art conspire to move your mind *E.C.* 531
Nay wits had pensions, and young Lords had *w*. *E.C.* 539
Such, without *w*., are Poets when they please *E.C.* 590
Who conquer'd Nature, should preside o'er *W*. *E.C.* 652
He, who supreme in judgment, as in *w*. *E.C.* 657
Fierce for the liberties of *w*., and bold *E.C.* 717
To him the *w*. of Greece and Rome was known *E.C.*727
With all the rash dexterity of *w*. (*rep*.) *E.M.* ii. 84
W., Spirit, Faculties, but make it worse *E.M.* ii. 146
What crops of *w*. and honesty appear *E.M.* ii. 285
Be Man the *W*. and Tyrant of the whole *E.M.* iii. 50
While still too wide or short is human *W*. *E.M.* iii. 90
Ere *W*. oblique had broke that steady light *E.M.*iii.231
A *W*.'s a feather, and a Chief's a rod *E.M.* iv. 247
And are, besides, too *moral* for a *W*. *E.S.* i. 4
Come Henley's Oratory, Osborne's *W*. *E.S.* i. 6*b*
The *W*. of Cheats, the Courage of a Whore *E.S.* i. 166
While Roman Spirit charms, and Attic *W*. *E.S.* ii. 84 85
Or P—ge pour'd forth the Torrent of his *W*. *E.S.* ii. 159
In *W*., a Man; Simplicity, a Child *Ep*. xi. 2
The sprightly *W*., the lively Eye *I.H.* i. 45
Tells me I have more Zeal than *W*. *I.H.* ii. 56 *s*
But show'd his Breeding and his *W*. *I.H.* ii. 172
Make but his Riches equal to his *W*. *I.H.* iii. 18
Faithless thro' Piety, and dup'd thro' *W*. *M.E.* i. 92
A Fool, with more of *W*. than half mankind *M.E.* i. 200
Less *W*. than Mimic, more a *W*. than wise *M.E.* ii. 48
She sins with Poets thro' pure Love of *W*. *M.E.* ii. 76
Flavia's a *W*., has too much sense to pray *M.E.* ii. 87
For true No-meaning puzzles more than *W*. *M.E.* ii. 114
So much the Fury still out-ran the *W*. *M.E.* ii. 127
The gen'rous God, who *W*. and Gold refines *M.E.* ii. 289
Yet was not Cotta void of *w*. or worth *M.E.* iii. 198
Whose table, *W*., or modest Merit share *M.E.* iii. 241
No *W*. to flatter left of all his store *M.E.* iii. 311
He pledg'd it to the knight; the knight had *w*. *M.E.*iii. 363
What late he call'd a Blessing, now was *W*. *M.E.*iii.377
But has the *w*. to make the most of little *Mi*. iii. 10
Seen with *W*., and Beauty seldom *Mi*. vi. 2
The mushrooms shew his *w*. was sudden *Mi*. xii. 11
Wisdom and *w*. in vain reclaim *O*. iii. 3
And curses *W*., and Poetry and Pope *P.S.* 26
Still to one Bishop Philips seem a *w*. *P.S.* 100
Yet *w*. ne'er tastes, and beauty ne'er enjoys *P.S.* 312
His *w*. all see-saw, between *that* and *this P.S.* 323
W. that can creep, and pride that licks the dust *P.S.*333
The damning critic, half approving *w*. *P.S.* 344
Yet soft by nature, more a dupe than *w*. *P.S.* 368
Parent of vapours and of female *w*. *R.L.* iv. 59
Sigh, while his Chloe blind to *W*. and Worth *S*. iv. 42
If Time improve our *W*. as well as Wine *S*. v. 49
I hold that *W*. a Classic, good in law *S*. v. 36
His Moral pleases, not his pointed *w*. *S*. v. 76

Of Shakespear's Nature, and of Cowley's *W. S.* v. 83
And call for pen and ink to show our *W. S.* v. 180
Let Ireland tell, how *W.* upheld her cause *S.* v. 221
And heals with Morals, what it hurts with *W. S.* vi. 262
W. grew polite, and Numbers learn'd to flow *S.* v. 266
How Van wants grace, who never wanted *w. S.* v. 289
There still remains to mortify a *W. S.* v. 304
How shall we fill a Library with *W. S.* v. 354
Repeat unask'd; lament, the *W.*'s too fine *S.* v. 366
But Kings in *W.* may want discerning Spirit *S.* v. 383
Oh but a *W.* can study in the streets *S.* vi. 98
And shook his head at Murray, as a *W. S.* vi. 132
Indeed, could wealth bestow or *w.* or merit *S.* vi. 226
He bought at thousands, what with better *w. S.* vi. 236
In pow'r, *w.*, figure, virtue, fortune plac'd *S.* vi. 302
Here a lean Bard, whose *w.* could never give *S.* vii. 13
Is he who makes his meal on others' *w. S.* vii. 30
His rank digestion makes it *w.* no more *S.* vii. 32
But turn a *w.*, and scribble verses too *S.* vii. 54
And "sweet Sir Fopling! you have so much *w.!*" (*rep.*) *S.* viii. 233
Howe'er what's now Apocrypha, my *W. S.* viii. 286
And, lest we err by W.*'s wild dancing light D.* i. 175
Or one vain *w.*, that might a hundred tire *E.C.* 45
Encourag'd thus, *W.* Titans brav'd the skies *E.C.* 552
And here restor'd *W.* fundamental laws *E.C.* 722
For *W.* false mirror held up Nature's light *E.M.* iv. 393
Blockheads with reason wicked w—s *abhor D.* iii. 175
W., who like owls, see only in the dark *D.* iii. 192
When Dulness smiling—" Thus revive the *W. D.* iv. 119
W. have short Memories, and Dunces none *D.* iv. 620
Ev'y rival *W.* did Voiture's death deplore *E.* v. 15
Some have at first for *W.*, then Poets past *E.C.* 36
Some neither can for *W.* nor Critics pass *E.C.* 38
But following *w.* from that intention stray'd *E.C.* 104
Great *w.* sometimes may gloriously offend *E.C.* 159
To teach vain *W.* a science little known *E.C.* 199
And but to mimic ancient *w.* at best *E.C.* 311
Contending *w.* become the sport of fools *E.C.* 517
Nay *w.* had pensions, and young Lords had wit *E.C.* 539
By *W.*, than Critics in as wrong Quotations *E.C.* 664
Judicious *W.* spread wide the Ridicule *E.S.* i. 61
Let Courtly *W.* to *W.* afford supply *E.S.* ii. 171
And to be kept in my right *w. I.H.* ii. 22
Turn then from *W.*; and look on Simo's Mate *M.E.* ii. 101
Not of the *W.* his foes, but Fools his friends *Mi.* iii. 14
Ev'n *Button's W.* to Worms shall turn *Mi.* iv. 39
While *W.* and Templars ev'ry sentence raise *P.S.* 211
I ne'er with *w.* or witlings pass'd my days *P.S.* 223
Received of *w.* an undistinguish'd race *P.S.* 237
What tho' no credit doubting *W.* may give *R.L.* i. 39
And *w.* take lodgings in the sound of Bow *R.L.* iv. 118
Weighs the Men's *w.* against the Lady's hair *R.L.* v. 72
At length the *w.* mount up, the hairs subside *R.L.* v. 74
There Hero's *w.* are kept in pond'rous vases *R.L.* v. 115
But for the *W.* of either Charles's days *S.* v. 107
Courts are too much for *w.* so weak as mine *S.* viii. 280

Witch
Did ever Proteus, Merlin, any *w. S.* iii. 152
In spite of w—es, *devils, dreams, and fire S.* vi. 313

Witchcraft
You give all royal *W.* to the Devil *S.* vi. 219

With, Within, Without.—*Passim.*

Withdraw
I get a whisper, and *w. I.H.* ii. 63 *s*
Blush, Grandeur, blush! proud Courts *w.* your blaze *M.E.* iii. 281

Withdrawn
The Guests *w.* had left the Treat *I.H.* ii. 196

Withdrew
W. his hand, and clos'd the pompous page *D.* iv. 114
Saw others happy, and with sighs *w. E.* v. 8
For, that sad moment, when the Sylphs *w. R.L.* iv. 11
So Rome's great founder to the heav'ns *w. R.L.* v. 125

Wither
Fade ev'ry blossom, *w.* ev'ry tree *A.* 33

Wither'd
Smote ev'ry Brain, and *w.* ev'ry Bay *D.* iv. 10

Starts from her trance, and trims her *w.* bays *E.C.* 698
Now nothing left, but *w.*, pale, and shrunk *Mi.* iii. 25
Their beauty *w.*, and their verdure lost *W.* 10

With'ring
Now warm in love, now *w.* in my bloom *E.A.* 37

Withers
Where wretch'd *W.*, Ward, and Gildon rest *D.* i. 296
Here, *W.* rest! thou bravest, gentlest mind *Ep.* ix. 1
W., adieu! yet not with thee remove *Ep.* ix. 7

Withheld
Foreseen by me, but ah! *w.* from mine *D.* iii. 276

Withhold
W. the pension, and set up the head *D.* iv. 96

Withstand
But, Madam, if the Fates *w.*, and you *E.* iv. 57
Prescient, the tides or tempests to *w. E.M.* iii. 101
No Pow'r, when Virtue claims it, can *w. E.S.* ii. 119
When Florio speaks what virgin could *w. R.L.* i. 97

Withstood
So long by watchful Ministers *w. M.E.* iii. 136

Witling
A Beau and *W.* perish'd in the throng *R.L.* v. 59
Those half-learn'd w—s, *num'rous in our isle E.C.* 40
I ne'er with wits or *w.* pass'd my days *P.S.* 223

Witness
Takes God to *w.* he affects your cause *S.* vii. 76
W., great Ammon! by whose horns I swore *D.* iv. 387

Witty
His time, the Muse, the *w.*, and the fair *E.* iv. 10
Handsome and *w.*, yet a Friend *Mi.* viii. 4
Whose buzz the *w.* and the fair annoys *P.S.* 311

Wizard
With that a *W.* OLD his Cup extends *D.* iv. 517
A *w.* told him in these words our fate *M.E.* iii. 134
And hence th' egregious *w.* shall foredoom *R.L.* v. 139
New w—s *rise! I see my Cibber there D.* iii. 266

Woe
Led thro' a sad variety of *w. E.A.* 36
Come! with thy looks, thy words, relieve my *w. E.A.* 119
Thro' dreary wastes, and weep each other's *w. E.A.* 242
Who fancy Bliss to Vice, to Virtue *W. E.* iv. 94
Lay Fortune-struck, a spectacle of *W. Mi.* ii. 3
Shrieks of *w. O.* i. 59
And wild Ambition well deserves its *w. P.C.* 12
Th' impending *w.* sat heavy on his breast *R.L.* ii. 54
On the rich quilt sinks with becoming *w. R.L.* ii. 35
For others' good, or melt at others' *w. U.L.* 46
And bear about the mockery of *w. U.L.* 57
Teach me to feel another's *W. U.P.* 37
That well-known name awakens all my w—s *E.A.* 30
Then, ages hence, when all my *w.* are o'er *E.A.* 345
The well-sung *w.* will soothe my pensive ghost *E.A.* 365
And helps, another creature's wants and *w. E.M.* iii. 52

Woful
What *w.* stuff this madrigal would be *E.C.* 418
If true, a *w.* likeness; and if lies *S.* v. 412

Wolves
W. gave thee suck, and savage Tigers fed *A.* 90
Silence, ye *W.!* while Ralph to Cynthia howls *D.* iii. 165
The lambs with *w.* shall graze the verdant mead *M.* 77
Loud as the *W.*, on Orcas' stormy steep *S.* v. 328

Wolsey
Sejanus, *W.*, hurt not honest Fleury *E.S.* i. 51
Call Verres, *W.*, any odious name *E.S.* ii. 137

Woman
Here rests a *W.*, good without pretence *Ep.* vi. 1
The Saint sustain'd it, but the *W.* died *Ep.* vi. 10
Europe a *W.*, Child, or Dotard rule *M.E.* i. 93
W. and Fool are two hard things to hit *M.E.* ii. 113
A *W.*'s seen in Private life alone *M.E.* ii. 200
But ev'ry *W.* is at heart a Rake *M.E.* ii. 216
W.'s at best a Contradiction still *M.E.* ii. 270
That *W.* is a Worm, we find *Mi.* iv. 9
I know a reasonable *W. Mi.* viii. 3

The *W*.'s deaf and does not hear *Mi*. viii. 12
Be this a W.'s *Fame : with this unblest* M.E. ii. 281
And once inclos'd in *W.* beauteous mould *R.L.* i. 48
Think not, when *W.* transient breath is fled *R.L.* i. 51
Scarecrow to boys, the breeding *w.* curse *S.* viii. 268
And value books, as w—en men, for Dress E.C. 306
Priests, Princes, *W.*, so dissemblers here *M.E.* i. 177
W. and fools must like him or he dies *M.E.* i. 183
Most *W.* have no Characters at all *M.E.* ii. 2
In *W.*, two almost divide the kind *M.E.* ii. 208
Oft, when the world imagine *w.* stray *R.L.* i. 91
Are, as when *w.*, wond'rous fond of place *R.L.* iii. 36
The other slights for *w.*, sports, and wines *S.* vi. 272

Womankind.
Severe to all, but most to *W. E.* iv. 32
Is gentle love, and charms all *w. E.M.* ii. 190
Scarce once herself, by turns all *W. M.E.* ii. 116

Won.
The race by vigour, not by vaunts is *w. D.* ii. 59
But when by Man's audacious labour *w. M.E.* iii. 11
At *Corticelli's* he the Raffle *w. Mi.* ix. 39
The *Knave w. Sonica*, which I had chose *Mi.* ix. 51
This hand, which *w.* it, shall for ever wear *R.L.* iv. 138
And Heav'n is *w.* by Violence of Song *S.* v. 240

Wonder.
And saints with *w.* heard the vows I made *E.A.* 114
The world's just *w.*, and ev'n thine, O Rome *E.C.* 248
What *w.* modes in Wit should take their turn *E.C.* 447
Alas what *w.!* Man's superior part *E.M.* ii. 39
Have I, in silent *w.*, seen such things *E.S.* i. 109
Wharton, the scorn and *w.* of our days *M.E.* i. 180
Dryden alone (what *w.!*) came not nigh *P.S.* 245
What *w.* then, fair nymph, thy hairs should feel *R.L.* iii. 177
W. of Kings! like whom, to mortal eyes *S.* v. 29
No *w.* then, when all was love and sport *S.* v. 151
No *w.* some folks bow, and think them Kings *S.* viii. 211
Or hush'd with *w.*, hearken from the sprays *W.* 56
What *w.* then, a beast or subject slain *W.F.* 57
Then thus the w—s of the deep declares D. ii. 330
Behold the *w.* of th' oblivious Lake *D.* iii. 44
"What pow'r," he cries, "what pow'r these *w.* wrought?" *D.* iii. 250
And are these *w.*, Son, to the unknown (*rep.*) *D.* iii. 273
They please as beauties, here as *w.* strike *M.E.* i. 144
Erect new *w.*, and the old repair *M.E.* iv. 192
Imperial *w.* rais'd on Nations spoil'd *M.E.* v. 5
And calls forth all the *w.* of her face *R.L.* i. 142
To w. at their Maker, not to serve D. iv. 458
I *w.* what some people mean *J.H.* ii. 104 *s*
A work to *w.* at—perhaps a STOWE *M.E.* iv. 70
But *w.* how the devil they got there *P.S.* 172
And *w.* with a foolish face of praise *P.S.* 212

Wonder'd.
And foes to virtue *w.* how they wept *P.C.* 8
And Nations *w.* while they dropp'd the sword *S.* v. 399
The forests *w.* at th' unusual grain *W.F.* 89

Wond'ring.
W. he gaz'd: When lo! a Sage appears *D.* iii. 35
He from the *w.* furrow call'd the food *E.M.* iii. 219
Tho' *w.* Senates hung on all he spoke *M.E.* i. 184
The *w.* forests soon shall dance again *Su.* 82
But see! where Daphne *w.* mounts on high *W.* 69

Wond'rous.
And learn, my sons, the *w.* pow'r of Noise *D.* ii. 222
Each with some *w.* gift approach'd the Pow'r *D.* iv. 399
Go, *w.* creature! mount where Science guides *E.M.* ii. 19
Thought *w.* honest, tho' of mean degree *Mi.* iii. 19
Are, as when women, *w.* fond of place *R.L.* iii. 36
A *w.* Bag she binds with both her hands *R.L.* iv. 81
Or Sloane or Woodward's *w.* shelves contain *S.* viii. 30
A *w.* Tree that sacred Monarchs bears *Sp.* 86

Wonders.
And no man *w.* he's not stung by Pug *S.* i. 88

Wont.
Such was her *w.* at early dawn to drop *D.* ii. 71
The dagger w. to pierce the Tyrant's breast D. iv. 38
Where Bentley late tempestuous *w.* to sport *D.* iv. 201

Woo.
And *w.* in language of the Pleas and Bench *S.* vii. 60
Reap their own fruits, and *w.* their sable loves *W.F.* 410

Wood.
One clasp'd in *w.*, and one in strong cow-hide *D.* i. 150
To that which warbles thro' the vernal *w. E.M.* i. 216
Who taught the nations of the field and *w. E.M.* iii. 99
Not Man alone, but all that roam the *w. E.M.* iii. 119
In the same temple, the resounding *w. E.M.* iii. 155
Of Land, set out to plant a *W. I.H.* ii. 6 *s*
The *W.* supports the Plain, the parts unite *M.E.* iv. 8 *t*
For all his Lordship knows, but they are *W. M.E.* iv. 138
Buy ev'ry stick of *w.* that lends them heat *S.* vi. 242
The trembling trees, in ev'ry plain and *w. W.* 63
Or wand'ring thoughtful in the silent *w. W.F.* 249
The winds to breathe, the waving w—s to move A. 41
Farewell, ye *w.!* adieu the light of day *A.* 94
Whales sport in *w.*, and Dolphins in the skies *D.* iii. 246
Love-whisp'ring *w.*, and lute-resounding waves *D.* iv. 306
And leave you in lone *w.*, or empty walls *E.* v. 40
And breathes a browner horror on the *w. E.A.* 170
Some safer world in depth of *w.* embrac'd *M.E.* i. 105
Man cares for all: to birds he gives his *w. E.M.* iii. 57
The *w.* recede around the naked seat *M.E.* iii. 209
Who hung with *w.* yon mountain's sultry brow *M.E.* iii. 253
Joins willing *w.*, and varies shades from shades *M.E.* iv. 62
Thro' his young *W.* how pleas'd Sabinus stray'd *M.E.* iv. 89
Huge Theatres that now unpeopled *W. M.E.* v. 7
Eurydice the *w. O.* i. 115
The walls, the *w.*, and long canals reply *R.L.* iii. 100
Slopes at its foot, the *w.* its sides embrace *S.* iii. 147
Those ancient *w.*, that shaded all the ground *S.* vii. 110
The *w.* shall answer, and their echo ring *Su.* 16
In *w.* bright Venus with Adonis stray'd *Su.* 61
The lonely lords of empty wilds and *w. W.* 48
Now range the hills, the gameful *w.* beset *W.F.* 95
The *w.* and fields their pleasing toils deny *W.F.* 120
The wat'ry landscape of the pendant *w. W.F.* 213
With joyful pride survey'st our lofty *w. W.F.* 220
Thy trees, fair Windsor! now shall leave their *w. W.F.* 385

Woodbine.
Now rise, and haste to yonder *w.* bow'rs *Sp.* 97

Woodcocks.
And lonely *w.* haunt the wat'ry glade *W.F.* 128

Wooden.
Who holds Dragoons and *w.* shoes in scorn *Mi.* ii. 20

Woodland.
Here hills and vales, the *w.* and the plain *W.F.* 11

Woodward.
Or Sloane or *W.'s* wond'rous shelves contain *S.* viii. 30
As one of *W.* patients, sick, and sore *S.* viii. 152

Woo'd.
Who could not win the mistress, *w.* the maid *E.C.* 105

Wool.
Next goes his *W.*—to clothe our valiant bands *M.E.* i. 211

Woollen.
Odious! in *w.!* 'twould a Saint provoke *M.E.* i. 246

Woolston.
In Toland's, Tindal's, and in *W.'s* days *D.* iii. 213

Word.
Here one poor *w.* an hundred clenches makes *D.* i. 63
And dies, when Dulness gives her Page the *w. D.* iv. 30
Or, impious, preach his *w.* without a call *D.* iv. 94
Light dies before thy uncreating *w. D.* iv. 654
But Appius reddens at each *w.* you speak *E.C.* 585
Just of thy *W.*, in ev'ry thought sincere *Ep.* vii. 5
'Tis true, my Lord, I gave my *w. I.H.* i. 1
A *w.*, pray, in your Honour's ear *I.H.* i. 42
And, Mr. Dean, one *w.* from you *I.H.* i. 82 *s*
But let it (in a *w.*) be said *I.H.* ii. 193
But fix'd his *w.*, his saving pow'r remains *M.* 107

WORE—WORLD.

You hold the *w.*, from Jove to Momus giv'n *M.E.* iii. 2
His *w.* would pass for more than he was worth *M.E.* iii. 344
"Live like yourself," was soon my Lady's *w. M.E.* iii. 359
And gave the harmless fellow a good *w. Mi.* iii. 6
Tho' Honour is the *w.* with Men below *R.L.* i. 78
At ev'ry *w.* a reputation dies *R.L.* iii. 16
The world's good *w.* is better than a song *S,* ii. 102
For Snug's the *w.;* my dear I we'll live in town *S.* iii. 147
Upon my *w.,* you must be rich indeed *S.* iv. 90
To do the Honours, and to give the *W. S.* iv. 100
Whose *W.* is Truth, as sacred and rever'd *S.* v. 298
We Poets are (upon a Poet's *w.*) *S.* v. 358
How barb'rous rage subsided at your *w. S.* v. 398
Take him with all his virtues, on my *w. S.* vi. 13
Their own strict Judges, not a *w.* they spare *S.* vi. 159
With mystic *w—s, the sacred Opium shed D.* i. 288
And empty *w.* she gave, and sounding strain *D.* ii. 45
Soft creeping, *w.* on *w.,* the sense compose *D.* ii. 389
Who sate the nearest, by the *w.* o'ercome *D.* ii. 402
Yet oh, my sons, a father's *w.* attend *D.* iii. 213
Then thus. "Since man from beast by *W.* is known (rep.) *D.* iv. 149
And keep them in the pale of *W.* till death *D.* iv. 160
Give law to *W.,* or war with *W.* alone *D.* iv. 178
'Tis true, on *W.* is still our whole debate *D.* iv. 219
But wherefore waste I *w.?* I see advance *D.* iv. 271
First slave to *W.,* then vassal to a Name *D.* iv. 501
Then gives a smacking buss, and cries, "No *w.!" E.* v. 26
W. are like Leaves; and where they most abound *E.C.* 309
A vile conceit in pompous *w.* express'd *E.C.* 320
Some by old *w.* to fame have made pretence *E.C.* 324
In *w.,* as fashions, the same rule will hold *E.C.* 333
And ten low *w.* oft creep in one dull line *E.C.* 347
The line too labours, and the *w.* move slow *E.C.* 371
Lie in three *w.,* Health, Peace, and Competence *E.M.* iv. 80
Why *w.* so flowing, thoughts so free *I.H.* iii. 39
Were the last *w.* that poor Narcissa spoke *M.E.* i. 247
A wizard told him in these *w.* our fate *M.E.* iii. 234
Hard *w.* or hanging, if your Judge be Page *S.* i. 82
Know there are *W.,* and Spells, which can control *S.* iii. 57
So take it in the very *w.* of Creech *S.* iv. 4
Grac'd as thou art, with all the Pow'r of *W. S.* iv. 48
Thinks that but *w.,* and this but brick and stones *S.* iv. 66
Command old *w.* that have long slept, to wake (rep.) *S.* vi. 167
Those *w.,* that would against them clear the doubt *S.* vii. 104
Nor sly informer watch these *w.* to draw *S.* vii. 127
"But the best *w.?"* "O Sir, the *Dictionary." S.* viii. 69
Each W.-catcher, that lives on syllables P.S. 166

Wore.

Known by the band and suit which Settle *w. D.* iii. 37
What the fine gentleman *w.* yesterday *E.C.* 330
On her white breast a sparkling Cross she *w. R.L.* ii. 7
Her great, grant, grandsire *w.* about his head *R.L.* v. 90
Which long she *w.,* and now Belinda wears *R.L.* v. 96
Ah what avail the beauties nature *w. W.* 35

Work.

Call'd to this *w.* by Dulness, Jove, and Fate *D.* i. 4
The op'ning clouds disclose each *w.* by turns *D.* i. 249
Instructive *w.!* whose wry-mouth'd portraiture *D.* ii. 145
Had reach'd the *W.,* the All that mortal can *D.* iv. 176
This small well-polish'd Gem, the *w.* of years *E.* iii. 40
A *w.* t' outlast immortal Rome design'd *E.C.* 131
And rules as strict his labour'd *w.* confine *E.C.* 177
A perfect Judge will read each *w.* of Wit *E.C.* 233
In ev'ry *w.* regard the writer's End *E.C.* 255
Pleas'd with a *w.* where nothing's just or fit *E.C.* 291
In grave Quintilian's copious *w.* we unite *E.C.* 669
But when his own great *w.* is but begun *E.M.* ii. 41
Yet, mix'd and soften'd, in his *w.* unite *E.M.* ii. 112
The worker from the *w.* distinct was known *E.M.* iii. 229
An honest Man's the noblest *w.* of God *E.M.* iv. 248
To Virtue's *w.* provoke the tardy Hall *E.S.* ii. 218
Its last best *w.,* but forms a softer Man *M.E.* ii. 272

The Tempter saw his time; the *w.* he ply'd *M.E.* iii. 369
A *W.* to wonder at, perhaps a Stowe *M.E.* iv. 70
The creature's at his dirty *w.* again *P.S.* 29
Verse cheers their leisure, Verse assists their *w. S.* v. 235
But fill their purse, our Poet's is done *S.* v. 294
Be call'd to Court to plan some *w.* divine *S.* v. 374
Four figures rising from the *w.* appear *Sp.* 37
Founds the whole pile, of all his w—s the base D. i. 160
Heav'n had decreed these *w.* a longer date *D.* i. 196
W. damn'd, or to be damn'd! (your Father's fault) *D.* i. 226
Here to her Chosen all her *w.* she shews *D.* i. 273
Fair as before her *w.* she stands confess'd *D.* ii. 139
If there be man, who o'er such *w.* can wake *D.* ii. 372
How oft our slowly-growing *w* impart *E.* iii. 19
New graces yearly like thy *w.* display *E.* iii. 65
In human *w.* tho' labour'd on with pain *E.A.* 53
Be Homer's *w.* your study and delight *E.C.* 124
For *w.* may have more wit than does 'em good *E.C.* 303
Some judge of author's names, not *w.,* and then *E.C.* 412
With him, most authors steal their *w.,* or buy *E.C.* 618
His Precepts teach but what his *w.* inspire *E.C.* 660
Here subterranean *w.,* and cities see *E.M.* iii. 181
Her *w.;* and dying, fears herself may die *Ep.* viii. 8
These are Imperial *W.,* and worthy Kings *M.E.* iv. 204
Imputes to me and my damn'd *w.* the cause *P.S.* 24
Sir, let me see you and your *w.* no more *P.S.* 68
Steel could the *w.* of mortal pride confound *R.L.* iii. 175
When *w.* are censur'd, not as bad but new *S.* v. 116
These as good *w.,* 'tis true, we all allow (rep.) *S.* vii. 121
And Temples rise, the beauteous *w.* of Peace *W.F.* 378
Nor could a BARROW *w. on ev'ry block D.* iv. 245
Plants as you plant, and as you *w.,* designs *M.E.* iv. 64
Go *w.,* hunt, exercise! (he thus began) *S.* ii. 11

Work'd.

Has God, thou fool! *w.* solely for thy good *E.M.* iii. 27

Worker.

The *w.* from the work distinct was known *E.M.* iii. 229

Working.

Wild Nature's vigor *w.* at the root *E.M.* ii. 184
See plastic Nature *w.* to this end *E.M.* iii. 9

Workmanship.

The Metal, and the *W.* divine *Mi.* ix. 36

Works.

Pity! the charm *w.* only in our wall *D.* iv. 165
W. without show, and without pomp presides *E.C.* 75
Each *w.* its end, to move or govern all *E.M.* ii. 56
Men prove with child, as pow'rful fancy *w. R.L.* iv. 53
Long, as to him who *w.* for debt, the day *S.* iii. 35

World.

Forsake mankind, and all the *w.*—but love *A.* 88
Rush to the *w.,* impatient for the day *D.* iii. 30
And all the western *w.* believe and sleep *D.* iii. 100
Thence a new *w.* to Nature's laws unknown *D.* iii. 241
Of dull and venal a new *W.* to mould *D.* iv. 15
For him thou oft hast bid the *W.* attend *E.* i. 71
Still to charm those who charm the *w.* beside *E.* iv. 80
Thus from the *w.,* fair Zephalinda flew *E.* v. 7
When, warm in youth, I bade the *w.* farewell *E.A.* 110
From the false *w.* in early youth they fled *E.A.* 131
The *w.* forgetting; by the *w.* forgot *E.A.* 208
And taught the *w.* with reason to admire *E.C.* 101
Where a new *w.* leaps out at his command *E.C.* 486
Whom, when they praise, the *w.* believes no more *E.C.* 594
Thence Arts o'er all the northern *w.* advance *E.C.* 711
And now a bubble burst, and now a *w. E.M.* i. 90
Some safer *w.* in depth of woods embrac'd *E.M.* i. 103
Being on Being wreck'd, and *w.* on *w. E.M.* i. 254
The glory, jest, and riddle of the *w. E.M.* ii. 18
Look round our *W.;* behold the chain of Love *E.M.* iii. 7
T' invert the *w.,* and counter-work its Cause *E.M.* iii. 244
With Heav'n's own thunders shook the *w.* below *E.M.* iii. 267
In Faith and Hope the *w.* will disagree *E.M.* iii. 307
But still this *w.*—(so fitted for the knave) *E.M.* iv. 131
WHATEVER IS, IS RIGHT.—This *w.,* 'tis true *E.M.* iv. 15
Sets half the *w.,* God knows, against the rest *E.S.* i. 58

WORLDLY—WORTHLESS. 361

In golden Chains the willing *W*. she draws *E.S* i. 147
Sweet to the *W*., and grateful to the Skies *E.S*. ii. 245
Who knew no wish but what the *w*. might hear *Ep*. vii. 6
What I desire the *w*. should know *I.H*. ii. 62 s
Peace o'er the *W*. her olive wand extend *M*. 19
No sigh, no murmur, the wide *w*. shall hear *M*. 45
How Trade increases and the *W*. goes well *M.E*. i. 159
Full sixty years the *W*. has been her Trade *M.E*. ii. 123
See how the *W*. its Veterans rewards *M.E*. ii. 243
Kept Dross for Duchesses, the *w*. shall know it *M.E.* ii. 291
Since then, my Lord, on such a *W*. we fall *M.E.* iii. 77
Not with those Toys the female *w*. admire *Mi*. v. 3
When all the *W*. conspires to praise her *Mi*. viii. 31
Steal from the *w*., and not a stone *O*. iv. 19
The *w*. recedes ; it disappears *O*. v. 13
The *w*. had wanted many an idle song *P.S*. 28
Thou stand'st unshook amidst a bursting *w*. *P.S*. 88
From these the *w*. will judge of men and books *P.S*. 145
Oft, when the *w*. imagine women stray *R.L*. i. 91
The various off'rings of the *w*. appear *R.L*. i. 130
Belinda smil'd, and all the *w*. was gay *R.L*. ii. 52
That single act gives half the *w*. the spleen *R.L*. iv. 78
Shall walk the *W*., in credit, to his grave *S*. i. 120
The *W*. beside may murmur or commend (*rep*.) *S*. i. 122
Mix with the *W*., and battle for the State *S*. iii. 28
But to the *w*., no bugbear is so great *S*. iii. 67
The balanc'd *W*., and open all the Main *S*. v. 2
Or Laws establish'd, and the *w*. reform'd *S*. v. 12
To thee, the *W*. its present homage pays *S*. v. 23
Should Ripley venture, all the *w*. would smile *S*. v. 186
Peace stole her wing, and wrapt the *w*. in sleep *S*. v. 401
My only son, I'd have him see the *w*. *S*. vi. 6
And carrying with you all the *w*. can boast *Sp*. 9
Cold is that breast which warm'd the *w*. before *U.L*. 33
Daphne, farewell, and all the *w*. adieu *W*. 92
But, as the *w*., harmoniously confus'd *W.F*. 14
She said ! the *w*. obey'd, and all was Peace *W.F*. 328
And the new *w*. launch forth to seek the old *W.F*. 402
Should at my feet the w.'s great master fall (*rep*.) *E.A.* 85
The *w*. just wonder, and ev'n thine, O Rome *E.C*. 248
And the *w*. victor stood subdu'd by sound *E.C*. 381
Such is the *W*. great harmony, that springs *E.M.*iii.295
Why risk the *W*. great empire for a Punk *M.E*. i. 131
Wise Peter saw the *W*. respect for Gold *M.E*. iii. 123
The *W*. great Victor pass'd unheeded by *P.C*. 34
The *w*. good word is better than a song *S*. ii. 102
The *W*. great Oracle in times to come *W.F*. 382
A matchless youth ! his nod these w—s controls D. iii. 255
And *w*. applaud that must not yet be found *E.C.* 194
Thro' *w*. unnumber'd tho' the God be known *E.M.* i. 21
See *w*. on *w*. compose one universe *E M*. i. 24
Heav'ns not his own, and *w*. unknown before *E.M.* iii. 106
Grasp the whole *w*. of Reason, Light, and Sense *E.M.* iv. 357
Hereditary Realms and *W*. of Gold *M.E*. iii. 130
Say, for such worth are other *w*. prepar'd *M.E*. iii. 335
Survey both *w*., intrepid and entire *S*. vi. 312
When thousand *w*. are round *U.P*. 24
O'er figur'd *w*. now travels with thine eye *W.F*. 246

Worldly.

And *W*. crying coals from street to street *M.E*. iii. 62
All W.'s *hens, nay partridge, sold to town S*. vi. 234

Worm.

Vile *w*.!—Oh Madness ! Pride ! Impiety ! *E.M*. i. 258
Learn of the mole to plough, the *w*. to weave *E.M*. iii. 176
Man is a very *W*. by birth *Mi*. iv. 5
That Woman is a *W*., we find *Mi*. iv. 9
That ancient *W*. the Devil *Mi*. iv. 12
First from a *W*. they take their Rise (*rep*.) *Mi*. iv. 19
That Statesmen have the *W*. is seen *Mi*. iv. 25
Their Conscience is a *W*. within *Mi*. iv. 27
The *W*. that never dies *Mi*. iv. 32
All Humankind are W—s Mi. iv. 4
Thus *W*. suit all Conditions *Mi*. iv. 22
Since *W*. shall eat ev'n thee *Mi*. iv. 36
Ev'n Button's Wits to *W*. shall turn *Mi*. iv. 39
Of hairs, or straws, or dirt, or grubs, or *w*. *P.S*. 170

Wormius.

On parchment scraps y-fed, and *W*. hight *D*. iii. 188

Wormwood.

The Doctor's *W*. style, the Hash of tongues *S*. viii. 52

Worn.

The garlands fade, the vows are *w*. away *A*. 69
As flow'ry bands in wantonness are *w*. *E*. iv. 65
Ye rugged rocks ! which holy knees have *w*. *E.A*. 19
If Faith itself has diff'rent dresses *w*. *E.C*. 446
W. out in public, weary ev'ry eye *M.E*. ii. 229

Worse.

There are who judge still *w*. than he can write *E.C*. 35
Wit, Spirit, Faculties, but make it *w*. *E.M*, ii. 146
But future views of better, or of *w*. *E.M*. iv. 72
But these less taste them, as they *w*. obtain *E M*. iv. 84
And there I'll die, no *w*. nor better *I.H*. i. 80
But an Inferior not dependant ? *w*. *M.E*. ii. 136
Resolve me, Reason, which of these is *w*. *M.E*. iii. 319
But foes like these—One Flatt'rer's *w*. than all *P.S*. 104
Alas ! 'tis ten times *w*. when they repent *P.S*. 108
You could not do a *w*. thing for your life *S*. i. 15
Surpris'd at better, or surpris'd at *w*. *S*. iv. 23
Believe me, many a German Prince is *w*. *S*. iv. 83
Nay *w*., to ask for Verse at such a time *S*. vi. 31
You only make the matter *w*. and *w*. *S*. viii. 121
Has yet a strange ambition to look *w*. *S*. viii. 269

Worship.

Against your *w*. when had S—k writ *E.S*. ii. 158
To *w*. *like his Fathers was his care S*. v. 165

Worshipful.

How pale each *W*. and Rev'rend guest *S*. ii. 75

Worshipper.

Not Fortune's *w*., nor Fashion's fool *P.S*. 334

Worsley.

And other Beauties envy *W*.'s eyes *E*. iii. 60

Worst.

And (last and *w*.) with all the cant of wit *D*. iv. 99
But the last Tyrant ever proves the *w*. *E*. iv. 40
Of all this servile herd the *w*. is he *E.C*. 414
But still the *w*. with most regret commend *E.C*. 518
For the *w*. avarice is that of sense *E.C*. 579
In the *w*. ina's *w*. room, with mat half-hung *M.E*. iii. 299
The *w*. of Madmen is a Saint run mad *S*. iv. 27
Adieu—if this advice appear the *w*. *S*. iv. 130
Chaucer's *w*. ribaldry is learn'd by rote *S*. v. 37

Worsted.

The very *w*. still look'd black and blue *D*. ii. 150

Worth.

Patrons, who sneak from living *w*. to dead *D*. iv. 95
A Soul as full of *W*., as void of Pride *E*. ii. 1
Whatever nature has in *w*. deny'd *E.C*. 205
W. makes the Man, the want of it the fellow *E.M*. iv. 203
But by your fathers' *w*. if yours you rate *E.M*. iv. 209
While Truth, *W*., Wisdom, daily they decry *E.S*. i. 169
Oh born to Arms ! O *W*. in Youth approv'd *Ep*. ix. 3
For their own *W*., or our own Ends *I.H*. ii. 150
Yet was not Cotta void of wit or *w*. *M.E*. iii. 178
To *W*. or Waat well-weigh'd, be Bounty giv'n *M.E*. iii. 229
Say, for such *w*. are other worlds prepar'd *M.E*. iii. 335
Britons, attend : be *w*. like this approv'd *P.C*. 37
Insults fall'n *w*., or Beauty in distress *P.S*. 288
Barnard, thou art a Cit, with all thy *w*. *S*. iii. 89
Sigh, while thy Chloe blind to Wit and *W*. *S*. iv. 42
A Man of wealth is dubb'd a Man of *w*. *S*. iv. 81
Foes to all living *w*. except your own *S*. v. 33
Proud Vice to brand, and injur'd *W*. adorn *S*. v. 227
*His word would pass for more than he was w. M.E.*iii. 344
And tho' no Science, fully *w*. the seven *M.E*. iv. 44
Who, if they have not, think not *w*. their care *S*. vii. 267
Poor, and disarm'd, and hardly *w*. your hate *S*. vi. 12

Worthier.

Bid Temples, *w*. of the God, ascend *M.E*. iv. 198

Worthless.

I scarce can think him such a *w*. thing *S*. v. 209
A senseless, *w*., and unhonour'd crowd *S*. v. 306

Worthy.
Well-purg'd, and w. Settle, Banks, and Broome *D.* i. 146
A shaggy Tap'stry, w. to be spread *D.* ii. 143
O w. thou of Ægypt's wise abodes *D.* iii. 207
W. to fill Pythagoras's place *D.* iv. 572
Oh fool! to think God hates the w. mind *E.M.* iv. 189
The w. Youth shall ne'er be in a rage *E.S.* i. 48
But does the Court a w. Man remove *E.S.* ii. 74
Mine, as a Friend to ev'ry w. mind *E.S.* ii. 203
But that the W. and the Good shall say *Ep.* xi. 11
These are Imperial Works, and w. Kings *M.E.* iv. 204
That tends to make one w. man my foe *P.S.* 284
How dar'st thou let one w. man be poor *S.* ii. 118
White gloves, and linen w. Lady Mary *S.* iii. 164
Or what remain'd, so w. to be read *S.* v. 137
A w. member, no small fool, a Lord *S.* vi. 185

Wot.
What is't to me (a passenger God w.) *S.* vi. 296

Would, Wouldst.—*Passim.*

Wound.
And Hell's grim Tyrant feel th' eternal w. *M.* 48
Like Gods they fight, nor dread a mortal w. *R.L.* v. 44
Short is his joy; he feels the fiery w. *W.F.* 113
Pours balm into the bleeding lover's w—s *O.* i. 29
W., Charms, and Ardors were no sooner read *R.L.* i. 119
Heav'ns, what new w.! and how her old have bled *W.F.* 322
This taste the honey, and not w. the flow'r *E.M.* ii. 90
Willing to w., and yet afraid to strike *P.S.* 203
The fewer still you name, you w. the more *S.* i. 43
The Poets learn'd to please, and not to w. *S.* v. 258

Wounded.
That, like a w. snake, drags its slow length along *E.C.* 357
Bleeds in the Forest like a w. hart *W.F.* 84

Wounds.
Yet absent, w. an honest author's fame *P.S.* 292
And with her dart the flying deer she w. *W.F.* 180

Wrangle.
And all the question (w. ne'er so long) *E.M.* i. 49

Wrangling.
A Scorn for w., yet a Zeal for Truth *Ep.* ii. 8

Wrap.
Not w. up Oranges, to pelt your sire *D.* i. 236
Receive, and w. me in eternal rest *E.A.* 302
W. my cold limbs, and shade my lifeless face *M.E.* i. 249
To w. me in the universal shade *S.* i. 96

Wraps.
W. in her veil, and frees from sense of shame *D.* iv. 336

Wrapt.
W. up in Self, a God without a Thought *D.* iv. 485
Peace stole her wing, and w. the world in sleep *S.* v. 401
But what, or where, the fates have w. in night *R.L.* ii. 104
W. in a gown, for sickness or for show *R.L.* iv. 36
There w. in clouds the blueish hills ascend *W.F.* 24

Wrath.
Or which must end me, a Fool's w. or love *P.S.* 30
To read in Greek the w. of Peleus' son *S.* ii. 53

Wreath.
Why rail they then, if but a W. of mine *E.S.* ii. 138
Not Waller's W. can hide the Nation's Scar *E.S.* ii. 230
That adds this w. of Ivy to thy Bays *Su.* 10
Accept the w. which you deserve alone *Su.* 57
Twin'd with the w—s Parnassian laurels yield *E.M.* iv. 11
See Nature hastes her earliest w. to bring *M.* 23
With golden crowns and w. of heav'nly flow'rs *R.L.* i. 34
Let w. of Triumph now my temples twine *R.L.* iii. 161
On Cooper's Hill eternal w. shall grow *W.F.* 265

Wreathe.
When Dukes and Butchers join to w. my crown *D.* i. 223

Wreath'd.
For this with tort'ring irons w. around *R.L.* iv. 100

Wreck'd.
Being on Being w., and world on world *E.M.* i. 254

Wren.
While W. with sorrow to the grave descends *D.* iii. 329

Wretch.
And lo the w.! whose vile, whose insect lust *D.* iv. 415
Ah w.! believ'd the spouse of God in vain *E.A.* 177
Wise W.! with Pleasures too refin'd to please *M.E.* ii. 95
The w. he starves"—and piously denies *M.E.* iii. 104
The W. that trusts them, or the Rogue that cheats *M.E.* iii. 238
The w., who living sav'd a candle's end *M.E.* iii. 292
Ungrateful w., with mimic airs grown pert *Mi.* ix. 65
W. that I was, how often have I swore *Mi.* ix. 67
Or, as Ixion fix'd, the w. shall feel *R.L.* ii. 133
Satire be kind, and let the w. alone *S.* iii. 135
Man! and for ever! W.! what would'st thou have *S.* vi. 252
Curs'd be the w., so venial and so vain *S.* vii. 63
Heav'n first taught letters for some w.'s aid *E.A.* 51
And w—es hang that jurymen may dine *R.L.* iii. 22

Wretched.
Where w. Withers, Ward, and Gildon rest *D.* i. 296
A vain, unquiet, glitt'ring, w. Thing *E.* iv. 54
We, w. subjects, tho' to lawful sway *E.M.* ii. 149
Mark by what w. steps their glory grows *M.E.* iv. 291
Arraign no mightier Thief than w. Wild *E.S.* ii. 39
And w. Shylock, spite of Shylock's Wife *M.E.* ii. 94
Thy life more w., Cutler, was confess'd *M.E.* iii. 321
Seiz'd and tied down to judge, how w. ! *P.S.* 33
A w. Sylph too fondly interpos'd *R.L.* iii. 150
" O w. maid!" she spread her hands and cry'd (*rep.*) *R.L.* iv. 95
With w. Av'rice, or as w. Love *S.* iii, 56
W. indeed! but far more w. yet *S.* vii. 29
Ah w. shepherd, what avails thy art *Su.* 33

Wrinkled.
Her w. form in black and white array'd *R.L.* iv. 28

Writ.
In time to come, may pass for holy w. *S.* viii. 287
Of ancient w. unlocks the learned store *W.F.* 247
In eldest time, ere mortals w. or read *D.* i. 9
That once so flutter'd, and that once so w. *D.* ii. 120
On Poets' Tombs see Benson's titles w. *D.* iii. 325
With the same spirit that its author w. *E.C.* 234
Jilts rul'd the state, and statesmen farces w. *E.C.* 538
Might boldly censure, as he boldly w. *E.C.* 658
You grow correct, that once with Rapture w. *E.S.* i. 4
Against your worship when had S—k w. *E.S.* ii. 158
W. not, and Chartres scarce could write or read *E.S.* ii. 186
W. underneath the Country signs *I.H.* ii. 92 e
There he stopp'd short, nor since has w. a tittle *Mi.* iii. 9
How Beaumont's judgment check'd what Fletcher w. *S.* v. 84
And ev'ry flow'ry Courtier w. Romance *S.* v. 146
What pert, low Dialogue has Farquhar w. *S.* v. 288
As Eusden, Philips, Settle w. of Kings *S.* v. 417

Write.
Shall this a *Pasquin*, that a *Grumbler* w. *D.* iii. 182
And w. about it, Goddess, and about it *D.* iv. 252
Few w. to those, and none can live to these *E.* iv. 30
I gave it you to w. again *E.* vi. 16
You'd w. as smooth again on glass *E.* vi. 21
O w. it not my hand—the name appears *E.A.* 13
Yet w., oh w. me all, that I may join *E.A.* 41
Ah, come not, w. not, think not once of me *E.A.* 291
These born to judge, as well as those to w. *E.C.* 14
Each burns alike, who can, or cannot w. *E.C.* 30
There are who judge still worse than he can w. *E.C.* 35
W. dull receipts how poems may be made *E.C.* 115
For who can rail so long as they can w. *E.C.* 599
Garth did not w. his own Dispensary *E.C.* 619
They judge with fury, but they w. with fle'me *E.C.* 662
Writ not, and Chartres scarce could w. or read *E.S.* ii. 186
But Pens can forge, my Friend, that cannot w. *E.S.* ii. 188

And *w.* next winter more *Essays on Man E.S.* ii. 255
'Tis well—but Artists ! who can paint or *w. M.E.* ii. 181
If foes, they *w.*, if friends, they read me dead *P.S.* 32
He'll *w.* a *Journal*, or he'll turn Divine *P.S.* 54
I too could *w.*, and I am twice as tall *P.S.* 103
Why did I *w.!* what sin to me unknown *P.S.* 125
And knowing *Walsh*, would tell me I could *w. P.S.* 136
And borne to *w.*, converse, and live with ease *P.S.* 196
I sought no homage from the Race that *w. P.S.* 219
Heav'ns ! was I born for nothing but to *w. P.S.* 272
And *w.* whate'er he pleas'd, except his Will *P.S.* 379
I'd *w.* no more—Not *w.?* but then I think *S.* i. 11
Fools rush into my head, and so I *w. S.* i. 14
Or if you needs must *w.*, *w.* CÆSAR's praise *S.* i. 21
Or whiten'd wall provoke the skew'r to *w. S.* i. 98
Such as a King might read, a Bishop *w. S.* i. 152
The men, who *w.* such verse as we can read *S.* v. 158
But those who cannot *w.*, and those who can *S.* v. 187
We needs will *w.* Epistles to the King *S.* v. 369
Besides, a fate attends on all I *w. S.* v. 408
I told you when I went, I could not *w. S.* vi. 28
To court applause by printing what I *w. S.* vi. 150
If such the plague and pains to *w.* by rule *S.* vi. 180
These *w.* to Lords, some mean reward to get *S.* vii. 25
Those *w.* because all *w.*, and so have still *S.* vii. 27
But let them *w.* for you, each rogue impairs *S.* vii. 99

Writer.

And all the *W.* lives in ev'ry line *E.* iv. 2
And while self-love each jealous *w.* rules *E.C.* 516
In ev'ry work regard the w.'s End E.C. 255
Some foreign w—s, some our own despise E.C. 394
My Liege ! why *W.* little claim your thought *S.* v. 356
" But Sir, of *w.!*" "Swift, for closer style *S.* viii. 72

Writes.

Ev'n Ralph repents, and Henley *w.* no more *D.* i. 216
Ten censure wrong, for one who *w.* amiss *E.C.* 6
Glows while he reads, but trembles as he *w. E.C.* 198
Plu— Plutarch, what's his name that *w.* his life *E.J.S.* 31
His Prince, that *w.* in Verse, and has his ear *E.S.* i. 46
Just *w.* to make his barrenness appear *P.S.* 181
Who *w.* a Libel, or who copies out *P.S.* 290

Writing.

For *w.* Pamphlets, and for roasting Popes *D.* iii. 284
Appear in *w.* or in judging ill *E.C.* 2
True ease in *w.* comes from art, not chance *E.C.* 362
Nature's chief Master-piece is *w.* well *E.C.* 724
But ease in *w.* flows from Art, not chance *S.* vi. 178
Excuse for *w.*, and for *w.* ill *S.* vii. 28
Are Fathers of the Church for *w.* less *S.* vii. 98
Nor *praise nor blame the w—s, but the men E.C.* 413
The morals blacken'd, when the *w.* 'scape *P.S.* 352

Written.

Already *w.*—wash it out, my tears *E.A.* 14
And censure freely who have *w.* well *E.C.* 16
To *w.* Wisdom, as another's, less *M.E.* i. 13

Wrong.

To cavil, censure, dictate, right or *w. D.* ii. 377
The RIGHT DIVINE of Kings to govern *w. D.* iv. 188
Till drown'd was Sense, and Shame, and Right, and *W. D.* iv. 625
Ten censure *w.* for one who writes amiss *E.C.* 6
And smooth or rough, with them is right or *w. E.C.* 338
By chance go right, they purposely go *w. E.C.* 427
Who, if once *w.*, will needs be always so *E.C.* 569
Nor suffers Horace more in *w.* Translations (rep.) *E.C.* 663
Is only this, if God has plac'd him *w.* (rep.) *E.M.* i. 50
Pleasure, or *w.* or rightly understood *E.M.* ii. 91
One must go right, the other may go *w. E.M.* iii. 94
And right, too rigid, harden into *w. E.M.* iii. 193
His can't be *w.* whose life is in the right *E.M.* iii. 306
Who risk the most, that take *w.* means or right *E.M.* iv. 86
And then mistook reverse of *w.* for right *M.E.* iii. 198
If *w.*, I smil'd ; if right, I kiss'd the rod *P.S.* 158
For faith, Lord Fanny, you are in the *w. S.* ii. 101
And, having once been *w.*, will be so still *S.* v. 130
Who felt the *w.*, or fear'd it, took th' alarm *S.* v. 255
To say too much, might do my honour *w. S.* vi. 12
If I am *w.*, oh teach my heart *U.P.* 31
Of w—s from Duchesses and Lady Maries D. ii. 136

Strange spleen to S—k ! Do I *w.* the Man *E.S.* ii. 62
This jealous, waspish, w.-head, rhyming race S. vi. 148

Wrote.—*See also* **Writ.**

Yet *w.* and flounder'd on in mere despair *D.* i. 120
The Mob of Gentlemen who *w.* with Ease *S.* v. 208

Wrought.

"What pow'r," he cries, "what pow'r these wonders *w.!* *D.* iii. 250
What flatt'ring scenes our wand'ring fancy *w. E.* iii. 23
Becomes the stuff of which our dream is *w. M.E.* i. 48
Behold this *Equipage*, by *Mathers w. Mi.* ix. 29
Behold the band that *w.* a Nation's cure *S.* v. 225

Wry-mouth'd.

Instructive work ! whose *w.* portraiture *D.* ii. 145

Wycherley.

How Shadwell hasty, *W.* was slow *S.* v. 85

Wyndham.

There truant *W.* ev'ry Muse gave o'er *D.* iv. 167
Or *W.*; just to Freedom and the Throne *E.S.* ii. 88
Where *British* sighs from dying *W.* stole *Mi.* x. 11

Wynkyn.

There Caxton slept, with *W.* at his side *D.* i. 149

Y.

The Flow'rs of Bubo, and the Flow of *Y—g E.S.* i. 68

Yawn.

And heard thy everlasting *y.* confess *D.* iv. 343
What Mortal can resist the *Y.* of Gods *D.* iv. 606
At ev'ry line, they stretch, they y., they doze D. ii. 390
Ready to cast, I *y.*, I sigh, and sweat *S.* viii. 157

Yawn'd.

More had she spoke, but *y.*—All Nature nods *D.* iv. 605
And Navies *y.* for Orders on the Main *D.* iv. 618

Yawning.

And all thy *y.* daughters cry, *encore D.* iv. 60

Ye.—*Passim.*

Year.

There sav'd by spice, like mummies, many a *y. D.* i. 151
And ev'ry *y.* be duller than the last *D.* iii. 296
Signs following signs lead on the mighty *y. D.* iii. 321
Till Westminster's whole *y.* be holiday *D.* iii. 336
Thence the full harvest of the golden *y. E.M.* iii. 39
Because he wants a thousand pounds a *y. E.M.* iv. 192
Go live ! for Heav'n's Eternal *Y.* is thine *Ep.* vii. 9
For life, six hundred pounds a *y. I.H.* ii. 2 s
Nor cross the Channel twice a *y. I.H.* ii. 31 s
This Phœbus promis'd (I forget the *y.*) *M.E.* ii. 283
What made Directors cheat in South-sea *y. M.E.* iii.117
This *y.* a Reservoir, to keep and spare *M.E.* iii. 173
This man possest five hundred pounds a *y. M.E.* iii. 280
Some joy still lost, as each vain *y.* runs o'er *Mi.* v. 7
'Tis but the Fun'ral of the former *y. Mi.* v. 10
Let day improve on day, and *y.* on *y. Mi.* v. 15
And strains, from hard-bound brains, eight lines a *y. P.S.* 182
They scarce can bear their *Laureate* twice a *y. S.* i. 34
On broccoli and mutton, round the *y. S.* ii. 138
The Chanc'ry takes your rents for twenty *y. S.* ii 172
To him commit the hour, the day, the *y. S.* iv. 9
Suppose he wants a *y.*, will you compound *S.* v. 57
We shall not quarrel for a *y.* or two *S.* v. 61
I pluck out *y.* by *y.*, and hair by hair *S.* v. 64
And estimating Authors by the *y. S.* v. 67
Sir, be's your slave for twenty pound a *y. S.* vi. 8
With rhymes of this *per cent.* and that *per y. S.* vii. 56
And lavish nature paints the purple *Y. Sp.* 28
The various seasons of the rolling *y. Sp.* 38
But blest with her, 'tis spring throughout the *y. Sp.* 84
Grieve for an hour, perhaps, then mourn a *y. U.L.* 56
There the first roses of the *y.* shall blow *U.L.* 66
A standing sermon at each y.'s expense M.E. vi. 21
Long as the *Y.* dull circle seems to run *S.* iii. 37
(His only suit) for twice three y—s before D. iii. 38

YEARLY—YOUTH.

And Pope's, ten *y.* to comment and translate *D.* iii. 332
This small well-polish'd Gem, the work of *y. E.* iii. 40
Blooms in thy colours for a thousand *y. E.* iii. 58
Whole *y.* neglected, for some months ador'd *E.* iv. 43
Condemn'd whole *y.* of absence to deplore *E.A.* 361
When Patriarch-wits surviv'd a thousand *y. E.C.* 479
When mellowing *y.* their full perfection give *E.C.* 490
As who began a thousand *y.* ago *E.M.* i. 76
One self-approving hour whole *y.* outweighs *E.M.* iv. 255
Strike? why the man was hang'd ten *y.* ago *E.S.* ii. 55
Else might he take to Virtue some *y.* hence *E.S.* ii. 60
'Tis (let me see) three *y.* and more *I.H.* ii. 83 *s*
Swift fly the *y.*, and rise th' expected morn *M.* 21
The Courtier smooth who forty *y.* had shin'd *M.E.* i. 252
Full sixty *y.* the World has been her Trade *M.E.* ii. 123
See the wide waste of all-devouring *y. M.E.* v. 1
The sacred rust of twice ten hundred *y. M.E.* v. 38
This more than pays whole *y.* of thankless pain *Mi.* i. 5
With added *y.* if Life bring nothing new *Mi.* v. 5
Hours, days, and *y.* slide soft away *O.* iv. 10
This saving counsel, "Keep your piece nine *y.*" (*rep.*) *P.S.* 40
Great Homer died three thousand *y.* ago *P.S.* 124
Full ten *y.* slander'd, did he once reply *P.S.* 374
With his broad sabre next, a chief in *y. R.L.* iii. 55
Who died, perhaps, an hundred *y.* ago (*rep.*) *S.* v. 52
With growing *y.* the pleasing license grew *S.* v. 249
Y. following *y.*, steal something ev'ry day *S.* vi. 72
To books and study gives seven *y.* complete *S.* vi. 117
Bright thro' the rubbish of some hundred *y. S.* vi. 166
Wicked as Pages, who in early *y. S.* vii. 39
Swears ev'ry place entailed for *y.* to come *S.* viii. 160
Dim lights of life, that burn a length of *y. U.L.* 19
Her cheerful head, and leads the golden *y. W.F.* 92
Behold Villario's ten y—*s' toil complete M.E.* iv. 79

Yearly.
New graces *y.* like thy works display *E.* iii. 65
Whose cheerful Tenants bless their *y.* toil *M.E.* iv. 183

Yellow.
Now blushing berries paint the *y.* grove *A.* 75
As all looks *y.* to the jaundic'd eye *E.C.* 559
Is *y.* dirt the passion of thy life *E.M.* iv. 279
Where tawdry *y.* strove with dirty red *M.E.* iii. 304
In *y.* meads of Asphodel *O.* i. 75
O'er sandy wilds were *y.* harvests spread *W.F.* 88
The *y.* carp, in scales bedropp'd with gold *W.F.* 144

Yea, Yea.—*Passim.*

Yesterday.
What the fine gentlemen wore *y. E.C.* 330
That leaves the load of *y.* behind *S.* i. 82
Thou who since *y.* hast roll'd o'er all *S.* viii. 202

Yet.—*Passim.*

Yews.
With all the mournful family of *Y. M.E.* iv. 96

Y-fed.
On parchment scraps *y.*, and Wormius hight *D.* iii. 188

Yield.
Just Gods! shall all things *y.* returns but love *A.* 76
Suck the thread in, then *y.* it out again *D.* iii. 58
Try what the open, what the covert *y. E.M.* i. 10
Learn from the birds what food the thickets *y. E.M.* iii. 173
Twin'd with the wreaths Parnassian laurels *y. E.M.* iv. 11
May *y.*, God knows, to strong temptation *I.H.* ii. 181
Nor yet shall Waller *y.* to time *I.H.* iv. 7
Their vines a shadow to their race shall *y. M.* 65
Ti'rd, not determin'd, to the last we *y. M.E.* i. 43
Love, if it makes her *y.*, must make her hate *M.E.* ii. 134
Ti'rd of the scene Parterres and Fountains *y. M.E.* iv. 87
I *y.* at once, and sink into his arms *Mi.* ix. 109
Attend, and *y.* to what I now decide *Mi.* ix. 109
Whose trees in summer *y.* him shade *O.* iv. 7
As many more Manillio forc'd to *y. R.L.* iii. 51
Thus far both armies to Belinda *y. R.L.* iii. 65
Blest Thames's shores the brightest beauties *y. Sp.* 63
Cynthus and Hybla *y.* to Windsor-shade *Sp.* 68
And crown'd with corn their thanks to Ceres *y. Su.* 66
And curs'd with hearts unknowing how to *y. U.L.* 42

So may kind rains their vital moisture *y. W.* 15
Nor fragrant herds their native incense *y. W.* 48

Yielding.
By Nature *y.*, stubborn but for fame *E.* iv. 35
Soft *y.* minds to Water glide away *R.L.* i. 61
And win my way by *y.* to the tide *S.* iii. 34
And *y.* Metal flow'd to human form *S.* v. 148

Yields.
The silenc'd Preacher *y.* to potent strain *S.* v. 237
The Thistle springs, to which the Lily *y. Sp.* 90
Not proud Olympus *y.* a nobler sight *W.F.* 33
The swain with tears his frustrate labour *y. W.F.* 55
He gathers health from herbs the forests *y. W.F.* 241

Yoke.
Cages for gnats and chains to *y.* a flea *R.L.* v. 121

Yon, Yonder.—*Passim.*

Yore.
But Satan now is wiser than of *y. M.E.* iii. 351
Where are those troops of Poor that throng'd of *y. S.* vii. 113

York.
Ask where's the North? at *Y.*, 'tis on the Tweed *E.M.* ii. 222

You, Your, Yours.—*Passim.*

Young.
And whisk 'em back to Evans, *Y.*, and Swift *D.* ii. 116
How *y. Lutetia, softer than the down D.* ii. 333
The *y.*, the old, who feel her inward sway *D.* iv. 73
Safe and unseen the *y.* Æneas past *D.* iv. 290
When first *y.* Maro in his boundless mind *E.C.* 130
Nay wits had pensions, and *y.* Lords had wit *E.C.* 539
Or turns *y.* Ammon loose to scourge mankind *E.M.* i. 160
The *y.* disease, that must subdue at length *E.M.* ii. 135
The *y.* dismiss'd to wander earth or air *E.M.* iii. 127
Go! and pretend your family is *y. E.M.* iv. 213
And what *y.* AMMON wish'd, but wish'd in vain *E.S.* ii. 117
Noble and *y.*, who strikes the heart *I.H.* iii. 11
Shall call the smiling Loves, and *y.* Desires *I.H.* iii. 26
Y. without Lovers, old without a Friend *M.E.* ii. 246
The *y.* who labour, and the old who rest *M.E.* iii. 268
Thro' his *y.* Woods how pleas'd Sabinus stray'd *M.E.* iv. 89
Instruct the eyes of *y.* Coquettes to roll *R.L.* i. 88
Alas *y.* man! your days can ne'er be long *S.* i. 102
Perhaps, *y.* men! our fathers had no nose *S.* ii. 92
Free as *y.* Littleton, her Cause pursue *S.* iii. 29
No *y.* divine, new-benefic'd, can be *S.* vii. 51

Youngest.
The eldest is a fool, the *y.* wise *S.* iii. 44

Youth.
A *y.* unknown to Phoebus, in despair *D.* ii. 213
Mark first that *y.* who takes the foremost place *D.* iii. 139
A matchless *y.!* his nod these worlds controls *D.* iii. 255
Plac'd at the door of Learning, *y.* to guide *D.* iv. 153
This glorious *Y.*, and add one Venus more *D.* iv. 359
So shall each *y.*, assisted by our eyes *D.* iv. 359
Each maid cry'd, Charming! and each *y.*, Divine *D.* iv. 410 & 414
Led up the *Y.*, and call'd the Goddess *Dame D.* iv. 498
When, warm in *y.*, I bade the world farewell *E.A.* 110
From the false world in early *y.* they fled *E.A.* 131
In fearless *y.* we tempt the heights of Arts *E.C.* 220
In *y.* alone its empty praise we boast *E.C.* 496
Some livelier plaything gives his *y.* delight *E.M.* ii. 277
That pointed back to *y.*, this on to age *E.M.* iii. 144
The worthy *Y.* shall ne'er be in a rage *E.S.* i. 48
Dear Sir, forgive the prejudice of *Y. E.S.* i. 63
Our *Y.*, all liv'ry'd o'er with foreign Gold *E.S.* i. 155
And how did, pray, the little *Y.* offend *E.S.* ii. 166
Fill'd with the Sense of Age, the Fire of *Y. Ep.* ii. 7
Go! fair example of untainted *y. Ep.* vii. 1
Oh born to Arms! O Worth in *Y.* approv'd *Ep.* ix. 3
If modest *Y.*, with cool Reflection crown'd *Ep.* xiv. 1
From loveless *y.* to unrespected age *M.E.* ii. 125
In *Y.* they conquer, with so wild a rage *M.E.* ii. 231
At last to follies *Y.* could scarce defend *M.E.* ii. 235
A *Y.* of Frolics, an old Age of Cards *M.E.* ii. 244

Long Health, long *Y*., long Pleasure, and a Friend *Mi.* v. 2
Mourn'd *Adonis*, darling *Y*. *Mi.* vii. 10
A *Y*. more glitt'ring than a Birth-night Beau *R.L.* i. 23
Ah cease rash *y.!* desist ere 'tis too late *R.L.* iii. 121
If our intemp'rate *Y*. the vessel drains *S.* ii. 90
Lov'd without *y.*, and follow'd without pow'r *S.* iii. 183
He, from the taste obscene reclaims our *y*. *S.* v. 217
Was velvet in the *y*. of good Queen *Bess S.* viii. 41
See! where the British *y*. engag'd no more *S.* viii. 212
Ye vig'rous swains! while *y*. ferments your blood *W.F.* 93
The *y*. rush eager to the sylvan war *W.F.* 148
See the bold *y*. strain up the threat'ning steep *W.F.* 155
On whom three hundred gold-capt y—s *await D.* iv. 117
There *Y*. and Nymphs, in concert gay *I.H.* iii. 29
By the *y*. that died for love *O.* i. 79
Fair Nymphs, and well-drest *Y*. around her shone *R.L.* ii. 5
And naked *y*. and painted chiefs admire *W.F.* 405

Youthful.
Not *y*. kings in battle seiz'd alive *R.L.* iv. 3
What mov'd my mind with *y*. Lords to roam *R.L.*iv.159

Y-pent.
But who is he, in closet close *y. D.* iii. 185

Z.

Zany.
Preacher at once, and Z. of thy age *D.* iii. 206

Zeal.
Shall I, like Curtins, desp'rate in my *z. D.* i. 209
But far the foremost, two, with earnest *z. D.* iv. 401
Not grace, or *z.*, love only was my call *E.A.* 117
See anger, *z*. and fortitude supply *E.M.* ii. 187
Z. then, not charity, became the guide *E.M.* iii. 261
Rev'rent I touch thee, but with honest *z. E.S.* ii. 216
A Scorn of wrangling, yet a Z. for Truth *Ep.* ii. 8
Tells me I have more Z. than Wit *I.H.* ii. 56 *s*
And shew their *z.*, and hide their want of skill *M.E.* ii. 186
And Z. for that great House which eats him up *M.E.* iii. 108

Barbarian blindness, Christian *z*. conspire *M.E.* v. 13
For Virtue's self may too much *z*. be had *S.* iv. 26
The Z. of Fools offends at any time (*rep.*) *S.* v. 406

Zealots.
For modes of Faith let graceless *z*. fight *E.M.* iii. 305

Zealous.
Once School-divines this *z*. isle o'er-spread *E.C.* 440
An ardent Judge, who *z*. in his trust *E.C.* 677
To failings mild, but *z*. for desert *E.C.* 731
No *z*. Pastor blame a failing Spouse *E.S.* ii. 193

Zembla.
Or gives to Z. fruits, to Barca flow'rs *D.* i. 74
At Greenland, Z., or the Lord knows where *E.M.* ii.224

Zenith.
I shun his Z., court his mild Decline *E.S.* ii. 76

Zephalinda.
Thus from the world fair Z. flew *E.* v. 7

Zephyr.
Soft is the strain when Z. gently blows *E.C.* 366
The whisp'ring Z. and the purling rill *E.M.* i. 204
Waves to the tepid Z—s *of the spring D.* iv. 422
Lull'd by soft Z. thro' the broken pane *P.S.* 42
Smooth flow the waves, the Z. gently play *R.L.* ii. 51
That seem'd but Z. to the train beneath *R.L.* ii. 58
The balmy Z., silent since her death *W.* 49

Zephyretta.
The flutt'ring fan be Z.'s care *R.L.* ii. 112

Zeuxis.
With Z.' Helen thy Bridgewater vie *E.* iii. 75

Zig-Zags.
That slipp'd thro' Cracks, and Z. of the Head *D.* i. 124

Zoilus.
Z. again would start up from the dead *E.C.* 465

Zone.
Ev'n those who dwell beneath its very *z. E.M.* ii. 227
But by the crescent and the golden *z. W.F.* 176

Z—nds.
Z.! damn the lock! 'fore Gad, you must be civil *R.L.*iv. 128

CORRIGENDA.

Page.	Heading.	Line.		Page.	Heading.	Line.	
3	Admiring		*should follow* "admires"	71	Delia	3	*insert* "(*rep.*)"
4	adust		*should precede* "advance"	73	desire	1	*for* "the" *read* "her"
5	age	21	*for* "339" *read* "389"	81	dreadful	9	*for* "S. vi." *read* "S. iv."
7	alley	1	*for* "to" *read* "at"	84	dust	3	*for* "must" *read* "shall"
9	ancestors	1	*for* "cast" *read* "casts"	85	ear	29	*for* "hang" *read* "hang"
11	Arabian	1	*for* "conq'ring" *read* "conqu'ring"	87	eat	17	*for* "yet" *read* "but"
				"	erstatic	1	*for* "his" *read* "her"
16	avarice	5	*for* "as *his*" *read* "and"	108	first (*after* 5)		*insert* "And you shall see the f. warm Weather *J. H.* i. 19"
17	bade	10	*for* "For" *read* "From"				
18	balm	2	*for* "the" *read* "their"	114	foreign	5	*for* "liv'ry'd" *read* "liv'ry'd o'er"
"	bard	9	*for* "began" *read* "begun"				
19	barrister	1	*for* "79" *read* "59"	118	*after* first		*insert* "Fretful—Lean and *f.*; would seem wise *Mi.* vi. 7"
20	beam (5 fr. bot.)		*for* "issu'd" *read* "issuing"				
"	bean	9	*for* "Or" *read* "And"	121	future	14	*for* "339" *read* "389"
23	bends	4	*for* "streams" *read* "steams"	124	*after* George		*insert* "George—There liv'd in *prime G.* (they record) *S.* vi. 184"
25	bidden	1	*for* "learn" *read* "know"				
26	bishop	8	*for* "seems" *read* "seem"				
"	black	2	*for* "shall look" *read* "still look'd"	70	giant	4	*for* "them" *read* "em"
				"	"	8	*for* "opes" *read* "ope"
29	blue	1	*for* "look" *read* "look'd"	126	globe	3	*for* "lurid" *read* "lucid"
31	book	12	*for* "women" *insert* "men," *and dele* "their"	128	God	39	*for* "Or" *read* "And"
				149	honour	2	*for* "To" *read* "And"
"	booth	4	*for* "297" *read* "299"	159	issuing	2	*for* "Then" *read* "Than"
33	brawn	1	*for* "the" *read* "their"	160	jaw	1	*for* "opes" *read* "ope"
37	brown	2	*for* "Merdameate" *read* "Merdamaste"	171	lean (*after* 2)		*insert* "*L.* and fretful; would seem wise *Mi.* vi. 7"
39	call	10	*for* "all" (3rd *time*) *read* "and"	172	learn	16	"*L.* from &c." *should come under* "learns"
"	"	27	*for* "Or" *read* "And"	173	left (5 fr. bot.)		*for* "the" *read* "a"
40	capacious	1	*for* "the" *read* "and"	174	level	3	*for* "In" *read* "With"
42	cast	5	*for* "Once" *read* "One"	151	loose	2	*for* "dun-night gown" *read* "dim night-gown"
43	caution	1	*for* "or" *read* "nor"				
44	cent		*add, "see also* Per"	189	man *under* "m.'s" *for* "*E.* i. 299 *read* "*E.* i. 29"		
48	chine	1	*for* "the" *read* "their"	199	moment	7	*for* "you see I" *read* "I see you"
"	Cibber	2	*for* "shall" *read* "shalt"				
51	coarse	2	*for* "To" *read* "So"	208	night (5 fr. bot.)		*for* "are" *read* "seem"
52	cock	1	*for* "spurts" *read* "spirts"	211	obsequious	1	*for* "it rolls" *read* "she runs"
60	court	12	*for* "Cares" *read* "Those cares"	217	order	8	*for* "far" *read* "from"
				239	pretend	3	*for* "339" *read* "389"
66	Daphne	5	*insert* "(*rep.*)"	258	rhyme	12	"Not plagu'd &c." *should follow* line 4
68	death (6 fr. bot.)		*for* "langour" *read* "languor"				
70	deep	1	*for* "fill" *read* "fills"	298	spoon	1	*for* "your" *read* "the"
"	"	31	*for* "hang" *read* "hang"				

LONDON:
BRADBURY, AGNEW, & CO., PRINTERS, WHITEFRIARS.

www.ingramcontent.com/pod-product-compliance
Lightning Source LLC
Chambersburg PA
CBHW030343230426
43664CB00007BA/513